MARTIN TAYLOR

D1491511

XML Bible

Gold Edition

Praise for Elliotte Rusty Harold's *XML Bible*

"Great book! I have about 10 XML books and this is by far the best."

—Edward Blair, Systems Analyst, AT&T

"I recommend the *XML Bible*. I found it to be really helpful, as I am a beginner myself. It is easy to understand, which I found most useful since I am not a 'tech-head'."

—Marius Holth Hanssen, Independent IT Consultant

"I don't know how to praise Elliotte Rusty Harold enough. When I read a technical book, I don't expect to ENJOY it in the pure sense. Oh, I expect to ENJOY increasing my knowledge or to ENJOY the experience of successfully understanding a particularly poorly written passage. Your text is enjoyable in the pure sense. It is fun to read. I don't have to force myself to pick up *XML Bible* — I jump for it because I know I will be finding something on each page to make me smile."

—Mike Maddux, Software Architect, Texas Department of Health

"Just wanted to take a minute and send you a big thank you for writing *XML Bible* and JavaBeans. Without those two books, my life would be so much harder!"

—Ove "Lime" Lindström, Java Consultant, Enea Realtime AB

XML Bible

Gold Edition

Elliotte Rusty Harold

Hungry Minds™

Best-Selling Books • Digital Downloads • e-Books • Answer Networks • e-Newsletters • Branded Web Sites • e-Learning

New York, NY ✦ Cleveland, OH ✦ Indianapolis, IN

XML Bible, Gold Edition

Published by
Hungry Minds, Inc.
909 Third Avenue
New York, NY 10022
www.hungryminds.com

Copyright © 2001 Hungry Minds, Inc. All rights reserved. No part of this book, including interior design, cover design, and icons, may be reproduced or transmitted in any form, by any means (electronic, photocopying, recording, or otherwise) without the prior written permission of the publisher.

Library of Congress Control Number: 2001093384

ISBN: 0-7645-4819-0

Printed in the United States of America

10 9 8 7 6 5 4 3 2 1

1P/RY/QZ/QR/IN

Distributed in the United States by Hungry Minds, Inc.

Distributed by CDG Books Canada Inc. for Canada; by Transworld Publishers Limited in the United Kingdom; by IDG Norge Books for Norway; by IDG Sweden Books for Sweden; by IDG Books Australia Publishing Corporation Pty. Ltd. for Australia and New Zealand; by TransQuest Publishers Pte Ltd. for Singapore, Malaysia, Thailand, Indonesia, and Hong Kong; by Gotop Information Inc. for Taiwan; by ICG Muse, Inc. for Japan; by Intersoft for South Africa; by Eyrolles for France; by International Thomson Publishing for Germany, Austria, and Switzerland; by Distribuidora Cuspide for Argentina; by LR International for Brazil; by Galileo Libros for Chile; by Ediciones ZETA S.C.R. Ltda. for Peru; by WS Computer Publishing Corporation, Inc., for the Philippines; by Contemporanea de Ediciones for Venezuela; by Express Computer Distributors for the Caribbean and West Indies; by Micronesia Media Distributor, Inc. for Micronesia; by Chips Computadoras S.A. de C.V. for Mexico; by Editorial Norma de Panama S.A. for Panama; by American Bookshops for Finland.

For general information on Hungry Minds' products and services please contact our Customer Care department within the U.S. at 800-762-2974, outside the U.S. at 317-572-3993 or fax 317-572-4002.

For sales inquiries and reseller information, including discounts, premium and bulk quantity sales, and foreign-language translations, please contact our Customer Care department at 800-434-3422, fax 317-572-4002 or write to Hungry Minds, Inc., Attn: Customer Care Department, 10475 Crosspoint Boulevard, Indianapolis, IN 46256.

For information on licensing foreign or domestic rights, please contact our Sub-Rights Customer Care department at 212-884-5000.

For information on using Hungry Minds' products and services in the classroom or for ordering examination copies, please contact our Educational Sales department at 800-434-2086 or fax 317-572-4005.

For press review copies, author interviews, or other publicity information, please contact our Public Relations department at 317-572-3168 or fax 317-572-4168.

For authorization to photocopy items for corporate, personal, or educational use, please contact Copyright Clearance Center, 222 Rosewood Drive, Danvers, MA 01923, or fax 978-750-4470.

LIMIT OF LIABILITY/DISCLAIMER OF WARRANTY: THE PUBLISHER AND AUTHOR HAVE USED THEIR BEST EFFORTS IN PREPARING THIS BOOK. THE PUBLISHER AND AUTHOR MAKE NO REPRESENTATIONS OR WARRANTIES WITH RESPECT TO THE ACCURACY OR COMPLETENESS OF THE CONTENTS OF THIS BOOK AND SPECIFICALLY DISCLAIM ANY IMPLIED WARRANTIES OF MERCHANTABILITY OR FITNESS FOR A PARTICULAR PURPOSE. THERE ARE NO WARRANTIES WHICH EXTEND BEYOND THE DESCRIPTIONS CONTAINED IN THIS PARAGRAPH. NO WARRANTY MAY BE CREATED OR EXTENDED BY SALES REPRESENTATIVES OR WRITTEN SALES MATERIALS. THE ACCURACY AND COMPLETENESS OF THE INFORMATION PROVIDED HEREIN AND THE OPINIONS STATED HEREIN ARE NOT GUARANTEED OR WARRANTED TO PRODUCE ANY PARTICULAR RESULTS, AND THE ADVICE AND STRATEGIES CONTAINED HEREIN MAY NOT BE SUITABLE FOR EVERY INDIVIDUAL. NEITHER THE PUBLISHER NOR AUTHOR SHALL BE LIABLE FOR ANY LOSS OF PROFIT OR ANY OTHER COMMERCIAL DAMAGES, INCLUDING BUT NOT LIMITED TO SPECIAL, INCIDENTAL, CONSEQUENTIAL, OR OTHER DAMAGES.

Netscape Communications Corporation has not authorized, sponsored, or endorsed, or approved this publication and is not responsible for its content. Netscape and the Netscape Communications Corporate Logos are trademarks and trade names of Netscape Communications Corporation.

Trademarks: All trademarks are property of their respective owners. Hungry Minds, Inc. is not associated with any product or vendor mentioned in this book.

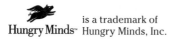

is a trademark of Hungry Minds, Inc.

Credits

Acquisitions Editor
Grace Buechlein

Project Editor
Sharon Nash

Technical Editors
Ken Cox
B. K. DeLong

Copy Editor
Richard H. Adin

Project Coordinator
Nancee Reeves

Graphics and Production Specialists
Heather Pope
Jill Piscitelli
Brian Torwelle

Quality Control Technicians
Laura Albert
Marianne Santy
Charles Spencer

Permissions Editor
Laura Moss

Media Development Specialist
Gregory Stephens

Media Development Coordinator
Marisa Pearman

Illustrators
Gabriele McCann
John Greenough

Proofreading and Indexing
TECHBOOKS Production Services

Cover Image
Lawrance Huck

About the Author

Elliotte Rusty Harold is an internationally respected writer, programmer, and educator, both on the Internet and off. He got his start writing FAQ lists for the Macintosh newsgroups on Usenet and has since branched out into books, Web sites, and newsletters. He's an adjunct professor of computer science at Polytechnic University in Brooklyn, New York. His Cafe con Leche Web site at `http://www.ibiblio.org/xml/` has become one of the most popular independent XML sites on the Internet.

Elliotte is originally from New Orleans, to which he returns periodically in search of a decent bowl of gumbo. However, he currently resides in the Prospect Heights neighborhood of Brooklyn with his wife Beth, and his cats Charm (named after the quark) and Marjorie (named after his mother-in-law). When not writing books, he enjoys working on genealogy, mathematics, free software, and quantum mechanics. His previous books include *The Java Developer's Resource, Java Network Programming, Java Secrets, JavaBeans, Java I/O, XML: Extensible Markup Language,* and *XML in a Nutshell.*

For Ma, a great grandmother

Preface

Welcome to the Gold Edition of the *XML Bible*. When the first edition was published about two years ago, XML was a promising technology with a small but growing niche. In the last two years, it has absolutely exploded. XML no longer needs to be justified as a good idea. In fact, the question developers are asking has changed from "Why XML?" to "Why not XML?". XML has become the data format of choice for fields as diverse as stock trading and graphic design. More new programs today are using XML than aren't. A solid understanding of just what XML is and how to use it has become a *sine qua non* for the computer literate.

The *XML Bible* is your introduction to the exciting and fast-growing world of XML. With this book, you'll learn how to write documents in XML and how to use style sheets to convert those documents into HTML so that legacy browsers can read them. You'll also learn how to use document type definitions (DTDs) and schemas to describe and validate documents. You'll encounter a variety of XML applications in many domains, ranging from finance to vector graphics to genealogy. And you'll learn how to take advantage of XML for your own unique projects, programs, and Web sites.

What's New in the Gold Edition

At more than 1,000 pages, the first edition of the *XML Bible* was the largest book I had written up to that point. My favorite reader comment about that edition was, "It would seem to me that if you asked the author to write 10,000 words about the color blue, he would be able to do it without breaking into a sweat." While I probably could write 10,000 words about blue, for the second edition I did try to restrain myself and write more concisely. I rewrote the book from the ground up, and while I retained the basic flavor and outline that proved so popular with the first edition, I tightened up the writing and cut many examples down to size.

However, technology never stands still for long, and there was a surfeit of new topics that deserved to be written about, including XML schemas, Scalable Vector Graphics (SVG), the Extensible Hypertext Markup Language (XHTML), and the Wireless Markup Language (WML); and this was only the beginning of the new material I wanted to cover. Although I made every effort to write more concisely, the second edition still grew to more than 1,200 pages. I simply could not fit in all the cool new technologies I wanted to write about. It was physically impossible to glue enough pages between two covers to adequately address SMIL, Canonical XML, CSS Level 3, and more. And when I was just about ready to despair of ever being able to say everything I wanted to say about XML, my editor at Hungry Minds broached the possibility of the hard cover edition you now hold in your hands.

The Gold edition starts with all the material you'll find in the paperback second edition, mostly unchanged. However, it adds more than 300 pages of new material covering many completely new topics including:

✦ Cascading Style Sheets Level 3

✦ XML Base

✦ XInclude

✦ Canonical XML

✦ The Resource Directory Description Language (RDDL)

✦ Modular XHTML

✦ Reading DTDs

In addition, the coverage of several existing topics such as schemas was expanded significantly. If you liked the first or second edition, you're going to like the Gold Edition even more. It's got everything you liked from the previous editions and more. I'm confident you'll find this an even more useful tutorial and reference.

Note

As I write these words, I can't help but think about the three chapters that didn't quite make the cut for this edition, not because they were poorly written or because what they discussed was unimportant, but simply because this time I hit the limit of the physical number of pages that could be sewn between two cloth covers. And certainly the flow of new XML specifications out of the W3C and other organizations continues unabated. Next year I expect to be working on XSLT 2.0, the XML Query Language, XML Digital Signatures, and probably some things that haven't even been invented yet. Barring radical new improvements in bookbinding technology, I have no idea how I'll possibly squeeze all this between the covers of future editions. *The XML Bible, Volume 2,* anyone?

Who You Are

Unlike most other XML books on the market, the *XML Bible* discusses XML from the perspective of a Web-page author, not from the perspective of a software developer. I don't spend a lot of time discussing BNF grammars or parsing element trees. Instead, I show you how you can use XML and existing tools today to more efficiently produce attractive, exciting, easy-to-use, easy-to-maintain Web sites that keep your readers coming back for more.

This book is aimed directly at Web-site developers. I assume you want to use XML to produce Web sites that are difficult to impossible to create with raw HTML. You'll be amazed to discover that in conjunction with style sheets and a few free tools, XML enables you to do things that previously required either custom software costing hundreds to thousands of dollars per developer or extensive knowledge of programming languages such as Perl. None of the software discussed in this book will cost you more than a few minutes of download time. None of the tricks require any programming.

What You Need to Know

XML does build on top of the underlying infrastructure of the Internet and the Web. Consequently, I will assume you know how to ftp files, send e-mail, and load URLs into your Web browser of choice. I will also assume you have a reasonable knowledge of HTML at about the level supported by Netscape 1.1. On the other hand, when I discuss newer aspects of HTML that are not yet in widespread use, such as Cascading Style Sheets, I discuss them in depth.

To be more specific, in this book I assume that you can:

◆ Write a basic HTML page, including links, images, and text, using a text editor.

◆ Place that page on a Web server.

On the other hand, I do not assume that you:

◆ Know SGML. In fact, this preface is almost the only place in the entire book you'll see the word SGML used. XML is supposed to be simpler and more widespread than SGML. It can't be that if you have to learn SGML first.

◆ Are a programmer, whether of Java, Perl, C, or some other language. XML is a markup language, not a programming language. You don't need to be a programmer to write XML documents.

What You'll Learn

This book has one primary goal: to teach you to write XML documents for the Web. Fortunately, XML has a decidedly flat learning curve, much like HTML (and unlike SGML). As you learn a little you can do a little. As you learn a little more, you can do a little more. Thus the chapters in this book build steadily on one another. They are meant to be read in sequence. Along the way you'll learn:

◆ How to author XML documents and deliver them to readers.

◆ How semantic tagging makes XML documents easier to maintain and develop than their HTML equivalents.

◆ How to post XML documents on Web servers in a form everyone can read.

◆ How to make sure your XML is well formed.

◆ How to write with international characters such as Ж and Æ.

◆ How to validate documents against DTDs and schemas.

◆ How to build large documents from smaller parts using entities and XInclude.

◆ How to embed non-XML data in your documents.

◆ How to merge different XML vocabularies with namespaces.

✦ How to format your documents with CSS and XSL style sheets.

✦ How to connect documents with XLinks and XPointers.

✦ How to write metadata for Web pages using RDF and RDDL.

In the final section of this book, you'll see several practical examples of XML being used for real-world applications, including:

✦ Web site design

✦ Schemas

✦ Push

✦ Vector graphics

✦ Genealogy

How the Book Is Organized

This book is divided into five parts:

I. Introducing XML

II. Document Type Definitions

III. Style Languages

IV. Supplemental Technologies

V. XML Applications

By the time you finish reading this book, you'll be ready to use XML to create compelling Web pages. The five parts are described below.

Part I: Introducing XML

Part I consists of Chapters 1 through 7. It begins with the history and theory behind XML and the goals XML is trying to achieve. It shows you how the different pieces of the XML equation fit together to enable you to create and deliver documents to readers. You'll see several compelling examples of XML applications that give you some idea of the wide applicability of XML, including Scalable Vector Graphics (SVG), the Resource Description Framework (RDF), the Mathematical Markup Language (MathML), the Extensible Forms Description Language (XFDL), and many others. Then you'll learn by example how to write XML documents with tags that you define so that they make sense for your document. You'll learn how to edit them in a text editor, attach style sheets to them, and load them into a Web browser such as Internet Explorer 5.0 or Mozilla. You'll even learn how you can write XML documents in languages other than English, even languages that are nothing like English, such as Chinese, Hebrew, and Russian.

Part II: Document Type Definitions

Part II (Chapters 8 through 13) focuses on document type definitions (DTDs). A DTD specifies which elements are and are not allowed in an XML document and the exact context and structure of those elements. A validating parser can read a document, compare it to its DTD, and report any mistakes it finds. DTDs enable document authors to ensure that their work meets any necessary criteria.

In Part II, you'll learn how to attach a DTD to a document, validate your documents against their DTDs, and write new DTDs that solve your own problems. You'll learn the syntax for declaring elements, attributes, entities, and notations. You'll learn how to use entity declarations and entity references to build both a document and its DTD from multiple, independent pieces. This allows you to make long, hard-to-follow documents much simpler by separating them into related modules and components. You'll learn how to integrate other forms of data like raw text and GIF image files in your XML document. And you'll learn how to use namespaces to mix together different XML vocabularies in one document.

Part III: Style Languages

Part III, consisting of Chapters 14 through 19, teaches you everything you need to know about style sheets. XML markup specifies only what's in a document. Unlike HTML, it does not say anything about what that content should look like. Information about an XML document's appearance when printed, viewed in a Web browser, or otherwise displayed is stored in a style sheet. Different style sheets can be used for the same document. You might, for instance, want to use one style sheet that specifies small fonts for printing, another one with larger fonts for on-screen presentation, and a third with absolutely humongous fonts to project the document on a wall at a seminar. You can change the appearance of an XML document by choosing a different style sheet without touching the document itself.

Part III describes in detail the two style sheet languages in broadest use today, Cascading Style Sheets (CSS) and the Extensible Stylesheet Language (XSL). CSS is a simple style-sheet language originally designed for use with HTML. It applies fixed style rules to the contents of particular elements. CSS exists in three versions: CSS Level 1, CSS Level 2, and CSS Level 3. CSS Level 1 provides basic information about fonts, color, positioning, and text properties and is reasonably well supported by current Web browsers for HTML and XML. CSS Level 2 is a more recent standard that adds support for aural style sheets, user interface styles, international and bidirectional text, and more. CSS Level 3 is the next generation of styles for both the Web and print. It adds many new features that are especially geared toward print media and non-Western languages, as well as filling in some of the gaps left by the earlier versions.

XSL, by contrast, is a more complicated and more powerful style language that can apply styles to the contents of elements as well as rearrange elements, add boiler-plate text, and transform documents in almost arbitrary ways. XSL is divided into two parts: a transformation language for converting XML trees to alternative trees, and a formatting language for specifying the appearance of the elements of an XML tree. Currently, many more tools support the transformation language than the for-matting language.

Part IV: Supplemental Technologies

Part IV consists of Chapters 20 through 25. It introduces some XML-based lan-guages and syntaxes that layer on top of basic XML to provide additional function-ality and features. XLinks provide multidirectional hypertext links that are far more powerful than the simple HTML <A> tag. XPointers introduce a new syntax you can attach to the end of URLs to link not only to particular documents but also to par-ticular parts of particular documents. XInclude enables you to build large XML doc-uments out of multiple smaller XML documents. XML Schemas provide a more complete validations language that includes data typing and range checking. RDF is an XML application used to embed metadata in XML and HTML documents. Metadata is information about a document, such as the author, date, and title of a work, rather than the work itself. Canonical XML is a standard form for XML docu-ments such that two documents whose canonical forms are byte-for-byte identical can be considered to be equal for most intents and purposes. All of these can be added to your own XML-based markup languages to extend their power and utility.

Part V: XML Applications

Part V, which consists of Chapters 26 to 34, demonstrates several practical uses of XML in different domains. XHTML is a reformulation of HTML 4.0 as valid XML. RDDL is an XHTML- and XLink-based language for documents containing meta-information placed at the end of namespace URLs. WML is an HTML-like language for serving Web content to cell phones, PDAs, pagers, and other memory, display, and bandwidth limited devices. Scalable Vector Graphics (SVG) is a standard XML format for drawings recommended by the World Wide Web Consortium (W3C). The Vector Markup Language (VML) is a Microsoft-proprietary XML application for vec-tor graphics used by Office 2000 and Internet Explorer 5.0. Microsoft's Channel Definition Format (CDF) is an XML-based markup language for defining channels that can push updated Web-site content to subscribers. Finally, a completely new application is developed for genealogical data to show you not just how to use XML tags and technologies, but why and when to choose them. Combining all of these different applications, you'll develop a good sense of how XML applications are designed, built, and used in the real world.

What You Need

XML is a platform-independent technology. Furthermore, most of the best software for working with XML is written in Java and can run on multiple platforms. Much of this is included on the CD in the back of the book or is freely available on the Internet. To make the best use of this book and XML, you need:

✦ A Web browser that supports XML such as Mozilla, Netscape 6.0, or Opera 5.0. Internet Explorer 5.0/5.5 also supports XML; but its built-in XML parser, MSXML, is out of date and more than a little buggy, so you'll need to upgrade it to MSXML 4.0 or later before you'll be able to use many of the techniques in this book.

✦ A Java 1.2 or later virtual machine. (Java 1.1 can do in a pinch.) You'll just need it to run programs written in Java. You won't need to write any programs to use this book.

How to Use This Book

This book is designed to be read more or less cover to cover. Each chapter builds on the material in the previous chapters in a fairly predictable fashion. Of course, you're always welcome to skim over material that's already familiar to you. I also hope you'll stop along the way to try out some of the examples and to write some XML documents of your own. It's important to learn not just by reading, but also by doing. Before you get started, I'd like to make a couple of notes about grammatical conventions used in this book.

Unlike HTML, XML is case sensitive. `<FATHER>` is not the same as `<Father>` or `<father>`. The `father` element is not the same as the `Father` element or the `FATHER` element. Unfortunately, case-sensitive markup languages have an annoying habit of conflicting with standard English usage. On rare occasion, this means that you may encounter sentences that don't begin with a capital letter. More commonly, you'll see capitalization used in the middle of a sentence where you wouldn't normally expect it. Please don't get too bothered by this. All XML and HTML code used in this book is placed in a `monospaced font`, so most of the time it will be obvious from the context what is meant.

I have also adopted the British convention of placing punctuation inside quote marks only when it belongs with the material quoted. Frankly, although I learned to write in the American educational system, I find the British system far more logical, especially when dealing with source code where the difference between a comma or a period and no punctuation at all can make the difference between perfectly correct and perfectly incorrect code.

What the Icons Mean

Throughout the book, I've used icons in the left margin to call your attention to points that are particularly important.

Note icons provide supplemental information about the subject at hand, but generally something that isn't quite the main idea. Notes are often used to elaborate on a detailed technical point.

Tip icons indicate a more efficient way of doing something, or a technique that may not be obvious.

CD-ROM icons tell you that software discussed in the book is available on the companion CD-ROM. This icon also tells you whether a longer example, discussed but not included in its entirety in the book, is on the CD-ROM.

Caution icons warn you of a common misconception or that a procedure doesn't always work quite like it's supposed to. The most common reason for a Caution icon in this book is to point out the difference between what a specification says should happen and what actually does.

The Cross-Reference icon refers you to other chapters that have more to say about a particular subject.

About the Companion CD-ROM

Glued to the inside of the back cover of this book is a CD-ROM that holds all numbered code listings from this book as well as some longer examples that couldn't fit into this book. The CD-ROM also contains the complete text of various XML specifications in XML and HTML. (Some of the specifications are also available in other formats like PDF.) Finally, you will find an assortment of useful software for working with XML documents. Many (though not all) of these programs are written in Java, so they'll run on any system with a reasonably compatible Java 1.2 or later virtual machine. Most of the programs that aren't written in Java are designed for Windows 95 or later, though there are also a few programs especially for Mac and Linux readers.

For a complete description of the CD-ROM contents, please read Appendix A. In addition, to get a complete description of what is on the CD-ROM, you can load the file index.html onto your Web browser. The files on the companion CD-ROM are not compressed, so you can access them directly from the CD.

Reach Out

Hungry Minds and I want your feedback. After you have had a chance to use this book, please take a moment to send us an e-mail at My2Cents@hungryminds.com. Be sure to include the title of this book in your e-mail. Please be honest in your evaluation. If you thought a particular chapter didn't tell you enough, let me know. Of course, I would prefer to receive comments like: "This is the best book I've ever read," "Thanks to this book, my Web site won Cool Site of the Year," or "Because I was reading this book on the beach, I met a stunning swimsuit model who thought I was the hottest thing on feet," but I'll take any comments I can get.

Feel free to send me specific questions regarding the material in this book. I'll do my best to help you out and answer your questions, but I can't guarantee a reply. The best way to reach me is by e-mail:

elharo@metalab.unc.edu

Also, I invite you to visit my Cafe con Leche Web site at http://www.ibiblio. org/xml/, which contains a lot of XML-related material and is updated almost daily. Despite my persistent efforts to make this book perfect, some errors have doubtless slipped by. Even more certainly, some of the material discussed here will change over time. I'll post any necessary updates and errata on my Web site at http://www.ibiblio.org/xml/books/bible/. Please let me know via e-mail of any errors that you find that aren't already listed.

Elliotte Rusty Harold

elharo@metalab.unc.edu

http://www.ibiblio.org/xml/

New York City, June 17, 2001

Acknowledgments

The folks at Hungry Minds have all been great. The acquisitions editors, John Osborn on the first edition and Grace Buechlein on this edition, deserve special thanks for arranging the unusual scheduling this book required to hit the moving target that XML presents, as well as for putting up with multiple missed deadlines. I'll do better on the third edition, guys, I promise! Sharon Nash shepherded this book through the development process. With poise and grace, she managed the constantly shifting outline and schedule that a book based on unstable specifications and software requires. Terri Varveris edited the first edition. Without her, there could never have been a second edition.

Steven Champeon brought his SGML experience to the book, and provided many insightful comments on the text. My brother Thomas Harold put his command of chemistry at my disposal when I was trying to grasp the Chemical Markup Language. Carroll Bellau provided me with the parts of my family tree, which you'll find in Chapter 20.

Piroz Mohseni and Heather Williamson served as technical editors on the first edition and corrected many of my errors. Ken Cox performed the same service for the second edition, and B. K. Delong stepped up to the plate for the this edition. Heather Williamson also wrote parts of the CSS, Namespaces, and VML chapters for the first edition. WandaJane Phillips wrote the original version of Chapter 33 on CDF that is adapted here. David Lerner, Shirq Eshed, and Reggie Dablo loaned me various uncommon hardware you'll see photographs of at various points in this book.

I also greatly appreciate all the comments, questions, and corrections sent in by readers of the first and second editions and *XML: Extensible Markup Language*. I hope that I've managed to address most of those comments in this book. They've definitely helped make the *XML Bible* a better book. Particular thanks are due to Michael Dyck, Alan Esenther, and Donald Lancon Jr. for their especially detailed comments.

The agenting talents of David and Sherry Rogelberg of the Studio B Literary Agency (http://www.studiob.com/) have made it possible for me to write more or less full-time. I recommend them highly to anyone thinking about writing computer books. And as always, thanks go to my wife, Beth, for her endless love and understanding.

Contents at a Glance

Contents

Chapter 6: Well-formedness **143**

Chapter 7: Foreign Languages and Non-Roman Text **175**

Part II: Document Type Definitions   209

Chapter 8: DTDs and Validity 211

Chapter 9: Element Declarations 227

Part III: Style Languages   351

Part IV: Supplemental Technologies   691

Introducing XML

An Eagle's Eye View of XML

This chapter introduces you to XML. It explains, in general terms, what XML is and how it is used. It shows you how the different pieces of the XML equation fit together, and how an XML document is created and delivered to readers.

What Is XML?

XML stands for Extensible Markup Language (often miscapitalized as *eXtensible Markup Language* to justify the acronym). XML is a set of rules for defining semantic tags that break a document into parts and identify the different parts of the document. It is a meta-markup language that defines a syntax in which other field-specific markup languages can be written.

XML is a meta-markup language

The first thing you need to understand about XML is that it isn't just another markup language like Hypertext Markup Language (HTML) or TeX. These languages define a fixed set of tags that describe a fixed number of elements. If the markup language you use doesn't contain the tag you need, you're out of luck. You can wait for the next version of the markup language, hoping that it includes the tag you need, but then you're really at the mercy of whatever the vendor chooses to include.

XML, however, is a meta-markup language. It's a language in which you make up the tags you need as you go along. These tags must be organized according to certain general principles, but they're quite flexible in their meaning. For instance, if you're working on genealogy and need to describe family names, personal names, dates, births, adoptions, deaths, burial sites, families, marriages, divorces, and so on, you can create tags for each of these. You don't have to force your data to fit into paragraphs, list items, table cells, and other very general categories.

The tags you create can be documented in a Document Type Definition (DTD). You'll learn more about DTDs in Part II of this book. For now, think of a *DTD* as a vocabulary and a syntax for certain kinds of documents. For example, the MOL.DTD in Peter Murray-Rust's Chemical Markup Language (CML) describes a vocabulary and a syntax for the molecular sciences: chemistry, crystallography, solid state physics, and the like. It includes tags for atoms, molecules, bonds, spectra, and so on. Many different people in the field can share this DTD. Other DTDs are available for other fields, and you can create your own.

XML defines the meta syntax that field-specific markup languages such as MusicML, MathML, and CML must follow. It specifies the rules for the low-level syntax, saying how markup is distinguished from content, how attributes are attached to elements, and so forth without saying what these tags, elements, and attributes are or what they mean. It specifies the patterns that elements must follow without giving the names of the elements. For instance, XML says that tags begin with a < and end with a >. However, XML does not tell you what names must go between the < and the >.

If an application understands this meta syntax, it at least partially understands all the languages built from this meta syntax. A browser does not need to know in advance each and every tag that might be used by thousands of different markup languages. Instead, it discovers the tags used by any given document as it reads the document or its DTD. The detailed instructions about how to display the content of these tags are provided in a separate style sheet that is attached to the document.

For example, consider the three-dimensional Schrödinger equation:

$$i\hbar\frac{\partial\psi(r,\,t)}{\partial t} = -\frac{\hbar^2}{2m}\nabla^2\psi(r,\,t) + V(r)\psi(r,\,t)$$

Scientific papers are full of equations like this, but scientists have been waiting eight years for the browser vendors to support the tags needed to write even the most basic math. Musicians are in a similar bind, because Netscape and Internet Explorer can't display sheet music.

XML means you don't have to wait for browser vendors to catch up with what you want to do. You can invent the tags you need, when you need them, and tell the browsers how to display these tags.

XML describes structure and semantics, not formatting

The second thing to understand about XML is that XML markup describes a document's structure and meaning. It does not describe the formatting of the elements on the page. Formatting can be added to a document with a style sheet. The document itself only contains tags that say what is in the document, not what the document looks like.

By contrast, HTML encompasses formatting, structural, and semantic markup. <B> is a formatting tag that makes its content bold. <STRONG> is a semantic tag that means its contents are especially important. <TD> is a structural tag that indicates that the contents are a cell in a table. In fact, some tags can have all three kinds of meaning. An <H1> tag can simultaneously mean 20-point Helvetica bold, a level 1 heading, and the title of the page.

For example, in HTML a song might be described using a definition title, definition data, an unordered list, and list items. But none of these elements actually have anything to do with music. The HTML might look something like this:

```
<dt>Hot Cop
<dd> by Jacques Morali, Henri Belolo, and Victor Willis
<ul>
<li> Jacques Morali
<li> PolyGram Records
<li> 6:20
<li> 1978
<li> Village People
</ul>
```

In XML the same data might be marked up like this:

```
<SONG>
   <TITLE>Hot Cop</TITLE>
   <COMPOSER>Jacques Morali</COMPOSER>
   <COMPOSER>Henri Belolo</COMPOSER>
   <COMPOSER>Victor Willis</COMPOSER>
   <PRODUCER>Jacques Morali</PRODUCER>
   <PUBLISHER>PolyGram Records</PUBLISHER>
   <LENGTH>6:20</LENGTH>
   <YEAR>1978</YEAR>
   <ARTIST>Village People</ARTIST>
</SONG>
```

Instead of generic tags such as <dt> and <li>, this example uses meaningful tags such as <SONG>, <TITLE>, <COMPOSER>, and <YEAR>. These tags didn't come from any preexisting standard or specification. I just made them up on the spot because they fit the information I was describing. Field-specific tagging has a number of advantages, not the least of which is that it's easier for a human to read the source code to determine what the author intended.

XML markup also makes it easier for nonhuman automated computer software to locate all of the songs in the document. A computer program reading HTML can't tell more than that an element is a dt. It cannot determine whether that dt represents a song title, a definition, or just some designer's favorite means of indenting text. In fact, a single document may well contain dt elements with all three meanings.

XML element names can be chosen such that they have extra meaning in additional contexts. For instance, they might be the field names of a database. XML is far more flexible and amenable to varied uses than HTML because a limited number of tags don't have to serve many different purposes. XML offers an infinite number of tags to fill an infinite number of needs.

Why Are Developers Excited About XML?

XML makes easy many Web-development tasks that are extremely difficult with HTML, and it makes tasks that are impossible with HTML, possible. Because XML is extensible, developers like it for many reasons. Which reasons most interest you depends on your individual needs; but once you learn XML, you're likely to discover that it's the solution to more than one problem you're already struggling with. This section investigates some of the generic uses of XML that excite developers. In Chapter 2, you'll see some of the specific applications that have already been developed with XML.

Design of field-specific markup languages

XML enables individual professions (e.g., music, chemistry, human resources) to develop their own field-specific markup languages. These languages make it possible for practitioners in the field to trade notes, data, and information without worrying about whether or not the person on the receiving end has the particular proprietary payware that was used to create the data. They can even send documents to people outside the profession with reasonable confidence that the people who receive them will at least be able to view the documents.

Furthermore, creating separate markup languages for different fields does not lead to bloatware or unnecessary complexity for those outside the profession. You may not be interested in electrical engineering diagrams, but electrical engineers are. You may not need to include sheet music in your Web pages, but composers do. XML lets the electrical engineers describe their circuits and the composers notate their scores, mostly without stepping on each other's toes. Neither field needs special support from the browser manufacturers or complicated plug-ins, as is true today.

Self-describing data

Much computer data from the last 40 years is lost, not because of natural disaster or decaying backup media (though those are problems, too — ones that XML doesn't solve), but simply because no one bothered to document how one actually reads the data media and formats. A Lotus 1-2-3 file on a 10-year-old 5.25-inch floppy disk may be irretrievable in most corporations today without a huge investment of time and resources. Data in a less-known binary format such as Lotus Jazz may be gone forever.

XML is, at a low level, an incredibly simple data format. It can be written in 100 percent pure ASCII text as well as in a few other well-defined formats. ASCII text is reasonably resistant to corruption. The removal of bytes or even large sequences of bytes does not noticeably corrupt the remaining text. This starkly contrasts with many other formats, such as compressed data or serialized Java objects, in which the corruption or loss of even a single byte can render the entire remainder of the file unreadable.

At a higher level, XML is self-describing. Suppose you're an information archaeologist in the twenty-third century and you encounter this chunk of XML code on an old floppy disk that has survived the ravages of time:

```
<PERSON ID="p1100" SEX="M">
  <NAME>
    <GIVEN>Judson</GIVEN>
    <SURNAME> McDaniel</SURNAME>
  </NAME>
  <BIRTH>
    <DATE>21 Feb 1834</DATE>  </BIRTH>
  <DEATH>
    <DATE>9 Dec 1905</DATE>  </DEATH>
</PERSON>
```

Even if you're not familiar with XML, assuming you speak a reasonable facsimile of twentieth-century English, you've got a pretty good idea that this fragment describes a man named Judson McDaniel, who was born on February 21, 1834 and died on December 9, 1905. In fact, even with gaps in, or corruption of the data, you could probably still extract most of this information. The same could not be said for a proprietary binary spreadsheet or word-processor format.

Furthermore, XML is very well documented. The World Wide Web Consortium (W3C)'s XML 1.0 specification and numerous paper books like this one tell you exactly how to read XML data. There are no secrets waiting to trip up the unwary.

Interchange of data among applications

Because XML is nonproprietary and easy to read and write, it's an excellent format for the interchange of data among different applications. XML is not encumbered by copyright, patent, trade secret, or any other sort of intellectual property restrictions. It has been designed to be extremely powerful, while at the same time being easy for both human beings and computer programs to read and write. Thus it's an obvious choice for exchange languages.

One such format is the Open Financial Exchange 2.0 (OFX, http://www.ofx.net/). OFX is designed to let personal finance programs such as Microsoft Money and Quicken trade data. The data can be sent back and forth between programs and exchanged with banks, brokerage houses, credit card companies, and the like.

 Cross-Reference   OFX is discussed in Chapter 2.

By choosing XML instead of a proprietary data format, you can use any tool that understands XML to work with your data. You can even use different tools for different purposes, one program to view and another to edit for instance. XML keeps you from getting locked into a particular program simply because that's what your data is already written in, or because that program's proprietary format is all your correspondent can accept.

For example, many publishers require submissions in Microsoft Word. This means that most authors have to use Word, even if they would rather use WordPerfect or Nisus Writer. This makes it extremely difficult for any other company to publish a competing word processor unless it can read and write Word files. To do so, a developer must reverse-engineer the undocumented Word file format, which requires a significant investment of limited time and resources. Most other word processors have a limited ability to read and write Word files, but they generally lose track of graphics, macros, styles, revision marks, and other important features. The problem is that Word's file format is undocumented, proprietary, and constantly changing. Word tends to end up winning by default, even when writers would prefer to use other, simpler programs. If a common word-processing format were developed in XML, writers could use the program of their choice.

Structured and integrated data

XML is ideal for large and complex documents because the data is structured. It not only lets you specify a vocabulary that defines the elements in the document; it also lets you specify the relations between elements. For example, if you're putting together a Web page of sales contacts, you can require that every contact have a phone number and an e-mail address. If you're inputting data for a database, you can make sure that no fields are missing. You can even provide default values to be used when no data is entered.

XML also provides a client-side include mechanism that integrates data from multiple sources and displays it as a single document. (In fact, it provides at least three different ways of doing this, which is a source of some confusion.) The data can even be rearranged on the fly. Parts of it can be shown or hidden depending on user actions. This is extremely useful when you're working with large information repositories like relational databases.

The Life of an XML Document

XML is, at its root, a document format. It is a series of rules about what XML documents look like. There are two levels of conformity to the XML standard. The first is *well-formedness* and the second is *validity*. Part I of this book shows you how to write well-formed documents. Part II shows you how to write valid documents.

HTML is a document format that is designed for use on the Internet and inside Web browsers. XML can certainly be used for that, as this book demonstrates. However, XML is far more broadly applicable. It can be used as a storage format for word processors, as a data interchange format for different programs, as a means of enforcing conformity with Intranet templates, and as a way to preserve data in a human-readable fashion.

However, like all data formats, XML needs programs and content before it's useful. Thus, it isn't enough to just understand XML itself. That's not much more than a specification for what data should look like. You also need to know how XML documents are created, written, and edited, how processors read XML documents and pass the information they read on to applications, and what these applications do with that data.

Editors

XML documents are most commonly created with an editor. This may be a basic text editor such as Notepad or vi that doesn't really understand XML at all. On the other hand, it may be a completely WYSIWYG (What You See Is What You Get) editor such as Adobe FrameMaker that insulates you almost completely from the details of the underlying XML format. Or it may be a structured editor such as Visual XML (`http://www.pierlou.com/visxml/`) that displays XML documents as trees. For the most part, the fancy editors aren't very useful yet, so this book concentrates on writing raw XML by hand in a text editor.

Other programs can also create XML documents. For example, later in this book, you'll see several XML documents whose data came straight out of a FileMaker database. In these cases, the data was first entered into the FileMaker database. Next, a FileMaker calculation field converted that data to XML. Finally, an AppleScript program extracted the data from the database and wrote it as an XML file. Similar processes can extract XML from MySQL, Oracle, and other databases by using Perl, Java, PHP, or any convenient language. In general, XML works extremely well with databases.

In any case, the editor or other program creates an XML document. More often than not, this document is an actual file on some computer's hard disk, but it doesn't absolutely have to be. For example, the document may be a record or a field in a database, or it may be a stream of bytes received from the network.

Parsers and processors

An XML parser (also known as an XML processor) reads the document and verifies that the XML it contains is well formed. It may also check that the document is valid, although this test is not required. The exact details of these tests are covered in Part II. If the document passes the tests, then the processor converts the document into a tree of elements.

Browsers and other applications

Finally, the parser passes the tree or individual nodes of the tree to the end application. If this application is a Web browser such as Mozilla, then the browser formats the data and shows it to the user. But other programs may also receive the data. For instance, a database might interpret an XML document as input data for new records; a MIDI program might see the document as a sequence of musical notes to play; a spreadsheet program might view the XML as a list of numbers and formulas. XML is extremely flexible and can be used for many different purposes.

The process summarized

To summarize, an XML document is created in an editor. The XML parser reads the document and converts it into a tree of elements. The parser passes the tree to the browser or other application that displays it. Figure 1-1 shows this process.

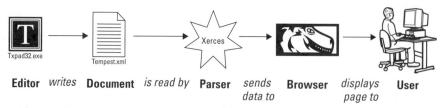

Figure 1-1: XML document life cycle

It's important to note that all of these pieces are independent of and decoupled from each other. The only thing that connects them is the XML document. You can change the editor program independently of the end application. In fact, you may not always know what the end application is. It may be an end-user reading your work; it may be a database sucking in data; or it may be something not yet invented. It may even be all of these. The document is independent of the programs that read and write it.

Note   HTML is also somewhat independent of the programs that read and write it, but it's really only suitable for browsing. Other uses, such as database input, are beyond its scope. For example, HTML does not provide a way to force an author to include certain required content. For instance, you can't say that every book must have an ISBN number. In XML, however, you can require this. You can even control the order in which particular elements appear (for example, that level 2 headers must always follow level 1 headers).

Related Technologies

XML doesn't operate in a vacuum. Using XML as more than a data format involves several related technologies and standards. These include:

✦ HTML for backward compatibility with legacy browsers

✦ The CSS and XSL style sheet languages to define the appearance of XML documents

✦ URLs (Uniform Resource Locaters) and URIs (Uniform Resource Identifiers) to specify the locations of XML documents

✦ XLinks to connect XML documents to each other

✦ The Unicode character set to encode the text of XML documents

HTML

Opera 4.0 and later, Internet Explorer 5.0 and later, Netscape 6.0 and Mozilla provide some (albeit incomplete) support for XML. However, it takes about two years from initial release before most users have upgraded to a particular browser version (in 2001, my wife still uses Netscape 1.1 on her Mac at work), so you're going to need to convert your XML content into classic HTML for some time to come.

Therefore, before you jump into XML, you should be completely comfortable with HTML. You don't need to be a hotshot graphical designer, but you should know how to link from one page to the next, how to include an image in a document, how to make text bold, and so forth. Since HTML is the most common output format of XML, the more familiar you are with HTML, the easier it will be to create the effects you want.

On the other hand, if you're accustomed to using tables or single-pixel GIFs to arrange objects on a page, or if you begin planning a Web site by sketching out its design in Photoshop, then you're going to have to unlearn some bad habits. As previously discussed, XML separates the content of a document from the appearance of the document. You develop the content first, then design a style sheet that formats the content. Separating content from presentation is an extremely effective technique that improves both the content and the appearance of the document. Among other things, it allows authors and designers to work more independently of each other. However, it does require a different way of thinking about the design of a Web site, and perhaps even the use of different project management techniques when multiple people are involved.

Cascading Style Sheets

Because XML allows arbitrary tags in a document, there is no way for the browser to know in advance how each element should be displayed. When you send a document to a user, you also need to send along a style sheet that tells the browser how to format the elements you've chosen. One kind of style sheet you can use is a Cascading Style Sheet.

CSS, initially invented for HTML, defines formatting properties such as font size, font family, font weight, paragraph indentation, paragraph alignment, and other styles that can be applied to particular elements. For example, CSS allows HTML documents to specify that all H1 elements should be formatted in 32-point, centered, Helvetica bold. Individual styles can be applied to most HTML elements that override the browser's defaults. Multiple style sheets can be applied to a single document, and multiple styles can be applied to a single element. The applied styles then cascade according to a particular set of rules.

Cross-Reference   CSS rules and properties are explored in more detail in Chapters 14, 15, 16, and 17.

It's easy to apply CSS rules to XML documents. You simply change the names of the tags to which you're applying the rules. Mozilla, Opera 4.0 and later, Netscape 6.0, and Internet Explorer 5.0 and later can display XML documents with associated CSS style sheets. They differ a little in how many CSS properties they support and how well they support them.

Extensible Stylesheet Language

The Extensible (or eXtensible) Stylesheet Language (XSL) is a more powerful style language designed specifically for XML documents. XSL style sheets are themselves well-formed XML documents. XSL is actually two different XML applications:

✦ XSL Transformations (XSLT)

✦ XSL Formatting Objects (XSL-FO)

Generally, an XSLT style sheet describes a transformation from an input XML document in one format to an output XML document in another format. That output format can be XSL-FO, but it can also be any other text format, XML or otherwise, such as HTML, plain text, or TeX.

An XSLT style sheet contains a series of rules that apply to particular patterns of XML elements. An XSLT processor reads an XML document and compares the elements it finds there to the patterns in the style sheet. When a pattern from the XSLT style sheet is recognized in the input XML document, the processor outputs a piece of text. Unlike cascading style sheets, this output text is not limited to the input text plus formatting information. The style sheet can add text that wasn't present in the original document or delete text that was.

CSS can only change the format of a particular element, and it can only do so on an element-wide basis. XSLT style sheets, on the other hand, can rearrange and reorder elements. They can hide some elements and display others. Furthermore, they can choose the style to use based not just on the element name, but also on the contents and attributes of the element, on the position of the element in the document relative to other elements, and on a variety of other criteria.

Cross-Reference   XSLT is explored in detail in Chapter 18.

XSL-FO is an XML application that describes the layout of a page. It specifies where particular text is placed on the page in relation to other items on the page. It also assigns styles such as italic or fonts such as Arial to individual items on the page. You can think of XSL-FO as a page description language such as PostScript (minus PostScript's built-in, Turing-complete programming language.)

Cross-Reference   XSL-FO is covered in Chapter 19.

Which style sheet language should you choose? CSS has the advantage of broader browser support. However, XSL is far more flexible and powerful, and better suited to XML documents. Furthermore, XML documents with XSLT style sheets can easily be converted to HTML documents with CSS style sheets. XSL-FO is a little past the bleeding edge, however; the specification is not yet finished. No browsers support it, and even third-party FO-to-PDF converters such as FOP don't support all of the current formatting object specification.

Which language you pick largely depends on your needs. If you want to serve clients XML files directly and have them use their CPU power to format the documents, then you really need to be using CSS (and even then, the clients had better have very up-to-date browsers). On the other hand, if you want to support older browsers, you're better off converting documents to HTML on the server using XSLT and sending the browsers pure HTML. For high-quality printing, you're better off with XSLT plus XSL-FO. One big advantage of XML is that it's quite easy to do all of this at the same time. You can change the style sheet and even the style sheet language you use without changing the XML documents that contain your content.

URLs and URIs

XML documents can live on the Web, just like HTML and other documents. When they do, they are referred to by Uniform Resource Locators (URLs), just like HTML files. For example, at the URL `http://www.hypermedic.com/style/xml/tempest.xml` you'll find the complete text of Shakespeare's *The Tempest* marked up in XML.

Although URLs are well understood and well supported, the XML specification uses Uniform Resource Identifiers (URIs) instead. URIs are a superset of URLs. A *URI* is a more general means of locating a resource; URIs focus a little more on the resource and a little less on the location. Furthermore, they aren't necessarily limited to resources on the Internet. For instance, the URI for this book is `uri:isbn:0764548190`. This doesn't refer to the specific copy you're holding in your hands. It refers to the almost-Platonic form of the *XML Bible, Gold Edition* shared by all individual copies.

In theory, a URI can find the closest copy of a mirrored document or locate a document that has been moved from one site to another. In practice, URIs are still an area of active research, and the only kinds of URIs that are actually supported by current software are URLs.

XLinks and XPointers

As long as XML documents are posted on the Internet, people will want to link them to each other. Standard HTML link tags can be used in XML documents, and HTML documents can link to XML documents. For example, this HTML link points to the aforementioned copy of *The Tempest* in XML:

```
<A HREF="http://www.hypermedic.com/style/xml/tempest.xml">
  The Tempest by Shakespeare
</A>
```

Note   Whether the browser can display this document if you follow the link, depends on just how well the browser handles XML files. Fourth generation and earlier browsers don't handle them very well.

However, XML lets you go further with XLinks for linking to documents and XPointers for addressing individual parts of a document.

XLinks enable any element to become a link, not just an A element. For example, in XML, the above link might be written like this:

```
<PLAY xlink:type="simple"
      xmlns:xlink="http://www.w3.org/1999/xlink"
  xlink:href="http://www.hypermedic.com/style/xml/tempest.xml">
  <TITLE>The Tempest</TITLE> by <AUTHOR>Shakespeare</AUTHOR>
</PLAY>
```

Furthermore, XLinks can be bidirectional, multidirectional, or even point to multiple mirror sites from which the nearest is selected. XLinks use normal URLs to identify the site they're linking to. As new URI schemes become available, XLinks will be able to use those, too.

Cross-Reference   XLinks are discussed in Chapter 20.

XPointers allow URLs to point not just to a particular document at a particular location, but to a particular part of a particular document. An XPointer can refer to a particular element of a document, to the first, the second, or the seventeenth such element, to the first element that's a child of a given element, and so on. XPointers provide extremely powerful connections between documents that do not require the targeted document to contain additional markup just so its individual pieces can be linked to from other documents.

Furthermore, unlike HTML anchors, XPointers don't just refer to a point in a document. They can point to ranges or spans. Thus, an XPointer might be used to select a particular part of a document, perhaps so that it can be copied or loaded into a program.

Cross-Reference   XPointers are discussed in Chapter 21.

The Unicode character set

The Web is international, yet most of the text you'll find on it is in English. XML is helping to change that. XML provides full support for the Unicode character set. This character set supports almost every character that is commonly used in every modern, non-fictional script on Earth.

Unfortunately, XML and Unicode alone are not enough to enable you to read and write Russian, Arabic, Chinese, and other languages written in non-Roman scripts. To read and write a language on your computer, you need three things.

1. A character set for the script the language is written in

2. A font for the character set

3. An operating system and application software that understand the character set

If you want to write in the script as well as read it, you'll also need an input method for the script. However, XML defines character references that allow you to use pure ASCII to encode characters not available in your native character set. This is sufficient for an occasional quote in Greek or Chinese, although you wouldn't want to rely on it to write a novel in another language.

Cross-Reference   Chapter 7 explores how international text is represented in computers, how XML understands text, and how you can use the software you have to read and write in languages other than English.

Putting the pieces together

XML defines the syntax for the tags you use to mark up a document. An XML document is marked up with XML tags. The default character set for XML documents is Unicode.

Among other things, an XML document may contain hypertext links to other documents and resources. These links are created according to the XLink specification. XLinks identify the documents that they're linking to with URIs (in theory) or URLs (in practice). An XLink may further specify the individual part of a document it's linking to. These parts are addressed via XPointers.

If an XML document is intended to be read by human beings — and not all XML documents are — then a style sheet provides instructions about how individual elements are formatted. The style sheet may be written in any of several style sheet languages. CSS and XSL are the two most popular style sheet languages, and the two best suited for XML.

Summary

In this chapter, you've seen a high-level overview of what XML is and what it can do for you. In particular, you learned that:

✦ XML is a meta-markup language that enables the creation of markup languages for particular documents and fields.

✦ XML tags describe the structure and semantics of a document's content, not the format of the content. The format is described in a separate style sheet.

✦ XML documents are created in an editor, read by a parser, and displayed by a browser.

✦ XML on the Web rests on the foundations provided by HTML, CSS, and URLs.

✦ Numerous supporting technologies layer on top of XML, including XSL style sheets, XLinks, and XPointers. These let you do more than you can accomplish with just CSS and URLs.

The next chapter shows you a number of XML applications that teach you some of the ways that XML is being used in the real world. Examples include vector graphics, music notation, mathematics, chemistry, human resources, webcasting, and more.

✦   ✦   ✦

XML Applications

◆   ◆   ◆   ◆

In This Chapter

XML applications

XML for XML

Behind-the-scene uses of XML

◆   ◆   ◆   ◆

T his chapter investigates many examples of XML applications: publicly standardized markup languages, XML applications that are used to extend and expand XML itself, and some behind-the-scene uses of XML. It is inspiring to see so many different uses to which XML has been put because it shows just how widely applicable XML is. Many more XML applications are being created or ported from other formats every day.

Don't try and understand every detail of every example in this chapter. Most of them are unimportant. The main purpose here is to give you a feel for both the many different uses to which XML is put and the many different ways XML documents can be designed. Once you've absorbed the flavor of XML in this chapter, you'll be better prepared to start working on your own XML applications in the next chapter.

Cross-Reference Part V covers some of the XML applications discussed in this chapter in more detail.

XML Applications

XML is a meta-markup language for designing domain-specific markup languages. Each specific XML-based markup language is called an *XML application*. This is not an application that uses XML, such as the Mozilla Web browser, the Gnumeric spreadsheet, or the XML Spy editor; rather, it is an application of XML to a specific field such as the Chemical Markup Language (CML) for chemistry or GedML for genealogy.

Each XML application has its own syntax and vocabulary. This syntax and vocabulary adheres to the fundamental rules of XML. This is much like human languages, each of which has its own vocabulary and grammar, while adhering to certain fundamental rules imposed by human anatomy and the structure of the brain.

XML is an extremely flexible format for text-based data. The reason XML was chosen as the foundation for the wildly different applications discussed in this chapter (aside from the hype factor) is that XML provides a sensible, well-documented format that's easy to read and write. By using this format for its data, a program can offload a great quantity of detailed processing to a few standard free tools and libraries. Furthermore, it's easy for such a program to layer additional levels of syntax and semantics on top of the basic structure XML provides.

Chemical Markup Language

Peter Murray-Rust's Chemical Markup Language (CML) may have been the first XML application. CML was originally developed as an SGML (Standard Generalized Markup Language) application, and gradually transitioned to XML as the XML standard developed. In its most simplistic form, CML is "HTML plus molecules," but it has applications far beyond the limited confines of the Web.

Molecular documents often contain thousands of different, very detailed objects. For example, a single medium-sized organic molecule may contain hundreds of atoms, each with at least one bond, and many with several bonds, to other atoms in the molecule. CML seeks to organize these complex chemical objects in a straightforward manner that can be understood, displayed, and searched by a computer. CML can be used for molecular structures and sequences, spectrographic analysis, crystallography, scientific publishing, chemical databases, and more. Its vocabulary includes molecules, atoms, bonds, crystals, formulas, sequences, symmetries, reactions, and other chemistry terms. For instance, Listing 2-1 is a basic CML document for water (H_2O):

Listing 2-1: The water molecule H_2O described in CML

```
<?xml version="1.0"?>
<CML>
  <MOL TITLE="Water">
    <ATOMS>
      <ARRAY BUILTIN="ELSYM">H O H</ARRAY>
    </ATOMS>
    <BONDS>
      <ARRAY BUILTIN="ATID1">1 2</ARRAY>
      <ARRAY BUILTIN="ATID2">2 3</ARRAY>
      <ARRAY BUILTIN="ORDER">1 1</ARRAY>
    </BONDS>
  </MOL>
</CML>
```

CML has several advantages over more traditional approaches to managing chemical data such as the Protein Data Bank (PDB) format or MDL Molfiles. First, CML is easier to search, especially for generic tools that don't understand all the intricacies of a particular format. It's also more easily integrated with Web sites, a crucial advantage at a time when Internet preprints and discussion groups are rapidly replacing traditional paper journals and scientific meetings. Finally, and most importantly, because the underlying XML is platform-independent, CML avoids the platform-dependency that has plagued the binary formats used by traditional chemical software and document formats. All chemists can read and write CML files, regardless of the hardware and software they've chosen to adopt.

Murray-Rust also created JUMBO, the first general-purpose XML browser. Figure 2-1 shows JUMBO displaying a CML file. JUMBO works by assigning each XML element to a Java class that knows how to render that element. To teach JUMBO how to display new elements, you simply write Java classes for those elements. JUMBO is distributed with classes for displaying the basic set of CML elements including molecules, atoms, and bonds, and is available at `http://www.xml-cml.org/`.

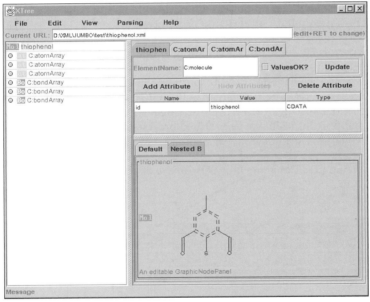

Figure 2-1: The JUMBO browser displaying a CML file

Mathematical Markup Language

Legend claims that Tim Berners-Lee invented the World Wide Web and HTML at CERN so that high-energy physicists could exchange papers and preprints. Personally, I've never believed that story. I grew up in physics, and while I've wandered back and forth between physics, applied math, astronomy, and computer science over the years, one thing the papers in all of these disciplines had in common was lots and lots of equations. Until now, 10 years after the Web was invented, there hasn't been any good way to include equations in Web pages.

There have been a few hacks — Java applets that parse a custom syntax, converters that turn LaTeX equations into GIF images, custom browsers that read TeX files — but none has produced high-quality results, and none has caught on with Web authors, even in scientific fields. XML is finally starting to change this.

The Mathematical Markup Language (MathML) is an XML application for mathematical equations. MathML is sufficiently expressive to handle most math — from grammar-school arithmetic through calculus and differential equations. It can handle many more advanced topics as well, although there are definite gaps in some of the more advanced and obscure notations used by certain subfields of mathematics. Although there are limits to MathML at the high end of pure mathematics and theoretical physics, it is eloquent enough to handle almost all educational, scientific, engineering, business, economics, and statistics needs. And MathML is likely to be expanded in the future, so even the purest of the pure mathematicians and the most theoretical of the theoretical physicists will be able to publish and do research on the Web. MathML completes the development of the Web into a serious tool for scientific research and communication (despite its long digression to make it suitable as a new medium for advertising brochures).

Netscape and Internet Explorer do not yet support MathML. However, plug-ins and Java applets that add this support are available, such as IBM's Tech Explorer (`http://www.software.ibm.com/techexplorer`) and Design Science's WebEQ (`http://www.webeq.com`). There's also an active effort to add MathML support to the open source Mozilla. The World Wide Web Consortium (W3C) has integrated some MathML support into Amaya, its test-bed browser. Figure 2-2 shows Amaya displaying the covariant form of Maxwell's equations written in MathML.

On the CD-ROM   Amaya is on the CD-ROM in the browsers/amaya directory.

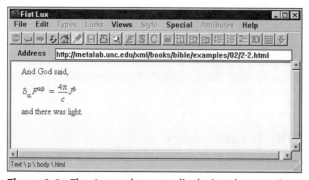

Figure 2-2: The Amaya browser displaying the covariant form of Maxwell's equations written in MathML

Listing 2-2 contains the document Amaya is displaying:

Listing 2-2: **Maxwell's equations in MathML**

```xml
<?xml version="1.0"?>
<html xmlns="http://www.w3.org/TR/REC-html40"
      xmlns:m="http://www.w3.org/TR/REC-MathML/"
>
<head>
<title>Fiat Lux</title>
<meta name="GENERATOR" content="amaya V1.3b" />
</head>
<body>

<p>And God said,</p>

<math>
  <m:mrow>
    <m:msub>
      <m:mi>&delta;</m:mi>
      <m:mi>&alpha;</m:mi>
    </m:msub>
    <m:msup>
      <m:mi>F</m:mi>
      <m:mi>&alpha;&beta;</m:mi>
    </m:msup>
    <m:mi></m:mi>
    <m:mo>=</m:mo>
    <m:mi></m:mi>
    <m:mfrac>
      <m:mrow>            <m:mn>4</m:mn>
        <m:mi>&pi;</m:mi>
      </m:mrow>
      <m:mi>c</m:mi>
    </m:mfrac>
    <m:mi></m:mi>
    <m:msup>
      <m:mi>J</m:mi>
      <m:mrow>
        <m:mi>&beta;</m:mi>
        <m:mo></m:mo>
      </m:mrow>
    </m:msup>
  </m:mrow>
</math>

<p>and there was light.</p>
</body>
</html>
```

Listing 2-2 is an example of a mixed HTML/XML page. The headers and paragraphs of text ("Fiat Lux," "Maxwell's Equations," "And God said," "and there was light") are given in classic HTML. The actual equations are written in MathML, an XML application.

In general, such mixed pages require special support from the browser, as is the case here, or perhaps plug-ins, ActiveX controls, or JavaScript programs that parse and display the embedded XML data. Ultimately, of course, you want a browser such as Mozilla that can parse and display pure XML files without an HTML intermediary.

Channel Definition Format

Microsoft's Channel Definition Format (CDF) is an XML application for defining channels. Web sites use channels to upload information to readers who subscribe to the site rather than waiting for them to come and get it. This is alternately called *webcasting* or *push*. CDF was first introduced in Internet Explorer 4.0.

A CDF document is an XML file, separate from, but linked to an HTML document on the site being pushed. The channel defined in the CDF document determines which pages are sent to the readers, how the pages are transported, and how often the pages are sent. Pages can either be pushed by sending notifications, or even whole Web sites, to subscribers, or pulled down by the readers at their convenience.

You can add CDF to your site without changing any of the existing content. You simply add a link to a CDF file on your home page. Then when a reader visits the page, the browser displays a dialog box asking if they want to subscribe to the channel. If the reader chooses to subscribe, then the browser downloads a copy of the CDF document describing the channel. The browser then combines the schedule information given in the CDF document with the user's own preferences to determine when to check back with the server for new content. This isn't true push because the client has to initiate the connection, but it still happens without an explicit request by the reader.

Listing 2-3 is a simple CDF document for IDG.net. It specifies that the channel contents should be loaded daily from `http://www.idg.net/` between August 11, 1999 and December 31, 2002. It also provides logos, icons, titles, and abstracts for the channel; and allows the channel to be used as a screensaver.

Listing 2-3: **A CDF Push Schedule for IDG.net**

```
<?xml version="1.0"?>
<CHANNEL HREF="http://www.idg.net/" BASE="http://www.idg.net">
  <TITLE>IDG Channel</TITLE>
  <ABSTRACT>
    IDG.net is the largest network of Web sites covering
    computer technology. IDG.net serves the needs of
    information technology decision-makers and personal
    computer users by providing local content, personalization,
    search, product information, news, and analysis.">
```

```
    </ABSTRACT>
    <USAGE VALUE="Channel"></USAGE>
    <LOGO HREF="/channel/images/start-channel-logo-80.gif"
          STYLE="IMAGE"/>
    <LOGO HREF="/channel/images/start-icon-32.gif" STYLE="ICON"/>
    <LOGO HREF="/channel/images/start-channel-logo-194.gif"
          STYLE="IMAGE-WIDE"/>
    <SCHEDULE STARTDATE="1999-08-11" ENDDATE="2002-12-31">
      <INTERVALTIME DAY="1"/> <LATESTTIME HOUR="2"/>
    </SCHEDULE>
    <ITEM HREF="http://www.idg.net/" PRECACHE="YES" LEVEL="0">
      <LOGO HREF="/channel/images/start-icon.gif" STYLE="ICON"/>
      <TITLE>IDG.net, the computer technology network</TITLE>
      <USAGE VALUE="Channel"></USAGE>
    </ITEM>
    <ITEM HREF="http://www.idg.net/" PRECACHE="YES" LEVEL="0">
      <USAGE VALUE="Screensaver"></USAGE>
    </ITEM>
    <USAGE VALUE="Channel"></USAGE>
  </CHANNEL>
```

Cross-Reference   CDF is covered in more detail in Chapter 33.

Classic literature

Jon Bosak has translated all of Shakespeare's plays into XML. XML markup in each document distinguishes between titles, subtitles, stage directions, speeches, lines, speakers, and more. A typical piece of a play is marked up like this extract from *Romeo and Juliet*.

```
<STAGEDIR>Enter ROMEO</STAGEDIR>

<SPEECH>
<SPEAKER>BENVOLIO</SPEAKER>
<LINE>See, where he comes: so please you, step aside;</LINE>
<LINE>I'll know his grievance, or be much denied.</LINE>
</SPEECH>

<SPEECH>
<SPEAKER>MONTAGUE</SPEAKER>
<LINE>I would thou wert so happy by thy stay,</LINE>
<LINE>To hear true shrift. Come, madam, let's away.</LINE>
</SPEECH>


<STAGEDIR>Exeunt MONTAGUE and LADY MONTAGUE</STAGEDIR>

<SPEECH>
<SPEAKER>BENVOLIO</SPEAKER>
```

```
<LINE>Good-morrow, cousin.</LINE>
</SPEECH>

<SPEECH>
<SPEAKER>ROMEO</SPEAKER>
<LINE>Is the day so young?</LINE>
</SPEECH>
```

On the CD-ROM   The complete set of Shakespeare's plays is on the CD-ROM in the examples/ shakespeare directory.

You may ask yourself what this offers over a book, or even a plain text file. To a human reader, the answer is not much. But to a computer doing textual analysis, it offers the opportunity to easily distinguish between the different elements into which the plays have been divided. For instance, it makes it quite simple for the computer to go through the text and extract all of Romeo's lines.

Furthermore, by altering the style sheet with which the document is formatted, an actor could easily print a version of the document in which all of his or her lines were formatted in bold face, and the lines immediately before and after were italicized. Anything else you might imagine that requires separating a play into the lines uttered by different speakers is much more easily accomplished with the XML-formatted versions than with the raw text.

Bosak has also marked up English translations of the old and new Testaments, the Koran, and the Book of Mormon in XML. For example, here's the first sura from the Koran:

```
<sura>
<bktlong>1. The Opening</bktlong>
<bktshort>1. The Opening</bktshort>
<v>In the name of Allah, the Beneficent, the Merciful.</v>
<v>All praise is due to Allah, the Lord of the Worlds.</v>
<v>The Beneficent, the Merciful.</v>
<v>Master of the Day of Judgment.</v>
<v>Thee do we serve and Thee do we beseech for help.</v>
<v>Keep us on the right path.</v>
<v>The path of those upon whom Thou hast bestowed favors. Not
(the path) of those upon whom Thy wrath is brought down, nor of
those who go astray.</v>
</sura>
```

The markup Bosak used for these religious texts is a little different than the ones he used for the plays of Shakespeare. For instance, it doesn't distinguish between speakers. Thus you couldn't use these particular XML documents to create a red-letter Bible, for example, although a different set of tags might allow you to do that. (A red-letter Bible prints words spoken by Jesus in red.) And because these files are in English rather than the original languages, they are not as useful for scholarly textual analysis. Still, time and resources permitting, those are exactly the sorts of things that XML would allow you to do if you desired. You'd simply need to invent a different vocabulary and syntax than the one Bosak used.

On the CD-ROM The XML-ized Bible, Koran, and Book of Mormon are all on the CD-ROM in the examples/religion directory.

Synchronized Multimedia Integration Language

The Synchronized Multimedia Integration Language (SMIL, pronounced "smile") is a W3C-recommended XML application for writing "TV-like" multimedia presentations for the Web. SMIL documents don't describe the actual multimedia content (that is the video and sound that are played). Instead, SMIL documents describe when and where particular video and audio clips are played.

For instance, a SMIL document might say that the browser should play the sound file beethoven9.mid, show the video file corange.mov, and display the HTML file clockwork.htm. Then, when it's done, it should play the video file 2001.mov, the audio file zarathustra.mid, and display the HTML file aclarke.htm. This eliminates the need to embed low bandwidth data such as text in high bandwidth data such as video just to combine them. Listing 2-4 is a simple SMIL file that does exactly this.

Listing 2-4: A SMIL film festival

```xml
<?xml version="1.0" encoding="ISO-8859-1"?>
<!DOCTYPE smil PUBLIC "-//W3C//DTD SMIL 1.0//EN"
  "http://www.w3.org/TR/REC-smil/SMIL10.dtd">
<smil>
  <body>
    <seq id="Kubrick">
      <audio src="beethoven9.mid"/>
      <video src="corange.mov"/>
      <text  src="clockwork.htm"/>
      <audio src="zarathustra.mid"/>
      <video src="2001.mov"/>
      <text  src="aclarke.htm"/>
    </seq>
  </body>
</smil>
```

Furthermore, as well as specifying the time sequencing of data, a SMIL document can position individual graphic elements on the display and attach links to media objects. For instance, at the same time as the movie and sound are playing, the text of the respective novels could be subtitling the presentation.

HTML+TIME

SMIL operates independently of the Web page. The streaming media pushed through SMIL has its own pane in the browser frame, but it doesn't really have any interaction with the content in the HTML on the rest of the page. For instance, SMIL only lets you time SMIL elements such as audio, video, and text. It doesn't let you add timing information to basic HTML elements such as P, LI, or IMG. Moreover, SMIL duplicates some aspects of HTML, such as how elements are positioned on the page.

Microsoft, along with Macromedia and Compaq, has proposed a semi-competitive XML application called Timed Interactive Multimedia Extensions for HTML (or HTML+TIME for short). HTML+TIME builds on SMIL to support timing for traditional HTML elements and features much closer integration with the HTML on the Web page. For example, HTML+TIME lets you write a countdown Web page such as Listing 2-5 that adds text to the page as time progresses.

Listing 2-5: **A countdown Web page using HTML+TIME**

```
<HTML>
  <HEAD>
  <STYLE>
      .time { behavior:url(#default#time); }
  </STYLE>
  </HEAD>
  <BODY>
  <P class="time" t:dur="1" t:begin="1">10</P>
  <P class="time" t:dur="1" t:begin="2">9</P>
  <P class="time" t:dur="1" t:begin="3">8</P>
  <P class="time" t:dur="1" t:begin="4">7</P>
  <P class="time" t:dur="1" t:begin="5">6</P>
  <P class="time" t:dur="1" t:begin="6">5</P>
  <P class="time" t:dur="1" t:begin="7">4</P>
  <P class="time" t:dur="1" t:begin="8">3</P>
  <P class="time" t:dur="1" t:begin="9">2</P>
  <P class="time" t:dur="1" t:begin="10">1</P>
  <P class="time" t:dur="1" t:begin="11">Blast Off!</P>
  </BODY>
</HTML>
```

This is useful for slide shows, timed quizzes, and the like. In HTML+TIME, the film festival example of Listing 2-4 looks like this:

```
<t:seq id="Kubrick">
  <t:audio src="beethoven9.mid"/>
  <t:video src="corange.mov"/>
  <t:textstream src="clockwork.htm"/>
  <t:audio src="zarathustra.mid"/>
  <t:video src="2001.mov"/>
  <t:textstream src="aclarke.htm"/>
</t:seq>
```

It's close to although not exactly the same as the SMIL version. The major difference is that the SMIL version is intended to be stored in separate files and rendered by special players such as RealPlayer, whereas the HTML+TIME version is supposed to be included in the Web page and rendered by the browser. Another key difference is that SMIL is being implemented by a plethora of browsers and other software such as RealPlayer, whereas HTML+TIME is only supported by Internet Explorer 5.0 and later.

There are some nice features and some good ideas in HTML+TIME. However, the W3C had already given its blessing to SMIL several months before Microsoft proposed HTML+TIME, and SMIL has a lot more momentum and support in the third-party, content-creator community. Consequently, there may be a lack of standards until these differences can be resolved.

Open Software Description

The Open Software Description (OSD) format is an XML application that was code-veloped by Marimba and Microsoft to update software automatically. *OSD* defines XML tags that describe software components. The description of a component includes the version of the component, its underlying structure, and its relationships to and dependencies on other components. This provides enough information to decide whether a user needs a particular update. If the update is needed, it can be automatically pushed to the user without requiring the usual manual download and installation. Listing 2-6 is an example of an OSD file for an update to the fictional product WhizzyWriter 1000:

Listing 2-6: An OSD file for an update to WhizzyWriter 1000

```xml
<?xml version="1.0"?>
<CHANNEL HREF="http://updates.whizzy.com/updateChannel.html">
  <TITLE>WhizzyWriter 1000 Update Channel</TITLE>
  <USAGE VALUE="SoftwareUpdate"/>
  <SOFTPKG HREF="http://updates.whizzy.com/updateChannel.html"
           NAME="{46181F7D-1C38-22A1-3329-00415C6A4D54}"
           VERSION="5,2,3,1"
           STYLE="MSAppLogo5"
           PRECACHE="yes">
    <TITLE>WhizzyWriter 1000</TITLE>
    <ABSTRACT>
      Abstract: WhizzyWriter 1000: now with tint control!
    </ABSTRACT>
    <IMPLEMENTATION>
     <CODEBASE HREF="http://updates.whizzy.com/tinupdate.exe"/>
    </IMPLEMENTATION>
  </SOFTPKG>
</CHANNEL>
```

Only information about the update is kept in the OSD file. The actual update files are stored in a separate CAB archive or executable and downloaded when needed. There is considerable controversy about whether or not this is actually a good thing. Many software companies, Microsoft not least among them, have a long history of releasing updates that cause more problems than they fix. Many users prefer to stay away from new software for awhile until other, more adventurous souls have given it a shakedown.

Cross-Reference OSD is discussed in Chapter 33.

Scalable Vector Graphics

Vector graphics are better than bitmaps for many kinds of pictures including flow charts, cartoons, assembly diagrams, blueprints, and more. However, the GIF and JPEG formats currently used on the Web are bitmap only; most traditional vector graphics formats, such as PDF, PostScript, and CGM, were designed with ink (or toner) on paper in mind rather than electrons on a screen. (This is one reason PDF on the Web is such an inferior replacement for HTML, despite PDF's much larger collection of graphics primitives.) A vector-graphics format for the Web should support a lot of features that don't make sense on paper, such as transparency, antialiasing, additive color, hypertext, animation, and metadata for search engines and audio renderers. None of these features are needed for the ink-on-paper world of PostScript and PDF. The W3C is developing a single, unified vector graphics format called Scalable Vector Graphics (SVG) to do for vector drawings what GIF, JPEG, and PNG do for bitmap images.

SVG is an XML application for describing two-dimensional graphics. It defines three basic types of graphics: shapes, images, and text. A shape is defined by its outline, also known as its path, and may have various strokes or fills. An image is a bitmap such as a GIF or a JPEG. Text is defined as a string of characters in a particular font, and may be attached to a path, so it's not restricted to horizontal lines of text as on this page. All three kinds of graphics can be positioned on the page at a particular location, rotated, scaled, skewed, and otherwise manipulated. Listing 2-7 shows an SVG document describing a pink triangle.

Listing 2-7: **A pink triangle in SVG**

```
<?xml version="1.0"?>
<svg xmlns="http://www.w3.org/2000/svg"
     width="12cm" height="8cm">
  <title>Example 2-7 from the XML Bible, 2nd Edition</title>
  <text x="10" y="15">This is SVG!</text>
  <polygon style="fill: pink" points="0,311 180,0 360,311" />
</svg>
```

Because SVG describes graphics rather than text — unlike most of the other XML applications discussed in this chapter — it requires special display software. All of the proposed style sheet languages assume that they're displaying fundamentally text-based data, and none of them can support the heavy graphics requirements of an application such as SVG. Adobe has published browser plug-ins that support SVG on Windows and the Mac (http://www.adobe.com/svg), and the XML Apache Project has published Batik (http://xml.apache.org/batik), an open source SVG viewer program written in Java that can that can display SVG documents and convert them to JPEGs. Figure 2-3 shows Listing 2-7 displayed by Batik. Native SVG support may be added to future browsers, especially to Mozilla since it's open source.

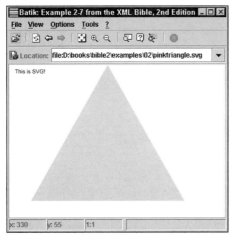

Figure 2-3: The pink triangle displayed in Batik

Batik is included on the CD-ROM in the directory utilities/batik. The most recent version can be downloaded from the Web at http://xml.apache.org/batik/.

For authoring, Adobe has published an Illustrator plug-in that enables Adobe Illustrator 8 to export drawings as SVG files. Adobe Illustrator 9 can save drawings as SVG files without any special plug-ins. Jasc Software (the Paint Shop Pro folks) are working on WebDraw, an SVG-native drawing program (http://www.jasc.com/webdraw.asp). Many other graphics software vendors have also announced plans to support SVG in future versions of their products.

Because SVG documents are pure text (like all XML documents), the SVG format is easy for programs to generate automatically; and it's easy for software to manipulate. In particular, you can combine SVG with DHTML (Dynamic HTML) and ECMAScript to make the pictures on a Web page animated and responsive to user action.

SVG is discussed in more detail in Chapter 31.

Vector Markup Language

Microsoft has developed its own XML application for vector graphics called the Vector Markup Language (VML). VML is supported by Internet Explorer 5.0/5.5 and Microsoft Office 2000. Listing 2-8 is an example of an HTML file with embedded VML that draws the pink triangle. Figure 2-4 shows this file displayed in Internet Explorer 5.5. However, VML is not nearly as ambitious a format as SVG, and leaves out many of the advanced features that SVG includes, such as clipping, masking, and compositing.

Listing 2-8: **The pink triangle in VML**

```
<html xmlns:vml="urn:schemas-microsoft-com:vml">
  <head>
    <title>
      A Pink Triangle, Listing 2-8 from the XML Bible
    </title>
    <object id="VMLRender"
      classid="CLSID:10072CEC-8CC1-11D1-986E-00A0C955B42E">
    </object>
    <style>
      vml\:* { behavior: url(#VMLRender) }
    </style>
  </head>
  <body>
    <div>

      <vml:polyline title="Example 2-8 from the XML Bible"
        style="width: 12cm; height: 8cm"
        stroked="false" fill="true" fillcolor="#FFCCCC"
        points="0,311 180,0 360,311">
        <vml:textbox>This is VML!</vml:textbox>
      </vml:polyline>

    </div>
  </body>
</html>
```

There's really no reason for there to be two separate, mutually incompatible vector graphics standards for the Web, and Microsoft will probably grudgingly support SVG in the end. Web artists would prefer to have a single standard, but having two is not unheard of (think GIF and JPEG). As long as the formats are documented and nonproprietary, it's not out of the question for Web browsers to support both. At the least, the underlying XML makes it easier for programmers to write converters that translate files from one format to the other.

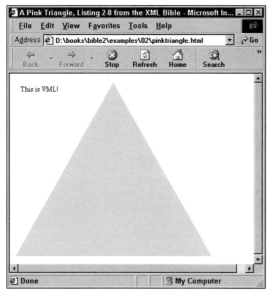

Figure 2-4: The pink triangle created with VML

 VML is discussed in more detail in Chapter 26.

MusicML

The Connection Factory has created an XML application for sheet music called MusicML. MusicML includes notes, beats, clefs, staffs, rows, rhythms, rests, beams, rows, chords, and more. Listing 2-9 shows the first bar from Beth Anderson's *Flute Swale* in MusicML.

Listing 2-9: **The first bar of Beth Anderson's *Flute Swale***

```
<?xml version="1.0"?>
<!DOCTYPE sheetmusic SYSTEM "music.dtd">
<sheetmusic>
 <musicrow size="one">

   <entrysegment>
     <entrypart cleff="bass" rhythm="fourquarter"
               position="one">
      <molkruis level="plus1" name="f" notetype="sharp"/>
      <molkruis level="plus1" name="c" notetype="sharp"/>
     </entrypart>
   </entrysegment>
```

Continued

Listing 2-9 *(continued)*

```
<segment>

 <subsegment position="one">
   <beam size="double">
     <note beat="sixteenth" name="a" level="zero"
           dynamics="mf"/>
     <note beat="sixteenth" name="b" level="zero"></note>
     <note beat="sixteenth" name="c" level="plus1"></note>
     <note beat="sixteenth" name="a" level="zero"></note>
   </beam>
   <beam size="single">
     <note beat="eighth" name="d" level="plus1"/>
     <note beat="eighth" name="c" level="plus1"/>
   </beam>
   <note beat="quarter" name="b" level="zero"/>
   <note beat="quarter" name="a" level="zero"/>
 </subsegment>

 </segment>

 </musicrow>
</sheetmusic>
```

The Connection Factory has also written a Java applet that can parse and display MusicML. Figure 2-5 shows the above example rendered by this applet. The applet has a few bugs (for instance the last note is missing), but overall it's a surprisingly good rendition.

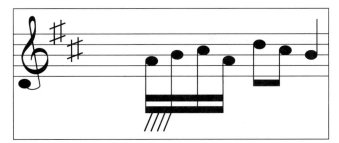

Figure 2-5: The first bar of Beth Anderson's *Flute Swale* in MusicML

MusicML isn't going to replace Finale or Nightingale anytime soon. And it really seems like more of a proof of concept than a polished product. MusicML has a lot of discrepancies that will drive musicians nuts (e.g., rhythm is misspelled, treble and bass clefs are reversed, segments should really be measures, and so forth). Nonetheless something like this is a reasonable output format for music notation programs that enable sheet music to be displayed on the Web. Furthermore, if the various notation programs all support MusicML or something like it, then it can be used as an interchange format to move data from one program to another, something composers desperately need to be able to do now.

Note Recordare has published MusicXML (`http://www.musicxml.org/xml.html`), an alternative XML application for music. This seems a lot more polished and likely to be adopted in the long run. However, as of mid–2001 there aren't yet any viewer programs or software to convert MusicXML into more established formats like Finale or Score.

VoiceXML

VoiceXML (`http://www.voicexml.org/`) is an XML application for the spoken word. In particular, it's intended for those annoying voice mail and automated phone response systems. ("If you found a boll weevil in Natural Goodness biscuit dough, please press one. If you found a cockroach in Natural Goodness biscuit dough, please press two. If you found an ant in Natural Goodness biscuit dough, please press 3. Otherwise, please stay on the line for the next available entomologist.")

VoiceXML enables the same data that's used on a Web site to be served up via telephone. It's particularly useful for information that's created by combining small nuggets of data, such as stock prices, sports scores, weather reports, airline schedules, and test results. From within the U.S., you can try out some VoiceXML-enabled services by calling 1-800-4-BVOCAL, 1-800-44-ANITA, or 1-800-555-TELL.

A small VoiceXML file for a shampoo manufacturer's automated phone response system might look something like Listing 2-10.

Listing 2-10: **A VoiceXML document**

```
<?xml version="1.0"?>
<vxml version="1.0">

  <form>
    <block>
      <prompt bargein="false">
        Welcome to TIC hair products division,
        home of Wonder Shampoo.
      </prompt>
      <goto next="#color_choice"/>
    </block>
  </form>

  <menu id="color_choice">
    <property name="inputmodes" value="dtmf"/>
```

Continued

Listing 2-10 *(continued)*

```
      <prompt>
        If Wonder Shampoo turned your hair green, please press 1.
        If Wonder Shampoo turned your hair purple, please press 2.
        If Wonder Shampoo made you bald, please press 3.
      </prompt>
      <choice dtmf="1" next="#green.vxml"/>
      <choice dtmf="2" next="#purple.vxml"/>
      <choice dtmf="3" next="#bald.vxml"/>
  </menu>

  <form id="green">
    <block>
      <prompt>
        If Wonder Shampoo turned your hair green and you wish
        to return it to its natural color, simply shampoo
        seven times with three parts soap, seven parts water,
        four parts kerosene, and two parts iguana bile.
      </prompt>
      <goto next="#bye"/>
    </block>
  </form>

  <form id="purple">
    <block>
      <prompt>
        If Wonder Shampoo turned your hair purple and you wish
        to return it to its natural color, please walk
        widdershins around your local cemetery
        three times while chanting "Surrender Dorothy."
      </prompt>
      <goto next="#bye"/>
    </block>
  </form>

  <form id="bald">
    <block>
      <prompt>
        If you went bald as a result of using Wonder Shampoo,
        please purchase and apply a three-month supply
        of our Magic Hair Growth Formula. Please do not
        consult an attorney as doing so would violate the
        license agreement printed on the inside fold of
        the Wonder Shampoo box in 3-point type, which you
        agreed to by opening the box.
      </prompt>
      <goto next="#bye"/>
    </block>
  </form>

  <form id="bye">
    <block>
```

```
      <prompt>
       Thank you for visiting TIC Corp. Goodbye.
      </prompt>
      <disconnect/>
    </block>
  </form>

</vxml>
```

I can't show you a screen shot of this example, because it's not intended to be shown in a Web browser. Instead, you would listen to it on a telephone.

Open Financial Exchange

As noted in the last chapter, the Open Financial Exchange 2.0 (OFX) is an XML application for describing consumer-level financial transactions. Personal finance products such as Microsoft Money or Quicken use OFX to provide online banking, stock trading, and other electronic business. Banks, stock brokers, and mutual funds use OFX to talk to their customer's computers. Because OFX is fully documented and nonproprietary (unlike the binary formats of Money, Quicken, and other programs), it's easy for programmers to write the code to understand OFX..

Listing 2-11 is an OFX document that tells MegaBank to transfer $10,000 from savings account #777777 to checking account #3333333. The account owner has the social security number 078-05-1120 and authenticates the transaction with the password "secret" (not an especially good choice). I can't show you a screen shot of this document because it's not intended for humans to read. It's just a convenient way for different computer programs on different platforms to exchange data.

Listing 2-11: **An OFX document requesting a $10,000 transfer from savings to checking**

```
<?xml version="1.0"?>
<?OFX OFXHEADER="200" VERSION="200" SECURITY="NONE"
      OLDFILEUID="NONE" NEWFILEUID="NONE"?>
<OFX>
  <SIGNONMSGSRQV1>
    <SONRQ>
      <DTCLIENT>20010106113254</DTCLIENT>
      <USERID>078-05-1120</USERID>
      <USERPASS>secret</USERPASS>
      <LANGUAGE>ENG</LANGUAGE>
      <FI>
        <ORG>MegaBank</ORG>
        <FID>666</FID>
```

Continued

Listing 2-11 *(continued)*

```
        </FI>
        <APPID>SuperFinance</APPID>
        <APPVER>1000</APPVER>
      </SONRQ>
    </SIGNONMSGSRQV1>
    <BANKMSGSRQV1>
      <INTRATRNRQ>
        <TRNUID>31415</TRNUID>
        <INTRARQ>
          <XFERINFO>
            <BANKACCTFROM>
              <BANKID>123456789</BANKID>
              <ACCTID>777777</ACCTID>
              <ACCTTYPE>SAVINGS</ACCTTYPE>
            </BANKACCTFROM>
            <BANKACCTTO>
              <BANKID>123456789</BANKID>
              <ACCTID>3333333</ACCTID>
              <ACCTTYPE>CHECKING</ACCTTYPE>
            </BANKACCTTO>
            <TRNAMT>10000.00</TRNAMT>
          </XFERINFO>
        </INTRARQ>
      </INTRATRNRQ>
    </BANKMSGSRQV1>
  </OFX>
```

Any program that understands OFX can exchange information with any other program that understands OFX. For instance, if a bank wants to deliver statements to customers electronically, it only has to write one program to encode the statements in the OFX format rather than several programs to encode the statement in Quicken's format, Money's format, Managing Your Money's format, and so forth. Looked at from the other direction, the Quicken developers can enable electronic banking for all banks by using OFX instead of writing different code for each separate bank's system.

The more programs that use a given format, the greater the savings in development cost and effort. For example, six programs reading and writing their own and each other's proprietary formats require 30 different converters. Six programs reading and writing the same OFX format require only six converters. Effort is reduced to $O(n)$ from $O(n^2)$. Figure 2-6 depicts six programs reading and writing their own and each other's proprietary binary formats. Figure 2-7 depicts the same six programs reading and writing a single, open OFX format. Every arrow represents a converter that has to trade files and data between programs. The XML-based exchange is much simpler and cleaner than the binary-format exchange.

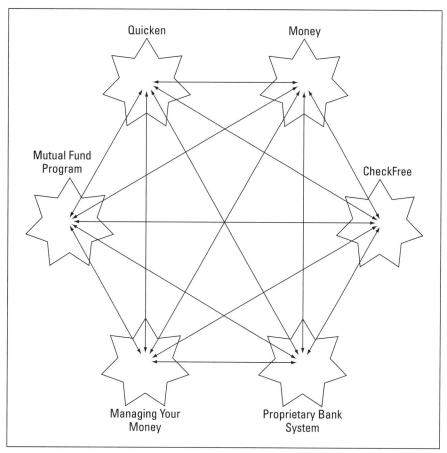

Figure 2-6: Six different programs reading and writing their own and each other's formats

Extensible Forms Description Language

Today I went to my local bookstore and bought a copy of Armistead Maupin's novel *Sure of You*. I paid for that purchase with a credit card, and when I did so, I signed a piece of paper agreeing to pay the credit card company $14.07 when billed. Eventually they will send me a bill for that purchase, and I'll pay it. If I refuse to pay it, then the credit card company can take me to court to collect, and they can use my signature on that piece of paper to prove to the court that on October 15, 1998 I really did agree to pay them $14.07.

The same day I also ordered Anne Rice's *The Vampire Armand* from the online bookstore amazon.com. Amazon charged me $16.17 plus $3.95 shipping and handling, and again I paid for that purchase with a credit card. But the difference is that Amazon never got a signature on a piece of paper from me. Eventually the credit card company will send me a bill for that purchase, and I'll pay it. But if I refuse to pay the bill, they don't have a piece of paper with my signature on it showing that I agreed to pay $20.12 on October 15, 1998. If I claim that I never made the purchase, the credit card company will bill the charges back to Amazon. Before Amazon or any other online or phone-order merchant is allowed to accept credit card purchases without a signature in ink on paper, the merchant has to agree that it will be responsible for all disputed transactions.

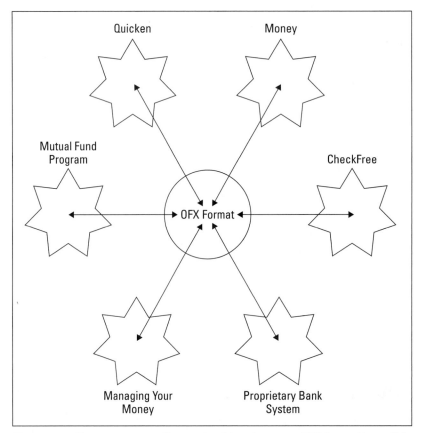

Figure 2-7: Six programs reading and writing the same OFX formatExtensible Forms Description Language

Exact numbers are hard to come by and, of course, vary from merchant to merchant, but probably around 2 percent of Internet transactions are billed back to the originating merchant because of credit card fraud or disputes. This is a *huge* amount, especially in an arena where margins are often negative to start with. Consumer businesses such as Amazon simply accept this as a cost of doing business on the Internet and work it into their price structure, but obviously this isn't acceptable for six-figure business-to-business transactions. Nobody wants to send out $200,000 of masonry supplies only to have the purchaser claim they never made the order. Before business-to-business transactions can move onto the Internet, a method needs to be developed that can verify that an order was in fact made by a particular person and that this person is who he or she claims to be. Furthermore, this has to be enforceable in court. (It's a sad fact of American business that many companies won't do business with anyone they can't sue.)

Part of the solution to the problem is digital signatures—the electronic equivalent of ink on paper. To digitally sign a document, you calculate a hash code for the document using a known algorithm, encrypt the hash code with your private key, and attach the encrypted hash code to the document. Correspondents can decrypt the hash code using your public key and verify that it matches the document. However, they can't sign documents on your behalf because they don't have your private key. The exact protocol followed is a little more complex in practice, but the bottom line is that your private key is merged with the data you're signing in a verifiable fashion. No one who doesn't know your private key can sign the document.

The scheme isn't foolproof—it's vulnerable to your private key being stolen, for example—but it's probably as hard to forge a digital signature as it is to forge a real ink-on-paper signature. However, there are also a number of less obvious attacks on digital signature protocols. One of the most important is changing the data that's signed. Changing the data that's signed should invalidate the signature, but it doesn't if the changed data wasn't included in the first place. For example, when you submit an HTML form, the only data the browser sends to the server are the values that you fill into the form's fields and the names of the fields. The rest of the HTML markup is not included. You may agree to pay $1500 for a new 1.8GHz Pentium IV PC, but the only thing sent on the form is the $1500. Signing this number signifies what you're paying, but not what you're paying for. The merchant can then send you two gross of flushometers and claim that's what you bought for your $1500. Obviously, if digital signatures are to be useful, all details of the transaction must be included. Nothing can be omitted.

The problem gets worse if you have to deal with the United States government. Government regulations for purchase orders and requisitions often spell out the contents of forms in minute detail, right down to the font face and type size. Failure to adhere to the exact specifications can lead to your invoice for $20,000,000 worth of depleted uranium artillery shells being rejected. Therefore, you not only need to establish exactly what was agreed to, you also need to establish that you met all legal requirements for the form. HTML's forms just aren't sophisticated enough to handle these needs.

XML, however, can. It is almost always possible to use XML to develop a markup language with the right combination of power and rigor to meet your needs, and this case is no exception. In particular, PureEdge has proposed an XML application called the Extensible Forms Description Language (XFDL, `http://www.pureedge.com/resources/xfdl.htm`) for forms with extremely tight legal requirements that are to be signed with digital signatures. XFDL further offers the option to do simple mathematics in the form, for instance, to automatically fill in the sales tax and shipping and handling charges, and then total the price.

Listing 2-12 is a simple XFDL document that asks the user to input the coefficients of a quadratic equation (that is, an equation in the form $\mathbf{a}x^2 + \mathbf{b}x + \mathbf{c} = 0$) and solves for the two roots of the equation. Regular Web browsers can't handle forms like these. Therefore, you have to use a special program that understands how to read them. Right now that means PureEdge's Internet Forms Viewer. Figure 2-8 shows this program displaying the quadratic equation form in Listing 2-12.

Listing 2-12: **An XFDL form that solves quadratic equations**

```
<?xml version="1.0"?>
<XFDL version="4.1.0">
  <page sid="QuadraticEquationSolver">
    <label>Quadratic Equation Form</label>
    <field sid="a">
      <label>Enter a: (coefficient of x^2)</label>
      <value>1</value>
    </field>
    <field sid="b">
      <label>Enter b: (coefficient of x^1)</label>
      <value>0</value>
    </field>
    <field sid="c">
      <label>Enter c: (coefficient of x^0)</label>
      <value>-1</value>
    </field>
    <field sid="x1">
      <label>Root 1</label>
      <editstate>readonly</editstate>
      <value content="compute">
        <compute>
          (-b.value
           + sqrt(b.value*b.value - "4"*a.value*c.value))
          /"2"*a.value
        </compute>
      </value>
    </field>
    <field sid="x2">
      <label>Root 2</label>
      <editstate>readonly</editstate>
        <compute>
          (-b.value
           - sqrt(b.value*b.value - "4"*a.value*c.value))
          /"2"*a.value
        </compute>
    </field>
  </page>
</XFDL>
```

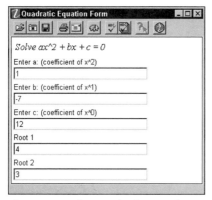

Figure 2-8: The quadratic equation form in the Internet Forms Viewer

PureEdge has submitted XFDL to the W3C, but it's really overkill for Web browsers, and probably won't be adopted there. The real benefit of XFDL, if it becomes widely adopted, is in business-to-business and business-to-government transactions. XFDL can become a key part of electronic commerce, which is not to say that it *will* become a key part of electronic commerce. It's still early, and there are other players in this space.

HR-XML

The HR-XML Consortium (http://www.hr-xml.org/) is a nonprofit organization with over 100 different members from various branches of the human resources industry including recruiters, temp agencies, and large employers. It's trying to develop standard XML applications that describe resumes, available jobs, and candidates. Listing 2-13 shows a job listing encoded in an HR-XML 1.0 document. This application defines elements matching the parts of a typical classified want ad such as companies, positions, skills, contact information, compensation, experience, and more.

Listing 2-13: **A job listing in HR-XML**

```
<?xml version="1.0"?>
<!DOCTYPE JobPositionPosting SYSTEM
"http://www.hr-xml.org/schemas/dtd/recruiting/JobPositionPosting-v1.0.dtd">

<JobPositionPosting status="inactive">
```

Continued

Listing 2-13 *(continued)*

```
<HiringOrg>
  <HiringOrgName>IDG Books</HiringOrgName>
  <WebSite>http://www.idgbooks.com</WebSite>
  <Industry><SummaryText>Publishing</SummaryText></Industry>
  <Contact>
    <PersonName>
      <GivenName>Dee</GivenName>
      <FamilyName>Harris</FamilyName>
    </PersonName>
    <PositionTitle>HR Manager</PositionTitle>
    <PostalAddress>
      <CountryCode>US</CountryCode>
      <PostalCode>94404</PostalCode>
      <Region>CA</Region>
      <Municipality>Foster City</Municipality>
      <DeliveryAddress>
        <AddressLine>919 E. Hillsdale Blvd.</AddressLine>
        <AddressLine>Suite 400</AddressLine>
      </DeliveryAddress>
    </PostalAddress>
    <VoiceNumber>
      <AreaCode>650</AreaCode>
      <TelNumber>655-3000</TelNumber>
    </VoiceNumber>
  </Contact>
</HiringOrg>

<JobPositionInformation>
  <JobPositionTitle>Web Development Manager</JobPositionTitle>
  <JobPositionDescription>
    <JobPositionPurpose>
      This position is responsible for the technical and
      production functions of the Online group as well as
      strategizing and implementing technology to improve
      the IDG Books Web sites. Skills must include
      C/C++, HTML, SQL, JavaScript, Windows NT 4, mod-
      perl, CGI, TCP/IP, Netscape servers, and Apache
      server.
    </JobPositionPurpose>
    <JobPositionLocation>
      <LocationSummary>
        <Municipality>Foster City</Municipality>
        <Region>CA</Region>
      </LocationSummary>
    </JobPositionLocation>
    <Classification>
      <DirectHireOrContract>
        <DirectHire/>
```

```
          </DirectHireOrContract>
          <Duration>
            <Regular/>
          </Duration>
        </Classification>
        <CompensationDescription>
          <Pay>
            <SalaryAnnual currency="USD">$60,000</SalaryAnnual>
          </Pay>
        </CompensationDescription>
      </JobPositionDescription>
      <JobPositionRequirements>
        <QualificationsRequired>
          <Qualification type="skill">Perl</Qualification>
          <Qualification type="skill">C</Qualification>
          <Qualification type="skill">C++</Qualification>
          <Qualification type="skill">HTML</Qualification>
          <Qualification type="skill">SQL</Qualification>
          <Qualification type="skill">JavaScript</Qualification>
          <Qualification type="skill">Windows NT4</Qualification>
          <Qualification type="skill">mod-perl</Qualification>
          <Qualification type="skill">CGI</Qualification>
          <Qualification type="skill">TCP/IP</Qualification>
          <Qualification type="skill">Netscape Server</Qualification>
          <Qualification type="skill">Apache Server</Qualification>
        </QualificationsRequired>
        <SummaryText>
          Must have excellent communication skills,
          project management, the ability to communicate
          technical solutions to non-technical people and
          management experience.
        </SummaryText>
      </JobPositionRequirements>
    </JobPositionInformation>

    <HowToApply distribute="external">
      <SummaryText>
        Qualified candidates should submit their resumes
        via e-mail in pure ASCII (no attachments) to Dee
        Harris at <Link mailTo="cajobs@idgbooks.com">
        cajobs@idgbooks.com</Link>.
      </SummaryText>
    </HowToApply>

    <EEOStatement>
      IDG Books is an equal opportunity employer.
    </EEOStatement>

</JobPositionPosting>
```

Although you could certainly define a style sheet for HR-XML documents, and use it to place job listings on Web pages, that's not its main purpose. Instead HR-XML is trying to automate the exchange of job information between companies, applicants, recruiters, job boards, and other interested parties. There are hundreds of job boards on the Internet today, as well as numerous Usenet newsgroups and mailing lists. It's impossible for one individual to search them all, and it's hard for a computer to search them all because they all use different formats for salaries, locations, benefits, and the like.

But if many sites adopt HR-XML, then it becomes relatively easy for a job seeker to search with criteria like "all the jobs for Java programmers in New York City paying more than $100,000 a year with full health benefits." The IRS could enter a search for all full-time, onsite, freelance openings so that it would know which companies to go after for failure to withhold tax and pay unemployment insurance.

In practice, these searches would likely be mediated through an HTML form just like current Web searches. The main difference is that such a search would return far more useful results because it can use the structure in the data and semantics of the markup rather than relying on imprecise English text.

Resource Description Framework

XML adds structure to documents. The Resource Description Framework (RDF) is an XML application that adds semantics. RDF can be used to specify anything from the author and abstract of a Web page to the version and dependencies of a software package to the director, screenwriter, and actors in a movie. What links all of these uses is that what's being encoded in RDF is not the data itself (the Web page, the software, the movie) but information about the data. This data about data is called *meta-data*, and is RDF's *raison d'être*.

An RDF vocabulary defines a set of elements and their permitted content that's appropriate for meta-data in a given domain. RDF enables communities of interest to standardize their vocabularies and share those vocabularies with others who may extend them. For example, the Dublin Core is a vocabulary specifically designed for meta-data about Web pages. Educom's Instructional Metadata System (IMS) builds on the Dublin Core by adding additional elements that are useful when describing school-related content such as learning level, educational objectives, and price.

Of course, although RDF can be used for print-publishing systems, videostore catalogs, automated software updates, and much more, it's likely to be adopted first for embedding meta-data in Web pages. RDF has the potential to synchronize the current hodge-podge of <META> tags used for site maps, content rating, automated indexing, and digital libraries into a unified collection that all of these tools understand. Once RDF meta-data becomes a standard part of Web pages, search engines will be able to return more focused, useful results. Intelligent agents can more easily traverse the Web to conduct business for you. The Web can evolve from its current state as an unordered sea of information to a structured, searchable, under-standable data library.

As the name implies, RDF describes *resources*. A resource is anything that can be addressed with a URI. The description of a resource is composed of a number of properties. Each property has a type and a value. For example, <dc:Format> text/html</dc:Format> has the type dc:Format and the value text/html. Values may be text strings, numbers, dates, and so forth, or they may be other resources. These other resources can have their own descriptions in RDF. For example, the code in Listing 2-14 uses the Dublin Core vocabulary to describe the Cafe con Leche Web site.

Listing 2-14: An RDF description of the Cafe con Leche home page using the Dublin Core vocabulary

```
<rdf:RDF
  xmlns:rdf="http://www.w3.org/1999/02/22-rdf-syntax-ns#"
  xmlns:dc="http://purl.org/dc/">

  <rdf:Description about="http://www.ibilio.org/xml/">
    <dc:Creator>Elliotte Rusty Harold</dc:Creator>
    <dc:Language>en-US</dc:Language>
    <dc:Format>text/html</dc:Format><dc:Date>2000-08-19</dc:date>
    <dc:Type>text</dc:Type>
    <dc:Title>Cafe con Leche</dc:Title>
  </rdf:Description>

</rdf:RDF>
```

RDF will be used for Platform for Privacy Preferences (P3P) and possibly for future versions of the Platform for Internet Content Selection (PICS), as well as for many other areas where meta-data is needed to describe Web pages and other kinds of content.

Cross-Reference   RDF is covered in more detail in Chapter 24.

XML for XML

XML is an extremely general-purpose format for text data. Some of the applications it's used for are further refinements of XML itself. These include the XSL style sheet language, the XLink hypertext language, and the XML Schema data description language.

XSL

XSL, the Extensible Stylesheet Language, is actually two XML applications. The first application is a vocabulary for transforming XML documents called XSL Transformations (XSLT). XSLT includes XML elements that represent nodes, patterns, templates, and other items needed for transforming XML documents from one markup vocabulary to another (or even to the same vocabulary with different data).

The second application is an XML vocabulary for formatting the transformed XML document produced by the first part. This application is called XSL Formatting Objects (XSL-FO). XSL-FO provides elements that describe the layout of a page including pagination, blocks, characters, lists, graphics, boxes, fonts, and more. A typical XSLT style sheet that transforms an input document into XSL formatting objects is shown in Listing 2-15:

Listing 2-15: **An XSL style sheet**

```
<?xml version="1.0"?>
<xsl:stylesheet version="1.0"
  xmlns:xsl="http://www.w3.org/1999/XSL/Transform"
  xmlns:fo="http://www.w3.org/1999/XSL/Format">

<xsl:output indent="yes"/>

<xsl:template match="/">
  <fo:root xmlns:fo="http://www.w3.org/1999/XSL/Format">

    <fo:layout-master-set>
      <fo:simple-page-master master-name="only">
        <fo:region-body/>
      </fo:simple-page-master>
    </fo:layout-master-set>

    <fo:page-sequence master-name="only">

      <fo:flow>
        <xsl:apply-templates select="//ATOM"/>
      </fo:flow>

    </fo:page-sequence>

  </fo:root>
</xsl:template>

<xsl:template match="ATOM">
  <fo:block font-size="20pt" font-family="serif"
            line-height="30pt">
```

```
        <xsl:value-of select="NAME"/>
      </fo:block>
    </xsl:template>

  </xsl:stylesheet>
```

Cross-Reference Chapters 18 and 19 explore XSL in great detail.

XLinks

XML makes possible a new, more general kind of link called an XLink. XLinks accomplish everything possible with HTML's URL-based hyperlinks and anchors. However, any element can become a link, not just A elements. For instance a footnote element can link directly to the text of the note like this:

```
<footnote xmlns:xlink="http://www.w3.org/1999/xlink"
          xlink:type="simple"
          xlink:href="footnote7.xml">7</footnote>
```

Furthermore, XLinks can do many things that HTML links cannot do. XLinks can be bidirectional so that readers can return to the page they came from. XLinks can link to arbitrary positions in a document. XLinks can embed text or graphic data inside a document rather than requiring the user to activate the link (much like HTML's <IMG> tag but more flexible). In short, XLinks make hypertext even more powerful.

Cross-Reference XLinks are covered in Chapter 20.

Schemas

XML's facilities for declaring how the contents of an XML element should be formatted are weak to nonexistent. For example, suppose as part of a date you set up MONTH elements like this:

```
<MONTH>9</MONTH>
```

All a DTD (Document Type Definition) can say is that the contents of the MONTH element should be character data. It cannot say that the month should be given as an integer between 1 and 12.

A number of schemes have been proposed to use XML itself to more tightly restrict what can appear in the content of any given element. The W3C has endorsed XML Schema for this purpose. For example, Listing 2-16 shows a schema that declares that MONTH elements may only contain an integer between 1 and 12:

Listing 2-16: **A schema for months**

```
<?xml version="1.0"?>
<xsd:schema xmlns:xsd="http://www.w3.org/2001/XMLSchema">

  <xsd:simpleType name="monthInt">
    <xsd:restriction base="xsd:integer">
      <xsd:minInclusive value="1"/>
      <xsd:maxInclusive value="12"/>
    </xsd:restriction>
  </xsd:simpleType>

  <xsd:element name="month" type="monthInt"/>

</xsd:schema>
```

Cross-Reference   Schemas are discussed in more detail in Chapter 23.

I could show you more examples of XML used for XML, but the ones I've already discussed demonstrate the basic point: XML is powerful enough to describe and extend itself. Among other things, this means that the XML specification can remain small and simple. There may well never be an XML 2.0 because any major additions that are needed can be built *from* XML rather than being built *into* XML. People and programs that need these enhanced features can use them. Others who don't need them can ignore them. You don't need to know about what you don't use. XML provides the bricks and mortar from which you can build simple huts or towering castles.

Note   There is a *second edition* of XML 1.0, and indeed this edition is precisely what this book is based on; but this is not at all the same thing as XML 2.0. The second edition of XML 1.0 merely rewrote the XML specification to clarify a number of points that confused people, and to correct a very small number of mistakes in the original specification. However, it did not change the definition of what is and is not a well-formed or valid XML document. The changes were editorial, not substantive.

Behind-the-Scene Uses of XML

Not all XML applications are public, open standards. Many software vendors are moving to XML for their own data simply because it's a well-understood, general-purpose format for structured data that can be easily manipulated with free tools.

Microsoft Office 2000

Microsoft Office 2000 promotes HTML to a coequal status with its native binary file formats. However, HTML 4.0 doesn't provide support for all of the features that Office requires, such as revision tracking, footnotes, comments, index and glossary entries, macros, and more. Additional data that can't be written as HTML is embedded in the file in small chunks of XML. Vector graphics created with the Office drawing tool are stored in VML. Other data can be encoded in custom vocabularies created just for this purpose. For example, here's one of those chunks taken from the HTML version of this very chapter.

```
<xml>
 <o:DocumentProperties>
  <o:Author>Elliotte Rusty Harold</o:Author>
  <o:Template>Bible2000.dot</o:Template>
  <o:LastAuthor>Elliotte Rusty Harold</o:LastAuthor>
  <o:Revision>2</o:Revision>
  <o:TotalTime>673</o:TotalTime>
  <o:LastPrinted>2000-05-08T20:55:00Z</o:LastPrinted>
  <o:Created>2000-05-23T23:05:00Z</o:Created>
  <o:LastSaved>2000-05-23T23:05:00Z</o:LastSaved>
  <o:Pages>29</o:Pages>
  <o:Words>8823</o:Words>
  <o:Characters>50295</o:Characters>
  <o:Company>IDG Books Worldwide</o:Company>
  <o:Bytes>28160</o:Bytes>
  <o:Lines>419</o:Lines>
  <o:Paragraphs>100</o:Paragraphs>
  <o:CharactersWithSpaces>61765</o:CharactersWithSpaces>
  <o:Version>9.2720</o:Version>
 </o:DocumentProperties>
 <o:OfficeDocumentSettings>
  <o:AllowPNG/>
  <o:TargetScreenSize>640x480</o:TargetScreenSize>
 </o:OfficeDocumentSettings>
</xml>
```

Netscape's What's Related

Netscape 6.0 supports direct display of XML in the Web browser, but Netscape actually started using XML internally as early as version 4.0.6. When you ask Netscape to show you a list of sites related to the current one you're looking at, your browser connects to a CGI program running on a Netscape server (http://www-rl1.netscape.com/wtgn through http://www-rl7.netscape.com/wtgn). The data the server sends back is in XML. Listing 2-17 shows the XML data for sites related to my Cafe au Lait site at http://metalab.unc.edu/javafaq/.

Listing 2-17: **XML data for sites related to http://metalab.unc.edu/javafaq/**

```
<RDF:RDF>
<RelatedLinks>
<child href= "http://info.netscape.com/fwd/rlstatic/
http://search.netscape.com/cgi-bin/search?search=unc"
name="Search on 'unc'"/>
<child instanceOf="Separator1"/>
<child href= "http://info.netscape.com/fwd/rlpaid/
http://excite.netscape.com/education" name="Teacher & student
resources" type=244/>
<child instanceOf="Separator1"/>
<child href= "http://info.netscape.com/fwd/rlstatic/
http://directory.netscape.com/Computers/Programming/Languages/
Java/News_and_Events" name="Computers: ...: News and Events"/>
<child href= "http://info.netscape.com/fwd/rlstatic/
http://directory.netscape.com/add.html" name="Submit a site to
the Open Directory..."/>
<child href= "http://info.netscape.com/fwd/rlstatic/
http://directory.netscape.com/about.html" name="Become an Open
Directory editor..."/>
<child instanceOf="Separator1"/>
<child href="http://info.netscape.com/fwd/rlurls/http://www.
km-cd.com/black_coffee" name="Black Coffee" priority="7"/>
<child href= "http://info.netscape.com/fwd/rlurls/
http://www.javaworld.com/" name="JavaWorld" priority="7"/>
<child href= "http://info.netscape.com/fwd/rlurls/
http://www.gamelan.com/" name="Gamelan" priority="7"/>
<child href= "http://info.netscape.com/fwd/rlurls/
http://www.apl.jhu.edu/~hall/java"
name="www.apl.jhu.edu/%7Ehall/java" priority="7"/>
<child href= "http://info.netscape.com/fwd/rlurls/
http://teamjava.com/" name="Teamjava Hq" priority="7"/>
<child href= "http://info.netscape.com/fwd/rlurls/
http://ncc.hursley.ibm.com/javainfo/hurindex.html" name="Ibm
Centre For Java Technology Deve" priority="7"/>
<child href=
"http://info.netscape.com/fwd/rlurls/http://java.sun.com/"
name="Java Home Page" priority="7"/>
<child href= "http://info.netscape.com/fwd/rlurls/
http://www.javasoft.com/" name="JavaSoft" priority="7"/>
<child href= "http://info.netscape.com/fwd/rlurls/
http://www.jars.com/" name="Java Review Service" priority="7"/>
<child href= "http://info.netscape.com/fwd/rlurls/
http://www.yahoo.com/Computers_and_Internet/Programming_
Languages/Java" name="Yahoo: Java" priority="7"/>
```

```
<child href="http://editorial.alexa.com/netscape_editor"
name="Suggest related links..."/>
<child instanceOf="Separator1"/>
<Topic name="Site info for metalab.unc.edu">
<child href="http://info.netscape.com/fwd/rlstatic/
http://home.netscape.com/escapes/related/faq.html" name="Owner:
MetaLab Projects"/>
<child href= "http://info.netscape.com/fwd/rlstatic/
http://home.netscape.com/escapes/related/faq.html" name="Date
established: 19-Feb-97"/>
<child href= "http://info.netscape.com/fwd/rlstatic/
http://home.netscape.com/escapes/related/faq.html"
name="Popularity: in top 1182 sites on web"/>
<child href= "http://info.netscape.com/fwd/rlstatic/
http://home.netscape.com/escapes/related/faq.html" name="Number
of pages on site: 7447"/>
<child href= "http://info.netscape.com/fwd/rlstatic/
http://home.netscape.com/escapes/related/faq.html" name="Number
of links to site on web: 225444"/>
</Topic>
<child instanceOf="Separator1"/>
<child href= "http://info.netscape.com/fwd/rlstatic/
http://home.netscape.com/escapes/related" name="Learn more
about What's Related"/>
<child href= "http://info.netscape.com/fwd/rlstatic/
http://home.netscape.com/escapes/keywords" name="Learn more
about Internet Keywords"/>
</RelatedLinks>
</RDF:RDF>
```

This all happens completely behind the scenes. The users never know that the data is being transferred in XML. The actual display is a menu in Netscape Navigator, shown in Figure 2-9, not an XML or HTML page.

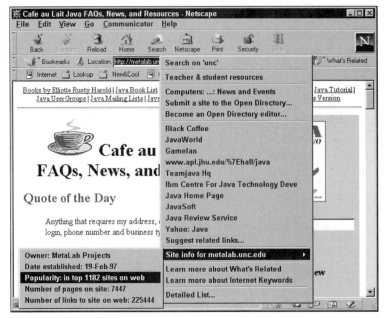

Figure 2-9: Netscape's What's Related menu

This really just scratches the surface of the use of XML for internal data. Many other projects that use XML are just getting started, and many more will be started over the next several years. Most of these won't receive any publicity or write-ups in the trade press, but they nonetheless have the potential to save their companies millions of dollars in development costs over the life of the project. The self-documenting nature of XML can be as useful for a company's internal data as for its external data. For instance, recently many companies were scrambling to try to figure out whether programmers who retired 20 years ago used two-digit or four-digit dates. If that were your job, would you rather be pouring over data that looked like this?

```
3c 79 65 61 72 3e 39 39 3c 2f 79 65 61 72 3e
```

Or that looked like this?

```
<YEAR>99</YEAR>
```

Binary file formats meant that programmers were stuck trying to clean up data in the first format. XML even makes the mistakes easier to find and fix.

Summary

This chapter has just begun to touch on the many and varied applications for which XML has been and will be used. Some of these applications, such as SVG, MathML, and MusicML, are clear extensions of HTML for Web browsers. Many others, however, such as OFX, XFDL, and HR-XML, go in completely new directions. And all of these applications have their own semantics and syntax that sits on top of the underlying XML. In some cases, the XML roots are obvious. In others, you could easily spend months working with them and only hear of XML tangentially. In this chapter, you explored the following applications in which XML has been put to use.

✦ Molecular sciences with CML

✦ Science and math with MathML

✦ Webcasting with CDF

✦ Classic literature

✦ Multimedia with SMIL and HTML+TIME

✦ Software updates through OSD

✦ Vector graphics with both SVG and VML

✦ Music notation in MusicML

✦ Automated voice responses with VoiceXML

✦ Financial data with OFX 2.0

✦ Legally binding forms with XFDL

✦ Job listings with HR-XML

✦ Meta-data through RDF

✦ Extending XML itself with XSL, XLink, and XML Schemas

✦ Internal use of XML by various companies, including Microsoft and Netscape

In the next chapter, you will begin writing your own XML documents and displaying them in a Web browser.

✦   ✦   ✦

Your First XML Document

✦ ✦ ✦ ✦

In This Chapter

Creating a simple
XML document

Exploring the simple
XML document

Assigning meaning to
XML tags

Writing style sheets
for XML documents

Attaching style sheets
to XML documents

✦ ✦ ✦ ✦

T his chapter teaches you how to create simple XML documents with tags that you define that make sense for your
document. You'll learn which tools and software you can use
to edit and save an XML document. You'll also learn how to
write a style sheet for the document that describes how the
content of those tags should be displayed. Finally, you'll learn
how to load the document into a Web browser so that it can
be viewed.

Since this chapter teaches you by example, it will not cross all
the *t*s and dot all the *i*s. Experienced readers may notice a few
exceptions and special cases that aren't discussed here. Don't
worry about these; the details will be covered over the course
of the next several chapters. For the most part, you don't
need to worry about the technical rules up front. As with
HTML, you can learn and do a lot by copying a few simple
examples that others have prepared and by modifying them
to fit your needs.

Toward that end I encourage you to follow along by typing in
the examples I give in this chapter and loading them into the
different programs discussed. This will give you a basic feel
for XML that will make the technical details in future chapters
easier to grasp in the context of these specific examples.

Hello XML

This section follows an old programmer's tradition of introducing a new language with a program that prints "Hello
World" on the console. XML is a markup language, not a programming language; but the basic principle still applies. It's
easiest to get started if you begin with a complete, working
example that you can build on, rather than starting with more
fundamental pieces that by themselves don't do anything. If

you do encounter problems with the basic tools, those problems are a lot easier to debug and fix in the context of the short, simple documents used here, rather than in the context of the more complex documents developed in the rest of the book.

Creating a simple XML document

In this section, you create a simple XML document and save it in a file. Listing 3-1 is about the simplest XML document I can imagine, so start with it. This document can be typed in any convenient text editor, such as Notepad, BBEdit, or emacs.

Listing 3-1: **Hello XML**

```
<?xml version="1.0"?>
<FOO>
Hello XML!
</FOO>
```

Listing 3-1 is not very complicated, but it is a good XML document. To be more precise, it is a *well-formed* XML document. (XML has special terms for documents that it considers "good" depending on exactly which set of rules they satisfy. "Well-formed" is one of those terms, but we'll get to that later.)

Cross-Reference   Well-formedness is covered in Chapter 6.

Saving the XML file

After you've typed in Listing 3-1, save it in a file called hello.xml, HelloWorld.xml, MyFirstDocument.xml, or some other name. The three-letter extension .xml is fairly standard. However, do make sure that you save it in plain-text format, and not in the native format of a word processor such as WordPerfect or Microsoft Word.

Note   If you're using Notepad to edit your files, be sure to enclose the filename in double quotes when saving the document; for example, "Hello.xml", not merely Hello.xml, as shown in Figure 3-1. Without the quotes, Notepad will append the .txt extension to your file name, naming it Hello.xml.txt, which is not what you want at all.

The Windows NT version of Notepad gives you the option to save the file in Unicode. This will also work, though for now you should stick to basic ASCII. XML files are written in Unicode or a compressed version of Unicode called UTF-8, which is a strict superset of ASCII; thus, pure ASCII files are also well-formed XML files.

Figure 3-1: An XML document saved in Notepad with the filename in quotes

UTF-8 and ASCII are discussed in more detail in Chapter 7.

Loading the XML file into a Web browser

Now that you've created your first XML document, you're going to want to look at it. The file can be opened directly in a browser that supports XML such as Internet Explorer 5.0. Figure 3-2 shows the result.

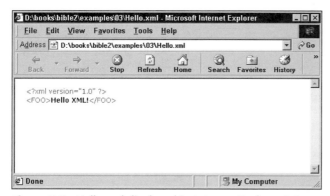

Figure 3-2: Hello.xml displayed in Internet Explorer 5.0

What you see will vary from browser to browser. In this case it's a nicely formatted and syntax-colored view of the document's source code. Mozilla, Netscape, and Opera will simply show you the string "Hello XML!" in the default font. Whatever the browser shows you, it's not likely to be particularly attractive. The problem is that the browser doesn't really know what to do with the FOO element. You have to tell the browser how to handle each element by adding a style sheet. You learn to do that shortly, but let's first look a little more closely at this XML document.

Exploring the Simple XML Document

The first line of the simple XML document in Listing 3-1 is the *XML declaration*:

```
<?xml version="1.0"?>
```

The XML declaration has a `version` attribute. An attribute is a name-value pair separated by an equals sign. The name is on the left side of the equals sign, and the value is on the right side between double quote marks.

Every XML document should begin with an XML declaration that specifies the version of XML in use. (Some XML documents omit this for reasons of backward compatibility, but you should include an XML declaration unless you have a specific reason to leave it out.) In the previous example, the `version` attribute says that this document conforms to the XML 1.0 specification. There isn't any version of XML except 1.0. This attribute just exists to allow the possibility of future revisions.

Now look at the next three lines of Listing 3-1:

```
<FOO>
Hello XML!
</FOO>
```

Collectively these three lines form a `FOO` *element*. Separately, `<FOO>` is a *start tag*; `</FOO>` is an *end tag*; and `Hello XML!` is the *content* of the `FOO` element. Divided another way, the start tag, end tag, and XML declaration are all *markup*. The text `Hello XML!` is *character data*.

You may be asking what the `<FOO>` tag means. The short answer is "whatever you want it to mean." Rather than relying on a few hundred predefined tags, XML lets you create the tags that you need when you need them. Therefore, the `<FOO>` tag has whatever meaning you assign it. The same XML document could have been written with different tag names, as Listings 3-2, 3-3, and 3-4 show.

Listing 3-2: **greeting.xml**

```
<?xml version="1.0"?>
<GREETING>
Hello XML!
</GREETING>
```

Listing 3-3: **paragraph.xml**

```
<?xml version="1.0"?>
<P>
Hello XML!
</P>
```

Listing 3-4: **document.xml**

```
<?xml version="1.0"?>
<DOCUMENT>
Hello XML!
</DOCUMENT>
```

The four XML documents in Listings 3-1 through 3-4 have tags with different names. However, they are all equivalent because they have the same structure and content.

Assigning Meaning to XML Tags

Markup can indicate three kinds of meaning: structural, semantic, or stylistic. Structure specifies the relations between the different elements in the document. Semantics relates the individual elements to the real world outside of the document itself. Style specifies how an element is displayed.

Structure merely expresses the form of the document, without regard for differences between individual tags and elements. For instance, the four XML documents shown in Listings 3-1 through 3-4 are structurally the same. They all specify documents with a single nonempty, root element that contains the same content. The different names of the tags have no structural significance.

Semantic meaning exists outside the document, in the mind of the author or reader, or in some computer program that generates or reads these files. For instance, a Web browser that understands HTML, but not XML, would assign the meaning "paragraph" to the tags <P> and </P> but not to the tags <GREETING> and </GREETING>, <FOO> and </FOO>, or <DOCUMENT> and </DOCUMENT>. An English-speaking human would be more likely to understand <GREETING> and </GREETING> or <DOCUMENT> and </DOCUMENT> than <FOO> and </FOO> or <P> and </P>. Meaning, like beauty, is in the mind of the beholder.

Computers, being relatively dumb machines, can't really be said to understand the meaning of anything. They simply process bits and bytes according to predetermined formulas (albeit very quickly). A computer is just as happy to use `<FOO>` or `<P>` as it is to use the more meaningful `<GREETING>` or `<DOCUMENT>` tags. Even a Web browser can't be said to really understand what a paragraph is. All the browser knows is that when it encounters the end of a paragraph it should place a blank line before the next element.

Naturally, it's better to pick tags that more closely reflect the meaning of the information they contain. Many disciplines, such as math and chemistry, are working on creating industry-standard tag sets. These should be used when appropriate. However, many tags are made up as you need them.

The third kind of meaning that can be associated with a tag is stylistic. Style says how the content of a tag is to be presented on a computer screen or other output device. Style says whether a particular element is bold, italic, green, two inches high, or what have you. Computers are better at understanding stylistic than semantic meaning. In XML, style is applied through style sheets.

Writing a Style Sheet for an XML Document

XML allows you to create any tags that you need. Of course, since you have almost complete freedom in creating tags, there's no way for a generic browser to anticipate your tags and provide rules for displaying them. Therefore, you also need to write a style sheet for the XML document that tells browsers how to display particular tags. Like tag sets, style sheets can be shared between different documents and different people, and the style sheets you create can be integrated with style sheets others have written.

As discussed in Chapter 1, there is more than one style sheet language to choose from. The one introduced in this chapter is Cascading Style Sheets (CSS). CSS has the advantage of being an established W3C standard, being familiar to many people from HTML, and being supported in the first wave of XML-enabled Web browsers.

Note   As noted in Chapter 1, another possibility is the Extensible Stylesheet Language. XSL is currently the most powerful and flexible style sheet language, and the only one designed specifically for use with XML. However, XSL is more complex than CSS, not yet as well supported, and not finished either.

Cross-Reference   XSL is discussed in Chapters 5, 18, and 19.

The greeting.xml example shown in Listing 3-2 only contains one tag, `<GREETING>`, so all you need to do is define the style for the GREETING element. Listing 3-5 is a very simple style sheet that specifies that the contents of the GREETING element should be rendered as a block-level element in 24-point bold type.

Listing 3-5: **greeting.xsl**

```
GREETING {display: block; font-size: 24pt; font-weight: bold}
```

Listing 3-5 should be typed in a text editor and saved in a new file called greeting.css in the same directory as Listing 3-2. The .css extension stands for Cascading Style Sheet. Again, the .css extension is important, although the exact filename is not important. However, if a style sheet is to be applied only to a single XML document, it's often convenient to give it the same name as that document with the extension .css instead of .xml.

Attaching a Style Sheet to an XML Document

Once you've written an XML document and a Cascading Style Sheet for that document, you need to tell the browser to apply the style sheet to the document. In the long-term, there are likely to be a number of different ways to do this, including browser-server negotiation via HTTP headers, naming conventions, and browser-side defaults. However, right now the only way that works is to include an `<?xml-stylesheet?>` processing instruction in the XML document to specify the style sheet to be used.

The `<?xml-stylesheet?>` processing instruction has two required attributes: type and href. The type attribute specifies the style sheet language used, and the href attribute specifies a URL, possibly relative, where the style sheet can be found. In Listing 3-6, the xml-stylesheet processing instruction specifies that the style sheet named greeting.css written in the CSS style sheet language is to be applied to this document.

Listing 3-6: **styledgreeting.xml with an xml-stylesheet processing instruction**

```
<?xml version="1.0"?>
<?xml-stylesheet type="text/css" href="greeting.css"?>
<GREETING>
Hello XML!
</GREETING>
```

Now that you've created your first XML document and style sheet, you want to look at it. All you have to do is load Listing 3-6 into an XML-enabled Web browser such as Mozilla, Opera 4.0 and 5.0, Internet Explorer 5.0 and 5.5, or Netscape 6. Figure 3-3 shows styledgreeting.xml in Mozilla for Windows.

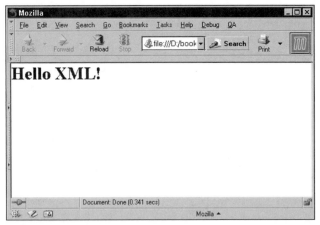

Figure 3-3: Styledgreeting.xml displayed in Mozilla 0.6

Summary

In this chapter, you learned to create a simple XML document. In particular, you learned:

✦ How to write and save simple XML documents.

✦ How to assign XML elements three kinds of meaning: structural, semantic, and stylistic.

✦ How to write a CSS style sheet for an XML document that tells browsers how to display particular elements.

✦ How to attach a CSS style sheet to an XML document with an `xml-stylesheet` processing instruction.

✦ How to load XML documents into a Web browser.

In the next chapter, we develop a much larger example of an XML document that demonstrates more of the practical considerations involved in choosing XML tags.

✦   ✦   ✦

Structuring Data

This chapter develops a longer example that shows how a large list of baseball statistics might be stored in XML. By following along with this example, you'll learn many useful techniques that you can apply to all kinds of data-heavy documents.

A document such as this has several potential uses. Most obviously, it can be displayed on a Web page. It can also be used as input to other programs that want to analyze particular seasons or lineups. As the example is developed, you'll learn, among other things, how to mark up data in XML, the principles for good XML element names, and how to prepare a CSS for a document.

Examining the Data

1998 was an astonishing year for baseball. The New York Yankees won their twenty-fourth World Series by sweeping the San Diego Padres in four games. The Yankees finished the regular season with an American League record 114 wins. The St. Louis Cardinals' Mark McGwire and the Chicago Cubs' Sammy Sosa dueled through September for the record, previously held by Roger Maris, for most home runs hit in a single season since baseball was integrated. (The all-time major league record for home runs in a single season is still held by catcher Josh Gibson who hit 75 home runs in the Negro league in 1931. Admittedly, Gibson didn't have to face the sort of pitching Sosa and McGwire faced in today's integrated league. Then again neither did Babe Ruth who was widely — and incorrectly — believed to have held the record until Roger Maris hit 61 in 1961.)

What exactly made 1998 such an exciting season? A cynic would tell you that 1998 was an expansion year with three new teams, and consequently much weaker pitching overall. This gave outstanding batters, such as Sosa and McGwire, and outstanding teams, such as the Yankees, a chance to really shine because, although they were as strong as they'd been in 1997, the average opponent they faced was a lot weaker. Of course, true baseball fanatics know the real reason — statistics.

That's a funny thing to say. In most sports you hear about heart, guts, ability, skill, determination, and more. Only in baseball do the fans get so worked up about raw numbers — batting average, earned run average, slugging average, on base average, fielding percentage, batting average against right-handed pitchers, batting average against left-handed pitchers, batting average against right-handed pitchers when batting left-handed, batting average against right-handed pitchers in Cleveland under a full moon, and so on.

Baseball fans are obsessed with numbers, the more numbers the better. Every season the Internet is host to thousands of rotisserie leagues in which avid netizens manage teams, trade players, and calculate how their fantasy teams are doing based on the real-world performance of the players on their fantasy rosters. STATS, Inc. tracks the results of each and every pitch made in a major league game, so it's possible to calculate statistics for excruciatingly specific situations. For instance, you can figure out whether a particular batter performs better or worse than average with players in scoring position.

In the next two sections, for the benefit of the less baseball-obsessed reader, I examine the commonly available statistics that describe an individual player's batting and pitching. Fielding statistics are also available, but I omit them to keep the examples to a more manageable size. The specific example I use is the New York Yankees, but the same statistics are available for any team.

Batters

A few years ago, Bruce Bukiet, Jose Palacios, and I wrote a paper called "A Markov Chain Approach to Baseball" (Operations Research, Volume 45, Number 1, January-February, 1997, pp. 14-23, http://m.njit.edu/~bukiet/Papers/ball.pdf). In this paper we analyzed all possible batting orders for all teams in the 1989 National League. The results of that paper were mildly interesting. The worst batter on the team, generally the pitcher, should bat eighth rather than the customary ninth position, at least in the National League. However, what concerns me here is the work that went into producing this paper. As low grad student on the totem pole, it was my job to manually rekey the complete batting history of each and every player in the National League. That summer would have been a lot more pleasant if I'd had the data available in a convenient format such as XML. In this chapter, I'm going to produce the data in that format. Typically this data is presented in rows of numbers as shown in Table 4-1 for the 1998 Yankees offense (batters). Because pitchers rarely bat in the American League, only players who actually batted are listed.

Table 4-1 The 1998 Yankees Offense												
Name	*P*	*G*	*AB*	*R*	*H*	*2B*	*3B*	*HR*	*RBI*	*BB*	*SO*	*HBP*
Scott BrosiusThird Base		152	530	86	159	34	0	19	98	52	97	10
Homer Bush Second Base		45	71	17	27	3	0	1	5	5	19	0
Chad CurtisOutfield		151	456	79	111	21	1	10	56	75	80	7
Chili Davis Designated Hitter		35	103	11	30	7	0	3	9	14	18	0
Mike Figga Catcher		1	4	1	1	0	0	0	0	0	1	0
Joe Girardi Catcher		78	254	31	70	11	4	3	31	14	38	2
Derek Jeter Shortstop		149	626	127	203	25	8	19	84	57	119	5
Chuck Knoblauch Second Base		150	603	117	160	25	4	17	64	76	70	18
Ricky Ledee Outfield		42	79	13	19	5	2	1	12	7	29	0
Mike Lowell Third Base		8	15	1	4	0	0	0	0	0	1	0
Tino Martinez First Base		142	531	92	149	33	1	28	123	61	83	6
Paul O'Neill Outfield		152	602	95	191	40	2	24	116	57	103	2
Jorge Posada Catcher		111	358	56	96	23	0	17	63	47	92	0
Tim Raines Outfield		109	321	53	93	13	1	5	47	55	49	3
Luis Sojo Shortstop		54	147	16	34	3	1	0	14	4	15	0
Shane Spencer Outfield		27	67	18	25	6	0	10	27	5	12	0
Darryl Strawberry Designated Hitter		101	295	44	73	11	2	24	57	46	90	3
Dale Sveum First base		30	58	6	9	0	0	0	3	4	16	0
Bernie Williams Outfield		128	499	101	169	30	5	26	97	74	81	1

Standard Abbreviations   TM: Team; P: Position; G: Games Played; GS: Games Started; AB: At Bats; R: Runs; H: Hits; 2B: Doubles; 3B: Triples; HR: Home Runs; RBI: Runs Batted In; SB: Stolen Bases; CS: Caught Stealing; SH: Sacrifice Hits; SF: Sacrifice Flies; Err: Errors; PB: Pitcher Balked; BB: Base on Balls (Walks); SO: Strike Outs; HBP: Hit By Pitch

Each column effectively defines an element. Thus, there need to be elements for player, position, games played, at bats, runs, hits, doubles, triples, home runs, runs batted in, and walks. Singles are generally not reported separately. Rather, they're calculated by subtracting the total number of doubles, triples, and home runs from the number of hits.

The above data and the pitcher data in the next section is actually a somewhat limited list that only begins to specify the data collected on a typical baseball game. There are a lot more elements, including number of times the pitcher balked (rare), fielding percentage, throwing arm, batting arm, college attended, height, weight, shoe size, ring size, preferred brand of chewing tobacco, and more. However, I stick to this basic information to keep the examples manageable.

Pitchers

Pitchers are not expected to be home-run hitters or base stealers. Indeed, a pitcher who can reach first on occasion is a surprise bonus for a team. Instead, pitchers are judged on a whole different set of numbers, which are shown in Table 4-2. Each column of this table also defines an element. Some of these elements, such as name and position, are the same for batters and pitchers. Others, such as saves and shutouts, only apply to pitchers. And a few — such as runs and home runs — have the same name as a batter statistic, but have different meanings. For instance, the number of runs for a batter is the number of runs the batter scored. The number of runs for a pitcher is the number of runs scored by the opposing teams against this pitcher.

Table 4-2
The 1998 Yankees Pitchers

Name	P	W	L	S	GP	GS	CG	SHO	ERA	IP	H	HR	Runs	ER	HB	WP	BK	WB	SO
Joe Borowski	Relief Pitcher	1	0	0	8	0	0	0	6.52	9.2	11	0	7	7	0	0	0	4	7
Ryan Bradley	Relief Pitcher	2	1	0	5	1	0	0	5.68	12.2	12	2	9	8	1	0	0	9	13
Jim Bruske	Relief Pitcher	1	0	0	3	1	0	0	3	9	9	2	3	3	0	0	0	1	3
Mike Buddie	Relief Pitcher	4	1	0	24	2	0	0	5.62	41.2	46	5	29	26	3	2	1	13	20
David Cone	Starting Pitcher	20	7	0	31	31	3	0	3.55	207.2	186	20	89	82	15	6	0	59	209
Todd Erdos	Relief Pitcher	0	0	0	2	0	0	0	9	2	5	0	2	2	0	0	0	1	0
Orlando Hernandez	Starting Pitcher	12	4	0	21	21	3	1	3.13	141	113	11	53	49	6	5	2	52	131
Darren Holmes	Relief Pitcher	0	3	2	34	0	0	0	3.33	51.1	53	4	19	19	2	1	0	14	31
Hideki Irabu	Starting Pitcher	13	9	0	29	28	2	1	4.06	173	148	27	79	78	9	6	1	76	126
Mike Jerzembeck	Starting Pitcher	0	1	0	3	2	0	0	12.79	6.1	9	2	9	9	0	1	1	4	1
Graeme Lloyd	Relief Pitcher	3	0	0	50	0	0	0	1.67	37.2	26	3	10	7	2	2	0	6	20

Continued

Table 4-2 (continued)

Name	P	W	L	S	GP	GS	CG	SHO	ERA	IP	H	HR	Runs	ER	HB	WP	BK	WB	SO
Ramiro Mendoza	Relief Pitcher	10	2	1	41	14	1	1	3.25	130.1	131	9	50	47	9	3	0	30	56
Jeff Nelson	Relief Pitcher	5	3	3	45	0	0	0	3.79	40.1	44	1	18	17	8	2	0	22	35
Andy Pettitte	Starting Pitcher	16	11	0	33	32	5	0	4.24	216.1	226	20	101	102	6	5	0	87	146
Mariano Rivera	Relief Pitcher	3	0	36	54	0	0	0	1.91	61.1	48	3	13	13	1	0	0	17	36
Mike Stanton	Relief Pitcher	4	1	6	67	0	0	0	5.47	79	71	13	51	48	4	0	0	26	69
Jay Tessmer	Relief Pitcher	1	0	0	7	0	0	0	3.12	8.2	4	1	3	3	0	1	0	4	6
David Wells	Starting Pitcher	18	4	0	30	30	8	5	3.49	214.1	195	29	86	83	1	2	0	29	163

Standard Abbreviations   P: Position; GP: Games Played; GS: Games Started; W: Wins; L: Losses; S: Saves; ERA: Earned Run Average; CG: Complete Games; SHO: Shut Outs; IP: Innings Pitched; H: Hits; HR: Home Runs; R: Runs; ER: Earned Runs; HB: Hit Batter; WP: Wild Pitch; BK: Balk; WB: Walked Batter; SO: Struck Out Batter

Organization of the XML data

XML is based on a containment model. Each XML element can contain text or other XML elements called children. A few XML elements may contain both text and child elements. This is called *mixed content*. However, in data heavy documents like the one being developed in this chapter, mixed content is bad form and should be avoided. Mixed content is a lot more common and useful in narrative documents like Web pages, letters, essays, and books.

However, there's often more than one way to organize the data, depending on your needs. One advantage of XML is that it makes it fairly straightforward to write a program that reorganizes the data in a different form. We discuss this when we talk about XSL transformations in Chapter 17.

To get started, the first question you have to address is what contains what? For instance, it is fairly obvious that a league contains divisions that contain teams that contain players. Although teams can change divisions when moving from one city to another, and players are routinely traded, at any given moment in time each player belongs to exactly one team, and each team belongs to exactly one division. Similarly, a season contains games, which contain innings, which contain at bats, which contain pitches or plays.

However, does a season contain leagues or does a league contain a season? The answer isn't so obvious, and indeed there isn't one unique answer. Whether it makes more sense to make season elements children of league elements or league elements children of season elements depends on the use to which the data will be put. You can even create a new root element that contains both seasons and leagues, neither of which is a child of the other (although doing so would require some advanced techniques that won't be discussed for several chapters yet).

Note Readers familiar with database theory may recognize XML's model as essentially a hierarchical database, and consequently recognize that it shares all the disadvantages (and a few advantages) of that data model. There are times when a table-based relational approach makes more sense. This example certainly looks like one of those times. However, XML doesn't follow a relational model.

On the other hand, it is completely possible to store the actual data in multiple tables in a relational database, and then generate the XML on the fly. Indeed, the larger examples on the CD-ROM were created in that fashion. This enables one set of data to be presented in multiple formats. Transforming the data with style sheets provides still more possible views of the data.

Because my personal interests lie in analyzing player performance within a single season, I'm going to choose season for the root of my documents. Each season will contain leagues, which will contain divisions, which will contain players. I'm not going to granularize my data all the way down to the level of individual games, innings, or plays, because while useful, such examples would be excessively long.

You, however, may have other interests. If you choose to divide the data in some other fashion, that works, too. There's almost always more than one way to organize data in XML. In fact, several upcoming chapters explore alternative markup vocabularies for this very example.

XMLizing the Data

Let's begin the process of marking up the data for the 1998 Major League season in XML. Remember that in XML you're allowed to make up the tags as you go along. We've already decided that the fundamental element of this document will be a season. Seasons will contain leagues. Leagues will contain divisions. Divisions will contain teams. Teams contain players. Players will have statistics including games played, at bats, runs, hits, doubles, triples, home runs, runs batted in, walks, and hits by pitch.

Starting the document: XML declaration and root element

XML documents may be recognized by the XML declaration. This is placed at the start of XML files to identify the version in use. The only version currently understood is 1.0.

```
<?xml version="1.0"?>
```

Every good XML document (where *good* has a very specific meaning to be discussed in Chapter 6) must have a root element. This is an element that completely contains all other elements of the document. The root element's start tag comes before all other elements' start tags, and the root element's end tag comes after all other elements' end tags. For the root element, we will use SEASON with a start tag of <SEASON> and an end tag of </SEASON>. The document now looks like this:

```
<?xml version="1.0"?>
<SEASON>
</SEASON>
```

The XML declaration is not an element or a tag. Therefore, it does not need to be contained inside the root element SEASON. But every element that you put in this document will go between the <SEASON> start tag and the </SEASON> end tag.

This choice of root element means that you will not be able to store multiple seasons in a single file. If you want to do that, however, you can define a new root element that contains seasons. For example,

Naming Conventions

Before I go any further, I'd like to say a few words about naming conventions. As you'll see in Chapter 6, XML element names are quite flexible and can contain any number of letters and digits in either upper- or lowercase. You have the option of writing XML tags that look like any of the following:

```
<SEASON>
```

```
<Season>
```

```
<season>
```

```
<season1998>
```

```
<Season98>
```

```
<season_98>
```

There are several thousand more variations. I don't really care (nor does XML) whether you use all uppercase, all lowercase, mixed-case with internal capitalization, or some other convention. However, I do recommend that you choose one convention and stick to it.

```
<?xml version="1.0"?>
<DOCUMENT>
  <SEASON>
  </SEASON>
  <SEASON>
  </SEASON>
</DOCUMENT>
```

Of course you will want to identify which season you're talking about. To do that, give the SEASON element a YEAR child element. For example:

```
<?xml version="1.0"?>
<SEASON>
  <YEAR>
    1998
  </YEAR>
</SEASON>
```

I've used indentation here and in other examples to indicate that the YEAR element is a child of the SEASON element and that the text 1998 is the content of the YEAR element. This is good coding style, but it is not required. White space in XML is normally not especially significant. The same example could have been written like this:

```
<?xml version="1.0"?>
<SEASON>
  <YEAR>1998</YEAR>
</SEASON>
```

Indeed, I often compress elements in this fashion when they'll fit and space is at a premium. You can compress the document still further, even down to a single line, but with a corresponding loss of clarity. For example:

```
<?xml version="1.0"?><SEASON><YEAR>1998</YEAR></SEASON>
```

Of course, this version is much harder to read and to understand, which is why I didn't write it that way in the first place. The tenth goal listed in the XML 1.0 specification is "Terseness in XML markup is of minimal importance." The baseball example reflects this principle throughout.

XMLizing league, division, and team data

Major league baseball in the United States is divided into two leagues, the American League and the National League. Each league has a name. The two names can be encoded like this:

```
<?xml version="1.0"?>
<SEASON>
  <YEAR>1998</YEAR>
  <LEAGUE>
    <LEAGUE_NAME>National League</LEAGUE_NAME>
  </LEAGUE>
  <LEAGUE>
    <LEAGUE_NAME>American League</LEAGUE_NAME>
  </LEAGUE>
</SEASON>
```

I've chosen to define the name of a league with a LEAGUE_NAME element, rather than simply a NAME element because NAME is too generic and likely to be used in other contexts. For instance, divisions, teams, and players also have names.

Cross-Reference

Elements from different XML applications with the same name can be combined using namespaces. Namespaces will be discussed in Chapter 13. However, even with namespaces, you wouldn't want to give multiple items in the same application (TEAM and LEAGUE in this example) the same name.

Each league can be divided into East, West, and Central divisions, which can be encoded as follows:

```
<LEAGUE>
  <LEAGUE_NAME>National League</LEAGUE_NAME>
  <DIVISION>
    <DIVISION_NAME>East</DIVISION_NAME>
  </DIVISION>
  <DIVISION>
```

```
      <DIVISION_NAME>Central</DIVISION_NAME>
    </DIVISION>
    <DIVISION>
      <DIVISION_NAME>West</DIVISION_NAME>
    </DIVISION>
  </LEAGUE>
  <LEAGUE>
    <LEAGUE_NAME>American League</LEAGUE_NAME>
    <DIVISION>
      <DIVISION_NAME>East</DIVISION_NAME>
    </DIVISION>
    <DIVISION>
      <DIVISION_NAME>Central</DIVISION_NAME>
    </DIVISION>
    <DIVISION>
      <DIVISION_NAME>West</DIVISION_NAME>
    </DIVISION>
  </LEAGUE>
```

The true value of an element depends on its parent; that is, the elements that contain it as well as itself. Both the American and National Leagues have an East division but these are not the same thing.

Each division is divided into teams. Each team has a name and a city. For example, data that pertains to the American League East can be encoded as follows:

```
<DIVISION>
  <DIVISION_NAME>East</DIVISION_NAME>
  <TEAM>
    <TEAM_CITY>Baltimore</TEAM_CITY>
    <TEAM_NAME>Orioles</TEAM_NAME>
  </TEAM>
  <TEAM>
    <TEAM_CITY>Boston</TEAM_CITY>
    <TEAM_NAME>Red Sox</TEAM_NAME>
  </TEAM>
  <TEAM>
    <TEAM_CITY>New York</TEAM_CITY>
    <TEAM_NAME>Yankees</TEAM_NAME>
  </TEAM>
  <TEAM>
    <TEAM_CITY>Tampa Bay</TEAM_CITY>
    <TEAM_NAME>Devil Rays</TEAM_NAME>
  </TEAM>
  <TEAM>
    <TEAM_CITY>Toronto</TEAM_CITY>
    <TEAM_NAME>Blue Jays</TEAM_NAME>
  </TEAM>
</DIVISION>
```

XMLizing player data

Each team is composed of players. Each player has a first name and a last name. It's important to separate the first and last names so that you can sort by either one. The data for the starting pitchers in the 1998 Yankees lineup can be encoded as follows:

```
<TEAM>
  <TEAM_CITY>New York</TEAM_CITY>
  <TEAM_NAME>Yankees</TEAM_NAME>
  <PLAYER>
    <GIVEN_NAME>Orlando</GIVEN_NAME>
    <SURNAME>Hernandez</SURNAME>
  </PLAYER>
  <PLAYER>
    <GIVEN_NAME>David</GIVEN_NAME>
    <SURNAME>Cone</SURNAME>
  </PLAYER>
  <PLAYER>
    <GIVEN_NAME>David</GIVEN_NAME>
    <SURNAME>Wells</SURNAME>
  </PLAYER>
  <PLAYER>
    <GIVEN_NAME>Andy</GIVEN_NAME>
    <SURNAME>Pettitte</SURNAME>
  </PLAYER>
  <PLAYER>
    <GIVEN_NAME>Hideki</GIVEN_NAME>
    <SURNAME>Irabu</SURNAME>
  </PLAYER>
</TEAM>
```

Note   The tags `<GIVEN_NAME>` and `<SURNAME>` are preferable to the more obvious `<FIRST_NAME>` and `<LAST_NAME>` or `<FIRST_NAME>` and `<FAMILY_NAME>`. Whether the family name or the given name comes first or last varies from culture to culture. Furthermore, surnames aren't necessarily family names in all cultures.

XMLizing player statistics

The next step is to provide statistics for each player. Statistics look a little different for pitchers and batters, especially in the American League where few pitchers bat. Below are Joe Girardi's 1998 statistics. He's a catcher so he has batting statistics:

```
<PLAYER>
  <GIVEN_NAME>Joe</GIVEN_NAME>
  <SURNAME>Girardi</SURNAME>
  <POSITION>Catcher</POSITION>
  <GAMES>78</GAMES>
  <GAMES_STARTED>76</GAMES_STARTED>
  <AT_BATS>254</AT_BATS>
```

```
      <RUNS>31</RUNS>
      <HITS>70</HITS>
      <DOUBLES>11</DOUBLES>
      <TRIPLES>4</TRIPLES>
      <HOME_RUNS>3</HOME_RUNS>
      <RBI>31</RBI>
      <STEALS>2</STEALS>
      <CAUGHT_STEALING>4</CAUGHT_STEALING>
      <SACRIFICE_HITS>8</SACRIFICE_HITS>
      <SACRIFICE_FLIES>1</SACRIFICE_FLIES>
      <ERRORS>3</ERRORS>
      <WALKS>14</WALKS>
      <STRUCK_OUT>38</STRUCK_OUT>
      <HIT_BY_PITCH>2</HIT_BY_PITCH>
   </PLAYER>
```

Terseness in XML Markup is of Minimal Importance

Throughout this example, I'm following the explicit XML principle that "Terseness in XML markup is of minimal importance." This certainly assists nonbaseball-literate readers who may not recognize baseball arcana such as the standard abbreviation for a walk—BB, base on balls, not W as you might expect. If document size is truly an issue, it's easy to compress the files with zip or any other compression tool.

However, this does mean that XML documents tend to be quite long, and relatively tedious to type by hand. I confess that this example sorely tempts me to use abbreviations, clarity be damned. If I were to do so, a typical PLAYER element might look like this:

```
      <PLAYER>
        <GIVEN_NAME>Joe</GIVEN_NAME>
        <SURNAME>Girardi</SURNAME>
        <P>C</P>
        <G>78</G>
        <AB>254</AB>
        <R>31</R>
        <H>70</H>
        <DO>11</DO>
        <TR>4</TR>
        <HR>3</HR>
        <RBI>31</RBI>
        <BB>14</BB>
        <SO>38</SO>
        <SB>2</SB>
        <CS>4</CS>
        <HBP>2</HBP>
      </PLAYER>
```

Now let's look at the statistics for a pitcher. Although pitchers occasionally bat in the American League, and frequently bat in the National League, they do so far less often than any other player. Pitchers are hired and fired, cheered and booed, based on their pitching performance. If they can actually hit the ball on occasion, that's pure gravy. Pitching statistics include games played, wins, losses, innings pitched, earned runs, shutouts, hits against, walks given up, and more. Here are Hideki Irabu's 1998 statistics encoded in XML.

```
<PLAYER>
  <GIVEN_NAME>Hideki</GIVEN_NAME>
  <SURNAME>Irabu</SURNAME>
  <POSITION>Starting Pitcher</POSITION>
  <GAMES>29</GAMES>
  <GAMES_STARTED>28</GAMES_STARTED>
  <WINS>13</WINS>
  <LOSSES>9</LOSSES>
  <SAVES>0</SAVES>
  <COMPLETE_GAMES>2</COMPLETE_GAMES>
  <SHUT_OUTS>1</SHUT_OUTS>
  <ERA>4.06</ERA>
  <INNINGS>173</INNINGS>
  <HITS_AGAINST>148</HITS_AGAINST>
  <HOME_RUNS_AGAINST>27</HOME_RUNS_AGAINST>
  <RUNS_AGAINST>79</RUNS_AGAINST>
  <EARNED_RUNS>78</EARNED_RUNS>
  <HIT_BATTER>9</HIT_BATTER>
  <WILD_PITCHES>6</WILD_PITCHES>
  <BALK>1</BALK>
  <WALKED_BATTER>76</WALKED_BATTER>
  <STRUCK_OUT_BATTER>126</STRUCK_OUT_BATTER>
</PLAYER>
```

Putting the XML document back together

Until now, I've been showing the XML document in pieces, element by element. However, it's now time to put all the pieces together and look at the complete document containing the statistics for the 1998 Major League season. Listing 4-1 demonstrates a complete XML document with 2 leagues, 6 divisions, 30 teams, and 9 players.

Listing 4-1: **A complete XML document**

```
<?xml version="1.0"?>
<SEASON>
  <YEAR>1998</YEAR>
  <LEAGUE>
    <LEAGUE_NAME>American League</LEAGUE_NAME>
    <DIVISION>
      <DIVISION_NAME>East</DIVISION_NAME>
```

```
<TEAM>
  <TEAM_CITY>Baltimore</TEAM_CITY>
  <TEAM_NAME>Orioles</TEAM_NAME>
    <PLAYER>
      <GIVEN_NAME>Doug</GIVEN_NAME>
      <SURNAME>Drabek</SURNAME>
      <POSITION>Starting Pitcher</POSITION>
      <GAMES>23</GAMES>
      <GAMES_STARTED>21</GAMES_STARTED>
      <WINS>6</WINS>
      <LOSSES>11</LOSSES>
      <SAVES>0</SAVES>
      <COMPLETE_GAMES>1</COMPLETE_GAMES>
      <SHUT_OUTS>0</SHUT_OUTS>
      <ERA>7.29</ERA>
      <INNINGS>108.2</INNINGS>
      <HITS_AGAINST>138</HITS_AGAINST>
      <HOME_RUNS_AGAINST>20</HOME_RUNS_AGAINST>
      <RUNS_AGAINST>90</RUNS_AGAINST>
      <EARNED_RUNS>88</EARNED_RUNS>
      <HIT_BATTER>5</HIT_BATTER>
      <WILD_PITCHES>1</WILD_PITCHES>
      <BALK>0</BALK>
      <WALKED_BATTER>29</WALKED_BATTER>
      <STRUCK_OUT_BATTER>55</STRUCK_OUT_BATTER>
    </PLAYER>
    <PLAYER>
      <GIVEN_NAME>Roberto</GIVEN_NAME>
      <SURNAME>Alomar</SURNAME>
      <POSITION>Second Base</POSITION>
      <GAMES>147</GAMES>
      <GAMES_STARTED>143</GAMES_STARTED>
      <AT_BATS>588</AT_BATS>
      <RUNS>86</RUNS>
      <HITS>166</HITS>
      <DOUBLES>36</DOUBLES>
      <TRIPLES>1</TRIPLES>
      <HOME_RUNS>14</HOME_RUNS>
      <RBI>56</RBI>
      <STEALS>18</STEALS>
      <CAUGHT_STEALING>5</CAUGHT_STEALING>
      <SACRIFICE_HITS>3</SACRIFICE_HITS>
      <SACRIFICE_FLIES>5</SACRIFICE_FLIES>
      <ERRORS>11</ERRORS>
      <WALKS>59</WALKS>
      <STRUCK_OUT>70</STRUCK_OUT>
      <HIT_BY_PITCH>2</HIT_BY_PITCH>
    </PLAYER>
    <PLAYER>
      <GIVEN_NAME>Brady</GIVEN_NAME>
      <SURNAME>Anderson</SURNAME>
      <POSITION>Outfield</POSITION>
```

Continued

Listing 4-1 *(continued)*

```
        <GAMES>133</GAMES>
        <GAMES_STARTED>121</GAMES_STARTED>
        <AT_BATS>479</AT_BATS>
        <RUNS>84</RUNS>
        <HITS>113</HITS>
        <DOUBLES>28</DOUBLES>
        <TRIPLES>3</TRIPLES>
        <HOME_RUNS>18</HOME_RUNS>
        <RBI>51</RBI>
        <STEALS>21</STEALS>
        <CAUGHT_STEALING>7</CAUGHT_STEALING>
        <SACRIFICE_HITS>4</SACRIFICE_HITS>
        <SACRIFICE_FLIES>1</SACRIFICE_FLIES>
        <ERRORS>4</ERRORS>
        <WALKS>75</WALKS>
        <STRUCK_OUT>78</STRUCK_OUT>
        <HIT_BY_PITCH>15</HIT_BY_PITCH>
    </PLAYER>
    <PLAYER>
        <GIVEN_NAME>Rich</GIVEN_NAME>
        <SURNAME>Becker</SURNAME>
        <POSITION>Outfield</POSITION>
        <GAMES>79</GAMES>
        <GAMES_STARTED>26</GAMES_STARTED>
        <AT_BATS>113</AT_BATS>
        <RUNS>22</RUNS>
        <HITS>23</HITS>
        <DOUBLES>1</DOUBLES>
        <TRIPLES>0</TRIPLES>
        <HOME_RUNS>3</HOME_RUNS>
        <RBI>11</RBI>
        <STEALS>2</STEALS>
        <CAUGHT_STEALING>0</CAUGHT_STEALING>
        <SACRIFICE_HITS>2</SACRIFICE_HITS>
        <SACRIFICE_FLIES>0</SACRIFICE_FLIES>
        <ERRORS>1</ERRORS>
        <WALKS>22</WALKS>
        <STRUCK_OUT>34</STRUCK_OUT>
        <HIT_BY_PITCH>2</HIT_BY_PITCH>
    </PLAYER>
    <PLAYER>
        <GIVEN_NAME>Mike</GIVEN_NAME>
        <SURNAME>Bordick</SURNAME>
        <POSITION>Shortstop</POSITION>
        <GAMES>151</GAMES>
        <GAMES_STARTED>144</GAMES_STARTED>
        <AT_BATS>465</AT_BATS>
        <RUNS>59</RUNS>
        <HITS>121</HITS>
        <DOUBLES>29</DOUBLES>
        <TRIPLES>1</TRIPLES>
```

```
    <HOME_RUNS>13</HOME_RUNS>
    <RBI>51</RBI>
    <STEALS>6</STEALS>
    <CAUGHT_STEALING>7</CAUGHT_STEALING>
    <SACRIFICE_HITS>15</SACRIFICE_HITS>
    <SACRIFICE_FLIES>4</SACRIFICE_FLIES>
    <ERRORS>7</ERRORS>
    <WALKS>39</WALKS>
    <STRUCK_OUT>65</STRUCK_OUT>
    <HIT_BY_PITCH>10</HIT_BY_PITCH>
</PLAYER>
<PLAYER>
    <GIVEN_NAME>Danny</GIVEN_NAME>
    <SURNAME>Clyburn</SURNAME>
    <POSITION>Outfield</POSITION>
    <GAMES>11</GAMES>
    <GAMES_STARTED>7</GAMES_STARTED>
    <AT_BATS>25</AT_BATS>
    <RUNS>6</RUNS>
    <HITS>7</HITS>
    <DOUBLES>0</DOUBLES>
    <TRIPLES>0</TRIPLES>
    <HOME_RUNS>1</HOME_RUNS>
    <RBI>3</RBI>
    <STEALS>0</STEALS>
    <CAUGHT_STEALING>0</CAUGHT_STEALING>
    <SACRIFICE_HITS>0</SACRIFICE_HITS>
    <SACRIFICE_FLIES>0</SACRIFICE_FLIES>
    <ERRORS>0</ERRORS>
    <WALKS>1</WALKS>
    <STRUCK_OUT>10</STRUCK_OUT>
    <HIT_BY_PITCH>0</HIT_BY_PITCH>
</PLAYER>
<PLAYER>
    <GIVEN_NAME>Charlie</GIVEN_NAME>
    <SURNAME>Greene</SURNAME>
    <POSITION>Catcher</POSITION>
    <GAMES>13</GAMES>
    <GAMES_STARTED>6</GAMES_STARTED>
    <AT_BATS>21</AT_BATS>
    <RUNS>1</RUNS>
    <HITS>4</HITS>
    <DOUBLES>1</DOUBLES>
    <TRIPLES>0</TRIPLES>
    <HOME_RUNS>0</HOME_RUNS>
    <RBI>0</RBI>
    <STEALS>0</STEALS>
    <CAUGHT_STEALING>0</CAUGHT_STEALING>
    <SACRIFICE_HITS>1</SACRIFICE_HITS>
    <SACRIFICE_FLIES>0</SACRIFICE_FLIES>
    <ERRORS>0</ERRORS>
    <WALKS>0</WALKS>
```

Continued

Listing 4-1 *(continued)*

```
            <STRUCK_OUT>8</STRUCK_OUT>
            <HIT_BY_PITCH>0</HIT_BY_PITCH>
          </PLAYER>
          <PLAYER>
            <GIVEN_NAME>Cal</GIVEN_NAME>
            <SURNAME>Ripken</SURNAME>
            <POSITION>Third Base</POSITION>
            <GAMES>161</GAMES>
            <GAMES_STARTED>161</GAMES_STARTED>
            <AT_BATS>601</AT_BATS>
            <RUNS>65</RUNS>
            <HITS>163</HITS>
            <DOUBLES>27</DOUBLES>
            <TRIPLES>1</TRIPLES>
            <HOME_RUNS>14</HOME_RUNS>
            <RBI>61</RBI>
            <STEALS>0</STEALS>
            <CAUGHT_STEALING>2</CAUGHT_STEALING>
            <SACRIFICE_HITS>1</SACRIFICE_HITS>
            <SACRIFICE_FLIES>2</SACRIFICE_FLIES>
            <ERRORS>8</ERRORS>
            <WALKS>51</WALKS>
            <STRUCK_OUT>68</STRUCK_OUT>
            <HIT_BY_PITCH>4</HIT_BY_PITCH>
          </PLAYER>
          <PLAYER>
            <GIVEN_NAME>Rafael</GIVEN_NAME>
            <SURNAME>Palmeiro</SURNAME>
            <POSITION>First Base</POSITION>
            <GAMES>162</GAMES>
            <GAMES_STARTED>161</GAMES_STARTED>
            <AT_BATS>619</AT_BATS>
            <RUNS>98</RUNS>
            <HITS>183</HITS>
            <DOUBLES>36</DOUBLES>
            <TRIPLES>1</TRIPLES>
            <HOME_RUNS>43</HOME_RUNS>
            <RBI>121</RBI>
            <STEALS>11</STEALS>
            <CAUGHT_STEALING>7</CAUGHT_STEALING>
            <SACRIFICE_HITS>0</SACRIFICE_HITS>
            <SACRIFICE_FLIES>4</SACRIFICE_FLIES>
            <ERRORS>9</ERRORS>
            <WALKS>79</WALKS>
            <STRUCK_OUT>91</STRUCK_OUT>
            <HIT_BY_PITCH>7</HIT_BY_PITCH>
          </PLAYER>
        </TEAM>
        <TEAM>
          <TEAM_CITY>Boston</TEAM_CITY>
          <TEAM_NAME>Red Sox</TEAM_NAME>
```

```
      </TEAM>
      <TEAM>
        <TEAM_CITY>New York</TEAM_CITY>
        <TEAM_NAME>Yankees</TEAM_NAME>
      </TEAM>
      <TEAM>
        <TEAM_CITY>Tampa Bay</TEAM_CITY>
        <TEAM_NAME>Devil Rays</TEAM_NAME>
      </TEAM>
      <TEAM>
        <TEAM_CITY>Toronto</TEAM_CITY>
        <TEAM_NAME>Blue Jays</TEAM_NAME>
      </TEAM>
  </DIVISION>
  <DIVISION>
      <DIVISION_NAME>Central</DIVISION_NAME>
      <TEAM>
        <TEAM_CITY>Chicago</TEAM_CITY>
        <TEAM_NAME>White Sox</TEAM_NAME>
      </TEAM>
      <TEAM>
        <TEAM_CITY>Kansas City</TEAM_CITY>
        <TEAM_NAME>Royals</TEAM_NAME>
      </TEAM>
      <TEAM>
        <TEAM_CITY>Detroit</TEAM_CITY>
        <TEAM_NAME>Tigers</TEAM_NAME>
      </TEAM>
      <TEAM>
        <TEAM_CITY>Cleveland</TEAM_CITY>
        <TEAM_NAME>Indians</TEAM_NAME>
      </TEAM>
      <TEAM>
        <TEAM_CITY>Minnesota</TEAM_CITY>
        <TEAM_NAME>Twins</TEAM_NAME>
      </TEAM>
  </DIVISION>
  <DIVISION>
      <DIVISION_NAME>West</DIVISION_NAME>
      <TEAM>
        <TEAM_CITY>Anaheim</TEAM_CITY>
        <TEAM_NAME>Angels</TEAM_NAME>
      </TEAM>
      <TEAM>
        <TEAM_CITY>Oakland</TEAM_CITY>
        <TEAM_NAME>Athletics</TEAM_NAME>
      </TEAM>
      <TEAM>
        <TEAM_CITY>Seattle</TEAM_CITY>
        <TEAM_NAME>Mariners</TEAM_NAME>
      </TEAM>
      <TEAM>
```

Continued

Listing 4-1 *(continued)*

```
            <TEAM_CITY>Texas</TEAM_CITY>
            <TEAM_NAME>Rangers</TEAM_NAME>
         </TEAM>
      </DIVISION>
   </LEAGUE>
   <LEAGUE>
      <LEAGUE_NAME>National League</LEAGUE_NAME>
      <DIVISION>
         <DIVISION_NAME>East</DIVISION_NAME>
           <TEAM>
             <TEAM_CITY>Atlanta</TEAM_CITY>
             <TEAM_NAME>Braves</TEAM_NAME>
           </TEAM>
           <TEAM>
             <TEAM_CITY>Florida</TEAM_CITY>
             <TEAM_NAME>Marlins</TEAM_NAME>
           </TEAM>
           <TEAM>
             <TEAM_CITY>Montreal</TEAM_CITY>
             <TEAM_NAME>Expos</TEAM_NAME>
           </TEAM>
           <TEAM>
             <TEAM_CITY>New York</TEAM_CITY>
             <TEAM_NAME>Mets</TEAM_NAME>
           </TEAM>
           <TEAM>
             <TEAM_CITY>Philadelphia</TEAM_CITY>
           <TEAM_NAME>Phillies</TEAM_NAME>
           </TEAM>
      </DIVISION>
      <DIVISION>
         <DIVISION_NAME>Central</DIVISION_NAME>
         <TEAM>
           <TEAM_CITY>Chicago</TEAM_CITY>
           <TEAM_NAME>Cubs</TEAM_NAME>
         </TEAM>
         <TEAM>
           <TEAM_CITY>Cincinatti</TEAM_CITY>
           <TEAM_NAME>Reds</TEAM_NAME>
         </TEAM>
         <TEAM>
           <TEAM_CITY>Houston</TEAM_CITY>
           <TEAM_NAME>Astros</TEAM_NAME>
         </TEAM>
         <TEAM>
           <TEAM_CITY>Milwaukee</TEAM_CITY>
           <TEAM_NAME>Brewers</TEAM_NAME>
         </TEAM>
```

```
            <TEAM>
              <TEAM_CITY>Pittsburgh</TEAM_CITY>
              <TEAM_NAME>Pirates</TEAM_NAME>
            </TEAM>
            <TEAM>
              <TEAM_CITY>St. Louis</TEAM_CITY>
              <TEAM_NAME>Cardinals</TEAM_NAME>
            </TEAM>
        </DIVISION>
        <DIVISION>
            <DIVISION_NAME>West</DIVISION_NAME>
            <TEAM>
              <TEAM_CITY>Arizona</TEAM_CITY>
              <TEAM_NAME>Diamondbacks</TEAM_NAME>
            </TEAM>
            <TEAM>
              <TEAM_CITY>Colorado</TEAM_CITY>
              <TEAM_NAME>Rockies</TEAM_NAME>
            </TEAM>
            <TEAM>
              <TEAM_CITY>Los Angeles</TEAM_CITY>
              <TEAM_NAME>Dodgers</TEAM_NAME>
            </TEAM>
            <TEAM>
              <TEAM_CITY>San Diego</TEAM_CITY>
              <TEAM_NAME>Padres</TEAM_NAME>
            </TEAM>
            <TEAM>
              <TEAM_CITY>San Francisco</TEAM_CITY>
              <TEAM_NAME>Giants</TEAM_NAME>
            </TEAM>
        </DIVISION>
      </LEAGUE>
    </SEASON>
```

Figure 4-1 shows this document loaded into Internet Explorer 5.0.

Even as large as it is, this document is incomplete. It only contains players from one team (the Baltimore Orioles) and only nine players from that team. Showing more than that would make the example too long to include in this book.

On the CD-ROM A more complete XML document called 1998fullstatistics.xml with statistics for all players in the 1998 Major League is on the CD-ROM in the examples\baseball directory.

Figure 4-1: The 1998 major league baseball statistics displayed in Internet Explorer 5.0.

Furthermore, I've limited the data included to make this a manageable example within the confines of this book. There are many more details you could add. I've already alluded to the possibility of arranging the data game by game, pitch by pitch. Even without going to that extreme, there are a lot of details that could be added to individual elements. Teams also have coaches, managers, owners (How can you think of the Yankees without thinking of George Steinbrenner?), home stadiums, and more.

I've also deliberately omitted numbers that can be calculated from other numbers given here, such as batting average (number of hits divided by number of at bats). Nonetheless, players have batting arms, throwing arms, heights, weights, birth dates, positions, numbers, nicknames, colleges attended, and much more. And, of course, there are many more players than I've shown here. All of this is equally easy to include in XML. However, I will stop the XMLization of the data here so that we can move on; first to a brief discussion of why this data format is useful, and then to the techniques that can be used for actually displaying it in a Web browser.

The Advantages of the XML Format

Tables 4-1 and 4-2 do a pretty good job of displaying the batting and pitching data for a team in a comprehensible and compact fashion. What exactly have we gained by rewriting those tables as the much longer XML document of Listing 4-1? There are several benefits. Among them:

✦ The data is self-describing.

✦ The data can be manipulated with standard tools.

✦ The data can be viewed with standard tools.

✦ Different views of the same data are easy to create with style sheets.

The first major benefit of the XML format is that the data is self-describing. The meaning of each number is clearly and unmistakably associated with the number itself. When reading the document, you know that the 183 in <HITS>183</HITS> refers to hits and not runs batted in or strikeouts. If the person typing in the document inadvertently leaves out a statistic, that doesn't mean that every number after it is misinterpreted. HITS is still HITS even if the preceding RUNS element is missing. Another common error in less-verbose formats is transposing values; for instance, using runs for hits and hits for runs. XML lets you transpose with abandon. As long as the markup is transposed along with the content, no information is lost or misunderstood.

Cross-Reference   In Part II you'll see that XML can even use document type definitions (DTDs) to enforce constraints that certain elements such as HITS or RUNS must be present. In Chapter 23, you'll learn to use schemas to restrict the contents of elements, so that, for example, you can specify that HITS or RUNS must be a nonnegative integer.

The second benefit of the XML format is that data can be manipulated in a wide range of XML-enabled tools, from expensive payware such as Adobe FrameMaker to free, open-source software such as Python and Perl. The data may be bigger, but the extra redundancy allows more tools to process it.

The same is true when the time comes to view the data. The XML document can be loaded into Internet Explorer, Mozilla, Jumbo, and many other tools, all of which provide unique, useful views of the data. The document can even be loaded into simple, bare-bone text editors such as vi, BBEdit, and TextPad. XML is at least marginally viewable on most platforms.

New software isn't the only way to get a different view of the data either. The next section develops a style sheet for baseball statistics that provides a completely different way of looking at the data than what you see in Figure 4-1. Each time you apply a different style sheet to the same document you see a different picture.

Lastly, you should ask yourself if the size is really that important. Modern hard drives are quite big and can a hold a lot of data, even if it's not stored very efficiently. Furthermore, XML files compress very well. The complete 1998 major league baseball statistics document is 718K. However, compressing the file with gzip reduces the file size to 63K, a greater than 90 percent reduction. Advanced

HTTP servers such as Jigsaw can actually send compressed files rather than the uncompressed files so that network bandwidth used by a document like this is fairly close to its actual information content. Finally, you should not assume that binary file formats, especially general-purpose ones, are necessarily more efficient. A Microsoft Excel 2000 file that contains the same data as 1998fullstatistics.xml actually takes up 663K, almost as much space as the uncompressed XML document. Although you can certainly create more efficient file formats to hold this data, in practice that simply isn't often necessary.

Preparing a Style Sheet for Document Display

The view of the raw XML document shown in Figure 4-1 is not bad for some uses. For instance, it allows you to collapse and expand individual elements so you see only those parts of the document you want to see. However, most of the time you'd probably like a more finished look, especially if you're going to display it on the Web. To provide a more polished look, you must write a style sheet for the document.

In this chapter, I use Cascading Style Sheets (CSS). A CSS style sheet defines formatting for each element of the document. The complete list of elements used in the XML document of Listing 4-1 is:

SEASON	LOSSES	HITS
YEAR	SAVES	DOUBLES
LEAGUE	COMPLETE_GAMES	TRIPLES
LEAGUE_NAME	SHUT_OUTS	HOME_RUNS
DIVISION	ERA	RBI
DIVISION_NAME	INNINGS	STEALS
TEAM	HITS_AGAINST	CAUGHT_STEALING
TEAM_NAME	HOME_RUNS_AGAINST	SACRIFICE_HITS
TEAM_CITY	RUNS_AGAINST	SACRIFICE_FLIES
PLAYER	EARNED_RUNS	ERRORS
GIVEN_NAME	WILD_PITCHES	WALKS
SURNAME	BALK	STRUCK_OUT
POSITION	WALKED_BATTER	HIT_BY_PITCH
GAMES	STRUCK_OUT_BATTER	HIT_BATTER
GAMES_STARTED	AT_BATS	
WINS	RUNS	

Generally, you'll want to follow an iterative procedure, adding style rules for each of these elements one at a time, checking that they do what you expect, then moving on to the next element. In this example, such an approach also has the advantage of introducing CSS properties one at a time for those who are not familiar with them.

Linking to a style sheet

The style sheet can be named anything you like. If it's only going to apply to one document, then it's customary to give it the same name as the document but with the three-letter extension .css instead of .xml. For instance, the style sheet for the XML document 1998shortstats.xml might be called 1998shortstats.css. On the other hand, if the same style sheet will be applied to many documents, then it should probably have a more generic name such as baseballstats.css.

Cross-Reference

Since CSS style sheets cascade, more than one can be applied to the same document. Thus it's possible that baseballstats.css would apply some general formatting rules, while 1998shortstats.css would override a few to handle specific details in the one document 1998shortstats.xml. We discuss this procedure in Chapter 14.

To attach a style sheet to the document, you simply add an `<?xml-stylesheet?>` processing instruction between the XML declaration and the root element like this:

```
<?xml version="1.0"
<?xml-stylesheet type="text/css" href="baseballstats.css"?>
<SEASON>
. . .
```

This tells a browser reading the document to apply the style sheet found in the file baseballstats.css to this document. This file is assumed to reside in the same directory and on the same server as the XML document itself. In other words, baseballstats.css is a relative URL. Absolute URLs may also be used. For example:

```
<?xml version="1.0"
<?xml-stylesheet type="text/css"
href="http://www.ibiblio.org/xml/examples/baseballstats.css"?>
<SEASON>
. . .
```

You can begin by simply placing an empty file named baseballstats.css in the same directory as the XML document. After you've done this and added the necessary processing instruction to 1998shortstats.xml (Listing 4-1), the document now appears as shown in Figure 4-2. Only the element content is shown. The collapsible outline view of Figure 4-1 is gone. The formatting of the element content uses the browser's defaults — black 12-point Verdana on a white background in this case.

Figure 4-2: The 1998 major league baseball statistics displayed after a blank style sheet is applied.

Note   Figure 4-2 is also very close to what you'd see if you loaded Listing 4-1 into Netscape, Mozilla, or Opera, because they don't provide a hierarchical source code view like Internet Explorer does. You'll also see something similar to Figure 4-2 in Internet Explorer if the style sheet named by the `xml-stylesheet` processing instruction can't be found in the specified location.

Assigning style rules to the root element

You do not have to assign a style rule to each element in the list. Many elements can rely on the styles of their parents cascading down. The most important style, therefore, is the one for the root element — SEASON in this example. This defines the default for all the other elements on the page. Computer monitors at roughly 72 dots per inch (dpi) don't have as high a resolution as paper at 300 or more dpi. Therefore, Web pages should generally use a larger point size than is customary. Let's make the default 14-point type, black on a white background, as shown below:

```
SEASON {font-size: 14pt; background-color: white;
        color: black; display: block}
```

Place this statement in a text file, save the file with the name baseballstats.css in the same directory as Listing 4-1, 1998shortstats.xml, and open 1998shortstats.xml in your browser. You should see something similar to what is shown in Figure 4-3.

Figure 4-3: Baseball statistics in 14-point type with a black on white background

The default font size changed between Figure 4-2 and Figure 4-3. The text color and background color did not. Indeed, it was not absolutely required to set them, because black foreground and white background are the defaults. Nonetheless, nothing is lost by being explicit about what you want.

Assigning style rules to titles

The YEAR element is more or less the title of the document. Therefore, let's make it appropriately large and bold — 32 points should be big enough. Furthermore, it should stand out from the rest of the document rather than simply running together with the rest of the content, so let's make it a centered block element. All of this can be accomplished by the following style rule.

```
YEAR {display: block; font-size: 32pt; font-weight: bold;
      text-align: center}
```

Figure 4-4 shows the document after this rule has been added to the style sheet. Notice in particular the line break after 1998. That's there because YEAR is now a block-level element. Everything else in the document is an inline element. Only block-level elements can be centered (or left-aligned, right-aligned, or justified).

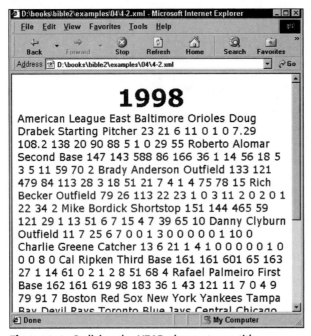

Figure 4-4: Stylizing the YEAR element as a title

1998 isn't the ideal title for this document. 1998 Major League Baseball would be better, but the phrase Major League Baseball isn't included in the XML document. CSS lets you add extra content from the style sheet either before or after particular elements using the :before and :after pseudoselectors. The text that you want to add is given as a string value of the content property. For example, to add the phrase " Major League Baseball" to the end of the YEAR element, add this rule to the style sheet:

```
YEAR:after {content: " Major League Baseball"}
```

Internet Explorer 5.0/5.5 doesn't support either the :before and :after pseudose-lectors or the content property. Therefore, Figure 4-5 shows the document after this rule has been added in Mozilla, which does support these.

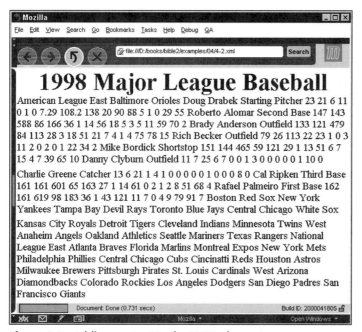

Figure 4-5: Adding content to the YEAR element

In this document, with these style rules, YEAR duplicates the functionality of HTML's H1 header element. Because this document is so neatly hierarchical, several other elements serve the role of H2 headers, H3 headers, and so on. These elements can be formatted by similar rules with only a slightly smaller font size.

For instance, SEASON is divided into two LEAGUE elements. The name of each LEAGUE — that is, the LEAGUE_NAME element — has the same role as an H2 element in HTML. Each LEAGUE element is divided into three DIVISION elements. The name of each DIVISION — that is, the DIVISION_NAME element — has the same role as an H3 element in HTML. These two rules format them accordingly.

```
LEAGUE_NAME {display: block; text-align: center; font-size:
28pt; font-weight: bold}
DIVISION_NAME {display: block; text-align: center; font-size:
24pt; font-weight: bold}
```

Figure 4-6 shows the resulting document.

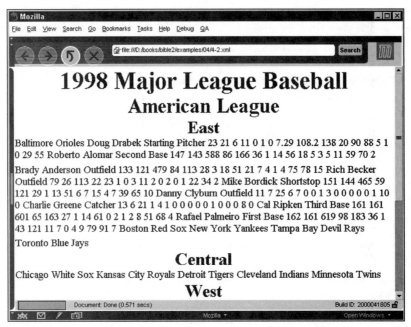

Figure 4-6: Stylizing the LEAGUE_NAME and DIVISION_NAME elements as headings

Divisions are divided into TEAM elements. Formatting these is a little trickier because the title of a team is not simply the TEAM_NAME element but rather the TEAM_CITY concatenated with the TEAM_NAME. Therefore these need to be inline elements rather than separate block-level elements. However, they are still titles, so we set them to bold, italic, 20-point type. Figure 4-7 shows the results of adding these two rules to the style sheet.

```
TEAM_CITY {font-size: 20pt; font-weight: bold;
           font-style: italic}
TEAM_NAME {font-size: 20pt; font-weight: bold;
           font-style: italic}
```

At this point, it would be nice to arrange the team names and cities as a combined block-level element. There are several ways to do this. You could, for instance, add an additional TEAM_TITLE element to the XML document whose sole purpose is merely to contain the TEAM_NAME and TEAM_CITY. For instance:

```
<TEAM>
  <TEAM_TITLE>
    <TEAM_CITY>Colorado</TEAM_CITY>
    <TEAM_NAME>Rockies</TEAM_NAME>
  </TEAM_TITLE>
</TEAM>
```

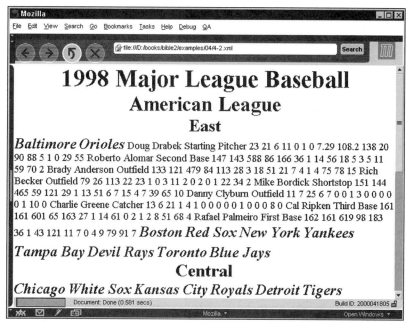

Figure 4-7: Stylizing team names

Next, you would add a style rule that applies block-level formatting to TEAM_TITLE:

```
TEAM_TITLE {display: block; text-align: center}
```

However, you really should never reorganize an XML document just to make the style sheet work easier. After all, the whole point of a style sheet is to keep formatting information out of the document itself. However, you can achieve much the same effect by making the immediately preceding and following elements block-level elements — that is, TEAM and PLAYER respectively. This places the TEAM_NAME and TEAM_CITY in an implicit block-level element of their own. Figure 4-8 shows the result.

```
TEAM {display: block}
PLAYER {display: block}
```

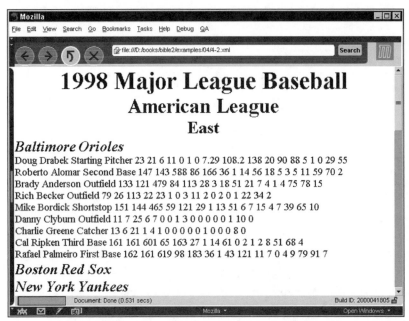

Figure 4-8: Stylizing team names and cities as headers

Assigning style rules to player and statistics elements

The trickiest formatting that this document requires is for the individual players and statistics. Each team has a couple of dozen players. Each player has statistics. You could think of a TEAM element as being divided into PLAYER elements, and place each player in his own block-level section as you did for previous elements. However, a more attractive and efficient way to organize this is to use a table. The style rules that accomplish this look like this:

```
TEAM {display: table}
TEAM_CITY {display: table-caption}
TEAM_NAME {display: table-caption}
PLAYER {display: table-row}
SURNAME {display: table-cell}
GIVEN_NAME {display: table-cell}
POSITION {display: table-cell}
GAMES {display: table-cell}
GAMES_STARTED {display: table-cell}
AT_BATS {display: table-cell}
RUNS {display: table-cell}
HITS {display: table-cell}
DOUBLES {display: table-cell}
TRIPLES {display: table-cell}
```

```
HOME_RUNS {display: table-cell}
RBI {display: table-cell}
STEALS {display: table-cell}
CAUGHT_STEALING {display: table-cell}
SACRIFICE_HITS {display: table-cell}
SACRIFICE_FLIES {display: table-cell}
ERRORS {display: table-cell}
WALKS {display: table-cell}
STRUCK_OUT {display: table-cell}
HIT_BY_PITCH {display: table-cell}
```

Unfortunately, Internet Explorer 5.0/5.5 does not support table properties. Mozilla, Netscape 6.0, and Opera 5.0 do support table formatting. Figure 4-9 shows the final result.

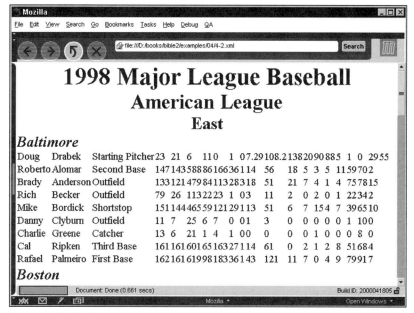

Figure 4-9: Stylizing player statistics as tables

Summing up

Listing 4-2 shows the finished style sheet. CSS style sheets don't have a lot of structure beyond the individual rules. In essence, this is just a list of all the rules that I introduced separately in the preceding material. Reordering them wouldn't make any difference as long as they're all present.

Listing 4-2: **baseballstats.css**

```
SEASON {font-size: 14pt; background-color: white;
        color: black; display: block}
YEAR {display: block; font-size: 32pt; font-weight: bold;
      text-align: center; }
YEAR:after {content: " Major League Baseball"}
LEAGUE_NAME {display: block; text-align: center;
             font-size: 28pt; font-weight: bold}
DIVISION_NAME {display: block; text-align: center;
               font-size: 24pt; font-weight: bold}
TEAM_CITY {font-size: 20pt; font-weight: bold;
           font-style: italic}
TEAM_NAME {font-size: 20pt; font-weight: bold;
           font-style: italic}
TEAM {display: table}
TEAM_CITY {display: table-caption}
TEAM_NAME {display: table-caption}
PLAYER {display: table-row}
GIVEN_NAME {display: table-cell}
SURNAME {display: table-cell}
POSITION {display: table-cell}
GAMES {display: table-cell}
GAMES_STARTED {display: table-cell}
WINS {display: table-cell}
LOSSES {display: table-cell}
SAVES {display: table-cell}
COMPLETE_GAMES {display: table-cell}
SHUT_OUTS {display: table-cell}
ERA {display: table-cell}
INNINGS {display: table-cell}
HITS_AGAINST {display: table-cell}
HOME_RUNS_AGAINST {display: table-cell}
RUNS_AGAINST {display: table-cell}
EARNED_RUNS {display: table-cell}
WILD_PITCHES {display: table-cell}
BALK {display: table-cell}
WALKED_BATTER {display: table-cell}
STRUCK_OUT_BATTER {display: table-cell}
AT_BATS {display: table-cell}
RUNS {display: table-cell}
HITS {display: table-cell}
DOUBLES {display: table-cell}
TRIPLES {display: table-cell}
HOME_RUNS {display: table-cell}
RBI {display: table-cell}
STEALS {display: table-cell}
CAUGHT_STEALING {display: table-cell}
SACRIFICE_HITS {display: table-cell}
SACRIFICE_FLIES {display: table-cell}
ERRORS {display: table-cell}
```

```
WALKS {display: table-cell}
STRUCK_OUT {display: table-cell}
HIT_BY_PITCH {display: table-cell}
HIT_BATTER {display: table-cell}
```

This completes the basic formatting for baseball statistics. However, work clearly remains to be done. Here are some things that you might want to add.

✦ The numbers are presented raw with no indication of what they represent. Instead, each number should be identified by a caption that names it, such as RBI or At Bats.

✦ Interesting data such as batting average that could be calculated from the data presented here is not included.

✦ Because pitcher statistics are so different from batter statistics, it would be nice to place them in a separate table for each team.

✦ You can't really provide two elements for a single table caption. That's why you only see the team cities and not the team names in Figure 4-9.

Many of these points could be addressed by adding more content to the document. For instance, captions can be added to the player stats by placing a phantom PLAYER element at the top of each roster, like this:

```
<PLAYER>
  <GIVEN_NAME>First Name</GIVEN_NAME>
  <SURNAME>Last Name</SURNAME>
  <POSITION>Position</POSITION>
  <GAMES>Games Played</GAMES>
  <GAMES_STARTED>Games Started</GAMES_STARTED>
  <AT_BATS>At Bats</AT_BATS>
  <RUNS>Runs</RUNS>
  <HITS>Hits</HITS>
  <DOUBLES>Doubles</DOUBLES>
  <TRIPLES>Triples</TRIPLES>
  <HOME_RUNS>Home Runs</HOME_RUNS>
  <RBI>Runs Batted In</RBI>
  <STEALS>Steals</STEALS>
  <CAUGHT_STEALING>Caught Stealing</CAUGHT_STEALING>
  <SACRIFICE_HITS>Sacrifice Hits</SACRIFICE_HITS>
  <SACRIFICE_FLIES>Sacrifice Flies</SACRIFICE_FLIES>
  <ERRORS>Errors</ERRORS>
  <WALKS>Walks</WALKS>
  <STRUCK_OUT>Struck Out</STRUCK_OUT>
  <HIT_BY_PITCH>Hit By Pitch</HIT_BY_PITCH>
</PLAYER>
```

Still, there's something fundamentally troublesome about such tactics. The caption At Bats is not the same as a number of at bats. (It's the difference between the name of a thing and the thing itself.) You can encode still more markup like this:

```
<TABLE_HEAD>
  <COLUMN_LABEL>Surname</COLUMN_LABEL>
  <COLUMN_LABEL>Given name</COLUMN_LABEL>>
  <COLUMN_LABEL>Position</COLUMN_LABEL>
  <COLUMN_LABEL>Games</COLUMN_LABEL>
  <COLUMN_LABEL>Games Started</COLUMN_LABEL>
  <COLUMN_LABEL>At Bats</COLUMN_LABEL>
  <COLUMN_LABEL>Runs</COLUMN_LABEL>
  <COLUMN_LABEL>Hits</COLUMN_LABEL>
  <COLUMN_LABEL>Doubles</COLUMN_LABEL>
  <COLUMN_LABEL>Triples</COLUMN_LABEL>
  <COLUMN_LABEL>Home Runs</COLUMN_LABEL>
  <COLUMN_LABEL>Runs Batted In</COLUMN_LABEL>
  <COLUMN_LABEL>Steals</COLUMN_LABEL>
  <COLUMN_LABEL>Caught Stealing</COLUMN_LABEL>
  <COLUMN_LABEL>Sacrifice Hits</COLUMN_LABEL>
  <COLUMN_LABEL>Sacrifice Flies</COLUMN_LABEL>
  <COLUMN_LABEL>Errors</COLUMN_LABEL>
  <COLUMN_LABEL>Walks</COLUMN_LABEL>
  <COLUMN_LABEL>Struck Out</COLUMN_LABEL>
  <COLUMN_LABEL>Hit By Pitch</COLUMN_LABEL>>
</TABLE_HEAD>
```

However, this basically reinvents HTML, and returns us to the point of using markup for formatting rather than meaning. Furthermore, we're still simply repeating the information that's already contained in the names of the elements. The full document is large enough as it is. I would prefer to not make it larger.

Adding batting and other averages is easy. Just include the data as additional elements. For example, here's a player with batting, slugging, and on-base averages.

```
<PLAYER>
  <GIVEN_NAME>Luis</GIVEN_NAME>
  <SURNAME>Ordaz</SURNAME>
  <POSITION>Shortstop</POSITION>
  <GAMES>57</GAMES>
  <GAMES_STARTED>47</GAMES_STARTED>
  <ON_BASE_AVERAGE>.253</ON_BASE_AVERAGE>
  <SLUGGING_AVERAGE>.233</SLUGGING_AVERAGE>
  <BATTING_AVERAGE>.204</BATTING_AVERAGE>
  <AT_BATS>153</AT_BATS>
  <RUNS>9</RUNS>
  <HITS>31</HITS>
  <DOUBLES>5</DOUBLES>
  <TRIPLES>0</TRIPLES>
  <HOME_RUNS>0</HOME_RUNS>
  <RBI>8</RBI>
  <STEALS>2</STEALS>
  <CAUGHT_STEALING>0</CAUGHT_STEALING>
```

```
      <SACRIFICE_HITS>4</SACRIFICE_HITS>
      <SACRIFICE_FLIES>0</SACRIFICE_FLIES>
      <ERRORS>13</ERRORS>
      <WALKS>12</WALKS>
      <STRUCK_OUT>18</STRUCK_OUT>
      <HIT_BY_PITCH>0</HIT_BY_PITCH>
</PLAYER>
```

However, this information is redundant because it can be calculated from the other information already included in a player's listing. Batting average, for example, is simply the number of base hits divided by the number of at bats; that is, HITS/AT_BATS. Redundant data makes maintaining and updating the document exponentially more difficult. A simple change or addition to a single element requires changes and recalculations in multiple locations.

What's really needed is a different style sheet language that enables you to add certain boilerplate content to elements and to perform transformations on the element content that is present. Such a language exists — the Extensible Stylesheet Language (XSL).

CSS is simpler than XSL. CSS works well for basic Web pages and reasonably straightforward documents. XSL is considerably more complex, but it is also more powerful. XSL builds on the simple CSS formatting that you learned in this chapter, but it also transforms the source document into various forms that the reader can view. It's often a good idea to make a first pass at a problem using CSS while you're still debugging your XML, and then move to XSL to achieve greater flexibility.

Cross-
Reference   XSL is discussed in Chapters 5, 17, and 18.

Summary

In this chapter, you saw an example of an XML document being built from scratch. This chapter was full of seat-of-the-pants/back-of-the-envelope coding. In particular you learned:

✦ How to identify the elements in the data to be included in the XML document.

✦ How to mark up the data with XML tags that you choose.

✦ The advantages of XML formats over traditional formats.

✦ How to write a style sheet that says how the document should be formatted and displayed.

In the next chapter, we explore some additional means of embedding information in XML documents, including attributes, comments, and processing instructions, and also look at an alternative way of encoding baseball statistics in XML.

✦   ✦   ✦

Attributes, Empty Tags, and XSL

There are an infinite number of ways to encode any given set of data in XML. There's no one right way to do it, although some ways are more right than others, and some are more appropriate for particular uses. This chapter explores a different solution to the problem of marking up baseball statistics in XML, carrying over the baseball example from the previous chapter. Specifically, you'll learn how to use attributes to store information and empty-element tags to define element positions. In addition, because CSS doesn't work well with content-less XML elements of this form, we examine an alternative and more powerful style sheet language called the Extensible Stylesheet Language (XSL).

Attributes

In the last chapter, all information was provided either in the form of a tag name or as the text content of an element. This is a straightforward and easy-to-understand approach, but it's not the only one possible. As in HTML, XML elements may have attributes. An attribute is a name-value pair associated with an element. The name and the value are each strings. You're already familiar with attribute syntax from HTML. For example, consider this `<IMG>` tag:

```
<IMG SRC=cup.gif WIDTH=89 HEIGHT=67 ALT="Cup
of coffee">
```

It has four attributes, the `SRC` attribute whose value is `cup.gif`, the `WIDTH` attribute whose value is `89`, the `HEIGHT` attribute whose value is `67`, and the `ALT` attribute whose value is `Cup of coffee`. However, in XML—unlike HTML—attribute values must always be quoted and start tags must have matching end tags. Thus, the XML equivalent of this tag is:

```
<IMG SRC="cup.gif" WIDTH="89" HEIGHT="67" ALT="Cup of coffee">
</IMG>
```

Note Another difference between HTML and XML is that XML assigns no particular meaning to the IMG element and its attributes. In particular, there's no guarantee that an XML browser will interpret this element as an instruction to load and display the image in the file cup.gif.

Attribute syntax fits the baseball example quite nicely. One advantage is that it makes the markup somewhat more concise. For example, instead of containing a YEAR child element, the SEASON element only needs a YEAR attribute:

```
<SEASON YEAR="1998">
</SEASON>
```

On the other hand, LEAGUE should be a child of the SEASON element rather than an attribute. For one thing, there are two leagues in a season. Anytime there's likely to be more than one of something, child elements are called for. Attribute names must be unique within an element. Thus, you cannot, for example, write a SEASON element like this:

```
<SEASON YEAR="1998" LEAGUE="National" League="American">
</SEASON>
```

The second reason LEAGUE is naturally a child element rather than an attribute is that it has substructure; that is, it, itself, is subdivided into DIVISION elements. Attribute values are flat text. XML elements can conveniently encode structure. Attribute values cannot.

However, the name of a league is unstructured, flat text; and there's only one name per league, so LEAGUE elements can easily have a NAME attribute instead of a LEAGUE_NAME child element:

```
<LEAGUE NAME="National League">
</LEAGUE>
```

Because an attribute is more closely tied to its element than a child element is, you don't run into problems by using NAME instead of LEAGUE_NAME for the name of the attribute. Divisions and teams can also have NAME attributes without any fear of confusion with the name of a league. Because an element can have more than one attribute (as long as the attributes have different names), you can also make a team's city an attribute, as shown here:

```
<LEAGUE NAME="American League">
  <DIVISION NAME="East">
   <TEAM NAME="Orioles"    CITY="Baltimore"></TEAM>
   <TEAM NAME="Red Sox"    CITY="Boston"></TEAM>
```

```
    <TEAM NAME="Yankees"    CITY="New York"></TEAM>
    <TEAM NAME="Devil Rays" CITY="Tampa Bay"></TEAM>
    <TEAM NAME="Blue Jays"  CITY="Toronto"></TEAM>
  </DIVISION>
</LEAGUE>
```

Players will have a lot of attributes if you choose to make each statistic an attribute. For example, here are Joe Girardi's 1998 statistics as attributes:

```
<PLAYER GIVEN_NAME="Joe" SURNAME="Girardi"
  POSITION="Catcher" GAMES="78" GAMES_STARTED="76"
  AT_BATS="254" RUNS="31" HITS="70"
  DOUBLES="11" TRIPLES="4" HOME_RUNS="3"
  RUNS_BATTED_IN="31" WALKS="14" STRUCK_OUT="38"
  STOLEN_BASES="2" CAUGHT_STEALING="4"
  SACRIFICE_FLIES="1" SACRIFICE_HITS="8"
  HIT_BY_PITCH="2" STEALS="2">
</PLAYER>
```

Listing 5-1 uses this new attribute style for a complete XML document containing the baseball statistics for the 1998 season. It contains the same information (i.e., 2 leagues, 6 divisions, 30 teams, and 9 players) as does Listing 4-1 in the last chapter. It is merely marked up differently. Figure 5-1 shows this document loaded into Internet Explorer 5.0 without a style sheet.

Listing 5-1: A complete XML document using attributes to store baseball statistics

```
<?xml version="1.0"?>
<SEASON YEAR="1998">
  <LEAGUE NAME="American League">
    <DIVISION NAME="East">
      <TEAM CITY="Baltimore" NAME="Orioles">
        <PLAYER GIVEN_NAME="Doug" SURNAME="Drabek"
          POSITION="Starting Pitcher" GAMES="23"
          GAMES_STARTED="21" WINS="6" LOSSES="11" SAVES="0"
          COMPLETE_GAMES="1" SHUT_OUTS="0" ERA="7.29"
          INNINGS="108.2" HITS_AGAINST="138"
          HOME_RUNS_AGAINST="20" RUNS_AGAINST="90"
          EARNED_RUNS="88" HIT_BATTER="5" WILD_PITCHES="1"
          BALK="0" WALKED_BATTER="29" STRUCK_OUT_BATTER="55">
        </PLAYER>
        <PLAYER GIVEN_NAME="Roberto" SURNAME="Alomar"
          POSITION="Second Base" GAMES="147"
          GAMES_STARTED="143" AT_BATS="588" RUNS="86"
          HITS="166" DOUBLES="36" TRIPLES="1" HOME_RUNS="14"
          RUNS_BATTED_IN="56" WALKS="59" STRUCK_OUT="70"
          STOLEN_BASES="18" CAUGHT_STEALING="5"
          SACRIFICE_FLIES="5" SACRIFICE_HITS="3"
```

Continued

Listing 5-1 *(continued)*

```
        HIT_BY_PITCH="2" STEALS="18">
</PLAYER>
<PLAYER GIVEN_NAME="Brady" SURNAME="Anderson"
    POSITION="Outfield" GAMES="133" GAMES_STARTED="121"
    AT_BATS="479" RUNS="84" HITS="113" DOUBLES="28"
    TRIPLES="3" HOME_RUNS="18" RUNS_BATTED_IN="51"
    WALKS="75" STRUCK_OUT="78" STOLEN_BASES="21"
    CAUGHT_STEALING="7" SACRIFICE_FLIES="1"
    SACRIFICE_HITS="4" HIT_BY_PITCH="15" STEALS="21">
</PLAYER>
<PLAYER GIVEN_NAME="Rich" SURNAME="Becker"
    POSITION="Outfield" GAMES="79" GAMES_STARTED="26"
    AT_BATS="113" RUNS="22" HITS="23" DOUBLES="1"
    TRIPLES="0" HOME_RUNS="3" RUNS_BATTED_IN="11"
    WALKS="22" STRUCK_OUT="34" STOLEN_BASES="2"
    CAUGHT_STEALING="0" SACRIFICE_FLIES="0"
    SACRIFICE_HITS="2" HIT_BY_PITCH="2" STEALS="2">
</PLAYER>
<PLAYER GIVEN_NAME="Mike" SURNAME="Bordick"
    POSITION="Shortstop" GAMES="151" GAMES_STARTED="144"
    AT_BATS="465" RUNS="59" HITS="121" DOUBLES="29"
    TRIPLES="1" HOME_RUNS="13" RUNS_BATTED_IN="51"
    WALKS="39" STRUCK_OUT="65" STOLEN_BASES="6"
    CAUGHT_STEALING="7" SACRIFICE_FLIES="4"
    SACRIFICE_HITS="15" HIT_BY_PITCH="10" STEALS="6">
</PLAYER>
<PLAYER GIVEN_NAME="Danny" SURNAME="Clyburn"
    POSITION="Outfield" GAMES="11" GAMES_STARTED="7"
    AT_BATS="25" RUNS="6" HITS="7" DOUBLES="0"
    TRIPLES="0" HOME_RUNS="1" RUNS_BATTED_IN="3"
    WALKS="1" STRUCK_OUT="10" STOLEN_BASES="0"
    CAUGHT_STEALING="0" SACRIFICE_FLIES="0"
    SACRIFICE_HITS="0" HIT_BY_PITCH="0" STEALS="0">
</PLAYER>
<PLAYER GIVEN_NAME="Charlie" SURNAME="Greene"
    POSITION="Catcher" GAMES="13" GAMES_STARTED="6"
    AT_BATS="21" RUNS="1" HITS="4" DOUBLES="1"
    TRIPLES="0" HOME_RUNS="0" RUNS_BATTED_IN="0"
    WALKS="0" STRUCK_OUT="8" STOLEN_BASES="0"
    CAUGHT_STEALING="0" SACRIFICE_FLIES="0"
    SACRIFICE_HITS="1" HIT_BY_PITCH="0" STEALS="0">
</PLAYER>
<PLAYER GIVEN_NAME="Cal" SURNAME="Ripken"
    POSITION="Third Base" GAMES="161"
    GAMES_STARTED="161" AT_BATS="601" RUNS="65"
    HITS="163" DOUBLES="27" TRIPLES="1"
    HOME_RUNS="14" RUNS_BATTED_IN="61" WALKS="51"
    STRUCK_OUT="68" STOLEN_BASES="0" CAUGHT_STEALING="2"
    SACRIFICE_FLIES="2" SACRIFICE_HITS="1"
    HIT_BY_PITCH="4" STEALS="0">
</PLAYER>
```

```
            <PLAYER GIVEN_NAME="Rafael" SURNAME="Palmeiro"
                POSITION="First Base" GAMES="162"
                GAMES_STARTED="161" AT_BATS="619" RUNS="98"
                HITS="183" DOUBLES="36" TRIPLES="1" HOME_RUNS="43"
                RUNS_BATTED_IN="121" WALKS="79" STRUCK_OUT="91"
                STOLEN_BASES="11" CAUGHT_STEALING="7"
                SACRIFICE_FLIES="4" SACRIFICE_HITS="0"
                HIT_BY_PITCH="7" STEALS="11">
            </PLAYER>
        </TEAM>
        <TEAM CITY="Boston"     NAME="Red Sox"></TEAM>
        <TEAM CITY="New York"   NAME="Yankees"></TEAM>
        <TEAM CITY="Tampa Bay"  NAME="Devil Rays"></TEAM>
        <TEAM CITY="Toronto"    NAME="Blue Jays"></TEAM>
      </DIVISION>
      <DIVISION NAME="Central">
        <TEAM CITY="Chicago"      NAME="White Sox"></TEAM>
        <TEAM CITY="Kansas City"  NAME="Royals"></TEAM>
        <TEAM CITY="Detroit"      NAME="Tigers"></TEAM>
        <TEAM CITY="Cleveland"    NAME="Indians"></TEAM>
        <TEAM CITY="Minnesota"    NAME="Twins"></TEAM>
      </DIVISION>
      <DIVISION NAME="West">
        <TEAM CITY="Anaheim" NAME="Angels"></TEAM>
        <TEAM CITY="Oakland" NAME="Athletics"></TEAM>
        <TEAM CITY="Seattle" NAME="Mariners"></TEAM>
        <TEAM CITY="Texas"   NAME="Rangers"></TEAM>
      </DIVISION>
    </LEAGUE>
    <LEAGUE NAME="National League">
      <DIVISION NAME="East">
        <TEAM CITY="Atlanta"       NAME="Braves"></TEAM>
        <TEAM CITY="Florida"       NAME="Marlins"></TEAM>
        <TEAM CITY="Montreal"      NAME="Expos"></TEAM>
        <TEAM CITY="New York"      NAME="Mets"></TEAM>
        <TEAM CITY="Philadelphia" NAME="Phillies"></TEAM>
      </DIVISION>
      <DIVISION NAME="Central">
        <TEAM CITY="Chicago"     NAME="Cubs"></TEAM>
        <TEAM CITY="Cincinnati"  NAME="Reds"></TEAM>
        <TEAM CITY="Houston"     NAME="Astros"></TEAM>
        <TEAM CITY="Milwaukee"   NAME="Brewers"></TEAM>
        <TEAM CITY="Pittsburgh"  NAME="Pirates"></TEAM>
        <TEAM CITY="St. Louis"   NAME="Cardinals"></TEAM>
      </DIVISION>
      <DIVISION NAME="West">
        <TEAM CITY="Arizona"        NAME="Diamondbacks"></TEAM>
        <TEAM CITY="Colorado"       NAME="Rockies"></TEAM>
        <TEAM CITY="Los Angeles"    NAME="Dodgers"></TEAM>
        <TEAM CITY="San Diego"      NAME="Padres"></TEAM>
        <TEAM CITY="San Francisco" NAME="Giants"></TEAM>
      </DIVISION>
    </LEAGUE>
  </SEASON>
```

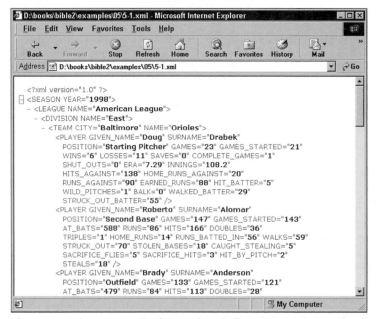

Figure 5-1: The 1998 major league baseball statistics using attributes for most information

Listing 5-1 uses only attributes for player information. Listing 4-1 used only element content. There are intermediate approaches as well. For example, you could make the player's name part of element content while leaving the rest of the statistics as attributes, like this:

```
<P>
   On Tuesday <PLAYER POSITION="Catcher" GAMES="78"
   GAMES_STARTED="76" AT_BATS="254" RUNS="31" HITS="70"
   DOUBLES="11" TRIPLES="4" HOME_RUNS="3" RUNS_BATTED_IN="31"
   WALKS="14" STRUCK_OUT="38" STOLEN_BASES="2"
   CAUGHT_STEALING="4" SACRIFICE_FLIES="1" SACRIFICE_HITS="8"
   HIT_BY_PITCH="2" STEALS="2">Joe Girardi</PLAYER> struck
   out twice and...
</P>
```

This would include Joe Girardi's name in the text of a page while still making his statistics available to readers who want to look deeper, perhaps as a hypertext footnote or a tool tip. There's always more than one way to encode the same data. Which one you pick depends on the needs of your specific application.

Attributes versus Elements

Last chapter's no-attribute approach was an extreme position. It's also possible to swing to the other extreme — storing all the information in the attributes and none in the content. In general, I don't recommend this approach. Storing all the information in element content is much easier to work with in practice. However, this chapter entertains the possibility of using only attributes for the sake of elucidation.

There are no hard and fast rules about when to use child elements and when to use attributes. Generally, you'll use whichever suits your application. With experience, you'll gain a feel for when attributes are easier than child elements and vice versa. Until then, one good rule of thumb is that the data itself should be stored in elements. Information about the data (metadata) should be stored in attributes. And when in doubt, put the information in the elements.

To differentiate between data and metadata, ask yourself whether someone reading the document would want to see a particular piece of information. If the answer is yes, then the information probably belongs in a child element. If the answer is no, then the information probably belongs in an attribute. If all tags were stripped from the document along with all the attributes, the basic information should still be present. Attributes are good places to put ID numbers, URLs, references, and other information not directly or immediately relevant to the reader. However, there are many exceptions to the basic principle of storing metadata as attributes. Reasons for making an exception include:

✦ Attributes can't hold structure well.

✦ Elements allow you to include meta-metadata (information about the information about the information).

✦ Not everyone always agrees on what is and isn't metadata.

✦ Elements are more extensible in the face of future changes.

Structured metadata

Elements can have substructure, attributes can't. This makes elements far more flexible, and may convince you to encode metadata as child elements. For example, suppose you're writing an article and you want to include a source for a fact. It might look something like this:

```
<FACT SOURCE="The Biographical History of Baseball,
Donald Dewey and Nicholas Acocella (New York: Carroll &amp;
Graf Publishers, Inc. 1995) p. 169">
  Josh Gibson is the only person in the history of baseball to
  hit a pitch out of Yankee Stadium.
</FACT>
```

Clearly, the information "The Biographical History of Baseball, Donald Dewey and Nicholas Acocella (New York: Carroll & Graf Publishers, Inc. 1995) p. 169" is metadata. It is not the fact itself. Rather it is information about the fact. However, the SOURCE attribute contains a lot of implicit substructure. You might find it more useful to organize the information like this:

```
<SOURCE>
  <AUTHOR>Donald Dewey</AUTHOR>
  <AUTHOR>Nicholas Acocella</AUTHOR>
  <BOOK>
    <TITLE>The Biographical History of Baseball</TITLE>
    <PAGES>169</PAGES>
    <YEAR>1995</YEAR>
    <PUBLISHER>Carroll &amp; Graf Publishers, Inc.</PUBLISHER>
    <CITY>New York</CITY>
  </BOOK>
</SOURCE>
```

Furthermore, using elements instead of attributes makes it straightforward to include additional information such as the authors' e-mail addresses, a URL where an electronic copy of the document can be found, the chapter title, and anything else that seems important.

Dates are another example. A common piece of metadata about scholarly articles is the date the article was first received. This is important for establishing priority of discovery and invention. It's easy to include a DATE attribute in an ARTICLE tag:

```
<ARTICLE DATE="10/11/2000">
  Polymerase Reactions in Organic Compounds
</ARTICLE>
```

However, the DATE attribute has substructure signified by the /. Getting that structure out of the attribute value is much more difficult than reading child elements of a DATE element, as shown below:

```
<DATE>
  <YEAR>2000</YEAR>
  <MONTH>10</MONTH>
  <DAY>11</DAY>
</DATE>
```

For instance, with CSS or XSL, it's easy to format the day and month invisibly so that only the year appears. For example, using CSS:

```
YEAR  {display: inline}
MONTH {display: none}
DAY   {display: none}
```

If the DATE is stored as an attribute, however, there's no easy way to access only part of it. You must write a separate program in a programming language such as ECMAScript or Java that can parse your date format. It's easier to use the standard XML tools and child elements.

Furthermore, the attribute syntax is ambiguous. What does the date "10/11/2000" signify? In particular, is it October 11th or November 10th? Readers from different countries will interpret this data differently. Even if your parser understands one format, there's no guarantee the people entering the data will enter it correctly. The XML form, by contrast, is unambiguous.

Finally, using DATE children rather than attributes allows more than one date to be associated with an element. For instance, scholarly articles are often returned to the authors for revisions. In these cases, it can also be important to note when the revised article was received. For example:

```
<ARTICLE>
  <TITLE>
    Maximum Projectile Velocity in an Augmented Railgun
  </TITLE>
  <AUTHOR>Elliotte Harold</AUTHOR>
  <AUTHOR>Bruce Bukiet</AUTHOR>
  <AUTHOR>William Peter</AUTHOR>
  <DATE>
    <YEAR>1992</YEAR>
    <MONTH>10</MONTH>
    <DAY>29</DAY>
  </DATE>
  <DATE>
    <YEAR>1993</YEAR>
    <MONTH>10</MONTH>
    <DAY>26</DAY>
  </DATE>
</ARTICLE>
```

As another example, consider the ALT attribute of an IMG tag in HTML. This is limited to a single string of text. However, given that a picture is worth a thousand words, you might well want to replace an IMG with marked up text. For instance, consider the pie chart shown in Figure 5-2.

The best description of this picture an ALT attribute can provide is:

```
<IMG SRC="05021.gif"
     ALT="Pie Chart of Positions in Major League Baseball"
     WIDTH="819" HEIGHT="623">
</IMG>
```

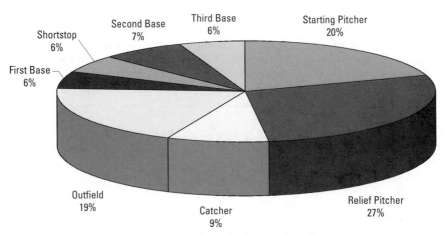

Figure 5-2: Distribution of positions in major league baseball

However, an ALT child element can include markup as well as text. For example, you might provide a table of the relevant numbers instead of a pie chart.

```
<IMG SRC="05021.gif" WIDTH="819" HEIGHT="623">
  <ALT>
    <TABLE>
      <TR>
        <TD>Starting Pitcher</TD> <TD>242</TD> <TD>20%</TD>
      </TR>
      <TR>
        <TD>Relief Pitcher</TD> <TD>336</TD> <TD>27%</TD>
      </TR>
      <TR>
        <TD>Catcher</TD> <TD>104</TD> <TD>9%</TD>
      </TR>
      <TR>
        <TD>Outfield</TD> <TD>235</TD> <TD>19%</TD>
      </TR>
      <TR>
        <TD>First Base</TD> <TD>67</TD> <TD>6%</TD>
      </TR>
      <TR>
        <TD>Shortstop</TD> <TD>67</TD> <TD>6%</TD>
      </TR>
      <TR>
        <TD>Second Base</TD> <TD>88</TD> <TD>7%</TD>
      </TR>
      <TR>
        <TD>Third Base</TD> <TD>67</TD> <TD>6%</TD>
```

```
      </TR>
    </TABLE>
  </ALT>
</IMG>
```

You might even provide the actual Postscript, Scalable Vector Graphics (SVG), or Vector Markup Language (VML) code to render the picture in the event that the bitmap image is not available.

Meta-metadata

Using elements for metadata also easily allows for meta-metadata, or information about the information about the information. For example, the author of a poem may be considered to be metadata about the poem. The language in which that author's name is written is data about the metadata about the poem. This isn't a trivial concern, especially for distinctly non-Roman languages. For instance, is the author of the *Odyssey* Homer or Ὅμηρος? Using elements, it's easy write.

```
<POET LANGUAGE="English">Homer</POET>
<POET LANGUAGE="Greek">Ὅμηρος</POET>
```

However, if POET is an attribute rather than a child element, you're stuck with unwieldy constructs such as this.

```
<POEM POET="Homer" POET_LANGUAGE="English"
 POEM_LANGUAGE="English">
   Tell me, O Muse, of the cunning man...
</POEM>
```

And it's even more bulky if you want to provide both the poet's English and Greek names.

```
<POEM POET_NAME_1="Homer" POET_LANGUAGE_1="English"
 POET_NAME_2="Ὅμηρος" POET_LANGUAGE_2="Greek"
 POEM_LANGUAGE="English">
   Tell me, O Muse, of the cunning man...
</POEM>
```

What's your metadata is someone else's data

"Metaness" is in the mind of the beholder. Who's reading your document and why they're reading it determines what they consider to be data and what they consider to be metadata. For example, if you're simply reading an article in a scholarly journal, then the name of the author of the article is tangential to the information it contains. However, if you're sitting on a tenure and promotions committee scanning a journal to see whose publishing and whose not, then the names of the authors and the number of articles they've published may be more important to you than what they wrote (sad but true).

In fact, you yourself may change your mind about what's meta and what's data. What's only tangentially relevant to you today may become crucial to you next week. You can use style sheets to hide unimportant elements today and change the style sheets to reveal them later. However, it's more difficult to later reveal information that was first stored in an attribute. This may require rewriting the document itself rather than simply changing the style sheet.

Elements are more extensible

Attributes are certainly convenient when you only need to convey one or two words of unstructured information. In these cases, there may genuinely be no current need for a child element. However, this doesn't preclude such a need in the future.

For instance, you may only need to store the name of the author of an article now, and you may not need to distinguish between the first and last names. However, in the future you may uncover a need to store first and last names, e-mail addresses, institutions, snail-mail addresses, URLs, and more. If you've stored the authors of the article as elements, then it's easy to add child elements to include this additional information.

Although any such change will probably require some revision of your documents, style sheets, and associated programs, it's still much easier to change a simple element to a tree of elements than it is to make an attribute a tree of elements. However, if you used an attribute, you're stuck. It's very difficult to extend attribute syntax beyond the region it was originally designed for.

Good times to use attributes

Having exhausted all the reasons why you should use elements instead of attributes, I feel compelled to point out that there are still times when using attributes makes sense. First of all, as previously mentioned, attributes are fully appropriate for very simple data without substructure that the reader is unlikely to want to see. One example is the HEIGHT and WIDTH attributes of an IMG element. Although the values of these attributes may change if the image changes, it's hard to imagine how the data in the attribute could be anything more than a very short string of text. HEIGHT and WIDTH are one-dimensional quantities (in more ways than one) so they work well as attributes.

Furthermore, attributes are appropriate for simple information about the document that has nothing to do with the content of the document. For example, it is often useful to assign an ID attribute to each element. The value of an ID attribute is a unique string possessed only by one element in the document. You can then use this string for a variety of tasks including linking to particular elements of the document, even if the elements move around as the document changes over time. For example:

```
<SOURCE ID="S1">
  <AUTHOR ID="A1">Donald Dewey</AUTHOR>
  <AUTHOR ID="A2">Nicholas Acocella</AUTHOR>
  <BOOK ID="B1">
    <TITLE ID="B2">
      The Biographical History of Baseball
    </TITLE>
    <PAGES ID="B3">169</PAGES>
    <YEAR ID="B4">1995</YEAR>
    <PUBLISHER>Carroll &amp; Graf Publishers, Inc.</PUBLISHER>
    <CITY>New York</CITY>
  </BOOK>
</SOURCE>
```

ID attributes make links to particular elements in the document possible. In this way, they can serve the same purpose as the NAME attribute of HTML's A elements. Other data associated with linking — HREFs to link to, SRCs to pull images and binary data from, and so forth — also work well as attributes.

Cross-Reference

You'll see more examples of attributes used to hold linking information in Chapter 20.

Attributes are also useful containers for document-specific style information. For example, if TITLE elements are normally rendered as bold text but you want to make just one TITLE element both bold and italic, you might write something similar to this.

```
<TITLE STYLE="font-style: italic">Significant Others</TITLE>
```

This allows the style information to be embedded without changing the tree structure of the document. Although ideally you'd prefer to use a separate element, this scheme gives document authors somewhat more control when they cannot add elements to the tag set that they're working with. For example, the webmasters of a site might require page authors and designers to use a particular XML vocabulary with a fixed list of elements and attributes. Nonetheless, they might want to allow designers to make minor adjustments to individual pages. Use this tactic with restraint, however, or you'll soon find yourself back in the HTML hell that XML was supposed to save you from, in which formatting is freely intermixed with meaning and documents are no longer maintainable.

The final reason to use attributes is to maintain compatibility with HTML. To the extent that you're using tags that at least look similar to HTML such as <IMG>, <P>, and <TD>, you might as well employ the standard HTML attributes for these tags. This has the double advantage of allowing legacy browsers to at least partially parse and display your document, and of being more familiar to the people writing the documents.

Empty Elements and Empty Element Tags

An element that contains no content is called an empty element. It can be written like this:

```
<PLAYER GIVEN_NAME="Rich" SURNAME="Becker"
  POSITION="Outfield" GAMES="79" GAMES_STARTED="26"
  AT_BATS="113" RUNS="22" HITS="23" DOUBLES="1"
  TRIPLES="0" HOME_RUNS="3" RUNS_BATTED_IN="11"
  WALKS="22" STRUCK_OUT="34" STOLEN_BASES="2"
  CAUGHT_STEALING="0" SACRIFICE_FLIES="0"
  SACRIFICE_HITS="2" HIT_BY_PITCH="2" STEALS="2"></PLAYER>
```

The end tag immediately follows the start tag. Rather than including both a start and an end tag you can include one empty-element tag. Empty-element tags are distinguished from start tags by a closing /> instead of simply a closing >. For instance, instead of <PLAYER></PLAYER> you would write <PLAYER/>. Rich Becker's PLAYER element can be written with an empty-element tag like this.

```
<PLAYER GIVEN_NAME="Rich" SURNAME="Becker"
  POSITION="Outfield" GAMES="79" GAMES_STARTED="26"
  AT_BATS="113" RUNS="22" HITS="23" DOUBLES="1"
  TRIPLES="0" HOME_RUNS="3" RUNS_BATTED_IN="11"
  WALKS="22" STRUCK_OUT="34" STOLEN_BASES="2"
  CAUGHT_STEALING="0" SACRIFICE_FLIES="0"
  SACRIFICE_HITS="2" HIT_BY_PITCH="2" STEALS="2"/>
```

XML parsers treat this single tag identically to its two-tag equivalent. This PLAYER element is precisely equal (though not identical) to the previous PLAYER element formed with an empty tag. The difference between <PLAYER></PLAYER> and <PLAYER/> is syntactic sugar and nothing more. If you don't like the empty-element tag syntax, or find it hard to read, you don't have to use it.

XSL

Attributes are visible in an XML source view of the document as shown in Figure 5-1. However, once a CSS style sheet is applied, the attributes disappear. Figure 5-3 shows Listing 5-1 after the baseball stats style sheet from the previous chapter is applied. It looks like a blank document because CSS styles only apply to element content, not to attributes. If you use CSS, any data that you want to display to the reader should be part of an element's content rather than one of its attributes.

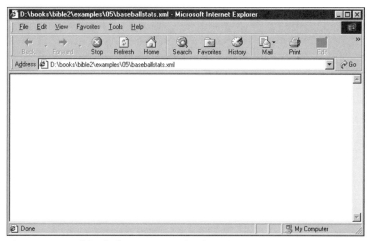

Figure 5-3: A blank document is displayed when a CSS style sheet is applied to an XML document whose elements do not contain any character data.

However, there is an alternative style sheet language that does allow you to access and display attribute data. This is the Extensible Stylesheet Language (XSL). XSL is divided into two parts, XSL Transformations (XSLT) and XSL Formatting Objects (XSL-FO). XSLT enables you to replace one element with another. You define rules that map your XML elements to standard HTML elements, to HTML elements plus CSS attributes, or to a non-HTML vocabulary like XSL-FO. XSLT can reorder elements in the document and even add additional content that was never present in the XML document.

Caution

At the time of this writing (January 2001) no browser supports XSLT as configured by default. This includes Netscape, Internet Explorer, Mozilla, Opera, Lynx, Mosaic, and HotJava.

Internet Explorer 5.0 and 5.5 do support a nonstandard version of a very early working draft of the XSLT specification, but do not support any part of the final version described in this chapter and this book. Version 3.0 of MSXML, Microsoft's XML parser/ XSLT processor, can add support for most (though still not quite all) of XSLT 1.0 to IE 5.0 and 5.5. However, MSXML 3.0 is not included in the default install of IE 5.0 or 5.5. You have to download it from Microsoft's Web site at `http://msdn.microsoft.com/xml/general/xmlparser.asp` and install it using the Windows Installer. Once that's done, you have to download and run another program, xmlinst.exe to actually replace the MSXML 2.x DLL that was bundled with IE with the MSXML 3.0 DLL. Otherwise, existing programs such as Internet Explorer will continue to use the old, non-standard, buggy parser. You can download xmlinst.exe from the same URL where you found MSXML 3.0.

Chapter 18 shows you some techniques that allow you to use XSLT even with browsers that don't support it directly. In the meantime, however, don't expect any of the examples in the rest of this chapter to work as advertised except in Internet Explorer 5.0 or later, and then only after you've successfully installed MSXML 3.0.

The formatting half of XSL defines an extremely powerful view of documents as pages. XSL-FO enables you to specify the appearance and layout of a page, including multiple columns, text flow around objects, line spacing, widow and orphan control, font faces, styles, and sizes, and more. It's designed to be powerful enough to layout documents for both the Web and print from the same source document. For example, suppose a local newspaper stores TV show times and advertisements in an XML document. Then they could use two different XSL style sheets to generate both the printed and online editions of the television listings from the same source document automatically. However, no Web browsers yet support XSL formatting objects. Therefore, this chapter focuses on XSLT, the more finished half of XSL.

XSL-FO is discussed in Chapter 19.

XSLT templates

An XSLT style sheet contains templates into which data from the XML document is poured. For example, a template might look like this:

```
<HTML>
  <HEAD>
    <TITLE>
      XSLT Instructions to get the title
    </TITLE>
  </HEAD>
  <BODY>
    <H1>XSLT Instructions to get the title</H1>
    XSLT Instructions to get the statistics
  </BODY>
</HTML>
```

The italicized sections will be replaced by particular XSLT elements that copy data from the underlying XML document into this template. You can apply this template to many different data sets. For instance, if the template is designed to work with the baseball example, then the same style sheet can display statistics from different seasons.

This may remind you of some server-side include schemes for HTML. In fact, this is very much like server-side includes. However, the actual transformation of the source XML document by the XSLT style sheet takes place on the client rather than on the server. Furthermore, the output document does not have to be HTML. It can be any well-formed XML.

Servers can be configured to perform the transformation on the server side instead. This is how you make XML documents with XSLT style sheets compatible with legacy browsers that don't support XSL.

XSLT instructions can retrieve any data in the XML document. This includes element content, element names, and, most importantly for this example, attributes. Particular elements are chosen by a pattern that considers the element's name, its value, its attributes' names and values, its absolute and relative position in the tree structure of the XML document, and more. Once the data is extracted from an element, it can be moved, copied, and manipulated in a variety of ways. This brief introduction doesn't discuss everything you can do with XSLT. However, you will learn to use XSLT to write some pretty amazing documents that can be displayed in a Web browser immediately.

Cross-Reference Chapter 18 covers XSLT in depth.

The body of the document

Let's begin by looking at a simple example and applying it to the baseball statistics document of Listing 5-1. Listing 5-2 is an XSLT style sheet. This style sheet provides the HTML mold into which XML data will be poured.

Listing 5-2: An XSLT style sheet

```
<?xml version="1.0"?>
<xsl:stylesheet version="1.0"
        xmlns:xsl="http://www.w3.org/1999/XSL/Transform">

  <xsl:template match="SEASON">
    <HTML>
      <HEAD>
        <TITLE>
          Major League Baseball Statistics
        </TITLE>
      </HEAD>
      <BODY>
        <H1>Major League Baseball Statistics</H1>

        <HR></HR>
        Copyright 2000
        <A HREF="http://www.macfaq.com/personal.html">
         Elliotte Rusty Harold
        </A>
        <BR />
        <A HREF="mailto:elharo@metalab.unc.edu">
         elharo@metalab.unc.edu
        </A>

      </BODY>
    </HTML>
  </xsl:template>

</xsl:stylesheet>
```

Listing 5-2 resembles an HTML file included inside an `xsl:template` element. In other words, its structure looks like this:

```
<?xml version="1.0"?>
<xsl:stylesheet version="1.0"
        xmlns:xsl="http://www.w3.org/1999/XSL/Transform">

  <xsl:template match="SEASON">
    HTML file goes here
  </xsl:template>

</xsl:stylesheet>
```

Listing 5-2 is not just an XSLT style sheet; it's also a well-formed XML document. It begins with an XML declaration. The root element of this document is `xsl:stylesheet`. This style sheet contains a single template for the XML data encoded as an `xsl:template` element. The `xsl:template` element has a `match` attribute with the value `SEASON`, and its content is a well-formed HTML document. It's not a coincidence that the output HTML is well-formed. Because the HTML must first be part of an XSLT style sheet, and because XSLT style sheets are well-formed XML documents, all the HTML included in an XSLT style sheet must be well formed.

The Web browser tries to match parts of the XML document against each `xsl:template` element. The SEASON template matches all SEASON elements in the document. Of course, in Listing 5-1 there's exactly one of those, the root element. When the browser reads the XML document, it matches this SEASON element to the SEASON template and inserts data from the XML document where indicated by XSLT instructions. However, this particular template contains no XSLT instructions, so its contents are merely copied verbatim into the Web browser, producing the output you see in Figure 5-4. Notice that Figure 5-4 does not display any data from the XML document, only from the XSLT template.

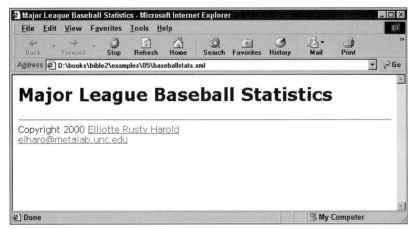

Figure 5-4: Baseball statistics after application of the XSL style sheet in Listing 5-2

To apply the XSLT style sheet of Listing 5-2 to the XML document in Listing 5-1, add an `xml-stylesheet` processing instruction with a `type` pseudo-attribute with value `text/xml` and an `href` pseudo-attribute that points to the style sheet between the XML declaration and the root element. For example:

```
<?xml version="1.0"?>
<?xml-stylesheet type="text/xml" href="5-2.xsl"?>
<SEASON YEAR="1998">
...
```

This is the same way you attach a CSS style sheet to a document. The only difference is that the `type` pseudo-attribute has the value `text/xml` instead of `text/css`.

Caution   Internet Explorer requires you to use the nonstandard and incorrect MIME media type `text/xsl` instead of `text/xml`. For maximum portability, you may want to include two `xml-stylesheet` processing instructions pointing to the same style sheet, one instruction with type `text/xsl` and the second instruction with type `text/xml`, like this:

```
<?xml version="1.0"?>
<?xml-stylesheet type="text/xml" href="5-2.xsl"?>
<?xml-stylesheet type="text/xsl" href="5-2.xsl"?>
<SEASON YEAR="1998">
...
```

The browser will pick whichever one it understands. In early 2001, the new MIME media type `application/xml+xslt` was standardized especially for XSLT style sheets. However, no browsers yet support this; and `text/xml` is still allowed, so I recommend using `text/xml` for the time being.

The title

Of course, there was something rather obvious missing from Figure 5-4 — the data! Although the style sheet in Listing 5-2 displays something (unlike the CSS style sheet of Figure 5-3) it doesn't show any data from the XML document. To add this, you need to use XSLT instruction elements to copy data from the source XML document into the output document. Listing 5-3 adds the necessary XSLT instructions to extract the `YEAR` attribute from the `SEASON` element and insert it into the `TITLE` and `H1` header of the resulting document. Figure 5-5 shows the rendered document.

> **Listing 5-3: An XSLT style sheet with instructions to extract the YEAR attribute of the SEASON element**

```
<?xml version="1.0"?>
<xsl:stylesheet version="1.0"
        xmlns:xsl="http://www.w3.org/1999/XSL/Transform">

   <xsl:template match="SEASON">
     <HTML>
       <HEAD>
         <TITLE>
           <xsl:value-of select="@YEAR"/>
           Major League Baseball Statistics
         </TITLE>
       </HEAD>
       <BODY>

       <H1>
         <xsl:value-of select="@YEAR"/>
         Major League Baseball Statistics
       </H1>

       <HR></HR>
       Copyright 2000
       <A HREF="http://www.macfaq.com/personal.html">
        Elliotte Rusty Harold
       </A>
       <BR/>
       <A HREF="mailto:elharo@metalab.unc.edu">
        elharo@metalab.unc.edu
       </A>

       </BODY>
     </HTML>
   </xsl:template>

</xsl:stylesheet>
```

The XSLT instruction that extracts the YEAR attribute from the SEASON element is:

```
<xsl:value-of select="@YEAR"/>
```

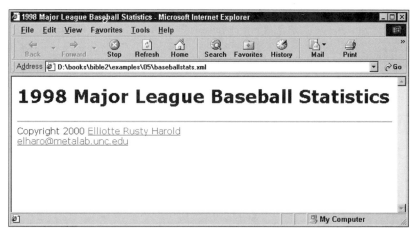

Figure 5-5: Listing 5-1 after application of the XSL style sheet in Listing 5-3

The `xsl:value-of` element copies the value of something from the input document into the output document. In this example, it copies the value of the `YEAR` attribute of the root `SEASON` element. It appears twice because the year should appear twice in the output document — once in the `H1` header and once in the `TITLE`. Each time it appears, this instruction does the same thing — it inserts the value of the `YEAR` attribute, the string "1998" in this example.

XSLT instructions are distinguished from output elements such as `HTML` and `H1` because the instructions are in the `http://www.w3.org/1999/XSL/Transform` namespace. In most cases, this namespace is associated with the prefix `xsl`. That is, the names of all XSLT elements begin with `xsl:`. The namespace is identified by the `xmlns:xsl` attribute of the root element of the style sheet. In Listings 5-2 and 5-3, and in all other examples in this book, the value of that attribute is `http://www.w3.org/1999/XSL/Transform`.

Caution

The prefix can and occasionally does change. However, the URI absolutely must be `http://www.w3.org/1999/XSL/Transform`, nothing else. Various early and outdated drafts of the XSLT specification used different namespace URIs. However, modern, up-to-date, specification-compliant software uses `http://www.w3.org/1999/XSL/Transform` and `http://www.w3.org/1999/XSL/Transform` only! If you use any other namespace URI, or make even a small typo in the URI, the results are likely to be very strange and hard to debug.

You should avoid any software that uses other namespaces because it's likely to be out-of-date and quite buggy. Furthermore, you should be wary of anybody who tries to tell you to use a different namespace. *They are not your friends!* (Yes, I'm talking about Microsoft here. Its trainers and evangelists have been promulgating a nonstandard, Microsoft-only version of XSLT that doesn't work with anything except Internet Explorer. This nonstandard XSLT can be identified by its use of the `http://www.w3.org/TR/WD-xsl` namespace URI. Treat this URI as a warning: Dangerous nonstandard Microsoft extensions ahead!) In this book, I will adhere strictly to W3C standard XSLT that works across all browsers and platforms.

Namespaces are discussed in depth in Chapter 13.

Leagues, divisions, and teams

Next, let's add some XSLT instructions to pull out the two LEAGUE elements. There's more than one of these, so we'll use the `xsl:for-each` instruction to iterate through all the leagues. An `xsl:value-of` element will extract the name of each league from its NAME attribute. Each name will be mapped to an H2 header. Listing 5-4 demonstrates the process; Figure 5-6 shows the document rendered with this style sheet.

Listing 5-4: An XSLT style sheet with instructions to extract LEAGUE elements

```
<?xml version="1.0"?>
<xsl:stylesheet version="1.0"
       xmlns:xsl="http://www.w3.org/1999/XSL/Transform">

  <xsl:template match="SEASON">
    <HTML>
      <HEAD>
        <TITLE>
          <xsl:value-of select="@YEAR"/>
          Major League Baseball Statistics
        </TITLE>
      </HEAD>
      <BODY>

      <H1>
        <xsl:value-of select="@YEAR"/>
        Major League Baseball Statistics
      </H1>

      <xsl:for-each select="LEAGUE">
        <H2 ALIGN="CENTER">
          <xsl:value-of select="@NAME"/>
        </H2>
      </xsl:for-each>

      <HR></HR>
      Copyright 2000
      <A HREF="http://www.macfaq.com/personal.html">
       Elliotte Rusty Harold
      </A>
      <BR />
```

```
<A HREF="mailto:elharo@metalab.unc.edu">
 elharo@metalab.unc.edu
</A>

</BODY>
</HTML>
</xsl:template>

</xsl:stylesheet>
```

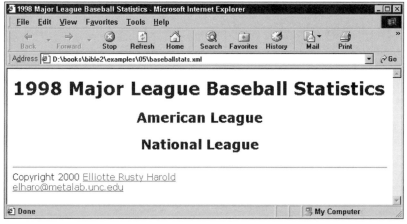

Figure 5-6: The league names are displayed as H2 headers when the XSLT style sheet in Listing 5-4 is applied.

The key new instruction is the xsl:for-each element

```
<xsl:for-each select="LEAGUE">
  <H2 ALIGN="CENTER">
    <xsl:value-of select="@NAME"/>
  </H2>
</xsl:for-each>
```

xsl:for-each loops through all the LEAGUE elements (more accurately, those LEAGUE elements that are children of the previously matched SEASON element, although in this document that's all the LEAGUE elements). As the XSLT processor visits each LEAGUE element, it outputs the value of its NAME attribute between <H2 ALIGN="CENTER"> and </H2>. Although there's only one xsl:for-each matching a LEAGUE element, it loops over all the LEAGUE elements that are immediate children of the SEASON element. Thus, this template works for anywhere from zero to an indefinite number of leagues.

The same technique can be used to assign H3 headers to divisions and H4 headers to teams. Listing 5-5 demonstrates the procedure and Figure 5-7 shows the document rendered with this style sheet. The names of the divisions and teams are read from the XML data.

Listing 5-5: An XSLT style sheet with instructions to extract DIVISION and TEAM elements

```
<?xml version="1.0"?>
<xsl:stylesheet version="1.0"
        xmlns:xsl="http://www.w3.org/1999/XSL/Transform">

  <xsl:template match="SEASON">
    <HTML>
      <HEAD>
        <TITLE>
          <xsl:value-of select="@YEAR"/>
          Major League Baseball Statistics
        </TITLE>
      </HEAD>
      <BODY>

      <H1>
        <xsl:value-of select="@YEAR"/>
        Major League Baseball Statistics
      </H1>

      <xsl:for-each select="LEAGUE">
        <H2 ALIGN="CENTER">
          <xsl:value-of select="@NAME"/>
        </H2>

        <xsl:for-each select="DIVISION">
          <H3 ALIGN="CENTER">
          <xsl:value-of select="@NAME"/>
          </H3>

          <xsl:for-each select="TEAM">
            <H4 ALIGN="CENTER">
              <xsl:value-of select="@CITY"/>
              <xsl:value-of select="@NAME"/>
            </H4>
          </xsl:for-each>

        </xsl:for-each>

      </xsl:for-each>

      <HR></HR>
      Copyright 2000
      <A HREF="http://www.macfaq.com/personal.html">
```

```
      Elliotte Rusty Harold
      </A>
      <BR />
      <A HREF="mailto:elharo@metalab.unc.edu">
      elharo@metalab.unc.edu
      </A>

      </BODY>
    </HTML>
  </xsl:template>

</xsl:stylesheet>
```

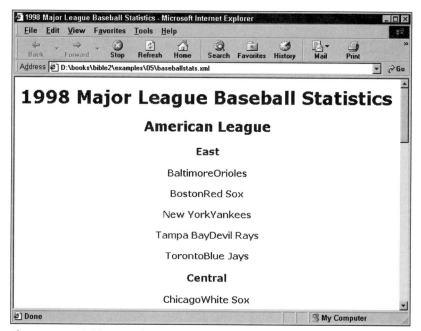

Figure 5-7: Divisions and team names are displayed after application of the XSL style sheet in Listing 5-5.

In the case of the TEAM elements, the values of both its CITY and NAME attributes are used as contents for the H4 header. Also notice that the nesting of the xsl:for-each elements that selects seasons, leagues, divisions, and teams mirrors the hierarchy of the document itself. That's not a coincidence. While other schemes are possible that don't require matching hierarchies, this is the simplest, especially for highly structured data like the baseball statistics of Listing 5-1.

Players

The next step is to add statistics for individual players on a team. The most natural way to do this is in a table. Listing 5-6 shows an XSLT style sheet that arranges the players and their stats in a table. No new XSLT elements are introduced. The same `xsl:for-each` and `xsl:value-of` elements are used on the PLAYER element and its attributes. The output contains standard HTML table tags. Figure 5-8 displays the results.

Listing 5-6: An XSLT style sheet that places players and their statistics in a table

```
<?xml version="1.0"?>
<xsl:stylesheet version="1.0"
      xmlns:xsl="http://www.w3.org/1999/XSL/Transform">

  <xsl:template match="SEASON">
    <HTML>
      <HEAD>
        <TITLE>
          <xsl:value-of select="@YEAR"/>
          Major League Baseball Statistics
        </TITLE>
      </HEAD>
      <BODY>

      <H1>
        <xsl:value-of select="@YEAR"/>
        Major League Baseball Statistics
      </H1>

      <xsl:for-each select="LEAGUE">
        <H2 ALIGN="CENTER">
          <xsl:value-of select="@NAME"/>
        </H2>

        <xsl:for-each select="DIVISION">
          <H3 ALIGN="CENTER">
          <xsl:value-of select="@NAME"/>
          </H3>

          <xsl:for-each select="TEAM">
            <H4 ALIGN="CENTER">
              <xsl:value-of select="@CITY"/>
              <xsl:value-of select="@NAME"/>
            </H4>

            <TABLE>
```

```
   <THEAD>
    <TR>
     <TH>Player</TH><TH>P</TH><TH>G</TH>
     <TH>GS</TH><TH>AB</TH><TH>R</TH><TH>H</TH>
     <TH>D</TH><TH>T</TH><TH>HR</TH><TH>RBI</TH>
     <TH>S</TH><TH>CS</TH><TH>SH</TH><TH>SF</TH>
     <TH>E</TH><TH>BB</TH><TH>SO</TH><TH>HBP</TH>
    </TR>
   </THEAD>
  <TBODY>
   <xsl:for-each select="PLAYER">
    <TR>
     <TD>
      <xsl:value-of select="@GIVEN_NAME"/>
      <xsl:value-of select="@SURNAME"/>
     </TD>
     <TD><xsl:value-of select="@POSITION"/></TD>
     <TD><xsl:value-of select="@GAMES"/></TD>
     <TD>
       <xsl:value-of select="@GAMES_STARTED"/>
     </TD>
     <TD><xsl:value-of select="@AT_BATS"/></TD>
     <TD><xsl:value-of select="@RUNS"/></TD>
     <TD><xsl:value-of select="@HITS"/></TD>
     <TD><xsl:value-of select="@DOUBLES"/></TD>
     <TD><xsl:value-of select="@TRIPLES"/></TD>
     <TD><xsl:value-of select="@HOME_RUNS"/></TD>
     <TD><xsl:value-of select="@RBI"/></TD>
     <TD><xsl:value-of select="@STEALS"/></TD>
     <TD>
      <xsl:value-of select="@CAUGHT_STEALING"/>
     </TD>
     <TD>
      <xsl:value-of select="@SACRIFICE_HITS"/>
     </TD>
     <TD>
      <xsl:value-of select="@SACRIFICE_FLIES"/>
     </TD>
     <TD><xsl:value-of select="@ERRORS"/></TD>
     <TD><xsl:value-of select="@WALKS"/></TD>
     <TD>
      <xsl:value-of select="@STRUCK_OUT"/>
     </TD>
     <TD>
      <xsl:value-of select="@HIT_BY_PITCH"/>
     </TD>
    </TR>
   </xsl:for-each>
  </TBODY>
</TABLE>
```

Continued

Listing 5-6 *(continued)*

```
        </xsl:for-each>

      </xsl:for-each>

    </xsl:for-each>

    <HR></HR>
    Copyright 2000
    <A HREF="http://www.macfaq.com/personal.html">
     Elliotte Rusty Harold
    </A>
    <BR />
    <A HREF="mailto:elharo@metalab.unc.edu">
     elharo@metalab.unc.edu
    </A>

    </BODY>
  </HTML>
 </xsl:template>

</xsl:stylesheet>
```

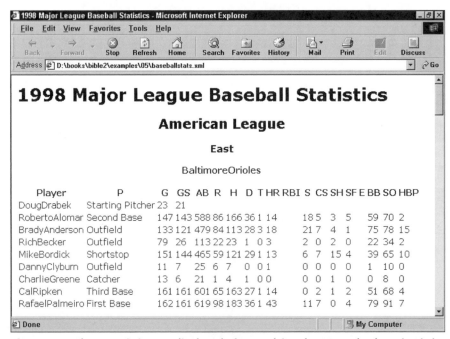

Figure 5-8: Player statistics are displayed after applying the XSL style sheet in Listing 5-6.

Separation of pitchers and batters

One discrepancy you may have noted in Figure 5-8 is that the pitchers aren't handled properly. Throughout this chapter and Chapter 4, the pitchers have had a completely different set of statistics, whether those stats were stored in element content or attributes. Therefore, the pitchers really need a table that is separate from the other players. Before putting a player into the table, you must test whether the player is or is not a pitcher. If his POSITION attribute contains the string "Pitcher", omit him. Then reverse the procedure in a second table that only includes pitchers — that is PLAYER elements whose POSITION attribute contains the string "Pitcher".

To do this, you have to include code in the xsl:for-each element that selects the players. You don't select all players. Instead, you select only those players whose POSITION attribute is not pitcher. The syntax looks like this.

```
<xsl:for-each select="PLAYER[(@POSITION != 'Pitcher')">
```

But because the XML document distinguishes between starting and relief pitchers, the true answer must test both cases.

```
<xsl:for-each select="PLAYER[(@POSITION != 'Starting Pitcher')
    and (@POSITION != 'Relief Pitcher')]">
```

For the table of pitchers, you logically reverse this to the position being equal to either "Starting Pitcher" or "Relief Pitcher". (It is not sufficient to just change *not equal* to *equal*. You also have to change *and* to *or*.) The syntax looks like this:

```
<xsl:for-each select="PLAYER[(@POSITION = 'Starting Pitcher')
    or (@POSITION = 'Relief Pitcher')]">
```

Note   Only a single equals sign is used to test for equality rather than the double equals sign used in C and Java. That's because XSLT does not have an assignment operator.

Listing 5-7 shows an XSLT style sheet separating the batters and pitchers into two different tables. The pitchers' table adds columns for all the usual pitcher statistics. Listing 5-1 encodes in attributes: wins, losses, saves, shutouts, and so on. Column labels are abbreviated to keep the table to a manageable width. Figure 5-9 shows the results.

Listing 5-7: An XSLT style sheet that separates batters and pitchers

```
<?xml version="1.0"?>
<xsl:stylesheet version="1.0"
      xmlns:xsl="http://www.w3.org/1999/XSL/Transform">

  <xsl:template match="SEASON">
    <HTML>
      <HEAD>
        <TITLE>
          <xsl:value-of select="@YEAR"/>
          Major League Baseball Statistics
        </TITLE>
      </HEAD>
      <BODY>

      <H1>
        <xsl:value-of select="@YEAR"/>
        Major League Baseball Statistics
      </H1>

      <xsl:for-each select="LEAGUE">
        <H2 ALIGN="CENTER">
          <xsl:value-of select="@NAME"/>
        </H2>

        <xsl:for-each select="DIVISION">
          <H3 ALIGN="CENTER">
          <xsl:value-of select="@NAME"/>
          </H3>

          <xsl:for-each select="TEAM">
            <H4 ALIGN="CENTER">
              <xsl:value-of select="@CITY"/>
              <xsl:value-of select="@NAME"/>
            </H4>

              <TABLE>
               <CAPTION><B>Batters</B></CAPTION>
               <THEAD>
                <TR>
                 <TH>Player</TH><TH>P</TH><TH>G</TH>
                 <TH>GS</TH><TH>AB</TH><TH>R</TH><TH>H</TH>
                 <TH>D</TH><TH>T</TH><TH>HR</TH><TH>RBI</TH>
                 <TH>S</TH><TH>CS</TH><TH>SH</TH><TH>SF</TH>
                 <TH>E</TH><TH>BB</TH><TH>SO</TH>
                 <TH>HBP</TH>
```

```
    </TR>
   </THEAD>
  <TBODY>
   <xsl:for-each select="PLAYER[(@POSITION
     != 'Starting Pitcher')
     and (@POSITION != 'Relief Pitcher')]">
    <TR>
     <TD>
      <xsl:value-of select="@GIVEN_NAME"/>
      <xsl:value-of select="@SURNAME"/>
     </TD>
     <TD><xsl:value-of select="@POSITION"/></TD>
     <TD><xsl:value-of select="@GAMES"/></TD>
     <TD>
       <xsl:value-of select="@GAMES_STARTED"/>
     </TD>
     <TD><xsl:value-of select="@AT_BATS"/></TD>
     <TD><xsl:value-of select="@RUNS"/></TD>
     <TD><xsl:value-of select="@HITS"/></TD>
     <TD><xsl:value-of select="@DOUBLES"/></TD>
     <TD><xsl:value-of select="@TRIPLES"/></TD>
     <TD>
       <xsl:value-of select="@HOME_RUNS"/>
     </TD>
     <TD><xsl:value-of select="@RBI"/></TD>
     <TD><xsl:value-of select="@STEALS"/></TD>
     <TD>
      <xsl:value-of select="@CAUGHT_STEALING"/>
     </TD>
     <TD>
      <xsl:value-of select="@SACRIFICE_HITS"/>
     </TD>
     <TD>
      <xsl:value-of select="@SACRIFICE_FLIES"/>
     </TD>
     <TD><xsl:value-of select="@ERRORS"/></TD>
     <TD><xsl:value-of select="@WALKS"/></TD>
     <TD>
      <xsl:value-of select="@STRUCK_OUT"/>
     </TD>
     <TD>
      <xsl:value-of select="@HIT_BY_PITCH"/>
     </TD>
    </TR>
   </xsl:for-each>
  </TBODY>
</TABLE>

<TABLE>
```

Continued

Listing 5-7 *(continued)*

```
      <CAPTION><B>Pitchers</B></CAPTION>
      <THEAD>
       <TR>
        <TH>Player</TH><TH>P</TH><TH>G</TH>
        <TH>GS</TH><TH>W</TH><TH>L</TH><TH>S</TH>
        <TH>CG</TH><TH>SO</TH><TH>ERA</TH>
        <TH>IP</TH><TH>HR</TH><TH>R</TH><TH>ER</TH>
        <TH>HB</TH><TH>WP</TH><TH>B</TH><TH>BB</TH>
        <TH>K</TH>
       </TR>
      </THEAD>
    <TBODY>
    <xsl:for-each select="PLAYER[(@POSITION
    = 'Starting Pitcher')
    or (@POSITION = 'Relief Pitcher')]">
    <TR>
     <TD>
      <xsl:value-of select="@GIVEN_NAME"/>
      <xsl:value-of select="@SURNAME"/>
     </TD>
     <TD><xsl:value-of select="@POSITION"/></TD>
     <TD><xsl:value-of select="@GAMES"/></TD>
     <TD>
       <xsl:value-of select="@GAMES_STARTED"/>
     </TD>
     <TD><xsl:value-of select="@WINS"/></TD>
     <TD><xsl:value-of select="@LOSSES"/></TD>
     <TD><xsl:value-of select="@SAVES"/></TD>
     <TD>
      <xsl:value-of select="@COMPLETE_GAMES"/>
     </TD>
     <TD>
      <xsl:value-of select="@SHUT_OUTS"/>
     </TD>
     <TD><xsl:value-of select="@ERA"/></TD>
     <TD><xsl:value-of select="@INNINGS"/></TD>
     <TD>
     <xsl:value-of select="@HOME_RUNS_AGAINST"/>
     </TD>
     <TD>
      <xsl:value-of select="@RUNS_AGAINST"/>
     </TD>
     <TD>
      <xsl:value-of select="@EARNED_RUNS"/>
     </TD>
     <TD>
```

```
                <xsl:value-of select="@HIT_BATTER"/>
              </TD>
              <TD>
                <xsl:value-of select="@WILD_PITCH"/>
              </TD>
              <TD><xsl:value-of select="@BALK"/></TD>
              <TD>
                <xsl:value-of select="@WALKED_BATTER"/>
              </TD>
              <TD>
                <xsl:value-of select="@STRUCK_OUT_BATTER"/>
              </TD>
            </TR>
          </xsl:for-each>
        </TBODY>
      </TABLE>

    </xsl:for-each>

  </xsl:for-each>

</xsl:for-each>

<HR></HR>
Copyright 2000
<A HREF="http://www.macfaq.com/personal.html">
 Elliotte Rusty Harold
</A>
<BR />
<A HREF="mailto:elharo@metalab.unc.edu">
 elharo@metalab.unc.edu
</A>

</BODY>
</HTML>
</xsl:template>

</xsl:stylesheet>
```

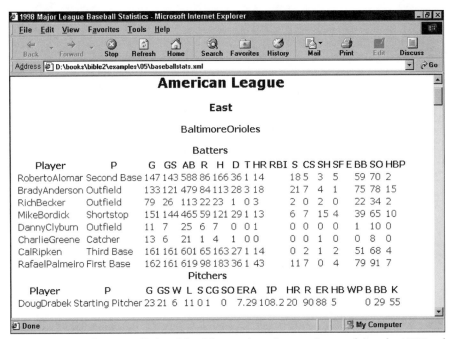

American League East table screenshot. The table contains:

American League

East

BaltimoreOrioles

Batters

Player	P	G	GS	AB	R	H	D	T	HR	RBI	S	CS	SH	SF	E	BB	SO	HBP
RobertoAlomar	Second Base	147	143	588	86	166	36	1	14		18	5	3	5		59	70	2
BradyAnderson	Outfield	133	121	479	84	113	28	3	18		21	7	4	1		75	78	15
RichBecker	Outfield	79	26	113	22	23	1	0	3		2	0	2	0		22	34	2
MikeBordick	Shortstop	151	144	465	59	121	29	1	13		6	7	15	4		39	65	10
DannyClyburn	Outfield	11	7	25	6	7	0	0	1		0	0	0	0		1	10	0
CharlieGreene	Catcher	13	6	21	1	4	1	0	0		0	0	1	0		0	8	0
CalRipken	Third Base	161	161	601	65	163	27	1	14		0	2	1	2		51	68	4
RafaelPalmeiro	First Base	162	161	619	98	183	36	1	43		11	7	0	4		79	91	7

Pitchers

Player	P	G	GS	W	L	S	CG	SO	ERA	IP	HR	R	ER	HB	WP	B	BB	K
DougDrabek	Starting Pitcher	23	21	6	11	0	1	0	7.29	108.2	20	90	88	5			0	29	55

Figure 5-9: Pitchers are distinguished from other players after applying the XSLT style sheet in Listing 5-7.

Element contents and the select attribute

In this chapter, I focused on using XSLT to format data stored in the attributes of an element because attributes aren't accessible from CSS. However, XSLT works equally well when you want to include an element's character data. To indicate that an element's text is to be copied into the output document, simply use the element's name as the value of the `select` attribute of the `xsl:value-of` element. For example, suppose the PLAYER elements were given as they were in Listing 4-1 where the statistics were child elements rather than attributes. In this case, a typical PLAYER element looks like this:

```
<PLAYER>
  <GIVEN_NAME>Roberto</GIVEN_NAME>
  <SURNAME>Alomar</SURNAME>
  <POSITION>Second Base</POSITION>
  <GAMES>147</GAMES>
  <GAMES_STARTED>143</GAMES_STARTED>
  <AT_BATS>588</AT_BATS>
  <RUNS>86</RUNS>
  <HITS>166</HITS>
  <DOUBLES>36</DOUBLES>
```

```
      <TRIPLES>1</TRIPLES>
      <HOME_RUNS>14</HOME_RUNS>
      <RBI>56</RBI>
      <STEALS>18</STEALS>
      <CAUGHT_STEALING>5</CAUGHT_STEALING>
      <SACRIFICE_HITS>3</SACRIFICE_HITS>
      <SACRIFICE_FLIES>5</SACRIFICE_FLIES>
      <ERRORS>11</ERRORS>
      <WALKS>59</WALKS>
      <STRUCK_OUT>70</STRUCK_OUT>
      <HIT_BY_PITCH>2</HIT_BY_PITCH>
  </PLAYER>
```

The major change needed to make the style sheet in Listing 5-7 work with documents in this format is to remove the @ in front of the statistic name. For example, instead of writing `<xsl:value-of select="@RUNS"/>` to insert the number of runs into the output document, you write `<xsl:value-of select="RUNS"/>`. Whereas `<xsl:value-of select="@RUNS"/>` inserts the value of the RUNS *attribute* of the matched element into the output, `<xsl:value-of select= "RUNS"/>` inserts the value of the RUNS *child element* of the matched element into the output. The value of an element is the text contained in the element after all tags have been stripped out. For instance, the value of the element `<RUNS>86</RUNS>` is 86. The value of the above PLAYER element is:

```
      Roberto
      Alomar
      Second Base
      147
      143
      588
      86
      166
      36
      1
      14
      56
      18
      5
      3
      5
      11
      59
      70
      2
```

White space is part of the value of an element and is not trimmed. Thus, the value of this PLAYER element includes all the indenting and line breaks of the original element.

Listing 5-8 is a complete XSLT style sheet designed for Listing 4-1 in the last chapter. The major difference between this style sheet and Listing 5-7 is the removal of a lot of @ signs which merely reflects the change from attributes to child elements. In a few cases, I also had to account for the difference between the name of an attribute and the name of an equivalent element (LEAGUE_NAME instead of NAME, TEAM_CITY instead of CITY, and so on). The output from this style sheet is almost identical to the output from the style sheet in Listing 5-7, aside from some insignificant extra white space that the browser will ignore.

Listing 5-8: An XSLT style sheet for element-based baseball statistics

```
<?xml version="1.0"?>
<xsl:stylesheet version="1.0"
      xmlns:xsl="http://www.w3.org/1999/XSL/Transform">

  <xsl:template match="SEASON">
    <HTML>
      <HEAD>
        <TITLE>
          <xsl:value-of select="YEAR"/>
          Major League Baseball Statistics
        </TITLE>
      </HEAD>
      <BODY>

      <H1>
        <xsl:value-of select="YEAR"/>
        Major League Baseball Statistics
      </H1>

      <xsl:for-each select="LEAGUE">
        <H2 ALIGN="CENTER">
          <xsl:value-of select="LEAGUE_NAME"/>
        </H2>

        <xsl:for-each select="DIVISION">
          <H3 ALIGN="CENTER">
          <xsl:value-of select="DIVISION_NAME"/>
          </H3>

          <xsl:for-each select="TEAM">
            <H4 ALIGN="CENTER">
              <xsl:value-of select="TEAM_CITY"/>
              <xsl:value-of select="TEAM_NAME"/>
            </H4>

            <TABLE>
            <CAPTION><B>Batters</B></CAPTION>
            <THEAD>
```

```
  <TR>
  <TH>Player</TH><TH>P</TH><TH>G</TH>
  <TH>GS</TH><TH>AB</TH><TH>R</TH><TH>H</TH>
  <TH>D</TH><TH>T</TH><TH>HR</TH><TH>RBI</TH>
  <TH>S</TH><TH>CS</TH><TH>SH</TH><TH>SF</TH>
  <TH>E</TH><TH>BB</TH><TH>SO</TH>
  <TH>HBP</TH>
  </TR>
 </THEAD>
<TBODY>
 <xsl:for-each select="PLAYER[(POSITION
   != 'Starting Pitcher')
  and (POSITION != 'Relief Pitcher')]">
  <TR>
   <TD>
    <xsl:value-of select="GIVEN_NAME"/>
    <xsl:value-of select="SURNAME"/>
   </TD>
   <TD><xsl:value-of select="POSITION"/></TD>
   <TD><xsl:value-of select="GAMES"/></TD>
   <TD>
     <xsl:value-of select="GAMES_STARTED"/>
   </TD>
   <TD><xsl:value-of select="AT_BATS"/></TD>
   <TD><xsl:value-of select="RUNS"/></TD>
   <TD><xsl:value-of select="HITS"/></TD>
   <TD><xsl:value-of select="DOUBLES"/></TD>
   <TD><xsl:value-of select="TRIPLES"/></TD>
   <TD>
     <xsl:value-of select="HOME_RUNS"/>
   </TD>
   <TD><xsl:value-of select="RBI"/></TD>
   <TD><xsl:value-of select="STEALS"/></TD>
   <TD>
    <xsl:value-of select="CAUGHT_STEALING"/>
   </TD>
   <TD>
    <xsl:value-of select="SACRIFICE_HITS"/>
   </TD>
   <TD>
    <xsl:value-of select="SACRIFICE_FLIES"/>
   </TD>
   <TD><xsl:value-of select="ERRORS"/></TD>
   <TD><xsl:value-of select="WALKS"/></TD>
   <TD>
    <xsl:value-of select="STRUCK_OUT"/>
   </TD>
   <TD>
    <xsl:value-of select="HIT_BY_PITCH"/>
   </TD>
  </TR>
```

Continued

Listing 5-8 *(continued)*

```
        </xsl:for-each>
      </TBODY>
    </TABLE>

    <TABLE>
      <CAPTION><B>Pitchers</B></CAPTION>
      <THEAD>
       <TR>
        <TH>Player</TH><TH>P</TH><TH>G</TH>
        <TH>GS</TH><TH>W</TH><TH>L</TH><TH>S</TH>
        <TH>CG</TH><TH>SO</TH><TH>ERA</TH>
        <TH>IP</TH><TH>HR</TH><TH>R</TH><TH>ER</TH>
        <TH>HB</TH><TH>WP</TH><TH>B</TH><TH>BB</TH>
        <TH>K</TH>
       </TR>
      </THEAD>
      <TBODY>
      <xsl:for-each select="PLAYER[(POSITION
      = 'Starting Pitcher')
      or (POSITION = 'Relief Pitcher')]">
       <TR>
        <TD>
         <xsl:value-of select="GIVEN_NAME"/>
         <xsl:value-of select="SURNAME"/>
        </TD>
        <TD><xsl:value-of select="POSITION"/></TD>
        <TD><xsl:value-of select="GAMES"/></TD>
        <TD>
          <xsl:value-of select="GAMES_STARTED"/>
        </TD>
        <TD><xsl:value-of select="WINS"/></TD>
        <TD><xsl:value-of select="LOSSES"/></TD>
        <TD><xsl:value-of select="SAVES"/></TD>
        <TD>
         <xsl:value-of select="COMPLETE_GAMES"/>
        </TD>
        <TD>
         <xsl:value-of select="SHUT_OUTS"/>
        </TD>
        <TD><xsl:value-of select="ERA"/></TD>
        <TD><xsl:value-of select="INNINGS"/></TD>
        <TD>
        <xsl:value-of select="HOME_RUNS_AGAINST"/>
        </TD>
        <TD>
         <xsl:value-of select="RUNS_AGAINST"/>
        </TD>
        <TD>
         <xsl:value-of select="EARNED_RUNS"/>
```

```
            </TD>
            <TD>
             <xsl:value-of select="HIT_BATTER"/>
            </TD>
            <TD>
              <xsl:value-of select="WILD_PITCH"/>
            </TD>
            <TD><xsl:value-of select="BALK"/></TD>
            <TD>
             <xsl:value-of select="WALKED_BATTER"/>
            </TD>
            <TD>
            <xsl:value-of select="STRUCK_OUT_BATTER"/>
            </TD>
           </TR>
         </xsl:for-each>
        </TBODY>
       </TABLE>

      </xsl:for-each>

    </xsl:for-each>

   </xsl:for-each>

   <HR></HR>
   Copyright 2000
   <A HREF="http://www.macfaq.com/personal.html">
    Elliotte Rusty Harold
   </A>
   <BR />
   <A HREF="mailto:elharo@metalab.unc.edu">
    elharo@metalab.unc.edu
   </A>

      </BODY>
    </HTML>
  </xsl:template>

</xsl:stylesheet>
```

In this case, within each PLAYER element, the contents of that element's
GIVEN_NAME, SURNAME, POSITION, GAMES, GAMES_STARTED, AT_BATS, RUNS, HITS,
DOUBLES, TRIPLES, HOME_RUNS, RBI, STEALS, CAUGHT_STEALING, SACRIFICE_HITS,
SACRIFICE_FLIES, ERRORS, WALKS, STRUCK_OUT, and HIT_BY_PITCH children are
extracted and copied to the output. Because this chapter's example uses the same
names for the attributes as last chapter's example used for the PLAYER child elements, this style sheet is very similar to Listing 5-7. The main difference is that the
@ signs are missing. They indicate an attribute rather than a child.

You can do even more with the `select` attribute. You can select elements in certain positions (for example, the first, second, last, seventeenth element, and so forth); elements with particular contents; elements with specific attribute values; or elements whose parents or children have certain content or attribute values. You can even apply a complete set of Boolean logical operators to combine different selection conditions. We will explore more of these possibilities when we return to XSLT in Chapter 18.

CSS or XSL?

CSS and XSL overlap to some extent. XSL is certainly more powerful than CSS. This chapter only touched on the basics of what you can do with XSL. However, XSL's power is matched by its complexity. It is definitely harder to learn and use than CSS. So the question is, "When should you use CSS and when should you use XSL?"

CSS is more broadly supported than XSL. Netscape 4 and Internet Explorer 4 support parts of CSS Level 1 for HTML elements (although there are many annoying differences between the two). Furthermore, most of CSS Level 1 and some of CSS Level 2 is supported by Internet Explorer 5.0 and 5.5, Opera 4.0 and 5.0, Netscape 6.0, and Mozilla for both XML and HTML. Thus, choosing CSS gives you more compatibility with a broader range of browsers.

However, XSL definitely lets you do more than CSS. CSS only allows you to apply formatting to element contents. It does not allow you to change or reorder those contents; choose different formatting for elements based on their contents or attributes; or add boilerplate text like a signature block. XSL is far more appropriate when the XML documents contain only the minimum of data and none of the HTML frou frou that surrounds the data.

XSL lets you separate the crucial data from everything else on the page, such as mastheads, navigation bars, and signatures. With CSS, you have to include all these pieces in your data documents. XML+XSL allows the data documents to live separately from the Web page documents. This makes XML+XSL documents more maintainable and easier to work with.

In the long run, XSL should become the preferred choice for data-intensive applications. CSS is more suitable for simple Web pages such as the ones grandparents write to post pictures of their grandchildren. But for these uses, HTML alone is sufficient. If you've really hit the wall with HTML, XML+CSS doesn't take you much further before you run into another wall. XML+XSL, by contrast, takes you far past the walls of HTML. You still need CSS to work with legacy browsers, but in the long-term, XSL is the way to go.

Summary

In this chapter, you saw examples of XML documents with attributes and XSLT style sheets that transformed them to HTML. Specifically, you learned that:

✦ An attribute is a name-value pair included in an element's start tag.

✦ Attributes typically hold meta-information about the element rather than the element's data.

✦ Attributes are less convenient to work with than the contents of an element.

✦ Attributes work well for very simple information that's unlikely to change form as the document evolves. In particular, style and linking information work well as attributes.

✦ Empty-element tags offer syntactic sugar for elements with no content.

✦ XSLT is a powerful language that enables you to transform documents from one XML vocabulary to other XML vocabularies or to non-XML vocabularies such as HTML or tab-delimited text.

The next chapter discusses the exact rules that well-formed XML documents must adhere to. It also explores some additional means of embedding information in XML documents, including comments and processing instructions.

✦   ✦   ✦

Well-formedness

HTML 4.0 has nearly 100 different elements. Most of these elements have a dozen or more possible attributes for several thousand different possible variations. Since XML is more powerful than HTML, you might think that you need to learn even more elements, but you don't. XML gets its power through simplicity and extensibility, not through a plethora of elements.

In fact, XML predefines no elements at all. Instead XML allows you to define your own elements as needed. However, these elements and the documents built from them are not completely arbitrary. Instead, they have to follow a specific set of rules elaborated in this chapter. A document that follows these rules is said to be *well-formed*. Well-formedness is the minimum criteria necessary for XML processors and browsers to read files. This chapter examines the rules for well-formed documents. It explores the different constructs that make up an XML document — tags, text, attributes, elements, and so on — and discusses the primary rules each of these must follow. Particular attention is paid to how XML differs from HTML. Along the way I introduce several new XML constructs, including comments, processing instructions, entity references, and CDATA sections. This chapter isn't an exhaustive discussion of well-formedness rules. Some of the rules I present here must be adjusted slightly for documents that have a document type definition (DTD), and there are additional rules for well-formedness that define the relationship between the document and its DTD, but we'll explore these in later chapters.

Well-formedness Rules

Although XML allows you to invent as many different elements and attributes as you need, these elements and attributes, as well as their contents and the documents that contain them, must all follow certain rules in order to be *well-formed*. If a document is not well-formed, any attempts to read it or render it will fail.

The XML specification strictly prohibits XML parsers from trying to fix and understand malformed documents. All a conforming parser is allowed to do is report the error. It may not fix the error. It may not make a best-faith effort to render what the author intended. It may not ignore the offending malformed markup. All it can do is report the error and exit.

> **Note** The objective here is to avoid the bug-for-bug compatibility wars that have hindered HTML, and that have made writing HTML parsers and renderers so difficult. Because Web browsers allow malformed HTML, Web-page designers don't make the extra effort to ensure that their HTML is correct. In fact, they even rely on bugs in individual browsers to achieve special effects. In order to properly display the huge installed base of HTML pages, every new Web browser must support every quirk of all the Web browsers that have come before. The marketplace would ignore any browser that strictly adhered to the HTML standard. It is to avoid this sorry state that XML processors are explicitly required to only accept well-formed XML.

To be well-formed, an XML document must follow more than 100 different rules. However, most of these rules simply forbid things that you're not very likely to do anyway if you follow the examples given in this book. For instance, one rule is that the name of the element must immediately follow the ⟨ of the element's start tag. For example, ⟨triangle⟩ is a legal start tag but ⟨ triangle⟩ isn't. On the other hand, the same rule says that it is OK to have extra space before the tag's closing angle bracket. That is, both ⟨triangle⟩ and ⟨triangle ⟩ are well-formed start tags. Another rule says that element names must have at least one character; that is, ⟨⟩ is not a legal start tag, and ⟨/⟩ is not a legal end tag. Chances are it never would have occurred to you to create an element with a zero-length name, but computers are dumber than human beings, and need to have constraints like this spelled out for them very formally. XML's well-formedness rules are designed to be understood by software rather than human beings, so quite a few of them are a little technical and won't present much of a problem in practice. The only source for the complete list of rules is the XML specification itself. However, if you follow the rules given here, and check your work with an XML parser such as Xerces before distributing your documents, they should be fine.

> **Cross-Reference** The XML specification itself is found in Appendix C. The formal syntax the XML specification uses is called the Extended Backus-Naur-Form, or EBNF for short. EBNF grammars are an outgrowth of compiler theory that very formally defines what is and is not a syntactically correct program or, in the case of XML, a syntactically correct document. A parser can compare any document to the XML EBNF

grammar character by character and determine definitively whether or not it satisfies the rules of XML. There are no borderline cases. BNF grammars, properly written, leave no room for interpretation. The advantage of this should be obvious to anyone who's had to struggle with HTML documents that display in one browser but not in another.

As well as matching the BNF grammar, a well-formed XML document must also meet various well-formedness constraints that specify conditions that can't be easily described in the BNF syntax. Well-formedness is the minimum level that a document must achieve to be parsed. Appendix B provides an annotated description of the complete XML 1.0 BNF grammar as well as all of the well-formedness constraints.

XML Documents

An XML document is made up of text that's divided between markup and character data. It is a sequence of characters with a fixed length that adheres to certain constraints. It may or may not be a file. For instance, an XML document may be:

✦ A CLOB field in an Oracle database

✦ The result of a query against a database that combines several records from different tables

✦ A data structure created in memory by a Java program

✦ A data stream created on the fly by a CGI program written in Perl

✦ Some combination of several different files, each of which is embedded in another

✦ One part of a larger file containing several XML documents

However, nothing essential is lost if you think of an XML document as a file, as long as you keep in the back of your mind that it might not really be a file on a hard drive.

XML documents are made up of storage units called *entities*. Each entity contains either text or binary data, never both. Text data is comprised of characters. Binary data is used for images and applets and the like.

Note   To use a concrete example, a raw HTML file that includes ‹IMG› tags is an entity but not a document. An HTML file plus all the pictures embedded in it with ‹IMG› tags is a complete document.

The XML declaration

In this and the next several chapters, I treat only simple XML documents that are made up of a single entity, the document itself. Furthermore, these documents only contain text data, not binary data such as images or applets. Such documents can be understood completely on their own without reading any other files. In other words, they stand alone. Such a document normally contains a `standalone` pseudo-attribute in its XML declaration with the value `yes`, similar to this one.

```
<?xml version="1.0" standalone="yes"?>
```

Note   I call this a *pseudo-attribute* because technically only elements can have attributes. The XML declaration is not an element. Therefore `standalone` is not an attribute even if it looks like one.

External entities and entity references can be used to combine multiple files and other data sources to create a single XML document. These documents cannot be parsed without reference to other files. Therefore, they normally have a `stand-alone` pseudo-attribute with the value `no`.

```
<?xml version="1.0" standalone="no"?>
```

If a document does not have an XML declaration, or if a document has an XML declaration but that XML declaration does not have a `standalone` pseudo-attribute, then the value `no` is assumed. That is, the document is assumed to be incapable of standing on its own, and the parser will prepare itself to read external pieces as necessary. If the document can, in fact, stand on its own, nothing is lost by the parser being ready to read an extra piece.

XML documents do not have to include XML declarations, although they should unless you've got a specific reason not to include them. If an XML document does include an XML declaration, then this declaration must be the first thing in the file (except possibly for an invisible Unicode byte order mark). XML processors determine which character set is being used (UTF-8, big-endian Unicode, or little-endian Unicode) by reading the first several bytes of a file and comparing those bytes against various encodings of the string `<?xml`. Nothing should come before this, including white space. For instance, this line is not an acceptable way to start an XML file because of the extra spaces at the front of the line.

```
     <?xml version="1.0" standalone="yes"?>
```

The root element

An XML document has a root element that completely contains all other elements of the document. This is also sometimes called the *document element*, although this element does not have to have the name `document` or `root`. Root elements are delimited by a start tag and an end tag, just like any other element. For instance, consider Listing 6-1.

Listing 6-1: **greeting.xml**

```
<?xml version="1.0" standalone="yes"?>
<GREETING>
Hello XML!
</GREETING>
```

In this document, the root element is GREETING. The XML declaration is not an element. Therefore, it does not have to be included inside the root element. Similarly, other nonelement data in an XML document, such as an xml-stylesheet processing instruction, a DOCTYPE declaration, or comments, do not have to be inside the root element. But all other elements (other than the root itself) and all raw character data must be contained in the root element.

Text in XML

An XML document is made up of text. Text is made up of characters. A character is a letter, a digit, a punctuation mark, a space or tab, or some similar thing. XML uses the Unicode character set which not only includes the usual letters and symbols from English and other Western European alphabets, but also the Cyrillic, Greek, Hebrew, Arabic, and Devanagari alphabets, as well as the most common Han ideographs for Chinese and Japanese, and the Hangul syllables for Korean. For now, I'll stick to the English language, the Roman script, and the ASCII character set; but I'll introduce many alternatives in the next chapter.

A document's text is divided into character data and markup. To a first approximation, markup describes a document's logical structure, while character data provides the basic information of the document. For example, in Listing 6-1, <?xml version="1.0" standalone="yes"?>, <greeting>, and </greeting> are markup. Hello XML!, along with its surrounding white space, is the character data. A big advantage of XML over other formats is that it clearly separates the actual data of a document from its markup.

To be more precise, markup includes all tags, processing instructions, DTDs, entity references, character references, comments, CDATA section delimiters, and the XML declaration. Everything else is character data. However, this is tricky because when a document is processed some of the markup turns into character data. For example, the markup > is turned into the greater than sign character (>). The character data that's left after the document is processed, and after all markup that refers to character data has been replaced by the actual character data, is called *parsed character data*, or PCDATA for short.

Elements and Tags

An XML document is a singly rooted hierarchical structure of elements. Each element is delimited by a start tag (also known as an opening tag) and an end tag (also known as a closing tag) or is represented by a single, empty-element tag. An XML tag has the same form as an HTML tag. That is, start tags begin with a ⟨ followed by the name of the element the tags start, and they end with the first ⟩ after the opening ⟨ (for example, ⟨GREETING⟩). End tags begin with a ⟨/ followed by the name of the element the tag finishes and are terminated by a ⟩ (for example, ⟨/GREETING⟩). Empty-element tags begin with a ⟨ followed by the name of the element and are terminated with a /⟩ (for example, ⟨GREETING/⟩).

Element names

Every element has a name made up of one or more characters. This is the name included in the element's start and end tags. Element names begin with a letter such as y or A or an underscore _. Subsequent characters in the name may include letters, digits, underscores, hyphens, and periods. They cannot include other punctuation marks such as %, ^, or &. They cannot include white space. (The underscore often substitutes for white space.) Both lower- and uppercase letters may be used in XML names. In this book, I mostly follow the convention of making my names uppercase, mainly because this makes them stand out better in the text. However, when I'm using a tag set that was developed by other people it is necessary to adopt their case convention. For example, the following are legal XML start tags with legal XML names:

```
<HELP>
<Book>
<volume>
<heading1>
<section.paragraph>
<Mary_Smith>
<_8ball>
```

Note   Colons are also technically legal in XML names. However, these are reserved for use with namespaces. Namespaces allow you to mix and match XML applications that may use the same element names. Chapter 13 introduces namespaces. Until then, you should not use colons in your element names.

The following are not legal start tags because they don't contain legal XML names:

```
<Book%7>
<volume control>
<3heading>
<Mary Smith>
<.employee.salary>
```

Note The rules for element names actually apply to names of many other things as well. The same rules are used for attribute names, ID attribute values, entity names, and a number of other constructs you'll encounter over the next several chapters.

Every start tag must have a corresponding end tag

Web browsers are relatively forgiving if you forget to close an HTML tag. For instance, if you include a `<B>` tag in your document but no corresponding `</B>` tag, the entire document after the `<B>` tag will be made bold. However, the document will still be displayed.

XML is not so forgiving. Every start tag must be closed with the corresponding end tag. If a document fails to close an element with the right end tag, the browser or renderer reports an error message and does not display any of the document's content in any form.

End tags have the same name as the corresponding start tag, but are prefixed with a / after the initial angle bracket. For example, if the start tag is `<FOO>`, the end tag is `</FOO>`. These are the end tags for the previous set of legal start tags.

```
</HELP>
</Book>
</volume>
</heading1>
</section.paragraph>
</Mary_Smith>
</_8ball>
```

XML names are case sensitive. This is different from HTML in which `<P>` and `<p>` are the same tag, and a `</p>` can close a `<P>` tag. The following are *not* end tags for the set of legal start tags we've been discussing:

```
</help>
</book>
</Volume>
</HEADING1>
</Section.Paragraph>
</MARY_SMITH>
</_8BALL>
```

Empty-element tags

Many HTML elements do not have closing tags. For example, there are no `</LI>`, `</IMG>`, `</HR>`, or `</BR>` tags in HTML. Some page authors do include `</LI>` tags after their list items, and some HTML tools also use `</LI>`. However, the HTML 4.0 standard specifically denies that this is required. Like all unrecognized tags in HTML, the presence of an unnecessary `</LI>` has no effect on the rendered output.

This is *not* the case in XML. The whole point of XML is to allow new elements and their corresponding tags to be discovered as a document is parsed. Thus, unrecognized tags may not be ignored. Furthermore, an XML processor must be capable of determining on the fly whether a tag it has never seen before does or does not have an end tag. It does this by looking for special empty-element tags that end in />.

Elements that are represented by a single tag without a closing tag are called *empty elements* because they have no content. Tags that represent empty elements are called *empty-element tags*. These empty-element tags are closed with a slash and a closing angle bracket (/>); for example, <BR/> or <HR/>. From the perspective of XML, these are the same as the equivalent syntax using both start and end tags with nothing in between them — for example,
</BR> and <HR></HR>.

However, empty-element tags can only be used when the element is truly empty, not when the end tag is simply omitted. For example, in HTML you might write an unordered list like this:

```
<UL>
<LI>I've a Feeling We're Not in Kansas Anymore
<LI>Buddies
<LI>Everybody Loves You
</UL>
```

In XML, you cannot simply replace the <LI> tags with <LI/> because the elements are not truly empty. Instead they contain text. In normal HTML the closing </LI> tag is omitted by the editor and filled in by the parser. This is not the same thing as the element itself being empty. The first LI element above contains the content I've a Feeling We're Not in Kansas Anymore. In XML, you must close these tags like this:

```
<UL>
<LI>I've a Feeling We're Not in Kansas Anymore</LI>
<LI>Buddies</LI>
<LI>Everybody Loves You</LI>
</UL>
```

On the other hand, a BR or HR or IMG element really is empty. It doesn't contain any text or child elements. Thus, in XML, you have two choices for these elements. You can either write them with a start and an end tag in which the end tag immediately follows the start tag — for example,   <HR></HR> — or you can write them with an empty-element tag as in <HR/>.

Note   Current Web browsers deal inconsistently with empty-element tags. For instance, some browsers will insert a line break when they see a <HR/> tag and some won't. Furthermore, the problem may arise even without empty-element tags. Some browsers insert two horizontal lines when they see <HR></HR> and some insert one horizontal line. The most generally compatible scheme is to use an extra attribute before the closing />. The class attribute is often a good choice — for example, <HR CLASS="empty"/>. XSLT offers a few more ways to maintain compatibility with legacy browsers. Chapter 18 discusses these methods.

Elements may nest but may not overlap

Elements may contain (and indeed often do contain) other elements. However, elements may not overlap. Practically, this means that if an element contains a start tag for an element, it must also contain the corresponding end tag. Conversely, an element may not contain an end tag without its matching start tag. For example, this is legal XML.

```
<H1><CITE>What the Butler Saw</CITE></H1>
```

However, the following is not legal XML because the closing </CITE> tag comes before the closing </H1> tag:

```
<H1><CITE>What the Butler Saw</H1></CITE>
```

Most HTML browsers can handle this case with ease. However, XML browsers are required to report an error for this construct.

Empty-element tags may appear anywhere, of course. For example,

```
<PLAYWRIGHTS>Oscar Wilde<HR/>Joe Orton</PLAYWRIGHTS>
```

This implies that for all nonroot elements, there is exactly one other element that contains the element, but which does not contain any other element containing the element. This immediate container is called the *parent* of the element. The contained element is called the *child* of the parent element. Thus each nonroot element always has exactly one parent, but a single element may have an indefinite number of children or no children at all.

Consider Listing 6-2. The root element is the PLAYS element. This contains two PLAY children. Each PLAY element contains three children: TITLE, AUTHOR, and YEAR. Each of these contains only character data, not more children.

Listing 6-2: **Parents and Children**

```
<?xml version="1.0" standalone="yes"?>
<PLAYS>
  <PLAY>
    <TITLE>What the Butler Saw</TITLE>
    <AUTHOR>Joe Orton</AUTHOR>
    <YEAR>1969</YEAR>
  </PLAY>
  <PLAY>
    <TITLE>The Ideal Husband</TITLE>
    <AUTHOR>Oscar Wilde</AUTHOR>
    <YEAR>1895</YEAR>
  </PLAY>
</PLAYS>
```

In programmer terms, this means that XML documents form a tree. Figure 6-1 shows why this structure is called a tree. It starts from the root and gradually bushes out to the leaves on the ends. Trees have a number of nice properties that make them congenial to programmatic traversal, although this doesn't matter so much to you as the author of the document.

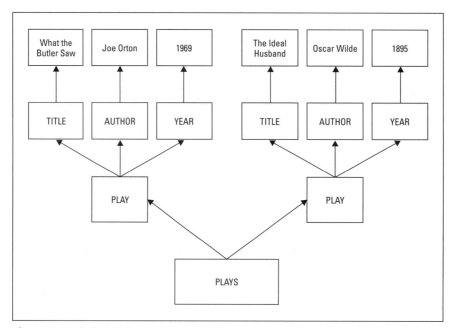

Figure 6-1: Listing 6-2's tree structure

Note   Trees are more commonly drawn from the top down. That is, the root of the tree is shown at the top of the picture rather than the bottom. While this looks less like a real tree, it doesn't affect the topology of the data structure in the least.

Attributes

Elements may have *attributes*. Each attribute of an element is encoded in the start tag of the element as a name-value pair separated by an equals sign (=) and, optionally, some extra white space. The attribute value is enclosed in single or double quotes. For example,

```
<GREETING LANGUAGE="English">
  Hello XML!
  <MOVIE SRC = 'WavingHand.mov'/>
</GREETING>
```

Here the GREETING element has a LANGUAGE attribute that has the value English. The MOVIE element has an SRC attribute with the value WavingHand.mov.

Attribute names

Attribute names are strings that follow the same rules as element names. That is, attribute names must contain one or more characters, and the first character must be a letter or the underscore (_). Subsequent characters in the name may include letters, digits, underscores, hyphens, and periods. They may not include white space or other punctuation marks.

The same element may not have two attributes with the same name. For example, this is illegal:

```
<RECTANGLE SIDE="8" SIDE="10"/>
```

Attribute names are case sensitive. The SIDE attribute is not the same as the side or the Side attribute. Therefore, the following is legal:

```
<BOX SIDE="8" side="10" Side="31"/>
```

However, this is extremely confusing, and I strongly urge you not to write markup that depends on case.

Attribute values

Attributes values are strings. Even when the string shows a number, as in the LENGTH attribute below, that number is the two characters 7 and 2, not the binary number 72.

```
<RULE LENGTH="72"/>
```

If you're writing a program to process XML, you'll need to convert the string to a number before performing arithmetic on it.

Unlike attribute names, there are few limits on the content of an attribute value. Attribute values may contain white space, begin with a number, or contain any punctuation characters (except, sometimes, for single and double quotes). The only characters an attribute value may not contain are the angle brackets < and >, though these can be included using the < and > entity references (discussed soon).

XML attribute values are delimited by quote marks. Unlike HTML attribute values, XML attribute values *must* be enclosed in quotes whether or not the attribute value includes spaces. For example,

```
<A HREF="http://www.ibiblio.org/">IBiblio</A>
```

Most people choose double quotes. However, you can also use single quotes, which is useful if the attribute value itself contains a double quote. For example,

```
<IMG SRC="sistinechapel.jpg"
    ALT='And God said, "Let there be light,"
        and there was light'/>
```

If the attribute value contains both single and double quotes, then the one that's not used to delimit the string must be replaced with the proper entity reference. I generally just go ahead and replace both, which is always legal. For example,

```
<RECTANGLE LENGTH='8&apos;7&quot;' WIDTH="10&apos;6&quot;"/>
```

Entity References

You're probably familiar with a number of entity references from HTML. For example, © inserts the copyright symbol © and ® inserts the registered trademark symbol ®. XML predefines the five entity references listed in Table 6-1. These predefined entity references are used in XML documents in place of specific characters that would otherwise be interpreted as part of markup. For instance, the entity reference < stands for the less than sign (<), which would otherwise be interpreted as beginning a tag.

Table 6-1
XML Predefined Entity references

Entity Reference	Character
&	&
<	<
>	>
"	"
'	'

Caution   In XML, unlike HTML, entity references must end with a semicolon. > is a correct entity reference; &gt is not.

XML assumes that the opening angle bracket always starts a tag, and that the ampersand always starts an entity reference. (This is often true of HTML as well, but most browsers are more forgiving.) For example, consider this line,

```
<H1>A Homage to Ben & Jerry's
    New York Super Fudge Chunk Ice Cream</H1>
```

Web browsers that treat this as HTML will probably display it correctly. However, XML parsers will reject it. You should escape the ampersand with & like this:

```
<H1>A Homage to Ben &amp; Jerry's New York Super Fudge Chunk
Ice Cream</H1>
```

The open angle bracket (<) is similar. Consider this common Java code embedded in HTML:

```
<CODE>    for (int i = 0; i <= args.length; i++ ) { </CODE>
```

Both XML and HTML consider the less than sign in <= to be the start of a tag. The tag continues until the next >. Thus a Web browser treating this fragment as HTML will render this line as

```
        for (int i = 0; i
```

rather than

```
        for (int i = 0; i <= args.length; i++ ) {
```

The = args.length; i++) { is interpreted as part of an unrecognized tag. Again, an XML parser will reject this line completely because it's malformed.

The less than sign can be included in text in both XML and HTML by writing it as <. For example,

```
<CODE>    for (int i = 0; i &lt;= args.length; i++ ) { </CODE>
```

Raw less than signs and ampersands in normal XML text are always interpreted as starting tags and entity references respectively. (The abnormal text is CDATA sections, described below.) Therefore, less than signs and ampersands that are text rather than markup must always be encoded as < and & respectively. Attribute values are text, too, and as you already saw, entity references may be used inside attribute values.

Greater than signs, double quotes, and apostrophes must be encoded when they would otherwise be interpreted as part of markup. However, it's easier just to get in the habit of encoding all of them rather than trying to figure out whether a particular use would or would not be interpreted as markup.

Other than the five entity references already discussed, you can only use an entity reference if you define it in a DTD first. Since you don't know about DTDs yet, if the ampersand character & appears anywhere in your document, it must be immediately followed by `amp;`, `lt;`, `gt;`, `apos;`, or `quot;`. All other uses violate well-formedness.

Cross-Reference   Chapter 10 teaches you how to define new entity references for other characters and longer strings of text using DTDs.

Comments

XML comments are almost exactly like HTML comments. They begin with `<!--` and end with `-->` . All data between the `<!--` and `-->` is ignored by the XML processor. It's as if it weren't there. This can be used to make notes to yourself or your coauthors, or to temporarily comment out sections of the document that aren't ready, as Listing 6-3 demonstrates.

Listing 6-3: **An XML document that contains a comment**

```
<?xml version="1.0" standalone="yes"?>
<!-- This is Listing 6-3 from The XML Bible -->
<GREETING>
Hello XML!
<!--Goodbye XML-->
</GREETING>
```

Since comments aren't elements, they may be placed before or after the root element. However, comments may not come before the XML declaration, which must be the very first thing in the document. For example, this is not a well-formed XML document:

```
<!-- This is Listing 6-3 from The XML Bible -->
<?xml version="1.0" standalone="yes"?>
<GREETING>
Hello XML!
<!--Goodbye XML-->
</GREETING>
```

Comments may not be placed inside a tag. For example, this is also illegal:

```
<?xml version="1.0" standalone="yes"?>
<GREETING>
Hello XML!
</GREETING <!--Goodbye--> >
```

However comments may surround and hide tags. In Listing 6-4, the
<ANTIGREETING> tag and all its children are commented out. They are not
shown when the document is rendered. It's as if they don't exist.

Listing 6-4: **A comment that comments out an element**

```
<?xml version="1.0" standalone="yes"?>
<DOCUMENT>
  <GREETING>
    Hello XML!
  </GREETING>
  <!--
  <ANTIGREETING>
    Goodbye XML!
  </ANTIGREETING>
  -->
</DOCUMENT>
```

Because comments effectively delete sections of text, you must take care to ensure
that the remaining text is still a well-formed XML document. For example, be careful
not to comment out essential tags, as in this malformed document:

```
<?xml version="1.0" standalone="yes"?>
<GREETING>
Hello XML!
<!--
</GREETING>
-->
```

Once the commented text is removed what remains is

```
<?xml version="1.0" standalone="yes"?>
<GREETING>
Hello XML!
```

Because the <GREETING> tag is no longer matched by a closing </GREETING> tag,
this is no longer a well-formed XML document.

There is one final constraint on comments. The two-hyphen string -- may not
occur inside a comment except as part of its opening or closing tag. For example,
this is an illegal comment:

```
<!-- The red door--that is, the second one--was left open -->
```

This means, among other things, that you cannot nest comments like this:

```
<?xml version="1.0" standalone="yes"?>
<DOCUMENT>
  <GREETING>
    Hello XML!
  </GREETING>
  <!--
  <ANTIGREETING>
    <!--Goodbye XML!-->
  </ANTIGREETING>
  -->
</DOCUMENT>
```

It also means that you may run into trouble if you're commenting out a lot of C, Java, or JavaScript source code that's full of expressions such as `i--` or `numberLeft--`. Generally, it's not too hard to work around this problem once you recognize it.

Processing Instructions

Processing instructions are like comments that are intended for computer programs reading the document rather than people reading the document. However, XML parsers are required to pass along the contents of processing instructions to the application on whose behalf they're parsing, unlike comments, which a parser is allowed to silently discard. The application that receives the information is free to ignore any processing instruction it doesn't understand.

Processing instructions begin with `<?` and end with `?>`. The starting `<?` is followed by an XML name called the *target,* which identifies the program that the instruction is intended for, followed by data for that program. For example, you saw this processing instruction in the last chapter.

```
<?xml-stylesheet type="text/xml" href="5-2.xsl"?>
```

The target of this processing instruction is `xml-stylesheet`, a standard name that means the data in this processing instruction is intended for any Web browser that can apply a style sheet to the document. `type="text/xml" href="5-2.xsl"` is the processing instruction data that will be passed to the application reading the document. If that application happens to be a Web browser that understands XSLT, then it will apply the style sheet 5-2.xsl to the document and render the result. If that application is anything other than a Web browser, it will simply ignore the processing instruction.

Note   Appearances to the contrary, the XML declaration is technically not a processing instruction. The difference is academic unless you're writing a program to read an XML document using an XML parser. In that case, the parser's API will provide different methods to get the contents of processing instructions and the contents of the XML declaration.

`xml-stylesheet` processing instructions are always placed in the document's prolog between the XML declaration and the root element start tag. Other processing instructions may also be placed in the prolog, or at almost any other convenient location in the XML document, either before, after, or inside the root element. For example, PHP processing instructions generally appear wherever you want the PHP processor to place its output. The only place a processing instruction may not appear is inside a tag or before the XML declaration.

The target of a processing instruction may be the name of the program it is intended for or it may be a generic identifier such as `xml-stylesheet` that many different programs recognize. The target name `xml` (or `XML`, `Xml`, `xMl`, or any other variation) is reserved for use by the World Wide Web Consortium. However, you're free to use any other convenient name for processing instruction targets. Different applications support different processing instructions. Most applications simply ignore any processing instruction whose target they don't recognize.

The `xml-stylesheet` processing instruction uses a very common format for processing instructions in which the data is divided into *pseudo-attributes*; that is, the data is passed as name-value pairs, and the values are delimited by quotes. However, as with the XML declaration, these are not true attributes because a processing instruction is not a tag. Furthermore, this format is optional. Some processing instructions will use this style; others won't. The only limit on the content of processing instruction data is that it may not contain the two-character sequence `?>` that signals the end of a processing instruction. Otherwise, it's free to contain any legal characters that may appear in XML documents. For example, this is a legal processing instruction.

```
<?html-signature
  Copyright 2001 <a href=http://www.macfaq.com/personal.html>
    Elliotte Rusty Harold</a><br>
    <a href=mailto:elharo@metalab.unc.edu>
      elharo@metalab.unc.edu</a><br>
    Last Modified May 3, 2001
?>
```

In this example, the target is `html-signature`. The rest of the processing instruction is data and contains a lot of malformed HTML that would otherwise be illegal in an XML document. Some programs might read this, recognize the `html-signature` target, and copy the data into the signature of an HTML page. Other programs that don't recognize the `html-signature` target will simply ignore it.

CDATA Sections

Suppose your document contains one or more large blocks of text that have a lot of `<`, `>`, `&`, or `"` characters but no markup. This would be true for a Java or HTML tutorial, for example. It would be inconvenient to have to replace each instance of one of these characters with the equivalent entity reference. Instead, you can include the block of text in a *CDATA section*.

CDATA sections begin with `<![CDATA[` and end with `]]>`. For example:

```
<![CDATA[
System.out.print("<");
if (x <= args.length && y > z) {
  System.out.println(args[x - y]);
}
System.out.println(">");
]]>
```

The only text that's not allowed within a CDATA section is the closing CDATA tag `]]>`. Comments may appear in CDATA sections, but do not act as comments. That is, both the comment tags and all the text they contain will be displayed.

Most of the time anything inside a pair of `<>` angle brackets is markup, and anything that's not is character data. However, in CDATA sections, all text is pure character data. Anything that looks like a tag or an entity reference is really just the text of the tag or the entity reference. The XML processor does not try to interpret it in any way. CDATA sections are used when you want all text to be interpreted as pure character data rather than as markup.

CDATA sections are extremely useful if you're trying to write about HTML or XML in XML. For example, this book contains many small blocks of XML code. The word processor I'm using doesn't care about that. But if I were to convert this book to XML, I'd have to painstakingly replace all the less than signs with `&lt;` and all the ampersands with `&amp;` like this:

```
&lt;?xml version="1.0" standalone="yes"?&gt;
&lt;greeting&gt;
Hello XML!
&lt;/greeting&gt;
```

To avoid having to do this, I can instead use a CDATA section to indicate that a block of text is to be presented as is with no translation. For example:

```
<![CDATA[<?xml version="1.0" standalone="yes"?>
<GREETING>
Hello XML!
</GREETING>]]>
```

Note   Because `]]>` may not appear in a CDATA section, CDATA sections cannot nest. This makes it relatively difficult to write about CDATA sections in XML. If you need to do this, you just have to bite the bullet and use the `&lt;` and `&amp;` escapes.

CDATA sections aren't needed that often, but when they are needed, they're needed badly.

Well-Formed HTML

You can practice your XML skills even before most Web browsers directly support XML by writing well-formed HTML. Well-formed HTML is HTML that adheres to XML's well-formedness constraints but only uses standard HTML tags. Well-formed HTML is easier to read than the sloppy HTML most humans and WYSIWYG tools such as FrontPage write. It's also easier for Web robots and automated search engines to understand. It's more robust, and less likely to break when you make a change. And it's less likely to be subject to annoying cross-browser and cross-platform differences in rendering. Furthermore, you can then use XML tools to work on your HTML documents, while still maintaining backward compatibility with browsers that don't support XML.

Rules for HTML

Real-world Web pages are extremely sloppy. Tags aren't closed. Elements overlap. Raw less than signs are included in pages. Semicolons are omitted from the ends of entity references. Web pages with these problems are technically incorrect, but most Web browsers accept them. Nonetheless, your Web pages will be cleaner, display faster, and be easier to maintain if you fix these problems.

Some of the common problems that you need to look for on Web pages include:

1. Start tags without matching end tags (unclosed elements)
2. End tags without start tags (orphaned tags)
3. Overlapping elements
4. Unquoted attributes
5. Unescaped <, >, and & signs
6. Documents without root elements
7. End tags in a different case than the corresponding start tag

I've listed these in rough order of importance. Exact details vary from tag to tag, however. For instance, an unclosed `<STRONG>` tag will turn all elements following it bold. However, an unclosed `<LI>` or `<P>` tag causes no problems at all.

There are also some rules that only apply to XML documents that might actually cause problems if you attempt to integrate them into your existing HTML pages. These XML-only constructs include:

8. Start documents with an XML declaration
9. Close empty element tags with a `/>`
10. Only use the `&amp;`, `&lt;`, `&gt;`, `&apos;`, and `&quot;` entity references

Fixing these problems isn't hard, but there are a few pitfalls to trip up the unwary. Let's explore them.

Close all elements

Any element that contains content, whether text or other child elements, should have a start tag and an end tag. HTML doesn't absolutely require this. For instance, `<P>`, `<DT>`, `<DD>`, and `<LI>` are often used in isolation. However, this relies on the Web browser to make a good guess at where the element ends, and browsers don't always do quite what authors want or expect. Therefore, it's best to explicitly close all start tags.

Probably the biggest change this requires to how you write HTML is thinking of `<P>` as a container rather than a simple paragraph break mark. For instance, previously you would have formatted these maxims from Oscar Wilde's *Phrases and Philosophies for the Use of the Young* like this:

```
Wickedness is a myth invented by good people to account for the
curious attractiveness of others.
<P>

Those who see any difference between soul and body have
neither.
<P>

Religions die when they are proved to be true. Science is the
record of dead religions.
<P>

The well-bred contradict other people. The wise contradict
themselves.
<P>
```

Now you have to format them like this instead:

```
<P>
Wickedness is a myth invented by good people to account for the
curious attractiveness of others.
</P>

<P>
Those who see any difference between soul and body have
neither.
</P>

<P>
Religions die when they are proved to be true. Science is the
record of dead religions.
</P>

<P>
The well-bred contradict other people. The wise contradict
themselves.
</P>
```

You've probably been taught to think of <P> as ending a paragraph. Now you have to think of it as beginning one. This does offer you some advantages though. For instance, you can easily assign a variety of formatting attributes to a paragraph. For example, here's the original HTML title of House Resolution 581 as seen on `http://thomas.loc.gov/home/hres581.html`:

```
<center>
<p><h2>House Calendar No. 272</h2>

<p><h1>105TH CONGRESS 2D SESSION H. RES. 581</h1>

<p>[Report No. 106-795]

<p><b>Authorizing and directing the Committee on the
Judiciary to investigate whether sufficient grounds
exist for the impeachment of William Jefferson Clinton,
President of the United States.</b>
</center>
```

Here's the same text, but using well-formed HTML. The `align` attribute now replaces the deprecated `center` element, and a CSS `style` attribute is used instead of the `<b>` tag.

```
<h2 align="center">House Calendar No. 272</h2>

<h1 align="center">105TH CONGRESS 2D SESSION H. RES. 581</h1>

<p align="center">[Report No. 106-795]</p>

<p align="center" style="font-weight: bold">
Authorizing and directing the Committee on the Judiciary to
investigate whether sufficient grounds exist for the
impeachment of William Jefferson Clinton,
President of the United States.
</p>
```

Delete orphaned end tags; don't let elements overlap

When editing pages, it's not uncommon to remove a start tag and forget to remove its associated end tag. In HTML, an orphaned end tag, such as a `</STRONG>` or `</TD>` that doesn't have any matching start tag, is unlikely to cause problems by itself. However, it does make the file longer than it needs to be, increases the time that it takes to download the document, and has the potential to confuse people or tools that are trying to understand and edit the HTML source. Therefore, you should make sure that each end tag is properly matched with a start tag.

However, more often an end tag that doesn't match any start tag means that elements incorrectly overlap. Most elements that overlap on Web pages are quite easy to fix. For instance, consider this common problem found on the White House home page (`http://www.whitehouse.gov/`, November 4, 1998).

```
<font size=2><b>
<!-- New Begin -->
<a href="/WH/New/html/19981104-12244.html">Remarks Of The
President Regarding Social Security</a>
<BR>
<!-- New End -->
 </font>
</b>
```

Because the b element starts inside the font element, it must end inside the font element. All that's needed to fix it is to swap the end tags like this:

```
<font size=2><b>
<!-- New Begin -->
<a href="/WH/New/html/19981104-12244.html">Remarks Of The
President Regarding Social Security</a>
<BR>
<!-- New End -->
</b>
</font>
```

Alternately, you can swap the start tags instead:

```
<b><font size=2>
<!-- New Begin -->
<a href="/WH/New/html/19981104-12244.html">Remarks Of The
President Regarding Social Security</a>
<BR>
<!-- New End -->
 </font>
</b>
```

Occasionally, you may have a tougher problem. For example, consider this larger fragment from the same page. I've emboldened the problem tags to make it easier to see the mistake:

```
<TD valign=TOP width=85>
<FONT size=+1>
<A HREF="/WH/New"><img border=0
src="/WH/images/pin_calendar.gif"
align=LEFT height=50 width=75 hspace=5 vspace=5></A><br> </TD>
<TD valign=TOP width=225>
<A HREF="/WH/New"><B>What's New:</B></A><br>
</FONT>
What's happening at the White <nobr>House - </nobr><br>
 <font size=2><b>
<!-- New Begin -->
<a href="/WH/New/html/19981104-12244.html">Remarks Of The
President Regarding Social Security</a>
<BR>
```

```
<!-- New End -->
 </font>
</b>
</TD>
```

Here the `<FONT size=+1>` element begins inside the first `<TD valign=TOP width=85>` element and continues past that element into the `<TD valign=TOP width=225>` element where it finishes. The proper solution in this case is to close the FONT element immediately before the first `</TD>` closing tag, and to then add a new `<FONT size=+1>` start tag immediately after the start of the second TD element, like this:

```
<TD valign=TOP width=85>
<FONT size=+1>
<A HREF="/WH/New"><img border=0
src="/WH/images/pin_calendar.gif"
align=LEFT height=50 width=75 hspace=5 vspace=5></A><br>
</FONT></TD>
<TD valign=TOP width=225>
<FONT size=+1>
<A HREF="/WH/New"><B>What's New:</B></A><br>
</FONT>
What's happening at the White <nobr>House - </nobr><br>
 <b><font size=2>
<!-- New Begin -->
<a href="/WH/New/html/19981104-12244.html">Remarks Of The
President Regarding Social Security</a>
<BR>
<!-- New End -->
 </font>
</b>
</TD>
```

Quote all attributes

HTML attributes only require quote marks if they contain embedded white space. Nonetheless, it doesn't hurt to include them. Furthermore, using quote marks may help in the future, if you later decide to change the attribute value to something that does include white space. It's quite easy to forget to add the quote marks later, especially if the attribute is something like an ALT in an `<IMG>` whose malformedness is not immediately apparent when viewing the document in a Web browser. For instance, consider this `<IMG>` tag:

```
<IMG SRC=cup.gif WIDTH=89 HEIGHT=67 ALT=Cup>
```

It should be rewritten like this:

```
<IMG SRC="cup.gif" WIDTH="89" HEIGHT="67" ALT="Cup">
```

The previous fragment from the White House home page has a lot of attributes that require quoting. When the quote marks are fixed, it looks like this:

```
<TD valign="TOP" width="85">
<FONT size="+1">
<A HREF="/WH/New"><img border="0"
src="/WH/images/pin_calendar.gif"
align="LEFT" height="50" width="75" hspace="5"
vspace="5"></A><br>
</FONT></TD>
<TD valign="TOP" width="225">
<FONT size="+1">
<A HREF="/WH/New"><B>What's New:</B></A><br>
</FONT>
What's happening at the White <nobr>House - </nobr><br>
 <b><font size="2">
<!-- New Begin -->
<a href="/WH/New/html/19981104-12244.html">Remarks Of The
President Regarding Social Security</a>
<BR>
<!-- New End -->
 </font>
</b>
</TD>
```

Escape <, >, and & signs

HTML is more forgiving of loose less than signs and ampersands than is XML. Nonetheless, even in pure HTML, they do cause trouble, especially if they're followed immediately by some other character. For instance, consider this e-mail address as it might easily be copied and pasted from the From: header in Eudora:

```
Elliotte Rusty Harold <elharo@metalab.unc.edu>
```

Were it to be rendered in HTML, this is all you would see:

```
Elliotte Rusty Harold
```

The e-mail address has been unintentionally hidden by the angle brackets. Anytime you want to include a raw less than sign or ampersand in HTML, you really should use the < and & entity references. The correct HTML for such a line would be:

```
From: Elliotte Rusty Harold &lt;elharo@metalab.unc.edu&gt;
```

You're slightly less likely to see problems with an unescaped greater than sign because this will only be interpreted as markup if it's preceded by an as yet unfinished tag. However, there may be such unfinished tags in a document, and a nearby greater than sign can mask their presence. For example, consider this fragment of Java code.

```
for (int i=0;i<10;i++) {
   for (int j=20;j>10;j--) {
```

It's likely to be rendered as

```
for (int i=0;i10;j--) {
```

If these are only 2 lines in a 100-line program, it's entirely possible you'll miss the problem when casually proofreading. On the other hand, if the greater than sign is escaped, the unescaped less than sign will probably obscure the rest of the program, and the problem will be much more obvious.

Use the same case for all tags

HTML isn't case sensitive, but XML is. If you open an element with `<TD>` you can't close it with `</td>`. When I went back to the White House home page for the second edition of this book, I found that they'd fixed the problems I noted above. However, this time I found a lot of elements like this:

```
<A href="/WH/Services"><B>Commonly Requested Federal
Services:</B></a>
```

The end tags need to at least match the case of the corresponding start tags. Thus in this example, `</a>` should be `</A>`, like this:

```
<A href="/WH/Services"><B>Commonly Requested Federal
Services:</B></A>
```

However, most of the time I'd go a little further. In particular, I recommend picking a single convention for tag case, either all uppercase or all lowercase, and sticking to it throughout the document. This is easier than trying to remember details of each tag. In this book, I'm mostly using all uppercase tags so that the tags will stand out in the text, but for HTML I normally use all lowercase because it's much easier to type and because, eventually, XHTML will require it. Thus, I'd rewrite the above fragment like this:

```
<a href="/WH/Services"><b>Commonly Requested Federal
Services:</b></a>
```

Cross-Reference

XHTML is discussed in Chapter 27 and 28.

Include a root element

The root element for HTML files is supposed to be `html`. Most browsers forgive a failure to include this. Nonetheless, it's definitely better to make the very first tag in your document `<html>` and the very last `</html>`. If any extra text or tags have gotten in front of `<html>` or behind `</html>`, move them between `<html>` and `</html>`.

One common manifestation of this problem is simply forgetting to include `</html>` at the end of the document. I always begin my documents by typing `<html>` and `</html>`, then type in between them, rather than waiting until I've finished writing the document and hoping that by that point, possibly days later, I still remember that I need to put in a closing `</html>` tag.

Close empty-element tags with a `/>`

Empty tags are the *bête noir* of converting HTML to well-formed XML. HTML does not formally recognize the XML `<elementname/>` syntax for empty tags. You can convert `<BR>` to `<BR/>`, `<HR>` to `<HR/>`, `<IMG>` to `<IMG/>`, and so on quite easily. However, it's a tossup whether any given browser will render the transformed tags properly or not.

Caution   Do not confuse truly empty elements such as `<BR>`, `<HR>`, and `<IMG>` with elements that do contain content but often only have a start tag in standard HTML, such as `<P>`, `<LI>`, `<DT>`, and `<DD>`.

The simplest solution, and the one approved by the XML specification, is to replace the empty tags with start tag/end tag pairs with no content. The browser should then ignore the unrecognized end tag. For example,

```
<BR></BR>
<HR></HR>
<IMG SRC="cup.gif" WIDTH="89" HEIGHT="67" ALT="Cup"></IMG>
```

This seems to work well in practice with one notable exception. Netscape treats `</BR>` the same as `<BR>`; that is, as a signal to break the line. Thus while `<BR>` is a single line break, `<BR></BR>` is a double line break, more akin to a paragraph mark in practice. Furthermore, Netscape ignores `<BR/>` completely. Web sites that must support legacy browsers (essentially all Web sites) thus cannot use either `<BR></BR>` or `<BR/>`. What does seem to work in practice for XML and legacy browsers is this:

```
<BR />
```

Note the space between `<BR` and `/>`. If the space bothers you, you can add an extra attribute like this:

```
<BR CLASS="empty"/>
```

Don't use any entity references other than &, <, >, ', and "

Many Web pages don't need entity references other than `&amp;`, `&lt;`, `&gt;`, `&apos;`, and `&quot;`. However, the HTML 4.0 specification does define many more including:

✦ `&trade;`, the trademark symbol (™)

✦ `&copy;`, the copyright symbol (©)

✦ `&infin;`, the infinity symbol ∞

✦ `&pi;`, the lowercase Greek letter π

There are several hundred others. These are just a sample. However, using any of these will make your document not well-formed. The real solution to this problem is to use a DTD. We discuss the effect that DTDs have on entity references in Chapter 10. In the meantime, there are several short-term solutions.

The simplest is to write your document in a character set that has all the symbols you need, and then use a `<META>` directive to specify the character set in use. For example, to specify that your document uses UTF-8 encoding, a character set discussed in the next chapter that contains all the characters you're likely to want, you would place this `<META>` directive in the head of your document.

```
<META http-equiv="Content-Type" content="text/html;
      charset=UTF-8"></META>
```

Alternately, you can simply configure your Web server to emit the necessary content type header. However, it's normally easier to use the `<META>` tag.

```
Content-Type: text/html; charset=UTF-8
```

The problem with this approach is that many browsers are not capable of displaying the UTF-8 character set. The same is true of most of the other character sets that you're likely to use to provide these special characters.

HTML 4.0 supports character entity references just like XML's; that is, you can replace a character with `&#` and the decimal or hexadecimal value of the character in Unicode. For example:

✦ `&#8482;` is the trademark symbol (™)

✦ `&#169;` is the copyright symbol (©)

✦ `&#8734;` is the infinity symbol ∞

✦ `&#960;` is the lowercase Greek letter π

Unfortunately, HTML 3.2 only officially supports the numeric character references between 0 and 255 (ISO Latin-1), and many commonly used Web browsers won't recognize character references outside this range.

If you're really desperate for well-formed XML that's backward compatible with HTML, you can include these characters as inline images. For example:

✦ `<img src="tm.gif" width="12" height="12" alt="TM"></img>` includes the trademark symbol (™)

✦ `<img src="copyright.gif" width="12" height="12" alt="Copyright"></img>` includes the copyright symbol (©)

✦ `img src="infinity.gif" width="12" height="12" alt="infinity"></img>` includes the infinity symbol ∞

✦ `<img src="pi.gif" width="12" height="12" alt="pi"></img>` includes the lowercase Greek letter π

In practice, however, I don't recommend using these characters as inline images. Well-formedness is not nearly so important in HTML that it justifies the added download and rendering time that using characters as inline images imposes on your readers.

Don't include an XML declaration

HTML documents don't need XML declarations. However, they can have them. Web browsers should simply ignore tags they don't recognize. From their perspective, the line

```
<?xml version="1.0" standalone="yes"?>
```

is just another tag. Because browsers that don't understand XML don't understand the `<?xml?>` tag, they quietly ignore it. However, I've encountered strange behaviors when different browsers are presented with an HTML document that includes an XML declaration. When faced with such a file, Internet Explorer 4.0 for the Mac tried to download the file rather than displaying it. Netscape Navigator 3.0 showed the declaration as text at the top of the document. Admittedly, these are older browsers, but they are still used by many millions of people. Consequently, since the XML declaration is not required for XML documents and since it doesn't really add a lot to XMLized HTML pages, I've removed it from my Web sites.

Tools

It is not particularly difficult to write well-formed XML documents that follow the rules described in this chapter. However, XML browsers are less forgiving of poor syntax than are HTML browsers, so you do need to be careful.

If you violate any well-formedness constraints, XML parsers and browsers will report a syntax error. Thus, the process of writing XML can be a little like the process of writing code in a real programming language. You write it; then you compile it; then when the compilation fails, you note the errors reported and fix them. In the case of XML you parse the document rather than compile it, but the pattern is the same.

Generally, this is an iterative process in which you go through several edit-parse cycles before you get your first look at the finished document. Despite this, there's no question that writing XML is a lot easier than writing C or Java source code. With a little practice, you'll get to the point where you have relatively few errors and can write XML almost as quickly as you can type.

There are several tools that will help you clean up your pages, most notably RUWF (Are You Well Formed?) from XML.COM and Tidy from Dave Raggett of the W3C.

RUWF

Any tool that can check XML documents for well-formedness can test well-formed HTML documents as well. One of the easiest to use is the RUWF well-formedness checker from XML.COM at `http://www.xml.com/pub/a/tools/ruwf/check.html`. Figure 6-2 shows this tester. Simply type in the URL of the page that you want to check, and RUWF returns the first several dozen errors on the page.

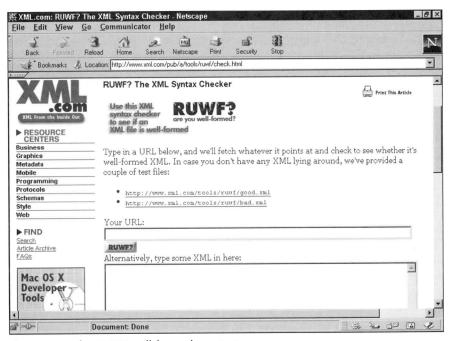

Figure 6-2: The RUWF well-formedness tester

Here's the first batch of errors RUWF found on the White House home page. Most of these errors are malformed XML, but legal (if not necessarily well styled) HTML. However, at least one error ("Line 55, column 30: Encountered </FONT> with no start-tag.") is a problem for both HTML and XML.

```
Line 28, column 7: Encountered </HEAD> expected </META>
...assumed </META> ...assumed </META> ...assumed </META>
...assumed </META>
Line 36, column 12, character 'O': after AttrName= in start-tag
Line 37, column 12, character 'O': after AttrName= in start-tag
Line 38, column 12, character 'O': after AttrName= in start-tag
Line 40, column 12, character 'O': after AttrName= in start-tag
Line 41, column 10, character 'A': after AttrName= in start-tag
Line 42, column 12, character 'O': after AttrName= in start-tag
Line 43, column 14: Encountered </CENTER> expected </br>
...assumed </br> ...assumed </br>
Line 51, column 11, character '+': after AttrName= in start-tag
Line 52, column 51, character 'O': after AttrName= in start-tag
Line 54, column 57: after &
Line 55, column 30: Encountered </FONT> with no start-tag.
Line 57, column 10, character 'A': after AttrName= in start-tag
Line 59, column 15, character '+': after AttrName= in start-tag
```

Tidy

After you've identified the problems, you'll want to fix them. Many common problems — for instance, putting quote marks around attribute values — can be fixed automatically. The most convenient tool for doing this is Dave Raggett's command line program HTML Tidy. Tidy is a character mode program written in ANSI C that can be compiled and run on most platforms, including Windows, UNIX, BeOS, and Mac.

On the CD-ROM Tidy is on the CD-ROM in the directory utilities\tidy. Binaries are included for Windows. Portable source is included for all platforms. The latest version is available from `http://www.w3.org/People/Raggett/tidy/`.

Tidy cleans up HTML files in several ways, not all of which are relevant to XML well-formedness. In fact, in its default mode Tidy tends to remove unnecessary (for HTML, but not for XML) end tags such as </LI>, and to make other modifications that break well-formedness. However, you can use the -asxml switch to specify that you want well-formed XML output. For example, to convert the file index.html to well-formed XML, you would type this command from a DOS window or shell prompt:

```
C:\> tidy -m -asxml index.html
```

The -m flag tells Tidy to convert the file in place. The -asxml flag tells Tidy to format the output as XML.

Summary

In this chapter, you learned about XML's well-formedness rules. In particular, you learned:

✦ XML documents are sequences of characters that meet certain well-formedness criteria.

✦ The text of an XML document is divided into character data and markup.

✦ An XML document is a tree structure made up of elements.

✦ Tags delimit elements.

✦ Start tags and empty tags may contain attributes, which describe elements.

✦ Entity references allow you to include ⟨, ⟩, &, ", and ' in your document.

✦ CDATA sections are useful for embedding text that contains a lot of ⟨, ⟩, and & characters.

✦ Comments can document your code for other people who read it, but parsers may ignore them. Comments can also hide sections of the document that aren't ready.

✦ Processing instructions allow you to pass application-specific information to particular applications.

✦ HTML documents can also be well-formed with a little extra effort.

The next chapter explores how to write XML in languages other than English, in particular in languages that don't look even remotely like English, such as Arabic, Chinese, and Greek.

✦　　✦　　✦

Foreign Languages and Non-Roman Text

The Web is international, yet most of the text that you find on it is English. XML is starting to change this. XML provides full support for the double-byte Unicode character set, as well as its more compact representations. This is good news for Web authors because Unicode supports almost every character commonly used in every modern script on Earth. For instance, this is a well-formed XML document:

```
<definition>
  <word>可擴展擴示語言</word>
  <translation>Extensible Markup Language</translation>
</definition>
```

Unicode isn't limited to character data either. Non-English characters can be used for markup as well. For example, this is also a well-formed XML document:

```
<資料>42</資料>
```

It's easy to read (or at least look at) these documents in this printed book, but if you were to try displaying them on your computer from the source files, you'd discover they're not quite so simple. You'd very likely end up looking at a screen full of gibberish. Typing them into a text editor would be even more challenging. In this chapter, you learn how international text is represented in computer applications, how XML understands text, and how you can take advantage of the software you already own to read and write in languages other than English.

Non-Roman Scripts on the Web

Although the Web is international, much of its text is in English. Because of the Web's expansiveness, however, you can still surf through Web pages in French, Spanish, Chinese, Arabic, Hebrew, Russian, Hindi, and other languages. Most of the time, though, these pages come out looking less than ideal. Figure 7-1 shows the October 1998 cover page of one of the United States Information Agency's propaganda journals, *Issues in Democracy* (`http://usinfo.state.gov/journals/itdhr/1098/ijdr/ijdr1098.htm`), in Russian translation viewed in an English encoding. The red Cyrillic text in the upper left is a bitmapped image file so it's legible (if you speak Russian) and so are a few words in English, such as Adobe Acrobat. However, the rest of the text is mostly a bunch of accented Roman vowels, not the Cyrillic letters they're supposed to be.

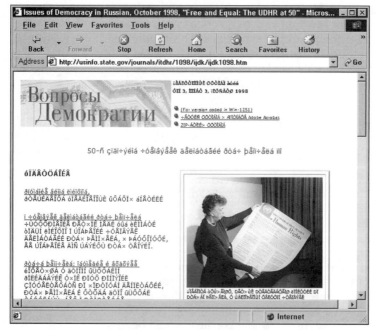

Figure 7-1: The Russian translation of the October 1998 issue of *Issues of Democracy* viewed in a Roman script

The quality of Web pages deteriorates even further when complex, non-Western scripts such as Chinese and Japanese are used. Figure 7-2 shows the home page for the Japanese translation of my book *JavaBeans* (IDG Books (now Hungry Minds), 1997, `http://www.ohmsha.co.jp/data/books/contents/4-274-06271-6.htm`) viewed in an English browser. Once again, the bitmapped images show the proper

Japanese (and English) text, but the rest of the text on the page looks like an almost-random collection of characters except for a few recognizable English words such as CD-ROM. The Kanji characters that you're supposed to see are completely absent.

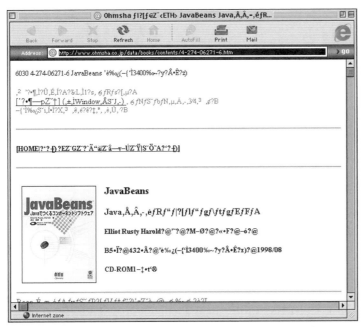

Figure 7-2: The Japanese translation of *JavaBeans* viewed in an English browser

These pages look as they're intended to look if viewed with the right encoding and application software, and if the correct font is installed. Figure 7-3 shows *Issues in Democracy* viewed with the Windows 1251 encoding of Cyrillic. As you can see, the text below the picture is now readable (assuming you can read Russian).

Figure 7-3: *Issues of Democracy* viewed in a Cyrillic script

You can select the encoding for a Web page from the View ➪ Encoding menu in Netscape Navigator or Internet Explorer. In an ideal world, the Web server would tell the Web browser what encoding to use, and the Web browser would listen. It would also be nice if the Web server could send the Web browser the fonts it needed to display the page. In practice, however, you often need to select the encoding manually, even trying several to find the exact right one when more than one encoding is available for a script. For instance, a Cyrillic page might be encoded in Windows 1251, ISO 8859-5, or KOI6-R. Picking the wrong encoding may make Cyrillic letters appear, but the words will be gibberish.

Even when you can identify the encoding, there's no guarantee that you have fonts available to display it. Figure 7-4 shows the Japanese home page for *JavaBeans* with Japanese encoding, but without a Japanese font installed on the computer. Most of the characters in the text are shown as a box, which indicates an unavailable character glyph.

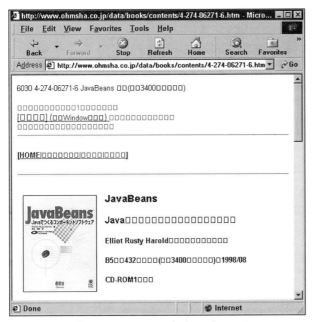

Figure 7-4: The Japanese translation of *JavaBeans* in Kanji without the necessary fonts installed

If your system does have Japanese fonts, you can see the text more or less as it was meant to be seen, as Figure 7-5 demonstrates. Generally speaking, fourth generation and later browsers running on MacOS 9 or Windows 2000 should have all the necessary fonts. Earlier versions of the operating systems generally require additional software such as Apple's Japanese Language Kit (about $99) or Microsoft's Japanese Language Pack (free download from the Microsoft Web site).

Figure 7-5: The Japanese translation of *JavaBeans* in Kanji with the necessary fonts installed

Note   Of course, the higher the quality of the fonts that you use, the better the text will look. Chinese and Japanese fonts tend to be quite large (there are over 50,000 characters in Chinese alone), and the distinctions between individual ideographs can be quite subtle. Japanese publishers generally use higher-quality paper and printing than Western publishers, so they can maintain the fine detail necessary to print Japanese letters. Regrettably a 72-dpi computer monitor can't do justice to most Japanese and Chinese characters unless they're displayed at almost obscenely large point sizes.

Because each page can only have a single encoding, it is difficult to write a Web page that integrates multiple scripts, such as an Arabic commentary on a Greek text. For reasons such as this, the Web community needs a single, universal character set to display all characters for all computers and Web browsers. We don't have such a character set yet, but XML and Unicode get pretty close to that ideal.

XML files are written in Unicode, a multi-byte character set that can represent most characters in most of the world's languages. If a Web page is written in Unicode, as XML pages are, and if the browser understands Unicode, as XML browsers should, then it's not a problem for characters from different languages to be included on the same page. As long as the multi-byte set has the space to hold all of the different characters, there's no need to use more than one character set.

Furthermore, the browser doesn't need to distinguish between different encodings such as Windows 1251, ISO 8859-5, or KOI8-R. It can just assume everything's written in Unicode. The XML parser will convert data in other encodings to Unicode as necessary before presenting it to the application. Therefore, there's no need for browsers to try to detect which character set is in use.

Scripts, Character Sets, Fonts, and Glyphs

Most modern human languages have written forms. The set of characters used to write a language is called a *script*. A script may be a phonetic alphabet, but it doesn't have to be. For instance, Chinese is written with ideographic characters that represent whole words. Different languages often share scripts, sometimes with slight variations. For instance, the modern Turkish alphabet is essentially the familiar Roman alphabet with three extra letters — ğ, š, and ı. Chinese and Japanese, on the other hand, share essentially the same 50,000 Han ideographs, although many characters have different meanings and almost all of them have different pronunciations in the different languages.

 Note   The word *script* is also often used to refer to programs written in weakly typed, interpreted languages such as JavaScript, Perl, and TCL. In this chapter, the word *script* always refers to the set of characters used to write a language and not to any sort of program.

Some languages can even be written in different scripts. Serbian and Croatian are virtually identical as spoken languages and are generally referred to as Serbo-Croatian. However, Serbian is written in a modified Cyrillic script, and Croatian is written in a modified Roman script. As long as a computer doesn't attempt to grasp the meaning of the words it processes, working with a script is equivalent to working with any language that can be written in that script.

Unfortunately, XML alone is not enough to read a script. For each script a computer processes, four things are required.

1. A character set for the script

2. A font for the character set

3. An input method for the character set

4. An operating system and application software that understand the character set

If any of these four elements are missing, you won't be able to work easily in the script, although XML does provide a workaround that's adequate for occasional use. If the only thing your application is missing is an input method, you'll be able to read text written in the script; you just won't be able to write in it.

A character set for the script

Computers only understand numbers. Before they can work with text, that text has to be encoded as numbers in a specified *character set*. For example, the popular ASCII character set encodes the capital letter A as 65; capital letter B as 66; capital letter C as 67, and so on.

These are semantic encodings that provide no style or font information. **C**, C, or even 𝕮 are all represented by the number 67. Information about how the character is drawn is stored elsewhere.

A font for the character set

A font is a collection of glyphs for a character set, generally in a specific size, face, and style. For example, **C**, C, and *C* are all the same character, but they are drawn with different glyphs. Nonetheless, their essential meaning is the same.

Exactly how the glyphs are stored varies from system to system. They may be bitmaps or vector drawings; they may even be hot lead on a printing press. The form they take doesn't concern us here. The key idea is that a font tells the computer how to draw each character in the character set.

An input method for the character set

An input method enables you to enter text. English speakers don't think much about input methods. We just type on our keyboards, and everything's hunky-dory. The same is true in most of Europe, where all that's needed is a slightly modified keyboard with a few extra umlauts, cedillas, or thorns (depending on the country). Figure 7-6 shows a French keyboard I bought in Quebec. It's close to the standard U.S. QWERTY layout. However, a number of the keys on the right and left have been changed to add French letters and diacritical marks like É and ¨. In addition several keys serve triple duty. The third symbol printed on the lower right hand corner of the key is accessed by holding down the AltGr (for "Alternate Graphic") key while pressing the key with the desired character.

Figure 7-6: A French keyboard

Radically different character sets, such as Cyrillic, Hebrew, Arabic, and Greek, are more difficult to input. There's a finite number of keys on the keyboard, generally not enough for Arabic and Roman letters, or Roman and Greek letters. Assuming both are needed though, a keyboard can have a Greek lock key that shifts the keyboard from Roman to Greek and back. Both Greek and Roman letters can be printed on the keys in different colors. The same scheme works for Hebrew, Arabic, Cyrillic, and other non-Roman alphabetic character sets. Figure 7-7 shows a keyboard that includes both Hebrew and Roman letters mapped onto the same basic keys.

Figure 7-7: A standard PC Hebrew keyboard

However, this scheme really breaks down when faced with ideographic scripts like Chinese and Japanese. Chinese keyboards can have more than 5000 different keys; and that still covers less than 10 percent of the language! Syllabic, phonetic, and radical representations exist that can reduce the number of keys — the most common Japanese keyboard layout only has 106 keys and some have even fewer as shown in Figure 7-8 — but it is questionable whether a keyboard is really an appropriate means of entering text in these languages. Reliable speech and handwriting recognition have even greater potential in Asia than in the West.

Figure 7-8: A Japanese keyboard on Macintosh PowerBook

Because speech and handwriting recognition still haven't reached the reliability of even a mediocre typist like myself, most input methods today map multiple sequences of keys on the keyboard to a single character. For example, to type the Chinese character for sheep, you might hold down the Alt key and type a tilde (~), then type *yang*, then hit the space bar. The input method would then present you with a list of words that are pronounced more or less like *yang*, as shown in Figure 7-9.

You would then type the number of or click the mouse on the character you wanted, 羊. The exact details of both the GUI and the transliteration system used to convert typed keys such as *yang* to the ideographic characters such as 羊 vary from program to program, operating system to operating system, and language to language.

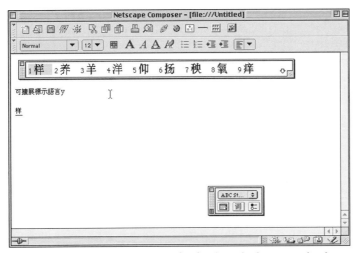

Figure 7-9: A Chinese input method using Pinyin Romanization

Operating system and application software

As of version 4.0, the major Web browsers do a surprisingly good job of displaying non-Roman scripts. Provided the underlying operating system supports a given script and has the right fonts installed, a Web browser can probably display it.

MacOS 9.0 and later can handle most common scripts in the world today, including right-to-left languages, such as Arabic and Hebrew, and ideographic scripts, such as Chinese, Japanese, and Korean. These aren't installed by default. To install them, run the installer on your MacOS 9.0 or System Install CD, pick the disk that you want to install them on, select Language Kits, choose Customized Installation, and then check the scripts that you want to use. Before MacOS 9.0, the base operating system only supported Western European languages. Chinese, Japanese, Korean, Arabic, Hebrew, and Cyrillic are still available as language kits that cost about $100 apiece. Each provides fonts and input methods for languages written in those scripts. There's also an Indian language kit, which handles the Devanagari, Gujarati, and Gurmukhu scripts common on the Indian subcontinent.

Windows NT 4.0 and Windows 2000 use Unicode as their native character set. NT 4.0 does a fairly good job with Roman languages, Cyrillic, Greek, Hebrew, and a few others. NT 4.0 bundles the Lucida Sans Unicode font which covers about 1300 of the most common of Unicode's approximately 50,000 characters. Windows 2000 adds fonts covering most of the Chinese-Japanese-Korean ideographs, as well as input methods for these scripts.

Microsoft's consumer operating systems, Windows 3.1, 95, 98, and Me, do not fully support Unicode. Instead, they rely on localized systems that can only handle basic English characters plus the localized script.

Microsoft Office 2000 includes fonts covering the full range of Unicode 2.0, including Chinese, Japanese, Korean, Arabic, and Hebrew, that you can install to read text in these languages on Windows operating systems from 95 to 2000. (Install International Support under Office Tools.) If you also want an input method for these scripts, you can get one with the *Microsoft Office 2000 Resource Kit* (Microsoft Press, ISBN 0-7356-0555-6) or download it from http://www.microsoft.com/Windows/ie/Features/ime.asp.

The major UNIX variants have varying levels of support for Unicode. Solaris 7 and later fully support Unicode and include the necessary fonts and input methods for most Latin-derived scripts, as well as for Greek, Cyrillic, Chinese, Japanese, Korean, Arabic, Hebrew, and Thai. Linux has embryonic support for Unicode, which may grow to something useful in the near future.

Legacy Character Sets

Different computers in different locales use different default character sets. Most modern computers use a superset of the ASCII character set. ASCII encodes the English alphabet and the most common punctuation and white-space characters.

In the United States, Macs use the MacRoman character set, Windows PCs use a character set called Cp1252, and most UNIX workstations use ISO 8859-1, a.k.a Latin-1. These are all extensions of ASCII that support additional characters such as ç and ¿ that are needed for Western European languages such as French and Spanish. In other locales, such as Japan, Greece, and Israel, computers use a still more confusing hodgepodge of character sets that mostly support ASCII plus the local language.

This doesn't work on the Internet. It's unlikely that while you're reading the *San Jose Mercury News* you'll turn the page and be confronted with several columns written in German or Chinese. However, on the Web it's entirely possible that a user will follow a link and end up staring at a page of Japanese. Even if the surfer can't read Japanese it would still be nice if they saw a correct version of the language, as seen in Figure 7-5, instead of a random collection of characters like those shown in Figure 7-2.

XML addresses this problem by moving beyond small, local character sets to one large set that's supposed to encompass all scripts used in all living languages (and a few dead ones) on planet Earth. This character set is called Unicode. As previously noted, Unicode is a multi-byte character set that provides representations of more than 90,000 different characters in dozens of scripts and hundreds of languages, and more will be added in the future. All XML processors are required to understand Unicode, even if they can't fully display it.

As you learned in Chapter 6, an XML document is divided into text and binary entities. Each text entity has an encoding. If the encoding is not explicitly specified in the entity's definition, then the default is UTF-8 — a compressed form of Unicode that leaves pure ASCII text unchanged. Thus, XML files that contain nothing but the common ASCII characters may be edited with tools that are unaware of the complications of dealing with multibyte character sets such as Unicode.

The ASCII character set

ASCII, the American Standard Code for Information Interchange, is one of the original character sets, and is by far the most common. It forms a sort of lowest common denominator for what a character set must support. It defines all the characters needed to write U.S. English, and essentially nothing else. The characters are encoded as the numbers 0 to 127. Table 7-1 presents the ASCII character set.

Table 7-1
The ASCII Character Set

Code	Character	Code	Character	Code	Character	Code	Character
0	null (Ctrl+@)	32	Space	64	@	96	`
1	start of heading (Ctrl+A)	33	!	65	A	97	a
2	start of text (Ctrl+B)	34	"	66	B	98	b
3	end of text (Ctrl+C)	35	#	67	C	99	c
4	end of transmission (Ctrl+D)	36	$	68	D	100	d
5	enquiry (Ctrl+E)	37	%	69	E	101	e
6	acknowledge (Ctrl+F)	38	&	70	F	102	f

continued

Table 7-1 *(continued)*

Code	Character	Code	Character	Code	Character	Code	Character
7	bell (Ctrl+G)	39	'	71	G	103	g
8	backspace (Ctrl+H)	40	(	72	H	104	h
9	tab (Ctrl+I)	41	)	73	I	105	i
10	linefeed (Ctrl+J)	42	*	74	J	106	j
11	vertical tab (Ctrl+K)	43	+	75	K	107	k
12	formfeed (Ctrl+L)	44	,	76	L	108	l
13	carriage return (Ctrl+M)	45	-	77	M	109	m
14	shift out (Ctrl+N)	46	.	78	N	110	n
15	shift in (Ctrl+O)	47	/	79	O	111	o
16	data link escape (Ctrl+P)	48	0	80	P	112	p
17	device control 1 (Ctrl+Q)	49	1	81	Q	113	q
18	device control 2 (Ctrl+R)	50	2	82	R	114	r
19	device control 3 (Ctrl+S)	51	3	83	S	115	s
20	device control 4 (Ctrl+T)	52	4	84	T	116	t
21	negative acknowledge (Ctrl+U)	53	5	85	U	117	u
22	synchronous idle (Ctrl+V)	54	6	86	V	118	v
23	end of transmission block (Ctrl+W)	55	7	87	W	119	w
24	cancel (Ctrl+X)	56	8	88	X	120	x
25	end of medium (Ctrl+Y)	57	9	89	Y	121	y
26	substitute (Ctrl+Z)	58	:	90	Z	122	z

Code	Character	Code	Character	Code	Character	Code	Character
27	escape (Ctrl+[)	59	;	91	[	123	{
28	file separator (Ctrl+\)	60	<	92	\	124	|
29	group separator (Ctrl+])	61	=	93	]	125	}
30	record separator (Ctrl+^)	62	>	94	^	126	~
31	unit separator (Ctrl+_)	63	?	95	_	127	delete

Characters 0 through 31 are nonprinting control characters. They include the carriage return, the linefeed, the tab, the bell, and similar characters. Many of these are leftovers from the days of paper-based Teletype terminals. For instance, carriage return used to literally mean move the carriage back to the left margin, as you would do on a typewriter. Linefeed moved the platen up one line. Aside from the few control characters mentioned, these aren't used much anymore.

Most other character sets that you're likely to encounter are supersets of ASCII. In other words, they define 0 though 127 exactly the same as ASCII, but add additional characters from 128 on up.

The ISO character sets

The A in ASCII stands for American, so it shouldn't surprise you that ASCII is only adequate for writing English, and strictly American English at that. ASCII does not contain the £, ü, ¿, or many other characters that you might want for writing in other languages or locales.

ASCII can be extended by assigning additional characters to numbers above 128. The International Standards Organization (ISO) has defined a number of different character sets based on ASCII that add additional characters needed for other languages and locales. The most prominent such character set is ISO 8859-1, commonly called Latin-1. Latin-1 includes enough additional characters to write in most Latin alphabet-based Western European languages. Characters 0 through 127 are the same as they are in ASCII. Characters 128 through 255 are given in Table 7-2. Again, the first 32 characters are mostly unused, nonprinting control characters.

Table 7-2
The Upper Half of the ISO 8859-1 Latin-1 Character Set

Code	Character	Code	Character	Code	Character	Code	Character
128	Undefined	160	nonbreaking space	192	À	224	à
129	Undefined	161	¡	193	Á	225	á
130	Break permitted here	162	¢	194	Â	226	â
131	No break permitted here	163	£	195	Ã	227	ã
132	Index	164	¤	196	Ä	228	ä
133	Next line	165	¥	197	Å	229	å
134	Start of selected area	166	¦	198	Æ	230	æ
135	End of selected area	167	§	199	Ç	231	ç
136	Character tabulation set	168	¨	200	È	232	è
137	Character tabulation with justification	169	©	201	É	233	é
138	Line tabulation set	170	ª	202	Ê	234	ê
139	Partial line down	171	«	203	Ë	235	ë
140	Partial line up	172	¬	204	Ì	236	ì
141	Reverse line feed	173	Discretionary hyphen	205	Í	237	í
142	Single shift 2	174	®	206	Î	238	î
143	Single shift 3	175	¯	207	Ï	239	ï
144	Device control string	176	°	208	Ð	240	ð
145	Private use 1	177	±	209	Ñ	241	ñ
146	Private use 2	178	²	210	Ò	242	ò
147	Set transmit state	179	³	211	Ó	243	ó
148	Cancel character	180	´	212	Ô	244	ô
149	Message waiting	181	>	213	Õ	245	õ
150	Start of guarded area	182	¶	214	Ö	246	ö
151	End of guarded area	183	·	215	×	247	÷
152	Start of string	184	¸	216	Ø	248	ø

Code	Character	Code	Character	Code	Character	Code	Character
153	Undefined	185	¹	217	Ù	249	ù
154	Single character introducer	186	º	218	Ú	250	ú
155	Control sequence indicator	187	»	219	Û	251	û
156	String terminator	188	1/4	220	Ü	252	ü
157	Operating system command	189	1/2	221	Ý	253	ý
158	Privacy message	190	3/4	222	Þ	254	þ
159	Application program command	191	¿	223	ß	255	ÿ

Latin-1 still lacks many useful characters including those needed for Greek, Cyrillic, Chinese, Turkish, and many other scripts and languages. You might think that these could just be moved into the numbers from 256 up. However, there's a catch. A single byte can only hold values from 0 to 255. To go beyond that, you need a multibyte character set. For historical reasons most software is written under the assumption that characters and bytes are identical, and tends to break when faced with multibyte character sets. Therefore, most current operating systems (Windows NT being the notable exception) use different, single-byte character sets rather than one large multibyte set. Latin-1 is the most common such set, but other sets are needed to handle additional languages.

ISO 8859 defines thirteen other character sets (8859-2 through 8859-10 and 8859-13 through 8859-16) suitable for different scripts, with one more, 8859-11, in active development. Table 7-3 lists the ISO character sets and the languages and scripts for which they can be used. All share the same ASCII characters from 0 to 127, and then each includes additional characters from 128 to 255.

Table 7-3
The ISO Character Sets

Character Set		Also Known As / Languages
ISO 8859-1	Latin-1	ASCII plus the characters required for most Western European languages including Albanian, Afrikaans, Basque, Catalan, Danish, Dutch, English, Faroese, Finnish, Flemish, Galician, German, Icelandic, Irish, Italian, Norwegian, Portuguese, Scottish, Spanish, and Swedish. However it omits the ligatures ij (Dutch), Œ (French), and German quotation marks.
ISO 8859-2	Latin-2	ASCII plus the characters required for most Central European languages including Czech, English, German, Hungarian, Polish, Romanian, Croatian, Slovak, Slovene, and Sorbian.
ISO 8859-3	Latin-3	ASCII plus the characters required for English, Esperanto, German, Maltese, and Galician.
ISO 8859-4	Latin-4	ASCII plus the characters required for the Baltic languages Latvian, Lithuanian, German, Greenlandic, and Lappish; superseded by ISO 8859-10, Latin-6.
ISO 8859-5		ASCII plus Cyrillic characters required for Byelorussian, Bulgarian, Macedonian, Russian, Serbian, and Ukrainian.
ISO 8859-6		ASCII plus Arabic.
ISO 8859-7		ASCII plus Greek.
ISO 8859-8		ASCII plus Hebrew.
ISO 8859-9	Latin-5	Latin-1 except that the Turkish letters İ, ı, Ş, ş, Ğ, and ğ take the place of the less commonly used Icelandic letters Ý, ý, Þ, þ, Ð, and ð.
ISO 8859-10	Latin-6	ASCII plus characters for the Nordic languages Lithuanian, Inuit (Greenlandic Eskimo), non-Skolt Sami (Lappish), and Icelandic.
ISO 8859-11		ASCII plus Thai.
ISO 8859-12		This may eventually be used for ASCII plus Devanagari (Hindi, Sanskrit, and so on), but no proposal is yet available.
ISO 8859-13	Latin-7	ASCII plus the Baltic Rim, particularly Latvian.
ISO 8859-14	Latin-8	ASCII plus Gaelic and Welsh.
ISO 8859-15	Latin-9, Latin-0	Essentially the same as Latin-1 but with the euro sign, €, instead of the international currency sign, ¤. Furthermore, the Finnish characters Š, š, Ž, ž replace the uncommon symbols ¦, ¨, and ´. Finally, the French Œ, œ, and Ÿ characters replace the fractions 1/4, 1/2, 3/4.

These sets often overlap. Several languages, most notably English and German, can be written in more than one of the character sets. To some extent the different sets are designed to allow different combinations of languages. For instance Latin-1 can combine most Western languages and Icelandic whereas Latin-5 combines most Western languages with Turkish instead of Icelandic. Thus, if you needed a document in English, French, and Icelandic, you'd use Latin-1. A document containing English, French, and Turkish would be written in Latin-5. However, a document that required English, Hebrew, and Turkish, would have to be written in Unicode because no single-byte character set handles all three languages and scripts.

A single-byte set is insufficient for Chinese, Japanese, and Korean. These languages have more than 256 characters apiece, so they must use multibyte character sets.

The MacRoman character set

The MacOS predates Latin-1 by several years. (The ISO 8859-1 standard was first adopted in 1987. The first Mac was released in 1984.) Unfortunately, this meant that Apple had to define its own extended character set called MacRoman. MacRoman is the same as ASCII and Latin-1 in the codes through the first 127 characters. From 128 through 255, MacRoman has most of the same extended characters as Latin-1 (except for the Icelandic letters Ý, ý, Þ, þ, Ð, and ð), but the characters are assigned to different numbers. This is one reason text files that use extended characters often look funny when moved from a PC to a Mac or vice versa. Table 7-4 lists the upper half of the MacRoman character set.

Table 7-4
The Upper Half of the MacRoman Character Set

Code	Character	Code	Character	Code	Character	Code	Character
128	Â	160	†	192	¿	224	‡
129	Å	161	°	193	¡	225	·
130	Ç	162	¢	194	¬	226	‚
131	É	163	£	195	√	227	„
132	Ñ	164	§	196	ƒ	228	‰
133	Ö	165	·	197	≈	229	Â
134	Ü	166	¶	198	∆	230	Ê
135	á	167	ß	199	«	231	Á
136	à	168	®	200	»	232	È
137	â	169	©	201	…	233	Ë

continued

Table 7-4   *(continued)*

Code	Character	Code	Character	Code	Character	Code	Character
138	ä	170	™	202	nonbreaking space	234	Í
139	ã	171	_	203	À	235	Î
140	å	172	¨	204	Ã	236	Ï
141	ç	173	≠	205	Õ	237	Ì
142	é	174	Æ	206	Œ	238	Î
143	è	175	Ø	207	œ	239	Ó
144	ê	176	∞	208	–	240	Ô
145	ë	177	±	209	_	241	🍎
146	í	178	≤	210	"	242	Ò
147	ì	179	≥	211	"	243	Û
148	î	180	¥	212	'	244	Ú
149	ï	181	>	213	'	245	ı
150	ñ	182	∂	214	÷	246	ˆ
151	ó	183	Σ	215	◊	247	˜
152	ò	184	Π	216	ÿ	248	¯
153	ô	185	π	217	Ÿ	249	˘
154	ö	186	∫	218	⁄	250	˙
155	õ	187	ª	219	€ (¤ in MacOS 8.1 and earlier)	251	°
156	ú	188	º	220	‹	252	¸
157	ù	189	Ω	221	›	253	˝
158	û	190	Æ	222	fi	254	˛
159	ü	191	Ø	223	fl	255	ˇ

The Windows ANSI character set

The first version of Windows to achieve widespread adoption followed the Mac by a few years, so it was able to adopt the Latin-1 character set. However, it replaced the nonprinting control characters between 130 and 159 with more printing characters to stretch the available range a little further. This modified version of Latin-1 is often called Windows ANSI (even though it was never standardized by ANSI or any other standards body) or, more properly, Cp1252. Table 7-5 lists the characters Cp1252 added to Latin-1.

Table 7-5
The Windows ANSI Character Set

Code	Character	Code	Character	Code	Character	Code	Character
128	Undefined	136	ˆ	144	Undefined	152	˜
129	Undefined	137	‰	145	'	153	™
130	,	138	Š	146	'	154	š
131	ƒ	139	‹	147	"	155	›
132	„	140	Œ	148	"	156	œ
133	…	141	Undefined	149	•	157	Undefined
134	†	142	Undefined	150	–	158	Undefined
135	‡	143	Undefined	151	—	159	Ÿ

The Unicode Character Set

Using different character sets for different scripts and languages works well enough as long as:

1. You don't need to work in more than one script at once.

2. You never trade files with anyone using a different character set.

Because Macs and PCs use different character sets, more people fail these criteria than not. Obviously what is needed is a single character set that everyone agrees on and that encodes all characters in all the world's scripts. Creating such a set is difficult. It requires a detailed understanding of hundreds of languages and their scripts. Getting software developers to agree to use that set once it's been created is even harder. Nonetheless work is ongoing to create exactly such a set called Unicode, and the major vendors (Microsoft, Apple, IBM, Sun, Be, and many others) are slowly moving toward complying with it. XML specifies Unicode as its default character set.

Unicode provides room for over one million different characters. Currently, a few more than 94,000 different Unicode characters are defined. Unicode characters 0 through 255 are identical to Latin-1 characters 0 through 255. About 70,000 of the characters are used for the Han ideographs and another 11,000 or so are used for the Korean Hangul syllables. The remainder encodes most of the rest of the world's languages. About 6000 more are earmarked for private use by vendors. The remaining million spaces are reserved for future extensions.

I'd love to show you a table of all the characters in Unicode, but if I did this book would consist entirely of that table and not much else. If you need to know more about the specific encodings of the different characters in Unicode, get a copy of *The Unicode Standard Version 3.0* (ISBN 0-201-61633-5, from Addison-Wesley). This 1000-page book includes the complete Unicode 3.0 specification, including character charts for all the different characters defined in Unicode 3.0. You can also find information online at the Unicode Consortium Web site at `http://www.unicode.org/`.

Table 7-6 lists the different scripts encoded by Unicode 3.0, which should give you some idea of Unicode's versatility. The characters of each script are generally encoded in a consecutive subrange (block) of Unicode. Most languages can be written with the characters in one of these blocks (for example, Russian can be written with the Cyrillic block), although some languages, such as Croatian or Turkish, may need to mix and match characters from the first four Latin blocks.

Table 7-6
Unicode 3.0 Script Blocks

Script	Range	Purpose
Basic Latin	0–127	ASCII, American English.
Latin-1 Supplement	126–255	Upper half of ISO Latin-1, in conjunction with the Basic Latin block can handle Danish, Dutch, English, Faroese, Flemish, German, Hawaiian, Icelandic, Indonesian, Irish, Italian, Norwegian, Portuguese, Spanish, Swahili, and Swedish.
Latin Extended-A	256–383	This block adds the characters from the ISO 8859 sets Latin-2, Latin-3, Latin-4, and Latin-5 that are not already found in the Basic Latin and Latin-1 blocks. In conjunction with those blocks, this block can encode Afrikaans, Breton, Basque, Catalan, Czech, Esperanto, Estonian, French, Frisian, Greenlandic, Hungarian, Latvian, Lithuanian, Maltese, Polish, Provençal, Rhaeto-Romanic, Romanian, Romany, Slovak, Slovenian, Sorbian, Turkish, and Welsh.

Script	Range	Purpose
Latin Extended-B	383–591	Mostly characters needed to extend the Latin script to handle languages not traditionally written in this script; includes many African languages, Croatian digraphs to match Serbian Cyrillic letters, the Pinyin transcription of Chinese, and the Sami characters from Latin-10.
IPA Extensions	592–687	The International Phonetic Alphabet.
Spacing Modifier Letters	686–767	Small symbols that somehow change (generally phonetically) the previous letter.
Combining Diacritical Marks	766–879	Diacritical marks, such as ~, ', and ˉ, that will somehow be combined with the previous character (most commonly, be placed on top of) rather than drawn as a separate character.
Greek	880–1023	Modern Greek; based on ISO 8859-7
Cyrillic	1024–1279	Russian and most other Slavic languages (Ukrainian, Byelorussian, and so forth), and many non-Slavic languages of the former Soviet Union (Azerbaijani, Ossetian, Kabardian, Chechen, Tajik, and so forth); based on ISO 8859-5. A few languages (Kurdish, Abkhazian) require both Latin and Cyrillic characters.
Armenian	1326–1423	Armenian.
Hebrew	1424–1535	Hebrew (classical and modern), Yiddish, Judezmo, early Aramaic.
Arabic	1536–1791	Arabic, Persian, Pashto, Sindhi, Kurdish, and classical Turkish.
Syriac	1792–1866	Syriac.
Thaana	1920–1969	The Dhivehi language of the Maldives.
Devanagari	2304–2431	Sanskrit, Hindi, Nepali, and other languages of the Indian subcontinent including Awadhi, Bagheli, Bhatneri, Bhili, Bihari, Braj Bhasha, Chhattisgarhi, Garhwali, Gondi, Harauti, Ho, Jaipuri, Kachchhi, Kanauji, Konkani, Kului, Kumaoni, Kurku, Kurukh, Marwari, Mundari, Newari, Palpa, and Santali.
Bengali	2432–2559	A North Indian script used in India's West Bengal state and Bangladesh; used for Bengali, Assamese, Daphla, Garo, Hallam, Khasi, Manipuri, Mizo, Naga, Munda, Rian, and Santali.
Gurmukhi	2560–2687	Punjabi.

continued

Table 7-6 *(continued)*

Script	Range	Purpose
Gujarati	2686–2815	Gujarati.
Oriya	2816–2943	Oriya, Khondi, and Santali.
Tamil	2944–3071	Tamil and Badaga, used in south India, Sri Lanka, Singapore, and parts of Malaysia.
Telugu	3072–3199	Telugu, Gondi, and Lambadi.
Kannada	3200–3327	Kannada and Tulu.
Malalayam	3326–3455	Malalayam.
Sinhala	3456–3583	Sinhala, the primary language of Sri Lanka. Also used for Pali and Sanskrit.
Thai	3584–3711	Thai, Kuy, Lavna, and Pali.
Lao	3712–3839	Lao.
Tibetan	3840–4031	Himalayan languages including Tibetan, Ladakhi, and Lahuli.
Myanmar	4096–4255	Burmese, as well as Shan, Mon, Pali, and Sanskrit.
Georgian	4256–4351	Georgian, the language of the former Soviet Republic of Georgia on the Black Sea.
Hangul Jamo	4352–4607	The alphabetic components of the Korean Hangul syllabary.
Ethiopic	4608–4991	Various central East African languages including Ge'ez, Amharic, Tigre, and Oromo.
Cherokee	5024–5119	The Cherokee syllabary designed by Sequoyah.
Canadian Aboriginal Syllabics	5120–5759	A unified version of several syllabaries used by aboriginal groups in Canada for languages in the Algonquian, Inuktitut, and Athapascan families.
Ogham	5760–5791	A script used for Irish and possibly Pictish, found on stone monuments in Ireland and the U.K.; died out around the sixteenth century.
Runic	5792–5887	An extinct script used from about the first to the nineteenth century for a number of Germanic languages including the ancestors of today's English, Swedish, and German.
Khmer	6016–6143	Cambodian.
Mongolian	6144–6319	Mongolian.

Script	Range	Purpose
Latin Extended Additional	7680–7935	Normal Latin letters like E and Y combined with diacritical marks, rarely used except for Vietnamese vowels.
Greek Extended	7936–8191	Greek letters combined with diacritical marks; used in polytonic and classical Greek.
General Punctuation	8192–8303	Assorted relatively uncommon punctuation marks such as ‰, †, and •.
Superscripts and Subscripts	8304–8351	Common subscripts and superscripts.
Currency Symbols	8352–8399	Currency symbols not already present in other blocks such as the Peseta sign Pts, the Lira sign £, and the euro sign €.
Combining Marks for Symbols	8400–8447	Used to make half of a diacritical mark that spans two or more characters.
Letter like Symbols	8446–8527	Symbols that look like letters, such as ™ and №.
Number Forms	8526–8591	Fractions and Roman numerals.
Arrows	8592–8703	Arrows.
Mathematical Operators	8704–8959	Mathematical operators that don't already appear in other blocks.
Miscellaneous Technical	8960–9039	Cropping marks, bra-ket notation from quantum mechanics, symbols needed for the APL programming language, and assorted other technical symbols.
Control Pictures	9216–9279	Pictures of the ASCII control characters; generally used in debugging and network-packet sniffing.
Optical Character Recognition	9280–9311	OCR-A and the MICR (magnetic ink character recognition) symbols used on printed checks.
Enclosed Alphanumerics	9312–9471	Letters and numbers in circles and parentheses.
Box Drawing	9472–9599	Characters for drawing boxes on monospaced terminals.
Block Elements	9600–9631	Monospaced terminal graphics as used in DOS and elsewhere.
Geometric Shapes	9632–9727	Squares, diamonds, triangles, and the like.
Miscellaneous Symbols	9726–9983	Cards, chess, astrology, and more.

continued

Table 7-6 *(continued)*

Script	Range	Purpose
Dingbats	9984–10175	Characters from the Zapf Dingbat font.
Braille	10240–10495	A writing system built out of raised dots and read by touch; used by blind people for many different languages.
CJK and KangXi Radicals	11904–12245	Fragments of ideographs used to sort dictionaries, indexes, and other word lists in Chinese, Japanese, and Korean.
Ideographic Description	12272–12283	Characters used to describe rare ideographs that are not included in Unicode.
CJK Symbols and Punctuation	12286–12351	Symbols and punctuation used in Chinese, Japanese, and Korean.
Hiragana	12352–12447	A cursive syllabary for Japanese.
Katakana	12446–12543	A noncursive syllabary used to write words imported from the West into Japanese, especially modern words like キーボード(keyboard).
Bopomofo	12544–12591, 12704–12727	A phonetic alphabet for Chinese used primarily for teaching.
Hangul Compatibility Jamo	12592–12687 5601	Korean characters needed for compatibility with the KSC encoding.
Kanbun	12688–12703	Marks used in Japanese to indicate the reading order of classical Chinese.
Enclosed CJK Letters and Months	12800–13055	Hangul and Katakana characters enclosed in circles and parentheses.
CJK Compatibility	13056–13311	Characters needed only for compatibility with the legacy encodings KSC 5601 and CNS 11643.
CJK Unified Ideographs	13312–40959	The Han ideographs used for Chinese, Japanese, and Korean.
Yi (a.k.a. Cuan, a.k.a Wei)	40960–42191	Yi, a minority language of China.
Hangul Syllables	44032–55203	The Korean syllabary.
Surrogates	55296–57343	Enables the extension of Unicode to over one million different characters by encoding characters as pairs of these values.

Script	Range	Purpose
Private Use	57344–63743	Software developers can include their custom characters here; not compatible across implementations.
CJK Compatibility Ideographs	63744–64255	A few extra Han ideographs needed only to maintain compatibility with existing standards such as KSC 5601.
Alphabetic Presentation Forms	64256–64335	Latin and Armenian Ligatures and Hebrew presentation forms.
Arabic Presentation Forms	64336–65023	Variants of assorted Arabic characters.
Combining Half Marks	65056–65071	Code points that represent only half of a combining diacritical mark that spans multiple characters.
CJK Compatibility Forms	65072–65103	Mostly vertical variants of Han ideographs used in Taiwan.
Small Form Variants	65104–65135	Smaller version of ASCII punctuation mostly used in Taiwan.
Additional Arabic Presentation Forms	65136–65279	More variants of assorted Arabic characters.
Half-width and Full-width Forms	65280–65519	Characters that allow conversion between different Chinese and Japanese encodings of the same characters.
Specials	65520–65535	The byte order mark and the zero-width, nonbreaking space often used to start Unicode files.

Unicode Encodings

The Unicode character set just assigns characters to numbers. It does not specify how those numbers are represented. This is done by an encoding scheme. Since Unicode 3.0 and earlier characters are assigned numbers less than 65,536, a two-byte, unsigned integer suffices for each character. The most naïve encoding of Unicode simply identifies each character by such a two-byte, unsigned integer in either big- or little-endian form. This encoding is called UCS-2. When new characters are assigned to numbers beyond 65,536 in Unicode 3.1, you'll need four bytes for each character. This encoding is called UCS-4.

When Unicode uses 2 bytes for each character, files of English text are about twice as large in Unicode as they would be in ASCII or Latin-1. UTF-8 is a compressed version of Unicode that uses only a single byte for the most common characters, that is the ASCII characters 0 to 127, at the expense of having to use 3 or more bytes for the less common characters, particularly the Hangul syllables and Han ideographs. If you're writing mostly in English, UTF-8 can reduce your file sizes by as much as 50 percent. On the other hand, if you're writing mostly in Chinese, Korean, or Japanese, UTF-8 can *increase* your file size by as much as 50 percent — so it should be used with caution. UTF-8 has mostly no effect on non-Roman, non-CJK scripts such as Greek, Arabic, Cyrillic, and Hebrew.

XML processors assume text data is in the UTF-8 format unless told otherwise. This means that they can read ASCII files, because ASCII is a strict subset of UTF-8. XML parsers can also recognize and process documents written in UCS-2 provided the document starts with either a byte order mark or an XML declaration or both. However, other formats like MacRoman or Latin-1 can cause parsers trouble. You'll see how to account for that shortly.

Unicode 3.1

Unicode has been criticized for not encompassing enough, especially in regard to East Asian languages. It only defines about 20,000 of the 50,000+ Han ideographs used amongst Chinese, Japanese, Korean, and historical Vietnamese. (Modern Vietnamese use a Roman alphabet.) Unicode 3.0 does not assign any characters to code points beyond 65,535. However, it's anticipated that a number of dead languages, such as Egyptian hieroglyphics and Gothic, will be added to this region in Unicode 3.1 and later, as will fictional scripts such as Cirth and Tengwar.

Unicode 3.1 uses 4 bytes per character (more precisely, 31 bits) to provide space for more than 2 billion different characters. This is large enough to easily cover every character ever used in any language in any script on the planet Earth with room left over for scripts from more than a few other planets as well. In practice, future versions of Unicode will encode at most about one million total characters, which is still enough to cover all of Earth's living and dead languages. Characters 0 through 65,536 can be encoded directly as 2-byte values, exactly as they are in Unicode 3.0. Characters from 65,537 to 1,048,575 will be encoded as 4-byte surrogate pairs using the surrogates block of Unicode. UCS-2 plus surrogate pairs is called UTF-16. As long as surrogate pairs aren't used then UCS-2 and UTF-16 are essentially the same encoding.

How to Write XML in Unicode

Unicode is the native character set of XML, and XML browsers do a pretty good job of displaying it, at least within the limits of the available fonts. Nonetheless, there simply aren't many, if any, text editors that support the full range of Unicode. Consequently, you'll probably have to tackle this problem in one of these ways.

1. Write in a localized character set such as Latin-3, and then convert your file to Unicode.

2. Include Unicode character references in the text that numerically identify particular characters.

The first option is preferable when you've got a large amount of text to enter in essentially one script, or one script plus ASCII. The second works best when you need to mix small portions of multiple scripts into your document.

Converting to and from Unicode

Application software that exports XML files, such as Adobe FrameMaker, handles the conversion to Unicode or UTF-8 automatically. Otherwise, you need to use a conversion tool. Sun's freely available Java Development Kit (http://java.sun.com/j2se/) includes a simple command-line utility called native2ascii that converts between many common and uncommon localized character sets and Unicode.

For example, the following command converts a text file named myfile.txt from the platform's default encoding to Unicode:

```
C:\> native2ascii myfile.txt myfile.uni
```

You can specify other encodings with the -encoding option.

```
C:\> native2ascii -encoding Big5 chinese.txt chinese.uni
```

You can also reverse the process to go from Unicode to a local encoding with the -reverse option.

```
C:\> native2ascii -encoding Big5 -reverse chinese.uni
chinese.txt
```

The native2ascii program also processes Java-style Unicode escapes, which are characters embedded as \u09E3. These are not in the same format as XML numeric character references, though they're similar. If you convert to Unicode using native2ascii, you can still use XML character references — the XML processor that eventually reads the document will still recognize them.

Word 2000 also does a pretty good job of saving files in various encodings of Unicode. Open the file you want to convert in Word, then select Save As from the File menu. From the Save as type: pop-up menu, select Encoded Text (*.txt) and click OK. Word will then bring up a dialog box, shown in Figure 7-10, that asks you to pick the character set to save the document in, as well as warning you about any characters that don't exist in your chosen encoding, although this shouldn't be a problem if you're saving to Unicode. Word gives you four options for Unicode, but for XML documents you should pick Unicode (UTF-8).

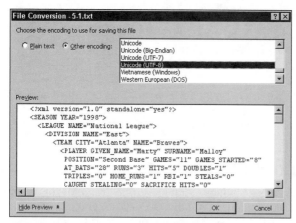

Figure 7-10: The Save As encoded text dialog box from Word 2000

Inserting characters in XML files with character references

Every Unicode character is a number between 0 and 1,114,111. If you do not have a text editor that can write in Unicode, you can always use a character reference to insert the character in your XML file instead.

A Unicode character reference consists of the two characters &# followed by the character code and a semicolon. For instance, the Greek letter π has Unicode value 960, so it may be inserted in an XML file as π. The Cyrillic character Ч has Unicode value 1206, so it can be included in an XML file with the character reference Ҷ.

Unicode character references may also be specified in hexadecimal (base 16). Although most people are more comfortable with decimal numbers, the Unicode specification gives character values as 2-byte hexadecimal numbers. It's often easier to use hex values directly rather than converting them to decimal.

All you need to do is include an x after the &# to signify that you're using a hexadecimal value. For example, π has hexadecimal value 3C0 so it may be inserted in an XML file as π. The Cyrillic character Ч has hexadecimal value 4B6 so it can be included in an XML file with the escape sequence `&#x04B6;`. Because 2 bytes always produce exactly four hexadecimal digits, it's customary (although not required) to include leading zeros in hexadecimal character references so they are rounded out to four digits.

Unicode character references, both hexadecimal and decimal, may be used to embed characters that would otherwise be interpreted as markup. For instance, the ampersand (&) is encoded as `&#38;` or `&#x0026;`. The less than sign (<) is encoded as `&#60;` or `&#x003C;`.

How to write XML in other character sets

Unless told otherwise, an XML processor assumes that all text entities are encoded in UTF-8. Because UTF-8 includes ASCII as a subset, XML processors can easily parse ASCII text too.

If you cannot convert your text into either UTF-8 or raw Unicode, you can leave the text in its native character set and tell the XML processor which set that is. This should be a last resort, though, because there's no guarantee that an arbitrary XML processor can process other encodings. The only character set other than UTF-8 that an XML processor is required to understand is the UTF-16 encoding of Unicode. Nonetheless, Netscape and Internet Explorer both do a pretty good job of interpreting the common character sets.

To warn the XML processor that you're using a non-Unicode encoding, you include an `encoding` attribute in the XML declaration at the start of the file. For example, to specify that the entire document uses Latin-1 by default (unless overridden by another processing instruction in a nested entity) you would use this XML declaration.

```
<?xml version="1.0" encoding="ISO-8859-1"?>
```

Table 7-7 lists the official names of the most common character sets used today, as they would be given in XML encoding attributes. For encodings not found in this list, consult the official list maintained by the Internet Assigned Numbers Authority (IANA) at `www.isi.edu/in-notes/iana/assignments/character-sets`.

Table 7-7
Names of Common Character Sets

Character Set Name	Languages/Countries
US-ASCII	English
UTF-8	Compressed Unicode
UTF-16	Compressed UCS
ISO-10646-UCS-2	Raw Unicode
ISO-10646-UCS-4	Raw UCS
ISO-8859-1	Latin-1, Western Europe
ISO-8859-2	Latin-2, Eastern Europe
ISO-8859-3	Latin-3, Southern Europe
ISO-8859-4	Latin-4, Northern Europe
ISO-8859-5	ASCII plus Cyrillic
ISO-8859-6	ASCII plus Arabic
ISO-8859-7	ASCII plus Greek
ISO-8859-8	ASCII plus Hebrew
ISO-8859-9	Latin-5, Turkish
ISO-8859-10	Latin-6, ASCII plus the Nordic languages
ISO-8859-11	ASCII plus Thai
ISO-8859-13	Latin-7, ASCII plus the Baltic Rim languages, particularly Latvian
ISO-8859-14	Latin-8, ASCII plus Gaelic and Welsh
ISO-8859-15	Latin-9, Latin-0; Western Europe
ISO-2022-JP	Japanese
Shift_JIS	Japanese, Windows
EUC-JP	Japanese, Unix
Big5	Traditional Chinese, Taiwan
GB2312	Simplified Chinese, mainland China
KOI6-R	Russian
ISO-2022-KR	Korean
EUC-KR	Korean, Unix
ISO-2022-CN	Chinese

Summary

In this chapter you learned:

- ✦ What a script is, how it relates to languages, and the four things a script requires.
- ✦ How scripts are used in computers with character sets, fonts, glyphs, and input methods.
- ✦ What character sets are commonly used on different platforms and that most are based on ASCII.
- ✦ How to write XML in Unicode without a Unicode editor (write the document in ASCII and include Unicode character references).
- ✦ When writing XML in other encodings, include an `encoding` attribute in the XML or text declaration.

This chapter concludes your exploration of basic, well-formed XML. The next chapter takes up Document Type Definitions (DTDs) and validity. A DTD defines a structure for a class of XML documents. It specifies what documents in that class must, must not, and may contain. By validating documents against DTDs, you can quickly and easily verify that your documents meet any necessary conditions.

✦　　✦　　✦

Document Type Definitions

DTDs and Validity

XML has been described as a meta-markup language —
that is, a language for describing markup languages. In
this chapter, you begin to learn how to document and
describe the new markup languages that you create. Such
markup languages (also known as *vocabularies* or *XML applications*) are defined with a document type definition (DTD).
Individual documents can be compared against DTDs in a process known as *validation*. If the document matches the constraints listed in the DTD, then the document is said to be
valid; if the document doesn't match the constraints, then the
document is said to be *invalid*.

Document Type Definitions

DTD is an acronym for *document type definition*. A document
type definition lists the elements, attributes, entities, and
notations that can be used in a document, as well as their possible relationships to one another. A DTD specifies a set of
rules for the structure of a document. For example, a DTD
may dictate that each BOOK element has exactly one ISBN
child, exactly one TITLE child, and one or more AUTHOR children, and it may or may not contain a single SUBTITLE. Each
such rule is given in a *declaration*.

Every valid XML document must specify the DTD it's valid
with respect to. This DTD can be included in the XML document it describes, or that document can link to it at an external URL. Such external DTDs can be shared by different
documents and Web sites. If the DTD is not directly included
in the document but is linked in from an external source,
changes made to the DTD automatically propagate to all documents using that DTD. On the other hand, backward compatibility is not guaranteed when a DTD is modified. Incompatible
changes can invalidate documents.

The real power of XML comes from common DTDs that are shared among many documents written by different people. DTDs provide a means for applications, organizations, and interest groups to agree upon, document, and enforce adherence to markup standards. For example, a publisher may want an author to adhere to a particular format because it makes it easier to lay out a book. An author may prefer writing words in a row without worrying about matching up each bullet point in the front of the chapter with a subhead inside the chapter. If the author writes in XML, it's easy for the publisher to check whether the author adhered to the predetermined format specified by the DTD, and even to find out exactly where and how the author deviated from the format. This is much easier than having human editors read through documents with the hope that they spot all the minor deviations from the format based on style alone.

DTDs also help ensure that different people and programs can read each other's files. For instance, if chemists agree on a single DTD for basic chemical notation, possibly via the intermediary of an appropriate professional organization such as the American Chemical Society, then they can rest assured that they can all read and understand one another's papers. The DTD defines exactly what is and is not allowed to appear inside a document. The DTD establishes a standard for the markup that viewing and editing software must support. Even more importantly, it establishes that extensions beyond those the DTD declares are invalid. Thus, it helps prevent software vendors from embracing and extending open protocols in order to lock users into their proprietary software.

Furthermore, a DTD shows how the different elements of a document are arranged. A DTD shows the generic structure of a document separate from the actual data in the individual document instances. This means that you can slap a lot of fancy styles and formatting onto the underlying structure without destroying it, much as you paint a house without changing its basic architectural plan. The reader of your page may not see or even be aware of the underlying structure, but as long as it's there, human authors and JavaScripts, CGIs, servlets, databases, and other computer programs can use it.

Element Declarations

Recall Listing 3-2 (greeting.xml) from Chapter 3. It is shown below:

Listing 3-2: **greeting.xml**

```
<?xml version="1.0"?>
<GREETING>
Hello XML!
</GREETING>
```

This XML document contains a single element, GREETING. (Remember, <?xml version="1.0"?> is the XML declaration, not an element.) A DTD for this document has to declare the GREETING element. It may declare other elements, too, including ones that aren't present in this particular document, but it must at least declare the GREETING element.

Elements are declared using element declarations. Each element declaration gives the name of the element and lists the elements and text that it can contain. This list is called the *content model*. For instance, this element declaration for the GREETING element says that elements with the name GREETING must contain only parsed character data:

```
<!ELEMENT GREETING (#PCDATA)>
```

Every declaration begins with <!. Element declarations begin with <!ELEMENT (case sensitive, as most things are in XML). This is followed by some white space and the name of the element being declared, GREETING in this example. Then there's some more white space and the content model for this element. This content model, (#PCDATA), says that the element must contain parsed character data. Parsed character data is essentially any text that's not markup. This also includes entity references, such as &, that are replaced by text when the document is parsed. In other words, GREETING elements can contain text but no child elements. A valid GREETING element must look like this:

```
<GREETING>
  various random text but no markup
</GREETING>
```

There's no restriction on what text the element can contain. It can be zero or more Unicode characters with any meaning. DTDs don't let you specify that an element must contain a year, such as 2001, or a floating point number like 3.14152. You can only say whether the element contains text, or child elements, or both. Thus a GREETING element can also look like this:

```
<GREETING>Hello!</GREETING>
```

Or even this:

```
<GREETING></GREETING>
```

However, a valid GREETING element may not look like this:

```
<GREETING>
  <SOME_TAG>various random text</SOME_TAG>
  <SOME_EMPTY_TAG/>
</GREETING>
```

Nor may it look like this:

```
<GREETING>
  <GREETING>various random text</GREETING>
</GREETING>
```

Each GREETING element must consist of nothing more and nothing less than parsed character data between an opening <GREETING> tag and a closing </GREETING> tag.

DTD Files

Declarations are placed in DTDs. Usually a DTD is a single file, separate from the document itself (although, as you'll soon see, other storage schemes are possible). Such a DTD can be saved in a text file using any standard text editor. By convention, this file will have the three-letter extension .dtd, although this isn't required. For instance, you might save a DTD describing only GREETING elements in a file called greeting.dtd, as shown in Listing 8-1.

Listing 8-1: **greeting.dtd**

```
<!ELEMENT GREETING (#PCDATA)>
```

Of course, DTDs are usually much longer and more complex and contain many more declarations than this trivial example.

Most of the time DTDs are written in either ASCII or UTF-8. If you use any other encoding, then the DTD must have a text declaration identifying the encoding used as discussed in the last chapter. For example, Listing 8-2 shows a DTD that uses the ISO-8859-5 encoding because it uses the Russian word for *greeting* as an element name:

Listing 8-2: **russian_greeting.dtd**

```
<?xml encoding="ISO-8859-5"?>
<!ELEMENT ПРИВЕТСТВИЕ (#PCDATA)>
```

Document Type Declarations

A document type declaration is placed in an XML document's prolog to say what DTD that document adheres to. It also specifies which element is the root element of the document. The document type declaration can either specify the DTD directly by including it inside the document type declaration or indirectly by giving the URL where the DTD is found. It may even do both, in which case the DTD has two parts, the internal and external subsets.

 Caution
A document type *declaration* is not the same thing as a document type *definition*. Only the document type definition is abbreviated *DTD*. A document type declaration must contain or refer to a document type definition, but a document type definition never contains a document type declaration. I agree that this is unnecessarily confusing. Unfortunately, XML is stuck with this terminology.

A document type declaration begins with <!DOCTYPE and ends with a >. In between is the name of the root element, followed by either a pair of square brackets containing the DTD itself, or the SYSTEM keyword and a URL where the DTD can be found (or, occasionally, both). Thus, a document type declaration has this basic form:

```
<!DOCTYPE name_of_root_element
    SYSTEM "URL of the external DTD subset" [
    internal DTD subset
]>
```

Here name_of_root_element is simply the name of the root element. The SYSTEM keyword indicates that what follows is a URL where the DTD is located. The square brackets enclose the internal subset of the DTD—that is, those declarations included inside the document itself. You can omit either the SYSTEM keyword and the URL to the external DTD subset or the square brackets and internal DTD subset, but you must have at least one of them. For example, this document type declaration only specifies an external DTD that can be found at the URL http://ibiblio.org/greeting.dtd:

```
<!DOCTYPE GREETING SYSTEM "http://ibiblio.org/greeting.dtd">
```

This document type declaration includes the DTD inside itself:

```
<!DOCTYPE GREETING [
  <!ELEMENT GREETING (#PCDATA)>
]>
```

Line breaks and extra white space are not significant in a DTD. The same document type declaration could be written on a single line like this:

```
<!DOCTYPE GREETING [ <!ELEMENT GREETING (#PCDATA)> ]>
```

In all cases, the document type declaration is placed in the document's prolog, after the XML declaration but before the root element. For instance, Listing 8-3 adds a document type declaration to the hello.xml document from Listing 3-2.

Listing 8-3: **Hello XML with DTD**

```
<?xml version="1.0"?>
<!DOCTYPE GREETING SYSTEM "greeting.dtd">
<GREETING>
Hello XML!
</GREETING>
```

Listing 8-3 uses a relative URL to locate the DTD so that it will be searched for in the same directory in which the document itself was found. You may also wish to locate DTDs relative to the Web server's document root or to the current directory. In general, any reference that forms a valid URL relative to the location of the document is acceptable. For example, these are all good document type declarations:

```
<!DOCTYPE SEASON SYSTEM "/xml/dtds/greeting.dtd">
<!DOCTYPE SEASON SYSTEM "dtds/greeting.dtd">
<!DOCTYPE SEASON SYSTEM "../greeting.dtd">
```

Note   A document can't have more than one document type declaration, that is, more than one `<!DOCTYPE>` tag. To use elements declared in more than one external DTD, you need to use external parameter entity references. These are discussed in Chapter 10.

Internal DTDs

Putting the entire DTD inside the document type declaration isn't as reusable or modular as locating it with a URL, but it sometimes helps when you're developing a new DTD and want to keep your example document and the DTD in sync. Moreover, it will have some important consequences when we discuss entities in a couple of chapters. Listing 8-4 shows a complete greeting document with an internal DTD.

Listing 8-4: **Hello XML with an internal DTD**

```
<?xml version="1.0"?>
<!DOCTYPE GREETING [
  <!ELEMENT GREETING (#PCDATA)>
]>
<GREETING>
Hello XML!
</GREETING>
```

You can load this document into an XML browser as usual. Figure 8-1 shows Listing 8-4 in Internet Explorer 5.5. The result is probably what you'd expect, a collapsible outline view of the document source. Internet Explorer indicates that a document type declaration is present by adding the line `<!DOCTYPE GREETING (View Source for full doctype...)>` in blue.

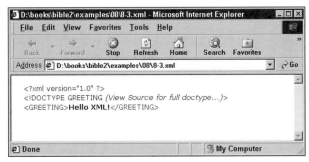

Figure 8-1: Hello XML with DTD displayed in Internet Explorer 5.5

Internal and external DTD subsets

Although most documents consist of easily defined pieces, not all documents use a common template. Many documents may need to use standard DTDs, such as the XHTML DTD, while adding custom elements for their own use. Other documents may use only standard elements, but need to reorder them. For instance, one HTML page may have a `BODY` that must contain exactly one `H1` header followed by a `DL` definition list, while another may have a `BODY` that contains many different headers, paragraphs, and images in no particular order. If a particular document has a different structure than other pages on the site, it can be useful to define its structure in the document itself rather than in a separate DTD. This approach also makes the document easier to edit.

To this end, a document can use both an internal and an external DTD subset. The internal declarations go in square brackets inside the document type declaration. For example, Listing 8-5 is an XML document whose root element is `DOCUMENT`. The `DOCUMENT` element contains a `GREETING` child `ELEMENT` followed by a `DATE` child element. This structure is declared by placing a comma between each element that must appear as a child element like this:

```
<!ELEMENT DOCUMENT (GREETING, DATE)>
```

The `DATE` element is also declared inside Listing 8-5's document type declaration. However, the declaration for the `GREETING` element is pulled from the file greeting.dtd, which forms the external DTD subset.

> **Listing 8-5: A document whose DTD has both an internal and an external subset**
>
> ```
> <?xml version="1.0"?>
> <!DOCTYPE DOCUMENT SYSTEM "greeting.dtd" [
>    <!ELEMENT DOCUMENT (GREETING, DATE)>
>    <!ELEMENT DATE (#PCDATA)>
> ]>
> <DOCUMENT>
>   <GREETING>Hello</GREETING>
>   <DATE>July 28, 2000</DATE>
> </DOCUMENT>
> ```

A conflict between elements of the same name in the internal and external DTD subsets is an error. The same element cannot be declared twice, whether in the internal or external DTD subsets or both.

Public DTDs

The SYSTEM keyword is intended for private DTDs used by a single author or group. Part of the promise of XML, however, is that broader organizations covering an entire industry, such as the ISO or the IEEE, can standardize public DTDs to cover their fields. This standardization saves people from having to reinvent tag sets for the same items, and makes it easier for users to exchange interoperable documents.

DTDs designed for writers outside the creating organization use the PUBLIC keyword instead of the SYSTEM keyword. Furthermore, the DTD gets a name. The syntax is:

```
<!DOCTYPE name_of_root_element PUBLIC "DTD_name" "DTD_URL">
```

Once again, name_of_root_element is the name of the root element. PUBLIC is an XML keyword that indicates that this DTD is intended for broad use and has a name. DTD_name is the name associated with this DTD. Some XML processors may attempt to use this name to retrieve the DTD from a central repository, although this behavior is purely theoretical at this point in time. Finally, DTD_URL is a relative or absolute URL where the DTD can be found if it cannot be retrieved by name from a well-known repository. In practice, all existing XML parsers retrieve the DTD from its URL.

DTD names follow different rules than most XML names. They can only contain the ASCII alphanumeric characters, the space, the carriage return, the linefeed, and these punctuation marks: -'()+,/:=?;!*#@$_%. Furthermore, the names of public DTDs follow a few conventions.

If a DTD is an ISO standard, its name begins with the string ISO. If a non-ISO standards body has approved the DTD, its name begins with a plus sign (+). If no standards body has approved the DTD, its name begins with a hyphen (-). These initial strings are followed by a double slash (//) and the name of the DTD's owner, which is followed by another double slash and the type of document the DTD describes. Then there's another double slash followed by an ISO 639 language identifier, such as EN for English. A complete list of ISO 639 identifiers is available at `http://www.ics.uci.edu/pub/ietf/http/related/iso639.txt`. For example, the greeting DTD can be named as follows:

```
-//Elliotte Rusty Harold//DTD Greetings and salutations//EN
```

This public identifier says that the DTD is not standards-body approved (-), belongs to Elliotte Rusty Harold, describes greetings and salutations, and is written in English. A full document type declaration pointing to this DTD with this name is:

```
<!DOCTYPE SEASON PUBLIC
  "-//Elliotte Rusty Harold//DTD Greetings and salutations//EN"
  "http://www.ibiblio.org/xml/dtds/greeting.dtd">
```

You may have noticed that many HTML editors such as BBEdit automatically place the following string at the beginning of every HTML file they create:

```
<!DOCTYPE HTML PUBLIC "-//W3C//DTD HTML//EN">
```

Now you know what this string means! It says the document follows a nonstandards-body-approved (-) DTD for HTML produced by the World Wide Web Consortium (W3C) in the English language.

Note Technically, the W3C is not a standards organization because its membership is limited to corporations that pay its fees rather than to official government-approved bodies. It only publishes *recommendations* instead of *standards*. In practice, the distinction is irrelevant.

DTDs and style sheets

A valid document with a DTD can be combined with a style sheet just as a well-formed document can be. Simply add the usual `<?xml-stylesheet?>` processing instruction to the prolog as shown in Listing 8-6.

Listing 8-6: Hello XML with a DTD and style sheet

```
<?xml version="1.0"?>
<?xml-stylesheet type="text/css" href="greeting.css"?>
<!DOCTYPE GREETING [
  <!ELEMENT GREETING (#PCDATA)>
]>
<GREETING>
Hello XML!
</GREETING>
```

Figure 8-2 shows the resulting Web page. In fact, this gives you *exactly* the same result as did the same document in Chapter 3 without the DTD. Formatting generally does not consider the DTD.

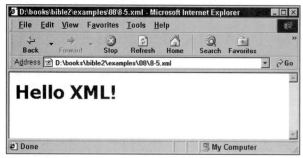

Figure 8-2: Hello XML with a DTD and style sheet displayed in Internet Explorer 5.5

After you add a style sheet, the three essential parts of the document are stored in three different files. The data is in the document file, the structure and semantics applied to the data is in the DTD file, and the formatting is in the style sheet. This structure enables you to inspect or change any or all of these relatively independently.

The DTD and the document are more closely linked than the document and the style sheet. Changing the DTD generally requires revalidating the document and may require edits to the document to bring it back into conformance with the DTD. The necessity of this sequence depends on your edits; adding elements is rarely an issue, although removing elements may be problematic.

Validating Against a DTD

To be considered *valid,* an XML document must satisfy four criteria:

1. It must be well formed.

2. It must have a document type declaration.

3. Its root element must be the one specified by the document type declaration.

4. It must satisfy all the constraints indicated by the DTD specified by the document type declaration.

Note   Not all XML documents have to be valid, and not all parsers check documents for validity. Often, it's enough to merely be well formed. In fact, most Web browsers, including Internet Explorer, Opera, Netscape, and Mozilla, do not check documents for validity.

Suppose we make a simple change to the hello.xml example by replacing the `<GREETING>` and `</GREETING>` tags with `<FOO>` and `</FOO>`, as shown in Listing 8-7. Listing 8-7 is *invalid*. It is a well-formed XML document, but it does not meet the constraints specified by the document type declaration and the DTD it contains.

Listing 8-7: This document is invalid because it does not satisfy the DTD's rules

```
<?xml version="1.0"?>
<!DOCTYPE GREETING SYSTEM "greeting.dtd">
<FOO>
Hello XML!
</FOO>
```

This document has two problems:

1. The root element is not `GREETING` as required by the document type declaration.

2. The `FOO` element has not been declared.

Command-line validators

In more complex documents, it's not so easy to just look at a document and its DTD and tell whether or not it's valid. Instead, you'll want to use a software tool that understands all the rules of XML to make the checks for you. A validating parser is such a tool. The parser's job is to divide the document into a tree structure and pass the nodes of the tree to the program that will display the data. This might be a Web browser such as Netscape or Internet Explorer. It might be a database. It might even be a custom program that you've written yourself. As the parser reads a document, it checks whether the document adheres to the rules specified by the document's DTD. If it does, the parser passes the data along to the application (such as a Web browser or a database). If the parser finds a mistake, then it reports the error. If you're writing XML by hand, you'll want to validate your documents before posting them so that you can be confident that readers won't encounter errors.

There are about a dozen different validating parsers available on the Web. Most of them are free. Most are libraries intended for programmers to incorporate into their own, more finished products, and they have minimal (if any) user interfaces. The one I chose for this book is the Apache XML Project's Xerces-J because it's free software and written in Java, so it runs on most major platforms. Versions of Xerces are also available in C and Perl.

On the CD-ROM Xerces-J 1.4.1 is included on the CD-ROM in the parsers directory. You can also download the latest version from `http://xml.apache.org/xerces-j/`.

Some of these class libraries also include stand-alone parsers that run from the command line. These are programs that read an XML document and report any errors found but do not display it. For example, Xerces includes `sax.SAXCount` for this purpose. To run this program, you first have to add the Xerces jar files to your Java class path or jre/lib/ext directory. You can then validate a file by opening a DOS Window or a shell prompt and passing the local name or remote URL of the file you want to validate to the `sax.SAXCount` program, like this:

```
C:\>java sax.SAXCount -v 8-7.xml
```

You can use a URL instead of a filename, as shown below:

```
C:\>java sax.SAXCount -v http://www.ibiblio.org/xml/8-7.xml
```

In either case, `sax.SAXCount` responds with a list of the errors it found. For example:

```
C:\books\bible2\examples\08>java sax.SAXCount -v 8-7.xml
[Error] 8-7.xml:3:6: Document root element "FOO", must match
DOCTYPE root "GREETING".
[Error] 8-7.xml:3:6: Element type "FOO" must be declared.
8-6.xml: 350 ms (1 elems, 0 attrs, 0 spaces, 12 chars)
```

You use `sax.SAXCount` or a similar tool first to find your mistakes so that you can fix them, and then to verify that you've written valid XML that other programs can handle. In essence, this is a proofreading or quality assurance phase, not finished output.

Caution Because Xerces is written in Java, it shares all the disadvantages of cross-platform Java programs. First, before you can run the parser you must have the Java Development Kit (JDK) or Java Runtime Environment (JRE) installed. Second, you need to add the Xerces jar files to your class path or your jre/lib/ext directory in Java 1.2 and later. Neither of these tasks is as simple as it should be. None of these tools were designed with an eye toward nonprogrammer end-users; they tend to be poorly designed and frustrating to use.

Web-based validators

Web-based validators are an alternative for documents that aren't particularly private and that can easily be placed on a public Web server. These validators only require you to enter the URL of your document into an HTML form. They have the distinct advantage of not requiring you to muck around with Java runtime software, class paths, and environment variables.

Richard Tobin's Web-hosted XML well-formedness checker and validator based on the RXP parser is shown in Figure 8-3. You'll find it at `http://www.cogsci.ed.ac.uk/%7Erichard/xml-check.html`. Figure 8-4 shows the errors displayed as a result of using this program to validate Listing 8-7.

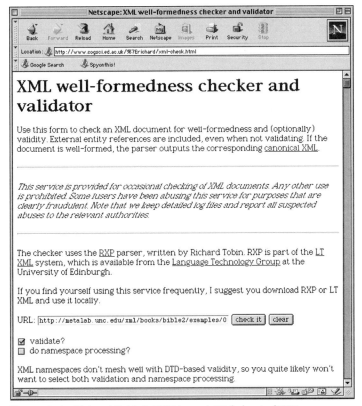

Figure 8-3: Richard Tobin's RXP-based, Web-hosted XML well-formedness checker and validator

Brown University's Scholarly Technology Group provides a validator at `http://www.stg.brown.edu/service/xmlvalid/` that's notable for allowing you to upload files from your computer instead of placing them on a public Web server. This validator is shown in Figure 8-5. Figure 8-6 shows the results of using this program to validate Listing 8-7.

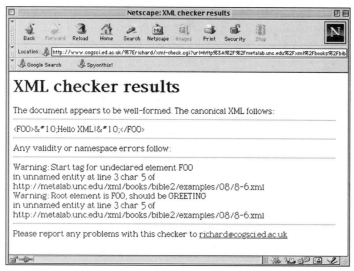

Figure 8-4: The errors in Listing 8-7, as reported by Richard Tobin's XML validator

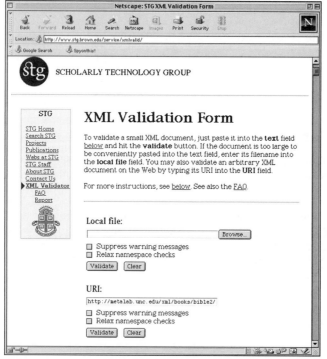

Figure 8-5: Brown University's Scholarly Technology Group's Web-hosted XML validator

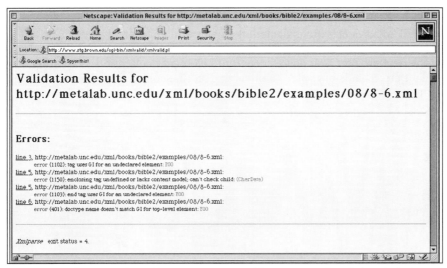

Figure 8-6: The errors in Listing 8-6, as reported by Brown University's Scholarly Technology Group's XML validator

Summary

In this chapter, you learned how to write a simple DTD and how to validate a document against that DTD. In particular you learned that:

✦ A document type definition (DTD) provides a list of the elements, attributes, entities, and notations that may be used in the document, and their relationships to one another.

✦ DTDs lay out the permissible tags and the structure of a document.

✦ DTDs help document and enforce markup standards.

✦ A document's prolog may contain a document type declaration that specifies the root element and either contains or refers to the DTD.

✦ External DTDs can be located using the `SYSTEM` keyword and a URL in the document type declaration.

✦ Standard DTDs can be identified using the `PUBLIC` keyword in the document type declaration.

✦ An internal DTD subset (which may be the complete DTD) can appear in the document type declaration surrounded by square brackets.

✦ A document that adheres to the rules of its DTD is said to be valid.

✦ Element declarations declare the name and children of an element.

In the next chapter, you delve deeper into element declarations, exploring how to use different kinds of content models to describe complicated structures applicable to many XML documents.

✦   ✦   ✦

Element Declarations

Elements form the primary structure of an XML document. In valid documents, these element structures are constrained by element declarations. An element declaration specifies what children in which orders and quantities an element of a certain type can have. In this chapter, you learn how to write DTDs that describe complex element structures.

Each element used in a valid XML document must be declared by an element declaration in the document's DTD. An element declaration specifies the name and possible contents of an element. The list of contents is called the *content model*. The content model uses a simple grammar to precisely specify what is and isn't allowed in an element of that type. This sounds complicated, but all it really means is that you attach punctuation marks such as *, ?, +, |, (, and) to element names to indicate where and how many times an element may appear.

Analyzing the Document

The first step to creating a DTD appropriate for a particular document is to understand the structure of the information that you'll encode. Sometimes information is quite structured, as in a contact list. At other times, it is relatively free-form, as in an illustrated short story or a magazine article.

It's often easier to begin if you have a concrete, well-formed example document in mind that uses all the elements you want in your DTD. This chapter uses a relatively structured document you're already familiar with as an example, the baseball statistics document first discussed in Chapter 4. Listing 9-1 is a trimmed-down version of Listing 4-1. Although it only has two players, it demonstrates all the essential features.

Listing 9-1: **A well-formed XML document for which a DTD will be written**

```
<?xml version="1.0"?>
<SEASON>
  <YEAR>1998</YEAR>
  <LEAGUE>
    <LEAGUE_NAME>National</LEAGUE_NAME>
    <DIVISION>
      <DIVISION_NAME>East</DIVISION_NAME>
      <TEAM>
        <TEAM_CITY>Florida</TEAM_CITY>
        <TEAM_NAME>Marlins</TEAM_NAME>
          <PLAYER>
            <GIVEN_NAME>Eric</GIVEN_NAME>
            <SURNAME>Ludwick</SURNAME>
            <POSITION>Starting Pitcher</POSITION>
            <GAMES>13</GAMES>
            <GAMES_STARTED>6</GAMES_STARTED>
            <WINS>1</WINS>
            <LOSSES>4</LOSSES>
            <SAVES>0</SAVES>
            <COMPLETE_GAMES>0</COMPLETE_GAMES>
            <SHUT_OUTS>0</SHUT_OUTS>
            <ERA>7.44</ERA>
            <INNINGS>32.2</INNINGS>
            <HITS_AGAINST>46</HITS_AGAINST>
            <HOME_RUNS_AGAINST>7</HOME_RUNS_AGAINST>
            <RUNS_AGAINST>31</RUNS_AGAINST>
            <EARNED_RUNS>27</EARNED_RUNS>
            <HIT_BATTER>0</HIT_BATTER>
            <WILD_PITCHES>2</WILD_PITCHES>
            <BALK>0</BALK>
            <WALKED_BATTER>17</WALKED_BATTER>
            <STRUCK_OUT_BATTER>27</STRUCK_OUT_BATTER>
          </PLAYER>
          <PLAYER>
            <GIVEN_NAME>Brian</GIVEN_NAME>
            <SURNAME>Daubach</SURNAME>
            <POSITION>First Base</POSITION>
            <GAMES>10</GAMES>
            <GAMES_STARTED>3</GAMES_STARTED>
            <AT_BATS>15</AT_BATS>
            <RUNS>0</RUNS>
            <HITS>3</HITS>
            <DOUBLES>1</DOUBLES>
            <TRIPLES>0</TRIPLES>
            <HOME_RUNS>0</HOME_RUNS>
            <RBI>3</RBI>
            <STEALS>0</STEALS>
            <CAUGHT_STEALING>0</CAUGHT_STEALING>
```

```
                    <SACRIFICE_HITS>0</SACRIFICE_HITS>
                    <SACRIFICE_FLIES>0</SACRIFICE_FLIES>
                    <ERRORS>0</ERRORS>
                    <WALKS>1</WALKS>
                    <STRUCK_OUT>5</STRUCK_OUT>
                    <HIT_BY_PITCH>1</HIT_BY_PITCH>
                </PLAYER>
            </TEAM>
            <TEAM>
                <TEAM_CITY>Montreal</TEAM_CITY>
                <TEAM_NAME>Expos</TEAM_NAME>
            </TEAM>
            <TEAM>
                <TEAM_CITY>New York</TEAM_CITY>
                <TEAM_NAME>Mets</TEAM_NAME>
            </TEAM>
            <TEAM>
                <TEAM_CITY>Philadelphia</TEAM_CITY>
                <TEAM_NAME>Phillies</TEAM_NAME>
            </TEAM>
        </DIVISION>
        <DIVISION>
            <DIVISION_NAME>Central</DIVISION_NAME>
            <TEAM>
                <TEAM_CITY>Chicago</TEAM_CITY>
                <TEAM_NAME>Cubs</TEAM_NAME>
            </TEAM>
        </DIVISION>
        <DIVISION>
            <DIVISION_NAME>West</DIVISION_NAME>
            <TEAM>
                <TEAM_CITY>Arizona</TEAM_CITY>
                <TEAM_NAME>Diamondbacks</TEAM_NAME>
            </TEAM>
        </DIVISION>
    </LEAGUE>
    <LEAGUE>
        <LEAGUE_NAME>American</LEAGUE_NAME>
        <DIVISION>
            <DIVISION_NAME>East</DIVISION_NAME>
            <TEAM>
                <TEAM_CITY>Baltimore</TEAM_CITY>
                <TEAM_NAME>Orioles</TEAM_NAME>
            </TEAM>
        </DIVISION>
        <DIVISION>
            <DIVISION_NAME>Central</DIVISION_NAME>
            <TEAM>
                <TEAM_CITY>Chicago</TEAM_CITY>
                <TEAM_NAME>White Sox</TEAM_NAME>
            </TEAM>
```

Continued

Listing 9-1 *(continued)*

```
    </DIVISION>
    <DIVISION>
       <DIVISION_NAME>West</DIVISION_NAME>
       <TEAM>
          <TEAM_CITY>Anaheim</TEAM_CITY>
          <TEAM_NAME>Angels</TEAM_NAME>
       </TEAM>
    </DIVISION>
  </LEAGUE>
</SEASON>
```

Adding a DTD to this document enables you to enforce constraints that were previously adhered to only by convention. For instance, you can require that a SEASON contain exactly two LEAGUE children, that every TEAM have a TEAM_CITY and a TEAM_NAME, and that the TEAM_CITY always precede the TEAM_NAME.

The DTD for this document should have one element declaration for each type of element that appears in the document. Each element declaration gives the name of the element and the children the element may have. For instance, this DTD will require that a LEAGUE element have exactly three DIVISION children. It will also require that the SURNAME element always be inside a PLAYER element, never outside. It will insist that a DIVISION have an indefinite number of TEAM elements but never less than one.

The DTD can require that a PLAYER has exactly one each of the GIVEN_NAME, SURNAME, and GAMES elements, but make it optional whether a PLAYER has an RBI or an ERA. Furthermore, it can require that the GIVEN_NAME, SURNAME, POSITION, and GAMES elements be used in a particular order. A DTD can also require that elements occur in a particular context. For instance, the GIVEN_NAME, SURNAME, POSITION, and GAMES may be used only inside a PLAYER element.

Table 9-1 lists the different elements in this particular XML application, as well as the conditions they must adhere to. Each element has a list of the elements it must contain and the elements it may contain. In some cases, an element may contain more than one child element of the same type. A SEASON contains one YEAR and two LEAGUE elements. A DIVISION generally contains more than one TEAM. Less obviously, some batters alternate between designated hitter and the outfield from game to game. Thus, a single PLAYER element might have more than one POSITION. In the table, a requirement for a particular number of children is indicated by prefixing the element with a number (for example, 2 LEAGUE), and the possibility of multiple children is indicated by adding (s) to the end of the element's name, such as PLAYER(s).

Listing 9-1 adheres to these conditions. It could be shorter if the two PLAYER elements and some TEAM elements were omitted. It could be longer if many other PLAYER elements were included. However, all the other elements are required to be in the positions in which they appear.

	Table 9-1	
	The Elements in the Baseball Statistics	
Element	*Required Children*	*Optional Children*
SEASON	YEAR, **2** LEAGUE	
YEAR	Text	
LEAGUE	LEAGUE_NAME, **3** DIVISION	
LEAGUE_NAME	Text	
DIVISION	DIVISION_NAME, TEAM	TEAM(**s**)
DIVISION_NAME	Text	
TEAM	TEAM_CITY, TEAM_NAME	PLAYER(**s**)
TEAM_CITY	Text	
TEAM_NAME	**Text**	
PLAYER	SURNAME, GIVEN_NAME, POSITION(**s**), GAMES	GAMES_STARTED, AT_BATS, RUNS, HITS, DOUBLES, TRIPLES, HOME_RUNS, RBI, STEALS, CAUGHT_STEALING, SACRIFICE_HITS, SACRIFICE_FLIES, ERRORS, WALKS, STRUCK_OUT, HIT_BY_PITCH, COMPLETE_GAMES, SHUT_OUTS, ERA, INNINGS, HITS_AGAINST, HOME_RUNS_AGAINST, RUNS_AGAINST, EARNED_RUNS, HIT_BATTER, WILD_PITCHES, BALK, WALKED_BATTER, STRUCK_OUT_BATTER
SURNAME	Text	
GIVEN_NAME	Text	
POSITION	Text	
GAMES	Text	
GAMES_STARTED	Text	

Continued

Table 9-1 *(continued)*

Element	Required Children	Optional Children
AT_BATS	Text	
RUNS	Text	
HITS	Text	
DOUBLES	Text	
TRIPLES	Text	
HOME_RUNS	Text	
RBI	Text	
STEALS	Text	
CAUGHT_STEALING	Text	
SACRIFICE_HITS	Text	
SACRIFICE_FLIES	Text	
ERRORS	Text	
WALKS	Text	
STRUCK_OUT	Text	
HIT_BY_PITCH	Text	
COMPLETE_GAMES	Text	
SHUT_OUTS	Text	
ERA	Text	
INNINGS	Text	
HITS_AGAINST	Text	
HOME_RUNS_AGAINST	Text	
RUNS_AGAINST	Text	
EARNED_RUNS	Text	
HIT_BATTER	Text	
WILD_PITCHES	Text	
BALK	Text	
WALKED_BATTER	Text	
STRUCK_OUT_BATTER	Text	

Note   Elements have two basic types in XML. Simple elements contain text, also known as parsed character data, #PCDATA or PCDATA in this context. Compound elements contain other elements or, less commonly, text and other elements. There are no integer, floating point, date, or other data types in standard XML. Thus, you can't use a DTD to say that the number of walks must be a nonnegative integer, or that the ERA must be a floating point number between 0.0 and 1.0, even though doing so would be useful in documents like this one.

The W3C has defined an XML Schema language that uses XML documents to describe information that might traditionally be encoded in a DTD, as well as data type information. Schemas will be explored in Chapter 23.

Now that you've identified the information that you're storing, and the optional and required relationships between these elements, you're ready to build a DTD for the document that concisely — if a bit opaquely — summarizes those relationships.

DTDs are conservative. Everything not explicitly permitted is forbidden. If an element has not been declared, it can't be used (at least not in a valid document), and this does sometimes make the development of DTDs rather tedious. However, DTD syntax does enable you to compactly specify relationships that are cumbersome to specify in sentences. For instance, DTDs make it easy to say that GIVEN_NAME must precede SURNAME, which must precede POSITION, which must precede GAMES, which must precede GAMES_STARTED, which must precede AT_BATS, which must precede RUNS, which must precede HITS, and that all of these elements may appear only inside a PLAYER element.

The ANY Content Model

It's easiest to build DTDs hierarchically, working from the outside in. This enables you to build a sample document at the same time that you build the DTD so that you can verify that the DTD is itself correct and actually describes the format you want. Thus, the root element is probably the first element you'll want to deal with. In the baseball example, SEASON is the root element. The document type declaration in the XML document specifies the name of this element:

```
<!DOCTYPE SEASON SYSTEM "baseball.dtd">
```

However, this merely says that the root element is SEASON. It does not say anything about what a SEASON element may or may not contain, which is why you must next declare the SEASON element in an element declaration inside the DTD. That's done with this line of code:

```
<!ELEMENT SEASON ANY>
```

All element declarations begin with <!ELEMENT (case sensitive) and end with >. They include the name of the element being declared (SEASON in this example), followed by the content model. In this declaration the content model is the keyword ANY (again case-sensitive). This says that all possible elements as well as parsed character data can be children of the SEASON element.

Using ANY is common for root elements — especially of unstructured documents — but should be avoided in most other cases. Generally, it's better to be as precise as possible about the contents of each element. DTDs are usually refined throughout their development, and tend to become less strict over time as they reflect uses and contexts unimagined in the first pass at the problem. Therefore, it's best to start out strict and loosen things up later.

The #PCDATA Content Model

Although any element may appear inside the document, elements that do appear must also be declared. The first one needed is YEAR. This is the element declaration for the YEAR element:

```
<!ELEMENT YEAR (#PCDATA)>
```

This declaration says that a YEAR may contain only parsed character data, that is, text that's not markup. It may not contain children of its own. Therefore, this YEAR element is valid:

```
<YEAR>1998</YEAR>
```

These YEAR elements are also valid:

```
<YEAR>98</YEAR>
<YEAR>1998 C.E.</YEAR>
<YEAR>
 The year of our Lord one thousand,
 nine hundred, &amp; ninety-eight
</YEAR>
```

Even this YEAR element is valid because XML does not attempt to validate the contents of PCDATA, only that it is text that doesn't contain markup.

```
<YEAR>Delicious, delicious, oh how boring</YEAR>
```

However, this YEAR element is invalid because it contains child elements:

```
<YEAR>
  <MONTH>January</MONTH>
  <MONTH>February</MONTH>
  <MONTH>March</MONTH>
  <MONTH>April</MONTH>
  <MONTH>May</MONTH>
  <MONTH>June</MONTH>
  <MONTH>July</MONTH>
  <MONTH>August</MONTH>
```

```
<MONTH>September</MONTH>
<MONTH>October</MONTH>
<MONTH>November</MONTH>
<MONTH>December</MONTH>
</YEAR>
```

There are now two declarations. Listing 9-2 puts them together into one DTD.

Listing 9-2: **A DTD that declares SEASON and YEAR elements**

```
<!ELEMENT SEASON ANY>
<!ELEMENT YEAR (#PCDATA)>
```

As usual, spacing and indentation are not significant. The order in which the element declarations appear isn't relevant either. Listing 9-3 is a DTD that means exactly the same thing as Listing 9-2.

Listing 9-3: **A DTD that declares SEASON and YEAR elements in a different order**

```
<!ELEMENT YEAR (#PCDATA)>
<!ELEMENT SEASON ANY>
```

Both DTDs say that a SEASON element may contain parsed character data and any number of any other declared elements in any order. The only other such declared element is YEAR, which may contain only parsed character data. Listing 9-4 shows one document that's valid according to this DTD:

Listing 9-4: **A valid document**

```
<?xml version="1.0"?>
<!DOCTYPE SEASON SYSTEM "9-3.dtd">
<SEASON>
  <YEAR>1998</YEAR>
</SEASON>
```

Because the SEASON element may also contain parsed character data, you can add additional text outside of the YEAR. Listing 9-5 demonstrates this.

Listing 9-5: A valid document that contains a YEAR and normal text

```
<?xml version="1.0"?>
<!DOCTYPE SEASON SYSTEM "9-3.dtd">
<SEASON>
  <YEAR>1998</YEAR>
  Major League Baseball
</SEASON>
```

Eventually the DTD will be modified to disallow documents such as this. However, for now it's legal because SEASON is declared to accept ANY content, which includes parsed character data. On the other hand, Listing 9-6 is invalid because the SEASON element contains an undeclared SPORT element. The problem is not that SEASON is not allowed to contain SPORT elements, but rather that the SPORT element has not been declared. The ANY content model really means any declared element, not any element at all.

Listing 9-6: An invalid document that contains a SPORT element

```
<?xml version="1.0"?>
<!DOCTYPE SEASON SYSTEM "9-3.dtd">
<SEASON>
  <YEAR>1998</YEAR>
  <SPORT>Major League Baseball</SPORT>
</SEASON>
```

You can attach a simple style sheet, such as the baseballstats.css style sheet developed in Chapter 4, to Listing 9-5 — as shown in Listing 9-7 — and load it into a Web browser, as shown in Figure 9-1. The baseballstats.css style sheet contains style rules for elements that aren't present in the DTD or the document part of Listing 9-7, but this is not a problem. Web browsers simply ignore any style rules for elements that aren't present in the document.

> **Listing 9-7: A valid document that contains a style sheet, a YEAR, and normal text**
>
> ```
> <?xml version="1.0"?>
> <?xml-stylesheet type="text/css" href="baseballstats.css"?>
> <!DOCTYPE SEASON SYSTEM "9-3.dtd">
> <SEASON>
>   <YEAR>1998</YEAR>
>   Major League Baseball
> </SEASON>
> ```

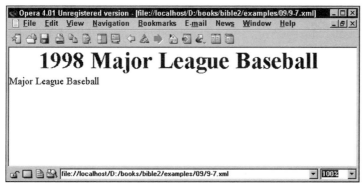

Figure 9-1: A valid document that contains a style sheet, a YEAR element, and normal text displayed in Opera 4.01.

Child Elements

Because the SEASON element was declared to accept any element as a child, elements could be tossed in willy-nilly. This is useful when you have text that's more or less unstructured, such as a magazine article in which paragraphs, sidebars, bulleted lists, numbered lists, graphs, photographs, and subheads may appear pretty much anywhere in the document. However, sometimes you may want to exercise more discipline and control over the placement of your data. For example, you could require that every LEAGUE have one LEAGUE_NAME, that every PLAYER have a GIVEN_NAME and a SURNAME, and that the GIVEN_NAME come before the SURNAME.

To declare that a LEAGUE must have a name, simply declare a LEAGUE_NAME element, and then include LEAGUE_NAME in parentheses at the end of the LEAGUE declaration, like this:

```
<!ELEMENT LEAGUE (LEAGUE_NAME)>
<!ELEMENT LEAGUE_NAME (#PCDATA)>
```

Each element should be declared in its own <!ELEMENT> declaration exactly once, even if it appears as a child in other <!ELEMENT> declarations. Here I've placed the declaration LEAGUE_NAME after the declaration of LEAGUE that refers to it, but that doesn't matter. XML allows forward references. It even allows circular references; that is, two elements A and B, either of which can be the child of the other. The order in which element declarations appear is irrelevant as long as all elements used in any content model are declared somewhere in the DTD.

You can add these two declarations to the DTD and then include LEAGUE and LEAGUE_NAME elements in the SEASON. Listing 9-8 shows the revised DTD. Listing 9-9 shows the revised document. Figure 9-2 shows the rendered document.

Listing 9-8: **A DTD that declares LEAGUE and LEAGUE_NAME elements**

```
<!ELEMENT YEAR (#PCDATA)>
<!ELEMENT SEASON ANY>
<!ELEMENT LEAGUE (LEAGUE_NAME)>
<!ELEMENT LEAGUE_NAME (#PCDATA)>
```

Listing 9-9: **A SEASON with two LEAGUE children**

```
<?xml version="1.0"?>
<?xml-stylesheet type="text/css" href="baseballstats.css"?>
<!DOCTYPE SEASON SYSTEM "9-8.dtd">
<SEASON>
  <YEAR>1998</YEAR>
  <LEAGUE>
    <LEAGUE_NAME>American League</LEAGUE_NAME>
  </LEAGUE>
  <LEAGUE>
    <LEAGUE_NAME>National League</LEAGUE_NAME>
  </LEAGUE>
</SEASON>
```

Figure 9-2: A valid document that contains a style sheet, a YEAR element, and two LEAGUE children.

Sequences

Let's restrict the SEASON element as well. A SEASON contains exactly one YEAR, followed by exactly two LEAGUE elements. Instead of saying that a SEASON can contain ANY elements, specify these three children by including them in SEASON's element declaration, enclosed in parentheses and separated by commas, as follows:

```
<!ELEMENT SEASON (YEAR, LEAGUE, LEAGUE)>
```

A list of child elements separated by commas is called a *sequence*. With this declaration, every valid SEASON element must contain exactly one YEAR element, followed by exactly two LEAGUE elements, and nothing else. The complete DTD now looks like Listing 9-10:

Listing 9-10: **A DTD that uses a SEQUENCE**

```
<!ELEMENT YEAR        (#PCDATA)>
<!ELEMENT LEAGUE      (LEAGUE_NAME)>
<!ELEMENT LEAGUE_NAME (#PCDATA)>
<!ELEMENT SEASON      (YEAR, LEAGUE, LEAGUE)>
```

The document part of Listing 9-9 does adhere to this DTD because its SEASON element contains one YEAR child followed by two LEAGUE children, and nothing else. However, if the document included only one LEAGUE, then the document, although well-formed, would be invalid. Similarly, if the LEAGUE came before the YEAR element instead of after it, or if the LEAGUE element had YEAR children, or if the document in any other way did not adhere to the DTD, then the document would be invalid and validating parsers would reject it.

It's straightforward to expand these techniques to cover divisions. As well as a LEAGUE_NAME, each LEAGUE has three DIVISION children. For example:

```
<!ELEMENT LEAGUE (LEAGUE_NAME, DIVISION, DIVISION, DIVISION)>
```

One or More Children

Each DIVISION has a DIVISION_NAME and between four and six TEAM children. Specifying the DIVISION_NAME is easy. This is demonstrated below:

```
<!ELEMENT DIVISION      (DIVISION_NAME)>
<!ELEMENT DIVISION_NAME (#PCDATA)>
```

However, the TEAM children are trickier. It's easy to say you want four TEAM children in a DIVISION, as shown below:

```
<!ELEMENT DIVISION (DIVISION_NAME, TEAM, TEAM, TEAM, TEAM)>
```

Five and six are not harder. But how do you say you want between four and six inclusive? In fact, XML doesn't provide an easy way to do this. But you can say that you want one or more of a given element by placing a plus sign (+) after the element name in the child list. For example:

```
<!ELEMENT DIVISION (DIVISION_NAME, TEAM+)>
```

This says that a DIVISION element must contain a DIVISION_NAME element followed by one or more TEAM elements.

Tip   XML schemas allow you to say that an element contains between four and six child elements. However there's no reasonable way to say this using only DTDs. There is a hard way to say that a DIVISION contains between four and six TEAM elements using only DTDs, but not three and not seven. After you finish reading this chapter, see if you can figure out how to do it.

Zero or More Children

Each TEAM should contain one TEAM_CITY, one TEAM_NAME, and an indefinite number of PLAYER elements. In reality, you need at least nine players for a baseball team. However, in the examples in this book, many teams are listed without players for reasons of space. Thus, we want to specify that a TEAM can contain zero or more PLAYER children. You do this by appending an asterisk (*) to the element name in the content model. For example:

```
<!ELEMENT TEAM (TEAM_CITY, TEAM_NAME, PLAYER*)>
<!ELEMENT TEAM_CITY (#PCDATA)>
<!ELEMENT TEAM_NAME (#PCDATA)>
```

Zero or One Child

The final elements in the document to be declared are the children of the PLAYER. All of these are simple elements that contain only text. Here are their declarations:

```
<!ELEMENT SURNAME             (#PCDATA)>
<!ELEMENT GIVEN_NAME          (#PCDATA)>
<!ELEMENT POSITION            (#PCDATA)>
<!ELEMENT GAMES               (#PCDATA)>
<!ELEMENT GAMES_STARTED       (#PCDATA)>
<!ELEMENT AT_BATS             (#PCDATA)>
<!ELEMENT RUNS                (#PCDATA)>
<!ELEMENT HITS                (#PCDATA)>
<!ELEMENT DOUBLES             (#PCDATA)>
<!ELEMENT TRIPLES             (#PCDATA)>
<!ELEMENT HOME_RUNS           (#PCDATA)>
<!ELEMENT RBI                 (#PCDATA)>
<!ELEMENT STEALS              (#PCDATA)>
<!ELEMENT CAUGHT_STEALING     (#PCDATA)>
<!ELEMENT SACRIFICE_HITS      (#PCDATA)>
<!ELEMENT SACRIFICE_FLIES     (#PCDATA)>
<!ELEMENT ERRORS              (#PCDATA)>
<!ELEMENT WALKS               (#PCDATA)>
<!ELEMENT STRUCK_OUT          (#PCDATA)>
<!ELEMENT HIT_BY_PITCH        (#PCDATA)>
<!ELEMENT ERA                 (#PCDATA)>
<!ELEMENT INNINGS             (#PCDATA)>
<!ELEMENT HITS_AGAINST        (#PCDATA)>
<!ELEMENT HOME_RUNS_AGAINST   (#PCDATA)>
<!ELEMENT RUNS_AGAINST        (#PCDATA)>
<!ELEMENT EARNED_RUNS         (#PCDATA)>
<!ELEMENT HIT_BATTER          (#PCDATA)>
<!ELEMENT WILD_PITCHES        (#PCDATA)>
<!ELEMENT BALK                (#PCDATA)>
<!ELEMENT WALKED_BATTER       (#PCDATA)>
<!ELEMENT STRUCK_OUT_BATTER   (#PCDATA)>
<!ELEMENT WINS                (#PCDATA)>
<!ELEMENT LOSSES              (#PCDATA)>
<!ELEMENT SAVES               (#PCDATA)>
<!ELEMENT COMPLETE_GAMES      (#PCDATA)>
<!ELEMENT SHUT_OUTS           (#PCDATA)>
```

Now we can write the declaration for the PLAYER element. All players have one
SURNAME, one GIVEN_NAME, one or more POSITIONs, one GAMES, and one
GAMES_STARTED element. We could declare that each PLAYER also has one AT_BATS,
RUNS, HITS, and so forth. However, I'm not sure it's accurate to list zero runs for a
pitcher who hasn't batted. This would likely lead to division by zero errors when
you start calculating batting averages and such. If a particular element doesn't
apply to a given player, or if it's not available, then the more sensible thing to do is
to omit the particular statistic from the player's information. Except for POSITION,
a given player doesn't have more than one of each statistic. Thus, we want zero or
one element of the given type. You indicate this in a child element list by appending
a question mark (?) to the element, as shown below:

```
<!ELEMENT PLAYER (
    GIVEN_NAME, SURNAME, POSITION+, GAMES, GAMES_STARTED,

    AT_BATS?, RUNS?, HITS?, DOUBLES?, TRIPLES?, HOME_RUNS?,
    RBI?, STEALS?, CAUGHT_STEALING?, SACRIFICE_HITS?,
    SACRIFICE_FLIES?, ERRORS?, WALKS?, STRUCK_OUT?,
    HIT_BY_PITCH?,

    WINS?, LOSSES?, SAVES?, COMPLETE_GAMES?, SHUT_OUTS?, ERA?,
    INNINGS?, HITS_AGAINST?, HOME_RUNS_AGAINST?, RUNS_AGAINST?,
    EARNED_RUNS?, HIT_BATTER?, WILD_PITCHES?, BALK?,
    WALKED_BATTER?, STRUCK_OUT_BATTER?
    )
>
```

This declaration says that every PLAYER has a GIVEN_NAME, SURNAME, one or more
POSITIONs, GAMES, and GAMES_STARTED elements in that order. Furthermore, each
player might or might not have a single AT_BATS, RUNS, HITS, DOUBLES, TRIPLES,
HOME_RUNS, RBI, STEALS, CAUGHT_STEALING, SACRIFICE_HITS, SACRIFICE_FLIES,
ERRORS, WALKS, STRUCK_OUT, HIT_BY_PITCH, WINS, LOSSES, SAVES, COMPLETE_GAMES,
SHUT_OUTS, ERA, INNINGS, HITS_AGAINST, HOME_RUNS_AGAINST, RUNS_AGAINST,
EARNED_RUNS, HIT_BATTER, WILD_PITCHES, BALK, WALKED_BATTER, and
STRUCK_OUT_BATTER element. Any of those elements that do appear must occur in
the order given here. You now have a complete DTD for baseball statistics. Review it in
its entirety in Listing 9-11.

Listing 9-11: **The complete baseball statistics DTD**

```
<!ELEMENT SEASON (YEAR, LEAGUE, LEAGUE)>
<!ELEMENT YEAR (#PCDATA)>

<!ELEMENT LEAGUE (LEAGUE_NAME, DIVISION, DIVISION, DIVISION)>
<!ELEMENT LEAGUE_NAME (#PCDATA)>

<!ELEMENT DIVISION_NAME (#PCDATA)>
<!ELEMENT DIVISION (DIVISION_NAME, TEAM+)>

<!ELEMENT TEAM (TEAM_CITY, TEAM_NAME, PLAYER*)>
<!ELEMENT TEAM_CITY (#PCDATA)>
```

```
<!ELEMENT TEAM_NAME (#PCDATA)>

<!ELEMENT PLAYER (
   GIVEN_NAME, SURNAME, POSITION+, GAMES, GAMES_STARTED,

   AT_BATS?, RUNS?, HITS?, DOUBLES?, TRIPLES?, HOME_RUNS?,
   RBI?, STEALS?, CAUGHT_STEALING?, SACRIFICE_HITS?,
   SACRIFICE_FLIES?, ERRORS?, WALKS?, STRUCK_OUT?,
   HIT_BY_PITCH?,

   WINS?, LOSSES?, SAVES?, COMPLETE_GAMES?, SHUT_OUTS?,
   ERA?, INNINGS?, HITS_AGAINST?, HOME_RUNS_AGAINST?,
   RUNS_AGAINST?, EARNED_RUNS?, HIT_BATTER?, WILD_PITCHES?,
   BALK?, WALKED_BATTER?, STRUCK_OUT_BATTER?
   )
>

<!ELEMENT SURNAME (#PCDATA)>
<!ELEMENT GIVEN_NAME (#PCDATA)>
<!ELEMENT POSITION (#PCDATA)>
<!ELEMENT GAMES (#PCDATA)>
<!ELEMENT GAMES_STARTED (#PCDATA)>
<!ELEMENT AT_BATS (#PCDATA)>
<!ELEMENT RUNS (#PCDATA)>
<!ELEMENT HITS (#PCDATA)>
<!ELEMENT DOUBLES (#PCDATA)>
<!ELEMENT TRIPLES (#PCDATA)>
<!ELEMENT HOME_RUNS (#PCDATA)>
<!ELEMENT RBI (#PCDATA)>
<!ELEMENT STEALS (#PCDATA)>
<!ELEMENT CAUGHT_STEALING (#PCDATA)>
<!ELEMENT SACRIFICE_HITS (#PCDATA)>
<!ELEMENT SACRIFICE_FLIES (#PCDATA)>
<!ELEMENT ERRORS (#PCDATA)>
<!ELEMENT WALKS (#PCDATA)>
<!ELEMENT STRUCK_OUT (#PCDATA)>
<!ELEMENT HIT_BY_PITCH (#PCDATA)>

<!ELEMENT ERA (#PCDATA)>
<!ELEMENT INNINGS (#PCDATA)>
<!ELEMENT HITS_AGAINST (#PCDATA)>
<!ELEMENT HOME_RUNS_AGAINST (#PCDATA)>
<!ELEMENT RUNS_AGAINST (#PCDATA)>
<!ELEMENT EARNED_RUNS (#PCDATA)>
<!ELEMENT HIT_BATTER (#PCDATA)>
<!ELEMENT WILD_PITCHES (#PCDATA)>
<!ELEMENT BALK (#PCDATA)>
<!ELEMENT WALKED_BATTER (#PCDATA)>
<!ELEMENT STRUCK_OUT_BATTER (#PCDATA)>
<!ELEMENT WINS (#PCDATA)>
<!ELEMENT LOSSES (#PCDATA)>
<!ELEMENT SAVES (#PCDATA)>
<!ELEMENT COMPLETE_GAMES (#PCDATA)>
<!ELEMENT SHUT_OUTS (#PCDATA)>
```

Grouping with Parentheses

Although the DTD in Listing 9-11 correctly describes PLAYER elements such as the ones in Listing 9-1, it's perhaps a little too loose. It also allows PLAYER elements you don't want to accept, such as a pitcher with a WINS element but no corresponding LOSSES element. And although white space is used to more clearly separate the batting, pitching, and common statistics, the declaration still allows players with a mix of batting and pitching statistics like this one:

```
<PLAYER>
  <GIVEN_NAME>Eric</GIVEN_NAME>
  <SURNAME>Daubach</SURNAME>
  <POSITION>Starting Pitcher</POSITION>
  <GAMES>13</GAMES>
  <GAMES_STARTED>3</GAMES_STARTED>
  <AT_BATS>15</AT_BATS>
  <HITS>3</HITS>
  <DOUBLES>1</DOUBLES>
  <HOME_RUNS>0</HOME_RUNS>
  <STEALS>0</STEALS>
  <SACRIFICE_HITS>0</SACRIFICE_HITS>
  <WALKS>1</WALKS>
  <HIT_BY_PITCH>1</HIT_BY_PITCH>
  <LOSSES>4</LOSSES>
  <COMPLETE_GAMES>0</COMPLETE_GAMES>
  <ERA>7.44</ERA>
  <HOME_RUNS_AGAINST>7</HOME_RUNS_AGAINST>
  <HIT_BATTER>0</HIT_BATTER>
  <BALK>0</BALK>
  <STRUCK_OUT_BATTER>27</STRUCK_OUT_BATTER>
</PLAYER>
```

Content models can be written in such a way as to prohibit these as well. Doing that requires grouping elements with parentheses so that you can say that each PLAYER has either a complete set of batting statistics or a complete set of pitching statistics.

Each set of parentheses combines several elements so that the combination is treated as a single unit when validating. This parenthesized unit can then be nested inside other parentheses in place of a single element. Furthermore, you could then affix a plus sign, an asterisk, or a question mark to it. You can group these parenthesized combinations into still larger parenthesized groups to produce quite complex structures. This is a very powerful technique.

For example, consider a list composed of two elements that must alternate with each other. This is essentially how HTML's definition list works. Each <DT> tag should match one <DD> tag. If you replicate this structure in XML, the declaration of the DL element looks like this:

```
<!ELEMENT DL (DT, DD)*>
```

The parentheses indicate that it's the matched `<DT><DD>` pair being repeated, not `<DD>` alone.

You can use parentheses in the baseball DTD to specify different sets of statistics for pitchers and batters. If a player has one statistic for a group, then he must have all the statistics for the group. The `PLAYER` declaration now looks like this:

```
<!ELEMENT PLAYER (
    GIVEN_NAME, SURNAME, POSITION+, GAMES, GAMES_STARTED,

    (AT_BATS, RUNS, HITS, DOUBLES, TRIPLES, HOME_RUNS,
    RBI, STEALS, CAUGHT_STEALING, SACRIFICE_HITS,
    SACRIFICE_FLIES, ERRORS, WALKS, STRUCK_OUT,
    HIT_BY_PITCH)?,

    (WINS, LOSSES, SAVES, COMPLETE_GAMES, SHUT_OUTS,
    ERA, INNINGS, HITS_AGAINST, HOME_RUNS_AGAINST,
    RUNS_AGAINST, EARNED_RUNS, HIT_BATTER, WILD_PITCHES,
    BALK, WALKED_BATTER, STRUCK_OUT_BATTER)?
    )
>
```

This says that each `PLAYER` element must contain a `GIVEN_NAME` element, a `SURNAME` element, one or more `POSITION` elements, a `GAMES` element, and a `GAMES_STARTED` element in that order. Then the `PLAYER` element may or may not contain the group of `AT_BATS`, `RUNS`, `HITS`, `DOUBLES`, `TRIPLES`, `HOME_RUNS`, `RBI`, `STEALS`, `CAUGHT_STEALING`, `SACRIFICE_HITS`, `SACRIFICE_FLIES`, `ERRORS`, `WALKS`, `STRUCK_OUT`, and `HIT_BY_PITCH` elements. However, if it contains any of them, then it must contain all of them. The question mark indicating that an element is optional has been moved from the individual batting statistics onto the group of batting statistics.

Finally, a `PLAYER` element may or may not contain the group of `WINS`, `LOSSES`, `SAVES`, `COMPLETE_GAMES`, `SHUT_OUTS`, `ERA`, `INNINGS`, `HITS_AGAINST`, `HOME_RUNS_AGAINST`, `RUNS_AGAINST`, `EARNED_RUNS`, `HIT_BATTER`, `WILD_PITCHES`, `BALK`, `WALKED_BATTER`, and `STRUCK_OUT_BATTER` elements. Again, if it contains any of them, then it must contain all of them.

This new `PLAYER` declaration still allows a `PLAYER` element to have both batting and pitching statistics as long as it has a complete set of each. While it's true that pitchers do bat in the National League, this application ignores that. Furthermore, this declaration also allows players to have neither pitching nor batting statistics, which you definitely do not want to allow. What you really want to say is that each player has either pitching or batting statistics, but not both. To do that you need to use a *choice*.

Choices

In general, a single parent element has many children. To indicate that the children must occur in sequence, they can be separated by commas. However, each such child element may be suffixed with a question mark, a plus sign, or an asterisk to adjust the number of times it appears in that place in the sequence.

So far, I've assumed that child elements appear or do not appear in a specific order. You, however, may wish to make your DTD more flexible, for instance by allowing document authors to choose between different elements in a given place. For example, in a DTD describing a purchase by a customer, each PAYMENT element might have either a CREDIT_CARD child or a CASH child providing information about the method of payment. However, an individual PAYMENT would not have both.

You can indicate that the document author needs to input either one or another element by separating child elements with a vertical bar (|) rather than with a comma (,) in the parent's element declaration. For example, this declaration says that the PAYMENT element must have a single child of type CASH or CREDIT_CARD.

```
<!ELEMENT PAYMENT (CASH | CREDIT_CARD)>
```

This sort of content specification is called a *choice*. You can separate any number of children with vertical bars when you want exactly one of them to be used. For example, the following says that the PAYMENT element must have a single child of type CASH, CREDIT_CARD, or CHECK.

```
<!ELEMENT PAYMENT (CASH | CREDIT_CARD | CHECK)>
```

The vertical bar is even more useful when you group elements with parentheses. You can group combinations of elements in parentheses, and then suffix the parentheses with asterisks, question marks, and plus signs to indicate that particular combinations of elements must occur zero or more, zero or one, or one or more times. For example, this final version of the PLAYER declaration now requires either pitching or batting statistics. However, the document author must pick one or the other. They cannot include both:

```
<!ELEMENT PLAYER (
    GIVEN_NAME, SURNAME, POSITION+, GAMES, GAMES_STARTED,

    ((AT_BATS, RUNS, HITS, DOUBLES, TRIPLES, HOME_RUNS,
    RBI, STEALS, CAUGHT_STEALING, SACRIFICE_HITS,
    SACRIFICE_FLIES, ERRORS, WALKS, STRUCK_OUT,
    HIT_BY_PITCH) |
    (WINS, LOSSES, SAVES, COMPLETE_GAMES, SHUT_OUTS,
    ERA, INNINGS, HITS_AGAINST, HOME_RUNS_AGAINST,
    RUNS_AGAINST, EARNED_RUNS, HIT_BATTER, WILD_PITCHES,
    BALK, WALKED_BATTER, STRUCK_OUT_BATTER))
    )
>
```

There are still a few things that are difficult to handle in element declarations. For example, there's no good way to say that a document must begin with a TITLE element and end with a SIGNATURE element, but may contain any other elements between those two. This is because ANY may not be combined with other child elements. And, in general, the less precise you are about where things appear, the less control you have over how many of them there are. For example, you can't say that a document should have exactly one TITLE element but that the TITLE may appear anywhere in the document.

Nonetheless, using parentheses to create blocks of elements, either in sequence with a comma or in parallel with a vertical bar, enables you to create complex structures with detailed rules for how different elements follow one another. Try not to go overboard with this, though. Simpler solutions are better solutions. The more complex your DTD is, the harder it is to write valid files that satisfy the DTD, to say nothing of the complexity of maintaining the DTD itself.

Mixed Content

You may have noticed that in most of the examples shown so far, elements either contained child elements or parsed character data, but not both. The only exceptions were the root elements in early examples when the full list of tags had not yet been developed. In these cases, because the root element could contain ANY data, it was allowed to contain both child elements and raw text.

You can declare tags that contain both child elements and parsed character data. This is called *mixed content.* You can use this to allow each TEAM to include an arbitrary block of text. For example:

```
<!ELEMENT TEAM (#PCDATA | TEAM_CITY | TEAM_NAME | PLAYER)*>
```

Mixing child elements with parsed character data severely restricts the structure you can impose on your documents. In particular, you can specify only the names of the child elements that can appear. You cannot constrain the order in which they appear, the number of each that appears, or whether they appear at all. In terms of DTDs, think of this as meaning that the child part of the DTD must look like this:

```
<!ELEMENT PARENT (#PCDATA | CHILD1 | CHILD2 | CHILD3 )* >
```

Almost everything else, other than changing the list of permitted child elements, is invalid. You cannot place the #PCDATA after the child elements. You cannot use commas, question marks, or plus signs in an element declaration that includes #PCDATA. A list of elements and #PCDATA separated by vertical bars is valid. Any other use is not. For example, the following is illegal:

```
<!ELEMENT TEAM (TEAM_CITY, TEAM_NAME, PLAYER*, #PCDATA)>
```

Thus, once you've said that a TEAM element can contain parsed character data, you can no longer say that it must have exactly one name and one city or nine or more players.

Mixed content is most common in narrative content such as Web pages and newspaper articles. While writing a paragraph, you might want to <EMPHASIZE>emphasize a phrase</EMPHASIZE> or note a <PERSON>person's name</PERSON>. On the other hand, most of the text of the paragraph or sentence or verse that surrounds the emphasized phrase or noted name is just text, with nothing special to distinguish it from all the other text of the paragraph, sentence, or verse. This structure is common to both written and spoken narratives.

More data-focused documents, such as the baseball example of this chapter, by contrast, should avoid mixed content whenever possible. Structured documents are easier to work with if all elements contain either other elements or unmarked-up text, but not both. You can always create a new element that holds parsed character data if you find you need it. For example, you can include a block of text at the end of each TEAM element by declaring a new BLURB element that holds only #PCDATA and adding it as the last child element of TEAM. Here's how this looks:

```
<!ELEMENT TEAM (TEAM_CITY, TEAM_NAME, PLAYER*, BLURB)>
<!ELEMENT BLURB (#PCDATA)>
```

This does not significantly change the structure of the document. All it does is add one more optional element to each TEAM element. However, human thought is not nearly so structured, and thus these strict forms of markup don't work as well in that domain. Articles, essays, novels, diaries, travelogues, short stories, speeches, and similar narratives are likely to make much heavier use of mixed content.

Empty Elements

As discussed in earlier chapters, it's occasionally useful to define an element that has no content. Examples in HTML include the image <IMG>, horizontal rule <HR>, and break <BR>. In XML, such empty-elements are identified by empty element tags that end with />, such as <IMG/>, <HR/>, and <BR/>.

Valid documents must declare both the empty and nonempty elements they use. Because empty elements by definition don't have children, they're easy to declare. Use an <!ELEMENT> declaration containing the name of the empty element as normal, but use the keyword EMPTY (case sensitive as all XML tags are) instead of a list of children. For example:

```
<!ELEMENT BR  EMPTY>
<!ELEMENT IMG EMPTY>
<!ELEMENT HR  EMPTY>
```

Listing 9-12 is a valid document that uses both empty and nonempty elements.

Listing 9-12: A valid document using empty elements

```xml
<?xml version="1.0"?>
<!DOCTYPE DOCUMENT [
  <!ELEMENT DOCUMENT (TITLE, SIGNATURE)>
  <!ELEMENT TITLE (#PCDATA)>
  <!ELEMENT COPYRIGHT (#PCDATA)>
  <!ELEMENT EMAIL (#PCDATA)>
  <!ELEMENT BR EMPTY>
  <!ELEMENT HR EMPTY>
  <!ELEMENT LAST_MODIFIED (#PCDATA)>
  <!ELEMENT SIGNATURE (HR, COPYRIGHT, BR, EMAIL,
      BR, LAST_MODIFIED)>
]>
<DOCUMENT>
  <TITLE>Empty Tags</TITLE>
  <SIGNATURE>
    <HR/>
    <COPYRIGHT>2000 Elliotte Rusty Harold</COPYRIGHT><BR/>
    <EMAIL>elharo@metalab.unc.edu</EMAIL><BR/>
    <LAST_MODIFIED>Thursday, July 27, 2000</LAST_MODIFIED>
  </SIGNATURE>
</DOCUMENT>
```

Declaring an element to be EMPTY requires that all instances of it be empty. However, an element that is declared to have PCDATA content or purely optional child elements may also be empty some of the time. For example, Listing 9-12 declares that the TITLE element contains parsed character data. Therefore, these are all valid TITLE elements according to that DTD:

```xml
<TITLE>Empty Tags</TITLE>
<TITLE></TITLE>
<TITLE/>
```

The empty-element tag syntax used in <TITLE/> is pure syntactic sugar for the longer form <TITLE></TITLE>. You can use <TITLE/> anywhere you can use <TITLE></TITLE>. The TITLE element does not need to be declared EMPTY in order to be represented by an empty-element tag.

Comments in DTDs

DTDs can contain comments, just like the rest of an XML document. These comments cannot appear inside a declaration, but they can appear outside one. Comments are often used to organize the DTD in different parts, to document the allowed content of particular elements, and to further explain what an element is.

For example, the element declaration for the YEAR element might have a comment such as this:

```
<!-- A four-digit year like 1999, 2000, or 2001 -->
<!ELEMENT YEAR (#PCDATA)>
```

As with all comments, this is only for the benefit of people reading the source code. XML processors will ignore it.

One possible use of comments is to define abbreviations used in the markup. For example, in this and previous chapters, I've avoided using abbreviations for baseball terms because they're simply not obvious to the casual fan. (Would you have guessed that the abbreviation for Walks is not *W*, which actually stands for *Wins*, but rather *BB* which stands for *Base on Balls*?) An alternative approach is to use abbreviations but define them with comments in the DTD. Listing 9-13 is similar to previous baseball examples, but uses DTD comments and abbreviated tags.

Listing 9-13: **A DTD for abbreviated baseball statistics elaborated with comments**

```
<!ELEMENT YEAR (#PCDATA)>
<!ELEMENT LEAGUE (LEAGUE_NAME, DIVISION, DIVISION, DIVISION)>

<!-- American or National -->
<!ELEMENT LEAGUE_NAME (#PCDATA)>

<!-- East, West, or Central -->
<!ELEMENT DIVISION_NAME (#PCDATA)>
<!ELEMENT DIVISION (DIVISION_NAME, TEAM+)>
<!ELEMENT SEASON (YEAR, LEAGUE, LEAGUE)>
<!ELEMENT TEAM (TEAM_CITY, TEAM_NAME, PLAYER*)>
<!ELEMENT TEAM_CITY (#PCDATA)>
<!ELEMENT TEAM_NAME (#PCDATA)>

<!ELEMENT PLAYER (
   GIVEN_NAME, SURNAME, P+, G, GS, (
   (AB, R, H, D, T, HR, RBI, SB, CS, SH, SF, E, BB, S, HBP) |
   (W, L, S, CG, SO, ERA, IP, HA, HRA, RA, ER, HB, WP, B, WB, K)
   ))
>

<!-- ======================== -->
<!-- Player Info -->
<!-- Player's last name -->
<!ELEMENT SURNAME (#PCDATA)>

<!-- Player's first name -->
<!ELEMENT GIVEN_NAME (#PCDATA)>

<!-- Position -->
```

```
<!ELEMENT P (#PCDATA)>

<!--Games Played -->
<!ELEMENT G (#PCDATA)>

<!--Games Started -->
<!ELEMENT GS (#PCDATA)>


<!-- ======================= -->
<!-- Batting Statistics -->
<!-- At Bats -->
<!ELEMENT AB (#PCDATA)>

<!-- Runs -->
<!ELEMENT R (#PCDATA)>

<!-- Hits -->
<!ELEMENT H (#PCDATA)>

<!-- Doubles -->
<!ELEMENT D (#PCDATA)>

<!-- Triples -->
<!ELEMENT T (#PCDATA)>

<!-- Home Runs -->
<!ELEMENT HR (#PCDATA)>

<!-- Runs Batted In -->
<!ELEMENT RBI (#PCDATA)>

<!-- Stolen Bases -->
<!ELEMENT SB (#PCDATA)>

<!-- Caught Stealing -->
<!ELEMENT CS (#PCDATA)>

<!-- Sacrifice Hits -->
<!ELEMENT SH (#PCDATA)>

<!-- Sacrifice Flies -->
<!ELEMENT SF (#PCDATA)>

<!-- Errors -->
<!ELEMENT E (#PCDATA)>

<!-- Walks (Base on Balls) -->
<!ELEMENT BB (#PCDATA)>

<!-- Struck Out -->
```

Continued

Listing 9-13 *(continued)*

```
<!ELEMENT S (#PCDATA)>

<!-- Hit By Pitch -->
<!ELEMENT HBP (#PCDATA)>

<!-- ======================== -->
<!-- Pitching Statistics -->
<!-- Complete Games -->
<!ELEMENT CG (#PCDATA)>

<!-- Shut Outs -->
<!ELEMENT SO (#PCDATA)>

<!-- ERA -->
<!ELEMENT ERA (#PCDATA)>

<!-- Innings Pitched -->
<!ELEMENT IP (#PCDATA)>

<!-- Hits Against -->
<!ELEMENT HA (#PCDATA)>

<!-- Home Runs Hit Against -->
<!ELEMENT HRA (#PCDATA)>

<!-- Runs Hit Against -->
<!ELEMENT RA (#PCDATA)>

<!-- Earned Runs -->
<!ELEMENT ER (#PCDATA)>

<!-- Hit Batter -->
<!ELEMENT HB (#PCDATA)>

<!-- Wild Pitches -->
<!ELEMENT WP (#PCDATA)>

<!-- Balk -->
<!ELEMENT B (#PCDATA)>

<!-- Walked Batter -->
<!ELEMENT WB (#PCDATA)>

<!-- Struck Out Batter -->
<!ELEMENT K (#PCDATA)>

<!-- ======================= -->
<!-- Fielding Statistics -->
<!-- Not yet supported -->
```

Listing 9-14 shows a sample collection of statistics encoded with the short tag names. When the entire Major League is encoded using abbreviated names instead of the full-length names, the resulting document shrinks from 699K with long tag names to 391K with short tag names, a reduction of 44 percent. The information content, however, is virtually the same. Consequently, the compressed sizes of the two documents are much closer, about 58K for the document with short tag names versus 66K for the document with long tag names using gzip on maximum compression.

Listing 9-14: **Baseball statistics with short element names**

```
<?xml version="1.0"?>
<!DOCTYPE SEASON SYSTEM "9-12.dtd">
<SEASON>
  <YEAR>1998</YEAR>
  <LEAGUE>
    <LEAGUE_NAME>National</LEAGUE_NAME>
    <DIVISION>
        <DIVISION_NAME>East</DIVISION_NAME>
          <TEAM>
            <TEAM_CITY>Atlanta</TEAM_CITY>
            <TEAM_NAME>Braves</TEAM_NAME>
          </TEAM>
          <TEAM>
            <TEAM_CITY>Florida</TEAM_CITY>
            <TEAM_NAME>Marlins</TEAM_NAME>
          </TEAM>
          <TEAM>
            <TEAM_CITY>Montreal</TEAM_CITY>
            <TEAM_NAME>Expos</TEAM_NAME>
          </TEAM>
          <TEAM>
            <TEAM_CITY>New York</TEAM_CITY>
            <TEAM_NAME>Mets</TEAM_NAME>
          </TEAM>
          <TEAM>
            <TEAM_CITY>Philadelphia</TEAM_CITY>
            <TEAM_NAME>Phillies</TEAM_NAME>
          </TEAM>
    </DIVISION>
    <DIVISION>
        <DIVISION_NAME>Central</DIVISION_NAME>
          <TEAM>
            <TEAM_CITY>Chicago</TEAM_CITY>
            <TEAM_NAME>Cubs</TEAM_NAME>
          </TEAM>
    </DIVISION>
    <DIVISION>
        <DIVISION_NAME>West</DIVISION_NAME>
          <TEAM>
            <TEAM_CITY>Arizona</TEAM_CITY>
```

Continued

Listing 9-14 *(continued)*

```
            <TEAM_NAME>Diamondbacks</TEAM_NAME>
          </TEAM>
        </DIVISION>
      </LEAGUE>
      <LEAGUE>
        <LEAGUE_NAME>American</LEAGUE_NAME>
        <DIVISION>
          <DIVISION_NAME>East</DIVISION_NAME>
          <TEAM>
            <TEAM_CITY>Baltimore</TEAM_CITY>
            <TEAM_NAME>Orioles</TEAM_NAME>
          </TEAM>
        </DIVISION>
        <DIVISION>
          <DIVISION_NAME>Central</DIVISION_NAME>
          <TEAM>
            <TEAM_CITY>Chicago</TEAM_CITY>
            <TEAM_NAME>White Sox</TEAM_NAME>
             <PLAYER>
              <GIVEN_NAME>Jeff</GIVEN_NAME>
              <SURNAME>Abbott</SURNAME>
              <P>Outfield</P>
              <G>89</G>
              <GS>61</GS>
              <AB>244</AB>
              <R>33</R>
              <H>68</H>
              <D>14</D>
              <T>1</T>
              <HR>12</HR>
              <RBI>41</RBI>
              <SB>3</SB>
              <CS>3</CS>
              <SH>2</SH>
              <SF>5</SF>
              <E>4</E>
              <BB>9</BB>
              <S>28</S>
              <HBP>0</HBP>
            </PLAYER>
          </TEAM>
        </DIVISION>
        <DIVISION>
          <DIVISION_NAME>West</DIVISION_NAME>
          <TEAM>
            <TEAM_CITY>Anaheim</TEAM_CITY>
            <TEAM_NAME>Angels</TEAM_NAME>
          </TEAM>
        </DIVISION>
      </LEAGUE>
    </SEASON>
```

There's no limit to the amount of information that you can or should include in comments. Including more does make your DTDs a little longer (and thus both harder to scan and slower to download). However, the increased clarity provided by using comments far outweighs these disadvantages. I recommend using comments liberally in all of your DTDs, but especially in those intended for public use.

Summary

In this chapter, you learned the complete syntax for element declarations that are used in DTDs. In particular, you learned that:

✦ Element declarations declare the name and content model of an element.

✦ The content model specifies what an element must, may, and may not contain.

✦ Child elements separated by commas in an element type declaration must appear in the same order in that element inside the document.

✦ A plus sign means one or more instances of the element may appear.

✦ An asterisk means zero or more instances of the element may appear.

✦ A question mark means zero or one instance of the child may appear.

✦ A vertical bar means one element or another is to be used.

✦ Parentheses group child elements to enable more detailed element declarations.

✦ An element with mixed content contains both child elements and parsed character data. However, declaring mixed content limits the structure that you can impose on the parent element.

✦ Empty elements are declared with the EMPTY keyword.

✦ Comments make DTDs much more legible.

In the next chapter, you learn more about DTDs, including how to define new entity references such as ©, α, and €. You also learn how to use multiple DTDs to describe a single document, and to divide one large document into many smaller parts.

✦   ✦   ✦

Entity Declarations

A single XML document may draw both data and declarations from many different sources, in many different files. In fact, some of the data may draw directly from databases, CGI scripts, or other nonfile sources. The items where the pieces of an XML document are stored, in whatever form they take, are called *entities*. Entity references load these entities into the main XML document. General entity references load data into the root element of an XML document, while parameter entity references load data into the document's DTD. `&lt;`, `&gt;`, `&apos;`, `&quote;`, and `&amp;` are predefined general entity references that refer to the text entities <, >, ', ", and &, respectively. However, you can also define new entities in your document's DTD.

What Is an Entity?

Logically speaking, an XML document is composed of a prolog followed by a root element that strictly contains all other elements; but in practice, the actual data of an XML document can be spread across multiple files. For example, each PLAYER element might appear in a separate file even though the root element contains all 1200 or so players in a league. The storage units that contain particular parts of an XML document are called *entities*. An entity may be a file, a database record, or any other item that contains data. For example, all the complete XML files in this book are entities.

The storage unit that contains the XML declaration, the document type declaration, and the root element is called the *document entity*. However, the root element and its descendents may also contain entity references pointing to additional data that should be inserted into the document. A validating XML parser combines all the different referenced entities into a single logical document before it passes the document onto the end application or displays the file.

Note   Nonvalidating parsers may, but do not have to, insert external entities. They must insert internal entities.

Entities hold content — well-formed XML, other forms of text, or binary data. The prolog and the document type declaration are part of the root entity of the document. An XSL style sheet qualifies as an entity, but only because it itself is a well-formed XML document. The entity that makes up the style sheet is not one of the entities that composes the XML document to which the style sheet applies. A CSS style sheet is not an entity at all.

Most entities have names by which you can refer to them. The only exception is the document entity — the main file containing the XML document (although there's no requirement that this be a file as opposed to a database record, the output of a CGI program, or something else). The document entity is the storage unit, in whatever form it takes, that holds the XML declaration, the document type declaration (if any), and the root element. Thus, every XML document has at least one entity.

There are two kinds of entities: internal and external. Internal entities are defined completely within the document entity. The document itself is one such entity, so all XML documents have at least one internal entity.

External entities, by contrast, draw their content from another source located with a URL. The main document only includes a reference to the URL where the actual content resides. In HTML, an IMG element represents an external entity (the actual image data), while the document itself contained between the <HTML> and </HTML> tags is an internal entity.

Entities fall into two categories: parsed and unparsed. Parsed entities contain well-formed XML text. Unparsed entities contain either binary data or non-XML text (such as an e-mail message). Currently, unparsed entities aren't well supported (if at all) by most XML processors. This chapter focuses on parsed entities exclusively.

Cross-Reference   Chapter 12 covers unparsed entities.

Internal General Entities

You can think of an internal general entity reference as an abbreviation for commonly used text or text that's hard to type. An <!ENTITY> declaration in the DTD defines an abbreviation and the text that the abbreviation stands for. For instance, instead of typing the same footer at the bottom of every page, you can simply define that text as the footer entity in the DTD and then type &footer; at the bottom of each page. Furthermore, if you decide to change the footer block (perhaps because your e-mail address changes), you only need to make the change once in the DTD instead of on every page that shares the footer.

General entity references begin with an ampersand (&) and end with a semicolon (;), with the entity's name between these two characters. For instance, < is a general entity reference for the less than sign (<). The name of this entity is lt. The replacement text of this entity is the one character string <. Entity names consist of any set of alphanumeric characters and the underscore. White space and other punctuation characters are prohibited. Like most everything else in XML, entity references are case sensitive.

Cross-Reference Although the colon (:) is technically permitted in entity names, this character is reserved for use with namespaces, which are discussed in Chapter 13.

Defining an internal general entity reference

Internal general entity references are defined in the DTD with an <!ENTITY> declaration, which has the following format:

```
<!ENTITY name "replacement text">
```

The *name* is the abbreviation for the *replacement text*. The replacement text must be enclosed in quotation marks because it may contain white space and XML markup. You type the name of the entity in the document, but the reader sees the replacement text.

For example, my name is the somewhat excessive Elliotte Rusty Harold (blame my parents for that one). Even with years of practice, I still make typos with that phrase. I can define a general entity reference for my name so that every time I type &ERH;, the reader will see Elliotte Rusty Harold. That definition is:

```
<!ENTITY ERH "Elliotte Rusty Harold">
```

Listing 10-1 demonstrates the &ERH; general entity reference. Figure 10-1 shows this document loaded into Internet Explorer. You see that the &ERH; entity reference in the source code is replaced by Elliotte Rusty Harold in the output.

Listing 10-1: **The ERH internal general entity reference**

```
<?xml version="1.0"?>
<!DOCTYPE DOCUMENT [

    <!ENTITY ERH "Elliotte Rusty Harold">

    <!ELEMENT DOCUMENT (TITLE, SIGNATURE)>
    <!ELEMENT TITLE (#PCDATA)>
    <!ELEMENT COPYRIGHT (#PCDATA)>
    <!ELEMENT EMAIL (#PCDATA)>
```

Continued

Listing 10-1 *(continued)*

```
    <!ELEMENT LAST_MODIFIED (#PCDATA)>
    <!ELEMENT SIGNATURE (COPYRIGHT, EMAIL, LAST_MODIFIED)>
]>
<DOCUMENT>
  <TITLE>&ERH;</TITLE>
  <SIGNATURE>
    <COPYRIGHT>2000 &ERH;</COPYRIGHT>
    <EMAIL>elharo@metalab.unc.edu</EMAIL>
    <LAST_MODIFIED>July 30, 2000</LAST_MODIFIED>
  </SIGNATURE>
</DOCUMENT>
```

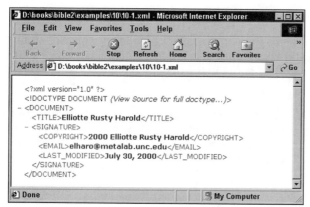

Figure 10-1: Listing 10-1 after the internal general entity reference has been replaced by the actual entity.

Notice that the general entity reference, &ERH; appears inside both the COPYRIGHT and TITLE elements even though these are declared to accept only #PCDATA as children. This arrangement is legal because the replacement text of the &ERH; entity reference is parsed character data. Validation occurs after the parser replaces the entity references with their values. The same thing happens when you use a style sheet. The styles are applied to the element tree as it exists after entity values replace the entity references.

However, validation is optional, even when the DTD defines entities that the document uses. A parser can read the DTD to find entity definitions but still not check for validity. For instance, Listing 10-2 provides the same basic data as Listing 10-1 even though it's invalid because the DTD doesn't include declarations for every element:

Listing 10-2: **An invalid document that uses a DTD solely to define a general entity reference**

```
<?xml version="1.0"?>
<!DOCTYPE DOCUMENT [
    <!ENTITY ERH "Elliotte Rusty Harold">
]>
<DOCUMENT>
  <TITLE>&ERH;</TITLE>
  <SIGNATURE>
    <COPYRIGHT>2000 &ERH;</COPYRIGHT>
    <EMAIL>elharo@metalab.unc.edu</EMAIL>
    <LAST_MODIFIED>July 30, 2000</LAST_MODIFIED>
  </SIGNATURE>
</DOCUMENT>
```

General entity values may not contain the three characters %, &, and " directly, although you can include them via character references; & and % may be included if they're starting an entity reference rather than simply representing themselves. An entity value may contain tags and may span multiple lines. For example, the following SIGNATURE entity is valid:

```
<!ENTITY SIGNATURE
  "<SIGNATURE>
     <COPYRIGHT>2000 Elliotte Rusty Harold</COPYRIGHT>
     <EMAIL>elharo@metalab.unc.edu</EMAIL>
     <LAST_MODIFIED>July 30, 2000</LAST_MODIFIED>
  </SIGNATURE>"
>
```

An entity value may also contain multiple elements. For example,

```
<!ENTITY SIGNATURE
  "<HR/>
   <COPYRIGHT>2000 Elliotte Rusty Harold</COPYRIGHT>
   <EMAIL>elharo@metalab.unc.edu</EMAIL>
   <LAST_MODIFIED>July 30, 2000</LAST_MODIFIED>"
>
```

However, if an entity value contains the start tag for an element it must also contain the end tag for the same element. That is, it cannot contain only part of an element. For example, these are both illegal, even if they're used in such a way that the resulting document would be well-formed:

```
<!ENTITY COPYYEAR "<COPYRIGHT>2000 ">
<!ENTITY COPYNAME "Elliotte Rusty Harold</COPYRIGHT>">
```

The same is true for comments, processing instructions, entity references, and anything else you might place inside an entity value. If it starts inside the entity, it must finish inside the entity.

One advantage of using entity references instead of the full text is that it's easier to change the text. This is especially useful when a single DTD is shared between multiple documents. For example, suppose I decide to use the e-mail address `eharold@solar.stanford.edu` instead of `elharo@metalab.unc.edu`. Rather than searching and replacing through multiple files, I simply change one line of the DTD as follows:

```
<!ENTITY SIGNATURE
  "<HR/>
  <COPYRIGHT>2000 Elliotte Rusty Harold</COPYRIGHT>
  <EMAIL>eharold@solar.stanford.edu</EMAIL>
  <LAST_MODIFIED>July 30, 2000</LAST_MODIFIED>"
>
```

The next obvious question is whether it's possible for entities to have parameters. Can you use the above `SIGNATURE` entity but change the date in each separate `LAST_MODIFIED` element on each page? The answer is no; entities are only for static replacement text. If you need to pass data to an entity, you should use an element along with the appropriate rendering instructions in the style sheet instead.

Using general entity references in the DTD

You may wonder whether it's possible to include one general entity reference inside another as follows:

```
<!ENTITY COPY2000 "Copyright 2000 &ERH;">
```

This example is legal because the `ERH` entity appears as part of the `COPY2000;` entity that itself will ultimately become part of the document's content. You can also use general entity references in other places in the DTD that ultimately become part of the document content (such as a default attribute value), although there are restrictions. The first restriction is that the declaration cannot contain a circular reference like this one:

```
<!ENTITY ERH "&COPY2000 Elliotte Rusty Harold">
<!ENTITY COPY2000 "Copyright 2000 &ERH;">
```

The second restriction: General entity references may not insert text that is only part of the DTD and that will not be used as part of the document content. For example, the following attempted shortcut fails:

```
<!ENTITY PCD    "(#PCDATA)">
<!ELEMENT ANIMAL &PCD;>
<!ELEMENT FOOD   &PCD;>
```

It's often useful, however, to have entity references merge text into a document's DTD. For this purpose, XML uses the parameter entity reference, which is discussed later in this chapter.

Predefined general entity references

XML predefines the five general entity references listed in Table 10-1. These five entity references appear in XML documents in place of specific characters that would otherwise be interpreted as markup. For instance, the entity reference < stands for the less than sign (<).

Table 10-1	
XML Predefined Entity References	
Entity Reference	*Character*
&amp;	&
&lt;	<
&gt;	>
&quot;	"
&apos;	'

For maximum compatibility, you should declare these references in your DTD if you plan to use them. Declaration is actually quite tricky because you must also escape the characters in the DTD without using recursion. To do this, use character references. Listing 10-3 shows the necessary declarations:

Listing 10-3: Declarations for the predefined general entity references

```
<!ENTITY lt    "&#38;#60;">
<!ENTITY gt    "&#62;">
<!ENTITY amp   "&#38;#38;">
<!ENTITY apos  "&#39;">
<!ENTITY quot  "&#34;">
```

Cross-Reference

Character references are discussed in Chapter 7.

External General Entities

Documents using only internal entities closely resemble the HTML model. The complete text of the document is available in a single file. Images, applets, sounds, and other non-HTML data may be linked to the file, but at least all the text is present. Of course, the HTML model has some problems. In particular, it's quite difficult to embed dynamic information in the file. CGI, Java applets, fancy database software, server-side includes, and various other technologies can all add this capability to HTML; but HTML alone only provides a static document. You have to go outside HTML to build a document from multiple pieces. Frames are perhaps the simplest HTML solution to this problem, but they are a nonstandard, user interface disaster that consistently confuse and annoy users.

XML allows you to embed both well-formed (though not valid) XML documents and document pieces inside other XML documents. Furthermore, XML defines the syntax whereby an XML parser can build a document out of multiple smaller XML documents and pieces thereof found either on local or remote systems. Documents may contain other documents, which may contain other documents. As long as there's no recursion (an error reported by the processor), the application only sees a single, complete document. In essence, this provides client-side includes.

External entities are data outside the main file containing the root element/document entity. External entity references let you embed these external entities in the parsed character data content of your document (though not in the attribute values), and thus build a single XML document from multiple independent files.

An external general entity reference such as &CalSmith; indicates where in the document the parser should insert the external entity. The text of the entity comes from a document at a given Uniform Resource Identifier (URI). This URI is specified in the entity's declaration in the DTD using this syntax:

```
<!ENTITY name SYSTEM "URI">
```

Note   URIs are similar to URLs but allow for more precise specification of the linked resource. In theory, URIs separate the resource from the location so that a Web browser can select the nearest or least congested of several mirrors without requiring an explicit link to that mirror. URIs are an area of active research and heated debate. Therefore, in practice, and certainly in this book, URIs are URLs for all purposes.

For example, you may want to put the same signature block on almost every page of a site. For the sake of definiteness, let's assume that the signature block is the XML code shown in Listing 10-4. This would be a well-formed XML document except that it doesn't have a root element.

Listing 10-4: **An XML external parsed entity**

```
<COPYRIGHT>2000 Elliotte Rusty Harold</COPYRIGHT>
<EMAIL>elharo@metalab.unc.edu</EMAIL>
<LAST_MODIFIED>July 30, 2000</LAST_MODIFIED>
<HR/>
```

Furthermore, let's assume that you can retrieve this code from the URL
http://www.ibiblio.org/xml/signature.xml. You associate this file with the
entity reference &SIG; by adding the following declaration to the DTD:

```
<!ENTITY SIG SYSTEM "http://www.ibiblio.org/xml/signature.xml">
```

You can also use a relative URL. For example,

```
<!ENTITY SIG SYSTEM "/xml/signature.xml">
```

If the file to be included is in the same directory as the file doing the including, you
only need to use the filename. For example,

```
<!ENTITY SIG SYSTEM "signature.xml">
```

With any of these declarations, you can include the contents of the signature file
in a document at any point merely by using &SIG;, as illustrated with the simple
document in Listing 10-5. Figure 10-2 shows the rendered document in Internet
Explorer 5.5.

Listing 10-5: **The SIG external general entity reference**

```
<?xml version="1.0" standalone="no"?>
<!DOCTYPE DOCUMENT [
   <!ELEMENT DOCUMENT
     (TITLE, COPYRIGHT, EMAIL, LAST_MODIFIED, HR?)>
   <!ELEMENT TITLE (#PCDATA)>
   <!ELEMENT COPYRIGHT (#PCDATA)>
   <!ELEMENT EMAIL (#PCDATA)>
   <!ELEMENT HR EMPTY>
   <!ELEMENT LAST_MODIFIED (#PCDATA)>
   <!ENTITY SIG SYSTEM "signature.xml">
]>
<DOCUMENT>
  <TITLE>Entity references</TITLE>
  &SIG;
</DOCUMENT>
```

The DTD declares both the internal elements, such as `TITLE`, and the external elements, such as `COPYRIGHT`. Validating parsers are required to resolve all entity references and replace them with their values before checking the document against its DTD.

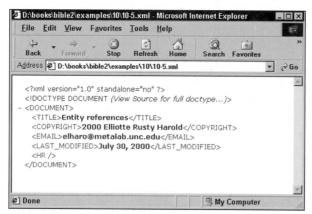

Figure 10-2: A document that uses an external general entity reference.

Text declarations

Because neither Listing 10-4 nor Listing 10-5 has an encoding declaration, the parser assumes both are encoded in the UTF-8 encoding of Unicode. However, in general, there's no guarantee or requirement that all the external parsed entities a document includes will use the same encoding. Indeed each external parsed entity may have a different encoding. To account for this, each external parsed entity can have its own text declaration. Text declarations look like XML declarations except that the `version` pseudo-attribute is optional, the `encoding` pseudo-attribute is required, and there's no `standalone` pseudo-attribute. For example, Listing 10-6 has a text declaration that says the entity is encoded in UTF-16 instead of the default UTF-8.

Listing 10-6: **An XML external parsed entity with a text declaration**

```
<?xml encoding="UTF-16"?>
<COPYRIGHT>2000 Elliotte Rusty Harold</COPYRIGHT>
<EMAIL>elharo@metalab.unc.edu</EMAIL>
<LAST_MODIFIED>July 30, 2000</LAST_MODIFIED>
<HR/>
```

If the external parsed entity has a root element, and if it either has a `version` pseudo-attribute in the text declaration or does not have a text declaration at all, then the external parsed entity may itself be a well-formed XML document. For example, it could be the signature block shown in Listing 10-7. However, while sometimes useful, this is not required.

Listing 10-7: **An external parsed entity that is also a well-formed XML document**

```
<?xml version="1.0" encoding="ISO-8859-1"?>
<SIGNATURE>
  <COPYRIGHT>2000 Elliotte Rusty Harold</COPYRIGHT>
  <EMAIL>elharo@metalab.unc.edu</EMAIL>
  <LAST_MODIFIED>July 30, 2000</LAST_MODIFIED>
</SIGNATURE>
```

Whether a well-formed XML document or not, an external parsed entity may not contain a document type declaration. This means an external parsed entity cannot be valid on its own. It can only be validated when it's inserted into a full XML document that does have a document type declaration. A document that uses external parsed entities can be valid as long as it properly declares all the elements and attributes used in both the document entity and all the other entities. Indeed, Listing 10-5 is valid, but it does not have to be. Well-formedness only requires that a document declare all the entities it uses. Listing 10-8 is an invalid but well-formed version of Listing 10-5.

Listing 10-8: **An invalid but well-formed document that uses an external general entity reference**

```
<?xml version="1.0" standalone="no"?>
<!DOCTYPE DOCUMENT [
   <!ENTITY SIG SYSTEM "signature.xml">
]>
<DOCUMENT>
  <TITLE>Entity references</TITLE>
  &SIG;
</DOCUMENT>
```

Nonvalidating parsers

All XML parsers resolve internal entity references. Nonvalidating processors may resolve external entity references, but they are not required to do so. Expat, the open source XML parser used by Mozilla, for instance, does not resolve external entity references. Most other parsers do resolve external entity references.

In the world of Web browsers, Mozilla, Netscape and Opera do not resolve external entity references. Internet Explorer does resolve external entity references.

Internal Parameter Entities

General entities become part of the document, not the DTD. They can be used in the DTD but only in places where they will become part of the document body. General entity references may not insert text that is only part of the DTD and will not be used as part of the document content. It's often useful, however, to have entity references in a DTD. For this purpose, XML provides the *parameter entity reference*.

Parameter entity references are very similar to general entity references except for these two key differences:

1. Parameter entity references begin with a percent sign (%) instead of an ampersand (&).

2. Parameter entity references can only appear in the DTD, not the document content.

Parameter entities are declared in the DTD like general entities with the addition of a percent sign before the name. The syntax looks like this:

```
<!ENTITY % name "replacement text">
```

The name is the abbreviation for the entity. The reader sees the replacement text, which must appear in quotes. For example:

```
<!ENTITY % ERH "Elliotte Rusty Harold">
<!ENTITY COPY2000 "Copyright 2000 %ERH;">
```

Our earlier failed attempt to abbreviate (#PCDATA) works when a parameter entity reference replaces the general entity reference:

```
<!ENTITY % PCD "(#PCDATA)">
<!ELEMENT ANIMAL %PCD;>
<!ELEMENT FOOD   %PCD;>
```

The real value of parameter entity references becomes apparent when you're sharing common lists of children and attributes between elements. The larger the block of text you're replacing and the more times you use it, the more useful parameter entity references become. For instance, suppose your DTD declares a number of block-level container elements such as PARAGRAPH, CELL, and HEADING. Each of these container elements may contain an indefinite number of inline elements such as PERSON, DEGREE, MODEL, PRODUCT, ANIMAL, INGREDIENT, and so forth. The element declarations for the container elements could appear as the following:

```
<!ELEMENT PARAGRAPH
   (PERSON | DEGREE | MODEL | PRODUCT | ANIMAL | INGREDIENT)*>
<!ELEMENT CELL
   (PERSON | DEGREE | MODEL | PRODUCT | ANIMAL | INGREDIENT)*>
<!ELEMENT HEADING
   (PERSON | DEGREE | MODEL | PRODUCT | ANIMAL | INGREDIENT)*>
```

The container elements all have the same content model. If you invent a new element such as EQUATION, CD, or ACCOUNT, this element must be declared as a possible child of all three container elements. Adding it to two, but forgetting to add it to the third element, may cause trouble. This problem multiplies when you have 30 or 300 container elements instead of 3.

DTDs are much easier to maintain if you don't give each container a separate content model. Instead, make the content model a parameter entity reference; then use that parameter entity reference in each of the container element declarations. For example:

```
<!ENTITY % inlines
   "(PERSON | DEGREE | MODEL | PRODUCT | ANIMAL | INGREDIENT)*">
<!ELEMENT PARAGRAPH %inlines;>
<!ELEMENT CELL      %inlines;>
<!ELEMENT HEADING   %inlines;>
```

To add a new element, you only have to change a single parameter entity declaration, rather than 3, 30, or 300 element declarations.

Parameter entity references must be declared before they're used. The following example is malformed because the %PCD; reference is not declared until it's already been used twice:

```
<!ELEMENT FOOD   %PCD;>
<!ELEMENT ANIMAL %PCD;>
<!ENTITY % PCD "(#PCDATA)">
```

Parameter entities can only be used to define content models, element names, and other *parts* of declarations in the external DTD subset. That is, when the replacement text is comething less than a complete declaration, the parameter entity references can only appear inside a declaration in the external DTD subset. The above examples are all illegal if they're used in an internal DTD subset — that is, inside the square brackets in a document type declaration.

Parameter entity references can be used in the internal DTD subset, but only if they provide whole declarations, not simply pieces of them. For example, the following declaration is legal in both the internal and external DTD subsets:

```
<!ENTITY % hr "<!ELEMENT HR EMPTY>">
%hr;
```

Of course, this really isn't any easier than declaring the HR element without parameter entity references:

```
<!ELEMENT HR EMPTY>
```

You'll mainly use parameter entity references in internal DTD subsets when they're referring to external parameter entities; that is, when they're pulling in declarations or parts of declarations from a different file. This is the subject of the next section.

External Parameter Entities

Up to this point, all the examples have used monolithic DTDs that defined all the elements used in the document. This technique becomes unwieldy with longer documents, however. Furthermore, you often want to use part of a DTD in many different places. For example, consider a DTD that describes a snail mail address. The definition of an address is quite general, and can easily be used in many different contexts. Similarly, the list of predefined entity references in Listing 10-2 is useful in many XML documents, but you'd rather not copy and paste it all the time.

External parameter entities enable you to build large DTDs from smaller ones; that is, one DTD may link to another and in so doing pull in the elements and entities declared in the first. Although cycles are prohibited — DTD 1 may not refer to DTD 2 if DTD 2 refers to DTD 1 — such nested DTDs can become large and complex.

At the same time, breaking a DTD into smaller, more manageable chunks makes the DTD easier to analyze. Many of the examples in the last chapter were unnecessarily large. Both the document and its DTD become much easier to understand when split into separate files.

Furthermore, using smaller, modular DTDs that only describe one set of elements makes it easier to mix and match DTDs created by different people or organizations. For instance, if you're writing a technical article about high temperature superconductivity, you can use a molecular sciences DTD to describe the molecules involved, a math DTD to write down your equations, a vector graphics DTD for the figures, and a basic HTML DTD to handle the explanatory text.

Note

In particular, you can use the mol.dtd DTD from Peter Murray-Rust's Chemical Markup Language, the MathML DTD from the World Wide Web Consortium (W3C)'s Mathematical Markup Language, the SVG DTD from the W3C's Scalable Vector Graphics, and the W3C's XHTML DTD.

You can probably think of more examples where you need to mix and match concepts (and therefore tags) from different fields. Human thought doesn't restrict itself to narrowly defined categories. It tends to wander all over the map. The documents you write will reflect this.

Let's see how to organize the baseball statistics DTD of the last chapter as a combination of several different DTDs. This example is extremely hierarchical. One possible division is to write separate DTDs for PLAYER, TEAM, and SEASON. This is far from the only way to divide the DTD into more manageable chunks, but it will serve as a reasonable example. Listing 10-9 shows a DTD solely for a player that can be stored in a file named player.dtd.

Listing 10-9: **A DTD for the PLAYER element and its children (player.dtd)**

```
<!ELEMENT PLAYER (
    GIVEN_NAME, SURNAME, POSITION+, GAMES, GAMES_STARTED,

    ((AT_BATS, RUNS, HITS, DOUBLES, TRIPLES, HOME_RUNS,
    RBI, STEALS, CAUGHT_STEALING, SACRIFICE_HITS,
    SACRIFICE_FLIES, ERRORS, WALKS, STRUCK_OUT,
    HIT_BY_PITCH) |
    (WINS, LOSSES, SAVES, COMPLETE_GAMES, SHUT_OUTS,
    ERA, INNINGS, HITS_AGAINST, HOME_RUNS_AGAINST,
    RUNS_AGAINST, EARNED_RUNS, HIT_BATTER, WILD_PITCHES,
    BALK, WALKED_BATTER, STRUCK_OUT_BATTER))
    )
```

Continued

Listing 10-9 *(continued)*

```
>

<!ELEMENT SURNAME              (#PCDATA)>
<!ELEMENT GIVEN_NAME           (#PCDATA)>
<!ELEMENT POSITION             (#PCDATA)>
<!ELEMENT GAMES                (#PCDATA)>
<!ELEMENT GAMES_STARTED        (#PCDATA)>

<!ELEMENT AT_BATS              (#PCDATA)>
<!ELEMENT RUNS                 (#PCDATA)>
<!ELEMENT HITS                 (#PCDATA)>
<!ELEMENT DOUBLES              (#PCDATA)>
<!ELEMENT TRIPLES              (#PCDATA)>
<!ELEMENT HOME_RUNS            (#PCDATA)>
<!ELEMENT RBI                  (#PCDATA)>
<!ELEMENT STEALS               (#PCDATA)>
<!ELEMENT CAUGHT_STEALING      (#PCDATA)>
<!ELEMENT SACRIFICE_HITS       (#PCDATA)>
<!ELEMENT SACRIFICE_FLIES      (#PCDATA)>
<!ELEMENT ERRORS               (#PCDATA)>
<!ELEMENT WALKS                (#PCDATA)>
<!ELEMENT STRUCK_OUT           (#PCDATA)>
<!ELEMENT HIT_BY_PITCH         (#PCDATA)>
<!ELEMENT ERA                  (#PCDATA)>
<!ELEMENT INNINGS              (#PCDATA)>
<!ELEMENT HITS_AGAINST         (#PCDATA)>
<!ELEMENT HOME_RUNS_AGAINST    (#PCDATA)>
<!ELEMENT RUNS_AGAINST         (#PCDATA)>
<!ELEMENT EARNED_RUNS          (#PCDATA)>
<!ELEMENT HIT_BATTER           (#PCDATA)>
<!ELEMENT WILD_PITCHES         (#PCDATA)>
<!ELEMENT BALK                 (#PCDATA)>
<!ELEMENT WALKED_BATTER        (#PCDATA)>
<!ELEMENT STRUCK_OUT_BATTER    (#PCDATA)>
<!ELEMENT WINS                 (#PCDATA)>
<!ELEMENT LOSSES               (#PCDATA)>
<!ELEMENT SAVES                (#PCDATA)>
<!ELEMENT COMPLETE_GAMES       (#PCDATA)>
<!ELEMENT SHUT_OUTS            (#PCDATA)>
```

By itself, this DTD doesn't enable you to create very interesting documents. Listing 10-10 shows a simple valid file that only uses the PLAYER DTD in Listing 10-9. This simple file is not important for its own sake; however, you can build other, more complex files out of these small parts.

Listing 10-10: **A valid document using the PLAYER DTD**

```
<?xml version="1.0" standalone="no"?>
<!DOCTYPE PLAYER SYSTEM "player.dtd">
<PLAYER>
  <GIVEN_NAME>Chris</GIVEN_NAME>
  <SURNAME>Hoiles</SURNAME>
  <POSITION>Catcher</POSITION>
  <GAMES>97</GAMES>
  <GAMES_STARTED>81</GAMES_STARTED>
  <AT_BATS>267</AT_BATS>
  <RUNS>36</RUNS>
  <HITS>70</HITS>
  <DOUBLES>12</DOUBLES>
  <TRIPLES>0</TRIPLES>
  <HOME_RUNS>15</HOME_RUNS>
  <RBI>56</RBI>
  <STEALS>0</STEALS>
  <CAUGHT_STEALING>1</CAUGHT_STEALING>
  <SACRIFICE_HITS>5</SACRIFICE_HITS>
  <SACRIFICE_FLIES>4</SACRIFICE_FLIES>
  <ERRORS>3</ERRORS>
  <WALKS>38</WALKS>
  <STRUCK_OUT>50</STRUCK_OUT>
  <HIT_BY_PITCH>4</HIT_BY_PITCH>
</PLAYER>
```

What other parts of the document can have their own DTDs? Obviously, a TEAM is a big part. You could write its DTD as follows:

```
<!ELEMENT TEAM (TEAM_CITY, TEAM_NAME, PLAYER*)>
<!ELEMENT TEAM_CITY (#PCDATA)>
<!ELEMENT TEAM_NAME (#PCDATA)>
```

On closer inspection, however, you should notice that something is missing: The definition of the PLAYER element. The definition is in the separate file player.dtd and needs to be connected to this DTD.

You connect DTDs with external parameter entity references. For a private DTD, this connection takes the following form:

```
<!ENTITY % name SYSTEM "URI">
%name;
```

For example:

```
<!ENTITY % player SYSTEM "player.dtd">
%player;
```

This example uses a relative URL (`player.dtd`) and assumes that the file player.dtd will be found in the same place as the linking DTD. If that's not the case, you can use a full URL as follows:

```
<!ENTITY % player SYSTEM
   "http://www.ibiblio.org/xml/dtds/player.dtd">
%player;
```

Listing 10-11 shows a completed TEAM DTD that includes a reference to the PLAYER DTD:

Listing 10-11: **The TEAM DTD (team.dtd)**

```
<!ELEMENT TEAM (TEAM_CITY, TEAM_NAME, PLAYER*)>
<!ELEMENT TEAM_CITY (#PCDATA)>
<!ELEMENT TEAM_NAME (#PCDATA)>
<!ENTITY % player SYSTEM "player.dtd">
%player;
```

By using this DTD, producing a valid team document whose root element is TEAM is straightforward. Listing 10-12 demonstrates one such valid team document whose root element is TEAM. This document uses both the elements declared in team.dtd and those declared in player.dtd.

Listing 10-12: **A valid team document**

```
<?xml version="1.0" encoding="ISO-8859-1"?>
<!DOCTYPE TEAM SYSTEM "team.dtd">
<TEAM>
  <TEAM_CITY>Florida</TEAM_CITY>
  <TEAM_NAME>Marlins</TEAM_NAME>
  <PLAYER>
    <GIVEN_NAME>Alex</GIVEN_NAME>
    <SURNAME>Gonzalez</SURNAME>
    <POSITION>Shortstop</POSITION>
    <GAMES>25</GAMES>
    <GAMES_STARTED>23</GAMES_STARTED>
    <AT_BATS>86</AT_BATS>
    <RUNS>11</RUNS>
    <HITS>13</HITS>
    <DOUBLES>2</DOUBLES>
    <TRIPLES>0</TRIPLES>
    <HOME_RUNS>3</HOME_RUNS>
    <RBI>7</RBI>
    <STEALS>0</STEALS>
    <CAUGHT_STEALING>0</CAUGHT_STEALING>
    <SACRIFICE_HITS>2</SACRIFICE_HITS>
```

```
        <SACRIFICE_FLIES>0</SACRIFICE_FLIES>
        <ERRORS>2</ERRORS>
        <WALKS>9</WALKS>
        <STRUCK_OUT>30</STRUCK_OUT>
        <HIT_BY_PITCH>1</HIT_BY_PITCH>
    </PLAYER>
    <PLAYER>
        <GIVEN_NAME>Brian</GIVEN_NAME>
        <SURNAME>Daubach</SURNAME>
        <POSITION>First Base</POSITION>
        <GAMES>10</GAMES>
        <GAMES_STARTED>3</GAMES_STARTED>
        <AT_BATS>15</AT_BATS>
        <RUNS>0</RUNS>
        <HITS>3</HITS>
        <DOUBLES>1</DOUBLES>
        <TRIPLES>0</TRIPLES>
        <HOME_RUNS>0</HOME_RUNS>
        <RBI>3</RBI>
        <STEALS>0</STEALS>
        <CAUGHT_STEALING>0</CAUGHT_STEALING>
        <SACRIFICE_HITS>0</SACRIFICE_HITS>
        <SACRIFICE_FLIES>0</SACRIFICE_FLIES>
        <ERRORS>0</ERRORS>
        <WALKS>1</WALKS>
        <STRUCK_OUT>5</STRUCK_OUT>
        <HIT_BY_PITCH>1</HIT_BY_PITCH>
    </PLAYER>
    <PLAYER>
        <GIVEN_NAME>Joe</GIVEN_NAME>
        <SURNAME>Fontenot</SURNAME>
        <POSITION>Starting Pitcher</POSITION>
        <GAMES>8</GAMES>
        <GAMES_STARTED>8</GAMES_STARTED>
        <WINS>0</WINS>
        <LOSSES>7</LOSSES>
        <SAVES>0</SAVES>
        <COMPLETE_GAMES>0</COMPLETE_GAMES>
        <SHUT_OUTS>0</SHUT_OUTS>
        <ERA>6.33</ERA>
        <INNINGS>42.2</INNINGS>
        <HITS_AGAINST>56</HITS_AGAINST>
        <HOME_RUNS_AGAINST>5</HOME_RUNS_AGAINST>
        <RUNS_AGAINST>34</RUNS_AGAINST>
        <EARNED_RUNS>30</EARNED_RUNS>
        <HIT_BATTER>5</HIT_BATTER>
        <WILD_PITCHES>6</WILD_PITCHES>
        <BALK>0</BALK>
        <WALKED_BATTER>20</WALKED_BATTER>
        <STRUCK_OUT_BATTER>24</STRUCK_OUT_BATTER>
    </PLAYER>
</TEAM>
```

A SEASON contains LEAGUE, DIVISION, and TEAM elements. Although LEAGUE and DIVISION could each have their own DTD, it doesn't pay to go overboard with splitting DTDs. Unless you expect you'll have some documents that contain LEAGUE or DIVISION elements that are not part of a SEASON, you might as well include all three in the same DTD. Listing 10-13 demonstrates.

Listing 10-13: **The SEASON DTD (season.dtd)**

```
<!ELEMENT YEAR (#PCDATA)>
<!ELEMENT LEAGUE (LEAGUE_NAME, DIVISION, DIVISION, DIVISION)>

<!-- American or National -->
<!ELEMENT LEAGUE_NAME (#PCDATA)>

<!-- East, West, or Central -->
<!ELEMENT DIVISION_NAME (#PCDATA)>
<!ELEMENT DIVISION (DIVISION_NAME, TEAM+)>
<!ELEMENT SEASON (YEAR, LEAGUE, LEAGUE)>
<!ENTITY % team SYSTEM "team.dtd">
%team;
```

It's now possible to write a document including all players and teams in the league. This document only refers to the SEASON DTD of Listing 10-13 using this document type declaration:

```
<!DOCTYPE TEAM SYSTEM "season.dtd">
```

It does not need to include the PLAYER or TEAM DTDs specifically because the SEASON DTD will pull them in. DTD inclusion has an indefinite number of levels. Although neither the league DTD nor the team DTD it imports declares the PLAYER element, you can still use PLAYER elements in the right places in a league document because the player DTD that the team DTD does import does declare the PLAYER element. Only after all parameter entity imports are fully resolved is the document checked against the DTD.

Building a Document from Pieces

The baseball examples have been quite large. Although only a truncated version with limited numbers of players appears in this book, the full document is more than half a megabyte, way too large to comfortably download or search, especially if the reader is only interested in a single team, player, or division. The techniques discussed in the previous section of this chapter allow you to split the document into many different, smaller, more manageable documents, one for each team, player, division, and league. External entity references connect the players to form teams, the teams to form divisions, the divisions to form leagues, and the leagues to form a season.

Unfortunately you cannot embed just any XML document as an external parsed entity. Consider, for example, Listing 10-14, ChrisHoiles.xml. This is a revised version of Listing 10-10. However, if you look closely you'll notice that the prolog is different. Listing 10-10's prolog is:

```
<?xml version="1.0" standalone="no"?>
<!DOCTYPE PLAYER SYSTEM "player.dtd">
```

Listing 10-14's prolog has a text declaration instead of an XML declaration. Furthermore, the document type declaration is completely omitted.

Listing 10-14: **ChrisHoiles.xml**

```
<?xml encoding="UTF-8"?>
<PLAYER>
  <GIVEN_NAME>Chris</GIVEN_NAME>
  <SURNAME>Hoiles</SURNAME>
  <POSITION>Catcher</POSITION>
  <GAMES>97</GAMES>
  <GAMES_STARTED>81</GAMES_STARTED>
  <AT_BATS>267</AT_BATS>
  <RUNS>36</RUNS>
  <HITS>70</HITS>
  <DOUBLES>12</DOUBLES>
  <TRIPLES>0</TRIPLES>
  <HOME_RUNS>15</HOME_RUNS>
  <RBI>56</RBI>
  <STEALS>0</STEALS>
  <CAUGHT_STEALING>1</CAUGHT_STEALING>
  <SACRIFICE_HITS>5</SACRIFICE_HITS>
  <SACRIFICE_FLIES>4</SACRIFICE_FLIES>
  <ERRORS>3</ERRORS>
  <WALKS>38</WALKS>
  <STRUCK_OUT>50</STRUCK_OUT>
  <HIT_BY_PITCH>4</HIT_BY_PITCH>
</PLAYER>
```

On the CD-ROM

I'll spare you the other 1200 or so players, although you'll find them all on the accompanying CD-ROM in the examples\baseball\players folder.

The examples in this chapter are all given in ASCII. Because ASCII is a strict subset of both Latin-1 and UTF-8, you could use either of these text declarations:

```
<?xml version="1.0" encoding="ISO-8859-1"?>
<?xml version="1.0" encoding="UTF-8"?>
```

Listing 10-15, mets.dtd, and Listing 10-16, mets.xml, show how you can use external parsed entities to put together a complete team. The DTD defines external entity references for each player on the team. The XML document loads the DTD using an external parameter entity reference in its internal DTD subset. Then, its document entity includes many external general entity references that load in the individual players. Notice in particular how compactly external entity references enable you to embed multiple players.

Listing 10-15: **The New York Mets DTD with entity references for players (mets.dtd)**

```
<!ENTITY AlLeiter          SYSTEM "mets/AlLeiter.xml">
<!ENTITY ArmandoReynoso    SYSTEM "mets/ArmandoReynoso.xml">
<!ENTITY BobbyJones        SYSTEM "mets/BobbyJones.xml">
<!ENTITY BradClontz        SYSTEM "mets/BradClontz.xml">
<!ENTITY DennisCook        SYSTEM "mets/DennisCook.xml">
<!ENTITY GregMcMichael     SYSTEM "mets/GregMcMichael.xml">
<!ENTITY HideoNomo         SYSTEM "mets/HideoNomo.xml">
<!ENTITY JohnFranco        SYSTEM "mets/JohnFranco.xml">
<!ENTITY JosiasManzanillo  SYSTEM "mets/JosiasManzanillo.xml">
<!ENTITY OctavioDotel      SYSTEM "mets/OctavioDotel.xml">
<!ENTITY RickReed          SYSTEM "mets/RickReed.xml">
<!ENTITY RigoBeltran       SYSTEM "mets/RigoBeltran.xml">
<!ENTITY WillieBlair       SYSTEM "mets/WillieBlair.xml">
```

Listing 10-16: **The New York Mets with players loaded from external entities (mets.xml)**

```
<?xml version="1.0" standalone="no"?>
<!DOCTYPE TEAM SYSTEM "team.dtd" [
  <!ENTITY % players SYSTEM "mets.dtd">
  %players;
]>
<TEAM>
  <TEAM_CITY>New York</TEAM_CITY>
  <TEAM_NAME>Mets</TEAM_NAME>
```

```
       &AlLeiter;
       &ArmandoReynoso;
       &BobbyJones;
       &BradClontz;
       &DennisCook;
       &GregMcMichael;
       &HideoNomo;
       &JohnFranco;
       &JosiasManzanillo;
       &OctavioDotel;
       &RickReed;
       &RigoBeltran;
       &WillieBlair;
   </TEAM>
```

Figure 10-3 shows Listing 10-16 loaded into Internet Explorer. Notice that the data for the players is present even though the main document only contains references to the entities where the player data resides. Internet Explorer resolves external references — not all XML parsers/browsers do.

Figure 10-3: The XML document displays all players on the 1998 New York Mets.

It would be nice to continue this procedure—building a division by combining team files, a league by combining divisions, and a season by combining leagues. Unfortunately, if you try this you rapidly run into a wall. The documents embedded via external entities cannot have their own document type declarations. At most, their prologs can contain text declarations. This means you can only have a single level of document embedding. This contrasts with DTD embedding in which DTDs can be nested arbitrarily deeply.

There are two roads around this problem. One is to include all teams, divisions, leagues, and seasons in a single document that refers to the many different player documents. This requires a few more than 1200 entity declarations (one for each player). The other is to remove the document type declarations from the individual team files. They will then no longer be able to parsed on their own. They will then only make sense when rendered as part of a document that does define all the various entity references they make use of.

In both cases, you need a DTD that defines entity references for each player. Because there's no limit to how deeply DTDs can nest (unlike XML documents), we begin with a DTD that pulls in DTDs containing entity definitions for all the teams. This is shown in Listing 10-17.

Listing 10-17: **The players DTD (players.dtd)**

```
<!ENTITY % angels SYSTEM "angels.dtd">
%angels;
<!ENTITY % astros SYSTEM "astros.dtd">
%astros;
<!ENTITY % athletics SYSTEM "athletics.dtd">
%athletics;
<!ENTITY % bluejays SYSTEM "bluejays.dtd">
%bluejays;
<!ENTITY % braves SYSTEM "braves.dtd">
%braves;
<!ENTITY % brewers SYSTEM "brewers.dtd">
%brewers;
<!ENTITY % cubs SYSTEM "cubs.dtd">
%cubs;
<!ENTITY % devilrays SYSTEM "devilrays.dtd">
%devilrays;
<!ENTITY % diamondbacks SYSTEM "diamondbacks.dtd">
%diamondbacks;
<!ENTITY % dodgers SYSTEM "dodgers.dtd">
%dodgers;
<!ENTITY % expos SYSTEM "expos.dtd">
%expos;
<!ENTITY % giants SYSTEM "giants.dtd">
%giants;
```

```
<!ENTITY % indians SYSTEM "indians.dtd">
%indians;
<!ENTITY % mariners SYSTEM "mariners.dtd">
%mariners;
<!ENTITY % marlins SYSTEM "marlins.dtd">
%marlins;
<!ENTITY % mets SYSTEM "mets.dtd">
%mets;
<!ENTITY % orioles SYSTEM "orioles.dtd">
%orioles;
<!ENTITY % padres SYSTEM "padres.dtd">
%padres;
<!ENTITY % phillies SYSTEM "phillies.dtd">
%phillies;
<!ENTITY % pirates SYSTEM "pirates.dtd">
%pirates;
<!ENTITY % rangers SYSTEM "rangers.dtd">
%rangers;
<!ENTITY % redsox SYSTEM "redsox.dtd">
%redsox;
<!ENTITY % reds SYSTEM "reds.dtd">
%reds;
<!ENTITY % rockies SYSTEM "rockies.dtd">
%rockies;
<!ENTITY % royals SYSTEM "royals.dtd">
%royals;
<!ENTITY % tigers SYSTEM "tigers.dtd">
%tigers;
<!ENTITY % twins SYSTEM "twins.dtd">
%twins;
<!ENTITY % whitesox SYSTEM "whitesox.dtd">
%whitesox;
<!ENTITY % yankees SYSTEM "yankees.dtd">
%yankees;
```

Listing 10-18 takes the first path. It pulls together all the player subdocuments and all the DTDs that define the entities for each player. It includes one entity reference for each player in the league. Although this document is much smaller than the monolithic document developed earlier (32K vs. 628K), it's still quite long, so not all players are included here. The full version of Listing 10-18 relies on 33 DTDs and more than 1000 XML files to produce the finished document. The largest problem with this approach is that if the document is served via HTTP, then browsers will need to make over 1000 separate connections to the Web server before the document can be displayed.

On the CD-ROM The full example is on the CD-ROM in the file examples\baseball\players\index.xml.

> ### Listing 10-18: **Master document for the 1998 season using external entity references for players**

```xml
<?xml version="1.0" standalone="no"?>
<!DOCTYPE SEASON SYSTEM "season.dtd" [
    <!ENTITY % players SYSTEM "players.dtd">
    %players;
]>
<SEASON>
  <YEAR>1998</YEAR>
  <LEAGUE>
    <LEAGUE_NAME>National</LEAGUE_NAME>
    <DIVISION>
      <DIVISION_NAME>East</DIVISION_NAME>
      <TEAM>
        <TEAM_CITY>Florida</TEAM_CITY>
        <TEAM_NAME>Marlins</TEAM_NAME>
      </TEAM>
      <TEAM>
        <TEAM_CITY>Montreal</TEAM_CITY>
        <TEAM_NAME>Expos</TEAM_NAME>
      </TEAM>
      <TEAM>
        <TEAM_CITY>New York</TEAM_CITY>
        <TEAM_NAME>Mets</TEAM_NAME>
          &RigoBeltran;
          &DennisCook;
          &SteveDecker;
          &JohnFranco;
          &MattFranco;
          &ButchHuskey;
          &BobbyJones;
          &MikeKinkade;
          &HideoNomo;
          &VanceWilson;
      </TEAM>
      <TEAM>
        <TEAM_CITY>Philadelphia</TEAM_CITY>
        <TEAM_NAME>Phillies</TEAM_NAME>
      </TEAM>
    </DIVISION>
    <DIVISION>
      <DIVISION_NAME>Central</DIVISION_NAME>
      <TEAM>
        <TEAM_CITY>Chicago</TEAM_CITY>
        <TEAM_NAME>Cubs</TEAM_NAME>
      </TEAM>
    </DIVISION>
    <DIVISION>
      <DIVISION_NAME>West</DIVISION_NAME>
      <TEAM>
```

```
            <TEAM_CITY>Arizona</TEAM_CITY>
            <TEAM_NAME>Diamondbacks</TEAM_NAME>
         </TEAM>
      </DIVISION>
   </LEAGUE>
   <LEAGUE>
      <LEAGUE_NAME>American</LEAGUE_NAME>
      <DIVISION>
         <DIVISION_NAME>East</DIVISION_NAME>
         <TEAM>
            <TEAM_CITY>Baltimore</TEAM_CITY>
            <TEAM_NAME>Orioles</TEAM_NAME>
         </TEAM>
      </DIVISION>
      <DIVISION>
         <DIVISION_NAME>Central</DIVISION_NAME>
         <TEAM>
            <TEAM_CITY>Chicago</TEAM_CITY>
            <TEAM_NAME>White Sox</TEAM_NAME>
            &JeffAbbott;
            &MikeCameron;
            &MikeCaruso;
            &LarryCasian;
            &TomFordham;
            &MarkJohnson;
            &RobertMachado;
            &JimParque;
            &ToddRizzo;
         </TEAM>
      </DIVISION>
      <DIVISION>
         <DIVISION_NAME>West</DIVISION_NAME>
         <TEAM>
            <TEAM_CITY>Anaheim</TEAM_CITY>
            <TEAM_NAME>Angels</TEAM_NAME>
         </TEAM>
      </DIVISION>
   </LEAGUE>
</SEASON>
```

You do have some flexibility in which levels you choose for your master document and embedded data. For instance, one alternative to the structure used by Listing 10-18 places the teams and all their players in individual documents, then combines those team files into a season with external entities as shown in Listing 10-19. This has the advantage of using a smaller number of XML files of more even sizes that place less load on the Web server and that would download and display more quickly. To be honest, however, the advantage of one approach over the other is minimal. Feel free to use whichever one more closely matches the organization of your data, or simply whichever you feel more comfortable with.

Listing 10-19: **The 1998 season using external entity references for teams**

```
<?xml version="1.0" standalone="no"?>
<!DOCTYPE SEASON SYSTEM "season.dtd" [

  <!ENTITY players       SYSTEM "players.dtd">
  %players;
  <!ENTITY angels        SYSTEM "angels.xml">
  <!ENTITY astros        SYSTEM "astros.xml">
  <!ENTITY athletics     SYSTEM "athletics.xml">
  <!ENTITY bluejays      SYSTEM "bluejays.xml">
  <!ENTITY braves        SYSTEM "braves.xml">
  <!ENTITY brewers       SYSTEM "brewers.xml">
  <!ENTITY cardinals     SYSTEM "cardinals.xml">
  <!ENTITY cubs          SYSTEM "cubs.xml">
  <!ENTITY devilrays     SYSTEM "devilrays.xml">
  <!ENTITY diamondbacks  SYSTEM "diamondbacks.xml">
  <!ENTITY dodgers       SYSTEM "dodgers.xml">
  <!ENTITY expos         SYSTEM "expos.xml">
  <!ENTITY giants        SYSTEM "giants.xml">
  <!ENTITY indians       SYSTEM "indians.xml">
  <!ENTITY mariners      SYSTEM "mariners.xml">
  <!ENTITY marlins       SYSTEM "marlins.xml">
  <!ENTITY mets          SYSTEM "mets.xml">
  <!ENTITY orioles       SYSTEM "orioles.xml">
  <!ENTITY padres        SYSTEM "padres.xml">
  <!ENTITY phillies      SYSTEM "phillies.xml">
  <!ENTITY pirates       SYSTEM "pirates.xml">
  <!ENTITY rangers       SYSTEM "rangers.xml">
  <!ENTITY redsox        SYSTEM "red sox.xml">
  <!ENTITY reds          SYSTEM "reds.xml">
  <!ENTITY rockies       SYSTEM "rockies.xml">
  <!ENTITY royals        SYSTEM "royals.xml">
  <!ENTITY tigers        SYSTEM "tigers.xml">
  <!ENTITY twins         SYSTEM "twins.xml">
  <!ENTITY whitesox      SYSTEM "whitesox.xml">
  <!ENTITY yankees       SYSTEM "yankees.xml">

]>
<SEASON>
  <YEAR>1998</YEAR>
  <LEAGUE>
    <LEAGUE_NAME>National</LEAGUE_NAME>
    <DIVISION>
      <DIVISION_NAME>East</DIVISION_NAME>
       &marlins;
       &braves;
       &expos;
```

```
            &mets;
            &phillies;
        </DIVISION>
        <DIVISION>
            <DIVISION_NAME>Central</DIVISION_NAME>
            &cardinals;
            &cubs;
            &reds;
            &astros;
            &brewers;
            &pirates;
        </DIVISION>
        <DIVISION>
            <DIVISION_NAME>West</DIVISION_NAME>
            &diamondbacks;
            &rockies;
            &dodgers;
            &padres;
            &giants;
        </DIVISION>
    </LEAGUE>
    <LEAGUE>
        <LEAGUE_NAME>American</LEAGUE_NAME>
        <DIVISION>
            <DIVISION_NAME>East</DIVISION_NAME>
            &orioles;
            &redsox;
            &yankees;
            &devilrays;
            &bluejays
        </DIVISION>
        <DIVISION>
            <DIVISION_NAME>Central</DIVISION_NAME>
            &whitesox;
            &indians;
            &tigers;
            &royals;
            &twins;
        </DIVISION>
        <DIVISION>
            <DIVISION_NAME>West</DIVISION_NAME>
            &angels;
            &athletics;
            &mariners;
            &rangers;
        </DIVISION>
    </LEAGUE>
</SEASON>
```

The individual team files that are being included in this example, such as mets.xml, will contain the data for the players on those teams. They can either contain the data directly or they can contain the entity references defined by players.dtd. Listing 10-20 shows what one such team document looks like. This is not by itself a complete or well-formed XML document. It does not define any of the entity references it uses, and it has a text declaration instead of an XML declaration. It can only be parsed when imported into a document that does define these entity references such as Listing 10-19. It is only a part of an XML document. The team documents are not usable on their own because the entity references they contain are not defined until they're aggregated into the master document.

Listing 10-20: The New York Mets with players loaded from external entities

```
<?xml encoding="ISO-8859-1"?>
<TEAM>
  <TEAM_CITY>New York</TEAM_CITY>
  <TEAM_NAME>Mets</TEAM_NAME>
  &AlLeiter;
  &ArmandoReynoso;
  &BobbyJones;
  &BradClontz;
  &DennisCook;
  &GregMcMichael;
  &HideoNomo;
  &JohnFranco;
  &JosiasManzanillo;
  &OctavioDotel;
  &RickReed;
  &RigoBeltran;
  &WillieBlair;
</TEAM>
```

It's truly unfortunate that only the top-level document is allowed to have a document type declaration. This somewhat limits the utility of external parsed entities.

New Feature

XInclude is a proposed standard that offers an alternative, non-DTD–based means of building an XML document out of smaller XML documents. However, XInclude is not part of the core XML standard and is not necessarily supported by any validating XML parser and Web browser, unlike the techniques of this chapter, which are supported. XInclude is discussed in Chapter 22.

Summary

In this chapter, you discovered that XML documents are built from both internal and external entities. In particular, you learned that:

✦ Entities are the physical storage units from which an XML document is assembled.

✦ An entity holds content: well-formed XML, other forms of text, or binary data.

✦ Internal entities are defined completely within the DTD.

✦ External entities draw their content from another resource located with a URL.

✦ General entity references have the form &name; and are used in a document's content.

✦ Internal general entity references are replaced by an entity value given in the entity declaration.

✦ External general entity references are replaced by the data at a URL specified in the entity declaration after the SYSTEM keyword.

✦ Internal parameter entity references have the form %name; and are used exclusively in DTDs.

✦ You can merge different DTDs with external parameter entity references.

✦ External entity references enable you to build large, compound documents out of small parts.

✦ Invalid documents can still use DTDs to define entity references.

When a document uses attributes, the attributes must also be declared in the DTD in order for the document to be valid. The next chapter shows how to declare attributes in DTDs, and how you can attach constraints to the attribute values.

✦　　✦　　✦

Attribute Declarations

Some XML elements have attributes, that is, name-value pairs containing information intended for the application. Attributes are intended for extra information associated with an element (such as an ID number) used only by programs that read and write the file, and not for the content of the element that's read and written by humans. In this chapter, you learn about the various attribute types and how to declare attributes in DTDs.

What Is an Attribute?

As first discussed in Chapter 5, start tags and empty-element tags may contain attributes — name-value pairs separated by an equals sign (=). For example,

```
<GREETING LANGUAGE="English">
   Hello XML!
   <MOVIE SOURCE="WavingHand.mov"/>
</GREETING>
```

In this example, the GREETING element has a LANGUAGE attribute, which has the value English. The MOVIE element has a SOURCE attribute, which has the value WavingHand.mov. The GREETING element's content is Hello XML!. The language in which the content is written is useful information about the content. The language, however, is not itself part of the content.

Similarly, the MOVIE element's content is the binary data stored in the file WavingHand.mov. The name of the file is not the content, although the name tells you where the content can be found. The attribute contains information about the content rather than the content itself.

Elements can possess more than one attribute. For example:

```
<RECTANGLE WIDTH="30" HEIGHT="45"/>
<SCRIPT LANGUAGE="javascript" ENCODING="8859_1">...</SCRIPT>
```

In this example, the LANGUAGE attribute of the SCRIPT element has the value javascript. The ENCODING attribute of the SCRIPT element has the value 8859_1. The WIDTH attribute of the RECTANGLE element has the value 30. The HEIGHT attribute of the RECTANGLE element has the value 45. These values are all strings, not numbers.

Declaring Attributes in DTDs

Like elements and entities, the attributes used in a document must be declared in the DTD in order for the document to be valid. The <!ATTLIST> construct declares attributes. <!ATTLIST> has the following form:

```
<!ATTLIST Element_name Attribute_name Type Default_value>
```

Element_name is the name of the element possessing this attribute. Attribute_name is the name of the attribute. Type is the kind of attribute — one of the ten types listed in Table 11-1. The most general type is CDATA. Finally, Default_value is the value the attribute takes on if no value is specified for the attribute.

Table 11-1
Attribute Types

Type	Meaning
CDATA	Character data — text that is not markup
Enumerated	A list of possible values from which exactly one will be chosen
ID	A unique name not shared by any other ID type attribute in the document
IDREF	The value of an ID type attribute of an element in the document
IDREFS	Multiple IDs of elements separated by white space
ENTITY	The name of an entity declared in the DTD
ENTITIES	The names of multiple entities declared in the DTD, separated by white space
NMTOKEN	An XML name token
NMTOKENS	Multiple XML name tokens separated by white space
NOTATION	The name of a notation declared in the DTD

For example, consider the following element:

```
<GREETING LANGUAGE="French">
  Bonjour!
</GREETING>
```

This element might be declared as follows in the DTD:

```
<!ELEMENT GREETING (#PCDATA)>
<!ATTLIST GREETING LANGUAGE CDATA "English">
```

The `<!ELEMENT>` declaration simply says that a `GREETING` element contains parsed character data. That's nothing new. The `<!ATTLIST>` declaration says that GREET-ING elements have an attribute with the name `LANGUAGE` whose value has the type `CDATA`, essentially the same as `#PCDATA` for element content. If you encounter a `GREETING` tag without a `LANGUAGE` attribute, the value `English` is used by default.

The attribute list is declared separately from the element itself. The name of the element to which the attribute belongs is included in the `<!ATTLIST>` declaration. This attribute declaration applies only to that element, `GREETING` in the preceding example. If other elements also have `LANGUAGE` attributes, they require separate `<!ATTLIST>` declarations.

As with most declarations, the exact order in which attribute declarations appear is not important. They can come before or after the element declaration with which they're associated. In fact, you can even declare an attribute more than once (although I don't recommend this practice), in which case the first such declaration takes precedence.

You can even declare attributes for elements that don't exist, although this is uncommon. Perhaps you could declare these nonexistent attributes as part of the initial editing of the DTD, with a plan to return later and declare the elements.

Declaring Multiple Attributes

Elements often have multiple attributes. HTML's `IMG` element can have `HEIGHT`, `WIDTH`, `ALT`, `BORDER`, `ALIGN`, and several other attributes. In fact, all HTML elements can have multiple attributes. XML elements can also have multiple attributes. For instance, a `RECTANGLE` element naturally needs both a `LENGTH` and a `WIDTH` attribute.

```
<RECTANGLE LENGTH="70cm" WIDTH="85cm"/>
```

You can declare these attributes in several attribute declarations, with one declaration for each attribute. For example:

```
<!ELEMENT RECTANGLE EMPTY>
<!ATTLIST RECTANGLE LENGTH CDATA "0cm">
<!ATTLIST RECTANGLE WIDTH  CDATA "0cm">
```

The preceding example says that RECTANGLE elements possess LENGTH and WIDTH attributes, each of which has the default value 0cm.

You can combine the two <!ATTLIST> tags into a single declaration like this:

```
<!ATTLIST RECTANGLE LENGTH CDATA "0cm"
                    WIDTH  CDATA "0cm">
```

This single declaration declares both the LENGTH and WIDTH attributes, each with type CDATA, and each with a default value of 0cm. You can also use this syntax when the attributes have different types or defaults, as shown below:

```
<!ATTLIST RECTANGLE LENGTH CDATA "15cm"
                    WIDTH  CDATA "34cm">
```

Specifying Default Values for Attributes

Instead of specifying an explicit default attribute value such as 0px, an attribute declaration can require the author to provide a value, allow the value to be omitted completely, or even always use the default value. These requirements are specified with the three keywords #REQUIRED, #IMPLIED, and #FIXED, respectively.

#REQUIRED

You may not always have a good option for a default value. For example, when writing a DTD for use on your intranet, you may want to require that all documents have at least one empty <AUTHOR/> element. This element might not be rendered, but it can identify the person who created the document. This element can have NAME, EMAIL, and EXTENSION attributes so that the author may be contacted. For example:

```
<AUTHOR NAME="Elliotte Rusty Harold"
   EMAIL="elharo@metalab.unc.edu" EXTENSION="3459"/>
```

Instead of providing default values for these attributes, suppose you want to force anyone posting a document on the Intranet to identify themselves. Although XML can't prevent someone from attributing authorship to Luke Skywalker, it can at least require that authorship be attributed to someone by using #REQUIRED as the default value. For example:

```
<!ELEMENT AUTHOR EMPTY>
<!ATTLIST AUTHOR NAME      CDATA #REQUIRED>
<!ATTLIST AUTHOR EMAIL     CDATA #REQUIRED>
<!ATTLIST AUTHOR EXTENSION CDATA #REQUIRED>
```

If the parser encounters an AUTHOR element that does not include one or more of these attributes, it returns an error.

You might also want to use #REQUIRED to force authors to give their IMG elements WIDTH, HEIGHT, and ALT attributes. For example:

```
<!ELEMENT IMG EMPTY>
<!ATTLIST IMG ALT    CDATA #REQUIRED>
<!ATTLIST IMG WIDTH  CDATA #REQUIRED>
<!ATTLIST IMG HEIGHT CDATA #REQUIRED>
```

Any attempt to omit these attributes (as all too many Web pages do) produces an invalid document. The XML parser notices the error and informs the application of the missing attributes.

#IMPLIED

Sometimes you may not have a good option for a default value, but you do not want to require the author of the document to include a value either. For example, suppose some of the people posting documents to your Intranet are offsite freelancers who have e-mail addresses but lack phone extensions. Therefore, you don't want to require them to include an extension attribute in their AUTHOR elements. For example:

```
<AUTHOR NAME="Elliotte Rusty Harold"
        EMAIL="elharo@metalab.unc.edu" />
```

You still don't want to provide a default value for the extension, but you do want to allow authors to include such an attribute. In this case, use #IMPLIED as the default value like this:

```
<!ELEMENT AUTHOR EMPTY>
<!ATTLIST AUTHOR EXTENSION CDATA #IMPLIED>
<!ATTLIST AUTHOR NAME      CDATA #REQUIRED>
<!ATTLIST AUTHOR EMAIL     CDATA #REQUIRED>
```

If the XML parser encounters an AUTHOR element without an EXTENSION attribute, it informs the application that no value is available. The application can act on this notification as it chooses. For example, if the application is feeding elements into a SQL database in which the attributes are mapped to fields, the application would probably insert a null into the corresponding database field.

#FIXED

Finally, you may want to provide a default value for the attribute without allowing the author to change it. For example, you may wish to specify an identical COMPANY attribute of the AUTHOR element for anyone posting documents to your Intranet like this:

```
<AUTHOR NAME="Elliotte Rusty Harold" COMPANY="TIC"
  EMAIL="elharo@metalab.unc.edu" EXTENSION="3459"/>
```

You can require that everyone use this value for the company name by specifying the default value as #FIXED, followed by the actual default. For example:

```
<!ELEMENT AUTHOR EMPTY>
<!ATTLIST AUTHOR COMPANY    CDATA #FIXED "TIC">
<!ATTLIST AUTHOR EXTENSION  CDATA #IMPLIED>
<!ATTLIST AUTHOR NAME       CDATA #REQUIRED>
<!ATTLIST AUTHOR EMAIL      CDATA #REQUIRED>
```

Document authors are not required to actually include the fixed attribute in their tags. If they don't include the fixed attribute, the default value will be used. If they do include the fixed attribute, however, they must use an identical value. Otherwise, the parser will return an error.

Attribute Types

All preceding examples have been CDATA type attributes. This is the most general type, but there are nine other types permitted for attributes. Altogether the ten types are:

- ✦ CDATA
- ✦ NMTOKEN
- ✦ NMTOKENS
- ✦ Enumerated
- ✦ ID
- ✦ IDREF
- ✦ IDREFS
- ✦ ENTITY
- ✦ ENTITIES
- ✦ NOTATION

Nine of the preceding types are constants used in the type field, while Enumerated is a special type that indicates the attribute must take its value from a list of possible values. Let's investigate each type in depth.

The CDATA attribute type

CDATA, the most general attribute type, means the attribute value may be any string of text not containing a less than sign (<) or quotation marks ("). These characters may be inserted using the usual entity references (< and ") or by character references (< and "). Furthermore, all raw ampersands (&) — that is ampersands that do not begin a character or entity reference — must also be escaped as & or &.

In fact, even if the value itself contains double quotes, they do not have to be escaped. Instead, you may use single quotes to delimit the attributes, as in the following example:

```
<RECTANGLE LENGTH='7"' WIDTH='8.5"'/>
```

If the attribute value contains single and double quotes, the one not used to delimit the value must be replaced with the entity reference ' (apostrophe) or " (double quote). For example:

```
<RECTANGLE LENGTH='8&apos;7"' WIDTH="10'6&quot;"/>
```

The NMTOKEN attribute type

The NMTOKEN attribute type restricts the value of the attribute to a valid XML name token. As discussed in Chapter 6, XML names must begin with a letter or an underscore (_), and subsequent characters in the name may include letters, digits, underscores, hyphens, and periods. They may not include white space. (The underscore often substitutes for white space.) Technically, names may contain colons, but you shouldn't use this character because it's reserved for use with namespaces. A name token is the same as an XML name except that it may begin with digits, hyphens, and periods rather than just letters and the underscore. Thus 73 and -red are legal XML name tokens even though they're not legal XML names. All names are name tokens, but not all name tokens are names.

The NMTOKEN attribute type helps when you need to pick from any large group of names that aren't specifically part of XML but do meet requirements for XML name tokens. The most significant of these requirements is the prohibition of white space. For example, NMTOKEN could be used for an attribute whose value had to map to an 8.3 DOS filename. On the other hand, it wouldn't work well for UNIX, Macintosh, or Windows NT filenames because those names often contain white space.

For example, suppose you want to require a STATE attribute in an ADDRESS element to be a two-letter abbreviation. You cannot force this characteristic with a DTD, but you can prevent people from entering New York or Puerto Rico with the following <!ATTLIST> declaration:

```
<!ATTLIST ADDRESS STATE NMTOKEN #REQUIRED>
```

However, California, Nevada, and other single-word states are still legal values. Of course, you could simply use an enumerated list with several dozen two-letter codes, but that approach results in more effort than most people want to expend. For that matter, do you even know the two-letter codes for all 50 U.S. states, all the territories and possessions, all foreign military postings, and all Canadian provinces? On the other hand, if you define this list once in a parameter entity reference in a DTD file, you can reuse the file many times over.

The NMTOKENS attribute type

The NMTOKENS attribute type is a rare plural form of NMTOKEN. It enables the value of the attribute to consist of multiple XML name tokens that are separated from each other by white space. Generally, you use NMTOKENS for the same reasons as NMTOKEN, but only when multiple tokens are required. For example, if you want to require multiple two-letter state codes for a STATES attribute, you can use the following declaration:

```
<!ATTLIST ADDRESS STATES NMTOKENS #REQUIRED>
```

Then, documents could contain an ADDRESS element like this one:

```
<ADDRESS STATES="MI NY LA CA"/>
```

Unfortunately, if you apply this technique, you're no longer ruling out states such as New York because each individual part of the state name qualifies as an NMTOKEN, as shown here:

```
<ADDRESS STATES="MI New York LA CA"/>
```

The enumerated attribute type

The enumerated type is not an XML keyword, but a list of possible values for the attribute, separated by vertical bars. Each value must be a valid XML name token. The document author can choose any member of the list as the value of the attribute. The default value must be one of the values in the list.

For example, suppose you want an element to be visible or invisible. You may assign the element to have a VISIBLE attribute, which can only have the values TRUE or FALSE. If that element is the simple P element, then the <!ATTLIST> declaration would look as follows:

```
<!ATTLIST P VISIBLE (TRUE | FALSE) "TRUE">
```

The preceding declaration says that a P element may or may not have a VISIBLE attribute. If it does have a VISIBLE attribute, then the value of that attribute must be either TRUE or FALSE. If it does not have such an attribute, then the value TRUE is assumed. For example,

```
<P VISIBLE="FALSE">You can't see me! Nyah! Nyah!</P>
<P VISIBLE="TRUE">You can see me.</P>
<P>You can see me too.</P>
```

By itself, this declaration is not a magic incantation that enables you to hide text. It still relies on the application to understand that it shouldn't display invisible elements. Whether the element is shown or hidden would probably be set through a style sheet rule applied to elements with VISIBLE attributes. For example, in XSLT,

```
<xsl:template match="P[@VISIBLE='FALSE']">
</xsl:template>

<xsl:template match="P[@VISIBLE='TRUE']">
  <xsl:apply-templates/>
</xsl:template>
```

The ID attribute type

An ID type attribute uniquely identifies an element in the document. Authoring tools and other applications commonly use ID to help identify the elements of a document without concern for their exact meaning or relationship to one another.

An attribute value of type ID must be a valid XML name — that is, it begins with a letter and is composed of alphanumeric characters and the underscore without white space. A particular name may not be used as an ID attribute of more than one tag. Using the same ID twice in one document causes the parser to return an error. Furthermore, each element may not have more than one attribute of type ID.

Typically, ID attributes exist solely for the convenience of programs that manipulate the data. In many cases, multiple elements can be effectively identical except for the value of an ID attribute. If you choose IDs in some predictable fashion, a program can enumerate all the different elements or all the different elements of one type in the document.

The ID type is incompatible with #FIXED. An attribute cannot be both fixed and have an ID type because a #FIXED attribute can only have a single value, whereas

each ID type attribute must have a different value. Most ID attributes use
#REQUIRED, as Listing 11-1 demonstrates.

Listing 11-1: **A required ID attribute type**

```
<?xml version="1.0"?>
<!DOCTYPE DOCUMENT [
   <!ELEMENT DOCUMENT (P*)>
   <!ELEMENT P (#PCDATA)>
   <!ATTLIST P PNUMBER ID #REQUIRED>
]>
<DOCUMENT>
  <P PNUMBER="p1">The quick brown fox</P>
  <P PNUMBER="p2">The quick brown fox</P>
</DOCUMENT>
```

The IDREF attribute type

The value of an attribute with the IDREF type is the ID of another element in the
document. For example, Listing 11-2 shows the IDREF and ID attributes used to
connect children to their parents.

Listing 11-2: **family.xml**

```
<?xml version="1.0"?>
<!DOCTYPE FAMILY [
   <!ELEMENT FAMILY (PERSON*)>
   <!ELEMENT PERSON   (#PCDATA)>
   <!ATTLIST PERSON PNUMBER ID #REQUIRED>
   <!ATTLIST PERSON FATHER IDREF #IMPLIED>
   <!ATTLIST PERSON MOTHER IDREF #IMPLIED>
]>
<FAMILY>
  <PERSON PNUMBER="a1">Susan</PERSON>
  <PERSON PNUMBER="a2">Jack</PERSON>
  <PERSON PNUMBER="a3" MOTHER="a1" FATHER="a2">Chelsea</PERSON>
  <PERSON PNUMBER="a4" MOTHER="a1" FATHER="a2">David</PERSON>
</FAMILY>
```

You generally use this uncommon but crucial type when you need to establish connections between elements that aren't reflected in the tree structure of the document. In Listing 11-2, each child is given FATHER and MOTHER attributes containing the ID attributes of its father and mother. However, based on the element structure alone, there are simply four PERSON elements. None is the parent or child of the other elements.

The IDREFS attribute type

You cannot easily and directly use an IDREF to link parents to their children in Listing 11-2 because each parent has an indefinite number of children. As a workaround, you could group all the children of the same parents into a SIBLINGS element and link to the SIBLINGS. Even this approach falters in the face of half-siblings who share only one parent. In short, IDREF works for many-to-one relationships, but not for one-to-many or many-to-many relationships.

If one attribute potentially needs to refer to more than one ID in the document you can declare it to have type IDREFS. The value of such an attribute is a white-space–separated list of XML names. Each name in the list must be the ID of some element somewhere in the same document.

Listing 11-3 demonstrates this by using a single PARENTS attribute of type IDREFS rather than separate FATHER and MOTHER attributes. This is a more realistic approach for a world in which families often don't come in neat packages of one father, one mother, and two children.

Listing 11-3: **alternative_family.xml**

```
<?xml version="1.0"?>
<!DOCTYPE FAMILY [
   <!ELEMENT FAMILY (PERSON*)>
   <!ELEMENT PERSON    (#PCDATA)>
   <!ATTLIST PERSON PNUMBER ID      #REQUIRED>
   <!ATTLIST PERSON PARENTS IDREFS #IMPLIED>
]>
<FAMILY>
  <PERSON PNUMBER="a1">Susan</PERSON>
  <PERSON PNUMBER="a2">Jack</PERSON>
  <PERSON PNUMBER="a3" PARENTS="a1 a2">Chelsea</PERSON>
  <PERSON PNUMBER="a4" PARENTS="a1 a2">David</PERSON>
</FAMILY>
```

The ENTITY attribute type

An ENTITY type attribute enables you to link external binary data — that is, an external unparsed general entity — into the document. The value of the ENTITY attribute is the name of an unparsed general entity declared in the DTD, which links to the external data.

The classic example of an ENTITY attribute is an image. The image consists of binary data available from another URL. Provided the XML browser can support it, you may include an image in an XML document with the following declarations in your DTD:

```
<!ELEMENT IMAGE EMPTY>
<!ATTLIST IMAGE SOURCE ENTITY #REQUIRED>
<!ENTITY  LOGO SYSTEM "logo.gif">
```

Then, at the desired image location in the document, insert the following IMAGE tag:

```
<IMAGE SOURCE="LOGO"/>
```

This approach is not a magic formula that all XML browsers automatically understand. It is simply one technique that browsers and other applications may or may not adopt to embed non-XML data in documents.

Cross-Reference   This technique is explored further in Chapter 12.

The ENTITIES attribute type

ENTITIES is a relatively rare plural form of ENTITY. The value of an ENTITIES type attribute consists of multiple unparsed entity names separated by white space. Each entity name refers to an external non-XML data source. One use for this approach is a slide show that rotates different pictures, as in the following example:

```
<!ELEMENT SLIDESHOW EMPTY>
<!ATTLIST SLIDESHOW SOURCES ENTITIES #REQUIRED>
<!ENTITY PIC1 SYSTEM "cat.gif">
<!ENTITY PIC2 SYSTEM "dog.gif">
<!ENTITY PIC3 SYSTEM "cow.gif">
```

Then, at the point in the document where you want the slide show to appear, insert the following tag:

```
<SLIDESHOW SOURCES="PIC1 PIC2 PIC3"/>
```

This is not a universal formula that all (or even any) XML browsers automatically understand; it is simply one method that browsers and other applications might adopt to embed non-XML data in documents.

The NOTATION attribute type

The NOTATION attribute type specifies that an attribute's value is the name of a notation declared in the DTD. The default value of this attribute must also be the name of a notation declared in the DTD. Notations are introduced in the next chapter. In brief, notations identify the format of non-XML data, for instance by specifying a helper application for an unparsed entity.

Cross-Reference

Chapter 12 covers notations.

For example, this PLAYER attribute of a SOUND element has type NOTATION and a default value of MP — the notation signifying a particular kind of sound file:

```
<!ATTLIST SOUND PLAYER NOTATION (MP) #REQUIRED>
<!NOTATION MP SYSTEM "mplay32.exe">
```

You can also offer a choice of different notations. One use for this is to specify different helper apps for different platforms. The browser can pick the one it has available. In this case, the NOTATION keyword is followed by a set of parentheses containing the list of allowed notation names separated by vertical bars. For example:

```
<!NOTATION MP SYSTEM "mplay32.exe">
<!NOTATION ST SYSTEM "soundtool">
<!NOTATION SM SYSTEM "Sound Machine">
<!ATTLIST SOUND PLAYER NOTATION (MP | SM | ST) #REQUIRED>
```

This says that the PLAYER attribute of the SOUND element may be set to MP, ST, or SM. We explore this further in the next chapter.

Note

At first glance, this approach may appear inconsistent with the handling of other list attributes, such as ENTITIES and NMTOKENS, but these two approaches are actually quite different. ENTITIES and NMTOKENS have a list of attributes in the actual element in the document but only one value in the attribute declaration in the DTD. NOTATION only has a single value in the attribute of the actual element in the document, however. The list of possible values occurs in the attribute declaration in the DTD.

Predefined Attributes

In a way, two attributes are predefined in XML. You must declare these attributes in your DTD for each element to which they apply, but you should only use these declared attributes for their intended purposes. Such attributes are identified by a name that begins with xml:.

These two attributes are xml:space and xml:lang. The xml:space attribute describes how white space is treated in the element. The xml:lang attribute describes the language (and, optionally, dialect and country) in which the element is written.

xml:space

In HTML, white space is relatively insignificant. Although the difference between one space and no space is significant, the difference between 1 space and 2 spaces, 1 space and a carriage return, or 1 space, 3 carriage returns, and 12 tabs is not important. For text in which white space is significant — computer source code, certain mainframe database reports, or the poetry of e. e. cummings, for example — you can use a PRE element to specify a monospaced font and preservation of white space.

XML, however, preserves white space by default. The XML processor passes all white space characters to the application unchanged. The application usually ignores the extra white space. However, the XML processor can tell the application that certain elements contain significant white space that should be preserved. The page author uses the xml:space attribute to indicate these elements to the application.

Note An XML parser always passes all white space to the application, regardless of whether xml:space's value is default or preserve. With a value of default, however, the application does what it would normally do with extra white space. With a value of preserve, the application treats the extra white space as significant. Significance depends somewhat on the eventual destination of the data. For instance, extra white space in Java source code is relevant to a source code editor but not to a compiler.

If an element contains significant white space, the DTD should have an <!ATTLIST> declaration for the xml:space attribute. This attribute will have an enumerated type with the two values, default and preserve, as shown in Listing 11-4.

Listing 11-4: Java source code with significant white space encoded in XML

```
<?xml version="1.0" standalone="yes"?>
<!DOCTYPE PROGRAM [
  <!ELEMENT PROGRAM (#PCDATA)>
  <!ATTLIST PROGRAM xml:space (default|preserve) 'preserve'>
]>
<PROGRAM xml:space="preserve">public class AsciiTable {

  public static void main (String[] args) {

    for (int i = 0; i &lt; 128; i++) {
      System.out.println(i + "    " + (char) i);
    }

  }

}
</PROGRAM>
```

Caution

The XML specification requires that when declared, the `xml:space` attribute "must be given as an enumerated type whose only possible values are 'default' and 'preserve.'" In other words, it must be declared like this:

```
<!ATTLIST PROG xml:space (default|preserve) 'preserve'>
```

Or perhaps like this:

```
<!ATTLIST PROG xml:space (default|preserve) 'default'>
```

However, it may not be declared like this, even though this would seem to be reasonable:

```
<!ATTLIST PROG xml:space CDATA #FIXED 'preserve'>
```

It can't even be declared like this:

```
<!ATTLIST PROG xml:space CDATA (preserve) 'preserve'>
```

You have to provide both possible values to the enumeration. In fact, the last declaration should be allowed. An erratum to the XML 1.0 specification, which was incorporated into the second edition of the XML specification, clarifies this point and explicitly allows declarations of `xml:space` with only one of the two possible enumerated values. However, not all parsers have been updated to take advantage of this erratum. For the time being you should only use the two-value enumeration.

Descendants (child elements and their children, and their children's children, and so on) of an element for which `xml:space` is defined are assumed to behave similarly to their parent (either preserving or not preserving space), unless they possess an `xml:space` attribute with a conflicting value.

xml:lang

The `xml:lang` attribute identifies the language in which the element's content is written. The value of this attribute can have type CDATA, NMTOKEN, or an enumerated list. Ideally, each of these attribute values should be one of the two-letter language codes defined by the original ISO-639 standard. The complete list of codes can be found on the Web at `http://www.ics.uci.edu/pub/ietf/http/related/iso639.txt`.

For instance, consider this sentence from Petronius's *Satyricon* in both Latin and English. A SENTENCE element encloses both versions, but the first SENTENCE element has an `xml:lang` attribute for Latin, while the second has an `xml:lang` attribute for English.

```
<SENTENCE xml:lang="la">
  Veniebamus in forum deficiente iam die, in quo notavimus
  frequentiam rerum venalium, non quidem pretiosarum sed tamen
  quarum fidem male ambulantem obscuritas temporis
  facillime tegeret.
</SENTENCE>
<SENTENCE xml:lang="en">
  We have come to the marketplace now when the day is failing,
  where we have seen many things for sale, not for the
  valuable goods but rather that the darkness of
  the time may most easily conceal their shoddiness.
</SENTENCE>
```

While an English-speaking reader can easily tell which is the original text and which is the translation, a computer can use the hint provided by the xml:lang attribute. This distinction enables a spell checker to determine whether to check a particular element and designate which dictionary to use. Search engines can inspect these language attributes to determine whether to index a page and return matches based on the user's preferences. The language applies to the element and all its children until one of its children declares a different language.

Country codes

The value of the xml:lang attribute may include additional subcode segments, separated from the primary language code by a hyphen. Most often, the first subcode segment is a two-letter country code specified by ISO 3166. You can retrieve the most current list of country codes from http://www.isi.edu/in-notes/iana/assignments/country-codes. For example:

```
<P xml:lang="en-US">Put the body in the trunk of the car.</P>
<P xml:lang="en-GB">Put the body in the boot of the car.</P>
```

By convention, language codes are written in lowercase and country codes are written in uppercase. However, this is merely a convention. This is one of the few parts of XML that is case insensitive, because of its heritage in the case-insensitive ISO standard.

IANA language codes

If no appropriate ISO code is available for the primary language, you can use one of the codes registered with the Internet Assigned Numbers Authority (IANA). Table 11-2 lists the additional codes registered with the IANA as of January 2001. You can find the most current list at http://www.iana.org/assignments/language-tags.

Table 11-2
The IANA Language Codes

Code	Language
no-bok	Norwegian "Book language"
no-nyn	Norwegian "New Norwegian"
i-navajo	Navajo, the language of the most populous Native American tribe, the Navajo tribe, which has about 150,000 speakers mostly located in Arizona, New Mexico, and Utah
i-mingo	The language of the Mingo tribe of West Virginia
i-default	The default language context
i-tsu	Tsou, a non-Chinese aboriginal language in Taiwan with about 5000 native speakers
i-hak	Hakka, a Chinese dialect with about 20 million speakers; see also zh-hak
i-klingon	Klingon, the fictional language used in Star Trek
i-tay	Tayal, a non-Chinese aboriginal language in Taiwan with about 63,000 native speakers
i-tao	Tao, Wobe, an African language spoken by about 156,000 people in Côte d'Ivoire
i-pwn	Paiwan, a non-Chinese aboriginal language in Taiwan with about 81,000 native speakers
i-bnn	Bunun, a non-Chinese aboriginal language in Taiwan with about 34,000 native speakers
i-ami	Amis, a non-Chinese aboriginal language in Taiwan with about 130,000 native speakers
i-lux	Luxembourgish, a.k.a. Letzeburgesh, the German dialect spoken in the Grand Duchy of Luxembourg
zh-guoyu	Mandarin, the Chinese dialect spoken by about two-thirds of Chinese speakers, approximately 800 million people
zh-hakka	Hakka, a Chinese dialect with about 20 million speakers
zh-min	The primary Chinese dialect of Taiwan spoken by about 45 million people, alternately known as Min, Fukienese, Fuzhou, Hokkien, Amoy, or Taiwanese
zh-wuu	Wu, a Chinese dialect spoken by about 50 million people in and south of Shanghai, a.k.a. Shanghaiese
zh-xiang	The Xiang or Hunanese dialect of Chinese with about 15 million speakers in China's Hunan province
zh-yue	Cantonese, the primary dialect of Hong Kong and the surrounding areas of southern China
zh-gan	Kan, a.k.a. Gan, a dialect of Chinese spoken by about 21 million people

Too Many Languages, Not Enough Codes

XML remains a little behind the times in this area. The original ISO-639 standard language codes were formed from two case-insensitive ASCII alphabetic characters. This standard allows no more than 26 × 26 or 676 different codes. About ten times that many different languages are spoken on Earth today (not even counting dead languages such as Etruscan). In practice, the reasonable codes are somewhat fewer than 676 because the language abbreviations should have some relation to the name of the language.

ISO-639, part two, uses three-letter language codes, which should handle all languages spoken on Earth. The XML standard specifically requires two-letter codes, however. On the other hand, because of some very technical details about how the XML specification is written (see the comments about production 33 in the Language identification section of Appendix B for details), parsers are not required to enforce this constraint. Unfortunately, some do and some do not, so documents really have to assume that two-letter codes are required.

IANA codes beginning with i-, such as i-navajo, represent new languages not currently included in two-letter form in ISO 639. IANA codes beginning with a two-letter ISO 639 code, such as zh-yue, represent a dialect of the primary language. Thus, zh is the ISO-639 code for Chinese; zh-yue is the IANA code for the Yue dialect of Chinese (more commonly known as Cantonese in English). The criteria for what qualifies as a language and what qualifies as a dialect are not particularly well defined. For instance, Swedish and Norwegian, two different languages, are mutually intelligible; but Cantonese and Mandarin, two different dialects of Chinese, are mutually unintelligible. To be perfectly honest, the best answer is that the people who speak different languages have their own armies and the people who speak different dialects don't.

For example, Listing 11-5 gives the national anthem of Luxembourg in both Letzeburgesh (i-lux) and English (en):

Listing 11-5: **The national anthem of Luxembourg in Letzeburgesh and English**

```
<?xml version="1.0" encoding="ISO-8859-1"?>
<!DOCTYPE DOCUMENT [
  <!ELEMENT DOCUMENT (SONG+)>
  <!ELEMENT SONG     (STANZA+)>
  <!ELEMENT STANZA   (VERSE+)>
  <!ELEMENT VERSE    (#PCDATA)>
  <!ATTLIST SONG xml:lang   NMTOKEN 'en'
                 LYRICIST   CDATA   #IMPLIED
                 COMPOSER   CDATA   #IMPLIED
                 TRANSLATOR CDATA   #IMPLIED
  >
]>
<DOCUMENT>
  <SONG xml:lang="i-lux"
```

```
               LYRICIST="Michel Lentz" COMPOSER="J.A. Zinnen">
        <STANZA>
          <VERSE>Wo d'Uelzecht duerch d'Wisen ze't,</VERSE>
          <VERSE>Dʊrch d'Fielzen d'Sauer brëcht,</VERSE>
          <VERSE>Wo' d'Ref lânscht d'Musel dofteg ble't,</VERSE>
          <VERSE>Den Himmel Wein ons mëcht:</VERSE>
          <VERSE>Dat ass onst Land, fir dat mer ge'f</VERSE>
          <VERSE>Heinidden alles won,</VERSE>
          <VERSE>Ons Hemeschtsland dat mir so' de'f</VERSE>
          <VERSE>An onsen Hierzer dron.</VERSE>
          <VERSE>Ons Hemeschtsland dat mir so' de'f</VERSE>
          <VERSE>An onsen Hierzer dron.</VERSE>
        </STANZA>
        <STANZA>
          <VERSE>O Du do uewen, dem seng Hand</VERSE>
          <VERSE>Durch d'Welt Natio'ne let,</VERSE>
          <VERSE>Behitt du d'Lëtzeburger Land</VERSE>
          <VERSE>Vum frieme Joch a Led;</VERSE>
          <VERSE>Du hues ons all als Kanner schon</VERSE>
          <VERSE>De freie Gêscht jo ginn,</VERSE>
          <VERSE>Loss viru blënken d'Freihetsonn,</VERSE>
          <VERSE>De' mir so' lâng gesinn.</VERSE>
          <VERSE>Loss viru blënken d'Freihetsonn,</VERSE>
          <VERSE>De' mir so' lâng gesinn.</VERSE>
        </STANZA>
      </SONG>
      <SONG xml:lang="en" TRANSLATOR="Nicholas E. Weydert">
        <STANZA>
          <VERSE>Where slow you see the Alzette flow,</VERSE>
          <VERSE>The Sura play wild pranks,</VERSE>
          <VERSE>Where lovely vineyards amply grow,</VERSE>
          <VERSE>Upon the Moselle's banks,</VERSE>
          <VERSE>There lies the land for which our thanks</VERSE>
          <VERSE>Are owed to God above,</VERSE>
          <VERSE>Our own, our native land which ranks</VERSE>
          <VERSE>Well foremost in our love.</VERSE>
          <VERSE>Our own, our native land which ranks</VERSE>
          <VERSE>Well foremost in our love.</VERSE>
        </STANZA>
        <STANZA>
          <VERSE>Oh Father in Heaven whose powerful hand</VERSE>
          <VERSE>Makes states or lays them low,</VERSE>
          <VERSE>Protect the Luxembourger land</VERSE>
          <VERSE>From foreign yoke and woe.</VERSE>
          <VERSE>God's golden liberty bestow</VERSE>
          <VERSE>On us now as of yore.</VERSE>
          <VERSE>Let Freedom's sun in glory glow</VERSE>
          <VERSE>For now and evermore.</VERSE>
          <VERSE>Let Freedom's sun in glory glow</VERSE>
          <VERSE>For now and evermore.</VERSE>
        </STANZA>
      </SONG>
    </DOCUMENT>
```

X-Codes

If neither the ISO nor the IANA has a code for the language you need, which is often the case for many aboriginal languages, you may define new language codes. These *x-codes* must begin with the string x- or X- to identify them as user-defined, private use codes. For example,

```
<P xml:lang="x-choctaw">
  Chahta imanumpa ish anumpola hinla ho?
</P>
<P xml:lang="en">Do you speak Choctaw?</P>
```

Declarations of xml:lang

Like all attributes used in DTDs for valid documents, the xml:lang attribute must be specifically declared for those elements to which it directly applies. (It indirectly applies to children of elements that have specified xml:lang attributes, but these children do not require separate declaration.) The declaration of the SENTENCE element can appear as follows:

```
<!ELEMENT SENTENCE (#PCDATA)>
<!ATTLIST SENTENCE xml:lang NMTOKEN "en">
```

You may not want to permit arbitrary values for xml:lang. The permissible values are also valid XML names, so the attribute is commonly given the NMTOKEN type. This restricts the value of the attribute to an XML name token. For example,

```
<!ELEMENT P (#PCDATA)>
<!ATTLIST P xml:lang NMTOKEN #IMPLIED "en">
```

Alternately, if only a few languages or dialects are permitted, you can use an enumerated type. For example, the following DTD says that the P element may be either English or Latin.

```
<!ELEMENT P (#PCDATA)>
<!ATTLIST P xml:lang (en | la) "en">
```

You can use a CDATA type attribute, but there's little reason to. Using NMTOKEN or an enumerated type helps catch some potential errors.

A DTD for Attribute-Based Baseball Statistics

Chapter 5 developed a well-formed XML document for the 1998 Major League Baseball Season that used attributes to store the YEAR of a SEASON, the NAME of leagues, divisions, and teams, the CITY in which a team plays, and the detailed statistics of individual players. Listing 11-6 presents a shorter version of Listing 5-1. It is a complete XML document with two leagues, six divisions, six teams, and two players. It serves to refresh your memory of which elements belong where and with which attributes.

Listing 11-6: **A complete XML document**

```
<?xml version="1.0"?>
<SEASON YEAR="1998">
  <LEAGUE NAME="American League">
    <DIVISION NAME="East">
      <TEAM CITY="Baltimore" NAME="Orioles">
        <PLAYER GIVEN_NAME="Doug" SURNAME="Drabek"
          POSITION="Starting Pitcher" GAMES="23"
          GAMES_STARTED="21" WINS="6" LOSSES="11" SAVES="0"
          COMPLETE_GAMES="1" SHUT_OUTS="0" ERA="7.29"
          INNINGS="108.2" HITS_AGAINST="138"
          HOME_RUNS_AGAINST="20" RUNS_AGAINST="90"
          EARNED_RUNS="88" HIT_BATTER="5" WILD_PITCHES="1"
          BALK="0" WALKED_BATTER="29" STRUCK_OUT_BATTER="55"/>
        <PLAYER GIVEN_NAME="Roberto" SURNAME="Alomar"
          POSITION="Second Base" GAMES="147"
          GAMES_STARTED="143" AT_BATS="588" RUNS="86"
          HITS="166" DOUBLES="36" TRIPLES="1" HOME_RUNS="14"
          RUNS_BATTED_IN="56" WALKS="59" STRUCK_OUT="70"
          STEALS="18" CAUGHT_STEALING="5" HIT_BY_PITCH="2"
          SACRIFICE_FLIES="5" SACRIFICE_HITS="3"/>
      </TEAM>
    </DIVISION>
    <DIVISION NAME="Central">
      <TEAM CITY="Chicago" NAME="White Sox"></TEAM>
    </DIVISION>
    <DIVISION NAME="West">
      <TEAM CITY="Anaheim" NAME="Angels"></TEAM>
    </DIVISION>
  </LEAGUE>
  <LEAGUE NAME="National League">
    <DIVISION NAME="East">
      <TEAM CITY="New York" NAME="Mets"></TEAM>
    </DIVISION>
    <DIVISION NAME="Central">
      <TEAM CITY="Chicago" NAME="Cubs"></TEAM>
    </DIVISION>
    <DIVISION NAME="West">
      <TEAM CITY="San Francisco" NAME="Giants"></TEAM>
    </DIVISION>
  </LEAGUE>
</SEASON>
```

To make this document valid, you need to provide a DTD. This DTD must declare both the elements and the attributes used in Listing 11-6. The element declarations resemble the ones used in the last chapter, except that there are fewer of them because most of the information has been moved into attributes:

```
<!ELEMENT SEASON (LEAGUE, LEAGUE)>
<!ELEMENT LEAGUE (DIVISION, DIVISION, DIVISION)>
<!ELEMENT DIVISION (TEAM+)>
<!ELEMENT TEAM (PLAYER*)>
<!ELEMENT PLAYER EMPTY>
```

Declaring SEASON attributes in the DTD

The SEASON element has a single attribute, YEAR. Although some semantic constraints determine what is and is not a year (1998 is a year; Steinbrenner is not), the DTD doesn't enforce these. Thus, the best approach declares that the YEAR attribute has the most similar attribute type, NMTOKEN. Furthermore, we want all seasons to have a year, so we'll make the YEAR attribute required.

```
<!ATTLIST SEASON YEAR NMTOKEN #REQUIRED>
```

Although you really can't restrict the form of the text authors enter in YEAR attributes, you can at least provide a comment that shows what's expected. For example, it may be a good idea to specify that four-digit years are required.

```
<!ATTLIST SEASON YEAR NMTOKEN #REQUIRED> <!-- e.g. 1998 -->
<!-- DO NOT USE TWO-DIGIT YEARS like 98, 99, 00!! -->
```

Note
The W3C XML Schema language uses XML documents to describe information that might traditionally be encoded in a DTD, as well as data type information. Schemas do allow you to express requirements such as "Each YEAR element must contain a four-digit year between 1845 and 9999". Schemas will be explored in Chapter 23.

Declaring LEAGUE and DIVISION attributes in the DTD

Next, consider LEAGUE and DIVISION. Each has a single NAME attribute. Again, the natural type is CDATA and the attribute will be required. Because these are two separate NAME attributes for two different elements, two separate <!ATTLIST> declarations are required.

```
<!ATTLIST LEAGUE   NAME CDATA #REQUIRED>
<!ATTLIST DIVISION NAME CDATA #REQUIRED>
```

A comment may help here to show document authors the expected form; for instance, whether or not to include the words *League* and *Division* as part of the name.

```
<!ATTLIST LEAGUE   NAME CDATA #REQUIRED>
<!-- e.g. "National League" -->

<!ATTLIST DIVISION NAME CDATA #REQUIRED>
<!-- e.g. "East" -->
```

Declaring TEAM attributes in the DTD

A TEAM has both a NAME and a CITY. Each is CDATA and each is required:

```
<!ATTLIST TEAM NAME CDATA #REQUIRED>
<!ATTLIST TEAM CITY CDATA #REQUIRED>
```

Alternately, you can declare both attributes in a single <!ATTLIST> declaration:

```
<!ATTLIST TEAM NAME CDATA #REQUIRED
               CITY CDATA #REQUIRED>
```

In either case, a comment may help to establish what isn't obvious to everyone; for instance, that the CITY attribute may actually be the name of a state.

```
<!ATTLIST TEAM NAME CDATA #REQUIRED>
<!ATTLIST TEAM CITY CDATA #REQUIRED>
<!-- e.g. "San Diego" as in "San Diego Padres"
     or "Texas" as in "Texas Rangers" -->
```

Declaring PLAYER attributes in the DTD

The PLAYER element boasts the most attributes. GIVEN_NAME and SURNAME, the first two, are simply CDATA and required:

```
<!ATTLIST PLAYER GIVEN_NAME CDATA #REQUIRED>
<!ATTLIST PLAYER SURNAME    CDATA #REQUIRED>
```

The next PLAYER attribute is POSITION. Because baseball positions are standardized, you might use the enumerated attribute type here. However First Base, Second Base, Third Base, Starting Pitcher, and Relief Pitcher all contain white space and are therefore not valid XML names. Consequently, the only attribute type that works is CDATA. There is no reasonable default value for the position so we make this attribute required as well.

```
<!ATTLIST PLAYER POSITION CDATA #REQUIRED>
```

Next come the various statistics: GAMES, GAMES_STARTED, AT_BATS, RUNS, HITS, WINS, LOSSES, SAVES, SHUTOUTS, and so forth. Each should be a single number. XML does not allow you to declare an attribute as integer or float, but you can at least require them to be name tokens so as to rule out a few invalid values. Because not all players have valid values for each of these, declare each one implied rather than required.

```
<!ATTLIST PLAYER GAMES                  NMTOKEN #IMPLIED>
<!ATTLIST PLAYER GAMES_STARTED          NMTOKEN #IMPLIED>

<!-- Batting Statistics -->
<!ATTLIST PLAYER AT_BATS                NMTOKEN #IMPLIED>
<!ATTLIST PLAYER RUNS                   NMTOKEN #IMPLIED>
<!ATTLIST PLAYER HITS                   NMTOKEN #IMPLIED>
<!ATTLIST PLAYER DOUBLES                NMTOKEN #IMPLIED>
<!ATTLIST PLAYER TRIPLES                NMTOKEN #IMPLIED>
<!ATTLIST PLAYER HOME_RUNS              NMTOKEN #IMPLIED>
<!ATTLIST PLAYER RUNS_BATTED_IN         NMTOKEN #IMPLIED>
<!ATTLIST PLAYER STEALS                 NMTOKEN #IMPLIED>
<!ATTLIST PLAYER CAUGHT_STEALING        NMTOKEN #IMPLIED>
<!ATTLIST PLAYER SACRIFICE_HITS         NMTOKEN #IMPLIED>
<!ATTLIST PLAYER SACRIFICE_FLIES        NMTOKEN #IMPLIED>
<!ATTLIST PLAYER ERRORS                 NMTOKEN #IMPLIED>
<!ATTLIST PLAYER WALKS                  NMTOKEN #IMPLIED>
<!ATTLIST PLAYER STRUCK_OUT             NMTOKEN #IMPLIED>
<!ATTLIST PLAYER HIT_BY_PITCH           NMTOKEN #IMPLIED>

<!-- Pitching Statistics -->
<!ATTLIST PLAYER WINS                   NMTOKEN #IMPLIED>
<!ATTLIST PLAYER LOSSES                 NMTOKEN #IMPLIED>
<!ATTLIST PLAYER SAVES                  NMTOKEN #IMPLIED>
<!ATTLIST PLAYER COMPLETE_GAMES         NMTOKEN #IMPLIED>
<!ATTLIST PLAYER SHUT_OUTS              NMTOKEN #IMPLIED>
<!ATTLIST PLAYER ERA                    NMTOKEN #IMPLIED>
<!ATTLIST PLAYER INNINGS                NMTOKEN #IMPLIED>
<!ATTLIST PLAYER HITS_AGAINST           NMTOKEN #IMPLIED>
<!ATTLIST PLAYER HOME_RUNS_AGAINST NMTOKEN #IMPLIED>
<!ATTLIST PLAYER RUNS_AGAINST           NMTOKEN #IMPLIED>
<!ATTLIST PLAYER EARNED_RUNS            NMTOKEN #IMPLIED>
<!ATTLIST PLAYER HIT_BATTER             NMTOKEN #IMPLIED>
<!ATTLIST PLAYER WILD_PITCHES           NMTOKEN #IMPLIED>
<!ATTLIST PLAYER BALK                   NMTOKEN #IMPLIED>
<!ATTLIST PLAYER WALKED_BATTER          NMTOKEN #IMPLIED>
<!ATTLIST PLAYER STRUCK_OUT_BATTER NMTOKEN #IMPLIED>
```

One disadvantage of this approach relative to the child elements that were used in the last chapter is that you can no longer separate out the pitching and batting statistics and treat them as a group. There's no way to say that all elements must have either Group X or Group Y or both. Whether one attribute is required, implied, or fixed is completely independent of the presence or absence of other attributes.

If you prefer, you can combine all the possible attributes of PLAYER into one monstrous <!ATTLIST> declaration:

```
<!ATTLIST PLAYER
  GIVEN_NAME          NMTOKEN #REQUIRED
  SURNAME             NMTOKEN #REQUIRED
  POSITION            NMTOKEN #REQUIRED
  GAMES               NMTOKEN #IMPLIED
  GAMES_STARTED       NMTOKEN #IMPLIED
  AT_BATS             NMTOKEN #IMPLIED
  RUNS                NMTOKEN #IMPLIED
  HITS                NMTOKEN #IMPLIED
  DOUBLES             NMTOKEN #IMPLIED
  TRIPLES             NMTOKEN #IMPLIED
  HOME_RUNS           NMTOKEN #IMPLIED
  RUNS_BATTED_IN      NMTOKEN #IMPLIED
  STEALS              NMTOKEN #IMPLIED
  CAUGHT_STEALING     NMTOKEN #IMPLIED
  SACRIFICE_HITS      NMTOKEN #IMPLIED
  SACRIFICE_FLIES     NMTOKEN #IMPLIED
  ERRORS              NMTOKEN #IMPLIED
  WALKS               NMTOKEN #IMPLIED
  STRUCK_OUT          NMTOKEN #IMPLIED
  HIT_BY_PITCH        NMTOKEN #IMPLIED

  WINS                NMTOKEN #IMPLIED
  LOSSES              NMTOKEN #IMPLIED
  SAVES               NMTOKEN #IMPLIED
  SHUT_OUTS           NMTOKEN #IMPLIED
  COMPLETE_GAMES      NMTOKEN #IMPLIED
  SHUTOUTS            NMTOKEN #IMPLIED
  ERA                 NMTOKEN #IMPLIED
  INNINGS             NMTOKEN #IMPLIED
  HITS_AGAINST        NMTOKEN #IMPLIED
  HOME_RUNS_AGAINST   NMTOKEN #IMPLIED
  RUNS_AGAINST        NMTOKEN #IMPLIED
  EARNED_RUNS         NMTOKEN #IMPLIED
  HIT_BATTER          NMTOKEN #IMPLIED
  WILD_PITCHES        NMTOKEN #IMPLIED
  BALK                NMTOKEN #IMPLIED
  WALKED_BATTER       NMTOKEN #IMPLIED
  STRUCK_OUT_BATTER   NMTOKEN #IMPLIED
>
```

One disadvantage of this approach is that it makes it impossible to include even simple comments next to the individual attributes because comments cannot appear inside declarations, only outside them.

The complete DTD for the baseball statistics example

Listing 11-7 shows the complete attribute-based baseball DTD.

Listing 11-7: The complete DTD for baseball statistics that uses attributes for most of the information

```
<!ELEMENT SEASON (LEAGUE, LEAGUE)>
<!ELEMENT LEAGUE (DIVISION, DIVISION, DIVISION)>
<!ELEMENT DIVISION (TEAM+)>
<!ELEMENT TEAM (PLAYER*)>
<!ELEMENT PLAYER EMPTY>

<!ATTLIST SEASON YEAR NMTOKEN #REQUIRED> <!-- e.g. 1998 -->
<!-- DO NOT USE TWO DIGIT YEARS like 98, 99, 00!! -->

<!ATTLIST LEAGUE   NAME CDATA #REQUIRED>
<!-- e.g. "National League" -->

<!ATTLIST DIVISION NAME CDATA #REQUIRED>
<!-- e.g. "East" -->

<!ATTLIST TEAM NAME CDATA #REQUIRED>
<!ATTLIST TEAM CITY CDATA #REQUIRED>
<!-- e.g. "San Diego" as in "San Diego Padres"
     or "Texas" as in "Texas Rangers" -->

<!ATTLIST PLAYER GIVEN_NAME CDATA #REQUIRED>
<!ATTLIST PLAYER SURNAME    CDATA #REQUIRED>
<!ATTLIST PLAYER POSITION   CDATA #REQUIRED>

<!ATTLIST PLAYER
  GIVEN_NAME       NMTOKEN #REQUIRED
  SURNAME          NMTOKEN #REQUIRED
  POSITION         NMTOKEN #REQUIRED
  GAMES            NMTOKEN #IMPLIED
  GAMES_STARTED    NMTOKEN #IMPLIED
  AT_BATS          NMTOKEN #IMPLIED
  RUNS             NMTOKEN #IMPLIED
  HITS             NMTOKEN #IMPLIED
  DOUBLES          NMTOKEN #IMPLIED
  TRIPLES          NMTOKEN #IMPLIED
  HOME_RUNS        NMTOKEN #IMPLIED
  RUNS_BATTED_IN   NMTOKEN #IMPLIED
  STEALS           NMTOKEN #IMPLIED
  CAUGHT_STEALING  NMTOKEN #IMPLIED
  SACRIFICE_HITS   NMTOKEN #IMPLIED
  SACRIFICE_FLIES  NMTOKEN #IMPLIED
```

```
ERRORS              NMTOKEN #IMPLIED
WALKS               NMTOKEN #IMPLIED
STRUCK_OUT          NMTOKEN #IMPLIED
HIT_BY_PITCH        NMTOKEN #IMPLIED

WINS                NMTOKEN #IMPLIED
LOSSES              NMTOKEN #IMPLIED
SAVES               NMTOKEN #IMPLIED
SHUT_OUTS           NMTOKEN #IMPLIED
COMPLETE_GAMES      NMTOKEN #IMPLIED
SHUTOUTS            NMTOKEN #IMPLIED
ERA                 NMTOKEN #IMPLIED
INNINGS             NMTOKEN #IMPLIED
HITS_AGAINST        NMTOKEN #IMPLIED
HOME_RUNS_AGAINST   NMTOKEN #IMPLIED
RUNS_AGAINST        NMTOKEN #IMPLIED
EARNED_RUNS         NMTOKEN #IMPLIED
HIT_BATTER          NMTOKEN #IMPLIED
WILD_PITCHES        NMTOKEN #IMPLIED
BALK                NMTOKEN #IMPLIED
WALKED_BATTER       NMTOKEN #IMPLIED
STRUCK_OUT_BATTER   NMTOKEN #IMPLIED>
```

To attach the above to Listing 11-6, use the following document type declaration, assuming of course that Listing 11-7 is stored in a file called baseballattributes.dtd:

```
<!DOCTYPE SEASON SYSTEM "baseballattributes.dtd">
```

Summary

In this chapter, you learned how to declare attributes in DTDs. In particular, you learned the following concepts:

+ Attributes are declared in an `<!ATTLIST>` tag in the DTD.

+ One `<!ATTLIST>` tag can declare an indefinite number of attributes for a single element.

+ Attributes normally have default values, but this condition can be changed by using the keywords `#REQUIRED`, `#IMPLIED`, or `#FIXED`.

+ There are ten attribute types: CDATA, Enumerated, `NMTOKEN`, `NMTOKENS`, `ID`, `IDREF`, `IDREFS`, `ENTITY`, `ENTITIES`, and `NOTATION`.

✦ The `xml:space` attribute determines whether white space in an element is significant.

✦ The `xml:lang` attribute specifies the language in which an element's content appears.

In the next chapter, you learn how notations, processing instructions, and unparsed external entities can be used to embed non-XML data in XML documents.

✦　　✦　　✦

Unparsed Entities, Notations, and Non-XML Data

Not all data in the world is XML. In fact, I'd venture to say that most of the world's accumulated data isn't XML. A heck of a lot is stored in plain text, HTML, and Microsoft Word, to name just three common non-XML formats. Although most of this data could theoretically be rewritten in XML—interest and resources permitting—not all of the world's data should be in XML. Encoding photographs in XML, for example, would be extremely inefficient.

XML provides three constructs for working with non-XML data: Notations, unparsed entities, and processing instructions. Notations describe the format of non-XML data. Unparsed entities provide links to the actual location of the non-XML data. Processing instructions give information about how to view the data.

Caution The material discussed in this chapter is controversial. Although everything I describe is part of the XML 1.0 specification, not everyone agrees that it should be. You can certainly write XML documents without using any notations or unparsed entities, and with only a few simple processing instructions. You may want to skip this chapter at first, and return to it later if you discover a need for it.

Notations

The first problem you encounter when working with non-XML data in an XML document is identifying the format of the data so that the XML application knows how to display the non-XML data. For example, it would be silly to try to draw an MP3 file on the screen.

To a limited extent, you can solve this problem within a single application by using a fixed set of elements for particular kinds of data. For instance, if all pictures are embedded through IMAGE elements and all sounds through AUDIO elements, then it's not hard to develop a browser that knows how to handle those two elements. In essence, this is the approach that HTML takes. However, this approach does prevent document authors from creating new tags that more specifically describe their content; for example, a PERSON element that happens to have a HEADSHOT attribute that points to a JPEG image of that person.

Furthermore, no application understands all possible file formats. Most Web browsers can recognize and read GIF, JPEG, PNG, and perhaps a few other kinds of image files; but they fail completely when faced with EPS files, TIFF files, FITS files, or any of the hundreds of other common and uncommon image formats. The dialog box in Figure 12-1 is probably all too familiar.

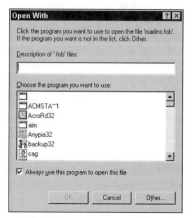

Figure 12-1: What happens when Netscape Navigator doesn't recognize a file type

Ideally, a document should tell the application what format an unparsed entity is in so that you don't have to rely on the application recognizing the file type by a magic number in the first few bytes of the file or a potentially unreliable filename extension. Furthermore, you'd like to give the application some hints about what program it can use to display the unparsed entity if it's unable to do so itself.

Notations provide a partial (although not always well-supported) solution to this problem. A notation describes one possible format for non-XML data through a `NOTATION` declaration in the Document Type Definition (DTD). Each notation declaration contains a name and an external identifier in the following syntax:

```
<!NOTATION name SYSTEM "externalID">
```

The *name* is an identifier for this particular format used in the document. The *externalID* contains a human-intelligible string that somehow identifies the notation. For instance, you might use MIME media types as in this notation for GIF images:

```
<!NOTATION GIF SYSTEM "image/gif">
```

You can also use a `PUBLIC` identifier instead of the `SYSTEM` identifier. To do this, you must provide both a public ID and a URL. For example,

```
<!NOTATION GIF PUBLIC
    "-//IETF//NONSGML Media Type image/gif//EN"
    "http://www.isi.edu/in-notes/iana/assignments/media-
types/image/gif">
```

Caution

There is *a lot* of debate about what exactly makes a good external identifier. MIME media types, such as image/gif or text/html, are one possibility. Another possibility is to use URLs or other locators for standards documents such as `http://www.w3.org/TR/REC-html40/`. A third possibility is the name of an official international standard such as ISO 8601 for representing dates and times. In some cases, an ISBN or Library of Congress catalog number for the paper document where the standard is defined might be more appropriate, and there are many more choices.

Which you choose may depend on the expected life span of your document. For instance, if you use an unusual format, you don't want to rely on a URL that changes from month to month. If you expect or hope that your document will still spark interest in 100 years, then you may want to consider identifiers that are likely to have meaning in 100 years, as opposed to those that are merely this decade's technical ephemera.

You can also use notations to describe data that does fit in an XML document. For instance, consider this `DATE` element:

```
<DATE>05-07-06</DATE>
```

What day, exactly, does 05-07-06 represent? Is it May 7, 1906 C.E.? Or is it July 5, 1906 C.E.? The answer depends on whether you read this in the United States or Europe. Maybe it's even May 7, 2006 C.E. or July 5, 2006 C.E. Or perhaps what's meant is May 7, 6 C.E., during the reign of the Roman emperor Augustus in the West and the Han dynasty in China. It's also possible that this date isn't in the "Common Era" at all but is given in the traditional Jewish, Muslim, or Chinese calendar. Without more information, you cannot determine the true meaning.

To avoid this type of confusion, ISO standard 8601 defines a precise means of representing dates. In this scheme, July 5, 2006 C.E. is written as 20060705 or, in XML, as follows:

```
<DATE>20060705</DATE>
```

This format doesn't match *anybody's* expectations; it's equally confusing to everybody and thus has the advantage of being more or less culturally neutral (although still biased toward the traditional Western calendar).

Notations are declared in the DTD and then used as the values of NOTATION-type attributes. To continue with the date example, Listing 12-1 defines two possible notations for dates in ISO 8601 and conventional U.S. formats. Then, a required FORMAT attribute of type NOTATION is added to each DATE element to describe the structure of the particular element.

Listing 12-1: DATE elements in an ISO 8601 and conventional U.S. formats

```
<?xml version="1.0" standalone="yes"?>
<!DOCTYPE SCHEDULE [

  <!NOTATION ISODATE SYSTEM
    "http://www.iso.ch/cate/d15903.html">
  <!NOTATION USDATE SYSTEM
    "http://www.boulder.nist.gov/timefreq/general/calendars/">

  <!ELEMENT SCHEDULE (APPOINTMENT*)>
  <!ELEMENT APPOINTMENT (NOTE, DATE, TIME?)>

  <!ELEMENT NOTE (#PCDATA)>
  <!ELEMENT DATE (#PCDATA)>
  <!ELEMENT TIME (#PCDATA)>

  <!ATTLIST DATE FORMAT NOTATION (ISODATE | USDATE) #IMPLIED>
]>
<SCHEDULE>
  <APPOINTMENT>
    <NOTE>Deliver presents</NOTE>
    <DATE FORMAT="USDATE">12-25-1999</DATE>
  </APPOINTMENT>
  <APPOINTMENT>
    <NOTE>Party like it's 1999</NOTE>
    <DATE FORMAT="ISODATE">19991231</DATE>
  </APPOINTMENT>
</SCHEDULE>
```

Notations can't force authors to use the format described by the notation. For that you need to use some sort of schema language in addition to basic XML — but it is sufficient for simple uses where you trust authors to correctly describe their data.

Unparsed Entities

XML is not an ideal format for all data, particularly nontext data. For instance, you could store each pixel of a bitmap image as an XML element like this:

```
<PIXEL X="232" Y="128" COLOR="FF5E32" />
```

This is hardly a good idea, though. Anything remotely like this would cause your image files to balloon to obscene proportions. Since you shouldn't encode all data in XML, XML documents must be capable of referring to data that is not currently XML and probably never will be.

A typical Web page may include GIF and JPEG images, Java applets, ActiveX controls, various kinds of sounds, and so forth. In XML, any block of non-XML data is called an *unparsed entity* because the XML parser won't attempt to understand it. At most, it informs the application of the entity's existence and provides the application with the entity's name and possibly (though not necessarily) its content.

HTML pages embed non-HTML entities through a variety of custom tags. Pictures are included with the `<IMG>` tag whose `SRC` attribute provides the URL of the image file. Java applets are embedded via the `<APPLET>` tag whose `CLASS` and `CODEBASE` attributes refer to the file and directory where the applet resides. The `<OBJECT>` tag uses its `CODEBASE` attribute for a Uniform Resource Identifier (URI) from which the object's data is retrieved. In each case, a particular predefined element represents a particular kind of content. A predefined attribute contains the URL for that content.

XML applications can work like this, but they don't have to. Instead, XML applications can use an unparsed entity to refer to the content. Unparsed entity declarations provide links to the actual location of the non-XML data. Then they use an `ENTITY`-type attribute to associate that entity with a particular element in the document.

Declaring unparsed entities

Recall from Chapter 10 that an external entity declaration looks like this:

```
<!ENTITY SIG SYSTEM "http://www.ibiblio.org/xml/signature.xml">
```

However, this form is only acceptable if the external entity that the URL names is well-formed XML. If the external entity is not XML, then you have to specify the entity's type using the NDATA keyword. For example, to associate the GIF file logo.gif with the name LOGO, you would place this ENTITY declaration in the DTD:

```
<!ENTITY LOGO SYSTEM "logo.gif" NDATA GIF>
```

The final word in the declaration, GIF in this example, must be the name of a notation declared in the DTD. For example, the notation for GIF might look like this:

```
<!NOTATION GIF SYSTEM "image/gif">
```

As usual, you can use absolute or relative URLs for the external entity as convenience dictates. For example,

```
<!ENTITY LOGO SYSTEM "http://www.ibiblio.org/xml/logo.gif"
   NDATA GIF>
<!ENTITY LOGO SYSTEM "/xml/logo.gif" NDATA GIF>
<!ENTITY LOGO SYSTEM "../logo.gif"   NDATA GIF>
```

Embedding unparsed entities

You cannot simply embed an unparsed entity at an arbitrary location in the document using a general entity reference as you can with parsed entities. For instance, Listing 12-2 is a malformed XML document because LOGO is an unparsed entity. If LOGO were a parsed entity, this example would be okay.

Listing 12-2: **A malformed XML document that tries to embed an unparsed entity with a general entity reference**

```
<?xml version="1.0" standalone="no"?>
<!DOCTYPE DOCUMENT [
  <!ELEMENT DOCUMENT ANY>
  <!ENTITY LOGO SYSTEM "http://www.ibiblio.org/xml/logo.gif"
     NDATA GIF>
  <!NOTATION GIF SYSTEM "image/gif">
]>
<DOCUMENT>
  &LOGO;
</DOCUMENT>
```

To embed unparsed entities, rather than using general entity references such as &LOGO;, you declare an element that serves as a placeholder for the unparsed entity (IMAGE, for example). Then you declare an ENTITY-type attribute for the IMAGE element (SOURCE, for example) that provides the name of the unparsed entity. Listing 12-3 demonstrates.

> **Listing 12-3: A valid XML document that correctly embeds an unparsed entity**

```
<?xml version="1.0" standalone="no"?>
<!DOCTYPE DOCUMENT [

  <!ELEMENT DOCUMENT ANY>
  <!ENTITY LOGO SYSTEM "http://www.ibiblio.org/xml/logo.gif"
     NDATA GIF>
  <!NOTATION GIF SYSTEM "image/gif">
  <!ELEMENT IMAGE EMPTY>
  <!ATTLIST IMAGE SOURCE ENTITY #REQUIRED>

]>
<DOCUMENT>
  <IMAGE SOURCE="LOGO" />
</DOCUMENT>
```

It is now up to the application reading the XML document to recognize the unparsed entity and display it. Applications may choose not to display the unparsed entity (just as a Web browser may choose not to load images when the user has disabled image loading).

These examples show empty elements as the containers for unparsed entities. That's not required, however. For instance, imagine an XML-based corporate ID system that a security guard uses to look up people entering a building. The PERSON element might have NAME, PHONE, OFFICE, and EMPLOYEE_ID children and a PHOTO ENTITY attribute. Listing 12-4 demonstrates.

> **Listing 12-4: A nonempty PERSON element with a PHOTO ENTITY attribute**

```
<?xml version="1.0" standalone="no"?>
<!DOCTYPE PERSON [
  <!ELEMENT  PERSON (NAME, EMPLOYEE_ID, PHONE, OFFICE)>
  <!ELEMENT  NAME         (#PCDATA)>
  <!ELEMENT  EMPLOYEE_ID  (#PCDATA)>
  <!ELEMENT  PHONE        (#PCDATA)>
  <!ELEMENT  OFFICE       (#PCDATA)>
  <!NOTATION JPEG SYSTEM "image/jpg">
  <!ENTITY   ROGER SYSTEM "rogers.jpg" NDATA JPEG>

  <!ATTLIST PERSON PHOTO ENTITY #REQUIRED>

]>
```

Continued

Listing 12-4 *(continued)*

```
<PERSON PHOTO="ROGER">
  <NAME>Jim Rogers</NAME>
  <EMPLOYEE_ID>4534</EMPLOYEE_ID>
  <PHONE>X396</PHONE>
  <OFFICE>RH 415A</OFFICE>
</PERSON>
```

This example may seem a little contrived. In practice, you'd be better advised to make an empty PHOTO element with a SOURCE attribute a child of a PERSON element rather than an attribute of PERSON. Furthermore, you'd probably separate the DTD into external and internal subsets. The external subset, shown in Listing 12-5, declares the elements, notations, and attributes. These are the parts likely to be shared among many different documents. The entity, however, changes from document to document. Thus, you can better place it in the internal DTD subset of each document as shown in Listing 12-6.

Listing 12-5: **The external DTD subset person.dtd**

```
<!ELEMENT   PERSON (NAME, EMPLOYEE_ID, PHONE, OFFICE, PHOTO)>
<!ELEMENT   NAME        (#PCDATA)>
<!ELEMENT   EMPLOYEE_ID (#PCDATA)>
<!ELEMENT   PHONE       (#PCDATA)>
<!ELEMENT   OFFICE      (#PCDATA)>
<!ELEMENT   PHOTO       EMPTY>
<!NOTATION JPEG SYSTEM "image/jpeg">
<!ATTLIST   PHOTO SOURCE ENTITY #REQUIRED>
```

Listing 12-6: **A document that uses an internal DTD subset to locate the unparsed entity**

```
<?xml version="1.0" standalone="no"?>
<!DOCTYPE PERSON [

  <!ENTITY % PERSON_DTD SYSTEM "person.dtd">
  %PERSON_DTD;
  <!ENTITY ROGER SYSTEM "rogers.jpg" NDATA JPEG>

]>
<PERSON>
```

```
        <NAME>Jim Rogers</NAME>
        <EMPLOYEE_ID>4534</EMPLOYEE_ID>
        <PHONE>X396</PHONE>
        <OFFICE>RH 415A</OFFICE>
        <PHOTO SOURCE="ROGER"/>
    </PERSON>
```

Embedding multiple unparsed entities

On rare occasions, you may need to refer to more than one unparsed entity in a single attribute, perhaps even an indefinite number. You can do this by declaring an attribute of the entity placeholder to have type ENTITIES. An ENTITIES-type attribute has a value part that consists of multiple unparsed entity names separated by white space. Each entity name refers to an external non-XML data source and must be declared in the DTD. For example, you might use this to write a slide show element that rotates different pictures. The DTD would require these declarations:

```
    <!ELEMENT   SLIDESHOW  EMPTY>
    <!ATTLIST   SLIDESHOW  SOURCES ENTITIES #REQUIRED>
    <!NOTATION  JPEG       SYSTEM "image/jpeg">
    <!ENTITY    CHARM      SYSTEM "charm.jpg"    NDATA JPEG>
    <!ENTITY    MARJORIE   SYSTEM "marjorie.jpg" NDATA JPEG>
    <!ENTITY    POSSUM     SYSTEM "possum.jpg"   NDATA JPEG>
    <!ENTITY    BLUE       SYSTEM "blue.jpg"     NDATA JPEG>
```

Then, at the point in the document where you want the slide show to appear, insert the following element:

```
    <SLIDESHOW SOURCES="CHARM MARJORIE POSSUM BLUE"/>
```

Caution   Once again, I must emphasize that this is not a magic formula that all (or even any) XML browsers automatically understand. It is simply one technique that browsers and other applications may or may not adopt to embed non-XML data in documents.

Processing Instructions

HTML comments are often abused to support proprietary extensions such as server-side includes, browser-specific scripting languages, database templates, and several dozen other items outside the purview of the HTML standard. The advantage of using comments for these purposes is that other systems simply ignore the data they don't understand. The disadvantage of this approach is that a document stripped of its comments may no longer be the same document, and that comments intended as mere documentation may be unintentionally processed as input to these proprietary extensions. To avoid this misuse of comments, XML provides the *processing instruction* — an explicit mechanism for embedding information in a file intended for applications that receive data from the XML parser rather than for the XML parser itself. Among other uses, processing instructions can provide additional information about how to view unparsed external entities.

A processing instruction is a string of text between <? and ?> marks. The only required syntax for the text inside the processing instruction is that it must begin with an XML name that is followed by white space that is then followed by data. The XML name may either be the actual name of the application (e.g., latex) or the name of a notation in the DTD that points to the application (e.g., LATEX) where LATEX is declared like this in the DTD:

```
<!NOTATION LATEX SYSTEM "/usr/local/bin/latex">
```

It may also be a general-purpose name, such as xml-stylesheet, that is recognized by many different applications.

The syntax of the processing instruction data is deliberately left unspecified. The details tend to be very specific to the application for which the processing instruction is intended. Indeed, most applications that rely on processing instructions will impose more structure on the contents of a processing instruction. For example, consider this processing instruction used in IBM's Bean Markup Language:

```
<?bmlpi register demos.calculator.EventSourceText2Int?>
```

The name of this processing instruction is bmlpi. Any application that recognizes this name will ask the parser for the data. This data is the string register demos.calculator.EventSourceText2Int, which happens to include the full package qualified name of a Java class. This tells the application named bmlpi to use the Java class demos.calculator.EventSourceText2Int to convert action events to integers. If bmlpi encounters this processing instruction while reading the document, it will load the class demos.calculator.EventSourceText2Int and use it to convert events to integers from that point on.

If this sounds fairly specific and detailed, that's because it is. Unless you're using the Bean Markup Language, you don't need to know it. Processing instructions are not part of the general structure of the document. They are intended to provide extra, detailed information for particular applications, not for every application that reads the document. If some other application encounters this instruction while reading a document, it will simply ignore the instruction.

Processing instructions may be placed almost anywhere in an XML document except inside a tag or a CDATA section. They may appear in the prolog or in the DTD, in the content of an element, or even after the root element's end tag. Because processing instructions are not elements, they do not affect the tree structure of a document. You do not need to open or close processing instructions, or worry about how they nest inside other elements. Processing instructions are not tags, and they do not delimit elements.

You're already familiar with one example of processing instructions, the xml-stylesheet processing instruction used to bind style sheets to documents:

```
<?xml-stylesheet type="text/xml" href="baseball.xsl"?>
```

Although this example appears in a document's prolog, in general processing instructions may appear anywhere in a document. You do not need to declare these instructions as child elements of the element they are contained in because they're not elements.

Processing instructions with the name xml , XML, XmL, and so forth, in any other combination of case, are reserved. Otherwise, you are free to use any name and any string of text inside a processing instruction other than the closing string ?>. For instance, the following examples are all legal processing instructions:

```
<?cocoon-process type="xslt"?>
<?gcc HelloWorld.c ?>
<?html
  <h2>Composers</h2>
  <ul>
    <li>John Cage
    <li>Ruth Anderson
    <li>Pauline Oliveros
  </ul>
?>
<?acrobat document="passport.pdf"?>
<?Dave Remember to replace this with the real data
      before publishing?>
```

Note   Remember that an XML parser won't necessarily do anything with these instructions. It merely passes them along to the application. The application decides what to do with the instructions. Most applications simply ignore processing instructions they don't understand.

Sometimes knowing the type of an unparsed external entity is insufficient. You may also need to know what program to run to view the entity and what parameters you need to provide that program. You can use a processing instruction to provide this information. Because processing instructions can contain fairly arbitrary data, it's relatively easy for them to contain instructions determining what action the external program listed in the notation should take.

Such a processing instruction can range from simply the name of a program that can view the file to several kilobytes of configuration information. Of course, the application and the document author must use the same means of determining which processing instructions belong with which unparsed external entities. Listing 12-7 shows one scheme that uses a processing instruction and a PDF notation to try to pass the PDF version of a physics paper to Acrobat Reader for display.

Listing 12-7: **Embedding a PDF document in XML**

```
<?xml version="1.0" standalone="yes"?>
<!DOCTYPE PAPER [

  <!NOTATION PDF PUBLIC
      "-//IETF//NONSGML Media Type application/pdf//EN"
      "http://www.isi.edu/in-notes/iana/assignments/media-
types/application/pdf">
    <!ELEMENT PAPER (TITLE, AUTHOR+)>
    <!ATTLIST PAPER CONTENTS ENTITY #IMPLIED>
    <!ENTITY P0007053 SYSTEM
        "http://xxx.lanl.gov/pdf/astro-ph/0007053?"
        NDATA PDF
    >

    <!ELEMENT AUTHOR (#PCDATA)>
    <!ELEMENT TITLE (#PCDATA)>

]>

<?PDF acroread?>
<PAPER CONTENTS="P0007053">
  <TITLE>
    Influence of the Magnetic Field on the Fermion
    Scattering off Bubble and Kink Walls
  </TITLE>
  <AUTHOR>P. Cea</AUTHOR>
  <AUTHOR>G. L. Fogli</AUTHOR>
  <AUTHOR>L. Tedesco</AUTHOR>
</PAPER>
```

As always, you have to remember that not every XML processor will treat this example in the way intended. In fact, it's entirely possible that no processor will. However, this is one possible scheme for how an application might support PDF files and other non-XML media types.

Conditional Sections in DTDs

When developing DTDs or documents, you may need to comment out parts of the DTD not yet reflected in the documents. In addition to using comments directly, you can omit a particular group of declarations in the DTD by wrapping it in an `IGNORE` directive. The syntax follows:

```
<![ IGNORE [
  declarations that are ignored
]]>
```

As usual, white space doesn't really affect the syntax, but you should keep the opening `<![ IGNORE [` and the closing `]]>` on separate lines for easy viewing.

You can ignore any declaration or combination of declarations — elements, entities, attributes, or even other `IGNORE` blocks — but you must ignore entire declarations. The `IGNORE` construct must completely enclose the entire declaration it removes from the DTD. You cannot ignore a piece of a declaration (such as the `NDATA GIF` in an unparsed entity declaration).

You can also specify that a particular section of declarations is included — that is, not ignored. The syntax for the `INCLUDE` directive is just like the `IGNORE` directive but with a different keyword:

```
<![ INCLUDE [
  declarations that are included
]]>
```

When an `INCLUDE` is inside an `IGNORE`, the `INCLUDE` and its declarations are ignored. When an `IGNORE` is inside an `INCLUDE`, the declarations inside the `IGNORE` block are still ignored. In other words, an `INCLUDE` never overrides an `IGNORE`.

Given these conditions, you may wonder why `INCLUDE` even exists. No DTD would change if all `INCLUDE` blocks were simply removed, leaving only their contents. `INCLUDE` appears to be completely extraneous. However, there is one neat trick with parameter entity references and both `IGNORE` and `INCLUDE` that you can't do with `IGNORE` alone. First, define a parameter entity reference as follows:

```
<!ENTITY % fulldtd "IGNORE">
```

You can ignore elements by wrapping them in the following construct:

```
<![ %fulldtd; [
  declarations
]]>
```

The `%fulldtd;` parameter entity reference evaluates to `IGNORE`, so the declarations are ignored. Now, suppose you make the one-word edit to change `fulldtd` from `IGNORE` to `INCLUDE` as follows:

```
<!ENTITY % fulldtd "INCLUDE">
```

Immediately, all the `IGNORE` blocks convert to `INCLUDE` blocks. In effect, you have a one-line switch to turn blocks on or off.

In this example, I've only used one switch, `fulldtd`. You can use this switch in multiple `IGNORE/INCLUDE` blocks in the DTD. You can also have different groups of `IGNORE/INCLUDE` blocks that you switch on or off based on different conditions.

You'll find this capability particularly useful when designing DTDs for inclusion in other DTDs. The ultimate DTD can change the behavior of the DTDs it embeds by changing the value of the parameter entity switch.

Summary

In this chapter, you learned how to integrate non-XML data into your XML documents through notations, unparsed entities, and processing instructions. In particular, you learned that:

✦ Notations define a data type for non-XML data using a `NOTATION` declaration.

✦ Unparsed entities are storage units containing non-XML text or binary data.

✦ Unparsed entities are defined in the DTD using an `ENTITY` declaration with an extra `NDATA` declaration identifying the type of the data through a notation name.

✦ Documents include unparsed entities using `ENTITY` or `ENTITIES` attributes.

✦ Processing instructions contain data passed along unchanged from the XML processor to the ultimate application.

✦ `INCLUDE` and `IGNORE` blocks specify that the enclosed declarations of the DTD are or are not (respectively) to be considered when parsing the document.

You'll see a lot more examples of documents with DTDs over the next several parts of this book, but as far as basic syntax and usage goes, this chapter concludes the exploration of DTDs. However, there's one more fundamental technology that you need to add to your toolbox before you've got a complete picture of XML itself. That technology is namespaces, a way of attaching prefixes and URIs to element and attribute names so that applications can tell the difference between elements and attributes from different XML vocabularies, even when they have the same names. The next chapter explores namespaces.

✦   ✦   ✦

Namespaces

♦ ♦ ♦ ♦

In This Chapter

The need for namespaces

Namespace syntax

Namespaces and validity

♦ ♦ ♦ ♦

No XML is an island. While documents that use a single markup vocabulary are useful (witness the baseball examples of Chapters 4 and 5), documents that mix and match markup from different XML applications are even more functional. For example, imagine you want to include a BIOG-RAPHY element in each PLAYER element. Since the biography consists basically of free-form, formatted text, it's convenient to write it in well-formed HTML without reinventing all the elements for paragraphs, line breaks, list items, boldface, and so forth from scratch.

The problem, however, is that when mixing and matching elements from different XML applications, you're likely to find the same name used for two different things. Is a TITLE the title of a page, the title of a book, or the title of a person? Is an ADDRESS the mailing address of a company or the e-mail address of a webmaster? Namespaces disambiguate these cases by associating a URI with each XML application and attaching a prefix to each element to indicate which URI it's associated with. Thus, you can have both BOOK:TITLE and HTML:TITLE elements or POSTAL:ADDRESS and HTML:ADDRESS elements instead of just one kind of TITLE or ADDRESS. This chapter shows you how to use namespaces.

Caution If you're familiar with namespaces as used in C++ and other programming languages, you need to put aside your preconceptions before reading further. XML namespaces are similar to, but not quite the same as, the namespaces used in programming. In particular, XML namespaces do not necessarily form a set (a collection with no duplicates).

The Need for Namespaces

XML enables developers to create their own markup languages for their own projects. These languages can be shared with people working on similar projects all over the world. One specific example of this is Scalable Vector Graphics

(SVG). SVG is an XML application that describes line art such as might be produced by CorelDRAW or Visio. SVG documents are embedded in HTML or XHTML documents to add vector graphics to Web pages. SVG elements include desc, title, metadata, defs, path, text, rect, circle, ellipse, line, polyline, polygon, use, image, svg, g, view, switch, a, altGlyphDef, script, style, symbol, marker, clipPath, mask, linearGradient, radialGradient, pattern, filter, cursor, font, animate, set, animateMotion, animateColor, animateTransform, color-profile, and font-face. Five of these — title, a, script, style, and font — happen to share names with HTML elements. Several others conflict with other XML vocabularies you might want to embed in an HTML document. For instance, MathML uses set to mean a mathematical set; the Resource Description Framework (RDF) uses title to refer to the title of a resource.

How is a browser reading a document that mixes HTML, SVG, and RDF supposed to know whether any given title element is an HTML title, an SVG title, or an RDF title? Perhaps the browser could have enough knowledge of where the different kinds of SVG pictures, RDF metadata, MathML equations, and other extra-HTML vocabularies are supposed to appear to be able to tell which is which. But what is the browser supposed to do when it encounters conflicts with nonstandard vocabularies that it hasn't seen before and of which it has no understanding? XML is designed to allow authors and developers to extend it with their own elements in an infinite variety of ways. When authors begin mixing and matching tag sets created by different developers, name conflicts are almost inevitable.

Namespaces are the solution. They allow each element and attribute in a document to be placed in a different namespace mapped to a particular URI. The XML elements that come from SVG are placed in the http://www.w3.org/2000/svg namespace. The XML elements that come from XHTML are placed in the http://www.w3.org/1999/xhtml namespace. MathML goes in the http://www.w3.org/1998/Math/MathML namespace. If you mix in elements from some vocabulary you created yourself, you can place that in another namespace, with a URI somewhere in a domain you own.

Note A URI (Uniform Resource Identifier) is an abstraction of a URL. Whereas a URL *locates* a resource, a URI *identifies* a resource. For instance, a URI for a person might include that person's social security number. This doesn't mean you can look the person up in a Web browser using a person URI. In practice, most URIs that are actually used today, including most URIs that are used for namespaces, are in fact URLs.

This URI doesn't even have to point at any particular file. The URI that defines a namespace is purely formal. Its only purpose is to group and disambiguate element and attribute names in the document. It does not necessarily point to anything. In particular, *there is no guarantee that the document at the namespace URI describes the syntax used in the document; or, for that matter, that any document exists at the*

URI. Most namespace URIs produce "404 Not Found" errors when you attempt to resolve them. Having said that, if there is a canonical URI for a particular XML application, then that URI is a good choice for the namespace definition.

Namespaces have been carefully crafted to layer on top of the XML 1.0 specification. Other than reserving the colon character to separate prefixes and local names, namespaces have no direct effect on standard XML syntax. An XML 1.0 processor that knows nothing about namespaces can still read a document that uses namespaces, and will not find any errors. Conversely, a document that uses namespaces must still be well-formed when read by a processor that knows nothing about namespaces. If the document is validated, then it must be validated without specifically considering the namespaces. To an XML processor, a document that uses namespaces is just a funny-looking document in which some of the element and attribute names have a single colon. Documents that use namespaces do not break existing XML parsers; and users don't have to wait for notoriously unpunctual software companies to release expensive upgrades before using namespaces.

Caution   *Namespaces in XML* is an official W3C recommendation. The W3C considers it complete, aside from possible minor errors and elucidations. Nonetheless, of all the finished XML specifications from the W3C, this one is the most controversial. Many people feel very strongly that this standard contains fundamental flaws. The main objection is that namespaces are, in practice, incompatible with DTDs. While I don't have a strong opinion on this one way or the other, I do question the wisdom of publishing a standard when nothing approaching a consensus has been reached. Namespaces are a crucial part of many XML-related specifications such as XSL and XHTML, so you need to understand them. Nonetheless, a lot of developers and authors have chosen to ignore this specification for their own work.

Namespace Syntax

Suppose you're a webmaster at a small agency in Hollywood that represents screenwriters. You want a Web page that describes the scripts currently available for auction from the agency's clients. The basic page that provides the list is written in HTML. The information about each client is given in some industry standard DTD for describing people that produces PERSON elements that look like this:

```
<PERSON>
  <FIRST>Larry</FIRST>
  <LAST>Smith</LAST>
  <TITLE>Mr.</TITLE>
</PERSON>
```

The information about screenplays is provided in SCRIPT elements that look like this:

```
<SCRIPT>
  <TITLE>New York Stories</TITLE>
  <AUTHOR>
    <PERSON>
      <FIRST>Larry</FIRST>
      <LAST>Smith</LAST>
      <TITLE>Mr.</TITLE>
    </PERSON>
  </AUTHOR>
  <SYNOPSIS>
    Six friends with no visible means of support nonetheless
    manage to live in improbably large apartments in
    Manhattan.
  </SYNOPSIS>
</SCRIPT>
```

The entire document might look something like Listing 13-1.

Listing 13-1: A well-formed XML document that uses HTML and two custom XML applications

```
<HTML>
  <HEAD><TITLE>Screenplays for Auction</TITLE></HEAD>
  <BODY>
    <H1>January 27, 2001 Auction</H1>

    <P>Pilot scripts for the Fall season:</P>

    <SCRIPT>
      <TITLE>Chicken Feathers</TITLE>
      <AUTHOR>
        <PERSON>
          <FIRST>William</FIRST>
          <LAST>Sanders</LAST>
          <TITLE>Col.</TITLE>
        </PERSON>
      </AUTHOR>
      <SYNOPSIS>
        Hijinks in a poultry factory
      </SYNOPSIS>
    </SCRIPT>

    <SCRIPT>
      <TITLE>Soft Copy</TITLE>
      <AUTHOR>
```

```
        <PERSON>
          <FIRST>Nora</FIRST>
          <LAST>Lessinger</LAST>
          <TITLE>Dr.</TITLE>
        </PERSON>
      </AUTHOR>
      <SYNOPSIS>Sex lives of the rich and famous</SYNOPSIS>
    </SCRIPT>

    Send inquiries to
    <PERSON>
      <TITLE>Mr.</TITLE>,
      <FIRST>Mikhail</FIRST>
      <LAST>Ovitsky</LAST>
      <COMPANY>Duplicative Artists Mismanagement</COMPANY>,
      <ADDRESS>135 Agents Row, Hollywood, CA 90123</ADDRESS>
    </PERSON>

  </BODY>
</HTML>
```

There are several problems with this document, even though it's well-formed XML. Some of the elements used as part of the custom vocabularies conflict with each other and with standard HTML. The first problem is that the TITLE element is used for three separate things: The title of the page, the title of a script, and the title of a person. The second problem may be even worse in practice. The SCRIPT element conflicts with the HTML SCRIPT element. A Web browser reading this document may try to interpret the contents of the SCRIPT element as a JavaScript program. Even though this particular page doesn't use any JavaScript, an HTML renderer, even one that supports XML embedded in HTML documents, is still going to think that a SCRIPT element contains JavaScript. These sorts of problems crop up all the time when you mix and match different XML vocabularies. In this case, the problem is the attempt to merge three different vocabularies — one for persons, one for scripts, and one for Web pages — that were designed without much concern for each other.

For that matter, even if you're lucky and the names don't conflict, how is an XML browser supposed to be able to distinguish between groups of elements from different vocabularies? For instance, a studio robot might want to collect script proposals from various agencies by harvesting all the SCRIPT elements that contain synopses while ignoring all the JavaScript. You can fix all these problems by adding name-spaces to the document. Namespaces identify which elements in the document belong to which XML vocabularies.

Defining namespaces with xmlns attributes

The script auction example uses elements from three different vocabularies, so three different namespaces are needed. Each namespace has a URI. You can choose any convenient absolute URI in a domain that you own for the namespace. In this example, I use the URI `http://ns.cafeconleche.org/people/` for the person application because I happen to own the cafeconleche.org domain.

> **Note**
>
> The URI you choose does not have to refer to anything. There does not have to be a DTD or a schema or any other page at all at the location identified by the namespace URI. In fact, there isn't even a host named ns.cafeconleche.org. A namespace URI is nothing more than a formal identifier that helps to distinguish between elements with the same name from different organizations. URIs were chosen for this purpose because they allow developers to choose their own namespace URIs without having to create yet another central registration authority.

However, URIs often contain characters that can't appear in XML element and attribute names. For example, `http://ns.cafeconleche.org/people:first` is not a legal name for an XML element because it contains forward slashes. Therefore you have to associate the URI with a prefix and put the prefix in the element name instead. The prefixes are generally some abbreviated form of the thing that the XML application describes. For the person application, you might choose the prefix P, p, or PE, or perhaps even `person` or `PEOPLE`. In this example, I use P as the prefix for the person vocabulary with the associated URI `http://ns.cafeconleche.org/people/`.

You associate a namespace URI with a prefix by adding an `xmlns:prefix` attribute to the elements they apply to. `prefix` is replaced by the actual prefix used for the namespace. The value of the attribute is the URI of the namespace. For example, this `xmlns:P` attribute associates the prefix P with the URI `http://ns.cafeconleche.org/people/`.

```
xmlns:P="http://ns.cafeconleche.org/people/"
```

Once this attribute is added to an element, the P prefix can then be attached to that element's name as well as the names of all its attributes and descendants. Within that element the P prefix identifies something as belonging to the `http://ns.cafeconleche.org/people/` namespace. The prefix is attached to the local name by a colon. Listing 13-2 demonstrates this by adding the P prefix to the PERSON, FIRST, and LAST elements, as well as those TITLE elements that come from the people application, but not to the TITLE elements that come from HTML or the script application.

Listing 13-2: **Placing the person application elements in a separate namespace**

```
<HTML>
  <HEAD><TITLE>Screenplays for Auction</TITLE></HEAD>
  <BODY>
    <H1>January 27, 2001 Auction</H1>

    <P>Pilot scripts for the Fall season:</P>

    <SCRIPT>
      <TITLE>Chicken Feathers</TITLE>
      <AUTHOR>
        <P:PERSON xmlns:P="http://ns.cafeconleche.org/people/">
          <P:FIRST>William</P:FIRST>
          <P:LAST>Sanders</P:LAST>
          <P:TITLE>Col.</P:TITLE>
        </P:PERSON>
      </AUTHOR>
      <SYNOPSIS>
        Hijinks in a poultry factory
      </SYNOPSIS>
    </SCRIPT>

    <SCRIPT>
      <TITLE>Soft Copy</TITLE>
      <AUTHOR>
        <P:PERSON xmlns:P="http://ns.cafeconleche.org/people/">
          <P:FIRST>Nora</P:FIRST>
          <P:LAST>Lessinger</P:LAST>
          <P:TITLE>Dr.</P:TITLE>
        </P:PERSON>
      </AUTHOR>
      <SYNOPSIS>Sex lives of the rich and famous</SYNOPSIS>
    </SCRIPT>

    Send inquiries to
    <P:PERSON xmlns:P="http://ns.cafeconleche.org/people/">
      <P:TITLE>Mr.</P:TITLE>,
      <P:FIRST>Mikhail</P:FIRST>
      <P:LAST>Ovitsky</P:LAST>
      <P:COMPANY>Duplicative Artists Mismanagement</P:COMPANY>,
      <P:ADDRESS>
        135 Agents Row, Hollywood, CA 90123
      </P:ADDRESS>
    </P:PERSON>

  </BODY>
</HTML>
```

It's now quite easy to distinguish between the title of the page and the title of a person. The first is represented by a TITLE element, while the second is represented by a P:TITLE element.

The elements with the P prefix are said to have *qualified names* beginning with the P prefix:

- ✦ P:PERSON
- ✦ P:TITLE
- ✦ P:FIRST
- ✦ P:LAST
- ✦ P:COMPANY
- ✦ P:ADDRESS

The part of the name after the colon is called the *local name*. These six elements have these six local names:

- ✦ PERSON
- ✦ TITLE
- ✦ FIRST
- ✦ LAST
- ✦ COMPANY
- ✦ ADDRESS

The prefix can change as long as the URI and the local names stay the same. The true names of these elements are based on the URI rather than on the prefix. Thus, the abstract true names of these six elements have a form like this:

- ✦ http://ns.cafeconleche.org/people/:PERSON
- ✦ http://ns.cafeconleche.org/people/:TITLE
- ✦ http://ns.cafeconleche.org/people/:FIRST
- ✦ http://ns.cafeconleche.org/people/:LAST
- ✦ http://ns.cafeconleche.org/people/:COMPANY
- ✦ http://ns.cafeconleche.org/people/:ADDRESS

However, you'll never use a name like this anywhere in an XML document. In essence, the shorter qualified names are mandatory nicknames that are used within the document because URIs often contain characters such as ~, %, and / that aren't legal in XML names.

A namespace prefix can be any legal XML name that does not contain a colon. Recall from Chapter 6 that a legal XML name must begin with a letter or an underscore (_). Subsequent letters in the name may include letters, digits, underscores, hyphens, and periods. They may not include white space.

Note Two prefixes are specifically disallowed, xml and xmlns. The xml prefix should only be used for the xml:space and xml:lang attributes defined in the XML 1.0 specification. The prefix xml is automatically mapped to the URI http://www.w3.org/XML/1998/namespace. The xmlns prefix is used to bind elements to namespaces, and is therefore not available as a prefix to be bound to.

Multiple namespaces

The difference between the title of a page and the title of a script is still up in the air, as is the difference between a screenplay SCRIPT and a JavaScript SCRIPT. To fix this, you need to add another namespace to the document. This time, I use the prefix SCR and the URI http://ns.cafeconleche.org/scripts/. Defining this mapping requires adding this attribute to all the SCRIPT elements:

```
xmlns:SCR="http://ns.cafeconleche.org/scripts/"
```

Alternately, instead of placing the declaration of the SCR namespace prefix on all SCRIPT elements, I can put it on one element that contains them all. There are two such elements in the example, HTML and BODY. When the namespace declaration is not placed directly on the start tag that begins the vocabulary, it's generally put on the root element. Listing 13-3 does exactly this.

Listing 13-3: Declaring a namespace on the root element

```
<HTML xmlns:SCR="http://ns.cafeconleche.org/scripts/">
  <HEAD><TITLE>Screenplays for Auction</TITLE></HEAD>
  <BODY>
    <H1>January 27, 2001 Auction</H1>

    <P>Pilot scripts for the Fall season:</P>

    <SCR:SCRIPT>
      <SCR:TITLE>Chicken Feathers</SCR:TITLE>
      <SCR:AUTHOR>
        <P:PERSON xmlns:P="http://ns.cafeconleche.org/people/">
          <P:FIRST>William</P:FIRST>
          <P:LAST>Sanders</P:LAST>
          <P:TITLE>Col.</P:TITLE>
```

Continued

Listing 13-3 *(continued)*

```
      </P:PERSON>
    </SCR:AUTHOR>
    <SCR:SYNOPSIS>
      Hijinks in a poultry factory
    </SCR:SYNOPSIS>
  </SCR:SCRIPT>

  <SCR:SCRIPT>
    <SCR:TITLE>Soft Copy</SCR:TITLE>
    <SCR:AUTHOR>
      <P:PERSON xmlns:P="http://ns.cafeconleche.org/people/">
        <P:FIRST>Nora</P:FIRST>
        <P:LAST>Lessinger</P:LAST>
        <P:TITLE>Dr.</P:TITLE>
      </P:PERSON>
    </SCR:AUTHOR>
    <SCR:SYNOPSIS>Sex lives of the rich and famous
    </SCR:SYNOPSIS>
  </SCR:SCRIPT>

  Send inquiries to
  <P:PERSON xmlns:P="http://ns.cafeconleche.org/people/">
    <P:TITLE>Mr.</P:TITLE>,
    <P:FIRST>Mikhail</P:FIRST>
    <P:LAST>Ovitsky</P:LAST>
    <P:COMPANY>Duplicative Artists Mismanagement</P:COMPANY>,
    <P:ADDRESS>
      135 Agents Row, Hollywood, CA 90123
    </P:ADDRESS>
  </P:PERSON>

  </BODY>
</HTML>
```

Whether you choose to declare a namespace on the root element or on some element further down the hierarchy is mostly a matter of personal preference and convenience in the document at hand. Some developers prefer to declare all namespaces on the root element. Others prefer to declare the namespaces closer to where they're actually used. XML doesn't care. For example, Listing 13-3 could have equally well been written as shown in Listing 13-4, with both the SCR and P prefixes declared on the root element.

Listing 13-4: **Declaring all namespaces on the root element**

```
<HTML xmlns:SCR="http://ns.cafeconleche.org/scripts/"
      xmlns:P="http://ns.cafeconleche.org/people/">
  <HEAD><TITLE>Screenplays for Auction</TITLE></HEAD>
  <BODY>
    <H1>January 27, 2001 Auction</H1>

    <P>Pilot scripts for the Fall season:</P>

    <SCR:SCRIPT>
      <SCR:TITLE>Chicken Feathers</SCR:TITLE>
      <SCR:AUTHOR>
        <P:PERSON>
          <P:FIRST>William</P:FIRST>
          <P:LAST>Sanders</P:LAST>
          <P:TITLE>Col.</P:TITLE>
        </P:PERSON>
      </SCR:AUTHOR>
      <SCR:SYNOPSIS>
        Hijinks in a poultry factory
      </SCR:SYNOPSIS>
    </SCR:SCRIPT>

    <SCR:SCRIPT>
      <SCR:TITLE>Soft Copy</SCR:TITLE>
      <SCR:AUTHOR>
        <P:PERSON>
          <P:FIRST>Nora</P:FIRST>
          <P:LAST>Lessinger</P:LAST>
          <P:TITLE>Dr.</P:TITLE>
        </P:PERSON>
      </SCR:AUTHOR>
      <SCR:SYNOPSIS>Sex lives of the rich and famous
      </SCR:SYNOPSIS>
    </SCR:SCRIPT>

    Send inquiries to
    <P:PERSON>
      <P:TITLE>Mr.</P:TITLE>,
      <P:FIRST>Mikhail</P:FIRST>
      <P:LAST>Ovitsky</P:LAST>
      <P:COMPANY>Duplicative Artists Mismanagement</P:COMPANY>,
      <P:ADDRESS>
        135 Agents Row, Hollywood, CA 90123
      </P:ADDRESS>
    </P:PERSON>

  </BODY>
</HTML>
```

In most cases (validation against a DTD being the notable exception), it's the URI that's important, not the prefix. The prefixes can change. As long as the URI stays the same the meaning of the document is unchanged. For example, Listing 13-5 uses the prefixes PERSON and SCRIPT instead of P and SCR. However, this document is effectively the same as Listing 13-4.

Listing 13-5: **Same document, different prefixes**

```
<HTML xmlns:SCRIPT="http://ns.cafeconleche.org/scripts/"
      xmlns:PERSON="http://ns.cafeconleche.org/people/">
  <HEAD><TITLE>Screenplays for Auction</TITLE></HEAD>
  <BODY>
    <H1>January 27, 2001 Auction</H1>

    <P>Pilot scripts for the Fall season:</P>

  <SCRIPT:SCRIPT>
    <SCRIPT:TITLE>Chicken Feathers</SCRIPT:TITLE>
    <SCRIPT:AUTHOR>
      <PERSON:PERSON>
        <PERSON:FIRST>William</PERSON:FIRST>
        <PERSON:LAST>Sanders</PERSON:LAST>
        <PERSON:TITLE>Col.</PERSON:TITLE>
      </PERSON:PERSON>
    </SCRIPT:AUTHOR>
    <SCRIPT:SYNOPSIS>
      Hijinks in a poultry factory
    </SCRIPT:SYNOPSIS>
  </SCRIPT:SCRIPT>

  <SCRIPT:SCRIPT>
    <SCRIPT:TITLE>Soft Copy</SCRIPT:TITLE>
    <SCRIPT:AUTHOR>
      <PERSON:PERSON>
        <PERSON:FIRST>Nora</PERSON:FIRST>
        <PERSON:LAST>Lessinger</PERSON:LAST>
        <PERSON:TITLE>Dr.</PERSON:TITLE>
      </PERSON:PERSON>
    </SCRIPT:AUTHOR>
    <SCRIPT:SYNOPSIS>Sex lives of the rich and famous
    </SCRIPT:SYNOPSIS>
  </SCRIPT:SCRIPT>

    Send inquiries to
  <PERSON:PERSON>
    <PERSON:TITLE>Mr.</PERSON:TITLE>,
    <PERSON:FIRST>Mikhail</PERSON:FIRST>
    <PERSON:LAST>Ovitsky</PERSON:LAST>
    <PERSON:COMPANY>Duplicative Artists Mismanagement
```

```
      </PERSON:COMPANY>
      <PERSON:ADDRESS>
        135 Agents Row, Hollywood, CA 90123
      </PERSON:ADDRESS>
    </PERSON:PERSON>

  </BODY>
</HTML>
```

In fact, it's even possible to redeclare prefixes so that one prefix refers to different URIs in different places in the document, or so that two different prefixes refer to the same URI. This is, however, needlessly confusing; and I strongly recommend that you don't do it. There are more than enough prefixes to go around, and almost no need to reuse them within the same document. The main importance of this is if two different documents from different authors that happen to reuse a similar prefix are being combined. This is a good reason to avoid short prefixes such as A, S, and X that are likely to be reused for different purposes.

Attributes

Because attributes belong to particular elements, they're more easily distinguished from similarly named attributes without namespaces. Consequently, it's not nearly as essential to add namespaces to attributes as to elements. For example, the XSLT specification requires that all XSL transformation elements fall in the http://www. w3.org/1999/XSL/Transform namespace. However, it does not require that the attributes of these elements be in any particular namespace. (In fact, it requires that they *not* be in any namespace.) Nonetheless, you can attach namespace prefixes to attributes if necessary. For example, all the attributes in this SCRIPT element and its children live in the http://namespaces.cafeconleche.org/scripts/ namespace.

```
<SCR:SCRIPT SCR:TYPE="Sitcom"
           SCR:COPYRIGHT="2001 William Sanders"
  xmlns:SCR="http://namespaces.cafeconleche.org/scripts/"
  xmlns:P="http://namespaces.cafeconleche.org/people/">
  <SCR:TITLE SCR:ALT="NO">Chicken Feathers</SCR:TITLE>
  <SCR:AUTHOR SCR:ID="A67Y">
    <P:PERSON>
      <P:FIRST>William</P:FIRST>
      <P:LAST>Sanders</P:LAST>
      <P:TITLE>Col.</P:TITLE>
    </P:PERSON>
  </SCR:AUTHOR>
  <SCR:SYNOPSIS SCR:LANG="English">
    Hijinks in a poultry factory
  </SCR:SYNOPSIS>
</SCR:SCRIPT>
```

This might occasionally prove useful if you need to combine attributes from two different XML applications on the same element. XLink uses prefixed attributes to allow any element to become a link.

Cross-Reference XLinks are discussed in Chapter 20.

It is possible (though mostly pointless) to associate the same namespace URI with two different prefixes. There's really no reason to do this. The only reason I bring it up here is simply to warn you that it is the true name of the attribute that must satisfy XML's rules for an element not having more than one attribute with the same name. For example, this code is illegal because SCR:ID and SCRIPT:ID are the same:

```
<SCR:SCRIPT SCR:TYPE="Sitcom"
           SCR:COPYRIGHT="2001 William Sanders"
  xmlns:SCR="http://namespaces.cafeconleche.org/scripts/"
  xmlns:SCRIPT="http://namespaces.cafeconleche.org/scripts/"
  xmlns:P="http://namespaces.cafeconleche.org/people/">
  <SCR:TITLE SCR:ID="A67Y" SCRIPT:ID="Y76A">
    Chicken Feathers
  </SCR:TITLE>
</SCR:SCRIPT>
```

On the other hand, the parser does not actually check the URI to see what it points to. The URIs http://ibiblio.org/xml/ and http://www.ibiblio.org/xml/ point to the same page. However, this code is legal:

```
<SCR:SCRIPT SCR:TYPE="Sitcom"
           SCR:COPYRIGHT="2001 William Sanders"
  xmlns:SCR="http://ibiblio.org/xml/"
  xmlns:SCRIPT="http://www.ibiblio.org/xml/"
  xmlns:P="http://namespaces.cafeconleche.org/people/">
  <SCR:TITLE SCR:ID="A67Y" SCRIPT:ID="Y76A">
    Chicken Feathers
  </SCR:TITLE>
</SCR:SCRIPT>
```

Default namespaces

In long documents with a lot of markup, all in the same namespace, you might find it inconvenient to add a prefix to each element name. You can attach a default namespace to an element and to its descendants using an xmlns attribute with no prefix. The element itself and all its descendants are considered to be in the defined namespace unless they have an explicit prefix.

For example, you may wish to place the HTML elements in the script auction example in a namespace of their own, but not to give them any prefixes so that legacy browsers will still recognize them. Listing 13-6 does exactly this.

Listing 13-6: **Placing the HTML elements in the same namespace**

```
<HTML xmlns="http://www.w3.org/1999/xhtml"
     xmlns:SCRIPT="http://ns.cafeconleche.org/scripts/"
     xmlns:PERSON="http://ns.cafeconleche.org/people/">
  <HEAD><TITLE>Screenplays for Auction</TITLE></HEAD>
  <BODY>
    <H1>January 27, 2001 Auction</H1>

    <P>Pilot scripts for the Fall season:</P>

    <SCRIPT:SCRIPT>
      <SCRIPT:TITLE>Chicken Feathers</SCRIPT:TITLE>
      <SCRIPT:AUTHOR>
        <PERSON:PERSON>
          <PERSON:FIRST>William</PERSON:FIRST>
          <PERSON:LAST>Sanders</PERSON:LAST>
          <PERSON:TITLE>Col.</PERSON:TITLE>
        </PERSON:PERSON>
      </SCRIPT:AUTHOR>
      <SCRIPT:SYNOPSIS>
        Hijinks in a poultry factory
      </SCRIPT:SYNOPSIS>
    </SCRIPT:SCRIPT>

    <SCRIPT:SCRIPT>
      <SCRIPT:TITLE>Soft Copy</SCRIPT:TITLE>
      <SCRIPT:AUTHOR>
        <PERSON:PERSON>
          <PERSON:FIRST>Nora</PERSON:FIRST>
          <PERSON:LAST>Lessinger</PERSON:LAST>
          <PERSON:TITLE>Dr.</PERSON:TITLE>
        </PERSON:PERSON>
      </SCRIPT:AUTHOR>
      <SCRIPT:SYNOPSIS>Sex lives of the rich and famous
      </SCRIPT:SYNOPSIS>
    </SCRIPT:SCRIPT>

    Send inquiries to
    <PERSON:PERSON>
      <PERSON:TITLE>Mr.</PERSON:TITLE>,
      <PERSON:FIRST>Mikhail</PERSON:FIRST>
      <PERSON:LAST>Ovitsky</PERSON:LAST>
      <PERSON:COMPANY>Duplicative Artists Mismanagement
      </PERSON:COMPANY>,
      <PERSON:ADDRESS>
        135 Agents Row, Hollywood, CA 90123
      </PERSON:ADDRESS>
    </PERSON:PERSON>

  </BODY>
</HTML>
```

From the perspective of most XML applications, a document that uses the default namespace is the same as a document that uses prefixes as long as the URIs associated with each element are the same. However, a legacy HTML browser will have a much easier time with the Listing 13-6 than with the equivalent version in Listing 13-7 that attaches the prefix HTML to all the HTML elements.

Listing 13-7: **Prefixing the HTML elements in the same namespace**

```
<HTML:HTML xmlns:HTML="http://www.w3.org/1999/xhtml"
     xmlns:SCRIPT="http://ns.cafeconleche.org/scripts/"
     xmlns:PERSON="http://ns.cafeconleche.org/people/">
  <HTML:HEAD>
    <HTML:TITLE>Screenplays for Auction</HTML:TITLE>
  </HTML:HEAD>
  <HTML:BODY>
    <HTML:H1>January 27, 2001 Auction</HTML:H1>

    <HTML:P>Pilot scripts for the Fall season:</HTML:P>

    <SCRIPT:SCRIPT>
      <SCRIPT:TITLE>Chicken Feathers</SCRIPT:TITLE>
      <SCRIPT:AUTHOR>
        <PERSON:PERSON>
          <PERSON:FIRST>William</PERSON:FIRST>
          <PERSON:LAST>Sanders</PERSON:LAST>
          <PERSON:TITLE>Col.</PERSON:TITLE>
        </PERSON:PERSON>
      </SCRIPT:AUTHOR>
      <SCRIPT:SYNOPSIS>
        Hijinks in a poultry factory
      </SCRIPT:SYNOPSIS>
    </SCRIPT:SCRIPT>

    <SCRIPT:SCRIPT>
      <SCRIPT:TITLE>Soft Copy</SCRIPT:TITLE>
      <SCRIPT:AUTHOR>
        <PERSON:PERSON>
          <PERSON:FIRST>Nora</PERSON:FIRST>
          <PERSON:LAST>Lessinger</PERSON:LAST>
          <PERSON:TITLE>Dr.</PERSON:TITLE>
        </PERSON:PERSON>
      </SCRIPT:AUTHOR>
      <SCRIPT:SYNOPSIS>Sex lives of the rich and famous
      </SCRIPT:SYNOPSIS>
    </SCRIPT:SCRIPT>
```

```
Send inquiries to
<PERSON:PERSON>
  <PERSON:TITLE>Mr.</PERSON:TITLE>,
  <PERSON:FIRST>Mikhail</PERSON:FIRST>
  <PERSON:LAST>Ovitsky</PERSON:LAST>
  <PERSON:COMPANY>Duplicative Artists Mismanagement
  </PERSON:COMPANY>,
  <PERSON:ADDRESS>
    135 Agents Row, Hollywood, CA 90123
  </PERSON:ADDRESS>
</PERSON:PERSON>

  </HTML:BODY>
</HTML:HTML>
```

A good time to use default namespaces is when you need to attach a namespace to every element in an existing document to which you're now going to add elements from a different language. For instance, if you place some MathML in an XHTML document, you only have to add prefixes to the MathML elements. You can put all the HTML elements in the XHTML namespace simply by adding an `xmlns` attribute to the start tag like this:

```
<html xmlns="http://www.w3.org/1999/xhtml">
```

You do not need to edit the rest of the file! The MathML tags you insert still need to be in the proper MathML namespace. However, as long as they aren't mixed up with a lot of HTML markup, you can simply declare an `xmlns` attribute on the root element of the MathML. This defines a default namespace for the MathML elements that overrides the default namespace of the document containing the MathML. Listing 13-8 demonstrates.

Listing 13-8: **A MathML math element embedded in a well-formed HTML document**

```
<?xml version="1.0"?>
<html xmlns="http://www.w3.org/1999/xhtml">
  <head>
    <title>Fiat Lux</title>
    <meta name="GENERATOR" content="amaya V1.3b" />
  </head>
  <body>

    <P>And God said,</P>

    <math xmlns="http://www.w3.org/1998/Math/MathML">
```

Continued

Listing 13-8 *(continued)*

```
        <mrow>
          <msub>
            <mi>&#x3B4;</mi>
            <mi>&#x3B1;</mi>
          </msub>
          <msup>
            <mi>F</mi>
            <mi>&#x3B1;&#x3B2;</mi>
          </msup>
          <mi></mi>
          <mo>=</mo>
          <mi></mi>
          <mfrac>
            <mrow>
              <mn>4</mn>
              <mi>&#x3C0;</mi>
            </mrow>
            <mi>c</mi>
          </mfrac>
          <mi></mi>
          <msup>
            <mi>J</mi>
            <mrow>
              <mi>&#x3B2;</mi>
              <mo></mo>
            </mrow>
          </msup>
        </mrow>
      </math>

    <P>and there was light</P>

  </body>
</html>
```

Here, `math`, `mrow`, `msub`, `mo`, `mi`, `mfrac`, `mn`, and `msup` are all in the `http://www.w3.org/1998/Math/MathML` namespace, even though the document that contains them uses the `http://www.w3.org/1999/xhtml` namespace.

Note   Attributes are never in a default namespace. They must be explicitly prefixed. An unprefixed attribute is in no namespace at all. Even if the element it is a part of is in some namespace, default or otherwise, the unprefixed attribute is still not in that or any other namespace.

Namespaces and Validity

Namespaces do not get any special exemptions from the normal rules of well-formedness and validity. Well-formedness is generally not a problem, but validity sometimes is. In order for a document that uses namespaces to be valid, you must declare the `xmlns` attributes in the DTD just like you'd declare any other attribute. Furthermore, you must declare the elements and attributes using the prefixes they use in the document. For instance, if a document uses a `PERSON:ADDRESS` element, then the DTD must declare a `PERSON:ADDRESS` element, not merely an `ADDRESS` element, like this:

```
<!ELEMENT PERSON:ADDRESS (#PCDATA)>
```

This means that if a DTD was written without namespace prefixes, then it must be rewritten using the namespace prefixes before it can be used to validate documents that use prefixed element and attribute names. For example, consider this element declaration:

```
<!ELEMENT SCRIPT (TITLE, AUTHOR, SYNOPSIS)>
```

You have to rewrite it like this if the elements are all given the `SCR` namespace prefix:

```
<!ELEMENT SCR:SCRIPT (SCR:TITLE, SCR:AUTHOR, SCR:SYNOPSIS)>
```

This means that you cannot use the same DTD for both documents with namespaces and documents without, even if they use essentially the same vocabulary. In fact you can't even use the same DTD for documents that use the same tag sets and namespaces, but different prefixes, because DTDs are tied to the actual prefixes rather than the URIs of the namespaces.

Tip   If you have a question about whether a document that uses namespaces is well-formed or valid, forget everything you know about namespaces. Simply treat the document as a normal XML document that happens to have some element and attribute names that contain colons. The document is as well-formed and valid as it is when you don't consider namespaces.

Default attribute values can help a little here. For example, this `ATTLIST` declaration places every `PERSON:ADDRESS` element in the `http://ns.cafeconleche.org/people/` namespace unless specified otherwise in the document.

```
<!ATTLIST PERSON:ADDRESS xmlns:PERSON
                    "http://ns.cafeconleche.org/people/" >
```

Default namespaces are especially useful in valid documents since they don't require you to add prefixes to all the elements. Adding prefixes to elements from an XML application whose DTD doesn't use prefixes breaks validity.

There are, however, clear limits to how far default namespaces will take you. In particular, they are not sufficient to differentiate between two elements that use an element name in incompatible ways. For example, if one DTD defines a HEAD as containing a TITLE and a META element, and another DTD defines a HEAD as containing #PCDATA, then you have to use prefixes in the DTD and the document to distinguish the two different HEAD elements.

Note   Two different development efforts are underway that may (or may not) eventually solve the problem of merging incompatible DTDs from different domains. XML schemas offers a namespace-aware alternative to DTDs for validation. XML fragments may enable different documents to be combined with more explicit acknowledgement of which parts come from where. However, for now, merging incompatible DTDs will probably require you to rewrite the DTD and your documents to use prefixes.

Summary

This chapter explained namespaces. In particular, you learned that:

✦ Namespaces distinguish between elements and attributes with the same name from different XML applications.

✦ In a document that mixes markup from multiple XML applications, namespaces identify which elements and attributes are part of which XML applications.

✦ Namespaces are declared by an xmlns attribute whose value is the URI of the namespace. The document referred to by this URI need not exist.

✦ The prefix associated with a namespace is the part of the name of the xmlns attribute that follows the colon, for example, xmlns:*prefix*.

✦ Prefixes are attached to all element and attribute names that belong to the namespace identified by the prefix.

✦ If an xmlns attribute has no prefix, it establishes a default namespace for that element and its descendants (but not for any attributes).

✦ DTDs must be written in such a fashion that a processor that knows nothing about namespaces can still parse and validate the document.

This completes Part II. You now have a solid grasp of XML fundamentals. In the next several parts, we'll investigate a number of supplementary technologies that layer on top of XML, as well as applications built with XML. Many of these applications use namespaces for one purpose or another. In particular, you'll learn how namespaces are used in the Extensible Stylesheet Language (XSL), the XML Linking Language (XLink), the Resource Description Framework (RDF), and several other XML applications.

✦   ✦   ✦

Style Languages

CSS Style Sheets

C SS is a very simple and straightforward language for applying styles to XML documents. Most of the styles CSS supports are familiar from any word processor. For example, you can choose the font, the font weight, the font size, the background color, the spacing of various elements, the borders around elements, and more. However, rather than being stored as part of the document itself, all the style information is placed in a separate document called a style sheet. A single XML document can be formatted in many different ways just by changing the style sheet. Different style sheets can be designed for different purposes — for print, the Web, presentations, and other uses — all with the styles appropriate for the specific medium, and all without changing any of the content in the document itself.

Caution

Netscape/Mozilla 6.0, Opera 4.0 and 5.0, and Internet Explorer 5.0 and 5.5 all implement some but not all parts of the CSS specification. Earlier versions of the major browsers, while perhaps supporting some form of CSS for HTML documents, do not support it at all for XML documents. To make matters worse, they all implement different subsets of the specification; and sometimes don't implement the same subsets for XML as they do for HTML. I'll try to indicate where one browser or another has a particular problem as we go along. However, if you find that something in this chapter doesn't work as advertised in your favorite browser (or in any browser), please complain to the browser vendor, not to me.

What Are Cascading Style Sheets?

Cascading Style Sheets (referred to as CSS from now on) is a declarative language introduced in 1996 as a standard means of adding information to HTML documents about style properties such as fonts and borders. However, CSS actually works better with XML than with HTML because HTML is burdened with backward-compatibility issues. For instance, properly supporting the CSS `nowrap` property requires eliminating the nonstandard but frequently used `NOWRAP` element in HTML. Since XML elements don't have any predefined formatting, they don't restrict which CSS styles can be applied to which elements.

A simple CSS style sheet

A CSS style sheet contains a list of rules. Each rule gives the names of the elements it applies to and the styles to apply to those elements. Consider Listing 14-1, a CSS style sheet for poems. Listing 14-1 can be typed in any text editor, saved as a text file, and named something like poem.css. The three letter extension .css is conventional, but not required.

Listing 14-1: **A CSS style sheet for poems**

```
POEM   { display: block }
TITLE  { display: block; font-size: 16pt; font-weight: bold }
POET   { display: block; margin-bottom: 10px }
STANZA { display: block; margin-bottom: 10px }
VERSE  { display: block }
```

This style sheet has five rules. Each rule has a *selector* — in this example the name of the element to which it applies — and a list of styles to apply to instances of that element. The first rule says that the contents of the POEM element should be displayed in a block by itself (`display: block`). The second rule says that the contents of the TITLE element should be displayed in a block by itself (`display: block`) in 16-point (`font-size: 16pt`) bold type (`font-weight: bold`). The third rule says that the POET element should be displayed in a block by itself (`display: block`) and should be set off from what follows it by 10 pixels (`margin-bottom: 10px`). The fourth rule is the same as the third rule except that it applies to STANZA elements. Finally, the fifth rule simply states that VERSE elements are also displayed in their own block.

Attaching style sheets to documents

To really make sense out of the style sheet in Listing 14-1, you have to give it an XML document to format. Listing 14-2 is a poem from Walt Whitman's classic book of poetry, *Leaves of Grass*, marked up in XML. The second line is the `xml-stylesheet` processing instruction that instructs the Web browser loading this document to apply the style sheet found in the file poem.css to this document. Figure 14-1 shows this document loaded into Mozilla.

Listing 14-2: *Darest Thou Now O Soul* marked up in XML

```
<?xml version="1.0"?>
<?xml-stylesheet type="text/css" href="poem.css"?>
<POEM>

  <TITLE>Darest Thou Now O Soul</TITLE>
  <POET>Walt Whitman</POET>

  <STANZA>
    <VERSE>Darest thou now O soul,</VERSE>
    <VERSE>Walk out with me toward the unknown region,</VERSE>
    <VERSE>Where neither ground is for the feet nor
            any path to follow?</VERSE>
  </STANZA>
  <STANZA>
    <VERSE>No map there, nor guide,</VERSE>
    <VERSE>Nor voice sounding, nor touch of
            human hand,</VERSE>
    <VERSE>Nor face with blooming flesh, nor lips,
            are in that land.</VERSE>
  </STANZA>
  <STANZA>
    <VERSE>I know it not O soul,</VERSE>
    <VERSE>Nor dost thou, all is blank before us,</VERSE>
    <VERSE>All waits undream'd of in that region,
            that inaccessible land.</VERSE>
  </STANZA>
  <STANZA>
    <VERSE>Till when the ties loosen,</VERSE>
    <VERSE>All but the ties eternal, Time and Space,</VERSE>
    <VERSE>Nor darkness, gravitation, sense,
            nor any bounds bounding us.</VERSE>
  </STANZA>
  <STANZA>
    <VERSE>Then we burst forth, we float,</VERSE>
    <VERSE>In Time and Space O soul,
            prepared for them,</VERSE>
    <VERSE>Equal, equipt at last, (O joy! O fruit of all!)
            them to fulfil O soul.</VERSE>
  </STANZA>

</POEM>
```

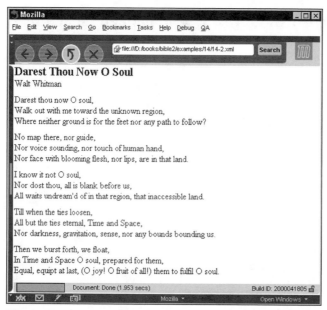

Figure 14-1: *Darest Thou Now O Soul* as rendered by Mozilla

The `type` pseudo-attribute in the `xml-stylesheet` processing instruction is the MIME media type of the style sheet you're using. Its value is `text/css` for CSS and `text/xml` for XSL.

Cross-Reference XSL is discussed in Chapters 5, 18 and 19.

The value of the `href` pseudo-attribute in the `xml-stylesheet` processing instruction is the URL, often relative, where the style sheet is located. If the style sheet can't be found, the Web browser will use its default style sheet instead.

You can apply the same style sheet to many documents. Indeed, you generally will. Thus, it's common to put your style sheets in some central location on your Web server where all of your documents can refer to them; a convenient location is a styles directory at the root level of the Web server.

```
<?xml-stylesheet type="text/css" href="/styles/poem.css"?>
```

You might even use an absolute URL to a style sheet on another Web site, though this does leave your site dependent on the status of the external Web site.

```
<?xml-stylesheet type="text/css"
      href="http://www.ibiblio.org/xml/styles/poem.css"?>
```

CSS in HTML

Although XML is the focus of this book, CSS style sheets also work with HTML documents. The main differences between CSS with HTML and CSS with XML are:

1. In HTML, the elements you can attach rules to are limited to standard HTML elements such as P, PRE, LI, DIV, and SPAN.

2. HTML browsers don't recognize processing instructions, so style sheets are attached to HTML documents using LINK tags in the HEAD element. Furthermore, per-document style rules can be included in the HEAD in a STYLE element. For example:

```
<LINK REL=STYLESHEET TYPE="text/css" HREF="/styles/poem.css" >
<STYLE TYPE="text/css">
  PRE { color: red }
</STYLE>
```

3. HTML browsers don't render CSS properties as faithfully as XML browsers because of the legacy formatting of elements. Tables are notoriously problematic in this respect.

You can even use multiple xml-stylesheet processing instructions to pull in rules from different style sheets. For example:

```
<?xml version="1.0"?>
<?xml-stylesheet type="text/css" href="/styles/poem.css"?>
<?xml-stylesheet type="text/css"
      href="http://www.ibiblio.org/xml/styles/poem.css"?>
<POEM>
...
```

Document Type Definitions and style sheets

Style sheets are more or less orthogonal to Document Type Definitions (DTDs). A document with a style sheet may or may not have a DTD, and a document with a DTD may or may not have a style sheet. However, DTDs do often serve as convenient lists of the elements that you need to provide style rules for.

In this and the next several chapters, most of the examples use documents that are well-formed but not valid. The lack of DTDs will make the examples shorter and the relevant parts more obvious. However, there's absolutely no reason why you can't attach a style sheet to a document that has a DTD. In either case, the style rules only apply to the content of the document, not to the DTD.

CSS1 versus CSS2

The first version of CSS was thrown together rather quickly, and left a lot to the imagination. It was quite limited in what it could accomplish. For instance, CSS could make an element red but couldn't make it the same color as the menu bar. It could make text bold, but couldn't make it shadowed. The underlying layout model only really worked for left-to-right Western languages such as English and Greek, and fell apart when faced with documents containing right-to-left languages such as Arabic or top-to-bottom languages such as Chinese. Many details were insufficiently specified and open to multiple incompatible interpretations. Most importantly for our purposes, CSS only really considered HTML; it didn't work well for XML. For example, it didn't provide table formatting because that could be done with HTML table tags.

In 1998, the World Wide Web Consortium (W3C) published a revised and expanded specification for CSS called CSS Level 2 (CSS2). At the same time, they renamed the original CSS to CSS Level 1 (CSS1). CSS2 is mostly a superset of CSS1, with a few minor exceptions. CSS2 incorporates many features that Web developers and designers have long requested from browser vendors. The specification has more than doubled in size from CSS1, and is not only a compilation of changes and new features, but a redraft of the original specification. This makes this specification a single source for all Cascading Style Sheet syntax, semantics, and rules. Of course, CSS2 fights the same backward compatibility battles with HTML that CSS1 fought. However, with XML, CSS2 can format content on both paper and the Web almost as well as a desktop publishing program such as PageMaker or QuarkXPress can.

On the CD-ROM The complete CSS Level 2 specification is available on the Web at `http://www.w3.org/TR/REC-CSS2` and on the CD-ROM in the specs/css2 folder. This is possibly the most readable specification document ever produced by the W3C and is well worth your time to read.

All browsers that can display XML documents support CSS Level 2, at least in part. Therefore, this chapter focuses on CSS Level 2 exclusively. The distinction between CSS Level 1 and Level 2 is really only important for older browsers that don't support XML at all.

CSS3

Work is ongoing to produce CSS Level 3. This is currently being developed by the W3C as several independent pieces including:

✦ Better page formatting including running headers and footers, page numbers, and automatically updated cross-references

✦ Styles for forms including input fields, checkboxes, radio buttons, buttons, list boxes, and more

✦ Math styles for equations and numbers

✦ Behavioral styles for tasks currently accomplished with JavaScript and DHTML

✦ More accurate color matching

✦ Multi-column layouts

✦ Selectors that operate by element content and relative position in the document

When all of these are done, they'll be rolled together with the existing CSS Level 2 specification to produce CSS Level 3. However, it's unlikely that this will be finished before late 2001, and it certainly won't be implemented by browsers in any large way until at least 2002.

Comments in CSS

CSS style sheets can include comments. CSS comments are similar to C's /* */ comments, but not to the <!-- --> XML and HTML comments. Listing 14-3 demonstrates this. This style sheet doesn't merely apply style rules to elements. It also describes, in English, the results those style rules are supposed to achieve.

Listing 14-3: **A style sheet for poems with comments**

```
/* Work around a Mozilla bug */
POEM { display: block }

/* Make the title look like an H1 header */
TITLE  { display: block; font-size: 16pt; font-weight: bold }
POET   { display: block; margin-bottom: 10 }

/* Put a blank line in-between stanzas,
   only a line break between verses */
STANZA { display: block; margin-bottom: 10 }
VERSE  { display: block }
```

CSS style sheets aren't nearly as convoluted as XML DTDs, or Java, C, or Perl programs, so comments aren't quite as necessary as they are in other languages. However, it's rarely a bad idea to include comments. They can only help someone who's trying to make sense out of a style sheet you wrote.

Selecting Elements

The part of a CSS rule that specifies which elements it applies to is called a *selector*. The most common kind of selector is simply the name of an element, for instance TITLE in this rule:

```
TITLE { display: block; font-size: 16pt; font-weight: bold }
```

However, selectors can also specify multiple elements, elements with a particular ID, and elements that appear in particular contexts relative to other elements. Indeed, a selector can be anything from a simple element name to a complex system of contextual patterns. Table 14-1 summarizes the selector patterns.

Table 14-1
CSS Selector Patterns

Syntax	Meaning
*	Matches all elements.
X	Matches every element with the name X; for example, the pattern STANZA matches all STANZA elements.
X Y	Matches every element with the name Y that is a descendent of an element with the name X; for example, POEM VERSE matches all VERSE descendents of POEM elements.
X > Y	Matches every element named Y that is a child of an element named X; for example, STANZA > VERSE matches all VERSE children of a STANZA element.
X + Y	Matches all elements named Y whose preceding sibling is an element named X. For example, STANZA + REFRAIN matches every REFRAIN element that is immediately preceded by a STANZA element. VERSE + VERSE matches every VERSE element that is immediately preceded by another VERSE element. In Listing 14-2 this matches all verses in each STANZA except the first.
X:first-child	Matches every element named X that is the first child of its parent element; for example, POEM:first-child matches the first child element of the POEM element. In Listing 14-2 this is the TITLE element.
X[A]	Matches all elements named X that have an A attribute, no matter what its value; for example, AUTHOR[NAME] matches every AUTHOR element with a NAME attribute.

Syntax	Meaning
X[A="M"]	Matches all elements named X whose A attribute has the value M; for example, AUTHOR[NAME="Walt Whitman"] matches every AUTHOR element whose NAME attribute has the value Walt Whitman.
X[A~="M"]	Matches all elements named X whose A attribute contains a space separated list of names one of which is M; for example, AUTHOR[NAME="Walt"] matches every AUTHOR element whose NAME attribute has the value Walt Whitman, Walt Smith, Walt Irving, or Irving Walt.
X[A|="M"]	Matches all elements named X whose A attribute contains a space separated list of names the first of which is M; for example, AUTHOR[NAME|="Walt"] matches every AUTHOR element whose NAME attribute has the value Walt Whitman but not those whose NAME attribute has the value Irving Walt.
X#M	Matches any elements named X whose ID is M as identified by an ID type attribute. Unfortunately, this selector does not work properly for XML in most Web browsers.
X:lang(*i*)	Matches all elements named X that are written in the natural language *i* as indicated by an xml:lang attribute.
X:link	Matches all elements named X that are inside a link whose target has not yet been visited.
X:visited	Matches all elements named X that are inside a link whose target has been visited.
X:active	Matches all elements named X that are currently selected.
X:hover	Matches all elements named X over which the cursor is currently positioned.
X:focus	Matches all elements named X that currently have the focus.

To demonstrate these selectors let's pick a poem with a slightly more complicated structure. Listing 14-4 shows Shakespeare's twenty-first sonnet. This has both STANZA and REFRAIN elements, each of which contains VERSE elements. The STANZA elements have NUMBER attributes of ID type as established by a document type definition. The POEM element has a TYPE attribute with the value SONNET.

Listing 14-4: **Shakespeare's twenty-first sonnet**

```
<?xml version="1.0"?>
<?xml-stylesheet type="text/css" href="sonnet.css"?>
<!DOCTYPE POEM [
  <!ATTLIST STANZA NUMBER ID #IMPLIED>
]>
<POEM TYPE="SONNET">
  <POET>William Shakespeare</POET>
  <TITLE>Sonnet 21</TITLE>
  <STANZA NUMBER="st1">
    <VERSE>So is it not with me as with that Muse</VERSE>
    <VERSE>Stirr'd by a painted beauty to his verse,</VERSE>
    <VERSE>Who heaven itself for ornament doth use</VERSE>
    <VERSE>And every fair with his fair doth rehearse;</VERSE>
  </STANZA>
  <STANZA NUMBER="st2">
    <VERSE>Making a couplement of proud compare</VERSE>
    <VERSE>With sun and moon, with earth and sea's rich
            gems,</VERSE>
    <VERSE>With April's first-born flowers, and all things
            rare</VERSE>
    <VERSE>That heaven's air in this huge rondure hems.</VERSE>
  </STANZA>
  <STANZA NUMBER="st3">
    <VERSE>O, let me, true in love, but truly write,</VERSE>
    <VERSE>And then believe me, my love is as fair</VERSE>
    <VERSE>As any mother's child, though not so bright</VERSE>
    <VERSE>As those gold candles fix'd in heaven's air.</VERSE>
  </STANZA>
  <REFRAIN>
    <VERSE>Let them say more that like of hearsay well,</VERSE>
    <VERSE>I will not praise that purpose not to sell.</VERSE>
  </REFRAIN>
</POEM>
```

The universal selector

The * symbol selects all elements in the document. This lets you set default styles for all elements. For example, this rule sets the default font to New York:

```
* { font-family: "New York" }
```

You can use * instead of an element name in other selector patterns to apply styles to all elements with a specific attribute, attribute value, role, and so forth. For example, this rule makes all elements whose TYPE attribute has the value SONNET italic:

```
*[TYPE="SONNET"] { font-style: italic }
```

There's only one such element in Listing 14-3, but other documents might have more of these, which may or may not be POEM elements.

Tip   If you are using the universal selector with just one other property specification, you can leave out the *. For example, the above rule could be rewritten as

```
[TYPE="SONNET"] { font-style: italic }
```

Grouping selectors

If you want to apply one set of properties to some but not all elements, list the element names in the selector separated by commas. For instance, in Listing 14-1 POET and STANZA were both styled as block display with a 10-pixel margin. You can combine these two rules like this:

```
POET, STANZA { display: block; margin-bottom: 10px }
```

You can add as many elements as you like. For example, this rule applies style to POET, STANZA and REFRAIN elements:

```
POET, STANZA, REFRAIN { display: block; margin-bottom: 10px }
```

Furthermore, more than one rule can apply styles to a single element. So you can combine some standard properties into a rule with many selectors, then use more specific rules to apply custom formatting to selected elements. For instance, in Listing 14-1 all the elements were listed as block display. This can be combined into one rule while additional formatting for the POET, STANZA, REFRAIN and TITLE elements is contained in separate rules, as shown in Listing 14-5.

Listing 14-5: **sonnet.css**

```
POEM, VERSE, TITLE, POET, STANZA, REFRAIN { display: block }
POET, STANZA, REFRAIN { margin-bottom: 10px }
TITLE {font-size: 16pt; font-weight: bold }
```

Hierarchy selectors

In XML, as in life, what you look like depends heavily on what your ancestors looked like. You can individually select elements that are children or descendants of a specified type of element with descendant, child, and sibling selectors.

Child selectors

A child selector uses the greater than sign > to select an element if and only if it's an immediate child of a specified parent. For instance, to apply a rule to VERSE elements that are children of STANZA elements but not to VERSE elements that are children of REFRAIN elements, you'd use the selector STANZA > VERSE. These rules make stanza verses bold but refrain verses italic:

```
STANZA  > VERSE {font-weight: bold }
REFRAIN > VERSE {font-style:  italic }
```

You can expand this to look at the parent of the parent, the parent of the parent of the parent, and so forth. For example, the following rule says that a VERSE element inside a STANZA element inside a POEM element should be rendered in a monospaced font:

```
POEM > REFRAIN > VERSE { font-family: Courier, monospaced }
```

In practice, this level of specificity is rarely needed. In cases in which it does seem to be needed, you can often rewrite your style sheet to rely more on inheritance, cascades, and relative units, and less on the precise specification of formatting.

Descendant selectors

A descendant selector chooses elements that are children, grandchildren, or other descendants of a specified element. For instance, you can specify one style for VERSE elements contained in a POEM element and a different style for VERSE elements contained in a BOOK element. To do this, prefix the name of the ancestor element to the name of the styled element separated by a space. For example, these rules make book verses bold, but poem verses italic:

```
BOOK VERSE {font-weight: bold }
POEM VERSE {font-style:  italic; font-weight: normal }
```

In the event of a conflict between two rules, the closer one takes precedence. For instance, if a BOOK contains a POEM that contains VERSE elements, then those VERSE elements will be italic and not bold. In case of a conflict between two equally specific rules, the last rule encountered in the style sheet takes precedence.

You can even give VERSE elements inside POEM elements inside BOOK elements a completely different style that is not shared by VERSE elements inside POEM elements that are not inside BOOK elements or VERSE elements that are not inside POEM elements but are inside BOOK elements. For instance, this rule makes such elements red:

```
BOOK POEM VERSE {color: red }
```

Not all styles conflict with each other. For instance, consider these three rules:

```
BOOK VERSE    {font-weight: bold }
POEM VERSE    {font-style: italic }
CHAPTER VERSE {color: red }
```

Together these say that every VERSE element contained inside a BOOK element will be bold; every VERSE element contained inside a POEM element will be italic; and every VERSE element contained inside a CHAPTER element will be red. A VERSE element that matches all three rules — that is, one that has a BOOK ancestor and a POEM ancestor and a CHAPTER ancestor — will have all three properties; that is, it will be bold, italic, and red.

In Listings 14-2 and 14-4, all VERSE elements are descendants of POEM elements, but not immediate children. Some VERSE elements are immediate children of STANZA elements and some are immediate children of the REFRAIN element. A descendant selector of the form POEM VERSE matches a VERSE element that is an arbitrary descendant of a SONNET element. In order to specify a minimum generation for a descendant, you can use the selector POEM * VERSE, which forces the VERSE element to be at least a grandchild, or lower descendant of the POEM element.

You can combine descendant and child selectors to find specific elements. For example, the following rule italicizes all VERSE elements that are children of a REFRAIN element that is in turn a descendant of a POEM element.

```
POEM REFRAIN>VERSE { font-style: italic }
```

Adjacent sibling selectors

A plus sign between two element names signifies that the left-hand element precedes the right-hand element at the same level of the hierarchy. The right-hand element is selected. For example, this rule finds all REFRAIN elements that share a parent with a STANZA element and that immediately follow a STANZA element:

```
STANZA+REFRAIN {color: red}
```

This rule finds all VERSE elements that are preceded by another VERSE element:

```
VERSE+VERSE {color: blue}
```

Applied to Listings 14-2 and 14-4 this has the effect of coloring all verses blue except the first one in the stanza.

Attribute selectors

Attribute selectors identify specific element/attribute combinations. Square brackets surround the name of the attribute being specified. For example, this rule specifies a script font for all `<POEM TYPE="x">` elements, but not plain `<POEM>` elements:

```
POEM[TYPE]  { font-family: "Zapf Chancery", cursive }
```

To distinguish between `<POEM TYPE="x">` and `<POEM TYPE="y">` elements, you can add an equals sign followed by the quoted attribute value. For example, this rule only applies to sonnets:

```
POEM[TYPE="SONNET"]  { font-style: italic }
```

You can use a ~= to indicate that the attribute value only needs to contain the specified word somewhere within it. For example, this rule italicizes all POEM elements whose TYPE attribute contains the word SONNET:

```
POEM[TYPE~="SONNET"]  { font-style: italic }
```

However, this would not find elements whose TYPE attribute contains the word SONNETS or UNISONNET. CSS only looks for complete words. It does not look for substrings.

You can use a |= to indicate that the attribute value needs to begin with the specified word. For example, this rule italicizes all POEM elements whose TYPE attribute begins with the word SONNET:

```
POEM[TYPE|="SONNET"]  { font-style: italic }
```

This would not find elements whose TYPE attribute had the value "HEXAMETER SONNET", but it would match a POEM with a TYPE attribute having the value "SONNET HEXAMETER".

ID selectors

Sometimes, a unique element needs a unique style. You need a rule that applies to exactly that one element. For instance, suppose you want to make one element in a list bold to really emphasize it in contrast to its siblings. In this case, you can write a rule that applies to an ID type attribute of the element. The selector is the name of the element, followed by a sharp sign # and the value of the ID attribute.

For example, this rule makes bold the first STANZA element, and only the first STANZA element, in Listing 14-4. Other STANZA elements appear with the default weight.

```
STANZA#st1 {font-weight: bold}
```

However, there's a catch. In order to tell which attributes have ID type and can therefore be selected by an ID selector, the browser must read the DTD. Most browsers, including Mozilla, Netscape, Opera, and Internet Explorer, do not read the DTD. Therefore they will not apply this style to the requested element. You're better off simply using an attribute selector that picks up the attribute by name like this:

```
STANZA[NUMBER="st1"] {font-weight: bold}
```

Pseudo-elements

Pseudo-elements are treated as elements in style sheets but are not necessarily particular-named elements in the document source code or the document tree. They are abstractions of certain parts of the rendered document after application of the style sheet; for example, the first line of a paragraph. Pseudo-elements address parts of the document that aren't normally identified as separate elements, but nonetheless often need separate styles. These include:

✦ The first line of an element

✦ The first letter of an element

✦ The position immediately before an element

✦ The position immediately after an element

Addressing the first letter

The most common reason to format the first letter of an element separately from the rest of the element is to insert a drop cap as shown in Figure 14-2. This is accomplished by writing a rule that is addressed with the element name and followed by :first-letter. For example:

```
CHAPTER:first-letter {
  font-size: 300%;
  float: left;
  vertical-align: text-top;
  margin-right: 12px
}
```

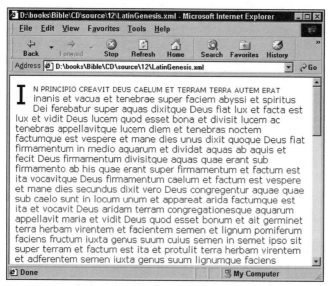

Figure 14-2: A drop cap on the first-letter pseudo-element with small caps used on the first-line pseudo-element

Addressing the first line

The first line of an element is also often formatted differently than subsequent lines. For instance, it may be printed in small caps instead of normal body text as shown in Figure 14-2. You can attach the :first-line selector to the name of an element to create a rule that only applies to the first line of the element. For example,

```
CHAPTER:first-line { font-variant: small-caps }
```

Exactly what this pseudo-element selects is relative to the current layout. If the window is larger and there are more words in the first line, then more words will be in small caps. If the window is made smaller or the font gets larger so that the text wraps differently and fewer words fit on the first line, then the words that are wrapped to the next line are no longer in small caps. The determination of which characters comprise the first-line pseudo-element is deferred until the document is actually displayed.

Before and after

The :before and :after pseudo-elements select the location immediately before and after the element that precedes them. The content property is used to put data into this location. For example, this rule places the string --------- between STANZA objects to help separate the stanzas. The line breaks are encoded as \A in the string literal:

```
STANZA:after  {content: "\A---------\A"}
STANZA:before {content: "\A---------\A"}
```

Content is the only property a :before or :after selector is allowed to have. In addition to including raw text, this can insert the value of an attribute, various kinds of quotation marks, or a file found at a particular URL.

Cross-Reference   The content property is discussed in more depth in the section on generated content in Chapter 16.

Pseudo-classes

Pseudo-classes select elements that have something in common, but do not necessarily have the same type. Pseudo-classes differ from regular classes in that they select elements based on aspects other than the name, attributes, or content of the element. Pseudo-classes differ from pseudo-elements in that they always select an entire element, never just a part of it.

For example, a pseudo-class may be based on the position of the mouse, the object that has the focus, or whether an object is a link. The :hover pseudo-class refers to whichever element the cursor is currently over, regardless of the element's type. An element may even change its pseudo-class as the reader interacts with the document. Some pseudo-classes are mutually exclusive, but most can be applied simultaneously to the same element, and can be placed anywhere within an element selector. CSS defines 10 pseudo-classes:

+ :first-child
+ :link
+ :visited
+ :active
+ :hover
+ :focus
+ :lang
+ :right
+ :left
+ :first

:first-child

The :first-child pseudo-class selects the first child of the named element, regardless of its type. For example, this rule makes the first verse of each stanza bold:

```
STANZA:first-child {font-style: bold}
```

:link, :visited, :active

The :link pseudo-class applies to all elements that the browser recognizes as hyperlinks that the user has not yet followed. In XML, this would apply to elements with an xlink:type attribute. The :visited pseudo-class applies to links the user has followed. The :active pseudo-class applies to links the user is following right this second.

Cross-Reference   XLinks are discussed in Chapter 20.

For example, the following code fragment assumes that the AUTHOR element has been designated as a link and alters the colors of the text depending on the current state of the link. An unvisited link will be colored red, a visited link will be colored gray, and an active link will be colored lime green:

```
AUTHOR:link     { color: "red" }
AUTHOR:visited  { color: "gray" }
AUTHOR:active   { color: "lime" }
```

In practice, these pseudo-classes don't work for XML documents because browsers don't yet recognize XLinks.

:hover

The :hover pseudo-class refers to elements that the mouse or other pointing device is pointing at, but without the mouse button depressed. For instance, this rule emboldens the STANZA element the cursor is pointing at:

```
STANZA:hover { font-weight: bold }
```

The STANZA element returns to its normal weight when the cursor is no longer positioned over it.

:focus

The :focus pseudo-class selects the element that has the focus. An element has the focus when it has been selected and is ready to receive some sort of input. The following rule makes whichever element has the focus bold.

```
*:focus { font-weight: "bold" }
```

:lang( )

The :lang() pseudo-class selects elements with a specified language. In XML, languages are specified with an xml:lang attribute. The following rule changes the direction of all VERSE elements written in Hebrew to read right to left, rather than left to right:

```
VERSE:lang(he) {direction: "rtl" }
```

Inheritance

CSS does not require that you define a rule giving a value for every property to every element. Some properties have default values that are used when no rule is specified. Even more importantly, most elements can simply inherit the value of a property from their parent element. For instance, if no rule explicitly specifies the font size of an element, then the element has the same font size as its parent. If no rule specifies the color of an element, then the element has the same color as its parent. The same is true of most CSS properties. In fact, the only properties that aren't inherited are the background and box properties. For example, consider these rules:

```
P      { font-weight: bold;
         font-size: 24pt;
         font-family: sans-serif}
BOOK   { font-style: italic; font-family: serif}
```

Now consider this XML fragment:

```
<P>
   According to the American Library Association,
   Michael Willhoite's <BOOK>Daddy's Roommate</BOOK> was
   the #2 most frequently banned book in the U.S. in the 1990s.
</P>
```

Although the BOOK element has not been specifically assigned a font-weight or a font-size, it will be rendered in 24-point bold because it is a child of the P element. It will also be italicized because that is specified in its own rule. BOOK *inherits* the font-weight and font-size of its parent P. If later in the document a BOOK element appears in the context of some other element, then it will inherit the font-weight and font-size of that element.

The font-family is a little trickier because both P and BOOK declare conflicting values for this property. Inside the BOOK element, the font-family declared by BOOK takes precedence. Outside the BOOK element, P's font-family is used. So, "Daddy's Roommate" is drawn in a serif font, while "most frequently banned book" is drawn in a sans serif font.

Often you want the child elements to inherit formatting from their parents so it's important not to overspecify the formatting of any element. For instance, suppose I had declared that BOOK was written in a 14-point font like this:

```
BOOK { font-style: italic; font-family: serif; font-size: 14pt}
```

Then the example would be rendered as shown in Figure 14-3, with the BOOK title being much smaller than the body text it's embedded in.

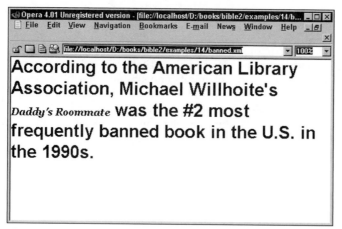

Figure 14-3: The BOOK title written in a 14-point font size

You could fix this with a special rule that uses a contextual selector to pick out BOOK elements inside P elements, but it's easier to simply inherit the parent's font-size.

One way to avoid problems like this, while retaining some control over the size of individual elements, is to use relative units such as ems and exs instead of absolute units such as points, picas, inches, and centimeters. An em is the width of the letter *m* in the current font. An ex is the height of the letter *x* in the current font. If the font gets bigger, so does everything measured in ems and exs.

A similar option that's available for some properties is to use percentage units. For example, the following rule sets the font size of the FOOTNOTE_NUMBER element to 80 percent of the font size of the parent element. If the parent element's font size increases or decreases, FOOTNOTE_NUMBER's font size scales similarly.

```
FOOTNOTE_NUMBER { font-size: 80% }
```

Exactly what the percentage is a percentage of varies from property to property. In the vertical-align property, the percentage is of the line height of the element itself. In a margin property, a percentage is a percentage of the element's width.

Cascades

There are several ways a CSS style sheet can be attached to an XML document:

1. The XML document can include an `<?xml-stylesheet?>` processing instruction in its prolog. In fact, there may be more than one of these.

2. The style sheet itself may import other style sheets, as discussed below.

3. The user may specify a style sheet for the document using mechanisms inside the browser.

4. The browser may provide a default style sheet.

Thus, a single document may have more than one style sheet. For instance, a browser may have a default style sheet which is added to the one that the designer provides for the page. In such a case, it's entirely possible that there will be multiple rules that apply to one element, and that these rules may conflict. Thus, it's important to determine in which order the rules are applied. This process is called a *cascade*, and is where Cascading Style Sheets get their name from.

When multiple style rules match a particular element, the most specific one is chosen. For example, these two rules say that verses have a plain font-style but that verses inside a refrain are italicized:

```
VERSE          {font-style: normal }
REFRAIN VERSE {font-style: italic }
```

In case of a conflict between two equally specific rules, the last rule encountered in the style sheet takes precedence.

Tip   Try to avoid depending on cascading order. It's rarely a mistake to specify as little style as possible and to let the browser preferences take control.

If there is more than one rule at a given level of specificity, the cascading order is resolved in the following order of preference:

1. Reader declarations marked important.

2. Author declarations marked important.

3. Reader declarations not marked important.

4. Author declarations not marked important.

5. The last rule in the style sheet that applies.

To mark a rule important, you add !important after the property value. For example, the following rule says that the TITLE element should be colored blue even if the author of the document requested a different color. On the other hand, the font-family should be serif only if the author rules don't disagree.

```
TITLE { color: blue !important; font-family: serif}
```

On the other hand, if no rule matches a given element, then that element inherits its properties from its parent. If there is no value to be inherited from the parent element, the default value is used. You can give most properties the value inherit to say explicitly that it inherits the value from its parent. However, because this is normally the default, this isn't done much in practice. Instead, the property is simply left unspecified.

Different Rules for Different Media

XML documents aren't just for Web pages. They can be shown on TV screens, printed on paper, bound in books, read by speech synthesizers, beamed to Palm Pilots, and projected onto movie screens. Each media type has its own customary styles and formats. Italics don't make much sense on a dumb terminal. A font that's easily readable on paper at 300 dpi may be illegible when displayed on a low-resolution computer screen.

CSS allows you to vary styles to match the medium in which the content is displayed. For example, text is easier to read onscreen if it uses a sans serif font, while text on paper is generally easiest to read if it is written in a serif font. You can enclose style rules intended for only one medium in an @media rule naming that medium. There can be as many @media rules in a document as there are media types to specify. For example, Listing 14-6 formats a POEM differently depending on whether it's being printed on paper or displayed onscreen.

Listing 14-6: A CSS style sheet with different styles for different media

```
@media print {
   POEM  { font-size: 10pt; font-family: Times, serif }
   TITLE { font-size: larger; font-weight: bold;
           font-family: Helvetica, sans-serif }
}
@media screen {
   POEM { font-size: 12pt;
          font-family: Geneva, Arial, sans-serif }
}
@media screen, print {
   VERSE { line-height: 1.2 }
}
POEM, VERSE, TITLE, POET, STANZA, REFRAIN { display: block }
POET, STANZA, REFRAIN { margin-bottom: 2mm }
TITLE {font-size: larger; font-weight: bold }
```

The first @media block defines styles that will only be used if the document is printed on paper. The second @media block defines styles that will only be used when the document is displayed on the screen. The screen rules pick a larger font than the print rules do. Because modern computer displays have much lower resolutions than modern printers, it's important to make the font larger on the screen than on the printout and to choose a font that's designed for the screen. The third @media block provides styles that apply to both of these media types. To designate style instructions for multiple media types simultaneously, you simply list them following the @media rule designator separated by a comma. The last three rules apply in all media: screen, print, or anything else.

The browser decides which rules make sense in its current context when it knows how it's going to display the document. CSS does not specify an all-inclusive list of media types, although it does provide a list of 10 possible values:

✦ all: all devices

✦ aural: speech synthesizers

✦ braille: Braille tactile feedback devices for the sight impaired

✦ embossed: paged Braille printers

✦ handheld: PDAs and other handheld devices such as Windows CE palmtops, Newtons, and Palm Pilots

✦ print: all printed, opaque material

✦ projection: presentation and slide shows, whether projected directly from a computer or printed on transparencies

✦ screen: bitmapped, color computer displays

✦ tty: dumb terminals and old PC monitors that use a fixed-pitch, monochromatic character grid

✦ tv: television-type devices; that is, low resolution, analog display, color

Some properties are only available with specific media types. For instance, the pitch property only makes sense with the aural media type.

Browsing software does not have to support all these types. Indeed I know of no single device that does support all of these. However, style sheet designers should probably assume that readers will use any or all of these types of devices to view their content.

Importing Style Sheets

The @import rule embeds a different style sheet into an existing style sheet. This allows you to build large style sheets from smaller, easier to understand pieces. An absolute or relative URL is used to identify the style sheets. For example, the following rule imports the file poetry.css.

```
@import url(poetry.css);
```

@import rules may specify a media type following the name of the style sheet, in which case the imported style sheet rules will only be used in the specified medium. For example, the following rule imports the file printmedia.css. However, the rules in this style sheet will only be applied to printouts and not to screen displays.

```
@import url(printmedia.css) print;
```

The next rule imports the file continuous.css that will be used for both computer monitors and/or television display:

```
@import url(continuous.css) tv, screen;
```

The @import directives must appear at the beginning of the style sheet, before any rules. Cycles (for example, poem.css imports stanza.css which imports poem.css) are prohibited.

Style sheets that are imported into other style sheets have lower precedence than the importing style sheet. This means that if sonnet.css imported poem.css and they declared conflicting rules for an element, the rules in sonnet.css would override those in poem.css.

Style Sheet Character Sets

CSS style sheets can be written in a multitude of encodings — ISO 8859-1, SJIS, UTF-8, and so on — just like XML documents. There are three ways to specify the character set in which a style sheet is written, and they take precedence in the following order.

1. The HTTP "charset" parameter in a "Content-Type" field.

2. An @charset rule in the style sheet itself.

3. The charset pseudo-attribute of the xml-stylesheet processing instruction that links the style sheet to the XML document.

Most of the time the @charset rule is the easiest one to use because it lets the person who writes the style sheet choose whatever encoding is convenient for them. Each style sheet can contain no more than one of these. If present, it must appear at the very beginning of the document, and cannot be preceded by any other characters. It's followed by the name of the character set in double quotes. For example, this rule says that the style sheet is written in the ISO 8859-1 character set, a.k.a. Latin-1:

```
@charset "ISO-8859-1"
```

The character set name specified in this statement must be a name as described in the IANA registry.

Cross-Reference   Character sets are discussed in great detail in Chapter 7, which contains a partial list of the IANA registered character set names.

Summary

This chapter showed you how to apply CSS styles to XML elements and documents. In this chapter, you learned that:

✦ CSS is a straightforward declarative language for applying styles to the contents of elements that works well with HTML and even better with XML.

✦ Browser implementations of CSS are limited. No browser comes close to implementing the full CSS Level 2 specification. Extensive testing is necessary before publishing a document and its style sheet.

✦ One or more processing instructions in the form `<?xml-stylesheet type="text/css" href="url"?>` in the prolog indicates which style sheets a browser should apply to the document.

✦ Selectors are a list of the elements that a rule applies to.

✦ Many (though not all) CSS properties are inherited by the children of the elements they apply to.

✦ If multiple rules apply to a single element, then the formatting properties cascade in a sensible way.

✦ You can include C-like `/* */` comments in a CSS style sheet.

✦ One style sheet can import another using an `@import` rule.

✦ An `@media` rule identifies in which media the given styles should be applied.

✦ An `@charset` rule identifies the character set in which the style sheet is encoded.

This chapter focused on how you choose the elements that you apply styles to. The next two chapters focus on the styles themselves. You'll learn about all the different CSS properties that let you specify borders, colors, margins, fonts, sizes, positions, and more.

✦   ✦   ✦

CSS Layouts

When a browser renders an XML document, it places the text from the individual elements on one or more pages. The text on each page is organized into nested boxes. Each paragraph is a box. Each line in the paragraph is a box. And these line boxes can contain still other boxes, which ultimately contain text. As well as paragraphs, there may be tables and lists and other items that are formed from boxes and that are subdivided into smaller boxes. Furthermore, the browser can create boxes to hold images, pull quotes, and other content that isn't part of the normal flow of the page. This chapter shows you how CSS arranges text on the page in boxes with different sizes, borders, margins, padding, and positions. You learn how to create boxes that are a certain size or that fall into a certain range of sizes. You also learn how to position the boxes at particular points on the page, as well as how to let the browser do the hard work for you.

◆ ◆ ◆ ◆

In This Chapter

CSS units

The display property

Box properties

Size

Positioning

Formatting pages

◆ ◆ ◆ ◆

Caution Netscape 6.0, Mozilla, Opera 4.0 and 5.0, and Internet Explorer 5.0 and later all implement only some parts of the CSS specification. Earlier versions of the major browsers, while perhaps supporting some form of CSS for HTML documents, do not support it at all for XML documents. To make matters worse, they all implement different subsets of the specification, and sometimes don't implement the same subsets for XML as they do for HTML. I'll note where one browser or another has a particular problem as we go along. However, if you find that something in this chapter doesn't work as advertised in your favorite browser, please complain to the browser vendor, not to me.

CSS Units

CSS properties have names and values. Table 15-1 lists a few of these property names and sample values.

Table 15-1
Sample Property Names and Values

Name	Value
display	none
font-style	italic
margin-top	0.5in
font-size	12pt
border-style	solid
color	#CC0033
background-color	white
background-image	url(http://www.idgbooks.com/images/paper.gif)
list-style-image	url(/images/redbullet.png)
line-height	120%

The names are all CSS keywords. However, the values are much more diverse. Some of them are keywords, such as the none in display: none or the solid in border-style: solid. Other values are numbers with units, such as the 0.5in in margin-top: 0.5in or the 12pt in font-size: 12pt. Still other values are URLs, such as url(http://www.idgbooks.com/images/paper.gif) in background-image: url(http://www.idgbooks.com/images/paper.gif); and still others are RGB colors such as the #CC0033 in color: #CC0033. Different properties permit different values. However, only five different kinds of values account for almost all properties. These types are:

✦ A length

✦ A URL

✦ A color

✦ A keyword

✦ A string

Keywords vary from property to property, but the other kinds of values are the same from property to property. That is, a length is a length is a length regardless of which property it's the value of. If you know how to specify the length of a border, you also know how to specify the length of a margin and a padding and an image and a font. This reuse of syntax makes working with different properties much easier.

Length values

In CSS, length is a scalar measure used for width, height, font-size, word and letter spacing, text indentation, line height, margins, padding, border widths, and many other properties. Lengths are given as a number followed by the abbreviation for one of these units:

Inches	`in`
Centimeters	`cm`
Millimeters	`mm`
Points	`pt`
Picas	`pc`
Pixels	`px`
Ems	`em`
Exs	`ex`

For example, this rule says that the font used for the `TITLE` element should be exactly one centimeter high:

```
TITLE {font-size: 1cm}
```

Although font sizes are normally given in points rather than centimeters, the browser will perform any necessary conversion between units.

The number may have a decimal point (for example, `margin-top: 0.3in`). Some properties allow negative values such as `-0.5in`, but not all do; and even those that do often place limits on how negative a length can be. It's best to avoid negative lengths for maximum cross-browser compatibility.

The units of length are divided into three classes:

✦ Absolute units: inches, centimeters, millimeters, points, and picas

✦ Relative units: pixels, ems, and exs

✦ Percentages

Absolute units of length

Absolute units of length are something of a misnomer because there's really no such thing as an absolute unit of length on a computer screen. Changing a monitor's resolution from 640×480 to 1600×1200 changes the length of everything on the screen, inches and centimeters included. Nonetheless, CSS supports five "absolute" units of length that at least don't change from one font to the next. These are listed in Table 15-2, along with the conversion factors between them.

Table 15-2 Absolute Units of Length					
	Inch (in)	Centimeters (cm)	Millimeters (mm)	Points (pt)	Picas (pc)
Inch	1.0	2.54	25.4	72	6
Centimeters	0.3937	1.0	10	28.3464	4.7244
Millimeters	0.03937	0.1	1.0	2.83464	0.47244
Points	0.01389	0.0352806	0.352806	1.0	0.83333
Picas	0.16667	0.4233	4.233	12	1.0

Relative units of length

CSS also supports three relative units for lengths. These are:

✦ em: the width of the letter m in the current font

✦ ex: the height of the letter x in the current font

✦ px: the size of a pixel (This assumes square pixels. Most common modern displays use square pixels although some older PC monitors, mostly now leaking lead into landfills, did not.)

For example, this rule sets the left and right borders of the PULLQUOTE element to twice the width of the letter m in the current font and the top and bottom borders to one and a half times the height of the letter x in the current font:

```
PULLQUOTE { border-right-width:  2em;
            border-left-width:   2em;
            border-top-width:    1.5ex;
            border-bottom-width: 1.5ex }
```

The normal purpose of using ems and exs is to set a width that's appropriate for a given font, without necessarily knowing how big the font is. For instance in the above rule, the font size is not known so the exact width of the borders is not known either. It can be determined at display time by comparison with the m and the x in the current font. Larger font sizes will have correspondingly larger ems and exs.

Lengths in pixels are relative to the height and width of a (presumably square) pixel on the monitor. Widths and heights of images are often given in pixels.

Caution

Pixel measurements are generally not a good idea. First, the size of a pixel varies widely with resolution. Most power users set their monitors at much too high a resolution, which makes the pixels far too small for legibility.

Second, within the next 10 years, 200-dpi and even 300-dpi monitors will become common, finally breaking away from the rough 72-pixels-per-inch (give or take 28 pixels) de facto standard that's prevailed since the first Macintosh in 1984. Documents that specify measurements in nonscreen-based units such as ems, exs, points, picas, and inches will be able to make the transition. However, documents that use pixel-level specifications will become illegibly small when viewed on high-resolution monitors.

Percentage units of length

Finally, lengths can be specified as a percentage of something. Generally, this is a percentage of the current value of a property. For instance, if the font-size of a STANZA element is 12 points, and the font-size of the VERSE the STANZA contains is set to 150 percent, then the font-size of the VERSE will be 18 points. Such a rule would look like this:

```
VERSE {font-size: 150%}
```

The exact size in this case does depend on the size of the font in the parent element. If the parent element font-size is bigger, the font-size of this element will be bigger. If the parent element font-size is smaller, the font-size of this element will be smaller.

URL values

Several CSS properties can have URL values, including background-image, content, and list-style-image. Furthermore, as you saw in the last chapter, the @import rule uses URL values. Literal URLs are placed inside url(). All forms of relative and absolute URLs are allowed. For example:

```
DOC    { background-image: url(http://www.mysite.com/bg.gif) }
LETTER { background-image: url(/images/paper.gif) }
GAME   { background-image: url(currentposition.gif)}
INSTRC { background-image: url(../images/screenshot.gif)}
```

You can enclose the URL in single or double quotes, although nothing is gained by doing so. For example:

```
DOC    { background-image: url("http://www.mysite.com/bg.gif")}
LETTER { background-image: url('/images/paper.gif') }
GAME   { background-image: url("currentposition.gif") }
INSTRC { background-image: url('../images/screenshot.gif') }
```

Any parentheses, apostrophes, white space, or quotation marks that appear inside the URL (uncommon except perhaps for the space character) should be replaced by URL standard % escapes. That is:

space   %20

,   %2C

'	%27
"	%22
(	%28
)	%29

Note CSS defines its own backslash escapes for these characters \(, \), \,, \', and \", but these only add an additional layer of confusion.

Color values

One of the most widely adopted uses of CSS over traditional HTML is applying foreground and background colors to elements on the page. Properties that take on color values include `color`, `background-color`, and `border-color`.

CSS provides four ways to specify color: by name, by hexadecimal components, by decimal components, and by percentages. Defining color by name is the simplest. CSS understands these 16 color names adopted from the Windows VGA palette:

✦ aqua	✦ gray	✦ navy	✦ silver
✦ black	✦ green	✦ olive	✦ teal
✦ blue	✦ lime	✦ purple	✦ white
✦ fuchsia	✦ maroon	✦ red	✦ yellow

Of course, the typical color monitor can display several million more colors. Other colors can be created by providing values for the red, green, and blue (RGB) components of the colors. CSS identifies colors as RGB values in the Standard Default Color Space for the Internet (sRGB). Different browsers and different monitors placed side-by-side may display visibly different hues for the same color. Indeed, even the ambient light in the room can change the exact appearance of a color. Nonetheless, this specification provides an unambiguous and objectively measurable definition of a color. Web browsers that conform to the standard perform a gamma correction on the colors identified by the CSS2 specification. sRGB specifies a display gamma of 2.2 under most viewing conditions. This means that for most computer hardware, the colors given through CSS properties will have to be adjusted for an effective display gamma of 2.2.

Note Only colors identified in CSS rules are affected. Colors used in images are expected to carry their own color-correction information.

CSS uses a 24-bit color model. Each primary color is stored in 8 bits. An 8-bit unsigned integer is a number between 0 and 255. This number may be given in either decimal or hexadecimal. Alternately, each component may be given as a percentage between 0 percent (0) and 100 percent (255). Table 15-3 lists some of the possible colors and their decimal, hexadecimal, and percentage RGB values.

Gamma correction

At its most basic, gamma correction controls the brightness of images so that they are displayed accurately on computer screens. Images that have not been properly corrected can appear bleached out or too dark on a monitor.

Most computer monitors have an innate gamma fairly close to 2.5. This means that the ratio of intensity to voltage roughly follows an exponential curve with the power 2.5. If you send your monitor a message for a specific pixel to have an intensity of x, that pixel will automatically have an intensity of $x^{2.5}$ applied to it. Because the range of voltage is between 0 and 1, this means that your pixel's intensity is lower than you wish. To correct this, the voltage to the monitor has to be "gamma corrected."

The easiest way to correct this problem is to increase the voltage before it gets to the monitor. Because the relationship between the voltage and the brightness is known, the signal can be adjusted to remove the effect of the monitor's gamma. When this is done properly, the computer display should accurately reflect the image input. Of course, when gamma correcting an image, the ambient light, brightness and contrast settings on the monitor, and personal taste also play a role.

When doing gamma correction for the Web, platform idiosyncrasies come into play. Some UNIX workstations automatically correct for gamma variance on their video card, just as the Macintosh does, but most PCs do not. This means that an image that looks good on a PC will be too light on a Mac; and when something looks good on a Mac, it will be too dark on a PC. If you are placing colored images or text on the Internet, you can't please all of the people all of the time. Currently, PNG is the only common graphic format used on the Web that can encode gamma-correction information.

Table 15-3
Sample CSS Colors

Color	Decimal RGB	Hexadecimal RGB	Percentage RGB
Pure red	rgb(255,0,0)	#FF0000	rgb(100%, 0%, 0%)
Pure green	rgb(0,255,0)	#00FF00	rgb(0%, 100%, 0%)
Pure blue	rgb(0,0,255)	#0000FF	rgb(0%, 0%, 100%)
White	rgb(255,255,255)	#FFFFFF	rgb(100%, 100%, 100%)
Black	rgb(0,0,0)	#000000	rgb(0%, 0%, 0%)
Light violet	rgb(255,204,255)	#FFCCFF	rgb(100%, 80%, 100%)
Medium gray	rgb(153,153,153)	#999999	rgb(60%, 60%, 60%)
Brown	rgb(153,102,51)	#996633	rgb(60%, 40%, 20%)
Pink	rgb(255,204,204)	#FFCCCC	rgb(100%, 80%, 80%)
Orange	rgb(255,204,204)	#FFCC00	rgb(100%, 80%, 80%)

Tip   Many people still use 256-color monitors. Some people even browse the Web in monochrome, especially on handheld devices such as Palm Pilots. Even on more capable systems, some colors are distinctly different on Macs and PCs. The most reliable colors are the 16 named colors.

The next most reliable colors are those formed using only the hexadecimal components 00, 33, 66, 99, CC, and FF (0, 51, 102, 153, 204, 255 in decimal; 0%, 20%, 40%, 60%, 80%, 100% in percentage units). For instance, 33FFCC is a "browser-safe" color because the red component is made from two threes, the green from two Fs, and the blue from two Cs.

If you specify a hexadecimal RGB color using only three digits, CSS duplicates them; for example, #FC0 is really #FFCC00 and #963 is really #996633.

System colors

CSS also allows you to specify colors by copying them from the local Graphical User Interface (GUI). These system colors can be used with all color-related properties. Style rules based on system colors take into account user preferences, and therefore offer some advantages, including:

✦ Pages that fit the user's preferred look and feel

✦ Greater accessibility for users whose default settings compensate for a disability

Table 15-4 lists system color keywords and their descriptions. Any of the color properties can take on these values.

Table 15-4
Additional System Colors Used with All Color-Related Properties

System Color Keywords	Description
ActiveBorder	The color of the border of the currently active window.
ActiveCaption	The color of the caption of the currently active window.
AppWorkspace	The background color of a multiple document interface window.
Background	Desktop background color.
ButtonFace	The foreground color for three-dimensional widgets.
ButtonHighlight	The shadow color for three-dimensional widgets (for edges facing away from the light source).
ButtonShadow	The shadow color for three-dimensional widgets.
ButtonText	Color of the text on push buttons.
CaptionText	Color of the text in captions, size boxes, and scrollbar arrow boxes.

System Color Keywords	Description
GrayText	The color of disabled text. This color is set to #000000 if the current display driver does not support a solid gray color.
Highlight	The color of items selected in a control.
HighlightText	The color with which selected text is highlighted.
InactiveBorder	The color of an inactive window border.
InactiveCaption	The color of an inactive window caption.
InactiveCaptionText	The color of the text of a caption of an inactive window.
InfoBackground	The background color for tooltip controls.
InfoText	The text color used in tooltip controls.
Menu	The background color of a menu.
MenuText	The color of text in menu items.
Scrollbar	The color of the scrollbar area.
ThreeDDarkShadow	The color of the dark shadow for three-dimensional widgets.
ThreeDFace	The face color for three-dimensional widgets.
ThreeDHighlight	The highlight color for three-dimensional widgets.
ThreeDLightShadow	The light color for three-dimensional widgets (for edges facing the light source).
ThreeDShadow	The color of the dark shadow for three-dimensional widgets.
Window	The color in the window background.
WindowFrame	The color of the window frame.
WindowText	The color of the text in the window.

For example, this rule sets the foreground and background colors of a VERSE to the same colors used for the foreground and background of the browser's window:

```
VERSE { color: WindowText; background-color: Window}
```

Keyword values

Keywords are not necessarily the same from property to property, but similar properties generally support similar keywords. For instance, the value of border-left-style can be any one of the keywords none, dotted, dashed, solid, double, groove, ridge, inset, or outset. The border-right-style, border-top-style, border-bottom-style, and border-style properties can also assume one of this set of values. The individual keywords are discussed in the sections about the individual properties.

Strings

A few CSS properties, such as font-family and content, have string values. In CSS, a string is a sequence of Unicode characters enclosed in either single or double quotes. If the string contains double quotes, then single quotes must be used to enclose the string and vice versa.

You can also use a backslash to escape otherwise illegal characters, typically single or double quotes. For instance, you can use \" to include a double quote mark inside a string that's surrounded by double quotes. Strings cannot contain line breaks. However, you can use \A to insert one. You can also include a raw line break if you prefix it by a backslash first. This is sometimes useful in the content property.

You can also use a backslash followed by the hexadecimal value of a Unicode character to insert a character that isn't easy to type. For example, to insert the Greek letter Θ, Unicode value 398 (in hexadecimal), you could simply use \398.

The Display Property

From the perspective of CSS, all elements are block elements, inline elements, table parts, or invisible. The display property specifies which one of these an element is. This property has 19 possible values given by keywords shown in Table 15-5.

Table 15-5
Values for the Display Property

Block Level	Inline Elements	Table Parts	Invisible
block	Inline	table-column	none
table	inline-table	table-cell	
list-item	marker	table-footer-group	
run-in	run-in	table-column-group	
compact	compact	table-row	
		table-header-group	
		table-row-group	
		table-caption	

Block elements are usually separated from other elements by placing a line break before and after each one. Table elements are parts of a grid. Inline elements are placed one after the other in a row. These are like words in a sentence. They move freely as text is added and deleted around them. Block elements are more fixed and at most move up and down but not left and right as content is added before and after them. Block elements include tables, lists, and list items. Most display types are just modifications of the main block or inline types.

A browser uses the distinction between these elements to make its first pass at laying out the document. It will place the text of any inline elements on the page moving from left to right, until it fills the line. If necessary, it will continue on the next line down. (The direction property lets you reverse the order so that elements are placed from right to left, useful if you're formatting Hebrew or Arabic.) However, when the browser comes to a block-level element, either the start or the end of one, it breaks the line and continues on the next line.

Consider Listing 15-1, which is a synopsis of William Shakespeare's *Twelfth Night*. The root element, SYNOPSIS, contains six top-level elements, one TITLE and five ACT elements. Each ACT contains an ACT_NUMBER and one or more SCENE children. Each SCENE contains a SCENE_NUMBER and a LOCATION. LOCATION elements contain mixed content, possibly including one or more CHARACTER elements.

Listing 15-1: **A synopsis of Shakespeare's *Twelfth Night* in XML**

```
<?xml version="1.0"?>
<?xml-stylesheet type="text/css" href="synopsis.css"?>
<SYNOPSIS>
  <TITLE>Twelfth Night</TITLE>

  <ACT>
    <ACT_NUMBER>Act 1</ACT_NUMBER>
    <SCENE>
      <SCENE_NUMBER>Scene 1</SCENE_NUMBER>
      <LOCATION><CHARACTER>Duke Orsino</CHARACTER>'s palace
      </LOCATION>
    </SCENE>
    <SCENE>
      <SCENE_NUMBER>Scene 2</SCENE_NUMBER>
      <LOCATION>The sea-coast</LOCATION>
    </SCENE>
    <SCENE>
      <SCENE_NUMBER>Scene 3</SCENE_NUMBER>
      <LOCATION><CHARACTER>Olivia</CHARACTER>'s house
      </LOCATION>
    </SCENE>
    <SCENE>
      <SCENE_NUMBER>Scene 4</SCENE_NUMBER>
      <LOCATION><CHARACTER>Duke Orsino</CHARACTER>'s palace.
      </LOCATION>
    </SCENE>
    <SCENE>
```

Continued

Listing 15-1 *(continued)*

```
      <SCENE_NUMBER>Scene 5</SCENE_NUMBER>
      <LOCATION><CHARACTER>Olivia</CHARACTER>'s house
      </LOCATION>
    </SCENE>
</ACT>

<ACT>
  <ACT_NUMBER>Act 2</ACT_NUMBER>
  <SCENE>
    <SCENE_NUMBER>Scene 1</SCENE_NUMBER>
    <LOCATION>The sea-coast</LOCATION>
  </SCENE>
  <SCENE>
    <SCENE_NUMBER>Scene 2</SCENE_NUMBER>
    <LOCATION>A street</LOCATION>
  </SCENE>
  <SCENE>
    <SCENE_NUMBER>Scene 3</SCENE_NUMBER>
    <LOCATION><CHARACTER>Olivia</CHARACTER>'s house
    </LOCATION>
  </SCENE>
  <SCENE>
    <SCENE_NUMBER>Scene 4</SCENE_NUMBER>
    <LOCATION><CHARACTER>Duke Orsino</CHARACTER>'s palace.
    </LOCATION>
  </SCENE>
  <SCENE>
    <SCENE_NUMBER>Scene 5</SCENE_NUMBER>
    <LOCATION><CHARACTER>Olivia</CHARACTER>'s garden
    </LOCATION>
  </SCENE>
</ACT>

<ACT>
  <ACT_NUMBER>Act 3</ACT_NUMBER>
  <SCENE>
    <SCENE_NUMBER>Scene 1</SCENE_NUMBER>
    <LOCATION><CHARACTER>Olivia</CHARACTER>'s garden
    </LOCATION>
  </SCENE>
  <SCENE>
    <SCENE_NUMBER>Scene 2</SCENE_NUMBER>
    <LOCATION><CHARACTER>Olivia</CHARACTER>'s house
    </LOCATION>
  </SCENE>
  <SCENE>
    <SCENE_NUMBER>Scene 3</SCENE_NUMBER>
    <LOCATION>A street</LOCATION>
  </SCENE>
  <SCENE>
```

```
      <SCENE_NUMBER>Scene 4</SCENE_NUMBER>
      <LOCATION><CHARACTER>Olivia</CHARACTER>'s garden
      </LOCATION>
    </SCENE>
  </ACT>

  <ACT>
    <ACT_NUMBER>Act 4</ACT_NUMBER>
    <SCENE>
      <SCENE_NUMBER>Scene 1</SCENE_NUMBER>
      <LOCATION><CHARACTER>Olivia</CHARACTER>'s front yard
      </LOCATION>
    </SCENE>
    <SCENE>
      <SCENE_NUMBER>Scene 2</SCENE_NUMBER>
      <LOCATION><CHARACTER>Olivia</CHARACTER>'s house
      </LOCATION>
    </SCENE>
    <SCENE>
      <SCENE_NUMBER>Scene 3</SCENE_NUMBER>
      <LOCATION><CHARACTER>Olivia</CHARACTER>'s garden
      </LOCATION>
    </SCENE>
  </ACT>

  <ACT>
    <ACT_NUMBER>Act 5</ACT_NUMBER>
    <SCENE>
      <SCENE_NUMBER>Scene 1</SCENE_NUMBER>
      <LOCATION><CHARACTER>Olivia</CHARACTER>'s front yard
      </LOCATION>
    </SCENE>
  </ACT>

</SYNOPSIS>
```

You can do a fair job of formatting this document using only display properties.
SYNOPSIS, TITLE, ACT, and SCENE are all block-level elements. ACT_NUMBER,
SCENE_NUMBER, LOCATION, and CHARACTER can remain inline elements. Listing 15-2
is a very simple style sheet that accomplishes this.

Listing 15-2: A very simple style sheet for the synopsis of a play

```
SYNOPSIS, TITLE, ACT, SCENE { display: block }
```

Figure 15-1 shows the synopsis of *Twelfth Night* loaded into Mozilla with the style sheet of Listing 15-2. Notice that in Listing 15-2 it is not necessary to explicitly specify that ACT_NUMBER, SCENE_NUMBER, LOCATION, and CHARACTER are all inline elements. This is the default unless otherwise specified. Children do not inherit the display property. Thus, just because SCENE is a block-level element does not mean that its children SCENE_NUMBER and LOCATION are also block-level elements.

Figure 15-1: The synopsis of *Twelfth Night* as displayed in Mozilla

Inline elements

Inline elements are laid out horizontally in a row starting from the top of the containing box of the surrounding page or block element, and moving from left to right. When a row fills up, a new row is started on the next line down. Words may be wrapped but only as necessary to fit the text on the screen. There are no hard line breaks. In HTML, EM, STRONG, B, I, and A are all inline elements. As another example, you can think of EM, STRONG, B, I, and A in this paragraph as inline code elements. They aren't separated out from the rest of the text. If no value is specified for the display property of an element, then the default is to make the element an inline element.

Block elements

Block-level elements are laid out vertically, one on top of the other. The first block is laid out in the top-left corner of the containing block, then the second block is placed below it, also flush against the left edge of the containing block. Each block-level element is separated from its sibling and parent elements, generally by placing a line break before and after it. The vertical distance between each block is defined by the individual block's margin and padding properties. In HTML P, BLOCKQUOTE, H1 through H6, and HR are all examples of block-level elements. The paragraphs and headings you see on this page are all block-level elements. Block-level elements may contain inline elements and other block-level elements, but inline elements should only contain other inline elements, not block-level elements, although this rule is not strictly enforced.

None

Setting display to none hides the element. An element whose display property is set to none is invisible and not rendered on the screen. It does not affect the position of other visible elements on the page. In HTML, TITLE, META, and HEAD would have a display property of none. In XML, display: none is often useful for meta-information in elements.

For example, suppose you wanted to list the locations in the synopsis but drop everything else. You could use the style sheet in Listing 15-3. This hides the TITLE, ACT_NUMBER, and SCENE_NUMBER elements by setting their display property to none. The LOCATION element is displayed as a block. Figure 15-2 shows the result of applying this style sheet to Listing 15-1.

Listing 15-3: A style sheet for the synopsis of a play that only shows the locations

```
TITLE, ACT_NUMBER, SCENE_NUMBER { display: none }
LOCATION { display: block}
```

Once you've hidden an element by using display: none you cannot then show any of its descendants. For example, consider these rules:

```
SYNOPSIS { display: none }
LOCATION { display: block}
```

Because the LOCATION element is contained inside the SYNOPSIS element, it is hidden even though its own display property is set to block.

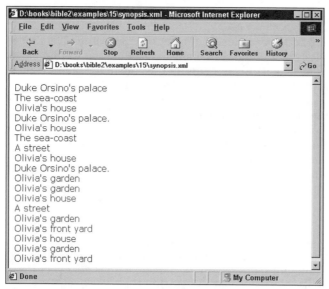

Figure 15-2: The synopsis of *Twelfth Night* showing only locations as displayed in Internet Explorer

Compact and run-in elements

The `compact` and `run-in` values of the `display` property identify an element as either a block or an inline box depending on context. Other properties declared as these types will treat them as either a block or inline element depending on what they eventually become.

A run-in box is a block-level element if the element that follows it is an inline element. It is an inline element if the element that follows it is a block-level element. In other words, it guarantees that there will be a line break before it but not after it. This is sometimes useful for headings.

A compact box will normally be a block-level element. However, if it's followed by a block-level element and it can fit in the margin of that element's box, then the browser will put it in the margin rather than making it a separate element.

Marker

Setting the `display` property to `marker` identifies a block that's formed by content generated in the style sheet rather than copied in from the XML document. This value is only used with the `:before` and `:after` pseudo-elements that have been attached to block-level elements. `marker` is discussed in more detail in the section on the `content` property in the next chapter.

Tables

CSS lets you format elements as parts of tables using these 10 values of the `display` property:

- ✦ `table`
- ✦ `inline-table`
- ✦ `table-row-group`
- ✦ `table-header-group`
- ✦ `table-footer-group`
- ✦ `table-row`
- ✦ `table-column-group`
- ✦ `table-column`
- ✦ `table-cell`
- ✦ `table-caption`

For example, setting the `display` property to `table` indicates that the selected element is a block-level container for various smaller children that will be arranged in a grid. The `inline-table` value forces the table to act as an inline element, allowing text to float along its sides, and allows multiple tables to be placed side by side.

The other eight values in this list identify particular parts of a table, and should only be used when the elements they're applied to are descendants of an element formatted as a table or inline table. The `table-caption` value formats an element as a table caption. The `table-row-group`, `table-header-group`, and `table-footer-group` values create groups of data cells that are formatted as a single row. The `table-column-group` creates a group of data cells that are formatted as a single column that was defined using the `table-column` value. XML elements that appear in table cells have — naturally enough — a `display` property with the value `table-cell`.

For example, if you were to build a table of the scenes and locations in the synopsis, each scene could be a row. Scene numbers and locations could be cells. Each act could be a row group. The title would be a header. Listing 15-4 demonstrates.

Listing 15-4: **A style sheet that formats synopses as tables**

```
SYNOPSIS {display: table}
TITLE {display: table-header}
SCENE { display: table-row}
ACT { display: table-row-group }
LOCATION, SCENE_NUMBER { display: table-cell }
```

Figure 15-3 shows the result of applying this style sheet to the *Twelfth Night* synopsis. By default, there are no grid lines or borders. These could be inserted using the border properties that you'll encounter shortly. It also wouldn't hurt to add a little padding around each cell.

Figure 15-3: A table-based synopsis layout

Caution   Internet Explorer 5.0 and 5.5 do not support table formatting using CSS.

List items

List-item elements are block-level elements with a list-item marker preceding them. In HTML, `LI` is a list-item element. If you simply set the `display` property to `list-item` and don't do anything else, then the element is formatted as a block-level element that may or may not have a bullet, called a *marker,* in front of it. However, you can set three additional properties that affect how list items are displayed. These are:

✦ `list-style-type`

✦ `list-style-image`

✦ `list-style-position`

There's also a shorthand `list-style` property that lets you set all three in a single rule.

Caution Internet Explorer 5.5 and Mozilla 0.9.2 and earlier do not yet support `display:`
`list-item`. Mozilla treats list items as simple block-level elements, while Internet
Explorer does even worse by treating them as inline elements. Opera 4.0.1 sup-
ports it, but has some weird bugs.

One thing CSS lists do not imply, however, is indentation. If you're accustomed to
using lists to indent items from HTML, you need to break yourself of that habit. In
CSS, indentation is provided by the margin and padding properties as well as the
`text-indent` property. List items are not automatically indented unless you set the
other properties necessary to indent something.

The list-style-type property

The `list-style-type` property determines the nature of the bullet character in
front of each list item. Possibilities include:

- `disc`: •
- `circle`: ◯
- `square`: ☐
- `decimal`: 1, 2, 3, 4, 5, and so on
- `decimal-leading-zero`: 01, 02, 03, 04, 05, and so on
- `lower-roman`: i, ii, iii, iv, and so on
- `upper-roman`: I, II, III, IV, and so on
- `lower-alpha`: a, b, c, and so on
- `upper-alpha`: A, B, C, and so on
- `lower-latin`: same as `lower-alpha`; a, b, c, and so on
- `upper-latin`: same as `upper-alpha`; A, B, C, and so on
- `lower-greek`: α, β, γ, δ, ε, and so on
- `hebrew`: א, ב, ג, ד, ה, and so on
- `armenian`: Ա, Բ, Գ, Դ, Ե and so on
- `georgian`: ა, ბ, გ, დ, ე, and so on
- `cjk-ideographic`: 一, 二, 三, and so on
- `hiragana`: あ, い, う, え, お, か, and so on
- `katakana`: ア, イ, ウ, エ, オ, カ, キ, and so on
- `hiragana-iroha`: い, ろ, は, に, ほ, へ, と, and so on
- `katakana-iroha`: イ, ロ, ハ, ニ, ホ, ヘ, ト, and so on
- `none`: no bullet character is used

I would not rely on a typical Western browser being capable of handling the more unusual of these. In that case, it will default to `decimal`. (European style numerals have pretty much replaced Hebrew, Han, and other traditional number systems in most of the world for day-to-day use.) If no value is set, the default is `disc`. For example, the style sheet in Listing 15-5 defines `ACT` and `SCENE` as list items. However, `ACT` is given no bullet, and `SCENE` is given a square bullet. Figure 15-4 shows the synopsis in Opera with this style sheet.

Listing 15-5: A style sheet for a play synopsis that uses list items

```
SYNOPSIS, TITLE { display: block }
ACT { display: list-item; list-style-type: none }
SCENE { display: list-item; list-style-type: square }
```

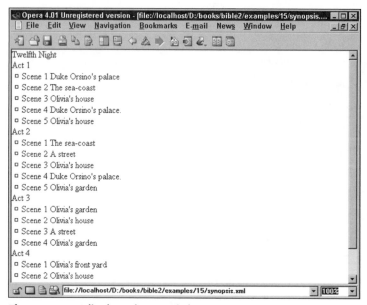

Figure 15-4: A list-based synopsis layout

The list-style-image property

Alternately, you can use a bitmapped image of your choice loaded from a file as the bullet. To do this you set the `list-style-image` property to the URL of the image. If both `list-style-image` and `list-style-type` are set, the `list-style-image` will be used, unless it can't be found, in which case the bullet specified by `list-style-type` will be used. For example, this rule uses a heart (♥) stored in the file heart.jpg as the bullet before each scene. (After all, *Twelfth Night* is a romantic comedy.) Figure 15-5 shows the result of adding this rule to the synopsis style sheet.

```
SCENE { display: list-item;
        list-style-image: url(heart.jpg);
        list-style-type: square
}
```

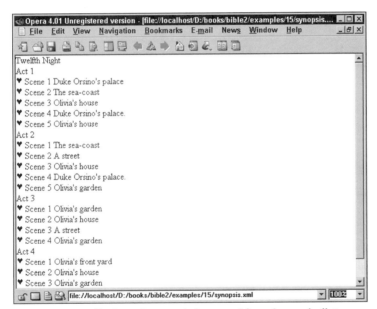

Figure 15-5: A list-based synopsis layout with an image bullet

The list-style-position property

The `list-style-position` property specifies whether the bullet is drawn inside or outside the text of the list item. The legal values are `inside` and `outside`. The default is `outside`. The difference is only obvious when the text wraps onto more than one line. This is inside:

♦ If music be the food of love, play on/Give me excess of it, that, surfeiting,/The appetite may sicken, and so die./That strain again! it had a dying fall:

This is outside:

✦ If music be the food of love, play on/Give me excess of it, that, surfeiting,/The appetite may sicken, and so die./That strain again! it had a dying fall:

The list-style shorthand property

Finally, the list-style property is a shorthand that allows you to set all three of the above-described properties simultaneously. For example, this rule says that a SCENE is displayed inside with a heart image and no bullet:

```
SCENE { display: list-item;
        list-style: none inside url(heart.jpg) }
```

Box Properties

CSS arranges text on a two-dimensional canvas. The elements drawn on this canvas are laid out in imaginary rectangles called boxes. Each box is given a size and a position as well as margins, borders, and padding. The box edges are always oriented parallel to the edges of the canvas. Box properties enable you to specify the width, height, margins, padding, and borders of the individual boxes. Figure 15-6 shows how these properties relate to each other.

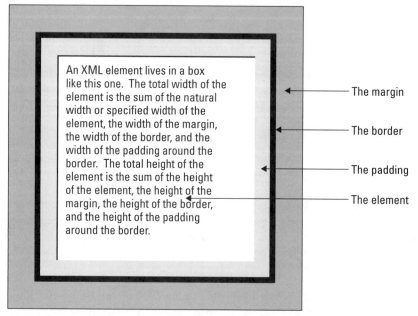

Figure 15-6: A CSS box with margin, border, and padding

These boxes stack together and wrap around each other so that the contents of each element are aligned in an orderly fashion, based upon the rules of the style sheets.

Margin properties

Margin properties specify the amount of space added to the box outside its border. This may be set separately for the top, bottom, right and left margins using the `margin-top`, `margin-bottom`, `margin-right`, and `margin-left` properties. Each margin may be given as an absolute length or as a percentage of the size of the parent element's width. For example, you can add a little extra space between each ACT element and the preceding element by setting ACT's `margin-top` property to 3ex as Listing 15-6 and Figure 15-7 demonstrate.

Listing 15-6: **Extra space on the top margin of each act**

```
ACT { margin-top: 3ex }
SYNOPSIS, TITLE, ACT, SCENE { display: block }
```

Figure 15-7: The top margin of the ACT element is larger

You can also set all four margins simultaneously using the shorthand `margin` property. For example, you can add extra white space around the entire *Twelfth Night* document by setting the margin property for the root-level element (SYNOPSIS in this example) as shown by the first rule of Listing 15-7 and in Figure 15-8.

Listing 15-7: Adding a one centimeter margin on each side of the SYNOPSIS

```
SYNOPSIS { margin: 1cm 1cm 1cm 1cm }
SYNOPSIS, TITLE, ACT, SCENE { display: block }
ACT { margin-top: 3ex }
```

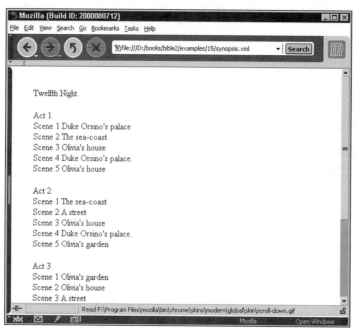

Figure 15-8: One centimeter of white space around the entire synopsis

In fact, this is the same as using a single value for margin, which CSS interprets as being applicable to all four sides.

```
SYNOPSIS { margin: 1cm }
```

Given two `margin` values, the first applies to top and bottom, the second to right and left. Given three `margin` values, the first applies to the top, the second to the right and left, and the third to the bottom. It's probably easier to just use the separate `margin-top`, `margin-bottom`, `margin-right`, **and** `margin-left` properties if you want to specify different margins for different sides.

Border properties

Most boxes don't have borders. They are invisible rectangles that affect the layout of their contents, but are not seen as boxes by the readers. However, you can make a box visible by drawing lines around it using the border properties. Border properties let you specify the style, width, and color of the border.

Border style

By default, no border is drawn around boxes regardless of the width and color of the border. To make a border visible you must change the `border-style` property of the box from its default value of `none` to one of these 10 values:

✦ `none`: no line

✦ `hidden`: an invisible line that still takes up space

✦ `dotted`: a dotted line

✦ `dashed`: a dashed line

✦ `solid`: a solid line

✦ `double`: a double solid line

✦ `grooved`: a line that appears to be drawn into the page

✦ `ridge`: a line that appears to be coming out of the page

✦ `inset`: the entire element (not just the line around the edge) appears pushed into the document

✦ `outset`: the entire element (not just the line around the edge) appears to be pushed out of the document

The `border-style` property can have between one and four values. As with the `margin` property, a single value applies to all four borders. Two values set the top and bottom borders to the first style, right and left borders to the second style. Three values set the top, right and left, and bottom border styles in that order. Four values set each border in the order top, right, bottom, and left. For example, Listing 15-8 adds a rule to enclose the entire SYNOPSIS in a solid border.

Listing 15-8: **Bordering the SYNOPSIS**

```
SYNOPSIS { border-style: solid }
SYNOPSIS { margin: 1cm 1cm 1cm 1cm }
SYNOPSIS, TITLE, ACT, SCENE { display: block }
ACT { margin-top: 3ex }
```

Figure 15-9 shows the result in Mozilla. In this case, the border has the secondary effect of making the margin more obvious. (Remember that the margin is outside the border.)

```
SYNOPSIS { border-style: solid }
```

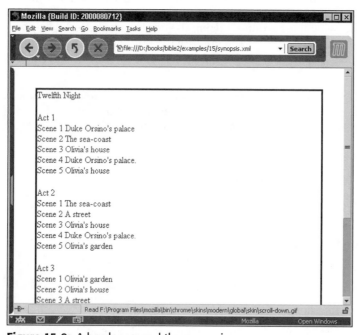

Figure 15-9: A border around the synopsis

Border width

Four border-width properties specify the width of the borderlines along the top, bottom, right, and left edges of the box. These are:

- ✦ `border-top-width`
- ✦ `border-right-width`
- ✦ `border-bottom-width`
- ✦ `border-left-width`

Each may be specified as an absolute length or as one of three keywords: `thin`, `medium`, or `thick`. Border widths cannot be negative, but can be zero.

For example, to enclose the `SYNOPSIS` element in a one-pixel wide solid border (the thinnest border any computer monitor can display), you could use the next rule to set these four properties:

```
SYNOPSIS { border-style:         solid;
           border-top-width:     1px;
           border-right-width:   1px;
           border-bottom-width:  1px;
           border-left-width:    1px }
```

If you want to set all or several borders to the same width, it's most convenient to use the `border-width` shorthand property. This property can have between one and four values. One value sets all four border widths. Two values set the top and bottom borders to the first value, right and left borders to the second value. Three values set the top, right, and left, and bottom widths in that order. Four values set each border in the order top, right, bottom, and left. For example, the following is equivalent to the previous rule:

```
SYNOPSIS { border-style: solid; border-width: 1px }
```

Border color

Most browsers draw borders in black by default, or possibly in shades of gray if necessary to produce 3D effects for the grooved, ridge, inset, and outset styles. However, you can use the border-color properties to change this for one or more sides of the box. These properties are:

✦ `border-top-color`

✦ `border-right-color`

✦ `border-bottom-color`

✦ `border-left-color`

There's also a `border-color` shorthand property that sets the color of all four borders. A single value sets all four border colors. Two values set the top and bottom borders to the first color, the right and left borders to the second color. Three values set the top, right and left, and bottom border colors in that order. Four values set each border in the order top, right, bottom, and left. The value can be any recognized color name or an RGB triplet. For example, to enclose the SYNOPSIS element in a one-pixel wide, solid red border, you'd use this rule:

```
SYNOPSIS { border-style: solid;
           border-width: 1px;
           border-color: red }
```

Because this book is printed in black and white, I'll spare you the picture.

Shorthand border properties

Five shorthand border properties let you set the width, style, and color of a border with one rule. These properties are:

- ✦ border-top
- ✦ border-right
- ✦ border-bottom
- ✦ border-left
- ✦ border

For instance, the border-top property provides a width, style, and color for the top border. The border-right, border-bottom, and border-left properties are similar. For example, the first rule of Listing 15-9 produces a two-pixel groove blue border (a horizontal rule if you will) below each act. Figure 15-10 shows the result.

Listing 15-9: **Using borders to produce horizontal rules**

```
ACT { border-bottom: 2px groove blue }
SYNOPSIS { border-style: solid }
SYNOPSIS { margin: 1cm 1cm 1cm 1cm }
SYNOPSIS, TITLE, ACT, SCENE { display: block }
ACT { margin-top: 3ex }
```

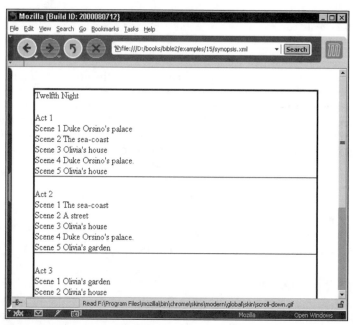

Figure 15-10: A two-pixel groove bottom border is similar to HTML's HR element

The border property sets all four sides to the specified width, style, and height. For example, this rule draws a three-pixel wide, solid, red border around a SYNOPSIS element.

```
SYNOPSIS { border: 3pt solid red }
```

Padding properties

The padding properties specify the amount of space on the *inside* of the border of the box. The border of the box, if shown, falls between the margin and the padding. Padding may be set separately for the top, bottom, right and left padding using the padding-top, padding-bottom, padding-right, and padding-left properties. Each padding may be given as an absolute length or be a percentage of the element's width. For example, you can set off the SYNOPSIS from its border by setting its padding properties as shown in this rule.

```
SYNOPSIS { padding-bottom: 1em;
           padding-top:    1em;
           padding-right:  1em;
           padding-left:   1em }
```

You can also set all four at once using the shorthand padding property. For example, this rule is the same as the previous one:

```
SYNOPSIS { padding: 1em 1em 1em 1em }
```

In fact, this is the same as using a single value for the padding property, which CSS interprets as applying to all four sides:

```
SYNOPSIS { padding: 1em }
```

Given two padding values, the first applies to the top and bottom, the second to the right and left. Given three padding values, the first applies to the top, the second to the right and left, and the third to the bottom. It's probably easier to use the separate padding-top, padding-bottom, padding-right, and padding-left properties.

The blue borders below the acts in the synopsis in Figure 15-10 seem a little too close, so let's add an ex of padding between the end of the act and the border with the padding-bottom property, as shown in the first rule of Listing 15-10. Figure 15-11 shows the result. Generally, it's a good idea to use a little padding around borders to make the text easier to read.

Listing 15-10: **Padding the border**

```
ACT { padding-bottom: 1ex }
ACT { border-bottom: 2px groove blue }
SYNOPSIS { border-style: solid }
SYNOPSIS { margin: 1cm 1cm 1cm 1cm }
SYNOPSIS, TITLE, ACT, SCENE { display: block }
ACT { margin-top: 3ex }
```

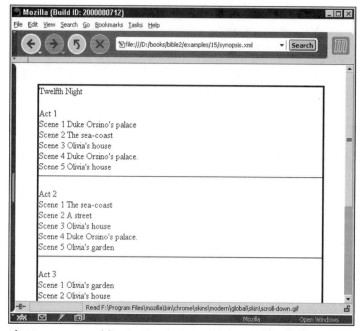

Figure 15-11: Padding makes borders easier on the eye

Size

CSS lets you choose exactly how big each element's box will be. By default, boxes are just big enough to contain their contents, borders, and padding. Inline and table elements that contain text always have these automatically calculated dimensions. However, you can make block-level elements either bigger or smaller than this default by using these six properties:

✦ height

✦ width

✦ min-width

✦ max-width

✦ min-height

✦ max-height

The width and height properties

Usually the browser decides how much space each element requires by adding up the total size of its contents, along with the size of any borders and padding; and usually this is exactly what you want it to do. However, you can force a block-level element to a predetermined size by setting its width and height properties. Consider Listing 15-11. The first rule says that every TITLE element will be exactly three inches wide and two inches high. Even if it doesn't use up all this space, other elements that follow it will leave the extra space empty.

Listing 15-11: **A style sheet that sets a fixed size for the TITLE element**

```
TITLE      { width: 3in; height: 2in }
SYNOPSIS, TITLE, ACT, SCENE { display: block }
TITLE      { border-style: solid }
SYNOPSIS { border-style: dotted }
ACT        { border-style: dashed }
SCENE      { border-style: groove }
ACT, SCENE, TITLE, SYNOPSIS { margin: 1ex }
```

Figure 15-12 demonstrates the effect of Listing 15-11. Borders are added to all the block level elements so you can see where their boxes are placed. All of them except for TITLE take up the minimum amount of vertical space they need to hold their contents and the maximum amount of horizontal space. However, because the TITLE element's width and height properties have been set, it's taller than it needs to be and narrower than it could be.

If the box size you specify is too small to hold what the box needs to hold, the contents will not be scaled to fit. By default the content will spill out of the box and overlap whatever follows. Figure 15-13 demonstrates this with a box that's too small for the actual title. However, you can clip or scroll the overflowed contents using the overflow property.

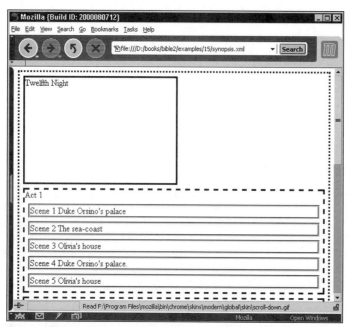

Figure 15-12: This TITLE element is exactly three inches wide and two inches high

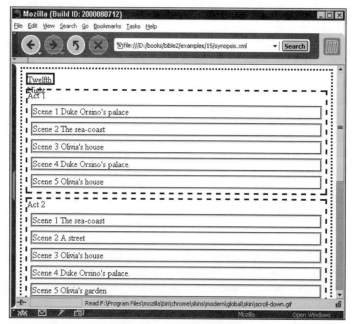

Figure 15-13: This TITLE element is exactly three ems wide and one em high, too small to hold the entire title

You do not have to set both `width` and `height`. You can set one or the other, or neither. The default setting for both is `auto`; that is, calculate the necessary size based on the contents and context of the box.

The min-width and min-height properties

If you want an element to take up at least a minimum amount of space, but you do want to allow it to grow larger if necessary to hold its contents, you can set the `min-height` and `min-width` properties. These specify the smallest dimensions that the element will use. For example, this rule says that a `TITLE` element must be at least one inch wide and one inch high:

```
TITLE { min-width: 1in; min-height: 1in }
```

If the title needs more space than that, the browser is free to make its box larger. If it takes up less space than that, then the browser will leave some empty space. `Min-height` and `min-width` should be preferred to `height` and `width` because you can never be sure exactly how much space any given string of text is going to occupy from one computer to the next. Using `min-height` and `min-width` instead of `height` and `width` will give you the same effect most of the time, and look much better in the occasional cases where you do need the extra space.

The `min-height` and `min-width` properties override `height` and `width`. If `height` is set to something smaller than `min-height`, then the value of the `min-height` property determines the height of the box, regardless of the value of `height`. The same is true for `width` and `min-width`.

The max-width and max-height properties

If you want an element to occupy no more than a certain amount of space, but you do want it to be smaller if its contents allow, you can set the `max-height` and `max-width` properties. Together, these specify the largest area that an element will occupy. For example, this rule says that a `TITLE` element must be no more than three inches wide and two inches high:

```
TITLE { max-width: 3in; max-height: 2in }
```

If the title needs less space than that, the browser is free to shrink its box. However, if it needs more space than that, then the browser will let some text fall outside the box, or otherwise handle it as specified by the `overflow` property. Because `max-height` and `max-width` can cause text to overlap other text in an unattractive fashion, just like `height` and `width` can, you should use it sparingly.

The `max-height` and `max-width` properties override `height` and `width`. If `height` is set to something larger than `max-height`, then the value of the `max-height` property determines the height of the box, regardless of the value of `height`. The same is true for `width` and `max-width`.

The overflow property

When the size of a box is precisely specified using `width` and `height` or limited by `max-width` and `max-height`, it's entirely possible that its contents may take up more area than the box actually has. The `overflow` property controls how the excess content is dealt with. This property can be set to one of four values:

✦ `visible`

✦ `hidden`

✦ `scroll`

✦ `auto`

The default is `visible`, which means let the text continue outside the box, on top of the text in other boxes if necessary. You saw an example of this in Figure 15-13. On the other hand, if `overflow` is set to `hidden`, then the visible text will be clipped to its containing box as shown for the `TITLE` element in Figure 15-14. This rule produces that effect:

```
TITLE { width: 3em; height: 1em; overflow: hidden}
```

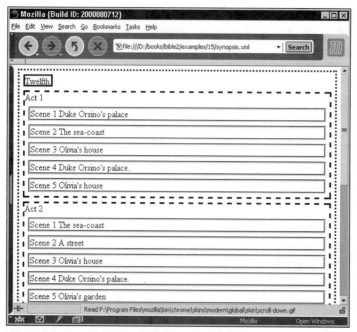

Figure 15-14: This TITLE element is exactly three ems wide and one em high, too small to hold the entire title, so the overflow is hidden

Another option that's useful, especially for relatively large blocks that contain still larger amounts of text, is to provide scroll bars. You can request this by setting overflow to scroll. To specify scroll bars only if they're actually needed — that is, only if the content does indeed overflow — choose the value auto.

Clipping

Clipping is a very unusual effect that shows only some of the content of a box. It does this by setting a clipping region using the clip property. By default, the clipping region is the content box itself. However, you can make it smaller so that only some of the box's content is shown. You can only clip elements whose overflow attribute is set to some value other than visible.

Caution Current Web browsers don't support the clip property very well, if at all.

For example, let's suppose you want to put the title in a two centimeter by two centimeter box. This rule does that:

```
TITLE {height: 2cm; width: 2cm}
```

Now suppose you only want to show the content in the middle one centimeter by one centimeter square of that box. You add this rule:

```
TITLE {clip: rect(0.5cm, 0.5cm, 0.5cm, 0.5cm) }
```

The first argument is the offset of the clipping region from the top of the box. The second argument is the offset of the clipping region from the bottom of the box. The third and fourth arguments are the offset of the clipping region from the left and right sides of the box respectively. Only content that appears in the clipping region will be shown. The major purpose of clipping is to choose what subset of the content will be shown when the block that's available to show it is smaller than the size of the content.

Positioning

For truly custom layouts, CSS lets you decide exactly where to put each element's box. By default, block-level elements contained inside the same parent element follow each other on the page. They do not line up side by side or wrap around each other. You can change this with judicious use of the float and clear properties. You can even make elements overlap each other, in which case the z-index property determines which element's on top and which is on bottom.

The position property

Element boxes can be positioned automatically by the browser, offset relative to their automatically calculated positions, or placed at a fixed position in the box that contains them or at a fixed position on the page. The position property determines which of these options the browser uses to position each element. It can have one of these four keyword values:

✦ static: the default layout

✦ relative: elements are offset from their static positions

✦ absolute: elements are placed at a specific position relative to the box they're contained in

✦ fixed: elements are placed at a specific point in the window or on the page

Relative positioning

As a document is being laid out, the formatter chooses positions for items according to the normal flow of elements and text. This is the default static formatting used by most documents. After this has been completed, the elements may be shifted relative to their natural, calculated positions. This adjustment in an element's position is known as *relative positioning*. Altering the position of an element in this manner does not affect the positions of other elements. Thus, boxes can overlap because relatively positioned boxes retain all of their normal flow sizes and spacing.

To relatively position an element you set its position property to relative. Then you give the length to offset the left edge of the element to the right of its normal position as the value of the left attribute and the length to offset the top edge of the element down from its normal position as the value of the top attribute. You can use negative numbers to offset to the left and up. For example, Listing 15-12 moves the TITLE element 50 pixels to the right and down from where it would normally be placed.

Listing 15-12: A style sheet that adjusts the position of the TITLE element

```
TITLE     { position: relative; left: 50px; top: 50px }
SYNOPSIS, TITLE, ACT, SCENE { display: block }
TITLE     { border-style: solid }
SYNOPSIS { border-style: dotted }
ACT       { border-style: dashed }
SCENE     { border-style: groove }
ACT, SCENE, TITLE, SYNOPSIS { margin: 1ex }
```

Figure 15-15 shows how this makes the TITLE element overlap some other elements on the page.

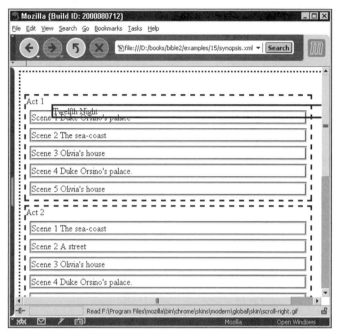

Figure 15-15: A relatively positioned TITLE element

You can use the right property to offset the right edge of the element from the right edge of its normal block; that is, to move it to the left. Similarly, you can set the bottom property to offset the bottom edge of the element from the bottom edge of its normal position and thus move it up. You should not set left at the same time as right or top at the same time as bottom.

Absolute positioning

An absolutely positioned element is placed at a specific point inside the block that contains it. For example, the coordinates of an absolutely positioned TITLE element are relative to the top-left corner of the SYNOPSIS block. If the SYNOPSIS block moves, then the TITLE element moves with it. However, if a sibling ACT element moves, the TITLE element won't move to accommodate it. The contents of absolutely positioned elements do not flow around other boxes, so absolute positioning may cause elements to overlap. In fact, absolutely positioned elements have no impact on the flow of their following siblings, so elements that follow the absolutely positioned one act as if it were not there.

The position of the upper-left corner of an absolutely positioned element is set by the top and left properties. The position of the lower-right corner of an absolutely positioned element is set by the bottom and right properties. Specifying all four positions fixes the height and width of the box. If one corner is omitted, the box is sized appropriately for its contents. For example, this rule places the TITLE element exactly one inch down and one inch to the right of the upper-left corner of its parent SYNOPSIS element:

```
TITLE { position: absolute;
        left: 1in; top: 1in; width: 3in; height: 2in}
```

Figure 15-16 shows the result. Notice that unlike a relatively positioned element, an absolutely positioned element does not reserve any space for itself. Unless everything on the page is absolutely positioned, it's almost certain that some elements will overlap each other.

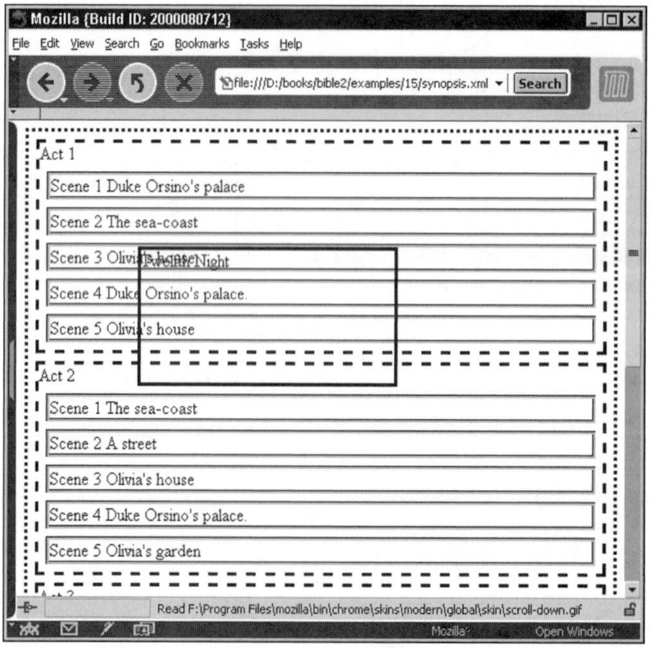

Figure 15-16: An absolutely positioned TITLE element

Most of the time, absolute positioning is a bad idea for the same reason that absolute sizes are a bad idea. Although an absolutely positioned element may look okay on your system, it probably won't on some of the systems that people will use to read the document.

Fixed positioning

Elements with fixed positions are placed at coordinates relative to the window in which they're displayed or the piece of paper on which they're printed. A fixed element does not move when the document is scrolled. When printed on paper, a fixed element appears in the same place on each page. This enables you to place a footer or header on a document, or a signature at the end of a series of one-page letters. For example, this rule puts the title near the top-center of the window even when the user has scrolled down to the bottom of the synopsis:

```
TITLE  { position: fixed; top: 0.1in; left: 2in}
```

Unfortunately, this isn't as useful as it might sound, because unless you also carefully apply a fixed position to everything else on the page, the elements will overlap as shown in Figure 15-17.

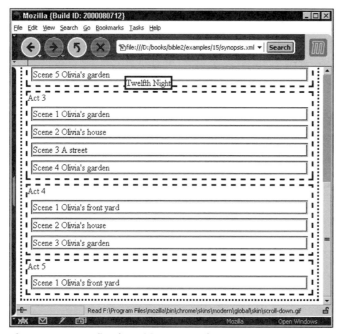

Figure 15-17: A fixed position TITLE element

Stacking elements with the z-index property

When boxes overlap, the z-index property determines which boxes are on top of which others. Elements with larger z-indexes are placed on top of elements with smaller z-indexes. Whether the elements on the bottom show through is a function of the background properties of the element on top of them. If the background is transparent, at least some of what's below will probably show through. For example, Figure 15-17 showed the title on top of the synopsis. You can change the z-index to put the title behind the synopsis using these rules:

```
TITLE     { z-index: 1}
SYNOPSIS  { z-index: 2}
```

Caution   Current Web browsers don't support the z-index property very well, if at all.

The float property

The float property, whose value is none by default, can be set to left or right. If the value is left, then the element is moved to the left side of the page and the text flows around it on the right. In HTML, this is how an IMG with ALIGN="LEFT" behaves. If the value is right, then the element is moved to the right side of the page and the text flows around it on the left. In HTML, this is how an IMG with ALIGN="RIGHT" behaves. For example, the first rule in Listing 15-13 lets text float to the right of the title as shown in Figure 15-18:

Listing 15-13: **A floating TITLE**

```
TITLE { float: left }
SYNOPSIS, TITLE, ACT, SCENE { display: block }
TITLE     { border-style: solid }
SYNOPSIS { border-style: dotted }
ACT      { border-style: dashed }
SCENE    { border-style: groove }
ACT, SCENE, TITLE, SYNOPSIS { margin: 1ex }
```

The clear property

The clear property specifies whether an element can have floating elements on its sides. If it cannot, the element will be moved below any floating elements that precede it. It's related to the HTML <BR CLEAR="ALL"> element. The possible values are:

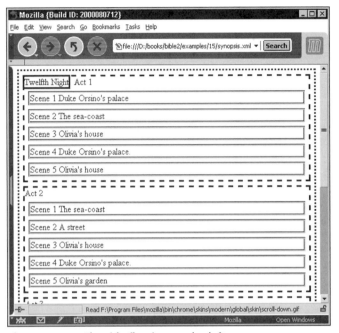

Figure 15-18: The title floating on the left

✦ none

✦ left

✦ right

✦ both

The default value, none, causes floating elements to appear on both sides of the element. The value left bans floating elements on the left side of the element. The value right bans floating elements on the right side of the element. The value both bans floating elements on the both sides of the element. For example, suppose you add this rule to the style sheet in Listing 15-13:

```
ACT { clear: left }
```

Now, although the TITLE element wants to float on the left of the first ACT, ACT doesn't allow that, as is shown in Figure 15-19. TITLE is still on the left, but now ACT is pushed down below the image.

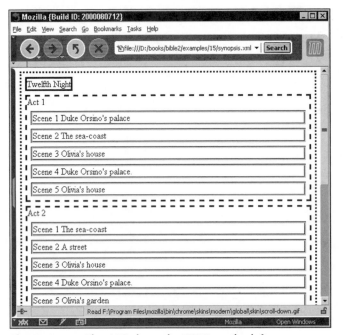

Figure 15-19: The ACT clears the TITLE on the left

Formatting Pages

CSS makes the reasonable assumption that pages are rectangular. A page can have most of the standard box properties including margins and size. However, a page box does not have borders or padding because these would fall off the actual page. The @page selector selects the page so you can set those properties that apply to the page itself rather than XML elements on the page. Pseudo-classes can specify different properties for the first page, right facing pages, and left facing pages.

@page

@page is a selector that refers to the page box. This is a rectangular area, roughly the size of a printed page, which contains the page area and the margin block. The page area contains the material to be displayed, and the edges of the box provide a container in which page layout occurs between page breaks. For example, this rule gives the page one-inch margins on all four sides:

```
@page  { margin-left:   1.0in;
         margin-right:  1.0in;
         margin-top:    1.0in;
         margin-bottom: 1.0in }
```

Because the @page rule is unaware of the page's content, including the fonts it uses, it can't understand measurements in ems and exs. All other units of measurement are acceptable, including percentages. Percentages used on margin settings are a percentage of the total page box size. Page boxes allow negative values for margins, which can place content outside of the area normally accessible by the application or printer. In most of these cases, the information is simply cut.

@page selects every page of a document. You can use one of the page pseudo-class selectors — :first, :left, or :right — to specify different properties for the first page of a document, for the left (generally even numbered) pages of a document, and for the right (generally odd numbered) pages of a document. For example, these rules specify one inch outside margins and half inch inside margins:

```
@page:right   { margin-left: 0.5in; margin-right: 1.0in }
@page:left    { margin-left: 1.0in; margin-right: 0.5in }
@page:first   { margin-left: 0.5in; margin-right: 1.0in }
```

The size property

In an @page rule, the size property specifies the height and width of the page. You can set the size as one or two absolute lengths or as one of the four keywords auto, portrait, landscape, or inherit. If only one length is given, the page will be a square. When both dimensions are given, the first is the width of the page, the second is the height. For example,

```
@page { size: 8.5in 11in }
```

The auto setting automatically sizes to the target screen or sheet. landscape forces the document to be formatted to fit the target page, but with long sides horizontal. The portrait setting formats the document to fit the default target page size, but with long sides vertical.

The margin property

The margin property determines the sizes of the margins of the page, the rectangular areas on all four sides in which nothing is printed. This property is used as a shorthand for setting the margin-top, margin-bottom, margin-right, and margin-left properties separately. These properties are the same as they are for boxes. For example, this rule describes an 8.5- by 11-inch page with one inch margins on all sides.

```
@page { size: 8.5in 11in; margin: 1.0in }
```

The mark property

The mark property places marks on the page delineating where the paper should be cut and/or how pages should be aligned. These marks appear in the margins outside of the page box. The software controls the rendering of the marks, which are only displayed on absolute page boxes. Absolute page boxes cannot be moved and are controlled by the general margins of the page. Relative page boxes are aligned against a target page, in most cases forcing the marks off the edge of the page. When aligning a relative page box, you are essentially looking at the page in your mind's eye and using `margin` and `padding` properties to move the printed area of that page about the physical paper.

The `mark` property has four possible values — `crop`, `cross`, `inherit`, and `none` — and can only be used with the @page element. Crop marks identify the cutting edges of paper. Cross marks, also known as registration marks, are used to align pages after printing. If set to `none`, no marks will be displayed on the document. For example, this rule specifies a page with both crop and cross marks:

```
@page { mark: crop cross}
```

The page property

As well as using the `@page` selector to specify page properties, you can attach page properties to individual elements using the `page` property. To do this you write an `@page` rule that specifies the page properties, give that `@page` rule a name, and then use the name as the value of the `page` property of a normal element rule. For example, these two rules together say that a `SYNOPSIS` will be printed in landscape orientation:

```
@page rotated { size: landscape}
SYNOPSIS       { page: rotated}
```

When using the `page` property, it's possible that different sibling elements will specify different page properties. If this happens, a page break will be inserted between the elements. If a child uses a different page layout than its parent, the child's layout takes precedence.

Controlling page breaks

When working in paged media, it's often useful to be able to specify that one or more elements are kept on the same page if possible. Conversely, you may want to suggest a good place to break a page. You can control page breaks with these five CSS properties:

- ✦ `page-break-before`
- ✦ `page-break-after`
- ✦ `page-break-inside`
- ✦ `orphans`
- ✦ `widows`

Generally, these properties are ignored in nonpaged media such as browser windows.

The `page-break-before` property controls whether pages are allowed, forbidden, or required before the selected element; the `page-break-after` property controls whether pages are allowed, forbidden, or required after the selected element; and the `page-break-inside` property determines whether pages are allowed, forbidden, or required inside the selected element. These can be used to keep paragraphs of related text, headings and their body text, images and their captions, or complete tables together on the same page. They can also be used to insert page breaks. `Page-break-before` and `page-break-after` can have any of these five values:

- ✦ `auto`
- ✦ `always`
- ✦ `avoid`
- ✦ `left`
- ✦ `right`

`Page-break-inside` is limited to `avoid` and `auto`.

The default for all three properties is `auto`, which means the formatter is free to put page breaks wherever it likes. The value `always` means that a page break is required in the specified place. The value `avoid` prevents a page break from occurring where indicated. Finally, the values `left` and `right` force either one or two page breaks, whichever is necessary to make the next page either a left- or right-hand page. This is useful at the end of a chapter in a book where chapters generally start on right-hand pages, even when that leaves blank pages.

The following rule inserts a page break before and after every SYNOPSIS element in a document but not inside a synopsis so that each synopsis appears on its own page.

```
SYNOPSIS { page-break-before: always;
           page-break-after:  always;
           page-break-inside: avoid }
```

This rule prevents page breaks inside acts but allows them if necessary, between acts:

```
ACT { page-break-before: auto;
      page-break-after:  auto;
      page-break-inside: avoid }
```

This keeps every act complete on one page. Of course, it is possible that one ACT element will simply be too large to fit on a single page. In this case, the formatter may break the page anyway.

Widows and orphans

Sometimes it's necessary to insert a page break in the middle of an element. For instance a paragraph may begin on one page and continue on the next. This avoids large runs of white space at the ends of pages. However, if too little of a paragraph is left on any one page, then the page looks ugly. For instance, you would normally prefer to avoid printing just the first line of a paragraph at the end of a page and the rest of the paragraph on the next page. It would be more aesthetic to leave a blank line at the bottom of the page and move the entire paragraph to the next page. Similarly, there should be more than one line of a paragraph at the top of any given page. If the normal line-breaking algorithm only places the last line of a paragraph at the top of the page, then the second-to-last line of the paragraph should be removed from the bottom of the previous page and placed at the top of the next page.

Single lines at the bottom of a page are called *orphans*. Single lines at the top of a page are called *widows*. You can set the orphans and widows properties of an element to specify the minimum number of lines of a block-level element that the formatter must place before and after each page break. For example, this rule says that if there's a page break in the middle of an ACT, then there must be at least two lines of the ACT on both sides of the break:

```
ACT {  orphans: 2; widows: 2 }
```

Summary

This chapter discussed CSS's layout model. In this chapter, you learned that:

✦ Lengths in CSS can be specified in relative or absolute units. Relative units are preferred.

✦ Color is given in a 24-bit RGB space using decimal, hexadecimal, or percentage components.

✦ The display property determines whether an element is a block element, inline element, list item, or table part.

✦ The text of XML elements are placed in rectangular boxes on one or more pages when rendered by a browser.

✦ Box properties let you adjust borders, margins, and padding around elements.

✦ Margins are extra white space inside an element's box and can be set separately for each side.

✦ Padding is extra white space inside an element's box and can be set separately for each side.

✦ A border is a line drawn between the margin and padding of a box and can be set separately for each side in a variety of styles, widths, and colors.

✦ The `height`, `width`, `min-height`, `min-width`, `max-height`, and `max-width` properties let you adjust the size of element boxes.

✦ The `position`, `left`, `right`, `top`, and `bottom` properties let you adjust where an element box is placed on the page.

✦ The `@page` rule lets you set the margins, size, and other properties of the pages on which the XML elements will be placed.

The documents in this chapter were rather dry. Elements moved around on the page, but they didn't have any *flare*. They weren't italic or bold or big or small or flashing neon. The next chapter shows you the CSS properties that adjust a variety of text styles including font weight, font size, alignment, and even pitch, volume, and speed.

✦　　✦　　✦

CSS Text Styles

The first part of each CSS rule is a selector that says which elements the rule applies to. The second part is a list of the properties that the rule applies to those elements. This chapter focuses on the properties that you can specify in a CSS style sheet. You learn how to change the font size, style, and weight; how to align text and order paragraphs; how to control the behavior of speech synthesizers reading the text; and more.

Caution Netscape 6.0, Mozilla, Opera 4.0 and 5.0, and Internet Explorer 5.0 and 5.5 all implement only some parts of the CSS specification. Earlier versions of the major browsers, while perhaps supporting some form of CSS for HTML documents, do not support it at all for XML documents. To make matters worse, they all implement different subsets of the specification and sometimes don't implement the same subsets for XML as they do for HTML. I'll note where one browser or another has a particular problem as we go along. However, if you find that something in this chapter doesn't work as advertised in your favorite browser (or in any browser), please complain to the browser vendor, not to me.

Font Properties

CSS supports seven basic properties that control the font used to draw the text. These are:

- ✦ font-family
- ✦ font-size
- ✦ font-size-adjust
- ✦ font-stretch
- ✦ font-style
- ✦ font-variant

✦ `font-weight`

In addition, there's a `font` shorthand property that can set most of these properties simultaneously.

Choosing the font family

The font family is the font in which the text is drawn. The value of the `font-family` property is a comma-separated list of font names such as Helvetica, Times, and Palatino. Font names that include white space, such as Times New Roman, should be enclosed in double quotes.

Names may also be one of the five generic names `serif`, `sans-serif`, `cursive`, `fantasy`, and `monospace`. The browser replaces these names with a font of the requested type installed on the local system. Table 16-1 demonstrates these fonts.

	Table 16-1 **Generic Fonts**		
Name	*Typical Families*	*Distinguishing Characteristic*	*Example*
Serif	Times, Times New Roman, Palatino	Curlicues on the edges of letters make serif text easier to read in small body type.	The quick brown fox jumped over the lazy dog.
Sans-serif	Geneva, Helvetica, Verdana	Block type, often used in headlines.	The quick brown fox jumped over the lazy dog.
Monospace	Courier, Courier New, Monaco, American Typewriter	A typewriter-like font in which each character has exactly the same width; commonly used for source code and e-mail.	The quick brown fox jumped over the lazy dog.
Cursive	ZapfChancery	Script font, a simulation of handwriting.	The quick brown fox jumped over the lazy dog.
Fantasy	Western, Critter	Text with special effects; for example, letters on fire, letters formed by tumbling acrobats, and letters made from animals.	THE QUICK BROWN FOX JUMPED OVER THE LAZY DOG.

Because there isn't a guarantee that any given font will be available or appropriate on a particular client system (10-point Times is practically illegible on a Macintosh, much less a Palm Pilot), you should provide a comma-separated list of choices for the font in the order of preference. The last choice in the list should always be one of the generic names. However, even if you don't specify a generic name and the fonts you do specify aren't available, the browser will pick something. It just may not be anything like what you wanted.

For example, Listing 16-1 is the style sheet for play synopses similar to Listing 15-1 of the last chapter. It has rules that make the TITLE element Helvetica with fallback positions of Verdana and any sans serif font, and the rest of the elements Times with fallback positions of Times New Roman, and any serif font.

Listing 16-1: A style sheet for the synopsis of a play

```
TITLE    { font-family: Helvetica, Verdana, sans-serif }
SYNOPSIS { font-family: Times, "Times New Roman", serif }
SYNOPSIS, TITLE, ACT, SCENE { display: block }
```

Figure 16-1 shows the synopsis loaded into Mozilla with this style sheet. Not a great deal has changed since Figure 15-1 in the last chapter. Times or something very close to it is commonly the default font. The most obvious difference is that the title is now in Helvetica.

Figure 16-1: The synopsis of *Twelfth Night* with the title in Helvetica

The `font-family` property is inherited by child elements. Thus, by setting SYNOPSIS's `font-family` to Times, all the child elements are also set to Times except for TITLE whose own `font-family` property overrides the one it inherits.

Choosing the font style

The `font-style` property has three possible values: `normal`, `italic`, and `oblique`. The regular text you're reading now is normal. The typical rendering of the HTML EM element is *italicized*. Oblique text is very similar to italicized text. However, a computer creates oblique text by algorithmically slanting normal text. A human designer creates italics by carefully handcrafting a font to look good in its slanted form. Listing 16-2 adds a rule to the synopsis style sheet that italicizes scene numbers.

Listing 16-2: **A style sheet that italicizes scene numbers**

```
TITLE     { font-family: Helvetica, Verdana, sans-serif }
SYNOPSIS { font-family: Times, "Times New Roman", serif }
SYNOPSIS, TITLE, ACT, SCENE { display: block }
SCENE_NUMBER { font-style: italic}
```

Figure 16-2 shows the synopsis loaded into Internet Explorer with this style sheet.

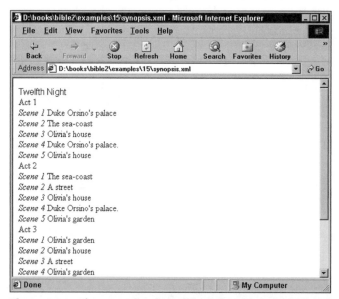

Figure 16-2: The synopsis of *Twelfth Night* with italic scene numbers

Small caps

The font-variant property has two possible values: normal and small-caps. The default is normal. Setting font-variant to small-caps replaces lowercase letters with capital letters in a smaller font size than the main body text.

You can get a very nice effect by combining the font-variant property with the first-letter pseudo-element. For example, define the ACT_NUMBER element to have the font-variant: small-caps. Next define the first letter of ACT_NUMBER to have font-variant: normal. This produces act numbers that look like this:

ACT 1

Here are the rules:

```
ACT_NUMBER                { font-variant: small-caps}
ACT_NUMBER:first-letter { font-variant: normal}
```

The second rule overrides the first, but only for the first letter of the act number.

Caution Internet Explorer 5.0 and 5.5 don't support the first-letter pseudo-element, though Mozilla and Opera 5.0 do.

Setting the font weight

The font-weight property determines how dark (bold) or light the text appears. There are 13 possible values for this property:

✦ normal

✦ bold

✦ bolder

✦ lighter

✦ 100

✦ 200

✦ 300

✦ 400

✦ 500

✦ 600

✦ 700

✦ 800

✦ 900

Weights range from 100 (the lightest) to 900 (the darkest). Intermediate, noncentury values such as 850 are not allowed. Normal weight is 400. Bold is 700. The `bolder` value makes an element bolder than its parent. The `lighter` value makes an element less bold than its parent. However, there's no guarantee that a particular font has as many as nine separate levels of boldness.

Here's a simple rule that makes the `TITLE` and `ACT_NUMBER` elements bold:

```
TITLE, ACT_NUMBER { font-weight: bold}
```

Figure 16-3 shows the effect of adding this rule to the synopsis style sheet.

Figure 16-3: The synopsis of *Twelfth Night* with bold title and act numbers

Setting the font size

The `font-size` property determines the height and the width of a typical character in the font. Larger sizes take up more space on the screen. The size may be specified as a keyword, a value relative to the font size of the parent, a percentage of the size of the parent element's font size, or an absolute number.

Keyword

Absolute size keywords are:

- ✦ xx-small
- ✦ x-small
- ✦ small
- ✦ medium
- ✦ large
- ✦ x-large
- ✦ xx-large

These keywords are the preferred way to set font sizes because they are relative to the base font size of the page. For instance, if the user has adjusted their default font size to 20 points because they're very nearsighted, a large font will be even larger and a small font will still be pretty large.

Although the exact values are up to the browser's best judgment, in general each size is 1.2 times larger than the next smallest size. The default is medium, so if a browser's default is 12 points, then large type will be 14.4 points, x-large type will be 17.28 points, and xx-large type will be 20.736 points. By contrast, small type will be 10 points, x-small type will be 8.33 points, and xx-small will be a possibly illegible 7 points. A browser may well choose to round these values to the nearest integer. Here's a simple rule that makes the TITLE extra large:

```
TITLE { font-size: x-large }
```

Figure 16-4 shows the results after this rule is added to the synopsis style sheet.

Value relative to parent's font size

You can also specify the size relative to the parent element as either larger or smaller. For instance, in the following, the SCENE_NUMBER will have a font size that is smaller than the font size of its parent SCENE.

```
SCENE_NUMBER { font-size: smaller }
```

Figure 16-5 shows the result of adding this rule to the synopsis style sheet.

Figure 16-4: The synopsis of *Twelfth Night* with an extra large title

Figure 16-5: The synopsis of *Twelfth Night* with a smaller scene number

There's no hard-and-fast rule for exactly how much smaller a smaller font will be or how much larger a larger font will be. Generally, the browser will attempt to move from medium to small, from small to x-small, and so forth. The same is true (in the other direction) for larger fonts. Thus, making a font larger should increase its size by about 20 percent, and making a font smaller should decrease its size by about 16.6 percent, but browsers are free to fudge these values in order to match the available font sizes.

Percentage of parent element's font size

If these options aren't precise enough, you can make finer adjustments by using a percentage of the parent element's font size. For example, this rule says that the font used for a SCENE_NUMBER is 50% of the size of the font for the SCENE.

```
SCENE_NUMBER { font-size: 50% }
```

Absolute lengths

Finally, you can specify a font size as an absolute length. Although you can use pixels, picas, centimeters, millimeters, or inches, the most common unit when measuring fonts is the point. For example, this rule sets the default font-size for the SYNOPSIS element and its children to 14 points.

```
SYNOPSIS { font-size: 14pt }
```

Caution

I urge you not to use absolute units to describe font sizes. It's extremely difficult (I'd argue impossible) to pick a font size that's legible across all the different platforms on which your page might be viewed, ranging from cell phones to the Sony Jumbotron in Times Square. Even when restricting themselves to standard personal computers, most designers usually pick a font that's too small. Any text that's intended to be read on the screen should be at least 12 points, possibly more.

Figure 16-6 shows the results after all these font rules have been added to the synopsis style sheet. The text of the scenes is not really bolder. It's just bigger. In any case, it's a lot easier to read.

Adjusting the aspect value

How legible a font is depends less on the size of the font than on its *aspect value*. This is the ratio of x-height to font size. The higher this number, the more legible a font is at smaller sizes. The lower the aspect value, the less legible the font will be as it is shrunk. When browsers rely solely on the font size when choosing substitute fonts, the likelihood that the chosen font will be too small to read is greatly increased. The font-size-adjust property controls the aspect value of elements to preserve the x-height of the first choice font in the substitute font when using the font-family property.

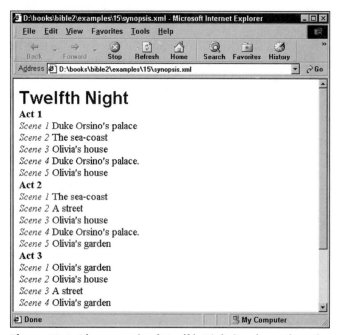

Figure 16-6: The synopsis of *Twelfth Night* in a larger font size

For example, Verdana has an aspect value of .58, while Times New Roman has an aspect value of .46. Therefore, Verdana will remain legible at smaller sizes than Times New Roman, but may appear too large if substituted directly for Times New Roman at the same font size.

If the value of the font-size-adjust property is none, the font's x-height is not preserved. If a number is specified, the value identifies the aspect value of the first choice font, and directs the software to scale any font it substitutes to match. This helps you ensure legibility across all platforms, and all supporting applications. The following rules use the font-size-adjust property to keep fonts legible while implementing a range of sizes.

```
TITLE    { font-size-adjust: ".58";
           font-family: Helvetica, Verdana, Arial, sans-serif }
SYNOPSIS { font-size-adjust: ".46";
           font-family: Times, "Times New Roman", serif }
```

The change when these rules are added is actually quite dramatic, as Figure 16-7 shows.

Figure 16-7: The synopsis of *Twelfth Night* with a different aspect ratio

Kerning a font

The font-stretch property controls the kerning of a font; that is, the amount of space between two characters in the font. There are nine possible values for this property. In order from tightest to loosest, they are:

- ✦ ultra-condensed
- ✦ extra-condensed
- ✦ condensed
- ✦ semi-condensed
- ✦ normal
- ✦ semi-expanded
- ✦ expanded
- ✦ extra-expanded
- ✦ ultra-expanded

The default is normal. The values ultra-condensed through ultra-expanded are organized from most condensed to least condensed. Each makes a small change in the horizontal spacing of the text. In addition you can specify this property as `wider` or `narrower` to change the `font-stretch` by one position up or down from the inherited value. The following style sheet rules use a variety of kernings.

```
TITLE          { font-stretch: "ultra-expanded" }
ACT            { font-stretch: "expanded" }
SCENE          { font-stretch: "ultra-condensed" }
SCENE_NUMBER   { font-stretch: "wider" }
```

Caution   Existing Web browsers really don't support the `font-stretch` property. You can use it if you want, but don't rely on it.

The font shorthand property

`Font` is a shorthand property that sets the font style, variant, weight, size, and family with one rule. For example, here are two rules for the TITLE and SCENE_NUMBER elements that combine the separate rules of the previous section:

```
TITLE { font: bold x-large Helvetica, sans-serif }
SCENE_NUMBER { font: italic smaller Times, serif }
```

Values must be given in the following order:

1. One each of style, variant, and weight, in any order, any of which may be omitted

2. Size, which may not be omitted

3. Optionally, a forward slash (/) and a line height

4. Family, which may not be omitted

Note   If this sounds complicated and hard to remember, that's because it is. I certainly can't remember the exact details for the order of these properties without looking them up. I prefer to just set the individual properties one at a time. It's questionable whether shorthand properties like this really save any time.

Listing 16-3 is the style sheet for the synopsis with all the rules devised so far, using the `font` shorthand properties. However, because a `font` property is exactly equivalent to the sum of the individual properties it represents, there's no change to the rendered document.

Listing 16-3: A style sheet for the synopsis with font shorthand

```
SYNOPSIS, TITLE, ACT, SCENE { display: block }
ACT_NUMBER { font-weight: bold}
SYNOPSIS { font-size: 14pt }
TITLE    { font-size-adjust: ".58";  }
```

```
SYNOPSIS { font-size-adjust: ".46" }
         font-family: Times, "Times New Roman", serif }
ACT_NUMBER    { font-variant: small-caps}
ACT_NUMBER:first-letter { font-variant: normal}
TITLE {
   font: bold x-large Helvetica, Verdana, Arial, sans-serif
}
SCENE_NUMBER { font: italic smaller Times, serif }
```

The font property may also have one of these six keyword values that match all of a font's properties to the properties of particular elements of the browser user interface or the users system:

✦ caption: the font that used for captioned widgets like buttons

✦ icon: the font that labels icons

✦ menu: the font used for menu items

✦ message-box: the font used for display text in dialog boxes

✦ small-caption: the font used for labels on small widgets

✦ status-bar: the font used in the browser's status bar

For example this rule says that a SYNOPSIS element will be formatted with the same font family, size, weight, and style as the font the browser uses in its status bar:

```
SYNOPSIS { font: status-bar }
```

The Color Property

CSS allows you to assign colors to almost any element on a page with the color property. The value of this color property may be one of 16 named color keywords, or an RGB triple in decimal, hexadecimal, or percentages. For instance, the following rules specify that every element in the SYNOPSIS is colored black except the SCENE_NUMBER, which is colored blue:

```
SYNOPSIS      { color: black }
SCENE_NUMBER { color: blue}
```

Children inherit the color property. Thus, all elements in the synopsis except for the SCENE_NUMBER elements will be colored black.

The following rules are all equivalent to the above two. I recommend using named colors when possible, and browser-safe colors when not.

```
SYNOPSIS      { color: #000000 }
SCENE_NUMBER { color: #0000FF}
SYNOPSIS      { color: rgb(0, 0, 0) }
SCENE_NUMBER { color: rgb(0, 0, 255)}
SYNOPSIS      { color: rgb(0%, 0%, 0%) }
SCENE_NUMBER { color: rgb(0%, 0%, 100%)}
```

The `color` property specifies the foreground color for the text content of an element. Color names include `aqua`, `black`, `blue`, `fuchsia`, `gray`, `green`, `lime`, `maroon`, `navy`, `olive`, `purple`, `red`, `silver`, `teal`, `white`, and `yellow`.

The following style rules apply color to three elements, using three methods of identifying color. It specifies the RGB hex value `#FF0000` for `SCENE_NUMBER` elements, all `TITLE` elements to appear in red, and all `ACT_NUMBER` elements to appear in `rgb(255,0,0)`.

```
SCENE_NUMBER  { color: #FF0000}
TITLE         { color: red}
ACT_NUMBER    { color: rgb(255,0,0) }
```

In fact, these are just three different ways of saying pure red; and all three elements will have the same color.

Text Properties

Ten properties affect the appearance of text, irrespective of font:

- ✦ `word-spacing`
- ✦ `letter-spacing`
- ✦ `text-decoration`
- ✦ `vertical-align`
- ✦ `text-transform`
- ✦ `text-align`
- ✦ `text-indent`
- ✦ `text-shadow`
- ✦ `line-height`
- ✦ `white-space`

Word spacing

The `word-spacing` property expands the text by adding additional space between words. A negative value removes space between words. The only reason I can think of to alter the word spacing on a Web page is if you are a student laboring under tight page-count limits who wants to make a paper look bigger or smaller than it is.

Note

Desktop publishers love to spend hours and hours tweaking these details pixel by pixel. The problem is that all the rules they've learned about how and when to adjust spacing are based on ink on paper and really don't work when transferred to the medium of electrons on phosphorus (a typical CRT monitor). You're almost always better off letting the browser make decisions about word and letter spacing for you.

If, on the other hand, your target medium *is* ink on paper, then there's a little more to be gained by adjusting these properties. The main difference is that with ink on paper you control the delivery medium. You know exactly how big the fonts are, how wide and high the display is, how many dots per inch are being used, and so forth. On the Web, you simply don't have enough information about the output medium available to control everything at this level of detail.

To change this from the default value of `normal`, you set a length for the property. For example,

```
SYNOPSIS { word-spacing: 1em }
```

Browsers are not required to respect this property, especially if it interferes with other properties like `align: justified`. Internet Explorer does not support `word-spacing`, but Mozilla and Opera do as shown in Figure 16-8.

Figure 16-8: The synopsis of *Twelfth Night* with one em of word spacing

Caution   Spacing words requires that the browser be able to figure out where the boundaries between words fall. While this is relatively straight-forward in most Western languages (just look for the white space) it's much more complex in some other languages such as Sanskrit and Japanese. I wouldn't count on most browsers being able to handle this property for the more typographically challenging languages.

The letter-spacing property

The `letter-spacing` property lets you expand text by adding additional space between letters. A negative value removes space between letters. Again, the only reason I can think of to do this on a Web page is to make a paper look bigger or smaller than it really is to meet a length requirement.

To change this from the default value of `normal`, set a length for the property. For example:

```
SYNOPSIS { letter-spacing: 0.3em }
```

Because justification works by adjusting the amount of space between letters, changing the letter spacing manually can prevent the browser from justifying text. However, browsers are not required to respect this property, especially if it interferes with other properties such as `align: justified`. Nonetheless, most browsers attempt to implement it as best they can within the restrictions of other rules as shown in Figure 16-9.

Figure 16-9: The SYNOPSIS element with 0.3 em letter spacing

The text-decoration property

The `text-decoration` property can have one of the following five values:

✦ `none`

✦ `underline`

✦ `overline`

✦ `line-through`

✦ `blink`

Except for `none`, which is the default, these values are not mutually exclusive. You may, for example, specify that a paragraph is underlined, overlined, struck through, and blinking. (I do not, however, recommend that you do this.)

Note   Browsers, fortunately, are not required to support blinking text.

For example, the next rule specifies that `CHARACTER` elements are underlined. Figure 16-10 shows the result of applying this rule to the synopsis of *Twelfth Night*.

```
CHARACTER { text-decoration: underline }
```

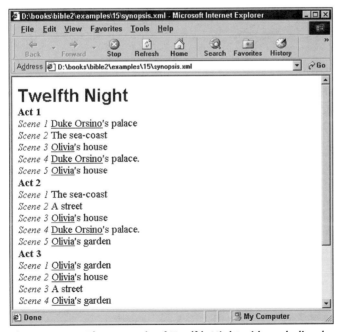

Figure 16-10: The synopsis of *Twelfth Night* with underlined characters

The vertical-align property

The `vertical-align` property controls the vertical alignment of text within an inline box. It specifies how an inline element is positioned relative to the baseline of the text. Valid values are:

- ✦ `baseline`: align the baseline of the inline box with the baseline of the block box (this is the default)

- ✦ `sub`: position the inline box as a subscript

- ✦ `super`: position the inline box as a superscript

- ✦ `top`: align the top of the inline box with the top of the line

- ✦ `middle`: align the midpoint of the inline box with the baseline of the block box, plus half of the x-height of the block box

- ✦ `bottom`: align the bottom of the inline box with the bottom of the line

- ✦ `text-top`: align the top of the inline box with the top of the parent element's font

- ✦ `text-bottom`: align the bottom of the inline box with the bottom of the parent element's font

You can also set the `vertical-align` property to a percentage that raises (positive value) or lowers (negative value) the box by the percentage of the line-height. A value of 0% is the same as the `baseline` value. Finally, you can set `vertical-align` to a signed length that will raise or lower the box by the specified distance. A value of 0cm is the same as the `baseline` value.

The `sub` value makes the element a subscript. The `super` value makes the element a superscript. The `text-top` value aligns the top of the element with the top of the parent element's font. The `middle` value aligns the vertical midpoint of the element with the baseline of the parent plus half the x-height. The `text-bottom` value aligns the bottom of the element with the bottom of the parent element's font. The `top` value aligns the top of the element with the tallest letter or element on the line. The `bottom` value aligns the bottom of the element with the bottom of the lowest letter or element on the line. The exact alignment changes as the height of the tallest or lowest letter changes.

For example, the rule for a footnote number might look like this one that superscripts the number and decreases its size by 20 percent.

```
FOOTNOTE_NUMBER { vertical-align: super; font-size: 80% }
```

The text-transform property

The `text-transform` property lets you specify that text should be rendered in all uppercase, all lowercase, or with initial letters capitalized. This is useful in headlines, for example. The valid values are:

+ `capitalize`
+ `uppercase`
+ `lowercase`
+ `none`

Capitalization Makes Only The First Letter Of Every Word Uppercase Like This Sentence. PLACING THE SENTENCE IN UPPERCASE, HOWEVER, MAKES EVERY LETTER IN THE SENTENCE UPPERCASE. The following rule converts the `TITLE` element in the *Twelfth Night* synopsis to uppercase.

```
TITLE { text-transform: uppercase }
```

Note   The `text-transform` property is somewhat language-dependent because many languages — Hebrew, modern Georgian, and Chinese, for example — don't have any concept of upper- and lowercase. Even worse, letters that have the same capital form in two languages may have different lowercase forms or vice versa.

The text-align property

The `text-align` property applies only to block-level elements. It specifies whether the text in the block is aligned with the left side, the right side, centered, or justified. The valid values are:

+ `left`
+ `right`
+ `center`
+ `justify`

The following rules center the `TITLE` element in the *Twelfth Night* synopsis and justify everything else. Figure 16-11 shows the synopsis after these rules have been applied. I also changed `SCENE` to `display: inline` so that there'd be enough text in a paragraph to extend across the browser window and show that the text is truly justified.

```
SCENE    { display: inline}
TITLE    { text-align: center }
SYNOPSIS { text-align: justify }
```

Figure 16-11: The TITLE in the synopsis is centered and the rest of the text is justified.

The text-indent property

The `text-indent` property, which only applies to block-level elements, specifies how far the first line of a block is indented with respect to the remaining lines of the block. It is given either as an absolute length or as a percentage of the width of the parent element. The value may be negative to create a hanging indent.

Tip   To indent all the lines of an element, rather than just the first, you use the box properties discussed in the last chapter to set an extra left margin on the element.

For example, the following rule indents the scenes in the synopsis by half an inch. Figure 16-12 shows the synopsis after this rule has been applied.

```
SCENE { text-indent: 0.5in }
```

The text-shadow property

The `text-shadow` property applies shadows to text. The value is a comma-separated list of shadow effects to control the order, color, and dimensions of the shadows that are overlaid on the text. Shadows do not extend the size of the block containing the text, but may extend over the boundaries of the block.

The value of the `text-shadow` includes a signed length for the offset of the shadow. It may also include a blur radius and a shadow color. The shadow offset is specified with two signed lengths that specify how far out from the text the shadow extends. The first length specifies the horizontal distance from the text; the second length specifies the vertical depth of the shadow. If you apply a negative value to the shadow offsets, the shadow will appear to the left and above the text, rather than below and to the right. An optional third signed length specifies the boundary of the blur effect. An optional fourth value specifies the color of the shadow. For example,

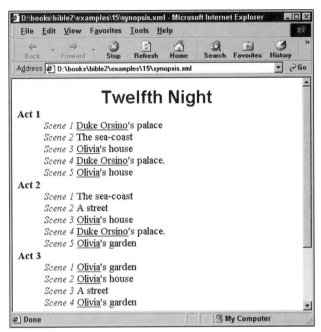

Figure 16-12: Each SCENE and its children in the synopsis are indented half an inch.

```
TITLE          { text-shadow: -5pt -5pt -2pt red }
SCENE_NUMBER   { text-shadow: 5pt 4pt 3pt green }
ACT_NUMBER     { text-shadow: none }
```

In practice, however, the text-shadow property isn't supported by any major browser.

The line-height property

The line-height property specifies the distance between the baselines of successive lines. It can be given as an absolute number, an absolute length, or a percentage of the font size. For instance, the following rule double-spaces the SYNOPSIS element. Figure 16-13 shows the *Twelfth Night* synopsis after this rule has been applied.

```
SYNOPSIS { line-height: 200% }
```

Double-spacing isn't particularly attractive, though, so I'll remove it. Listing 16-4 summarizes the additions made in this and the previous sections to the synopsis style sheet (minus the double-spacing).

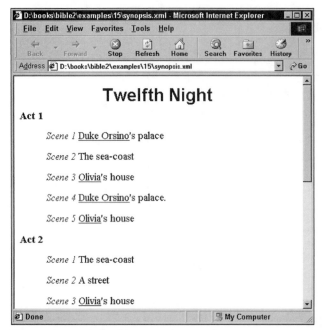

Figure 16-13: A double-spaced synopsis

Listing 16-4: **The synopsis style sheet with text properties**

```
SYNOPSIS, TITLE, ACT, SCENE { display: block }
ACT_NUMBER { font-weight: bold}
SYNOPSIS { font-size: 14pt }
SYNOPSIS { word-spacing: 1em }
SYNOPSIS { letter-spacing: 0.3em }
SCENE_NUMBER {   color: #FF0000}
TITLE        {   color: red}
ACT_NUMBER   {   color: rgb(255,0,0) }
ACT_NUMBER   {   font-variant: small-caps}
CHARACTER { text-decoration: underline }
SCENE_NUMBER {   vertical-align: subscript}
TITLE    { font-size-adjust: ".58";  }
SYNOPSIS { font-size-adjust: ".46"
           font-family: Times, "Times New Roman", serif }
TITLE {
font: normal bold x-large Helvetica, Verdana, Arial, sans-serif
}
SCENE_NUMBER { font: italic smaller Times, serif }
TITLE    { text-align: center }
SYNOPSIS { text-align: justify }
SCENE { text-indent: 0.5in }
```

The white-space property

The `white-space` property determines how significant white space (spaces, tabs, line breaks) is within an element. The allowable values are:

✦ `normal`

✦ `pre`

✦ `nowrap`

The default value, `normal`, simply means that runs of white space are condensed to a single space and words are wrapped to fit on the screen or page. This is the way white space is normally handled in both HTML and XML.

The `pre` value acts like the `PRE` (preformatted) element in HTML. All white space in the input document is considered significant and faithfully reproduced on the output device. It may be accompanied by a shift to a monospaced font. This would be useful for much computer source code or some poetry. Listing 16-5 is a poem, *The Altar* by George Herbert, in which spacing is important. In this poem, the lines form the shape of the poem's subject.

Listing 16-5: *The Altar* in XML

```
<?xml version="1.0"?>
<?xml-stylesheet type="text/css" href="16-6.css"?>
<POEM>

<TITLE>The Altar</TITLE>
<POET>George Herbert</POET>

<VERSE>    A broken ALTAR, Lord, thy servant rears,</VERSE>
<VERSE>    Made of a heart, and cemented with tears:</VERSE>
<VERSE>     Whose parts are as thy hand did frame;</VERSE>
<VERSE>     No workman's tool hath touched the same.</VERSE>
<VERSE>     No workman's tool hath touched the same.</VERSE>
<VERSE>          A     HEART      alone</VERSE>
<VERSE>          Is   such    a    stone,</VERSE>
<VERSE>          As    nothing     but</VERSE>
<VERSE>          Thy   power   doth   cut.</VERSE>
<VERSE>          Wherefore   each   part</VERSE>
<VERSE>          Of   my    hard    heart</VERSE>
<VERSE>          Meets in  this  frame,</VERSE>
<VERSE>          To   praise   thy   name:</VERSE>
<VERSE>    That  if  I  chance  to  hold  my  peace,</VERSE>
<VERSE>    These stones to praise thee may not cease.</VERSE>
<VERSE>    O let  thy  blessed  SACRIFICE  be  mine,</VERSE>
<VERSE>    And  sanctify  this  ALTAR  to  be  thine.</VERSE>

</POEM>
```

Listing 16-6 is a style sheet that uses `white-space: pre` to preserve this form. Figure 16-14 shows the result in Mozilla.

Caution

Internet Explorer 5.0 and 5.5 do not correctly implement the `white-space` property. Mozilla and Opera do.

Listing 16-6: **A style sheet for white space-sensitive poetry**

```
POEM    { display: block }
TITLE   { display: block; font-size: 16pt; font-weight: bold }
POET    { display: block; margin-bottom: 10px }
STANZA  { display: block; margin-bottom: 10px }
VERSE   { display: block;
          white-space: pre; font-family: monospace }
```

Figure 16-14: *The Altar* by George Herbert with white-space: pre

Finally, the `nowrap` value is a compromise that breaks lines exactly where there's an explicit break in the source text, but condenses other runs of space to a single space. This might be useful when you're trying to faithfully reproduce the line breaks in a classical manuscript or some other poetry where the line breaks are significant but the space between words isn't.

Background Properties

The background of an element can be set to a color or an image. If it's set to an image, the image can be positioned differently relative to the content of the element. This is accomplished with the following five basic properties:

- ✦ background-color
- ✦ background-image
- ✦ background-repeat
- ✦ background-attachment
- ✦ background-position

Finally, there's a background shorthand property that allows you to set some or all of these five properties in one rule.

Caution   Fancy backgrounds are vastly overused. Anything other than a very light background color only makes your page harder to read and annoys users. I list these properties here for the sake of completeness, but I recommend that you use them sparingly, if at all.

None of the background properties is inherited. Each child element must specify the background it wants. However, it may appear as if background properties are inherited because the default is for the background to be transparent. The background of whatever element is drawn below an element will show through. Most of the time this is the background of the parent element.

The background-color property

The background-color property may be set to the same values as the color property. However, rather than changing the color of the element's contents, it changes the color of the element's background on top of which the contents are drawn. For example, to draw a SIGN element with yellow text on a blue background, you would use this rule:

```
SIGN { color: yellow; background-color: blue}
```

You can also set the background-color to the keyword transparent (the default) which simply means that the background takes on the color or image of whatever the element is laying on top of, generally the parent element.

The background-image property

The background-image property is either none (the default) or a URL (generally relative) where a bitmapped image file can be found. If it's a URL, then the browser will load the image and use it as the background, much like the BACKGROUND attribute of the BODY element in HTML. For example, here's how you attach the file shakespeare.jpg (shown in Figure 16-15) as the background for a SYNOPSIS element.

```
SYNOPSIS { background-image: url(shakespeare.jpg) }
```

Figure 16-15: The original, untiled, uncropped background image for the synopsis

The image referenced by the background-image property is drawn underneath the specified element, *not* underneath the browser pane like the BACKGROUND attribute of HTML's BODY element. Background images will generally not be the exact same size as the contents of the page. If the image is larger than the element's box, the image will be cropped. If the image is smaller than the element's box, it will be tiled vertically and horizontally. Figure 16-16 shows a background image that has tiled exactly far enough to cover the underlying content.

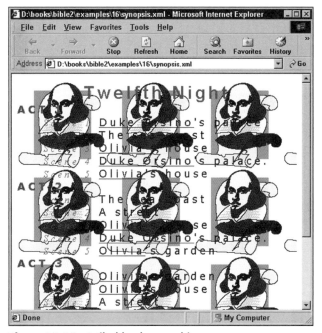

Figure 16-16: A tiled background image

Tiling takes place across the element whose `background-image` property is set; *not* across the browser window. You can set background images for nonroot elements like the `ACT` or the `SCENE` if you like.

The background-repeat property

The `background-repeat` property adjusts how background images are tiled across the screen. You can specify that background images are not tiled or are only tiled horizontally or vertically. Possible values for this property are:

- ✦ `repeat`
- ✦ `repeat-x`
- ✦ `repeat-y`
- ✦ `no-repeat`

For example, to show only a single picture of Shakespeare, you would set the `background-repeat` of the `SYNOPSIS` element to `no-repeat` like this:

```
SYNOPSIS { background-image:  url(shakespeare.jpg);
          background-repeat: no-repeat }
```

Figure 16-17 shows the result.

Figure 16-17: An untiled background image

To tile across but not down the page, set `background-repeat` to `repeat-x`, like this:

```
SYNOPSIS { background-image:  url(shakespeare.jpg);
          background-repeat: repeat-x }
```

The result is shown in Figure 16-18:

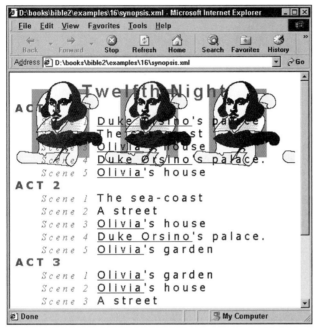

Figure 16-18: A background image tiled across but not down

To tile down but not across the page, set `background-repeat` to `repeat-y` like this:

```
SYNOPSIS { background-image: url(shakespeare.jpg);
          background-repeat: repeat-y }
```

Figure 16-19 shows the effect.

Figure 16-19: A background image tiled down but not across

The background-attachment property

In HTML, the background image is attached to the document. When the document is scrolled, the background image scrolls with it. With the `background-attachment` property, you can specify that the background be attached to the window instead. Possible values are `scroll` and `fixed`. The default is `scroll`; that is, the background is attached to the document rather than the window.

However, with `background-attachment` set to `fixed`, the document scrolls but the background image doesn't. This might be useful in conjunction with an image that's big enough for a typical browser window but not big enough to be a backdrop for a large document when you don't want to tile the image. You would code that request like this:

```
SYNOPSIS { background-image: url(shakespeare.jpg);
          background-attachment: fixed;
          background-repeat: no-repeat }
```

Figure 16-20 shows the effect after a little scrolling.

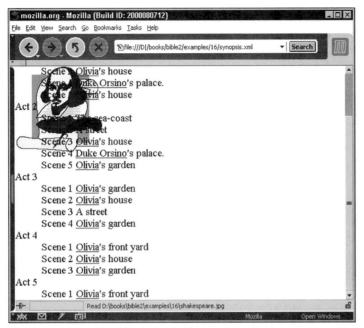

Figure 16-20: A fixed background image stays in the same position in the window even as the document scrolls.

Caution Internet Explorer does not support fixed background images; Mozilla and Opera do.

The background-position property

By default, the upper-left corner of a background image is aligned with the upper-left corner of the element it's attached to. (See Figure 16-17 for an example.) Most of the time this is exactly what you want. However, for those rare times when you want something else, the `background-position` property allows you to move the background relative to the element.

You can specify the offset by using percentages of the width and height of the parent element, by using absolute lengths, or by using two of these six keywords:

✦ top

✦ center

✦ bottom

✦ left

✦ center

✦ right

Percentages of parent element's width and height

Percentages enable you to pin different parts of the background to the corresponding part of the element. The *x* coordinate is given as a percentage ranging from 0% (left side) to 100% (right side). The *y* coordinate is given as a percentage ranging from 0% (top) to 100% (bottom). For example, this rule places the upper-right corner of the image in the upper-right corner of the SYNOPSIS element. Figure 16-21 shows the result.

```
SYNOPSIS { background-image: url(shakespeare.jpg);
          background-repeat: no-repeat;
          background-position: 100% 0% }
```

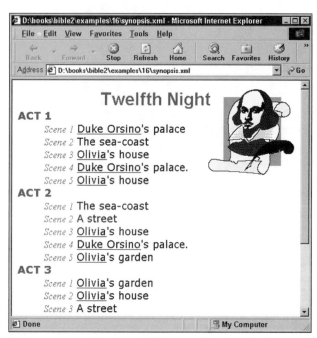

Figure 16-21: A background image aligned with the upper-right corner of the content

Absolute lengths

Setting background-position to a length positions the upper-left corner of the background at an absolute position in the element. The next rule places the upper-left corner of the background image shakespeare.jpg one centimeter to the right and two centimeters below the upper-left corner of the element. Figure 16-22 shows the result.

```
SYNOPSIS { background-image: url(shakespeare.jpg);
          background-repeat: no-repeat;
          background-position: 1cm 2cm }
```

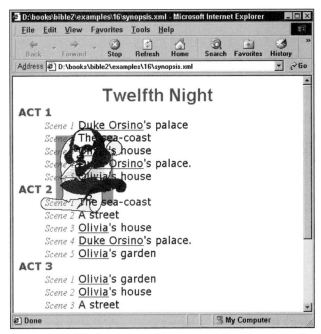

Figure 16-22: A background image positioned one centimeter to the right and two centimeters below the left corner of the element

Keywords

The top left and left top keywords are the same as 0% 0%. The top, top center, and center top are the same as 50% 0%. The right top and top right keywords are the same as 100% 0%. The left, left center, and center left keywords are the same as 0% 50%. The center and center center keywords are the same as 50% 50%. The right, right center, and center right keywords are the same as 100% 50%. The bottom left and left bottom keywords are the same as 0% 100%. The bottom, bottom center, and center bottom mean the same as 50% 100%. The bottom right and right bottom keywords are the same as 100% 100%. Figure 16-23 shows the positions for the different values.

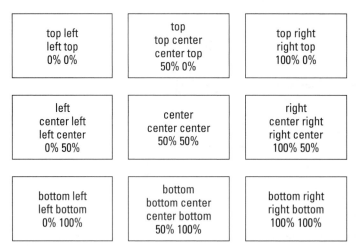

Figure 16-23: Relative positioning of background images

For instance, this rule positions the image in the top center of the synopsis, as shown in Figure 16-24:

```
SYNOPSIS { background-image: url(shakespeare.jpg);
           background-repeat: no-repeat;
           background-position: center top }
```

Figure 16-24: An untiled background image pinned to the top center of the SYNOPSIS element

If the `background-attachment` property has the value `fixed`, then the image is placed relative to the windowpane instead of the element.

The background shorthand property

The `background` property is shorthand for setting the `background-color`, `background-image`, `background-repeat`, `background-attachment`, and `background-position` properties in a single rule. For example, to set `background-color` to `white`, `background-image` to shakespeare.jpg, `background-repeat` to `no-repeat`, and `background-attachment` to `fixed` in the SYNOPSIS element, you can use this rule:

```
SYNOPSIS {
   background: url(shakespeare.jpg) white no-repeat fixed
}
```

The foregoing rule means exactly the same thing as this longer but more legible rule:

```
SYNOPSIS { background-image: url(shakespeare.jpg);
           background-color: white;
           background-repeat: no-repeat;
           background-attachment: fixed }
```

When using the `background` shorthand property, values for any or all of the five properties may be given in any order. However, none may occur more than once. For example, the upper-right corner alignment rule used for Figure 16-21 could have been written like this instead:

```
SYNOPSIS { background: url(shakespeare.jpg) no-repeat 100% 0% }
```

Visibility

The `visibility` property controls whether the contents of an element are seen. The three possible values of this property are:

- ✦ `visible`
- ✦ `hidden`
- ✦ `collapse`

If `visibility` is set to `visible`, the contents of the box, including all borders, are shown. This is the default. If `visibility` is set to `hidden`, the box's contents and border are not drawn. However, unlike an element whose `display` property is set to `none`, invisible boxes still take up space and affect the layout of the document. Setting `visibility` to `hidden` is not the same as setting `display` to `none`.

The `collapse` value is the same as `hidden` for most elements, except for table rows and columns. For table rows and columns, `collapse` hides the row or column, but it does not otherwise change the layout of the `table` as `hidden` would. That is, it acts almost exactly like `display: none`. However, you can't set `display` to both `none` and `table-row` or `table-column` so for these elements you have to use `visibility: collapse` instead.

For example, this rule hides the SCENE_NUMBER elements:

```
SCENE_NUMBER {visibility: hidden}
```

Figure 16-25 shows the result. Notice that the locations of each scene are still pushed over to the right in pretty much the same position they were in Figure 16-24. That's because the space on the left is taken up by the invisible SCENE_NUMBER elements.

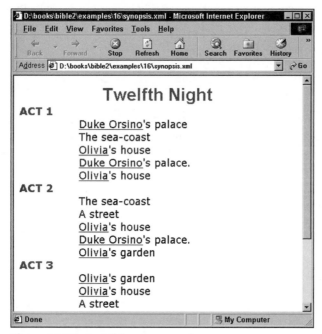

Figure 16-25: Invisible scene numbers

Caution Mozilla and Opera only recognize the `visibility` property when it's applied to block-level elements, not when it's applied to inline elements.

Cursors

The cursor is the arrow/hand/insertion bar/other icon that indicates the position of the pointer on the screen. The `cursor` property specifies the cursor the browser should display when a reader moves the pointer over a particular element. CSS allows these 16 cursor values:

✦ `auto`: the browser chooses a cursor based on the current context. This is the default value

✦ `crosshair`: a simple cross hair cursor such as ✚

✦ `default`: the platform-dependent default cursor, usually an arrow; for example ⇖

✦ `hand`: a hand such as ☞

✦ `move`: a symbol that indicates something is to be moved such as ⊹

✦ `n-resize`: north (up is north) pointing arrow such as ⇡

✦ `e-resize`: east (right) pointing arrow such as ⇨

✦ `s-resize`: south (down) pointing arrow such as ⇩

✦ `w-resize`: west (left) pointing arrow such as ⇦

✦ `ne-resize`: northeast pointing arrow such as ⤢

✦ `nw-resize`: northwest pointing arrow such as ⤢

✦ `se-resize`: southeast pointing arrow such as ⤡

✦ `sw-resize`: southwest pointing arrow such as ⤡

✦ `text`: I-beam such as I

✦ `wait`: stop watch, spinning beach ball, hourglass, or other icon indicating the passage of time such as ⧖

✦ `help`: question mark such as ？

The following rule uses the `cursor` property to specify that the hand cursor should be used over individual verses.

```
VERSE { cursor: hand }
```

You can also use a custom cursor that's loaded from an image file by giving a URL for the image. Generally, you provide cursors in several formats in a comma-separated list, the last of which is the name of a generic cursor. For example:

```
VERSE { cursor: url("poetry.cur"), url("poetry.gif"), text }
```

The Content Property

The content property places data from the style sheet into the output document at a position indicated by a :before or :after pseudo-element. The value of the content property may be a string enclosed in quote marks. For example, this rule places an asterisk before and after each SCENE element:

```
SCENE:after  { content: "*"}
SCENE:before { content: "*"}
```

Caution Mozilla, Internet Explorer, and Opera currently only support the content property on block-level elements. This would not work (although it should) for inline elements such as SCENE_NUMBER.

Figure 16-26 shows the result. The asterisks are just part of the display. They do not become part of the XML document itself, so even if you added characters or strings with special meaning to XML, < or & for example, this would not make the document malformed because the document is never changed.

Figure 16-26: Asterisks have been added by the content property

You can add more than a single character to the content. You can even add multiple lines of text. The line breaks are encoded as \A in the string literal. For example, this rule places two rows of asterisks after each act:

```
ACT:after   {content: "\A*********\A*********\A"}
```

Caution   Mozilla, Internet Explorer, and Opera do not yet support \A.

Quotes

Instead of a string literal, the value may be the keyword `open-quote` to insert an opening quote like " or `close-quote` to insert a closing quote character like". By default, the straight double quote " is used to quote items. However, you can change this with the `quotes` property. The value of this element is the quote pair to be used. For example, this rule says that if a `LOCATION` is quoted, the left quote should be " and the right quote should be ":

```
LOCATION {quotes: """ """}
```

The quotes can be anything you want. For instance, you could use the French guillemets « and » like this:

```
LOCATION {quotes: "«" "»"}
```

You could do e-mail-style quoting by setting the left quote to > and the right quote to nothing at all like this:

```
LOCATION {quotes: ">" ""}
```

There's not even any requirement that you actually use any sort of quote marks. For example, this rule uses these properties to put a right parenthesis after each `SCENE_NUMBER` element:

```
SCENE_NUMBER {quotes: "" ")"}
SCENE_NUMBER:before {content: open-quote}
SCENE_NUMBER:after {content: close-quote}
```

If quotes are likely to nest, then you can specify multiple quote combinations. For example, this says that a quote inside a quote would be quoted with single quotation marks:

```
LOCATION {quotes: '"' '"' "'" "'"}
```

You have to match each open quote with a close quote, but if for some reason you don't want to show one or the other you can use `no-open-quote` instead of `open-quote` and `no-close-quote` where you would normally use `close-quote`. The `no-open-quote` and `no-close-quote` keywords do not insert any characters; they just increment or decrement the level of nesting as if quotes had been used.

Attributes

Normally, the only content the reader sees is character data that came from element content in the XML document. However, you can use the `attr()` function as the value of the `content` property to insert an attribute value into the displayed document. For example, this rule inserts the content of the `POEM` element's `TYPE` attribute:

```
POEM:before {content: "A " + attr(type)}
```

URIs

One of the most interesting values of the `content` property is a URI (Uniform Resource Identifier). The URI is given in the same syntax used for the `background-image` property, and it means much the same thing: load the document at the specified URI and display it in the specified location. The browser is allowed to load and embed any kind of document it understands. For example, this rule says that the picture found at the URI `http://www.example.com/shakespeare.jpg` should be inserted before the `TITLE` element:

```
TITLE:before {
  content: uri(http://www.example.com/shakespeare.jpg)
}
```

This can be used for any kind of content that the browser understands: images, text files, PDFs, other XML documents, sound recordings, and more. For example, this rule suggests that a sound file should be played before the `TITLE` element:

```
TITLE:before {
  content: uri(http://www.example.com/12th_night.mp3)
}
```

Unfortunately, current Web browsers don't yet let you use the `content` property to embed the contents of an arbitrary URI, even though this use is endorsed by the CSS specification.

Counters

The final thing you can offer as the value of the `content` property is a *counter*. This is a running total of some type of element from the input document. This enables you to make simple numbered lists, to create outlines that are properly indented with different numbering systems for each level of the outline, to assign numbers to each part, chapter, and section, and more. Numbers can be recalculated on the fly whenever a document changes, rather than having to be painstakingly inserted by hand.

The `counter-increment` property creates and adds to the value of a named counter. The `counter()` function inserts the current value of a specified counter into the output. There's also a `counter-reset property` that returns a counter to its starting point. For example, suppose your XML document did not contain built-in scene numbers or act numbers; that is, suppose it looked like Listing 16-7:

Listing 16-7: A synopsis of Shakespeare's *Twelfth Night* in XML without explicit act or scene numbers

```
<?xml version="1.0"?>
<?xml-stylesheet type="text/css" href="counters.css"?>
<SYNOPSIS>
  <TITLE>Twelfth Night</TITLE>

  <ACT>
    <SCENE>
      <LOCATION><CHARACTER>Duke Orsino</CHARACTER>'s palace
      </LOCATION>
    </SCENE>
    <SCENE>
      <LOCATION>The sea-coast</LOCATION>
    </SCENE>
    <SCENE>
      <LOCATION><CHARACTER>Olivia</CHARACTER>'s house
      </LOCATION>
    </SCENE>
    <SCENE>
      <LOCATION><CHARACTER>Duke Orsino</CHARACTER>'s palace.
      </LOCATION>
    </SCENE>
    <SCENE>
      <LOCATION><CHARACTER>Olivia</CHARACTER>'s house
      </LOCATION>
    </SCENE>
  </ACT>

  <ACT>
    <SCENE>
      <LOCATION>The sea-coast</LOCATION>
    </SCENE>
    <SCENE>
      <LOCATION>A street</LOCATION>
    </SCENE>
    <SCENE>
      <LOCATION><CHARACTER>Olivia</CHARACTER>'s house
      </LOCATION>
    </SCENE>
    <SCENE>
      <LOCATION><CHARACTER>Duke Orsino</CHARACTER>'s palace.
```

Continued

Listing 16-7 *(continued)*

```
      </LOCATION>
    </SCENE>
    <SCENE>
      <LOCATION><CHARACTER>Olivia</CHARACTER>'s garden
      </LOCATION>
    </SCENE>
  </ACT>

  <ACT>
    <SCENE>
      <LOCATION><CHARACTER>Olivia</CHARACTER>'s garden
      </LOCATION>
    </SCENE>
    <SCENE>
      <LOCATION><CHARACTER>Olivia</CHARACTER>'s house
      </LOCATION>
    </SCENE>
    <SCENE>
      <LOCATION>A street</LOCATION>
    </SCENE>
    <SCENE>
      <LOCATION><CHARACTER>Olivia</CHARACTER>'s garden
      </LOCATION>
    </SCENE>
  </ACT>

  <ACT>
    <SCENE>
      <LOCATION><CHARACTER>Olivia</CHARACTER>'s front yard
      </LOCATION>
    </SCENE>
    <SCENE>
      <LOCATION><CHARACTER>Olivia</CHARACTER>'s house
      </LOCATION>
    </SCENE>
    <SCENE>
      <LOCATION><CHARACTER>Olivia</CHARACTER>'s garden
      </LOCATION>
    </SCENE>
  </ACT>

  <ACT>
    <SCENE>
      <LOCATION><CHARACTER>Olivia</CHARACTER>'s front yard
      </LOCATION>
    </SCENE>
  </ACT>

</SYNOPSIS>
```

You can still insert scene numbers using counters. First, add a rule that increments a counter named "scene" by 1 with each SCENE element:

```
SCENE {counter: scene}
```

Next, add a rule that inserts the current value of the scene counter as well as the word "Scene" and a colon before each SCENE element:

```
SCENE:before {content: "Scene " counter(scene) ": "}
```

Finally, reset the scene counter to zero at the beginning of each act so that scenes start over from 1 in each act rather than counting continuously throughout the play:

```
ACT {counter-reset:scene 0}
```

It's not any harder to add an act counter. In fact, it's a little easier because you don't have to reset it. These two rules suffice:

```
ACT {counter-increment: act}
ACT:before {content: "Act " counter(act) ": "}
```

Caution   Internet Explorer, Mozilla, and Opera all have different bugs in handling counters. Regrettably, counters are not very reliable at the present time.

You can increment by a number other than 1 by adding a second value to the counter-increment property. For example, this rule increments the act counter by 2 with each act:

```
ACT {counter-increment: act 2}
```

By default, counters are decimal numbers. However, you can provide an optional second argument to the counter() function that changes the numbering style. The options are:

✦ disc: ●
✦ circle: ○
✦ square: ❏
✦ decimal: 1, 2, 3, 4, 5, and so on
✦ decimal-leading-zero: 01, 02, 03, 04, 05, and so on
✦ lower-roman: i, ii, iii, iv, and so on
✦ upper-roman: I, II, III, IV, and so on
✦ lower-alpha: a, b, c, and so on
✦ upper-alpha: A, B, C, and so on
✦ lower-latin: same as lower-alpha; a, b, c, and so on

- ✦ `upper-Latin`: same as `upper-alpha`; A, B, C, and so on

- ✦ `lower-greek`: α, β, γ, δ, ε, and so on

- ✦ `hebrew`: א, ב, ג, ד, ה, and so on

- ✦ `armenian`: Ա₂ Բ₂ Գ₂ Դ₂ Ե₂, and so on

- ✦ `georgian`: ⴼ, Ⴋ, Ⴓ, Ⴊ, Ⴇ, and so on (same as the Georgian alphabet)

- ✦ `cjk-ideographic`: 一, 二, 三, and so on

- ✦ `hiragana`: あ, い, う, え, お, か, and so on

- ✦ `katakana`: ア, イ, ウ, エ, オ, カ, キ, and so on

- ✦ `hiragana-iroha`: い, ろ, は, に, ほ, へ, と, and so on

- ✦ `katakana-iroha`: イ, ロ, ハ, ニ, ホ, ヘ, ト, and so on

- ✦ `none`: no bullet character is used

I would not rely on a typical Western browser being able to handle the more unusual of these characters. In that case, the browser will default to `decimal`.

If you'd like to use generated content as the list bullet instead of the standard bullet, set the `display` property of the `:before` or `:after` pseudo-element to marker. This must occur inside an element whose `display` property is set to `list-item`. For example, Listing 16-8 uses generated content as a marker for both ACT and SCENE lists.

Listing 16-8: Using scene numbers as list bullets

```
SYNOPSIS, TITLE { display: block }
TITLE { font-family: Helvetica, Verdana, sans-serif;
        font-size: x-large; text-align: center }
SYNOPSIS { font-family: Times, "Times New Roman", serif; font-
size: 14pt; text-align: justify }
ACT, SCENE, TITLE, SYNOPSIS { margin: 1ex }
SCENE {display: list-item; counter-increment: scene}
ACT {display: list-item; counter-increment: act}
SCENE:before {display: marker;
              content: "Scene " counter(scene) ": "}
ACT {counter-reset: scene 0}
ACT:before {content: "Act " counter(act) ": "}
```

Caution

Existing Web browsers don't yet support `display: marker`. I'd stick to the more standard list-item bullets for the time being, or simply generate the markers manually using the appropriate `:before` and `:after` rules, indentation, and the `content` property.

Aural Style Sheets

Visually impaired users already have special software that reads Web pages. In the future, such use is likely to expand to sighted people browsing the Web while talking on cell phones, driving their cars, washing the dishes, and performing other activities in which the eyes and hands have to be directed elsewhere. As well as the visual properties you've encountered up to this point that say how elements are printed or shown on a screen, CSS provides aural properties to describe how elements should be read out loud as well. Listing 16-9 is an aural style sheet that identifies specific ways to speak information in the SYNOPSIS example.

Listing 16-9: An aural style sheet for a synopsis

```
SYNOPSIS {speak: normal}

TITLE, AUTHOR, ACT, SCENE {
        voice-family: Bruce, male;
        stress: 20;
        richness: 90;
        cue-before: url("ping.au")
}

ACT    { pause: 30ms 40ms } /* pause-before: 30ms;
                                pause-after: 40ms */

SCENE { pause-after: 10ms;
        cue-before: url("bell.aiff");
        cue-after: url("dong.wav") }
```

The speak property

The speak property determines whether text will be rendered aurally, and if so, how. If speak has the value normal, words are spoken using the best available speech synthesis. If speak has the value spell-out, words are spelled out letter-by-letter, which might be useful for unusual or foreign words a speech synthesizer probably can't handle. The default value is none (that is, just render the content visually and forget about speech synthesis).

The volume property

The volume property controls the average volume of the speaking voice of the speech synthesizer. This is only an average. A highly inflected voice at a volume of 50 might peak at 75. The minimum volume is 0. The maximum volume is 100. Percentage values can also be used, as can any of these six keywords:

✦ silent: no sound

✦ x-soft: 0, the minimum audible volume

✦ soft: about 25

✦ medium: about 50

✦ loud: about 75

✦ x-loud: 100, the maximum comfortable hearing level

Pause properties

Pauses are the aural equivalent of commas. They can be used to provide drama, or just to help separate one speaker's voice from another's. They're set with the pause, pause-before, and pause-after properties.

The pause-before property specifies the length of time the speech synthesizer should pause before speaking an element's contents. The pause-after property specifies the length of time the speech synthesizer should pause after speaking an element's contents. Each can be set as an absolute time or as a percentage of the speech-rate property. The pause property is a shorthand for setting both pause-before and pause-after. When two values are supplied, the first is applied to pause-before and the second is applied to pause-after. When only one value is given, it applies to both properties. For example,

```
SCENE { pause-after: 10ms }

/* pause-before: 30ms; pause-after: 40ms */
ACT   { pause: 30ms 40ms }
```

Cue properties

Cues are audible clues that alert the listener to a specific event that is about to occur, or has just occurred. The cue properties let you specify a URL for a sound file that will be played before or after an element is spoken. The cue-before property plays a sound before an element is read. The cue-after property plays a sound after an element is read. Both use a URI to specify the cue to play.

The cue property is a shorthand for setting both cue-before and cue-after. When two values are supplied, the first is applied to cue-before and the second is applied to cue-after. When only one value is given, it applies to both properties. For example:

```
ACT, SCENE { cue-before: url("ping.au") }
SCENE      { cue-before: url("bell.aiff");
             cue-after:  url("dong.wav") }
```

Play-during property

The play-during property specifies a sound to be played in the background while an element's content is spoken. The value of the property is URL to the sound file. You can also add one or both of the keywords mix and repeat to the value. Mix tells the speech synthesizer to mix in the parent's play-during sound. Repeat tells the speech synthesizer to loop the sound continuously until the entire element has been spoken. The default value is none.

Spatial properties

The spatial properties specify where the sound should appear to be coming from. For example, you can have a document read to you from 3 feet away in a ditch or from 100 feet away on a cliff. This is, of course, limited by the capabilities of the speech synthesizer and audio hardware.

The azimuth property

The azimuth property controls the horizontal angle from which the sound appears to emanate. When you listen to audio through good stereo speakers, you seem to hear a lateral sound stage. The azimuth property can be used with this type of stereo system to create angles to the sound you hear. When you add a total surround sound system using either a binaural headphone or a five-speaker home theatre setup, the azimuth property becomes very noticeable.

The azimuth is specified as an angle between –360 degrees and 360 degrees. A value of 0deg means that the sound is directly in front of the listener (as are -360deg and 360deg). A value of 180deg means that the sound is directly behind the listener. (In CSS terminology deg replaces the more common ° degree symbol.) Angles are counted clockwise to the listener's right. You can also use one of these nine keywords to specify the azimuth angle:

✦ center: 0 deg

✦ center-right: 20deg

✦ right: 40deg

✦ far-right: 60deg

✦ right-side: 90deg

✦ left-side: 270deg

✦ far-left: 300deg

✦ left: 320deg

✦ center-left: 340deg

You can add the keyword behind to any of these values to subtract 180deg from the values. For example, left behind is the same as -140deg, which is the same as 220deg.

A value of leftwards moves the sound an additional 20 degrees to the left, relative to the current angle. This is most easily understood as turning the sound counter-clockwise. So, even if the sound is already behind the listener, it will continue to move "left" around the circle. A value of rightwards moves the sound an additional 20 degrees to the right (clockwise) from the current angle.

The elevation property

The elevation property controls the apparent height of the speaker above the listener's position. Because you cannot predetermine the number and location of speakers in use by the document reader, this attribute simply identifies the desired result. As the document author, you can't really force a specific result in all cases, anymore than you can guarantee that a reader has a color monitor. The elevation is specified as an angle between –90 degrees and 90 degrees. It can also be given as one of these five keywords:

✦ below: –90deg

✦ level: 0deg

✦ above: 90deg

✦ higher: 10deg above the current elevation

✦ lower: 10deg below the current elevation

Voice characteristics

Adjusting the rate of speech controls the individual characteristics of the synthesizer's "voice," the voice-family used, the pitch, and the richness of the voice.

The speech-rate property

The speech-rate property specifies the speech synthesizer's speed as an approximate number of average-sized words per minute. You can supply an integer or one of these five keywords:

✦ x-slow: 80 words per minutes

✦ slow: 120 words per minute

✦ medium: 180 to 200 words per minute

✦ fast: 300 words per minute

✦ x-fast: 500 words per minute

You can also use the keyword faster to add 40 words per minute to the rate of the parent element or slower to subtract 40 words per minute from the rate of the parent element.

The voice-family property

The voice-family property is a comma-separated, prioritized list of voice family names that chooses the voice used for reading the text of the document. It's like the font-family property, but with voices instead of type faces.

Generic voice values include male, female, and child. Specific names are as diverse as font names and include Agnes, Bruce, Good News, Hysterical, Victoria, Whisper, and many more. Just as with font families, there's no guarantee that any of these voices is installed on any given system. And just as with font families, these names must be quoted if they consist of more than one word. For example, if you were marking up a play, you might choose different voices for each actor but fall back to the generics if necessary, like this:

```
LINE[speaker="Olivia"]     { voice-family: Victoria, female }
LINE[speaker="Viola"]      { voice-family: Agnes, female }
LINE[speaker="Antonio"]    { voice-family: Bruce, male }
LINE[speaker="Sebastian"]  { voice-family: David, male }
```

The pitch property

The pitch property specifies the frequency that the speech synthesizer uses for a particular type of object. To some degree, this controls whether a voice sounds male or female. However, it's better to use an appropriate voice-family instead. The value is given in hertz, that is, in cycles per second. Female voices are about 210 Hz, while typical male voices fall in the ballpark of 120 Hz. You can also use these keywords to adjust the pitch:

✦ x-low

✦ low

✦ medium

✦ high

✦ x-high

The exact values of these keywords in hertz depend on the user's environment and selected voice.

The pitch-range property

The pitch-range property specifies the acceptable variations in the speaker's average pitch as a number between 0 and 100. This controls the inflection and variation of the voice used by the speech synthesizer. A value of 0 creates a flat, monotone voice, while 50 is a normal voice, and values above 50 create an exceptionally animated voice. For example,

```
LINE[speaker="Tuvok"]   { pitch-range: 10 }
LINE[speaker="Seven"]   { pitch-range: 20 }
LINE[speaker="Janeway"] { pitch-range: 50 }
LINE[speaker="Paris"]   { pitch-range: 70 }
```

The stress property

The `stress` property specifies the level of assertiveness or emphasis that's used in the speaking voice. The default is 50. For example,

```
LINE[speaker="Tuvok"]    { stress: 40 }
LINE[speaker="Seven"]    { stress: 90 }
LINE[speaker="Janeway"]  { stress: 60 }
LINE[speaker="Kim"]      { stress: 30 }
```

This attribute has a different effect in different languages. When used with languages such as English, which use stresses on sentence position, you can select primary, secondary, and tertiary stress points to control the inflection that is applied to these areas of the sentence.

The richness property

The `richness` property specifies the "brightness" of the voice used by the speech synthesizer. The richer the voice, the better its carrying capacity. Smooth voices don't carry far because they're not as deeply pitched as rich voices. The value is a number between 1 and 100, with a default of 50. Higher values produce voices that carry better, while lower values produce softer, easier-to-listen-to voices. For example,

```
LINE[speaker="Tuvok"]    { richness: 45 }
LINE[speaker="Seven"]    { richness: 65 }
LINE[speaker="Janeway"]  { richness: 70 }
LINE[speaker="Neelix"]   { richness: 25 }
```

Speech properties

These properties control how the speech synthesizer interprets punctuation and numbers. There are two such properties: `speak-punctuation` and `speak-numeral`.

The speak-punctuation property

By default, punctuation is spoken literally. A statement such as "The cat, Charm, ate all of his food." is read as "The cat comma Charm comma ate all of his food period". However, by setting the `speak-punctuation` property to `none`, the punctuation will not be spoken. It will, however, be paused for, as in a natural speaking voice. For example, "The cat <pause> Charm <pause> ate all of his food <silence>".

The speak-numeral property

By default, numbers are spoken as a full string. For example, the number 102 would be read as "one hundred and two." If, however, you set the `speak-numeral` property to `digits`, each number will be spoken individually such as "one zero two." You can return to the default by setting `speak-numeral` property to `continuous`.

Summary

This chapter discussed CSS's text and character-oriented properties. In this chapter, you learned that:

✦ The font-family property specifies the face in which the text is drawn. Its value is a comma separated list of family names such as Helvetica and "Times New Roman" and generic names such as sans-serif, serif, cursive, monospace, and fantasy.

✦ The font-size property specifies how big text is as either an absolute length such as 12pt, an absolute keyword such as small, a relative keyword such as smaller, or a percentage of the parent element's font size such as 80%.

✦ The font-size-adjust property sets the aspect value of text. This is the ratio of x-height to font size.

✦ The font-stretch property determines how loose or tight a font is; that is, how close the letters are together. Possible values include normal (the default), wider, narrower, ultra-condensed, extra-condensed, condensed, semi-condensed, semi-expanded, expanded, extra-expanded, and ultra-expanded.

✦ The font-style property can be set to normal (the default), italic, or oblique.

✦ The font-variant property can be set to normal (the default) or small-caps.

✦ The font-weight property determines how bold a font is. Possible values include the keywords normal, bold, bolder, and lighter as well as the numeric levels from 100 (the lightest) to 900 (the darkest).

✦ The color property can be set to a named color such as fuchsia, a hexadecimal triple such as #FF00FF, or a decimal triple such as rgb(255, 0, 255) to indicate the color of the foreground object.

✦ The word-spacing property gives a length to be used as extra space between each pair of words.

✦ The letter-spacing property gives a length to be used as extra space between each pair of characters.

✦ The text-decoration property can be set to none (the default), underline, overline, line-through, and/or blink.

✦ The vertical-align property determines where an object is placed between the top and bottom of its containing box. It can be set to an absolute length, a percentage of the vertical height of the box, or one of the keywords baseline, sub, super, top, text-top, middle, bottom, and text-bottom.

✦ The `text-transform` property can be set to `none` (the default), `capitalize`, `uppercase`, or `lowercase`.

✦ The `text-align` property can be set to `left`, `right`, `center`, or `justify`.

✦ The `text-indent` property specifies how far to indent the first line of a paragraph using either an absolute length or a percentage of the width of the paragraph.

✦ The `text-shadow` property places a shadow of a specified color, length, width, and blur radius on one corner of an element.

✦ The `line-height` property determines the vertical extension of a line box. It can be set to an absolute length or a percentage of the font size.

✦ The `white-space` property determines how whitespace is handled inside the element. Allowed values include `normal` (the default), `pre`, and `nowrap`.

✦ The `background-color` property sets the color of the background of an element using the same values the `color` property uses for the foreground color.

✦ The background of an element can be set to an image using the `background-image`, `background-repeat`, `background-attachment`, and `background-position` properties.

✦ The `visibility` property controls whether the contents of an element are seen. It has three possible values: `visible`, `hidden`, and `collapse`.

✦ The `cursor` property specifies the arrow, hand, insertion bar, or other icon the browser uses to indicate the position of the pointer on the screen within a particular element.

✦ The `content` property places data from the style sheet into the output document at a position indicated by a `:before` or `:after` pseudo-element. The value of the `content` property can be a literal string, an attribute value loaded with the `attr()` function, an opening or closing quote mark defined by the `quotes` property, the value of a counter, or the document at a URI.

✦ Aural style sheets specify properties such as `speak-punctuation`, `volume`, `pause-before`, `cue-after`, and `voice` that determine how a document should be read by a speech synthesizer.

Although CSS Level 2 is quite powerful when fully implemented, there are some limits to what you can achieve with it. For one thing, it's static. CSS2 only describes what elements look like, not how they behave. It's intended mostly for Web browsers, and thus doesn't support many features important for print such as multicolumn layouts. It relies on HTML to provide forms and user input, which works well for HTML but fails with more free-form XML documents. In addition, CSS2 focuses mostly on Western languages such as English, Greek, and Turkish; it doesn't have all the features it needs for more typographically challenging languages such as Hebrew and Japanese. The next chapter explores CSS Level 3, a developing standard that adds all these features and more to CSS.

✦   ✦   ✦

CSS Level III

CSS Level 2 (CSS2), as described in the last three chapters, is quite powerful. It allows you to specify text styles, colors, page layouts, and more. However, there are still some missing pieces. Some common tasks that you cannot accomplish with CSS2 include:

✦ Multicolumn layouts

✦ Transparency

✦ Copy fitting, autosizing, and autospacing

✦ Ruby text for Japanese and Chinese

✦ Running headers and footers

✦ Cross-references

✦ Positioning floating objects in particular places on the page

✦ Forms

✦ Web pages in full-screen kiosk mode

✦ Animation

✦ Accepting user input through the mouse and keyboard

✦ Selectors that depend on namespace URIs instead of prefixes

✦ Content from attributes as well as elements

CSS Level 3 (CSS3) expands on CSS2 to add these capabilities and more. CSS3 is particularly useful for documents printed on paper, such as this book, rather than displayed in a browser window. CSS3 allows you to define multicolumn layouts such as you see in most newspapers and many magazines. It lets you assign running headers and footers at the top and bottom of each page. Page numbers can be placed in the header or footer and used to identify cross-references from one page to the next (e.g. "For more on this topic see p. 525").

CSS Level 3 leaves the familiar syntax of CSS Levels 1 and 2 unchanged. Styles are still applied by rules with a selector identifying the elements to style followed by a list of styles in curly braces. The styles are still given as names and values separated by colons. The old styles still mean what they meant in CSS Level 2. However, the list of available selectors and styles has been expanded to add more power and greater flexibility.

Caution

I must warn you that at the time of this writing (August 2001), CSS3 is very bleeding-edge technology. The individual specifications that comprise CSS3 are still undergoing significant development and modification. This chapter is based on the following working draft specifications from the W3C:

Introduction to CSS 3 — May 23 2001 Working Draft

CSS3 module: W3C selectors — January 26 2001 Last Call Working Draft

CSS3 module: Color — March 5 2001 Working Draft

CSS3 module: Ruby — February 16 2001 Working Draft

CSS3 module: Text — May 17 2001 Working Draft

CSS3 module: Media Queries — May 17 2001 Working Draft

CSS Namespace Enhancements — June 25 1999 Working Draft

User Interface for CSS3 — February 16 2000 Working Draft

Behavioral Extensions to CSS — August 4 1999 Working Draft

Paged Media Properties for CSS3 — September 28 1999 Working Draft

Multi-column layout in CSS — January 18 2001 Working Draft

Values and Units — July 13 2001 Working Draft

Cascading and inheritance — July 13 2001 Working Draft

By the time you're reading this, the exact syntax is likely to have changed, perhaps a little, perhaps a lot.

Furthermore, no browsers yet implement any of the selectors and properties discussed here. This chapter gives you a pretty good idea of what you can expect in CSS3, but it is not a final description of exactly how you'll use it.

Modularization

CSS3 divides CSS into different modules: a color module, a layout module, a selectors module, a positioning module, a background module, and so forth. Some of the modules — the *Fonts* and *Tables* modules, for example — describe functionality that was already present in CSS2. Other modules, such as *Columns,* offer completely new functionality. Each module is published as its own specification. This makes the entire CSS language easier to digest and develop. Twenty-six modules are planned for CSS3:

✦ The Syntax/grammar module describes the basic syntax of CSS irrespective of the detailed names — for example, that a rule is a selector followed by a list of properties enclosed in curly braces; that property names are separated from property values by colons; that properties are separated from each other by semicolons; and so forth.

✦ The Selectors module defines the syntax of the selectors used to choose which XML and HTML elements a given rule applies to.

✦ The Values & units module defines the units used in CSS such as inches, centimeters, points, pixels, colors, URLs, and so forth.

✦ The Value assignment / cascade / inheritance module specifies how properties declared for different elements and by different rules interact to assign styles to each element.

✦ The Box model / vertical module describes those properties that determine where elements are laid out on a page in normal text flow; that is, it describes how words are placed on lines, how lines are accumulated into paragraphs, and how paragraphs are placed one after the other inside the margins.

✦ The Positioning module defines properties like `float` and `position` that enable the designer to override the usual flow of text to place specific blocks at particular positions on the page.

✦ The Color / gamma / color profiles module defines a sophisticated way to perform gamma correction and other operations necessary to produce consistent color across platforms.

✦ The Colors and Backgrounds module defines the actual properties used to assign colors and background patterns to elements.

✦ The Line box model module describes how inline elements are laid out.

✦ The Text module describes how text is laid out, including text in non-left-to-right languages such as Arabic and Chinese.

✦ The Fonts module defines the basic font properties such as `font-family`, `font-weight`, and `font-size`.

✦ The Ruby module defines properties for the rendering of the Ruby text used in Chinese and Japanese to indicate pronunciation of ideographic characters.

✦ The Generated content / markers module describes properties that tell a browser to display content that doesn't come from the input document, for instance the bullets in a bulleted list like this one.

✦ The Replaced content module defines new properties to allow the content of an element to be replaced by other content.

✦ The Paged media module defines properties for controlling the layout of a printed page, including floats, gutters, running headers and footers, and page numbers.

✦ The User interface module describes how elements can be styled as check-boxes, buttons, and other GUI widgets.

✦ The WebFonts module endeavors to provide better font control for Web pages.

✦ The ACSS module endeavors to make Web pages more accessible to readers who have limited or no use of hands, hearing, and/or vision. It includes the aural properties used in CSS2, such as `pitch`, `richness`, `voice-family`, and so forth.

✦ The Tables module defines properties for associating elements with parts of tables and laying out tabular data.

✦ The Columns module defines properties such as `column-count` and `column-width` for breaking up elements into more than one column.

✦ The SMIL module tries to make CSS fit well with the Synchronized Multimedia Integration Language.

✦ The SVG module defines properties that are useful for styling nontext vector graphics.

✦ The Math module defines properties that are useful for styling mathematical equations.

✦ The BECSS module defines properties for specifying the dynamic behavior of elements and the connections between XML elements and scripting languages such as JavaScript.

✦ The Media queries module provides ways to associate style rules with particular media types, ranging from the very generic (computer monitors, printed pages) to the quite specific (8.5- by 11-inch paper printed on a 300-dpi black-and-white printer).

✦ The Test Suite module does not define any properties, selectors, or @ rules. Instead, it defines tests that implementers must pass in order to be CSS3 compliant.

Different devices and environments can implement only those modules that make sense for their particular environment. For instance, a VoiceXML browser might implement the ACSS, selector, and syntax modules, but leave out the modules that are concerned with visual formatting such as color and tables. A Web browser for a Palm Pilot might implement the basic box model module but omit the more advanced layout modules for tables and columns.

Selectors

The basic selector syntax of CSS2 remains unchanged in CSS3. All existing selectors continue to work as described in the last three chapters. However, CSS3 adds several new selectors with a special focus on what's needed for XML (as opposed to HTML) documents including:

✦ Namespace selectors for elements and attributes

✦ Substring selectors for attribute values

✦ Many new pseudo-classes, including :target, `:enabled`, `:disabled`, `:checked`, `:indeterminate`, `:root pseudo-class`, `:nth-child()`, `:nth-last-child()`, `:nth-of-type()`, `:nth-last-of-type()`, `:first-of-type`, `:last-of-type`, `:only-child`, `:only-of-type`, `:empty`, `:contains()`, and `:not()`

✦ A `::selection` pseudo-element

✦ The ~ combinator to select according to an element's siblings

Namespaces

Because CSS documents are not XML documents, they have no way to bind a namespace prefix to a namespace URI. Therefore CSS2 style sheets can only select elements and attributes by their prefixed names. If you change the prefix in the XML documents, you also have to change the prefix used in the style sheets. This violates the fundamental principle of namespaces: that it's only the URI that matters, not the prefix.

CSS3 introduces the @namespace rule to map prefixes to URLs. For example, this rule binds the prefix person to the `http://ns.cafeconleche.org/people/` namespace URI:

```
@namespace person url(http://ns.cafeconleche.org/people/);
```

Given this rule, you can use the prefix person in your style sheet, even if the styled document uses a different prefix. However, because the colon is reserved for pseudo-classes in CSS, you must use a vertical bar to separate the prefix from the local name. This looks a little confusing at first, but doesn't cause any problems in practice. For example, this rule specifies that person:TITLE elements should be written in 24-point Helvetica:

```
person|TITLE {font-size: 24pt; font-family: Helvetica, sans}
```

You can use the asterisk wild card to match either any namespace or any local name. For instance, the first rule below makes all TITLE elements red regardless of namespace, whereas the second rule makes all elements in the http://ns.cafeconleche.org/people/ namespace red:

```
*|TITLE   {color: red}
person|*  {color: red}
```

The first rule also matches all TITLE elements that are not in any namespace.

To only select elements that don't have a namespace, use a vertical bar without any prefix in front of it. For example, this rule colors TITLE elements without a namespace green, but not TITLE elements in the http://ns.cafeconleche.org/people/ namespace:

```
|TITLE {color: green}
```

An `@namespace` rule without a prefix defines the default namespace for the stylesheet. This namespace URI applies to all elements in the style sheet that don't have a prefix. For example, this rule declares that the default namespace is `http://ns.cafeconleche.org/people/`:

```
@namespace url(http://ns.cafeconleche.org/people/);
```

Given this rule, unprefixed names such as `TITLE`, `FIRST`, and `PERSON` are all assumed to be in this namespace. However, if the style sheet doesn't have an `@namespace` rule that defines a default namespace, then raw element names used in selectors match all elements with that local name, regardless of what namespace they're in.

Tip   You can still use a prefix in the style sheet even if you use no prefix in the input document. Furthermore, just because you use a namespace in the styled document doesn't mean you have to use a namespace in the stylesheet. It's still acceptable to have selectors that exactly match element names.

Substring matching in attribute selectors

CSS2 defines a number of selectors that match on attribute names and values, including:

✦ `E[foo]` selects all `E` elements that have a `foo` attribute, regardless of its value

✦ `E[foo="bar"]` selects all `E` elements that have a `foo` attribute with the value `bar`

✦ `E[foo~="bar"]` selects all `E` elements that have a `foo` attribute whose value contains the entire word `bar` (not just the substring `bar`)

CSS3 adds three more attribute selectors:

✦ `E[foo^="bar"]` selects all `E` elements whose `foo` attribute begins with the string `bar`

✦ `E[foo$="bar"]` selects all `E` elements whose `foo` attribute ends with the string `bar`

✦ `E[foo*="bar"]` selects all `E` elements whose `foo` attribute contains the substring `bar`; this will be a superset of the elements selected by `E[foo~="bar"]`

Combinators

A combinator is a binary operator that separates two elements. The last element is selected only if the first element is also matched and has the relationship to the second element indicated by the particular combinator. For example, consider this CSS2 rule:

```
BOOK > TITLE {font-size: 24pt; font-weight: bold}
```

The greater than sign between BOOK and TITLE is a combinator that indicates a child relationship. This rule only applies to TITLE elements that are immediate children of BOOK elements. It does not apply to TITLE elements that are children of MOVIE or PERSON elements. Nor does it apply to BOOK elements. CSS2 also has combinators for ancestor and immediate preceding sibling relationships. The latter is indicated by a plus sign. For example, this rule applies to all AUTHOR elements that are immediately preceded by a sibling TITLE element:

```
TITLE + AUTHOR {font-size: 20pt; font-weight: bold}
```

CSS3 adds a tilde combinator for preceding sibling relationships, regardless of whether or not the sibling is the previous sibling. For example, this CSS3 rule colors blue all AUTHOR elements that are preceded by a sibling TITLE element even if there's an intervening SUBTITLE element first:

```
TITLE ~ AUTHOR {color: blue}
```

Pseudo-elements

A pseudo-element selects something that isn't necessarily a single identifiable element in XML such as the first line of a paragraph or the first letter of a sentence. Pseudo-element selectors in CSS2 include:

✦ :first-letter

✦ :first-line

✦ :before

✦ :after

For instance, in CSS2 you'd make the first line of a CHAPTER element small caps with a large initial drop cap by using the first-line and first-letter pseudo-element selectors like this:

```
CHAPTER:first-line { font-variant: small-caps }
CHAPTER:first-letter {
  font-size: 300%;
  float: left;
  vertical-align: text-top;
  margin-right: 12px
}
```

CSS3 changes the syntax of pseudo-element selectors so that they're separated from the actual element name by two colons rather than one. Thus, in CSS3, the above rules are written like this instead:

```
CHAPTER::first-line { font-variant: small-caps }
CHAPTER::first-letter {
  font-size: 300%;
  float: left;
  vertical-align: text-top;
  margin-right: 12px
}
```

The goal here is to more clearly distinguish between pseudo-element selectors and pseudo-class selectors. In CSS3, pseudo-class selectors use one colon and pseudo-element selectors use two colons. However, for backwards compatibility, browsers should still recognize the one-colon pseudo-element selectors.

In addition to changing the syntax of pseudo-element selectors from one colon to two, CSS3 adds one new pseudo-element selector, `::selection`. This pseudo-element identifies the fragment of the document selected by the user with the mouse. For example, this rule says that the selection should be colored white on a blue background:

```
*::selection { color: white; background-color: blue}
```

New pseudo-classes

A pseudo-class selects something that is a complete element, but not by element type or attribute name or value alone. CSS2 pseudo-class selectors include:

- ✦ `:first-child`
- ✦ `:link`
- ✦ `:visited`
- ✦ `:active`
- ✦ `:hover`
- ✦ `:focus`
- ✦ `:lang`
- ✦ `:right`
- ✦ `:left`
- ✦ `:first`

CSS3 defines 17 more pseudo-class selectors:

- ✦ `:target`
- ✦ `:enabled`
- ✦ `:disabled`

- ✦ :indeterminate
- ✦ :checked
- ✦ :root
- ✦ :nth-child()
- ✦ :nth-last-child()
- ✦ :nth-of-type()
- ✦ :nth-last-of-type()
- ✦ :first-of-type()
- ✦ last-of-type()
- ✦ :only-child
- ✦ :last-child
- ✦ :empty
- ✦ :contains
- ✦ :not

The :target pseudo-class

URLs may contain fragment identifiers that point to a specific part of an HTML or XML document. A fragment identifier is attached to the end of the URL after a sharp sign #. For example, the URL http://www.cafeaulait.org/index.shtml#today has the fragment identifier today pointing to the Today's News section of the whole page at http://www.cafeaulait.org/index.shtml. In this particular case, the HTML uses an a element with a name attribute to identify the targeted section:

```
<h2><a name="today">Today's News</a></h2>
```

Most browsers will position the targeted a element at the top of the browser window when they load this URL.

HTML 4 and XHTML let you put an id attribute on any element and link to the value of that id attribute instead, like this:

```
<h2 id="today">Today's News</h2>
```

Whether you use the old style with a elements and name attributes or the new style with id attributes, the fragment identifier syntax in URLs is the same. To link to XML documents, you can also use an XPointer in the fragment identifier like this:

```
http://www.cafeaulait.org/index.shtml#xpointer(//td[1]/h2[2])
```

This has the advantage of not requiring you to modify the targeted document just so other documents can link to it.

Cross-Reference   XPointers are discussed in detail in Chapter 21.

Regardless of the kind of fragment identifier you use, and regardless of the syntax used inside the document being linked to, you can use the :target pseudo-class to apply special styles to the elements pointed at by the fragment identifier. For example, this rule colors targeted h2 elements blue but other h2 elements red:

```
h2         {color: red}
h2:target {color: blue}
```

Whether any given h2 element is colored blue depends on how the reader gets there. If they follow a link to that specific h2 element, then the element's text will be colored blue. However, if they follow a link to the entire page and just scroll down until they encounter that h2 element, the element will be colored red.

User interaction pseudo-classes

CSS2 defines several pseudo-classes that select particular elements depending on whether and how the user has interacted with them. These pseudo-classes include:

✦ :active

✦ :focus

✦ :hover

CSS3 adds four more pseudo-classes, although these are more useful for HTML than XML:

✦ :enabled: the user can interact with this element in some away

✦ :disabled: the user cannot interact with this element in any away

✦ :checked: the element is currently checked; only really applies to elements that are styled as checkboxes and radio buttons

✦ :indeterminate: the element is neither checked nor unchecked; only really applies to elements that are styled as checkboxes and radio buttons

Structural pseudo-classes

The structural pseudo-classes match elements according to their position in the tree; for instance, whether an element is the first child of its parent, the second child of its parent, the only child of its parent, or the last child of its parent. CSS2 has one such selector, :first-child; CSS3 adds ten more selectors:

✦ :root: the unique root element of the document.

✦ :nth-child(an+b): every element that's the *an+bth* child element of its parent element, for fixed nonnegative integer values of *a* and *b* and any nonnegative integer value of n.

✦ `:nth-last-child(`*an+b*`)`: every element that's the *an+bth* child element of its parent element counting backwards from the last child, for fixed nonnegative integer values of *a* and *b* and any nonnegative integer value of n.

✦ `:nth-of-type(`*an+b*`)`: every element that's the *an+bth* child element of its parent element with the previous type, for fixed non-negative integer values of *a* and *b* and any non-negative integer value of n.

✦ `:nth-last-of-type(`*an+b*`)`: every element that's the *an+bth* child element of its parent element counting backwards from the last child with the type specified by the previous part of the selector, for fixed nonnegative integer values of *a* and *b* and any nonnegative integer value of n.

✦ `:first-of-type()`: the first child element with a specified type.

✦ `last-of-type()`: the last child element with a specified type.

✦ `last-child()`: the last child element of its parent.

✦ `:only-child`: elements with no siblings.

✦ `:empty`: elements with no content.

This rule uses the `:root` pseudo-class to match a `SEASON` element only if it's the root element:

```
SEASON:root {font-size: 14pt; color: black; display: block}
```

This rule uses an asterisk wild card and the `:root` pseudo-class to match the root element, whatever its name:

```
*:root {font-size: 14pt; color: black; display: block}
```

The `nth-child()` pseudo-class can be used with an integer to select a particular child element of its parent. For example, this rule selects the seventh `SON` element in every `FAMILY`:

```
FAMILY>SON:nth-child(7): {font-style: italic}
```

Caution   This can be a little confusing. Remember this matches `SON` elements that are the seventh child of a `FAMILY` element, *not* the seventh child of a `SON` element that's a child of a `FAMILY` element. `SON` elements themselves are matched, not the children of the `SON`. The `nth-child()` and similar selectors do not change the type of the element that's selected.

However, `:nth-child()` can also be used with a more complex syntax to indicate every seventh element, or every seventh element counting from the second element, and so forth. To do this, use the form `:nth-child(`*an+b*`)` where *a* and *b* are variables that you'll replace by specific nonnegative integers such as 0, 3, 7, or 12. However n is not replaced. Instead, the browser calculates the value of this formula for n=0, n=1, n=2, and so on. This pseudo-class matches the *an+bth* elements for any nonnegative integer value of n. In other words, this formula calculates which child elements it applies to.

For example, this set of rules colors the first row of a table green, the second row and every subsequent third row blue, the third row and every subsequent third row red, and the fourth row and every third row after that yellow.

```
TR:first-child     {background-color: green}
TR:nth-child(3n+2) {background-color: blue}
TR:nth-child(3n+3) {background-color: red}
TR:nth-child(3n+4) {background-color: yellow}
```

You can also use the keywords odd and even to match only even- and odd-numbered child elements. These are the same as 2n+1 and 2n+0, respectively. For example, these rules alternate gray and white backgrounds in table rows:

```
TR:nth-child(odd)  {background-color: #666666}
TR:nth-child(even) {background-color: #FFFFFF}
```

The :nth-last-child() pseudo-element is similar except that it counts backward from the end of the parent element rather than forward from the start of the parent element. For example, in a table with four rows these rules produce gray-white-gray-white:

```
TR:nth-last-child(2n+1) {background-color: #666666}
TR:nth-last-child(2n+0) {background-color: #FFFFFF}
```

However, if you change nth-last-child() to nth-child(), the sequence is reversed: white-gray-white-gray.

The :nth-of-type() pseudo-class works similarly to :nth-child() except that only children of the type specified by its preceding selector are counted. For instance the above rules assume that a TABLE contains only TR elements but no CAPTION or THEAD elements. The following rules, however, still work even if the table also contains a CAPTION or a THEAD.

```
TR:first-child       {background-color: green}
TR:nth-of-type(3n+2) {background-color: blue}
TR:nth-of-type(3n+3) {background-color: red}
TR:nth-of-type(3n+4) {background-color: yellow}
```

The :nth-last-of-type(an+b) pseudo-class behaves similarly except that it counts backwards from the end of the parent element like :nth-last-child(an+b).

The :first-of-type pseudo-class selects the first child element of the type specified by the previous part of the selector. For example, this rule colors the first TR element green:

```
TR:first-of-type {background-color: green}
```

The :last-of-type pseudo-class selects the last child element of the type speci-fied by the previous part of the selector. For example, this rule colors the last TR element green:

```
TR:last-of-type {background-color: green}
```

The :last-child pseudo-class only selects the specified element of the type speci-fied if it's the last element in its parent, regardless of type. For example, this rule colors the last TR element green only if it is not followed by a TFOOT or an element of some other type:

```
TR:last-child {background-color: green}
```

The :only-child pseudo-class simply selects elements with no siblings. For exam-ple, this rule only applies to rows in a table with exactly one row:

```
TR:only-child {background-color: yellow}
```

Finally, the :empty pseudo-class selects elements with no content, whether repre-sented by a start tag and an end tag or an empty element tag. For example, this rule replaces empty PLAYER elements with the content of their GIVEN_NAME and SUR-NAME attributes:

```
PLAYER:empty:before {
  content: attr(GIVEN_NAME) " " attr(SURNAME)
}
```

This example uses the attr() function introduced in CSS2 to extract the values of attributes and to show them to the reader.

The :contains() pseudo-class

The :contains() pseudo-class selects elements based on their text content. For example, this rule colors red all TITLE elements that contain the substring "Bible":

```
TITLE:contains("Bible") {color: red}
```

The :contains() pseudo-class matches substrings. For instance, P:contains("Hyper") selects all P elements that contain the string Hypertext, HyperCard, and UltraHyper.

The substring is matched against the complete text content of the element includ-ing any content in descendants. Tags, comments, and processing instructions are not considered and indeed are stripped out before the substring is matched. Entity references are resolved. Thus, P:contains("Ben & Jerry's") would select P elements that contain the string Ben & Jerry's or the markup <PERSON>Ben</PERSON> & <PERSON>Jerry</PERSON>'s.

The :not() pseudo-class

The `:not()` pseudo-class selects nodes that are not something. For example, this CSS rule makes everything except `TITLE` elements bold:

```
*:not(TITLE) {font-weight: bold}
```

You can only apply `not()` to simple selectors; you cannot use it with selectors that use combinators such as >, +, and ~. For example, this attempt to make everything that is not a child of a `PLAYER` element bold is illegal:

```
*:not(PLAYER > *)
```

Color

CSS2 defines several color properties, including:

✦ `color`

✦ `background-color`

✦ `border-color`

✦ `outline-color`

Each of these properties may be specified as a color name taken from the 16 colors of the VGA palette such as `pink`, or an RGB triple in hexadecimal, such as `#FFCCCC`, in decimal, such as `rgb(255,204,204)`, or as a percentage, such as `rgb(100%,80%,80%)`. CSS3 also allows the value of the color to be read from an attribute in the input document. This allows more convenient coloring of individual elements rather than all elements of a certain type. For example, imagine you have this P element in the input document:

```
<P COLOR="#000000">
  The quick brown fox jumped over the lazy dog.
</P>
<P COLOR="#FF0000">
  Thy quack brawn fix jumper ever thy hazy dig.
</P>
```

This single rule marks the first sentence black but the second red:

```
P {color: attr(COLOR, color)}
```

CSS3 adds several new color properties, including:

✦ `opacity`

✦ `color-profile`

✦ `rendering-intent`

Finally, CSS3 adds many new keywords for color names taken from X Windows.

The opacity property

The opacity property defines how transparent something is. Its value ranges from the default 1.0 (fully opaque; completely hides everything underneath the colored object) to 0.0 (fully transparent; colored object is totally invisible). For example, these rules say that an IMAGE is rendered at 0.5 opacity whereas TEXT has 1.0 opacity. The CSS2 z-index property says that the IMAGE is on top of the text.

```
IMAGE {opacity: 0.5; z-index: 2}
TEXT  {opacity: 1.0; z-index: 1}
```

Figure 17-1 shows the effect this might produce, as mocked up in Photoshop. However, I wouldn't count on any browsers supporting this anytime soon.

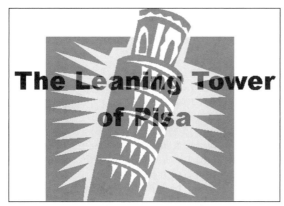

Figure 17-1: A 50 percent opaque image on top of 100 percent opaque text

The color-profile property

The International Color Consortium (ICC, http://www.color.org) color profile is a standard non-XML, binary file format used to characterize the color capabilities of different devices such as scanners, monitors, and printers. Intelligent software can compare ICC color profiles for different devices to make sure that if you take a picture of a flower, scan it into your computer, crop, rotate, and resize the picture in Photoshop, and then print it out on your color inkjet printer, the final print is as close as reasonably possible to the actual color of the flower in the light where the photo was taken.

The CSS3 `color-profile` property identifies the ICC color profile that should be applied to an image by providing a URL to the location where the profile is stored. Alternately, you can use the keyword `sRGB` to indicate that the standard Default Color Space for the Internet (sRGB, `http://www.w3.org/Graphics/Color/sRGB.html`) color profile should be used. If the `color-profile` property is not set, then images with embedded color profiles use their embedded profiles, and images without embedded color profiles use sRGB.

For example, this rule says that `IMG` elements should use the color profile at `http://www.cafeconleche.org/profiles/darker.icm`:

```
IMG { color-profile:
  url("http://www.cafeconleche.org/profiles/darker.icm")
}
```

Relative URLs can also be used, of course. This rule says that `IMG` elements should use the color profile in the file `darker.icm` in the profiles directory:

```
IMG { color-profile: url("profiles/darker.icm") }
```

The rendering-intent property

The `rendering-intent` property specifies what the browser, printer, or other renderer should do when faced with an image whose ICC color profile can't be perfectly reproduced on the output device. Possible values are:

✦ `perceptual`: Compress or expand the full gamut of colors in the color profile as necessary to fill the gamut of the destination device. This scheme may shift individual colors, but it does a decent job of ensuring that distinct colors remain as distinct as possible. It prevents the brightest and darkest shades in an image from all becoming a single color when a device tries to perform the closest possible match on each color but doesn't have as much range as the image it's matching.

✦ `relative-colorimetric`: Adjust the white point so that white is the color of the paper being used. In practice, paper is normally a slightly off-white as compared to the pure white you can get on a good computer display. Hold a blank piece of white paper up to a white page on your monitor to see the difference. Otherwise, match colors exactly.

✦ `saturation`: Using a hue-saturation-brightness color model, preserve the saturation of each pixel even if that makes it necessary to change the hue and brightness.

✦ `absolute-colorimetric`: Try to match each pixel in the image to the nearest color the output device can present. The more colors and the broader gamut of the output device the better this works.

✦ `inherit`: Use the same profile the parent element uses.

✦ `auto`: Make a best guess based on the content type of the image.

The default is `auto`.

New color names

CSS3 adds 140 named colors to the 16 CSS2 named colors. The names are taken from X-Windows. Table 17-1 lists the new color names and their values.

Table 17-1
New Color Names in CSS3

Color Name	Hex RGB	Decimal RGB
AliceBlue	#F0F8FF	rgb(240,248,255)
AntiqueWhite	#FAEBD7	rgb(250,235,215)
Aqua	#00FFFF	rgb(0,255,255)
Aquamarine	#7FFFD4	rgb(127,255,212)
Azure	#F0FFFF	rgb(240,255,255)
Beige	#F5F5DC	rgb(245,245,220)
Bisque	#FFE4C4	rgb(255,228,196)
Black	#000000	rgb(0,0,0)
BlanchedAlmond	#FFEBCD	rgb(255,235,205)
Blue	#0000FF	rgb(0,0,255)
BlueViolet	#8A2BE2	rgb(138,43,226)
Brown	#A52A2A	rgb(165,42,42)
BurlyWood	#DEB887	rgb(222,184,135)
CadetBlue	#5F9EA0	rgb(95,158,160)
Chartreuse	#7FFF00	rgb(127,255,0)
Chocolate	#D2691E	rgb(210,105,30)
Coral	#FF7F50	rgb(255,127,80)
CornflowerBlue	#6495ED	rgb(100,149,237)
Cornsilk	#FFF8DC	rgb(255,248,220)
Crimson	#DC143C	rgb(220,20,60)
Cyan	#00FFFF	rgb(0,255,255)

Continued

Table 17-1 (continued)		
Color Name	*Hex RGB*	*Decimal RGB*
DarkBlue	#00008B	rgb(0,0,139)
DarkCyan	#008B8B	rgb(0,139,139)
DarkGoldenrod	#B8860B	rgb(184,134,11)
DarkGray	#A9A9A9	rgb(169,169,169)
DarkGreen	#006400	rgb(0,100,0)
DarkKhaki	#BDB76B	rgb(189,183,107)
DarkMagenta	#8B008B	rgb(139,0,139)
DarkOliveGreen	#556B2F	rgb(85,107,47)
DarkOrange	#FF8C00	rgb(255,140,0)
DarkOrchid	#9932CC	rgb(153,50,204)
DarkRed	#8B0000	rgb(139,0,0)
DarkSalmon	#E9967A	rgb(233,150,122)
DarkSeaGreen	#8FBC8F	rgb(143,188,143)
DarkSlateBlue	#483D8B	rgb(72,61,139)
DarkSlateGray	#2F4F4F	rgb(47,79,79)
DarkTurquoise	#00CED1	rgb(0,206,209)
DarkViolet	#9400D3	rgb(148,0,211)
DeepPink	#FF1493	rgb(255,20,147)
DeepSkyBlue	#00BFFF	rgb(0,191,255)
DimGray	#696969	rgb(105,105,105)
DodgerBlue	#1E90FF	rgb(30,144,255)
FireBrick	#B22222	rgb(178,34,34)
FloralWhite	#FFFAF0	rgb(255,250,240)
ForestGreen	#228B22	rgb(34,139,34)
Fuchsia	#FF00FF	rgb(255,0,255)
Gainsboro	#DCDCDC	rgb(220,220,220)
GhostWhite	#F8F8FF	rgb(248,248,255)
Gold	#FFD700	rgb(255,215,0)
Goldenrod	#DAA520	rgb(218,165,32)
Gray	#808080	rgb(128,128,128)
Green	#008000	rgb(0,128,0)

Color Name	Hex RGB	Decimal RGB
GreenYellow	#ADFF2F	rgb(173,255,47)
Honeydew	#F0FFF0	rgb(240,255,240)
HotPink	#FF69B4	rgb(255,105,180)
IndianRed	#CD5C5C	rgb(205,92,92)
Indigo	#4B0082	rgb(75,0,130)
Ivory	#FFFFF0	rgb(255,255,240)
Khaki	#F0E68C	rgb(240,230,140)
Lavender	#E6E6FA	rgb(230,230,250)
LavenderBlush	#FFF0F5	rgb(255,240,245)
LawnGreen	#7CFC00	rgb(124,252,0)
LemonChiffon	#FFFACD	rgb(255,250,205)
LightBlue	#ADD8E6	rgb(173,216,230)
LightCoral	#F08080	rgb(240,128,128)
LightCyan	#E0FFFF	rgb(224,255,255)
LightGoldenrodYellow	#FAFAD2	rgb(250,250,210)
LightGreen	#90EE90	rgb(144,238,144)
LightGrey	#D3D3D3	rgb(211,211,211)
LightPink	#FFB6C1	rgb(255,182,193)
LightSalmon	#FFA07A	rgb(255,160,122)
LightSeaGreen	#20B2AA	rgb(32,178,170)
LightSkyBlue	#87CEFA	rgb(135,206,250)
LightSlateGray	#778899	rgb(119,136,153)
LightSteelBlue	#B0C4DE	rgb(176,196,222)
LightYellow	#FFFFE0	rgb(255,255,224)
Lime	#00FF00	rgb(0,255,0)
LimeGreen	#32CD32	rgb(50,205,50)
Linen	#FAF0E6	rgb(250,240,230)
Magenta	#FF00FF	rgb(255,0,255)
Maroon	#800000	rgb(128,0,0)
MediumAquamarine	#66CDAA	rgb(102,205,170)
MediumBlue	#0000CD	rgb(0,0,205)

Continued

Table 17-1 *(continued)*

Color Name	Hex RGB	Decimal RGB
MediumOrchid	#BA55D3	rgb(186,85,211)
MediumPurple	#9370DB	rgb(147,112,219)
MediumSeaGreen	#3CB371	rgb(60,179,113)
MediumSlateBlue	#7B68EE	rgb(123,104,238)
MediumSpringGreen	#00FA9A	rgb(0,250,154)
MediumTurquoise	#48D1CC	rgb(72,209,204)
MediumVioletRed	#C71585	rgb(199,21,133)
MidnightBlue	#191970	rgb(25,25,112)
MintCream	#F5FFFA	rgb(245,255,250)
MistyRose	#FFE4E1	rgb(255,228,225)
Moccasin	#FFE4B5	rgb(255,228,181)
NavajoWhite	#FFDEAD	rgb(255,222,173)
Navy	#000080	rgb(0,0,128)
OldLace	#FDF5E6	rgb(253,245,230)
Olive	#808000	rgb(128,128,0)
OliveDrab	#6B8E23	rgb(107,142,35)
Orange	#FFA500	rgb(255,165,0)
OrangeRed	#FF4500	rgb(255,69,0)
Orchid	#DA70D6	rgb(218,112,214)
PaleGoldenrod	#EEE8AA	rgb(238,232,170)
PaleGreen	#98FB98	rgb(152,251,152)
PaleTurquoise	#AFEEEE	rgb(175,238,238)
PaleVioletRed	#DB7093	rgb(219,112,147)
PapayaWhip	#FFEFD5	rgb(255,239,213)
PeachPuff	#FFDAB9	rgb(255,218,185)
Peru	#CD853F	rgb(205,133,63)
Pink	#FFC0CB	rgb(255,192,203)
Plum	#DDA0DD	rgb(221,160,221)
PowderBlue	#B0E0E6	rgb(176,224,230)
Purple	#800080	rgb(128,0,128)
Red	#FF0000	rgb(255,0,0)

Color Name	Hex RGB	Decimal RGB
RosyBrown	#BC8F8F	rgb(188,143,143)
RoyalBlue	#4169E1	rgb(65,105,225)
SaddleBrown	#8B4513	rgb(139,69,19)
Salmon	#FA8072	rgb(250,128,114)
SandyBrown	#F4A460	rgb(244,164,96)
SeaGreen	#2E8B57	rgb(46,139,87)
Seashell	#FFF5EE	rgb(255,245,238)
Sienna	#A0522D	rgb(160,82,45)
Silver	#C0C0C0	rgb(192,192,192)
SkyBlue	#87CEEB	rgb(135,206,235)
SlateBlue	#6A5ACD	rgb(106,90,205)
SlateGray	#708090	rgb(112,128,144)
Snow	#FFFAFA	rgb(255,250,250)
SpringGreen	#00FF7F	rgb(0,255,127)
SteelBlue	#4682B4	rgb(70,130,180)
Tan	#D2B48C	rgb(210,180,140)
Teal	#008080	rgb(0,128,128)
Thistle	#D8BFD8	rgb(216,191,216)
Tomato	#FF6347	rgb(255,99,71)
Turquoise	#40E0D0	rgb(64,224,208)
Violet	#EE82EE	rgb(238,130,238)
Wheat	#F5DEB3	rgb(245,222,179)
White	#FFFFFF	rgb(255,255,255)
WhiteSmoke	#F5F5F5	rgb(245,245,245)
Yellow	#FFFF00	rgb(255,255,0)
YellowGreen	#9ACD32	rgb(154,205,50)

Columns

CSS2 supports strictly unicolumn layouts. Multicolumn layouts have to be faked with tables, which is a bit of a hack. For one thing, the text does not automatically flow between adjacent cells in a table. The breaks have to be inserted manually, which tends to be problematic when the exact amount of text that fits in any one cell depends heavily on the reader's font preferences. Netscape supports a proprietary `MULTICOL` element in HTML, but this is nonstandard and has never been adopted into HTML, and it certainly doesn't help with pure XML documents.

CSS3 adds ten properties to arrange true multicolumn layouts. These properties specify the number of columns on a page, the width of the columns, the space between columns, the flow of text through columns, and more. These ten properties are:

✦ `column-count`

✦ `column-width`

✦ `column-gap`

✦ `column-width-policy`

✦ `column-space-distribution`

✦ `column-rule-color`

✦ `column-rule-style`

✦ `column-rule-width`

✦ `column-rule`

✦ `column-span`

Block-level elements can be divided into columns using these properties. Note that it is an element that is divided into columns, not a page. Columns add a new kind of box to the standard CSS layout model, the column box. Column boxes both contain and are contained in block boxes. Unlike other boxes, column boxes do not have backgrounds, borders, padding, or margins. However, between any two columns there is a column gap that contains a column rule. Figure 17-2 diagrams how this fits together for two columns. The extension to more than two columns is straightforward.

For example, to specify that an `ARTICLE` should be set in three columns, set `display` to `block` and `column-count` to 3 as in this rule:

```
ARTICLE { display: block; column-count: 3 }
```

The browser will pick a width for the columns that allows them to fit on the page. Alternately, you could specify a certain width for the column with the `column-width` property and allow the browser to figure out how many columns will fit on the page. For example, this rule says that the `ARTICLE` will be flowed into three-inch wide columns:

```
ARTICLE { display: block; column-width: 3in}
```

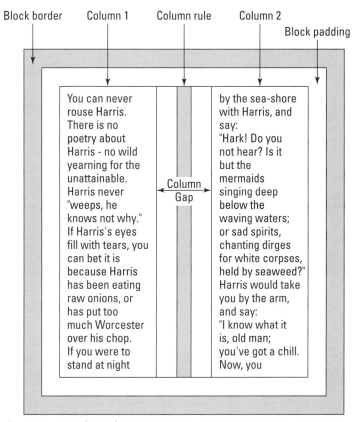

Figure 17-2: Column boxes

You can set both the width and the number of columns. However, in this case, there's no guarantee that all the columns will fit on one page. For example, the next rule specifies three three-inch columns which wouldn't fit on a standard 8.5 by 11-inch piece of paper.

```
ARTICLE { display: block; column-count: 3; column-width: 3in}
```

Generally speaking, parallel columns are not placed immediately next to each other. Instead, there's a certain gap between them. The size of this gap is set by the `column-gap` property, whose value is a length. For example, this rule says an `ARTICLE` is divided into two columns with a one-centimeter gap between them:

```
ARTICLE { display: block; column-count: 2; column-gap: 1.0cm}
```

You can also place a vertical line called the column rule between each pair of columns. This column rule has a style, a width, and a color, just like borders around elements. Indeed, the three `column-rule-style`, `column-rule-width`, and `column-rule-color` properties have the same possible values and defaults as `border-rule-style`, `border-rule-width`, and `border-rule-color`. For example, this rule says there's a two pixel solid blue rule between each pair of columns in an article:

```
ARTICLE { column-rule-style: solid;
          column-rule-width: 2px;
          column-rule-color: blue
}
```

As with the border properties, there's also a shorthand `column-rule` property that sets all three values at once. For example, the above rule could instead have been written like this:

```
ARTICLE { column-rule: 2px solid blue }
```

Every column in an element has the same width, and every pair of adjacent columns has the same gap and rule. You cannot, for example, make the left column of an `ARTICLE` two inches wide and the right column of an `ARTICLE` three inches wide.

On the other hand, you can specify that an element spans multiple columns. For instance, the `ARTICLE` element might be three columns wide, but the `TITLE` of the article might be set across all three columns. To specify this behavior, give the child of the multicolumn element a `column-span` property whose value is the number of columns to span. For example,

```
ARTICLE       { display: block; column-count: 3}
ARTICLE TITLE { column-span: 3}
```

You can also set `column-span` to `all` to indicate that it should span every column the multicolumn ancestor uses.

At other times you might want to emphasize an element by making it span more than one but less than the full number of columns. For example,

```
ARTICLE H2 { column-span: 2 }
```

An element that spans columns breaks the normal flow of text through the columns, similar to the headline of a newspaper article. All the text that comes before the spanning element appears above it in multiple columns. All the text that comes after the spanning element appears below it in multiple columns. The text does not flow through the spanning element. Figure 17-3 demonstrates. Text before the title spanning two columns initially flows into column 1, section A. When that fills up text continues into column 2, section B. The two sections together are exactly big enough to hold all the text that comes before the title (perhaps on additional previous pages if necessary). Then the title is placed, breaking both columns. The text that comes after the title starts in column 1, section B, continues in column 2, section B, and if necessary continues on the next page.

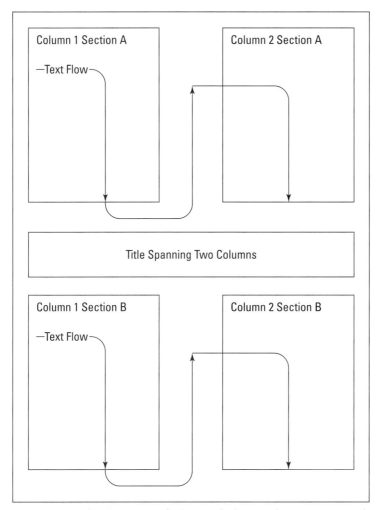

Figure 17-3: The flow of text before and after a column-spanning element

An element that spans columns occupies the full width of the columns it spans. Sometimes, however, pull quotes, photographs, and other out-of-line elements are placed inside or in-between two columns. These elements should not break the normal flow of text because the text can flow around on one side or another. CSS3 allows this, not by defining a new property, but rather by adding two more values to the CSS2 `float` property, `in-column` and `mid-column`. An `in-column` element floats in a single column, and a `mid-column` object floats centered between two columns, overlapping equal amounts of space in both columns. On the left side, text flows to the left; on the right side, it flows to the right. Unlike a `column-span` element, an element floating inside a column or columns does not break the flow of the rest of the text. For example, these rules say that a `PULLQUOTE` floats between the two columns of an article, overlapping both the gap and an inch on each side. Figure 17-4 diagrams this.

```
ARTICLE { display: block;
          column-count: 2;
          column-width: 3.5in;
          column-gap: 1.0in }
ARTICLE PULLQUOTE { float: mid-column;
                    width: 3in }
```

Column 1

IT was Lady Windermere's last reception before Easter, and Benlinck House was even more crowded than usual. Six Cabinet Ministers had come on from the Speaker's Levee in their stars and ribands, all the pretty women wore their smartest dresses, and at the end of the picture-gallery stood the Princess Sophia of Carlsuhe, a heavy Tartar-looking lady, with tiny black eyes and wonderful emeralds, talking bad French at the top of her voice, and laughing immoderately at everything that was said to her. It was certainly a wonderful medley of people. Gorgeous peeresses chatted affably to violent Radicals, popular preachers brushed coat-tails with eminent sceptics, a perfect bevy of bishops kept following a stout prima-donna from room to room, on the staircase stood several Royal Academicians,

Midcolumn pullquote or picture

Column 2

disguised as artists, and it was said that at one time the supper-room was absolutely crammed with geniuses. In fact, it was one of Lady Windermere's best nights, and the Princess stayed till nearly half-past eleven.

As soon as she had gone Lady Windermere returned to the picture gallery, where a celebrated political economist was solemnly explaining the scientific theory of music to an indignant virtuoso from Hungary, and began to talk to the Duchess of Paisley. She looked wonderfully beautiful with her grand ivory throat, her large blue forget-me-not eyes, and her heavy coils of golden hair. OR PUR they were-not that pale straw colour that nowadays usurps the gracious name of gold, but such gold as is woven into sunbeams or hidden in strange amber; and

Figure 17-4: The flow of text around a mid-column element

The total width of all the columns and the gaps between the columns is limited by the width of the parent element that contains the columns. If the parent element is too small to hold the number of columns of the specified size requested by the column properties, then the browser removes some of the columns and reflows the text accordingly.

It's also possible that the parent element is too wide for the columns; that is, it has more space than the columns need. In this case, the column-width-policy property specifies what to do. The default value of this property is flexible, which allows the columns to expand to fill the available space. However, you can also set it to strict to indicate that you want the widths you asked for, even if that leaves extra white space on one side.

If the column-width-policy is strict and there is extra space, then the column-space-distribution property determines where to place the extra space. There are five possible values for this property:

- ✦ end: after the end of the columns; the right side in left-to-right languages such as English.

- ✦ start: before the start of the columns; the left side in left-to-right languages such as English.

- ✦ inner: the side closest to the page binding; right on left pages and left on right pages.

- ✦ outer: the side furthest from the page binding; left on left pages and right on right pages.

- ✦ between: distribute the space equally between all columns.

Behavior

CSS2 styles are mostly static. With the sole exception of blinking text (which browsers are fortunately not required to support), no CSS2 style indicates any change in time. CSS2 lets you change colors, sizes, fonts, and more; but nothing moves. Movement is possible using Dynamic HTML and JavaScript, but this doesn't work in the XML domain. Furthermore, depending on how a page is authored, movement can really mix up page content with presentation. For example, a headline that flies in from the left or a bullet point that doesn't appear until the reader presses the space bar is really just another style. These don't change the information stored in the page at all. They just change how and when it's presented to the reader.

CSS3 is not Turing complete and it's not going to replace JavaScript, nor does it attempt to. However, CSS3 does offer some more maintainable alternatives for attaching scripts to individual elements in the document. The association between a script and an element can be placed in the style sheet rather than in the document itself. This offers the same flexibility for scripting that the rest of CSS offers for static presentation.

The @script rule

If you want to use scripting in your stylesheets, the first thing you need to do is select the scripting language. You can choose JavaScript, VBScript, Python, Perl, or something else, depending on what the browser supports. JavaScript is the most common choice, and the most widely supported across browsers, but CSS itself is language neutral.

The @script rule allows you to embed a script directly in the stylesheet. This script is run the first time the style sheet is applied to the document. This is the equivalent of an onload script in standard HTML. The @script keyword is followed by the MIME media type of the script. Then the script code itself is enclosed in curly braces. For example, this is a variation of a script I use on some of my Web sites to make sure that the document is not unintentionally mirrored:

```
@script "text/javascript" {
  if (location.host.toLowerCase().indexOf("cafeaulait") < 0)
  {
    location.href="http://www.cafeaulait.org/";
  }
}
```

When a browser applies a style sheet containing this @script rule to a document, it looks at the host the document came from. If that host contains the string cafeaulait as it does at the home site, www.cafeaulait.org, nothing happens. However, if somebody has copied the page to a different mirror site, then the browser will load the page from the official location at http://www.cafeaulait.org instead.

The content of the script block depends on the language. However, regardless of the language, all rules for CSS must still be followed. In particular, parentheses (( )), square brackets ([ ]), curly braces ({ }), and single (') and double straight quotes (") must always occur in matching pairs. This isn't a big problem. Most scripting languages require this anyway, at least most of the time. However, if there are any unmatched single occurrences of these characters, for instance in a string literal, then they must be escaped using the standard CSS backslash escape. For example:

```
@script "text/javascript" {
  alert("You must escape your square brackets such as \[.");
}
```

In most cases, it's better design to keep the script code separate from the style sheet, especially if graphic designers are writing the style sheets and programmers are writing the scripts. In this case, you can provide a URL, possibly relative, to the script instead of including the script inline. For example, if the above script was placed in a single JavaScript document named redirector.js at http://www.cafeaulait.org/scripts/, then you could use this @script rule instead:

```
@script "text/javascript"
  url("http://www.cafeaulait.org/scripts/redirector.js")
```

Among its other advantages, external scripts don't require you to escape characters such as (and " when their use in the scripting language conflicts with their use in CSS.

An @script rule followed by a MIME media type without any script block specifies the default scripting language for all scripts used in a style sheet. For example, this rule specifies that the default is JavaScript:

```
@script "text/javascript";
```

You can then omit the MIME media type on individual scripts. For example,

```
@script {
  if (location.host.toLowerCase().indexOf("cafeaulait") < 0)
  {
    location.href="http://www.cafeaulait.org/";
  }
}
@script url("http://www.cafeaulait.org/scripts/redirector.js")
```

The default language can still be overridden by explicit specification of the MIME media type in individual @script rules.

Event handler properties

CSS3 also enables you to attach scripts to specific events on particular elements. The events it supports are defined in the Document Object Model (DOM) level 2 events specification (http://www.w3.org/TR/DOM-Level-2-Events/events.html) and include:

✦ DOMActivate: the user chose the element

✦ DOMFocusIn: the element gained focus

✦ DOMFocusOut: the element lost focus

✦ mousedown: the user pressed the mouse button down on the element, but has not yet released it

✦ mouseup: the user released the mouse button while focus was on the element

✦ click: the user clicked on the element (mousedown followed by mouseup on the same element)

✦ mouseover: the user moved the cursor into the element

✦ mousemove: the user moved the cursor inside the element

✦ mouseout: the user moved the cursor from inside the element to outside the element

Each of these is a possible property of an element. The value of this property is a string containing a script written in the default scripting language of the style sheet. For example, these style sheet rules pop up a dialog box containing the text "You clicked me!" as shown in Figure 17-5, when the user clicks a BUTTON element:

```
@script "text/javascript";
BUTTON { click: "alert('You clicked me!')"}
```

Figure 17-5: A dialog box produced by JavaScript

Note   The event properties really aren't as well thought out as the @script rule for onload scripts. First, they don't let an individual script override the default script type. Second, they require scripts to be embedded directly in the style sheet, rather than being referenced by a URL. I suspect both of these problems will be fixed with a syntax more similar to @script in a future draft.

User Interfaces

The CSS3 User Interfaces module is a relatively limited-ambition extension of the user interface styles of CSS2. As you may recall, CSS2 let you set the cursor, specify the outline around a widget, check which element has the focus and whether or not an element is active, and magnify the page. CSS3 merely expands on this with more cursors, a few more pseudo-classes representing different states of user interface components, a couple of extra pseudo-elements, and a few properties to control whether and how the user is allowed to interact with an element. It is not a full-featured language for designing arbitrary GUIs such as Mozilla's XUL (XML-based User Interface Language, pronounced "zuul"; http://www.mozilla.org/xpfe). Nonetheless, it does have some neat uses for Web pages that interact with the user.

User interface pseudo-classes

CSS2 defines several pseudo-classes that select particular elements depending on whether and how the user has interacted with them. These include:

✦ :active

✦ :focus

✦ :hover

CSS3 adds four more pseudo-classes, although these are more useful for HTML than XML:

✦ :enabled: the user can interact with this element in some way

✦ :disabled: the user cannot interact with this element in any way

✦ :checked: the element is currently checked; only applies to elements whose content property identifies them as a checkbox or radio button

✦ :indeterminate: the element is neither checked nor unchecked; only applies to elements whose content property identifies them as a checkbox or radio button

Kiosk mode

Most Web browsers, including Opera and Netscape Navigator 4, can run in kiosk mode. In this mode, all menus, scroll bars, task bars, tools bars, location bars, and other artifacts of the GUI outside the page are hidden. All that's shown is the pane that contains the HTML or XML document itself. Navigation is limited to what's provided on the page. In some contexts, other ways of accessing additional functionality, such as Ctrl-+W to Close the window, or Alt+Tab to switch to another application, or even the three-fingered salute (Ctrl+Alt+Delete) so familiar to Windows users may be disabled. In fact, it's often true that both keyboard and mouse are removed and the user navigates through a strictly restricted space by touching the screen. This enables the page author to completely control the user experience.

This is called kiosk mode because it's often used on general purpose PCs placed in public locations such as airports and hotels. The Brooklyn Museum of Art uses a kiosk to tell visitors about local attractions. U.S. Airways uses kiosks to assign boarding passes to frequent fliers with e-tickets and no baggage to check. Science museums use kiosks to present interactive exhibits. Polytechnic University uses the kiosk shown in Figure 17-6 to greet visitors when they come in the front door. Traditionally kiosk applications have been written using HyperCard, Macromedia Director, or other proprietary programs. However, increasingly they're being written in HTML and XML, using a browser in kiosk mode as the engine. Indeed, this is how the kiosk shown in Figure 17-6 runs.

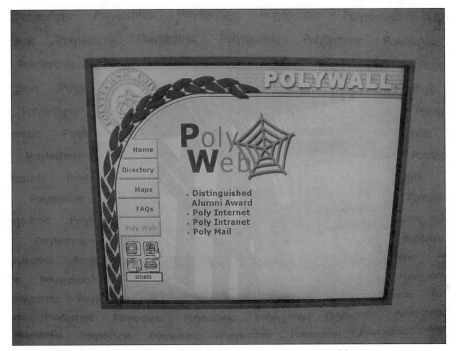

Figure 17-6: A welcome kiosk at Polytechnic University in Brooklyn

Needless to say kiosk mode is a special environment for Web pages. Kiosks don't really fit any of the CSS2 media types — screen, print, tv, braille, and so on. Kiosks look a lot like a browser screen, except that the scroll bars are normally hidden, so the screen type is probably closest. Still, a new type is really needed.

CSS3 adds one new media type specifically to indicate kiosk mode applications — presentation. For example, this rule indicates that it only applies in kiosk mode:

```
@media presentation {
   font-family: Helvetica, sans;
   font-size: 14pt;
   font-weight: bold
}
```

CSS3 does not add any new properties or selectors just for kiosks, nor does it give you a means of switching the browser into kiosk mode. You still have to do that in a browser-dependent fashion. It merely allows you to provide different style rules for kiosks than you do for normal Web pages.

Presentation preferences

The type of stylesheet desired for an XML document in a particular medium can be indicated by the `media` pseudo-attribute of an `xml-stylesheet` processing instruction. For example, this group of `xml-stylesheet` processing instructions identifies different style sheets to be used for onscreen display, print outs, and dumb terminals:

```
<?xml-stylesheet type="text/css" media="screen" href="sc.css"?>
<?xml-stylesheet type="text/css" media="print"  href="pr.css"?>
<?xml-stylesheet type="text/css" media="tty"    href="tty.css"?>
```

These would all be placed in the prolog of an XML document that used these style sheets. In CSS3, it's also possible for the style sheet itself to say what medium it's best suited for. This is done via an `@preference` rule. This rule has a `media` property whose value is a comma-separated list of media types. For example, this rule says that the style sheet that contains it is designed for kiosk presentations, computer monitors, and television-like devices:

```
@preference { media: presentation, screen, tv }
```

If the browser has any choice of which medium to display the document in, then it should pick from this list in the order specified. However, most browsers and other renderers are limited to a single medium, and will render in that medium regardless of what the `@preference` rule says.

Cursors

The cursor is the arrow/hand/insertion bar/other icon that indicates the position of the pointer on the screen. The `cursor` property specifies the cursor a user's software should display when a reader moves the pointer over a particular element. CSS2 defines 15 different cursors that indicate different states: `crosshair`, `default`, `hand`, `move`, `n-resize`, `e-resize`, `s-resize`, `w-resize`, `ne-resize`, `nw-resize`, `se-resize`, `sw-resize`, `text`, `wait`, and `help`.

CSS3 adds ten new cursors:

✦ `copy`: Indicates something is to be copied; possibly drawn as the default arrow cursor with a small plus sign next to it.

✦ `alias`: An alias of/shortcut to something is to be created; possibly drawn as the default arrow cursor with a small curved arrow next to it.

✦ `context-menu`: The object pointed at by the cursor has a context menu, which is generally accessed via the right mouse button on Windows and Linux, or by holding down the Ctrl key while pressing the mouse button on a Mac; possibly drawn as the default arrow cursor with a small picture of a menu next to it.

✦ cell: A cell or group of cells may be selected; often used in spreadsheets; sometimes drawn as a thick, outlined plus-sign with a dot in the middle.

✦ grab: The object pointed at by the cursor can be grabbed; often used for panning an image as in Acrobat and Photoshop; sometimes drawn as an open hand.

✦ grabbing: The object pointed at by the cursor has been grabbed; drawn as a closed hand in Acrobat but an open hand (same as grab) in Photoshop.

✦ spinning: Similar to the CSS2 wait cursor; however, it indicates that although the program is busy processing the user can still interact with it.

✦ count-up: The program is counting up.

✦ count-down: The program is counting down.

✦ count-up-down: The program is counting up and then back down.

System colors

CSS2 defines 27 color names that map to the colors of particular pieces of the user interface on the host platform, rather than to specific named colors. These range from ActiveBorder (the color of the border of the currently active window) to WindowText (the color of text in the window).

CSS3 pretty much throws these out and starts over from scratch. It begins by defining five different user interface widgets that it expects most renderers to understand:

✦ Icons

✦ Windows

✦ Buttons

✦ Menus

✦ Fields

Each of these is assumed to be drawn with three main colors: a background color, a text color, and a border color. For icons, the background color is Icon, the text color is IconText, and the border color is IconBorder. For windows, the background color is Window, the text color is WindowText, and the border color is WindowBorder. The same pattern is followed for the other three types of widget.

However, several widgets have different subtypes, each of which may use different colors. For instance, as well as plain-vanilla windows, there are also five other kinds of windows:

✦ Document windows

✦ Workspace windows

✦ Desktop windows

✦ Info windows (tool tips)

✦ Dialog windows

Each of these also uses three colors: `Document`, `DocumentText`, `DocumentBorder`; `Workspace`, `WorkspaceText`, `WorkspaceBorder`; and so forth. Icons and fields don't have any subtypes. Button has one subtype, the `DefaultButton`. Menu has three: `PulldownMenu`, `PopupMenu`, and `List`. Altogether there are 14 kinds of widgets with three colors each for a total of 42 named system colors. Of course, most of the time some of these colors are the same. For instance, on the system on which I'm typing this, almost all the text colors are pure black.

This still isn't all the colors. Each widget can be in one of four states: enabled, disabled, active, or hover. Most of the time, changing state changes the appearance of the widget, possibly changing its color. To get the color of the widget in a particular state, just prefix the name of the state to the normal color. For example, different parts of info windows (tool tips) in different states may use the colors `Info`, `InfoText`, `InfoBorder`, `EnabledInfo`, `EnabledInfoText`, `EnabledInfoBorder`, `DisabledInfo`, `DisabledInfoText`, `DisabledInfoBorder`, `ActiveInfo`, `ActiveInfoText`, `ActiveInfoBorder`, `HoverInfo`, `HoverInfoText`, and `HoverInfoBorder`. Thus there are actually 42×5, or 210 different named system colors, although, again, there are probably many duplicates in the list.

System fonts

Just as particular widgets may have particular colors on a user's system, so, too, may particular widgets have particular fonts. CSS3 defines symbolic font names that match the fonts used by the same widgets:

✦ `window`

✦ `document`

✦ `workspace`

✦ `desktop`

✦ `info`

✦ `dialog`

✦ `button`

✦ `pull-down-menu`

✦ `list`

✦ `field`

For example, this rule says that the text of an `INPUT` element whose `TYPE` attribute has the value `SUBMIT`, should be drawn with the font normally used for buttons:

```
INPUT[TYPE="SUBMIT"] {font: button}
```

User input

One of the most exciting possibilities CSS3 offers XML authors is the ability to format arbitrary elements as form parts, including buttons, text fields, checkboxes, radio buttons, and more. Although CSS3 lets you say that elements should be formatted as these form components and even lets you define how the user interacts with them, it stops short of fully defining how a browser is supposed to use this information to communicate with CGI programs on the server. More work in this area is needed, but because it's not strictly presentational, it's going on under the auspices of the XForms Working Group.

Widgets

CSS3 allows the content property to be set to any of three dozen named constants that identify specific user interface widgets and icons, particularly radio buttons and checkboxes as drawn in various states. Each radio button or checkbox can be on (checked) or off (unchecked). Furthermore, it can be enabled (the user can change its state), disabled (the user cannot change its state), active (the user is changing its state), or hovered over (the user has moved the mouse over the icon but not yet pushed down the mouse button). These content values are:

- check
- diamond
- menu-check
- menu-diamond
- radio
- radio-on
- radio-off
- radio-ind
- enabled-radio-on
- enabled-radio-off
- enabled-radio-ind
- disabled-radio-on
- disabled-radio-off
- disabled-radio-ind
- active-radio-off
- active-radio-on
- active-radio-ind
- hover-radio-off

- hover-radio-on
- hover-radio-ind
- checkbox
- checkbox-on
- checkbox-off
- checkbox-ind
- enabled-checkbox-on
- enabled-checkbox-off
- enabled-checkbox-ind
- disabled-checkbox-on
- disabled-checkbox-off
- disabled-checkbox-ind
- active-checkbox-on
- active-checkbox-off
- active-checkbox-ind
- hover-checkbox-on
- hover-checkbox-off
- hover-checkbox-ind

Not all browsers draw all of these differently. For instance, Netscape does not distinguish between active and inactive checkboxes; but IE does by drawing a dotted line around the active checkbox.

For example, this rule places an unchecked but enabled checkbox before each TODO element:

```
TODO:before {content: enabled-checkbox-off}
```

In CSS3, these same 36 values can also be used as the values of the list-style-type property. This allows you to create lists whose bullet is a radio button or a checkbox. For example, this CSS rule says that a group of TODO elements is styled as a list of checkboxes:

```
TODO {
    display: list-item;
    list-style-type: checkbox;
}
```

User input

CSS3 defines six properties that specify whether or not a user can somehow activate and input into the element, whether with the mouse or the keyboard. These are:

- ✦ user-input: Determines whether an element can either currently or ever accept user input.

- ✦ user-modify: Specifies whether the user is allowed to copy the text of and/or change the text of an element.

- ✦ user-select: Determines what combinations of the element's content the user is allowed to select.

- ✦ user-focus: Specifies what happens to the element when the user gives it the focus.

- ✦ user-focus-key: Determines what happens to the element when the user gives it the focus via the keyboard.

- ✦ user-focus-pointer: Determines what happens to the element when the user gives it the focus via the mouse, track pad, track ball. or other pointing device.

These properties are primarily intended for HTML forms. Their meaning for XML elements is still up in the air. However, it's tantalizing to surmise that you might be able to style arbitrary XML elements as form components.

The user-input property can be set to none, enabled, or disabled. Most elements will have the value none; that is, the element does not accept user input and never will. However, for an element that is ready to accept user input, this can have the value enabled. For example, this rule says that the user can type into an ADDRESS element:

```
ADDRESS {user-input: enabled}
```

Of course, no browsers yet support this; but eventually it might be one way to embed forms in XML documents without requiring page authors to use a single form vocabulary.

Finally, user-input can have the value disabled to indicate that this is an input element, but that the user cannot interact with it at this moment; they might be able to do so in the future.

The user-modify property determines whether the user is allowed to edit an element; that is, to change its text, such as by typing over it. It can have the values read-only, read-write, or write-only. With read access the user is allowed to copy the text. With write access the user can change the text. The default is read-only. For example, this rule says that P elements can be copied to another application but cannot be changed in the browser windows, whereas the user is allowed to click the mouse in an LI element and retype its text:

```
P  {user-modify: read-only  }
LI {user-modify: read-write }
```

This only applies, however, in a context where the browser allows the user to modify elements, such as in form fields.

To indicate that an element cannot be written or read, you have to set user-modify to read-only to prevent writing and set user-input to disabled to prevent writing. For example,

```
P  {user-modify: write-only; user-input: disabled}
```

The user-select property determines how its contents may be selected. The possible values are none, text, toggle, element, elements, and all. The default value of user-select is text, which just means that words and letters in the element can be selected individually or in a contiguous block like normal. If user-select is set to none, the element may not be selected and thus cannot be copied, pasted, cut, or have any other operation performed on it that first requires it to be selected. If user-select is set to toggle, then its contents behave like a group of radio buttons, exactly one of which can be selected at any time. If user-select is set to element, then at most one element can be selected at any time, but it must be selected as a unit. That is, you can't select half the text of an element. If user-select is set to elements, then one or more element can be selected at any time, but each one must be selected in its entirety, so you can select one, two, or three elements but not two-and-a-half elements. If user-select is set to all, then the contents must be completely selected or not at all selected.

The `user-focus` property specifies what happens when the element receives the focus, such as by having the user click on it or tab into it (see the `tab-index` property later in this chapter). The `user-focus` property can have any of these seven values:

✦ `auto`: do whatever the browser normally does

✦ `normal`: the element acquires the focus but nothing else changes; neither the existing selection nor the position of the insertion point is changed

✦ `select-all`: select the entire content of the element

✦ `select-before`: place the insertion point before the start of the element's content but select nothing

✦ `select-after`: place the insertion point after the start of the element's content but select nothing

✦ `select-same`: the selection becomes the same thing it was the last time the element had the focus

There are also `user-focus-key` and `user-focus-pointer` properties. These have the same possible seven values as `user-focus`. However, `user-focus-key` only applies when the user gives the element the focus by using the tab key. The `user-focus-pointer` property only applies when the user uses the mouse to assign the focus.

Toggle groups

A toggle group is a collection of elements, no more than one of which can be checked at any instant of time. The `group-reset` property creates a toggle group and assigns it a name. The `toggle-group` property uses one of these names to indicate that an element is a member of that toggle group. Generally, members of toggle groups are adjacent to each other; but they don't absolutely have to be.

For example, these rules style the `CASH`, `CHECK`, and `CHARGE` elements as three separate radio buttons, only one of which can be selected at any given time:

```
PAYMENT { group-reset: payment }
CASH, CHECK, CHARGE {
  toggle-group: payment;
  display: inline-block;
  color: ButtonText;
  background: Button;
  border-color: ButtonBorder;
  font: button;
  cursor: arrow;
  user-input: enabled;
  user-modify: read-only;
  user-select: toggle;
```

```
  }
CASH:before    { content: radio }
CHECK:before   { content: radio }
CHARGE:before  { content: radio }
```

Keyboard equivalents

The key-equivalent property determines which keyboard key or keys the user can press to activate an element. The default value of this property is none. It can also be set to one of these 20 keywords that map to the standard keyboard shortcut on the user's platform:

- ✦ system-new: Ctrl+N on Windows, Command+N on the Macintosh
- ✦ system-open: Ctrl+O on Windows, Command+O on the Macintosh
- ✦ system-close: Ctrl+W on Windows, Command+W on the Macintosh
- ✦ system-save: Ctrl+S on Windows, Command+S on the Macintosh
- ✦ system-print: Ctrl+P on Windows, Command+P on the Macintosh
- ✦ system-quit: Alt-X on Windows, Command+Q on the Macintosh
- ✦ system-terminate-operation: Ctrl+C on Unix
- ✦ system-undo: Ctrl+Z on Windows, Command+Z on the Macintosh
- ✦ system-redo: Ctrl+Y on Windows, Command+Y on the Macintosh
- ✦ system-cut: Ctrl+X on Windows, Command+X on the Macintosh
- ✦ system-copy: Ctrl+C on Windows, Command+C on the Macintosh
- ✦ system-paste: Ctrl+V on Windows, Command+V on the Macintosh
- ✦ system-clear: Delete key on Windows, Delete key on the Macintosh
- ✦ system-duplicate: no standard assignments
- ✦ system-select-all: Ctrl+A on Windows, Command+A on the Macintosh
- ✦ system-find: Ctrl+F on Windows, Command+F on the Macintosh
- ✦ system-find-again: Ctrl+G on Windows, Command+G on the Macintosh
- ✦ system-ok: Enter on Windows, Return on the Macintosh
- ✦ system-cancel: Esc key on Windows, Command+. (period) on the Macintosh
- ✦ system-apply: no standard assignments

Linux bindings tend to be mostly the same as on Windows.

For example, this rule maps the FINISH element to Command+Q on a Mac but to Alt+X on Windows:

```
FINISH { key-equivalent: system-quit }
```

If you want to select a specific key combination, such as Ctrl+H or Command+Shift+F12, to activate an element, you can. Simply use the key names in the list below and separate them by hyphens.

- ✦ cmd: Command (a.k.a. clover leaf, Apple) key
- ✦ rcmd: right Command key
- ✦ lcmd: left Command key
- ✦ opt: either Option key
- ✦ ropt: right Option key
- ✦ lopt: left Option key
- ✦ ctrl: either Ctrl key
- ✦ rctrl: right Ctrl key
- ✦ lctrl: left Ctrl key
- ✦ shift: either Shift key
- ✦ rshift: the right Shift key
- ✦ lshift: the left Shift key
- ✦ alt: either Alt key
- ✦ ralt: right Alt key
- ✦ lalt: the left Alt key
- ✦ win: either Windows key
- ✦ rwin: the right Windows key
- ✦ lwin: the left Windows key
- ✦ meta: the Meta key; often mapped to the Esc key
- ✦ rmeta: the right Meta key
- ✦ lmeta: the left Meta key
- ✦ fn: the Fn key is typically used on notebook keyboards to squeeze multiple functions onto certain keys
- ✦ caps: the Caps Lock key
- ✦ f1: the F1 key
- ✦ f2: the F2 key
- ✦ f3: the F3 key
- ✦ f4: the F4 key
- ✦ f5: the F5 key
- ✦ f6: the F6 key

✦ f7: the F7 key

✦ f8: the F8 key

✦ f9: the F9 key

✦ f10: the F10 key

✦ f11: the F11 key

✦ f12: the F12 key

✦ f13: the F13 key

✦ f14: the F14 key

✦ f15: the F15 key

✦ tab: the Tab key

✦ esc: the Esc key

✦ enter: the Enter key

✦ return: the Return key

✦ menu: the menu key

✦ help: Help key

✦ up: the up-arrow key

✦ down: the down-arrow key

✦ left: the left-arrow key

✦ right: the right-arrow key

✦ home: the Home key

✦ end: the End key

✦ pgup: the Page Up key

✦ pgdn: the Page Down key

✦ bs: the Backspace key

✦ del: the Delete key

✦ ins: the Insert key

✦ undo: the Undo key found on some Sun keyboards

✦ cut: the Cut key found on some Sun keyboards

✦ copy: the Copy key found on some Sun keyboards

✦ paste: the Paste key found on some Sun keyboards

✦ prtsc: the Print Screen key

✦ sysrq: the SysRq key on many PC keyboards

- ✦ `scrlock`: the Screen Lock key
- ✦ `pause`: the Pause key
- ✦ `brk`: the Break key
- ✦ `numlock`: the Num Lock key
- ✦ `pwr`: the Power key
- ✦ `fcn`: the FCN key available on some cell phones
- ✦ `namemenu`: the NAME MENU key found on some cell phone keypads
- ✦ `rcl`: the RCL key found on some cell phone keypads
- ✦ `snd`: the SND key found on some cell phone keypads
- ✦ `clr`: the CLR key found on some cell phone keypads
- ✦ `sto`: the STO key found on some cell phone keypads

Of course, there are some caveats when using these. First, not all keyboards have all these keys. For instance you'll only find a Command key on a Mac keyboard and a Windows key on a relatively modern PC keyboard. Second, not all operating systems and hardware are capable of distinguishing between the left and right versions of keys such as Shift and Ctrl. Finally, some of these keys may be occupied by other functions. For instance, if you press the Power key on a Macintosh keyboard, the system asks you if you want to shut down, restart, or put the computer to sleep. You can't remap this key to something else. Still, if you keep the normal system-supplied key bindings in mind, it's not too hard to attach reasonable key equivalents to elements. For example, if you wanted to map the `FINISH` element to Ctrl+F, this rule would do the trick:

```
FINISH { key-equivalent: ctrl-f }
```

There may be times when you want to offer multiple key combinations for different platforms. For instance, you might want to specify Command+F for platforms that have a command key (Macintoshes) and Ctrl+F for other platforms. In this case, you give the `key-equivalent` property multiple values separated by commas, like this:

```
FINISH { key-equivalent: cmd-F, ctrl-F }
```

An alternate approach that works with even more platforms is to use the constant `accesskey` instead, which signifies the default key for accessing menu shortcuts on the local platform. For example, `accesskey-F` means the Command+F on a Mac and Ctrl+F on Windows or Linux. For example,

```
FINISH { key-equivalent: accesskey-F }
```

The character — for example, `F`, `C`, or `X` — is always written in uppercase whereas the modifier key mnemonics — for example, `ctrl` and `accesskey` — are always written in lowercase.

Tabbing

The `tab-index` property determines in which order the tab key moves between enabled elements. The semantics are deliberately similar to HTML 4.0's `TABINDEX` attribute. The value of this property is a nonnegative integer. The first time you hit the tab key you move into the element with tab-index 1. The second time you hit the tab key you move into the element with tab-index 2. The third time you hit the tab key you move into the element with tab-index 3, and so on. If any number is missing, you just skip to the next highest number. Surprisingly, 0 is a legal value; but it comes last, after everything else, rather than first. For example, these rules establish a tab order that goes from NAME to ADDRESS to CITY to STATE to ZIP to COUNTRY to ENTER. As always, however, users are free to use the mouse to move around in any order they please.

```
NAME    {tab-index: 1;   user-input: enabled }
ADDRESS {tab-index: 4;   user-input: enabled }
CITY    {tab-index: 8;   user-input: enabled }
STATE   {tab-index: 12;  user-input: enabled }
ZIP     {tab-index: 16;  user-input: enabled }
COUNTRY {tab-index: 20;  user-input: enabled }
ENTER   {tab-index: 0;   user-input: enabled }
```

Even though these rules are written in order of the tab-index, the ordering of the individual rules within the style sheet doesn't have any particular significance. Only the values identified by the `tab-index` property matter. This variation has the same meaning as the above one:

```
COUNTRY {tab-index: 20; user-input: enabled }
NAME    {tab-index: 1;  user-input: enabled }
CITY    {tab-index: 8;  user-input: enabled }
ZIP     {tab-index: 16; user-input: enabled }
ADDRESS {tab-index: 4;  user-input: enabled }
ENTER   {tab-index: 0;  user-input: enabled }
STATE   {tab-index: 12; user-input: enabled }
```

The resize box

The `resizer` property allows you to control the behavior of the window that contains the element. This property is normally only applied to the root element. It determines in which direction the user is and is not allowed to resize the window. The possibilities are:

✦ `auto`: use the browser's defaults

✦ `horizontal`: allow horizontal resizing but not vertical resizing

✦ `vertical`: allow vertical resizing but not horizontal resizing

✦ `both`: allow resizing in both directions

✦ `none`: do not allow the element to be resized

For example, this rule says that the SEASON element should be displayed in a nonre-sizable 10-centimeter by 8-centimeter window with scroll bars if there's too much content to fit in this space:

```
SEASON { width: 10cm; height: 8cm;
        resizer: none;
        overflow: scroll
}
```

Paged Media

CSS was originally designed for documents meant to be displayed in Web browser windows. Printed pages were an afterthought. However, people do print Web pages, and XML is used a lot more broadly than merely on the Web. Thus CSS3 adds several properties, functions, and @ rules specifically intended for printouts on paper. These new features have little use when the output medium is a browser window.

Note   The current draft specification of paged media properties hasn't answered all the questions regarding printing to paper. In particular, several planned features, such as footnotes and endnotes, are not yet designed. For the latest information, see http://www.w3.org/TR/css3-page.

Page margins

The header of this page contains the page number and either the part number and part title (on even pages) or chapter number and chapter title (on odd pages). Some books (though not this one) place the page number and other content at the bottom of the page. Magazines and newspapers often include the date as well. And it's also common to include notes in the left and right margins. In a book, such marginal notes would probably be placed only on the outside of the pages, the left margin on left-hand pages and the right margin on right-hand pages.

Caution   I'm going way out on a limb in this section. The syntax for all these properties is very hypothetical at this point in time, and definitely subject to change. This section will give you a general idea of what will be possible in the future, but please don't accept it as accurate in every detail without confirming it with actual implementations and the finished specification.

CSS3 allows you to identify the margins of the page by using four new @ rules:

✦ @top: the top margin

✦ @bottom: the bottom margin

✦ @left: the left margin

✦ @right: the right margin

These may only appear inside @page rules. All the CSS box properties, such as background, padding, border, and even margin, can be applied to the page margins. For example this rule, uses the border-top property to put a horizontal line at the bottom of each page by setting the bottom margin's border-top properties:

```
@page { size: 8.5in 11in;
        margin: 10%;
        @bottom { border-top-style: solid;
                  border-top-color: black;
                  border-top-width: 2px }
}
```

To actually place content in the margins, you use the content property. For example, this style rule centers the words "The XML Bible" in the top margin of each page:

```
@page { size: 8.5in 11in;
        margin: 10%;
        @top { text-align: center;
            content: "The XML Bible" }
}
```

Page numbers

To include the page number in the margins, you can increment a named counter inside the @page rule to the pages and use the counter() function to access its value. For example,

```
@page { size: 8.5in 11in;
        margin: 10%;
        counter-increment: pages;
        @top { text-align: center;
            content: "The XML Bible Page " counter(pages)
            }
}
```

CSS3 introduces the pages() function to provide the total number of pages in a document. For example, this rule would put page numbers in the form Page 1 of 1600, Page 2 of 1600, Page 3 of 1600, and so forth in the top margin:

```
@page { size: 8.5in 11in;
        margin: 10%;
        counter-increment: pages;
        @top { text-align: center;
            content: "Page " counter(pages) " of " pages()
            }
}
```

String variables

As well as counters and string literals, CSS3 allows you to use a `string-set()` function to set a variable to the text content of a particular element or attribute. For example, this rule creates a string variable named `chapter` every time a `TITLE` child element of a `CHAPTER` element is encountered:

```
CHAPTER TITLE {string-set: chapter content()}
```

Then you can place the name of the current chapter in the top page margins with this rule that references the `chapter` variable:

```
@page { size: 8.5in 11in;
        margin: 10%;
        @top { text-align: center;
               content: chapter }
}
```

Every time a new `TITLE` of a `CHAPTER` is encountered, the `chapter` variable is set to a new value, which is used from that point forward. It's possible, however, depending on how the document is structured and where page breaks are placed, that a single page could contain multiple `TITLE` elements or could otherwise reset the `chapter` variable in the middle of a page. In such a case, it's not clear which value of `chapter` should be used, the one in effect at the top of the page or the one in effect at the bottom.

You can choose which variable you want to use by defining a `page-policy` property for the variable to either `start` or `last`. An `@string` rule selects the named variable. For example, this rule says that the first value of the chapter element found on a page should be used:

```
@string chapter { page-policy: start }
```

Tip   This technique isn't strictly limited to content for the page margins. You can set string variables by using the `string-set` property at the top of a document and then reuse the value of that string later in the document by using a `content` property. This isn't as powerful as XSLT, but it does give you some limited ability to reorder the content of an XML document before presenting it to the reader.

Cross-References

Throughout this book you've seen cross-references similar to this one:

Cross-Reference   XPointers are discussed in detail in Chapter 21.

All these cross-references only point to the chapter in question, not to a specific page. While it would occasionally be useful to point to a specific page or pages, the tools used to produce this book (Microsoft Word and QuarkXPress) don't make cross-referencing very easy. In fact, even keeping track of the chapter numbers in the cross-references as new chapters are added, deleted, and moved is more work than we like.

CSS3 adds new `target-counter()` and `target-content()` functions that let you calculate values for cross-references that are resolved when the document is displayed or printed. The cross-references can use chapter numbers, as in this book, chapter titles, or even page numbers. They identify the thing to be cross-referenced by a URL, normally a relative URL that has only a fragment identifier.

For example, suppose the document you wanted to cross-reference looked something like this:

```
<?xml version="1.0"?>
<BOOK>
  <TITLE>XML Bible</TITLE>
  <CHAPTER ID="c1">
    <TITLE ID="t1">An Eagles' Eye View of XML</TITLE>
    ...
  </CHAPTER>
  <CHAPTER ID="c2">
    <TITLE ID="t2">An Introduction to XML Applications</TITLE>
    ...
  </CHAPTER>
  ...
  <CHAPTER ID="c20">
    <TITLE ID="t20">XLinks</TITLE>
    ...
  </CHAPTER>
  <CHAPTER ID="c21">
    <TITLE ID="t21">XPointers</TITLE>
    ...
  </CHAPTER>
  <CHAPTER ID="c22">
    <TITLE ID="t22">XInclude</TITLE>
    ...
  </CHAPTER>
</BOOK>
```

Now, imagine that in another chapter, you want to include a cross-reference to the XPointers chapter. You don't know what page it starts on or what chapter number it will have when you're done writing the book. The cross-reference is probably marked up a little like this:

```
<CROSS_REFERENCE>
XPointers are discussed in detail <SEE TARGET="#t21"/>.
</CROSS_REFERENCE>
```

If you want cross-references by chapter number in the style used in this book, "XPointers are discussed in more detail in Chapter 21," you could use these rules:

```
TITLE { counter-increment: ChapterNumber}
SEE[TARGET] {
  content: "in Chapter " target-counter(TARGET, ChapterNumber)
}
```

The TITLE rule creates a counter on TITLE elements named ChapterNumber and increments it with each TITLE element encountered. This counter is then referenced inside the rule that matches SEE elements with TARGET attributes by making target-counter() part of the value of a content property.

On the other hand, suppose you wanted to use the chapter titles, as in "XPointers are discussed in more detail in the chapter *XPointers*." Then you'd use the target-content() function to get the text of the title:

```
SEE[TARGET] {
  content: "in the chapter " target-content(TARGET)
}
```

Finally, if you actually want to include the page number, then you need to set a counter on pages using an @page rule and reference that inside target-counter(), like this:

```
@page { counter-increment: page }
SEE[TARGET] {
  content: "starting on p. " target-counter(TARGET, page)
}
```

This produces cross-references such as "XPointers are discussed in detail starting on p. 731."

You can combine any or all of these as needed. For example, suppose you want cross-references to include the chapter number, chapter title, and page number. Then you would use these rules:

```
@page { counter-increment: page }
TITLE { counter-increment: ChapterNumber}
SEE[TARGET] {
  content: "in Chapter "
            target-counter(TARGET, ChapterNumber)
            ", "
            target-content(TARGET)
            ", starting on p. "
            target-counter(TARGET, page)
}
```

This produces cross-references that read, "XPointers are discussed in detail in Chapter 21, XPointers, starting on p. 731."

Summary

In this chapter, you learned about CSS Level 3, a group of more than 20 W3C specifications covering every aspect of declarative styling for XML documents, ranging from fonts to tables to columns to behavior. In particular, you learned that:

✦ CSS3 is in a very early stage of development and is not yet supported by any browsers.

✦ CSS3 adds many new pseudo-classes including `:target`, `:enabled`, `:disabled`, `:checked`, `:indeterminate`, `:root pseudo-class`, `:nth-child()`, `:nth-last-child()`, `:nth-of-type()`, `:nth-last-of-type()`, `:first-of-type`, `:last-of-type`, `:only-child`, `:only-of-type`, `last-child()`, `:empty`, `:contains()`, and `:not()`.

✦ CSS3 can select elements based on their namespace URIs instead of just their qualified names.

✦ CSS3 can select elements based on substrings in attribute values.

✦ CSS3 uses a double colon (`::`) to distinguish pseudo-elements from pseudo-classes. It introduces one new pseudo-element, `::selection`, to indicate the range the user has selected with the mouse.

✦ CSS3 adds the ~ combinator to select according to an element's preceding siblings.

✦ CSS3 enables you to specify the transparency of an element through a new `opacity` property.

✦ CSS3 lets you perform sophisticated color matching by using ICC color profiles and the `color-profile` and `rendering-intent` properties.

✦ CSS3 adds many new named colors ranging from `AliceBlue` to `YellowGreen`.

✦ CSS3 allows you to split an element into columns with the `column-number` and `column-width` properties. The formatting of columns can be controlled via the `column-gap`, `column-width-policy`, `column-space-distribution`, `column-rule-color`, `column-rule-style`, `column-rule-width`, `column-rule`, and `column-span` properties.

✦ The `@script` rule lets you embed scripts in the stylesheet that are run when the browser applies the style sheet to the document.

✦ The `DOMActivate`, `DOMFocusIn`, `DOMFocusOut`, `mousedown`, `mouseup`, `click`, `mouseover`, `mousemove`, and `mouseout` properties attach scripts to specific events on an element.

✦ CSS3 can format arbitrary elements as form parts including checkboxes and radio buttons but stops short of fully defining how a browser is supposed to use this to communicate with CGI programs on the server.

✦ The `user-input`, `user-modify`, `user-select`, `user-focus`, `user-focus-key`, and `user-focus-pointer` properties specify whether and how a user can activate and type into an element.

✦ The `key-equivalent` property determines which key or keys on the keyboard the user can press to activate an element.

✦ CSS3 lets you place content in the page margins using `@top`, `@bottom`, `@left`, and `@right`.

✦ CSS3 supports page numbering and cross-referencing via the `@page` rule and the `pages()` function.

✦ The `target-counter()` and `target-content()` functions calculate values for cross-references that are resolved when the document is displayed or printed.

Although CSS3 is quite powerful when fully implemented, there are still some limits to what you can achieve with it. First, CSS can only attach styles to content that already appears in the document. It can only add very limited content to the document, and it cannot transform the content in any way, such as by sorting or reordering it. These needs are addressed by XSL, the Extensible Stylesheet Language. However, a more severe limitation is that you're limited to those parts of CSS that are reliably implemented across multiple browsers, a depressingly small subset of standard CSS. XSL, by contrast, can be implemented on the server side, so that you're not restricted to only those parts that browsers actually implement. The next chapter explores XSL transformations and shows you how much farther they can take you.

✦   ✦   ✦

XSL Transformations

The Extensible Stylesheet Language (XSL) includes both a transformation language and a formatting language. Each of these, naturally enough, is an XML application. The transformation language provides elements that define rules for how one XML document is transformed into another XML document. The transformed XML document may use the markup and DTD of the original document, or it may use a completely different set of elements. In particular, it may use the elements defined by the second part of XSL, the formatting objects. This chapter discusses the transformation language half of XSL.

What Is XSL?

The transformation and formatting halves of XSL can function independently of each other. For instance, the transformation language can transform an XML document into a well-formed HTML file, and completely ignore XSL formatting objects. This is the style of XSL previewed in Chapter 5 and emphasized in this chapter. Furthermore, it's not absolutely required that a document written in XSL formatting objects be produced by using the transformation part of XSL on another XML document. For example, it's easy to imagine a converter written in Java that reads TeX or PDF files and translates them into XSL formatting objects (though no such converters exist as of 2001).

In essence, XSL is two languages, not one. The first language is a transformation language, the second a formatting language. The transformation language is useful independent of the formatting language. Its ability to move data from one XML representation to another makes it an important component of XML-based electronic commerce, electronic data interchange, metadata exchange, and any application that needs to convert between different XML representations of the same information.

A word of caution about XSL

XSL is still under development. The language has changed radically in the past, and will almost certainly change again in the future. This chapter is based on the November 16, 1999 XSLT 1.0 Recommendation. Because XSLT is now an official Recommendation of the World Wide Web Consortium (W3C), I'm hopeful that any changes that do occur will simply add to the existing syntax without invalidating style sheets that adhere to the 1.0 spec. Indeed the W3C has just begun work on XSLT 2.0, and it does seem likely that all legal XSLT 1.0 documents will still be legal XSLT 2.0 documents.

Not all software has caught up to the 1.0 Recommendation, however. In particular, Version 5.5 and earlier of Internet Explorer only implement a very old working draft of XSLT that looks almost nothing like the finished standard. You should not expect most of the examples in this chapter to work with IE, even after substantial tweaking. Conversely, the language that IE does implement is not XSLT; and any book or person that tells you otherwise is telling you an untruth. Both Microsoft's live presentations and the written documentation it posts on its Web site are notorious for teaching nonstandard Microsoft versions of XSLT (and other languages) without clearly distinguishing which parts are real XSLT and which are Microsoft extensions to (some would say perversions of) standard XSLT.

In November 2000 Microsoft released MSXML 3.0, an XML parser/XSLT processor for IE that does come much closer to supporting XSLT 1.0. You can download it from `http://msdn.microsoft.com/xml/general/xmlparser.asp`. However, there are still some bugs and areas where Microsoft did not follow the specification, so this is not quite a complete implementation of XSLT 1.0. More importantly, MSXML 3.0 is not bundled with IE5.5; and even if you install it, it does not automatically replace the earlier, non-standard-compliant version of MSXML that is bundled. To replace the old version, you have to download and run a separate program called xmlinst.exe, which you can get from the same page where you found MSXML 3.0.

These uses are also united by their lack of concern with rendering data on a display for humans to read. They are purely about moving data from one computer system or program to another.

Consequently, many early implementations of XSL focus exclusively on the transformation part and ignore the formatting objects. These are incomplete implementations, but nonetheless useful. Not all data must ultimately be rendered on a computer monitor or printed on paper.

Cross-Reference   Chapter 19 discusses the XSL formatting language.

Overview of XSL Transformations

In an XSL transformation, an XSLT processor reads both an XML document and an XSLT style sheet. Based on the instructions the processor finds in the XSLT style sheet, it outputs a new XML document or fragment thereof. There's also special support for outputting HTML. With some effort most XSLT processors can also be made to output essentially arbitrary text, though XSLT is designed primarily for XML-to-XML and XML-to-HTML transformations.

Trees

As you learned in Chapter 6, every well-formed XML document is a tree. A tree is a data structure composed of connected nodes beginning with a top node called the root. The root is connected to its child nodes, each of which is connected to zero or more children of its own, and so forth. Nodes that have no children of their own are called *leaves*. A diagram of a tree looks much like a genealogical descendant chart that lists the descendants of a single ancestor. The most useful property of a tree is that each node and its children also form a tree. Thus, a tree is a hierarchical structure of trees in which each tree is built out of smaller trees.

For the purposes of XSLT, elements, attributes, namespaces, processing instructions, and comments are counted as nodes. Furthermore, the root of the document must be distinguished from the root element. Thus, XSLT processors model an XML document as a tree that contains seven kinds of nodes:

✦ The root

✦ Elements

✦ Text

✦ Attributes

✦ Namespaces

✦ Processing instructions

✦ Comments

The Document Type Definition (DTD) and document type declaration are specifically not included in this tree. However, a DTD may add default attribute values to some elements, which then become additional attribute nodes in the tree.

For example, consider the XML document in Listing 18-1. This shows part of the periodic table of the elements. I'll be using this as an example in this chapter.

On the CD-ROM   The complete periodic table appears on the CD-ROM in the file allelements.xml in the examples/periodic_table directory.

The root `PERIODIC_TABLE` element contains `ATOM` child elements. Each `ATOM` element contains several child elements providing the atomic number, atomic weight, symbol, boiling point, and so forth. A `UNITS` attribute specifies the units for those elements that have units.

Note ELEMENT would be a more appropriate name here than ATOM. However, writing about ELEMENT elements and trying to distinguish between chemical elements and XML elements might create confusion. Thus, at least for the purposes of this chapter, ATOM seemed like the more legible option.

Listing 18-1: An XML periodic table with two atoms: hydrogen and helium

```
<?xml version="1.0"?>
<?xml-stylesheet type="text/xml" href="18-2.xsl"?>
<PERIODIC_TABLE>

  <ATOM STATE="GAS">
    <NAME>Hydrogen</NAME>
    <SYMBOL>H</SYMBOL>
    <ATOMIC_NUMBER>1</ATOMIC_NUMBER>
    <ATOMIC_WEIGHT>1.00794</ATOMIC_WEIGHT>
    <BOILING_POINT UNITS="Kelvin">20.28</BOILING_POINT>
    <MELTING_POINT UNITS="Kelvin">13.81</MELTING_POINT>
    <DENSITY UNITS="grams/cubic centimeter">
      <!-- At 300K, 1 atm -->
      0.0000899
    </DENSITY>
  </ATOM>

  <ATOM STATE="GAS">
    <NAME>Helium</NAME>
    <SYMBOL>He</SYMBOL>
    <ATOMIC_NUMBER>2</ATOMIC_NUMBER>
    <ATOMIC_WEIGHT>4.0026</ATOMIC_WEIGHT>
    <BOILING_POINT UNITS="Kelvin">4.216</BOILING_POINT>
    <MELTING_POINT UNITS="Kelvin">0.95</MELTING_POINT>
    <DENSITY UNITS="grams/cubic centimeter"><!-- At 300K -->
      0.0001785
    </DENSITY>
  </ATOM>

</PERIODIC_TABLE>
```

Figure 18-1 displays a tree diagram of this document. It begins at the top with the root node (not the same as the root element!) which contains two child nodes, the xml-stylesheet processing instruction and the root element PERIODIC_TABLE. (The XML declaration is not visible to the XSLT processor and is not included in the tree the XSLT processor operates on.) The PERIODIC_TABLE element contains two child nodes, both ATOM elements. Each ATOM element has an attribute node for its STATE attribute, and a variety of child element nodes. Each child element contains a node for its contents, as well as nodes for any attributes, comments, and processing instructions it possesses. Notice in particular that many nodes are something other than elements. There are nodes for text, attributes, comments, namespaces and processing instructions. Unlike CSS, XSL is not limited to working only with whole elements. It has a much more granular view of a document that enables you to base styles on comments, attributes, processing instructions, element content, and more.

> **Note** Like the XML declaration, an internal DTD subset or DOCTYPE declaration is not part of the tree. However, it may have the effect of adding attribute nodes to some elements through `<!ATTLIST>` declarations that use `#FIXED` or default attribute values.

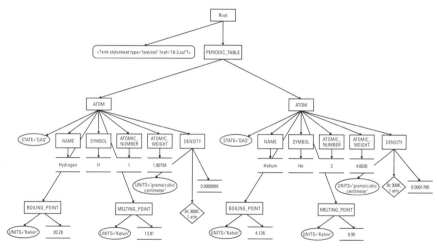

Figure 18-1: Listing 18-1 as a tree diagram

XSLT operates by transforming one XML tree into another XML tree. More precisely, an XSLT processor accepts as input a tree represented as an XML document and produces as output a new tree, also represented as an XML document. Consequently, the transformation part of XSL is also called the tree construction part. The XSL transformation language contains operators for selecting nodes from the tree, reordering the nodes, and outputting nodes. If one of these nodes is an element node, then it may be an entire tree itself. Remember that all these operators, both for input and output, are designed for operation on a tree.

The input must be an XML document. You cannot use XSLT to transform from non-XML formats such as PDF, TeX, Microsoft Word, PostScript, MIDI, or others. HTML and SGML are borderline cases because they're so close to XML. XSLT can work with HTML and SGML documents that satisfy XML's well-formedness rules. However, XSLT cannot handle the wide variety of non-well-formed HTML and SGML that you encounter on most Web sites and document production systems. XSLT is not a general-purpose regular expression language for transforming arbitrary data.

Most of the time the output of an XSLT transformation is also an XML document. However, it can also be a result tree fragment that could be used as an external parsed entity in another XML document. (That is, it would be a well-formed XML document if it were enclosed in a single root element.) In other words, the output may not necessarily be a well-formed XML document, but it will at least be a plausible part of a well-formed XML document. An XSLT transformation cannot output text that is malformed XML such as

```
<B><I>Tag Mismatch!</B></I>
```

Tip   The `xsl:output` element and `disable-output-escaping` attribute discussed below loosen this restriction somewhat.

Most XSLT processors also support output as HTML and/or raw text, although the standard does not require them to do so. To some extent this allows you to transform to non-XML formats like TeX, RTF, or PostScript. However XSLT is not designed to make these transformations easy. It is designed for XML-to-XML transformations. If you need a non-XML output format, it will probably be easier to use XSLT to transform the XML to an intermediate format like TeXML (`http://www.alphaworks.ibm.com/tech/texml`) and then use additional, non-XSLT software to transform that into the format you want.

XSLT style sheet documents

An XSLT document contains template rules. A template rule has a pattern specifying the nodes it matches and a template to be instantiated and output when the pattern is matched. When an XSLT processor transforms an XML document under the control of an XSLT style sheet, it walks the XML document tree starting at the root, and from there following an order defined by the template rules. As the processor visits each node in the XML document, it compares that node with the pattern of each template rule in the style sheet. When it finds a node that matches a template rule's pattern, it outputs the rule's template. This template generally includes some markup, some new data, some data copied out of the source XML document, as well as some directions about which nodes to process next.

XSLT uses XML to describe these rules, templates, and patterns. The root element of the XSLT document is either a `stylesheet` or a `transform` element in the `http://www.w3.org/1999/XSL/Transform` namespace. By convention this namespace is mapped to the `xsl` prefix, but you're free to pick another prefix if you prefer. In this chapter, I always use the `xsl` prefix. From this point forward it should be understood that the prefix `xsl` is mapped to the `http://www.w3.org/1999/XSL/Transform` namespace.

Tip   If you get the namespace URI wrong, either by using a URI from an older draft of the specification, such as `http://www.w3.org/TR/WD-xsl`, or simply by making a typo in the normal URI, the XSLT processor will output the style sheet document itself instead of the transformed input document. This is the result of the interaction between several obscure sections of the XSLT 1.0 specification. The details aren't important. What is important is that this very unusual behavior looks very much like a bug in the processor if you aren't familiar with it. If you are familiar with it, fixing it is trivial; just correct the namespace URI to `http://www.w3.org/1999/XSL/Transform`.

Each template rule is an `xsl:template` element. The pattern of the rule is placed in the `match` attribute of the `xsl:template` element. The output template is the content of the `xsl:template` element. All instructions in the template for doing things such as selecting parts of the input tree to include in the output tree are performed by one or another XSLT elements. These are identified by the `xsl:` prefix on the element names. Elements that do not have an `xsl:` prefix are part of the result tree.

Listing 18-2 shows a very simple XSLT style sheet with two template rules. The first template rule matches the root element `PERIODIC_TABLE`. It replaces this element with an `html` element. The contents of the `html` element are the results of applying the other templates in the document to the contents of the `PERIODIC_TABLE` element.

The second template matches `ATOM` elements. It replaces each `ATOM` element in the input document with a `P` element in the output document. The `xsl:apply-templates` rule inserts the text of the matched source element into the output document. Thus, the contents of a `P` element will be the text (but not the markup) contained in the corresponding `ATOM` element.

The `xsl:stylesheet` root element has two required attributes, `version` and `xmlns:xsl`, each of which must have exactly the values shown here (`1.0` for `version` and `http://www.w3.org/1999/XSL/Transform` for `xmlns:xsl`). I'll discuss the exact syntax of all these elements and attributes below.

Listing 18-2: An XSLT style sheet for the periodic table with two template rules

```
<?xml version="1.0"?>
<xsl:stylesheet version="1.0"
          xmlns:xsl="http://www.w3.org/1999/XSL/Transform">

  <xsl:template match="PERIODIC_TABLE">
    <html>
      <xsl:apply-templates/>
    </html>
  </xsl:template>

  <xsl:template match="ATOM">
    <P>
      <xsl:apply-templates/>
    </P>
  </xsl:template>

</xsl:stylesheet>
```

The `xsl:transform` element can be used in place of `xsl:stylesheet` if you prefer. This is an exact synonym with the same syntax, semantics, and attributes. For example,

```
<?xml version="1.0"?>
<xsl:transform version="1.0"
        xmlns:xsl="http://www.w3.org/1999/XSL/Transform">
  <!-- templates go here -->
</xsl:transform>
```

In this book, I will stick to `xsl:stylesheet`.

Where does the XML transformation happen?

There are three primary ways to transform XML documents into other formats, such as HTML, with an XSLT style sheet:

1. The XML document and associated style sheet are both served to the client (Web browser), which then transforms the document as specified by the style sheet and presents it to the user.

2. The server applies an XSLT style sheet to an XML document to transform it to some other format (generally HTML) and sends the transformed document to the client (Web browser).

3. A third program transforms the original XML document into some other format (often HTML) before the document is placed on the server. Both server and client only deal with the transformed document.

Each of these three approaches uses different software, although they all use the same XML documents and XSLT style sheets. An ordinary Web server sending XML documents to Internet Explorer is an example of the first approach. A servlet-compatible Web server using the IBM alphaWorks' XML Enabler (`http://www.alphaworks.ibm.com/tech/xmlenabler`) is an example of the second approach. A human using Michael Kay's command line SAXON program (`http://saxon.sourceforge.net/`) to transform XML documents to HTML documents, then placing the HTML documents on a Web server is an example of the third approach. However, these all use (at least in theory) the same XSLT language.

In this chapter, I emphasize the third approach, primarily because at the time of this writing, specialized converter programs such as Michael Kay's SAXON and the XML Apache Project's Xalan (`http://xml.apache.org/xalan/`) provide the most complete and accurate implementations of the XSLT specification. Furthermore, this approach offers the broadest compatibility with legacy Web browsers and servers, whereas the first approach requires a more recent browser than most users use, and the second approach requires special Web server software. In practice, though, requiring a different server is not nearly as onerous as requiring a particular client. You, yourself, can install your own special server software; but you cannot rely on your visitors to install particular client software.

On the CD-ROM Xalan is on the CD-ROM in the directory utilities/xalan. SAXON is on the CD-ROM in the directory utilities/saxon.

How to use Xalan

Xalan is a Java 1.1 character mode application. To use it, you'll need a Java 1.1-compatible virtual machine such as Sun's Java Development Kit (JDK), or Java Runtime Environment (JRE), Apple's Macintosh Runtime for Java 2.2 (MRJ), or Microsoft's virtual machine. You'll need to set your CLASSPATH environment variable to include both the xalan.jar and xerces.jar files (both included in the Xalan distribution). On Unix/Linux you can set this in your .cshrc file if you use csh or tcsh or in your .profile file if you use sh, ksh or bash. On Windows 95/98 you can set it in AUTOEXEC. BAT. In Windows NT/2000, set it with the System Control Panel Environment tab.

Tip If you're using the JRE 1.2 or later, you can just put the xalan.jar and xerces.jar files in your jre/lib/ext directory instead of mucking around with the CLASSPATH environment variable. If you've installed the JDK instead of the JRE on Windows, you may have two jre/lib/ext directories, one somewhere like C:\jdk1.3\jre\lib\ext and the other somewhere like C:\Program Files\Javasoft\jre\1.3\lib\ext. You need to copy the jar archive into both ext directories. Putting one copy in one directory and an alias into the other directory does not work. You must place complete, actual copies into each ext directory.

Note Although I primarily use Xalan in this chapter, the examples should work with SAXON or any other XSLT processor that implements the November 16, 1999 XSLT 1.0 recommendation.

The Java class containing the main method for Xalan is org.apache.xalan.xslt. Process. You can run Xalan by typing the following at the shell prompt or in a DOS window:

```
C:\> java org.apache.xalan.xslt.Process -in 18-1.xml -xsl
18-2.xsl -out 18-3.html
```

This line runs the java interpreter on the Java class containing the Xalan program's main() method, org.apache.xalan.xslt.Process. The source XML document following the -in flag is 18-1.xml. The XSLT style sheet follows the -xsl flag and is 18-2.xsl here; and the output HTML file follows the -out argument and is named 18-3.html. If the -out argument is omitted, the transformed document will be printed on the console. If the -xsl argument is omitted, Xalan will attempt to use the style sheet named by the xml-stylesheet processing instruction in the prolog of the input XML document.

Listing 18-2 transforms input documents to well-formed HTML files as discussed in Chapter 6. However, you can transform from any XML application to any other as long as you can write a style sheet to support the transformation. For example, you can imagine a style sheet that transforms from Vector Markup Language (VML) documents to Scalable Vector Graphics (SVG) documents:

```
% java org.apache.xalan.xslt.Process -in pinktriangle.vml
  -xsl VmlToSVG.xsl -out pinktriangle.svg
```

Most other command line XSLT processors behave similarly, though of course they'll have different command line arguments and options. They may prove slightly easier to use if they're not written in Java since there won't be any need to configure the CLASSPATH.

Tip   If you're using Windows, you can use a stand-alone executable version of SAXON called Instant SAXON (http://users.iclway.co.uk/mhkay/saxon/instant.html) instead. This is a little easier to use because it doesn't require you to mess around with CLASSPATH environment variables. To transform a document with this program, simply place the saxon.exe file in your path and type:

```
C:\> saxon -o 18-3.html 18-1.xml 18-2.xsl
```

Listing 18-3 shows the output of running Listing 18-1 through Xalan with the XSLT style sheet in Listing 18-2. Notice that Xalan does not attempt to clean up the HTML it generates, which has a lot of white space. This is not important since ultimately you want to view the file in a Web browser that trims white space. Figure 18-2 shows Listing 18-3 loaded into Netscape Navigator 4.6. Because Listing 18-3 is standard HTML, you don't need an XML-capable browser to view it.

Listing 18-3: **The HTML produced by applying the style sheet in Listing 18-2 to the XML in Listing 18-1**

```
<html>

  <P>
    Hydrogen
    H
    1
    1.00794
    20.28
    13.81


       0.0000899

  </P>

  <P>
    Helium
    He
    2
    4.0026
```

```
        4.216
        0.95

            0.0001785

    </P>

</html>
```

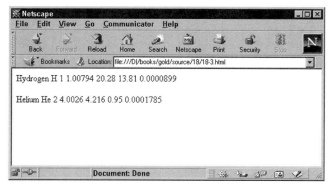

Figure 18-2: The page produced by applying the style sheet in Listing 18-2 to the XML document in Listing 18-1

Direct display of XML files with XSLT style sheets

Instead of preprocessing the XML file, you can send the client both the XML file and the XSLT file that describes how to render it. The client is responsible for applying the style sheet to the document and rendering it accordingly. This is more work for the client, but places much less load on the server. In this case, the XSLT style sheet must transform the document into an XML application the client understands. HTML is a likely choice, though in the future some browsers may understand XSL formatting objects as well.

Attaching an XSLT style sheet to an XML document is easy. Simply insert an `xml-stylesheet` processing instruction in the prolog immediately after the XML declaration. This processing instruction should have a `type` attribute with the value `text/xml` and an `href` attribute whose value is a URL pointing to the style sheet. For example:

```
<?xml version="1.0"?>
<?xml-stylesheet type="text/xml" href="18-2.xsl"?>
```

This is also how you attach a CSS style sheet to a document. The only difference here is that the `type` attribute has the value `text/xml` instead of `text/css`.

Note   In the future the more specific MIME media type `application/xslt+xml` will be available to distinguish XSLT documents from all other XML documents. Once XSLT processors are revised to support this, you will be able to write the `xml-stylesheet` processing instruction like this instead:

```
<?xml-stylesheet type="application/xslt+xml"
href="18-2.xsl"?>
```

Internet Explorer 5.0 and 5.5's XSLT support differs from the November 16, 1999 recommendation in several ways. First, it expects that XSLT elements live in the `http://www.w3.org/TR/WD-xsl` namespace instead of the `http://www.w3.org/1999/XSL/Transform` namespace, although the `xsl` prefix is still used. Second, it expects the non-standard MIME media type `text/xsl` in the `xml-stylesheet` processing instruction rather than `text/xml`. Finally, it does not implement the default rules for elements that match no template. Consequently, you need to provide a template for each element in the hierarchy starting from the root before trying to view a document in Internet Explorer. Listing 18-4 demonstrates. The three rules match the root node, the root element `PERIODIC_TABLE`, and the `ATOM` elements in that order. Figure 18-3 shows the XML document in Listing 18-1 loaded into Internet Explorer 5.5 with this style sheet.

Listing 18-4: The style sheet of Listing 18-2 adjusted to work with Internet Explorer 5.0 and 5.5

```
<?xml version="1.0"?>
<!-- This is a non-standard style sheet designed just for
     Internet Explorer. It will not work with any standards
     compliant XSLT processor. -->
<xsl:stylesheet version="1.0"
  xmlns:xsl="http://www.w3.org/TR/WD-xsl">

  <xsl:template match="/">
    <html>
      <xsl:apply-templates/>
    </html>
  </xsl:template>

  <xsl:template match="PERIODIC_TABLE">
    <xsl:apply-templates/>
  </xsl:template>

  <xsl:template match="ATOM">
    <P>
      <xsl:value-of select="."/>
```

```
      </P>
    </xsl:template>

  </xsl:stylesheet>
```

Caution　Ideally, you would use the same XML document both for direct display and for pre-rendering to HTML. Unfortunately, that would require Microsoft to actually support the real XSLT specification. Microsoft has repeatedly promised to support this, and they have just as repeatedly reneged on those promises.

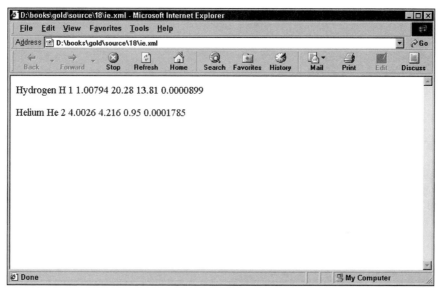

Figure 18-3: The page produced in Internet Explorer 5.5 by applying the style sheet in Listing 18-4 to the XML document in Listing 18-1

Internet Explorer also fails to support many other parts of standard XSLT, while offering a number of nonstandard extensions. If you've successfully installed MSXML3 in replace mode, then IE5 can handle most of XSLT 1.0 including the `http://www.w3.org/1999/XSL/Transform` namespace. However, even this version still has a few bugs, including expecting the `text/xsl` MIME media type instead of `text/xml`. In the rest of this chapter, I use only standard XSLT and simply prerender the file in HTML before loading it into a Web browser. If you find something in this chapter doesn't work in Internet Explorer, please complain to Microsoft, not to me.

XSL Templates

Template rules defined by xsl:template elements are the most important part of an XSLT style sheet. These associate particular output with particular input. Each xsl:template element has a match attribute that specifies which nodes of the input document the template is instantiated for.

The content of the xsl:template element is the actual template to be instantiated. A template may contain both text that will appear literally in the output document and XSLT instructions that copy data from the input XML document to the result. Because all XSLT instructions are in the http://www.w3.org/1999/XSL/Transform namespace, it's easy to distinguish between the elements that are literal data to be copied to the output and instructions. For example, here is a template that is applied to the root node of the input tree:

```
<xsl:template match="/">
  <html>
    <head>
    </head>
    <body>
    </body>
  </html>
</xsl:template>
```

When the XSLT processor reads the input document, the first node it sees is the root. This rule matches that root node and tells the XSLT processor to emit this text:

```
<html>
  <head>
  </head>
  <body>
  </body>
</html>
```

This text is well-formed HTML. Because the XSLT document is itself an XML document, its contents — templates included — must be well-formed XML.

If you were to use the above rule, and only the above rule, in an XSLT style sheet, the output would be limited to the above six tags. That's because no instructions in the rule tell the formatter to move down the tree and look for further matches against the templates in the style sheet.

The xsl:apply-templates element

To get beyond the root, you have to tell the formatting engine to process the children of the root. In general, to include content in the child nodes, you have to recursively process the nodes through the XML document. The element that does this is `xsl:apply-templates`. By including `xsl:apply-templates` in the output template, you tell the formatter to compare each child of the matched source element against the templates in the style sheet, and, if a match is found, output the template for the matched node. The template for the matched node may itself contain `xsl:apply-templates` elements to search for matches for its children. When the formatting engine processes a node, the node is treated as a complete tree. This is the advantage of the tree structure. Each part can be treated the same way as the whole. For example, Listing 18-5 is an XSLT style sheet that uses the `xsl:apply templates` element to process the child nodes.

Listing 18-5: An XSLT style sheet that recursively processes the children of the root

```
<?xml version="1.0"?>
<xsl:stylesheet version="1.0"
  xmlns:xsl="http://www.w3.org/1999/XSL/Transform">

  <xsl:template match="/">
    <html>
      <xsl:apply-templates/>
    </html>
  </xsl:template>

  <xsl:template match="PERIODIC_TABLE">
    <body>
      <xsl:apply-templates/>
    </body>
  </xsl:template>

  <xsl:template match="ATOM">
    An Atom
  </xsl:template>

</xsl:stylesheet>
```

When this style sheet is applied to Listing 18-1, here's what happens:

1. The root node is compared with all template rules in the style sheet. It matches the first one.

2. The `<html>` tag is written out.

3. The `xsl:apply-templates` element causes the formatting engine to process the child nodes of the root node of the input document.

    A. The first child of the root, the `xml-stylesheet` processing instruction, is compared with the template rules. It doesn't match any of them, so no output is generated.

    B. The second child of the root node of the input document, the root element `PERIODIC_TABLE`, is compared with the template rules. It matches the second template rule.

    C. The `<body>` tag is written out.

    D. The `xsl:apply-templates` element in the `body` element causes the formatting engine to process the child nodes of `PERIODIC_TABLE`.

        a. The first child of the `PERIODIC_TABLE` element, that is the Hydrogen `ATOM` element, is compared with the template rules. It matches the third template rule.

        b. The text "An Atom" is output.

        c. The second child of the `PERIODIC_TABLE` element, that is the Helium `ATOM` element, is compared with the template rules. It matches the third template rule.

        d. The text "An Atom" is output.

    E. The `</body>` tag is written out.

4. The `</html>` tag is written out.

5. Processing is complete.

The end result is:

```
<html>
<body>


    An Atom



    An Atom


</body>
</html>
```

The select attribute

To replace the text "An Atom" with the name of the ATOM element as given by its NAME child, you need to specify that templates should be applied to the NAME children of the ATOM element. To choose a particular set of children instead of all children you supply xsl:apply-templates with a select attribute designating the children to be selected. For example:

```
<xsl:template match="ATOM">
  <xsl:apply-templates select="NAME"/>
</xsl:template>
```

The select attribute uses the same kind of patterns as the match attribute of the xsl:template element. For now, I'll stick to simple names of elements; but in the section on patterns for matching and selecting later in this chapter, you'll see many more possibilities for both select and match. If no select attribute is present, all child element, text, comment, and processing instruction nodes are selected. (Attribute and namespace nodes are not selected.)

The result of adding this rule to the style sheet of Listing 18-5 and applying it to Listing 18-1 is this:

```
<html>
<body>

  Hydrogen

  Helium

</body>
</html>
```

Computing the Value of a Node with xsl:value-of

The xsl:value-of element computes the value of something (most of the time, though not always, something in the input document) and copies it into the output document. The select attribute of the xsl:value-of element specifies exactly which something's value is being computed.

For example, suppose you want to replace the literal text An Atom with the name of the ATOM element as given by the contents of its NAME child. You can replace An Atom with <xsl:value-of select="NAME"/> like this:

```
<xsl:template match="ATOM">
  <xsl:value-of select="NAME"/>
</xsl:template>
```

Then, when you apply the style sheet to Listing 18-1, this text is generated:

```
<html>
<body>

   Hydrogen

   Helium

</body>
</html>
```

The item whose value is selected, the NAME element in this example, is relative to the current node. The current node is the item matched by the template, the particular ATOM element in this example. Thus, when the Hydrogen ATOM is matched by `<xsl:template match="ATOM">`, the Hydrogen ATOM's NAME is selected by `xsl:value-of`. When the Helium ATOM is matched by `<xsl:template match="ATOM">`, the Helium ATOM's NAME is selected by `xsl:value-of`.

The value of a node is always a string, possibly an empty string. The exact contents of this string depend on the type of the node. The most common type of node is element, and the value of an element node is particularly simple. It's the concatenation of all the character data (but not markup!) between the element's start tag and end tag. For example, the first ATOM element in Listing 18-1 is as follows:

```
<ATOM STATE="GAS">
  <NAME>Hydrogen</NAME>
  <SYMBOL>H</SYMBOL>
  <ATOMIC_NUMBER>1</ATOMIC_NUMBER>
  <ATOMIC_WEIGHT>1.00794</ATOMIC_WEIGHT>
  <BOILING_POINT UNITS="Kelvin">20.28</BOILING_POINT>
  <MELTING_POINT UNITS="Kelvin">13.81</MELTING_POINT>
  <DENSITY UNITS="grams/cubic centimeter">
    <!-- At 300K, 1 atm -->
    0.0000899
  </DENSITY>
</ATOM>
```

The value of this element is shown below:

```
Hydrogen
H
1
1.00794
1
20.28
13.81


  0.0000899
```

I calculated this value by stripping out all the tags and comments. Everything else including white space was left intact. The values of the other six node types are calculated similarly, mostly in obvious ways. Table 18-1 summarizes.

**Table 18-1
Values of Nodes**

Node Type	Value
Root	The value of the root element
Element	The concatenation of all parsed character data contained in the element, including character data in any of the descendants of the element
Text	The text of the node; essentially the node itself
Attribute	The normalized attribute value as specified by Section 3.3.3 of the XML 1.0 recommendation; basically the attribute value after entities are resolved and leading and trailing white space is stripped; does not include the name of the attribute, the equals sign, or the quotation marks
Namespace	The URI of the namespace
Processing instruction	The data in the processing instruction; does not include the target, `<?` or `?>`
Comment	The text of the comment, `<!--` and `-->` not included

Processing Multiple Elements with xsl:for-each

The `xsl:value-of` element should only be used in contexts where it is obvious which node's value is being taken. If there are multiple possible items that could be selected, then only the first one will be chosen. For instance, this is a poor rule because a typical `PERIODIC_TABLE` element contains more than one `ATOM`:

```
<xsl:template match="PERIODIC_TABLE">
  <xsl:value-of select="ATOM"/>
</xsl:template>
```

There are two ways of processing multiple elements in turn. The first method you've already seen. Simply use `xsl:apply-templates` with a `select` attribute that chooses the particular elements that you want to include, like this:

```
<xsl:template match="PERIODIC_TABLE">
  <xsl:apply-templates select="ATOM"/>
</xsl:template>

<xsl:template match="ATOM">
  <xsl:value-of select="."/>
</xsl:template>
```

The select="." in the second template tells the formatter to take the value of the matched element, ATOM in this example.

The second option is xsl:for-each. The xsl:for-each element processes each element chosen by its select attribute in turn. However, no additional template is required. For example:

```
<xsl:template match="PERIODIC_TABLE">
  <xsl:for-each select="ATOM">
    <xsl:value-of select="."/>
  </xsl:for-each>
</xsl:template>
```

Patterns for Matching Nodes

The match attribute of the xsl:template element supports a complex syntax that allows you to express exactly which nodes you do and do not want to match. The select attribute of xsl:apply-templates, xsl:value-of, xsl:for-each, xsl:copy-of, and xsl:sort supports an even more powerful superset of this syntax called XPath that allows you to express exactly which nodes you do and do not want to select. Various patterns for matching and selecting nodes are discussed below.

Matching the root node

In order that the output document be well-formed, the first thing output from an XSL transformation should be the output document's root element. Consequently, XSLT style sheets generally start with a rule that applies to the root node. To specify the root node in a rule, you give its match attribute the value "/". For example:

```
<xsl:template match="/">
  <DOCUMENT>
    <xsl:apply-templates/>
  </DOCUMENT>
</xsl:template>
```

This rule applies to the root node and only the root node of the input tree. When the root node is read, the tag <DOCUMENT> is output, the children of the root node are processed, then the </DOCUMENT> tag is output. This rule overrides the default rule for the root node. Listing 18-6 shows a style sheet with a single rule that applies to the root node.

Listing 18-6: An XSLT style sheet with one rule for the root node

```xml
<?xml version="1.0"?>
<xsl:stylesheet version="1.0"
  xmlns:xsl="http://www.w3.org/1999/XSL/Transform">

    <xsl:template match="/">
      <html>
        <head>
          <title>Atomic Number vs. Atomic Weight</title>
        </head>
        <body>
          <table>
            Atom data will go here
          </table>
        </body>
      </html>
    </xsl:template>

</xsl:stylesheet>
```

Because this style sheet only provides a rule for the root node, and because that rule's template does not specify any further processing of child nodes, only literal output that's included in the template is inserted in the resulting document. In other words, the result of applying the style sheet in Listing 18-6 to Listing 18-1 (or any other well-formed XML document) is this:

```html
<html>
<head>
<title>Atomic Number vs. Atomic Weight</title>
</head>
<body>
<table>
          Atom data will go here
        </table>
</body>
</html>
```

Matching element names

As previously mentioned, the most basic pattern contains a single element name that matches all elements with that name. For example, this template matches ATOM elements and makes their ATOMIC_NUMBER children bold:

```
<xsl:template match="ATOM">
  <b><xsl:value-of select="ATOMIC_NUMBER"/></b>
</xsl:template>
```

Listing 18-7 demonstrates a style sheet that expands on Listing 18-6. First, an `xsl:apply-templates` element is included in the template rule for the root node. This rule uses a `select` attribute to ensure that only PERIODIC_TABLE elements are processed.

Second, a rule that only applies to PERIODIC_TABLE elements is created using `match="PERIODIC_TABLE"`. This rule sets up the header for the table, and then applies templates to form the body of the table from ATOM elements.

Finally, the ATOM rule specifically selects the ATOM element's NAME, ATOMIC_NUMBER, and ATOMIC_WEIGHT child elements with `<xsl:value-of select="NAME"/>`, `<xsl:value-of select="ATOMIC_NUMBER"/>`, and `<xsl:value-of select="ATOMIC_WEIGHT"/>`. These are wrapped up inside HTML's `tr` and `td` elements, so that the end result is a table of atomic numbers matched to atomic weights. Figure 18-4 shows the output of applying the style sheet in Listing 18-7 to the complete periodic table document displayed in Netscape Navigator.

One thing you may wish to note about this style sheet: The exact order of the NAME, ATOMIC_NUMBER, and ATOMIC_WEIGHT elements in the input document is irrelevant. They appear in the output in the order they were selected; that is, first number, then weight. Conversely, the individual atoms are sorted in alphabetical order as they appear in the input document. Later, you'll see how to use an `xsl:sort` element to change that so you can arrange the atoms in the more conventional atomic number order.

Listing 18-7: Templates applied to specific classes of element with select

```
<?xml version="1.0"?>
<xsl:stylesheet version="1.0"
  xmlns:xsl="http://www.w3.org/1999/XSL/Transform">

  <xsl:template match="/">
    <html>
      <head>
        <title>Atomic Number vs. Atomic Weight</title>
      </head>
      <body>
        <xsl:apply-templates select="PERIODIC_TABLE"/>
      </body>
    </html>
  </xsl:template>
```

```
<xsl:template match="PERIODIC_TABLE">
  <h1>Atomic Number vs. Atomic Weight</h1>
  <table>
    <th>Element</th>
    <th>Atomic Number</th>
    <th>Atomic Weight</th>
      <xsl:apply-templates select="ATOM"/>
  </table>
</xsl:template>

<xsl:template match="ATOM">
  <tr>
    <td><xsl:value-of select="NAME"/></td>
    <td><xsl:value-of select="ATOMIC_NUMBER"/></td>
    <td><xsl:value-of select="ATOMIC_WEIGHT"/></td>
  </tr>
</xsl:template>

</xsl:stylesheet>
```

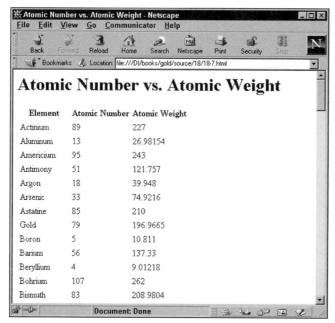

Figure 18-4: A table showing atomic number versus atomic weight in Netscape Navigator

Wild cards

Sometimes you want a single template to apply to more than one element. You can indicate that a template matches all elements by using the asterisk wildcard (*) in place of an element name in the match attribute. For example this template says that all elements should be wrapped in a P element:

```
<xsl:template match="*">
  <P>
    <xsl:value-of select="."/>
  </P>
</xsl:template>
```

Of course this is probably more than you want. You'd like to use the template rules already defined for PERIODIC_TABLE and ATOM elements as well as the root node and only use this rule for the other elements. Fortunately you can. In the event that two rules both match a single node, then by default the more specific one takes precedence. In this case that means that ATOM elements will use the template with match="ATOM" instead of a template that merely has match="*". However, NAME, BOILING_POINT, ATOMIC_NUMBER and other elements that don't match a more specific template will cause the match="*" template to activate.

You can place a namespace prefix in front of the asterisk to indicate that only elements in a particular namespace should be matched. For example this template matches all SVG elements, presuming that the prefix svg is mapped to the normal SVG URI http://www.w3.org/2000/svg in the style sheet.

```
<xsl:template match="svg:*">
  <DIV>
    <xsl:value-of select="."/>
  </DIV>
</xsl:template>
```

Of course in Listing 18-1, there aren't any elements from this namespace, so this template wouldn't produce any output. However, it might when applied to a different document that did include some SVG.

Matching children with /

You're not limited to the children of the current node in match attributes. You can use the / symbol to match specified hierarchies of elements. Used alone, the / symbol refers to the root node. However, you can use it between two names to indicate that the second is the child of the first. For example, ATOM/NAME refers to NAME elements that are children of ATOM elements.

In xsl:template elements, this enables you to match only some of the elements of a given kind. For example, this template rule marks SYMBOL elements that are children of ATOM elements strong. It does nothing to SYMBOL elements that are not direct children of ATOM elements.

```
<xsl:template match="ATOM/SYMBOL">
  <strong><xsl:value-of select="."/></strong>
</xsl:template>
```

Caution Remember that this rule selects SYMBOL elements that are children of ATOM elements, not ATOM elements that have SYMBOL children. In other words, the . in `<xsl:value-of select="."/>` refers to the SYMBOL and not to the ATOM.

You can specify deeper matches by stringing patterns together. For example, PERIODIC_TABLE/ATOM/NAME selects NAME elements whose parent is an ATOM element whose parent is a PERIODIC_TABLE element.

You can also use the * wild card to substitute for an arbitrary element name in a hierarchy. For example, this template rule applies to all SYMBOL elements that are grandchildren of a PERIODIC_TABLE element.

```
<xsl:template match="PERIODIC_TABLE/*/SYMBOL">
  <strong><xsl:value-of select="."/></strong>
</xsl:template>
```

Finally, as you saw above, a / by itself selects the root node of the document. For example, this rule applies to all PERIODIC_TABLE elements that are root elements of the document:

```
<xsl:template match="/PERIODIC_TABLE">
  <html><xsl:apply-templates/></html>
</xsl:template>
```

While / refers to the root node, /* refers to the root element, whatever it is. For example, this template doesn't care whether the root element is PERIODIC_TABLE, DOCUMENT, or SCHENECTADY. It produces the same output in all cases.

```
<xsl:template match="/*">
  <html>
    <head>
      <title>Atomic Number vs. Atomic Weight</title>
    </head>
    <body>
      <xsl:apply-templates/>
    </body>
  </html>
</xsl:template>
```

Matching descendants with //

Sometimes, especially with an uneven hierarchy, you may find it easier to bypass intermediate nodes and simply select all the elements of a given type, whether they're immediate children, grandchildren, great-grandchildren, or what have you. The double slash, //, refers to a descendant element at an arbitrary level. For example, this template rule applies to all `NAME` descendants of `PERIODIC_TABLE`, no matter how deep:

```
<xsl:template match="PERIODIC_TABLE//NAME">
  <i><xsl:value-of select="."/></i>
</xsl:template>
```

The periodic table example is fairly shallow, but this trick becomes more important in deeper hierarchies, especially when an element can contain other elements of its type (for example, an `ATOM` contains an `ATOM`).

The `//` operator at the beginning of a pattern selects any descendant of the root node. For example, this template rule processes all `ATOMIC_NUMBER` elements while completely ignoring their location:

```
<xsl:template match="//ATOMIC_NUMBER">
  <i><xsl:value-of select="."/></i>
</xsl:template>
```

Matching by ID

You may want to apply a particular style to a particular single element without changing all other elements of that type. The simplest way to do this in XSLT is to attach a style to the element's ID type attribute. This is done with the `id()` selector, which contains the ID value in single quotes. For example, this rule makes the element with the ID `e47` bold:

```
<xsl:template match="id('e47')">
  <b><xsl:value-of select="."/></b>
</xsl:template>
```

This assumes, of course, that the elements that you want to select in this fashion have an attribute declared as type `ID` in the source document's DTD. This may not be the case, however. For one thing, many documents do not have DTDs. They're merely well-formed, not valid. And even if they have a DTD, there's no guarantee that any element has an `ID` type attribute.

Cross-Reference ID-type attributes are not simply attributes with the name `ID`. ID type attributes are discussed in Chapter 11.

Matching attributes with @

As you saw in Chapter 5, the @ sign matches against attributes and selects nodes according to attribute names. Simply prefix the name of the attribute that you want to select with the @ sign. For example, this template rule matches `UNITS` attributes, and wraps them in an `I` element.

```
<xsl:template match="@UNITS">
  <I><xsl:value-of select="."/></I>
</xsl:template>
```

However, merely adding this rule to the style sheet will not automatically produce italicized units in the output because attributes are not children of the elements that contain them. Therefore by default when an XSLT processor is walking the tree it does not see attribute nodes. You have to explicitly process them using `xsl:apply-templates` with an appropriate `select` attribute. Listing 18-8 demonstrates with a style sheet that outputs a table of atomic numbers versus melting points. Not only is the value of the `MELTING_POINT` element written out, so is the value of its `UNITS` attribute. This is selected by `<xsl:apply-templates-of select="@UNITS"/>` in the template rule for `MELTING_POINT` elements.

Listing 18-8: An XSLT style sheet that selects the UNITS attribute with @

```
<?xml version="1.0"?>
<xsl:stylesheet version="1.0"
  xmlns:xsl="http://www.w3.org/1999/XSL/Transform">

    <xsl:template match="/PERIODIC_TABLE">
      <html>
        <body>
          <h1>Atomic Number vs. Melting Point</h1>
          <table>
            <th>Element</th>
            <th>Atomic Number</th>
            <th>Melting Point</th>
            <xsl:apply-templates/>
          </table>
        </body>
      </html>
    </xsl:template>

    <xsl:template match="ATOM">
      <tr>
        <td><xsl:value-of select="NAME"/></td>
        <td><xsl:value-of select="ATOMIC_NUMBER"/></td>
        <td><xsl:apply-templates select="MELTING_POINT"/></td>
      </tr>
    </xsl:template>

    <xsl:template match="MELTING_POINT">
      <xsl:value-of select="."/>
      <xsl:apply-templates select="@UNITS"/>
    </xsl:template>

    <xsl:template match="@UNITS">
      <I><xsl:value-of select="."/></I>
```

```
        </xsl:template>

    </xsl:stylesheet>
```

Recall that the value of an attribute node is simply the normalized string value of the attribute. Once you apply the style sheet in Listing 18-8, ATOM elements come out formatted like this:

```
    <tr>
<td>Hydrogen</td><td>1</td><td>13.81<I>Kelvin</I></td>
    </tr>

    <tr>
<td>Helium</td><td>2</td><td>0.95<I>Kelvin</I></td>
    </tr>
```

You can combine attributes with elements using the various hierarchy operators. For example, the pattern BOILING_POINT/@UNITS refers to the UNITS attribute of a BOILING_POINT element. ATOM/*/@UNITS matches any UNITS attribute of a child element of an ATOM element. This is especially helpful when matching against attributes in template rules. You must remember that what's being matched is the attribute node, not the element that contains it. It's a very common mistake to implicitly confuse the attribute node with the element node that contains it. For example, consider this rule, which attempts to apply templates to all child elements that have UNITS attributes:

```
<xsl:template match="ATOM">
  <xsl:apply-templates select="@UNITS"/>
</xsl:template>
```

What it actually does is apply templates to the nonexistent UNITS attributes of ATOM elements.

You can also use the @* wild card to match all attributes of an element, for example BOILING_POINT/@* to match all attributes of BOILING_POINT elements. You can also add a namespace prefix after the @ to match all attributes in a declared namespace. For instance, @xlink:* matches all the XLink attributes, such as xlink:show, xlink:type, and xlink:href, assuming the xlink prefix is mapped to the http://www.w3.org/1999/xlink XLink namespace URI.

Matching comments with comment()

Most of the time you should simply ignore comments in XML documents. Making comments an essential part of a document is a very bad idea. Nonetheless, XSLT does provide a means to match a comment if you absolutely have to.

To match a comment, use the `comment()` pattern. Although this pattern has function-like parentheses, it never actually takes any arguments. For example, this template rule italicizes all comments:

```
<xsl:template match="comment()">
  <i><xsl:value-of select="."/></i>
</xsl:template>
```

To distinguish between different comments, you have to look at the comments' parent and ancestors. For example, recall that a `DENSITY` element looks like this:

```
<DENSITY UNITS="grams/cubic centimeter">
  <!-- At 300K, 1 atm -->
  0.0000899
</DENSITY>
```

You can use the hierarchy operators to select particular comments. For example, this rule only matches comments that occur inside `DENSITY` elements:

```
<xsl:template match="DENSITY/comment()">
  <i><xsl:value-of select="."/></i>
</xsl:template>
```

The only reason Listing 18-1 uses a comment to specify conditions instead of an attribute or element is precisely for this example. In practice, you should never put important information in comments. The real reason XSLT allows you to select comments is so that a style sheet can transform from one XML application to another while leaving the comments intact. Any other use indicates a poorly designed original document. The following rule matches all comments, and copies them back out again using the `xsl:comment` element.

```
<xsl:template match="comment()">
  <xsl:comment><xsl:value-of select="."/></xsl:comment>
</xsl:template>
```

Matching processing instructions with processing-instruction()

When it comes to writing structured, intelligible, maintainable XML, processing instructions aren't much better than comments. However, there are occasional genuine needs for them, including attaching style sheets to documents.

The `processing-instruction()` function matches processing instructions. The argument to `processing-instruction()` is a quoted string giving the target of the processing instruction to select. If you do not include an argument, all processing instructions are matched. For example, this rule matches the processing instruction children of the root node (most likely the `xml-stylesheet` processing instruction). The `xsl:processing-instruction` element inserts a processing instruction with the specified name and value in the output document.

```
<xsl:template match="/processing-instruction()">
  <xsl:processing-instruction name="xml-stylesheet">
    type="text/xml" value="auto.xsl"
  </xsl:processing-instruction>
</xsl:template>
```

This rule also matches the `xml-stylesheet` processing instruction, but by its name:

```
<xsl:template
  match="processing-instruction('xml-stylesheet')">
  <xsl:processing-instruction name="xml-stylesheet">
    <xsl:value-of select="."/>
  </xsl:processing-instruction>
</xsl:template>
```

In fact, one of the primary reasons for distinguishing between the root element and the root node is so that processing instructions from the prolog can be read and processed. Although the `xml-stylesheet` processing instruction uses a name = value syntax, XSL does not consider these to be attributes because processing instructions are not elements. The value of a processing instruction is simply everything between the white space following its name and the closing `?>`.

Matching text nodes with text()

Text nodes are generally ignored as nodes, although their values are included as part of the value of a selected element. However, the `text()` operator does enable you to specifically select the text child of an element. Despite the parentheses, this operator takes no arguments. For example, this rule emboldens all text:

```
<xsl:template match="text()">
  <b><xsl:value-of select="."/></b>
</xsl:template>
```

The main reason this operator exists is for the default rules. XSLT processors must provide the following default rule whether the author specifies it or not:

```
<xsl:template match="text()">
  <xsl:value-of select="."/>
</xsl:template>
```

This means that whenever a template is applied to a text node, the text of the node is output. If you do not want the default behavior, you can override it. For example, including the following empty template rule in your style sheet will prevent text nodes from being output unless specifically matched by another rule.

```
<xsl:template match="text()">
</xsl:template>
```

Using the or operator |

The vertical bar (|) allows a template rule to match multiple patterns. If a node matches one pattern or the other, it will activate the template. For example, this template rule matches both `ATOMIC_NUMBER` and `ATOMIC_WEIGHT` elements:

```
<xsl:template match="ATOMIC_NUMBER|ATOMIC_WEIGHT">
  <B><xsl:apply-templates/></B>
</xsl:template>
```

You can include white space around the | if that makes the code clearer. For example,

```
<xsl:template match="ATOMIC_NUMBER | ATOMIC_WEIGHT">
  <B><xsl:apply-templates/></B>
</xsl:template>
```

You can also use more than two patterns in sequence. For example, this template rule applies to `ATOMIC_NUMBER`, `ATOMIC_WEIGHT`, and `SYMBOL` elements (that is, it matches `ATOMIC_NUMBER`, `ATOMIC_WEIGHT` and `SYMBOL` elements):

```
<xsl:template match="ATOMIC_NUMBER | ATOMIC_WEIGHT | SYMBOL">
  <B><xsl:apply-templates/></B>
</xsl:template>
```

The / operator is evaluated before the | operator. Thus, the following template rule matches an `ATOMIC_NUMBER` child of an `ATOM`, or an `ATOMIC_WEIGHT` of unspecified parentage, not an `ATOMIC_NUMBER` child of an `ATOM` or an `ATOMIC_WEIGHT` child of an `ATOM`.

```
<xsl:template match="ATOM/ATOMIC_NUMBER|ATOMIC_WEIGHT">
  <B><xsl:apply-templates/></B>
</xsl:template>
```

Testing with [ ]

So far, I've merely tested for the presence of various nodes. However, you can test for more details about the nodes that match a pattern using [ ]. You can perform many different tests including:

- ✦ Whether an element contains a given child, attribute, or other node
- ✦ Whether the value of an attribute is a certain string
- ✦ Whether the value of an element contains a string
- ✦ What position a given node occupies in the hierarchy

For example, seaborgium, element 106, has only been created in microscopic quantities. Even its most long-lived isotope has a half-life of only 30 seconds. With such a hard-to-create, short-lived element, it's virtually impossible to measure the density, melting point, and other bulk properties. Consequently, the periodic table document omits the elements describing the bulk properties of seaborgium and similar atoms because the data simply doesn't exist. If you want to create a table of atomic number versus melting point, you should omit those elements with unknown melting points. To do this, you can provide one template for ATOM elements that have MELTING_POINT children and another one for elements that don't, like this:

```
<!-- Include nothing for arbitrary atoms -->
<xsl:template match="ATOM" />

<!-- Include a table row for atoms that do have
     melting points. This rule will override the
     previous one for those atoms that do have
     melting points. -->
<xsl:template match="ATOM[MELTING_POINT]">
  <tr>
    <td><xsl:value-of select="NAME"/></td>
    <td><xsl:value-of select="MELTING_POINT"/></td>
  </tr>
</xsl:template>
```

Note here, that it is the ATOM element being matched, not the MELTING_POINT element as in the case of ATOM/MELTING_POINT.

The test brackets can contain more than simply a child-element name. In fact, they can contain any XPath expression. (XPath expressions are a superset of match patterns that are discussed in the next section.) If the specified element has a child matching that expression, it is considered to match the total pattern. For example, this template rule matches ATOM elements with NAME or SYMBOL children.

```
<xsl:template match="ATOM[NAME | SYMBOL]">
</xsl:template>
```

This template rule matches ATOM elements with a DENSITY child element that has a UNITS attribute:

```
<xsl:template match="ATOM[DENSITY/@UNITS]">
</xsl:template>
```

To revisit an earlier example, to correctly find all child elements that have UNITS attributes, use * to find all elements and [@UNITS] to winnow those down to the ones with UNITS attributes, like this:

```
<xsl:template match="ATOM">
  <xsl:apply-templates select="*[@UNITS]"/>
</xsl:template>
```

One type of pattern testing that proves especially useful is string equality. An equals sign (=) can test whether the value of a node identically matches a given string. For example, this template finds the ATOM element that contains an ATOMIC_NUMBER element whose content is the string 10 (Neon).

```
<xsl:template match="ATOM[ATOMIC_NUMBER='10']">
  This is Neon!
</xsl:template>
```

Testing against element content may seem extremely tricky because of the need to get the value exactly right, including white space. You may find it easier to test against attribute values since those are less likely to contain insignificant white space. For example, the style sheet in Listing 18-9 applies templates only to those ATOM elements whose STATE attribute value is the three letters GAS.

Listing 18-9: An XSLT style sheet that selects only those ATOM elements whose STATE attribute has the value GAS

```
<?xml version="1.0"?>
<xsl:stylesheet version="1.0"
  xmlns:xsl="http://www.w3.org/1999/XSL/Transform">

  <xsl:template match="PERIODIC_TABLE">
    <html>
      <head><title>Gases</title></head>
      <body>
        <xsl:apply-templates/>
      </body>
    </html>
  </xsl:template>

  <xsl:template match="ATOM"/>

  <xsl:template match="ATOM[@STATE='GAS']">
    <P><xsl:value-of select="."/></P>
  </xsl:template>

</xsl:stylesheet>
```

You can use other XPath expressions for more complex matches. For example, you can select all elements whose names begin with "A" or all elements with an atomic number less than 100.

XPath Expressions for Selecting Nodes

The select attribute is used in xsl:apply-templates, xsl:value-of, xsl:for-each, xsl:copy-of, xsl:variable, xsl:param, and xsl:sort to specify exactly which nodes are operated on. The value of this attribute is an *expression* written in the XPath language. The XPath language provides a means of identifying a particular element, group of elements, text fragment, or other part of an XML document. The XPath syntax is used both for XSLT and XPointer.

Cross-Reference   XPointers are discussed in Chapter 21. XPath is discussed further in that chapter as well.

Expressions are a superset of the match patterns discussed in the last section. That is, all match patterns are expressions, but not all expressions are match patterns. Recall that match patterns enable you to match nodes by element name, child elements, descendants, and attributes, as well as by making simple tests on these items. XPath expressions allow you to select nodes through all these criteria but also by referring to ancestor nodes, parent nodes, sibling nodes, preceding nodes, and following nodes. Furthermore, expressions aren't limited to producing merely a list of nodes, but can also produce booleans, numbers, and strings.

Node axes

Expressions are not limited to specifying the children and descendants of the current node. XPath provides a number of axes that you can use to select from different parts of the tree relative to some particular node in the tree called the context node. In XSLT, the context node is normally initialized to the current node that the template matches, though there are ways to change this. Table 18-2 summarizes the axes and their meanings.

Table 18-2 Expression Axes	
Axis	**Selects From**
ancestor	The parent of the context node, the parent of the parent of the context node, the parent of the parent of the parent of the context node, and so forth back to the root node
ancestor-or-self	The ancestors of the context node and the context node itself
attribute	The attributes of the context node
child	The immediate children of the context node
descendant	The children of the context node, the children of the children of the context node, and so forth
descendant-or-self	The context node itself and its descendants
following	All nodes that start after the end of the context node, excluding attribute and namespace nodes
following-sibling	All nodes that start after the end of the context node and have the same parent as the context node

Axis	Selects From
namespace	The namespace of the context node
parent	The unique parent node of the context node
preceding	All nodes that finish before the beginning of the context node, excluding attribute and namespace nodes
preceding-sibling	All nodes that start before the beginning of the context node and have the same parent as the context node
self	The context node

Choosing an axis limits the expression so that it only selects from the set of nodes indicated in the second column of Table 18-2. The axis is generally followed by a double colon (::) and a node test that further winnows down this node set. For example, a node test may contain the name of the element to be selected as in the following template rule:

```
<xsl:template match="ATOM">
  <tr>
    <td>
      <xsl:value-of select="child::NAME"/>
    </td>
    <td>
      <xsl:value-of select="child::ATOMIC_NUMBER"/>
    </td>
    <td>
      <xsl:value-of select="child::ATOMIC_WEIGHT"/>
    </td>
  </tr>
</xsl:template>
```

The template rule matches ATOM elements. When an ATOM element is matched, that element becomes the context node. A NAME element, an ATOMIC_NUMBER element, and an ATOMIC_WEIGHT element are all selected from the children of that matched ATOM element and output as table cells. (If there's one more than one of these desired elements — for example, three NAME elements — then all are selected but only the value of the first one is taken.)

The child axis doesn't let you do anything that you can't do with element names alone. In fact select="ATOMIC_WEIGHT" is just an abbreviated form of select="child::ATOMIC_WEIGHT". However, the other axes are a little more interesting.

Referring to the parent element is illegal in match patterns, but not in expressions. To refer to the parent, you use the parent axis. For example, this template matches BOILING_POINT elements but outputs the value of the parent ATOM element:

```
<xsl:template match="BOILING_POINT">
  <P><xsl:value-of select="parent::ATOM"/></P>
</xsl:template>
```

Some radioactive atoms such as polonium have half-lives so short that bulk properties such as the boiling point and melting point can't be measured. Therefore, not all ATOM elements necessarily have BOILING_POINT child elements. The above rule enables you to write a template that only outputs those elements that actually have boiling points. Expanding on this example, Listing 18-10 matches the MELTING_POINT elements but actually outputs the parent ATOM element using parent::ATOM.

Listing 18-10: **A style sheet that outputs only those elements with known melting points**

```
<?xml version="1.0"?>
<xsl:stylesheet version="1.0"
  xmlns:xsl="http://www.w3.org/1999/XSL/Transform">

    <xsl:template match="/">
      <html>
        <body>
          <xsl:apply-templates select="PERIODIC_TABLE"/>
        </body>
      </html>
    </xsl:template>

    <xsl:template match="PERIODIC_TABLE">
      <h1>Elements with known Melting Points</h1>
      <xsl:apply-templates select=".//MELTING_POINT"/>
    </xsl:template>

    <xsl:template match="MELTING_POINT">
      <p>
        <xsl:value-of select="parent::ATOM"/>
      </p>
    </xsl:template>

</xsl:stylesheet>
```

Once in a while, you may need to select the nearest ancestor of an element with a given type. The ancestor axis does this. For example, this rule inserts the value of the nearest PERIODIC_TABLE element that contains the matched SYMBOL element.

```
<xsl:template match="SYMBOL">
  <xsl:value-of select="ancestor::PERIODIC_TABLE"/>
</xsl:template>
```

The `ancestor-or-self` **axis** behaves like the `ancestor` axis except that if the context node passes the node test, then it will be returned as well. For example, this rule matches all elements. If the matched element is a `PERIODIC_TABLE`, then that very `PERIODIC_TABLE` is selected in `xsl:value-of`.

```
<xsl:template match="*">
  <xsl:value-of select="ancestor-or-self::PERIODIC_TABLE"/>
</xsl:template>
```

Node tests

Instead of the name of a node, the axis may be followed by one of these four node-type functions:

✦ `comment()`

✦ `text()`

✦ `processing-instruction()`

✦ `node()`

The `comment()` function selects a comment node. The `text()` function selects a text node. The `processing-instruction()` function selects a processing instruction node, and the `node()` function selects any type of node. (The * wild card only selects element nodes.) The `processing-instruction()` node type can also contain an optional argument specifying the name of the processing instruction to select.

Hierarchy operators

You can use the / and // operators to string expressions together. For example, Listing 18-11 prints a table of element names, atomic numbers, and melting points for only those elements that have melting points. It does this by selecting the parent of the `MELTING_POINT` element, then finding that parent's `NAME` and `ATOMIC_NUMBER` children with `select="parent::*/child::NAME)"`.

Listing 18-11: **A table of melting point versus atomic number**

```
<?xml version="1.0"?>
<xsl:stylesheet version="1.0"
  xmlns:xsl="http://www.w3.org/1999/XSL/Transform">

    <xsl:template match="/PERIODIC_TABLE">
      <html>
        <body>
          <h1>Atomic Number vs. Melting Point</h1>
          <table>
            <th>Element</th>
```

Continued

Listing 18-11 *(continued)*

```
            <th>Atomic Number</th>
            <th>Melting Point</th>
            <xsl:apply-templates select="child::ATOM"/>
          </table>
        </body>
      </html>
    </xsl:template>

    <xsl:template match="ATOM">
      <xsl:apply-templates
        select="child::MELTING_POINT"/>
    </xsl:template>

    <xsl:template match="MELTING_POINT">
        <tr>
         <td>
           <xsl:value-of select="parent::*/child::NAME"/>
         </td>
         <td>
           <xsl:value-of
          select="parent::*/child::ATOMIC_NUMBER"/>
         </td>
         <td>
           <xsl:value-of select="self::*"/>
           <xsl:value-of select="attribute::UNITS"/>
         </td>
        </tr>
    </xsl:template>

  </xsl:stylesheet>
```

This is not the only way to solve the problem. Another possibility is to use the preceding-sibling and following-sibling axes, or both if the relative location (preceding or following) is uncertain. The necessary template rule for the MELTING_POINT element looks like this:

```
  <xsl:template match="MELTING_POINT">
    <tr>
     <td>
       <xsl:value-of
        select="preceding-sibling::NAME
              | following-sibling::NAME"/>
     </td>
     <td>
       <xsl:value-of
        select="preceding-sibling::ATOMIC_NUMBER
              | following-sibling::ATOMIC_NUMBER"/>
```

```
      </td>
      <td>
        <xsl:value-of select="self::*"/>
        <xsl:value-of select="attribute::UNITS"/>
      </td>
    </tr>
</xsl:template>
```

Abbreviated syntax

The various axes in Table 18-2 are a bit too wordy for comfortable typing. XPath also defines an abbreviated syntax that can substitute for the most common of these axes and is more used in practice. Table 18-3 shows the full and abbreviated equivalents.

Table 18-3
Abbreviated Syntax for XPath Expressions

Abbreviation	Full
.	self::node()
..	parent::node()
name	child::name
@name	attribute::name
//	/descendant-or-self::node()/

Listing 18-12 demonstrates by rewriting Listing 18-11 using the abbreviated syntax. The output produced by the two style sheets is exactly the same, however.

Listing 18-12: A table of melting point versus atomic number using the abbreviated syntax

```
<?xml version="1.0"?>
<xsl:stylesheet version="1.0"
  xmlns:xsl="http://www.w3.org/1999/XSL/Transform">

    <xsl:template match="/PERIODIC_TABLE">
      <html>
        <body>
          <h1>Atomic Number vs. Melting Point</h1>
          <table>
            <th>Element</th>
```

Continued

Listing 18-12 *(continued)*

```
            <th>Atomic Number</th>
            <th>Melting Point</th>
            <xsl:apply-templates select="ATOM"/>
          </table>
        </body>
      </html>
    </xsl:template>

    <xsl:template match="ATOM">
      <xsl:apply-templates
        select="MELTING_POINT"/>
    </xsl:template>

    <xsl:template match="MELTING_POINT">
        <tr>
          <td>
            <xsl:value-of
              select="../NAME"/>
          </td>
          <td>
            <xsl:value-of
            select="../ATOMIC_NUMBER"/>
          </td>
          <td>
            <xsl:value-of select="."/>
            <xsl:value-of select="@UNITS"/>
          </td>
        </tr>
    </xsl:template>

</xsl:stylesheet>
```

Match patterns can only use the abbreviated syntax and the `child` and `attribute` axes. The full syntax using the axes of Table 18-2 is restricted to expressions.

Expression types

Every expression evaluates to a single value. For example, the expression $3 + 2$ evaluates to the value 5. The expressions used so far have all evaluated to node sets. However, there are five types of expressions in XSLT:

✦ Node sets

✦ Booleans

✦ Numbers

✦ Strings

✦ Result tree fragments

Node sets

A node set is an unordered group of nodes from the input document. The axes in Table 18-2 all return a node set containing the nodes they match. Which nodes are in the node set depends on the context node, the node test, and the axis.

For example, when the context node is the `PERIODIC_TABLE` element of Listing 18-1, the XPath expression `select="child::ATOM"` returns a node set that contains both `ATOM` elements in that document. The XPath expression `select="child::ATOM/child::NAME"` returns a node set containing the two element nodes `<NAME>Hydrogen</NAME>` and `<NAME>Helium</NAME>` when the context node is the `PERIODIC_TABLE` element of Listing 18-1.

The context node is a member of the *context node list*. The context node list is that group of elements that all match the same rule at the same time, generally as a result of one `xsl:apply-templates` or `xsl:for-each` call. For instance, when Listing 18-12 is applied to Listing 18-1, the `ATOM` template is invoked twice, first for the hydrogen atom, then for the helium atom. The first time it's invoked, the context node is the hydrogen `ATOM` element. The second time it's invoked, the context node is the helium `ATOM` element. However, both times the context node list is the set containing both the helium and hydrogen `ATOM` elements.

Table 18-4 lists a number of functions that operate on node sets, either as arguments or as the context node.

Table 18-4
Functions That Operate on or Return Node Sets

Function	Return Type	Returns
`position()`	number	The position of the context node in the context node list; the first node in the list has position 1.
`last()`	number	The number of nodes in the context node list; this is the same as the position of the last node in the list.
`count(node-set)`	number	The number of nodes in `node-set`.
`id(string1 string2 string3...)`	node set	A node set containing all the elements anywhere in the same document that have an ID named in the argument list; the empty set if no element has the specified ID.

Continued

Table 18-4 *(continued)*		
Function	**Return Type**	**Returns**
key(*string name*, *Object value*)	node set	A node set containing all nodes in this document that have a key with the specified value. Keys are set with the top-level xsl:key element.
document(*string URI*, *string base*)	node set	A node set in the document referred to by the URI; the nodes are chosen from the named anchor or XPointer used by the URI. If there is no named anchor or XPointer, then the root element of the named document is the node set. Relative URIs are relative to the base URI given in the second argument. If the second argument is omitted, then relative URIs are relative to the URI of the style sheet (not the source document!).
local-name(*node-set*)	string	The local name (everything after the namespace prefix) of the first node in the *node set* argument; can be used without any arguments to get the local name of the context node.
namespace-uri(*node-set*)	string	The URI of the namespace of the first node in the node set; can be used without any arguments to get the URI of the namespace of the context node; returns an empty string if the node is not in a namespace.
name(*node-set*)	string	The qualified name (both prefix and local part) of the first node in the *node set* argument; can be used without an argument to get the qualified name of the context node.
generate-id(*node-set*)	string	A unique identifier for the first node in the argument *node set*; can be used without any argument to generate an ID for the context node.

If an argument of the wrong type is passed to one of these functions, then XSLT will attempt to convert that argument to the correct type; for instance, by converting the number 12 to the string "12". However, no arguments may be converted to node sets.

The position() function can be used to determine an element's position within a node set. Listing 18-13 is a style sheet that prefixes the name of each atom's name with its position in the document using <xsl:value-of select="position()"/>.

Listing 18-13: A style sheet that numbers the atoms in the order they appear in the document

```
<?xml version="1.0"?>
<xsl:stylesheet version="1.0"
  xmlns:xsl="http://www.w3.org/1999/XSL/Transform">

  <xsl:template match="/PERIODIC_TABLE">
    <HTML>
      <HEAD><TITLE>The Elements</TITLE></HEAD>
      <BODY>
        <xsl:apply-templates select="ATOM"/>
      </BODY>
    </HTML>
  </xsl:template>

  <xsl:template match="ATOM">
    <P>
      <xsl:value-of select="position()"/>.
      <xsl:value-of select="NAME"/>
    </P>
  </xsl:template>

</xsl:stylesheet>
```

When this style sheet is applied to Listing 18-1, the output is this:

```
<HTML>
<HEAD>
<TITLE>The Elements</TITLE>
</HEAD>
<BODY>
<P>1.
     Hydrogen</P>
<P>2.
     Helium</P>
</BODY>
</HTML>
```

Booleans

A boolean has one of two values: true or false. XSLT allows any kind of data to be transformed into a boolean. This is often done implicitly when a string or a number or a node set is used where a boolean is expected, as in the `test` attribute of an `xsl:if` element. These conversions can also be performed by the `boolean()` function which converts an argument of any type to a boolean according to these rules:

✦ A number is false if it's zero or NaN (a special symbol meaning Not a Number, used for the result of dividing by zero and similar illegal operations); true otherwise.

✦ An empty node set is false. All other node sets are true.

✦ An empty result tree fragment is false. All other result tree fragments are true.

✦ A zero length string is false. All other strings are true.

Booleans are also produced as the result of expressions involving these operators:

✦ `=`   equal to

✦ `!=`   not equal to

✦ `<`   less than (really `&lt;`)

✦ `>`   greater than

✦ `<=`   less than or equal to (really `&lt;=`)

✦ `>=`   greater than or equal to

> **Caution**
>
> The `<` sign is illegal in attribute values. Consequently, it must be replaced by `&lt;` even when used as the less-than operator.

These operators are most commonly used in predicate tests to determine whether a rule should be invoked. An XPath expression can contain not only a pattern that selects certain nodes, but also a predicate that further filters the set of nodes selected. For example, `child::ATOM` selects all the `ATOM` children of the context node. However, `child::ATOM[position()=1]` selects only the first `ATOM` child of the context node. `[position()=1]` is a predicate on the node test `ATOM` that returns a boolean result: True if the position of the `ATOM` is equal to one; false otherwise. Each node test can have any number of predicates. However, more than one is unusual.

For example, this template rule applies to the first `ATOM` element in the periodic table, but not to subsequent ones, by testing whether or not the position of the element equals 1.

```
<xsl:template match="PERIODIC_TABLE/ATOM[position()=1]">
  <xsl:value-of select="."/>
</xsl:template>
```

This template rule applies to all `ATOM` elements that are not the first child element of the `PERIODIC_TABLE` by testing whether the position is greater than 1:

```
<xsl:template match="PERIODIC_TABLE/ATOM[position()>1]">
  <xsl:value-of select="."/>
</xsl:template>
```

The keywords and and or logically combine two boolean expressions according to the normal rules of logic. For example, suppose you want a template that matches an ATOMIC_NUMBER element that is both the first and last child of its parent element; that is, it is the only element of its parent. This template rule uses and to accomplish that:

```
<xsl:template
 match="ATOMIC_NUMBER[position()=1 and position()=last()]">
  <xsl:value-of select="."/>
</xsl:template>
```

If the first condition is false, then the complete and expression is guaranteed to be false. Consequently, the second condition won't be checked.

This template matches both the first and last ATOM elements in their parent by matching when the position is 1 or when the position is equal to the number of elements in the set:

```
<xsl:template match="ATOM[position()=1 or position()=last()]">
  <xsl:value-of select="."/>
</xsl:template>
```

This is logical or, so it will also match if both conditions are true. That is, it will match an ATOM that is both the first and last child of its parent. If the first condition is true, then the complete or expression is guaranteed to be true. Consequently, the second condition won't be checked.

The not() function reverses the result of an operation. For example, this template rule matches all ATOM elements that are not the first child of their parents:

```
<xsl:template match="ATOM[not(position()=1)]">
  <xsl:value-of select="."/>
</xsl:template>
```

The same template rule could be written using the not equal operator != instead:

```
<xsl:template match="ATOM[position()!=1]">
  <xsl:value-of select="."/>
</xsl:template>
```

This template rule matches all ATOM elements that are neither the first nor last ATOM child of their parent:

```
<xsl:template match =
 "ATOM[not(position()=1 or position()=last())]">
  <xsl:value-of select="."/>
</xsl:template>
```

XSLT does not have an exclusive or operator. However, one can be formed by judicious use of not(), and, and or. For example, this rule selects those ATOM elements that are either the first or last child, but not both:

```
<xsl:template
 match="ATOM[(position()=1 or position()=last())
                and not(position()=1 and position()=last())]">
  <xsl:value-of select="."/>
</xsl:template>
```

There are three remaining functions that return booleans:

✦ true() always returns true

✦ false() always returns false

✦ lang(*code*) returns true if the current node has the same language (as given by the xml:lang attribute) as the *code* argument

Numbers

XPath numbers are 64-bit IEEE 754 floating-point doubles. Even numbers like 42 or -7000 that look like integers are stored as doubles. Nonnumber values such as strings and booleans are converted to numbers automatically as necessary, or at user request through the number() function using these rules:

✦ Booleans are 1 if true; 0 if false.

✦ A string is trimmed of leading and trailing white space, then converted to a number in the fashion you would expect; for example, the string "12" is converted to the number 12. If the string cannot be interpreted as a number, then it is converted to the special symbol NaN, which stands for Not a Number.

✦ Node sets and result tree fragments are converted to strings; the string is then converted to a number.

For example, this template only outputs the nonnaturally occurring transuranium elements; that is, those elements with atomic numbers greater than 92 (the atomic number of uranium). The node set produced by ATOMIC_NUMBER is implicitly converted to the string value of the current ATOMIC_NUMBER node. This string is then converted into a number.

```
<xsl:template match="/PERIODIC_TABLE">
  <HTML>
    <HEAD><TITLE>The Transuranium Elements</TITLE></HEAD>
    <BODY>
      <xsl:apply-templates select="ATOM[ATOMIC_NUMBER>92]"/>
    </BODY>
  </HTML>
</xsl:template>
```

XPath provides the standard four arithmetic operators:

- ✦ + for addition
- ✦ - for subtraction
- ✦ * for multiplication
- ✦ div for division (the more common / is already used for other purposes in XPath)

For example, `<xsl:value-of select="2+2"/>` inserts the string "4" into the output document. These operations are more commonly used as part of a test. For example, this rule selects those elements whose atomic weight is more than twice their atomic number:

```
<xsl:template match="/PERIODIC_TABLE">
  <HTML>
    <BODY>
      <H1>High Atomic Weight to Atomic Number Ratios</H1>
      <xsl:apply-templates
        select="ATOM[ATOMIC_WEIGHT > 2 * ATOMIC_NUMBER]"/>
    </BODY>
  </HTML>
</xsl:template>
```

This template actually prints the ratio of atomic weight to atomic number:

```
<xsl:template match="ATOM">
  <p>
    <xsl:value-of select="NAME"/>
    <xsl:value-of select="ATOMIC_WEIGHT div ATOMIC_NUMBER"/>
  </p>
</xsl:template>
```

XPath also provides the less-familiar mod binary operator, which takes the remainder of two numbers. When used in conjunction with position() this operator lets you perform tasks such as outputting every second ATOM or alternating colors between rows in a table. Just define templates that apply different styles when the position mod two is one and when it's zero. For example, these two rules use different colors for alternate rows of a table:

```
<xsl:template match="ATOM[position() mod 2 = 1]">
    <tr>
      <td><xsl:value-of select="NAME"/></td>
      <td><xsl:value-of select="ATOMIC_NUMBER"/></td>
      <td><xsl:apply-templates select="MELTING_POINT"/></td>
    </tr>
</xsl:template>

<xsl:template match="ATOM[position() mod 2 = 0]">
    <tr style="color: #666666">
```

```
            <td><xsl:value-of select="NAME"/></td>
            <td><xsl:value-of select="ATOMIC_NUMBER"/></td>
            <td><xsl:apply-templates select="MELTING_POINT"/></td>
          </tr>
      </xsl:template>
```

You can change the divisor to 3 to apply different styles to every third element, to 4 to apply different styles to every fourth element, and so forth.

Finally, XPath includes four functions that operate on numbers:

✦ `floor()` returns the greatest integer less than or equal to the number

✦ `ceiling()` returns the smallest integer greater than or equal to the number

✦ `round()` rounds the number to the nearest integer

✦ `sum()` returns the sum of its arguments

For example, this template rule estimates the number of neutrons in an atom by subtracting the atomic number (the number of protons) from the atomic weight (the weighted average over the natural distribution of isotopes of the number of neutrons plus the number of protons) and rounding to the nearest integer:

```
<xsl:template match="ATOM">
  <p>
    <xsl:value-of select="NAME"/>
    <xsl:value-of
      select="round(ATOMIC_WEIGHT - ATOMIC_NUMBER)"/>
  </p>
</xsl:template>
```

This rule calculates the average atomic weight of all the atoms in the table by adding all the atomic weights, and then dividing by the number of atoms:

```
<xsl:template match="/PERIODIC_TABLE">
  <HTML>
    <BODY>
    <H1>Average Atomic Weight</H1>
      <xsl:value-of
        select="sum(descendant::ATOMIC_WEIGHT)
                div count(descendant::ATOMIC_WEIGHT)"/>
    </BODY>
  </HTML>
</xsl:template>
```

Strings

A string is a sequence of Unicode characters. Other data types can be converted to strings using the `string()` function according to these rules:

✦ Node sets are converted to strings by using the value of the first node in the set as calculated by the xsl:value-of element according to the rules given in Table 18-1.

✦ Result tree fragments are converted by acting as if they're contained in a single element, and then taking the value of that imaginary element. Again, the value of this element is calculated by the xsl:value-of element according to the rules given in Table 18-1. That is, all the result tree fragment's text (but not markup) is concatenated.

✦ A number is converted to a European-style number string like -12 or 3.1415292.

✦ Boolean false is converted to the English word false. Boolean true is converted to the English word true.

Besides string(), XSLT contains 10 functions that manipulate strings. These are summarized in Table 18-5.

Table 18-5 XPath String Functions		
Function	**Return Type**	**Returns**
starts-with(*main_string*, *prefix_string*)	Boolean	True if *main_string* starts with *prefix_string*; false otherwise
contains(*containing_string*, *contained_string*)	Boolean	True if the *contained_string* is part of the *containing_string*; false otherwise
substring(*string*, *offset*, *length*)	String	*length* characters from the specified *offset* in *string*; or all characters from the *offset* to the end of the *string* if *length* is omitted; *length* and *offset* are rounded to the nearest integer if necessary
substring-before(*string*, *marker-string*)	String	The part of the *string* from the first character up to (but not including) the first occurrence of *marker-string*
substring-after(*string*, *marker-string*)	String	The part of the *string* from the end of the first occurrence of *marker-string* to the end of *string*; the first character in the string is at offset 1

Continued

Table 18-5 *(continued)*

Function	Return Type	Returns
`string-length(string)`	Number	The number of characters in *string*
`normalize-space(string)`	String	The *string* after leading and trailing white space is stripped and runs of white space are replaced with a single space; if the argument is omitted the string value of the context node is normalized
`translate(string, replaced_text, replacement_text)`	String	Returns *string* with occurrences of characters in *replaced_text* replaced by the corresponding characters from *replacement_text*
`concat(string1, string2, . . . )`	String	Returns the concatenation of as many strings as are passed as arguments in the order they were passed
`format-number(number, format-string, locale-string)`	String	Returns the string form of *number* formatted according to the specified *format-string* as if by Java 1.1's `java.text.DecimalFormat` class (see `http://java.sun.com/products/jdk/1.1/docs/api/java.text.DecimalFormat.html`); the *locale-string* is an optional argument that provides the name of the `xsl:decimal-format` element used to interpret the *format-string*

Result tree fragments

A result tree fragment is a portion of an XML document that is not a complete node or set of nodes. For instance, using the `document()` function with a URI that points into the middle of an element might produce a result tree fragment. Result tree fragments may also be returned by some extension functions (functions unique to a particular XSLT implementation or installation).

Because result tree fragments aren't well-formed XML, you can't do much with them. In fact, the only allowed operations are to convert them to a string or a boolean using `string()` and `boolean()`, respectively.

The Default Template Rules

Having to carefully map the hierarchy of an XML document in an XSLT style sheet may be inconvenient. This is especially true if the document does not follow a stable, predictable order like the periodic table, but rather throws elements together willy-nilly like many Web pages. In those cases, you should have general rules that can find an element and apply templates to it regardless of where it appears in the source document.

To make this process easier, XSLT defines several default template rules that are implicitly included in all style sheets. The first default rule matches root and element nodes, and applies templates to all child nodes. The second default rule matches text nodes and attributes, copying their values onto the output stream. Together these two rules mean that even a blank XSLT style sheet with just one empty `xsl:stylesheet` element will still produce the raw character data of the input XML document as output.

The default rule for elements

The first default rule applies to element nodes and the root node:

```
<xsl:template match="*|/">
  <xsl:apply-templates/>
</xsl:template>
```

`*|/` is XPath shorthand for "any element node or the root node." The purpose of this rule is to ensure that all elements are recursively processed even if they aren't reached by following the explicit rules. That is, unless another rule overrides this one (especially for the root element), all element nodes will be processed.

However, once an explicit rule for any parent of an element is present, this rule will not be activated for the child elements unless the template rule for the parent has an `xsl:apply-templates` child. For instance, you can stop all processing by matching the root element and neither applying templates nor using `xsl:for-each` to process the children like this:

```
<xsl:template match="/">
</xsl:template>
```

The default rule for text nodes and attributes

Exceptionally observant readers may have noted several of the examples seem to have output the contents of some elements without actually taking the value of the element they were outputting! These contents were provided by XSLT's default rule for text and attribute nodes. This rule is:

```
<xsl:template match="text()|@*">
  <xsl:value-of select="."/>
</xsl:template>
```

This rule matches all text and attribute nodes (match="text()|@*") and outputs the value of the node (<xsl:value-of select="."/>). In other words, it copies the text from the input to the output. This rule ensures that at the very least an element's text is output, even if no rule specifically matches it. Another rule can override this one for specific elements where you want either more or less than the text content of an element.

This rule also copies attribute values (but not names). However, they turn from attributes in the input to simple text in the output. Because there's no default rule that ever applies templates to attributes, this rule won't be activated for attributes unless you specifically add a nondefault rule somewhere in the style sheet that does apply templates to attributes of one or more elements.

The default rule for processing instructions and comments

There's also a default rule for processing instructions and comments. It simply says to do nothing; that is, drop the processing instructions and comments from the output as if they didn't exist. It looks like this:

```
<xsl:template match="processing-instruction()|comment()"/>
```

You can, of course, replace this with your own rule for handling processing instructions and comments if you want to.

Implications of the default rules

Together, the default rules imply that applying an empty style sheet with only an xsl:stylesheet or xsl:transform element but no children (such as Listing 18-14) to an XML document copies all the #PCDATA out of the elements in the input to the output. However, this method produces no markup. These are, however, extremely low priority rules. Consequently, any other matches take precedence over the default rules.

Listing 18-14: **An empty XML style sheet**

```
<?xml version="1.0"?>
<xsl:stylesheet version="1.0"
          xmlns:xsl="http://www.w3.org/1999/XSL/Transform">

</xsl:stylesheet>
```

Caution   One of the most common sources of confusion about XSLT in Internet Explorer 5.5 and earlier is that IE does not provide any of these default rules. You have to make sure that you explicitly match any node whose contents (including descendants) you want to output.

Deciding What Output to Include

It's often necessary to defer decisions about what markup to emit until the input document has been read. For instance, you may want to change the contents of a FILENAME element into the HREF attribute of an A element, or replace one element type in the input with several different element types in the output depending on the value of an attribute. This is accomplished with xsl:element, xsl:attribute, xsl:processing-instruction, xsl:comment, and xsl:text elements. XSLT instructions are used in the contents of these elements and attribute value templates are used in the attribute values of these elements to vary their output.

Attribute value templates

Attribute value templates copy data from the input document to attribute values in the output. For example, suppose you want to convert the periodic table into empty ATOM elements with this attribute-based form:

```
<ATOM NAME="Vanadium"
  ATOMIC_WEIGHT="50.9415"
  ATOMIC_NUMBER="23"
/>
```

To do this, you need to extract the contents of elements in the input document and place those in attribute values in the output document. The first thing you're likely to attempt is something similar to this:

```
<xsl:template match="ATOM">
  <ATOM NAME="<xsl:value-of select='NAME'/>"
    ATOMIC_WEIGHT="<xsl:value-of select='ATOMIC_WEIGHT'/>"
    ATOMIC_NUMBER="<xsl:value-of select='ATOMIC_NUMBER'/>"
  />
</xsl:template>
```

But this is malformed XML. You can't use the < character inside an attribute value. Furthermore, it's extremely difficult to write software that can parse this in its most general case.

Instead, inside attribute values, curly braces {} take the place of the `xsl:value-of` element. The correct way to write the above template is like this:

```
<xsl:template match="ATOM">
  <ATOM NAME="{NAME}"/>
    ATOMIC_WEIGHT="{ATOMIC_WEIGHT}"
    ATOMIC_NUMBER="{ATOMIC_NUMBER}"
  />
</xsl:template>
```

In the output, {NAME} is replaced by the value of the NAME child element of the matched ATOM. {ATOMIC_WEIGHT} is replaced by the value of the ATOMIC_WEIGHT child element of the matched ATOM. {ATOMIC_NUMBER} is replaced by the value of the ATOMIC_NUMBER child element, and so on.

Attribute value templates can have more complicated patterns than merely an element name. In fact, you can use any XPath expression in an attribute value template. For example, this template rule selects DENSITY elements in the form used in Listing 18-1.

```
<xsl:template match="DENSITY">
  <BULK_PROPERTY
    NAME="DENSITY"
    ATOM="{../NAME}"
    VALUE="{normalize-space(.)}"
    UNITS="{@UNITS}"
  />
</xsl:template>
```

It converts them into BULK_PROPERTY elements that look like this:

```
<BULK_PROPERTY NAME="DENSITY" ATOM="Helium"
  VALUE="0.0001785" UNITS="grams/cubic centimeter"/>
```

Attribute values are not limited to a single attribute value template. You can combine an attribute value template with literal data or with other attribute value templates. For example, this template rule matches ATOM elements and replaces them with their name formatted as a link to a file in the format H.html, He.html, and so on. The filename is derived from the attribute value template {SYMBOL}, while the literal data provides the period and extension.

```
<xsl:template match="ATOM">
  <A HREF="{SYMBOL}.html">
    <xsl:value-of select="NAME"/>
  </A>
</xsl:template>
```

More than one attribute value template can be included in an attribute value. For example, this template rule includes the density units as part of the `VALUE` attribute rather than making them a separate attribute:

```
<xsl:template match="DENSITY">
  <BULK_PROPERTY
    NAME="DENSITY"
    ATOM="{../NAME}"
    VALUE="{normalize-space(.)} {@UNITS}"
  />
</xsl:template>
```

You can use attribute value templates in many attributes in an XSLT style sheet. This is particularly important in `xsl:element`, `xsl:attribute`, and `xsl:processing-instruction` elements where attribute value templates allow the designer to defer the decision about exactly what element, attribute, or processing instruction appears in the output until the input document is read. You cannot use attribute value templates as the value of a `select` or `match` attribute, an `xmlns` attribute, an attribute that provides the name of another XSLT instruction element, or an attribute of a top-level element (one that's an immediate child of `xsl:stylesheet`).

Inserting elements into the output with xsl:element

Elements are usually included in the output document simply by including the literal start and end tags in template content. For instance, to insert a `P` element you merely type `<P>` and `</P>` at the appropriate points in the style sheet. However, occasionally you need to use details from the input document to determine which element to place in the output document. This might happen, for example, when making a transformation from a source vocabulary that uses attributes for information to an output vocabulary that uses elements for the same information.

The `xsl:element` element inserts an element into the output document. The name of the element is given by an attribute value template in the `name` attribute of `xsl:element`. The content of the element derives from the content of the `xsl:element` element, which may include `xsl:attribute`, `xsl:processing-instruction`, and `xsl:comment` instructions (all discussed below) to insert these items.

For example, suppose you want to replace the `ATOM` elements with `GAS`, `LIQUID`, and `SOLID` elements, depending on the value of the `STATE` attribute. Using `xsl:element`, a single rule can do this by converting the value of the `STATE` attribute to an element name. This is how it works:

```
<xsl:template match="ATOM">
  <xsl:element name="{@STATE}">
    <NAME><xsl:value-of select="NAME"/></NAME>
    <!-- rules for other children -->
  </xsl:element>
</xsl:template>
```

By using more complicated attribute value templates, you can perform most of the calculations that you might need.

Inserting attributes into the output with xsl:attribute

You can include attributes in the output document simply by typing the literal attributes themselves. For instance, to insert a DIV element with an ALIGN attribute bearing the value CENTER, you merely type <DIV ALIGN="CENTER"> and </DIV> at the appropriate points in the style sheet. However, you frequently have to rely on data that you read from the input document to determine an attribute value and sometimes even to determine the attribute name.

For example, suppose you want a style sheet that selects atom names and formats them as links to files named H.html, He.html, Li.html, and so forth like this:

```
<LI><A HREF="H.html">Hydrogen</A></LI>
<LI><A HREF="He.html">Helium</A></LI>
<LI><A HREF="Li.html">Lithium</A></LI>
```

Each different element in the input will have a different value for the HREF attribute. The xsl:attribute element calculates an attribute name and value and inserts it into the output. Each xsl:attribute element is a child of either an xsl:element element or a literal result element. The attribute calculated by xsl:attribute will be attached to the element calculated by its parent in the output. The name of the attribute is specified by the name attribute of the xsl:attribute element. The value of the attribute is given by the contents of the xsl:attribute element. For example, this template rule produces the output shown above:

```
<xsl:template match="ATOM">
  <LI><A>
    <xsl:attribute name="HREF">
      <xsl:value-of select="SYMBOL"/>.html
    </xsl:attribute>
    <xsl:value-of select="NAME"/>
  </A></LI>
</xsl:template>
```

All xsl:attribute elements must come before any other content of their parent element. You can't add an attribute to an element after you've already started writing out its content. For example, this template is illegal:

```
<xsl:template match="ATOM">
  <LI><A>
    <xsl:value-of select="NAME"/>
    <xsl:attribute name="HREF">
      <xsl:value-of select="SYMBOL"/>.html
    </xsl:attribute>
  </A></LI>
</xsl:template>
```

Defining attribute sets

You often need to apply the same group of attributes to many different elements, of either the same or different classes. For instance, you might want to apply a `style` attribute to each cell in an HTML table. To make this simpler, you can define one or more attributes as members of an attribute set at the top level of the style sheet with `xsl:attribute-set`, and then include that attribute set in an element with an `xsl:use-attribute-sets` attribute.

For example, this `xsl:attribute-set` element defines an element named `cellstyle` with a `font-family` attribute of `New York, Times New Roman, Times, serif` and a `font-size` attribute of `12pt`.

```
<xsl:attribute-set name="cellstyle">
  <xsl:attribute name="font-family">
    New York, Times New Roman, Times, serif
  </xsl:attribute>
  <xsl:attribute name="font-size">12pt</xsl:attribute>
</xsl:attribute-set>
```

This template rule then applies those attributes to `td` elements in the output.

```
<xsl:template match="ATOM">
  <tr>
    <td xsl:use-attribute-sets="cellstyle">
      <xsl:value-of select="NAME"/>
    </td>
    <td xsl:use-attribute-sets="cellstyle">
      <xsl:value-of select="ATOMIC_NUMBER"/>
    </td>
  </tr>
</xsl:template>
```

An element can use more than one attribute set by specifying the names of all the sets in a white space separated list in the value of the `xsl:use-attribute-sets` attribute. All attributes from all the sets are applied to the element. For example, this `td` element possesses attributes from both the `cellstyle` and the `numberstyle` attribute sets.

```
<td xsl:use-attribute-sets="cellstyle numberstyle">
  <xsl:value-of select="ATOMIC_NUMBER"/>
</td>
```

If more than one attribute set defines the same attribute, then the last attribute set mentioned is used. If there is more than one attribute set with the same name (as may happen when one style sheet imports another), then the attributes in the sets are merged. If the identically named attribute sets define the same attribute, then the value from the set with higher importance is chosen. A style sheet in which multiple attribute sets of the same importance with the same name define the same attribute is in error.

You can also include attribute sets in particular elements by adding a `use-attribute-sets` element to an `xsl:element`, `xsl:copy`, or `xsl:attribute-set` element. For example,

```
<xsl:element name="td" use-attribute-sets="cellstyle">
  <xsl:value-of select="ATOMIC_NUMBER"/>
</xsl:element>
```

The `xsl:` prefix is unnecessary (and in fact prohibited) when `use-attribute-sets` is an attribute of an XSLT element rather than an element from the result set.

Generating processing instructions with xsl:processing-instruction

The `xsl:processing-instruction` element places a processing instruction in the output document. The target of the processing instruction is specified by a required name attribute. The contents of the `xsl:processing-instruction` element become the contents of the processing instruction. For example, this rule replaces `PROGRAM` elements with a `gcc` processing instruction:

```
<xsl:template match="PROGRAM">
  <xsl:processing-instruction name="gcc"> -04
  </xsl:processing-instruction>
</xsl:template>
```

`PROGRAM` elements in the input are replaced by this processing instruction in the output:

```
<?gcc -04
  ?>
```

The contents of the `xsl:processing-instruction` element can include `xsl:value-of` elements and `xsl:apply-templates` elements, provided the result of these instructions is pure text. For example,

```
<xsl:template match="PROGRAM">
  <xsl:processing-instruction name="gcc">-04
    <xsl:value-of select="NAME"/>
  </xsl:processing-instruction>
</xsl:template>
```

The `xsl:processing-instruction` element may not contain `xsl:element` and other instructions that produce elements and attributes in the result. Furthermore, `xsl:processing-instruction` may not include any instructions or literal text that insert a `?>` in the output because that would prematurely end the processing instruction.

Generating comments with xsl:comment

The `xsl:comment` element inserts a comment in the output document. It has no attributes. Its contents are the text of the comment. For example,

```
<xsl:template match="ATOM">
  <xsl:comment>There was an atom here once.</xsl:comment>
</xsl:template>
```

This rule replaces `ATOM` nodes with this comment:

```
<!--There was an atom here once.-->
```

The contents of the `xsl:comment` element can include `xsl:value-of` elements and `xsl:apply-templates` elements, provided the results of these instructions are pure text. It may not contain `xsl:element` and other instructions that produce elements and attributes in the result. Furthermore, `xsl:comment` may not include any instructions or literal text that inserts a double hyphen in the comment. This would result in a malformed comment in the output.

Generating text with xsl:text

The `xsl:text` element inserts its contents into the output document as literal text. For example, this rule replaces each `ATOM` element with the string "There was an atom here once."

```
<xsl:template match="ATOM">
  <xsl:text>There was an atom here once.</xsl:text>
</xsl:template>
```

The `xsl:text` element isn't much used because most of the time it's easier to simply type the text. However, `xsl:text` does have a couple of advantages. The first is that it preserves white space exactly, even if the node contains nothing but white space. By default, XSLT processors delete all text nodes from the style sheet that contain only white space. This is useful when dealing with poetry, computer source code, or other text in which white space is significant.

The second advantage is that it enables you to insert unescaped < and & into your output document that are not converted to < and &. To do this, place the general entity reference for the symbol (< or &) in an `xsl:text` element; then set the `xsl:text` element's `disable-output-escaping` attribute to `yes`. This can be useful when you need to include JavaScript source code in the output document. For example,

```
<xsl:template match="SCRIPT">
  <script language="javascript">
    <xsl:text disable-output-escaping="yes">
      &lt;!-- if (
```

```
            location.host.tolowercase().indexof("ibiblio")
            &lt; 0) {
               location.href="http://www.ibiblio.org/xml/";
            }
          } // --&gt;
       </xsl:text>
     </script>
   </xsl:template>
```

This may produce output that is not well-formed XML. (Indeed, that's the case here.) However, if you're trying to write a non-XML format such as HTML or TeX this may be what you want. Note, however, that the style sheet and the input document are both still well-formed XML.

Copying the Context Node with xsl:copy

The xsl:copy element copies the source node into the output tree. Child elements, attributes, and other content are not automatically copied. However, the contents of the xsl:copy element are an xsl:template element that can select these things to be copied as well. This is often useful when transforming a document from one markup vocabulary to the same or a closely related markup vocabulary. For example, this template rule strips the attributes and child elements off an ATOM and replaces it with the value of its contents enclosed in a b element:

```
<xsl:template match="ATOM">
   <xsl:copy>
     <b><xsl:value-of select="."/></b>
   </xsl:copy>
</xsl:template>
```

One useful template xsl:copy makes possible is the identity transformation; that is, a transformation from a document into itself. Such a transformation looks like this:

```
<xsl:template
   match="*|@*|comment()|processing-instruction()|text()">
   <xsl:copy>
     <xsl:apply-templates
       select="*|@*|comment()|processing-instruction()|text()"/>
   </xsl:copy>
</xsl:template>
```

You can adjust the identity transformation a little to produce similar documents. For example, Listing 18-15 is a style sheet that strips comments from a document, leaving the document otherwise untouched. It resulted from leaving the comment() node out of the match and select attribute values in the identity transformation.

Listing 18-15: **An XSLT style sheet that strips comments from a document**

```
<?xml version="1.0"?>
<xsl:stylesheet version="1.0"
  xmlns:xsl="http://www.w3.org/1999/XSL/Transform">

  <xsl:template
    match="*|@*|processing-instruction()|text()">
    <xsl:copy>
      <xsl:apply-templates
        select="*|@*|processing-instruction()|text()"/>
    </xsl:copy>
  </xsl:template>

</xsl:stylesheet>
```

xsl:copy only copies the source node. You can copy other nodes, possibly more than one of them, using xsl:copy-of. The select attribute of xsl:copy-of chooses the nodes to be copied. For example, Listing 18-16 is a style sheet that uses xsl:copy-of to strip out elements without melting points from the periodic table by copying only ATOM elements that have MELTING_POINT children.

Listing 18-16: **A style sheet that copies only ATOM elements that have MELTING_POINT children**

```
<?xml version="1.0"?>
<xsl:stylesheet version="1.0"
  xmlns:xsl="http://www.w3.org/1999/XSL/Transform">

    <xsl:template match="/PERIODIC_TABLE">
      <PERIODIC_TABLE>
        <xsl:apply-templates select="ATOM"/>
      </PERIODIC_TABLE>
    </xsl:template>

    <xsl:template match="ATOM">
      <xsl:apply-templates select="MELTING_POINT"/>
    </xsl:template>

  <xsl:template match="MELTING_POINT">
    <xsl:copy-of select=".."/>
  </xsl:template>

</xsl:stylesheet>
```

Note Listings 18-15 and 18-16 are examples of XSL transformations from a source vocabulary to the same vocabulary. Unlike most of the examples in this chapter, they do not transform to well-formed HTML.

Counting Nodes with xsl:number

The `xsl:number` element inserts a formatted integer into the output document. The value of the integer is given by the `value` attribute. This contains a number, which is rounded to the nearest integer, then formatted according to the value of the `format` attribute. Reasonable defaults are provided for both these attributes. For example, consider the style sheet for the `ATOM` elements in Listing 18-17.

Listing 18-17: **An XSLT style sheet that counts atoms**

```
<?xml version="1.0"?>
<xsl:stylesheet version="1.0"
  xmlns:xsl="http://www.w3.org/1999/XSL/Transform">

    <xsl:template match="PERIODIC_TABLE">
      <html>
        <head><title>The Elements</title></head>
        <body>
          <table>
            <tr><xsl:apply-templates select="ATOM"/></tr>
          </table>
        </body>
      </html>
    </xsl:template>

    <xsl:template match="ATOM">
      <td><xsl:number value="ATOMIC_NUMBER"/></td>
      <td><xsl:value-of select="NAME"/></td>
    </xsl:template>

</xsl:stylesheet>
```

When this style sheet is applied to Listing 18-1, the output appears like this:

```
<html>
<head>
<title>The Elements</title>
</head>
<body>
<table>
```

```
<tr>
<td>1</td><td>Hydrogen</td><td>2</td><td>Helium</td>
</tr>
</table>
</body>
</html>
```

Each element is matched with its atomic number. The `value` attribute can contain any data that XPath knows how to convert to a number. In this case, the `ATOMIC_NUMBER` child element of the matched `ATOM` is converted.

Default numbers

If you use the `value` attribute to calculate the number, that's all you need. However, if the `value` attribute is omitted, then the position of the current node in the context node list is used as the number. For example, consider Listing 18-18, which produces a table of atoms that have boiling points less than or equal to the boiling point of nitrogen.

Listing 18-18: **An XSLT style sheet that counts atoms**

```
<?xml version="1.0"?>
<xsl:stylesheet version="1.0"
  xmlns:xsl="http://www.w3.org/1999/XSL/Transform">

    <xsl:template match="PERIODIC_TABLE">
      <html>
        <head><title>The Elements</title></head>
        <body>
          <table>
            <tr>
              <td>Name</td>
              <td>Position</td>
              <td>Default Number</td>
              <td>Boiling Point</td>
            </tr>
            <xsl:apply-templates
              select="ATOM[BOILING_POINT &lt;= 77.344]"/>
          </table>
        </body>
      </html>
    </xsl:template>

    <xsl:template match="ATOM">
      <tr>
        <td><xsl:value-of select="NAME"/></td>
        <td><xsl:number value="position()"/></td>
        <td><xsl:number/></td>
```

Continued

Listing 18-18 *(continued)*

```
        <td><xsl:number value="BOILING_POINT"/></td>
    </tr>
</xsl:template>

</xsl:stylesheet>
```

Figure 18-5 shows the finished table produced by applying this stylesheet to the complete periodic table. This shows that the default value calculated by `xsl:number` is the position of the node among other sibling nodes of the same type (ATOM elements in this case). This is not the same as the number returned by the `position()` function, which only calculates position relative to other nodes in the context node list (the nodes which the template matched—hydrogen, helium, nitrogen, and neon in this example). You can change what `xsl:number` counts using these three attributes:

✦ `level`

✦ `count`

✦ `from`

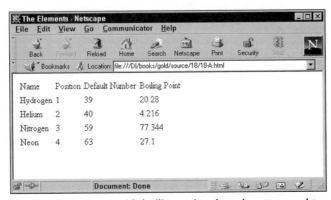

Figure 18-5: Atoms with boiling points less than or equal to nitrogen's

The level attribute

By default, with no `value` attribute, `xsl:number` counts siblings of the source node with the same type. For instance, if the ATOMIC_NUMBER elements were numbered instead of ATOM elements, none would have a number higher than 1 because an

ATOM never has more than one ATOMIC_NUMBER child. Although the document contains more than one ATOMIC_NUMBER element, these are not siblings.

Setting the level attribute of xsl:number to any counts all of the elements of the same kind as the current node in the document. This includes not just the ones in the current node list, but all nodes of the same type. Even if you select only the atomic numbers of the gases, for example, the solids and liquids would still count, even if they weren't output. Consider these rules:

```
<xsl:template match="ATOM">
  <tr><xsl:apply-templates select="NAME"/></tr>
</xsl:template>

<xsl:template match="NAME">
  <td><xsl:number level="any"/></td>
  <td><xsl:value-of select="."/></td>
</xsl:template>
```

Because level is set to any, these templates produce output like this that doesn't start from 1 with each new NAME element:

```
<tr>
<td>1</td><td>Hydrogen</td>
</tr>
<tr>
<td>2</td><td>Helium</td>
</tr>
```

If you remove the level attribute or set it to its default value of single, then the output looks like this:

```
<tr>
<td>1</td><td>Hydrogen</td>
</tr>
<tr>
<td>1</td><td>Helium</td>
</tr>
```

A slightly less useful option sets the level attribute of xsl:number to multiple to specify that both the siblings of the current node and its ancestors (but not their children that aren't siblings of the current node) should be counted.

The count attribute

By default, with no value attribute, only elements of the same type as the element of the current node get counted. However, you can set the count attribute of xsl:number to an expression that specifies what to count. For instance, this rule matches all the child elements of an ATOM. It places a number in front of each one that represents its position among all the children of that ATOM.

```
<xsl:template match="ATOM/*">
  <td><xsl:number count="*"/></td>
  <td><xsl:value-of select="."/></td>
</xsl:template>
```

The output from this template looks like this:

```
<td>1</td><td>Hydrogen</td>
<td>2</td><td>H</td>
<td>3</td><td>1</td>
<td>4</td><td>1.00794</td>
<td>5</td><td>20.28</td>
<td>6</td><td>13.81</td>
<td>7</td><td>

  0.0000899
</td>

<td>1</td><td>Helium</td>
<td>2</td><td>He</td>
<td>3</td><td>2</td>
<td>4</td><td>4.0026</td>
<td>5</td><td>4.216</td>
<td>6</td><td>0.95</td>
<td>7</td><td>

  0.0001785
</td>
```

The from attribute

The `from` attribute contains an XPath expression that specifies which element the counting begins with in the input tree. However, the counting still begins from 1, not 2 or 10 or some other number. The `from` attribute only changes which element is considered to be the first element. This attribute is only considered when `level="any"`. Other times it has no effect.

Number to string conversion

Until now, I've implicitly assumed that numbers looked like 1, 2, 3, and so on; that is, a European numeral starting from 1 and counting by 1. However, that's not the only possibility. For instance, the page numbers in the preface and other front matter of books often appear in small Roman numerals like i, ii, iii, iv, and so on. And different countries use different conventions to group the digits, separate the integer and fractional parts of a real number, and represent the symbols for the various digits. These are all adjustable through four attributes of `xsl:number`:

✦ `format`

✦ `letter-value`

✦ grouping-separator

✦ grouping-size

The format attribute

You can adjust the numbering style used by xsl:number using the format attribute. This attribute generally has one of the following values:

✦ i: the lowercase Roman numerals i, ii, iii, iv, v, vi, . . .

✦ I: the uppercase Roman numerals I, II, III, IV, V, VI, . . .

✦ a: the lowercase letters a, b, c, d, e, f, . . .

✦ A: the uppercase letters A, B, C, D, E, F, . . .

For example, this rule numbers the atoms with capital Roman numerals:

```
<xsl:template match="ATOM">
  <P>
    <xsl:number value="position()" format="I"/>
    <xsl:value-of select="."/>
  </P>
</xsl:template>
```

You can specify decimal numbering with leading zeroes by including the number of leading zeroes you want in the format attribute. For instance, setting format="01", produces the sequence 01, 02, 03, 04, 05, 06, 07, 08, 09, 10, 11, 12, ... You might find this useful when lining numbers up in columns.

The letter-value attribute

The letter-value attribute distinguishes between letters interpreted as numbers and letters interpreted as letters. For instance, if you want to use format="I" to start the sequence I, J, K, L, M, N, . . . instead of I, II, III, IV, V, VI, . . . you would set the letter-value attribute to the keyword alphabetic. The keyword traditional specifies a numeric sequence. For example,

```
<xsl:template match="ATOM">
  <P>
    <xsl:number value="position()"
                format="I" letter-value="alphabetic"/>
    <xsl:value-of select="."/>
  </P>
</xsl:template>
```

Grouping attributes

In the United States, we tend to write large numbers with commas grouping every three digits; for example, 4,567,302,000. However, in many languages and countries, a period or a space separates the groups instead; for instance, 4.567.302.000 or

4 567 302 000. Furthermore, in some countries it's customary to group large numbers every four digits instead of every three; for example, 4,5673,0000. If you're dealing with very long lists that may contain a thousand or more items, you need to worry about these issues.

The `grouping-separator` attribute specifies the grouping separator used between groups of digits. The `grouping-size` attribute specifies the number of digits used in a group. Generally, you'd make these attributes contingent on the language. For example,

```
<xsl:number grouping-separator=" " grouping-size="3"/>
```

Sorting Output Elements

The `xsl:sort` element sorts the output elements into a different order than they appear in the input. An `xsl:sort` element appears as a child of an `xsl:apply-templates` element or `xsl:for-each` element. The `select` attribute of the `xsl:sort` element defines the key used to sort the element's output by `xsl:apply-templates` or `xsl:for-each`.

By default, sorting is performed in alphabetical order of the keys. If more than one `xsl:sort` element is present in a given `xsl:apply-templates` or `xsl:for-each` element, then the elements are sorted first by the first key, then by the second key, and so on. If any elements still compare equally, they are output in the order they appear in the source document.

For example, suppose you have a file full of `ATOM` elements arranged alphabetically. To sort by atomic number, you can use the style sheet in Listing 18-19.

Listing 18-19: An XSLT style sheet that sorts by atomic number

```
<?xml version="1.0"?>
<xsl:stylesheet version="1.0"
  xmlns:xsl="http://www.w3.org/1999/XSL/Transform">

    <xsl:template match="PERIODIC_TABLE">
      <html>
        <head>
          <title>Atomic Number vs. Atomic Weight</title>
        </head>
        <body>
          <h1>Atomic Number vs. Atomic Weight</h1>
          <table>
            <th>Element</th>
```

```
            <th>Atomic Number</th>
            <th>Atomic Weight</th>
            <xsl:apply-templates>
              <xsl:sort select="ATOMIC_NUMBER"/>
            </xsl:apply-templates>
          </table>
        </body>
      </html>
    </xsl:template>

    <xsl:template match="ATOM">
      <tr>
        <td><xsl:apply-templates select="NAME"/></td>
        <td><xsl:apply-templates select="ATOMIC_NUMBER"/></td>
        <td><xsl:apply-templates select="ATOMIC_WEIGHT"/></td>
      </tr>
    </xsl:template>

</xsl:stylesheet>
```

Figure 18-6 shows the limits of alphabetical sorting. Hydrogen, atomic number 1, is the first element. However, the second element is not helium, atomic number 2, but rather neon, atomic number 10. Although 10 sorts after 9 numerically, alphabetically 10 falls before 2.

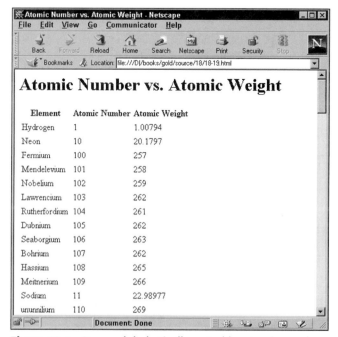

Figure 18-6: Atoms alphabetically sorted by atomic number

You can, however, adjust the order of the sort by setting the optional `data-type` attribute to the value `number`. For example,

```
<xsl:sort data-type="number" select="ATOMIC_NUMBER"/>
```

Figure 18-7 shows the elements sorted properly.

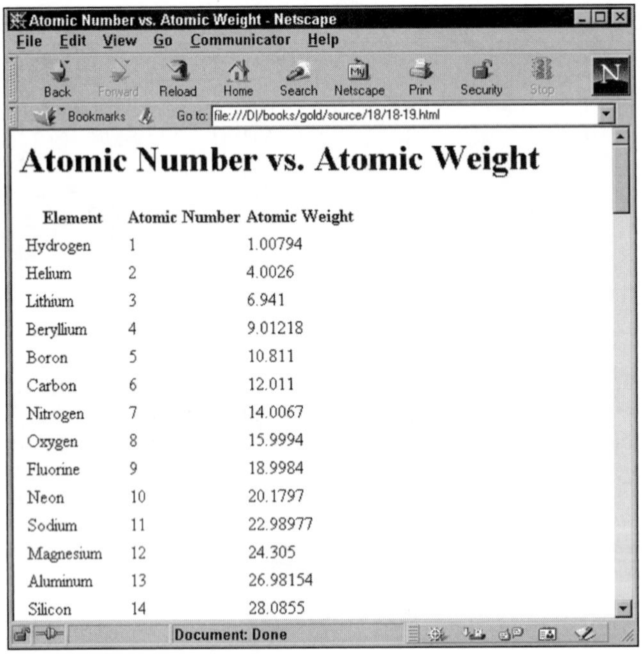

Figure 18-7: Atoms numerically sorted by atomic number

You can change the order of the sort from the default ascending order to descending by setting the `order` attribute to `descending` like this:

```
<xsl:sort order="descending"
          data-type="number"
          select="ATOMIC_NUMBER"/>
```

This sorts the elements from the largest atomic number to the smallest so that hydrogen now appears last in the list.

Alphabetical sorting naturally depends on the alphabet. The `lang` attribute can set the language of the keys. The value of this attribute should be an ISO 639 language code such as `en` for English. However, processors are not required to know how to sort in all the different languages that might be encountered in XML. While English sorting is fairly straight-forward, many other languages require much more complicated algorithms. Indeed a few languages actually have multiple standard ways of sorting based on different criteria. The `lang` attribute is ignored if `data-type` is `number`.

Cross-Reference
These are the same values supported by the `xml:lang` attribute discussed in Chapter 11.

Finally, you can set the `case-order` attribute to one of the two values `upper-first` or `lower-first` to specify whether uppercase letters sort before lowercase letters or vice versa. The default depends on the language.

Modes

Sometimes you want to include the same content from the source document in the output document multiple times. That's easy to do simply by applying templates multiple times, once in each place where you want the data to appear. However, suppose you want the data to be formatted differently in different locations? That's a little trickier.

For example, suppose you want the output of processing the periodic table to be a series of 100 links to more detailed descriptions of the individual atoms. In this case, the output document would start like this:

```
<UL>
<LI><A HREF="#Ac">Actinium</A></LI>
<LI><A HREF="#Al">Aluminum</A></LI>
<LI><A HREF="#Am">Americium</A></LI>
<LI><A HREF="#Sb">Antimony</A></LI>
<LI><A HREF="#Ar">Argon</A></LI>
   .  .  .
```

Later in the document, the actual atom descriptions would appear, formatted like this:

```
<H3>
<A NAME="H">Hydrogen</A>
</H3>
<P>
    Hydrogen
    H
    1
    1.00794
    20.28
    13.81

       0.0000899

</P>
```

This sort of application is common anytime you automatically generate a table of contents or an index. The NAME of the atom must be formatted differently in the table of contents than in the body of the document. You need two different rules that both apply to the ATOM element at different places in the document. The solution is to give each of the different rules a mode attribute. Then you can choose which template to apply by setting the mode attribute of the xsl:apply-templates element. Listing 18-20 demonstrates.

Listing 18-20: An XSLT style sheet that uses modes to format the same data differently in two different places

```
<?xml version="1.0"?>
<xsl:stylesheet version="1.0"
  xmlns:xsl="http://www.w3.org/1999/XSL/Transform">

  <xsl:template match="/PERIODIC_TABLE">
    <HTML>
      <HEAD><TITLE>The Elements</TITLE></HEAD>
      <BODY>

        <H2>Table of Contents</H2>
        <UL>
          <xsl:apply-templates select="ATOM" mode="toc"/>
        </UL>

        <H2>The Elements</H2>
        <xsl:apply-templates select="ATOM" mode="full"/>

      </BODY>
    </HTML>
  </xsl:template>

  <xsl:template match="ATOM" mode="toc">
    <LI><A>
      <xsl:attribute name="HREF">#<xsl:value-of
        select="SYMBOL"/></xsl:attribute>
      <xsl:value-of select="NAME"/>
    </A></LI>
  </xsl:template>

  <xsl:template match="ATOM" mode="full">
    <H3><A>
      <xsl:attribute name="NAME">
        <xsl:value-of select="SYMBOL"/>
      </xsl:attribute>
      <xsl:value-of select="NAME"/>
    </A></H3>
      <P>
```

```
            <xsl:value-of select="."/>
        </P>
    </xsl:template>

</xsl:stylesheet>
```

The default template rule for nodes preserves modes. That is, for every mode n you declare in your style sheet, the XSLT processor adds one template rule that applies specifically to that mode and looks like this:

```
<xsl:template match="*|/" mode="n">
    <xsl:apply-templates mode="n"/>
</xsl:template>
```

As usual, you are free to override this default rule with one of your own design.

Defining Constants with xsl:variable

Named constants help clean up code. They can replace commonly used boilerplate text with a simple name and reference. They can also make it easy to adjust boilerplate text that appears in multiple locations by simply changing the constant definition.

The `xsl:variable` element defines a named string for use elsewhere in the style sheet via an attribute value template. It has a single attribute, `name`, which provides a name by which the variable can be referred to. The contents of the `xsl:variable` element provide the replacement text. For example, this `xsl:variable` element defines a variable with the name `copy01` and the value `Copyright 2001 Elliotte Rusty Harold`:

```
<xsl:variable name="copy01">
    Copyright 2001 Elliotte Rusty Harold
</xsl:variable>
```

To access the value of this variable, you prefix a dollar sign to the name of the variable. To insert this in an attribute, use an attribute value template. For example:

```
<BLOCK COPYRIGHT="{$copy01}">
</BLOCK>
```

You can use `xsl:value-of` to insert the variable's replacement text into the output document as text:

```
<xsl:value-of select="$copy01"/>
```

The contents of the `xsl:variable` can contain markup including other XSLT instructions. This means that you can calculate the value of a variable based on other information, including the value of other variables. However, a variable may not refer to itself recursively, either directly or indirectly. For instance, the following example is in error:

```
<xsl:variable name="GNU">
  <xsl:value-of select="$GNU"/>'s not Unix
</xsl:variable>
```

Similarly, two variables may not refer to each other in a circular fashion like this:

```
<xsl:variable name="Thing1">
  Thing1 loves <xsl:value-of select="$Thing2"/>
</xsl:variable>

<xsl:variable name="Thing2">
  Thing2 loves <xsl:value-of select="$Thing1"/>
</xsl:variable>
```

`xsl:variable` elements can either be top-level children of the `xsl:stylesheet` root element or they can be included inside template rules. A variable present at the top level of a style sheet can be accessed anywhere in the style sheet. It's a global variable. By contrast, a variable that's declared inside a template rule is only accessible by its following sibling elements and their descendants (the *scope* of the variable). It's a local variable. Local variables override global variables with the same name. Local variables can also override other local variables. In the event of a conflict between two variables with the same name, the closest local variable with the same name is used.

Named Templates

Variables are limited to basic text and markup. XSLT provides a more powerful macro facility that can wrap standard markup and text around changing data. For example, suppose you want an atom's atomic number, atomic weight, and other key values formatted as a table cell in small, bold Times in blue. In other words, you want the output to look like this:

```
<td>
  <font face="Times, serif" color="blue" size="2">
    <b>52</b>
  </font>
</td>
```

You can certainly include all that in a template rule like this:

```
<xsl:template match="ATOMIC_NUMBER">
  <td>
    <font face="Times, serif" color="blue" size="2">
      <b>
        <xsl:value-of select="."/>
      </b>
    </font>
  </td>
</xsl:template>
```

This markup can be repeated inside other template rules. When the detailed markup grows more complex, and when it appears in several different places in a style sheet, you may elect to turn it into a named template. Named templates resemble variables. However, they enable you to include data from the place where the template is applied, rather than merely inserting fixed text.

The xsl:template element can have a name attribute by which it can be explicitly invoked, even when it isn't applied indirectly. For example, this shows a sample named template for the above pattern:

```
<xsl:template name="ATOM_CELL">
  <td>
    <font face="Times, serif" color="blue" size="2">
      <b>
        <xsl:value-of select="."/>
      </b>
    </font>
  </td>
</xsl:template>
```

The <xsl:value-of select="."/> element in the middle of the named template will be replaced by the contents of the current node from which this template was called.

The xsl:call-template element appears in the contents of a template rule. It has a required name argument that names the template it will call. When processed, the xsl:call-template element is replaced by the contents of the xsl:template element it names. For example, you can now rewrite the ATOMIC_NUMBER rule like this by using the xsl:call-template element to call the ATOM_CELL named template:

```
<xsl:template match="ATOMIC_NUMBER">
  <xsl:call-template name="ATOM_CELL"/>
</xsl:template>
```

This fairly simple example only saves a few lines of code, but the more complicated the template, and the more times it's reused, the greater the reduction in complexity of the style sheet. Named templates also have the advantage, like variables, of factoring out common patterns in the style sheet so that you can edit them as one.

For instance, if you decide to change the color of atomic number, atomic weight, and other key values from blue to red, you only need to change it once in the named template. You do not have to change it in each separate template rule. This facilitates greater consistency of style.

Passing Parameters to Templates

Each separate invocation of a template can pass parameters to the template to customize its output. This is done the same way for named templates and unnamed templates. In the `xsl:template` element, the parameters are represented as `xsl:param` child elements. In `xsl:call-template` or `xsl:apply-templates` elements, parameters are represented as `xsl:with-param` child elements.

For example, suppose you also want to include a link to a particular file for each atom cell. The output should look something like this:

```
<td>
  <font face="Times, serif" color="blue" size="2">
    <b>
      <a href="atomic_number.html">52</a>
    </b>
  </font>
</td>
```

The trick is that the value of the `href` attribute has to be passed in from the point where the template is invoked because it changes for each separate invocation of the template. For example, atomic weights will have to be formatted like this:

```
<td>
  <font face="Times, serif" color="blue" size="2">
    <b>
      <a href="atomic_weight.html">4.0026</a>
    </b>
  </font>
</td>
```

The template that supports this looks like this:

```
<xsl:template name="ATOM_CELL">
  <xsl:param name="file">index.html</xsl:param>
  <td>
    <font face="Times, serif" color="blue" size="2">
      <b>
        <a href="{$file}"><xsl:value-of select="."/></a>
      </b>
    </font>
  </td>
</xsl:template>
```

The name attribute of the xsl:param element gives the parameter a name (important if there are multiple arguments) and the contents of the xsl:param element supplies a default value for this parameter to be used if the invocation doesn't provide a value. (This can also be given as a string expression by using a select attribute.)

When this template is called, an xsl:with-param child of the xsl:call-template element provides the value of the parameter using its name attribute to identify the parameter and its contents to provide a value for the parameter. For example:

```
<xsl:template match="ATOMIC_NUMBER">
  <xsl:call-template name="ATOM_CELL">
    <xsl:with-param
              name="file">atomic_number.html</xsl:with-param>
    <xsl:value-of select="."/>
  </xsl:call-template>
</xsl:template>
```

Again, this is a simple example. However, much more complex named templates exist. For instance, you could define header and footer templates for pages on a Web site for importing by many different style sheets, each of which would only have to change a few parameters for the name of the page author, the title of the page, and the copyright date.

Stripping and Preserving White Space

You may have noticed that most of the examples of output have been formatted a little strangely. The reason the examples appeared strange is that the source document needed to break long elements across multiple lines to fit between the margins of this book. Unfortunately, the extra white space added to the input document carried over into the output document. For a computer, the details of insignificant white space aren't important, but for a person they can be distracting.

The default behavior for text nodes read from the input document, such as the content of an ATOMIC_NUMBER or DENSITY element, is to preserve all white space. A typical DENSITY element looks like this:

```
<DENSITY UNITS="grams/cubic centimeter">
  <!-- At 300K, 1 atm -->
  0.0000899
</DENSITY>
```

When its value is taken, the leading and trailing white space is included, like this, even though it's really only there to help fit on this printed page and isn't at all significant:

```
0.0000899
```

You can use the `normalize-space()` function to strip the leading and trailing white space from this or any other string. For example, instead of writing `<xsl:value-of select="DENSITY"/>`, you would write `<xsl:value-of select="normalize-space(DENSITY)"/>`.

You can also automatically delete white-space only nodes in the input document by using `xsl:strip-space`. The `elements` attribute of this top-level element contains a list of elements from which text nodes that contain nothing but white space should be deleted. For example, this element says that nodes containing only white space should be stripped from `DENSITY`, `NAME`, `SYMBOL`, and `BOILING_POINT` elements:

```
<xsl:strip-space elements="DENSITY NAME SYMBOL BOILING_POINT"/>
```

You can strip space-only nodes in all elements by using the `*` wildcard, like this:

```
<xsl:strip-space elements="*"/>
```

There's also an `xsl:preserve-space` element with a similar syntax but opposite meaning. However, since preserving space is the default, this element isn't much used. Its main purpose is to override `xsl:strip-space` elements imported from other style sheets or to specify a few elements where space is preserved when the default has been reset to stripping by `<xsl:strip-space elements="*"/>`.

White space only text nodes in the style sheet, as opposed to the input document, are another matter. They are stripped by default. If you want to preserve one, you attach an `xml:space` attribute with the value `preserve` to its parent element or to another one of its ancestors.

 Cross-Reference The `xml:space` attribute was discussed in Chapter 11.

Sometimes the easiest way to include significant white space in a style sheet is to wrap it in an `xsl:text` element. Space inside an `xsl:text` element is treated literally and never stripped.

Making Choices

XSLT provides two elements that allow you to change the output based on the input. The `xsl:if` element either does or does not output a given fragment of XML depending on what patterns are present in the input. The `xsl:choose` element picks one of several possible XML fragments, depending on what patterns are present in the input. Most of what you can do with `xsl:if` and `xsl:choose` can also be done by a suitable application of templates. However, sometimes the solution with `xsl:if` or `xsl:choose` is simpler and more obvious.

xsl:if

The `xsl:if` element provides a simple facility for changing the output based on a pattern. The `test` attribute of `xsl:if` contains an expression that evaluates to a boolean. If the expression is true, the contents of the `xsl:if` element are output. Otherwise, they're not. For example, this template writes out the names of all `ATOM` elements. A comma and a space is added after all except the last element in the list.

```
<xsl:template match="ATOM">
  <xsl:value-of select="NAME"/>
  <xsl:if test="position()!=last()">, </xsl:if>
</xsl:template>
```

This ensures that the list looks like "Hydrogen, Helium" and not "Hydrogen, Helium,".

There are no `xsl:else` or `xsl:else-if` elements. The `xsl:choose` element provides this functionality.

xsl:choose

The `xsl:choose` element selects one of several possible outputs depending on several possible conditions. Each condition and its associated output template is provided by an `xsl:when` child element. The `test` attribute of the `xsl:when` element is an XPath expression with a boolean value. If multiple conditions are true, only the first true one is instantiated. If none of the `xsl:when` elements are true, the `xsl:otherwise` child element is instantiated. For example, this rule changes the color of the output based on whether the `STATE` attribute of the `ATOM` element is `SOLID`, `LIQUID`, or `GAS`:

```
<xsl:template match="ATOM">
  <xsl:choose>
    <xsl:when test="@STATE='SOLID'">
      <P style="color: black">
        <xsl:value-of select="."/>
      </P>
    </xsl:when>
    <xsl:when test="@STATE='LIQUID'">
      <P style="color: blue">
        <xsl:value-of select="."/>
      </P>
    </xsl:when>
    <xsl:when test="@STATE='GAS'">
      <P style="color: red">
```

```
            <xsl:value-of select="."/>
        </P>
      </xsl:when>
      <xsl:otherwise>
        <P style="color: green">
          <xsl:value-of select="."/>
        </P>
      </xsl:otherwise>
    </xsl:choose>
  </xsl:template>
```

Merging Multiple Style Sheets

A single XML document may use many different markup vocabularies described in many different DTDs. You may wish to use different standard style sheets for those different vocabularies. However, you'll also want style rules for particular documents as well. The xsl:import and xsl:include elements enable you to merge multiple style sheets so that you can organize and reuse style sheets for different vocabularies and purposes.

Importing with xsl:import

The xsl:import element is a top-level element whose href attribute provides the URI of a style sheet to import. All xsl:import elements must appear before any other top-level element in the xsl:stylesheet root element. For example, these xsl:import elements import the style sheets genealogy.xsl and standards.xsl.

```
<xsl:stylesheet version="1.0"
  xmlns:xsl="http://www.w3.org/1999/XSL/Transform">
  <xsl:import href="genealogy.xsl"/>
  <xsl:import href="standards.xsl"/>
  <!-- other child elements follow -->
</xsl:stylesheet>
```

Rules in the imported style sheets may conflict with rules in the importing style sheet. If so, rules in the importing style sheet take precedence. If two rules in different imported style sheets conflict, then the rule in the last style sheet imported (standards.xsl above) takes precedence.

The xsl:apply-imports element is a slight variant of xsl:apply-templates that only uses imported rules. It does not use any rules from the importing style sheet. This allows access to imported rules that would otherwise be overridden by rules in the importing style sheet. Other than the name, it has identical syntax to xsl:apply-templates. The only behavioral difference is that it only matches template rules in imported style sheets.

Inclusion with xsl:include

The xsl:include element is a top-level element that copies another style sheet into the current style sheet at the point where it occurs. (More precisely, it copies the contents of the xsl-stylesheet or xsl:transform element in the remote document into the current document.) Its href attribute provides the URI of the style sheet to include. An xsl:include element can occur anywhere at the top level after the last xsl:import element.

Unlike rules included by xsl:import elements, rules included by xsl:include elements have the same precedence in the including style sheet that they would have if they were copied and pasted from one style sheet to the other. As far as the XSLT processor is concerned, there is no difference between an included rule and a rule that's physically present.

Embedding with xsl:stylesheet

You can directly include an XSLT style sheet in the XML document it applies to. I don't recommend this in practice, and browsers and XSLT processors are not required to support it. Nonetheless, a few do. To use this, the xsl:stylesheet element must appear as a child of the document element, rather than as a root element itself. It would have an id attribute giving it a unique name, and this id attribute would appear as the value of the href attribute in the xml-stylesheet processing instruction, following the fragment identifier separator #. Listing 18-21 demonstrates.

Listing 18-21: **An XSLT style sheet embedded in an XML document**

```
<?xml version="1.0"?>
<?xml-stylesheet type="text/xml" href="#id(mystyle)"?>
<PERIODIC_TABLE>

  <xsl:stylesheet version="1.0"
    xmlns:xsl="http://www.w3.org/1999/XSL/Transform"
    id="mystyle">

  <xsl:template match="/">
    <html>
      <xsl:apply-templates/>
    </html>
  </xsl:template>

  <xsl:template match="PERIODIC_TABLE">
    <xsl:apply-templates select="ATOM"/>
  </xsl:template>
```

Continued

Listing 18-21 *(continued)*

```
<xsl:template match="ATOM">
  <P>
    <xsl:value-of select="."/>
  </P>
</xsl:template>

<!--Don't display the style sheet itself
    or its descendants-->
<xsl:template match="xsl:stylesheet"/>

</xsl:stylesheet>

<ATOM>
  <NAME>Actinium</NAME>
  <ATOMIC_WEIGHT>227</ATOMIC_WEIGHT>
  <ATOMIC_NUMBER>89</ATOMIC_NUMBER>
  <OXIDATION_STATES>3</OXIDATION_STATES>
  <BOILING_POINT UNITS="Kelvin">3470</BOILING_POINT>
  <MELTING_POINT UNITS="Kelvin">1324</MELTING_POINT>
  <SYMBOL>Ac</SYMBOL>
  <DENSITY UNITS="grams/cubic centimeter"><!-- At 300K -->
    10.07
  </DENSITY>
  <ELECTRONEGATIVITY>1.1</ELECTRONEGATIVITY>
  <ATOMIC_RADIUS UNITS="Angstroms">1.88</ATOMIC_RADIUS>
</ATOM>

</PERIODIC_TABLE>
```

Output Methods

Most of the examples in this chapter have focused on transforming XML into well-formed HTML. However, most XSLT processors actually support three different output methods:

✦ XML

✦ HTML

✦ Text

The XSLT processor behaves differently depending on which of these output methods it uses. The XML format is the default and in many ways the simplest. The output is mostly exactly what you request in your style sheet. Because well-formed XML does not permit raw less-than signs and ampersands, if you use a character reference such as < or the entity reference < to insert the < character, the formatter will output < or perhaps <. If you use a character reference such as & or the entity reference & to insert the & character, the formatter will insert & or perhaps &. There are ways to disable this escaping, though, as you'll see later.

The HTML output method is designed to output standard HTML 4.0. This is not the well-formed HTML used in this book, but rather traditional HTML in which empty tags look like <HR> and <IMG> instead of <HR/> and <IMG/>, processing instructions are terminated with a > instead of ?>, and < signs used in JavaScript are not converted to <. This makes it much easier to output HTML that works across many browsers and platforms without odd effects such as double lines where a single line is expected or other detritus caused by forcing HTML into the XML mold. The HTML output method is automatically selected when the formatter notices that the root output element is html, HTML, HtMl, or any other combination of case that still spells Hypertext Markup Language.

The final output method is pure text. The text output method operates by first forming a full result tree as per the XML output method, but then only outputting the string value of that tree. This is useful for transforming to non-XML formats such as RTF or TeX. The primary benefit of the text output format is that less than signs are not converted to < or < and ampersands are not converted to & or &. This allows you to output effectively arbitrary text.

xsl:output

By default an XSLT processor will use the XML output method, unless it recognizes the output root element as HTML, in which case it uses the HTML output method. You can change this by using a top-level xsl:output element. The method attribute of the xsl:output element specifies which output method to use and normally has one of these three values:

✦ xml

✦ html

✦ text

Formatting engines may support other values as well. For example, to specify that you want pure well-formed HTML as output, with all the empty tags properly indicated, all less than signs escaped, and so forth, you would use this xsl:output element at the top level of your style sheet:

```
<xsl:output method="xml"/>
```

To indicate that you want regular HTML output even though you aren't using an html root element, you'd put this xsl:output element at the top level of your style sheet:

```
<xsl:output method="html"/>
```

The `xsl:output` element also has a number of other allowed attributes that modify how XML is output. These allow you to change the prolog of the document, how the output is indented with insignificant white space, and which elements use `CDATA` sections rather than escaping < and & characters.

XML declaration

Four attributes of `xsl:output` format the XML declaration used in your document. This assumes the output method is xml. These attributes are:

- ✦ `omit-xml-declaration`
- ✦ `version`
- ✦ `encoding`
- ✦ `standalone`

The `omit-xml-declaration` attribute has the value `yes` or `no`. If `yes`, then an XML declaration is not included in the output document. If `no`, then it is. For example, to insert a very basic `<?xml version="1.0"?>` XML declaration in the output document you would use this `xsl:output` element at the top level of your style sheet:

```
<xsl:output method="xml" omit-xml-declaration="no"/>
```

You could also include it as two separate `xsl:output` elements like this:

```
<xsl:output method="xml"/>
<xsl:output omit-xml-declaration="no"/>
```

The default value of the `version` attribute of the XML declaration is 1.0. Currently, that's the only value allowed. If at some point in the future that changes, then the `version` attribute of `xsl:output` will allow you to change the version used in the XML declaration. For example,

```
<xsl:output version="1.1"/>
```

You can set the `standalone` attribute of the XML declaration to the value `yes` or `no` using the `standalone` attribute of the `xsl:output` element. For example, this `xsl:output` element would insert the XML declaration `<?xml version="1.0" standalone="yes"?>`:

```
<xsl:output method="xml"
            omit-xml-declaration="no" standalone="yes"/>
```

The final possible piece of an XML declaration is the `encoding` declaration. As you probably guessed this can be set with the encoding attribute of the `xsl:output` element. The value can be any legal encoding name registered with the Internet Assigned Numbers Authority as discussed in Chapter 7. For example, to insert the

XML declaration `<?xml version="1.0" encoding="ISO-8859-1"?>`, you'd use this `xsl:output` element:

```
<xsl:output method="xml"
            omit-xml-declaration="no" encoding="ISO-8859-1"/>
```

This also changes the encoding the XSLT processor uses for the output document from its default UTF-8. However, not all processors support all possible encodings. Those written in Java are likely to support the most encodings because Java's rich class library makes it almost trivial to support several dozen popular encodings.

Document type declaration

XSLT does not provide any elements for building an internal DTD subset for the output document with `<!ELEMENT>`, `<!ATTLIST>`, `<!ENTITY>`, and `<!NOTATION>` declarations. However, it does provide two attributes of the `xsl:output` element you can use to include a `DOCTYPE` declaration that points to an external DTD. These are `doctype-system` and `doctype-public`. The first inserts a `SYSTEM` identifier for the DTD; the second a `PUBLIC` identifier. For example, suppose you want this `DOCTYPE` declaration in your output document:

```
<!DOCTYPE PERIODIC_TABLE SYSTEM "chemistry.dtd">
```

Then you would use this `xsl:output` element at the top level of your style sheet:

```
<xsl:output doctype-system="chemistry.dtd"/>
```

The XSLT processor determines the proper root element for the document type declaration by looking at the root element of the output tree. Using a full URL instead of a relative URL is equally easy:

```
<xsl:output
   doctype-system="http://www.example.com/chemistry.dtd"/>
```

On the other hand, suppose you want this `DOCTYPE` declaration in your output document:

```
<!DOCTYPE html PUBLIC "-//W3C//DTD HTML 4.0 Transitional//EN"
          "http://www.w3.org/TR/REC-html40/loose.dtd">
```

Then you would use both `doctype-system` and `doctype-public` attributes so your `DOCTYPE` declaration will have both a `PUBLIC` and a `SYSTEM` identifier. For example,

```
<xsl:output
   doctype-system="http://www.w3.org/TR/REC-html40/loose.dtd"
   doctype-public="-//W3C//DTD HTML 4.0 Transitional//EN"/>
```

Indentation

The indentation of most of the output examples in this chapter has been more than a little flaky. It's certainly not as neat as the carefully hand-coded indentation of the input documents. However, if white space isn't particularly significant in your output document, you can change this and ask the formatter for "pretty printed" XML with the nesting of different elements indicated by the indentation. This is accomplished by the indent attribute of the xsl:output element. If this attribute has the value yes (the default is no), then the processor is allowed (but not required) to insert (but not remove) extra white space into the output to try to "pretty print" the output. This may include indentation and line breaks. For example,

```
<xsl:output indent="yes"/>
```

You cannot, however, specify how much you want each level indented (for example, by two spaces or one tab). That's up to the formatter. Together, the xsl:strip-space and the indent attribute of the xsl:output element allow you to produce output that's almost as attractive as the most painstakingly hand-crafted XML.

CDATA sections

Standard XSLT does not allow you to insert CDATA sections at arbitrary locations in XML documents produced by XSL transformations. However, you can specify that the text contents of a particular element be placed in a CDATA section. In this case the < and & symbols are not encoded as < and & as they would normally be. To do this, place the name of the element whose text contents should be wrapped in CDATA delimiters in the cdata-section-elements attribute of the xsl:output element. For example, this xsl:output element says that the contents of the SCRIPT element should be wrapped in a CDATA section:

```
<xsl:output cdata-section-elements="SCRIPT"/>
```

You can enclose multiple names of elements whose text contents should be wrapped in CDATA delimiters in one cdata-section-elements attribute simply by separating the names with white space. For example, this xsl:output element says that the contents of both the SCRIPT and CODE elements should be wrapped in a CDATA section:

```
<xsl:output cdata-section-elements="SCRIPT CODE"/>
```

Alternately, you can just use multiple xsl:output elements, each naming one element. For example:

```
<xsl:output cdata-section-elements="SCRIPT"/>
<xsl:output cdata-section-elements="CODE"/>
```

Media type

One final `xsl:output` attribute specifies the MIME media type of the output document. This is `media-type`. Mostly this will have the value `text/xml`, but it might be `text/html` for the HTML output method, `text/plain` for the text output method, or even something else such as `text/rtf`. You should not specify a charset parameter for the media type. The formatting engine should determine this from the `encoding` attribute of the `xsl:output` element. For example, this `xsl:output` element specifies that the output encoding uses the text/rtf MIME type:

```
<xsl:output media-type="text/rtf"/>
```

Depending on external context, this may determine the filename extension, the icon of the file, how an HTTP server handles the file, or something else. Then again, it might have no effect at all. The XSLT processor might ignore this request and output the same byte stream or XML tree regardless of media type. This is something that's important to the environment in which the XML document exists, but not so important to the XML document itself.

Summary

In this chapter, you learned about XSL transformations. In particular, you learned that:

✦ The Extensible Stylesheet Language (XSL) comprises two separate XML applications for transforming and formatting XML documents.

✦ An XSL transformation applies rules to a tree read from an XML document to transform it into an output tree written out as an XML document.

✦ An XSL template rule is an `xsl:template` element with a `match` attribute. Nodes in the input tree are compared against the patterns of the `match` attributes of the different template elements. When a match is found, the contents of the template are output.

✦ The value of a node is a pure text (no markup) string containing the contents of the node. This can be calculated by the `xsl:value-of` element.

✦ You can process multiple elements in two ways: the `xsl:apply-templates` element and the `xsl:for-each` element.

✦ The value of the `match` attribute of the `xsl:template` element is a match pattern specifying which nodes the template matches.

✦ XPath expressions (or simply expressions) are a superset of match patterns used by the `select` attribute of `xsl:apply-templates`, `xsl:value-of`, `xsl:for-each`, `xsl:copy-of`, `xsl:variable`, `xsl:param`, `xsl:with-param`, and `xsl:sort` elements.

✦ Default rules apply templates to element nodes and take the value of text nodes and attributes.

✦ The `xsl:element`, `xsl:attribute`, `xsl:processing-instruction`, `xsl:comment`, and `xsl:text` elements output elements, attributes, processing instructions, comments, and text calculated from data in the input document.

✦ The `xsl:attribute-set` element defines a common group of attributes that can be applied to multiple elements in different templates with the `xsl:use-attribute-sets`.

✦ The `xsl:copy` element copies the current node from the input into the output.

✦ The `xsl:number` element inserts the number specified by its `value` attribute into the output using a specified number format given by the `format` attribute.

✦ The `xsl:sort` element can reorder the input nodes before copying them to the output.

✦ Modes can apply different templates to the same element from different locations in the style sheet.

✦ The `xsl:variable` element defines named constants that can clarify your code.

✦ Named templates help you reuse common template code.

✦ White space is maintained by default unless an `xsl:strip-space` element or `xml:space` attribute says otherwise.

✦ The `xsl:if` element produces output if, and only if, its `test` attribute is true.

✦ The `xsl:choose` element outputs the template of the first one of its `xsl:when` children whose `test` attribute is true, or the template of its `xsl:otherwise` element if no `xsl:when` element has a `true` `test` attribute.

✦ The `xsl:import` and `xsl:include` elements merge rules from different style sheets.

✦ The `xsl:stylesheet` element allows you to include a style sheet directly in the document it applies to.

✦ Various attributes of the `xsl:output` element allow you to specify the output document's format, XML declaration, document type declaration, indentation, encoding, and MIME media type.

The next chapter takes up the second half of XSL: the formatting objects vocabulary. Formatting objects are an extremely powerful way of specifying the precise layout you want your pages to have. XSL transformations are used to transform an XML document into an XSL formatting objects document.

✦   ✦   ✦

XSL Formatting Objects

XSL Formatting Objects (XSL-FO) are the second half of the Extensible Stylesheet Language (XSL). XSL-FO is an XML application that describes how pages will look when presented to a reader. A style sheet uses the XSL transformation language to transform an XML document in a semantic vocabulary into a new XML document that uses the XSL-FO presentational vocabulary. While one can hope that Web browsers will one day know how to directly display data marked up with XSL formatting objects, for now an additional step is necessary in which the output document is further transformed into some other format, such as Adobe's PDF.

Formatting Objects and Their Properties

XSL-FO provides a more sophisticated visual layout model than HTML+CSS. Formatting supported by XSL-FO, but not supported by HTML+CSS, includes right-to-left and top-to-bottom text, footnotes, margin notes, page numbers in cross-references, and more. In particular, while CSS (Cascading Style Sheets) is primarily intended for use on the Web, XSL-FO is designed for broader use. You should, for instance, be able to write an XSL style sheet that uses formatting objects to lay out an entire printed book. A different style sheet should be able to transform the same XML document into a Web site.

There are exactly 56 XSL formatting object elements. These are placed in the `http://www.w3.org/1999/XSL/Format` namespace. At least 99 percent of the time, the chosen prefix is `fo`. In this chapter, I use the `fo` prefix to indicate this namespace without further comment.

Of the 56 elements, most signify various kinds of rectangular areas. Most of the rest are containers for rectangular areas and spaces. In alphabetical order, these formatting objects are:

```
fo:basic-link                      fo:multi-toggle
fo:bidi-override                   fo:page-number
fo:block                           fo:page-number-citation
fo:block-container                 fo:page-sequence
fo:character                       fo:page-sequence-master
fo:color-profile                   fo:region-after
fo:conditional-page-              fo:region-before
master-reference
                                   fo:region-body
fo:declarations
                                   fo:region-end
fo:external-graphic
                                   fo:region-start
fo:float
                                   fo:repeatable-page-master-
fo:flow                            alternatives
fo:footnote                        fo:repeatable-page-master-reference
fo:footnote-body                   fo:retrieve-marker
fo:initial-property-set            fo:root
fo:inline                          fo:simple-page-master
fo:inline-container                fo:single-page-master-reference
fo:instream-foreign-object         fo:static-content
fo:layout-master-set               fo:table
fo:leader                          fo:table-and-caption
fo:list-block                      fo:table-body
fo:list-item                       fo:table-caption
fo:list-item-body                  fo:table-cell
fo:list-item-label                 fo:table-column
fo:marker                          fo:table-footer
fo:multi-case                      fo:table-header
fo:multi-properties                fo:table-row
fo:multi-property-set              fo:title
fo:multi-switch                    fo:wrapper
```

A Word of Caution about XSL Formatting Objects

XSL is still under development. The XSL language has changed radically in the past, and will change again in the future. This chapter is based on the November 21, 2000 Candidate Recommendation of the XSL specification. By the time you are reading this book, this draft of XSL will probably have been superseded and the exact syntax of XSL-FO will have changed. If you do encounter something that doesn't seem to work quite right, you should compare the examples in this book against the most current specification.

To make matters worse, no software implements all of the Candidate Recommendation of XSL. In fact, so far there are only a few standalone programs that convert XSL-FO documents into PDF files. There are no Web browsers that can display a document written with XSL formatting objects. Eventually, of course, this should be straightened out as the standard evolves toward its final incarnation and more vendors implement XSL formatting objects.

The XSL formatting model is based on rectangular boxes called *areas* that can contain text, empty space, images, or other formatting objects. As with CSS boxes, an area has borders and padding on each of its sides, although CSS's margins are replaced by XSL's space-before and space-after. An XSL formatter reads the formatting objects to determine which areas to place where on the page. Many formatting objects produce single areas (at least most of the time), but because of page breaks, word wrapping, hyphenation, and other details that must be taken into account when fitting a potentially infinite amount of text into a finite amount of space, some formatting objects do occasionally generate more than one area.

The formatting objects differ primarily in what they represent. For example, the `fo:list-item-label` formatting object is a box that contains a bullet, a number, or another indicator placed in front of a list item. A `fo:list-item-body` formatting object is a box that contains the text, sans label, of the list item. And a `fo:list-item` formatting object is a box that contains both the `fo:list-item-label` and `fo:list-item-body` formatting objects.

When processed, the formatting objects document is broken up into pages. A Web browser window will normally be treated as one very long page. A print format will often contain many individual pages. Each page contains a number of areas. There are four primary kinds of areas:

1. regions
2. block areas
3. line areas
4. inline areas

These form a rough hierarchy. Regions contain block areas. Block areas contain other block areas, line areas, and content. Line areas contain inline areas. Inline areas contain other inline areas and content. More specifically:

✦ A region is the highest-level container in XSL-FO. You can think of a page of this book as containing three regions: the header, the main body of the page, and the footer. Formatting objects that produce regions include `fo:region-body`, `fo:region-before`, `fo:region-after`, `fo:region-start`, and `fo:region-end`.

✦ A block area represents a block-level element, such as a paragraph or a list item. Although block areas may contain other block areas, there should always be a line break before the start and after the end of each block area. A block area, rather than being precisely positioned by coordinates, is placed sequentially in the area that contains it. As other block areas are added and deleted before it or within it, the block area's position shifts as necessary to make room. A block area may contain parsed character data, inline areas, line areas, and other block areas that are sequentially arranged in the containing block area. Formatting objects that produce block areas include `fo:block`, `fo:table-and-caption`, and `fo:list-block`.

✦ A line area represents a line of text inside a block. For example, each of the lines in this list item is a line area. Line areas can contain inline areas and inline spaces. There are no formatting objects that correspond to line areas. Instead, the formatting engine calculates the line areas as it decides how to wrap lines inside block areas.

✦ Inline areas are parts of a line such as a single character, a footnote reference, or a mathematical equation. Inline areas can contain other inline areas and raw text. Formatting objects that produce inline areas include `fo:character`, `fo:external-graphic`, `fo:inline`, `fo:instream-foreign-object`, `fo:leader`, and `fo:page-number`.

Formatting properties

When taken as a whole, the various formatting objects in an XSL-FO document specify the order in which content is to be placed on pages. However, *formatting properties* specify the details of formatting such as size, position, font, color, and a lot more. Formatting properties are represented as attributes on the individual formatting object elements.

The details of many of these properties should be familiar from CSS. Work is ongoing to ensure that CSS and XSL-FO use the same names to mean the same things. For example, the CSS `font-family` property means the same thing as the XSL `font-family` property; and although the syntax for assigning values to properties is different in CSS and XSL-FO, the meaning of the values themselves is the same. To indicate that the `fo:block` element is formatted in some approximation of Times, you might use this CSS rule:

```
fo:block {font-family: 'New York', 'Times New Roman', serif}
```

The XSL-FO equivalent is to include a `font-family` attribute in the `fo:block` start tag in this way:

```
<fo:block font-family="'New York', 'Times New Roman', serif">
```

Although this is superficially different, the style name (`font-family`) and the style value (`'New York'`, `'Times New Roman'`, `serif`) are the same. CSS's `font-family` property is specified as a list of font names, separated by commas, in order from first choice to last choice. XSL-FO's `font-family` property is specified as a list of font names, separated by commas, in order from first choice to last choice. Both CSS and XSL-FO quote font names that contain white space. Both CSS and XSL-FO understand the keyword `serif` to mean an arbitrary serif font.

Of course, XSL formatting objects support many properties that have no CSS equivalent, such as `destination-placement-offset`, `block-progression-dimension`, `character`, and `hyphenation-keep`. You need to learn these to take full advantage of XSL. The standard XSL-FO properties follow:

absolute-position	border-after-precedence
active-state	border-after-style
alignment-adjust	border-after-width
alignment-baseline	border-before-color
auto-restore	border-before-precedence
azimuth	border-before-style
background	border-before-width
background-attachment	border-bottom
background-color	border-bottom-color
background-image	border-bottom-style
background-position	border-bottom-width
background-position-horizontal	border-collapse
	border-color
background-position-vertical	border-end-color
	border-end-precedence
background-repeat	border-end-style
baseline-shift	border-end-width
blank-or-not-blank	border-left
block-progression-dimension	border-left-color
border	border-left-style
border-after-color	border-left-width

border-right

border-right-color

border-right-style

border-right-width

border-separation

border-spacing

border-start-color

border-start-precedence

border-start-style

border-start-width

border-style

border-top

border-top-color

border-top-style

border-top-width

border-width

bottom

break-after

break-before

caption-side

case-name

case-title

character

clear

clip

color

color-profile-name

column-count

column-gap

column-number

column-width

content-height

content-type

content-width

country

cue

cue-after

cue-before

destination-placement-offset

direction

display-align

dominant-baseline

elevation

empty-cells

end-indent

ends-row

extent

external-destination

float

flow-name

font

font-family

font-selection-strategy

font-size

font-size-adjust

font-stretch

font-style

font-variant

font-weight

force-page-count

format

glyph-orientation-horizontal

glyph-orientation-vertical

grouping-separator

grouping-size

height

hyphenate

hyphenation-character

hyphenation-keep

hyphenation-ladder-count

hyphenation-push-character-count

hyphenation-remain-character-count

id

indicate-destination

initial-page-number

inline-progression-dimension

internal-destination

keep-together

keep-with-next

keep-with-previous

language

last-line-end-indent

leader-alignment

leader-length

leader-pattern

leader-pattern-width

left

letter-spacing

letter-value

linefeed-treatment

line-height

line-height-shift-adjustment

line-stacking-strategy

margin

margin-bottom

margin-left

margin-right

margin-top

marker-class-name

master-name

max-height

maximum-repeats

max-width

media-usage

min-height

min-width

number-columns-repeated

number-columns-spanned

number-rows-spanned

odd-or-even

orphans

overflow

padding

padding-after

padding-before

padding-bottom

padding-end

padding-left

padding-right

padding-start

padding-top

page-break-after

page-break-before

page-break-inside

page-height

page-position

page-width

pause

pause-after

pause-before

pitch

pitch-range

play-during

position

precedence

provisional-distance-between-starts

provisional-label-separation

reference-orientation

ref-id

region-name

relative-align

relative-position

rendering-intent

retrieve-boundary

retrieve-class-name

retrieve-position

richness

right

role

rule-style

rule-thickness

scaling

scaling-method

score-spaces

script

show-destination

size

source-document

space-after

space-before

space-end

space-start

space-treatment

span

speak

speak-header

speak-numeral

speak-punctuation

speech-rate

src

start-indent

starting-state

starts-row

stress

suppress-at-line-break

switch-to

table-layout

table-omit-footer-at-break

table-omit-header-at-break

target-presentation-context

target-processing-context

target-stylesheet

text-align

text-align-last

text-altitude

text-decoration

text-depth

text-indent

text-shadow

text-transform

top

treat-as-word-space

```
unicode-bidi              widows

vertical-align            width

visibility                word-spacing

voice-family              wrap-option

volume                    writing-mode

white-space               xml:lang

white-space-collapse      z-index
```

Transforming to formatting objects

XSL-FO is a complete XML vocabulary for laying out text on a page. An XSL-FO document is simply a well-formed XML document that uses this vocabulary. That means it has an XML declaration, a root element, child elements, and so forth. It must adhere to all the well-formedness rules of any XML document, or formatters will not accept it. By convention, a file that contains XSL formatting objects has the three-letter extension .fob or the two-letter extension .fo. However, it might have the suffix .xml because it also is a well-formed XML file.

Listing 19-1 is a simple document marked up using XSL formatting objects. The root of the document is `fo:root`. This element contains a `fo:layout-master-set` and a `fo:page-sequence`. The `fo:layout-master-set` element contains `fo:simple-page-master` child elements. Each `fo:simple-page-master` describes a kind of page on which content will be placed. Here there's only one very simple page, but more complex documents can have different master pages for first, right, and left, body pages, front matter, back matter, and more, each with a potentially different set of margins, page numbering, and other features.

Content is placed on copies of the master page using a `fo:page-sequence`. The `fo:page-sequence` has a `master-name` attribute specifying the master page to be used. Its `fo:flow` child element holds the actual content to be placed on the pages. The content here is given as two `fo:block` children, each with a `font-size` property of 20 points, a `font-family` property of `serif`, and a line-height of 30 points.

Listing 19-1: **A simple XSL-FO document**

```
<?xml version="1.0"?>
<fo:root xmlns:fo="http://www.w3.org/1999/XSL/Format">

  <fo:layout-master-set>
    <fo:simple-page-master master-name="only">
      <fo:region-body/>
```

Continued

Listing 19-1 *(continued)*

```
    </fo:simple-page-master>
  </fo:layout-master-set>

  <fo:page-sequence master-name="only">

    <fo:flow flow-name="xsl-region-body">
      <fo:block font-size="20pt" font-family="serif"
                line-height="30pt">
        Hydrogen
      </fo:block>
      <fo:block font-size="20pt" font-family="serif"
                line-height="30pt" >
        Helium
      </fo:block>
    </fo:flow>

  </fo:page-sequence>

</fo:root>
```

Although you could write a document such as Listing 19-1 by hand, doing so would lose all the benefits of content-format independence achieved by XML. Normally, you write an XSLT style sheet that transforms an XML source document into XSL-FO. Listing 19-2 is the XSLT style sheet that produced Listing 19-1 by transforming the previous chapter's Listing 17-1.

Listing 19-2: **A transformation from a source vocabulary to XSL formatting objects**

```
<?xml version="1.0"?>
<xsl:stylesheet version="1.0"
  xmlns:xsl="http://www.w3.org/1999/XSL/Transform"
  xmlns:fo="http://www.w3.org/1999/XSL/Format">

  <xsl:output indent="yes"/>

  <xsl:template match="/">
    <fo:root xmlns:fo="http://www.w3.org/1999/XSL/Format">

      <fo:layout-master-set>
        <fo:simple-page-master master-name="only">
          <fo:region-body/>
```

```
      </fo:simple-page-master>
    </fo:layout-master-set>

    <fo:page-sequence master-name="only">

      <fo:flow flow-name="xsl-region-body">
        <xsl:apply-templates select="//ATOM"/>
      </fo:flow>

    </fo:page-sequence>

  </fo:root>
</xsl:template>

<xsl:template match="ATOM">
  <fo:block font-size="20pt" font-family="serif"
            line-height="30pt">
    <xsl:value-of select="NAME"/>
  </fo:block>
</xsl:template>

</xsl:stylesheet>
```

Using FOP

At the time of this writing, no browser can directly display XML documents transformed into XSL formatting objects. However, there are several applications that can convert an XSL-FO document into a viewable format such as PDF or TeX. The one used here is the XML Apache project's open source FOP. FOP is a command-line Java program that converts FO (formatting object) documents to Adobe Acrobat PDF files. At the time of this writing, the most recent version of FOP is 0.18.1, which incompletely supports a subset of the formatting objects and properties in the XSL Candidate Recommendation. You can download the latest version of FOP from `http://xml.apache.org/fop/`.

FOP is included on the CD-ROM in the directory utilities/fop. However, chances are good that a version that supports XSL-FO more completely will have been released by the time you're reading this, so you should try to get it from the Web if you can.

FOP is a Java program that should run on any platform with a reasonably compatible Java 1.1 virtual machine. To install it, just add the fop.jar, xerces.jar, and w3c.jar archives included with the FOP distribution to your CLASSPATH. If you're running Java 1.2 or later, you can just drop them in your jre/lib/ext directory.

Caution   If you've installed the JDK (rather than the JRE) on Windows, make sure to put fop.jar, xerces.jar, and w3c.jar in both of your jre/lib/ext directories. One of these is in the directory you selected when you installed the JDK, such as C:\jdk\jre\lib\ext. The other one is somewhere like C:\Program Files\JavaSoft\jre\1.3\lib\ext.

Also, make sure you use the w3c.jar file included with the FOP distribution rather than one included with other Apache products like Batik. The different versions are often incompatible.

The `org.apache.fop.apps.CommandLine` class contains the `main()` method for this program. Run it from the command line with arguments specifying the input and output files. For example,

```
C:\> java org.apache.fop.apps.CommandLine 19-1.fo 19-1.pdf
```

The output will look something like this:

```
java org.apache.fop.apps.CommandLine 19-1.fo 19-1.pdf
FOP 0.17.0 DEV
using SAX parser org.apache.xerces.parsers.SAXParser
using renderer org.apache.fop.render.pdf.PDFRenderer
using element mapping org.apache.fop.fo.StandardElementMapping
using element mapping org.apache.fop.svg.SVGElementMapping
using element mapping
org.apache.fop.extensions.ExtensionElementMapping
using property list mapping
org.apache.fop.fo.StandardPropertyListMapping
using property list mapping
org.apache.fop.svg.SVGPropertyListMapping
using property list mapping
org.apache.fop.extensions.ExtensionPropertyListMapping
building formatting object tree
setting up fonts
formatting FOs into areas
 [1]
rendering areas to PDF
writing out PDF
```

Here 19-1.fo is the input XML file that uses the formatting object vocabulary. 19-1.pdf is the output PDF file that can be displayed and printed by Adobe Acrobat or other programs that read PDF files.

Although PDF files are themselves ASCII text, this isn't a book about PostScript, so there's nothing to be gained by showing you the exact output of the above command. If you're curious, open the PDF file in any text editor. Instead, Figure 19-1 shows the rendered file displayed in Netscape Navigator using the Acrobat plug-in.

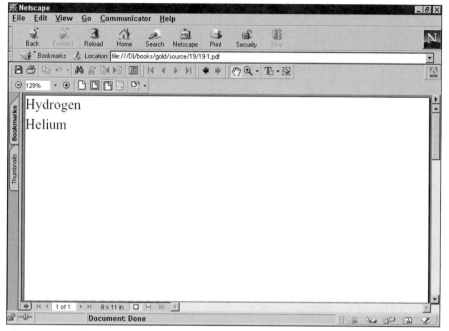

Figure 19-1: The PDF file displayed in Netscape Navigator

PDF files are not the only or even the primary eventual destination format for XML documents styled with XSL formatting objects. Certainly, one would hope that Web browsers will directly support XSL formatting objects in the not too distant future. For now, PDF files are the only convenient format, so that's what I show in this chapter. Eventually, more software will be able to read and display these files.

Page Layout

The root element of a formatting objects document is `fo:root`. This element contains one `fo:layout-master-set` element and one or more `fo:page-sequence` elements. The `fo:page-sequence` elements contain content; that is, text and images to be placed on the pages. The `fo:layout-master-set` contains templates for the pages that will be created. When the formatter reads an XSL-FO document, it creates a page based on the first template in the `fo:layout-master-set`. Then it fills it with content from the `fo:page-sequence`. When it's filled the first page, it instantiates a second page based on a template and fills it with content. The process continues until the formatter runs out of content.

The root element

The fo:root element generally has an xmlns:fo attribute with the value http://www.w3.org/1999/XSL/Format and may (though it generally does not) have an id attribute. The fo:root element exists just to declare the namespace and be the document root. It has no direct effect on page layout or formatting.

Simple page masters

The page templates are called *page masters*. Page masters are similar in purpose to QuarkXPress master pages or PowerPoint slide masters. Each defines a general layout for a page including its margins, the sizes of the header, footer, and body area of the page, and so forth. Each actual page in the rendered document is based on one master page and inherits certain properties like margins, page numbering, and layout from that master page. XSL-FO 1.0 defines exactly one kind of page master, the fo:simple-page-master, which represents a rectangular page. The fo:layout-master-set contains one or more fo:simple-page-master elements that define master pages.

Note   Future versions of XSL-FO will add other kinds of page masters, possibly including nonrectangular pages.

Each master page is represented by a fo:simple-page-master element. A fo:simple-page-master element defines a page layout, including the size of its before region, body region, after region, end region, and start region. Figure 19-2 shows the typical layout of these parts. One thing that may not be obvious from this picture is that the body region overlaps the other four regions (though not the page margins); that is, the body is everything inside the thick black line including the start, end, before, and after regions.

Note   In normal English text, the end region is the right side of the page and the start region is the left side of the page. This is reversed in Hebrew or Arabic text, because these languages are written from right to left. In almost all modern languages, the before region is the header and the after region is the footer, but this could be reversed in a language that wrote from bottom to top.

Simple page master properties

The fo:simple-page-master element has three main attributes:

- ✦ master-name: the name by which page sequences will reference this master page
- ✦ page-height: the height of the page
- ✦ page-width: the width of the page

If the page-height and page-width are not provided, then the formatter chooses a reasonable default based on the media in use (for example, 8.5" × 11").

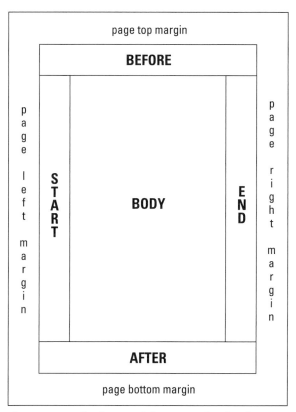

Figure 19-2: The layout of the parts of a simple page of English text

Other attributes commonly applied to page masters include:

✦ The `margin-bottom`, `margin-left`, `margin-right`, and `margin-top` attributes, or the shorthand `margin` attribute

✦ The `writing-mode` attribute that determines which direction text flows on the page, for example, left-to-right or right-to-left or top-to-bottom

✦ The `reference-orientation` attribute that specifies in 90-degree increments whether and how much the content is rotated

For example, here is a `fo:layout-master-set` containing one `fo:simple-page-master` named `US-Letter`. It specifies an 8.5 × 11-inch page with half-inch margins on each side. It contains a single region, the body, into which all content will be placed.

```
<fo:layout-master-set>
  <fo:simple-page-master    master-name="US-Letter"
      page-height="11in"    page-width="8.5in"
      margin-top="0.5in"    margin-bottom="0.5in"
```

```
        margin-left="0.5in"  margin-right="0.5in">
      <fo:region-body/>
   </fo:simple-page-master>
</fo:layout-master-set>
```

Regions

The designer sets the size of the body (center) region, header, footer, end region, and start region, as well as the distances between them, by adding region child elements to the `fo:simple-page-master`. These are:

- ✦ `fo:region-before`
- ✦ `fo:region-after`
- ✦ `fo:region-body`
- ✦ `fo:region-start`
- ✦ `fo:region-end`

The `fo:region-before` and `fo:region-after` elements each have an `extent` attribute that gives the height of these regions. Their width extends from the left side of the page to the right side. The `fo:region-start` and `fo:region-end` elements each have an `extent` attribute that specifies their widths. Their height extends from the bottom of the start region to the top of the end region. (This assumes normal Western text. Details would be rotated in Chinese or Hebrew or some other non-right-to-left–top-to-bottom script.)

The `fo:region-body` does not have an `extent` attribute. Instead, the size of the body is everything inside the page margins. Thus, the region body overlaps the other four regions on the page. If you place text into the body and the other four regions, text will be drawn on top of other content. To avoid this, you must set the left margin of the body to be as large or larger than the extent of the start region, the top margin of the body to be as large or larger than the extent of the before region, and so on.

Each of the five regions of a simple page master may be filled with content from a `fo:flow` or `fo:static-content` element when the document is processed. However, these elements do not contain that content. Instead, they simply give the dimensions of the boxes the formatter will build to put content in. They are blueprints for the boxes, not the boxes themselves.

For example, this `fo:simple-page-master` creates pages with one-inch before and after regions. The region body will extend vertically from the bottom of the before region to the top of the after region. It will extend horizontally from the left side of the page to the right side of the page because there is no start or end region.

```
<fo:simple-page-master master-name="table_page">
  <fo:region-before extent="1.0in"/>
  <fo:region-body margin-top="1.0in" margin-bottom="1.0in"/>
  <fo:region-after extent="1.0in"/>
</fo:simple-page-master>
```

For another example, here is a `fo:layout-master-set` that makes all outer regions one inch. Furthermore, the page itself has a half-inch margin on all sides.

```
<fo:layout-master-set>
  <fo:simple-page-master    master-name="only"
      page-width="8.5in"    page-height="11in"
      margin-top="0.5in"    margin-bottom="0.5in"
      margin-left="0.5in"   margin-right="0.5in">
    <fo:region-start   extent="1.0in"/>
    <fo:region-before  extent="1.0in"/>
    <fo:region-body    margin="1.0in"/>
    <fo:region-end     extent="1.0in"/>
    <fo:region-after   extent="1.0in"/>
  </fo:simple-page-master>
</fo:layout-master-set>
```

The body regions from pages based on this page master will be 5.5 inches wide and 8 inches high. That's calculated by subtracting the sum of the body region's margins and the page margins from the size of the page.

Page sequences

In addition to a `fo:layout-master-set`, each formatting object document contains one or more `fo:page-sequence` elements. Each page in the sequence has an associated page master that defines how the page will look. Which page master this is, is determined by the `master-name` attribute `fo:page-sequence` element. This must match the name of a page master in the `fo:layout-master-set`. Listing 19-1 used a `fo:simple-master-page` named `only` to fill this role, but it is not uncommon to have more than one master page. In this case, the master pages might be grouped as part of a `fo:page-sequence-master` instead. For instance, you could have one master page for the first page of each chapter, a different one for all the subsequent left-hand pages, and a third for all the subsequent right-hand pages. Or, there could be one simple page master for a table of contents, another for body text, and a third for the index. In this case, you use one page sequence each for the table of contents, the body text, and the index.

Each page sequence contains three child elements in this order:

1. An optional `fo:title` element containing inline content that can be used as the title of the document. This would normally be placed in the title bar of the browser window like the `TITLE` element in HTML.

2. Zero or more `fo:static-content` elements containing text to be placed on every page.

3. One `fo:flow` element containing data to be placed on each page in turn.

The main difference between a `fo:flow` and a `fo:static-content` is that text from the flow isn't placed on more than one page, whereas the static content is. For example, the words you're reading now are flow content that only appear on this page, whereas the part and chapter titles at the top of the page are static content that is repeated from page to page.

The `fo:flow` element contains, in order, the elements to be placed on the page. As each page fills with elements from the flow, a new page is created with the next master page in the page sequence master for the elements that remain in the flow. With a simple page master, the same page will be instantiated repeatedly, as many times as necessary to hold all the content.

The `fo:static-content` element contains information to be placed on each page. For instance, it may place the title of a book in the header of each page. Static content can be adjusted depending on the master page. For instance, the part title may be placed on left-hand pages, and the chapter title on right-hand pages. The `fo:static-content` element can also be used for items such as page numbers that have to be calculated from page to page. In other words, what's static is not the text, but the calculation that produces the text.

Flows

The `fo:flow` object holds the actual content, which will be placed on the instances of the master pages. This content is composed of a sequence of `fo:block`, `fo:block-container`, `fo:table-and-caption`, `fo:table`, and `fo:list-block` elements. This section sticks to basic `fo:block` elements, which are roughly equivalent HTML's `DIV` elements. Later in this chapter, you learn more block-level elements that a flow can contain.

For example, here is a basic flow containing the names of several atoms, each in its own block:

```
<fo:flow flow-name="xsl-region-body">
  <fo:block>Actinium</fo:block>
  <fo:block>Aluminum</fo:block>
  <fo:block>Americium</fo:block>
</fo:flow>
```

The `flow-name` attribute of the `fo:flow`, here with the value `xsl-region-body`, specifies which of the five regions of the page this flow's content will be placed in. The allowed values are:

✦ `xsl-region-body`

✦ `xsl-region-before`

✦ `xsl-region-after`

✦ `xsl-region-start`

✦ `xsl-region-end`

For example, a `flow` for the header has a `flow-name` value of `xsl-region-before`. A flow for the body would have a `flow-name` of `xsl-region-body`. There can't be two flows with the same name in the same page sequence. Thus, each `fo:page-sequence` can contain at most five `fo:flow` children, one for each of the five regions on the page.

You can now put together a complete style sheet that lays out the entire periodic table. Listing 19-3 demonstrates this with an XSLT style sheet that converts the periodic table into XSL formatting objects. The flow grabs all the atoms and places each one in its own block. A simple page master named `only` defines an A4-sized master page in landscape mode with half-inch margins on each side.

Listing 19-3: **A basic style sheet for the periodic table**

```xml
<?xml version="1.0"?>
<xsl:stylesheet version="1.0"
  xmlns:xsl="http://www.w3.org/1999/XSL/Transform"
  xmlns:fo="http://www.w3.org/1999/XSL/Format">

  <xsl:template match="/">
    <fo:root xmlns:fo="http://www.w3.org/1999/XSL/Format">

      <fo:layout-master-set>

        <fo:simple-page-master master-name="A4"
          page-width="297mm"  page-height="210mm"
          margin-top="0.5in"  margin-bottom="0.5in"
          margin-left="0.5in" margin-right="0.5in">
          <fo:region-body/>
        </fo:simple-page-master>

      </fo:layout-master-set>

      <fo:page-sequence master-name="A4">

        <fo:flow flow-name="xsl-region-body">
          <xsl:apply-templates select="//ATOM"/>
        </fo:flow>

      </fo:page-sequence>

    </fo:root>
  </xsl:template>

  <xsl:template match="ATOM">
    <fo:block><xsl:value-of select="NAME"/></fo:block>
  </xsl:template>

</xsl:stylesheet>
```

Figure 19-3 shows the resulting document after Listing 19-3 has been run through an XSLT processor to produce an XSL-FO document, and that document has been run through FOP to produce a PDF file.

Figure 19-3: The output of Listing 19-3

Static content

Whereas each piece of the content of a `fo:flow` element appears on one page, each piece of the content of a `fo:static-content` element appears on every page. For instance, if this book were laid out in XSL-FO, then the header at the top of the page would have been produced by `fo:static-content` elements. You do not have to use `fo:static-content` elements, but if you do use them they must appear before all the `fo:flow` elements in the page sequence.

`fo:static-content` elements have the same attributes and contents as a `fo:flow`. However, because a `fo:static-content` cannot break its contents across multiple pages if necessary, it generally has less content than a `fo:flow`. For example, Listing 19-4 uses a `fo:static-content` to place the words "The Periodic Table" in the header of each page.

Listing 19-4: **Using fo:static-content to generate a header**

```xml
<?xml version="1.0"?>
<xsl:stylesheet version="1.0"
  xmlns:xsl="http://www.w3.org/1999/XSL/Transform"
  xmlns:fo="http://www.w3.org/1999/XSL/Format">

  <xsl:template match="/">
    <fo:root xmlns:fo="http://www.w3.org/1999/XSL/Format">

      <fo:layout-master-set>

        <fo:simple-page-master master-name="A4"
          page-width="297mm"    page-height="210mm"
          margin-top="0.5in"  margin-bottom="0.5in"
          margin-left="0.5in" margin-right="0.5in">
         <fo:region-before extent="1.0in"/>
         <fo:region-body margin-top="1.0in"/>
        </fo:simple-page-master>

      </fo:layout-master-set>

      <fo:page-sequence master-name="A4">

        <fo:static-content flow-name="xsl-region-before">
          <fo:block>The Periodic Table</fo:block>
        </fo:static-content>

        <fo:flow flow-name="xsl-region-body">
          <xsl:apply-templates select="//ATOM"/>
        </fo:flow>

      </fo:page-sequence>

    </fo:root>
  </xsl:template>

  <xsl:template match="ATOM">
    <fo:block><xsl:value-of select="NAME"/></fo:block>
  </xsl:template>

</xsl:stylesheet>
```

Figure 19-4 shows the last page of the PDF file ultimately produced by Listing 19-4. The same text, "The Periodic Table," appears on all four pages of the document.

The Periodic Table

Thallium
Thulium
Uranium
ununbium
unumilium
unununium
Vanadium
Tungsten
Xenon
Yttrium
Ytterbium
Zinc
Zirconium

Figure 19-4: Static content in the header

Page numbering

The fo:page-sequence element has eight optional attributes that define page numbers for the sequence. These are:

- ✦ initial-page-number
- ✦ force-page-count
- ✦ format
- ✦ letter-value
- ✦ country
- ✦ language
- ✦ grouping-separator
- ✦ grouping-size

The initial-page-number attribute gives the number of the first page in this sequence. The most likely value for this attribute is 1, but it could be a larger number if the previous pages are in a different fo:page-sequence or even a different document. It can also be set to one of these three key words:

- ✦ auto: 1 unless pages from a preceding fo:page-sequence have pushed that up. This is the default.
- ✦ auto-odd: Same as auto, but add 1 if that value is an even number; that is, start on an odd page.
- ✦ auto-even: Same as auto, but add 1 if that value is an odd number; that is, start on an even page.

The `force-page-count` attribute is used to require the document to have an even or odd number of pages or to end on an even or odd page. This is sometimes necessary for printed books. The `force-page-count` attribute can have one of these six keyword values:

✦ `auto`: Make the last page an odd page if the `initial-page-number` of the next `fo:page-sequence` is even. Make the last page an even-page if the initial-page-number of the next page-sequence is odd. If there is no next `fo:page-sequence` or if the next `fo:page-sequence` does not specify an `initial-page-number`, then let the last page fall where it may.

✦ `even`: Require an even number of pages, inserting an extra blank page if necessary to make it so.

✦ `odd`: Require an odd number of pages, inserting an extra blank page if necessary to make it so.

✦ `end-on-even`: Require the last page to have an even page number, inserting an extra blank page if necessary to make it so.

✦ `end-on-odd`: Require the last page to have an odd page number, inserting an extra blank page if necessary to make it so.

✦ `no-force`: Do not require either an even or odd number of pages.

The `country` attribute should be set to an RFC 1766 country code. The `language` attribute should be set to an RFC 1766 language code (`http://www.ietf.org/rfc/rfc1766.txt`). For instance, you would use `en` to indicate English and `us` to indicate the United States.

Cross-Reference
These are essentially the same as the legal values for `xml:lang` that were discussed in Chapter 11, except that the country code and language codes are placed in two separate attributes rather than in one attribute.

The remaining four attributes have exactly the same syntax and meaning as when used as attributes of the `xsl:number` element from XSLT, so I won't repeat that discussion here.

Cross-Reference
The `xsl:number` element and the `format`, `letter-value`, `grouping-separator`, and `grouping-size` attributes are discussed in the "Number to String Conversion" section in Chapter 18.

The `fo:page-number` formatting object is an empty inline element that inserts the number of the current page. The formatter is responsible for determining what that number is. This element can have a variety of formatting attributes common to inline elements such as `font-family` and `text-decoration`. For example, Listing 19-5 uses `fo:static-content` and `fo:page-number` to put the page number at the bottom of every page:

Listing 19-5: Using fo:page-number to place the page number in the footer

```xml
<?xml version="1.0"?>
<xsl:stylesheet version="1.0"
  xmlns:xsl="http://www.w3.org/1999/XSL/Transform"
  xmlns:fo="http://www.w3.org/1999/XSL/Format">

  <xsl:template match="/">
    <fo:root xmlns:fo="http://www.w3.org/1999/XSL/Format">

      <fo:layout-master-set>

        <fo:simple-page-master master-name="A4"
          page-width="297mm"   page-height="210mm"
          margin-top="0.5in"  margin-bottom="0.5in"
          margin-left="0.5in" margin-right="0.5in">
          <fo:region-before extent="1.0in"/>
          <fo:region-body margin-top="1.0in"
                          margin-bottom="1.0in"/>
          <fo:region-after  extent="1.0in"/>
        </fo:simple-page-master>

      </fo:layout-master-set>

      <fo:page-sequence master-name="A4"
        initial-page-number="1" language="en" country="us">

        <fo:static-content flow-name="xsl-region-before">
          <fo:block>The Periodic Table</fo:block>
        </fo:static-content>

        <fo:static-content flow-name="xsl-region-after">
          <fo:block>p. <fo:page-number/></fo:block>
        </fo:static-content>

        <fo:flow flow-name="xsl-region-body">
          <xsl:apply-templates select="//ATOM"/>
        </fo:flow>

      </fo:page-sequence>

    </fo:root>
  </xsl:template>

  <xsl:template match="ATOM">
    <fo:block><xsl:value-of select="NAME"/></fo:block>
  </xsl:template>

</xsl:stylesheet>
```

Figure 19-5 shows the second page of the PDF file generated from Listing 19-5. The page number appears at the bottom of this and every other page in the document.

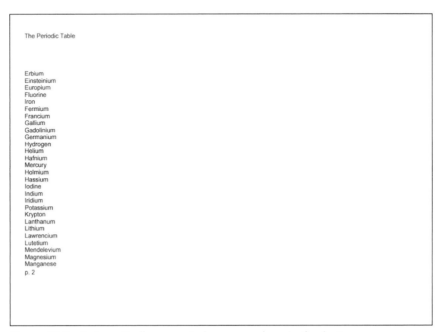

The Periodic Table

Erbium
Einsteinium
Europium
Fluorine
Iron
Fermium
Francium
Gallium
Gadolinium
Germanium
Hydrogen
Helium
Hafnium
Mercury
Holmium
Hassium
Iodine
Indium
Iridium
Potassium
Krypton
Lanthanum
Lithium
Lawrencium
Lutetium
Mendelevium
Magnesium
Manganese
p. 2

Figure 19-5: Automatically generated page numbers in the footer

Page sequence masters

Each page the formatter creates is associated with a master page from the `fo:layout-master-set` that defines how the page will look. Which master page this is, is determined by the `master-name` attribute `fo:page-sequence` element. Listings 19-3 through 19-5 used a single `fo:simple-master-page` named A4 to fill this role, but it is not uncommon to have more than one master page. For instance, you could use one master page for the first page of each chapter, a different one for all the subsequent left-hand pages, and a third for all the subsequent right-hand pages. In this case, the master pages might be grouped as part of a `fo:page-sequence-master` instead.

The `fo:page-sequence-master` element is a child of the `fo:layout-master-set` that lists the order in which particular master pages will be instantiated using one or more of these three child elements:

✦ `fo:single-page-master-reference`

✦ `fo:repeatable-page-master-reference`

✦ `fo:repeatable-page-master-alternatives`

Each of these elements has a `master-name` attribute that determines which master pages are used when.

fo:single-page-master-reference

The simplest is `fo:single-page-master-reference` whose `master-name` attribute identifies one master page to be instantiated. For example, this `fo:layout-master-set` contains a `fo:page-sequence-master` element named `contents` that says that all text should be placed on a single instance of the master page named A4:

```
<fo:layout-master-set>

  <fo:simple-page-master master-name="A4"
      page-width="297mm"  page-height="210mm"
      margin-top="0.5in"  margin-bottom="0.5in"
      margin-left="0.5in" margin-right="0.5in">
    <fo:region-body/>
  </fo:simple-page-master>

  <fo:page-sequence-master master-name="contents">
    <fo:single-page-master-reference master-name="A4"/>
  </fo:page-sequence-master>

</fo:layout-master-set>
```

This page sequence master only allows the creation of a single page. Technically, it's an error if there's more content than can fit on this one page. However, in practice most formatters simply repeat the last page used until they have enough pages to hold all the content.

Now consider this page sequence master:

```
<fo:page-sequence-master master-name="contents">
  <fo:single-page-master-reference master-name="A4"/>
  <fo:single-page-master-reference master-name="A4"/>
</fo:page-sequence-master>
```

This provides for up to two pages, each based on the master page named A4. If the first page fills up, a second is created. If that page fills up, then the formatter may throw an error, or it may create extra pages.

The same technique can be used to apply different master pages. For example, this sequence specification bases the first page on the master page named `front` and the second on the master page named `back`:

```
<fo:page-sequence-master master-name="contents">
  <fo:single-page-master-reference master-name="front"/>
  <fo:single-page-master-reference master-name="back"/>
</fo:page-sequence-master>
```

The first page the formatter creates will be based on the master page named front. The second page created will be based on the master page named back. If the second page fills up, the formatter may throw an error, or it may create extra pages based on back, the last master page instantiated.

fo:repeatable-page-master-reference

Of course, you usually don't know in advance exactly how many pages there will be. The fo:repeatable-page-master-reference element lets you specify that as many pages as necessary will be used to hold the content, all based on a single master page. The master-name attribute identifies which master page will be repeated. For example, this page sequence master will use as many copies of the master page named A4 as necessary to hold all the content:

```
<fo:page-sequence-master master-name="contents">
  <fo:repeatable-page-master-reference master-name="A4"/>
</fo:page-sequence-master>
```

Alternately, you can set the maximum-repeats attribute of the fo:repeatable-page-master-reference element to limit the number of pages that will be created. For instance, this fo:page-sequence-master generates at most ten pages per document:

```
<fo:page-sequence-master master-name="contents">
  <fo:repeatable-page-master-reference master-name="A4"
                                       maximum-repeats="10"/>
</fo:page-sequence-master>
```

This also lets you do things like using one master for the first two pages, another for the next three pages, and a third master for the next ten pages.

fo:repeatable-page-master-alternatives

The fo:repeatable-page-master-alternatives element specifies different master pages for the first page, even pages, odd pages, blank pages, last even page, and last odd page. This is more designed for a chapter of a printed book where the first and last pages, as well the even and odd pages, traditionally have different margins, headers, and footers.

Because a fo:repeatable-page-master-alternatives element needs to refer to more than one master page, it can't use a master-name attribute such as fo:single-page-master-reference and fo:repeatable-page-master-reference. Instead, it has fo:conditional-page-master-reference child elements. Each of these has a master-name attribute that identifies the master page to instantiate given that condition. The conditions themselves are determined by three attributes:

✦ page-position: This attribute can be set to first, last, rest, or any to identify it as applying only to the first page, last page, any page except the first, or any page, respectively.

✦ odd-or-even: This attribute can be set to odd, even, or any to identify it as applying only to odd pages, only to even pages, or to all pages, respectively.

✦ blank-or-not-blank: This attribute can be set to blank, not-blank, or any to identify it as applying only to blank pages, only to pages that contain content, or to all pages, respectively.

For example, this page sequence master says that the first page should be based on the master page named letter_first but that all subsequent pages should use the master page named letter:

```
<fo:page-sequence-master master-name="contents">
  <fo:repeatable-page-master-alternatives>
    <fo:conditional-page-master-reference
      page-position="first" master-name="letter_first"/>
    <fo:conditional-page-master-reference
      page-position="rest"  master-name="letter"/>
  </fo:repeatable-page-master-alternatives>
</fo:page-sequence-master master-name="contents">
```

If the content overflows the first page, the remainder will be placed on a second page. If it overflows the second page, a third page will be created. As many pages as needed to hold all the content will be constructed.

Content

The content (as opposed to markup) of an XSL-FO document is mostly text. Non-XML content such as GIF and JPEG images can be included in a fashion similar to the IMG element of HTML. Other forms of XML content, such as MathML and SVG, can be embedded directly inside the XSL-FO document. This content is stored in several kinds of elements including:

✦ Block-level formatting objects

✦ Inline formatting objects

✦ Table formatting objects

✦ Out-of-line formatting objects

All of these different kinds of elements are descendants of either a fo:flow or a fo:static-content element. They are never placed directly on page masters or page sequences.

Block-level formatting objects

A block-level formatting object is drawn as a rectangular area separated by a line break and possibly extra white space from any content that precedes or follows it.

Blocks may contain other blocks, in which case the contained blocks are also separated from the containing block by a line break and perhaps extra white space. Block-level formatting objects include:

✦ `fo:block`

✦ `fo:block-container`

✦ `fo:table-and-caption`

✦ `fo:table`

✦ `fo:list-block`

The `fo:block` element is the XSL-FO equivalent of `display: block` in CSS or `DIV` in HTML. Blocks may be contained in `fo:flow` elements, other `fo:block` elements, and `fo:static-content` elements. `fo:block` elements may contain other `fo:block` elements, other block-level elements such as `fo:table` and `fo:list-block`, and inline elements such as `fo:inline` and `fo:page-number`. Block-level elements may also contain raw text. For example:

```
<fo:block>The Periodic Table, Page <fo:page-number/></fo:block>
```

The block-level elements generally have attributes for both area properties and text-formatting properties. The text-formatting properties are inherited by any child elements of the block unless overridden.

Caution As of version 0.18.1, FOP does not support `fo:block-container` or `fo:table-and-caption`.

Inline formatting objects

An inline formatting object is also drawn as a rectangular area that may contain text or other inline areas. However, inline areas are most commonly arranged in lines running from left to right. When a line fills up, a new line is started below the previous one. The exact order in which inline elements are placed depends on the writing mode. For example, when working in Hebrew or Arabic, inline elements are first placed on the right and then fill to the left. Inline formatting objects include:

✦ `fo:bidi-override`

✦ `fo:character`

✦ `fo:external-graphic`

✦ `fo:initial-property-set`

✦ `fo:instream-foreign-object`

✦ `fo:inline`

✦ `fo:inline-container`

✦ `fo:leader`

✦ `fo:page-number`

✦ `fo:page-number-citation`

Caution   As of version 0.18.1, FOP does not support `fo:bidi-override`, `fo:initial-property-set`, or `fo:inline-container`.

Table formatting objects

The table formatting objects are the XSL-FO equivalents of CSS2 table properties. However, tables do work somewhat more naturally in XSL-FO than in CSS. For the most part, an individual table is a block-level object, while the parts of the table aren't really either inline or block level. However, an entire table can be turned into an inline object by wrapping it in a `fo:inline-container`.

There are nine XSL table formatting objects:

✦ `fo:table-and-caption`

✦ `fo:table`

✦ `fo:table-caption`

✦ `fo:table-column`

✦ `fo:table-header`

✦ `fo:table-footer`

✦ `fo:table-body`

✦ `fo:table-row`

✦ `fo:table-cell`

The root of a table is either a `fo:table` or a `fo:table-and-caption` that contains a `fo:table` and a `fo:caption`. The `fo:table` contains a `fo:table-header`, `fo:table-body`, and `fo:table-footer`. The table body contains `fo:table-row` elements that are divided up into `fo:table-cell` elements.

Caution   FOP 0.18.1 has limited support for the table formatting objects, and none at all for `fo:table-and-caption` and `fo:table-caption`.

Out-of-line formatting objects

There are three "out-of-line" formatting objects:

✦ `fo:float`

✦ `fo:footnote`

✦ `fo:footnote-body`

Out-of-line formatting objects "borrow" space from existing inline or block objects. On the page, they do not necessarily appear between the same elements that they appeared between in the input formatting object XML tree.

Caution   FOP 0.18.1 does not support fo:float.

Leaders and Rules

A rule is a block-level horizontal line inserted into text similar to the line below the chapter title on the first page of this chapter. The HR element in HTML produces a rule. A leader is a line that extends from the right side of left-aligned text in the middle of a line to the left side of some right-aligned text on the same line. It's most commonly made up of dots, although other characters can be used. Leaders are commonly seen in menus and tables of contents. In fact, if you flip back to the table of contents at the beginning of this book, you'll see leaders between chapter and section titles and the page numbers.

In XSL-FO both leaders and rules are produced by the fo:leader element. This is an inline element that represents a leader, although it can easily serve as a rule by placing it inside a fo:block.

Six attributes describe the appearance of a leader:

✦ leader-alignment: This can be set to reference-area or page to indicate that the start edge of the leader should be aligned with the start edge of the named item. It can also be set to none or inherit.

✦ leader-length: The length of the leader, such as 12pc or 5in.

✦ leader-pattern: This can be set to space, rule, dots, use-content, or inherit. The use-content value means that the leader characters should be read from the content of the fo:leader element.

✦ leader-pattern-width: This property can be set to a specific length such as 2mm or to use-font-metrics, which indicates that the leader should simply be as big as it would naturally be. This is not the length of the entire leader (which is set by leader-length); it is the length of each repeating pattern in the leader. If necessary, white space will be added to stretch each pattern out to the requested length.

✦ rule-style: This property has the same values as the CSS border-style properties; that is, none, dotted, dashed, solid, double, groove, ridge, and inherit.

✦ rule-thickness: This property is the thickness (width) of the rule; 1pt by default.

In addition, a number of other common properties apply to leaders. For instance, you can use the `font-family` property to change the font in which a leader is drawn or the `color` property to change the color in which a leader is drawn. For example, this is a green horizontal line that's 7.5 inches long and 2 points thick:

```
<fo:block>
  <fo:leader leader-length="7.5in" leader-pattern="rule"
             rule-thickness="2pt" color="green"/>
</fo:block>
```

Listing 19-6 uses `fo:leader` to place a rule at the top of each page footer.

Listing 19-6: Using fo:leader to separate the footer from the body with a horizontal line

```
<?xml version="1.0"?>
<xsl:stylesheet version="1.0"
  xmlns:xsl="http://www.w3.org/1999/XSL/Transform"
  xmlns:fo="http://www.w3.org/1999/XSL/Format">

<xsl:template match="/">
  <fo:root xmlns:fo="http://www.w3.org/1999/XSL/Format">

    <fo:layout-master-set>

      <fo:simple-page-master master-name="A4"
        page-width="297mm"   page-height="210mm"
        margin-top="0.5in"   margin-bottom="0.5in"
        margin-left="0.5in"  margin-right="0.5in">
        <fo:region-before extent="1.0in"/>
        <fo:region-body margin-top="1.0in"
                        margin-bottom="1.0in"/>
        <fo:region-after  extent="1.0in"/>
      </fo:simple-page-master>

    </fo:layout-master-set>

    <fo:page-sequence master-name="A4"
      initial-page-number="1" language="en" country="us">

      <fo:static-content flow-name="xsl-region-before">
        <fo:block>The Periodic Table</fo:block>
      </fo:static-content>

      <fo:static-content flow-name="xsl-region-after">
        <fo:block><fo:leader leader-pattern="rule"
                             leader-length="18cm" />
        </fo:block>
        <fo:block>p. <fo:page-number/></fo:block>
      </fo:static-content>
```

```
                <fo:flow flow-name="xsl-region-body">
                  <xsl:apply-templates select="//ATOM"/>
                </fo:flow>

            </fo:page-sequence>

          </fo:root>
       </xsl:template>

       <xsl:template match="ATOM">
         <fo:block><xsl:value-of select="NAME"/></fo:block>
       </xsl:template>

     </xsl:stylesheet>
```

Figure 19-6 shows the third page of the PDF file generated from Listing 19-6. The rule appears at the bottom of this and every other page in the document.

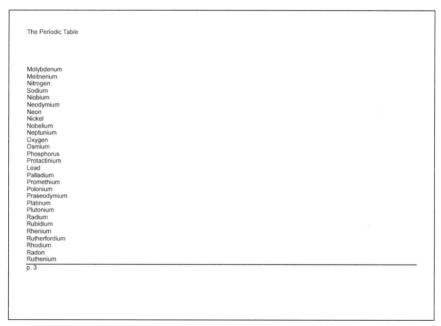

Figure 19-6: Automatically generated rules in the footer

Graphics

XSL-FO provides two elements for embedding pictures in a rendered document. The `fo:external-graphic` element inserts a non-XML graphic, such as a JPEG image.

The `fo:instream-foreign-object` element inserts an XML document that is not an XSL-FO document, such as an SVG picture or a MathML equation.

fo:external-graphic

The `fo:external-graphic` element provides the equivalent of an HTML `IMG` element. That is, it loads an image, probably in a non-XML format, from a URL. `fo:external-graphic` is always an empty element with no children. The `src` attribute contains a URI identifying the location of the image to be embedded. For example, consider this standard HTML `IMG` element:

```
<IMG SRC="cup.gif">
```

The `fo:external-graphic` equivalent looks like this:

```
<fo:external-graphic src="cup.gif"/>
```

Of course, you can use an absolute URL if you like:

```
<fo:external-graphic src="http://www.ibiblio.org/xml/cup.gif"/>
```

Just as with Web browsers and HTML, there's no guarantee that any particular formatting engine recognizes and supports any particular graphic format. Currently, FOP supports GIF and JPEG images. More formats may be added in the future.

`fo:external-graphic` is an inline element. You can make it a block-level picture simply by wrapping it in a `fo:block` element like this:

```
<fo:block><fo:external-graphic src="cup.gif"/></fo:block>
```

Listing 19-7 shows a style sheet that loads the image at `http://www.ibiblio.org/xml/images/atom.jpg` and puts it in the header of all the pages. In this case, the URI of the image is hard coded in the style sheet. In general, however, it would be read from the input document.

Listing 19-7: **An XSL style sheet that references an external graphic**

```
<?xml version="1.0"?>
<xsl:stylesheet version="1.0"
  xmlns:xsl="http://www.w3.org/1999/XSL/Transform"
  xmlns:fo="http://www.w3.org/1999/XSL/Format">

  <xsl:template match="/">
    <fo:root xmlns:fo="http://www.w3.org/1999/XSL/Format">
```

```
    <fo:layout-master-set>

      <fo:simple-page-master master-name="A4"
         page-width="297mm"  page-height="210mm"
         margin-top="0.5in"  margin-bottom="0.5in"
         margin-left="0.5in" margin-right="0.5in">
        <fo:region-before extent="1.0in"/>
        <fo:region-body margin-top="1.0in"
                        margin-bottom="1.0in"/>
        <fo:region-after  extent="1.0in"/>
      </fo:simple-page-master>

    </fo:layout-master-set>

    <fo:page-sequence master-name="A4"
       initial-page-number="1" language="en" country="us">

      <fo:static-content flow-name="xsl-region-before">
        <fo:block>
          <fo:external-graphic
          src="http://www.ibiblio.org/xml/images/atom.jpg"/>
          The Periodic Table
        </fo:block>
      </fo:static-content>

      <fo:static-content flow-name="xsl-region-after">
        <fo:block>
          <fo:leader leader-pattern="rule"
                     leader-length="18cm"/>
        </fo:block>
        <fo:block>p. <fo:page-number/></fo:block>
      </fo:static-content>

      <fo:flow flow-name="xsl-region-body">
        <xsl:apply-templates select="//ATOM"/>
      </fo:flow>

    </fo:page-sequence>

  </fo:root>
</xsl:template>

<xsl:template match="ATOM">
  <fo:block><xsl:value-of select="NAME"/></fo:block>
</xsl:template>

</xsl:stylesheet>
```

Figure 19-7 shows the first page of the PDF file generated from Listing 19-7. The picture appears at the top of this and every other page in the document.

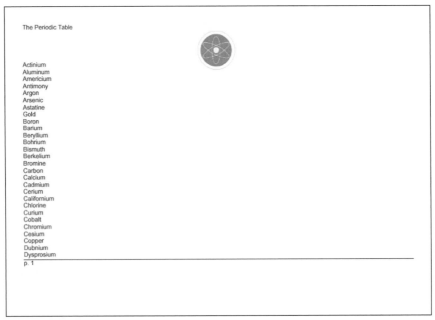

Figure 19-7: Inserting an external graphic in the header

fo:instream-foreign-object

The `fo:instream-foreign-object` inserts a graphic element that is described in XML and that is included directly in the XSL-FO document. For example, a `fo:instream-foreign-object` element might contain an SVG picture. The formatter would render the picture in the finished document. Listing 19-8 is an XSL-FO document that places the pink triangle SVG example from Chapter 2 on the header of each page:

Listing 19-8: An XSL style sheet that contains an instream SVG picture

```
<?xml version="1.0"?>
<xsl:stylesheet version="1.0"
  xmlns:xsl="http://www.w3.org/1999/XSL/Transform"
  xmlns:fo="http://www.w3.org/1999/XSL/Format">

  <xsl:template match="/">
    <fo:root xmlns:fo="http://www.w3.org/1999/XSL/Format">

      <fo:layout-master-set>
```

```
        <fo:simple-page-master master-name="A4"
           page-width="297mm"  page-height="210mm"
           margin-top="0.5in"  margin-bottom="0.5in"
           margin-left="0.5in" margin-right="0.5in">
          <fo:region-before extent="1.0in"/>
          <fo:region-body    margin-top="1.0in"/>
        </fo:simple-page-master>

    </fo:layout-master-set>

    <fo:page-sequence master-name="A4"
      initial-page-number="1" language="en" country="us">

      <fo:static-content flow-name="xsl-region-before">
        <fo:block> The Periodic Table
          <fo:instream-foreign-object>
            <svg xmlns="http://www.w3.org/2000/svg"
                width="1.5cm" height="1cm">
      <polygon style="fill:#FFCCCC" points="0,31 18,0 36,31"/>
            </svg>
          </fo:instream-foreign-object>
        </fo:block>
      </fo:static-content>

      <fo:flow flow-name="xsl-region-body">
        <xsl:apply-templates select="//ATOM"/>
      </fo:flow>

    </fo:page-sequence>

  </fo:root>
 </xsl:template>

 <xsl:template match="ATOM">
   <fo:block><xsl:value-of select="NAME"/></fo:block>
 </xsl:template>

</xsl:stylesheet>
```

Figure 19-8 shows the first page of the PDF file generated from Listing 19-8. The triangle appears at the top of this and every other page in the document.

Not all formatters support all possible XML graphics formats. For instance, FOP does not support MathML at all, and only supports a subset of SVG. Still this is a useful technique, especially when you want XSLT to generate pictures at runtime. For instance, you could write an XSLT style sheet that produced nicely formatted annual reports, including all the charts and graphics, simply by transforming some of the input document into XSL-FO and other parts of the input document into SVG.

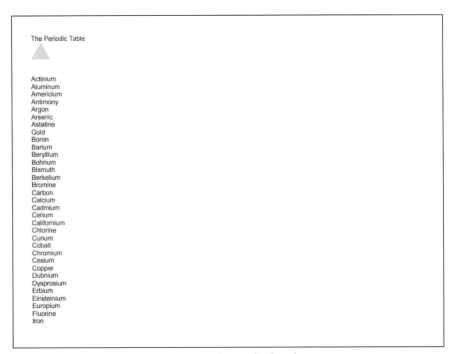

Figure 19-8: Inserting an instream graphic in the header

Graphic properties

`fo:external-graphic` and `fo:instream-foreign-object` share a number of properties designed to scale, position, crop, align, and otherwise adjust the appearance of the image on the page.

Content type

The `content-type` attribute specifies the type of the graphic. You can give this as a MIME media type, such as image/jpg or image/svg-xml, by prefixing the actual type with `content-type:`. For example, to specify that the `fo:external-graphic` element refers to a GIF image you would write it as

```
<fo:external-graphic content-type="content-type:image/gif"
                     src="cup.gif" />
```

This can also be given in terms of a namespace prefix by using a value in the form `namespace-prefix:`*prefix*. For example, to specify that the `fo:instream-foreign-object` includes an SVG picture you write it as

```
<fo:instream-foreign-object
    xmlns:svg="http://www.w3.org/2000/svg"
    content-type="namespace-prefix:svg">
```

The namespace prefix does not have to be declared on the `fo:instream-foreign-object` element. It simply needs to be declared somewhere in the ancestors of the element.

Size

The `height` and `width` attributes specify the vertical and horizontal size of the rectangle set aside on the page for the image. Either or both of these can be set to the keyword `auto`, rather than to an absolute length, to indicate that the size of the image itself should be used.

The `content-height` and `content-width` attributes specify the vertical and horizontal size of the image itself. If either or both of these is not the same as `height` and `width`, respectively, then the image has to be scaled.

Scaling

The `scaling` attribute can be set to either `uniform` or `non-uniform`. Uniform scaling maintains the height-to-width ratio of the image as it's scaled. This is the default. Non-uniform scaling may scale the height and width differently, so that the image is distorted.

You can also choose the algorithm by which scaling occurs by using the `scaling-method` attribute. This can be set to `auto`, `integer-pixels`, or `resample-any-method`. Integer scaling maintains an integral ratio between original and scaled images such as 2:1 or 3:1, but not 1.5:1. In most cases, integer-scaled images are smaller than images scaled by `resample-any-method`, but won't require dithering. The value `auto` lets the formatter decide what to do.

In addition, you can set a variety of common properties for inline elements. These include the common accessibility, aural, background, border, padding, and margin properties. Because graphics shouldn't be split across multiple pages, they don't support the usual break properties, but they do support `keep-with-next` and `keep-with-previous`.

Links

The `fo:basic-link` element encodes HTML-style hyperlinks in XSL-FO documents. This is an inline formatting object that the user can click on to move to a different document, or to a different place in the same document. This doesn't offer much for print, but it might be useful when and if Web browsers support XSL-FO directly. The link behavior is controlled by these eight attributes:

- ✦ `external-destination`
- ✦ `internal-destination`
- ✦ `indicate-destination`

- ✦ show-destination
- ✦ destination-placement-offset
- ✦ target-presentation-context
- ✦ target-processing-context
- ✦ target-stylesheet

A link to a remote document target specifies the URI through the value of the external-destination attribute. The browser should replace the current document with the document at this URI when the reader activates the link. In most GUI environments, the user activates the link by clicking on its contents. For example:

```
<fo:block> Be sure to visit the
   <fo:basic-link
     external-destination="http://www.ibiblio.org/xml/">
     Cafe con Leche Web site!
   </fo:basic-link>
</fo:block>
```

You can also link to another node in the same document by using the internal-destination attribute. The value of this attribute is not a URI, but rather the ID of the element you're linking to. You can often use the generate-id() function of XSLT to produce both the IDs on the output elements and the links to those elements inside the XSL-FO output. You should not specify both the internal and external destination for one link.

The three other destination attributes affect the appearance and behavior of the link. The indicate-destination attribute has a boolean value (true or false; false by default) that specifies whether, when the linked item is loaded, it should somehow be distinguished from nonlinked parts of the same document. For example, if you follow a link to one ATOM element in a table of 100 atoms, the specific atom you were connecting to might be in boldface while the other atoms are in normal type. The exact details are system dependent.

The show-destination attribute has two possible values: replace (the default) and new. With a value of replace, when a link is followed, the target document replaces the existing document in the same window. With a value of new, when the user activates a link, the browser opens a new window in which to display the target document.

When a browser follows an HTML link into the middle of a document, generally the specific linked element is positioned at the tip-top of the window. The destination-placement-offset attribute specifies how far down the browser should scroll the linked element in the window. It's given as a length such as 3in or 156px.

The three target properties describe how the document at the other end of the link will be displayed. The `target-presentation-context` attribute contains a URI that generally indicates some subset of the external destination that should actually be presented to the user. For instance, an XPointer could be used here to say that although an entire book is loaded only the seventh chapter will be shown.

The `target-processing-context` attribute contains a URI that serves as a base URI in the event that the external destination contains a relative URI. Otherwise, that would be considered relative to the current document.

Finally, the `target-stylesheet` attribute contains a URI that points to a style sheet that should be used when the targeted document is rendered. This overrides any style sheet that the targeted document itself specifies, whether through an `xml-stylesheet` processing instruction, a `LINK` element in HTML, or an HTTP header.

In addition, the link may have the usual accessibility, margin, background, border, padding, and aural properties.

Lists

The `fo:list-block` formatting object element describes a block-level list element. (There are no inline lists.) A list may or may not be bulleted, numbered, indented, or otherwise formatted. Each `fo:list-block` element contains either a series of `fo:list-item` elements or `fo:list-item-label` `fo:list-item-body` pairs. (It cannot contain both.) A `fo:list-item` must contain a `fo:list-item-label` and a `fo:list-item-body`. The `fo:list-item-label` contains the bullet, number, or other label for the list item as a block level element. The `fo:list-item-body` contains block-level elements holding the actual content of the list item. To summarize, a `fo:list-block` contains `fo:list-item` elements. Each `fo:list-item` contains a `fo:list-item-label` and `fo:list-item-body`. However, the `fo:list-item` elements can be omitted. For example:

```
<fo:list-block>
  <fo:list-item>
    <fo:list-item-label><fo:block>*</fo:block>
    </fo:list-item-label>
    <fo:list-item-body>
      <fo:block>Actinium</fo:block>
    </fo:list-item-body>
  </fo:list-item>
  <fo:list-item>
    <fo:list-item-label><fo:block>*</fo:block>
```

```
            </fo:list-item-label>
          <fo:list-item-body>
            <fo:block>Aluminum</fo:block>
          </fo:list-item-body>
        </fo:list-item>
      </fo:list-block>
```

Or, with the `fo:list-item` tags removed:

```
<fo:list-block>
    <fo:list-item-label>
      <fo:block>*</fo:block>
    </fo:list-item-label>
    <fo:list-item-body>
        <fo:block>Actinium</fo:block>
    </fo:list-item-body>
    <fo:list-item-label>
      <fo:block>*</fo:block>
    </fo:list-item-label>
    <fo:list-item-body>
      <fo:block>Aluminum</fo:block>
    </fo:list-item-body>
</fo:list-block>
```

The `fo:list-block` element has two special attributes that control list formatting:

✦ `provisional-label-separation`: The distance between the list item label and the list item body, given as a triplet of *maximum;minimum;optimum*, such as `2mm;0.5mm;1mm`

✦ `provisional-distance-between-starts`: The distance between the start edge of the list item label and the start edge of the list item body

`fo:list-block` also has the usual accessibility, aural, border, padding, background, margin, and keeps and breaks properties. The `fo:list-item` element has the standard block-level properties for backgrounds, position, aural rendering, borders, padding, margins, line and page breaking. The `fo:list-item-label` and `fo:list-item-body` elements only have the accessibility properties: `id` and `keep-together`. The rest of their formatting is controlled either by the parent elements (`fo:list-item` and `fo:list-item-block`) or the child elements they contain.

Listing 19-9 formats the periodic table as a list in which the atomic numbers are the list labels and the names of the elements are the list bodies. Figure 19-9 shows the second page of output produced by this style sheet.

Listing 19-9: An XSL style sheet that formats the periodic table as a list

```
<?xml version="1.0"?>
<xsl:stylesheet version="1.0"
  xmlns:xsl="http://www.w3.org/1999/XSL/Transform"
  xmlns:fo="http://www.w3.org/1999/XSL/Format">

  <xsl:template match="/">
    <fo:root xmlns:fo="http://www.w3.org/1999/XSL/Format">

      <fo:layout-master-set>

        <fo:simple-page-master master-name="A4"
          page-width="297mm"  page-height="210mm"
          margin-top="0.5in"  margin-bottom="0.5in"
          margin-left="0.5in" margin-right="0.5in">
          <fo:region-body/>
        </fo:simple-page-master>

      </fo:layout-master-set>

      <fo:page-sequence master-name="A4">

        <fo:flow flow-name="xsl-region-body">
          <fo:list-block>
            <xsl:apply-templates select="//ATOM">
              <xsl:sort data-type="number"
                        select="ATOMIC_NUMBER"/>
            </xsl:apply-templates>
          </fo:list-block>
        </fo:flow>

      </fo:page-sequence>

    </fo:root>
  </xsl:template>

  <xsl:template match="ATOM">
    <fo:list-item>
      <fo:list-item-label><fo:block>
        <xsl:value-of select="ATOMIC_NUMBER"/>
      </fo:block></fo:list-item-label>
      <fo:list-item-body><fo:block>
        <xsl:value-of select="NAME"/>
      </fo:block></fo:list-item-body>
    </fo:list-item>
  </xsl:template>

</xsl:stylesheet>
```

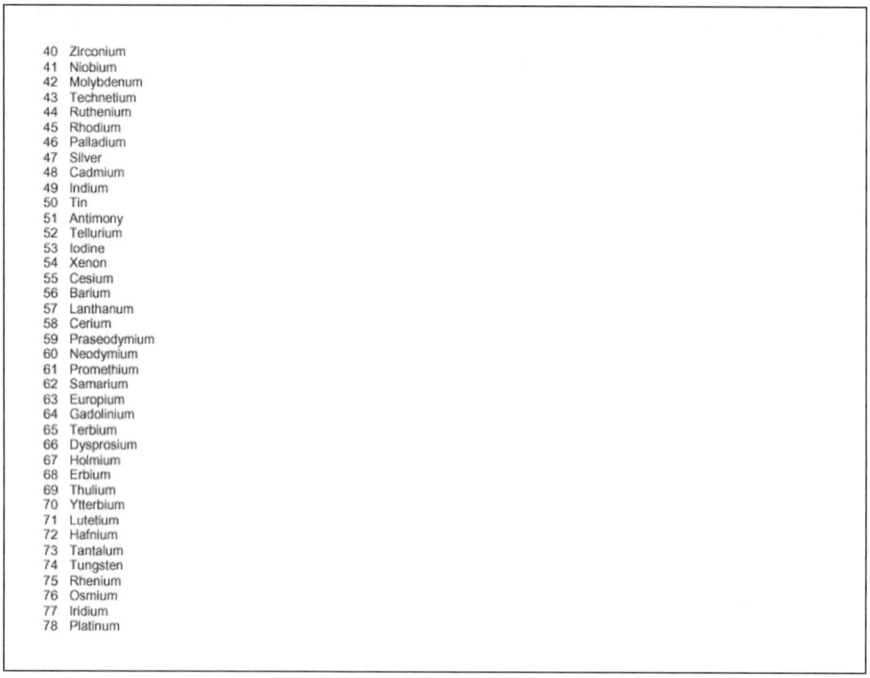

```
40   Zirconium
41   Niobium
42   Molybdenum
43   Technetium
44   Ruthenium
45   Rhodium
46   Palladium
47   Silver
48   Cadmium
49   Indium
50   Tin
51   Antimony
52   Tellurium
53   Iodine
54   Xenon
55   Cesium
56   Barium
57   Lanthanum
58   Cerium
59   Praseodymium
60   Neodymium
61   Promethium
62   Samarium
63   Europium
64   Gadolinium
65   Terbium
66   Dysprosium
67   Holmium
68   Erbium
69   Thulium
70   Ytterbium
71   Lutetium
72   Hafnium
73   Tantalum
74   Tungsten
75   Rhenium
76   Osmium
77   Iridium
78   Platinum
```

Figure 19-9: The periodic table formatted as a list

In HTML a list item implies a certain level of indenting. However, as you can see in Figure 19-9, no such indenting is implied by any of the XSL-FO list elements. If you want list items to be indented, you can use the start-indent and end-indent attributes on the fo:list-item-label and fo:list-item-body elements. Each of these is set to a length. However, because the list item body normally starts on the same line as the list item label, its start indent is often given by the special XSL-FO body-start() function. This returns the combined length of the start-indent and the provisional-distance-between-starts. For example,

```
<xsl:template match="ATOM">
  <fo:list-item>
    <fo:list-item-label start-indent="1.0cm"
                        end-indent="1.0cm">
      <fo:block>
        <xsl:value-of select="ATOMIC_NUMBER"/>
      </fo:block>
    </fo:list-item-label>
    <fo:list-item-body start-indent="body-start()">
      <fo:block>
        <xsl:value-of select="NAME"/>
      </fo:block>
    </fo:list-item-body>
  </fo:list-item>
</xsl:template>
```

Tables

The fundamental table element in XSL is `fo:table-and-caption`. This is a block-level object that contains a `fo:table` and a `fo:caption`. If your table doesn't need a caption, you can just use a raw `fo:table` instead. The XSL-FO table model is quite close to HTML's table model. Table 19-1 shows the mapping between HTML 4.0 table elements and XSL formatting objects:

Table 19-1 HTML Tables vs. XSL Formatting Object Tables	
HTML Element	*XSL FO Element*
TABLE	fo:table-and-caption
no equivalent	fo:table
CAPTION	fo:table-caption
COL	fo:table-column
COLGROUP	no equivalent
THEAD	fo:table-header
TBODY	fo:table-body
TFOOT	fo:table-footer
TD	fo:table-cell
TR	fo:table-row

Each `fo:table-and-caption` contains an optional `fo:table-caption` element and one `fo:table` element. The caption can contain any block-level elements you care to place in the caption. By default captions are placed before the table, but this can be adjusted by setting the `caption-side` property of the `table-and-caption` element to one of these eight values:

✦ `before`

✦ `after`

✦ `start`

✦ `end`

✦ `top`

✦ `bottom`

✦ `left`

✦ `right`

For example, here's a table with a caption on the bottom:

```
<fo:table-and-caption caption-side="bottom">
  <fo:table-caption>
    <fo:block font-weight="bold"
              font-family="Helvetica, Arial, sans"
              font-size="12pt">
      Table 19-1: HTML Tables vs. XSL Formatting Object Tables
    </fo:block>
  </fo:table-caption>
  <fo:table>
    <!-- table contents go here -->
  </fo:table>
</fo:table-and-caption>
```

The `fo:table` element contains `fo:table-column` elements, an optional `fo:table-header`, an optional `fo:table-footer`, and one or more `fo:table-body` elements. The `fo:table-body` is divided into `fo:table-row` elements. Each `fo:table-row` is divided into `fo:table-cell` elements. The `fo:table-header` and `fo:table-footer` can either be divided into `fo:table-cell` or `fo:table-row` elements. For example, here's a simple table that includes the first three rows of Table 19-1 above.

```
<fo:table>
  <fo:table-header>
    <fo:table-cell>
      <fo:block font-family="Helvetica, Arial, sans"
                font-size="11pt" font-weight="bold">
        HTML Element
      </fo:block>
    </fo:table-cell>
    <fo:table-cell>
      <fo:block font-family="Helvetica, Arial, sans"
                font-size="11pt" font-weight="bold">
        XSL FO Element
      </fo:block>
    </fo:table-cell>
  </fo:table-header>
  <fo:table-body>
    <fo:table-row>
      <fo:table-cell>
        <fo:block font-family="Courier, monospace">
          TABLE
        </fo:block>
      </fo:table-cell>
      <fo:table-cell>
        <fo:block font-family="Courier, monospace">
          fo:table-and-caption
        </fo:block>
      </fo:table-cell>
```

```
      </fo:table-row>
      <fo:table-row>
        <fo:table-cell>
          <fo:block>no equivalent</fo:block>
        </fo:table-cell>
        <fo:table-cell>
          <fo:block font-family="Courier, monospace">
            fo:table
          </fo:block>
        </fo:table-cell>
      </fo:table-row>
    </fo:table-body>
  </fo:table>
```

You can make table cells span multiple rows and columns by setting the `number-columns-spanned` and/or `number-rows-spanned` attributes to an integer giving the number of rows or columns to span. The optional `column-number` attribute can change which column the spanning begins in. The default is the current column.

Borders can be drawn around table parts using the normal border properties. The `empty-cells` attribute has the value `show` or `hide`; `show` if borders are to be drawn around cells with no content, `hide` if not. The default is `show`.

When a long table extends across multiple pages, sometimes the header and footer are repeated on each page. You can alter this behavior with the `table-omit-header-at-break` and `table-omit-footer-at-break` attributes of the `fo:table` element. The value `false` indicates that the header or footer is to be repeated from page to page. The value `true` indicates that it is not. The default is `false`.

The optional `fo:table-column` element is an empty element that specifies properties for all cells in a particular column. The cells it applies to are identified by the `column-number` attribute or by the position of the `fo:table-column` element itself. `fo:table-column` does not actually contain any cells. A `fo:table-column` can apply properties to more than one consecutive column by setting the `number-columns-spanned` property to an integer greater than one. The most common property to set in a `fo:table-column` is `column-width` (a signed length) but the standard border, padding, and background properties (discussed below and mostly the same as in CSS) can also be set.

Caution   FOP 0.18.1 only has limited table support. In particular, it does not support `fo:table-caption` or `fo:table-and-caption`. Furthermore, FOP requires you to explicitly specify the column widths using a `fo:table-column` element. You can't let it choose suitable widths as you might let a Web browser do.

For example, Listing 19-10 lays out all the properties of the elements in a table. Figure 19-10 shows the first page of output produced by this style sheet.

Hydrogen	H	1	1.00794	1	0.0899	1s1	2.1	2.08	14.1	14.304	14.304	0.1815
Helium	He	2	4.0026		0.1785	1s2	0		31.8	5.193	5.193	0.152
Lithium	Li	3	6.941	1	0.53	1s2 2s1	0.98	1.55	13.1	3.582	3.582	84.7
Beryllium	Be	4	9.01218	2	1.85	1s2 2s2	1.57	1.12	5	1.825	1.825	200
Boron	B	5	10.811	3	2.34	1s2 2s2 p1	2.04	0.98	4.6	1.026	1.026	27
Carbon	C	6	12.011	+/-4, 2	2.26	1s2 2s2 p2	2.55	0.91	5.3	0.709	0.709	155
Nitrogen	N	7	14.0067	+/-3, 5, 4, 2	1.251	1s2 2s2 p3	3.04	0.92	17.3	1.042	1.042	0.02598
Oxygen	O	8	15.9994	-2	1.429	1s2 2s2 p4	3.44	0.65	14	0.92	0.92	0.2674
Fluorine	F	9	18.9984	-1	1.696	1s2 2s2 p5	3.98	0.57	17.1	0.824	0.824	0.0279
Neon	Ne	10	20.1797		0.900	1s2 2s2 p6	0	0.51	16.9	1.03	1.03	0.0493
Sodium	Na	11	22.98977	1	0.97	[Ne] 3s1	0.93	1.9	23.7	1.23	1.23	141
Magnesium	Mg	12	24.305	2	1.74	[Ne] 3s2	1.31	1.6	14	1.02	1.02	156
Aluminum	Al	13	26.98154	3	2.7	[Ne] 3s2 p1	1.61	1.43	10	0.9	0.9	237
Silicon	Si	14	28.0855	4	2.33	[Ne] 3s2 p2	1.9	1.32	12.1	0.70	0.70	148
Phosphorus	P	15	30.97376	+/-3, 5, 4	1.82	[Ne] 3s2 p3	2.19	1.28	17	0.769	0.769	0.235
Sulfur	S	16	32.066	+/-2, 4, 6	2.07	[Ne] 3s2 p4	2.58	1.27	15.5	0.71	0.71	0.269
Chlorine	Cl	17	35.4527	+/-1, 3, 5, 7	3.214	[Ne] 3s2 p5	3.16	0.97	18.7	0.48	0.48	0.0089
Argon	Ar	18	39.948		1.784	[Ne] 3s2 p6	0	0.88	24.2	0.52	0.52	0.0177
Potassium	K	19	39.0983	1	0.86	[Ar] 4s1	0.82	2.35	45.3	0.757	0.757	102.5
Calcium	Ca	20	40.078	2	1.55	[Ar] 4s2	1	1.97	29.9	0.647	0.647	200
Scandium	Sc	21	44.9559	3	2.99	[Ar] 3d1 4s2	1.36	1.62	15	0.568	0.568	15.8
Titanium	Ti	22	47.88	4, 3	4.54	[Ar] 3d2 4s2	1.54	1.45	10.6	0.523	0.523	21.9
Vanadium	V	23	50.9415	5, 4, 3, 2	6.11	[Ar] 3d3 4s2	1.63	1.34	8.35	0.489	0.489	30.7
Chromium	Cr	24	51.996	6, 3, 2	7.19	[Ar] 3d5 4s1	1.66	1.3	7.23	0.449	0.449	93.7
Manganese	Mn	25	54.938	7, 6, 4, 2, 3	7.44	[Ar] 3d5 4s2	1.55	1.35	7.39	0.48	0.48	7.82
Iron	Fe	26	55.847	2, 3	7.874	[Ar] 3d6 4s2	1.83	1.26	7.1	0.449	0.449	80.2
Cobalt	Co	27	58.9332	2, 3	8.9	[Ar] 3d7 4s2	1.88	1.25	6.7	0.421	0.421	100
Nickel	Ni	28	58.6934	2, 3	8.9	[Ar] 3d8 4s2	1.91	1.24	6.6	0.444	0.444	90.7
Copper	Cu	29	63.546	2, 1	8.96	[Ar] 3d10 4s1	1.9	1.28	7.1	0.385	0.385	401
Zinc	Zn	30	65.39	2	7.13	[Ar] 3d10 4s2	1.65	1.38	9.2	0.388	0.388	116
Gallium	Ga	31	69.723	3	5.91	[Ar] 3d10 4s2 p1	1.81	1.41	11.8	0.371	0.371	40.6
Germanium	Ge	32	72.61	4	5.32	[Ar] 3d10 4s2 p2	2.01	1.37	13.6	0.32	0.32	59.9
Arsenic	As	33	74.9216	+/-3, 5	5.78	[Ar] 3d10 4s2 p3	2.18	1.39	13.1	0.33	0.33	50
Selenium	Se	34	78.96	-2, 4, 6	4.79	[Ar] 3d10 4s2 p4	2.55	1.4	16.5	0.32	0.32	2.04
Bromine	Br	35	79.904	+/-1, 5	3.12	[Ar] 3d10 4s2 p5	2.96	1.12	23.5	0.226	0.226	0.122
Krypton	Kr	36	83.8		3.75	[Ar] 3d10 4s2 p6	0	1.03	32.2	0.248	0.248	0.00949
Rubidium	Rb	37	85.4678	1	1.532	[Kr] 5s1	0.82	2.48	55.9	0.363	0.363	58.2
Strontium	Sr	38	87.62	2	2.54	[Kr] 5s2	0.95	2.15	33.7	0.3	0.3	35.3
Yttrium	Y	39	88.9059	3	4.47	[Kr] 4d1 5s2	1.22	1.78	19.8	0.3	0.3	17.2

Figure 19-10: The periodic table formatted as a table

Listing 19-10: **An XSL style sheet that formats the elements as a table**

```
<?xml version="1.0"?>
<xsl:stylesheet version="1.0"
  xmlns:xsl="http://www.w3.org/1999/XSL/Transform"
  xmlns:fo="http://www.w3.org/1999/XSL/Format">

  <xsl:template match="/">
    <fo:root xmlns:fo="http://www.w3.org/1999/XSL/Format">

      <fo:layout-master-set>

        <fo:simple-page-master master-name="A4"
          page-width="297mm"  page-height="210mm"
          margin-top="0.5in"  margin-bottom="0.5in"
          margin-left="0.5in" margin-right="0.5in">
          <fo:region-body/>
        </fo:simple-page-master>

      </fo:layout-master-set>

      <fo:page-sequence master-name="A4">
```

```
          <fo:flow flow-name="xsl-region-body">
            <fo:table>
              <fo:table-column column-width="30mm"/>
              <fo:table-column column-width="12mm"/>
              <fo:table-column column-width="12mm"/>
              <fo:table-column column-width="25mm"/>
              <fo:table-column column-width="27mm"/>
              <fo:table-column column-width="18mm"/>
              <fo:table-column column-width="49mm"/>
              <fo:table-column column-width="16mm"/>
              <fo:table-column column-width="16mm"/>
              <fo:table-column column-width="16mm"/>
              <fo:table-column column-width="21mm"/>
              <fo:table-column column-width="21mm"/>
              <fo:table-column column-width="21mm"/>
              <fo:table-body>
                <xsl:apply-templates select="//ATOM">
                  <xsl:sort data-type="number"
                    select="ATOMIC_NUMBER"/>
                </xsl:apply-templates>
              </fo:table-body>
            </fo:table>
          </fo:flow>

      </fo:page-sequence>

  </fo:root>
</xsl:template>

<xsl:template match="ATOM">
  <fo:table-row>
    <fo:table-cell>
      <fo:block><xsl:value-of select="NAME"/></fo:block>
    </fo:table-cell>
    <fo:table-cell>
      <fo:block><xsl:value-of select="SYMBOL"/></fo:block>
    </fo:table-cell>
    <fo:table-cell>
      <fo:block>
        <xsl:value-of select="ATOMIC_NUMBER"/>
      </fo:block>
    </fo:table-cell>
    <fo:table-cell>
      <fo:block>
        <xsl:value-of select="ATOMIC_WEIGHT"/>
      </fo:block>
    </fo:table-cell>
    <fo:table-cell>
      <fo:block>
        <xsl:value-of select="OXIDATION_STATES"/>
      </fo:block>
```

Continued

Listing 19-10 *(continued)*

```
      </fo:table-cell>
      <fo:table-cell>
        <fo:block><xsl:value-of select="DENSITY"/></fo:block>
      </fo:table-cell>
      <fo:table-cell>
        <fo:block>
          <xsl:value-of select="ELECTRON_CONFIGURATION"/>
        </fo:block>
      </fo:table-cell>
      <fo:table-cell>
        <fo:block>
          <xsl:value-of select="ELECTRONEGATIVITY"/>
        </fo:block>
      </fo:table-cell>
      <fo:table-cell>
        <fo:block>
          <xsl:value-of select="ATOMIC_RADIUS"/>
        </fo:block>
      </fo:table-cell>
      <fo:table-cell>
        <fo:block>
          <xsl:value-of select="ATOMIC_VOLUME"/>
        </fo:block>
      </fo:table-cell>
      <fo:table-cell>
        <fo:block>
          <xsl:value-of select="SPECIFIC_HEAT_CAPACITY"/>
        </fo:block>
      </fo:table-cell>
      <fo:table-cell>
        <fo:block>
          <xsl:value-of select="SPECIFIC_HEAT_CAPACITY"/>
        </fo:block>
      </fo:table-cell>
      <fo:table-cell>
        <fo:block>
          <xsl:value-of select="THERMAL_CONDUCTIVITY"/>
        </fo:block>
      </fo:table-cell>
    </fo:table-row>
  </xsl:template>

</xsl:stylesheet>
```

Inlines

The `fo:inline` element has no particular effect on the layout of the page. Rather it's an element on which you can hang formatting attributes such as `font-style` or `color` for application to the inline's contents. The `fo:inline` formatting object is a container that groups inline objects together. It cannot contain block-level elements. For example, you can use `fo:inline` elements to add style to various parts of the footer, like this:

```
<fo:static-content flow-name="xsl-region-after">
  <fo:block font-weight="bold" font-size="10pt"
            font-family="Arial, Helvetica, sans">
      <fo:inline font-style="italic" text-align="start">
        The XML Bible
      </fo:inline>
      <fo:inline text-align="centered">
        Page <fo:page-number/>
      </fo:inline>
      <fo:inline text-align="right">
        Chapter 18: XSL Formatting Objects
      </fo:inline>
  </fo:block>
</fo:static-content>
```

Footnotes

The `fo:footnote` element creates a footnote. The author places the `fo:footnote` element in the flow exactly where the footnote reference such as [1] or [*] will occur. The `fo:footnote` element contains both the reference text and a `fo:footnote-body` block-level element containing the text of the footnote. However, only the footnote reference is inserted inline. The formatter places the note text in the after region (generally the footer) of the page.

For example, this footnote uses an asterisk as a footnote marker and refers to "*JavaBeans*, Elliotte Rusty Harold (IDG Books, Foster City, 1998), p. 147." Standard properties such as `font-size` and `vertical-align` are used to format both the note marker and the text in the customary fashion.

```
<fo:footnote>
  <fo:inline font-size="smaller" vertical-align="super">*
  </fo:inline>
  <fo:footnote-body font-size="smaller">
    <fo:inline font-size="smaller" vertical-align="super">
      *
    </fo:inline>
    <fo:inline font-style="italic">JavaBeans</fo:inline>,
```

```
                Elliotte Rusty Harold
                (IDG Books, Foster City, 1998), p. 147
        </fo:footnote-body>
</fo:footnote>
```

Tip   XSL-FO doesn't provide any means of automatically numbering and citing footnotes, but this can be done by judicious use of `xsl:number` in the transformation
style sheet. XSL Transformations make end notes easy as well.

Floats

A `fo:float` produces a floating box anchored to the top of the region where it
occurs. A `fo:float` is most commonly used for graphics, charts, tables, or other
out-of-line content that needs to appear somewhere on the page, although precisely
where it appears is not particularly important. For example, this `fo:block` includes
a floating graphic with a caption:

```
<fo:block>
    Although PDF files are themselves ASCII text,
    this isn't a book about PostScript, so there's
    nothing to be gained by showing you the exact
    output of the above command. If you're curious,
    open the PDF file in any text editor.
    Instead, Figure 19-1
    <fo:float float="before">
        <fo:external-graphic src="4760-7fg1801.jpg"
                             height="485px" width="623px" />
        <fo:block font-family="Helvetica, sans">
            <fo:inline font-weight="bold">
                Figure 19-1:
            </fo:inline>
            The PDF file displayed in Netscape Navigator
        </fo:block>
    </fo:float>
    shows the rendered file displayed in
    Netscape Navigator using the Acrobat plug-in.
</fo:block>
```

The formatter tries to place the graphic somewhere on the same page where the
content surrounding the `fo:float` appears. However, it may not always be able to
find room on that page. If it can't, it moves the object to a subsequent page. Within
those limits, it's free to place it anywhere on the page.

The value of the `float` attribute indicates on which side of the page the `fo:float`
floats. It can be set to `before`, `start`, `end`, `left`, `right`, `none`, or `inherit`.

The `clear` attribute can be set on elements near the floating object to indicate
whether they'll flow around the side of the float or whether they'll move below the
float. It can have the values `start` (the start edge of the object must not be adjacent

to a floating object), end (the end edge of the object must not be adjacent to a floating object), left (the left edge of the object must not be adjacent to a floating object), right (the right edge of the object must not be adjacent to a floating object), both (neither the left nor the right edge of the object may be adjacent to a floating object), none, or inherit.

Caution   FOP 0.18.1 does not support the fo:float formatting object.

Formatting Properties

By themselves, formatting objects say relatively little about how content is formatted. They merely put content in abstract boxes, which are placed in particular parts of a page. Attributes on the various formatting objects determine how the content in those boxes is styled.

As already mentioned, there are more than 200 different formatting properties. Not all properties can be attached to all elements. For instance, there isn't much point to specifying the font-style of a fo:external-graphic. Most properties, however, can be applied to more than one kind of formatting object element. (The few that can't, such as src and provisional-label-separation, were discussed above with the formatting objects they apply to.) When a property is common to multiple formatting objects, it shares the same syntax and meaning across the objects. For example, you use identical code to format a fo:title in 14-point Times bold as you do to format a fo:block in 14-point Times bold.

Many of the XSL-FO properties are similar to CSS properties. The value of a CSS font-family property is the same as the value of an XSL-FO font-family attribute. If you've read about CSS in Chapters 14 through 16, you're already more than half finished learning XSL-FO properties.

The id property

The id property can be applied to any element. This is an XML ID-type attribute. The value of this property must, therefore, be an XML name that's unique within the style sheet and within the output formatting object document. The last requirement is a little tricky because it's possible that one template rule in the style sheet may generate several hundred elements in the output document. The generate-id() function of XSLT can be useful here.

The language property

The language property specifies the language of the content contained in either a fo:block or a fo:character element. Generally, the value of this property is an ISO 639 language code such as en (English) or la (Latin). It may also be the keyword none or use-document. The latter means to simply use the language of the input as specified by the xml:lang attribute. For example, consider the first verse of Caesar's *Gallic Wars*:

```
<fo:block id="verse1.1.1" language="la">
   Gallia est omnis divisa in partes tres,
   quarum unam incolunt Belgae, aliam Aquitani,
   tertiam qui ipsorum lingua Celtae, nostra Galli appellantur
</fo:block>
```

Although the language property has no direct effect on formatting, it may have an indirect effect if the formatter selects layout algorithms depending on the language. For instance, the formatter should use different default writing modes for Arabic and English text. This carries over into determination of the start and end regions and the inline and block progression directions.

Paragraph properties

Paragraph properties are styles that normally are thought of as applying to an entire block of text in a traditional word processor, although perhaps *block-level text properties* is a more appropriate name here. For example, indentation is a paragraph property, because you can indent a paragraph, but you can't indent a single word.

Break properties

The break properties specify where page breaks are and are not allowed. There are five loosely related break properties:

- ✦ keep-with-next
- ✦ keep-with-previous
- ✦ keep-together
- ✦ break-before
- ✦ break-after

The keep-with-next property determines how much effort the formatter will expend to keep this formatting object on the same page as the following formatting object. The keep-with-previous property determines how much effort the formatter will expend to keep this formatting object on the same page as the preceding formatting object. And the keep-together property determines how much effort the formatter will expend to keep the contents of this formatting object on one page. These are not hard and fast rules because it's always possible that a formatting object is just too big for one page. Each of these properties can be set to an integer giving the strength of the effort to keep the objects on the same page (larger integers are stronger) or to the keywords always or auto. always means maximum effort; auto means let the breaks fall where they may.

By contrast, the `break-before` property and `break-after` properties mandate some kind of break. What exactly is broken is determined by the value of the property. This can be one of these five values:

✦ `column`: Break the current column and move to the next column.

✦ `page`: Break the current page and move to the next page.

✦ `even-page`: Break the current page and move to the next even-numbered page, inserting a blank page if the current page is itself an even-numbered page.

✦ `odd-page`: Break the current page and move to the next odd-numbered page, inserting a blank page if the current page is itself an odd-numbered page.

✦ `auto`: Let the formatter decide where to break; the default.

For example, this template rule ensures that each `ATOM` of sufficiently small size is printed on a page of its own:

```
<xsl:template match="ATOM">
  <fo:block break-before="page" break-after="page">
    <xsl:apply-templates/>
  </fo:block>
</xsl:template>
```

Finally, the `inhibit-line-breaks` property is a boolean that can be set to `true` to indicate that not even a line break is allowed, much less a page break.

XSL-FO also defines three shorthand page-break properties: `page-break-after`, `page-break-before`, and `page-break-inside`. These are not absolutely necessary because their effects can be achieved by appropriate combinations of the keep and break properties. For example, to specify a page break after an element, you'd set `break-before` to `page` and `keep-with-previous` to `auto`.

Hyphenation properties

The hyphenation properties determine where hyphenation is allowed and how it should be used. These properties apply only to soft or "optional" hyphens such as the ones sometimes used to break long words at the end of a line. They do not apply to hard hyphens such as the ones in the word *mother-in-law*, although hard hyphens may affect where soft hyphens are allowed. There are six hyphenation properties. They are:

✦ `hyphenate`: Automatic hyphenation is allowed only if this property has the value `true`.

✦ `hyphenation-character`: The Unicode character used to hyphenate words, such as – in English.

✦ `hyphenation-keep`: One of the four keywords (`column`, `none`, `page`, `inherit`) that specify where and whether hyphenation is allowed. The default is not to hyphenate.

✦ hyphenation-ladder-count: A nonnegative integer that specifies the maximum number of hyphenated lines that may appear in a row.

✦ hyphenation-push-character-count: A nonnegative integer that specifies the minimum number of characters that must follow an automatically inserted hyphen. (Short syllables look bad in isolation.)

✦ hyphenation-remain-character-count: A nonnegative integer specifying the minimum number of characters that must precede an automatically inserted hyphen.

For example:

```
<fo:block hyphenate="true"
          hyphenation-character="-"
          hyphenation-keep="none"
          hyphenation-ladder-count="2"
          hyphenation-push-character-count="4"
          hyphenation-remain-character-count="4" >
    some content...
</fo:block>
```

XSL-FO does not specify a word-breaking algorithm to determine where a soft hyphen may be applied. Even when these properties allow hyphenation, it's still completely up to the formatter to figure out how to hyphenate individual words. Indeed, basic formatters may not attempt to hyphenate words at all.

Indent properties

The indent properties specify how far lines are indented from the edge of the text. There are four of these:

✦ start-indent

✦ end-indent

✦ text-indent

✦ last-line-end-indent

The start-indent property offsets all lines from the start edge (left edge in English). The end-indent property offsets all lines from the end edge (right edge in English). The text-indent property offsets only the first line from the start edge. The last-line-end-indent property offsets only the last line from the start edge. Values are given as a signed length. For example, a standard paragraph with a half-inch, first-line indent might be formatted this way:

```
<fo:block text-indent="0.5in">
   The first line of this paragraph is indented
</fo:block>
```

A block quote with a one-inch indent on all lines on both sides is formatted like this:

```
<fo:block start-indent="1.0in" end-indent="1.0in">
  This text is offset one inch from both edges.
</fo:block>
```

Because the `text-indent` is added to the `start-indent` to get the total indentation of the first line, using a positive value for `start-indent` and a negative value for `text-indent` creates hanging indents. For example, all lines except the first in this paragraph are indented by one inch. The first line is only indented half an inch:

```
<fo:block text-indent="-0.5in" start-indent="1.0in">
  This paragraph uses a hanging indent.
</fo:block>
```

Character properties

Character properties describe the qualities of individual characters. They are applied to elements that contain characters such as `fo:block` and `fo:list-item-body` elements. These include color, font, style, weight, and similar properties.

The color property

The `color` property sets the foreground color of the contents using the same syntax as the CSS `color` property. For example, this `fo:inline` colors the text "Lions and tigers and bears, oh my!" pink:

```
<fo:inline color="#FFCCCC">
  Lions and tigers and bears, oh my!
</fo:inline>
```

Colors are specified in much the same way as they are in CSS; that is, as hexadecimal triples in the form #RRGGBB or as one of the 16 named colors `aqua`, `black`, `blue`, `fuchsia`, `gray`, `green`, `lime`, `maroon`, `navy`, `olive`, `purple`, `red`, `silver`, `teal`, `white`, and `yellow`.

Font properties

Any formatting object that holds text can have a wide range of font properties. Most of these are familiar from CSS, including:

- ✦ `font-family`: A list of font names in order of preference
- ✦ `font-size`: A signed length
- ✦ `font-size-adjust`: The preferred ratio between the x-height and size of a font, specified as an unsigned real number or as `none`
- ✦ `font-stretch`: The "width" of a font, given as one of the keywords `condensed`, `expanded`, `extra-condensed`, `extra-expanded`, `narrower`, `normal`, `semi-condensed`, `semi-expanded`, `ultra-condensed`, `ultra-expanded`, **or** `wider`

✦ font-style: The style of font specified as one of the keywords italic, normal, oblique, reverse-normal, or reverse-oblique

✦ font-variant: Either normal or small-caps

✦ font-weight: The thickness of the strokes that draw the font, given as one of the keywords 100, 200, 300, 400, 500, 600, 700, 800, 900, bold, bolder, lighter, or normal

Text properties

The text properties apply styles to text that are more or less independent of the font chosen. These include:

✦ text-transform

✦ text-shadow

✦ text-decoration

✦ score-spaces

The text-transform property defines how text is capitalized, and is identical to the CSS property of the same name. The four possible values are:

✦ none: Don't change the case (the default)

✦ capitalize: Make the first letter of each word uppercase and all subsequent letters lowercase

✦ uppercase: Make all characters uppercase

✦ lowercase: Make all characters lowercase

This property is somewhat language specific. (Chinese and Hebrew, for example, don't have separate upper- and lowercases.) Formatters are free to ignore the case recommendations when they're applied to non-Roman text.

The text-shadow property applies a shadow to text. This is similar to a background color, but differs in that the shadow attaches to the text itself rather than to the box containing the text. The value of text-shadow can be the keyword none or a named or RGB color. For example:

```
<fo:inline text-shadow="FFFF66">
  This sentence has a yellow shadow.
</fo:inline>
```

The text-decoration property is similar to the CSS text-decoration property. Like that property, it has these five possible values:

✦ none: No decoration, the default

✦ underline: <u>Underlining</u>

- ✦ `overline`: A line above the text
- ✦ `line-through`: ~~Strike through~~
- ✦ `blink`: The notorious blinking text introduced by Netscape

In addition to the five values that are familiar from CSS, XSL-FO also adds four values that turn off decoration that is simply inherited from a parent element:

- ✦ `no-underline`
- ✦ `no-overline`
- ✦ `no-line-through`
- ✦ `no-blink`

Scoring is a catchall word for <u>underlining</u>, ~~line through~~, double strike-through, and so forth. The `score-space` property determines whether white space is scored. <u>For example, if `score-spaces` is `true`, an underlined sentence looks like this. If `score-spaces` is `false`, an <u>underlined</u> <u>sentence</u> <u>looks</u> <u>like</u> <u>this</u>.</u>

Sentence properties

Sentence properties apply to groups of characters, that is, a property that makes sense only for more than one letter at a time, such as how much space to place between letters or words.

Letter spacing properties

Kerning of text is a slippery measure of how much space separates two characters. It's not an absolute number. Most formatters adjust the space between letters based on local necessity, especially in justified text. Furthermore, high-quality fonts use different amounts of space between different glyphs. However, you can make text looser or tighter overall.

The `letter-spacing` property adds additional space between each pair of glyphs, beyond that provided by the kerning. It's given as a signed length specifying the desired amount of extra space to add. For example:

```
<fo:block letter-spacing="2px">
  This is fairly loose text.
</fo:block>
```

The length may be negative to tighten up the text. Formatters, however, generally impose limits on how much extra space they allow to be added to or removed from the space between letters.

Word spacing properties

The word-spacing property adjusts the amount of space between words. Otherwise, it behaves much like the letter spacing properties. The value is a signed length giving the amount of extra space to add between two words. For example:

```
<fo:block word-spacing="0.3cm">
  This is pretty loose text.
</fo:block>
```

Line spacing properties

An XSL-FO formatting engine divides block areas into line areas. You cannot create line areas directly from XSL-FO. However, with these five properties you can affect how they're vertically spaced:

✦ line-height: The minimum height of a line

✦ line-height-shift-adjustment: consider-shifts if subscripts and superscripts should expand the height of a line; disregard-shifts if they shouldn't

✦ line-stacking-strategy: line-height (the CSS model and the default); font-height (make the line as tall as the font height after addition of text-altitude and text-depth); or max-height (distance between the maximum ascender height and maximum descender depth)

✦ text-depth: A signed length specifying additional vertical space added after each line; can also be the keyword use-font-metrics (the default) to indicate that this depends on the font

✦ text-altitude: A signed length specifying the minimum additional vertical space added before each line; can also be the keyword use-font-metrics (the default) to indicate that this depends on the font

The line height also depends largely on the size of the font in which the line is drawn. Larger font sizes will naturally have taller lines. For example, the following opening paragraph from Mary Wollstonecraft's *A Vindication of the Rights of Woman* is effectively double-spaced:

```
<fo:block font-size="12pt" line-height="24pt">
  In the present state of society it appears necessary to go
  back to first principles in search of the most simple truths,
  and to dispute with some prevailing prejudice every inch of
  ground. To clear my way, I must be allowed to ask some plain
  questions, and the answers will probably appear as
  unequivocal as the axioms on which reasoning is built;
  though, when entangled with various motives of action, they
  are formally contradicted, either by the words or conduct
  of men.
</fo:block>
```

Text alignment properties

The text-align and text-align-last properties specify how the inline content is horizontally aligned within its box. The eight possible values are:

✦ start: Left-aligned in left-to-right languages like English

✦ center: Centered

✦ end: Right-aligned in left-to-right scripts

✦ justify: Expanded with extra space as necessary to fill out the line

✦ left: Align with the left side of the page regardless of the writing direction

✦ right: Align with the right side of the page regardless of the writing direction

✦ inside: Align with the inside edge of the page; that is, the right edge on the left page of two facing pages or the left edge on the right page of two facing pages

✦ outside: Align with the outside edge of the page; that is, the left edge on the left page of two facing pages or the right edge on the right page of two facing pages

The text-align-last property enables you to specify a different value for the last line in a block. This is especially important for justified text, where the last line often doesn't have enough words to be attractively justified. The possible values are the same as for text-align plus relative. A relatively aligned last line will line up the same way as all other lines unless text-align is justified, in which case the last line will align with the start edge instead.

White space properties

The space-treatment property specifies what the formatting engine should do with white space that's still present after the original source document is transformed into formatting objects. It can be set to either preserve (the default) or ignore. If you set it to ignore, leading and trailing white space will be thrown away.

The white-space-collapse property can be set to true (the default) or false. When true, runs of white space are replaced by a single space. When false, they're left unchanged.

The wrap-option property determines how text that's too long to fit on a line is handled. This property can be set to wrap (the default) or no-wrap. When set to wrap, this allows the formatter to insert line breaks as necessary to fit the text.

Area properties

Area properties are applied to boxes. These may be either block-level or inline boxes. Each of these boxes has:

✦ A background

✦ Margins

✦ Borders

✦ Padding

✦ A size

Background properties

The background properties are identical to the CSS background properties. There are five:

✦ The `background-color` property specifies the color of the box's background. Its value is either a color such as `red` or `#FFCCCC` or the keyword `transparent`.

✦ The `background-image` property gives the URI of an image to be used as a background. The value can also be the keyword `none`.

✦ The `background-attachment` property specifies whether the background image is attached to the window or the document. Its value is one of the two keywords `fixed` or `scroll`.

✦ The `background-position` property specifies where the background image is placed in the box. Possible values include `center`, `left`, `right`, `bottom`, `middle`, `top`, or a coordinate.

✦ The `background-repeat` property specifies how and whether a background image is tiled if it is smaller than its box. Possible values include `repeat`, `no-repeat`, `repeat-x`, and `repeat-y`.

The following block shows the use of the `background-image`, `background-position`, `background-repeat`, and `background-color` properties:

```
<fo:block background-image="/bg/paper.gif"
          background-position="0,0"
          background-repeat="repeat"
          background-color="white">
  Two strings walk into a bar...
</fo:block>
```

Caution   The only background property FOP 0.18.1 supports is `background-color`. The others will probably be added in future releases.

Border properties

The border properties describe the appearance of a border around the box. They are mostly the same as the CSS border properties. However, as well as `border-XXX-bottom`, `border-XXX-top`, `border-XXX-left`, and `border-XXX-right` properties, the XSL versions also have `border-XXX-before`, `border-XXX-after`, `border-XXX-start`, and `border-XXX-end` versions. There are 31 border properties in all. These are:

✦ Color: `border-color`, `border-before-color`, `border-after-color`, `border-start-color`, `border-end-color`, `border-top-color`, `border-bottom-color`, `border-left-color`, and `border-right-color`. The default color is black.

✦ Width: `border-width`, `border-before-width`, `border-after-width`, `border-start-width`, `border-end-width`, `border-top-width`, `border-bottom-width`, `border-left-width`, and `border-right-width`. The default width is `medium`.

✦ Style: `border-style`, `border-before-style`, `border-after-style`, `border-start-style`, `border-end-style`, `border-top-style`, `border-bottom-style`, `border-left-style`, `border-right-style`. The default style is `none`.

✦ Shorthand properties: `border`, `border-top`, `border-bottom`, `border-left`, `border-right`, `border-color`, `border-style`, `border-width`.

For example, this block has a two-pixel-wide blue border:

```
<fo:block border-before-color="blue"  border-before-width="2px"
          border-after-color="blue"   border-after-width="2px"
          border-start-color="blue"   border-start-width="2px"
          border-end-color="blue"     border-end-width="2px">
  You have been selected for special high intensity training.
</fo:block>
```

Padding properties

The padding properties specify the amount of space between the border of the box and the contents of the box. The border of the box, if shown, falls between the margin and the padding. The padding properties are mostly the same as the CSS padding properties. However, as well as `padding-bottom`, `padding-top`, `padding-left`, and `padding-right`, the XSL-FO versions also have `padding-before`, `padding-after`, `padding-start`, and `padding-end` versions. Thus in total there are eight padding properties, each of which has a signed length for a value. These are:

✦ `padding-after`

✦ `padding-before`

✦ `padding-bottom`

✦ `padding-end`

- padding-left
- padding-start
- padding-right
- padding-top

For example, this block has half a centimeter of padding on each side:

```
<fo:block padding-before="0.5cm" padding-after="0.5cm"
          padding-start="0.5cm"  padding-end="0.5cm">
  Did you hear the one about the dyslexic agnostic?
</fo:block>
```

Margin properties for blocks

There are five margin properties, each of whose values is given as an unsigned length. These are:

- margin-top
- margin-bottom
- margin-left
- margin-right
- margin

However, these properties are only here for compatibility with CSS. In general, it's recommended that you use these four properties instead because they fit better in the XSL-FO formatting model:

- space-before
- space-after
- start-indent
- end-indent

The space-before and space-after properties are equivalent to the margin-top and margin-bottom properties, respectively. The start-indent property is equivalent to the sum of padding-left, border-left-width, and margin-left. The end-indent property is equivalent to the sum of padding-right, border-right-width, and margin-right. Figure 19-11 should make this clearer.

For example, this block has a half centimeter margin at its start and end sides:

```
<fo:block start-indent="0.5cm" end-indent="0.5cm">
  Two strings walk into a bar...
</fo:block>
```

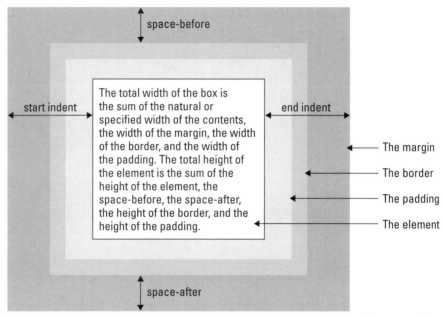

Figure 19-11: Padding, indents, borders, and space before and after for an XSL box

However, unlike margins, space properties are given as space specifiers that contain more than one value. In particular, they contain a preferred value, a minimum value, a maximum value, a conditionality, and a precedence. This allows the formatter somewhat more freedom in laying out the page. The formatter is free to pick any amount of space between the minimum and maximum to fit the constraints of the page.

Each of the space values is a length. The conditionality is one of the two keywords discard or retain. This determines what happens to extra space at the end of a line. The default is to discard it. The precedence can either be an integer or the keyword force. The precedence determines what happens when the space-end of one inline area conflicts with the space-start of the next. The area with higher precedence wins. The default precedence is 0. Semicolons separate all five values.

For example, consider this fo:block element:

```
<fo:block space-before="0in;0.5in;0.166in;discard;force">
  It goes to 11.
</fo:block>
```

It says that ideally the formatter should add a sixth of an inch of space before this element. However, it can add as little as no space at all and as much as half an inch if necessary. Because the precedence is set to force, this will override any other space specifiers that conflict with it. Finally, if there's any extra space that's left over at the end, it will be discarded.

Margin properties for inline boxes

Two margin properties apply only to inline elements:

✦ space-end

✦ space-start

Their values are space specifiers that give a range of extra space to be added before and after the element. The actual spaces may be smaller or larger. Because the space is not part of the box itself, one box's end space can be part of the next box's start space.

Size properties

Six properties specify the height and width of the content area of a box. These are:

✦ height

✦ width

✦ max-height

✦ max-width

✦ min-height

✦ min-width

These properties do not specify the total width and height of the box, which also includes the margins, padding, and borders. This is only the width and height of the content area. As well as an unsigned length, the height and width properties may be set to the keyword auto, which chooses the height and width based on the amount of content in the box. However, in no case are the height and width larger than the values specified by the max-height and max-width or smaller than the min-height and min-width. For example:

```
<fo:block height="2in" width="2in">
   Two strings walk into a bar...
</fo:block>
```

The overflow properties

The overflow property determines what happens when there's too much content to fit within a box of a specified size. This may be an explicit specification using the size properties or an implicit specification based on page size or other constraints. There are six possibilities, each of which is represented by a keyword:

✦ auto: Use scrollbars if there is overflow; don't use them if there isn't. If scroll bars aren't available (for example, on a printed page) then add a new page for flow content and generate an error for static content. This is the default.

✦ hidden: Don't show any content that runs outside the box.

✦ scroll: Attach scroll bars to the box so the reader can scroll to the additional content.

✦ visible: The complete contents are shown; if necessary, by overriding the size constraints on the box.

✦ error-if-overflow: The formatter should give up and display an error message if content overflows its box.

✦ paginate: If the object overflowed is a page, then create a new page to hold the excess content.

The clip property specifies the shape of the clipping region if the overflow property does not have the value visible. The default clipping region is simply the box itself. However, you can change this by specifying a particular rectangle like this:

```
clip=rect(top_offset  right_offset  bottom_offset  left_offset)
```

Here top_offset, right_offset, bottom_offset, and left_offset are signed lengths giving the offsets of the clipping region from the top, right, bottom, and left sides of the box. This allows you to make the clipping region larger or smaller than the box itself.

The reference-orientation property

The reference-orientation property allows you to specify that the content of a box is rotated relative to its normal orientation. The only valid values are 90-degree increments, which are measured counterclockwise, that is 0, 90, 180, and 270. You can also specify -90, -180, and -270. For example, here's a 90-degree rotation:

```
<fo:block reference-orientation="90">
   Bottom to Top
</fo:block>
```

Writing mode properties

The writing mode specifies the direction of text in the box. This has important implications for the ordering of formatting objects in the box. Most of the time, speakers of English and other Western languages assume a left-to-right, top-to-bottom writing mode, such as this:

```
A B C D E F G
H I J K L M N
O P Q R S T U
V W X Y Z
```

However, in the Hebrew and Arabic-speaking worlds, a right-to-left, top-to-bottom ordering such as this one seems more natural:

```
G F E D C B A
N M L K J I H
U T S R Q P O
Z Y X W V
```

In Taiwan, a top-to-bottom, left-to-right order is conventional:

```
A E I M Q U Y
B F J N R V Z
C G K O S W
D H L P T X
```

In XSL-FO, the writing mode doesn't just affect text. It also affects how objects in a flow or sequence are laid out, how wrapping is performed, and more. You've already noticed that many properties are organized in start, end, before, and after variations instead of left, right, top, and bottom. Specifying style rules in terms of start, end, before, and after, instead of left, right, top, and bottom, produces more robust, localizable style sheets.

The `writing-mode` property specifies the writing mode for an area. This property can have 1 of 13 keyword values. These are:

✦ `bt-lr`: Bottom-to-top, left-to-right

✦ `bt-rl`: Bottom-to-top, right-to-left

✦ `lr-alternating-rl-bt`: Left-to-right lines alternating with right-to-left lines, bottom-to-top

✦ `lr-alternating-rl-tb`: Left-to-right lines alternating with right-to-left lines, top-to-bottom

✦ `lr-bt`: Left-to-right, bottom-to-top

✦ `lr-inverting-rl-bt`: Left to right, then move up to the next line and go right to left (that is, snake up the page like a backward S)

✦ `lr-inverting-rl-tb`: Left to right, then move down to the next line and go right to left (that is, snake down the page like a backward S)

✦ `lr-tb`: Left to right, top to bottom

✦ `rl-bt`: Right to left, bottom to top

✦ `rl-tb`: Right to left, top to bottom

✦ `tb-lr`: Top to bottom, left to right

✦ `tb-rl`: Top to bottom, right to left

✦ `tb-rl-in-rl-pairs`: Text is written in two character, right-to-left pairs; the pairs are then laid out top-to-bottom to form a line; lines are laid out from right-to-left

Orphans and widows

To a typesetter, an orphan is a single line of a paragraph at the bottom of a page. A widow is a single line of a paragraph at the top of a page. Good typesetters move an extra line from the previous page to the next page or from the next page to the previous page as necessary to avoid orphans and widows. You can adjust the number of lines considered an orphan by setting the orphans property to an unsigned integer. You can adjust the number of lines considered a widow by setting the widows property to an unsigned integer. For instance, if you want to make sure that every partial paragraph at the end of a page has at least three lines, set the orphans property to 3. For example:

```
<fo:simple-page-master master-name="even"
    orphans="3" page-height="11in" page-width="8.5in"
/>
```

Aural properties

XSL-FO supports the full collection of CSS2 aural style properties including:

- ✦ azimuth
- ✦ cue
- ✦ cue-after
- ✦ cue-before
- ✦ elevation
- ✦ pause
- ✦ pause-after
- ✦ pause-before
- ✦ pitch
- ✦ pitch-range
- ✦ play-during
- ✦ richness
- ✦ speak
- ✦ speak-header
- ✦ speak-numeral
- ✦ speak-punctuation
- ✦ speech-rate
- ✦ stress
- ✦ voice-family
- ✦ volume

Of course, these probably won't be relevant in most of the output mediums that XSL-FO currently supports. When and if XSL-FO is implemented directly in Web browsers, these will become more important.

Cross-Reference The aural style properties are discussed in the last section of Chapter 16. They have the same semantics and syntax in XSL-FO as they do in CSS2.

Summary

In this chapter, you learned about XSL formatting objects. In particular, you learned that:

✦ An XSL processor follows the instructions in an XSLT style sheet to transform an XML source document into a new XML document marked up in the XSL formatting object vocabulary.

✦ Most XSL formatting objects generate one or more rectangular areas. Pages contain regions. Regions contain block areas. Block areas contain block areas and line areas. Line areas contain inline areas. Inline areas contain other inline areas and character areas.

✦ The root element of a formatting object document is `fo:root`. This contains `fo:layout-master-set` elements and `fo:page-sequence` elements.

✦ Each `fo:layout-master-set` element contains one or more `fo:simple-page-master` elements, each of which defines the layout of a particular kind of page by dividing it into five regions (before, after, start, end, and body) and assigning properties to each one. It may also contain one or more `fo:page-sequence-master` elements.

✦ Each `fo:page-sequence` element contains zero or one `fo:title` elements, zero or more `fo:static-content` elements, one or more `fo:flow` elements, and a `master-name` attribute. The contents of the `fo:flow` are copied onto instances of the master pages in the order specified by the `fo:page-sequence-master` element identified by the `master-name` attribute. The contents of the `fo:static-content` elements are copied onto every page that's created.

✦ The `fo:external-graphic` element loads an image from a URL and displays it inline.

✦ The `fo:instream-foreign-object` element displays an image encoded in a non-XSL-FO XML application such as SVG or MathML embedded in the XSL-FO document.

✦ The `fo:basic-link` element creates a hypertext link to a URL.

✦ A list is a block-level element created by a `fo:list-block` element. It contains block-level `fo:list-item` elements. Each `fo:list-item` contains a `fo:list-item-label` and `fo:list-item-body`, and each of these contains block-level elements.

✦ The `fo:page-number` element inserts the current page number.

✦ The `fo:inline` element is a container used to attach properties to the text and areas it contains.

✦ The `fo:footnote` element inserts an out-of-line footnote and an inline footnote reference into the page.

✦ The `fo:float` element inserts an out-of-line block-level element such as a figure or a pull quote onto the page. The `float` property determines which side of the page it floats on and the `clear` property determines whether and where other elements are allowed to float around it.

✦ There are more than 200 separate XSL formatting properties, many of which are identical to CSS properties of the same name. These are attached to XSL formatting object elements as attributes.

✦ The keeps and breaks properties describe where page breaks are and are not allowed. These include `keep-with-next`, `keep-with-previous`, `keep-together`, `break-before`, `break-after`, `widows`, and `orphans`.

✦ The hyphenation properties describe whether and how to insert soft hyphens. These include `hyphenate`, `hyphenation-character`, `hyphenation-keep`, `hyphenation-ladder-count`, `hyphenation-push-character-count`, and `hyphenation-remain-character-count`.

✦ The indent properties specify how far lines are indented from the edge of the text. There are four of these: `start-indent`, `end-indent`, `text-indent`, and `last-line-end-indent`.

✦ Character properties describe attributes of individual characters and include `color`, `font-family`, `font-size`, `font-size-adjust`, `font-stretch`, `font-style`, `font-variant`, `font-weight`, `text-transform`, `text-shadow`, `text-decoration`, and `score-space`.

✦ Sentence properties describe formatting that only makes sense for groups of letters and words and include `letter-spacing`, `word-spacing`, `line-height`, `line-height-shift-adjustment`, `line-stacking-strategy`, `text-depth`, `text-altitude`, `text-align`, `text-align-last`, `space-treatment`, `white-space-collapse`, and `wrap-option`.

✦ Area properties describe attributes of boxes produced by various formatting objects, and include the background, border, padding, and margin properties.

✦ XSL-FO supports the full complement of aural styles defined in CSS2 for reading documents aloud.

The next chapter introduces XLinks, a more powerful linking syntax than the standard HTML A element hyperlinks and XSL's `fo:basic-link`.

✦   ✦   ✦

Supplemental Technologies

XLinks

Hypertext in XML is divided into multiple parts: XLink, XML Base, XPointer, and XInclude. XLink, the XML Linking Language, defines how one document links to another document. XML Base defines how the base URL of a document against which relative URLs are resolved is set. XPointer, the XML Pointer Language, defines how individual parts of a document are addressed. XInclude defines how one document can be built out of different pieces of other documents.

An XLink points to a URI (in practice, a URL) that specifies a particular resource. If this URI is relative, then the base URI is established by XML Base. Relative or not, this URI may have a fragment identifier that more specifically identifies the desired part of the targeted document. When the URI points to an XML document, the syntax of the fragment identifier is an XPointer. This chapter explores XLink and XML base. The next two chapters explore XPointer and XInclude.

XLinks versus HTML Links

The Web conquered the more established gopher protocol for one main reason: HTML made it possible to embed hypertext links in documents. These links could insert images or let the user to jump from inside one document to another document or another part of the same document. To the extent that XML is rendered into HTML for viewing, the same syntax that HTML uses for linking can be used in XML documents. Alternate syntaxes can be converted into HTML syntax using XSLT.

Cross-Reference XSLT, including several examples of converting XML markup to HTML links, is discussed in Chapter 18.

However, HTML linking has limits. For one thing, URLs are limited to pointing at a single document. More granularity than that, such as linking to the third sentence of the seventeenth paragraph in a document, requires you to manually insert named anchors in the targeted document. It can't be done without write access to the document to which you're linking.

Furthermore, HTML links don't maintain any sense of history or relations between documents. Although browsers may track the path you've followed through a series of documents, such tracking isn't very reliable. From inside the HTML, there's no way to know from where a reader came. Links are purely one-way. The linking document knows to whom it's linking, but the linked document does not know who's linking to it.

XLink is a proposal for more powerful links between documents designed especially for use with XML. XLink achieves everything possible with HTML's URL-based hyperlinks and anchors. Beyond this, however, it supports multidirectional links where the links run in more than one direction. Any element can become a link, not just the A element. Links do not even have to be stored in the same file as the documents they connect. These features make XLinks more suitable not only for new uses, but for things that can be done only with considerable effort in HTML, such as cross-references, footnotes, end notes, and more.

Caution   Only Mozilla and Netscape 6.0 have any support for XLinks, and that support is incomplete. Internet Explorer 5.5 and Opera 5.11 and earlier have absolutely no support for any kind of XLink. There are no general-purpose applications that support arbitrary XLinks. That's because XLinks have a much broader base of applicability than HTML links. XLinks are not just used for hypertext connections and embedding images in documents. They can be used by any custom application that needs to establish connections between documents and parts of documents, for any reason. Thus, even when XLinks are fully implemented in browsers, they may not always be blue underlined text that you click to jump to another page. They can be that, but they can also be both more and less, depending on your needs.

Linking Elements

In HTML, a link is defined with the `<A>` tag. However, just as XML is more flexible with tags that describe elements, it is more flexible with tags that refer to external resources. In XML, any element can be a link or part of a link. XLink elements are identified by an `xlink:type` attribute with one of these seven values:

- ✦ `simple`
- ✦ `extended`
- ✦ `locator`
- ✦ `arc`
- ✦ `resource`
- ✦ `title`
- ✦ `none`

The xlink prefix must be bound to the http://www.w3.org/1999/xlink name-space URI. As usual, the prefix can change as long as the URI remains the same. The xlink prefix is customary and should be used unless you've got a really good reason to change it. In this chapter, I assume that the prefix xlink has been bound to the http://www.w3.org/1999/xlink URI.

XLinks elements whose xlink:type attribute has the value simple or extended are called *linking elements*. For example, these are three linking elements:

```
<COMPOSER xmlns:xlink="http://www.w3.org/1999/xlink"
          xlink:type="simple"
          xlink:href="http://users.rcn.com/beand/">
    Beth Anderson
</COMPOSER>
<FOOTNOTE xmlns:xlink="http://www.w3.org/1999/xlink"
          xlink:type="simple"
          xlink:href="footnote7.xml">7</FOOTNOTE>
<IMAGE xmlns:xlink="http://www.w3.org/1999/xlink"
       xlink:type="simple" xlink:href="logo.gif"
       xlink:actuate="onLoad" xlink:show="embed"/>
```

Notice that the elements have semantic names that describe the content they contain rather than how the elements behave. The information that these elements are links is included in the attributes, not the element names. Attributes define the linking behavior.

These three examples are simple XLinks. Simple XLinks are similar to standard HTML links and are the only kind of link supported by today's Web browsers, so I'll begin with them. Later, I'll talk about the more complex (and more powerful) extended links.

In the COMPOSER example above, the xlink:href attribute defines the target of the link. The value of this attribute is the absolute URL http://users.rcn.com/beand/. This linking element describes a connection from the COMPOSER element in the current document with the content "Beth Anderson" to the remote document at http://users.rcn.com/beand/. If you were to include this element in an XML document and load that document into an XLink-aware Web browser such as Mozilla or Netscape 6, then the browser would underline the link, color it blue, and let the user click on it to jump to the page http://users.rcn.com/beand/.

However, you can also interpret this link more abstractly, as simply defining a one-way connection from one resource, the COMPOSER element, to another resource, the Web page at http://users.rcn.com/beand/. Figure 20-1 diagrams this connection. This connection does not really imply any particular semantics or behavior. It's up to the application reading the document to decide what this abstract link means to it.

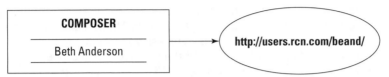

Figure 20-1: A link from the COMPOSER element to http://users.rcn.com/beand/

In the FOOTNOTE example, the link target attribute's name is xlink:href. Its value is the relative URL footnote7.xml. This describes a connection from the FOOTNOTE element in the current document with the content "7" to the document named footnote7.xml on the same server in the same directory as the document in which this link appears.

In the third example above, the value of the xlink:href attribute is the relative URL logo.gif. Again, the protocol, host, and directory of this document are taken from the protocol, host, and directory of the document in which this link appears. However, this element requests slightly different behavior. Instead of waiting for the user to activate the link, the xlink:actuate attribute asks that the link be activated automatically as soon as the document is loaded. The xlink:show attribute requests that the result be embedded in the current document instead of replacing the current document.

Declaring XLink attributes in document type definitions

If the document has a DTD, these attributes should be declared like any other. For example, declarations of the FOOTNOTE, COMPOSER, and IMAGE elements might look like this:

```
<!ELEMENT FOOTNOTE (#PCDATA)>
<!ATTLIST FOOTNOTE
    xmlns:xlink CDATA  #FIXED "http://www.w3.org/1999/xlink"
    xlink:type  CDATA  #FIXED "simple"
    xlink:href  CDATA  #REQUIRED
>
<!ELEMENT COMPOSER (#PCDATA)>
<!ATTLIST COMPOSER
    xmlns:xlink CDATA  #FIXED "http://www.w3.org/1999/xlink"
    xlink:type  CDATA  #FIXED "simple"
    xlink:href  CDATA  #REQUIRED
>
<!ELEMENT IMAGE EMPTY>
<!ATTLIST IMAGE
    xmlns:xlink    CDATA  #FIXED "http://www.w3.org/1999/xlink"
    xlink:type     CDATA  #FIXED "simple"
```

```
      xlink:href    CDATA  #REQUIRED
      xlink:show    CDATA  #FIXED "onLoad"
      xlink:actuate CDATA  #FIXED "embed"
  >
```

With these declarations, the `xlink:type`, `xmlns:xlink`, `xlink:show`, and `xlink:actuate` attributes have fixed values. Therefore they do not need to be included in the instances of the elements, which you may now write more compactly like this:

```
<FOOTNOTE xlink:href="footnote7.xml">7</FOOTNOTE>
<COMPOSER xlink:href="http://users.rcn.com/beand/">
  Beth Anderson
</COMPOSER>
<IMAGE xlink:href="logo.gif"/>
```

Making an element a link doesn't impose any restriction on other attributes or contents of the element. An XLink element may contain arbitrary children or other attributes, always subject to the restrictions of the DTD, of course. For example, a more realistic `IMAGE` element would look like this:

```
<IMAGE ALT="Cafe con Leche Logo of a coffee cup"
       WIDTH="89" HEIGHT="67"
       xmlns:xlink="http://www.w3.org/1999/xlink"
       xlink:type="simple" xlink:href="logo.gif"
       xlink:actuate="onLoad" xlink:show="embed"/>
```

Half of the attributes don't have anything to do with linking. The declaration in the DTD would then look like this:

```
<!ELEMENT IMAGE EMPTY>
<!ATTLIST IMAGE
    xmlns:xlink    CDATA  #FIXED "http://www.w3.org/1999/xlink"
    xlink:type     CDATA  #FIXED "simple"
    xlink:href     CDATA  #REQUIRED
    xlink:show     CDATA  #FIXED "onLoad"
    xlink:actuate  CDATA  #FIXED "embed"
    ALT            CDATA  #REQUIRED
    ALIGN          CDATA  #IMPLIED
    HEIGHT         CDATA  #REQUIRED
    WIDTH          CDATA  #REQUIRED
  >
```

In fact, a linking element may even have children that are themselves linking elements! That is, a linking element may contain another linking element or elements. This doesn't have any special meaning. As far as links go, each linking element is treated in isolation.

Descriptions of the Remote Resource

A linking element may have optional `xlink:role` and `xlink:title` attributes that describe the remote resource; that is, the document or other resource to which the link points. The title contains plain text that describes the resource. The role contains an absolute URI pointing to a document that more fully describes the resource. For example, the title might describe what a page does and the role might point to a help page for the page:

```
<SEARCH xlink:type="simple"
        xlink:href="http://www.google.com/advanced_search"
        xlink:title="Search with Google"
        xlink:role="http://www.google.com/help.html">
   Search the Web with Google
</SEARCH>
```

Both the role and title describe the remote resource, not the local element. The remote resource in the above example is the document at `http://www.google.com/advanced_search`. It's not uncommon, though it's not required, for the `xlink:title` to be the same as the contents of the `TITLE` element of the page to which you are linking.

Another possibility used in some XML applications is to have the role point to some form of identifier URL for the format of the data found at the `xlink:href`. This may be a MIME media type, a namespace URI, or the location of a prose specification, DTD, schema, or stylesheet. For example, to indicate that the search page is written in HTML you might set the role to the URL of the HTML 4.0 specification:

```
<SEARCH xlink:type="simple"
        xlink:href="http://www.google.com/advanced_search"
        xlink:title="Search with Google"
        xlink:role="http://www.w3.org/TR/html4/">
   Search the Web with Google
</SEARCH>
```

Alternately, you could use the URL for the HTML MIME media type, `http://www.isi.edu/in-notes/iana/assignments/media-types/text/html`, the URL for the XHTML namespace, `http://www.w3.org/1999/xhtml`, or the URL for the HTML 3.2 DTD, `http://www.w3.org/TR/REC-html32#dtd`. You could even use a mailto URL giving the e-mail address of the person who wrote the page. Other values are possible. XLink does not define any rules for how applications should interpret the value of an xlink:role, beyond simply stating that it must be an absolute URI.

XLink does not define the user interface by which link roles and titles are presented to users. For instance, Mozilla shows the user the title of the link in a tool tip when the cursor is hovering over the link, and does nothing with the role. A different application might choose to put the title in the status bar of the browser window, or do both, or neither. How or whether any particular application makes use of the role and title is completely up to it.

As with all other attributes, the xlink:title and xlink:role attributes should be declared in the DTD for all the elements to which they belong. For example, this is a reasonable declaration for the above SEARCH element:

```
<!ELEMENT SEARCH (#PCDATA)>
<!ATTLIST SEARCH
    xmlns:xlink CDATA   #FIXED "http://www.w3.org/1999/xlink"
    xlink:type  CDATA   #FIXED "simple"
    xlink:href  CDATA   #REQUIRED
    xlink:title CDATA   #IMPLIED
    xlink:role  CDATA   #IMPLIED
>
```

Link Behavior

Linking elements can contain two more optional attributes that suggest to applications how the link behaves when activated. These are:

✦ xlink:show

✦ xlink:actuate

The xlink:show attribute suggests *how* the content should be displayed when the link is activated, for example, by opening a new window to hold the remote resource or by loading the remote resource into the current window. The xlink:actuate attribute suggests *when* the link should be activated; for instance, as soon as the document is loaded or only after a specific user request. Behavior is application dependent, however, and applications are free to ignore the suggestions.

The xlink:show attribute

The xlink:show attribute has five possible values:

✦ replace

✦ new

✦ embed

✦ other

✦ none

If the value of xlink:show is replace, then when the link is activated (generally by clicking on it, at least in GUI browsers), the target of the link replaces the current document in the same window. This is the default behavior of HTML links. For example:

```
<COMPOSER xlink:type="simple"
          xlink:show="replace"
          xlink:href="http://users.rcn.com/beand/">
    Beth Anderson
</COMPOSER>
```

If the value of xlink:show is new, activating the link opens a new window in which the targeted resource is displayed. This is similar to the behavior of HTML links when the target attribute is set to _blank. For example:

```
<WEBSITE xlink:type="simple"
         xlink:show="new"
         xlink:href="http://www.quackwatch.com/">
   Check this out, but don't leave our site completely!
</WEBSITE>
```

Caution   Readers do not expect a new window to open after clicking a link. They expect that when they click a link, the new page will load into the current window, unless they specifically ask that the link open in a new window. Some Web sites are so self-important that they find it impossible to believe that any user would ever want to leave. Thus they "help" the readers by opening new windows. Most of the time this only serves to confuse and annoy. Don't change the behavior users expect without a very good reason. The thin hope that a reader might spend an additional two seconds on your site or view one more page and see one more ad is not a good enough reason.

If the value of xlink:show is embed, activating the link inserts the targeted resource into the existing document. Exactly what this means is application dependent. Mostly, it implies that the application should somehow render the linked content and display it as part of the finished document. This is how the IMG, APPLET, and OBJECT elements behave in HTML. For example, an element like this one might be used to indicate that a JPEG image should be embedded in the document:

```
<PHOTO xlink:type="simple"
       xlink:href="images/nypride.jpg"
       xlink:show="embed"
       ALT="Marchers on 5th Avenue, June 2000"/>
```

If the value of xlink:show is other, then the application is supposed to look for other markup in the document that explains what to do. Generally this would be used when a particular XML application used different, non-XLink elements or attributes to describe the link behavior. For example, many Web pages have a LINK element in their header that references a style sheet and looks similar to this:

```
<LINK REL="stylesheet" TYPE="text/css"
      HREF="http://www.w3.org/StyleSheets/TR/W3C-WD" />
```

This is a link, but what's at the end of the link does not replace the existing document; it does not embed itself into the existing document; it is not displayed in a new window. In XML documents, you might agree that this behavior was implied whenever a STYLESHEET element was encountered. Because this is not one of the three predetermined link behaviors, you'd set xlink:show to other.

```
<STYLESHEET xlink:show="other"
            xlink:href="http://www.w3.org/StyleSheets/TR/W3C-WD"
/>
```

Finally, you can set xlink:show to none to indicate that the document contains no information to help the application decide what, if anything, to do with the link. It's completely up to the application reading the document to make its own choices.

Regardless of what behavior xlink:show suggests, the browser or other application reading the document is free to do whatever it wants when the link is activated, including nothing at all. For instance, a browser with "Automatically load images" turned off might well choose to ignore xlink:show="embed".

Like all attributes in valid documents, the xlink:show attribute must be declared in a <!ATTLIST> declaration for the linking element. For example:

```
<!ELEMENT WEBSITE (#PCDATA)>
<!ATTLIST WEBSITE
    xmlns:xlink CDATA  #FIXED "http://www.w3.org/1999/xlink"
    xlink:type  CDATA  #FIXED "simple"
    xlink:href  CDATA  #REQUIRED
    xlink:show (new | replace | embed) #IMPLIED "replace"
>
```

This particular DTD fragment doesn't allow the xlink:show attribute to have the value other or none. That's OK, too. Not all linking elements necessarily support all possible values of xlink:show.

The xlink:actuate attribute

A linking element's xlink:actuate attribute has four possible values:

✦ onRequest

✦ onLoad

✦ other

✦ none

The value onRequest specifies that the link should be traversed only when and if the user requests it. This is the behavior of a normal HTML link. For example, this link jumps to the FatBrain bookstore when the user specifically requests that action:

```
<PURCHASE xlink:type="simple" xlink:actuate="onRequest"
          xlink:href="http://www.fatbrain.com/">
  Buy from FatBrain
</PURCHASE>
```

On the other hand, if the linking element's xlink:actuate attribute is set to onLoad, the link is traversed as soon as the document containing the link is loaded. For example, you might set the actuate attribute to onLoad for an image or other piece of external content that's to be embedded in the linking document. This way the user doesn't have to click the link to follow it. The code might look like this:

```
<IMAGE xlink:type="simple"    xlink:href="logo.gif"
       xlink:actuate="onLoad" xlink:show="embed"/>
```

If the linking element's xlink:actuate attribute value is other, then the application should look at other markup, not defined by XLink, to decide when to traverse the link. For instance, a browser might define a PRELOAD element as indicating that a document or image is not used on this page, but will likely soon be used. For example,

```
<PRELOAD xlink:type="simple"    xlink:href="logo.gif"
         xlink:actuate="other" xlink:show="none"/>
```

Therefore, if the browser has extra bandwidth available while the user is reading the page, it should load the document and cache it. Otherwise, it waits until the user actually actuates the link. Applications that don't recognize the PRELOAD element would simply ignore it. (I should warn you that this is a purely hypothetical example that is not yet and probably never will be implemented by any actual browser.)

Finally, setting xlink:actuate to none leaves it completely up to the application to decide when or if to traverse the link.

Like all attributes in valid documents, the xlink:actuate attribute must be declared in the DTD in an <!ATTLIST> declaration for the linking elements in which it appears. For example:

```
<!ELEMENT IMAGE EMPTY>
<!ATTLIST IMAGE
    xmlns:xlink CDATA  #FIXED "http://www.w3.org/1999/xlink"
    xlink:type  CDATA  #FIXED "simple"
    xlink:href  CDATA  #REQUIRED
    xlink:show    (new | replace | embed) #IMPLIED "embed"
    xlink:actuate (onLoad)                 #FIXED "onLoad"
>
```

This particular DTD fragment doesn't allow the xlink:actuate attribute to have the values onRequest, other, or none. That's OK, too. Not all linking elements necessarily support all possible values of xlink:actuate.

A Shortcut for the DTD

Because the attribute names and types are standardized, it's often convenient to make the attribute declarations a parameter entity reference and simply repeat that in the declaration of each linking element if there is more than one linking element in a document. For example:

```
<!ENTITY % link-attributes
"xlink:type    CDATA  #FIXED 'simple'
 xlink:role    CDATA  #IMPLIED
 xlink:title   CDATA  #IMPLIED

 xmlns:xlink   CDATA  #FIXED 'http://www.w3.org/1999/xlink'
 xlink:href    CDATA  #REQUIRED
 xlink:show    (new|replace|embed|other|none) #IMPLIED 'replace'
 xlink:actuate (onRequest|onLoad|other|none) #IMPLIED 'onRequest'
"
>

<!ELEMENT COMPOSER (#PCDATA)>
<!ATTLIST COMPOSER
    %link-attributes;
>
<!ELEMENT AUTHOR (#PCDATA)>
<!ATTLIST AUTHOR
    %link-attributes;
>
<!ELEMENT WEBSITE (#PCDATA)>
<!ATTLIST WEBSITE
    %link-attributes;
>
```

Extended Links

Simple links behave more or less like the standard links you're accustomed to from HTML. A simple link connects one element in the linking document to one target document. Furthermore, the link is one-way, from the source to the target.

Extended links, however, go substantially beyond HTML links to include multidirectional links between many documents and out-of-line links. An extended link consists of a set of resources and a set of the connections between them. The resources may be local (part of the extended link element) or remote (not part of the extended link element, and generally, though not necessarily, in another document). Each resource may be either a target or a source of a link or both. If a link does not contain any local resources, only remote resources, then it's called an *out-of-line link*.

In computer science terms, an extended link is a directed, labeled graph in which the resources are vertices and the links between resources are edges. Thought of abstractly like this, an extended link is really just an XML format for a directed graph. The tricky part comes in deciding exactly what any particular application is supposed to do with such a data structure. For now, I can only speculate about what applications might do with extended links and what sort of user interfaces they might provide.

An extended link is represented in an XML document as an element of some arbitrary type such as COMPOSER or TEAM that has an xlink:type attribute with the value extended. As usual the xlink prefix is associated with the http://www.w3.org/1999/xlink namespace URI. For example,

```
<WEBSITE xmlns:xlink="http://www.w3.org/1999/xlink"
         xlink:type="extended">
  ...
</WEBSITE>
```

Extended Link Syntax

Extended links generally point to more than one target and from more than one source. Both sources and targets are called by the more generic word *resource*. In fact, whether a resource is a source or a target can change depending on which link is being followed and in which direction.

Resources are divided into *remote resources* and *local resources*. A local resource is actually contained inside the extended link element. It is the content of an element of arbitrary type that has an xlink:type attribute with the value resource.

A remote resource exists outside the extended link element, very possibly in another document. The extended link element contains locator child elements that point to the remote resource. These are elements with any name that have an xlink:type attribute with the value locator. Each locator element has an xlink:href attribute whose value is a URI locating the remote resource.

Caution   The terminology is unnecessarily confusing here. Both xlink:type="locator" and xlink:type="resource" elements locate resources. An xlink:type= "locator" element locates a remote resource. An xlink:type="resource" element locates a local resource. Personally, I think xlink:type="local" and xlink:type="remote" would be better choices here, but xlink:type= "resource" and xlink:type="locator" are what the standard has given us.

For example, suppose you're writing a page of links to Java sites. One of the sites you want to link to is Cafe au Lait at http://ibiblio.org/javafaq/. However, there are also three mirrors of that site in three other countries. Some people coming to your site will want to access the home site while others will want to go to one of the mirror sites. With HTML links or simple XLinks you have to write four different links, one for the home site and one for each mirror and let the user pick. However with an extended XLink you can provide one link that connects all four sites as well as the page you're linking from. The browser can choose the one closest to the user when the link is activated (though I feel compelled to reiterate here that browser support for this is strictly hypothetical). The four remote sites are identified by locator elements. The text that will be shown to the user on your page is identified by a resource element. Here's the XML:

```
<WEBSITE xmlns:xlink="http://www.w3.org/1999/xlink"
         xlink:type="extended">
  <NAME xlink:type="resource">Cafe au Lait</NAME>
  <HOMESITE xlink:type="locator"
            xlink:href="http://www.cafeaulait.org/"/>
  <MIRROR xlink:type="locator"
          xlink:href="http://sunsite.kth.se/javafaq"/>
  <MIRROR xlink:type="locator"
          xlink:href="http://ibiblio.org/javafaq/"/>
  <MIRROR xlink:type="locator"
          xlink:href="http://sunsite.cnlab-switch.ch/javafaq"/>
</WEBSITE>
```

This `WEBSITE` element describes an extended link with five resources:

✦ The text `Cafe au Lait`, a local resource

✦ The document at `http://www.cafeaulait.org/`, a remote resource

✦ The document at `http://sunsite.kth.se/javafaq`, a remote resource

✦ The document at `http://ibiblio.org/javafaq/`, a remote resource

✦ The document at `http://sunsite.cnlab-switch.ch/javafaq`, a remote resource

Figure 20-2 shows the `WEBSITE` extended link element and five resources. The `WEBSITE` element contains one resource and refers to the other four by URLs. However, this just describes these resources. No connections are implied between them.

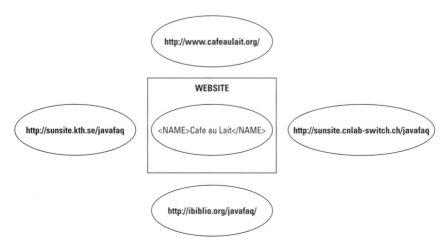

Figure 20-2: An extended link with one local and four remote resources

Another Shortcut for the DTD

If you have many extended link, resource, and locator elements, it may be advantageous to define the common attributes in parameter entities in the DTD, which you can reuse in different elements. For example:

```
<!ENTITY % extended.att
  "xlink:type    CDATA      #FIXED 'extended'
   xmlns:xlink   CDATA      #FIXED 'http://www.w3.org/1999/xlink'
   xlink:role    CDATA      #IMPLIED
   xlink:title   CDATA      #IMPLIED"
>

<!ENTITY % resource.att
  "xlink:type (resource) #FIXED  'resource'
   xlink:href    CDATA    #REQUIRED
   xlink:role    CDATA    #IMPLIED
   xlink:title   CDATA    #IMPLIED"
>

<!ENTITY % locator.att
  "xlink:type (locator)  #FIXED  'locator'
   xlink:href    CDATA    #REQUIRED
   xlink:role    CDATA    #IMPLIED
   xlink:title   CDATA    #IMPLIED"
>

<!ELEMENT WEBSITE (HOMESITE, MIRROR*) >
<!ATTLIST WEBSITE
   %extended.att;
>

<!ELEMENT NAME (#PCDATA)>
<!ATTLIST NAME
   %resource.att;
>

<!ELEMENT HOMESITE (#PCDATA)>
<!ATTLIST HOMESITE
   %locator.att;
>

<!ELEMENT MIRROR (#PCDATA)>
<!ATTLIST MIRROR
   %locator.att;
>
```

Both the extended link element itself and the individual locator children may have descriptive attributes such as xlink:role and xlink:title. The xlink:role and xlink:title attributes of the extended link element provide default roles and titles for each of the individual locator child elements. Individual resource and locator elements may override these defaults with xlink:role and xlink:title attributes of their own. Listing 20-1 demonstrates:

Listing 20-1: **An extended link with one local and four remote resources**

```
<WEBSITE xmlns:xlink="http://www.w3.org/1999/xlink"
         xlink:type="extended" xlink:title="Cafe au Lait">
  <NAME xlink:type="resource"
        xlink:role="http://www.cafeaulait.org/">
    Cafe au Lait
  </NAME>
  <HOMESITE xlink:type="locator"
            xlink:href="http://www.cafeaulait.org/"
            xlink:role="http://www.cafeaulait.org/"/>
  <MIRROR xlink:type="locator"
          xlink:title="Cafe au Lait Swedish Mirror"
          xlink:role="http://sunsite.kth.se/"
          xlink:href="http://sunsite.kth.se/javafaq"/>
  <MIRROR xlink:type="locator"
          xlink:title="Cafe au Lait U.S. Mirror"
          xlink:role="http://ibiblio.org/"
          xlink:href="http://ibiblio.org/javafaq/"/>
  <MIRROR xlink:type="locator"
          xlink:title="Cafe au Lait Swiss Mirror"
          xlink:role="http://sunsite.cnlab-switch.ch/"
          xlink:href="http://sunsite.cnlab-switch.ch/javafaq"/>
</WEBSITE>
```

As always, in valid documents, the XLink elements and all their possible attributes must be declared in the DTD. For example, Listing 20-2 is a DTD that declares the WEBSITE, HOMESITE, NAME, and MIRROR elements as used in the example above, as well as their attributes:

Listing 20-2: **A DTD that declares the WEBSITE, NAME, HOMESITE, and MIRROR elements**

```
<!ELEMENT WEBSITE (NAME, HOMESITE, MIRROR*) >
<!ATTLIST WEBSITE
  xmlns:xlink  CDATA     #FIXED  "http://www.w3.org/1999/xlink"
```

Continued

Listing 20-2 *(continued)*

```
  xlink:type   (extended) #FIXED  "extended"
  xlink:title  CDATA      #IMPLIED
  xlink:role   CDATA      #IMPLIED
>

<!ELEMENT NAME (#PCDATA)>
<!ATTLIST NAME
   xlink:type   (resource) #FIXED    "resource"
   xlink:role   CDATA      #IMPLIED
   xlink:title  CDATA      #IMPLIED
>

<!ELEMENT HOMESITE (#PCDATA)>
<!ATTLIST HOMESITE
   xlink:type   (locator)  #FIXED    "locator"
   xlink:href   CDATA      #REQUIRED
   xlink:role   CDATA      #IMPLIED
   xlink:title  CDATA      #IMPLIED
>

<!ELEMENT MIRROR (#PCDATA)>
<!ATTLIST MIRROR
   xlink:type   (locator)  #FIXED    "locator"
   xlink:href   CDATA      #REQUIRED
   xlink:role   CDATA      #IMPLIED
   xlink:title  CDATA      #IMPLIED
>
```

Arcs

The `xlink:show` and `xlink:actuate` attributes of a simple link define how and when a link is traversed. Extended links are a little more complicated because they provide many different possible traversal paths. For example in an extended link with three resources, A, B, and C, there are nine different possible traversals. These are:

✦ A → A

✦ B → B

✦ C → C

✦ A → B

✦ B → A

✦ A → C

✦ C → A

✦ B → C

✦ C → B

Each of these possible paths between resources can have different rules for when the link is traversed and what happens when it's traversed. These potential traversals are called *arcs*, and they're represented in XML by elements that have an xlink:type attribute with the value arc. Traversal rules are specified by attaching xlink:actuate and xlink:show attributes to arc elements. These attributes have the same values and meanings as they do for simple links. Applications can use arc elements to determine which traversals are and are not allowed and when a link is traversed.

An arc element also has an xlink:from attribute and an xlink:to attribute. The xlink:from attribute says which resource or resources the arc comes from. The xlink:to attribute says which resource or resources the arc goes to. They do this by matching the value of the xlink:label attributes on the various resources in the extended link. Each xlink:label should contain an XML name token. For instance, if the xlink:from attribute has the value A, and the xlink:to attribute has the value B, then the arc goes from the resource whose xlink:label has the value A to the resource whose xlink:label has the value B. Listing 20-3 demonstrates with labels that contain two-letter country codes and state abbreviations mapped to the geographical location of each resource.

Listing 20-3: **An extended link with arcs**

```
<WEBSITE xmlns:xlink="http://www.w3.org/1999/xlink"
         xlink:type="extended" xlink:title="Cafe au Lait">

  <NAME xlink:type="resource" xlink:label="source">
    Cafe au Lait
  </NAME>

  <HOMESITE xlink:type="locator"
            xlink:href="http://www.cafeaulait.org/"
            xlink:label="ny"/>

  <MIRROR xlink:type="locator"
          xlink:title="Cafe au Lait Swedish Mirror"
          xlink:label="se"
          xlink:href="http://sunsite.kth.se/javafaq"/>

  <MIRROR xlink:type="locator"
          xlink:title="Cafe au Lait U.S. Mirror"
          xlink:label="nc"
          xlink:href="http://ibiblio.org/javafaq/"/>
```

Continued

Listing 20-3 *(continued)*

```
<MIRROR xlink:type="locator"
        xlink:title="Cafe au Lait Swiss Mirror"
        xlink:label="ch"
        xlink:href="http://sunsite.cnlab-switch.ch/javafaq"/>

<CONNECTION xlink:type="arc" xlink:from="source"
            xlink:to="ch"    xlink:show="replace"
            xlink:actuate="onRequest"/>
<CONNECTION xlink:type="arc" xlink:from="source"
            xlink:to="ny"    xlink:show="replace"
            xlink:actuate="onRequest"/>
<CONNECTION xlink:type="arc" xlink:from="source"
            xlink:to="se"    xlink:show="replace"
            xlink:actuate="onRequest"/>
<CONNECTION xlink:type="arc" xlink:from="source"
            xlink:to="nc"    xlink:show="replace"
            xlink:actuate="onRequest"/>

</WEBSITE>
```

The first CONNECTION element above defines an arc from the resource with the label "source" to the resource with the label "ch." The second CONNECTION element defines an arc from the resource with the label "source" to the resource with the label "ny," and so on. Figure 20-3 diagrams this link with ovals representing the resources and arrows representing the arcs. This is the same as Figure 20-2, but now connections have been added between resources as specified by the arc elements.

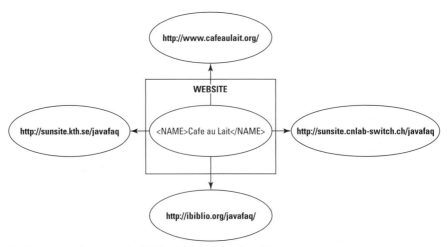

Figure 20-3: An extended link with one local and four remote resources and arcs going from the local resource to each of the remote resources

In this case, each `xlink:arc` element defines exactly one connection because the target and source labels aren't shared by multiple resources. However, this isn't necessarily the case. Each arc goes from exactly one resource to exactly one other resource. However, a single arc element may actually describe multiple arcs. If more than one resource has the `xlink:label` A, then `xlink:from="A"` and `xlink:to="B"` defines multiple arcs from all resources with the label A to the resource with label B. If more than one resource has the label B, then arcs go from all resources with the label A to all resources with label B. For instance, consider the `WEBSITE` element in Listing 20-4:

Listing 20-4: **Labels can be shared between resources**

```
<WEBSITE xmlns:xlink="http://www.w3.org/1999/xlink"
         xlink:type="extended" xlink:title="Cafe au Lait">

  <NAME xlink:type="resource" xlink:label="source">
    Cafe au Lait
  </NAME>

  <HOMESITE xlink:type="locator"
            xlink:href="http://www.cafeaulait.org/"
            xlink:label="home"/>

  <MIRROR xlink:type="locator"
          xlink:title="Cafe au Lait Swedish Mirror"
          xlink:label="mirror"
          xlink:href="http://sunsite.kth.se/javafaq"/>

  <MIRROR xlink:type="locator"
          xlink:title="Cafe au Lait U.S. Mirror"
          xlink:label="mirror"
          xlink:href="http://ibiblio.org/javafaq/"/>

  <MIRROR xlink:type="locator"
          xlink:title="Cafe au Lait Swiss Mirror"
          xlink:label="mirror"
          xlink:href="http://sunsite.cnlab-switch.ch/javafaq"/>

  <CONNECTION xlink:type="arc"  xlink:from="source"
              xlink:to="mirror" xlink:show="replace"
              xlink:actuate="onRequest"/>

</WEBSITE>
```

Here, the "mirror" label is shared by three different elements and the single arc element defines three arcs: One from the source to the Swedish mirror, one from the source to the Swiss mirror, and one from the source to the German mirror. Figure 20-4 diagrams this. It's very similar to Figure 20-3 except that the link between the NAME element and the home site at http://www.cafeaulait.org/ is missing. Because the HOMESITE has a different label, it isn't connected by the single arc element.

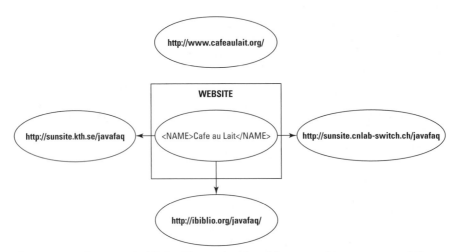

Figure 20-4: An extended link with one local and four remote resources and three arcs going from the local resource to each of the mirror resources

Although I don't recommend it, you can omit either the xlink:from attribute, the xlink:to attribute, or both from an arc element. In this case, all resources participating in the link, both local and remote, take the place of the missing attribute. For instance, consider the WEBSITE element in Listing 20-5.

Listing 20-5: **An omitted to attribute**

```
<WEBSITE xmlns:xlink="http://www.w3.org/1999/xlink"
         xlink:type="extended" xlink:title="Cafe au Lait">

  <NAME xlink:type="resource" xlink:label="source">
    Cafe au Lait
  </NAME>

  <HOMESITE xlink:type="locator"
            xlink:href="http://www.cafeaulait.org/"
            xlink:label="home"/>

  <MIRROR xlink:type="locator"
          xlink:title="Cafe au Lait Swedish Mirror"
          xlink:label="mirror"
          xlink:href="http://sunsite.kth.se/javafaq"/>
```

```
<MIRROR xlink:type="locator"
        xlink:title="Cafe au Lait U.S. Mirror"
        xlink:label="mirror"
        xlink:href="http://ibiblio.org/javafaq/"/>

<MIRROR xlink:type="locator"
        xlink:title="Cafe au Lait Swiss Mirror"
        xlink:label="mirror"
        xlink:href="http://sunsite.cnlab-switch.ch/javafaq"/>

<xlink:arc from="source" show="new" actuate="onRequest"/>

<CONNECTION xlink:type="arc" xlink:from="source"
            xlink:show="replace" xlink:actuate="onRequest"/>

</WEBSITE>
```

Its single arc element is missing the xlink:to attribute. Consequently this extended link includes five arcs — one from the source to the home site, three from the source to each of the mirrors, and one from the source to itself. All arcs start at the NAME element because the xlink:from attribute is present and so specifies. Figure 20-5 diagrams this. It's very similar to Figure 20-3 except that there's now an extra circular arc from the NAME element to itself.

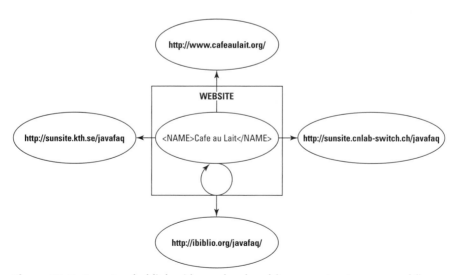

Figure 20-5: An extended link with one local and four remote resources and five arcs going from the local resource to each of the resources, including to itself

As usual, to be valid all the attributes and elements must be fully declared in the document's DTD. Listing 20-6 is a DTD fragment that describes the above WEBSITE element.

Listing 20-6: A DTD for the WEBSITE extended link

```
<!ELEMENT WEBSITE (HOMESITE, MIRROR*, xlink:arc*) >
<!ATTLIST WEBSITE
  xmlns:xlink  CDATA  #FIXED "http://www.w3.org/1999/xlink"
  xlink:type  (extended) #FIXED  "extended"
  xlink:title CDATA     #IMPLIED
  xlink:role  CDATA     #IMPLIED
>

<!ELEMENT HOMESITE (#PCDATA)>
<!ATTLIST HOMESITE
  xlink:type    (locator) #FIXED  "locator"
  xlink:href    CDATA     #REQUIRED
  xlink:label   CDATA     #IMPLIED
  xlink:role    CDATA     #REQUIRED
  xlink:title   CDATA     #IMPLIED
>

<!ELEMENT MIRROR (#PCDATA)>
<!ATTLIST MIRROR
  xlink:type    (locator) #FIXED  "locator"
  xlink:href    CDATA     #REQUIRED
  xlink:label   CDATA     #IMPLIED
  xlink:role    CDATA     #REQUIRED
  xlink:title   CDATA     #IMPLIED
>

<!ELEMENT CONNECTION EMPTY>
<!ATTLIST CONNECTION
  xlink:type   (arc)                  #FIXED    "arc"
  xlink:from   CDATA                  #IMPLIED
  xlink:to     CDATA                  #IMPLIED
  xlink:show   (replace)              #IMPLIED "replace"
  xlink:actuate (onRequest | onLoad) #IMPLIED "onRequest"
>
```

Out-of-Line Links

Inline links, such as the familiar A element from HTML, are themselves part of the source or target of the link. Generally, they link from the document that they're part of to some other document. However, they can also link to a different part of the same document. The source of the link, that is the blue underlined text, is included inside the A element that defines the link. Most simple links are inline.

Extended links can also be out-of-line. An out-of-line link does not contain any part of any of the resources it connects. Instead, the links are stored in a separate document called the *linkbase*. For example, you might use a linkbase to maintain a slide show where each slide requires next and previous links. By changing the order of the slides in the linkbase, you can change the targets of the previous and next links on each page without having to edit the slides themselves.

Out-of-line links also allow you to add links to and from documents that can't be modified, such as a page on someone else's Web site. For instance, media watchdog groups such as FAIR (`http://www.fair.org/`) and AIM (`http://www.aim.org/`) could put out-of-line links from the *New York Times* editorial page to analyses of those editorials. The links would only be visible to users who loaded the right linkbase, however.

Finally, out-of-line links allow you to add links to different parts of non-XML content. For instance, you could link to the third minute of a QuickTime movie, even though the movie doesn't contain any attributes or elements that would normally be used to identify the linked position.

For example, a list of mirror sites for a document such as Listing 20-6 might be stored in a separate file on a Web server in a known location where browsers can find and query it to determine the nearest mirror of a page they're looking for. The out-of-line-ness, however, is that this element does not appear in the document from which the link is activated.

This expands the abstraction of style sheets into the linking domain. A style sheet is completely separate from the document it describes and yet provides rules that modify how the document is presented to the reader. A linkbase containing out-of-line links is separated from the documents it connects, yet it provides the necessary links to the reader. This has several advantages, including keeping more presentation-oriented markup separate from the document and allowing the linking of read-only documents.

Caution   I feel compelled to note that application support for out-of-line links is at best hypothetical at the time of this writing. Although I can show you how to create such links, their actual implementation and support is almost certainly some time away. Some of the details remain to be defined and likely will be implemented in vendor-specific fashions, at least initially. Still, they hold the promise of enabling more sophisticated linking than can be achieved with HTML.

For example, I've put the notes for a Java course I teach on my Web site. Figure 20-6 shows the introductory page. This particular course consists of 13 classes, each of which contains between 30 and 60 individual pages of notes. A table of contents page for each class is then provided that links to each note page used in that class.

Each of the several hundred pages making up the entire site has links to the previous document (Previous link), the next document (Next link), and the table of contents (Top link) for the week, as shown in Figure 20-7. Putting it all together, this amounts to more than a thousand interconnections among this set of documents.

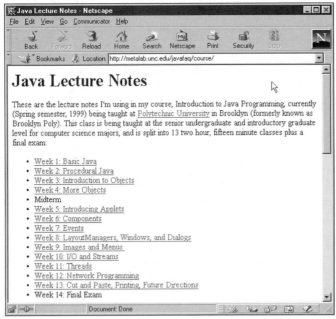

Figure 20-6: The introductory page for my class Web site shows 13 weeks of lecture notes.

The possible interconnections grow exponentially with the number of documents. Every time a document is moved, renamed, or divided into smaller pieces, the links need to be adjusted on that page, on the page before it and after it in the set, and on the table of contents for the week. Quite frankly, this is a lot more work than it should be, and it tends to discourage necessary modifications and updates to the course notes.

The sensible thing to do, if HTML supported it, would be to store the connections in a separate document. Pages could then be reorganized by editing that one document. HTML links don't support this, but extended XLinks do. Listing 20-7 demonstrates one such a document. This document describes links from the main index page to the individual classes and vice versa.

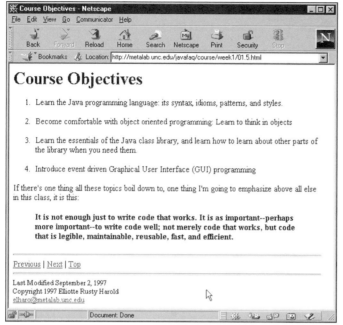

Figure 20-7: One page of lecture notes displaying the Previous, Next, and Top links

Listing 20-7: **An out-of-line extended link**

```
<COURSE xmlns:xlink="http://www.w3.org/1999/xlink"
        xlink:type="extended">

  <TOC xlink:type="locator" xlink:href="index.xml"
       xlink:label="index"/>

  <CLASS xlink:type="locator" xlink:href="week1.xml"
         xlink:label="class"/>
  <CLASS xlink:type="locator" xlink:href="week2.xml"
         xlink:label="class"/>
  <CLASS xlink:type="locator" xlink:href="week3.xml"
         xlink:label="class"/>
  <CLASS xlink:type="locator" xlink:href="week4.xml"
         xlink:label="class"/>
  <CLASS xlink:type="locator" xlink:href="week5.xml"
         xlink:label="class"/>
  <CLASS xlink:type="locator" xlink:href="week6.xml"
         xlink:label="class"/>
  <CLASS xlink:type="locator" xlink:href="week7.xml"
         xlink:label="class"/>
```

Continued

Listing 20-7 *(continued)*

```
<CLASS xlink:type="locator" xlink:href="week8.xml"
       xlink:label="class"/>
<CLASS xlink:type="locator" xlink:href="week9.xml"
       xlink:label="class"/>
<CLASS xlink:type="locator" xlink:href="week10.xml"
       xlink:label="class"/>
<CLASS xlink:type="locator" xlink:href="week11.xml"
       xlink:label="class"/>
<CLASS xlink:type="locator" xlink:href="week12.xml"
       xlink:label="class"/>
<CLASS xlink:type="locator" xlink:href="week13.xml"
       xlink:label="class"/>

<CONNECTION xlink:type="arc" from="index" to="class"/>
<CONNECTION xlink:type="arc" from="class" to="index"/>

</COURSE>
```

Listing 20-8 demonstrates another possible out-of-line extended link. This one provides previous and next links between the 13 classes.

Listing 20-8: An out-of-line extended link

```
<COURSE xmlns:xlink="http://www.w3.org/1999/xlink"
        xlink:type="extended">

<CLASS xlink:type="locator" xlink:href="week1.xml"
       xlink:label="1"/>
<CLASS xlink:type="locator" xlink:href="week2.xml"
       xlink:label="2"/>
<CLASS xlink:type="locator" xlink:href="week3.xml"
       xlink:label="3"/>
<CLASS xlink:type="locator" xlink:href="week4.xml"
       xlink:label="4"/>
<CLASS xlink:type="locator" xlink:href="week5.xml"
       xlink:label="5"/>
<CLASS xlink:type="locator" xlink:href="week6.xml"
       xlink:label="6"/>
<CLASS xlink:type="locator" xlink:href="week7.xml"
       xlink:label="7"/>
<CLASS xlink:type="locator" xlink:href="week8.xml"
       xlink:label="8"/>
<CLASS xlink:type="locator" xlink:href="week9.xml"
       xlink:label="9"/>
<CLASS xlink:type="locator" xlink:href="week10.xml"
       xlink:label="10"/>
```

```
<CLASS xlink:type="locator" xlink:href="week11.xml"
       xlink:label="11"/>
<CLASS xlink:type="locator" xlink:href="week12.xml"
       xlink:label="12"/>
<CLASS xlink:type="locator" xlink:href="week13.xml"
       xlink:label="13"/>

<!-- Previous Links -->
<CONNECTION xlink:type="arc" xlink:from="2"  xlink:to="1"/>
<CONNECTION xlink:type="arc" xlink:from="3"  xlink:to="2"/>
<CONNECTION xlink:type="arc" xlink:from="4"  xlink:to="3"/>
<CONNECTION xlink:type="arc" xlink:from="5"  xlink:to="4"/>
<CONNECTION xlink:type="arc" xlink:from="6"  xlink:to="5"/>
<CONNECTION xlink:type="arc" xlink:from="7"  xlink:to="6"/>
<CONNECTION xlink:type="arc" xlink:from="8"  xlink:to="7"/>
<CONNECTION xlink:type="arc" xlink:from="9"  xlink:to="8"/>
<CONNECTION xlink:type="arc" xlink:from="10" xlink:to="9"/>
<CONNECTION xlink:type="arc" xlink:from="11" xlink:to="10"/>
<CONNECTION xlink:type="arc" xlink:from="12" xlink:to="11"/>
<CONNECTION xlink:type="arc" xlink:from="13" xlink:to="12"/>

<!-- Next Links -->
<CONNECTION xlink:type="arc" xlink:from="1"  xlink:to="2"/>
<CONNECTION xlink:type="arc" xlink:from="2"  xlink:to="3"/>
<CONNECTION xlink:type="arc" xlink:from="3"  xlink:to="4"/>
<CONNECTION xlink:type="arc" xlink:from="4"  xlink:to="5"/>
<CONNECTION xlink:type="arc" xlink:from="5"  xlink:to="6"/>
<CONNECTION xlink:type="arc" xlink:from="6"  xlink:to="7"/>
<CONNECTION xlink:type="arc" xlink:from="7"  xlink:to="8"/>
<CONNECTION xlink:type="arc" xlink:from="8"  xlink:to="9"/>
<CONNECTION xlink:type="arc" xlink:from="9"  xlink:to="10"/>
<CONNECTION xlink:type="arc" xlink:from="10" xlink:to="11"/>
<CONNECTION xlink:type="arc" xlink:from="11" xlink:to="12"/>
<CONNECTION xlink:type="arc" xlink:from="12" xlink:to="13"/>

</COURSE>
```

Now the topics can be reordered simply by rearranging what's connected to what in the out-of-line extended link. The course notes themselves don't have to be touched. However, there are a couple of pieces missing from this puzzle. The first is some notion of how or where in the individual week documents the links will be displayed. It would be easy enough to add `<PREVIOUS/>` and `<NEXT/>` tags to the individual week pages. The XPointers you'll learn about in the next chapter would allow you to select these elements in particular as the sources of outgoing links rather than the entire document.

A single XML document may contain multiple out-of-line extended links. Listings 20-7 and 20-8 could be combined into a single document. However, the XLink specification is relatively silent on exactly what the format of such a compound document should look like. About all it says is that such a document must be a well-formed XML document. An XLink processor would presumably read the entire document and extract and store any extended links it found there.

The final thing that's missing is some way for a browser or other application that's reading the individual pages to be informed that there is a separate linkbase elsewhere that it should read and parse so that it can show the links to the user. This is probably the area in which the specification is weakest. Ideally, it would be handled through some external mechanism such as HTTP headers. However, the only currently defined way to do this (which still isn't supported by any browsers or other software) is to add an extended link inside the documents the out-of-line link connects.

One of the arcs in this extended link has an `xlink:arcrole` attribute with the value `http://www.w3.org/1999/xlink/properties/linkbase`. The `xlink:to` attribute of this arc should identify a locator element that gives the URL of the linkbase. The `xlink:actuate` attribute of the arc determines whether the links are loaded automatically or whether a user request is required. For example, if Listing 20-7 and Listing 20-8 were found in a file at the URL `http://ibiblio.org/javafaq/course/courselinks.xml`, then this element might be included in the main page for the Java course notes:

```
<LINKBASE xlink:type="xlink:extended"
          xmlns:xlink="http://www.w3.org/1999/xlink">
  <SOURCE xlink:type="resource" xlink:label="source"/>
  <LINKS xlink:type="locator" xlink:label="linkbase"
         xlink:href=
          "http://ibiblio.org/javafaq/course/courselinks.xml"/>
  <LOAD  xlink:type="arc"
         xlink:arcrole=
          "http://www.w3.org/1999/xlink/properties/linkbase"
         xlink:from="source" xlink:to="linkbase"
         xlink:actuate="onLoad" />
</LINKBASE>
```

Of course, the problem with this approach is that it requires that you to modify the documents before you can link them. At least in this case, however, it may be enough for the browser to load one such document to find the linkbase, so you may not need to modify every document the linkbase connects.

XML Base

Documents on the Web have an annoying tendency to move. Authors edit pages on their local systems or staging servers before uploading them to the Web server. Readers save copies on their hard drives. Fans make copies of entire sites, both licit and illicit. Google caches almost the entire Web on its servers. Given this, authors really can't assume that documents are in fact where they put them. It's entirely possible that a document will be somewhere else. For example, I just used AltaVista to search for a phrase in a document I published on my Web site and found it had somehow duplicated itself onto twelve different servers in five different countries, my copyright notices notwithstanding.

Given all this and more, using relative URLs in a Web document is a little risky; and that's true whether the URLs are stored in HTML, XML, XHTML, XLinks, XPointers, XInclude, RDF, schemas, RDDL, or any of the other myriad languages that somewhere contain URLs. HTML solves this problem by including an empty BASE element in the HEAD that identifies the base URL via an HREF attribute.

For example, Listing 20-9 is a very simple home page for a fictional San Francisco plant nursery called God's Green Earth. This page is normally found at http://www. geocities.com/godsgreenearthsf/. Because of the BASE element in the HEAD, it has the base URL http://www.geocities.com/godsgreenearthsf/ even if you load it from the CD included with this book. The logo image is loaded from GeoCities, even if the page has been moved to a different server. Links that point to relative URLs are relative to http://www.geocities.com/godsgreenearthsf/. Indeed anything in this page that uses a relative URL will be loaded from http://www.geocities.com/.

Listing 20-9: **Setting the base URL with a BASE element in HTML**

```
<HTML>
  <HEAD>
    <TITLE>God's Green Earth</TITLE>
    <BASE HREF="http://www.geocities.com/godsgreenearthsf/" />
  </HEAD>
  <BODY>
    <H1>God's Green Earth</H1>
    <IMG SRC="/clipart/m/s/appleblossoms.gif" />
    <UL>
      <LI><A HREF="flowers.html">Flowers</A></LI>
      <LI><A HREF="seeds.html">Seeds</A></LI>
      <LI><A HREF="fertilizer.html">Fertilizer</A></LI>
      <LI><A HREF="sod.html">Sod</A></LI>
    </UL>
  </BODY>
</HTML>
```

There are five relative URLs in Listing 20-9, one in an IMG element and four in A elements. When any of these links are activated, the relative URLs are combined with the absolute URL in the base before the link is followed. The five URLs in Listing 20-9 become:

✦ http://www.geocities.com/clipart/m/s/appleblossoms.gif

✦ http://www.geocities.com/godsgreenearthsf/flowers.htm

✦ http://www.geocities.com/godsgreenearthsf/seeds.html

✦ http://www.geocities.com/godsgreenearthsf/fertilizer.html

✦ http://www.geocities.com/godsgreenearthsf/sod.html

The first URL in this list comes from GeoCities, but not from the godsgreenearthsf directory because the relative URL in the IMG element begins with a forward slash and thus starts from the root of the Web server. It's relative to the host but not to the directory. The remaining four URLs do not begin with a forward slash and are all loaded from the godsgreenearthsf directory on www.geocities.com.

Similar approaches work in XHTML, but in most XML-based vocabularies there's no convenient place to put a BASE element. The BASE element could even be needed for something else entirely, such as the location of a military base or the length of the base of a triangle.

Instead in XML you can use an xml:base attribute to establish a base URL. The value of this attribute contains the base URL for that element and all its descendants. For example, Listing 20-10 also has the base URL http://www.geocities.com/godsgreenearthsf/ even if you load it from the CD included with this book. There are five XLinks in this document. Each XLink contains a relative URL, and each is relative to http://www.geocities.com/godsgreenearthsf/. Once again, anything in this page that uses a relative URL will be loaded from http://www.geocities.com/.

Listing 20-10: **Setting the base URL with an xml:base attribute in XML**

```
<?xml version="1.0"?>
<BUSINESS xml:base="http://www.geocities.com/godsgreenearthsf/"
        xmlns:xlink="http://www.w3.org/1999/xlink">
    <NAME>God's Green Earth</NAME>
    <LOGO xlink:type="simple"
          xlink:show="embed"
          xlink:actuate="onLoad"
          xlink:href="/clipart/m/s/appleblossoms.gif" />
    <PRODUCTS>
        <PRODUCT xlink:type="simple"
                 xlink:show="replace"
                 xlink:actuate="onRequest"
                 xlink:href="flowers.html">Flowers</PRODUCT>
        <PRODUCT xlink:type="simple"
                 xlink:show="replace"
                 xlink:actuate="onRequest"
                 xlink:href="seeds.html">Seeds</PRODUCT>
        <PRODUCT xlink:type="simple"
                 xlink:show="replace"
                 xlink:actuate="onRequest"
                 xlink:href="fertilizer.html">
            Fertilizer
```

```
        </PRODUCT>
        <PRODUCT xlink:type="simple"
                 xlink:show="replace"
                 xlink:actuate="onRequest"
                 xlink:href="sod.html">Sod</PRODUCT>
      </PRODUCTS>
    </BUSINESS>
```

When activated the five XLinks in Listing 20-10 resolve to the same five URLs as before:

✦ http://www.geocities.com/clipart/m/s/appleblossoms.gif

✦ http://www.geocities.com/godsgreenearthsf/flowers.htm

✦ http://www.geocities.com/godsgreenearthsf/seeds.html

✦ http://www.geocities.com/godsgreenearthsf/fertilizer.html

✦ http://www.geocities.com/godsgreenearthsf/sod.html

Caution   Only Mozilla and Netscape 6.0 support `xml:base`. Internet Explorer 5.5 and Opera 5.11 and earlier do not support `xml:base` at all.

In Listing 20-10 all the URLs to which the base is attached are in XLinks. The `xml:base` attribute is more general than that, however. It also applies to URLs found in XInclude `include` elements, processing instructions, W3C Schema Language `schemaLocation` attributes, and more.

The one common kind of URL that `xml:base` does not apply to is the namespace URL. `xml:base` attributes are not considered when processing a namespace URL, even a relative one. However, relative namespace URLs are highly discouraged and you should not use them in your own work, so this shouldn't be much of an issue in practice.

Listing 20-10 is well-formed and namespace well-formed, though the latter may be a little surprising because Listing 20-10 appears to be using an undeclared namespace prefix, `xml`. Nowhere do you see an `xmlns:xml` declaration that binds the prefix `xml` to some namespace URI. This is because the prefix `xml` is special. Out of all possible namespace prefixes, only this one does need to be declared. All namespace-aware parsers pre-bind it to the URI `http://www.w3.org/XML/1998/namespace`. This is a special case accounted for in the namespaces specification to allow namespace aware parsers to be backwardly compatible with documents that use the `xml:space` and `xml:lang` attributes defined in XML 1.0. You can declare the `xml` prefix if you feel a need to, but if so it must be set to that URL like this:

```
<BUSINESS xml:base="http://www.geocities.com/godsgreenearthsf/"
          xmlns:xml="http://www.w3.org/XML/1998/namespace"
          xmlns:xlink="http://www.w3.org/1999/xlink">
```

Most authors don't bother to declare it.

Listing 20-10 is not valid because it doesn't have a document type declaration, but it could be if you provided one. The DTD would have to declare the `xml:base` attribute just like any other attribute:

```
<!ATTLIST BUSINESS
     xml:base     CDATA #IMPLIED
     xmlns:xlink CDATA #FIXED  "http://www.w3.org/1999/xlink"
>
```

Most commonly the `xml:base` attribute is attached to the root element so that it establishes a base URL for the entire document. However, it can be applied to non-root elements in which case it only applies to the element and its descendants, but not to other elements elsewhere in the tree. For example, Listing 20-11 moves it to the PRODUCTS element:

Listing 20-11: **An xml:base attribute on a non-root element**

```
<?xml version="1.0"?>
<BUSINESS xmlns:xlink="http://www.w3.org/1999/xlink">
  <NAME>God's Green Earth</NAME>
  <LOGO xlink:type="simple"
        xlink:show="embed"
        xlink:actuate="onLoad"
        xlink:href="/clipart/m/s/appleblossoms.gif" />
  <PRODUCTS
        xml:base="http://www.geocities.com/godsgreenearthsf/">
    <PRODUCT xlink:type="simple"
             xlink:show="replace"
             xlink:actuate="onRequest"
             xlink:href="flowers.html">Flowers</PRODUCT>
    <PRODUCT xlink:type="simple"
             xlink:show="replace"
             xlink:actuate="onRequest"
             xlink:href="seeds.html">Seeds</PRODUCT>
    <PRODUCT xlink:type="simple"
             xlink:show="replace"
             xlink:actuate="onRequest"
             xlink:href="fertilizer.html">
      Fertilizer
    </PRODUCT>
    <PRODUCT xlink:type="simple"
             xlink:show="replace"
             xlink:actuate="onRequest"
             xlink:href="sod.html">Sod</PRODUCT>
  </PRODUCTS>
</BUSINESS>
```

In this position it only applies to the PRODUCT links. It does not apply to the LOGO link. The logo URL /clipart/m/s/appleblossoms.gif is now relative to the physical location of this document. A different image will load if you pull it in from a local drive than from one on a remote Web server.

There can even be multiple xml:base attributes on different elements in the document so that different elements are relative to different URLs. If an element has multiple ancestors with xml:base attributes, then the closest one takes precedence. Consider Listing 20-12. Here the root elements set the base URL to http://www.geocities.com/godsgreenearthsf/ and the PRODUCTS element sets the base URL to http://www.seedgrow.com/.

Listing 20-12: **Multiple xml:base attributes**

```
<?xml version="1.0"?>
<BUSINESS xmlns:xlink="http://www.w3.org/1999/xlink"
        xml:base="http://www.geocities.com/godsgreenearthsf/">
    <NAME>God's Green Earth</NAME>
    <LOGO xlink:type="simple"
          xlink:show="embed"
          xlink:actuate="onLoad"
          xlink:href="/clipart/m/s/appleblossoms.gif" />
    <PRODUCTS xml:base="http://www.seedgrow.com/">
      <PRODUCT xlink:type="simple"
               xlink:show="replace"
               xlink:actuate="onRequest"
               xlink:href="flowers.html">Flowers</PRODUCT>
      <PRODUCT xlink:type="simple"
               xlink:show="replace"
               xlink:actuate="onRequest"
               xlink:href="seeds.html">Seeds</PRODUCT>
      <PRODUCT xlink:type="simple"
               xlink:show="replace"
               xlink:actuate="onRequest"
               xlink:href="fertilizer.html">
        Fertilizer
      </PRODUCT>
      <PRODUCT xlink:type="simple"
               xlink:show="replace"
               xlink:actuate="onRequest"
               xlink:href="sod.html">Sod</PRODUCT>
    </PRODUCTS>
</BUSINESS>
```

When activated the five XLinks in Listing 20-12 resolve to these five URLs:

✦ http://www.geocities.com/clipart/m/s/appleblossoms.gif

✦ http://www.seedgrow.com/flowers.htm

✦ http://www.seedgrow.com/seeds.html

✦ http://www.seedgrow.com/fertilizer.html

✦ http://www.seedgrow.com/sod.html

On occasion it may be useful to use relative URLs in xml:base attributes. In this case, that URL is itself relative to the URL of the closest ancestor with an xml:base attribute. If there is no such ancestor, then the URL is relative to the actual URL of the document. For example, Listing 20-13 sets the base URL of the root element to http://www.geocities.com/godsgreenearthsf/ like before. However, an xml:base attribute on the PRODUCTS element sets the base URL to products.

Listing 20-13: Relative URLs in xml:base attributes

```
<?xml version="1.0"?>
<BUSINESS xmlns:xlink="http://www.w3.org/1999/xlink"
xml:base="http://www.geocities.com/godsgreenearthsf/">
   <NAME>God's Green Earth</NAME>
   <LOGO xlink:type="simple"
         xlink:show="embed"
         xlink:actuate="onLoad"
         xlink:href="/clipart/m/s/appleblossoms.gif" />
   <PRODUCTS xml:base="products">
     <PRODUCT xlink:type="simple"
              xlink:show="replace"
              xlink:actuate="onRequest"
              xlink:href="flowers.html">Flowers</PRODUCT>
     <PRODUCT xlink:type="simple"
              xlink:show="replace"
              xlink:actuate="onRequest"
              xlink:href="seeds.html">Seeds</PRODUCT>
     <PRODUCT xlink:type="simple"
              xlink:show="replace"
              xlink:actuate="onRequest"
              xlink:href="fertilizer.html">
        Fertilizer
     </PRODUCT>
     <PRODUCT xlink:type="simple"
              xlink:show="replace"
              xlink:actuate="onRequest"
              xlink:href="sod.html">Sod</PRODUCT>
   </PRODUCTS>
</BUSINESS>
```

When activated the five XLinks in Listing 20-13 resolve to these five URLs:

✦ http://www.geocities.com/clipart/m/s/appleblossoms.gif

✦ http://www.geocities.com/godsgreenearthsf/products/flowers.htm

✦ http://www.geocities.com/godsgreenearthsf/products/seeds.html

✦ http://www.geocities.com/godsgreenearthsf/products/fertilizer.html

✦ http://www.geocities.com/godsgreenearthsf/products/sod.html

The disadvantage to the element-wide scope of xml:base, as opposed to the document-wide scope of the BASE element in HTML, is that the base URL can never be applied to things outside the root element. Specifically, it does not change the location of a stylesheet referenced in an xml-stylesheet processing instruction. For example, consider Listing 20-14. The browser will look for the document business.css in the same directory where it found the XML document, regardless of what xml:base says.

Listing 20-14: **URLs outside the root element**

```
<?xml version="1.0"?>
<?xml-stylesheet type="text/css" href="business.css"?>
<BUSINESS xmlns:xlink="http://www.w3.org/1999/xlink"
  xml:base="http://www.geocities.com/godsgreenearthsf/">
  <NAME>God's Green Earth</NAME>
  <LOGO xlink:type="simple"
        xlink:show="embed"
        xlink:actuate="onLoad"
        xlink:href="/clipart/m/s/appleblossoms.gif" />
  <PRODUCTS>
    <PRODUCT xlink:type="simple"
             xlink:show="replace"
             xlink:actuate="onRequest"
             xlink:href="flowers.html">Flowers</PRODUCT>
    <PRODUCT xlink:type="simple"
             xlink:show="replace"
             xlink:actuate="onRequest"
             xlink:href="seeds.html">Seeds</PRODUCT>
    <PRODUCT xlink:type="simple"
             xlink:show="replace"
             xlink:actuate="onRequest"
             xlink:href="fertilizer.html">
      Fertilizer
    </PRODUCT>
    <PRODUCT xlink:type="simple"
             xlink:show="replace"
             xlink:actuate="onRequest"
             xlink:href="sod.html">Sod</PRODUCT>
  </PRODUCTS>
</BUSINESS>
```

Likewise, `xml:base` has no effect on URIs used inside DTDs and document type declarations, whether in the internal or external DTD subsets.

Summary

In this chapter, you learned about XLinks. In particular, you learned that:

✦ XLinks can do everything HTML links can do and quite a bit more, but they aren't well supported by current applications.

✦ XLink elements are all defined by attributes attached to the existing elements in other XML applications.

✦ XLink attributes of all types are placed in the `http://www.w3.org/1999/xlink` namespace, normally with the `xlink` prefix.

✦ Simple links behave much like HTML links, but they are not restricted to a single `<A>` tag.

✦ XLink elements are identified by `xlink:type` attributes.

✦ Simple link elements are identified by `xlink:type` attributes with the value `simple`.

✦ Simple link elements have an `xlink:href` whose value is the URI the link points to.

✦ Linking elements can describe the resource they're linking to with `xlink:title` and `xlink:role` attributes. The value of the `xlink:role` attribute must be a URI.

✦ Linking elements can use the `xlink:show` attribute to tell the application how the content should be displayed when the link is activated, for example, by opening a new window.

✦ Linking elements can use the `xlink:actuate` attribute to tell the application whether the link should be traversed without a specific user request.

✦ Extended link elements are identified by `xlink:type` attributes with the value `extended`.

✦ Extended links can contain multiple locators, resources, and arcs.

✦ Local resource elements are identified by `xlink:type` attributes with the value `resource`. The resource is the content of the resource element.

✦ Remote resource locator elements are identified by `xlink:type` attributes with the value `locator`.

✦ A locator element has an `xlink:href` attribute whose value is the URI of the resource it locates.

✦ Both resource and locator elements have an `xlink:label` attribute that contains an XML name token as a label for the resource.

✦ Arc elements are identified by `xlink:type` attributes with the value `arc`.

✦ Arc elements have `xlink:from` and `xlink:to` attributes that identify the resources they connect by their labels.

✦ Arc elements may have `xlink:show` and `xlink:actuate` attributes to determine when and how traversal of the link occurs.

✦ An out-of-line link is a link that does not contain any local resources.

✦ A linkbase is a document containing multiple out-of-line, extended link elements.

✦ A linkbase is found when a document with an extended link whose `xlink:arcrole` has the value `http://www.w3.org/1999/xlink/properties/linkbase` is read.

✦ An `xml:base` attribute on any element sets the URL against which relative URLs in that element and its descendants are relative.

In the next chapter, you learn how XPointers can be used to link not only to remote documents, but also to very specific elements in remote documents.

✦   ✦   ✦

XPointers

XPointer, the XML Pointer Language, defines an addressing scheme for individual parts of an XML document. These addresses can be used by any application that needs to identify parts of or locations in an XML document. For instance, an XML editor could use an XPointer to identify the current position of the insertion point or the range of the selection. An XInclude processor can use an XPointer to determine what part of a document to include. And the URI in an XLink can include an XPointer fragment identifier that locates one particular element in the targeted document. XPointers use the same XPath syntax that you're familiar with from XSL transformations to identify the parts of the document they point to, along with a few additional pieces.

Caution This chapter is based on the January 8, 2001, XPointer Last Call Working Draft, the November 16, 1999, XPath 1.0 specification. The broad picture presented here is likely to be correct, but the details are subject to change. You can find the latest XPointer specification at `http://www.w3.org/TR/xptr`. Furthermore, no mainstream browsers have any support for XPointers. You can use URLs with XPointer fragment identifiers in Web pages, but browsers will mostly ignore them.

Why Use XPointers?

Traditional URLs are simple and easy to use, but they're also quite limited. For one thing, a URL only points at a single, complete document. More granularity than that, such as linking to the third sentence of the seventeenth paragraph in a document, requires the author of the targeted document to manually insert named anchors at the targeted location. The author of the document doing the linking can't do this unless he or she also has write access to the document being linked to. Even if the author doing the linking can insert named anchors into the targeted document, it's almost always inconvenient.

It would be more useful to be able to link to a particular element or group of elements on a page without having to change the document you're linking to. For example, given a large document such as the complete baseball statistics of Chapters 4 and 5, you might want to link to only one team or one player. There are several parts to this problem. The first part is addressing the individual elements. This is the part that XPointers solve. XPointers enable you to target a given element by number, name, type, or relation, to other elements in the document.

The second part of the problem is the protocol by which a browser asks a Web server to send only part of a document rather than the whole thing. This is an area of active research. More work is needed. XPointers do little to solve this problem, except for providing a foundation on which such systems can build. For instance, the best efforts to date are the so-called "byte range extensions to HTTP" available in HTTP 1.1. So far these have not achieved widespread adoption, mostly because Web authors aren't comfortable specifying a byte range in a document. Furthermore, byte ranges are extremely fragile. Trivial edits to a document, even simple reformatting, can destroy byte range links. HTTP 1.1 does allow other range units besides raw bytes (for example, XML elements), but does not require Web servers or browsers to support such units. Much work remains to be done.

The third part of the problem is making sure that the retrieved document makes sense without the rest of the document to go along with it. In the context of XML, this effectively means the linked part is well formed, or perhaps valid. This is a tricky proposition, because most XML documents, especially ones with nontrivial prologs, don't decompose well. Again, XPointers don't address this. The W3C XML Fragment Working Group is addressing this issue, but work here is far from finished.

For the moment, therefore, an XPointer can be used as an index into a complete document, the whole of which is loaded and then positioned at the location identified by the XPointer, and even this much is more than most browsers can handle. In the long-term, extensions to XML, XLink, HTTP, and other protocols may allow more sophisticated uses of XPointers. For instance, XInclude will let you quote a remote document by using an XPointer to tell browsers where to copy the quote in the original document, rather than retyping the text of the quote. You could include cross-references inside a document that automatically update themselves as the document is revised. These uses, however, will have to wait for the development of several next-generation technologies. For now, you must be content with precisely identifying the part of a document you want to jump to when following an XLink.

XPointer Examples

HTML links generally point to one particular document. Additional granularity — that is, pointing to a particular section, chapter, or paragraph of a particular document —

isn't well supported. Provided you control both the linking and the linked document, you can insert a named anchor into an HTML file at the position to which you want to link. For example:

```
<H2><A NAME="xtocid20.2">XPointer Examples</A></H2>
```

You can then link to this position in the file by adding a # and the name of the anchor to the URL. The piece of the URL after the # is called the *fragment identifier*. For example, in this link the fragment identifier is xtocid20.2.

```
<A HREF="http://www.ibiblio.org/xml/bible/20.html#xtocid20.2">
  XPointer Examples
</A>
```

However, this solution is kludgy. It's not always possible to modify the target document so that the source document can link to it. The target document may be on a different server controlled by someone other than the author of the source document. And the author of the target document may change or move it without notifying the author of the source.

Furthermore, named anchors violate the principle of separating markup from content. Placing a named anchor in a document says nothing about the document or its content. It's just a marker for other documents to refer to. It adds nothing to the document's own content.

XPointers allow much more sophisticated connections between parts of documents. An XPointer can refer to any element of a document; to the first, second, or seventeenth element; to the seventh element named P, to the first element that's a child of the second DIV element, and so on. XPointers provide very precisely targeted addresses of particular parts of documents. They do not require the targeted document to contain additional markup just so its individual pieces can be linked to.

Furthermore, unlike HTML anchors, XPointers don't point to just a single point in a document. They can point to entire elements, to possibly discontiguous sets of elements, or to the range of text between two points. Thus, you can use an XPointer to select a particular part of a document, perhaps so it can be copied or loaded into a program.

Here are a few examples of XPointers:

```
xpointer(id("ebnf"))
xpointer(descendant::language[position()=2])
ebnf
xpointer(/child::spec/child::body/child::*/child::language[2])
xpointer(/spec/body/*/language[2])
/1/14/2
xpointer(id("ebnf"))xpointer(id("EBNF"))
```

Each of these selects a particular element in a document. The first finds the element with the ID `ebnf`. The second finds the second `language` element in the document. The third is a shorthand form of finding the element with the ID `ebnf`. The fourth and fifth both specify the second `language` child element of any child element of the `body` child elements of the `spec` child of the root node. The sixth finds the second child element of the fourteenth child element of the root element. The final URI also points to the element with the ID `ebnf`. However, if no such element is present, it then finds the element with the ID `EBNF`.

The document is not specified by the XPointer; rather, the URI that precedes the XPointer specifies the document. This URI may be contained in an XLink linking element, in an XInclude include element, or in something else. The XLinks and URIs you saw in the previous chapter did not contain XPointers, but it isn't hard to add XPointers to them. Most of the time you simply append the XPointer to the URI separated by a #, just as you do with named anchors in HTML. For example, the above list of XPointers could be suffixed to URLs and come out looking similar to the following:

```
http://www.w3.org/TR/1998/REC-xml-
19980210.xml#xpointer(id("ebnf"))
http://www.w3.org/TR/1998/REC-xml-
19980210.xml#xpointer(descendant::language[position()=2])
http://www.w3.org/TR/1998/REC-xml-19980210.xml#ebnf
http://www.w3.org/TR/1998/REC-xml-
19980210.xml#xpointer(/child::spec/child::body/child::*/child::
language[2])
http://www.w3.org/TR/1998/REC-xml-
19980210.xml#xpointer(/spec/body/*/language[2])
http://www.w3.org/TR/1998/REC-xml-19980210.xml#/1/14/2
http://www.w3.org/TR/1998/REC-xml-
19980210.xml#xpointer(id("ebnf"))xpointer(id("EBNF"))
```

In fact, these URIs are just six different ways of pointing to the same element of the document at `http://www.w3.org/TR/1998/REC-xml-19980210.xml`. Normally such URIs are values of the `xlink:href` attribute of a linking element. For example:

```
<SPECIFICATION xmlns:xlink="http://www.w3.org/1999/xlink"
  xlink:type="simple"
  xlink:href="http://www.w3.org/TR/1998/REC-xml-
19980210.xml#xpointer(id('ebnf'))"
  xlink:actuate="onRequest" xlink:show="replace">
  Extensible Markup Language (XML) 1.0
</SPECIFICATION>
```

XPointers don't have any special exemptions from the rules of URIs. In particular, if the XPointer contains characters that are not allowed in URLs (for example, Ω or ^) then these characters must be encoded in UTF-8, and the bytes of the UTF-8 encoding must be hex-escaped using a percent sign. For example, the capital Greek letter Omega is Unicode character 3A9 in hexadecimal. When encoded in UTF-8, this character is the two bytes 206 and 169. In hexadecimal, that's CE and A9. Therefore, the XPointer `xpointer(id("Ω"))` would be encoded in a URL as `xpointer(id("%CE%A9"))`. The

caret is Unicode character 5E in hexadecimal. The equals sign is Unicode character 3D in hexadecimal. The colon is Unicode
character 3A in hexadecimal. Because these three characters are part of the ASCII character set, their UTF-8 encodings are simply their values. Therefore `xpointer(descendant::*[.='^'])` would be encoded in a URL as `xpointer(descendant%3A%3A*[.%3D'%5E'])`. Modern Web browsers allow the square brackets [and] in URLs. However, some older browsers do not, so for maximum compatibility you should escape these characters as %5B and %5D, respectively. Thus the above XPointer would become
`xpointer(descendant%3A%3A*%5B.%3D'%5E'%5D)`.

A Concrete Example

To demonstrate the different types of XPointers, it's useful to have a concrete example in mind. Listing 21-1 is a simple, valid document that should be self-explanatory. It contains information about two related families and their members. The root element is FAMILYTREE. A FAMILYTREE can contain PERSON and FAMILY elements. Each PERSON and FAMILY element has a required ID attribute. Persons contain a name, birth date, death date and spouse. Families contain a husband, a wife, and zero or more children. The individual persons are referred to from the family by reference to their IDs.

Cross-Reference This XML application is revisited in Chapter 34.

Listing 21-1: **A family tree**

```
<?xml version="1.0"?>
<!DOCTYPE FAMILYTREE [

  <!ELEMENT FAMILYTREE (PERSON | FAMILY)*>

  <!-- PERSON elements -->
  <!ELEMENT PERSON (NAME*, BORN*, DIED*, SPOUSE*)>
  <!ATTLIST PERSON
    ID      ID      #REQUIRED
    FATHER  CDATA   #IMPLIED
    MOTHER  CDATA   #IMPLIED
  >
  <!ELEMENT NAME (#PCDATA)>
  <!ELEMENT BORN (#PCDATA)>
  <!ELEMENT DIED  (#PCDATA)>
  <!ELEMENT SPOUSE EMPTY>
  <!ATTLIST SPOUSE IDREF IDREF #REQUIRED>
```

Continued

Listing 21-1 *(continued)*

```
<!--FAMILY-->
<!ELEMENT FAMILY (HUSBAND?, WIFE?, CHILD*) >
<!ATTLIST FAMILY ID ID #REQUIRED>

<!ELEMENT HUSBAND EMPTY>
<!ATTLIST HUSBAND IDREF IDREF #REQUIRED>
<!ELEMENT WIFE EMPTY>
<!ATTLIST WIFE IDREF IDREF #REQUIRED>
<!ELEMENT CHILD EMPTY>
<!ATTLIST CHILD IDREF IDREF #REQUIRED>

]>
<FAMILYTREE>

  <PERSON ID="p1">
    <NAME>Domeniquette Celeste Baudean</NAME>
    <BORN>21 Apr 1836</BORN>
    <DIED>Unknown</DIED>
    <SPOUSE IDREF="p2"/>
  </PERSON>

  <PERSON ID="p2">
    <NAME>Jean Francois Bellau</NAME>
    <SPOUSE IDREF="p1"/>
  </PERSON>

  <PERSON ID="p3" FATHER="p2" MOTHER="p1">
    <NAME>Elodie Bellau</NAME>
    <BORN>11 Feb 1858</BORN>
    <DIED>12 Apr 1898</DIED>
    <SPOUSE IDREF="p4"/>
  </PERSON>

  <PERSON ID="p4">
    <NAME>John P. Muller</NAME>
    <SPOUSE IDREF="p3"/>
  </PERSON>

  <PERSON ID="p7">
    <NAME>Adolf Eno</NAME>
    <SPOUSE IDREF="p6"/>
  </PERSON>

  <PERSON ID="p6" FATHER="p2" MOTHER="p1">
    <NAME>Maria Bellau</NAME>
    <SPOUSE IDREF="p7"/>
  </PERSON>

  <PERSON ID="p5" FATHER="p2" MOTHER="p1">
    <NAME>Eugene Bellau</NAME>
  </PERSON>
```

```
<PERSON ID="p8" FATHER="p2" MOTHER="p1">
  <NAME>Louise Pauline Bellau</NAME>
  <BORN>29 Oct 1868</BORN>
  <DIED>3 May 1938</DIED>
  <SPOUSE IDREF="p9"/>
</PERSON>

<PERSON ID="p9">
  <NAME>Charles Walter Harold</NAME>
  <BORN>about 1861</BORN>
  <DIED>about 1938</DIED>
  <SPOUSE IDREF="p8"/>
</PERSON>

<PERSON ID="p10" FATHER="p2" MOTHER="p1">
  <NAME>Victor Joseph Bellau</NAME>
  <SPOUSE IDREF="p11"/>
</PERSON>

<PERSON ID="p11">
  <NAME>Ellen Gilmore</NAME>
  <SPOUSE IDREF="p10"/>
</PERSON>

<PERSON ID="p12" FATHER="p2" MOTHER="p1">
  <NAME>Honore Bellau</NAME>
</PERSON>

<FAMILY ID="f1">
  <HUSBAND IDREF="p2"/>
  <WIFE IDREF="p1"/>
  <CHILD IDREF="p3"/>
  <CHILD IDREF="p5"/>
  <CHILD IDREF="p6"/>
  <CHILD IDREF="p8"/>
  <CHILD IDREF="p10"/>
  <CHILD IDREF="p12"/>
</FAMILY>

<FAMILY ID="f2">
  <HUSBAND IDREF="p7"/>
  <WIFE IDREF="p6"/>
</FAMILY>

</FAMILYTREE>
```

In the sections that follow, this document is assumed to be present at the URL `http://www.theharolds.com/genealogy.xml`. This isn't a real URL, but the emphasis here is on selecting individual parts of a document rather than a document as a whole.

Location Paths, Steps, and Sets

Many (though not all) XPointers are *location paths*. These are the same location paths used by XSLT and discussed in Chapter 17. Consequently, much of the syntax should already be familiar to you.

Location paths are built from *location steps*. Each location step specifies a point in the targeted document, always relative to some other well-known point such as the start of the document or the previous location step. This well-known point is called the *context node*. In general, a location step has three parts: the *axis*, the *node test*, and an optional *predicate*. These are combined in this form:

```
axis::node-test[predicate]
```

For example, in the location step `child::PERSON[position()=2]`, the axis is `child`, the node-test is `PERSON`, and the predicate is `[position()=2]`. This location step selects the second `PERSON` element along the child axis, starting from the context node or, less formally, the second `PERSON` child element of the context node. Of course, which element this actually is depends on what the context node is. Consequently, this is what's referred to as a *relative location step*. There are also absolute location steps that do not depend on the context node.

The axis tells you in what direction to search from the context node. For instance, an axis can say to look at things that follow the context node, things that precede the context node, things that are children of the context node, things that are attributes of the context node, and so forth.

The node test tells you which nodes to consider along the axis. The most common node test is simply an element name. However the node test may also be the asterisk (*) wild card to indicate that any element is to be matched, or one of several functions for selecting comments, text, attributes, processing instructions, points, and ranges. The group of nodes along the given axis that satisfy the node test form a *location set*.

The predicate is a boolean expression (exactly like the expressions you learned about in XSLT) that tests each node in that set. If that expression returns false, then the node is removed from the set.

Often, after the entire location step — axis, node test, and predicate — has been evaluated, what's left is a single, unique node. A location set like this with only one node is called a *singleton*. However, not all location steps produce singletons. In some cases, you may finish with multiple nodes in the final location set. On occasion, there may be no nodes in the location set; in other words, the location set is the empty set.

A single location step is often not enough to identify the node you want. Commonly, location steps are strung together, separated by slashes, to form a *location path*.

Each location step's location set becomes the context node set for the next step in the path. For example, consider this XPointer:

```
xpointer(/child::FAMILYTREE/child::PERSON[position()=3])
```

The location path of this XPointer is `/child::FAMILYTREE/child::PERSON[position()=3]`. It is built from two location steps:

- ✦ `/child::FAMILYTREE`
- ✦ `child::PERSON[position()=3]`

The first location step is an absolute step that selects all child elements of the root node whose name is `FAMILYTREE`. When applied to Listing 21-1, there's exactly one such element. The second location step is then applied relative to the `FAMILYTREE` element returned by the first location step. All of its child nodes are considered. Those that satisfy the node test — that is, elements whose name is `PERSON` — are returned. There are 12 of these nodes. Each of these 12 nodes is then compared against the predicate to see if its position is equal to 3. This turns out to be true for only one node, Elodie Bellau's `PERSON` element, so that is the single node this XPointer points to.

It is not always the case, however, that an XPointer points to exactly one node. For instance, consider this XPointer:

```
xpointer(/child::FAMILYTREE/child::PERSON[position()>3])
```

This is exactly the same as before except that the equals sign has been changed to a greater than sign. Now when each of the 12 `PERSON` elements are compared, the predicate returns true for 9 of them. Each of these nine is included in the location set that this XPointer returns. This XPointer points to nine nodes, not to one.

The Root Node

Although Listing 21-1 includes ID attributes for most elements, and although they are convenient, they are not required for linking into the document. You can select any element in the document simply by working your way down from the root node. An initial `/` indicates the root node.

The root node of the document is not the same as the root element. Rather it is an abstract node that contains the entire document including the XML declaration, the document type declaration, any comments or processing instructions that come before or after the root element such as `xml-stylesheet`, and the root element itself. For example, to select the root node of the XML 1.0 specification at `http://www.w3.org/TR/REC-xml` you can use this URI:

```
http://www.w3.org/TR/REC-xml#xpointer(/)
```

For another example, Domeniquette Celeste Baudean is the first person in Listing 21-1. Therefore to point at her name, you can get the first element child of the root node (that is, the root element of the document, FAMILYTREE), then count one PERSON down from the root element, and then count one NAME down from that like this:

```
/child::*/child::PERSON[position()=1]/child::NAME
```

This location path says to find the root node, then find all element children of the root node (which in a well-formed XML document will be exactly the root element), then find the first PERSON element that's an immediate child of that element, and then find its NAME child elements.

Axes

XPath defines 13 axes along which an XPointer may search for nodes, all from the same XPath syntax used for XSLT. These depend on context to determine exactly what they point to. For instance, consider this location path:

```
id("p6")/child::NAME
```

It begins with the id() function that returns a node set containing the element with the ID type attribute whose value is p6. This provides a context node for the following location step along the relative child axis. Other axes include ancestor, descendant, self, ancestor-or-self, descendant-or-self, attribute, and more. Each serves to select a particular subset of the elements in the document. For instance, the following axis selects from nodes that come after the context node. The preceding axis selects from nodes that come before the context node. Table 21-1 summarizes the 13 axes.

Table 21-1 **Location Step Axes**	
Axis	*Selects From*
child	All nodes contained in the context node, but not contained in any other nodes the context node contains
parent	The unique node that contains the context node but that does not contain any other nodes that also contain the context node
self	The context node
ancestor	The parent of the context node, the parent of the parent of the context node, the parent of the parent of the parent of the context node, and so forth, back to the root node

Axis	Selects From
ancestor-or-self	The ancestors of the context node and the context node itself
attribute	The attributes of the context node
descendant	The children of the context node, the children of the children of the context node, and so forth
descendant-or-self	The context node itself and its descendants
following	All nodes that start after the end of the context node, excluding attribute and namespace nodes
following-sibling	All nodes that start after the end of the context node and have the same parent as the context node
namespace	All namespaces defined for the context node
preceding	All nodes that finish before the beginning of the context node, excluding attribute and namespace nodes
preceding-sibling	All nodes that start before the beginning of the context node and have the same parent as the context node

The child axis

The child axis selects from the children of the context node. For example, consider this XPointer:

```
xpointer(/child::FAMILYTREE/child::PERSON[position()=3]/child::
NAME)
```

Reading from right to left, it selects the NAME child elements of the third PERSON element that's a child of the FAMILYTREE element that's a child of the root of the document. In this example, there's only one such element; but if there are more than one, then all are returned. For instance, consider this XPointer:

```
xpointer(/child::FAMILYTREE/child::PERSON/child::NAME)
```

This selects all NAME children of PERSON elements that are children of FAMILYTREE elements that are children of the root. There are a dozen of these in Listing 21-1.

It's important to note that the child axis only selects from the *immediate* children of the context node. For example, consider this URI:

```
http://www.theharolds.com/genealogy.xml#xpointer(/child::NAME)
```

This points nowhere because there are no NAME elements in the document that are direct, immediate children of the root node. There are a dozen NAME elements that are indirect children. If you'd like to refer to these, you should use the descendant axis instead of child.

As in XSLT, the child axis is implied if no explicit axis name is present. For instance, the above three XPointers would more likely be written in this abbreviated form:

```
xpointer(/FAMILYTREE/PERSON[position()=3]/NAME)
xpointer(/FAMILYTREE/PERSON/NAME)
xpointer(/NAME)
```

The descendant axis

The descendant axis searches through all the descendants of the context node, not just the immediate children. For example, /descendant::BORN selects all the BORN elements in the document. /descendant::BORN[position()=3] selects the third BORN element encountered in a depth-first search of the document tree. (Depth first is the order you get if you simply read through the XML document from top to bottom.) In Listing 21-1, that selects Louise Pauline Bellau's birthday, <BORN>29 Oct 1868</BORN>.

The descendant axis can be abbreviated by using a double slash in place of a single slash. For example, //BORN[position()=3] also selects the third BORN element encountered in a depth-first search of the document tree. //NAME selects all NAME elements in the document. //PERSON/NAME selects all NAME children of PERSON elements.

The descendant-or-self axis

The descendant-or-self axis searches through all the descendants of the context node and the context node itself. For example, id("p11")/descendant-or-self::PERSON refers to all PERSON children of the element with ID p11 as well as that element itself, because it is of type PERSON. There is no abbreviation for descendant-or-self.

The parent axis

The parent axis refers to the node that's the immediate parent of the context node. For example, /descendant::HUSBAND[position()=1]/parent::* refers to the parent element of the first HUSBAND element in the document. In Listing 21-1, this is the FAMILY element with ID f1.

Without a node test the parent axis can be abbreviated by a .. as in //HUSBAND[position()=1]/...

The self axis

The `self` axis selects the context node. It's sometimes useful when making relative links. For example, `/self::node()` selects the root node of the document (which is not the same as the root element of the document; that would be selected by `/child::*` or, in this example, `/child::FAMILYTREE`). It can be abbreviated by a single period. However, this axis is rarely used in XPointers. It's more useful for XSLT select expressions.

The ancestor axis

The `ancestor` axis selects all nodes that contain the context node, starting with its parent. For example, `/descendant::BORN[position()=2]/ancestor::*[position()=1]` selects the element that contains the second BORN element. Applied to Listing 21-1, it selects Elodie Bellau's PERSON element. There's no abbreviation for the `ancestor` axis.

The ancestor-or-self axis

The `ancestor-or-self` axis selects the context node and all nodes that contain it. For example, `id("p1")/ancestor-or-self::*` identifies a node set that includes Domeniquette Celeste Baudean's PERSON element, that has ID p1, and its parent, the FAMILYTREE element, and its parent, the root node. There's also no abbreviation for the `ancestor-or-self` axis.

The preceding axis

The `preceding` axis selects all nodes that finish before the context node. The first time it encounters an element's start tag or empty element tag, moving backwards from the start of the context node, it counts that element. For example, consider this rule:

```
/descendant::BORN[position()=3]/preceding::*[position()=5]
```

This says go to the third BORN element from the root, Louise Pauline Bellau's birthday, `<BORN>29 Oct 1868</BORN>`, and then move back five elements. This lands on Maria Bellau's NAME element. There's no abbreviation for the `preceding` axis.

The following axis

The `following` axis selects all elements that occur after the context node's closing tag. The first time it encounters an element's start tag or empty element tag, it counts that element. For example, consider this rule:

```
/descendant::BORN[position()=2]/following::*[position()=5]
```

This says go to Elodie Bellau's birthday, `<BORN>11 Feb 1858</BORN>`, and then move forward five elements. This lands on John P. Muller's `SPOUSE` element, `<SPOUSE IDREF="p3" />`, after passing through Elodie Bellau's `DIED` element, Elodie Bellau's `SPOUSE` element, John P. Muller's `PERSON` element and John P. Muller's `NAME` element, in this order. There's no abbreviation for the `following` axis.

The preceding-sibling axis

The `preceding-sibling` axis selects elements that precede the context node in the same parent element. For example,
`/descendant::BORN[position()=2]/preceding-sibling::*[position()=1]`
selects Elodie Bellau's `NAME` element, `<NAME>Elodie Bellau</NAME>`.
`/descendant::BORN[position()=2]/preceding-sibling::*[position()=2]`
doesn't point to anything because there's only one sibling of Elodie Bellau's `BORN` element before it. There's no abbreviation for the `preceding-sibling` axis.

The following-sibling axis

The `following-sibling` axis selects elements that follow the context node in the same parent element. For example, `/descendant::BORN[position()=2] /following-sibling::*[position()=1]` selects Elodie Bellau's `DIED` element, `<DIED>12 Apr 1898</DIED>`. `/descendant::BORN[position()=2]/following-sibling::*[position()=3]` doesn't point to anything because there are only two sibling elements following Elodie Bellau's `BORN` element. There's no abbreviation for the `following-sibling` axis.

The attribute axis

The `attribute` axis selects attributes of the context node. For example, the location path `/descendant::SPOUSE/attribute::IDREF` selects all `IDREF` attributes of all `SPOUSE` elements in the document. The `attribute` axis can be abbreviated by an @ sign. Thus, `//SPOUSE/@IDREF` also selects all `IDREF` attributes of all `SPOUSE` elements in the document. `@*` is a general abbreviation for an attribute with any name. Thus `//SPOUSE/@*` indicates all attributes of all `SPOUSE` elements.

For another example, to find all `PERSON` elements in the document `http://www.theharolds.com/genealogy.xml` whose `FATHER` attribute is Jean Francois Bellau (ID p2), you could write `//PERSON[@FATHER="p2"]`.

The `xmlns` and `xmlns:prefix` attributes used to declare namespaces are not attribute nodes. To get information about namespaces, you have to use the `namespace` axis instead.

The namespace axis

The `namespace` axis contains the namespaces in scope on the context node. It only applies to element nodes. There is one namespace node for each prefix that is mapped to a URI on that element (whether the prefix is used or not, and whether the `xmlns:prefix` attribute that created the mapping is on the element itself or one of its ancestors). Furthermore, if the element is in a default, nonprefixed name-space, then there is also a namespace node for the default namespace.

Namespace nodes are very slippery and hard to grab hold of. Although the element is the parent of the namespace node, the namespace node is not the child of the element. A simple walk of the tree or asking for the children of the element will not find the namespaces of the element. Instead, you have to walk the `namespace` axis explicitly. The only node test that applies to namespace nodes is `node()`.

Fortunately, there's very little reason to point to a namespace node with an XPointer. This axis is more useful for XSLT and not much used in XPointer.

Node Tests

Most of the time the node test part of a location step is simply an element or attribute name like `PERSON` or `@IDREF`. However, there are nine other possibilities:

✦ `*`

✦ *prefix*:`*`

✦ `@`*prefix*:`*`

✦ `node()`

✦ `text()`

✦ `comment()`

✦ `processing-instruction()`

✦ `point()`

✦ `range()`

An asterisk stands for any element. For example, `id("p1")/child::*` selects all the child elements of the element with the ID p1 regardless of their type. This does, however, select only element nodes. It omits comment nodes, text nodes, process-ing instruction nodes, and attribute nodes. If you want to select absolutely any kind of node, use the `node()` node test instead.

A prefix followed by an asterisk selects all elements in the namespace that match the prefix. For example, if the `svg` prefix is mapped to the `http://www.w3.org/2000/svg` URI, then `svg:*` matches all SVG elements. Similarly, `@`*prefix*`:*` matches all attributes in the specified namespace. For instance, if `xlink` is mapped to the URI `http://www.w3.org/1999/xlink`, then `@xlink:*` matches all XLink attributes in the document such as `xlink:type`, `xlink:show`, `xlink:actuate`, `xlink:href`, `xlink:role`, and so forth.

Determining which namespace URIs a prefix is mapped to can be tricky. If the XPointer is used in an XML document, then the normal `xmlns:prefix` attributes in scope where the XPointer is used determine which namespace URI a prefix maps to. However, XPointers can also be used in non-XML documents. For instance, an XPointer may be included as a URL fragment identifier in a link to an XML document from an HTML page. HTML has no means of associating prefixes with URIs. In this case, you can prefix the `xpointer()` part with one or more an `xmlns(prefix=URI)` parts that establish a prefix mapping.

For example, suppose you want to point at the MathML `math` element in the document at `http://www.example.com/equations.xml`. You know that this element is in the `http://www.w3.org/1998/Math/MathML` namespace, but you don't know what prefix is used in the document. Regardless of what prefix the target document uses, you can use the prefix `mml` as long as you use an `xmlns(mml=http://www.w3.org/1998/Math/MathML)` part to associate it with the right URI. For example,

```
xmlns(mml=http://www.w3.org/1998/Math/MathML)
xpointer(//mml:math[1])
```

The `text()` node test specifically refers to the parsed character data content of an element. It's most commonly used with mixed content. Despite the parentheses, the `text()` node test does not actually take any arguments. For instance `/descendant::text()` refers to all of the text but none of the markup of a document. For another example, consider this `CITATION` element:

```
<CITATION CLASS="TURING" ID="C2">
  <AUTHOR>Turing, Alan M.</AUTHOR>
  "<TITLE>On Computable Numbers,
    With an Application to the Entscheidungs-problem</TITLE>"
  <JOURNAL>
    Proceedings of the London Mathematical Society</JOURNAL>,
  <SERIES>Series 2</SERIES>,
  <VOLUME>42</VOLUME>
  (<YEAR>1936</YEAR>):
  <PAGES>230-65</PAGES>.
</CITATION>
```

The following location path refers to the quotation mark before the `TITLE` element.

```
id("C2")/child::text()[position()=2]
```

The first text node in this fragment is the white space between `<CITATION CLASS="TURING" ID="C2">` and `<AUTHOR>`. Technically, this location path refers to all text between `</AUTHOR>` and `<TITLE>`, including the white space and not just the quotation mark.

Caution XPointers that point to text nodes are tricky. I recommend that you avoid them if possible. Of course, you may not always be able to.

Because character data does not contain any child nodes, child, descendant, descendant-or-self, and attribute relative location steps may not be attached to an XPath that selects a text node.

The comment() node test specifically refers to comments. For example, this XPointer points to the third comment in the document:

```
xpointer(/descendant::comment()[position()=3])
```

Because comments do not contain attributes or elements, you cannot add an additional child, descendant, or attribute relative location step after the first term that selects a comment. Despite the parentheses, the comment() node test does not actually take any arguments.

Finally, the processing-instruction() node test selects any processing instructions that occur along the chosen axis. You can use it without any arguments to select all processing instructions, or with an argument to specify the targets of the particular processing instructions you want to select. For example, /descendant:: processing-instruction() selects all processing instructions in the document. However, /descendant::processing-instruction('xml-stylesheet') only finds processing instructions that begin <?xml-stylesheet ./descendant:: processing-instruction("php") only finds processing instructions intended for PHP. As with comments, because processing instructions do not contain attributes or elements, you cannot add an additional child, descendant, or attribute relative location step after the first step that selects a processing instruction.

The point() and range() node tests refer to new ways of dividing an XML document that only work in XPointer, not in other standards that use XPath, such as XSLT. They will be discussed below.

Predicates

Each location step can contain zero or more predicates that further restrict which nodes an XPointer points to. In many cases a predicate is necessary to pick the one node from a node set that you want. This uses the same syntax as you already learned about from XSLT. Each predicate contains an expression in square brackets ([]). This allows an XPointer to select nodes according to many different criteria. For example, you can select:

- ✦ All elements that have a color attribute
- ✦ All elements that have a width attribute with the value 100
- ✦ The first element in the document that contains a LIMIT element
- ✦ The second element whose text content includes the word "Gale"
- ✦ All elements that are not the first or last children of their parents

✦ All elements whose value is 42

✦ All elements whose value is a number greater than 100

These are just a small sampling of the selections that predicates make possible.

The result of a predicate expression is ultimately converted to a boolean after all calculations are finished. Nonboolean results are converted as follows:

✦ A number is compared against the position of the node in the context node list. If it matches, then the result is true; otherwise, the result is false. (More about this shortly.)

✦ An empty node set is false; all other node sets are true.

✦ A zero-length string is false; all other strings are true (including the string "false").

The predicate expression is evaluated for each node in the context node list. Each node for which the expression ultimately evaluates to false is removed from the list. Thus only those nodes that satisfy the predicate remain. I will not repeat the discussion of the operators and functions available to use expressions here. However, I will show you a few examples of predicates using the expression syntax as it's likely to be used in XPointers.

Cross-Reference   Expression syntax is covered in Chapter 18.

Probably the most frequently used function in XPointer predicates is position(). This returns the index of the node in the context node list. This enables you to find the first, second, third, or other indexed node. You can compare positions using the relational operators ⟨, ⟩, =, !=, ⟩=, and ⟨=.

For instance, in Listing 21-1 the root FAMILYTREE element has 14 immediate children, 12 PERSON elements, and 2 FAMILY elements. In order, they are:

```
xpointer(/child::FAMILYTREE/child::*[position()=1])
xpointer(/child::FAMILYTREE/child::*[position()=2])
xpointer(/child::FAMILYTREE/child::*[position()=3])
xpointer(/child::FAMILYTREE/child::*[position()=4])
xpointer(/child::FAMILYTREE/child::*[position()=5])
xpointer(/child::FAMILYTREE/child::*[position()=6])
xpointer(/child::FAMILYTREE/child::*[position()=7])
xpointer(/child::FAMILYTREE/child::*[position()=8])
xpointer(/child::FAMILYTREE/child::*[position()=9])
xpointer(/child::FAMILYTREE/child::*[position()=10])
xpointer(/child::FAMILYTREE/child::*[position()=11])
xpointer(/child::FAMILYTREE/child::*[position()=12])
xpointer(/child::FAMILYTREE/child::*[position()=13])
xpointer(/child::FAMILYTREE/child::*[position()=14])
```

In fact, this test is so common that XPath offers a shorthand notation for it. Instead of writing [position=X] where X is a number, you can simply enclose the number or an XPath expression that returns the number in the square brackets like this:

```
xpointer(/child::FAMILYTREE/child::*[1])
xpointer(/child::FAMILYTREE/child::*[2])
xpointer(/child::FAMILYTREE/child::*[3])
xpointer(/child::FAMILYTREE/child::*[4])
xpointer(/child::FAMILYTREE/child::*[5])
xpointer(/child::FAMILYTREE/child::*[6])
xpointer(/child::FAMILYTREE/child::*[7])
xpointer(/child::FAMILYTREE/child::*[8])
xpointer(/child::FAMILYTREE/child::*[9])
xpointer(/child::FAMILYTREE/child::*[10])
xpointer(/child::FAMILYTREE/child::*[11])
xpointer(/child::FAMILYTREE/child::*[12])
xpointer(/child::FAMILYTREE/child::*[13])
xpointer(/child::FAMILYTREE/child::*[14])
```

Greater numbers, such as /child::FAMILYTREE/child::*[15], don't point to anything. They're just dangling.

To count all elements in the document, not just the immediate children of the root, you can use the descendant axis instead of child. Table 21-2 shows the first four descendant XPointers for the document element FAMILYTREE of Listing 21-1, and what they point to. Note especially that /child::FAMILYTREE/descendant:: *[position()=1] points to the entire first PERSON element, including its children, and not just the <PERSON> start tag.

Table 21-2
The First Four Descendants of the Document Element

XPointer	Points To
/child::FAMILYTREE/descendant::*[position()=1]	<PERSON ID="p1">
	<NAME>Domeniquette Celeste Baudean </NAME>
	<BORN>11 Feb 1858 </BORN>
	<DIED>12 Apr 1898 </DIED>
	<SPOUSE IDREF="p2"/>
	</PERSON>

Continued

Table 21-2 (continued)	
XPointer	**Points To**

`/child::FAMILYTREE/descendant::*[position()=2]`	`<NAME>Domeniquette`
	`Celeste Baudean`
	`</NAME>`

`/child::FAMILYTREE/descendant::*[position()=3]`	`<BORN>21 Apr 1836` `</BORN>`
`/child::FAMILYTREE/descendant::*[position()=4]`	`<DIED>` `Unknown</DIED>`

Functions That Return Node Sets

XPointers are not limited to location paths. In fact they can use any expression that returns a node set. In particular, they can use functions that return node sets. There are three of these:

✦ `id()`

✦ `here()`

✦ `origin()`

The last two, `here()` and `origin()`, are XPointer extensions to XPath that are not available in XSLT.

id()

The `id()` function is one of the simplest and most robust means of identifying an element node. It selects the element in the document that has an ID type attribute with a specified value. For example, consider this URI:

```
http://www.theharolds.com/genealogy.xml#xpointer(id("p12"))
```

If you look at Listing 21-1, you find this element:

```
<PERSON ID="p12" FATHER="p2" MOTHER="p1">
  <NAME>Honore Bellau</NAME>
</PERSON>
```

Because ID type attributes are unique, you know there aren't any other elements that match this XPointer. Therefore, `http://www.theharolds.com/genealogy.xml#xpointer(id("p12"))` must refer to Honore Bellau's `PERSON` element. Note that the XPointer points to the entire element to which it refers, including all its children, not just the start tag.

Since ID pointers are so common and so useful, there's also a shortcut for this. If all you want to do is point to a particular element with a particular ID, you can skip all the `xpointer(id(""))` frou frou and just use the bare ID after the # like this:

```
http://www.theharolds.com/genealogy.xml#p12
```

You can only do this if all you want is the particular element with the particular ID. You cannot add additional relative location steps to a URI that uses this shortcut to select children of the element with ID p12 or the third attribute of the element with ID p12. If you want to do that, you have to use the full `xpointer(id("p12"))` syntax.

The disadvantage of the `id()` function is that it requires assistance from the targeted document. If the element you want to point to does not have an ID type attribute, you're out of luck. If other elements in the document have ID type attributes, you may be able to point to one of them and use a relative location step to point to the one you really want. Nonetheless, ID type attributes work best when you control both the targeted document and the linking document, so that you can ensure that the IDs match the links even as the documents evolve and change over time.

If the document does not have a DTD, then it cannot have any ID type attributes, although it may have attributes named `ID`. In this case, you can't point at anything using the `id()` function.

One possibility is to first use an `id()`-based XPointer, but back it up with an XPointer that looks for the attribute with the specific name anywhere in the document, `ID` in this example. Simply append the second XPointer to the first like this:

```
xpointer(id("p12"))xpointer(//*[@ID="p12"])
```

XPointers are evaluated from left to right. The first match found is returned, so the backup is only used if an ID type attribute with the value p12 can't be found.

here()

The second node set returning function is `here()`. However, it's only useful when used in conjunction with one or more relative location steps. In intradocument links, that is, links from one point in a document to another point in the same document, it's often necessary to refer to "the next element after this one," or "the parent element of this element." The `here()` function refers to the node that contains the XPointer so that such references are possible.

Consider Listing 21-2, a simple slide show. In this example, `here()/../following::SLIDE[1]` refers to the next slide in the show. `here()/../preceding::SLIDE[1]` refers to the previous slide in the show. Presumably, this would be used in conjunction with a style sheet that showed one slide at a time.

Listing 21-2: **A slide show**

```
<?xml version="1.0"?>
<SLIDESHOW xmlns:xlink="http://www.w3.org/1999/xlink">
  <SLIDE>
    <H1>Welcome to the slide show!</H1>
    <BUTTON xlink:type="simple"
            xlink:href="here()/../following::SLIDE[1]">
      Next
    </BUTTON>
  </SLIDE>
  <SLIDE>
    <H1>This is the second slide</H1>
    <BUTTON xlink:type="simple"
            xlink:href="here()/../preceding::SLIDE[1]">
      Previous
    </BUTTON>
    <BUTTON xlink:type="simple"
            xlink:href="here()/../following::SLIDE[1]">
      Next
    </BUTTON>
  </SLIDE>
  <SLIDE>
    <H1>This is the third slide</H1>
    <BUTTON xlink:type="simple"
            xlink:href="here()/../preceding::SLIDE[1]">
      Previous
    </BUTTON>
    <BUTTON xlink:type="simple"
            xlink:href="here()/../following::SLIDE[1]">
      Next
    </BUTTON>
  </SLIDE>
  ...
  <SLIDE>
    <H1>This is the last slide</H1>
    <BUTTON xlink:type="simple"
            xlink:href="here()/../preceding::SLIDE[1]">
      Previous
    </BUTTON>
  </SLIDE>

</SLIDESHOW>
```

Generally, the here() function is only used in fully relative URIs in XLinks. If any URI part is included, it must be the same as the URI of the current document.

origin()

The origin() function is much the same as here(); that is, it refers to the source of a link. However, origin() is used in out-of-line links where the link is not actually present in the source document. It points to the element in the source document from which the user activated the link.

Points

Selecting a particular element or node is almost always good enough for pointing into well-formed XML documents. However, on occasion you may need to point into XML data in which large chunks of non-XML text are embedded via CDATA sections, comments, processing instructions, or some other means. In these cases, you may need to refer to particular ranges of text in the document that don't map onto any particular markup element. Or, you may need to point into non-XML substructure in the text content of particular elements; for example the month in a BORN element that looks like this:

```
<BORN>11 Feb 1858</BORN>
```

An XPath expression can identify an element node, an attribute node, a text node, a comment node, or a processing instruction node. However, it can't indicate the first two characters of the BORN element (the date) or the substring of text between the first space and the last space in the BORN element (the month).

XPointer generalizes XPath to allow identifiers like this. An XPointer can address points in the document and ranges between points. These may not correspond to any one node. For instance, the place between the X and the P in the word *XPointer* at the beginning of this paragraph is a point. The place between the t and the h in the word *this* at the end of the first sentence of this paragraph is another point. The text fragment "Pointer generalizes XPath to allow pointers like t" between those two points is a range.

Every point is either between two nodes or between two characters in the parsed character data of a document. To make sense of this, you have to remember that parsed character data is part of a text node. For instance, consider this very simple but well-formed XML document:

```
<GREETING>
  Hello
</GREETING>
```

There are exactly 3 nodes and 14 distinct points in this document. The nodes are the root node, which contains the GREETING element node, which contains a text node. In order the points are:

1. The point before the root node

2. The point before the GREETING element node

3. The point before the text node containing the text "Hello" (as well as assorted white space)

4. The point before the white space between <GREETING> and Hello

5. The point before the first *H* in Hello

6. The point between the *H* and the *e* in Hello

7. The point between the *e* and the *l* in Hello

8. The point between the *l* and the *l* in Hello

9. The point between the *l* and the *o* in Hello

10. The point after the *o* in Hello

11. The point after the white space between Hello and </GREETING>

12. The point after the text node containing the text "Hello"

13. The point after the GREETING element

14. The point after the root node

The exact details of the white space in the document are not considered here. XPointer collapses all runs of white space to a single space.

Points allow XPointers to indicate arbitrary positions in the parsed character data of a document. They do not, however, enable pointing at a position in the middle of a tag. In essence, what points add is the ability to break up the text content into smaller nodes, one for each character.

A point is selected by using the string-range() function to select a range, then using the start-point () or end-point () function to extract the first or last point from the range. For example, this XPointer selects the point immediately before the *D* in Domeniquette Celeste Baudean's NAME element:

```
xpointer(start-point(string-range
(id('p1')/NAME,"Domeniquette")))
```

This XPointer selects the point after the last *e* in *Domeniquette*:

```
xpointer(end-point(string-range(id('p1')/NAME,"Domeniquette")))
```

You can also take the start-point () or end-point () of an element, text, comment, processing instruction, or root node to get the first or last point in that node.

Ranges

Some applications need to specify a range across a document rather than a particular point in the document. For instance, the selection a user makes with a mouse is not necessarily going to match up with any one element or node. It may start in the middle of one paragraph, extend across a heading and a picture, and then into the middle of another paragraph two pages down.

Any such contiguous area of a document can be described with a *range*. A range begins at one point and continues until another point. The start and end points are each identified by a location path. If the starting path points to a node set rather than a point, then range-to() will return multiple ranges, one starting from the first point of each node in the set.

To specify a range, you append /range-to(*end-point*) to a location path specifying the start point of the range. The parentheses contain a location path specifying the end point of the range. For example, suppose you want to select everything between the <first <PERSON> start tag and the <last</PERSON> end tag in Listing 21-1. This XPointer accomplishes that:

```
xpointer(/child::FAMILYTREE/child::PERSON[position()=
1]/range-
to(/child::FAMILYTREE/child::PERSON[position()=last()]))
```

Range functions

XPointer includes several functions specifically for working with ranges. Most of these operate on *location sets*. A location set is just a node set that can also contain points and ranges, as well as nodes.

The range(location-set) function returns a location set containing one range for each location in the argument. The range is the minimum range necessary to cover the entire location. In essence, this function converts locations to ranges.

The range-inside(location-set) function returns a location set containing the interiors of each of the locations in the input. That is, if one of the locations is an element, then the location returned is the content of the element (but not including the start and end tags). However, if the input location is a range or point, then the interior of the location is just the same as the range or point.

The start-point(location-set) function returns a location set that contains the first point of each location in the input location set. For example, start-point (//PERSON[1]) returns the point immediately after the first <PERSON> start tag in the document. start-point(//PERSON) returns the set of points immediately after each <PERSON> start tag.

The end-point(location-set) function acts the same as start-point() except that it returns the points immediately after each location in its input.

String ranges

XPointer provides some very basic string-matching capabilities through the `string-range()` function. This function takes as an argument a location set to search and a substring to search for. It returns a location set containing one range for each nonoverlapping matching substring. You can also provide optional `index` and `length` arguments indicating how many characters after the match the range should start and how many characters after the start the range should continue. The basic syntax is:

```
string-range(location-set, substring, index, length)
```

The first argument is an XPath expression that returns a location set specifying which part of the document to search for a matching string. The second substring argument is the actual string to search for. By default, the range returned starts before the first matched character and encompasses all the matched characters. However, the `index` argument can give a positive number to start after the beginning of the match. For instance, setting it to 2 indicates that the range starts with the second character after the first matched character. The `length` argument can specify how many characters to include in the range.

A string range points to an occurrence of a specified string, or a substring of a given string in the text (not markup) of the document. For example, this XPointer finds all occurrences of the string Harold:

```
xpointer(string-range(/,"Harold"))
```

You can change the first argument to specify what nodes you want to look in. For example, this XPointer finds all occurrences of the string Harold in NAME elements:

```
xpointer(string-range(//NAME,"Harold"))
```

String ranges may have predicates. For example, this XPointer finds only the first occurrence of the string Harold in the document:

```
xpointer(string-range(/,"Harold")[position()=1])
```

This targets the position immediately preceding the word *Harold* in Charles Walter Harold's NAME element. This is not the same as pointing at the entire NAME element as an element-based selector would do.

A third numeric argument targets a particular position in the string. For example, this targets the point between the *l* and *d* in the first occurrence of the string *Harold* because *d* is the sixth letter:

```
xpointer(string-range(/,"Harold",6)[position()=1])
```

An optional fourth argument specifies the number of characters to select. For example, this URI selects the *old* from the first occurrence of the entire string *Harold*:

```
xpointer(string-range(/,"Harold",4,3)[position()=1])
```

If the first string argument in the node test is the empty string, then relevant positions in the context node's text contents are selected. For example, the following XPointer targets the first six characters of the document's parsed character data:

```
xpointer(string-range(/,""1,6)[position()=1])
```

For another example, let's suppose that you want to find the year of birth for all people born in the nineteenth century. The following will accomplish that:

```
xpointer(string-range(//BORN, " 18", 2, 4))
```

This says to look in all `BORN` elements for the string " 18". (The initial space is important to avoid accidentally matching someone born in 1918 or on the 18th day of the month.) When it's found, move one character ahead (to skip the space) and return a range covering the next four characters.

When matching strings, case is considered. Markup characters are ignored.

Child Sequences

The two most common ways to identify an element in an XML document are by ID and by location. Identifying an element by ID is accomplished through the `id()` function. Identifying an element by location is generally accomplished by counting children down from the root. For example, the following URIs both point to John P. Muller's `PERSON` element:

```
http://www.theharolds.com/genealogy.xml#xpointer(id("p4"))
http://www.e.com/genealogy.xml#xpointer(/child::*[position()=1]
/child::*[position()=4])
```

A *child sequence* is a shortcut for XPointers, like the second example above — that is, an XPointer that consists of nothing but a series of child relative location steps counting down from the root node, each of which selects a particular child by position only. The shortcut is to use only the position number and the slashes that separate individual elements from each other, like this:

```
http://www.theharolds.com/genealogy.xml#/1/4
```

/1/4 is a child sequence that selects the fourth child element of the first child element of the root. This syntax can be extended for any depth of child elements. For example these two URIs point to John P. Muller's NAME and SPOUSE elements, respectively:

```
http://www.theharolds.com/genealogy.xml#/1/4/1
http://www.theharolds.com/genealogy.xml#/1/4/2
```

Child sequences may include an initial ID. In that case, the counting begins from the element with that ID rather than from the root. For example, John P. Muller's PERSON element has an ID attribute with the value p4. Consequently xpointer(p4/1) points to his NAME element and xpointer(p4/2) points to his SPOUSE element.

Each child sequence always points to a single element. You cannot use child sequences with any other relative location steps. You cannot use them to select elements of a particular type. You cannot use them to select attributes or strings. You can only use them to select a single element by its relative location in the tree.

Summary

In this chapter, you learned about XPointers. In particular you learned that:

✦ XPointers refer to particular parts of or locations in XML documents.

✦ The syntax of an XPointer is the keyword xpointer, followed by parentheses containing an XPath expression that returns a node set.

✦ The id() function points to an element with a specified value for an ID type attribute.

✦ Each location step contains an axis, a node test, and zero or more predicates.

✦ Location steps can be chained to make location paths.

✦ Relative location steps select nodes in a document based on their relationship to a context node.

✦ The self axis points to the context node. It can be abbreviated as a period (.).

✦ The parent axis points to the node that contains the context node. It can be abbreviated as a double period (..).

✦ The child axis includes the immediate children of the context node. It can be abbreviated simply by a node test.

✦ The descendant axis includes all nodes contained in the context node. It can effectively be abbreviated as a double slash (//).

✦ The descendant-or-self axis includes all nodes contained in the context node as well as the context node itself.

✦ The ancestor axis includes all element nodes that contain the context node, as well as the root node.

✦ The ancestor-or-self axis includes all nodes that contain the context node, as well as the context node itself.

✦ The preceding axis includes all nodes that finish before the context node.

✦ The following axis includes all nodes that start after the context node.

✦ The preceding-sibling axis selects from nodes that precede the context node with the same parent node as the context node.

✦ The following-sibling axis selects from nodes that follow the context node with the same parent node as the context node.

✦ The attribute axis points to attributes of the context node. It can be abbreviated as an @ sign.

✦ The node test of a relative location step is normally an element or attribute name, but may also be the * wild card to select all elements or one of the keywords comment( ), text( ), processing-instruction( ), node( ), point( ), or range( ).

✦ The optional predicate of a relative location step is a boolean XPath expression enclosed in square brackets that further narrows the node set that the XPointer refers to.

✦ A point indicates a position preceding or following a node or a character.

✦ A range identifies the XML text between two points.

✦ The string-range( ) function points to a specified block of text.

✦ A child sequence points to an element by counting children from the root.

In this chapter, you saw XPointers used in XLinks. In the next chapter, you'll see them used in XInclude, the third leg in the XML hypertext tripod. XInclude is an element-based syntax for building large XML documents out of smaller XML documents that are themselves complete, well-formed, possibly valid XML documents. The individual pieces out of which the complete document is built are located via URLs. These URLs can have XPointer parts to indicate that only part of a targeted document should be included in the master document.

✦   ✦   ✦

XInclude

XML documents can grow extremely large. Some real world examples have already crossed the gigabyte threshold and are much bigger than can comfortably be stored in a normal file system. These documents need to be broken up into multiple separate files. In other cases it's simply more useful to store a document in multiple pieces. For instance, co-authors of a book would like to be able to work on different chapters of a book or different sections of a chapter simultaneously. This isn't possible if the entire book is stored in a single file.

XInclude is an element based syntax for building large XML documents out of smaller XML documents that are themselves complete, well-formed, possibly valid XML documents. For instance, a book might be built from chapters which are themselves built from sections. Each chapter and section can also be a complete, well-formed XML document.

XInclude uses URIs (in practice, URLs) to locate the individual parts that make up the complete document. The URIs can have XPointer fragment identifiers to indicate that only some piece of a part document will be included in the composed document. The individual part documents can be used in multiple different composed documents, or even multiple times in the same document. And the individual part documents can stand on their own and remain well formed and valid as well.

Caution

I must warn you that at the time of this writing (June 2001), XInclude is still bleedingedge technology. The specification is still undergoing significant development and modification. There's some experimental software that implements it, but it isn't yet built into any XML parsers like Xerces. This chapter is based on the May 16, 2001 Last Call Working Draft of the XInclude specification. By the time you're reading this, the exact syntax is likely to have changed, perhaps a little, perhaps a lot. This chapter should give you a pretty good idea of when, where, and how you can use XInclude; but it is not a final description of the exact syntax.

Use Cases for XInclude

Consider this book. It's made up of more than 30 chapters, several appendixes, a preface, a table of contents and other front matter, an index, front and back covers, and more. Each chapter is divided into sections. Some of the sections have subsections. Almost all the chapters have numerous code listings showing actual examples of XML documents. Not surprisingly, this book was not written as a single flowing stream of text starting with the first word on the front cover and finishing with the last word on the back cover. Instead individual chapters were written in a very roughly beginning-to-end fashion. However, I didn't hesitate to jump from one chapter to the next; nor did I always write in a linear order. As I type these words, I've already finished Chapters 1 through 16 and the appendixes. Chapter 17 has barely been begun. Chapters 18 through 21 are mostly done, but a couple of sections in those chapters remain to be written. Chapters 22 through 34 are in varying stages of completion. The preface hasn't been started and is probably the very last thing I will write.

When I complete a chapter, I e-mail it to Sharon Nash, the development editor. She makes her comments and passes it on to both the technical and copy editors for review. The technical editor checks it for factual mistakes. The copy editor checks the spelling and grammar as well as tightens up the prose. When they're done, each sends their comments back to her. She merges all the comments into a single manuscript and sends the document back to me for author review. When I've reviewed the manuscript, I e-mail the document back to Sharon who gives it to Hungry Minds' layout department for conversion to Quark XPress. This process can be going on in parallel for multiple chapters, each of which can be in a different stage of development. One chapter can be in layout while two chapters are in copy edit, seven more are in technical review, three are being author reviewed, and several are in early incomplete draft stages on my hard drive.

The only reason this all works is that the chapters reside in single files that can be written, reviewed, edited, and laid out more or less independently of each other. Nonetheless before the finished book you hold in your hands can be printed, all these diverse files must be integrated into a single unit to which page numbers can be applied and from which cross-references can be resolved. Depending on which part of the process we're in, we need different views of the entire document. When the technical editor is checking my code examples, he just wants to see the actual XML source code files and ignore the rest of the text completely. When the copy editor is checking my spelling, grammar, and usage, he needs to see a complete chapter with all text in place. When the indexing service is generating the index, they need to see the complete book with all page numbers in place.

This book was actually written in Microsoft Word and laid out in Quark XPress. These tools are a little too weak to make the process as seamless as it should be. For instance, the source code examples have to be manually copied and pasted from the source text files into the manuscript Word document. If I later discover a bug in an example, I have to remember to change both the source document and the chapter manuscript. Needless to say, sometimes a change gets made in one place and not the other and consequently the examples tend to get out of sync.

Note

Yes, I know there are features in Word that are supposed to allow you to do all of these things. Trust me when I tell you that these are notoriously buggy and unusable for 1500-page books. Authors and publishers have long since learned from brutal experience to avoid master documents, OLE, cross-references, auto-numbering, and other features of Word that are supposed to allow you to build documents from their component parts.

Data-oriented documents need to be built out of multiple pieces just as frequently, perhaps more frequently, than narrative documents like this book do. For instance, consider the baseball examples in Chapters 4, 5, 9, 10, and 11. Here a rather large document covering the entire league was built up out pieces containing individual teams. Each team contained individual players. It would be nice if each of those pieces could be a well-formed, valid XML document on its own. Something close to this was achieved in Chapter 10 with external entities. However, not all the pieces could stand on their own. The teams were only well formed when considered in the context of the entire document, not when considered in isolation. The player documents were individually well formed, but not valid.

The problem begins with more than a thousand PLAYER documents such as the one in Listing 22-1. I want to combine these into a TEAM document like Listing 22-2. Then I want to combine the team documents into division documents, the divisions, into leagues, and the leagues into a season. Maybe I even want to combine the statistics for all years into one humongous document listing all statistics for all Major League players since records started being kept.

Listing 22-1: **A valid document describing a single player**

```
<?xml version="1.0" encoding="UTF-8" standalone="yes"?>
<!DOCTYPE PLAYER "player.dtd">
<PLAYER>
  <GIVEN_NAME>Al</GIVEN_NAME>
  <SURNAME>Lieter</SURNAME>
  <POSITION>Starting Pitcher</POSITION>
  <GAMES>28</GAMES>
  <GAMES_STARTED>28</GAMES_STARTED>
  <WINS>17</WINS>
  <LOSSES>6</LOSSES>
  <SAVES>0</SAVES>
  <COMPLETE_GAMES>4</COMPLETE_GAMES>
  <SHUT_OUTS>2</SHUT_OUTS>
  <ERA>2.47</ERA>
  <INNINGS>193</INNINGS>
  <HITS_AGAINST>151</HITS_AGAINST>
  <HOME_RUNS_AGAINST>8</HOME_RUNS_AGAINST>
  <RUNS_AGAINST>55</RUNS_AGAINST>
  <EARNED_RUNS>53</EARNED_RUNS>
  <HIT_BATTER>11</HIT_BATTER>
```

Continued

Listing 22-1 *(continued)*

```
    <WILD_PITCHES>4</WILD_PITCHES>
    <BALK>1</BALK>
    <WALKED_BATTER>71</WALKED_BATTER>
    <STRUCK_OUT_BATTER>174</STRUCK_OUT_BATTER>
</PLAYER>
```

Listing 22-2: A valid team document

```
<?xml version="1.0" standalone="yes"?>
<!DOCTYPE TEAM SYSTEM "team.dtd">
<TEAM>
  <TEAM_CITY>New York</TEAM_CITY>
  <TEAM_NAME>Mets</TEAM_NAME>
  <PLAYER>
    <GIVEN_NAME>Al</GIVEN_NAME>
    <SURNAME>Lieter</SURNAME>
    <POSITION>Starting Pitcher</POSITION>
    <GAMES>28</GAMES>
    <GAMES_STARTED>28</GAMES_STARTED>
    <WINS>17</WINS>
    <LOSSES>6</LOSSES>
    <SAVES>0</SAVES>
    <COMPLETE_GAMES>4</COMPLETE_GAMES>
    <SHUT_OUTS>2</SHUT_OUTS>
    <ERA>2.47</ERA>
    <INNINGS>193</INNINGS>
    <HITS_AGAINST>151</HITS_AGAINST>
    <HOME_RUNS_AGAINST>8</HOME_RUNS_AGAINST>
    <RUNS_AGAINST>55</RUNS_AGAINST>
    <EARNED_RUNS>53</EARNED_RUNS>
    <HIT_BATTER>11</HIT_BATTER>
    <WILD_PITCHES>4</WILD_PITCHES>
    <BALK>1</BALK>
    <WALKED_BATTER>71</WALKED_BATTER>
    <STRUCK_OUT_BATTER>174</STRUCK_OUT_BATTER>
  </PLAYER>
  <PLAYER>
    <GIVEN_NAME>Armando</GIVEN_NAME>
    <SURNAME>Reynoso</SURNAME>
    <POSITION>Starting Pitcher</POSITION>
    <GAMES>11</GAMES>
    <GAMES_STARTED>11</GAMES_STARTED>
    <WINS>7</WINS>
    <LOSSES>3</LOSSES>
    <SAVES>0</SAVES>
    <COMPLETE_GAMES>0</COMPLETE_GAMES>
    <SHUT_OUTS>0</SHUT_OUTS>
```

```
      <ERA>3.82</ERA>
      <INNINGS>68.1</INNINGS>
      <HITS_AGAINST>64</HITS_AGAINST>
      <HOME_RUNS_AGAINST>4</HOME_RUNS_AGAINST>
      <RUNS_AGAINST>31</RUNS_AGAINST>
      <EARNED_RUNS>29</EARNED_RUNS>
      <HIT_BATTER>5</HIT_BATTER>
      <WILD_PITCHES>2</WILD_PITCHES>
      <BALK>2</BALK>
      <WALKED_BATTER>32</WALKED_BATTER>
      <STRUCK_OUT_BATTER>40</STRUCK_OUT_BATTER>
   </PLAYER>
   <!-- A few dozen more players...-->
</TEAM>
```

The most straightforward solution is to copy and paste each file into the next level up in the hierarchy. However, it's always a bad idea to store the same information in multiple places. If you later discover a mistake, for instance that the last name of the starting pitcher for the New York Mets is spelled "Leiter" instead of "Lieter," then you need to correct the mistake in multiple places. Quite often you'll miss a place, and the information will get out of sync. Instead, it's better to store each unit of information in exactly one physical storage location (e.g., one file) and then reference that information from all the other documents that need it.

Non-Solutions

There are several half-solutions that almost solve the problem. These solutions include:

✦ External parsed entities in DTDs

✦ Simple XLinks with `xlink:show="embed"`

✦ Server side includes

However, none of these do everything you need; and you can't mix and match them to get full functionality. What's needed is a fourth option that operates at the parser level and that's orthogonal to validation.

DTDs

Referring to each player document as an external parsed entity is probably the closest XML 1.0 comes to the desired functionality. External parsed entities do allow you to build one document out of multiple smaller parts, do allow you to validate the merged document, and do allow you to treat the merged document as a unit. This approach was demonstrated in Chapter 10 as Listing 22-3 recalls:

> **Listing 22-3: The New York Mets with players loaded from external entities**
>
> ```
> <?xml version="1.0" standalone="no"?>
> <!DOCTYPE TEAM SYSTEM "team.dtd" [
>   <!ENTITY % players SYSTEM "mets.dtd">
>   %players;
> ]>
> <TEAM>
>   <TEAM_CITY>New York</TEAM_CITY>
>   <TEAM_NAME>Mets</TEAM_NAME>
>   &AlLeiter;
>   &ArmandoReynoso;
>   &BobbyJones;
>   &BradClontz;
>   &DennisCook;
>   &GregMcMichael;
>   &HideoNomo;
>   &JohnFranco;
>   &JosiasManzanillo;
>   &OctavioDotel;
>   &RickReed;
>   &RigoBeltran;
>   &WillieBlair;
> </TEAM>
> ```

However, there are some strict and inconvenient rules about what may and may not appear in the external parsed entity files themselves. For instance these files can have a text declaration but not an XML declaration. They may have a root element so they can be well formed, but they cannot have a document type declaration so they cannot be valid. For example, if the team documents look like Listing 22-3, you can't combine them into a league document. The document type declaration gets in the way. If you go the other direction and take out the document type declaration so you can combine the team documents, each team document is no longer well formed on its own because the entity references that point to players such as &RigoBeltran; are no longer defined. External parsed entities only really work for single level hierarchies where only the top-most level needs to be valid. Deeper hierarchies than that require another approach.

Embedded XLinks

XLinks allow you to embed one XML document inside another by setting the xlink:show attribute to embed. For example, Listing 22-4 tries to create a full team document by linking to the individual player documents:

Listing 22-4: **The New York Mets with players loaded from XLinks**

```xml
<?xml version="1.0"?>
<!DOCTYPE TEAM SYSTEM "team.dtd">
<TEAM>
  <TEAM_CITY>New York</TEAM_CITY>
  <TEAM_NAME>Mets</TEAM_NAME>
  <PLAYER xlink:type="simple" xlink:show="embed"
    xlink:href="AlLeiter.xml"/>
  <PLAYER xlink:type="simple" xlink:show="embed"
    xlink:href="ArmandoReynoso.xml"/>
  <PLAYER xlink:type="simple" xlink:show="embed"
    xlink:href="BobbyJones.xml"/>
  <PLAYER xlink:type="simple" xlink:show="embed"
    xlink:href="BradClontz.xml"/>
  <PLAYER xlink:type="simple" xlink:show="embed"
    xlink:href="DennisCook.xml"/>
  <PLAYER xlink:type="simple" xlink:show="embed"
    xlink:href="GregMcMichael.xml"/>
  <PLAYER xlink:type="simple" xlink:show="embed"
    xlink:href="HideoNomo.xml"/>
  <PLAYER xlink:type="simple" xlink:show="embed"
    xlink:href="JohnFranco.xml"/>
  <PLAYER xlink:type="simple" xlink:show="embed"
    xlink:href="JosiasManzanillo.xml"/>
  <PLAYER xlink:type="simple" xlink:show="embed"
    xlink:href="OctavioDotel.xml"/>
  <PLAYER xlink:type="simple" xlink:show="embed"
    xlink:href="RickReed.xml"/>
  <PLAYER xlink:type="simple" xlink:show="embed"
    xlink:href="RigoBeltran.xml"/>
  <PLAYER xlink:type="simple" xlink:show="embed"
    xlink:href="WillieBlair.xml"/>
</TEAM>
```

However, `xlink:show="embed"` does something a little different than is needed here. It does not actually combine the XML documents the links point to. Instead, when a browser loads Listing 22-4, it sets aside space in the window for each of the individual player documents such as WillieBlair.xml. It then loads each of these documents separately, figures out how to render it, and embeds the *graphical representation* of the player document inside the *graphical representation* of the team document. Only the pictures are combined, not the documents themselves.

This has a number of implications. First among them is that Listing 22-4 is invalid, because a validator will see empty PLAYER elements with XLink attributes instead of PLAYER elements with child statistics elements as declared in the DTD. Secondly, a style sheet processor needs to operate on each of the ten documents separately.

It can't take advantage of the relationships between information in the individual documents. For instance, it cannot color each player with his team's colors. The information in the individual documents is not conveniently available to a program reading the team document. It has to resolve the URLs in the XLinks and parse those documents separately. It has no information to help it determine the relationship between the player documents and the team document that contains them.

Server side includes

Even before XML, many Web servers let authors build HTML documents out of multiple component parts using server side includes. Typically, when the Web server receives a request for a document that contains server side includes (normally such documents are identified by a .shtml file name extension) it first reads the document looking for special comments that look something like this:

```
<!--#include file="RickReed.html" -->
```

It builds a new document that replaces these comments with the contents of the referenced files.

The biggest problem with this approach is that it ties your pages to a particular Web server. While server side include syntax is similar on most Web servers, both syntax and functionality do change somewhat from server to server, even when you're doing something as simple as include files in different directories. If you switch Web servers, you need to change all your server side includes too. For example, if you're using Apache, then a document that uses server side includes looks something like Listing 22-5. However, if you use a different Web server, then it may be some other syntax.

Listing 22-5: **The New York Mets with players loaded via server side includes**

```
<HTML>
  <HEAD>
    <TITLE>New York Mets</TITLE>
  </HEAD>
  <BODY>
    <H1>New York Mets</H1>

  <!--#include file="AlLeiter.html" -->
  <!--#include file="ArmandoReynoso.html" -->
  <!--#include file="BobbyJones.html" -->
  <!--#include file="BradClontz.html" -->
  <!--#include file="DennisCook.html" -->
  <!--#include file="GregMcMichael.html" -->
  <!--#include file="HideoNomo.html" -->
  <!--#include file="JohnFranco.html" -->
```

```
<!--#include file="JosiasManzanillo.html" -->
<!--#include file="OctavioDotel.html" -->
<!--#include file="RickReed.html" -->
<!--#include file="RigoBeltran.html" -->
<!--#include file="WillieBlair.html" -->

</BODY>
</HTML>
```

The second disadvantage of this approach should be obvious from Listing 22-5: it's HTML-only, at least on most Web servers. Web servers can't process an XML document that uses an arbitrary, non-HTML vocabulary. And of course this approach assumes you're using a Web server. That's not always the case. For instance, an XML document containing a book made up of multiple chapters may be meant to be printed after application of an appropriate style sheet. There's no Web server anywhere in sight.

There are some other disadvantages even if you're using a Web server and serving XHTML. Notice that the document to include is identified by a `file` attribute, not an `href` attribute. Most Web servers can only include local documents from the local file system. They can't include a document served by a different Web server at a different URL. They often can't include a document served by the same Web server if that document is produced dynamically by a CGI or a servlet instead of being read from a static file on a hard drive.

Furthermore, even when the included document is a local file, it's included in its entirety almost as if by copy and paste. You can't say that you want just the contents of the root element, but not the root element itself. In the HTML and XHTML world where every document has exactly one `html` root element that may not contain other `html` elements, this means an included document can't be served al a carte without first being merged with some other master document. Similarly you can't say that you just want to include the second section of a document or all sections that have the word "Barbara" in their title. Inclusion is an all or nothing operation.

The next issue can be either an advantage or a disadvantage, depending on your point of view. Supporting server side includes is a lot of work. Typically that work is done by the server (hence the name). The client has a lot less work to do. Sometimes this is what you want, especially if the server is a raging beast of Pentium-fueled power and the clients are 98MHz weaklings. However, in practice it's much more common that the clients have CPU cycles to spare, while the server is maxed out. In particular, if you're on a local area network in an intranet environment where bandwidth isn't much of an issue, it may make a lot more sense to just burst all the documents to the clients, and let them do the work of parsing and merging them.

Still, despite all these issues, server side includes are actually the approach that is closest in spirit to the XInclude solution I discuss next. The syntax, environment, and tools, however, are quite different.

The xinclude:include Element

XInclude enables you to include one document in another by using a single xinclude:include element. This element has an href attribute whose value is a URL pointing to the document to be included. The xinclude prefix is mapped to the URI http://www.w3.org/2001/XInclude. The shorter prefix xi is also commonly used instead of xinclude. As always the prefix can change as long as the URI remains the same.

Caution   If there is one thing in this chapter that I fear will change between the time I'm writing these words and the time you're reading them, it is this namespace URI. You can find out the current namespace URI by consulting the current version of the XInclude specification at http://www.w3.org/TR/xinclude/.

Listing 22-6 demonstrates the syntax by building the New York Mets team document using xinclude:include elements. Each href attribute of such an element contains a relative URL pointing to the location of each player document. An XInclude processor will remove the XML declaration and document type declaration from each of the player documents and insert what remains into the including document.

Listing 22-6: The New York Mets with players included by XInclude

```
<?xml version="1.0"?>
<!DOCTYPE TEAM SYSTEM "team.dtd">
<TEAM xmlns:xinclude="http://www.w3.org/2001/XInclude">
  <TEAM_CITY>New York</TEAM_CITY>
  <TEAM_NAME>Mets</TEAM_NAME>
  <xinclude:include href="AlLeiter.xml"/>
  <xinclude:include href="ArmandoReynoso.xml"/>
  <xinclude:include href="BobbyJones.xml"/>
  <xinclude:include href="BradClontz.xml"/>
  <xinclude:include href="DennisCook.xml"/>
  <xinclude:include href="GregMcMichael.xml"/>
  <xinclude:include href="HideoNomo.xml"/>
  <xinclude:include href="JohnFranco.xml"/>
  <xinclude:include href="JosiasManzanillo.xml"/>
  <xinclude:include href="OctavioDotel.xml"/>
  <xinclude:include href="RickReed.xml"/>
  <xinclude:include href="RigoBeltran.xml"/>
  <xinclude:include href="WillieBlair.xml"/>
</TEAM>
```

Each of the `xinclude:include` elements in Listing 22-6 is replaced by the referenced player document. However, the XML declaration and document type declaration of the player document, if any, are not included in the merged document. This means that both the player and team documents can be valid because both can contain document type declarations. This is not the case when using external entity references to connect the files.

On occasion, one of the document type declarations in an included document may affect the content of the document. In particular, the document type declaration may reference a DTD that defines entity references used in the document instance, or it may provide default values for certain attributes. In this case, these entity values are resolved and the default attribute values added to the elements to which they apply before the document is included, even though the document type declaration that includes these things is not carried over into the included document. Ninety-nine percent of the time this is exactly the behavior you want. It means you can include documents based solely on their logical structure, without worrying about the details of the physical structure. The only time this is likely to surprise you is when one of the included documents contains an entity reference such as `&copy;`. In this case, the XInclude processor will probably replace it with the actual character such as © or a numeric character reference such as `&#xA9;`. Differences like this are only relevant when you're viewing a document as a text file in an editor without parsing it. An XML parser treats all these structures as the same single character.

Note   Technically, this behavior comes about because XInclude merges the infosets of the various documents rather than copying and pasting text strings.

When you're building a document out of multiple files like this, it's always possible there'll be a problem with one of the files. For instance, somebody might have deleted, renamed, or moved BradClontz.xml. Or perhaps you edited one of the included documents and made a mistake so it's no longer well formed. In these cases, the XInclude processor will give up and report an error when it detects the problem.

In Listing 22-6, relative URLs like `RigoBeltran.xml` are used to locate the player documents. However, absolute URLs are equally acceptable. For example, Listing 22-7 uses absolute URLs. Notice that this means you can build one document out of multiple documents stored on many different Web sites. This is something server side includes cannot do.

Listing 22-7: The New York Mets with players referenced by absolute URLs

```
<?xml version="1.0"?>
<!DOCTYPE TEAM SYSTEM "team.dtd">
<TEAM xmlns:xinclude="http://www.w3.org/2001/XInclude">
  <TEAM_CITY>New York</TEAM_CITY>
  <TEAM_NAME>Mets</TEAM_NAME>
  <xinclude:include
    href="http://ibiblio.org/xml/players/AlLeiter.xml"
  />
  <xinclude:include
    href="http://ibiblio.org/xml/players/ArmandoReynoso.xml"
  />
  <xinclude:include
    href="http://ibiblio.org/xml/players/BobbyJones.xml"
  />
  <xinclude:include
    href="http://ibiblio.org/xml/players/BradClontz.xml"
  />
  <xinclude:include
    href="http://ibiblio.org/xml/players/DennisCook.xml"
  />
  <xinclude:include
    href="http://ibiblio.org/xml/players/GregMcMichael.xml"
  />
  <xinclude:include
    href="http://ibiblio.org/xml/players/HideoNomo.xml"
  />
  <xinclude:include
    href="http://ibiblio.org/xml/players/JohnFranco.xml"
  />
  <xinclude:include
    href="http://ibiblio.org/xml/players/JosiasManzanillo.xml"
  />
  <xinclude:include
    href="http://ibiblio.org/xml/players/OctavioDotel.xml"
  />
  <xinclude:include
    href="http://ibiblio.org/xml/players/RickReed.xml"
  />
  <xinclude:include
    href="http://ibiblio.org/xml/players/RigoBeltran.xml"
  />
  <xinclude:include
    href="http://ibiblio.org/xml/players/WillieBlair.xml"
  />
</TEAM>
```

Other forms of relative URLS such as `mets/RigoBeltran.xml` or `../players/mets/RigoBeltran.xml` are also OK. If an `xml:base` attribute is present on the `xinclude:include` element or one of its ancestors, then the relative URL is resolved relative to that base URL. Otherwise it's resolved relative to the actual URL of the document.

Included documents may themselves include other documents. In other words, includes can nest. There's no limit to the depth. For example, Listing 22-8 builds a division by including teams. Listing 22-9 builds a league by including divisions, and Listing 22-10 builds the entire major league system by including the two leagues. The only restriction is that includes may not be circular. Document A may not include document B if document B includes, directly or indirectly, document A.

Listing 22-8: **A division includes teams**

```
<?xml version="1.0" encoding="ISO-8859-1"?>
<DIVISION xmlns:xinclude="http://www.w3.org/2001/XInclude">
  <xinclude:include href="Braves.xml"/>
  <xinclude:include href="Marlins.xml"/>
  <xinclude:include href="Expos.xml"/>
  <xinclude:include href="Mets.xml"/>
  <xinclude:include href="Phillies.xml"/>
  <xinclude:include href="Pirates.xml"/>
  <xinclude:include href="DevilRays.xml"/>
</DIVISION>
```

Listing 22-9: **A league includes divisions**

```
<?xml version="1.0"?>
<!DOCTYPE LEAGUE SYSTEM "league.dtd">
<LEAGUE xmlns:xinclude="http://www.w3.org/2001/XInclude">
  <LEAGUE_NAME>American League</LEAGUE_NAME>
  <xinclude:include href="American_League_East.xml"/>
  <xinclude:include href="American_League_Central.xml"/>
  <xinclude:include href="American_League_West.xml"/>
</LEAGUE>
```

Listing 22-10: **Major League Baseball has two leagues**

```
<?xml version="1.0"?>
<!DOCTYPE SEASON SYSTEM "baseball.dtd">
<SEASON xmlns:xinclude="http://www.w3.org/2001/XInclude">
  <YEAR>1998</YEAR>
  <xinclude:include href="national_league.xml"/>
  <xinclude:include href="american_league.xml"/>
</SEASON>
```

On the CD-ROM

The complete documents including all 1200 included players can be found on the accompanying CD-ROM in the examples\baseball\XInclude folder. Listing 22-10 is in the file 1998IncludedStatistics.xml.

Validating Documents That Use XInclude

Listings 22-6 through 22-10 all had document type declarations that denoted the root element for that document and located a DTD against which the instance document could be validated. This is allowed, but is certainly not required. XInclude works equally well in well-formed but invalid documents. However, if a DTD is referenced then XInclude processors are allowed to read it in order to resolve external entity references and supply default attribute values.

If a processor wants to take the next step and actually validate the document, it can. XInclude is deliberately orthogonal to validation. Validation can happen before or after the xinclude:include elements are replaced by the documents they refer to. Depending on when you want the validation to happen, you would structure your DTD in one of two ways. If you want to validate before inclusion, then your DTD must declare the xinclude:include element in the appropriate place. Listing 22-11 demonstrates with a team DTD for pre-inclusion validation.

Listing 22-11: **A DTD for pre-inclusion team documents**

```
<!ELEMENT TEAM (TEAM_CITY, TEAM_NAME, xinclude:include+)>
<!ATTLIST TEAM xmlns:xinclude CDATA #FIXED
               "http://www.w3.org/2001/XInclude">

<!ELEMENT TEAM_CITY (#PCDATA)>
<!ELEMENT TEAM_NAME (#PCDATA)>

<!ELEMENT xinclude:include EMPTY>
<!ATTLIST xinclude:include href CDATA #REQUIRED>
```

On the other hand, if you want to validate the document after all inclusions are resolved, then you have to write a DTD that fits the merged document. XInclude can only be used in instance documents, not DTDs; but you can use parameter entity references to split DTDs into multiple parts. This allows you to match the DTD modularity to the document modularity. For instance, assuming that a document called player.dtd contains a proper DTD for PLAYER elements, Listing 22-12 is an acceptable DTD for post-inclusion validation.

Cross-Reference One such player.dtd is found in Listing 10-9 in Chapter 10.

Listing 22-12: **A DTD for post-inclusion team documents**

```
<!ENTITY player.dtd % SYSTEM "player.dtd">
%player.dtd;

<!ELEMENT TEAM (TEAM_CITY, TEAM_NAME, PLAYER+)>
<!ATTLIST TEAM xmlns:xinclude CDATA #FIXED
                    "http://www.w3.org/2001/XInclude">

<!ELEMENT TEAM_CITY (#PCDATA)>
<!ELEMENT TEAM_NAME (#PCDATA)>
```

With a little effort, it isn't even hard to define a DTD that can validate both the pre- and post-inclusion versions. Just put a choice in the content model that allows either PLAYER or xinclude:include elements. Listing 22-13 demonstrates:

Listing 22-13: **A DTD for both pre- and post-inclusion team documents**

```
<!ENTITY player.dtd % SYSTEM "player.dtd">
%player.dtd;

<!ELEMENT TEAM
  (TEAM_CITY, TEAM_NAME, (PLAYER | xinclude:include)+)>
<!ATTLIST TEAM xmlns:xinclude CDATA #FIXED
                    "http://www.w3.org/2001/XInclude">

<!ELEMENT TEAM_CITY (#PCDATA)>
<!ELEMENT TEAM_NAME (#PCDATA)>

<!ELEMENT xinclude:include EMPTY>
<!ATTLIST xinclude:include href CDATA #REQUIRED>
```

In fact, the DTD in Listing 22-13 actually allows a `TEAM` element to contain both `PLAYER` and `xinclude:include` elements so that some players can be linked in from other files while others are typed directly into the team document.

XPointers in XInclude

In the examples so far, the URLs in the `xinclude:include` elements have all pointed to complete documents. However, this isn't necessarily the only or even the primary way XInclude will be used in practice. The URL in the `href` attribute value may have a fragment identifier, and this fragment identifier may contain an XPointer. The XPointer may select something other than the root element. For instance, it might select only the name of a player rather than all the player's statistics. It might select all `NAME` elements in the document. It might even select something that isn't an element at all such as a text node.

For example, suppose you just want to list the surnames of the players. Then from each player document you'd extract just the `SURNAME` elements. The XPointer that does this looks like this:

```
xpointer(/PLAYER/SURNAME)
```

You can use this as a fragment identifier in the URLs you store in the `href` attribute of the `xinclude:include` elements. Listing 22-14 demonstrates:

Listing 22-14: **The surnames of New York Mets players referenced by relative URLs with XPointer fragment identifiers**

```
<?xml version="1.0"?>
<!DOCTYPE TEAM SYSTEM "team.dtd">
<TEAM xmlns:xinclude="http://www.w3.org/2001/XInclude">
  <TEAM_CITY>New York</TEAM_CITY>
  <TEAM_NAME>Mets</TEAM_NAME>
  <xinclude:include
    href="AlLeiter.xml#xpointer(/PLAYER/SURNAME)"/>
  <xinclude:include
    href="ArmandoReynoso.xml#xpointer(/PLAYER/SURNAME)"/>
  <xinclude:include
    href="BobbyJones.xml#xpointer(/PLAYER/SURNAME)"/>
  <xinclude:include
    href="BradClontz.xml#xpointer(/PLAYER/SURNAME)"/>
  <xinclude:include
    href="DennisCook.xml#xpointer(/PLAYER/SURNAME)"/>
  <xinclude:include
    href="GregMcMichael.xml#xpointer(/PLAYER/SURNAME)"/>
  <xinclude:include
```

```
    href="HideoNomo.xml#xpointer(/PLAYER/SURNAME)"/>
  <xinclude:include
    href="JohnFranco.xml#xpointer(/PLAYER/SURNAME)"/>
  <xinclude:include
    href="JosiasManzanillo.xml#xpointer(/PLAYER/SURNAME)"/>
  <xinclude:include
    href="OctavioDotel.xml#xpointer(/PLAYER/SURNAME)"/>
  <xinclude:include
    href="RickReed.xml#xpointer(/PLAYER/SURNAME)"/>
  <xinclude:include
    href="RigoBeltran.xml#xpointer(/PLAYER/SURNAME)"/>
  <xinclude:include
    href="WillieBlair.xml#xpointer(/PLAYER/SURNAME)"/>
</TEAM>
```

After the `xinclude:include` elements are replaced, this document becomes
Listing 22-15:

Listing 22-15: **The surnames of New York Mets players**

```
<?xml version="1.0"?>
<!DOCTYPE TEAM SYSTEM "team.dtd">
<TEAM>
  <TEAM_CITY>New York</TEAM_CITY>
  <TEAM_NAME>Mets</TEAM_NAME>
  <PLAYER>
      <SURNAME>Leiter</SURNAME>
  </PLAYER>
  <PLAYER>
      <SURNAME>Reynoso</SURNAME>
  </PLAYER>
  <PLAYER>
    <SURNAME>Jones</SURNAME>
  </PLAYER>
  <PLAYER>
    <SURNAME>Clontz</SURNAME>
  </PLAYER>
  <PLAYER>
    <SURNAME>Cook</SURNAME>
  </PLAYER>
  <PLAYER>
      <SURNAME>McMichael</SURNAME>
  </PLAYER>
  <PLAYER>
    <SURNAME>Nomo</SURNAME>
  </PLAYER>
  <PLAYER>
```

Continued

Listing 22-15 *(continued)*

```
   <SURNAME>Franco</SURNAME>
  </PLAYER>
  <PLAYER>
   <SURNAME>Manzanillo</SURNAME>
  </PLAYER>
  <PLAYER>
   <SURNAME>Dotel</SURNAME>
  </PLAYER>
  <PLAYER>
   <SURNAME>Reed</SURNAME>
  </PLAYER>
  <PLAYER>
   <SURNAME>Beltran</SURNAME>
  </PLAYER>
  <PLAYER>
   <SURNAME>Blair</SURNAME>
  </PLAYER>
</TEAM>
```

By using more complicated XPath expressions, along with XPointers that point to text nodes, it's possible to put together still more complex documents. For example, suppose you want PLAYER elements that look like this:

```
<PLAYER>
  Beltran
</PLAYER>
```

You'd need to point to the text nodes inside the SURNAME elements of each PLAYER element like this:

```
xpointer(/PLAYER/SURNAME/SURNAME/text())
```

Or suppose you wanted to include both the first and last names like this:

```
<PLAYER>
  Rigo
  Beltran
</PLAYER>
```

Then you need to point at the text nodes inside both the GIVEN_NAME and SURNAME elements of the PLAYER node using a vertical bar like this:

```
xpointer(/PLAYER/SURNAME/GIVEN_NAME/text() |
/PLAYER/SURNAME/SURNAME/text())
```

Furthermore, you'd need to include the PLAYER start and end tags in the master document, and give it an xinclude:include child element, as demonstrated in Listing 22-16:

Listing 22-16: The full names of New York Mets players referenced by relative URLs with XPointer fragment identifiers

```xml
<?xml version="1.0"?>
<!DOCTYPE TEAM SYSTEM "team.dtd">
<TEAM xmlns:xinclude="http://www.w3.org/2001/XInclude">
  <TEAM_CITY>New York</TEAM_CITY>
  <TEAM_NAME>Mets</TEAM_NAME>
  <PLAYER>
    <xinclude:include href=
    "AlLeiter.xml#xpointer(/PLAYER/GIVEN_NAME/text() |
      /PLAYER/SURNAME/text())"/>
  </PLAYER>
  <PLAYER>
    <xinclude:include href=
    "ArmandoReynoso.xml#xpointer(/PLAYER/GIVEN_NAME/text() |
      /PLAYER/SURNAME/text())"/>
  </PLAYER>
  <PLAYER>
    <xinclude:include href=
    "BobbyJones.xml#xpointer(/PLAYER/GIVEN_NAME/text() |
      /PLAYER/SURNAME/text())"/>
  </PLAYER>
  <PLAYER>
    <xinclude:include href=
    "BradClontz.xml#xpointer(/PLAYER/GIVEN_NAME/text() |
      /PLAYER/SURNAME/text())"/>
  </PLAYER>
  <PLAYER>
    <xinclude:include href=
    "DennisCook.xml#xpointer(/PLAYER/GIVEN_NAME/text() |
      /PLAYER/SURNAME/text())"/>
  </PLAYER>
  <PLAYER>
    <xinclude:include href=
    "GregMcMichael.xml#xpointer(/PLAYER/GIVEN_NAME/text() |
      /PLAYER/SURNAME/text())"/>
  </PLAYER>
  <PLAYER>
    <xinclude:include href=
    "HideoNomo.xml#xpointer(/PLAYER/GIVEN_NAME/text() |
      /PLAYER/SURNAME/text())"/>
  </PLAYER>
  <PLAYER>
```

Continued

Listing 22-16 *(continued)*

```
    <xinclude:include href=
    "JohnFranco.xml#xpointer(/PLAYER/GIVEN_NAME/text() |
        /PLAYER/SURNAME/text())"/>
  </PLAYER>
  <PLAYER>
    <xinclude:include href=
    "JosiasManzanillo.xml#xpointer(/PLAYER/GIVEN_NAME/text() |
        /PLAYER/SURNAME/text())"/>
  </PLAYER>
  <PLAYER>
    <xinclude:include href=
    "OctavioDotel.xml#xpointer(/PLAYER/GIVEN_NAME/text() |
        /PLAYER/SURNAME/text())"/>
  </PLAYER>
  <PLAYER>
    <xinclude:include href=
    "RickReed.xml#xpointer(/PLAYER/GIVEN_NAME/text() |
        /PLAYER/SURNAME/text())"/>
  </PLAYER>
  <PLAYER>
    <xinclude:include href=
    "RigoBeltran.xml#xpointer(/PLAYER/GIVEN_NAME/text() |
        /PLAYER/SURNAME/text())"/>
  </PLAYER>
  <PLAYER>
    <xinclude:include href=
    "WillieBlair.xml#xpointer(/PLAYER/GIVEN_NAME/text() |
        /PLAYER/SURNAME/text())"/>
  </PLAYER>
</TEAM>
```

An XPointer that selects a point or a group of points has no effect when included. Points are non-dimensional so including a point doesn't really change the document at all. Ranges are a different matter. If an XPointer selects a range, then the complete contents of the range are included. Furthermore, if a range partially selects an element (e.g., it covers the start tag but not the end tag or vice versa) then the entire element that is only partially selected is included, not just the fraction of the element that is pointed to.

There are, however, some limits on what the XPointer can point to. In particular it is not allowed to point to anything that, when included, would make the including document malformed. For instance, an `xinclude:include` element can be the root element of the document; but if so it must be replaced by a node set containing exactly one element that can serve as the new root. It can't be replaced by a text node or two element nodes. Similarly the XPointer in an `xinclude:include` element should never point to an attribute or a namespace node because replacing an element with an attribute or namespace makes no sense. If an XPointer does point to any of these items, then the XInclude processor will signal an error and give up.

Unparsed Text

The examples up till this point have all included other well-formed XML documents or pieces thereof. If an included document is not well formed, then the XInclude processor stops processing and reports the error. However, it would be useful to be able to include documents that aren't XML documents, and that aren't well formed. For instance, you might want to include a plain text document such as an e-mail message. If you were writing a tutorial about Python programming, you'd like to be able to include the text of your programs. Perhaps the URL you're including actually points to a CGI query against a database that returns a SQL result set as ASCII text. However, in all these and many more cases, the text documents you want to include may contain characters that would make an XML document malformed such < and &. Such characters can be represented in XML documents using entity references, character references, or CDATA sections. However, you still need some way of telling the XInclude processor that it should escape these characters when it reads them in a referenced document rather than treating them as malformed markup and throwing an error.

To indicate that the included document is plain text that should not be parsed, rather than another XML document, you add a `parse="text"` attribute to the `xinclude:include` element that includes it. For example, this `xinclude:include` element references a Java source code file named HelloWorld.java:

```
<xinclude:include href="HelloWorld.java" parse="text"/>
```

You can also set the value of `parse` to `xml` to indicate that the referenced document is XML, and should be parsed. For example, the previous baseball examples could easily have been written like this:

```
<xinclude:include href="GregMcMichael.xml" parse="xml"/>
```

However, since `parse="xml"` is the default, this is rarely done explicitly.

I often use `parse="text"` when I want to include an XML document as an example in a larger document. That way the unresolved markup is shown. For instance, if this very chapter were written in XML, then it might be marked up like this:

```
<P>
Included documents may themselves include other documents.
In other words. includes can nest. There's no limit to the
depth. For example, Listing 22-8 builds a division by including
teams. Listing 22-9 builds a league by including divisions, and
Listing 22-10 builds the entire major league system by
```

```
including the two leagues. The only restriction is that
includes may not be circular. Document A may not include
document B if document B includes, directly or indirectly,
document A.
</P>
<LISTING>
  <LISTING_NUMBER>22-8</LISTING_NUMBER>
  <LISTING_CAPTION>A division includes teams</LISTING_CAPTION>
  <LISTING_BODY>
  <xinclude:include href="source/22/22-8.xml" parse="text"/>
  </LISTING_BODY>
</LISTING>
<LISTING>
  <LISTING_NUMBER>22-9</LISTING_NUMBER>
  <LISTING_CAPTION>A league includes
divisions</LISTING_CAPTION>
  <LISTING_BODY>
  <xinclude:include href="source/22/22-9.xml" parse="text"/>
  </LISTING_BODY>
</LISTING>
<LISTING>
  <LISTING_NUMBER>22-10</LISTING_NUMBER>
  <LISTING_CAPTION>
    Major League Baseball has two leagues
  </LISTING_CAPTION>
  <LISTING_BODY>
  <xinclude:include href="source/22/22-10.xml" parse="text"/>
  </LISTING_BODY>
</LISTING>
```

Note   There is no standard way to specify how illegal characters in plain text are escaped in XInclude documents; that is to say whether you want character references or entity references or CDATA sections to be used. Some XInclude processors may provide non-standard ways of doing this.

XInclude Tools

So far I've told you what an XInclude processor does, but I haven't shown you any examples of actually using one. That's because at the time of this writing (July, 2001) XInclude isn't particularly well supported by browsers, parsers, or other tools. The ultimate goal is that XInclude become a standard feature of XML parsers, just like namespaces became and schemas are becoming now. At most you'd turn on a switch for your parser, pass it the document, and the parser would automatically resolve all includes without any further effort on your part. A browser whose underlying parser supported XInclude could have a similar switch the user could set via a normal user interface like a checkbox in the preferences dialog.

For now, all that's available in terms of actual implementations are a few experimental programs. I've written one myself in Java called XIncluder. You can download the latest version from http://www.ibiblio.org/xml/XInclude/. This program reads an XML document that uses xinclude:include elements, replaces all those elements with the things they refer to, and then writes the merged document back out again onto stdout. Once you've installed the program, you just run it from the shell or DOS prompt like this:

```
C:\>java com.macfaq.xml.XIncluder 22-7.xml
<?xml version="1.0" encoding="UTF-8"?>
<!DOCTYPE TEAM SYSTEM "team.dtd">
<TEAM>
  <TEAM_CITY>New York</TEAM_CITY>
  <TEAM_NAME>Mets</TEAM_NAME>
  <PLAYER>
    <GIVEN_NAME>Al</GIVEN_NAME>
    <SURNAME>Leiter</SURNAME>
    <POSITION>Starting Pitcher</POSITION>
    <GAMES>28</GAMES>
    <GAMES_STARTED>28</GAMES_STARTED>
    <WINS>17</WINS>
    <LOSSES>6</LOSSES>
    <SAVES>0</SAVES>
    <COMPLETE_GAMES>4</COMPLETE_GAMES>
    <SHUT_OUTS>2</SHUT_OUTS>
    <ERA>2.47</ERA>
    <INNINGS>193</INNINGS>
    <HITS_AGAINST>151</HITS_AGAINST>
    <HOME_RUNS_AGAINST>8</HOME_RUNS_AGAINST>
    <RUNS_AGAINST>55</RUNS_AGAINST>
    <EARNED_RUNS>53</EARNED_RUNS>
    <HIT_BATTER>11</HIT_BATTER>
    <WILD_PITCHES>4</WILD_PITCHES>
    <BALK>1</BALK>
    <WALKED_BATTER>71</WALKED_BATTER>
    <STRUCK_OUT_BATTER>174</STRUCK_OUT_BATTER>
  </PLAYER>
  ...
```

If you prefer, you can use the shell redirection operator > to put the output in a different file rather than printing it on stdout. As well as this simple command line user interface, there's an API you can use to integrate it with your own programs. Versions are available for both DOM and JDOM.

The XML Apache Project supports XInclude in their open source Cocoon application server (http://xml.apache.org/cocoon/). Cocoon enables you to place XML documents with xinclude:include elements on your server and have all the pieces folded in before the document is sent to the client. To indicate that you want Cocoon to perform this merging, simply add this processing instruction to the prolog of every document in which xinclude:include elements should be resolved:

```
<?cocoon-process type="xinclude"?>
```

Cocoon does a lot more than just this for instance, it can also apply XSLT style sheets to the merged document to transform it to HTML before presenting it to a browser and it's probably overkill if all you want to do is experiment with XInclude. However, if you're already committed to Apache and Cocoon it can be an easy way to get started with XInclude.

Summary

In this chapter, you learned about XInclude, a W3C standard for building large XML documents out of smaller, more manageable XML documents that are themselves complete, well-formed, possibly valid XML documents. In particular, you learned that:

✦ Previous means of building large documents out of smaller parts including external general entities, server side includes, and XLinks all have significant limitations.

✦ An XInclude processor or an XInclude aware XML parser replaces each `xinclude:include` element with the document identified by the `xinclude:include` element's `href` attribute.

✦ This `href` attribute contains a relative or absolute URL. This URL can have an XPointer fragment identifier to indicate that only a part of the remote document should be included.

✦ The `xinclude:include` element can have an optional `parse="text"` attribute to indicate that the document at the remote URL should be treated as plain text rather than a parsed XML document.

✦ XInclude software is still beta quality at best, but improving. XInclude is not yet supported by any Web browsers.

This chapter addressed modular XML document instances. The next chapter explores the W3C XML Schema language, which, among other advantages, offers modular XML content models. The W3C XML Schema language is an XML application for defining the permissible contents of documents adhering to a particular XML application. Schemas let you specify element and attribute structures, much as DTDs do; but they do it using an XML instance document syntax. Furthermore, schemas let you impose constraints on the text content of XML elements and attributes, such as specifying that a `SHOE_SIZE` element must contain a number between 1 and 15 or that an `ABSTRACT` element must contain between 100 and 512 characters.

✦ ✦ ✦

Schemas

What's Wrong with DTDs?

Document Type Definitions (DTDs) are an outgrowth of XML's heritage in the Standardized General Markup Language (SGML). SGML was always intended for narrative-style documents: books, reports, technical manuals, brochures, Web pages, and the like. DTDs were designed to serve the needs of these sorts of documents, and indeed they serve them very well. DTDs let you state very simply and straightforwardly that every book must have one or more authors, that every song has exactly one title, that every PERSON element has an ID attribute, and so forth. Indeed for narrative documents that are intended for human beings to read from start to finish, that are more or less composed of words in a row, there's really no need for anything beyond a DTD. However, XML has gone well beyond the uses envisioned for SGML. XML is being used for object serialization, stock trading, remote procedure calls, vector graphics, and many more things that look nothing like traditional narrative documents; and it is in these new arenas that DTDs are showing some limits.

The limitation most developers notice first is the almost complete lack of data typing, especially for element content. DTDs can't say that a PRICE element must contain a number, much less a number that's greater than zero with two decimal digits of precision and a dollar sign. There's no way to say that a MONTH element must be an integer between 1 and 12. There's no way to indicate that a TITLE must contain between 1 and 255 characters. None of these are particularly important things to do for the narrative documents SGML was aimed at; but they're very common things to want to do with data formats intended for computer-to-computer exchange of information rather than computer-to-human communication. Humans are very good at handling fuzzy systems where expected data is missing, or perhaps in not quite the right format; computers are not. Computers need to know that when they expect an element to contain an integer between 1 and 12, the element really contains an integer in that range and nothing else.

The second problem is that DTDs have an unusual non-XML syntax. You actually need separate parsers and APIs to handle DTDs than you do to handle XML documents themselves. For instance, consider this common element declaration:

```
<!ELEMENT TITLE (#PCDATA)>
```

This is not a legal XML element. You can't begin an element name with an exclamation point. TITLE is not an attribute. Neither is (#PCDATA). This is a very different way of describing information than is used in XML document instances. One would expect that if XML were really powerful enough to live up to all its hype then it would be powerful enough to describe itself. You shouldn't need two different syntaxes: one for the information and one for the meta-information detailing the structure of the information. XML element and attribute syntax should suffice for both information and meta-information.

The third problem is that DTDs are only marginally extensible and don't scale very well. It's difficult to combine independent DTDs together in a sensible way. You can do this with parameter entity references. Indeed, SMIL 2.0 and modular XHTML are based on this idea. However, the modularized DTDs are very messy and very hard to follow. The largest DTDs in use today are in the ballpark of 10,000 lines of code, and it's questionable whether much larger XML applications can be defined before the entire DTD becomes completely unmanageable and incomprehensible. By contrast, the largest computer programs in existence today, which are much more intrinsically complex than even the most ambitious DTDs, easily reach sizes of 1,000,000 lines of code and more; sometimes even 10,000,000 lines of code or more.

Perhaps most annoyingly, DTDs are only marginally compatible with namespaces. The first principle of namespaces is that only the URI matters. The prefix does not. The prefix can change as long as the URI remains the same. However, validation of documents that use namespace prefixes works only if the DTD declares the prefixed names. You cannot use namespace URIs in a DTD. You must use the actual prefixes. If you change the prefixes in the document but don't change the DTD, then the document immediately ceases to be valid. There are some tricks that you can perform with parameter entity references to make DTDs less dependent on the actual prefix, but they're complicated and not well understood in the XML community. And even when they are understood, these tricks simply feel far too much like a dirty hack rather than a clean, maintainable solution.

Finally, there are a number of annoying minor limitations where DTDs don't allow you to do things that it really feels like you ought to be able to do. For instance, DTDs cannot enforce the order or number of child elements in mixed content. That is, you can't make statements such as each PARAGRAPH element must begin with exactly one SUMMARY element that is followed by plain text. Similarly you can't enforce the number of child elements without also enforcing their order. For instance, you cannot easily say that a PERSON element must contain a FIRST_NAME child, a `MIDDLE_NAME` child, and a `LAST_NAME` child, but that you don't care what order they appear in. Again, there are workarounds; but they grow combinatorially complex with the number of possible child elements.

Schemas are an attempt to solve all these problems by defining a new XML-based syntax for describing the permissible contents of XML documents that includes:

✦ Powerful data typing including range checking

✦ Namespace-aware validation based on namespace URIs rather than on prefixes

✦ Extensibility and scalability

However, schemas are not a be-all and end-all solution. In particular, *schemas do not replace DTDs!* You can use both schemas and DTDs in the same document. DTDs can do several things that schemas cannot do, most importantly declaring entities. And of course, DTDs still work very well for the classic sort of narrative documents they were originally designed for. Indeed, for these types of documents, a DTD is often considerably easier to write than an equivalent schema. Parsers and other software will continue to support DTDs for as long as they support XML.

What Is a Schema?

The word *schema* derives from the Greek word σχημα, meaning form or shape. It was first popularized in the Western world by Immanuel Kant in the late 1700s. According to the 1933 edition of the *Oxford English Dictionary*, Kant used the word *schema* to mean, "Any one of certain forms or rules of the 'productive imagination' through which the understanding is able to apply its 'categories' to the manifold of sense-perception in the process of realizing knowledge or experience." (And you thought computer science was full of unintelligible technical jargon!)

Schemas remained the province of philosophers for the next 200 years, until the word *schema* entered computer science, probably through database theory. Here, *schema* originally meant any document that described the permissible content of a database. More specifically, a schema was a description of all the tables in a database and the fields in the table. A schema also described what type of data each field could contain: CHAR, INT, CHAR[32], BLOB, DATE, and so on.

The word *schema* has grown from that source definition to a more generic meaning of any document that describes the permissible contents of other documents, especially if data typing is involved. Thus, you'll hear about different kinds of schemas from different technologies, including vocabulary schemas, RDF schemas, organizational schemas, X.500 schemas, and, of course, XML schemas.

You say schemas, I say schemata

Probably no single topic has been more controversial in the schema world than the proper plural form of the word *schema*. The original Greek plural is σχηματα, *schemata* in Latin transliteration; and this is the form which Kant used and which you'll find in most dictionaries. This was fine for the 200 years when only people with PhDs in philosophy actually used the word. However, as often happens when words from other languages are adopted into popular English, its plural changed to something that sounds more natural to an Anglophone ear. In this case, the plural form *schemata* seems to be rapidly dying out in favor of the simpler *schemas*. In fact, the three World Wide Web Consortium (W3C) schema specifications all use the plural form *schemas*. I follow this convention in this book.

Since schemas is such a generic term, it shouldn't come as any surprise to you that there's more than one schema language for XML. In fact there are many, each with its own unique advantages and disadvantages. These include Murata Makoto's Relax (`http://www.xml.gr.jp/relax/`), Rick Jelliffe's Schematron (`http://www.ascc.net/xml/resource/schematron/schematron.html`), James Clark's TREX - Tree Regular Expressions for XML (`http://www.thaiopensource.com/trex/`), the Document Definition Markup Language (DDML, also known as XSchema, `http://purl.oclc.org/NET/ddml`), and the W3C's misleadingly, generically titled XML Schema language. In addition, traditional XML DTDs can be considered to be yet another schema language.

There are also a number of dead XML schema languages that have been abandoned by their manufacturers in favor of other languages. These include Document Content Description (DCD), Commerce One's Schema for Object-Oriented XML (SOX), and Microsoft's XML-Data Reduced (XDR). None of these are worth your time or investment at this point. They never achieved broad adoption, and their vendors are now moving to the W3C XML Schema language instead.

This chapter focuses almost exclusively on the W3C XML Schema language. Nonetheless, TREX, Relax, and Schematron are definitely worthy of your attention as well. In particular, if you find W3C schemas to be excessively complex (and many people do so find them) and if you want a simpler schema language that still offers a complete set of extensible data types, you should consider Relax. Relax adopts the less controversial data types half of the W3C XML Schema recommendation, but replaces the much more complex and much less popular structures half with a much simpler language. Relax also has the advantage of being an official JIS and ISO standard.

Most schema languages, including W3C schemas, Relax, TREX, DDML, and DTDs, take the approach that you must carefully specify what is allowed in the document. They are conservative: Everything not permitted is forbidden. If, on the other hand, you're looking for a less-restrictive schema language in which everything not forbidden is permitted, you should consider Schematron. Schematron is based on XPath, which allows it to make statements none of the other major schema languages can, such as "An a element cannot have another a element as a descendant, even though an a element can contain a strong element which can contain an a element if it itself is not a descendant of an a element." This isn't a theoretical example. This is a real restriction in XHTML that has to be made in the prose of the specification because neither DTDs nor schemas are powerful enough to say it. What it means is that links can't nest; that is, a link cannot contain another link.

From this point forward, I will use the unqualified word *schema* to refer to the W3C's XML schema language; but please keep in mind that alternatives that are equally deserving of the appellation do exist.

The W3C XML Schema Language

The W3C XML Schema language was created by the W3C XML Schema Working Group based on many different submissions from a variety of companies and individuals. It is a very large specification designed to handle a broad range of use cases. In fact, the schema specification is considerably larger and more complex than the XML 1.0 specification. It is an open standard, free to be implemented by any interested party. There are no known patent, trademark, or other intellectual property restrictions that would prevent you from doing anything you might reasonably want to do with schemas. (which unfortunately is not quite the same thing as saying that there are no known patent, trademark, or other intellectual property restrictions that would prevent you from doing anything you might reasonably want to do. The U.S. Patent Office has been a little out of control lately, granting patents left and right for inventions that really don't deserve it, including a lot of software and business processes. I would not be surprised to learn of an as yet unnoticed patent that at least claims to cover some or all of the W3C XML Schema language).

Caution This chapter is based on the May 2, 2001 Recommendation of XML Schemas. At the time of this writing (July 2001) no software yet implements all of the final Recommendation. In fact, only one parser, Xerces-J, currently supports most of the W3C XML Schema language. Eventually, of course, this should be less of an issue as the standard evolves toward its final incarnation and more vendors implement the full schema language described here. In the meantime, if you do encounter something that doesn't seem to work quite right, please report the problem to your parser vendor, not to me.

Hello Schemas

Let's begin our exploration of schemas with the ubiquitous Hello World example. Recall, once again, Listing 3-2 (greeting.xml) from Chapter 3. It is shown below:

Listing 3-2: **greeting.xml**

```
<?xml version="1.0"?>
<GREETING>
Hello XML!
</GREETING>
```

This XML document contains a single element, GREETING. (Remember that <?xml version="1.0"?> is the XML declaration, not an element.) This element contains parsed character data. A schema for this document has to declare the GREETING element. It may declare other elements too, including ones that aren't present in this particular document, but it must at least declare the GREETING element.

The greeting schema

Listing 23-1 is a very simple schema for GREETING elements. By convention it would be stored in a file with the three-letter extension .xsd, greeting.xsd for example, but that's not required. It is an XML document so it has an XML declaration. It can be written and saved in any text editor that knows how to save Unicode files. As always, you can use a different character set if you declare it in an encoding declaration. Schema documents are XML documents and have all the privileges and responsibilities of other XML documents. They can even have DTDs, DOCTYPE declarations, and style sheets if that seems useful to you, although in practice most do not.

Listing 23-1: **greeting.xsd**

```
<?xml version="1.0"?>
<xsd:schema xmlns:xsd="http://www.w3.org/2001/XMLSchema">

  <xsd:element name="GREETING" type="xsd:string"/>

</xsd:schema>
```

The root element of this and all other schemas is schema. This must be in the http://www.w3.org/2001/XMLSchema namespace. Normally, this namespace is bound to the prefix xsd or xs, although this can change as long as the URI stays the same. The other common approach is to make this URI the default namespace, although that generally requires a few extra attributes to help separate out the names from the XML application the schema describes from the names of the schema elements themselves. You'll see this when namespaces are discussed at the end of this chapter.

Elements are declared using xsd:element elements. Listing 23-1 includes a single such element declaring the GREETING element. The name attribute specifies which element is being declared, GREETING in this example. This xsd:element element also has a type attribute whose value is the data type of the element. In this case the type is xsd:string, a standard type for elements that can contain any amount of text in any form but not child elements. It's equivalent to a DTD content model of #PCDATA. That is, this xsd:element says that a valid GREETING element must look like this:

```
<GREETING>
  various random text but no markup
</GREETING>
```

There's no restriction on what text the element can contain. It can be zero or more Unicode characters with any meaning. Thus a GREETING element can also look like this:

```
<GREETING>Hello!</GREETING>
```

Or even this:

```
<GREETING></GREETING>
```

However, a valid GREETING element may not look like this:

```
<GREETING>
  <SOME_TAG>various random text</SOME_TAG>
  <SOME_EMPTY_TAG/>
</GREETING>
```

Nor may it look like this:

```
<GREETING>
  <GREETING>various random text</GREETING>
</GREETING>
```

Each GREETING element must consist of nothing more and nothing less than parsed character data between an opening <GREETING> tag and a closing </GREETING> tag.

Validating the document against the schema

Before a document can be validated against a DTD, the document itself must contain a document type declaration pointing to the DTD it should be validated against. You cannot easily receive a document from a third party and validate it against your own DTD. You have to validate it against the DTD that the document's author specified. This is excessively limiting.

For example, imagine you're running an e-commerce business that accepts orders for products using SOAP or XML-RPC. Each order comes to you over the Internet as an XML document. Before accepting that order the first thing you want to do is check that it's valid against a DTD you've defined to make sure that it contains all the necessary information. However, if DTDs are all you have to validate with, then there's nothing to prevent a hacker sending you a document whose DOCTYPE declaration points to a different DTD. Then your system may report that the document is valid according to the hacked DTD, even though it would be invalid when compared to the correct DTD. If your system accepts the invalid document, it could introduce corrupt data that crashes the system or lets the hacker order goods they haven't paid for, all because the person authoring the document got to choose which DTD to validate against rather than the person validating the document.

Schemas are more flexible. The schema specification specifically allows for a variety of different means for associating documents with schemas. For instance, one possibility is that both the name of the document to validate and the name of the schema to validate it against could be passed to the validator program on the command line like this:

```
C:\>validator greeting.xml greeting.xsd
```

Parsers could also let you choose the schema by setting a SAX property or an environment variable. Many other schemes are possible. The schema specification does not mandate any one way of doing this. However, it does define one particular way to associate a document with a schema. As with DOCTYPE declarations and DTDs, this requires modifying the instance document to point to the schema. The difference is that with schemas, unlike with DTDs, this is not the only way to do it. Parser vendors are free to develop other mechanisms if they want to.

To attach a schema to a document, add an xsi:noNamespaceSchemaLocation attribute to the document's root element. (You can also add it to the first element in the document that the schema applies to, but most of the time adding it to the root element is simplest.) The xsi prefix is mapped to the http://www.w3.org/2001/XMLSchema-instance URI. As always, the prefix can change as long as the URI stays the same. Listing 23-2 demonstrates.

Listing 23-2: **valid_greeting.xml**

```
<?xml version="1.0"?>
<GREETING xsi:noNamespaceSchemaLocation="greeting.xsd"
  xmlns:xsi="http://www.w3.org/2001/XMLSchema-instance">
Hello XML!
</GREETING>
```

You can now run the document through any parser that supports schema validation. One such parser is Xerces Java 1.4.1 from the XML Apache Project. In fact, you can use the same SAXCount program you learned about in Chapter 8 to validate against schemas as well as DTDs. When you set the -v flag, SAXCount validates the documents it parses against a DTD if it sees a DOCTYPE declaration and against a schema if it finds an xsi:noNamespaceSchemaLocation attribute. Assuming SAXCount finds no errors, it simply returns the amount of time that was required to parse the document:

```
C:\XML>java sax.SAXCount -v valid_greeting.xml
valid_greeting.xml: 701 ms (1 elems, 1 attrs, 0 spaces, 12
chars)
```

Note   This chapter uses Xerces Java 1.4.1, which provides partial support for the May 2, 2001 Recommendation of XML Schema. Furthermore, earlier versions of Xerces Java support earlier drafts of the W3C XML Schema language that use different namespace URIs. In particular, they support the http://www.w3.org/2000/10/XMLSchema- and http://www.w3.org/1999/XMLSchema namespaces. You can download the latest version of Xerces from http://xml.apache.org/xerces-j/.

Now let's suppose you have a document that's not valid, such as Listing 23-3. This document uses a P element that hasn't been declared in the schema.

Listing 23-3: **invalid_greeting.xml**

```
<?xml version="1.0"?>
<GREETING
  xmlns:xsi="http://www.w3.org/2001/XMLSchema-instance"
  xsi:noNamespaceSchemaLocation="greeting.xsd">
  <P>Hello XML!</P>
</GREETING>
```

Running it through sax.SAXCount, you now get this output showing you what the problems are:

```
C:\XML>java sax.SAXCount -v invalid_greeting.xml
[Error] invalid_greeting.xml:5:6: Element type "P" must be
declared.
[Error] invalid_greeting.xml:6:13: Datatype error: In element
'GREETING' : Can not have element children within a simple type
content.
invalid_greeting.xml: 1292 ms (2 elems, 2 attrs, 0 spaces, 14
chars)
```

The validator found two problems. The first is that the P element is used but is not, itself, declared. The second is that the GREETING element is declared to have type xsd:string, one of several "simple" types that cannot have any child elements. However, in this case, the GREETING element does contain a child element: the P element.

Complex Types

The W3C XML Schema language divides elements into complex and simple types. A simple type element is one like GREETING that can only contain text and does not have any attributes. It cannot contain any child elements. It may, however, be more limited in the kind of text it can contain. For instance, a schema can say that a simple element contains an integer, a date, or a decimal value between 3.76 and 98.24. Complex elements can have attributes and can have child elements.

Most documents need a mix of both complex and simple elements. For example, consider Listing 23-4. This document describes the song *Yes I Am* by Melissa Etheridge. The root element is SONG. This element has a number of child elements giving the title of the song, the composer, the producer, the publisher, the duration of the song, the year it was released, the price, and the artist who sang it. Except for SONG itself, these are all simple elements that can have type xsd:string. You might see documents like this used in CD databases, MP3 players, Gnutella clients, or anything else that needs to store information about songs.

Listing 23-4: **yesiam.xml**

```
<?xml version="1.0"?>
<SONG xmlns:xsi="http://www.w3.org/2001/XMLSchema-instance"
      xsi:noNamespaceSchemaLocation="song.xsd">
  <TITLE>Yes I Am</TITLE>
  <COMPOSER>Melissa Etheridge</COMPOSER>
  <PRODUCER>Hugh Padgham</PRODUCER>
  <PUBLISHER>Island Records</PUBLISHER>
```

```
  <LENGTH>4:24</LENGTH>
  <YEAR>1993</YEAR>
  <ARTIST>Melissa Etheridge</ARTIST>
  <PRICE>$1.25</PRICE>
</SONG>
```

Now you need a schema that describes this and all other reasonable song documents. Listing 23-5 is the first attempt at such a schema.

Listing 23-5: **song.xsd**

```
<?xml version="1.0"?>
<xsd:schema xmlns:xsd="http://www.w3.org/2001/XMLSchema">

  <xsd:element name="SONG" type="SongType"/>

  <xsd:complexType name="SongType">
    <xsd:sequence>
      <xsd:element name="TITLE"     type="xsd:string"/>
      <xsd:element name="COMPOSER"  type="xsd:string"/>
      <xsd:element name="PRODUCER"  type="xsd:string"/>
      <xsd:element name="PUBLISHER" type="xsd:string"/>
      <xsd:element name="LENGTH"    type="xsd:string"/>
      <xsd:element name="YEAR"      type="xsd:string"/>
      <xsd:element name="ARTIST"    type="xsd:string"/>
      <xsd:element name="PRICE"     type="xsd:string"/>
    </xsd:sequence>
  </xsd:complexType>

</xsd:schema>
```

The root element of this schema is once again xsd:schema, and once again the prefix xsd is mapped to the namespace URI http://www.w3.org/2001/XMLSchema. This will be the case for all schemas in this chapter, and indeed all schemas that you write. I won't note it again.

This schema declares a single *top-level element*. That is, there is exactly one element declared in an xsd:element declaration that is an immediate child of the root xsd:schema element. This is the SONG element. Only top-level elements can be the root elements of documents described by this schema, though in general they do not have to be the root element.

The SONG element is declared to have type SongType. The W3C Schema Working Group wasn't prescient. They built a lot of common types into the language, but they didn't know that I was going to need a song type, and they didn't provide one.

Indeed, they could not reasonably have been expected to predict and provide for the numerous types that schema designers around the world were ever going to need. Instead, they provided facilities to allow users to define their own types. `SongType` is one such user-defined type. In fact, you can tell it's not a built-in type because it doesn't begin with the prefix `xsd`. All built-in types are in the `http://www.w3.org/2001/XMLSchema` namespace.

The `xsd:complexType` element defines a new type. The `name` attribute of this element names the type being defined. Here that name is `SongType`, which matches the type previously assigned to the `SONG` element. Forward references (for example, `xsd:element` using the `SongType` type before it's been defined) are perfectly acceptable in schemas. Circular references are okay, too. Type A can depend on type B which depends on type A. Schema processors sort all this out without any difficulty.

The contents of the `xsd:complexType` element specify what content a `SongType` element must contain. In this example, the schema says that every `SongType` element contains a sequence of eight child elements: TITLE, COMPOSER, PRODUCER, PUBLISHER, LENGTH, YEAR, PRICE, and ARTIST. Each of these is declared to have the built-in type `xsd:string`. Each `SongType` element must contain exactly one of each of these in exactly that order. The only other content it may contain is insignificant white space between the tags.

minOccurs and maxOccurs

You can validate Listing 23-4, yesiam.xml, against the song schema, and it does, indeed, prove valid. Are you done? Is song.xsd now an adequate description of legal song documents? Suppose you instead wanted to validate Listing 23-6, a song document that describes *Hot Cop* by the Village People. Is it valid according to the schema in Listing 23-5?

Listing 23-6: **hotcop.xml**

```
<?xml version="1.0"?>
<SONG xmlns:xsi="http://www.w3.org/2001/XMLSchema-instance"
      xsi:noNamespaceSchemaLocation="song.xsd">
  <TITLE>Hot Cop</TITLE>
  <COMPOSER>Jacques Morali</COMPOSER>
  <COMPOSER>Henri Belolo</COMPOSER>
  <COMPOSER>Victor Willis</COMPOSER>
  <PRODUCER>Jacques Morali</PRODUCER>
  <PUBLISHER>PolyGram Records</PUBLISHER>
  <LENGTH>6:20</LENGTH>
  <YEAR>1978</YEAR>
  <ARTIST>Village People</ARTIST>
</SONG>
```

The answer is no, it is not. The reason is that this song was a collaboration between three different composers and the existing schema only allows a single composer. Furthermore, the price is missing. If you looked at other songs, you'd find similar problems with the other child elements. *Under Pressure* has two artists, David Bowie and Queen. *We Are the World* has dozens of artists. Many songs have multiple producers. A garage band without a publisher might record a song and post it on Napster in the hope of finding one.

The song schema needs to be adjusted to allow for varying numbers of particular elements. This is done by attaching minOccurs and maxOccurs attributes to each xsd:element element. These attributes specify the minimum and maximum number of instances of the element that may appear at that point in the document. The value of each attribute is an integer greater than or equal to zero. The maxOccurs attribute may also have the value unbounded to indicate that an unlimited number of the particular element may appear. Listing 23-7 demonstrates.

Listing 23-7: **minOccurs and maxOccurs**

```xml
<?xml version="1.0"?>
<xsd:schema xmlns:xsd="http://www.w3.org/2001/XMLSchema">

  <xsd:element name="SONG" type="SongType"/>

  <xsd:complexType name="SongType">
    <xsd:sequence>
      <xsd:element name="TITLE"     type="xsd:string"
                   minOccurs="1"    maxOccurs="1"/>
      <xsd:element name="COMPOSER"  type="xsd:string"
                   minOccurs="1"    maxOccurs="unbounded"/>
      <xsd:element name="PRODUCER"  type="xsd:string"
                   minOccurs="0"    maxOccurs="unbounded"/>
      <xsd:element name="PUBLISHER" type="xsd:string"
                   minOccurs="0"    maxOccurs="1"/>
      <xsd:element name="LENGTH"    type="xsd:string"
                   minOccurs="1"    maxOccurs="1"/>
      <xsd:element name="YEAR"      type="xsd:string"
                   minOccurs="1"    maxOccurs="1"/>
      <xsd:element name="ARTIST"    type="xsd:string"
                   minOccurs="1"    maxOccurs="unbounded"/>
      <xsd:element name="PRICE"     type="xsd:string"
                   minOccurs="0"    maxOccurs="1"/>
    </xsd:sequence>
  </xsd:complexType>

</xsd:schema>
```

This schema says that every SongType element must have, in order,

- ✦ Exactly one TITLE (minOccurs="1" maxOccurs="1")

- ✦ At least one, and possibly a great many, COMPOSERs (minOccurs="1" maxOccurs="unbounded")

- ✦ Any number of PRODUCERs, although possibly no producer at all (minOccurs="0" maxOccurs="unbounded")

- ✦ Either one PUBLISHER or no PUBLISHER at all (minOccurs="0" maxOccurs="1")

- ✦ Exactly one LENGTH (minOccurs="1" maxOccurs="1")

- ✦ Exactly one YEAR (minOccurs="1" maxOccurs="1")

- ✦ At least one ARTIST, possibly more (minOccurs="1" maxOccurs="unbounded")

- ✦ An optional PRICE, (minOccurs="0" maxOccurs="1")

This is much more flexible and easier to use than the limited ?, *, and + that are available in DTDs. It is very straightforward to say, for example, that you want between 4 and 7 of a given element. Just set minOccurs to 4 and maxOccurs to 7.

If minOccurs and maxOccurs are not present, then the default value of each is 1. Taking advantage of this, the song schema can be written a little more compactly as shown in Listing 23-8.

Listing 23-8: **Taking advantage of the default values of minOccurs and maxOccurs**

```
<?xml version="1.0"?>
<xsd:schema xmlns:xsd="http://www.w3.org/2001/XMLSchema">

  <xsd:element name="SONG" type="SongType"/>

  <xsd:complexType name="SongType">
    <xsd:sequence>
      <xsd:element name="TITLE"     type="xsd:string"/>
      <xsd:element name="COMPOSER"  type="xsd:string"
                   maxOccurs="unbounded"/>
      <xsd:element name="PRODUCER"  type="xsd:string"
                   minOccurs="0"    maxOccurs="unbounded"/>
      <xsd:element name="PUBLISHER" type="xsd:string"
                   minOccurs="0"/>
      <xsd:element name="LENGTH"    type="xsd:string"/>
```

```
        <xsd:element name="YEAR"      type="xsd:string"/>
        <xsd:element name="ARTIST"    type="xsd:string"
                     maxOccurs="unbounded"/>
        <xsd:element name="PRICE"     type="xsd:string"
                     minOccurs="0"/>
      </xsd:sequence>
    </xsd:complexType>

  </xsd:schema>
```

Element content

The examples so far have all been relatively flat. That is, a SONG element contained other elements; but those elements only contained parsed character data, not child elements of their own. Suppose, however, that some child elements do contain other elements, as in Listing 23-9. Here the COMPOSER and PRODUCER elements each contain NAME elements.

Listing 23-9: **A deeper hierarchy**

```
<?xml version="1.0"?>
<SONG xmlns:xsi="http://www.w3.org/2001/XMLSchema-instance"
      xsi:noNamespaceSchemaLocation="23-10.xsd">
  <TITLE>Hot Cop</TITLE>
  <COMPOSER>
    <NAME>Jacques Morali</NAME>
  </COMPOSER>
  <COMPOSER>
    <NAME>Henri Belolo</NAME>
  </COMPOSER>
  <COMPOSER>
    <NAME>Victor Willis</NAME>
  </COMPOSER>
  <PRODUCER>
    <NAME>Jacques Morali</NAME>
  </PRODUCER>
  <PUBLISHER>PolyGram Records</PUBLISHER>
  <LENGTH>6:20</LENGTH>
  <YEAR>1978</YEAR>
  <ARTIST>Village People</ARTIST>
</SONG>
```

Because the COMPOSER and PRODUCER elements now have complex content, you can no longer use one of the built-in types such as xsd:string to declare them. Instead you have to define a new ComposerType and ProducerType using top-level xsd:complexType elements. Listing 23-10 demonstrates.

Listing 23-10: Defining separate ComposerType and ProducerType types

```
<?xml version="1.0"?>
<xsd:schema xmlns:xsd="http://www.w3.org/2001/XMLSchema">

  <xsd:element name="SONG" type="SongType"/>

  <xsd:complexType name="ComposerType">
    <xsd:sequence>
      <xsd:element name="NAME" type="xsd:string"/>
    </xsd:sequence>
  </xsd:complexType>

  <xsd:complexType name="ProducerType">
    <xsd:sequence>
      <xsd:element name="NAME" type="xsd:string"/>
    </xsd:sequence>
  </xsd:complexType>

  <xsd:complexType name="SongType">
    <xsd:sequence>
      <xsd:element name="TITLE"     type="xsd:string"/>
      <xsd:element name="COMPOSER"  type="ComposerType"
                   maxOccurs="unbounded"/>
      <xsd:element name="PRODUCER"  type="ProducerType"
                   minOccurs="0" maxOccurs="unbounded"/>
      <xsd:element name="PUBLISHER" type="xsd:string"
                   minOccurs="0"/>
      <xsd:element name="LENGTH" type="xsd:string"/>
      <xsd:element name="YEAR"     type="xsd:string"/>
      <xsd:element name="ARTIST" type="xsd:string"
                   maxOccurs="unbounded"/>
      <xsd:element name="PRICE" type="xsd:string"
                   minOccurs="0"/>
    </xsd:sequence>
  </xsd:complexType>

</xsd:schema>
```

Sharing content models

You may have noticed that PRODUCER and COMPOSER are very similar. Each contains a single NAME child element and nothing else. In a DTD you'd take advantage of this shared content model via a parameter entity reference. In a schema, it's much easier. Simply given them the same type. While you could declare that the PRODUCER has ComposerType or vice versa, it's better to declare that both have a more generic PersonType. Listing 23-11 demonstrates.

Listing 23-11: Using a single PersonType for both COMPOSER and PRODUCER

```
<?xml version="1.0"?>
<xsd:schema xmlns:xsd="http://www.w3.org/2001/XMLSchema">

  <xsd:element name="SONG" type="SongType"/>

  <xsd:complexType name="PersonType">
    <xsd:sequence>
      <xsd:element name="NAME" type="xsd:string"/>
    </xsd:sequence>
  </xsd:complexType>

  <xsd:complexType name="SongType">
    <xsd:sequence>
      <xsd:element name="TITLE"    type="xsd:string"/>
      <xsd:element name="COMPOSER" type="PersonType"
                   maxOccurs="unbounded"/>
      <xsd:element name="PRODUCER" type="PersonType"
                   minOccurs="0" maxOccurs="unbounded"/>
      <xsd:element name="PUBLISHER" type="xsd:string"
                   minOccurs="0"/>
      <xsd:element name="LENGTH" type="xsd:string"/>
      <xsd:element name="YEAR"   type="xsd:string"/>
      <xsd:element name="ARTIST" type="xsd:string"
                   maxOccurs="unbounded"/>
      <xsd:element name="PRICE" type="xsd:string"
                   minOccurs="0"/>
    </xsd:sequence>
  </xsd:complexType>

</xsd:schema>
```

Anonymous types

Suppose you wanted to divide the NAME elements into separate GIVEN and FAMILY elements like this:

```
<NAME>
  <GIVEN>Victor</GIVEN>
  <FAMILY>Willis</FAMILY>
</NAME>
<NAME>
  <GIVEN>Jacques</GIVEN>
  <FAMILY>Morali</FAMILY>
</NAME>
```

To declare this, you could use an xsd:complexType element to define a new NameType element like this:

```
<xsd:complexType name="NameType">
  <xsd:sequence>
    <xsd:element name="GIVEN"  type="xsd:string"/>
    <xsd:element name="FAMILY" type="xsd:string"/>
  </xsd:sequence>
</xsd:complexType>
```

Then the PersonType would be defined like this:

```
<xsd:complexType name="PersonType">
  <xsd:sequence>
    <xsd:element name="NAME" type="NameType"/>
  </xsd:sequence>
</xsd:complexType>
```

However, the NAME element is only used inside PersonType elements. Perhaps it shouldn't be a top-level definition. For instance, you may not want to allow NAME elements to be used as root elements, or to be children of things that aren't PersonType elements. You can prevent this by defining a name with an *anonymous type*. To do this, instead of assigning the NAME element a type with a type attribute on the corresponding xsd:element element, you give it an xsd:complexType child element to define its type. Listing 23-12 demonstrates.

Listing 23-12: **Anonymous types**

```
<?xml version="1.0"?>
<xsd:schema xmlns:xsd="http://www.w3.org/2001/XMLSchema">

  <xsd:element name="SONG" type="SongType"/>

  <xsd:complexType name="PersonType">
```

```
    <xsd:sequence>
      <xsd:element name="NAME">
        <xsd:complexType>
          <xsd:sequence>
            <xsd:element name="GIVEN"  type="xsd:string"/>
            <xsd:element name="FAMILY" type="xsd:string"/>
          </xsd:sequence>
        </xsd:complexType>
      </xsd:element>
    </xsd:sequence>
  </xsd:complexType>

  <xsd:complexType name="SongType">
    <xsd:sequence>
      <xsd:element name="TITLE"     type="xsd:string"/>
      <xsd:element name="COMPOSER"  type="PersonType"
                   maxOccurs="unbounded"/>
      <xsd:element name="PRODUCER"  type="PersonType"
                   minOccurs="0" maxOccurs="unbounded"/>
      <xsd:element name="PUBLISHER" type="xsd:string"
                   minOccurs="0"/>
      <xsd:element name="LENGTH" type="xsd:string"/>
      <xsd:element name="YEAR"   type="xsd:string"/>
      <xsd:element name="ARTIST" type="xsd:string"
                   maxOccurs="unbounded"/>
      <xsd:element name="PRICE" type="xsd:string"
                   minOccurs="0"/>
    </xsd:sequence>
  </xsd:complexType>

</xsd:schema>
```

Defining the element types inside the xsd:element elements that are themselves children of xsd:complexType elements is a very powerful technique. Among other things, it enables you to give elements with the same name different types when used in different elements. For example, you can say that the NAME of a PERSON contains GIVEN and FAMILY child elements while the NAME of a MOVIE contains an xsd:string and the NAME of a VARIABLE contains a string containing only alphanumeric characters from the ASCII character set.

Mixed content

Schemas offer much greater control over mixed content than DTDs do. In particular, schemas let you enforce the order and number of elements appearing in mixed content. For example, suppose you wanted to allow extra text to be mixed in with the names to provide middle initials, titles, and the like as shown in Listing 23-13.

Caution   The format used here is purely for illustrative purposes. In practice, I'd recommend that you make the middle initials and titles separate elements as well.

Listing 23-13: **Mixed content**

```
<?xml version="1.0"?>
<SONG xmlns:xsi="http://www.w3.org/2001/XMLSchema-instance"
      xsi:noNamespaceSchemaLocation="23-14.xsd">
  <TITLE>Hot Cop</TITLE>
  <COMPOSER>
<NAME>
      Mr. <GIVEN>Jacques</GIVEN> <FAMILY>Morali</FAMILY> Esq.
    </NAME>
  </COMPOSER>
  <COMPOSER>
    <NAME>
      Mr. <GIVEN>Henri</GIVEN> L. <FAMILY>Belolo</FAMILY>, M.D.
    </NAME>
  </COMPOSER>
  <COMPOSER>
    <NAME>
      Mr. <GIVEN>Victor</GIVEN> C. <FAMILY>Willis</FAMILY>
    </NAME>
  </COMPOSER>
  <PRODUCER>
    <NAME>
      Mr. <GIVEN>Jacques</GIVEN> S. <FAMILY>Morali</FAMILY>
    </NAME>
  </PRODUCER>
  <PUBLISHER>PolyGram Records</PUBLISHER>
  <LENGTH>6:20</LENGTH>
  <YEAR>1978</YEAR>
  <ARTIST>Village People</ARTIST>
</SONG>
```

It's very easy to declare that an element has mixed content in schemas. First, set up the `xsd:complexType` exactly as you would if the element only contained child elements. Then add a `mixed` attribute to it with the value `true`. Listing 23-14 demonstrates. It is almost identical to Listing 23-12 except for the addition of the `mixed="true"` attribute.

Listing 23-14: Declaring mixed content in a schema

```
<?xml version="1.0"?>
<xsd:schema xmlns:xsd="http://www.w3.org/2001/XMLSchema">

  <xsd:element name="SONG" type="SongType"/>

  <xsd:complexType name="PersonType">
    <xsd:sequence>
      <xsd:element name="NAME">
        <xsd:complexType mixed="true">
          <xsd:sequence>
            <xsd:element name="GIVEN"  type="xsd:string"/>
            <xsd:element name="FAMILY" type="xsd:string"/>
          </xsd:sequence>
        </xsd:complexType>
      </xsd:element>
    </xsd:sequence>
  </xsd:complexType>

  <xsd:complexType name="SongType">
    <xsd:sequence>
    <xsd:element name="TITLE"    type="xsd:string"/>
      <xsd:element name="COMPOSER"  type="PersonType"
                   maxOccurs="unbounded"/>
      <xsd:element name="PRODUCER"  type="PersonType"
                   minOccurs="0" maxOccurs="unbounded"/>
      <xsd:element name="PUBLISHER" type="xsd:string"
                   minOccurs="0"/>
      <xsd:element name="LENGTH" type="xsd:string"/>
      <xsd:element name="YEAR"   type="xsd:string"/>
      <xsd:element name="ARTIST" type="xsd:string"/>
                   maxOccurs="unbounded"/>
      <xsd:element name="PRICE" type="xsd:string"
                   minOccurs="0"/>
    </xsd:sequence>
  </xsd:complexType>

</xsd:schema>
```

Grouping

So far, all the schemas you've seen have held that order mattered; for example, that it would be wrong to put the COMPOSER before the TITLE or the PRODUCER after the ARTIST. Given these schemas, the document shown below in Listing 23-15 is clearly invalid. But should it be? Element order often does matter in narrative documents such as books and Web pages. However, it's not nearly as important in data-centric documents like the examples in this chapter. Do you really care whether the TITLE comes first or not, as long as there is a TITLE? After all, if the document's going to be shown to a human being, it will probably first be transformed with an XSLT style sheet that can easily place the contents in any order it likes.

Listing 23-15: A song document that places the elements in a different order

```
<?xml version="1.0"?>
<SONG xmlns:xsi="http://www.w3.org/2001/XMLSchema-instance"
      xsi:noNamespaceSchemaLocation="song.xsd">
  <ARTIST>Village People</ARTIST>
  <TITLE>Hot Cop</TITLE>
  <COMPOSER>
    <NAME><GIVEN>Jacques</GIVEN> <FAMILY>Morali</FAMILY></NAME>
  </COMPOSER>
  <PUBLISHER>PolyGram Records</PUBLISHER>
  <COMPOSER>
    <NAME><FAMILY>Belolo</FAMILY> <GIVEN>Henri</GIVEN></NAME>
  </COMPOSER>
  <YEAR>1978</YEAR>
  <COMPOSER>
    <NAME><FAMILY>Willis</FAMILY> <GIVEN>Victor</GIVEN></NAME>
  </COMPOSER>
  <PRODUCER>
    <NAME><GIVEN>Jacques</GIVEN> <FAMILY>Morali</FAMILY></NAME>
  </PRODUCER>
  <PRICE>$1.25</PRICE>
</SONG>
```

The W3C XML Schema language provides three grouping constructs that specify whether and how ordering of individual elements is important. These are:

✦ The xsd:all group requires that each element in the group must occur at most once, but that order is not important.

✦ The xsd:choice group specifies that any one element from the group should appear. It can also be used to say that between N and M elements from the group should appear in any order.

✦ The xsd:sequence group requires that each element in the group appear exactly once, in the specified order.

Unfortunately, these constructs are not everything you might desire. In particular, you can't specify constraints such as those that would be required to really handle Listing 23-14. In particular, you can't specify that you want a SONG to have exactly one TITLE, one or more COMPOSERs, zero or more PRODUCERs, one or more ARTISTs, but that you don't care in what order the individual elements occur.

The xsd:all group

You can specify that you want each NAME element to have exactly one GIVEN child and one FAMILY child, but that you don't care what order they appear in. The xsd:all group accomplishes this. For example,

```
<xsd:complexType name="PersonType">
  <xsd:sequence>
    <xsd:element name="NAME">
      <xsd:complexType>
        <xsd:all>
          <xsd:element name="GIVEN" type="xsd:string"
                       minOccurs="1" maxOccurs="1"/>
          <xsd:element name="FAMILY" type="xsd:string"
                       minOccurs="1" maxOccurs="1"/>
        </xsd:all>
      </xsd:complexType>
    </xsd:element>
  </xsd:sequence>
</xsd:complexType>
```

The extension to handle what you want for Listing 23-15 seems obvious. It would look like this:

```
<xsd:complexType name="SongType">
  <xsd:all>
    <xsd:element name="TITLE" type="xsd:string"
                 minOccurs="1" maxOccurs="1"/>
    <xsd:element name="COMPOSER" type="PersonType"
                 minOccurs="1" maxOccurs="unbounded"/>
    <xsd:element name="PRODUCER" type="PersonType"
                 minOccurs="0" maxOccurs="unbounded"/>
    <xsd:element name="PUBLISHER" type="xsd:string"
                 minOccurs="0" maxOccurs="1"/>
    <xsd:element name="LENGTH" type="xsd:string"
                 minOccurs="1" maxOccurs="1"/>
    <xsd:element name="YEAR" type="xsd:string"
                 minOccurs="1" maxOccurs="1"/>
    <xsd:element name="ARTIST" type="xsd:string"
                 minOccurs="1" maxOccurs="unbounded"/>
    <xsd:element name="PRICE" type="xsd:string" minOccurs="0"/>
  </xsd:all>
</xsd:complexType>
```

Unfortunately, the W3C XML Schema language restricts the use of minOccurs and maxOccurs inside xsd:all elements. In particular, each one's value must be 0 or 1. You cannot set it to 4 or 7 or unbounded. Therefore the above type definition is invalid. Furthermore, xsd:all can only contain individual element declarations. It cannot contain xsd:choice or xsd:sequence elements. xsd:all offers somewhat more expressivity than DTDs do, but probably not as much as you want.

Choices

The xsd:choice element is the schema equivalent of the | in DTDs. When xsd:element elements are combined inside an xsd:choice, then exactly one of those elements must appear in instance documents. For example, the choice in this xsd:complexType requires either a PRODUCER or a COMPOSER, but not both.

```
<xsd:complexType name="SongType">
  <xsd:sequence>
    <xsd:element name="TITLE" type="xsd:string"/>
    <xsd:choice>
      <xsd:element name="COMPOSER" type="PersonType"/>
      <xsd:element name="PRODUCER" type="PersonType"/>
    </xsd:choice>
    <xsd:element name="PUBLISHER" type="xsd:string"
              minOccurs="0"/>
    <xsd:element name="LENGTH" type="xsd:string"/>
    <xsd:element name="YEAR"   type="xsd:string"/>
    <xsd:element name="ARTIST" type="xsd:string"
              maxOccurs="unbounded"/>
    <xsd:element name="PRICE" type="xsd:string" minOccurs="0"/>
  </xsd:sequence>
</xsd:complexType>
```

The xsd:choice element itself can have minOccurs and maxOccurs attributes that establish exactly how many selections may be made from the choice. For example, setting minOccurs to 1 and maxOccurs to 6 would indicate that between one and six elements listed in the xsd:choice should appear. Each of these can be any of the elements in the xsd:choice. For example, you could have six different elements, three of the same element and three of another, or up to six of the same element. This next xsd:choice allows for any number of artists, composers, and producers. However, in order to require that there be at least one ARTIST element and at least one COMPOSER element, rather than allowing all spaces to be filled by PRODUCER elements, it's necessary to place xsd:element declarations for these two outside the choice. This has the unfortunate side effect of locking in more order than is really needed.

```
<xsd:complexType name="SongType">
  <xsd:sequence>
    <xsd:element name="TITLE" type="xsd:string"/>
    <xsd:element name="COMPOSER" type="PersonType"/>
    <xsd:choice minOccurs="0" maxOccurs="unbounded">
      <xsd:element name="PRODUCER" type="PersonType"/>
      <xsd:element name="COMPOSER" type="PersonType"/>
      <xsd:element name="ARTIST"   type="xsd:string"/>
    </xsd:choice>
    <xsd:element name="ARTIST" type="xsd:string"/>
    <xsd:element name="PUBLISHER" type="xsd:string"
              minOccurs="0"/>
```

```
        <xsd:element name="LENGTH" type="xsd:string"/>
        <xsd:element name="YEAR"   type="xsd:string"/>
        <xsd:element name="PRICE" type="xsd:string" minOccurs="0"/>
      </xsd:sequence>
</xsd:complexType>
```

Sequences

An xsd:sequence element requires each member of the sequence to appear in the
same order in the instance document as in the xsd:sequence element. I've used
this frequently as the basic group for xsd:complexType elements in this chapter so
far. The number of times each element is allowed to appear can be controlled by
the xsd:element's minOccurs and maxOccurs attributes. You can add minOccurs
and maxOccurs attributes to the xsd:sequence element to specify the number of
times the sequence should repeat.

Simple Types

Until now I've focused on writing schemas that validate the element structures in
an XML document. However, there's also a lot of non-XML structure in the song documents. The YEAR element isn't just a string. It's an integer, and maybe not just any
integer either, but a positive integer with four digits. The PRICE element is some
sort of money. The LENGTH element is a duration of time. DTDs have absolutely
nothing to say about such non-XML structures that are inside the parsed character
data content of elements and attributes. Schemas, however, do let you make all
sorts of statements about what forms the text inside elements may take and what it
means. Schemas provide much more sophisticated semantics for documents than
DTDs do.

Listing 23-16 is a new schema for song documents. It's based on Listing 23-8, but
read closely and you should notice that a few things have changed.

Listing 23-16: **A schema with simple data types**

```
<?xml version="1.0"?>
<xsd:schema xmlns:xsd="http://www.w3.org/2001/XMLSchema">

  <xsd:element name="SONG" type="SongType"/>

  <xsd:complexType name="SongType">
    <xsd:sequence>
      <xsd:element name="TITLE"    type="xsd:string"/>
      <xsd:element name="COMPOSER" type="xsd:string"
                   maxOccurs="unbounded"/>
```

Continued

Listing 23-16 *(continued)*

```
        <xsd:element  name="PRODUCER"   type="xsd:string"
                      minOccurs="0"     maxOccurs="unbounded"/>
        <xsd:element  name="PUBLISHER"  type="xsd:string"
                      minOccurs="0"/>
        <xsd:element  name="LENGTH"     type="xsd:duration"/>
        <xsd:element  name="YEAR"       type="xsd:gYear"/>
        <xsd:element  name="ARTIST"     type="xsd:string"
                      maxOccurs="unbounded"/>
        <xsd:element  name="PRICE"      type="xsd:string"
                      minOccurs="0"/>
      </xsd:sequence>
    </xsd:complexType>

  </xsd:schema>
```

Did you spot the changes? The values of the `type` attributes of the LENGTH and YEAR declarations are no longer `xsd:string`. Instead, LENGTH has the type `xsd:duration` and YEAR has the type `xsd:gYear`. These declarations say that it's no longer okay for the YEAR and LENGTH elements to contain just any old string of text. Instead they must contain strings in particular formats. In particular, the YEAR element must contain a year; and the LENGTH element must contain a recognizable length of time. When you check a document against this schema, the validator will check that these elements contain the proper data. It's not just looking at the elements. It's looking at the content inside the elements!

Let's actually validate hotcop.xml against this schema and see what we get:

```
C:\XML>java sax.SAXCount -v hotcop.xml
[Error] hotcop.xml:10:25: Datatype error: In element 'LENGTH' :
Value '6:20' is not legal value for current datatype.
hotcop.xml: 1783 ms (10 elems, 2 attrs, 28 spaces, 98 chars)
```

That's unexpected! The problem is that 6:20 is not in the proper format for time durations, at least not the format that the W3C XML Schema language uses and that schema validators know how to check. Schema validators expect that time types are expressed in the format defined in ISO standard 8601, *Representations of dates and times* (http://www.iso.ch/markete/8601.pdf). This standard says that time durations should have the form PnYnMnDTnHnMdS, where *n* is an integer and *d* is a decimal number. *P* stands for "Period". *nY* gives the number of years; the first *nM* gives the number of months; and *nD* gives the number of days. *T* separates the date from the time. Following the T, *nH* gives the number of hours; the second *nM* gives the number of minutes; and *dS* gives the number of seconds. If *d* has a fraction part, then the duration can be specified to an arbitrary level of precision.

In this format, a duration of 6 minutes and 20 seconds should be written as P0Y0M0DT0H6M20S. If you prefer, the zero pieces can be left out, so you can write this more compactly as PT6M20S. Listing 23-17 shows the fixed version of hotcop.xml with the LENGTH in the right format.

Listing 23-17: **Fixed hotcop.xml**

```
<?xml version="1.0"?>
<SONG xmlns:xsi="http://www.w3.org/2001/XMLSchema-instance"
      xsi:noNamespaceSchemaLocation="23-16.xsd">
  <TITLE>Hot Cop</TITLE>
  <COMPOSER>Jacques Morali</COMPOSER>
  <COMPOSER>Henri Belolo</COMPOSER>
  <COMPOSER>Victor Willis</COMPOSER>
  <PRODUCER>Jacques Morali</PRODUCER>
  <PUBLISHER>PolyGram Records</PUBLISHER>
  <LENGTH>P0YT6M20S</LENGTH>
  <YEAR>1978</YEAR>
  <ARTIST>Village People</ARTIST>
</SONG>
```

Admittedly the ISO 8601 format for time durations is a little obtuse, if precise. You may well be asking whether there's a type that you can specify for the LENGTH that would make lengths such as 6:20 and 4:24 legal. In fact, there's no such type built-in to the W3C XML Schema language; but you can define one yourself. You'll learn how to do that soon, but first let's explore some of the other data types that are built-in to the W3C XML Schema language.

There are 44 built-in simple types in the W3C XML Schema language. These can be unofficially divided into seven groups:

✦ Numeric types

✦ Time types

✦ XML types

✦ String types

✦ The boolean type

✦ The URI reference type

✦ The binary types

Numeric data types

The most obvious data types, and the ones most familiar to programmers, are the numeric data types. Among computer scientists, there's quite a bit of disagreement about how numbers should be represented in computer systems. The W3C XML Schema language tries to make everyone happy by providing almost every numeric type imaginable including:

✦ Integer and floating-point numbers

✦ Finite size numbers similar to those in Java and C and infinitely precise, unlimited-size numbers similar to those in Eiffel and Java's `java.math` package

✦ Signed and unsigned numbers

You'll probably only use a subset of these. For instance, you wouldn't use both the arbitrarily large `xsd:integer` type and the four-byte limited `xsd:int` type. Table 23-1 summarizes the different numeric types.

Table 23-1
Schema Numeric Types

Name	Type	Examples
xsd:float	IEEE 754 32-bit floating-point number, or as close as you can get using a base 10 representation; same as Java's `float` type	-INF, -1E4, -0, 0, 12.78E-2, 12, INF, NaN
xsd:double	IEEE 754 64-bit floating-point number, or as close as you can get using a base 10 representation; same as Java's `double` type	-INF, 1.401E-90, -1E4, -0, 0, 12.78E-2, 12, INF, NaN, 3.4E42
xsd:decimal	Arbitrary precision, decimal numbers; same as `java.math.BigDecimal`	-2.7E400, 5.7E-444, -3.1415292, 0, 7.8, 90200.76, 3.4E1024
xsd:integer	An arbitrarily large or small integer; same as `java.math.BigInteger`	-5000000000000000000000000, -9223372036854775809, -126789, -1, 0, 1, 5, 23, 42, 126789, 9223372036854775808, 45673498732498326498736 24958
xsd: nonPositiveInteger	An integer less than or equal to zero	0, -1, -2, -3, -4, -5, -6, -7, -8, -9, . . .
xsd: negativeInteger	An integer strictly less than zero	-1, -2, -3, -4, -5, -6, -7, -8, -9, . . .

Name	Type	Examples
xsd:long	An eight-byte two's complement integer such as Java's long type	-9223372036854775808, -9223372036854775807, . . . -6, -5, -4, -3, -2, -1, 0, 1, 2, 3, 4, 5, 6, 7, 8, 9, 10, 11, 12, 13, 14, . . ., 2147483645, 2147483646, 2147483647, 2147483648, . . .9223372036854775806, 9223372036854775807
xsd:int	An integer that can be represented as a four-byte, two's complement number such as Java's int type	-2147483648, -2147483647, -2147483646, 2147483645, . . .-6, -5, -4, -3, -2, -1, 0, 1, 2, 3, 4, 5, 6, 7, 8, 9, 10, 11, 12, 13, 14, . . ., 2147483645, 2147483646, 2147483647
xsd:short	An integer that can be represented as a two-byte, two's complement number such as Java's short type	-32768, -32767, -32766, . . ., -6, -5, -4, -3, -2, -1, 0, 1, 2, 3, 4, 5, 6, 7, 8, 9, 10, 11, 12, 13, 14, 15, . . . 32765, 32766, 32767
xsd:byte	An integer that can be represented as a one-byte, two's complement number such as Java's byte type	-128, -127, -126, -125, . . ., -3, -2, -1, 0, 1, 2, 3, 4, 5, 6, 7, 8, 9, 10, 11, 12, 13, 14, 15, 16, . . .121, 122, 123, 124, 125, 126, 127
xsd:nonNegativeInteger	An integer greater than or equal to zero	0, 1, 2, 3, 4, 5, 6, 7, 8, 9, 10, 11, 12, 13, 14, 15, . . .
xsd:unsignedLong	An eight-byte unsigned integer	0, 1, 2, 3, 4, 5, 6, 7, 8, 9, 10, 11, 12, . . .18446744073709551614, 18446744073709551615
xsd:unsignedInt	A four-byte unsigned integer	0, 1, 2, 3, 4, 5, . . .4294967294, 4294967295
xsd:unsignedShort	A two-byte unsigned integer	0, 1, 2, 3, 4, 5, 6, 7, 8, 9, 10, 11, 12, 13, 14, . . .65533, 65534, 65535
xsd:unsignedByte	A one-byte unsigned integer	0, 1, 2, 3, 4, 5, 6, 7, 8, 9, 10, 11, 12, 13, 14, . . . 252, 253, 254, 255
xsd:positiveInteger	An integer strictly greater than zero	1, 2, 3, 4, 5, 6, 7, 8, 9, 10, 11, 12, 13, 14, . . .

Time data types

The next set of simple types the W3C XML Schema language provides are more familiar to database designers than to procedural programmers; these are the time types. These can represent times of day, dates, or durations of time. The formats, shown in Table 23-2, are all based on the ISO standard 8601, *Representations of dates and times* (http://www.iso.ch/markete/8601.pdf). Time zones are given as offsets from Coordinated Universal Time (Greenwich Mean Time to laypeople) or as the letter Z to indicate Coordinated Universal Time.

	Table 23-2	
	XML Schema Time Types	
Name	*Type*	*Examples*
xsd:dateTime	A particular moment in Coordinated Universal Time, up to an arbitrarily small fraction of a second	1999-05-31T13:20:00.000-05:00, 1999-05-31T18:20:00.000Z, 1999-05-31T13:20:00.000, 1999-05-31T13:20:00.000-05:00.321
xsd:date	A specific day in history	-0044-03-15, 0001-01-01, 1969-06-27, 2000-10-31, 2001-11-17
xsd:time	A specific time of day that recurs every day	14:30:00.000, 09:30:00.000-05:00, 14:30:00.000Z
xsd:gDay	A day in no particular month, or rather in every month	--01, --02, . . . --09, --10, --11, --12, . . ., --28, --29, --30, --31
xsd:gMonth	A month in no particular year	--01--, --02--, --03--, ---04--, . . . --09--, --10--, --11--, --12--
xsd:gYear	A given year	. . . -0002, -0001, 0001, 0002, 0003, . . .1998, 1999, 2000, 2001, 2002, . . . 9997, 9998, 9999
xsd:gYearMonth	A specific month in a specific year	1999-12, 2001-04, 1968-07
xsd:gMonthDay	A date in no particular year, or rather in every year	--10-31, --02-28, --02-29
xsd:duration	A length of time, without fixed endpoints, to an arbitrary fraction of a second	P2000Y10M31DT09H32M7.4312S

Notice in particular that in all the date formats the year comes first, followed by the month, then the day, then the hour, and so on. The largest unit of time is on the left and the smallest unit is on the right. This helps avoid questions such as whether 2001–02–11 is February 11, 2000 or November 2, 2001.

XML data types

The next batch of schema data types should be quite familiar. These are the types related to XML constructs themselves. Most of these types match attribute types in DTDs such as NMTOKENS or IDREF. The difference is that with schemas these types can be applied to both elements and attributes. These also include four new types related to other XML constructs: xsd:language, xsd:Name, xsd:QName, and xsd:NCName. Table 23-3 summarizes the different types.

Table 23-3
XML Schema XML Types

Name	Type	Examples
xsd:ID	XML 1.0 ID attribute type; any XML name that's unique among ID type attributes and elements	p1, p2, ss123-45-6789, _92, red, green, NT-Decl, seventeen
xsd:IDREF	XML 1.0 IDREF attribute type;any XML name that's used as the value of an ID type attribute or element elsewhere in the document	p1, p2, ss123-45-6789, _92, p1, p2, red, green, NT-Decl, seventeen
xsd:ENTITY	XML 1.0 ENTITY attribute type; any XML name that's declared as an unparsed entity in the DTD	PIC1, PIC2, PIC3, cow_movie, MonaLisa, Warhol
xsd:NOTATION	XML 1.0 NOTATION attribute type; any XML name that's declared as a notation name in the schema using xsd:notation	GIF, jpeg, TIF, pdf, TeX
xsd:IDREFS	XML 1.0 IDREFS attribute type; a white space-separated list of XML names that are used as values of ID type attributes or elements elsewhere in the document	1 p2, ss123-45-6789 _92, pred green NT-Decl seventeen
xsd:ENTITIES	XML 1.0 ENTITIES attribute type; a white space-separated list of ENTITY names	PIC1 PIC2 PIC3

Continued

	Table 23-3 *(continued)*	
Name	**Type**	**Examples**
`xsd:NMTOKEN`	XML 1.0 `NMTOKEN` attribute type	`12 are you ready 199`

`xsd:NMTOKENS`	XML 1.0 `NMTOKENS` attribute type, a white space-separated list of name tokens	`MI NY LA CA`
		`p1 p2 p3 p4 p5 p6`
		`1 2 3 4 5 6`

`xsd:language`	Valid values for `xml:lang` as defined in XML 1.0	`en, en-GB, en-US, fr, i-lux,` `ama, ara, ara-EG, x-choctaw`

`xsd:Name`	An XML 1.0 Name, with or without colons	`set, title, rdf, math,`
		`math123, xlink:href,`
		`song:title`

`xsd:QName`	A namespace qualified name	`song:title, math:set,` `xsd:element`
`xsd:NCName`	A local name without any colons	`set, title, rdf, math, tei.2,` `href`

 For more details on the permissible values for elements and attributes declared to have these types, see Chapter 11.

String data types

You've already encountered the `xsd:string` type. It's the most generic simple type. It requires a sequence of Unicode characters of any length, but this is what all XML element content and attribute values are. There are also two very closely related types: `xsd:token` and `xsd:CDATA`. These are the same as `xsd:string` except that they limit the amount, location, and type of white space that can be used. Table 23-4 summarizes the string data types.

	Table 23-4 **XML Schema String Types**	
Name	**Type**	**Examples**

`xsd:string`	A sequence of zero or more Unicode characters that are allowed in an XML document; essentially the only forbidden characters are most of the C0 controls, surrogates, and the byte-order mark	`p1, p2, 123 45 6789,`
		`^*&^*&_92, red green blue,`
		`NT-Decl, seventeen; Mary`
		`had a little lamb, The`
		`love of money is the root`
		`of all Evil., Would you`
		`paint the lily? Would you`
		`gild gold?`

Name	Type	Examples
xsd:normalizedString	A string that does not contain any tabs, carriage returns, or linefeeds	PIC1, PIC2, PIC3, cow_movie, MonaLisa, Hello World , Warhol, red green
xsd:token	A string with no leading or trailing white space, no tabs, no linefeeds, and not more than one consecutive space	p1 p2, ss123 45 6789, _92, red, green, NT Decl, seventeenp1, p2, 123 45 6789, ^*&^*&_92, red green blue, NT-Decl, seventeen; Mary had a little lamb, The love of money is the root of all Evil.

Binary types

It's impossible to include arbitrary binary files in XML documents because they might contain illegal characters such as a form feed or a null that would make the XML document malformed. Therefore, any such data must first be encoded in legal characters. The W3C XML Schema Language supports two such encodings, xsd:base64Binary and xsd:hexBinary.

Hexadecimal binary encodes each byte of the input as two hexadecimal digits — 00, 01, 02, 03, 04, 05, 06, 07, 08, 09, 0A, 0B, 0C, 0D, 0E, 0F, 10, 11, 12, and so on. Thus, an entire file can be encoded using only the digits 0 through 9 and the letters A through F. (Lowercase letters are also allowed, but uppercase letters are customary.) On the other hand, each byte is replaced by two bytes so this encoding doubles the size of the data. It's not a very efficient encoding. Hexadecimal binary encoded data tends to look like this:

```
A4E345EC54CC8D52198000FFEA6C807F41F332127323432147A89979EEF3
```

Base64 encoding uses a more complex algorithm and a larger character set, 65 ASCII characters chosen for their ability to pass through almost all gateways, mail relays, and terminal servers intact, as well as their existence in ASCII, EBCDIC, and most other common character sets. Base64 encodes every three bytes as four characters, typically only increasing file size by a third, so it's somewhat more efficient than xsd:hexBinary. Base64 encoded data tends to look something like this:

```
6jKpNnmkkWeArsn50eeg2njcz+nXdkOf9kZI892dd1R8Lg1aMhPeFTYuoq3I6n
BjWzuktNZKiXYBfKsSTB8UO9dTiJo2ir3HJuY7eW/p89osKMfixPQsp9vQMgzph
6Qa 1Y7j4MB7y5ROJYsTr1/fFwmj/yhkHwpbpzed1LE=
```

XML Digital Signatures use Base64 encoding to encode the binary signatures before wrapping them in an XML element.

Caution   I really discourage you from using either of these if at all possible. If you have binary data, it's much more efficient and much less obtuse to link to it using XLink or unparsed entities rather than encoding it in Base64 or hexadecimal binary.

Miscellaneous data types

There are two types left over that don't fit neatly into the previous categories: xsd:boolean, and xsd:anyURI. The xsd:boolean type represents something similar to C++'s bool data type. It has four legal values: 0, 1, true, and false. 0 is considered to be the same as false, and 1 is considered the same as true.

The final schema simple type is xsd:anyURI. An element of this type contains a relative or absolute URI, possibly a URL, such as urn:isbn:0764547607, http://www.w3.org/TR/2000/WD-xmlschema-2-20000407/#timeDuration, /javafaq/reports/JCE1.2.1.htm, /TR/2000/WD-xmlschema-2-20000407/, or ../index.html.

Deriving Simple Types

You're not limited to the 44 simple types that the W3C XML Schema Language defines. As in object-oriented programming languages, you can create new data types by deriving from the existing types. The most common such derivation is to restrict a type to a subset of its normal values. For instance, you can define an integer type that only holds numbers between 1 and 20 by deriving from xsd:positiveInteger. You can create enumerated types that only allow a finite list of fixed values. You can create new types that join together the ranges of existing types through a union. For instance you can derive a type that can hold either an xsd:date or an xsd:int.

New simple types are created by xsd:simpleType elements, just as new complex types are created by xsd:complexType elements. The name attribute of xsd:simpleType assigns a name to the new type by which it can be referred to in xsd:element type attributes. The allowed content of elements and attributes with the new type can be specified by one of three child elements:

✦ xsd:restriction to select a subset of the values allowed by the base type

✦ xsd:union to combine multiple types

✦ xsd:list to specify a list of elements of an existing simple type

Deriving by restriction

To create a new type by restricting from an existing type you give the xsd:simpleType element an xsd:restriction child element. The base attribute of this element specifies what type you're restricting. For example, this xsd:simpleType element creates a new type named phonoYear that's derived from xsd:gYear:

```
<xsd:simpleType name="phonoYear">
  <xsd:restriction base="xsd:gYear">
  </xsd:restriction>
</xsd:simpleType>
```

With this declaration any legal xsd:gYear is also a legal phonoYear, and any illegal year is also an illegal phonoYear. You can limit phonoYear to a subset of the normal year values by using *facets* to specify which values are and are not allowed. For instance, the minInclusive facet defines the minimum legal value for a type. This facet is added to a restriction as an xsd:minInclusive child element. The value attribute of the xsd:minInclusive element sets the minimum allowed value for the year:

```
<xsd:simpleType name="phonoYear">
  <xsd:restriction base="xsd:gYear">
    <xsd:minInclusive value="1877"/>
  </xsd:restriction>
</xsd:simpleType>
```

Here the value of xsd:minInclusive is set to 1877, the year Thomas Edison invented the phonograph. Thus, 1877 is a legal phonoYear, 1878 is a legal phonoYear, 2001 is a legal phonoYear, and 3005 is a legal phonoYear. However, 1876, 1875, 1874, and earlier years are not legal phonoYears, even though they are legal xsd:gYears.

Once the phonoYear type has been defined, you can use it just like one of the built-in types. For example, in the SONG schema, you'd declare that the year element has the type phonoYear like this:

```
<xsd:element type="phonoYear"/>
```

minInclusive is not the only facet you can apply to xsd:gYear. Other facets of xsd:gYear are:

- ✦ xsd:minExclusive: the minimum value that all instances must be strictly greater than

- ✦ xsd:maxInclusive: the maximum value that all instances must be less than or equal to

- ✦ xsd:maxExclusive: the maximum value that all instances must be strictly less than

✦ `xsd:enumeration`: a list of all legal values

✦ `xsd:whiteSpace`: how white space is treated within the element

✦ `xsd:pattern`: a regular expression to which the instance is compared

Each facet is represented as an empty element inside an `xsd:restriction` element. Each facet has a `value` attribute giving the value of that facet. One restriction can contain more than one facet. For example, this `xsd:simpleType` element defines a `phonoYear` as any year between 1877 and 2100, inclusive:

```
<xsd:simpleType name="phonoYear">
  <xsd:restriction base="xsd:gYear">
    <xsd:minInclusive value="1877"/>
    <xsd:maxInclusive value="2100"/>
  </xsd:restriction>
</xsd:simpleType>
```

It's possible that multiple facets may conflict. For instance, the `minInclusive` value could be 2100 and the `maxInclusive` value could be 1877. While this is probably a design mistake, it is syntactically legal. It would just mean that the set of `phonoYears` was the empty set, and `phonoYear` type elements could not actually be used in instance documents.

Facets

Facets are shared among many types. For instance, the `minInclusive` facet can constrain essentially any well-ordered type, including not only xsd:gYear, but also xsd:byte, xsd:unsignedByte, xsd:integer, xsd:positiveInteger, xsd:negativeInteger, xsd:nonNegativeInteger, xsd:nonPositiveInteger, xsd:int, xsd:unsignedInt, xsd:long, xsd:unsignedLong, xsd:short, xsd:unsignedShort, xsd:decimal, xsd:float, xsd:double, xsd:time, xsd:dateTime, xsd:duration, xsd:date, xsd:gMonth, xsd:gYearMonth, and xsd:gMonthDay. The complete list of constraining facets that can be applied to different types is:

✦ `xsd:minInclusive`: the value that all instances must be greater than or equal to

✦ `xsd:minExclusive`: the value that all instances must be strictly greater than

✦ `xsd:maxInclusive`: the value that all instances must be less than or equal to

✦ `xsd:maxExclusive`: the value that all instances must be strictly less than

✦ `xsd:enumeration`: a list of all legal values

✦ `xsd:whiteSpace`: how white space is treated within the element

✦ `xsd:pattern`: a regular expression to which the instance is compared

✦ `xsd:length`: the exact number of characters in the element

✦ `xsd:minLength`: the minimum number of characters allowed in the element

✦ `xsd:maxLength`: the maximum number of characters allowed in the element

✦ `xsd:totalDigits`: the maximum number of digits allowed in the element

✦ `xsd:fractionDigits`: the maximum number of digits allowed in the fractional part of the element

Not all facets apply to all types. For instance it doesn't make much sense to talk about the minimum value of an `xsd:NMTOKEN` or the number of fraction digits in an `xsd:gYear`. However, when the same facet is shared by different types, it has the same syntax and basic meaning for all the types.

Facets for strings: length, minLength, maxLength

The three length facets — `xsd:length`, `xsd:minLength`, and `xsd:maxLength` — apply to the `xsd:string` type and its subtypes: `xsd:normalizedString`, `xsd:token`, `xsd:hexBinary`, `xsd:base64Binary`, `xsd:QName`, `xsd:NCName`, `xsd:ID`, `xsd:IDREF`, `xsd:IDREFS`, `xsd:language`, `xsd:anyURI`, `xsd:ENTITY`, `xsd:ENTITIES`, `xsd:NOTATION`, `xsd:NOTATIONS`, `xsd:NMTOKEN`, and `xsd:NMTOKENS`. These facets specify the number of characters allowed in the element or attribute value. The `value` attribute of each of these facets must contain a nonnegative integer. `xsd:length` sets the exact number of characters in the value, whereas `xsd:minLength` sets the minimum length and `xsd:maxLength` sets the maximum length.

For example, the schema in Listing 23-18 uses the `xsd:minLength` and `xsd:maxLength` facets to derive a new Str255 data type from `xsd:string`. Whereas `xsd:string` allows strings of any length from zero on up, Str255 requires each string to have a minimum length of 1 and a maximum length of 255. The schema then assigns this data type to all the names and titles to indicate that each must contain between 1 and 255 characters:

> ## Listing 23-18: **A schema that derives a Str255 data type from xsd:string**

```
<?xml version="1.0"?>
<xsd:schema xmlns:xsd="http://www.w3.org/2001/XMLSchema">

  <xsd:simpleType name="Str255">
    <xsd:restriction base="xsd:string">
      <xsd:minLength value="1"/>
      <xsd:maxLength value="255"/>
    </xsd:restriction>
  </xsd:simpleType>

  <xsd:element name="SONG" type="SongType"/>
```

Continued

Listing 23-18 *(continued)*

```
<xsd:complexType name="SongType">
  <xsd:sequence>
    <xsd:element name="TITLE"      type="Str255"/>
    <xsd:element name="COMPOSER"   type="Str255"
                 maxOccurs="unbounded"/>
    <xsd:element name="PRODUCER"   type="Str255"
                 minOccurs="0"      maxOccurs="unbounded"/>
    <xsd:element name="PUBLISHER"  type="Str255"
                 minOccurs="0"/>
    <xsd:element name="LENGTH"     type="xsd:duration"/>
    <xsd:element name="YEAR"       type="xsd:gYear"/>
    <xsd:element name="ARTIST"     type="Str255"
                 maxOccurs="unbounded"/>
    <xsd:element name="PRICE"      type="xsd:string"
                 minOccurs="0"/>
  </xsd:sequence>
</xsd:complexType>

</xsd:schema>
```

The whiteSpace facet

The whiteSpace facet is unusual. Unlike the other 11 facets, xsd:whiteSpace does not in any way constrain the allowed content of elements. Instead, it suggests what the application should do with any white space that it finds in the instance document. It says how significant that white space is. However, it does not in any way say that any particular kind of white space is legal or illegal.

The xsd:whiteSpace facet has three possible values:

✦ preserve: The white space in the input document is unchanged.

✦ replace: Each tab, carriage return, and linefeed is replaced with a single space.

✦ collapse: Each tab, carriage return, and linefeed is replaced with a single space. Furthermore, after this replacement is performed, all runs of multiple spaces are condensed to a single space. Leading and trailing white space is deleted.

Again, these are all just hints to the application. None of them have any effect on validation.

The whiteSpace facet can only be applied to xsd:string, xsd:normalizedString, and xsd:token types. Furthermore, it only fully applies to elements. XML 1.0 requires that parsers replace all white space in attributes, and collapse white space in attributes whose type is anything other than CDATA, regardless of what the schema says.

The schema in Listing 23-19 uses the xsd:whiteSpace facets to derive a new CollapsedString data type from xsd:string. Then it assigns this data type to all the names and titles to indicate that white space should be collapsed in these elements:

Listing 23-19: A schema that suggests collapsing white space in elements

```
<?xml version="1.0"?>
<xsd:schema xmlns:xsd="http://www.w3.org/2001/XMLSchema">

  <xsd:element name="SONG" type="SongType"/>

  <xsd:simpleType name="CollapsedString">
    <xsd:restriction base="xsd:string">
      <xsd:whiteSpace value="collapse"/>
    </xsd:restriction>
  </xsd:simpleType>

  <xsd:complexType name="SongType">
    <xsd:sequence>
      <xsd:element name="TITLE"     type="CollapsedString"/>
      <xsd:element name="COMPOSER"  type="CollapsedString"
        maxOccurs="unbounded"/>
      <xsd:element name="PRODUCER"  type="CollapsedString"
        minOccurs="0" maxOccurs="unbounded"/>
      <xsd:element name="PUBLISHER" type="CollapsedString"
        minOccurs="0"/>
      <xsd:element name="LENGTH"    type="xsd:duration"/>
      <xsd:element name="YEAR"      type="xsd:gYear"/>
      <xsd:element name="ARTIST"    type="CollapsedString"
        maxOccurs="unbounded"/>
      <xsd:element name="PRICE"     type="xsd:string"
                   minOccurs="0"/>
    </xsd:sequence>
  </xsd:complexType>

</xsd:schema>
```

Facets for decimal numbers: totalDigits and fractionDigits

When formatting numbers, it's useful to be able to specify how many digits should be used in the entire number, the integer parts, and the fraction parts. Schemas don't go as far in this regard as the `printf()` function in C or the `java.text.DecimalFormat` class in Java, but they do offer you some control.

The `xsd:totalDigits` facet specifies the maximum number of decimal digits in a number. It applies to most numeric types including `xsd:byte`, `xsd:unsignedByte`, `xsd:integer`, `xsd:positiveInteger`, `xsd:negativeInteger`, `xsd:nonNegativeInteger`, `xsd:nonPositiveInteger`, `xsd:int`, `xsd:unsignedInt`, `xsd:long`, `xsd:unsignedLong`, `xsd:short`, `xsd:unsignedShort`, and `xsd:decimal`. The only exceptions are the IEEE 754 types that occupy a fixed number of bytes; that is, `xsd:float` and `xsd:double`. The value of this facet must be a positive integer.

The `xsd:fractionDigits` facet specifies the maximum number of decimal digits to the right of the decimal point. (There is no facet that allows you to specify the minimum number of digits or fraction digits.) This only really applies to `xsd:decimal`. Technically, it applies to all the integer types too, but for those types it's fixed to the value zero; that is, no fraction digits at all. You're only allowed to change it for `xsd:decimal`. The value of this facet must be a nonnegative integer.

The enumeration facet

Rather than setting some sort of range on legal values, the `xsd:enumeration` facet simply lists all allowed values. It applies to every simple type except `xsd:boolean`. The syntax is a little unusual. Each possible value gets its own `xsd:enumeration` element as a child of the `xsd:restriction` element.

Listing 23-20 uses an enumeration to derive a `PublisherType` from `xsd:string`. It requires that the publisher be one of the oligopoly that controls 90 percent of all U.S. music (Warner-Elektra-Atlantic, Universal Music Group, Sony Music Entertainment, Inc., Capitol Records, Inc., and BMG Music).

Listing 23-20: **A schema that uses an enumeration to derive a type from xsd:string**

```
<?xml version="1.0"?>
<xsd:schema xmlns:xsd="http://www.w3.org/2001/XMLSchema">

  <xsd:element name="SONG" type="songType"/>

  <xsd:simpleType name="PublisherType">
```

```
      <xsd:restriction base="xsd:string">
        <xsd:enumeration value="Warner-Elektra-Atlantic"/>
        <xsd:enumeration value="Universal Music Group"/>
        <xsd:enumeration value="Sony Music Entertainment, Inc."/>
        <xsd:enumeration value="Capitol Records, Inc."/>
        <xsd:enumeration value="BMG Music"/>
      </xsd:restriction>
    </xsd:simpleType>

    <xsd:complexType name="songType">
      <xsd:sequence>
        <xsd:element name="TITLE"     type="xsd:string"/>
        <xsd:element name="COMPOSER"  type="xsd:string"
          maxOccurs="unbounded"/>
        <xsd:element name="PRODUCER"  type="xsd:string"
          minOccurs="0" maxOccurs="unbounded"/>
        <xsd:element name="PUBLISHER" type="PublisherType"
          minOccurs="0"/>
        <xsd:element name="LENGTH"    type="xsd:duration"/>
        <xsd:element name="YEAR"      type="xsd:gYear"/>
        <xsd:element name="ARTIST"    type="xsd:string"
          maxOccurs="unbounded"/>
        <xsd:element name="PRICE"     type="xsd:string"
                     minOccurs="0"/>
      </xsd:sequence>
    </xsd:complexType>

  </xsd:schema>
```

xsd:string is far from the only type you can derive from via enumeration. You can
derive from xsd:int, xsd:NMTOKEN, xsd:date, and, indeed, from all simple types
except xsd:boolean. Of course, the enumerated values all have to be legal
instances of the base type.

The pattern facet

There's one element in the song examples that clearly deserves a data type, but so
far doesn't have one — PRICE. However none of the built-in data types really match
the format for prices. Recall that PRICE elements look like this:

```
<PRICE>$1.25</PRICE>
```

This isn't an integer of any kind, because it has a decimal point. It could be a floating-point number, but that wouldn't account for the currency sign. You could drop
off the currency sign like this:

```
<PRICE>1.25</PRICE>
```

However, then you'd have to assume you were working in dollars. What if you wanted to sell songs priced in pounds or yen or lira? Perhaps you could make the currency sign part of a separate element, like this:

```
<PRICE>
  <CURRENCY>$</CURRENCY>
  <AMOUNT>1.25</AMOUNT>
</PRICE>
```

AMOUNT could be an xsd:float, and CURRENCY could be an xsd:string. However, this still isn't perfect. You want to limit the CURRENCY to exactly one character, and that character must be a currency sign. You don't want to allow it to contain any arbitrary string. Furthermore, you'd like to limit the precision of the AMOUNT to exactly two decimal places. You probably don't want to sell songs that cost $1.1 or $1.99999.

The solution to this problem, and to all similar problems where the values you want to allow don't quite fit any of the existing types, is to use the xsd:pattern facet whose value attribute contains a regular expression that matches all legal values and doesn't match any illegal values.

The regular expressions used in schemas are similar to the regular expressions you might be familiar with from Perl, grep, or other languages. You use statements like [A-Z]+ to mean "a string containing one or more of the capital letters from A to Z" or (club)* to mean "a string composed of zero or more repetitions of the word club."

Table 23-5 summarizes the grammar of XML schema regular expressions. In this table *A* and *B* represent some string or another regular expression particle from elsewhere in the table; that is, they will be replaced by something else when actually used in a regular expression. *n* and *m* represent some integer that will be replaced by a specific number.

Table 23-5
Regular Expression Symbols for XML Schema

Symbol	Meaning
A?	Zero or one occurrences of *A*
A*	Zero or more occurrences of *A*
A+	One or more occurrences of *A*
A{n,m}	Between *n* and *m* occurrences of *A*
A{n}	Exactly *n* occurrences of *A*
A{n,}	At least *n* occurrences of *A*
A|B	Either *A* or *B*
AB	*A* followed by *B*

Symbol	Meaning
.	Any one character
\p{A}	One character from Unicode character class *A*
[abcdefg]	A single occurrence of any of the characters contained in the brackets
[^abcdefg]	A single occurrence of any of the characters *not* contained in the brackets
[a-z]	A single occurrence of any character from *a* to *z* inclusive
[^a-z]	A single occurrence of any character *except* those from *a* to *z* inclusive
\n	Linefeed
\r	Carriage return
\t	Tab
\\	The backward slash \
|	The vertical bar	
\.	The period .
\-	The hyphen -
\^	The caret ^
\?	The question mark ?
*	The asterisk *
\+	The plus sign +
\{	The open brace {
\}	The closing brace }
\(	The open parenthesis (
\)	The closing parenthesis)
\[	The open bracket [
\]	The close bracket]

For the most part, these symbols have exactly the same meanings that they have in Perl. The schema regular expression syntax is somewhat weaker than Perl's, but then whose isn't? In any case, this should be sufficient power to meet any reasonable needs that schemas have.

Schema regular expressions do have one important feature that isn't available prior to Perl 5.6 and is unfamiliar to most developers — you can use \p{} to stand in for a character in a particular Unicode character class. For instance, N is the Unicode character class for numbers. This doesn't just include the European digits 0 through 9, but also the Arabic-Indic digits, the Devanagari digits, the Thai digits, and many more besides. Therefore \p{N} represents any digit defined anywhere in Unicode. \p{N}+ represents a string consisting of one or more Unicode digits. Table 23-6 lists the various Unicode character classes you can take advantage of in regular expressions. For the money regular expression, you need the Sc class for currency indicators and the Nd class for decimal digits. This is a little more restrictive than the N class, which includes nondecimal digits, such as the Roman numerals and the Han ideograph representing 100,000,000.

Table 23-6
Unicode Character Classes

Abbreviation	Includes	Examples
Letters		
L	All Letters	a, b, c, A, B, C, ü, Ü, ç, Ç, ζ, θ, Z, Θ, a, б, в, А, Б, В, א, ב, ג, dz, Dz, DZ
Lu	Uppercase letters	A, B, C, Ü, Ç, Z, Θ, A, Б, В, DZ
Ll	Lowercase letters	a, b, c, ü, ç, ζ, θ, a, б, в, dz
Lt	Title case letters	Dz
Lm	Modifier letters; letters that are attached to the previous characters somehow	ʰ, ʲ, ʳ, ʷ
Lo	Other letters; typically ones from languages that don't distinguish upper- and lowercase	א, ב, ג, Japanese Katakana and Hiragana, most Han ideographs
Marks		
M	All Marks	
Mn	Nonspacing marks; mostly accent marks that are attached to the previous character on the top or bottom, and thus do not change the amount of space the character occupies	◌̀, ◌́, ◌̈, ◌̄
Mc	Spacing combining marks; accent marks that are attached to the previous character on the left or right, and thus do change the amount of space the character occupies	◌ᵀ, Gurmukhi vowel sign AA
Me	Enclosing marks that completely surround a character	The Cyrillic hundred thousands and millions signs

Abbreviation	Includes	Examples
Numbers		
N	All numbers	0, 1, 2, 3, ¼, ½, ², ³, ·, ٩, I, II, III, IV, V, Ⅰ, Ⅱ, Ⅲ, Ⅹ
Nd	Decimal digits; characters that represent one of the numbers 0 through 9	0, 1, 2, 3, ·, ٩,
Nl	Numbers based on letters	I, II, III, IV, Ⅰ, Ⅱ, Ⅲ, Ⅹ
No	Other numbers	¼, ½, ², ³
Punctuation		
P	All punctuation	-, _, •, (, [, {,),], }, ', ", «, ', ", », !, ?, @, *, ¡, ¿, ·
Pc	Connectors	_, •
Pd	Dashes	Hyphens, soft hyphens, em dashes, en dashes, etc.
Ps	Opening punctuation	(, [, {
Pe	Closing punctuation	),], }
Pi	Initial quote marks	', ", «
Pf	Final quote marks	', ", »
Po	Other punctuation marks	!, ?, @, *, ¡, ¿, ·
Separators		
Z	All separators	
Zs	Space	Space, nonbreaking space, en space, em space
Zl	Line separators	Unicode character 2028, the line separator
Zp	Paragraph separators	Unicode character 2029, the paragraph separator
Symbols		
S	All Symbols	∂, Δ, Π, $, ¥, £, ~, ¯, ¨, ¡, ©, ®, °, ‖▲, ☺
Sm	Mathematical symbols	∂, Δ, Π, Σ, √, ≠, ≤, ≥, ≈

Continued

Table 23-6 *(continued)*		
Abbreviation	**Includes**	**Examples**
Symbols		
Sc	Currency signs	$, ¥, £, ¤, €, F, £, Pts, ₪, ₫
Sk	Modifier symbols	~, ¯, ¨
So	Other symbols	@ @i, ©, ®, °, §, ¶, ↔, ‰, ℓ, @ @N, ⌐, ¬, ‖▲, ☺, ♀, ♂, ♠, ♪, Braille, Han radicals
Other		
C	All Others	
Cc	Control characters	Carriage return, line feed, tab and the C1 controls
Cf	Format characters	The left-to-right and right-to-left marks used to indicate change of direction in bidirectional text
Co	Private use characters; code points which may be used for a program's internal purposes	
Cn	Unassigned; code points which, while legal in XML, the Unicode specification has not yet assigned a character to.	

You're now ready to put together a regular expression that describes money strings such as $1.25. What you want to say is that each such string contains:

1. A currency symbol

2. One or more decimal digits

3. An optional fractional part which, if present at all, consists of a decimal point and two decimal digits

Here's the regular expression that says that:

```
\p{Sc}\p{Nd}+(\.\p{Nd}\p{Nd})?
```

It begins with \p{Sc} to indicate a currency symbol such as $, ¥, £, or ¤.

This is followed by \p{Nd}+. \p{Nd} represents any decimal digit character. The + indicates one or more of these characters.

Next there's a parenthesized expression followed by a question mark, `(\.\p{Nd}\p{Nd})?`. The question mark indicates the parenthesized expression is optional. However, if it does appear its entire contents must be present, not just part. In other words, the question mark stands for zero or one, just as it does in DTDs. The contents of the parentheses are `\.\p{Nd}\p{Nd}`, which represents a period followed by two decimal digits, for example .35. Normally a period in a regular expression means any character at all, so here it's escaped with a preceding backslash to indicate that we really do want the actual period character.

Now that you have a regular expression that represents money, you're ready to define a money type. As for the other facets, this is done with the `xsd:simpleType` and `xsd:restriction` elements. Putting these together with the regular expression produces this type definition:

```
<xsd:simpleType name="money">
  <xsd:restriction base="xsd:string">
    <xsd:pattern value="\p{Sc}\p{Nd}+(\.\p{Nd}\p{Nd})?"/>
  </xsd:restriction>
</xsd:simpleType>
```

Listing 23-21 provides the complete song schema including this type definition. Take special note of the XML comment used to elucidate the regular expression. Regular expressions can be quite opaque, and a comment like this one can go a long way toward making the schema more understandable.

Listing 23-21: A schema that defines a custom money type

```
<?xml version="1.0"?>
<xsd:schema xmlns:xsd="http://www.w3.org/2001/XMLSchema">

  <xsd:element name="SONG" type="SongType"/>

  <xsd:simpleType name="money">
    <xsd:restriction base="xsd:string">
      <xsd:pattern value="\p{Sc}\p{Nd}+(\.\p{Nd}\p{Nd})?"/>
      <!--
        Regular Expression:
        \p{Sc}                Any Unicode currency indicator;
                              e.g., $, &#xA5, &#xA3, &#xA4, etc.
        \p{Nd}                A Unicode decimal digit character
        \p{Nd}+               One or more Unicode decimal digits
        \.                    The period character
        (\.\p{Nd}\p{Nd})
        (\.\p{Nd}\p{Nd})?  Zero or one strings of the form .35

        This works for any decimalized currency.

      -->
```

Continued

Listing 23-21 *(continued)*

```
      </xsd:restriction>
    </xsd:simpleType>

    <xsd:complexType name="SongType">
      <xsd:sequence>
        <xsd:element name="TITLE"    type="xsd:string"/>
        <xsd:element name="COMPOSER" type="PersonType"
                     maxOccurs="unbounded"/>
        <xsd:element name="PRODUCER" type="PersonType"
                     minOccurs="0" maxOccurs="unbounded"/>
        <xsd:element name="PUBLISHER" type="xsd:string"
                     minOccurs="0"/>
        <xsd:element name="LENGTH"   type="xsd:duration"/>
        <xsd:element name="YEAR"     type="xsd:gYear"/>
        <xsd:element name="ARTIST"   type="xsd:string"
                     maxOccurs="unbounded"/>
        <xsd:element name="PRICE" type="money" maxOccurs="1"/>
      </xsd:sequence>
    </xsd:complexType>

    <xsd:complexType name="PersonType">
      <xsd:sequence>
        <xsd:element name="NAME">
          <xsd:complexType>
            <xsd:all>
              <xsd:element name="GIVEN"  type="xsd:string"/>
              <xsd:element name="FAMILY" type="xsd:string"/>
            </xsd:all>
          </xsd:complexType>
        </xsd:element>
      </xsd:sequence>
    </xsd:complexType>

  </xsd:schema>
```

Unions

Restriction is not the only way to create a new simple type, although it is the most common way. You can also combine types using unions. For example, you could combine the built-in `xsd:decimal` type with the `money` type just defined to create a type that could contain either a decimal or a money value. To do this, give the `xsd:simpleType` element an `xsd:union` child element instead of an `xsd:restriction` child element. The `xsd:union` element contains more `xsd:simpleType` elements identifying the types you're combining in the union. For example, this is the above described `money`/`xsd:decimal` combined type:

```
<xsd:simpleType name="MoneyOrDecimal">
  <xsd:union>
    <xsd:simpleType>
      <xsd:restriction base="xsd:decimal">
      </xsd:restriction>
    </xsd:simpleType>
    <xsd:simpleType>
      <xsd:restriction base="xsd:string">
        <xsd:pattern value="\p{Sc}\p{Nd}+(\.\p{Nd}\p{Nd})?"/>
      </xsd:restriction>
    </xsd:simpleType>
  </xsd:union>
</xsd:simpleType>
```

Lists

Schemas can also specify that an element or attribute contains a list of a particular simple type. For example, this YEARS element contains a list of years:

```
<YEARS>1987 1999 1992    2002</YEARS>
```

Elements such as this can be specified using an xsd:list in the xsd:simpleType. The itemType attribute says what type of strings may appear in the list. For example:

```
<xsd:simpleType name="YearList">
  <xsd:list itemType="xsd:gYear"/>
</xsd:simpleType>
```

requires that elements with type YearList contain a white space-separated list of legal xsd:gYear values.

Caution

I must admit that I'm not very fond of list types, especially for elements. It seems to me that if you're going to have a list of different items, each of those items should be a separate element, possibly a child element of some parent element, but still its own element. Lists make a little more sense for attributes, but if there's a lot of substructure in the text, you should probably be using an element instead of an attribute anyway.

You can derive another list type from an existing list type. When so doing, you can restrict it according to the length, minLength, maxLength, and enumeration facets. In this case, the values of the three length facets refer to the number of items in the list rather than the number of characters in the content. For example, this xsd:simpleType element derives a DoubleYear list type that must hold exactly two years from the YearList type defined above:

```
<xsd:simpleType name="DoubleYear">
  <xsd:restriction base="YearList">
    <xsd:length value="2"/>
  </xsd:restriction>
</xsd:simpleType>
```

Empty Elements

Empty elements are those that cannot contain any child elements or parsed character data. This is the same as using the `EMPTY` content model in a DTD. As an example of this technique I'll define an empty `PHOTO` element. This will be used in the next section when attributes are introduced.

To create an empty element, you define it as a type, but don't give it an `xsd:sequence`, `xsd:all`, or `xsd:choice` child. Thus, you don't actually provide any child elements. For example:

```
<!-- An empty element -->
<xsd:complexType name="PhotoType">
</xsd:complexType>
```

Caution   This does not require the `PHOTO` element to be defined with an empty-element tag such as `<PHOTO/>`. The start-tag-end-tag pair `<PHOTO></PHOTO>` is also acceptable. In fact, the XML 1.0 specification says these two forms are equivalent. Schemas change nothing about XML 1.0. An XML 1.0 parser that knows nothing about schemas will have no trouble reading a document that uses schemas.

Attributes

In the examples so far, two XML constructs have been conspicuous by their absence: entities and attributes. The omission of entities was quite deliberate. Schemas cannot declare entities. If you need entities, you must use a DTD. (Of course, you can use a schema as well as the DTD.) However, schemas are fully capable of declaring attributes. Indeed they do a much better job of it than DTDs do because schemas can use the full set of data types like `xsd:float` and `xsd:anyURI`.

Note   You may not have noticed my avoidance of attributes because the examples all used `xmlns:xsi` and `xsi:noNamespaceSchemaLocation` attributes on the root element. However, as far as a schema validator is concerned, attributes used to declare namespaces, or to attach documents to schemas, "don't count." You do not have to, and indeed should not, declare these attributes. However, you do have to declare all the other attributes you use.

As a concrete example, let's consider how you might add an empty `PHOTO` element to the `SONG` documents. This element would be similar to the `IMG` element in HTML, and have an `SRC` attribute that contained a URL pointing to the photo's location, an `ALT` attribute containing some text in the event that the `PHOTO` can't be displayed, and `WIDTH` and `HEIGHT` attributes that together give the size of the image in pixels. Listing 23-22 demonstrates:

Listing 23-22: The PHOTO element has several attributes of different types

```xml
<?xml version="1.0"?>
<SONG xmlns:xsi="http://www.w3.org/2001/XMLSchema-instance"
      xsi:noNamespaceSchemaLocation="23-23.xsd">
  <TITLE>Yes I Am</TITLE>
  <PHOTO ALT="Melissa Etheridge holding a guitar"
         WIDTH="100" HEIGHT="300"
         SRC="guitar.jpg"/>
  <COMPOSER>
    <NAME>
      <GIVEN>Melissa</GIVEN>
      <FAMILY>Etheridge</FAMILY>
    </NAME>
  </COMPOSER>
  <PRODUCER>
    <NAME>
      <GIVEN>Hugh</GIVEN>
      <FAMILY>Padgham</FAMILY>
    </NAME>
  </PRODUCER>
  <PRODUCER>
    <NAME>
      <GIVEN>Melissa</GIVEN>
      <FAMILY>Etheridge</FAMILY>
    </NAME>
  </PRODUCER>
  <PUBLISHER>Island Records</PUBLISHER>
  <LENGTH>P0YT4M24S</LENGTH>
  <YEAR>1993</YEAR>
  <ARTIST>Melissa Etheridge</ARTIST>
  <PRICE>$1.25</PRICE>
</SONG>
```

Even though the PHOTO element is empty, because it has attributes it has a complex type. You define a PhotoType just as you previously defined a PersonType and a SongType. However, where those types used xsd:element to declare child elements, this type will use xsd:attribute to declare attributes.

```xml
<xsd:complexType name="PhotoType">
  <xsd:attribute name="SRC"    type="xsd:anyURI"/>
  <xsd:attribute name="WIDTH"  type="xsd:positiveInteger"/>
  <xsd:attribute name="HEIGHT" type="xsd:positiveInteger"/>
  <xsd:attribute name="ALT"    type="xsd:string"/>
</xsd:complexType>
```

Because the SRC attribute should contain a URL, it's been given the type xsd:anyURI. Because the HEIGHT and WIDTH attributes should each be an integer greater than zero, they're given the type xsd:positiveInteger. Finally, because the ALT attribute can contain essentially any string of text of any length, it's set to the most general type, xsd:string.

In this particular example, all the elements either have child elements or attributes, not both. However, that's certainly not required. In general, elements can have both child elements and attributes. Just use both xsd:element and xsd:attribute in the same xsd:complexType element. The xsd:attribute elements must come after the xsd:sequence, xsd:choice, or xsd:all group that forms the body of the element. For example, this xsd:element says that a PERSON element may have an optional attribute named ID with type ID:

```
<xsd:complexType name="PersonType">
  <xsd:sequence>
    <xsd:element name="NAME">
      <xsd:complexType>
        <xsd:all>
          <xsd:element name="GIVEN"  type="xsd:string"/>
          <xsd:element name="FAMILY" type="xsd:string"/>
        </xsd:all>
      </xsd:complexType>
    </xsd:element>
  </xsd:sequence>
  <xsd:attribute name="ID" type="xsd:ID"/>
</xsd:complexType>
```

Attributes can also be attached to elements that can only contain text such as an xsd:string or an xsd:gYear. The details are a little more complex, because an element with attributes by definition has a complex type. To make this work, you derive a new complex type from a simple type by giving the xsd:complexType element an xsd:simpleContent child element instead of an xsd:sequence, xsd:choice, or xsd:all. The xsd:simpleContent element itself has an xsd:extension child element whose base attribute identifies the simple type to extend such as xsd:string. The xsd:attribute elements are placed inside the xsd:extension element.

For example, suppose you want to allow the TITLE elements to have ID attributes like this:

```
<TITLE ID="test">Yes I Am</TITLE>
```

Previously TITLE was defined with type xsd:string. Instead let's derive a new type called StringWithID from xsd:string like this:

```
<xsd:complexType name="StringWithID">
  <xsd:simpleContent>
    <xsd:extension base="xsd:string">
      <xsd:attribute name="ID" type="xsd:ID"/>
```

```
        </xsd:extension>
      </xsd:simpleContent>
    </xsd:complexType>
```

The `StringWithID` type can then be applied to the `TITLE` element in the usual way like this:

```
<xsd:element name="TITLE" type="StringWithID"/>
```

By default attributes declared in schemas are optional (#IMPLIED in DTD terminology). However, an `xsd:attribute` can have a `use` attribute with the value `required` to indicate that the element must occur. In this case, you probably do want to insist that each of the four attributes be present. Therefore the declaration of `PhotoType` becomes this:

```
<xsd:complexType name="PhotoType">
  <xsd:attribute name="SRC"    type="xsd:anyURI"
                 use="required" />
  <xsd:attribute name="WIDTH"  type="xsd:positiveInteger"
                 use="required" />
  <xsd:attribute name="HEIGHT" type="xsd:positiveInteger"
                 use="required" />
  <xsd:attribute name="ALT"    type="xsd:string"
                 use="required" />
</xsd:complexType>
```

The `use` attribute can also have the value `optional` to indicate that it may or may not be present. (This is also the default if there is no `use` attribute.) If `optional`, then `xsd:attribute` may also have a `default` attribute giving the value the parser will provide if it doesn't find one in the instance document. If there is no default attribute, then this is the same as #IMPLIED in ATTLIST declarations in DTDs. Instead of a `use` attribute, `xsd:attribute` can have a `fixed` attribute whose value is the constant value for the attribute, whether present in the instance document or not. This has the same effect as #FIXED in DTDs. Listing 23-23 puts this all together in a complete schema for songs, including a PHOTO element with several required attributes.

Listing 23-23: **A SONG schema that declares attributes**

```
<?xml version="1.0"?>
<xsd:schema xmlns:xsd="http://www.w3.org/2001/XMLSchema">

  <xsd:element name="SONG" type="SongType"/>

  <xsd:complexType name="PhotoType">
    <xsd:attribute name="SRC"    type="xsd:anyURI"
                   use="required" />
    <xsd:attribute name="WIDTH"  type="xsd:positiveInteger"
```

Continued

Listing 23-23 *(continued)*

```
                      use="required" />
   <xsd:attribute name="HEIGHT" type="xsd:positiveInteger"
                      use="required" />
   <xsd:attribute name="ALT"    type="xsd:string"
                      use="required" />
 </xsd:complexType>

 <xsd:complexType name="SongType">
   <xsd:sequence>
     <xsd:element name="TITLE"     type="xsd:string"/>
     <xsd:element name="PHOTO"     type="PhotoType"/>
     <xsd:element name="COMPOSER"  type="PersonType"
                      maxOccurs="unbounded"/>
     <xsd:element name="PRODUCER"  type="PersonType"
                      minOccurs="0" maxOccurs="unbounded"/>
     <xsd:element name="PUBLISHER" type="xsd:string"
                      minOccurs="0"/>
     <xsd:element name="LENGTH"    type="xsd:duration"/>
     <xsd:element name="YEAR"      type="xsd:gYear"/>
     <xsd:element name="ARTIST"    type="xsd:string"
                      maxOccurs="unbounded"/>
     <xsd:element name="PRICE" type="money"/>
   </xsd:sequence>
 </xsd:complexType>

 <xsd:simpleType name="money">
   <xsd:restriction base="xsd:string">
     <xsd:pattern value="\p{Sc}\p{Nd}+(\.\p{Nd}\p{Nd})?"/>
     <!--
        Regular Expression:
        \p{Sc}              Any Unicode currency indicator;
                            e.g., $, &#xA5, &#xA3, &#A4, etc.
        \p{Nd}              A Unicode decimal digit character
        \p{Nd}+             One or more Unicode decimal digits
        \.                  The period character
        (\.\p{Nd}\p{Nd})
        (\.\p{Nd}\p{Nd})?   Zero or one strings of the form .35

        This works for any decimalized currency.

     -->
   </xsd:restriction>
 </xsd:simpleType>

 <xsd:complexType name="PersonType">
   <xsd:sequence>
     <xsd:element name="NAME">
       <xsd:complexType>
         <xsd:all>
```

```
                    <xsd:element name="GIVEN"  type="xsd:string"/>
                    <xsd:element name="FAMILY" type="xsd:string"/>
                  </xsd:all>
                </xsd:complexType>
              </xsd:element>
            </xsd:sequence>
          </xsd:complexType>

       </xsd:schema>
```

Namespaces

So far the example song documents have been blissfully namespace-free. Adding namespaces to the documents, and designing a schema that applies to the namespace-qualified documents is not particularly difficult. Namespaces add some important features, such as the ability to write schemas and validate documents that use elements and attributes from multiple XML applications. However, the terminology is a little on the confusing side. Some words, such as *qualified*, don't mean quite the same thing in schemas as they do in other XML technologies, so you do need to pay close attention and read what follows carefully.

Schemas for default namespaces

Let's begin with a simple example in which the XML application described by the schema uses a single default, nonprefixed namespace. Most of the time each namespace URI maps to exactly one schema (though later you'll learn several techniques to break large schemas into parts using xsd:import and xsd:include).

The schema for elements that are not in any namespace is identified by an xsi:noNamespaceSchemaLocation attribute. The schemas for elements that are in namespaces are identified by an xsi:schemaLocation attribute. This attribute contains a list of namespace URI/schema URI pairs. Each namespace URI is followed by one schema URI. The namespace URI is almost always absolute, but the schema URI is almost always a URL and often a relative URL.

Listing 23-24 demonstrates. This is the familiar hotcop.xml document that you've seen several times already, though it's been simplified a bit to keep the examples smaller. All the elements in this document are in the http://ibiblio.org/xml/namespace/song namespace defined by the xmlns attribute on the root element. The attributes in this document are not in any namespace because they don't have prefixes. There are two things you need to remember here:

1. Attributes without prefixes are never in any namespace, no matter what namespace their parent element is in, no matter what default namespace the document uses.

2. For purposes of schema validation, namespace declaration attributes, such as `xmlns` and `xmlns:xsi`, and schema attachment attributes, such as `xsi:schemaLocation`, don't count. You do not need to declare these in your schema.

In this case, all the elements are in the `http://ibiblio.org/xml/namespace/song` namespace, so an `xsi:schemaLocation` attribute is needed to associate this namespace with a URL where the schema can be found, `namespace_song.xsd` for this example.

Listing 23-24: A SONG document in the http://ibiblio.org/xml/namespace/song namespace

```
<?xml version="1.0" encoding="UTF-8" standalone="no"?>
<SONG xmlns="http://ibiblio.org/xml/namespace/song"
      xmlns:xsi="http://www.w3.org/2001/XMLSchema-instance"
      xsi:schemaLocation =
       "http://ibiblio.org/xml/namespace/song
        namespace_song.xsd"
>
  <TITLE>Hot Cop</TITLE>
  <!-- I've temporarily dropped the SRC attribute on this
       element. I'm going to replace it with XLinks shortly.
     -->
  <PHOTO ALT="Victor Willis in Cop Outfit" WIDTH="100"
         HEIGHT="200"/>
  <COMPOSER>Jacques Morali</COMPOSER>
  <COMPOSER>Henri Belolo</COMPOSER>
  <COMPOSER>Victor Willis</COMPOSER>
  <PRODUCER>Jacques Morali</PRODUCER>
  <PUBLISHER>PolyGram Records</PUBLISHER>
  <LENGTH>P0YT6M2OS</LENGTH>
  <YEAR>1978</YEAR>
  <ARTIST>Village People</ARTIST>
</SONG>
```

What does namespace_song.xsd look like? Listing 23-25 shows you. It's much the same schema as before, although I've dropped the `MoneyType` and `PersonType` to save a little room.

Listing 23-25: A schema for SONG documents in the http:// ibiblio.org/xml/namespace/song namespace

```xml
<?xml version="1.0"?>
<xsd:schema xmlns:xsd="http://www.w3.org/2001/XMLSchema"
  xmlns="http://ibiblio.org/xml/namespace/song"
  targetNamespace="http://ibiblio.org/xml/namespace/song"
  elementFormDefault="qualified"
  attributeFormDefault="unqualified"
>

  <xsd:element name="SONG" type="SongType"/>

  <xsd:complexType name="PhotoType">
    <xsd:attribute name="WIDTH"  type="xsd:positiveInteger"
                   use="required" />
    <xsd:attribute name="HEIGHT" type="xsd:positiveInteger"
                   use="required" />
    <xsd:attribute name="ALT"    type="xsd:string"
                   use="required" />
  </xsd:complexType>

  <xsd:complexType name="SongType">
    <xsd:sequence>
      <xsd:element name="TITLE"     type="xsd:string"/>
      <xsd:element name="PHOTO"     type="PhotoType"/>
      <xsd:element name="COMPOSER"  type="xsd:string"
                   maxOccurs="unbounded"/>
      <xsd:element name="PRODUCER"  type="xsd:string"
                   minOccurs="0" maxOccurs="unbounded"/>
      <xsd:element name="PUBLISHER" type="xsd:string"
                   minOccurs="0"/>
      <xsd:element name="LENGTH"    type="xsd:duration"/>
      <xsd:element name="YEAR"      type="xsd:gYear"/>
      <xsd:element name="ARTIST"    type="xsd:string"
                   maxOccurs="unbounded"/>
    </xsd:sequence>
  </xsd:complexType>

</xsd:schema>
```

The main body of the schema is much the same as before. However, the xsd:schema **start tag has several new attributes. It looks like this:**

```xml
<xsd:schema xmlns:xsd="http://www.w3.org/2001/XMLSchema"
  xmlns="http://ibiblio.org/xml/namespace/song"
  targetNamespace="http://ibiblio.org/xml/namespace/song"
  elementFormDefault="qualified"
  attributeFormDefault="unqualified"
>
```

The first `xmlns` attribute establishes the default namespace for this schema, which is, after all, an XML document itself. It sets the namespace to `http://ibiblio.org/xml/namespace/song`, the same as in the instance documents you're trying to model. This says that the unprefixed element names used in this schema such as `PhotoType` are in the `http://ibiblio.org/xml/namespace/song` namespace.

The second attribute says that this schema applies to documents in the `http://ibiblio.org/xml/namespace/song` namespace; that is, the elements identified by name attributes such as `SONG`, `PHOTO`, and `TITLE` are in the `http://ibiblio.org/xml/namespace/song` namespace.

The third attribute, `elementFormDefault`, has the value `qualified`. This means that the elements being described in this document are in fact in a namespace; specifically they're in the target namespace given previously by the `targetNamespace` attribute. This does not mean that the elements being modeled necessarily have prefixes, merely that they are in some namespace.

Finally, the fourth attribute, `attributeFormDefault`, has the value `unqualified`. This means that the attributes described by this schema are not in a namespace.

Schemas have one major advantage over DTDs when working with documents with namespaces. They validate against the local name and the namespace URIs of the elements and attributes, not the prefix and the local name like DTDs do. This means the prefixes do not have to match in the schema and in the instance documents. Indeed one might use prefixes and the other might use the default namespace.

For instance, consider Listing 23-26. This is the same as Listing 23-24 except that it uses the `song` prefix rather than the default namespace to indicate the `http://ibiblio.org/xml/namespace/song` namespace. However, it can use the *exact same schema!* The schema does not need to change just because the prefix (or lack thereof) has changed. As long as the namespace URI stays the same, the schema is happy.

Listing 23-26: **A SONG document in the http://ibiblio.org/ xml/namespace/song namespace with prefixes**

```
<?xml version="1.0" encoding="UTF-8" standalone="no"?>
<song:SONG
      xmlns:song="http://ibiblio.org/xml/namespace/song"
      xmlns:xsi="http://www.w3.org/2001/XMLSchema-instance"
      xsi:schemaLocation =
       "http://ibiblio.org/xml/namespace/song
        namespace_song.xsd"
>
   <song:TITLE>Hot Cop</song:TITLE>
   <!-- I've temporarily dropped the SRC attribute on this
        element. I'm going to replace it with XLinks shortly.
      -->
```

```
      <song:PHOTO ALT="Victor Willis in Cop Outfit" WIDTH="100"
            HEIGHT="200"/>
      <song:COMPOSER>Jacques Morali</song:COMPOSER>
      <song:COMPOSER>Henri Belolo</song:COMPOSER>
      <song:COMPOSER>Victor Willis</song:COMPOSER>
      <song:PRODUCER>Jacques Morali</song:PRODUCER>
      <song:PUBLISHER>PolyGram Records</song:PUBLISHER>
      <song:LENGTH>P0YT6M20S</song:LENGTH>
      <song:YEAR>1978</song:YEAR>
      <song:ARTIST>Village People</song:ARTIST>
  </song:SONG>
```

Multiple namespaces, multiple schemas

Now let's consider the case in which one document mixes markup from different vocabularies. In particular, let's suppose that you want to use XLink to connect the PHOTO element to the actual JPEG image rather than application-specific markup such as SRC. You need to set xlink:type, xlink:href, xlink:show, and xlink:actuate attributes on the PHOTO element to give it the proper meaning and behavior like this:

```
<PHOTO xlink:type="simple" xlink:href="hotcop.jpg"
       xlink:show="embed"   xlink:actuate="onLoad"
       ALT="Victor Willis in Cop Outfit"
       WIDTH="100" HEIGHT="200"/>
```

 Cross-Reference XLinks are discussed in Chapter 20.

Now the document uses two main namespaces, the http://ibiblio.org/xml/namespace/song namespace for songs and the http://www.w3.org/1999/xlink namespace for XLinks. Thus, it needs two schemas. However, because the root element can have only one xsi:schemaLocation attribute, it has to serve double duty and declare both. Listing 23-27 demonstrates.

Listing 23-27: **A SONG document that uses XLink to embed photos**

```
<?xml version="1.0" encoding="UTF-8" standalone="no"?>
<SONG xmlns="http://ibiblio.org/xml/namespace/song"
      xmlns:xlink="http://www.w3.org/1999/xlink"
      xmlns:xsi="http://www.w3.org/2001/XMLSchema-instance"
      xsi:schemaLocation =
      "http://ibiblio.org/xml/namespace/song 23-29.xsd
```

Continued

Listing 23-27 *(continued)*

```
          http://www.w3.org/1999/xlink xlink.xsd"
>
  <TITLE>Hot Cop</TITLE>
  <PHOTO xlink:type="simple" xlink:href="hotcop.jpg"
         xlink:show="embed"  xlink:actuate="onLoad"
         ALT="Victor Willis in Cop Outfit"
         WIDTH="100" HEIGHT="200"/>
  <COMPOSER>Jacques Morali</COMPOSER>
  <COMPOSER>Henri Belolo</COMPOSER>
  <COMPOSER>Victor Willis</COMPOSER>
  <PRODUCER>Jacques Morali</PRODUCER>
  <PUBLISHER>PolyGram Records</PUBLISHER>
  <LENGTH>POYT6M20S</LENGTH>
  <YEAR>1978</YEAR>
  <ARTIST>Village People</ARTIST>
</SONG>
```

Listing 23-28 shows the XLink schema. It only declares attributes, no elements at all. You haven't seen an example of this yet, but it's not hard. Just use xsd:attribute elements at the top-level, that is, as direct children of the xsd:schema element. The other difference between these top-level xsd:attribute elements and the ones you've seen before is that three of the attributes have fixed values, and don't even need to be explicitly included in the instance document. Only the xlink:href attribute asks the author to supply a value. However, this is rather specific to this particular use of XLink. Almost anything else you'd do with an XLink other than embedding an image or other non-XML content into the document would require a different schema that used different defaults.

Listing 23-28: **xlink.xsd: An XLink schema**

```
<?xml version="1.0" encoding="UTF-8" standalone="no"?>
<xsd:schema xmlns:xsd="http://www.w3.org/2001/XMLSchema"
  xmlns="http://www.w3.org/1999/xlink"
  targetNamespace="http://www.w3.org/1999/xlink"
  attributeFormDefault="unqualified"
>

  <xsd:attribute name="type"    type="xsd:string"
                 fixed="simple"/>
  <xsd:attribute name="href"    type="xsd:anyURI"/>
  <xsd:attribute name="actuate" type="xsd:string"
                 fixed="onLoad"/>
```

```
        <xsd:attribute name="show"     type="xsd:string"
                            fixed="embed"/>

</xsd:schema>
```

This schema doesn't actually apply these attributes to any elements. Therefore, the schema that does describe the PHOTO element needs to import xlink.xsd in order to reference these declarations. This is done with an xsd:import element. The xsd:import's schemaLocation attribute tells the processor where to find the schema to import. The namespace attribute says which elements and attributes the schema declares. Once this schema has been imported, you can add those attributes to any xsd:complexType by giving it an xsd:attribute child whose ref attribute identifies the attribute to be attached. Listing 23-29 demonstrates.

Listing 23-29: **A SONG schema that imports the XLink schema**

```
<?xml version="1.0"?>
<xsd:schema xmlns:xsd="http://www.w3.org/2001/XMLSchema"
  xmlns="http://ibiblio.org/xml/namespace/song"
  xmlns:xlink="http://www.w3.org/1999/xlink"
  targetNamespace="http://ibiblio.org/xml/namespace/song"
  elementFormDefault="qualified"
  attributeFormDefault="unqualified"
>

  <xsd:import namespace="http://www.w3.org/1999/xlink"
              schemaLocation="xlink.xsd"/>

  <xsd:element name="SONG" type="SongType"/>

  <xsd:complexType name="PhotoType">
    <xsd:attribute name="WIDTH"  type="xsd:positiveInteger"
                   use="required" />
    <xsd:attribute name="HEIGHT" type="xsd:positiveInteger"
                   use="required" />
    <xsd:attribute name="ALT"    type="xsd:string"
                   use="required" />
    <xsd:attribute ref="xlink:type"/>
    <xsd:attribute ref="xlink:href" use="required"/>
    <xsd:attribute ref="xlink:actuate"/>
    <xsd:attribute ref="xlink:show"/>
  </xsd:complexType>

  <xsd:complexType name="SongType">
```

Continued

Listing 23-29 *(continued)*

```
    <xsd:sequence>
      <xsd:element name="TITLE"     type="xsd:string"/>
      <xsd:element name="PHOTO"     type="PhotoType"/>
      <xsd:element name="COMPOSER"  type="xsd:string"
                   maxOccurs="unbounded"/>
      <xsd:element name="PRODUCER"  type="xsd:string"
                   minOccurs="0" maxOccurs="unbounded"/>
      <xsd:element name="PUBLISHER" type="xsd:string"
                   minOccurs="0"/>
      <xsd:element name="LENGTH"    type="xsd:duration"/>
      <xsd:element name="YEAR"      type="xsd:gYear"/>
      <xsd:element name="ARTIST"    type="xsd:string"
                   maxOccurs="unbounded"/>
    </xsd:sequence>
  </xsd:complexType>

</xsd:schema>
```

Annotations

At some point in this chapter, it's likely to have occurred to you that schemas can get rather large and rather complex. If that hasn't occurred to you yet, just imagine a schema not for the very small and simple song documents demonstrated in this chapter, but for much larger XML applications such as Scalable Vector Graphics, XHTML, and DocBook.

You can certainly use regular XML comments to describe schemas, and I encourage you to do so, especially when you're doing something less than obvious in the schema. The W3C XML Schema language also provides a more formal mechanism for annotating schemas. Both the top-level `xsd:schema` element itself and the various other schema elements (`xsd:complexType`, `xsd:all`, `xsd:element`, `xsd:attribute`, and so on) can contain `xsd:annotation` child elements that describe that part of the schema for human readers or for other computer programs. This element has two kinds of child elements:

✦ The `xsd:documentation` child element describes the schema for human readers. It often contains copyright and similar information.

✦ The `xsd:appInfo` child element describes the schema for computer programs. For instance, it might contain instructions about what style sheets to apply to the schema.

Each `xsd:annotation` element can contain any number of either of these. However, no special syntax has been defined for the content of these elements. You can put anything in there you find convenient, including other XML markup, subject only to the usual well-formedness constraints. Thus an `xsd:documentation` element might contain XHTML and an `xsd:appInfo` element might contain XSLT. Then again either or both might simply contain plain, unmarked-up text. For example, this annotation could be added to the song schemas developed in this chapter:

```
<xsd:annotation>
 <xsd:documentation>
  Song schema for Chapter 23 of the XML Bible, Gold Edition
  Copyright 2001 Elliotte Rusty Harold.
  elharo@metalab.unc.edu
 </xsd:documentation>
</xsd:annotation>
```

Summary

In this chapter, you learned that:

✦ Schemas address a number of perceived limitations of DTDs, including a strange, non-XML syntax, namespace incompatibility, lack of data typing, and limited extensibility and scalability.

✦ There are multiple XML schema languages including Relax, Schematron, TREX, and the W3C XML Schema language described in this chapter.

✦ An XML document can indicate the schema that applies to its non-namespace-qualified elements via an `xsi:noNamespaceSchemaLocation` attribute, which is normally placed on the root element.

✦ An XML document can indicate the schema that applies to its namespace qualified elements via an `xsi:schemaLocation` attribute, which is normally placed on the root element.

✦ Schemas declare elements with `xsd:element` elements.

✦ The `type` attribute of `xsd:element` specifies the data type of that element.

✦ Elements with complex types can have attributes and child elements.

✦ Elements with simple types only contain parsed character data.

✦ The `xsd:complexType` element defines a new type for an element that can contain child elements, attributes, and/or mixed content.

✦ The `xsd:group`, `xsd:all`, `xsd:choice`, and `xsd:sequence` elements let you specify particular combinations of elements in an element's content model.

✦ The `minOccurs` and `maxOccurs` attributes of `xsd:element` determine how many of a given element are allowed in the instance document at that point. The default for each is 1. `maxOccurs` can be set to `unbounded` to indicate that any number of the element may appear.

✦ There are 44 built-in simple types, including many numeric, string, time, and XML types.

✦ The `xsd:simpleType` element defines a new type for an element or attribute that can only contain character data.

✦ You can define your own simple types by restricting an existing type such as `xsd:string` with the `xsd:restriction` element. The `base` attribute of the `xsd:restriction` child specifies what type you're deriving from.

✦ Each `xsd:restriction` element contains one or more child elements representing facets: `xsd:minInclusive`, `xsd:minExclusive`, `xsd:maxInclusive`, `xsd:maxExclusive`, `xsd:enumeration`, `xsd:whiteSpace`, `xsd:pattern`, `xsd:length`, `xsd:minLength`, `xsd:maxLength`, `xsd:totalDigits`, and/or `xsd:fractionDigits`.

✦ An `xsd:simpleType` element can create a new type by unifying the value spaces of existing types. Each existing type combined into the new type is identified by an `xsd:union` child element.

✦ A list type can hold one or more white space-separated instances of an existing type. Such a type is defined by the `xsd:list` child of an `xsd:simpleType` element.

✦ Schemas declare attributes with `xsd:attribute` elements.

✦ The `xsd:import` element imports declarations for elements and attributes in a different namespace from another schema document.

✦ Adding `xsd:annotation` elements helps make your schemas more readable.

✦ The `xsd:documentation` child of an `xsd:annotation` element provides information for human readers.

✦ The `xsd:appInfo` child of an `xsd:annotation` element provides information for software programs reading the schema, though schema validators ignore it.

In the next chapter, we explore another standard XML application from the W3C, the Resource Description Framework (RDF). RDF is an XML application for encoding meta-data and information structures.

✦   ✦   ✦

The Resource Description Framework

◆ ◆ ◆ ◆

In This Chapter

What is RDF?

RDF statements

Basic RDF syntax

Abbreviated RDF syntax

Containers

◆ ◆ ◆ ◆

The Resource Description Framework (RDF) is an XML application for encoding metadata. It's particularly well suited for describing Web sites and Web pages so that search engines can not only index them but also understand what they're indexing. Once RDF and standard RDF vocabularies become prevalent on the Web, search engines will be able to determine whether a page titled Homer is talking about the father of Western literature or the father of Bart Simpson. This chapter discusses the nature of the resources RDF describes and the statements it describes those resources with.

What Is RDF?

Metadata is data about data—information about information. For example, the text of a book is its data. The name of the author, the address of the publisher, the copyright date, and so forth is metadata about the book. Metadata has many uses on the Web, including organizing, searching, filtering, and personalizing Web sites. Accurate metadata should make it much easier to find the Web sites you want while ignoring the Web sites you don't want.

To achieve these benefits, however, Web sites, search engines, and directories must agree to use a standard format for metadata. The Resource Description Framework is a World Wide Web Consortium (W3C)-recommended XML application for encoding, exchanging, and reusing structured metadata. RDF vocabularies can describe rating systems, site maps, privacy preferences, collaborative services, licensing restrictions, and more.

In general, metadata vocabularies must be customized for each individual knowledge domain. However, RDF strives to create a convention that controls how the semantics, syntax, and structure of metadata are formulated in the separate domains, so that metadata formats developed for one domain can be merged with formats developed for a second domain and used in a third domain without losing any of the clarity of the original statements. RDF is designed to make it easy for software to understand enough about a Web site so that it can discover resources on a site, catalog the site's content, rate that content, figure out who owns the content, learn under what terms and at what cost it may be used, and do other things a Web spider or intelligent agent might want to do.

RDF Statements

An RDF document or element makes *statements* about *resources*. A statement says that a certain resource has one or more properties. Each property has a type (that is, a name) and a value. The value of a property may be a literal, such as a string, number, or date; or it may be another resource.

A statement can be thought of as a triple composed of three items: resource, property type, and property value. For example, an RDF statement might say, "The book *XML Bible, Gold Edition* (ISBN: 0-7645-4819-0) has the author Elliotte Rusty Harold." Here the resource is "The book *XML Bible, Gold Edition* (ISBN: 0-7645-4819-0)," and the author property of this resource has the value "Elliotte Rusty Harold." Figure 24-1 is a pictorial description of this RDF statement.

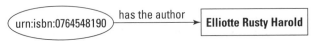

Figure 24-1: An RDF statement

A resource can be anything that can have a Uniform Resource Identifier (URI). URIs are a superset of the more common Uniform Resource Locators (URLs). As well as Web pages, URIs can identify books, television shows, individual people, and more. In the above example, an ISBN is used as a URI for a book. Thus, a resource might be an entire Web site (`http://www.norml.org/`), a single Web page (`http://www.mozilla.org/rdf/doc/index.html`), a specific HTML or XML element on a Web page identified with an XPointer (`http://ibiblio.org/xml/mailinglists.html#xpointer(/descendant::dt[7])`), a book (`urn:isbn:0764548190`), a person (`mailto:elharo@metalab.unc.edu`), or just about anything else—as long as a URI can be constructed for it. The only requirement for being a resource is a unique URI. This URI does not have to be a URL; it can be something else, such as an ISBN.

Resources are described with *properties*. A property is a specific characteristic, attribute, or relationship of a resource. Each property has a meaning that can be identified by the property's name and the associated schema. The schema should be found at the URI used for the property's namespace. The schema identifies the values, or value ranges, that are permitted for the property, and the types of resources it can describe.

Caution

RDF schemas (which should not be confused with the XML schemas described in Chapter 23) are still in the development stages, so don't be too surprised if you don't actually find a schema where one is supposed to be. Also note that a namespace URI pointing to a schema is an RDF requirement, not a requirement of namespaces in general. In fact, the namespaces specification specifically denies any such requirement.

RDF only defines an XML syntax for encoding these resource-property type-property value triples in XML. It does not define the actual vocabularies used to describe resources and properties. Eventually this will need to be addressed as well, at least if RDF is to be useful beyond a local intranet. Efforts are underway to produce standard vocabularies for content rating (PICS 2.0), personal information (P3P), news syndication (RSS), and digital library catalogs (Dublin Core). Others can be invented as needed.

An RDF statement combines a specific resource with a named property and its value. These three parts of the statement are called, respectively, the *subject*, the *predicate*, and the *object*. The resource being described is the subject, the property used to describe the resource is the predicate, and the value of the property is the statement's object.

Here's a normal, human readable statement:

Elliotte Rusty Harold is the creator of the Web site at the URL
`http://ibiblio.org/xml/`.

This same statement can be written in several other ways in English. For example:

The Web site at the URL `http://ibiblio.org/xml/` has the creator Elliotte Rusty Harold.

The Web site at the URL `http://ibiblio.org/xml/` was created by Elliotte Rusty Harold.

The creator of the Web site at the URL `http://ibiblio.org/xml/` is Elliotte Rusty Harold.

Elliotte Rusty Harold created the Web site at the URL
`http://ibiblio.org/xml/`.

However, all five versions mean exactly the same thing. In each version, the subject is the Web site at the URL `http://ibiblio.org/xml/`. The predicate is the creator property. The object is the value of the creator property, Elliotte Rusty Harold. Figure 24-2 diagrams this statement as RDF understands it.

Figure 24-2: The statement in diagram form

Note   The RDF subject, object, and predicate do not correspond to the common use of those terms in English grammar. Indeed, part of the purpose of RDF is to separate the meaning of subject, object, and predicate in an idea from their roles in any given sentence because the same idea can be expressed in multiple sentences, in each of which the grammatical subject, object, and predicate change places.

Basic RDF Syntax

The purpose of RDF is to write meaningful statements such as, "Elliotte Rusty Harold is the creator of the Web site at the URL `http://ibiblio.org/xml/`" in a standard XML format that computers can parse.

The RDF root element

The root element of an RDF document is `RDF`. This and all other RDF elements are placed in the `http://www.w3.org/1999/02/22-rdf-syntax-ns#` namespace. (As strange as it looks, the `#` is not a typo. It's there so that when an element name is added to the namespace URI, the result is a correct URL.) This namespace is usually either given the prefix `rdf` or set as the default namespace. For example, with an explicit prefix, an empty `RDF` element looks like this:

```
<rdf:RDF
  xmlns:rdf="http://www.w3.org/1999/02/22-rdf-syntax-ns#">
  <!-- rdf:Description elements will go here -->
</rdf:RDF>
```

With the default namespace, it looks like this:

```
<RDF xmlns="http://www.w3.org/1999/02/22-rdf-syntax-ns#">
  <!-- rdf:Description elements will go here -->
</RDF>
```

The Description element

An RDF statement is encoded in XML as a `Description` element. Each property of the resource being described is a child element of the `Description` element. The content of the child element is the value of the property. For example, Listing 24-1 translates the statement "Elliotte Rusty Harold created the Web site at the URL `http://ibiblio.org/xml/`" into RDF.

Listing 24-1: **The statement translated into RDF**

```
<rdf:RDF
  xmlns:rdf="http://www.w3.org/1999/02/22-rdf-syntax-ns#">
  <rdf:Description about="http://ibiblio.org/xml/">
    <Creator>Elliotte Rusty Harold</Creator>
  </rdf:Description>
</rdf:RDF>
```

This `rdf:RDF` element contains a single statement. The statement is encoded as an `rdf:Description` element. The resource this statement is about (the subject) is `http://ibiblio.org/xml/`. The predicate of this statement is the content of the `rdf:Description` element, `<Creator>Elliotte Rusty Harold</Creator>`. The object of this statement is the content of the `Creator` element, `Elliotte Rusty Harold`. In short, the statement says that the resource at `http://ibiblio.org/xml/` has a `Creator` property whose value is the literal string `Elliotte Rusty Harold`.

Namespaces

Namespaces are used to distinguish between RDF elements and elements from other vocabularies in property types and values. The `http://www.w3.org/1999/02/22-rdf-syntax-ns#` namespace is used for RDF elements, generally with an `rdf` prefix. In Listing 24-1, the `Creator` element is not in any namespace. However, the descriptions may (and should) come from a specified namespace. For instance, the `RDF` element in Listing 24-2 uses the Dublin Core vocabulary and the `http://purl.org/dc/elements/1.1/` namespace.

Listing 24-2: **Elements from the Dublin Core vocabulary are in the http://purl.org/dc/elements/1.1/ namespace**

```
<rdf:RDF
  xmlns:rdf="http://www.w3.org/1999/02/22-rdf-syntax-ns#"
  xmlns:dc="http://purl.org/dc/elements/1.1/">
  <rdf:Description about="http://ibiblio.org/xml/">
    <dc:creator>Elliotte Rusty Harold</dc:creator>
  </rdf:Description>
</rdf:RDF>
```

The Dublin Core

The Dublin Core (http://purl.org/dc/) is a collection of elements designed to help researchers find electronic resources in a manner similar to using a library card catalog. Dublin Core elements include basic cataloging information. In particular:

- ✦ TITLE: The name of the resource.

- ✦ CREATOR: The person or organization that created most of the resource, for example, the author of a novel or the photographer who took a picture.

- ✦ SUBJECT: The topic of the resource.

- ✦ DESCRIPTION: A brief description of the resource, such as an abstract.

- ✦ PUBLISHER: The person or organization making the resource available, for example, IDG Books, Claremont University, or Apple Computer.

- ✦ CONTRIBUTOR: A non-CREATOR who contributed to the resource, for example, the illustrator or editor of a novel.

- ✦ DATE: The date the resource was made available in its present form, generally in the format YYYY-MM-DD, such as 1969-06-29.

- ✦ TYPE: The category of the resource, for example, Web page, short story, poem, article, or photograph. Work is ongoing to produce a definitive list of acceptable resource categories. The current draft list (http://dublincore.org/documents/dcmi-type-vocabulary/) includes collection, dataset, event, image, interactive resource, service, software, sound, and text. These will likely be divided into subtypes in the future.

- ✦ FORMAT: The format of the resource, such as PDF, HTML, or JPEG. This would most likely be given as a MIME media type, such as application/pdf, text/html, or image/jpeg.

- ✦ IDENTIFIER: A unique string or number for the resource, for example, a URL or an ISBN.

- ✦ SOURCE: A string or number that uniquely identifies the work from which the resource was derived. For instance, a Web page with the text of Jerome K. Jerome's nineteenth century novel *Three Men in a Boat* might use this to note the specific edition from which text was scanned.

- ✦ LANGUAGE: The primary language in which the resource is written as ISO 639 language code, such as en for English.

- ✦ RELATION: An identifier for a different resource that is somehow related to this resource, probably by using an identifier string like the IDENTIFIER property. For example, if the resource were a newspaper story about a company, then this property might include the URI of that company's home page or a mailto URL for the author of the article.

✦ COVERAGE: The coverage property identifies the scope of applicability of the resource in time, space, jurisdiction, or some other dimension. For example, if the resource were a decision by the United States Court of Appeals for the Ninth Circuit, then the coverage might be California, Oregon, Washington, Arizona, Montana, Idaho, Nevada, Alaska, Hawaii, Guam, and the Northern Mariana Islands. If the resource were a volume of an encyclopedia, then the coverage might be the letter *A*.

✦ RIGHTS: Copyright and other intellectual property notices specifying the conditions under which the resource may or may not be used.

The Dublin Core is used throughout the examples in this chapter. However, you are by no means limited to using only these elements. You are free to use different standard and nonstandard vocabularies and namespaces for properties as long as you put them in a namespace.

Multiple properties and statements

A single `Description` element can specify more than one property of a resource. For instance, what's missing from the previous statement is the name of the site, Cafe con Leche. A statement that includes this is, "Elliotte Rusty Harold is the author of the Cafe con Leche Web site at the URL `http://ibiblio.org/xml/`." Rewritten in more stilted, RDF-like syntax, this becomes "The Web site at the URL `http://ibiblio.org/xml/` has the name Cafe con Leche and was created by Elliotte Rusty Harold." Figure 24-3 diagrams this statement. Listing 24-3 shows how to add the property name to the RDF serialization in a natural way as simply one more child of `rdf:Description`, `dc:title`.

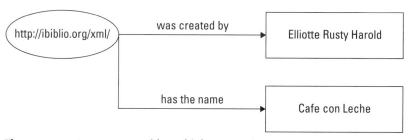

Figure 24-3: A statement with multiple properties

Listing 24-3: **A statement with multiple properties in RDF serialization form**

```
<rdf:RDF
  xmlns:rdf="http://www.w3.org/1999/02/22-rdf-syntax-ns#"
  xmlns:dc="http://purl.org/dc/elements/1.1/">

  <rdf:Description about="http://ibiblio.org/xml/">
    <dc:creator>Elliotte Rusty Harold</dc:creator>
    <dc:title>Cafe con Leche</dc:title>
  </rdf:Description>

</rdf:RDF>
```

A single RDF element can contain any number of Description elements, allowing it to make any number of statements. For example, suppose you want to make the two separate statements "Elliotte Rusty Harold is the author of the Cafe con Leche Web site at the URL http://ibiblio.org/xml/" and "Elliotte Rusty Harold is the author of the Cafe au Lait Web site at the URL http://www.cafeaulait.org/." These are two statements about two different resources. Listing 24-4 shows how these are encoded in RDF.

Listing 24-4: **Two separate statements encoded in RDF**

```
<rdf:RDF
  xmlns:rdf="http://www.w3.org/1999/02/22-rdf-syntax-ns#"
  xmlns:dc="http://purl.org/dc/elements/1.1/">

  <rdf:Description about="http://ibiblio.org/xml/">
    <dc:creator>Elliotte Rusty Harold</dc:creator>
    <dc:title>Cafe con Leche</dc:title>
  </rdf:Description>

  <rdf:Description about="http://www.cafeaulait.org/">
    <dc:creator>Elliotte Rusty Harold</dc:creator>
    <dc:title>Cafe au Lait</dc:title>
  </rdf:Description>

</rdf:RDF>
```

Resource valued properties

A slightly more complicated example is the statement, "The Cafe con Leche Web site at the URL `http://ibiblio.org/xml/` has the creator Elliotte Rusty Harold, whose e-mail address is `elharo@metalab.unc.edu`." The e-mail address is the key. It provides a unique identifier for an individual, specifically the URL `mailto:elharo@metalab.unc.edu`. Thus, the individual becomes a resource rather than simply a literal. This resource is the value of the creator property of the `http://ibiblio.org/xml/` resource. Figure 24-4 diagrams this statement.

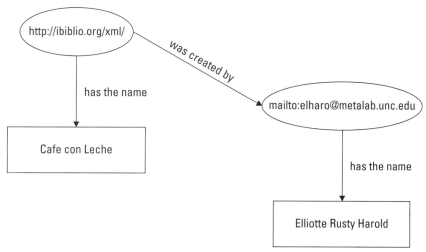

Figure 24-4: A statement with a resource valued property

Encoding this statement in RDF is straightforward. Simply give the `dc:creator` element a `Description` child that describes the `mailto:elharo@metalab.unc.edu` resource, as in Listing 24-5.

Listing 24-5: A statement encoded in RDF with nested Description elements

```
<RDF xmlns="http://www.w3.org/1999/02/22-rdf-syntax-ns#"
     xmlns:dc="http://purl.org/dc/elements/1.1/">

  <Description about="http://ibiblio.org/xml/">
    <dc:title>Cafe con Leche</dc:title>
    <dc:creator>
      <Description about="mailto:elharo@metalab.unc.edu">
        <dc:title>Elliotte Rusty Harold</dc:title>
      </Description>
```

Continued

Listing 24-5 *(continued)*

```
    </dc:creator>
   </Description>
</RDF>
```

There's no limit to the depth to which descriptions can be nested, nor is there any limit to the number of properties that can be applied to a `Description` element, nested or unnested.

RDF also provides an alternate syntax in which `Description` elements are not nested inside each other. Instead, the resource being described contains an `rdf:resource` attribute that points to the URI of the `Description` element. For example, Listing 24-6 is an equivalent serialization of the statement "The Cafe con Leche Web site at the URL `http://ibiblio.org/xml/` has the creator Elliotte Rusty Harold, whose e-mail address is `elharo@metalab.unc.edu`."

Listing 24-6: Descriptions by reference using the resource attribute

```
<rdf:RDF
  xmlns:rdf="http://www.w3.org/1999/02/22-rdf-syntax-ns#"
  xmlns:dc="http://purl.org/dc/elements/1.1/">

  <rdf:Description about="http://ibiblio.org/xml/">
    <dc:title>Cafe con Leche</dc:title>
    <dc:creator rdf:resource="mailto:elharo@metalab.unc.edu"/>
  </rdf:Description>

  <rdf:Description about="mailto:elharo@metalab.unc.edu">
    <dc:title>Elliotte Rusty Harold</dc:title>
  </rdf:Description>

</rdf:RDF>
```

Although this syntax is harder for a human reader to parse, it doesn't present any significant difficulties to a computer program. The primary advantage of this form is that it allows the same property to be attached to multiple resources. For example, consider the statement, "Elliotte Rusty Harold, whose e-mail address is `elharo@metalab.unc.edu`, created both the Cafe con Leche Web site at the URL `http://ibiblio.org/xml/` and the Cafe au Lait Web site at the URL `http://ibiblio.org/javafaq/`", which is diagrammed in Figure 24-5. This is easily serialized, as shown in Listing 24-7. The description of the resource `mailto:elharo@ metalab.unc.edu` does not have to be repeated.

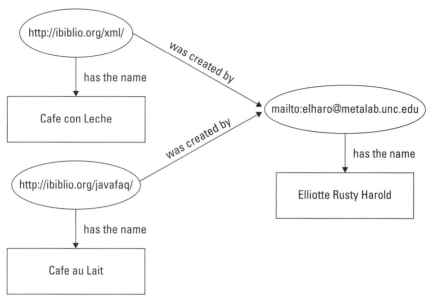

Figure 24-5: A statement with the same property attached to multiple resources

Listing 24-7: A statement with the same property attached to multiple resources

```
<rdf:RDF
  xmlns:rdf="http://www.w3.org/1999/02/22-rdf-syntax-ns#"
  xmlns:dc="http://purl.org/dc/elements/1.1/">

  <rdf:Description about="http://ibiblio.org/xml/">
    <dc:title>Cafe con Leche</dc:title>
    <dc:creator rdf:resource="mailto:elharo@metalab.unc.edu"/>
  </rdf:Description>

  <rdf:Description about="http://ibiblio.org/javafaq/">
    <dc:title>Cafe au Lait</dc:title>
    <dc:creator rdf:resource="mailto:elharo@metalab.unc.edu"/>
  </rdf:Description>

  <rdf:Description about="mailto:elharo@metalab.unc.edu">
    <dc:title>Elliotte Rusty Harold</dc:title>
  </rdf:Description>

</rdf:RDF>
```

XML valued properties

Property values are most commonly either pure text or resources. However, they may also contain well-formed XML markup that is not itself RDF markup. In this case, the property element must have a `parseType` attribute with the value `Literal`, as shown in Listing 24-8.

Listing 24-8: **A literal property value that uses XML markup**

```
<rdf:RDF
  xmlns:rdf="http://www.w3.org/1999/02/22-rdf-syntax-ns#"
  xmlns:dc="http://purl.org/dc/elements/1.1/"
  xmlns:nm="http://ibiblio.org/xml/names/">

  <rdf:Description about="http://ibiblio.org/xml/">
    <dc:creator parseType="Literal">
      <nm:FirstName>Elliotte</nm:FirstName>
      <nm:MiddleName>Rusty</nm:MiddleName>
      <nm:LastName>Harold</nm:LastName>
    </dc:creator>
  </rdf:Description>

</rdf:RDF>
```

Without `parseType="Literal"`, the value of a property must be a resource or parsed character data only. It must not contain any embedded markup.

Abbreviated RDF Syntax

As well as the basic syntax used above, RDF also defines an abbreviated syntax that uses attributes instead of parsed character data content. This is convenient when RDF data is embedded in an HTML page, because a Web browser can simply ignore the RDF tags without any effect on the rendered page. The two syntaxes are completely equivalent from the perspective of an RDF (as opposed to HTML) parser.

In abbreviated syntax, each property becomes an attribute of the `Description` element. The name of the property is the name of the attribute. If the property has a literal value, the value of the property is the value of the attribute. If the property has a resource value, the value of the property is the URI of the resource, and a separate `Description` element describes the resource. Because the `Description` element no longer has a variety of child elements, it does not need a closing tag and is normally written using an empty-element tag.

The simple statement "Elliotte Rusty Harold created the Web site `http://ibib-lio.org/xml/`" is written like this in abbreviated form:

```
<RDF xmlns="http://www.w3.org/1999/02/22-rdf-syntax-ns#"
    xmlns:dc="http://purl.org/dc/elements/1.1/">
  <Description about="http://ibiblio.org/xml/"
    dc:creator="Elliotte Rusty Harold" />
</RDF>
```

The statement "Elliotte Rusty Harold created the Cafe con Leche Web site `http://ibiblio.org/xml/`" is written like this in abbreviated form:

```
<RDF xmlns="http://www.w3.org/1999/02/22-rdf-syntax-ns#"
    xmlns:dc="http://purl.org/dc/elements/1.1/">
  <Description about="http://ibiblio.org/xml/"
    dc:creator="Elliotte Rusty Harold"
    dc:title="Cafe con Leche" />
</RDF>
```

Resource valued properties are trickier to abbreviate. The statement, "The Cafe con Leche Web site at the URL `http://ibiblio.org/xml/` has the creator Elliotte Rusty Harold, whose e-mail address is `elharo@metalab.unc.edu`" can be abbreviated like this:

```
<rdf:RDF
  xmlns:rdf="http://www.w3.org/1999/02/22-rdf-syntax-ns#"
  xmlns:dc="http://purl.org/dc/elements/1.1/">
  <rdf:Description about="http://ibiblio.org/xml/"
                  dc:title="Cafe con Leche">
    <dc:creator rdf:resource="mailto:elharo@metalab.unc.edu"
      dc:title="Elliotte Rusty Harold" />
  </rdf:Description>
</rdf:RDF>
```

Here the `Description` element is nonempty because it has a `dc:creator` child. However, it still doesn't contain any character data except white space.

Containers

When an RDF element describes a resource with multiple properties of the same type, for example, to say that a document was written by multiple people or to list mirror sites where a Web page can be found, a container can group the property values. Every item in the group is a property value of the same type (property name). This allows you to describe the group as a whole rather than merely describe individual items in the container. RDF defines three kinds of containers:

✦ Bag: A group of unordered properties

✦ Seq: A sequence (ordered list) of properties

✦ Alt: A list of alternative properties from which a single one is chosen

The Bag container

A bag is a list of property values (resources and literals), in no particular order, all of which share the same property name (type). This allows you to declare a property that has more than one value. This would be useful, for instance, if you were specifying the author property of a book with multiple authors, or the member property of a committee. A bag may contain duplicate values.

A bag of properties is represented by a Bag element. Each item in the bag is an li child element of the Bag. The Bag itself is a child of the Description to which it applies.

For example, consider the statement, "The Cafe con Leche Web site at http://ibiblio.org/xml/ was created by Elliotte Rusty Harold to provide XML news, XML mailing lists, XML conferences, and XML books." This is diagrammed in Figure 24-6. The four main subjects of the site can be collected in a Bag, as shown in Listing 24-9.

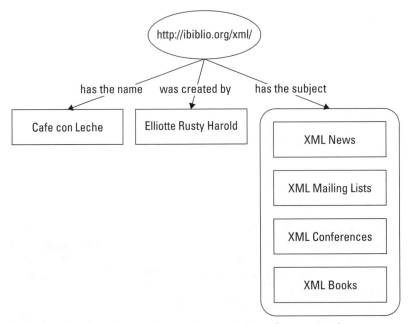

Figure 24-6: The statement uses a bag containing four properties

Listing 24-9: **A bag with four members**

```
<rdf:RDF
  xmlns:rdf="http://www.w3.org/1999/02/22-rdf-syntax-ns#"
  xmlns:dc="http://purl.org/dc/elements/1.1/">

  <rdf:Description about="http://ibiblio.org/xml/">
    <dc:title>Cafe con Leche</dc:title>
    <dc:creator>Elliotte Rusty Harold</dc:creator>
    <dc:subject>
      <rdf:Bag>
        <rdf:li>XML News</rdf:li>
        <rdf:li>XML Mailing lists</rdf:li>
        <rdf:li>XML Conferences</rdf:li>
        <rdf:li>XML Books</rdf:li>
      </rdf:Bag>
    </dc:subject>
  </rdf:Description>

</rdf:RDF>
```

If the members of the bag are resources rather than literals, they're identified with a resource attribute whose value is a URI for the resource. For example, Listing 24-10 provides a simple site map for Cafe con Leche.

Listing 24-10: **A simple site map for Cafe con Leche in a Bag**

```
<rdf:RDF
  xmlns:rdf="http://www.w3.org/1999/02/22-rdf-syntax-ns#"
  xmlns:dc="http://purl.org/dc/elements/1.1/">

  <rdf:Description about="http://ibiblio.org/xml/">
    <dc:title>Cafe con Leche</dc:title>
    <dc:creator>Elliotte Rusty Harold</dc:creator>
    <dc:subject>
      <rdf:Bag>
        <rdf:li
          resource="http://ibiblio.org/xml/news2001.html"/>
        <rdf:li
          resource="http://ibiblio.org/xml/mailinglists.html"/>
        <rdf:li
          resource="http://ibiblio.org/xml/books.html"/>
        <rdf:li
          resource="http://ibiblio.org/xml/tradeshows.html"/>
      </rdf:Bag>
```

Continued

Listing 24-10 *(continued)*

```
      </dc:subject>
    </rdf:Description>

    <rdf:Description
      about="http://ibiblio.org/xml/news2001.html">
      <dc:title>XML News from 2001</dc:title>
    </rdf:Description>

    <rdf:Description
      about="http://ibiblio.org/xml/books.html">
      <dc:title>XML Books</dc:title>
    </rdf:Description>

    <rdf:Description
      about="http://ibiblio.org/xml/mailinglists.html">
      <dc:title>XML Mailing Lists</dc:title>
    </rdf:Description>

    <rdf:Description
      about="http://ibiblio.org/xml/tradeshows.html">
      <dc:title>XML Trade Shows and Conferences</dc:title>
    </rdf:Description>

  </rdf:RDF>
```

The Seq container

A sequence container is similar to a bag container. However, it guarantees that the order of the contents is maintained. Sequences are written exactly like bags, except that the Seq element replaces the Bag element. For example, this sequence guarantees that when the Subject is read out by an RDF parser, it comes out in the order XML News, XML Mailing Lists, XML Conferences, XML Books, and not some other order, such as XML Books, XML Conferences, XML Mailing Lists, XML News.

```
<dc:subject>
  <rdf:Seq>
    <rdf:li>XML News</rdf:li>
    <rdf:li>XML Mailing lists</rdf:li>
    <rdf:li>XML Conferences</rdf:li>
    <rdf:li>XML Books</rdf:li>
  </rdf:Seq>
</dc:subject>
```

In practice, the order of properties in a container is rarely important, so sequences aren't used as much as bags and alternatives.

The Alt container

An `Alt` container holds one or more items from which a single one is picked. For example, this might be used to describe the mirrors of a Web site. Consider the statement The Cafe au Lait Web site at `http://www.cafeaulait.org/` created by Elliotte Rusty Harold is mirrored at ibiblio (`http://www.ibiblio.org/javafaq/`), Sunsite Sweden (`http://sunsite.kth.se/javafaq/`), and Sunsite Switzerland (`http://sunsite.cnlab-switch.ch/javafaq/`). Because only one of these mirror sites is desired, they can be placed in an alternative list. Listing 24-11 shows the RDF serialization.

Listing 24-11: **Mirror sites of Cafe au Lait in an Alt**

```
<rdf:RDF
  xmlns:rdf="http://www.w3.org/1999/02/22-rdf-syntax-ns#"
  xmlns:dc="http://purl.org/dc/elements/1.1/">

  <rdf:Description about="http://www.cafeaulait.org/">
    <dc:title>Cafe au Lait</dc:title>
    <dc:creator>Elliotte Rusty Harold</dc:creator>
    <dc:publisher>
      <rdf:Alt>
        <rdf:li resource =
         "http://www.ibiblio.org/javafaq/" />
        <rdf:li resource =
         "http://sunsite.kth.se/javafaq/" />
        <rdf:li resource =
         "http://sunsite.cnlab-switch.ch/javafaq/" />
      </rdf:Alt>
    </dc:publisher>
  </rdf:Description>

  <rdf:Description
    about="http://www.ibiblio.org/javafaq/">
    <dc:publisher>ibiblio</dc:publisher>
  </rdf:Description>

  <rdf:Description
    about="http://sunsite.cnlab-switch.ch/javafaq/">
    <dc:publisher>Sunsite Switzerland</dc:publisher>
  </rdf:Description>

  <rdf:Description
    about="http://sunsite.kth.se/javafaq/">
    <dc:publisher>Sunsite Sweden</dc:publisher>
  </rdf:Description>

</rdf:RDF>
```

Statements about containers

Statements can be made about a container as a whole, separate from statements about individual items in the container. You may want to say that a particular person developed a Web site without implying that he or she personally wrote each and every page on the site. Or, perhaps you want to claim a copyright on a collection of links without claiming a copyright on the pages to which you're linking. (For example, the market values Yahoo's collection of links and descriptions at around ten billion dollars, even though Yahoo owns essentially none of the pages to which it links.) In fact, the individual members of the container might have different copyrights than the container itself. Figure 24-7 diagrams this.

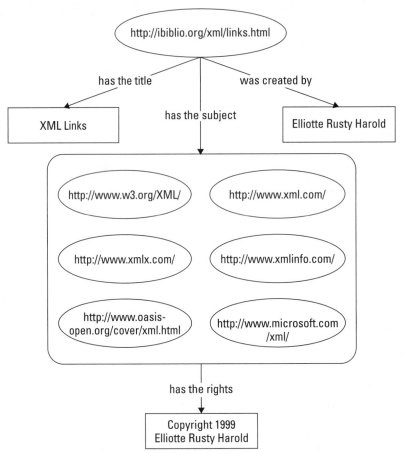

Figure 24-7: A Bag whose rights information is different than the rights information of the individual members of the Bag

To encode this in RDF, give the container (Bag, Seq, or Alt) an ID attribute. Description elements with about attributes, whose value is a relative URL pointing to the container ID, describe the container. This is shown in Listing 24-12.

Listing 24-12: **A description of a container encoded in RDF**

```
<rdf:RDF
  xmlns:rdf="http://www.w3.org/1999/02/22-rdf-syntax-ns#"
  xmlns:dc="http://purl.org/dc/elements/1.1/">

  <rdf:Description
    about="http://ibiblio.org/xml/links.html">
    <dc:title>XML Links</dc:title>
    <dc:creator>Elliotte Rusty Harold</dc:creator>
    <dc:subject>
      <rdf:Bag ID="links">
        <rdf:li resource="http://www.w3.org/XML/"/>
        <rdf:li resource="http://www.xml.com/"/>
        <rdf:li resource="http://www.xmlinfo.com/"/>
        <rdf:li resource="http://www.microsoft.com/xml/"/>
        <rdf:li
          resource="http://www.oasis-open.org/cover/xml.html"/>
        <rdf:li resource="http://www.xmlx.com/"/>
      </rdf:Bag>
    </dc:subject>
  </rdf:Description>

  <rdf:Description about="#links">
    <dc:rights>
      Copyright 1999 Elliotte Rusty Harold
    </dc:rights>
  </rdf:Description>

  <rdf:Description about="http://www.w3.org/XML/">
    <dc:title>The W3C</dc:title>
    <dc:rights>
      Copyright 1997 W3C (MIT, INRIA, Keio)
    </dc:rights>
  </rdf:Description>

  <rdf:Description about="http://www.xml.com/">
    <dc:title>xml.com</dc:title>
    <dc:rights>
      Copyright 1998-1999 Seybold Publications
      and O'Reilly &amp; Associates, Inc.
    </dc:rights>
  </rdf:Description>
```

Continued

Listing 24-12 *(continued)*

```
<rdf:Description about="http://www.xmlinfo.com/">
  <dc:title>XML Info</dc:title>
  <dc:creator>James Tauber</dc:creator>
</rdf:Description>

<rdf:Description about="http://www.microsoft.com/xml/">
  <dc:title>Microsoft's XML Page</dc:title>
  <dc:rights>Copyright 1999 Microsoft Corporation</dc:rights>
</rdf:Description>

<rdf:Description
  about="http://www.oasis-open.org/cover/xml.html">
  <dc:title>Robin Cover's XML Web Page</dc:title>
  <dc:rights>
    Copyright Robin Cover and OASIS, 1994-98
  </dc:rights>
</rdf:Description>

<rdf:Description about="http://www.xmlx.com/">
  <dc:title>XML Exchange</dc:title>
  <dc:publisher>CommerceNet</dc:publisher>
</rdf:Description>

</rdf:RDF>
```

Statements about container members

Sometimes you do want to make a statement about each member of a container, but you don't want to repeat the same description three or four times. For example, you may want to specify that the title and creator of each of the mirror sites is Cafe au Lait and Elliotte Rusty Harold, respectively, as shown in Figure 24-8.

You can include an ID attribute in the Bag, Seq, or Alt element whose value is a name by which descriptions can be applied to all the members of the container. For example, suppose you want to apply a copyright notice to each page in a Bag. Listing 24-13 accomplishes this.

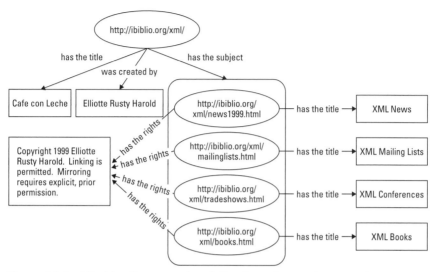

Figure 24-8: Attaching the same description to each page in a container

---

Listing 24-13: **A description of each element in a Bag container**

```
<rdf:RDF
  xmlns:rdf="http://www.w3.org/1999/02/22-rdf-syntax-ns#"
  xmlns:dc="http://purl.org/dc/elements/1.1/">

  <rdf:Description about="http://ibiblio.org/xml/">
    <dc:title>Cafe con Leche</dc:title>
    <dc:creator>Elliotte Rusty Harold</dc:creator>
    <dc:subject>
      <rdf:Bag ID="pages">
        <rdf:li
          resource="http://ibiblio.org/xml/news1999.html"/>
        <rdf:li
        resource="http://ibiblio.org/xml/mailinglists.html"/>
        <rdf:li
          resource="http://ibiblio.org/xml/books.html"/>
        <rdf:li
        resource="http://ibiblio.org/xml/tradeshows.html"/>
      </rdf:Bag>
    </dc:subject>
  </rdf:Description>
```

Continued

Listing 24-13 *(continued)*

```
<rdf:Description aboutEach="#pages">
  <dc:rights>
    Copyright 1999 Elliotte Rusty Harold
    Linking is permitted.
    Mirroring requires explicit, prior permission.
  </dc:rights>
</rdf:Description>

<rdf:Description
  about="http://ibiblio.org/xml/news1999.html">
  <dc:title>XML News from 1999</dc:title>
</rdf:Description>

<rdf:Description about="http://ibiblio.org/xml/books.html">
  <dc:title>XML Books</dc:title>
</rdf:Description>

<rdf:Description
  about="http://ibiblio.org/xml/mailinglists.html">
  <dc:title>XML Mailing Lists</dc:title>
</rdf:Description>

<rdf:Description
  about="http://ibiblio.org/xml/tradeshows.html">
  <dc:title>XML Trade Shows and Conferences</dc:title>
</rdf:Description>

</rdf:RDF>
```

Statements about implied bags

Sometimes you want to make a statement about a group of resources that may or may not be members of the same container. For example, suppose you want to specify that every page on the Web site http://www.cafeaulait.org is Copyright 2001 Elliotte Rusty Harold. You can do this with a Description element that applies to all resources whose URI begins with the string http://www.cafeaulait.org. This Description element must have an aboutEachPrefix attribute whose value is the URI prefix of the resources to which the description applies. For example:

```
<rdf:Description aboutEachPrefix="http://www.cafeaulait.org">
  <dc:rights>Copyright 2001 Elliotte Rusty Harold</dc:rights>
</rdf:Description>
```

This `Description` element creates an implicit bag whose members are the resources matching the prefix. These resources may or may not be members of other containers in the RDF file, and they may or may not be sibling elements. The members of this implied bag are gathered from wherever they reside.

URI prefixes can be used to select only a subtree of a Web site. For example, this description claims that all pages at ibiblio.org in the /xml hierarchy are Copyright 2001 Elliotte Rusty Harold. However, it does not apply to other pages outside that hierarchy such as `http://ibiblio.org/id/asiasylum` or `http://ibiblio.org/stats/`.

```
<rdf:Description
  aboutEachPrefix="http://ibiblio.org/xml/">
  <dc:rights>Copyright 2001 Elliotte Rusty Harold</dc:rights>
</rdf:Description>
```

For another example, consider ISBNs that are assigned by publishers. All books from Hungry Minds have an ISBN that begins 07645. Thus, this `Description` element creates an implicit `Bag` containing only books published by Hungry Minds and assigns a `Publisher` property to each member:

```
<rdf:Description aboutEachPrefix="urn:isbn:07645">
  <dc:publisher>Hungry Minds</dc:publisher>
</rdf:Description>
```

RDF Schemas

Although there's no guarantee that a generic XML namespace URI points to anything in particular, RDF is stricter than that. Any namespace URI used in RDF should point to a schema for the vocabulary. The schema describes the semantics and allowed syntax of a particular element. For instance, the schema may say that the contents of a `DATE` element must be in the form `1999-12-31` and not in the form `December 31, 1999`. A schema may also make DTD-like statements, such as that each `BOOK` element must contain one or more `AUTHOR` child elements.

Exactly how a schema makes statements such as this is a subject of debate, and, in fact, RDF does not mandate any one schema language. You are free to use DTDs, W3C XML Schemas, RELAX schemas, or something else. In practice, current RDF schemas are mostly written in prose that human beings read. For example, part of the Dublin Core "schema" is shown in Figure 24-9. (In the long run, a more formal and complete schema for the Dublin Core is likely to be developed.)

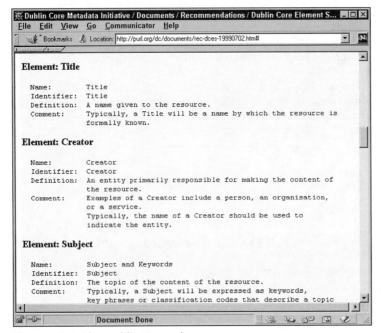

Figure 24-9: The Dublin Core schema

Eventually schemas will be written in a more formal syntax that computers can understand. In particular, the W3C RDF Schema Working Group is attempting to develop an RDF schema specification that writes RDF schemas in RDF. This will enable an RDF processor to validate a particular RDF document against the schemas it uses. However, this work is not finished as of June 2001. If you're curious about this project, you can retrieve the current draft of the RDF schema specification from http://www.w3.org/TR/rdf-schema/.

Summary

This chapter discussed the Resource Description Framework. In particular, you learned that:

✦ The Resource Description Framework (RDF) is an XML application for structured metadata. Metadata is information about information.

✦ An RDF document or element makes statements about resources.

✦ Each statement specifies a resource, a property of that resource, and the value of that property.

✦ A resource is anything that has a Uniform Resource Identifier (URI). Uniform Resource Locators (URLs) are just one form of URI.

✦ The value of a property may be plain text, another resource, or XML markup.

✦ All RDF elements are in the `http://www.w3.org/1999/02/22-rdf-syntax-ns#` namespace.

✦ The root element of an RDF document is `RDF`.

✦ An `RDF` element contains `Description` elements that make statements about resources.

✦ Each `Description` element contains either a literal property or a `resource` attribute whose value is the URI of the property value.

✦ RDF also defines an abbreviated syntax in which properties may be replaced by attributes of the same name on the `Description` element.

✦ The `Bag`, `Seq`, and `Alt` elements provide containers for multiple resources. Properties can be applied to the container as a whole, the individual elements of the container, or both.

✦ The namespace URI for each vocabulary used in an RDF document should point to a schema for the vocabulary.

RDF is a very abstract XML application. The information structures it describes are very high level. Indeed, RDF can almost be defined without any reference to XML at all. That's why I talked about RDF serialization as XML. Other encodings of the RDF model are possible. In the next chapter, I move in the opposite direction — to an XML application that is concerned with the most trivial details of low-level syntax, Canonical XML. Canonical XML is a standard serialization form for XML documents that resolves insignificant differences such as which encoding is used, what kind of quotes surround attributes, whether or not empty elements are represented by empty element tags, and so forth. For most intents and purposes, two documents with the same canonical form should be considered the same. Canonical XML is useful for standardizing XML documents before passing them to non-XML aware tools such as compressors and digital signature verifiers.

✦   ✦   ✦

Canonical XML

Although XML documents are text, really understanding one requires a substantial understanding of XML itself. A tool such as grep or wc that merely processes files is unlikely to be able to handle XML documents properly. For example, it won't know to look at the encoding declaration to determine the character set the document uses nor will it know how to resolve external entity references. Software that needs to compare two documents for equality really can't work without a deep understanding of XML. For instance, a program such as diff that merely compares two documents byte by byte won't realize that & and < represent the same character or that <HR/> is just syntax sugar for <HR></HR>.

Nonetheless there are many useful tools that work with binary and text documents without considering their contents: compression software such as zip, gzip, and StuffIt; encryption software such as PGP, crypt, and GnuPG; and text processing software such as wc, grep, and sed. To allow these tools to work with potentially complex XML documents that may be stored in multiple files, use various character sets and encodings, and be sweetened with any number of syntactic sugars such as CDATA sections and empty-element tags, you need to first translate the XML documents to a standard form that doesn't require a lot of complicated XML parsing to handle.

Canonical XML is such a format. Any XML document can be converted to canonical XML according to a deterministic algorithm. Two documents that are byte-for-byte identical when converted to canonical XML can be considered to be the same for almost all practical purposes. That is, they encode the same information. Differences between the original forms are purely matters of syntax and are insignificant from a semantic point of view. On the other hand, two documents whose canonical forms are not byte-for-byte identical may not be the same. They contain different information.

Canonical XML has many practical uses including archiving, transmission, and storage of XML documents. However, it is absolutely essential for calculating digital signatures for XML documents.

Four Documents

Consider the XML document in Listing 25-1. This is a fairly standard document, the likes of which you've seen many times in this book:

Listing 25-1: **An XML document that describes an order**

```
<?xml version="1.0" encoding="ISO-8859-1" standalone="yes"?>
<?xml-stylesheet type="text/css" href="order.css"?>
<!DOCTYPE ORDER [

  <!ATTLIST ORDER xmlns CDATA #FIXED
    "http://ns.macfaq.com/orders">
  <!ATTLIST CUSTOMER ID   ID       #REQUIRED>
  <!ATTLIST PRODUCT  SKU NMTOKEN #REQUIRED>
  <!ATTLIST PRICE     CURRENCY CDATA "$">
  <!ATTLIST SHIPPING CURRENCY CDATA "$">

]>
<ORDER xmlns="http://ns.macfaq.com/orders">
  <CUSTOMER ID=" c3475 ">Ace &amp; Gary, Ltd.</CUSTOMER>
  <PRODUCT SKU=" 57333 ">QuarkXPress 4.1</PRODUCT>
  <PRICE DISCOUNT="10%">819.95</PRICE>
  <SHIPPING>8.95</SHIPPING>
  <EXPEDITE/>
</ORDER>
<!-- Bob, this order's going to the boss's nephew.
     Please make sure it goes out ASAP. Thanks.
     Ed -->
```

Now consider Listing 25-2. This is very similar to Listing 25-1. Indeed, it seems to contain the same information. Is this in fact an equivalent document?

Listing 25-2: **An alternative XML document that describes the same order**

```
<?xml version='1.0' encoding='UTF-8'?>
<?xml-stylesheet type='text/xml' href='order.xsl'?>
<OP:ORDER
  xmlns:OP='http://ns.macfaq.com/orders'>
  <OP:CUSTOMER ID='c3475'>Ace &#38; Gary, Ltd.</OP:CUSTOMER>
  <OP:PRODUCT SKU='57333'>QuarkXPress 4.1</OP:PRODUCT>
  <OP:PRICE CURRENCY='$' DISCOUNT='10%'>819.95</OP:PRICE>
```

```
   <OP:SHIPPING CURRENCY='$'>8.95</OP:SHIPPING>
   <OP:EXPEDITE ></OP:EXPEDITE>
</OP:ORDER>
<!-- Bob, this customer's in no particular hurry.
     Take your time filling this order.
     Ed -->
```

Clearly both Listings 25-1 and 25-2 describe an order for QuarkXPress 4.1 from a company named Ace & Gary, Ltd. for $819.95 and $8.95 shipping and handling. However, the details are quite different between the two documents. Among others:

✦ Listing 25-1 has an internal DTD subset that provides some default attributes; Listing 25-2 includes those attributes directly in the instance document.

✦ Listing 25-1 uses a CSS style sheet; Listing 25-2 uses an XSLT style sheet.

✦ In Listing 25-1, the ID attribute of the CUSTOMER element and the SKU attribute of the PRODUCT element have some extra white space that isn't present in the same attributes in Listing 25-2.

✦ In Listing 25-1, the EXPEDITE element uses an empty-element tag; in Listing 25-2, it uses a start tag-end tag pair.

✦ Listing 25-1 places double quote marks around attribute values; Listing 25-2 uses single quotes.

✦ Listing 25-1 uses entity references to escape characters that would otherwise be interpreted as markup such as & and <; Listing 25-2 uses character references.

✦ The namespace is http://ns.macfaq.com/orders in both documents, but Listing 25-1 makes this the default namespace. Listing 25-2 binds this URI to the OP prefix.

✦ The comments after the root element end tag are quite different.

There might even be some differences that aren't apparent in the printed form in this book, such as whether lines end with a carriage return, a linefeed, or a carriage return/linefeed pair. Yet none of these differences seem important somehow. The content of the two documents is the same although the expression of that content is quite different.

Next consider Listing 25-3. This is yet another XML document describing an order for QuarkXPress 4.1 from Ace & Gary, Ltd. for $819.95 plus $8.95 shipping and handling. However, the element and attribute names use lowercase letters. Furthermore, the elements are indented differently and the order of the elements is mixed up. This time there's no style sheet at all. Still, this document seems to describe more or less the same information.

> **Listing 25-3: A second alternative XML document that describes the order**
>
> ```
> <?xml version="1.0"?>
> <order xmlns="http://ns.macfaq.com/orders">
>   <customer id='c3475'>
>     Ace &#x26; Gary, Ltd.
>   </customer>
>   <product sku='57333'>
>     QuarkXPress 4.1
>   </product>
>   <price discount='10%' currency="$">
>     819.95
>   </price>
>   <shipping currency="$" >
>     8.95
>   </shipping>
>   <expedite xmlns="http://ns.macfaq.com/orders"/>
> </order>
> ```

Now consider Listing 25-4. This is still another way to encode the order. It feels a lot like Listing 25-1. However, the character encoding is ISO-10646-UCS-2 instead of ISO-8859-1, so each character in this document occupies two bytes rather than one. There's also no standalone document declaration, so standalone has the default value no instead of the explicit value yes it had in Listing 25-1. Indeed this document cannot stand alone because it uses the external DTD shown in Listing 25-5, rather than an internal DTD subset; and this external DTD does provide default attribute values including the xmlns attribute that establishes the default namespace on the root element. Furthermore, for no apparent reason, the xmlns attribute is repeated in the EXPEDITE element's ATTLIST declaration. Finally, this DTD also includes all declarations necessary to make this document valid instead of merely well formed, unlike the DTD in Listing 25-1.

In the instance document, there's some extra white space used inside the tags to line up attribute values. Finally, Listing 25-4 uses a CDATA section to escape the ampersand in Ace & Gary, Ltd. rather than a character reference or an entity reference.

> **Listing 25-4: An XML document with an external DTD that describes an order**
>
> ```
> <?xml version="1.0" encoding="ISO-10646-UCS-2"?>
> <?xml-stylesheet type="text/css" href="order.css"?>
> <!DOCTYPE ORDER SYSTEM "order.dtd">
> <ORDER>
>   <CUSTOMER  ID="c3475"><![CDATA[Ace & Gary, Ltd.]]></CUSTOMER>
>   <PRODUCT SKU='57333'>QuarkXPress 4.1</PRODUCT>
> ```

```
<PRICE   DISCOUNT='10%' CURRENCY="$" >819.95</PRICE>
<SHIPPING>8.95</SHIPPING>
<EXPEDITE/>
</ORDER>
<!-- Bob, this order's going to the boss's nephew.
     Please make sure it goes out ASAP. Thanks.
     Ed -->
```

Listing 25-5: **A DTD for orders**

```
<!ELEMENT ORDER
     (CUSTOMER, PRODUCT, PRICE, SHIPPING, EXPEDITE?)>
<!ELEMENT CUSTOMER (#PCDATA)>
<!ELEMENT PRODUCT  (#PCDATA)>
<!ELEMENT PRICE    (#PCDATA)>
<!ELEMENT SHIPPING (#PCDATA)>
<!ELEMENT EXPEDITE EMPTY>

<!ATTLIST ORDER xmlns CDATA #FIXED
  "http://ns.macfaq.com/orders">
<!ATTLIST CUSTOMER ID   ID      #REQUIRED>
<!ATTLIST PRODUCT  SKU NMTOKEN #REQUIRED>
<!ATTLIST PRICE    CURRENCY CDATA "$"
                   DISCOUNT CDATA #IMPLIED>
<!ATTLIST SHIPPING CURRENCY CDATA "$">
<!ATTLIST EXPEDITE xmlns CDATA #FIXED
    "http://ns.macfaq.com/orders">
```

Are these four documents the same or different? Clearly, if you simply compare them byte-by-byte or character-by-character, then they are in fact different. But are those differences important to a client application reading them through an XML parser? Or will the parser simply report the same information regardless of the exact form this information takes in the XML document? If the documents are different, then which of the low-level differences are important and which aren't?

There is no one answer to these questions. To a large extent, what's considered significant and insignificant depends on the uses to which the document will be put. An order-processing system that automatically rejects invalid documents would accept Listing 25-4 and reject Listings 25-1, 25-2, and 25-3. However, a system that didn't require validity, but which did expect uppercase tags might accept Listings 25-1, 25-2, and 25-4, but would generate an error when presented with Listing 25-3. And a system that didn't care about case or white space might accept all four.

The Canonicalization Algorithm

Canonical XML is a standard serialization format for XML documents such that two documents with byte-for-byte identical canonical forms can reasonably be considered to be the same document. Canonicalization completely resolves differences in physical structure between documents such as which entity any given character is part of. It unifies various forms of syntactic sugar to a default representation. Furthermore, it makes some value judgments about whether certain parts of an XML document such as comments, processing instructions, and document type declarations should or should not be considered. The resulting canonical form is particularly well suited for use by tools such as diff and grep that are completely unaware of the normal processing behavior of an XML parser.

The canonicalization algorithm

The W3C-recommended algorithm for canonicalization of XML documents consists of 15 steps:

1. Encode the document in the UTF-8 encoding of Unicode without a byte order mark.

2. Change each line break to a single linefeed.

3. Normalize attribute values as a validating processor would do.

4. Replace character and parsed entity references with their actual replacement text.

5. Replace CDATA sections with their character content.

6. Delete the XML declaration and the document type declaration.

7. Convert empty-element tags to start tag-end tag pairs.

8. Normalize white space outside of the document element.

9. Normalize white space inside tags.

10. Retain all white space in character content.

11. Change all attribute value delimiters to double quote marks.

12. Replace illegal characters in attribute values and character content with entity references.

13. Add default attributes to each element.

14. Remove all unnecessary namespace declarations.

15. Sort the attributes (including namespace declarations) in each tag in a standard way.

Furthermore, you can choose whether or not to delete all comments. However, this step is not required. In essence there are two canonical forms, one with comments and one without.

After you've performed these steps, you can compare the documents byte by byte to decide whether or not they're equal. Let's explore the 15 steps by applying this algorithm to each of the four forms of the software order given in Listings 25-1 through 25-4.

Note   This is not the only way to define canonicalization. The Canonical XML specification actually uses a more technical description that is somewhat better suited for implementers rather than users. Any variation of the basic algorithm is acceptable provided that it produces the same results in the end.

1. Encode the document in the UTF-8 encoding of Unicode

XML documents can be written in a variety of character sets. However, the parser always converts these different character sets to Unicode when it reads the document. Since Unicode is a superset of almost all modern character sets, this works well. However, there are multiple encodings of Unicode with both fixed and variable numbers of bytes for character. For instance, UCS-4 uses four bytes for each character while UTF-8 uses between one and six bytes per character. For canonicalization, one such encoding must be chosen, and UTF-8 is the most efficient and the most broadly supported.

Documents encoded in Unicode, especially in the UTF-16, UCS-2, or UCS-4 encodings of Unicode, often begin with a byte order mark to establish the endianness of the document. If such a mark is present, it is deleted in this step since UTF-8 encoding does not depend on the byte-order of the host platform.

Cross-Reference   Chapter 7 discusses byte order marks and the various encodings of Unicode.

2. Change all line breaks to a linefeed

On Unix systems, lines end with a linefeed, Unicode, and ASCII character 10. On Macs, lines end with a carriage return, Unicode, and ASCII character 13. On Windows systems, lines typically end with both a carriage return and a linefeed in that order. Depending on where a document was created, it may use any or all of these conventions. However, no one really cares which line ending convention is used. Therefore XML parsers can read all three with equal facility.

Since the difference between these three conventions isn't really important or significant, canonical XML picks one. Specifically, it picks the linefeed. Every carriage return-linefeed pair in an XML document will be converted to a single linefeed. Every carriage return that is not part of a carriage return-linefeed pair is also converted to a single linefeed. Single linefeeds are left alone. Most of the time this change is invisible.

Note   Actually, this behavior is required of any XML parser. The step is just included here in case someone is writing software to canonicalize XML documents that for some strange reason does not use an XML parser.

Since this step is performed on input, before the document is even parsed, it does not affect any linefeeds or carriage returns that are encoded in the document with character references such as
 or . These are resolved at a later step.

3. Normalize all attribute values as a validating processor would do.

When an XML parser reads an attribute value, it throws away some of the space the attribute value contains and converts character and entity references to their replacement text. This process is called *normalization*. The algorithm for normalization is actually defined in XML 1.0 as follows:

1. Replace each character reference by the actual character it refers to.

2. Replace each entity reference by its normalized replacement text. (That is, recursively apply the normalization algorithm to any entities the attribute value uses.)

3. Replace each actual tab, carriage return, and linefeed (but not those that were included by a character reference such
, , or 	) with a single space.

Furthermore, if type of the attribute is not CDATA, then all leading and trailing spaces must be trimmed, and all runs of space inside the normalized value must be replaced by a single space. All attribute values have type CDATA, unless a DTD assigns a different type to them.

For example, Listing 25-1 contains these two elements:

```
<CUSTOMER ID=" c3475 ">Ace &amp; Gary, Ltd.</CUSTOMER>
<PRODUCT SKU=" 57333 ">QuarkXPress 4.1</PRODUCT>
```

After attribute normalization is performed, the extra white space around the edges is stripped like this:

```
<CUSTOMER ID="c3475">Ace &amp; Gary, Ltd.</CUSTOMER>
<PRODUCT SKU="57333">QuarkXPress 4.1</PRODUCT>
```

This only happens because the ID attribute is declared to have type ID and the SKU attribute is declared to have type NMTOKEN. If they had type CDATA, or if they were not explicitly declared to have a type, then the extra space in the attribute value would be retained.

If the document is serialized at this point of the process, the result may not be well-formed because attribute values may contain characters that are illegal in context such as ', ", &, and <. However, the canonicalization algorithm is not designed to produce well-formed XML at each step in the process. It is an entire process that must be followed. The intermediate states are not intended as anything more than input for the next step in the chain.

4. Replace all character and parsed entity references with their actual replacement text.

This step replaces all character references such as © and entity references such as & in element content with the actual characters they represent such as © and &. Characters in attribute content were already replaced in step 3. As with step 3, this may result in a malformed document.

This affects the customer element in three of the example documents. In Listing 25-1 the customer element was originally written like this:

```
<CUSTOMER ID="c3475">Ace &amp; Gary, Ltd.</CUSTOMER>
```

In canonical form it becomes this:

```
<CUSTOMER ID="c3475">Ace & Gary, Ltd.</CUSTOMER>
```

In Listing 25-2 the customer element was originally written like this:

```
<OP:CUSTOMER ID='c3475'>Ace &#38; Gary, Ltd.</OP:CUSTOMER>
```

In canonical form it becomes this:

```
<OP:CUSTOMER ID='c3475'>Ace & Gary, Ltd.</OP:CUSTOMER>
```

Listing 25-3 encoded the customer information like this:

```
<customer id='c3475'>
  Ace &#x26; Gary, Ltd.
</customer>
```

In canonical form it becomes this:

```
<customer id='c3475'>
  Ace & Gary, Ltd.
</customer>
```

The elements still aren't byte-for-byte identical, but the first three different ways of encoding the single character & have all been reconciled. The fourth way is reconciled in the next step.

5. Replace all CDATA sections with their character content.

Step 5 has the effect of removing the CDATA section delimiters, while leaving the contents intact. This may or may not produce malformed XML, depending on what was inside the CDATA section. For example, a CDATA section such as this

```
<![CDATA[Ace & Gary, Ltd.]]>
```

is changed into this:

```
Ace & Gary, Ltd.
```

Although this may look like XML markup, it is still just character data; and it will be further processed in step 11.

This step changes the customer information in Listing 25-4 into this:

```
<CUSTOMER ID="c3475">Ace & Gary, Ltd.</CUSTOMER>
```

6. Delete the XML declaration and the document type declaration

This step is straightforward. It simply removes the XML declaration (if any) and `DOCTYPE` declaration (if any). It does not remove any white space between or after these constructs, which tends to leave some excess blank lines. Processing instructions and comments before and after the root element are not touched in this step. However, any comments or processing instructions in the internal DTD subset are removed.

After this is done, Listing 25-1 becomes Listing 25-6; Listing 25-2 becomes Listing 25-7; Listing 25-3 becomes Listing 25-8; and Listing 25-4 becomes Listing 25-9.

Listing 25-6: Listing 25-1 after step 6

```
<?xml-stylesheet type="text/css" href="order.css"?>

<ORDER xmlns="http://ns.macfaq.com/orders">
  <CUSTOMER ID="c3475">Ace & Gary, Ltd.</CUSTOMER>
  <PRODUCT SKU='57333'>QuarkXPress 4.1</PRODUCT>
  <PRICE DISCOUNT='10%'>819.95</PRICE>
  <SHIPPING>8.95</SHIPPING>
  <EXPEDITE/>
</ORDER>
<!-- Bob, this order's going to the boss's nephew.
     Please make sure it goes out ASAP. Thanks.
     Ed -->
```

Listing 25-7: **Listing 25-2 after step 6**

```
<?xml-stylesheet type='text/xml' href='order.xsl'?>
<OP:ORDER
  xmlns:OP='http://ns.macfaq.com/orders'>
  <OP:CUSTOMER ID='c3475'>Ace & Gary, Ltd.</OP:CUSTOMER>
  <OP:PRODUCT SKU='57333'>QuarkXPress 4.1</OP:PRODUCT>
  <OP:PRICE CURRENCY='$' DISCOUNT='10%'>819.95</OP:PRICE>
  <OP:SHIPPING CURRENCY='$'>8.95</OP:SHIPPING>
  <OP:EXPEDITE ></OP:EXPEDITE>
</OP:ORDER>
<!-- Bob, this customer's in no particular hurry.
     Take your time filling this order.
  Ed -->
```

Listing 25-8: **Listing 25-3 after step 6**

```
<order xmlns="http://ns.macfaq.com/orders">
  <customer id='c3475'>
    Ace & Gary, Ltd.
  </customer>
  <product sku='57333'>
    QuarkXPress 4.1
  </product>
  <price discount='10%' currency="$">
    819.95
  </price>
  <shipping currency="$">
    8.95
  </shipping>
  <expedite xmlns="http://ns.macfaq.com/orders"/>
</order>
```

Listing 25-9: **Listing 25-4 after step 6**

```
<?xml-stylesheet type="text/css" href="order.css"?>

<ORDER>
```

Continued

Listing 25-9 *(continued)*

```
    <CUSTOMER  ID="c3475">Ace & Gary, Ltd.</CUSTOMER>
    <PRODUCT SKU='57333'>QuarkXPress 4.1</PRODUCT>
    <PRICE    DISCOUNT='10%' CURRENCY="$" >819.95</PRICE>
    <SHIPPING>8.95</SHIPPING>
    <EXPEDITE/>
  </ORDER>
  <!-- Bob, this order's going to the boss's nephew.
       Please make sure it goes out ASAP. Thanks.
       Ed -->
```

On the one hand, these documents are now a little more similar because all differences between the XML declarations and document type declarations have been eliminated. On the other hand, default attributes that were added from the DTD are no longer included in Listings 25-6 and 25-9. However, these will be added back in step 12.

7. Convert empty-element tags to start-end tag pairs.

Canonical XML standardizes empty-element syntax as two tags rather than one. For example, `<EXPEDITE/>` in Listings 25-1 and 25-4 is changed into `<EXPEDITE></EXPEDITE>`. In Listing 25-3, `<expedite xmlns="http://ns.mac-faq.com/orders"/>` is replaced by `<expedite xmlns="http://ns.macfaq.com/orders"></expedite>`. Listing 25-2 never used empty-element tags so it isn't changed by this step.

This emphasizes the point that there really shouldn't be any logical difference between `<A/>` and `<A></A>`. I have occasionally seen developers try to use this difference to signify the difference between an empty string value and a null value. However, this usage is not supported by XML or most XML parsers. If you need null values, the right way to indicate them is by adding an extra attribute to the empty element indicating that the value is null.

Tip The W3C XML schema language defines an `xsi:nil` attribute that can identify elements whose content is null. Simply add it to the elements that you want to specify as null and give it the value true, as in `<EXPEDITE xsi:nil="true"/>`. The `xsi` prefix should be mapped to the `http://www.w3.org/2001/XMLSchema-instance` namespace URI.

8. Normalize all white space outside of the document element.

The only things that should be left outside of the root element at this point are comments, processing instructions, and white space. In this step, all the white space outside the document element is thrown away. Then a single linefeed is placed after each comment or processing instruction outside the document element, except for the last one after the root element. The first goal here is to ensure that the canonical form of an XML document always begins with a ‹ character. The second goal is to place each comment and processing instruction on its own line.

For example, after step 6, the prolog of Listing 25-1 was this:

```
<?xml-stylesheet type="text/css" href="order.css"?>
```

After step 8, the blank lines have been removed, leaving:

```
<?xml-stylesheet type="text/css" href="order.css"?>
```

9. Normalize all white space inside tags.

Inside the angle brackets that delimit a tag, though outside any attribute values the tag contains, all line breaks are converted to spaces. (This means that multiline tags may become quite long.) All runs of space are compressed to a single space. Any space around the equals signs between attribute names and values is removed. Attribute values are not touched in this step.

For example, after step 7, the ORDER element of Listing 25-4 looked like this:

```
<ORDER>
  <CUSTOMER  ID="c3475">Ace & Gary, Ltd.</CUSTOMER>
  <PRODUCT SKU='57333'>QuarkXPress 4.1</PRODUCT>
  <PRICE    DISCOUNT='10%' CURRENCY="$" >819.95</PRICE>
  <SHIPPING>8.95</SHIPPING>
  <EXPEDITE></EXPEDITE>
</ORDER>
```

The extra spaces are now removed from each tag, leaving this:

```
<ORDER>
  <CUSTOMER ID="c3475">Ace & Gary, Ltd.</CUSTOMER>
  <PRODUCT SKU='57333'>QuarkXPress 4.1</PRODUCT>
  <PRICE DISCOUNT='10%' CURRENCY="$" >819.95</PRICE>
  <SHIPPING>8.95</SHIPPING>
  <EXPEDITE></EXPEDITE>
</ORDER>
```

In Listing 25-2, the OP:ORDER start tag appeared on two lines like this:

```
<OP:ORDER
  xmlns:OP="http://ns.macfaq.com/orders">
```

That is now compressed to a single line like this:

```
<OP:ORDER xmlns:OP="http://ns.macfaq.com/orders">
```

Listing 25-2 also had some extra space inside `OP:EXPEDITE` start tag. This element is now changed from this:

```
<OP:EXPEDITE ></OP:EXPEDITE>
```

to this:

```
<OP:EXPEDITE></OP:EXPEDITE>
```

10. Retain all white space in character content.

This rule is an unusual one because it tells you what not to do, rather than what to do. It says that white space in element content should be retained. Runs of spaces should not be changed to a single space. Tabs should not be converted to spaces or vice versa.

The reason this rule is here is to avoid some common misconceptions. Document authors, especially of data-oriented documents, often add extra space around tags to indent and prettify the markup. For example, in Listing 25-3 you find this element:

```
<price discount='10%' currency="$">
  819.95
</price>
```

This step says that you cannot convert that element into this one:

```
<price discount='10%' currency="$">819.95</price>
```

Canonically, they are not the same. Some applications may choose to treat them the same way and automatically trim the extra white space off of the first element. However, that's an application-level decision. XML parsers do not remove such excess white space for you, and it is retained in the canonical form.

The same is true of "ignorable white space," an unfortunate turn of phrase that refers to text nodes containing nothing but white space such as typically occurs between two tags. For example, in Listing 25-3, you also find this fragment:

```
</customer>
<product sku='57333'>
  QuarkXPress 4.1
</product>
<price discount='10%' currency="$">
```

You cannot place the start tags next to the end tags even though there's only ignorable white space between them. In other words, this is not canonically the same:

```
</customer><product sku='57333'>
  QuarkXPress 4.1
</product><price discount='10%' currency="$">
```

Again, an application that wants to ignore ignorable white space may treat the two as the same. However, that is a decision for the application to make, not the XML parser or canonicalizer.

11. Change all attribute value delimiters to double quote marks.

Most XML applications really don't care whether or not attribute values use single or double quotes; indeed, few parsers would even let an application know which was used. Canonical XML just picks the most common one, double quotes.

In this chapter's examples, Listings 25-1 and 25-4 only use double quotes, so they're unchanged. Listing 25-2 uses single quotes, so they must be shifted as shown in Listing 25-10.

Listing 25-10: **Listing 25-2 after step 10**

```
<?xml-stylesheet type='text/xml' href='order.xsl'?>
<OP:ORDER xmlns:OP="http://ns.macfaq.com/orders">
  <OP:CUSTOMER ID="c3475">Ace & Gary, Ltd.</OP:CUSTOMER>
  <OP:PRODUCT SKU="57333">QuarkXPress 4.1</OP:PRODUCT>
  <OP:PRICE CURRENCY="$" DISCOUNT="10%">819.95</OP:PRICE>
  <OP:SHIPPING CURRENCY="$">8.95</OP:SHIPPING>
  <OP:EXPEDITE></OP:EXPEDITE>
</OP:ORDER>
<!-- Bob, this customer's in no particular hurry.
     Take your time filling this order.
     Ed -->
```

Notice especially that this step only affects the quotes around attributes of elements, not any quotes that may be present around the pseudoattributes of an `xml-stylesheet` or other processing instruction. In Listing 25-10, these remain single quotes. XML parsers are not expected to understand the syntax or meaning of processing instruction data. (Indeed, processing instruction data is intended precisely for programs that are not XML parsers.) Therefore an XML canonicalizer should not change this data. For the same reason, it doesn't change any single quote that may be found inside comments, attribute values, or element content, only those which delimit attribute values.

Listing 25-3 uses both single and double quotes on different attributes. This step changes all the single quotes to double quotes and the double quotes are retained as shown in Listing 25-11.

> ### Listing 25-11: **Listing 25-3 after step 10**
>
> ```
> <order xmlns="http://ns.macfaq.com/orders">
>   <customer id="c3475">
>     Ace & Gary, Ltd.
>   </customer>
>   <product sku="57333">
>     QuarkXPress 4.1
>   </product>
>   <price discount="10%" currency="$">
>     819.95
>   </price>
>   <shipping currency="$">
>     8.95
>   </shipping>
>   <expedite xmlns="http://ns.macfaq.com/orders"></expedite>
> </order>
> ```

Of course, this means that an attribute whose value includes one or more double quotes is now malformed. However, that will be fixed in step 12.

12. Replace illegal characters in attribute values and character content with character references.

After the manipulations in steps 4, 5, and 11, it's entirely possible that attribute values and element content now contain characters they're not allowed to contain, including unescaped less than signs, ampersands, and greater than signs. The standard entity references <, &, and > are substituted for these characters. In addition, any carriage returns that remain are replaced by the character reference . Finally, any double quote marks that occur in attribute values (but not element content) are replaced by ".

In this chapter's examples, the only place this occurs is in the customer elements where there's an unescaped ampersand. In all four cases, the phrase:

```
Ace & Gary, Ltd.
```

is changed to:

```
Ace &amp; Gary, Ltd.
```

13. Add default attributes to each element.

In this step, all attributes that were not explicitly included in the instance document, but which were added as defaults in an ATTLIST declaration in the DTD, are explicitly added to the elements. The attribute value is always double quoted, and the content is escaped in the same way as attributes that are included in the instance document.

Naturally, this only affects documents that had a DTD (whether they were valid or invalid). In our examples, that's Listings 25-1 and 25-4. After applying default attribute values, Listing 25-1 becomes Listing 25-12, and Listing 25-4 becomes Listing 25-13.

Listing 25-12: **Listing 25-1 after step 12**

```
<?xml-stylesheet type="text/css" href="order.css"?>
<ORDER xmlns="http://ns.macfaq.com/orders">
  <CUSTOMER ID="c3475">Ace & Gary, Ltd.</CUSTOMER>
  <PRODUCT SKU="57333">QuarkXPress 4.1</PRODUCT>
  <PRICE CURRENCY="$" DISCOUNT="10%'>819.95</PRICE>
  <SHIPPING CURRENCY="$">8.95</SHIPPING>
  <EXPEDITE></EXPEDITE>
</ORDER>
<!-- Bob, this order's going to the boss's nephew.
     Please make sure it goes out ASAP. Thanks.
     Ed -->
```

Listing 25-13: **Listing 25-4 after step 6**

```
<?xml-stylesheet type="text/css" href="order.css"?>
<ORDER xmlns="http://ns.macfaq.com/orders">
  <CUSTOMER ID="c3475">Ace &amp; Gary, Ltd.</CUSTOMER>
  <PRODUCT SKU="57333">QuarkXPress 4.1</PRODUCT>
  <PRICE DISCOUNT="10%" CURRENCY="$">819.95</PRICE>
  <SHIPPING CURRENCY="$">8.95</SHIPPING>
  <EXPEDITE xmlns="http://ns.macfaq.com/orders"></EXPEDITE>
</ORDER>
<!-- Bob, this order's going to the boss's nephew.
     Please make sure it goes out ASAP. Thanks.
     Ed -->
```

As you can see, Listings 25-1 and 25-4 are getting very close to each other after 13 steps. But there are still a couple of differences that remain. On the other hand, Listings 25-2 and 25-3 are much farther away from these two and each other.

14. Remove all unnecessary namespace declarations.

This one's the trickiest step, although perhaps the least important step in practice. It simply means that if a namespace prefix or default namespace is unnecessarily redeclared on a descendant of an element in that same namespace that uses the same prefix (or no prefix at all), then the lower-level namespace declaration is removed. This occurred explicitly in the `expedite` element of Listing 25-3 and implicitly through a default attribute value in the DTD in Listing 25-4. The latter, however, was revealed in step 13 in Listing 25-13.

The concern is this. The `EXPEDITE` element is now set up like this:

```
<EXPEDITE xmlns="http://ns.macfaq.com/orders"></EXPEDITE>
```

However, that namespace declaration is superfluous because `EXPEDITE`'s parent element `ORDER` also declares that the default namespace is `http://ns.macfaq.com/orders`. This rule says that any attributes declaring a namespace when it's already in scope should be deleted. Thus, Listing 25-4 becomes Listing 25-14.

Listing 25-14: **Listing 25-4 after step 13**

```
<?xml-stylesheet type="text/css" href="order.css"?>
<ORDER xmlns="http://ns.macfaq.com/orders">
  <CUSTOMER ID="c3475">Ace &amp; Gary, Ltd.</CUSTOMER>
  <PRODUCT SKU="57333">QuarkXPress 4.1</PRODUCT>
  <PRICE DISCOUNT="10%" CURRENCY="$">819.95</PRICE>
  <SHIPPING CURRENCY="$">8.95</SHIPPING>
  <EXPEDITE></EXPEDITE>
</ORDER>
<!-- Bob, this order's going to the boss's nephew.
     Please make sure it goes out ASAP. Thanks.
     Ed -->
```

This is almost the same as Listing 25-1 after step 12, as shown in Listing 25-12. However, there is one remaining difference, the order of the attributes in the `PRICE` element. Listing 25-14 has them in the order `DISCOUNT`, then `CURRENCY`, whereas Listing 25-12 has `CURRENCY`, then `DISCOUNT`. This difference is accounted for in the next and final step.

However, canonicalization does not change namespace prefixes or the lack thereof. Thus the `OP` prefix in Listing 25-2 remains, and this document will be considered to be different from Listings 25-1, 25-3, and 25-4, which do not use prefixes.

Note   To some extent this violates one's natural sensibility about namespaces because the prefix (or lack thereof) isn't supposed to matter as long as the URI is the same. The problem is that namespace prefixes occur not just in element and attribute names but also in attribute values (think of the `match` attribute of an `xsl: template` element) and even occasionally in element content. A canonicalizer cannot reliably identify when a particular string of letters is a namespace prefix and when it's just a string of letters. This is one of many flaws in XML namespaces, but it is a flaw that XML canonicalization has to live with.

Furthermore, canonicalization does not move `xmlns` and `xmlns:prefix` attributes from elements that possess them to elements that do not; it just makes sure that no namespace is declared twice for any one element. It does not produce the minimal possible set of namespace declarations for a document. Canonicalization is not a compression algorithm.

15. Sort the attributes (including namespace declarations) in each tag in order of their Unicode character codes.

Attribute order doesn't matter in XML documents, but, again, the canonicalization algorithm has to pick something. Sorting in Unicode is an extremely difficult proposition given the many languages and scripts that may be involved. Fortunately, since how things are sorted doesn't really matter as long as the sort order is reproducible, a very naïve algorithm suffices here. Characters are ordered from first to last according to their Unicode value. Thus the Latin letter *a* comes before the French letter *á* which comes before the Greek letter α which comes before the Cyrillic letter *a*.

Tip   As long as the language is English, sorting is straightforward. The main thing you may have to remember is that all uppercase letters sort before all lowercase letters. For example, *W*, *Y*, and *Z* all sort before *a*, *b*, and *c*.

In this chapter's examples, only the price elements have multiple attributes, so they're the only elements that have to be sorted. In Listing 25-14, the `PRICE` element looked like this:

```
<PRICE DISCOUNT="10%" CURRENCY="$">819.95</PRICE>
```

C comes before D, so this gets reversed, like so:

```
<PRICE CURRENCY="$" DISCOUNT="10%">819.95</PRICE>
```

Similarly in Listing 25-11, this

```
<price discount="10%" currency="$">
   819.95
</price>
```

gets changed to this:

```
<price currency="$" discount="10%">
   819.95
</price>
```

Listing 25-12 was already in the correct order so it does not need to be changed.

Namespaces make this procedure a little more complicated. Attributes that declare namespaces, whether prefixed or default, sort before regular attributes. For example, `xmlns:OP="http://ns.macfaq.com/orders"` sorts before `currency="$"`

even though *x* comes after *c*. An `xmlns` attribute that declares the default name-space always sorts first.

Most of the time attributes are not in any namespace. However, if an attribute is in a namespace by virtue of a namespace prefix such as `xlink:`, then the attribute sorts first by namespace URI, then by local name. Thus, `xlink:type` sorts after `xlink:href` (both bound to `http://www.w3.org/1999/xlink`). `xlink:type` also sorts before `xml:space` (bound to `http://www.w3.org/XML/1998/namespace`) because `1999` comes before `XML`. However, `xsi:nil` (bound to `http://www.w3.org/2001/XMLSchema-instance`) sorts before `xml:space` because `2001` sorts before `XML`. This is true even though sorting by qualified name would place `xml:space` before `xsi:nil`.

Four Canonical XML Documents

We've now applied the complete algorithm to all four documents and are ready to compare them. Listing 25-15 is the canonical form of Listing 25-1; Listing 25-16 is the canonical form of Listing 25-2; Listing 25-17 is the canonical form of Listing 25-3; and Listing 25-18 is the canonical form of Listing 25-4.

Listing 25-15: **The canonical form of Listing 25-1**

```
<?xml-stylesheet type="text/css" href="order.css"?>
<ORDER xmlns="http://ns.macfaq.com/orders">
  <CUSTOMER ID="c3475">Ace &amp; Gary, Ltd.</CUSTOMER>
  <PRODUCT SKU="57333">QuarkXPress 4.1</PRODUCT>
  <PRICE CURRENCY="$" DISCOUNT="10%">819.95</PRICE>
  <SHIPPING CURRENCY="$">8.95</SHIPPING>
  <EXPEDITE></EXPEDITE>
</ORDER>
<!-- Bob, this order's going to the boss's nephew.
     Please make sure it goes out ASAP. Thanks.
     Ed -->
```

Listing 25-16: **The canonical form of Listing 25-2**

```
<?xml-stylesheet type='text/xml' href='order.xsl'?>
<OP:ORDER xmlns:OP="http://ns.macfaq.com/orders">
  <OP:CUSTOMER ID="c3475">Ace &amp; Gary, Ltd.</OP:CUSTOMER>
  <OP:PRODUCT SKU="57333">QuarkXPress 4.1</OP:PRODUCT>
  <OP:PRICE CURRENCY="$" DISCOUNT="10%">819.95</OP:PRICE>
  <OP:SHIPPING CURRENCY="$">8.95</OP:SHIPPING>
  <OP:EXPEDITE></OP:EXPEDITE>
</OP:ORDER>
```

```
<!-- Bob, this order's going to the boss's nephew.
     Please make sure it goes out ASAP. Thanks.
     Ed -->
```

Listing 25-17: **The canonical form of Listing 25-3**

```
<order xmlns="http://ns.macfaq.com/orders">
  <customer id="c3475">
    Ace &amp; Gary, Ltd.
  </customer>
  <product sku="57333">
    QuarkXPress 4.1
  </product>
  <price currency="$" discount="10%">
    819.95
  </price>
  <shipping currency="$">
    8.95
  </shipping>
  <expedite></expedite>
</order>
```

Listing 25-18: **The canonical form of Listing 25-4**

```
<?xml-stylesheet type="text/css" href="order.css"?>
<ORDER xmlns="http://ns.macfaq.com/orders">
  <CUSTOMER ID="c3475">Ace &amp; Gary, Ltd.</CUSTOMER>
  <PRODUCT SKU="57333">QuarkXPress 4.1</PRODUCT>
  <PRICE CURRENCY="$" DISCOUNT="10%">819.95</PRICE>
  <SHIPPING CURRENCY="$">8.95</SHIPPING>
  <EXPEDITE></EXPEDITE>
</ORDER>
<!-- Bob, this order's going to the boss's nephew.
     Please make sure it goes out ASAP. Thanks.
     Ed -->
```

You can now look at them and tell, canonically, that Listings 25-1 and 25-4 are the same document, whereas Listings 25-2 and 25-3 are not. Of course, this is only one way of looking at it. In specific contexts, it may well be true that all four are treated identically and produce the same data when processed. To some extent the definition of sameness depends on the context in which sameness is evaluated. However, canonical XML is one strong and useful definition of sameness.

It is more important what Canonical XML says is the same than what it says is different. If two XML documents have different canonical forms, they may only differ in unimportant details such as which namespace prefix is used. However, if two XML documents have the same canonical form, then it's a bad idea to design any processing algorithm that would treat the two original documents as different. For instance, it is a very bad idea to:

✦ Claim that `<EXPEDITE></EXPEDITE>` is the empty string, while `<EXPEDITE/>` is null

✦ Say that a dollar sign starts a variable but that `&#x24;` does not

✦ Use a CDATA section to delimit embedded HTML

✦ Require the first attribute of an element to be processed first, the second attribute second, and so on

These are all differences that are eliminated by canonicalization. To a large extent, they are eliminated by ordinary XML parsers as well. Most XML parsers do not tell the application on whose behalf they're parsing whether the dollar sign they saw in text content was provided by a literal $ character or the `&#x24;` character reference. They do not tell it whether any particular run of text came from a CDATA section or from a text node, or where the boundaries of the CDATA section were. They may provide the attributes in a different order than they appeared in the start tag.

Step 16: Removing comments

There's actually one more step you can take if you want, but it is not required and is often not recommended. This is the stripping of comments. There are actually two forms of canonical XML, canonical XML with comments and canonical XML without comments. So far I've been implicitly assuming canonical XML with comments. However, if you don't think comments matter, then you are free to leave them out.

In canonical XML without comments, all comments are deleted from the document. They are not replaced by white space or anything else. They are just gone. Listing 25-3 doesn't have any comments so its canonical form is the same with or without comments. Listings 25-1, 25-2, and 25-4 do have comments so they have different canonical forms without comments. These are shown in Listings 25-19, 25-20, and 25-21.

Listing 25-19: **The canonical form of Listing 25-1 without comments**

```
<?xml-stylesheet type="text/css" href="order.css"?>
<ORDER xmlns="http://ns.macfaq.com/orders">
  <CUSTOMER ID="c3475">Ace &amp; Gary, Ltd.</CUSTOMER>
  <PRODUCT SKU="57333">QuarkXPress 4.1</PRODUCT>
  <PRICE CURRENCY="$" DISCOUNT="10%">819.95</PRICE>
```

```
  <SHIPPING CURRENCY="$">8.95</SHIPPING>
  <EXPEDITE></EXPEDITE>
</ORDER>
```

Listing 25-20: The canonical form of Listing 25-2 without comments

```
<?xml-stylesheet type='text/xml' href='order.xsl'?>
<OP:ORDER xmlns:OP="http://ns.macfaq.com/orders">
  <OP:CUSTOMER ID="c3475">Ace &amp; Gary, Ltd.</OP:CUSTOMER>
  <OP:PRODUCT SKU="57333">QuarkXPress 4.1</OP:PRODUCT>
  <OP:PRICE CURRENCY="$" DISCOUNT="10%">819.95</OP:PRICE>
  <OP:SHIPPING CURRENCY="$">8.95</OP:SHIPPING>
  <OP:EXPEDITE></OP:EXPEDITE>
</OP:ORDER>
```

Listing 25-21: The canonical form of Listing 25-4 without comments

```
<?xml-stylesheet type="text/css" href="order.css"?>
<ORDER xmlns="http://ns.macfaq.com/orders">
  <CUSTOMER ID="c3475">Ace &amp; Gary, Ltd.</CUSTOMER>
  <PRODUCT SKU="57333">QuarkXPress 4.1</PRODUCT>
  <PRICE CURRENCY="$" DISCOUNT="10%">819.95</PRICE>
  <SHIPPING CURRENCY="$">8.95</SHIPPING>
  <EXPEDITE></EXPEDITE>
</ORDER>
```

With or without comments the canonical forms of Listings 25-1 and 25-4 are identical.

Things canonicalization does not resolve

Canonical XML is almost a minimal set of the things you don't care about. However, it is possible that in the context of any given application there may be more things that don't really matter when considering whether or not two documents are equal. It's certainly possible to argue that Listings 25-1 through 25-4 all contain the same information even though they don't all have the same canonical form.

Here are some of the things that Canonical XML does consider to be significant, and that it does not combine:

✦ Ignorable white space in element content

✦ Extra white space in element content used solely for purposes of indentation

✦ Upper- and lowercase letters, whether used in tags or character data

✦ Different namespace prefixes that map to the same URI

✦ Processing instructions

✦ Different Unicode representations of the same underlying character (for example, the single Unicode character *é* is different from an *e* followed by a combining accent acute)

You may be able to think of more examples. Again, canonical XML is a minimal set of rules for determining what should certainly be considered equal to a particular document. It is a conservative set of rules, though. If it does not seem likely that all plausible applications would be willing to treat two documents the same, it will not resolve all their differences.

Canonicalization Tools

The purpose of the last 20 pages was not so much to teach you how to canonicalize as it was to show you what canonicalization involves and what it means. To actually canonicalize a document, you almost always use some software program. Several are available. At the time of this writing, my favorite is the XML Security Suite from IBM's alphaWorks (http://www.alphaworks.ibm.com/tech/xmlsecuritysuite). This is a Java program with all the strengths (wide cross-platform compatibility) and weaknesses (hard to install and poor user interface) of your typical Java program.

The XML Security Suite is actually a Java class library that provides implementations of Canonical XML and several other specifications, such as XML Digital Signatures and XML encryption, that sit on top of canonical XML. For now, the part that you need is the c14n.C14nDOM program. This is a simple Java class that reads an XML document from stdin and writes the canonical form of that document on stdout. Before you can use it, you need to copy the xss4j.jar archive included with the distribution into your jre/lib/ext directory. Then you have to add the xss4j/samples directory to your CLASSPATH environment variable. (Because this is really just a class library designed to be used by other programs rather than an end-user tool, the user interface classes in xss4j/samples are not included in xss4j.jar.) After you've done this, you can produce canonical XML by passing the original XML document in on stdin. You'll have to use the shell input redirection operator < to read data from a file.

```
C:\>java c14n.C14nDOM < 25-1.xml
Use REC-xml-c14n-20010315.
ERROR: Element type "ORDER" must be declared.
ERROR: Element type "CUSTOMER" must be declared.
ERROR: Element type "PRODUCT" must be declared.
ERROR: Element type "PRICE" must be declared.
ERROR: Attribute "DISCOUNT" must be declared for element type
"PRICE".
ERROR: Element type "SHIPPING" must be declared.
ERROR: Element type "EXPEDITE" must be declared.
<?xml-stylesheet type="text/css" href="order.css"?>
<ORDER xmlns="http://namespaces.macfaq.com/orders">
  <CUSTOMER ID="c3475">Ace &amp; Gary, Ltd.</CUSTOMER>
  <PRODUCT SKU="57333">QuarkXPress 4.1</PRODUCT>
  <PRICE CURRENCY="$" DISCOUNT="10%">819.95</PRICE>
  <SHIPPING CURRENCY="$">8.95</SHIPPING>
  <EXPEDITE></EXPEDITE>
</ORDER>
```

There are numerous error messages, but these all just say that the document isn't valid. That's no great surprise and not a real problem; the DTD for that document was not meant for validation in the first place. There's no particular reason for a canonicalizer to validate or to report validity errors. This one simply chooses to do so, but it's certainly not required.

If you pass in the valid Listing 25-4 instead, then all of the error messages go away, and all that's left is a note that the program is using the March 15, 2001, version of Canonical XML and the canonical XML itself:

```
C:\>java c14n.C14nDOM < 25-4.xml
Use REC-xml-c14n-20010315.
<?xml-stylesheet type="text/css" href="order.css"?>
<ORDER xmlns="http://namespaces.macfaq.com/orders">
  <CUSTOMER ID="c3475">Ace &amp; Gary, Ltd.</CUSTOMER>
  <PRODUCT SKU="57333">QuarkXPress 4.1</PRODUCT>
  <PRICE CURRENCY="$" DISCOUNT="10%">819.95</PRICE>
  <SHIPPING CURRENCY="$">8.95</SHIPPING>
  <EXPEDITE></EXPEDITE>
</ORDER>
```

The key in both cases is the output canonical XML. You can see that the comments have been stripped and that this program only produces canonical XML without comments.

If you'd rather output the canonical XML into a separate file, just use the shell redirection operator > like this:

```
C:\>java c14n.C14nDOM < 25-1.xml > 25-19.xml
Use REC-xml-c14n-20010315.
ERROR: Element type "ORDER" must be declared.
ERROR: Element type "CUSTOMER" must be declared.
ERROR: Element type "PRODUCT" must be declared.
ERROR: Element type "PRICE" must be declared.
ERROR: Attribute "DISCOUNT" must be declared for element type
"PRICE".
ERROR: Element type "SHIPPING" must be declared.
ERROR: Element type "EXPEDITE" must be declared.
```

The error messages still show up on the console.

Something even stranger happens if you run Listing 25-2 or Listing 25-3 through c14n.C14nDOM:

```
C:\>java c14n.C14nDOM < 25-3.xml > 25-20.xml
Use REC-xml-c14n-20010315.
ERROR: General Schema Error: Grammar with uri 2:
http://ns.macfaq.com/orders , can not found.
ERROR: Element type "order" must be declared.
ERROR: Element type "customer" must be declared.
ERROR: Element type "product" must be declared.
ERROR: Element type "price" must be declared.
ERROR: Element type "shipping" must be declared.
ERROR: Element type "expedite" must be declared.
```

Even though this document has neither a document type declaration nor an xsi:schemaLocation attribute indicating a DTD or a schema against which it should be validated, c14n.C14nDOM takes it upon itself to validate the document nonetheless. It even looks for a schema at the namespace URI, which is a behavior the *Namespaces in XML Recommendation* specifically warns against. However, it still produces the correct canonical form of the input document and the errors are easy to ignore.

Summary

In this chapter, you learned about Canonical XML, a W3C Recommendation for an algorithm to convert an XML document into a single stand-alone file that can be compared byte-for-byte with other canonical XML documents. In particular, you learned that:

✦ Canonicalization follows a 15-step process for converting any namespace well-formed XML document into a sequence of bytes that can be stored in a single file.

✦ Two documents that have identical canonical forms can be considered equal for almost all intents and purposes.

✦ In some cases, two documents that have different canonical forms may still be considered equal by some applications.

✦ Canonical XML documents are encoded in the UTF-8 encoding of Unicode without a byte order mark.

✦ All line breaks are converted to Unicode (and ASCII) character 10, the line-feed, when canonicalizing a document.

✦ Attribute values in a canonical XML document are normalized, just as a validating processor would do.

✦ All character references, parsed entity references, and CDATA sections are replaced by the text they represent when a document is canonicalized.

✦ Canonicalization replaces all ampersands, less than signs, greater than signs, and double quotes inside attribute values with the predefined entity references `&amp;`, `&gt;`, `&lt;`, and `&quot;`, regardless of how they were originally represented in the document.

✦ The XML declaration and the document type declaration are deleted during canonicalization. Any default attribute values provided by the DTD are explicitly added to the instance document.

✦ All empty elements are represented by two tags — a start tag and an end tag — in a canonical XML document. No empty-element tags are used.

✦ Canonical XML normalizes all white space outside of the document element and inside tags.

✦ Canonicalization does not change in any way the white space in character content.

✦ All attribute values are delimited by double quote marks.

✦ Unnecessary namespace declarations are deleted from the canonical form.

✦ Namespace declaration attributes are sorted in order of Unicode character value according to the prefixes they declare. A default namespace declaration is sorted first.

✦ Nonnamespace declaration attributes are sorted in order of Unicode character value, first by namespace URI, and then by local name. These attributes are placed after the `xmlns` and `xmlns:prefix` attributes that declare namespaces.

✦ There are actually two canonical forms — with comments and without. It's important to specify which form you're using.

✦ IBM's alphaWorks XML Security Suite includes a command line Java program called c14n.C14nDOM that can convert a document to its canonical form, even if it's a bit overly aggressive about validation.

This completes your training in core XML technologies. The next part begins several case studies of different XML applications in different vertical domains. First out of the gate is a chapter on learning to read and interpret someone else's DTD. The specific DTD explored is the modular SMIL 2.0 DTD. SMIL, the Synchronized Multimedia Integration Language, is a W3C-recommended XML application for multimedia presentations, including slide shows, subtitled video, animation, and more.

✦   ✦   ✦

XML
Applications

Reading DTDs

In an ideal world, every markup language created with XML would come with copious documentation and examples showing you the exact meaning and use of every element and attribute. In practice, most DTD authors, like most programmers, consider documentation an unpleasant and unnecessary chore, one best left to tech writers if it's to be done at all. Not surprisingly, therefore, the DTD that contains sufficient documentation is the exception, not the rule. Consequently, it's important to learn to read raw DTDs written by others.

There's a second good reason for learning to read DTDs. When you read good DTDs, you can often learn tricks and techniques that you can use in your own DTDs. For example, no matter how much theory I may mumble about the proper use of parameter entities for common attribute lists in DTDs, nothing proves quite as effective for learning that as really digging into a DTD that uses the technique. Reading other designers' DTDs teaches you by example how you can design your own.

This chapter picks apart the modularized DTD for SMIL 2.0 from the W3C. This DTD is quite complex and relatively well written. By studying it closely, you can pick up a lot of good techniques for developing your own DTDs. You'll see what its designers did right, and a few things they did wrong (IMHO). I'll explore some different ways the same thing could have been accomplished, and the advantages and disadvantages of each. You will also learn some common tricks in XML DTDs and techniques for developing your own DTDs.

The Importance of Reading DTDs

Some XML applications are very precisely defined by standards documents. MathML is one such application. It's been the subject of several person-years of work by a dedicated committee with representatives from across the computer mathematics community. It's been through several levels of peer review, and the committee has been quite responsive to problems discovered both in the language and in the documentation of that language. Consequently, a full DTD is available accompanied by an extensive prose specification.

Other XML applications are not as well documented. Microsoft more or less completely created CDF in-house. CDF is documented informally on the Microsoft Developer Network in a set of poorly organized Web pages, but no current DTD is available. Microsoft may update and add to CDF in the future, but exactly what the updates will be is more or less a mystery to everyone else in the industry.

Cross-Reference   CDF is discussed in Chapter 33.

CML, the Chemical Markup Language invented by Peter Murray-Rust, is hardly documented at all. It contains a DTD, but it leaves a lot to the imagination. For instance, the DTD defines a `bondArray` element, but the only thing it tells you about the contents of the `bondArray` element is that it contains `#PCDATA`. There's no further description of what sort of data should appear in a `bondArray` element.

Other times, there may be both a DTD and a prose specification. Microsoft and Marimba's Open Software Description (OSD format) is one example. However, the problem with prose specifications is that they leave pieces out. For instance, the spec for OSD generally neglects to say how many of a given child element may appear in a parent element or in what order. The DTD makes that clear. Conversely, the DTD can't really say that a `SIZE` attribute is given in the format KB-number. That's left to the prose part of the specification.

Note   Actually, this sort of information could and should appear in a comment in the DTD, but the XML parser can't validate such restrictions. That has to be left to a higher layer of processing. In any case, simple comments can make the DTD more intelligible for humans, if nothing else. Currently, OSD does not have a solid DTD.

These are all examples of more or less public XML applications. However, many corporations, government agencies, Web sites, and other organizations have internal, private XML applications they use for their own documents. These are even less likely to be well documented and well written than the public XML applications. As an XML specialist, you may well find yourself trying to reverse engineer a DTD originally written by someone long gone that's grown haphazardly through accretion of new elements over several years.

Clearly, the more documentation you have for an XML application, and the better written the documentation is, the easier it will be to learn and use that application. However it's an unfortunate fact of life that documentation is often an afterthought. Frequently, the only thing you have to work with is a DTD. You're reduced to reading the DTD, trying to understand what it says, and writing and validating test documents to try to figure out what is and isn't permissible. Consequently, it's important to be able to read DTDs and create examples of permissible markup based on those DTDs.

In this chapter, you'll explore the SMIL 2.0 DTD from the W3C. This is actually one of the better documented DTDs I've seen. However, in this chapter I'm going to pretend that it isn't. Instead of paraphrasing the prose specification, I'm going to show you the actual DTD files. You'll explore the techniques you can use to understand those DTDs, even in the absence of a prose specification.

What is SMIL?

The Synchronized Multimedia Integration Language (SMIL, pronounced "smile") is a W3C recommended XML application for writing "TV-like" multimedia presentations for the Web. SMIL documents don't describe the actual multimedia content (that is the video and sound that are played) but rather when and where they are played. For instance, a SMIL document might list the pictures included in a slide show, the order in which to show them, the amount of time to display each one for, and the captions to place under each picture. Listing 26-1 is a simple valid SMIL 2.0 document describing such a show. This would normally have the file name extension .smil and the MIME type application/smil. It can be played in a SMIL-savvy program such as RealPlayer 8 as shown in Figure 26-1.

Listing 26-1: **A SMIL 2.0 document describing a slide show**

```
<?xml version="1.0"?>
<!DOCTYPE smil PUBLIC "-//W3C//DTD SMIL 2.0//EN"
                      "SMIL20.dtd">
<smil xmlns="http://www.w3.org/2001/SMIL20/PR/">
  <head>
    <layout>
      <root-layout width="300" height="347"
                   background-color="white"/>
      <region id="image_region" left="0" top="0"
              width="300" height="297" />
      <region id="caption_region" left="0" top="297"
              width="300" height="50" />
    </layout>
  </head>
  <body>
    <seq>
      <par dur="20s">
        <img src="charm.jpg" alt="My cat Charm"
             region="image_region"/>
        <text src="charm.txt" region="caption_region"/>
      </par>
      <par dur="20s">
        <img src="marjorie.jpg" alt="My cat Marjorie"
             region="image_region"/>
        <text src="marjorie.txt" region="caption_region"/>
```

Continued

Listing 26-1 *(continued)*

```
      </par>
      <par dur="20s">
        <img src="possum.jpg" alt="My cat Possum"
             region="image_region" />
        <text src="possum.txt" region="caption_region"/>
      </par>
    </seq>
  </body>
</smil>
```

Figure 26-1: Listing 26-1 in RealPlayer 8

Currently, the latest draft is from June 5, 2001. You can download this particular version from http://www.w3.org/TR/2001/PR-smil20-20010605/. The status of this version is, as given by the W3C:This is the W3C Proposed Recommendation of the Synchronized Multimedia Integration Language (SMIL) 2.0 specification. This document is a revision of the W3C Working Draft 01 March 2001, incorporating comments and suggestions received during the Last Call review. Also refer to the changes to this SMIL 2.0 Specification since Last Call.

The SYMM Working Group [*members only*] considers that all features in the SMIL 2.0 specification have been implemented at least twice in an interoperable way. The

SYMM Working Group Charter [members only] defines this as the implementations having been developed independently by different organizations and each test in the SMIL 2.0 test suite has at least two passing implementations. The Implementation results are publicly released and are intended solely to be used as proof of SMIL 2.0 implementability. It is only a snap shot of the actual implementation behaviors at one moment of time, as these implementations may not be immediately available to the public. The interoperability data is not intended to be used for assessing or grading the performance of any individual implementation.

This document enters a Proposed Recommendation review period. W3C Advisory Committee Members are invited to send formal review comments until 05 July 2001 to w3t-smil2@w3.org, visible only to the W3C Team.

The public is invited to send comments on this document to the public mailing list www-smil@w3.org - (public archives).

After the review, the Director will announce the document's disposition: it may become a W3C Recommendation (possibly with minor changes). This announcement should not be expected sooner than 14 days after the end of the review.

The [XHTML+SMIL] Profile which appeared in previous working drafts is still in progress. It continues to be updated and will be published as a separate document when it is ready.

There are patent disclosures and license commitments associated with the SMIL 2.0 specification, these may be found on the SYMM Patent Statement page in conformance with W3C policy.

This document has been produced as part of the W3C Synchronized Multimedia Activity of the W3C User Interface Domain. The goals of the SYMM Working Group are discussed in the SYMM Working Group charter [*members only*], (revised July 2000 from original charter version).

The authors of this document are the SYMM Working Group members. Different modules of the SMIL 2.0 have different editors.

The W3C staff contact for work on SMIL is Thierry MICHEL.

Publication as a Proposed Recommendation does not imply endorsement by the W3C membership. This is still a draft document and may be updated, replaced or obsoleted by other documents at any time. It is inappropriate to cite W3C Proposed Recommendations as other than "work in progress."

Since this chapter is more concerned with learning to read DTDs than with using SMIL to embed multimedia in Web pages, any changes between this draft and the final recommendation shouldn't be too relevant for the purposes of this chapter. Nonetheless, if you do want to learn more about SMIL's intended purpose and how to use it to present multimedia on the Web, you can find the most current version of the specification at http://www.w3.org/TR/smil20.

Caution   One thing that is almost guaranteed to change in the final version of SMIL 2.0 is the namespace URI. It will most likely be changed to http://www.w3.org/2001/SMIL20/ or http://www.w3.org/2001/SMIL20/Language, but that is not certain.

The Structure of the SMIL DTDs

SMIL 2.0 is a moderately complex XML application. The SMIL DTD is divided into 15 different files and about 2000 lines of code. Individual developers can add their own extensions to and variations of SMIL on top of the basic framework. All these files are connected through parameter entities. By splitting the DTD into these different files, it's easier to understand the individual pieces. Furthermore, common pieces can be shared by both versions of the SMIL DTD as well as by other DTDs that just need a piece of SMIL but not the whole thing.

SMIL 2.0 is organized into 15 different DTD fragments which are mixed and matched to form a complete DTD. The SMIL DTD fragments are divided into four types:

✦ Module DTDs

✦ The Modularization framework

✦ Driver DTDs

✦ Document models

Module DTDs

Each module DTD declares a related subset of SMIL elements and attributes. Some modules can be used independently of the other modules. For example, you can add a basic timing vocabulary to your own XML application by importing the timing and synchronization module into your DTD.

The module DTDs include:

✦ The Animation Module: elements and attributes for specifying animation along a time line. These include `animate`, `set`, `animateMotion`, `animateColor` and `target`.

✦ The Content Control Module: elements that allow the content to be chosen at playtime and content delivery to be optimized. These include `switch`, `prefetch`, `customAttributes` and `customTest`.

✦ The Layout Module: elements and attributes used to position images, video clips and text at certain points in the window as well as control audio volume. These elements include `layout`, `region` and `root-layout`.

✦ The Linking Module: elements used for hypertext including `a` and `area`.

✦ The Media Object Module: elements and attributes that represent various media types including ref, animation, audio, img, text, textstream and video.

✦ The Metainformation Module: the meta and metadata elements used to store meta-information in the header of a SMIL document.

✦ The Structure Module: basic structure of SMIL instance documents, specifically the root smil element and its two children, head and body.

✦ The Timing and Synchronization Module: elements and attributes that determine when and for how long a clip plays, including par, seq, and excl.

✦ The Transition Effects Module: elements used for transitioning from one media to another including transition and transitionFilter.

The Modularization Framework

The framework modules do not declare any elements or attributes. Instead, they define numerous parameter entity references on which many elements and attributes in different modules depend. For example, the data types module defines %Number.datatype; as an alias for CDATA. Any time an attribute in one of the above nine modules declares an attribute that must be a number, it uses the %Number.datatype; parameter entity reference. These framework modules are:

✦ The common datatypes module defines parameter entity references used to more precisely identify attribute types.

✦ The common attributes module defines attributes like id, class, and xml:lang applied to almost all SMIL elements.

✦ The qualified names module defines the namespace URI and prefix for SMIL elements and attributes.

✦ The framework module links the other three framework modules and the document model module.

The Document Model

The document model is a DTD fragment that defines common content models for both elements and attributes used elsewhere in the document. For instance, it defines the media-object entity used to provide content models for all the elements that can contain one or more media objects. Thus it establishes which media objects are allowed.

There are two document models for SMIL 2.0, the full Language Profile document model and the basic profile that omits the Animation, Transition, and Metainformation modules. The second is a simplified subset of the first targeted at small devices like Palm Pilots, cell phones, Blackberry pagers and other devices with limited memory, disk space, and CPU power. It contains only the fundamental pieces needed for layout, linking, media objects, structures, and timing. The full profile adds many other pieces including animation, transitions, and meta-information. In addition, if your needs aren't precisely met by either of these two, you have the option to build your own profile that only includes precisely those modules and that functionality which you need.

The version of the SMIL specification shown in this chapter only provides DTD fragments for the full profile (even though it defines both the full and basic profiles). The full profile is a superset of the basic profile so this isn't too big a problem in practice. A SMIL Basic document can be validated against the full DTD. However, to keep the examples simpler and smaller I will offer a DTD fragment for the basic document profile below.

The Driver DTD

The driver DTD is the final piece that pulls all the other pieces together. This is the DTD you actually reference from your instance documents using a document type declaration. It imports all the other necessary modules using external parameter entity references. SMIL 2.0 only provides a driver DTD for the full version of SMIL. I'll provide DTDs for the basic profile below.

The SMIL 2.0 Basic Language Profile

SMIL 2.0 Basic is intended for resource constrained environments like cell phones, pagers, and Sony Watchmen. It includes only the most important SMIL modules: basic layout, linking, media object, structure, and timing. It does not support animation, metadata or transitions. Both the SMIL Basic DTD and the full DTD have the same format:

1. A comment containing title, copyright, namespace, formal public identifier and other information for people who use this DTD.

2. Revised parameter entity declarations that will override parameter entities declared in the modules.

3. External parameter entity references to import the modules and entity sets.

Since the SMIL 2.0 Basic Language Profile has the same structure as the larger SMIL 2.0 Language Profile, it's easiest to begin with the basic version, then expand it to include the other pieces. SMIL 2.0 Basic documents can use the driver DTD shown in Listing 26-2.

To understand the permissible markup start at the top of this driver DTD and then work down to see what other DTD subsets it includes with parameter entity references, as well as what declarations it makes itself. Some of the other subsets it imports may also define the parameter entity definitions given in the main document. In that case, remember that the first definition encountered takes precedence. Parsers read the documents from top to bottom and replace the entities as they find them (that is, a parser reads the entire imported DTD subset before it finishes reading the importing DTD). Read this DTD now and see what it declares and what it imports.

Listing 26-2: **SMIL20Basic.dtd: The SMIL Basic Language Profile DTD**

```
<!-- ............................................. -->
<!-- SMIL 2.0 Basic DTD
.................................... -->
<!-- file: SMIL20Basic.dtd -->
<!-- SMIL 2.0 Basic DTD

     This is SMIL 2.0 Basic.

     Copyright 1998-2000 World Wide Web Consortium
         (Massachusetts Institute of Technology, Institut
          National de Recherche en Informatique et en
          Automatique, Keio University).
         All Rights Reserved.

     Permission to use, copy, modify and distribute the SMIL
     2.0 DTD and its accompanying documentation for any purpose
     and without fee is hereby granted in perpetuity, provided
     that the above copyright notice and this paragraph appear
     in all copies.  The copyright holders make no
     representation about the suitability of the DTD for any
     purpose.

     It is provided "as is" without expressed or implied
     warranty.

       Author:    Jacco van Ossenbruggen, Kenichi Kubota
       Revision:  $Id: SMIL20Basic.dtd,v 1.3 2000/09/21
                  11:16:46 jvanoss Exp $

     The W3C stopped publishing separate DTDs for SMIL Basic
     and full SMIL after the working draft of September 21,
     2001. Elliotte Rusty Harold derived this by combining parts
     of the SMIL Basic DTD in that draft with parts of the full
     DTD from the June 5, 2001 Proposed Recommendation.

-->
<!-- This is the driver file for the SMIL 2.0 Basic DTD.

     This DTD module is identified by the PUBLIC and SYSTEM
```

Continued

Listing 26-2 *(continued)*

```
      identifiers:

      PUBLIC "-//W3C//DTD SMIL 2.0 Basic//EN"
      SYSTEM "SMIL20Basic.dtd"
-->

<!ENTITY % NS.prefixed "IGNORE" >
<!ENTITY % SMIL.prefix "" >

<!-- Define the Content Model -->
<!ENTITY % smil-model.mod
PUBLIC "-//W3C//ENTITIES SMIL 2.0 Basic Document Model 1.0//EN"
      "smilbasic-model-1.mod" >

<!-- Modular Framework Module
.................................. -->
<!ENTITY % smil-framework.module "INCLUDE" >
<![%smil-framework.module;[
<!ENTITY % smil-framework.mod
   PUBLIC "-//W3C//ENTITIES SMIL 2.0 Modular Framework 1.0//EN"
          "smil-framework-1.mod" >
%smil-framework.mod;]]>

<!--  The SMIL 2.0 Basic Profile supports the lightweight
      multimedia features defined in SMIL language. This
      profile includes the following SMIL modules:

   SMIL 2.0 BasicLayout Module
   SMIL 2.0 BasicLinking Module
   SMIL 2.0 BasicMedia and MediaClipping Modules
   SMIL 2.0 Structure Module
   SMIL 2.0 BasicInlinTiming, SyncbaseTiming, EventTiming,
            MinMaxTiming and BasicTimeContainers Modules
   SMIL 2.0 BasicContentControl and SkipContentControl Modules
-->

<!ENTITY % control-mod
  PUBLIC "-//W3C//ELEMENTS SMIL 2.0 Content Control//EN"
  "SMIL-control.mod">
<!ENTITY % layout-mod
  PUBLIC "-//W3C//ELEMENTS SMIL 2.0 Layout//EN"
  "SMIL-layout.mod">
<!ENTITY % link-mod
  PUBLIC "-//W3C//ELEMENTS SMIL 2.0 Linking//EN"
  "SMIL-link.mod">
<!ENTITY % media-mod
  PUBLIC "-//W3C//ELEMENTS SMIL 2.0 Media Objects//EN"
  "SMIL-media.mod">
<!ENTITY % struct-mod
  PUBLIC "-//W3C//ELEMENTS SMIL 2.0 Document Structure//EN"
```

```
  "SMIL-struct.mod">
<!ENTITY % timing-mod
  PUBLIC "-//W3C//ELEMENTS SMIL 2.0 Timing//EN"
  "SMIL-timing.mod">

%struct-mod;
%control-mod;
%layout-mod;
%link-mod;
%media-mod;
%timing-mod;
```

Comments

The file begins with a comment identifying which file this is, and a basic copyright statement. That's followed by these very important words:

> Permission to use, copy, modify and distribute the SMIL 2.0 DTD and its accompanying documentation for any purpose and without fee is hereby granted in perpetuity, provided that the above copyright notice and this paragraph appear in all copies. The copyright holders make no representation about the suitability of the DTD for any purpose.

A statement like this is *very* important for any DTD that you want to be broadly adopted. In order for people outside your organization to use your DTD, they must be allowed to copy it, put it on their Web servers, send it to other people with their own documents, reprint it in its entirety in books like this one, and do a variety of other things normally prohibited by copyright. Including a simple statement like "Copyright 2001 XYZ Corp." with no further elucidation prevents many people from using your DTD.

The name of the authors and the date and version of the file are also given. This is good, but ideally it should also include the author's email addresses and the URL for the location of the SMIL specification. After all, this file may have moved between many different servers before the user ever got to see it. It would be nice if readers had a straight-forward way to figure out where it came from, and how to report errors in or comment on this DTD. For example, something like this would be preferable:

```
Authors:       Jacco van Ossenbruggen
               Kenichi Kubota
               www-smil@w3.org
Revision:      $Id: SMIL20Basic.dtd,v 1.3 2000/09/21
               11:16:46 jvanoss Exp $
Specification: Synchronized Multimedia Integration Language 2.0
               http://www.w3.org/TR/smil20/
```

Next comes a comment containing detailed information about how this DTD should be used including its formal public identifier and preferred file name. Still, a couple of things are missing here that would be useful including the preferred namespace and an example of how to begin a file that uses this DTD. For example,

```
<!-- This is the driver file for the SMIL Basic DTD.
     The root element is smil. This is normally placed in the
     http://www.w3.org/TR/REC-smil/2000/SMIL20/Basic
     namespace.

     Please use this formal public identifier to identify it:

         "-//W3C//DTD SMIL 2.0 Basic//EN"

     For example,

     <!DOCTYPE smil PUBLIC "-//W3C//DTD SMIL 2.0 Basic//EN"
                           "SMIL20Basic.dtd">
-->
```

There's no particular format for this information. Just use whatever seems most likely to help out people reading your DTDs.

White Space

Although Listing 26-1 is just a monospaced text file, it's still relatively attractively formatted. Some of the modules that follow are going to look even better. This is mostly achieved through judicious use of white space and indenting. There aren't any standard conventions for indenting in DTDs like there are in most programming languages. Use whatever seems to best reflect your structure and is easiest to read. Still. indenting is not just simply a matter of aesthetics. Properly indented code is *much* easier to read and much kinder to anyone who has to try to make sense out of your DTD.

When typing, keep in mind that you really have no idea what text editor someone will use to view your code. You do not know what size their window is and thus do not know how many columns they can see simultaneously. You do not know whether or where the viewer will wrap the lines. You do not know where their tab stops are. Thus you should use white space that provides a reasonable least common denominator for most people on most platforms.

The SMIL 2.0 modules are set at 80 characters. No line extends past that. 80 characters is a little wide, especially when you consider the possibility that DTDs might be passed around in e-mail messages where they might be quoted multiple times. 72 characters is a better default. For this book, I actually had to edit the DTDs down to 64 characters per line to make them fit, but that's a little too short for me to insist on.

Tabs are also quite tricky and should be avoided. There is absolutely nothing you can do with tabs you can't do with spaces. Space characters have the advantage that a space is a space is a space, no matter who's looking at it where. Tabs, by contrast, can vary quite a bit from editor to editor depending on where the user has set the tab stops. The SMIL DTDs actually do use tabs rather inconsistently, which makes them look quite funky when opened up raw. As best I can tell, some of the original authors set their tabs to eight spaces, others to four, and others to two. The resulting DTDs are virtually guaranteed to be misaligned when opened, no matter where you've set your own tab stops. When I edited the DTDs for this book, I had to clean up a lot of funky tabs and take my best guess at what the authors intended. Tabs are a mechanical artifact of typewriters. They have no place in computer source code whether XML or otherwise.

Parameter Entities

You should have noticed that Listing 26-1 only defines and dereferences parameter entities. It does not actually declare *any* elements or attributes. Every element and attribute is declared in a module imported through a parameter entity reference. By redefining the parameter entity references in the internal DTD subset of a document (which is the first part of the DTD the parser reads), you can change the source for each imported module. You could, for example, change the URL for each module to point to a local copy on a local server; or you could point to a different version of the module. The indirection the parameter entities offer is a very powerful lever. You'll see parameter entities used in this way again and again.

The first two parameter entities establish whether a prefix is used (`NS.prefixed`) and which prefix is used (`SMIL.prefix`). `NS.prefixed` is set to `IGNORE` and `SMIL.prefix.` is set to an empty string. Thus by default SMIL documents do not use any prefixes for SMIL elements. However, both these entities can be overridden in another part of the DTD to turn on prefixes. Or you can simply change them here in your local copy of the DTD like this:

```
<!ENTITY % NS.prefixed "INCLUDE" >
<!ENTITY % SMIL.prefix "smil" >
```

You'll see the effect this has shortly when you see the other DTDs where the parameter entities are dereferenced.

Next, the `smil-model.mod` parameter entity is defined. Its value is a `PUBLIC` identifier for the content model module to be used. This can be the basic model, the full model, or a home grown model that's somewhere in-between. Here it's pointed at the file smilbasic-model-1.mod, which I discuss soon. However, it is not actually loaded yet, merely defined. It will be loaded from the framework module.

The framework module is included in a very strange way. First a parameter entity named `smil-framework.module` is defined with the replacement text `INCLUDE`. Then the actual framework module is imported:

```
<!ENTITY % smil-framework.module "INCLUDE" >
<![%smil-framework.module;[
<!ENTITY % smil-framework.mod
    PUBLIC "-//W3C//ENTITIES SMIL 2.0 Modular Framework 1.0//EN"
           "smil-framework-1.mod" >
%smil-framework.mod;]]>
```

Since `%smil-framework.module;` resolves to the word `INCLUDE`, this is the same as this:

```
<![INCLUDE[
<!ENTITY % smil-framework.mod
    PUBLIC "-//W3C//ENTITIES SMIL 2.0 Modular Framework 1.0//EN"
           "smil-framework-1.mod" >
%smil-framework.mod;]]>
```

However, the effect of an `INCLUDE` block like this is simply to say that its contents are included in the DTD. This is exactly what would happen there were no `INCLUDE` block in the first place like this:

```
<!ENTITY % smil-framework.mod
    PUBLIC "-//W3C//ENTITIES SMIL 2.0 Modular Framework 1.0//EN"
           "smil-framework-1.mod" >
%smil-framework.mod;
```

Therefore you're probably wondering why the DTD doesn't just use this form in the first place. What's the point of the extra parameter entity reference and `INCLUDE` block? The reason is that by redefining `smil-framework.module` to the word `IGNORE` in the internal DTD subset, you can switch off the framework module. That is, in a particular document instance you can choose whether or not to include the framework module. You'll see this trick repeated many times below when including other modules.

Cross-Reference   `INCLUDE` and `IGNORE` blocks are discussed at the end of Chapter 12, *Unparsed Entities, Notations, and Non-XML Data.*

Finally you get to the meat of the DTD: six external parameter entity definitions and references that import the modules used to form the complete DTD. Here's the last one in the file:

```
<!ENTITY % timing-mod
    PUBLIC "-//W3C//ELEMENTS SMIL 2.0 Timing//EN"
    "SMIL-timing.mod">
```

All six share the same basic structure. First a `PUBLIC` ID identifies the module to be imported; then the module is actually imported using the parameter entity reference. If the public ID is not recognized, then a relative URL is used instead.

You can diagram the structure of this DTD as follows based on which files import which other files:

```
SMIL20Basic.dtd
   |
   +--smil-framework.mod
   |
   +--SMIL-struct.mod
   |
   +--SMIL-control.mod
   |
   +--SMIL-layout.mod
   |
   +--SMIL-link.mod
   |
   +--SMIL-media.mod
   |
   +--SMIL-timing.mod
```

As we investigate the contents of these files, we'll expand on this structure by adding additional levels. Since each of the modules may depend on the declarations in modules that precede it in the import sequence, it's important to work in order, so we'll begin with the SMIL 2.0 Framework Module.

The Modular Framework Module

The SMIL Modular Framework Module shown in Listing 26-3 uses parameter entity references to pull in the four support modules that will be needed by other modules.

Listing 26-3: smil-framework-1.mod: The SMIL Modular Framework Module DTD

```
<!-- ................................................... -->
<!-- SMIL 2.0 Modular Framework Module  ................. -->
<!-- file: smil-framework-1.mod

     This is SMIL 2.0.
     Copyright 1998-2000 W3C (MIT, INRIA, Keio), All Rights
     Reserved.
```

Continued

Listing 26-3 *(continued)*

```
    This DTD module is identified by the PUBLIC and SYSTEM
    identifiers:

    PUBLIC "-//W3C//ENTITIES SMIL 2.0 Modular Framework 1.0//EN"
    SYSTEM "smil-framework-1.mod"

    Revision: $Id: smil-DTD.html,v 1.1 2001/06/05 09:16:20
              jigsaw Exp $
    .............................................. -->

<!-- Modular Framework

    This required module instantiates the modules needed
    to support the SMIL 2.0 modularization model, including:

        + datatypes
        + namespace-qualified names
        + common attributes
        + document model
-->

<!ENTITY % smil-datatypes.module "INCLUDE" >
<![%smil-datatypes.module;[
<!ENTITY % smil-datatypes.mod
     PUBLIC "-//W3C//ENTITIES SMIL 2.0 Datatypes 1.0//EN"
            "smil-datatypes-1.mod" >
%smil-datatypes.mod;]]>

<!ENTITY % smil-qname.module "INCLUDE" >
<![%smil-qname.module;[
<!ENTITY % smil-qname.mod
     PUBLIC "-//W3C//ENTITIES SMIL 2.0 Qualified Names 1.0//EN"
            "smil-qname-1.mod" >
%smil-qname.mod;]]>

<!ENTITY % smil-attribs.module "INCLUDE" >
<![%smil-attribs.module;[
<!ENTITY % smil-attribs.mod
     PUBLIC "-//W3C//ENTITIES SMIL 2.0 Common Attributes
1.0//EN"
            "smil-attribs-1.mod" >
%smil-attribs.mod;]]>

<!ENTITY % smil-model.module "INCLUDE" >
<![%smil-model.module;[
<!-- A content model MUST be defined by the driver file -->
%smil-model.mod;]]>

<!-- end of smil-framework-1.mod -->
```

Comments

This module also begins with a comment identifying which file this is, and a basic copyright statement. Indeed pretty much all the modules you'll see have this structure. For the most part I won't mention this from this point forward. However, I do want to point out one thing that's a little different from the introductory comments in Listing 26-2. That's this:

```
This DTD module is identified by the PUBLIC and SYSTEM
identifiers:

PUBLIC "-//W3C//ENTITIES SMIL 2.0 Modular Framework 1.0//EN"
SYSTEM "smil-framework-1.mod"
```

I've noticed that this confuses a number of people who don't have the XML BNF grammar at the tip of their tongue. The specific problem is that it tends to suggest that you need a document type declaration that looks like this:

```
<!DOCTYPE smil
    PUBLIC "-//W3C//ENTITIES SMIL 2.0 Modular Framework 1.0//EN"
    SYSTEM "smil-framework-1.mod"
>
```

In fact, that's malformed. You do not use both the PUBLIC and SYSTEM keywords in the same document type declaration. You use both public and system *identifiers*, but not both *keywords*. The proper document type declaration is this:

```
<!DOCTYPE smil
    PUBLIC "-//W3C//ENTITIES SMIL 2.0 Modular Framework 1.0//EN"
           "smil-framework-1.mod"
>
```

Parameter Entities

The framework module uses parameter entity references to pull in the support modules that will be needed by other modules. These are:

✦ The datatypes module

✦ The namespace-qualified names module

✦ The common attributes module

✦ The document model module

Once these have been imported, the nested structure of modules now looks like this:

```
SMIL20Basic.dtd
   |
   +--smil-framework.mod
   |      |
   |      +--smil-datatypes-1.mod
   |      |
   |      +--smil-qname-1.mod
   |      |
   |      +--smil-attribs-1.mod
   |      |
   |      +--smilbasic-model-1.mod
   |
   +--SMIL-struct.mod
   |
   +--SMIL-control.mod
   |
   +--SMIL-layout.mod
   |
   +--SMIL-link.mod
   |
   +--SMIL-media.mod
   |
   +--SMIL-timing.mod
```

The modules this module imports are fundamental, and it's unlikely you'll want to delete them. However, if you need to you can. The technique used is this. In each case the DTD to be defined is wrapped in an INCLUDE block like this:

```
<![INCLUDE[
<!ENTITY % smil-attribs.mod
    PUBLIC "-//W3C//ENTITIES SMIL 2.0 Common Attributes 1.0//EN"
           "smil-attribs-1.mod" >
%smil-attribs.mod;]]>
```

However, the word INCLUDE is replaced by a parameter entity reference to the name of the module, suffixed with .module like this:

```
<!ENTITY % smil-attribs.module "INCLUDE" >
<![%smil-attribs.module;[
<!ENTITY % smil-attribs.mod
    PUBLIC "-//W3C//ENTITIES SMIL 2.0 Common Attributes 1.0//EN"
           "smil-attribs-1.mod" >
%smil-attribs.mod;]]>
```

Thus if you'd like to exclude the common attributes module all you have to do is redefine the `smil-attribs.module` parameter entity to the word IGNORE like this, typically in the internal DTD subset:

```
<!ENTITY % smil-attribs.module "IGNORE" >
```

Now all the definitions that import the common attributes module are ignored.

The last import is slightly different:

```
<!ENTITY % smil-model.module "INCLUDE" >
<![%smil-model.module;[
<!-- A content model MUST be defined by the driver file -->
%smil-model.mod;]]>
```

Here the module uses the `%smil-model.mod;` parameter entity reference but does not actually define it. It must already have been defined in the driver DTD, Listing 26-2 for our example. Looking back at Listing 26-2, you see that `%smil-model.mod;` was defined like this:

```
<!ENTITY % smil-model.mod
PUBLIC "-//W3C//ENTITIES SMIL 2.0 Basic Document Model 1.0//EN"
       "smilbasic-model-1.mod" >
```

This allows the driver DTD to change the model. However, the document model can still make use of the datatypes, qualified names, and common attributes defined in the first three framework modules.

The Datatypes Module

The SMIL 2.0 Datatypes Module defines more descriptive names for XML's limited attribute types. It allows you, for example, to specify that a certain attribute contains a URI or a language code or a number. This is far more descriptive of what the document should actually contain than the customary CDATA, even if DTDs don't allow validation of these more descriptive types.

Note   The SMIL 2.0 specification also includes implementations of the modules as schemas. Unlike DTDs, schema modules do allow data type validation.

Listing 26-4 shows the SMIL Datatypes Module.

Listing 26-4: smil-datatypes-1.mod: The SMIL Datatypes Module DTD

```
<!-- ............................................. -->
<!-- SMIL 2.0 Datatypes Module  ........................... -->
<!-- file: smil-datatypes-1.mod

     This is SMIL 2.0.
     Copyright 1998-2000 W3C (MIT, INRIA, Keio), All Rights
     Reserved.
     Revision: $Id: smil-DTD.html,v 1.1 2001/06/05 09:16:20
                 jigsaw Exp $

     This DTD module is identified by the PUBLIC and SYSTEM
     identifiers:

     PUBLIC "-//W3C//ENTITIES SMIL 2.0 Datatypes 1.0//EN"
     SYSTEM "smil-datatypes-1.mod"


     ............................................. -->

<!-- Datatypes

     defines containers for the following datatypes, many of
     these imported from other specifications and standards.
-->

<!ENTITY % Character.datatype "CDATA">
<!-- a single character from [ISO10646] -->
<!ENTITY % ContentType.datatype "CDATA">
<!-- media type, as per [RFC2045] -->
<!ENTITY % LanguageCode.datatype "NMTOKEN">
<!-- a language code, as per [RFC1766] -->
<!ENTITY % LanguageCodes.datatype "CDATA">
<!--comma-separated list of language codes, as per [RFC1766]-->
<!ENTITY % Number.datatype "CDATA">
<!-- one or more digits -->
<!ENTITY % Script.datatype "CDATA">
<!-- script expression -->
<!ENTITY % Text.datatype "CDATA">
<!-- used for titles etc. -->
<!ENTITY % TimeValue.datatype "CDATA">
<!-- a Number, possibly with its dimension, or a reserved
        word like 'indefinite' -->
<!ENTITY % URI.datatype "CDATA" >
<!-- used for URI references -->
```

DTDs aren't optimized for human legibility, even when relatively well written like this one – even less so when thrown together and poorly commented as is all too often the case. One of the most effective tricks for developing an understanding of a DTD is to reorganize it in a less formal but more legible fashion. Table 26-1 sorts out the Datatypes section into a three-column table corresponding to the parameter entity name, the parameter entity value, and the comment associated with each parameter entity. This table form makes it clearer that the primary responsibility of this module is to provide parameter entities for use as element content models.

Table 26-1
Summary of Imported Names Section

Parameter Entity Name	Parameter Entity Value	Comment Associated with Parameter Entity
Character.datatype	CDATA	a single character from [ISO10646]
ContentType.datatype	CDATA	media type, as per [RFC2045]
LanguageCode.datatype	NMTOKEN	a language code, as per [RFC1766]
LanguageCodes.datatype	CDATA	comma-separated list of language codes, as per [RFC1766]
Number.datatype	CDATA	one or more digits
Script.datatype	CDATA	script expression
Text.datatype	CDATA	used for titles etc.
TimeValue.datatype	CDATA	a Number, possibly with its dimension, or a reserved word like 'indefinite'
URI.datatype	CDATA	used for URI references

What really jumps out from this summary table is the number of synonyms for CDATA. In fact, all but one of these parameter entities is just a different synonym for CDATA. Why is that? It's certainly no easier to type %TimeValue.datatype; than CDATA, even leaving aside the issue of how much time it takes to remember all these different parameter entities.

The answer is that although each of these parameter entity references resolves to simply CDATA, the use of the more descriptive parameter entity names like TimeValue.datatype, URI.datatype, or LanguageCode.datatype makes it more obvious to the reader of the DTD exactly what should go in a particular element or attribute value. Furthermore, the author of the DTD may be looking forward to schemas allowing more detailed requirements to be imposed on attribute values.

These parameter entities are used in place of `CDATA` or `NMTOKEN` in content models in other modules. For example, the `repeatCount` attribute of the `animate` element is an integer specifying the number of times to repeat an animation before stopping. It can now be declared like this:

```
<!ATTLIST animate repeatCount %Number; #IMPLIED>
```

Once all the parameter entities are resolved this is exactly the same as this declaration with only CDATA types:

```
<!ATTLIST animate repeatCount CDATA #IMPLIED>
```

However, the former is a little clearer to humans reading the document. Given the obfuscated nature of most DTDs, this is an important consideration.

The Qualified Names Module

The Qualified Names module does two things:

✦ It defines the namespace URIs and prefixes used in SMIL documents.

✦ It defines parameter entity references for the qualified (prefixed) names.

Together, this allows the document to use non-standard prefixes (and even URIs) simply by overriding a few parameter entity definitions in the internal DTD subset. It even allows a document to use the default namespace instead of prefixes and vice versa. DTDs were not designed with this in mind. Consequently, the techniques used to achieve this are something of a hack. Nonetheless they do work.

Listing 26-5 shows the SMIL qualified names module. The first part, Section A, is very well commented and explains exactly what it's doing and why it's doing it, so read it carefully. The second section defines entity references for element names used elsewhere in the SMIL DTD.

Listing 26-5: **smil-qname-1.mod: The SMIL Qualified Names Module DTD**

```
<!-- ............................................... -->
<!-- SMIL Qualified Names Module  ..................... -->
<!-- file: smil-qname-1.mod

     This is SMIL.
     Copyright 1998-2000 W3C (MIT, INRIA, Keio), All Rights
     Reserved.
     Revision: $Id: smil-DTD.html,v 1.1 2001/06/05 09:16:20
               jigsaw Exp $ SMI
```

This DTD module is identified by the PUBLIC and SYSTEM identifiers:

```
PUBLIC "-//W3C//ENTITIES SMIL Qualified Names 1.0//EN"
SYSTEM "smil-qname-1.mod"
```

```
. . . . . . . . . . . . . . . . . . . . . . . . . . . . . . . . . . . . . . . . . . . . . . . . . . -->
```

```
<!-- SMIL Qualified Names
```

This module is contained in two parts, labeled Section 'A' and 'B':

Section A declares parameter entities to support namespace-qualified names, namespace declarations, and name prefixing for SMIL and extensions.

Section B declares parameter entities used to provide namespace-qualified names for all SMIL element types:

```
%animation.qname; the xmlns-qualified name for <animation>
%video.qname;     the xmlns-qualified name for <video>
...
```

SMIL extensions would create a module similar to this one, using the '%smil-qname-extra.mod;' parameter entity to insert it within Section A. A template module suitable for this purpose ('template-qname-1.mod') is included in the XHTML distribution.
```
-->
```

```
<!-- Section A: SMIL XML Namespace Framework ::::::::::::::: -->
```

```
<!-- 1. Declare the two parameter entities used to support
        XLink, first the parameter entity container for the URI
        used to identify the XLink namespace:
-->
<!ENTITY % XLINK.xmlns "http://www.w3.org/1999/xlink" >
```

```
<!-- This contains the XLink namespace declaration attribute.
-->
<!ENTITY % XLINK.xmlns.attrib
    "xmlns:xlink  %URI.datatype;       #FIXED '%XLINK.xmlns;'"
>
```

```
<!-- 2. Declare parameter entities (eg., %SMIL.xmlns;)
        containing the namespace URI for the SMIL namespace,
        and any namespaces included by SMIL:
-->
```

Continued

Listing 26-5 *(continued)*

```
<!ENTITY % SMIL.xmlns  "http://www.w3.org/2001/SMIL20/PR/" >

<!-- 3. Declare parameter entities (eg., %SMIL.prefix;)
        containing the default namespace prefix string(s) to
        use when prefixing is enabled. This may be overridden
        in the DTD driver or the internal subset of a document
        instance.

     NOTE: As specified in [XMLNAMES], the namespace prefix
     serves as a proxy for the URI reference, and is not in
     itself significant.
-->
<!ENTITY % SMIL.prefix   "" >

<!-- 4. Declare a %SMIL.prefixed; conditional section keyword,
        used to activate namespace prefixing. The default value
        should inherit '%NS.prefixed;' from the DTD driver, so
        that unless overridden, the default behaviour follows
        the overall DTD prefixing scheme.
-->
<!ENTITY % NS.prefixed "IGNORE" >
<!ENTITY % SMIL.prefixed "%NS.prefixed;" >

<!-- 5. Declare parameter entities (eg., %SMIL.pfx;) containing
        the colonized prefix(es) (eg., '%SMIL.prefix;:') used
        when prefixing is active, an empty string when it is
        not.
-->
<![%SMIL.prefixed;[
<!ENTITY % SMIL.pfx   "%SMIL.prefix;:" >
]]>
<!ENTITY % SMIL.pfx   "" >


<!-- declare qualified name extensions here -->
<!ENTITY % smil-qname-extra.mod "" >
%smil-qname-extra.mod;

<!-- 6. The parameter entity %SMIL.xmlns.extra.attrib; may be
        redeclared to contain any non-SMIL namespace
        declaration attributes for namespaces embedded in SMIL.
        The default is an empty string.  XLink should be
        included here if used in the DTD and not already
        included by a previously-declared
        %*.xmlns.extra.attrib;.
-->
<!ENTITY % SMIL.xmlns.extra.attrib "" >
```

```
<!-- 7. The parameter entity %NS.prefixed.attrib; is defined to
        be the prefix for SMIL elements if any and whatever is
        in SMIL.xmlns.extra.attrib.
-->
<![%SMIL.prefixed;[
<!ENTITY % NS.prefixed.attrib
  "xmlns:%SMIL.prefix;%URI.datatype;      #FIXED '%SMIL.xmlns;'
  %SMIL.xmlns.extra.attrib; " >
]]>
<!ENTITY % NS.prefixed.attrib "%SMIL.xmlns.extra.attrib;" >


<!-- Section B: SMIL Qualified Names
:::::::::::::::::::::::::::::::: -->

<!-- This section declares parameter entities used to provide
     namespace-qualified names for all SMIL element types.
-->

<!ENTITY % animate.qname "%SMIL.pfx;animate" >
<!ENTITY % set.qname "%SMIL.pfx;set" >
<!ENTITY % animateMotion.qname "%SMIL.pfx;animateMotion" >
<!ENTITY % animateColor.qname "%SMIL.pfx;animateColor" >

<!ENTITY % switch.qname "%SMIL.pfx;switch" >
<!ENTITY % customTest.qname "%SMIL.pfx;customTest" >
<!ENTITY % customAttributes.qname "%SMIL.pfx;customAttributes"
>
<!ENTITY % prefetch.qname "%SMIL.pfx;prefetch" >

<!ENTITY % layout.qname "%SMIL.pfx;layout" >
<!ENTITY % region.qname "%SMIL.pfx;region" >
<!ENTITY % root-layout.qname "%SMIL.pfx;root-layout" >
<!ENTITY % topLayout.qname "%SMIL.pfx;topLayout" >
<!ENTITY % regPoint.qname "%SMIL.pfx;regPoint" >

<!ENTITY % a.qname "%SMIL.pfx;a" >
<!ENTITY % area.qname "%SMIL.pfx;area" >
<!ENTITY % anchor.qname "%SMIL.pfx;anchor" >

<!ENTITY % ref.qname "%SMIL.pfx;ref" >
<!ENTITY % audio.qname "%SMIL.pfx;audio" >
<!ENTITY % img.qname "%SMIL.pfx;img" >
<!ENTITY % video.qname "%SMIL.pfx;video" >
<!ENTITY % text.qname "%SMIL.pfx;text" >
<!ENTITY % textstream.qname "%SMIL.pfx;textstream" >
<!ENTITY % animation.qname "%SMIL.pfx;animation" >
<!ENTITY % param.qname "%SMIL.pfx;param" >
<!ENTITY % brush.qname "%SMIL.pfx;brush" >
```

Continued

Listing 26-5 *(continued)*

```
<!ENTITY % meta.qname "%SMIL.pfx;meta" >
<!ENTITY % metadata.qname "%SMIL.pfx;metadata" >

<!ENTITY % smil.qname "%SMIL.pfx;smil" >
<!ENTITY % head.qname "%SMIL.pfx;head" >
<!ENTITY % body.qname "%SMIL.pfx;body" >

<!ENTITY % seq.qname "%SMIL.pfx;seq" >
<!ENTITY % par.qname "%SMIL.pfx;par" >
<!ENTITY % excl.qname "%SMIL.pfx;excl" >

<!ENTITY % transition.qname "%SMIL.pfx;transition" >
<!ENTITY % transitionFilter.qname "%SMIL.pfx;transitionFilter"
>

<!-- end of smil-qname-1.mod -->
```

Section A defines the `%SMIL.pfx;` parameter entity references as being equivalent to the empty string. However, if you prefer to use a prefix like `smil` rather than the default namespace, you can override this definition. You might think that it would be enough to declare elements like this so they could either be or not be prefixed:

```
<!ELEMENT %SMIL.pfx;head (layout)>
```

However, when expanding parameter entity references inside element declarations, the processor places extra white space around each resolved entity. For example, suppose `%SMIL.pfx;` is defined as `smil`. Then the element declaration that actually comes out is this:

```
<!ELEMENT  smil: head (layout)>
```

This is not well-formed because of the space between the colon and the local name. On the other hand, the processor does not add extra white space around parameter entities that are expanded inside the replacement text of other entity definitions. Thus this entity declaration:

```
<!ENTITY % head.qname "%SMIL.pfx;head" >
```

resolves to this after the `%SMIL.pfx;` entity reference is expanded:

```
<!ENTITY % head.qname "smil:head" >
```

Now the `%head.qname;` entity reference can be used in element declarations. Since this is the complete name which must have white space around it anyway, it doesn't matter if the processor adds a couple of extra spaces around its replacement text when substituting for it. In other words,

```
<!ELEMENT %head.qname;head (layout)>
```

expands to

```
<!ELEMENT  smil:head  (layout)>
```

This is perfectly well-formed. Double indirection is being used here just to make the prefixes on element names optional.

One thing that I think could be handled a little better in this module is the white space. I admit I'm a white space fanatic. Nonetheless, which would you prefer? This:

```
<!ENTITY % animate.qname "%SMIL.pfx;animate" >
<!ENTITY % set.qname "%SMIL.pfx;set" >
<!ENTITY % animateMotion.qname "%SMIL.pfx;animateMotion" >
<!ENTITY % animateColor.qname "%SMIL.pfx;animateColor" >
```

Or this?

```
<!ENTITY % animate.qname        "%SMIL.pfx;animate" >
<!ENTITY % set.qname            "%SMIL.pfx;set" >
<!ENTITY % animateMotion.qname  "%SMIL.pfx;animateMotion" >
<!ENTITY % animateColor.qname   "%SMIL.pfx;animateColor" >
```

Almost everyone would agree that the latter is an improvement. Once again, this is not simply a matter of aesthetics. A DTD that looks better is easier to read and easier to comprehend. While I don't recommend spending a lot of effort on polishing the white space in a DTD at the earliest stages of development, it's certainly worth doing as part of the final touch-ups.

The Common Attributes Module

The Common Attributes Module declares attributes that are shared between many different elements in SMIL; for instance, `id` and `system-screen-size`. By declaring them as parameter entities here and then dereferencing these parameter entities in the actual `ATTLIST` declarations, this module helps maintain consistency between all the different elements. Adding attributes to, subtracting attributes from, or modifying any group of attributes can be done in this one DTD rather than in many separate places. Listing 26-6 shows the SMIL common attributes module:

Listing 26-6: smil-attribs-1.mod: The SMIL Common Attributes Module DTD

```
<!-- ........................................................ -->
<!-- SMIL 2.0 Common Attributes Module  ................... -->
<!-- file: smil-attribs-1.mod

     This is SMIL 2.0.
     Copyright 2000 W3C (MIT, INRIA, Keio), All Rights
     Reserved.
     Revision: $Id: smil-attribs-1.mod,v 1.40 2001/04/12
               09:48:38 jvanoss Exp $

     This DTD module is identified by the PUBLIC and SYSTEM
     identifiers:

     PUBLIC "-//W3C//ENTITIES SMIL 2.0 Common Attributes 1.0//EN"
     SYSTEM "smil-attribs-1.mod"

     .................................................... -->

<!-- Common Attributes

     This module declares the common attributes for the SMIL
     DTD Modules.
-->

<!ENTITY % SMIL.pfx "">

<!ENTITY % Id.attrib
 "%SMIL.pfx;id             ID                   #IMPLIED"
>

<!ENTITY % Class.attrib
 "%SMIL.pfx;class          CDATA                #IMPLIED"
>

<!ENTITY % Title.attrib
 "%SMIL.pfx;title          %Text.datatype;      #IMPLIED"
>

<!ENTITY % Longdesc.attrib
 "%SMIL.pfx;longdesc       %URI.datatype;       #IMPLIED"
>

<!ENTITY % Alt.attrib
 "%SMIL.pfx;alt            %Text.datatype;      #IMPLIED"
>

<!ENTITY % Accessibility.attrib "
 %Longdesc.attrib;
 %Alt.attrib;
```

```
">

<!ENTITY % Core.extra.attrib "" >
<!ENTITY % Core.attrib "
  xml:base %URI.datatype; #IMPLIED
  %Id.attrib;
  %Class.attrib;
  %Title.attrib;
  %Accessibility.attrib;
  %Core.extra.attrib;
">

<!ENTITY % I18n.extra.attrib "" >
<!ENTITY % I18n.attrib "
  xml:lang %LanguageCode.datatype; #IMPLIED
  %I18n.extra.attrib;"
>

<!ENTITY % Description.attrib "
 %SMIL.pfx;abstract         %Text.datatype;    #IMPLIED
 %SMIL.pfx;author           %Text.datatype;    #IMPLIED
 %SMIL.pfx;copyright        %Text.datatype;    #IMPLIED
">

<!ENTITY % Tabindex.attrib "
 %SMIL.pfx;tabindex         %Number.datatype;  #IMPLIED
">

<!-- ================== BasicLayout ======================= -->
<!ENTITY % Region.attrib "
 %SMIL.pfx;region           CDATA #IMPLIED
">

<!ENTITY % Fill.attrib "
 %SMIL.pfx;fill (remove|freeze|hold|transition|auto|default)
  'default'
">

<!ENTITY % FillDefault.attrib "
 %SMIL.pfx;fillDefault
(remove|freeze|hold|transition|auto|inherit) 'inherit'
">

<!-- ================== HierarchicalLayout ================ -->
<!ENTITY % BackgroundColor.attrib "
 %SMIL.pfx;backgroundColor    CDATA      #IMPLIED
">
<!ENTITY % BackgroundColor-deprecated.attrib "
 %SMIL.pfx;background-color    CDATA      #IMPLIED
">

<!ENTITY % Sub-region.attrib "
```

Continued

Listing 26-6 *(continued)*

```
%SMIL.pfx;top      CDATA     'auto'
%SMIL.pfx;bottom   CDATA     'auto'
%SMIL.pfx;left     CDATA     'auto'
%SMIL.pfx;right    CDATA     'auto'
%SMIL.pfx;height   CDATA     'auto'
%SMIL.pfx;width    CDATA     'auto'
%SMIL.pfx;z-index CDATA      #IMPLIED
">

<!ENTITY % Fit.attrib "
 %SMIL.pfx;fit         (hidden|fill|meet|scroll|slice)   #IMPLIED
">

<!-- === Registration Point attribute for media elements == -->
<!-- integrating language using HierarchicalLayout must include
     regPoint   -->
<!-- attribute on media elements for regPoint elements to be
     useful     -->

<!ENTITY % RegPoint.attrib "
 %SMIL.pfx;regPoint  CDATA    #IMPLIED
">

<!ENTITY % RegAlign.attrib "
 %SMIL.pfx;regAlign  (topLeft|topMid|topRight|midLeft|center|
          midRight|bottomLeft|bottomMid|bottomRight) #IMPLIED
">

<!ENTITY % RegistrationPoint.attrib "
 %RegPoint.attrib;
 %RegAlign.attrib;
">

<!--==================== Content Control =====================-->
<!-- customTest Attribute -->
<!ENTITY % CustomTest.attrib "
      %SMIL.pfx;customTest                IDREF       #IMPLIED
">

<!-- ========================== SkipContentControl Module == -->
<!ENTITY % SkipContent.attrib "
  %SMIL.pfx;skip-content    (true|false)  'true'
">

<!-- Content Control Test Attributes -->

<!ENTITY % Test.attrib "
  %SMIL.pfx;systemBitrate            CDATA    #IMPLIED
  %SMIL.pfx;systemCaptions           (on|off) #IMPLIED
  %SMIL.pfx;systemLanguage           CDATA    #IMPLIED
  %SMIL.pfx;systemOverdubOrSubtitle (overdub|subtitle) #IMPLIED
```

```
    %SMIL.pfx;systemRequired          CDATA      #IMPLIED
    %SMIL.pfx;systemScreenSize        CDATA      #IMPLIED
    %SMIL.pfx;systemScreenDepth       CDATA      #IMPLIED
    %SMIL.pfx;systemAudioDesc         (on|off)   #IMPLIED
    %SMIL.pfx;systemOperatingSystem   NMTOKEN    #IMPLIED
    %SMIL.pfx;systemCPU               NMTOKEN    #IMPLIED
    %SMIL.pfx;systemComponent         CDATA      #IMPLIED

    %SMIL.pfx;system-bitrate          CDATA      #IMPLIED
    %SMIL.pfx;system-captions         (on|off)   #IMPLIED
    %SMIL.pfx;system-language         CDATA      #IMPLIED
  %SMIL.pfx;system-overdub-or-caption (overdub|caption) #IMPLIED
    %SMIL.pfx;system-required         CDATA      #IMPLIED
    %SMIL.pfx;system-screen-size      CDATA      #IMPLIED
    %SMIL.pfx;system-screen-depth     CDATA      #IMPLIED
">

<!-- SMIL Animation Module   ================================ -->
<!ENTITY % BasicAnimation.attrib "
    %SMIL.pfx;values    CDATA #IMPLIED
    %SMIL.pfx;from      CDATA #IMPLIED
    %SMIL.pfx;to        CDATA #IMPLIED
    %SMIL.pfx;by        CDATA #IMPLIED
">

<!-- SMIL Timing Module   ================================= -->
<!ENTITY % BasicInlineTiming.attrib "
   %SMIL.pfx;dur                   %TimeValue.datatype; #IMPLIED
   %SMIL.pfx;repeatCount           %TimeValue.datatype; #IMPLIED
   %SMIL.pfx;repeatDur             %TimeValue.datatype; #IMPLIED
   %SMIL.pfx;begin                 %TimeValue.datatype; #IMPLIED
   %SMIL.pfx;end                   %TimeValue.datatype; #IMPLIED
">

<!ENTITY % MinMaxTiming.attrib "
   %SMIL.pfx;min              %TimeValue.datatype; '0'
   %SMIL.pfx;max              %TimeValue.datatype; 'indefinite'
">

<!ENTITY % BasicInlineTiming-deprecated.attrib "
   %SMIL.pfx;repeat           %TimeValue.datatype; #IMPLIED
">

<!ENTITY % Endsync.attrib "
   %SMIL.pfx;endsync               CDATA 'last'
">

<!-- endsync has a different default when applied to media
     elements -->
<!ENTITY % Endsync.media.attrib "
  %SMIL.pfx;endsync                CDATA 'media'
```

Continued

Listing 26-6 *(continued)*

```
">

<!ENTITY % TimeContainerAttributes.attrib "
  %SMIL.pfx;timeAction           CDATA #IMPLIED
  %SMIL.pfx;timeContainer        CDATA #IMPLIED
">

<!ENTITY % RestartTiming.attrib "
  %SMIL.pfx;restart (always|whenNotActive|never|default)
   'default'
">

<!ENTITY % RestartDefaultTiming.attrib "
  %SMIL.pfx;restartDefault (inherit|always|never|whenNotActive)
   'inherit'
">

<!ENTITY % SyncBehavior.attrib "
  %SMIL.pfx;syncBehavior (canSlip|locked|independent|default)
    'default'
  %SMIL.pfx;syncTolerance %TimeValue.datatype;   'default'
">

<!ENTITY % SyncBehaviorDefault.attrib "
  %SMIL.pfx;syncBehaviorDefault
  (canSlip|locked|independent|inherit) 'inherit'
  %SMIL.pfx;syncToleranceDefault %TimeValue.datatype; 'inherit'
">

<!ENTITY % SyncMaster.attrib "
  %SMIL.pfx;syncMaster    (true|false)                'false'
">

<!-- ================== Time Manipulations ================ -->
<!ENTITY % TimeManipulations.attrib "
  %SMIL.pfx;accelerate  %Number.datatype; '0'
  %SMIL.pfx;decelerate  %Number.datatype; '0'
  %SMIL.pfx;speed       %Number.datatype; '1.0'
  %SMIL.pfx;autoReverse (true|false)      'false'
">

<!-- ================= Media Objects ===================== -->
<!ENTITY % MediaClip.attrib "
  %SMIL.pfx;clipBegin     CDATA   #IMPLIED
  %SMIL.pfx;clipEnd       CDATA   #IMPLIED
">
<!ENTITY % MediaClip.attrib.deprecated "
  %SMIL.pfx;clip-begin    CDATA   #IMPLIED
  %SMIL.pfx;clip-end      CDATA   #IMPLIED
">
```

```
<!-- =================== Streaming Media =================== -->
<!ENTITY % Streaming-media.attrib "
  %SMIL.pfx;port                     CDATA    #IMPLIED
  %SMIL.pfx;rtpformat                CDATA    #IMPLIED
  %SMIL.pfx;transport                CDATA    #IMPLIED
">

<!ENTITY % Streaming-timecontainer.attrib "
  %SMIL.pfx;control                  CDATA    #IMPLIED
">

<!-- ================== Transitions Media ================== -->
<!ENTITY % Transition.attrib "
  %SMIL.pfx;transIn                  CDATA         #IMPLIED
  %SMIL.pfx;transOut                 CDATA         #IMPLIED
">
```

What's provided here are not the actual ATTLIST declarations themselves, but rather entities that can be used in ATTLIST declarations for different elements elsewhere in the DTD.

Some of these entities define single attribute, like this one used to declare the id attribute:

```
<!ENTITY % Id.attrib
  "%SMIL.pfx;id            ID            #IMPLIED"
>
```

Others define a single attribute, but allow the author to add to the list by redefining an extra parameter entity reference. For example, the I18n.attrib entity is used to declare the xml:lang attribute:

```
<!ENTITY % I18n.extra.attrib "" >
<!ENTITY % I18n.attrib "
  xml:lang %LanguageCode.datatype; #IMPLIED
  %I18n.extra.attrib;"
>
```

However, you can add additional attributes to the I18N group by redefining I18n.extra.attrib like this:

```
<!ENTITY % I18n.extra.attrib "
  country NMTOKEN #IMPLIED
  "
>
```

Note   If you're curious why I18N is the abbreviation for *internationalization*, count the number of letters between the first *i* and last *n* in *internationalization*.

Still others actually do declare multiple attributes. For example, the last declaration in the common attributes module defines an entity named `Transition.attrib` whose replacement text is, assuming no prefix is being used:

```
transIn  IDREF        #IMPLIED
transOut IDREF        #IMPLIED
```

This is used like this in the transitions module (Listing 26-17):

```
<!ATTLIST %transition.qname; %transition.attrib;
    startProgress CDATA              "0.0"
    endProgress   CDATA              "1.0"
    direction     (forward|reverse)  "forward"
>
```

When the parameter entities are resolved, it becomes this:

```
<!ATTLIST transition
    transIn  IDREF            #IMPLIED
    transOut IDREF            #IMPLIED
    startProgress CDATA               "0.0"
    endProgress   CDATA               "1.0"
    direction     (forward|reverse)   "forward"
>
```

(I've taken a few liberties with the white space here, but that's not significant in this context.)

The attribute names are all declared using the `%SMIL.pfx;` parameter entity reference defined in the qualified names module of Listing 26-4. This way it can be decided at runtime whether or not to use prefixes on the attributes; that is, whether attribute names should be written like `transOut` or `smil:transOut`. This is the same trick that was used in Listing 26-4 to define element names with optional prefixes.

Caution While using a doubly indirected parameter entity reference to make namespace prefixes on elements optional is a very useful hack for element names, it doesn't work nearly so well for attribute names. The reason is that attributes, unlike elements, are only in a namespace when they have a prefix. An unprefixed attribute is never in any namespace, whether the default namespace or the namespace of the element it belongs to. Thus adding a prefix to an attribute moves the attribute from no namespace at all to the http://www.w3.org/2001/SMIL20/PR/. That has the potential to confuse parsers that are correctly looking for attributes that don't belong to any namespace.

I recommend that you not give your attributes optional prefixes. An attribute should either be required to have a prefix or not to have a prefix. Both cases should not be allowed. Of course if you do require your attributes to have prefixes, then you can still use this trick to change what prefix is used in any given document. However, you should not use this trick to turn off prefixing completely.

One common attribute declaration is a little funny because it's provided twice:

```
<!ENTITY % Endsync.attrib "
  %SMIL.pfx;endsync               CDATA 'last'
">

<!-- endsync has a different default when applied to media
     elements -->
<!ENTITY % Endsync.media.attrib "
  %SMIL.pfx;endsync               CDATA 'media'
">
```

Since this is very unusual, it's good that there's a comment to explain what's going on. Most elements that use the `endsync` attribute will use the `%Endsync.attrib;` parameter entity reference; but the media elements will use `%Endsync.media.attrib;` instead. The symmetry breaking here is a little disturbing, but not overwhelmingly so. It's an unfortunate necessity because it's not possible for the a module to override a definition of an entity made previously. All entities are defined exactly once, and subsequent definitions are ignored.

The Basic Profile Document Model

The final piece the framework module imports is the content model for the document. This module is responsible for defining parameter entity references for content models of the elements and attributes that will be declared in other modules. Using parameter entities instead of directly declaring content models offers two benefits:

✦ The same content models can be used for multiple elements, automatically maintaining consistency between them.

✦ By overriding the parameter entity definitions elsewhere, especially in the internal DTD subset, you can change the names and content models of the elements and attributes. This is particularly important when adding namespace prefixes to elements.

Listing 26-7 shows a Document Model Module for SMIL 2.0 Basic.

Listing 26-7: **smilbasic-model-1.mod: The SMIL Basic Document Model DTD**

```
<!-- =========================================================  -->
<!-- SMIL 2.0 Document Model Module ========================  -->
<!-- file: smil-model-1.mod

     This is SMIL 2.0.
     Copyright 1998-2000 W3C (MIT, INRIA, Keio), All Rights
     Reserved.

     This DTD module is identified by the PUBLIC and SYSTEM
     identifiers:

PUBLIC "-//W3C//ENTITIES SMIL 2.0 Basic Document Model 1.0//EN"
SYSTEM "smilbasic-model-1.mod"

Author: Kenichi Kubota, Warner ten Kate,
        Jacco van Ossenbruggen, Aaron Cohen
Revision: $Id: smil-DTD.html,v 1.13 2000/09/21 01:39:23 tmichel
             Exp $

     The W3C stopped publishing separate DTDs for SMIL Basic
     and full SMIL after the working draft of September 21,
     2001. Elliotte Rusty Harold derived this DTD by combining
     parts of the SMIL Basic DTD in that draft with parts of
     the full DTD from the June 5, 2001 Proposed Recommendation.


     ========================================================= -->

<!--
        This file defines the SMIL 2.0 Language Document Model.
        All attributes and content models are defined in the
        second half of this file.  We first start with some
        utility definitions.  These are mainly used to simplify
        the use of Modules in the second part of the file.

-->

<!-- ================== Util: Head ======================= -->
<!ENTITY % head-layout.content     "layout">

<!--==================== Util: Body - Content Control ====== -->
<!ENTITY % content-control "switch">
<!ENTITY % content-control-attrs
    "%Test.attrib; %CustomTest.attrib; %SkipContent.attrib;">

<!--==================== Util: Body - Media =============== -->

<!ENTITY % media-object "audio|video|text|img|textstream|ref">

<!--==================== Util: Body - Timing =========== -->
```

```
<!ENTITY % BasicTimeContainers.class "par|seq">
<!ENTITY % timecontainer.class "%BasicTimeContainers.class;">
<!ENTITY % timecontainer.content
 "%timecontainer.class;|%media-object;|%content-control;|a">

<!ENTITY % smil-basictime.attrib "
 %BasicInlineTiming.attrib;
 %MinMaxTiming.attrib;
">

<!ENTITY % timecontainer.attrib "
 %BasicInlineTiming.attrib;
 %MinMaxTiming.attrib;
 %RestartTiming.attrib;
 %RestartDefaultTiming.attrib;
 %FillDefault.attrib;
">

<!-- ======================================================== -->
<!-- ======================================================== -->
<!-- ======================================================== -->

<!--
    The actual content model and attribute definitions for
    each module sections follow below.
-->

<!-- ================== Content Control =================== -->
<!ENTITY % BasicContentControl.module  "INCLUDE">
<!ENTITY % SkipContentControl.module   "INCLUDE">

<!ENTITY % switch.content "((%timecontainer.class;|
    %media-object;|%content-control;|a|area|anchor)*|layout*)">

<!ENTITY % switch.attrib    "%Test.attrib; %CustomTest.attrib;">

<!ENTITY % customAttributes.attrib
    "%Test.attrib; %SkipContent.attrib;">
<!ENTITY % customTest.attrib
    "%SkipContent.attrib;">

<!-- ================== Layout ============================ -->
<!ENTITY % BasicLayout.module          "INCLUDE">

<!ENTITY % layout.content "(region|topLayout|
root-layout|regPoint)*">
<!ENTITY % region.content "(region)*">
<!ENTITY % topLayout.content "(region)*">
<!ENTITY % rootlayout.content "EMPTY">
<!ENTITY % regPoint.content "EMPTY">

<!ENTITY % layout.attrib               "%Test.attrib;
```

Continued

Listing 26-7 *(continued)*

```
%CustomTest.attrib;">
<!ENTITY % rootlayout.attrib      "%content-control-attrs;">
<!ENTITY % topLayout.attrib       "%content-control-attrs;">
<!ENTITY % region.attrib          "%content-control-attrs;">
<!ENTITY % regPoint.attrib        "%content-control-attrs;">

<!-- ================= Linking =========================== -->
<!ENTITY % LinkingAttributes.module "INCLUDE">
<!ENTITY % BasicLinking.module      "INCLUDE">

<!ENTITY % a.content     "(%timecontainer.class;|%media-object;|
                          %content-control;)*">
<!ENTITY % area.content   "EMPTY">
<!ENTITY % anchor.content "EMPTY">

<!ENTITY % a.attrib       "%smil-basictime.attrib; %Test.attrib;
%CustomTest.attrib;">
<!ENTITY % area.attrib    "%smil-basictime.attrib; %content-
control-attrs;">
<!ENTITY % anchor.attrib "%smil-basictime.attrib; %content-
control-attrs;">

<!-- ================= Media  =========================== -->
<!ENTITY % BasicMedia.module                    "INCLUDE">

<!ENTITY % media-object.content "(switch|anchor|area|param)*">
<!ENTITY % media-object.attrib "
  %BasicInlineTiming.attrib;
  %MinMaxTiming.attrib;
  %SyncBehavior.attrib;
  %SyncBehaviorDefault.attrib;
  %Endsync.media.attrib;
  %Fill.attrib;
  %FillDefault.attrib;
  %Test.attrib;
  %CustomTest.attrib;
  %Region.attrib;
  %Transition.attrib;
  %BackgroundColor.attrib;
  %Sub-region.attrib;
  %RegistrationPoint.attrib;
  %Fit.attrib;
  %Tabindex.attrib;
">

<!ENTITY % param.attrib          "%content-control-attrs;">

<!-- ================= Structure ========================= -->
<!ENTITY % Structure.module "INCLUDE">
<!ENTITY % smil.content "(head?,body?)">
<!ENTITY % head.content "(
```

```
                (%head-layout.content;)?
)">
<!ENTITY % body.content "(%timecontainer.class;|%media-object;|
                        %content-control;|a)*">

<!ENTITY % smil.attrib "%Test.attrib;">
<!ENTITY % body.attrib "
        %timecontainer.attrib;
        %Description.attrib;
        %Fill.attrib;
">

<!-- ================== Timing ============================ -->
<!ENTITY % BasicInlineTiming.module     "INCLUDE">
<!ENTITY % MinMaxTiming.module          "INCLUDE">
<!ENTITY % BasicTimeContainers.module   "INCLUDE">
<!ENTITY % RestartTiming.module         "INCLUDE">

<!ENTITY % par.attrib "
        %Endsync.attrib;
        %Fill.attrib;
        %timecontainer.attrib;
        %Test.attrib;
        %CustomTest.attrib;
        %Region.attrib;
">
<!ENTITY % seq.attrib "
        %Fill.attrib;
        %timecontainer.attrib;
        %Test.attrib;
        %CustomTest.attrib;
        %Region.attrib;
">
<!ENTITY % par.content  "(%timecontainer.content;)*">
<!ENTITY % seq.content  "(%timecontainer.content;)*">

<!ENTITY % priorityClass.attrib  "%content-control-attrs;">
<!ENTITY % priorityClass.content "(%timecontainer.content;)*">

<!-- ================== End of smilbasic-model-1.mod ====== -->
```

The SMIL 2.0 Basic Content Model Module shown in Listing 26-7 does not declare any elements or attributes. Nor does it use any external parameter entity references to pull in other modules that do declare elements and attributes. Instead this module declares internal parameter entities that will be used to define the content models of elements and attributes elsewhere in the document. For example, the area.content entity contains the content model for area elements. The body.content entity contains the content model for body elements. Attribute lists are similar. The area.attrib entity contains the attribute list for area elements. The body.attrib entity contains the attribute type for body elements, and so on.

Some of the entities declared here are quite straight-forward. For instance, `layout.content` is defined as `"(region|topLayout|root-layout|regPoint)*"`. That doesn't leave a lot of room for interpretation. However, many others are defined in terms of multiple other entities, which are themselves defined in terms of still other entities. To decode these it's easiest to work backwards. To grasp this section, let's use a different trick. Pretend you're cheating on one of those fast food restaurant menu mazes, and work backwards from the goal rather than forwards from the start. For example, let's start by looking at the `body.content` entity:

```
<!ENTITY % body.content "(%timecontainer.class;|%media-object;|
                          %content-control;|a)*">
```

As you can see this depends on three other entities: `timecontainer.class`, `media-object`, and `content-control`.

The `media-object` and `content-control` entities are defined near the beginning of Listing 26-7 using static replacement text:

```
<!ENTITY % media-object "audio|video|text|img|textstream|ref" >
<!ENTITY % content-control "switch">
```

Therefore, these are easy to substitute straight into the definition of `body.content`:

```
<!ENTITY % body.content "(%timecontainer.class;|
audio|video|text|img|textstream|ref|switch|a)*">
```

The one remaining entity is `timecontainer.class`. This is defined a little further down in Listing 26-7 like this:

```
<!ENTITY % timecontainer.class "%BasicTimeContainers.class;">
```

Luckily, the `BasicTimeContainers.class` entity is defined right above like so:

```
<!ENTITY % BasicTimeContainers.class "par|seq">
```

Thus `timeContainer` is really `par|seq`. Plugging this into the definition of `body.content`, you get:

```
<!ENTITY % body.content "(par|seq|text|img|audio|video|
text|img|textstream|ref|switch|a)*">
```

In other words, a `body` element can contain any number of `par`, `seq`, `text`, `img`, `audio`, `video`, `animation`, `textstream`, `ref`, `switch`, `a`, `anchor`, and `area` elements in any order.

Note I've been a little cavalier with whitespace in this example. The true expansion of `%body.content;` isn't so nicely formatted. However, whitespace is insignificant in declarations so this isn't really important, and you should feel free to manually adjust whitespace to line columns up or insert line breaks when manually expanding a parameter entity reference to see what it says.

One technique I find useful when reading modules like this one that define multiple parameter entity references on top of each other is to make a list of the all the entities defined and their fully resolved meaning. Since entities must be defined before they can be referenced, it's straight-forward to start at the top of the file and work down with each entity. The easiest way to do this is to copy the entire module into a blank text file and edit it repeatedly. For example, I begin with this first declaration:

```
<!ENTITY % head-layout.content     "layout">
```

I delete the markup and put a tab in between the entity name and the replacement text, like this (The tabs are shown as arrows.):

```
head-layout.content → layout
```

The next entity in Listing 26-7 is equally straight-forward:

```
<!ENTITY % content-control "switch">
```

After deleting the markup and inserting tabs I now have this:

```
content-control → switch
```

The next entity is a little more complicated because it refers to previous entities:

```
<!ENTITY % content-control-attrs
    "%Test.attrib; %CustomTest.attrib; %SkipContent.attrib;">
```

These were actually declared in a previous module so I leave them untouched here:

```
content-control-attrs → %Test.attrib; %CustomTest.attrib;
%SkipContent.attrib;
```

If these entities had been previously declared in this module, I'd replace them by their actual replacement text.

I contiunue this process until the end of the DTD fragment has been reached. I generally don't bother to include entities like `BasicContentControl.module` that only serve to determine whether a particular group of declarations is inlcuded or ignored. What's left is a table of entity names and the replacement text of each. Table 26-2 shows the final result of this process when applied to Listing 26-7.

Table 26-2
Entities and their replacement text

Parameter Entity	Replacement Text
head-layout.content	layout
content-control	switch
content-control-attrs	%Test.attrib; %CustomTest.attrib; %SkipContent.attrib;
media-object	audio|video|text|img|textstream|ref
BasicTimeContainers.class	par|seq
timecontainer.class	par|seq
timecontainer.content	par|seq|audio|video|text|img| textstream|ref|switch|a
smil-basictime.attrib	%BasicInlineTiming.attrib; %MinMaxTiming.attrib;
timecontainer.attrib	%BasicInlineTiming.attrib; %MinMaxTiming.attrib; %RestartTiming.attrib; %RestartDefaultTiming.attrib; %FillDefault.attrib;
switch.content	((par|seq|audio|video|text|img| textstream|ref|switch|a|area|anchor)* |layout*)
switch.attrib	%Test.attrib; %CustomTest.attrib;
customAttributes.attrib	%Test.attrib; %SkipContent.attrib;
customTest.attrib	%SkipContent.attrib;
layout.content	(region|topLayout|root- layout|regPoint)*
region.content	(region)*
topLayout.content	(region)*
rootlayout.content	EMPTY
regPoint.content	EMPTY
layout.attrib	%Test.attrib; %CustomTest.attrib;
rootlayout.attrib	%Test.attrib; %CustomTest.attrib; %SkipContent.attrib;
topLayout.attrib	%Test.attrib; %CustomTest.attrib; %SkipContent.attrib;

Parameter Entity	Replacement Text
region.attrib	%Test.attrib; %CustomTest.attrib; %SkipContent.attrib;
regPoint.attrib	%Test.attrib; %CustomTest.attrib; %SkipContent.attrib;
a.content	(par|seq|audio|video|text|img| textstream|ref|switch)*">
area.content	EMPTY
anchor.content	EMPTY
a.attrib	%BasicInlineTiming.attrib; %MinMaxTiming.attrib; %Test.attrib; %CustomTest.attrib;
area.attrib	%BasicInlineTiming.attrib; %MinMaxTiming.attrib; %Test.attrib; %CustomTest.attrib; %SkipContent.attrib;
anchor.attrib	%BasicInlineTiming.attrib; %MinMaxTiming.attrib; %Test.attrib; %CustomTest.attrib; %SkipContent.attrib;
media-object.content	(switch|anchor|area|param)*
media-object.attrib	%BasicInlineTiming.attrib; %MinMaxTiming.attrib; %SyncBehavior.attrib; %SyncBehaviorDefault.attrib; %Endsync.media.attrib; %Fill.attrib; %FillDefault.attrib; %Test.attrib; %CustomTest.attrib; %Region.attrib; %Transition.attrib; %BackgroundColor.attrib; %Sub-region.attrib; %RegistrationPoint.attrib; %Fit.attrib; %Tabindex.attrib;
param.attrib	%Test.attrib; %CustomTest.attrib; %SkipContent.attrib;
smil.content	(head?,body?)
head.content	((layout)?)
body.content	(par|seq|audio|video|text|img| textstream|ref|switch|a)*

Continued

Table 26-2 *(continued)*	
Parameter Entity	***Replacement Text***
`smil.attrib`	`%Test.attrib;`

`% body.attrib`	`%BasicInlineTiming.attrib;`
	 `%MinMaxTiming.attrib;`
	 `%RestartTiming.attrib;`
	 `%RestartDefaultTiming.attrib;`
	 `%FillDefault.attrib;`
	 `%Description.attrib; %Fill.attrib;`

`par.attrib`	`%Endsync.attrib; %Fill.attrib;`
	 `%timecontainer.attrib; %Test.attrib;`
	 `%CustomTest.attrib; %Region.attrib;`

`seq.attrib`	`%Fill.attrib; %timecontainer.attrib;`
	 `%Test.attrib; %CustomTest.attrib;`
	 `%Region.attrib;`

`par.content`	`(par|seq|audio|video|text|img|` `textstream|ref|switch|a)*`
`seq.content`	`(par|seq|audio|video|text|img|` `textstream|ref|switch|a)*`
`priorityClass.attrib`	`%Test.attrib; %CustomTest.attrib;` `%SkipContent.attrib;`
`priorityClass.content`	`(par|seq|audio|video|text|img|` `textstream|ref|switch|a)*`

You'll note that some of these entities cannot be resolved fully solely within Listing 26-7. Many of them depend on entities defined in other modules such as Listing 26-6, common attributes. If it seems useful you can merge those entities into this table as well. However, even if you do that, you should start with resolving the entities within a single file as shown in Table 26-2.

The Layout Module

Just to refresh your memory, the SMIL Basic profile is divided into DTD fragments like this. The bold ones are the ones you've seen.

```
SMIL20Basic.dtd
  |
  +--smil-framework.mod
  |    |
  |    +--smil-datatypes-1.mod
  |    |
```

```
    |      +--smil-qname-1.mod
    |      |
    |      +--smil-attribs-1.mod
    |      |
    |      +--smilbasic-model-1.mod
    |
    +--SMIL-struct.mod
    |
    +--SMIL-control.mod
    |
    +--SMIL-layout.mod
    |
    +--SMIL-link.mod
    |
    +--SMIL-media.mod
    |
    +--SMIL-timing.mod
```

Up till now, I've just been setting up the framework on top of which the rest of modules will be built. Many parameter entities have been declared representing element content models, attribute content models, element and attribute names, and namespace URIs and prefixes. However, none of these have actually been used. Up till this point exactly *zero* elements and attributes have been declared. That changes now. The next six modules all declare elements and attributes. Each module declares elements and attributes for one particular part of SMIL such as timing or the different media types that can be played by a SMIL player.

The Layout module defines those elements and attributes for specifying where to place particular media in particular windows such as layout, region and root-layout. Listing 26-8 shows the SMIL Layout Module DTD:

Listing 26-8: **SMIL-layout.mod: The SMIL Layout Module DTD**

```
<!-- ============================================================ -->
<!-- SMIL 2.0 Layout Modules ================================ -->
<!-- file: SMIL-layout.mod

        This is SMIL 2.0.
        Copyright 2000 W3C (MIT, INRIA, Keio), All Rights
        Reserved.

        Authors:  Jacco van Ossenbruggen, Aaron Cohen
        Revision: $Id: SMIL-layout.mod,v 1.23 2001/03/29
                  16:20:29 jvanoss Exp $

        This DTD module is identified by the PUBLIC and SYSTEM
        identifiers:

        PUBLIC "-//W3C//ELEMENTS SMIL 2.0 Layout//EN"
```

Continued

Listing 26-8 *(continued)*

```
        SYSTEM "SMIL-layout.mod"

        ================================================== -->

<!-- ================= BasicLayout ====================== -->
<!-- ================= BasicLayout Profiling Entities ==== -->
<!ENTITY % layout.attrib      "">
<!ENTITY % region.attrib      "">
<!ENTITY % rootlayout.attrib  "">
<!ENTITY % layout.content     "EMPTY">
<!ENTITY % region.content     "EMPTY">
<!ENTITY % rootlayout.content "EMPTY">

<!-- ================= BasicLayout Entities ============== -->
<!ENTITY % common-layout-attrs "
        height              CDATA     'auto'
        width               CDATA     'auto'
        %BackgroundColor.attrib;
">

<!ENTITY % region-attrs "
        bottom              CDATA     'auto'
        left                CDATA     'auto'
        right               CDATA     'auto'
        top                 CDATA     'auto'
        z-index             CDATA     #IMPLIED
   showBackground        (always|whenActive) 'always'
   %Fit.attrib;
">

<!-- ================= BasicLayout Elements ============== -->
<!--
    Layout contains the region and root-layout elements
    defined by smil-basic-layout or other elements defined an
    external layout mechanism.
-->

<!ENTITY % layout.qname "layout">
<!ELEMENT %layout.qname; %layout.content;>
<!ATTLIST %layout.qname; %layout.attrib;
        %Core.attrib;
        %I18n.attrib;
        type CDATA 'text/smil-basic-layout'
>

<!-- ================= Region Element =======================-->
<!ENTITY % region.qname "region">
<!ELEMENT %region.qname; %region.content;>
<!ATTLIST %region.qname; %region.attrib;
        %Core.attrib;
        %I18n.attrib;
```

```
        %BackgroundColor-deprecated.attrib;
        %common-layout-attrs;
        %region-attrs;
        regionName CDATA #IMPLIED
>

<!-- ================== Root-layout Element ================-->
<!ENTITY % root-layout.qname "root-layout">
<!ELEMENT %root-layout.qname; %rootlayout.content; >
<!ATTLIST %root-layout.qname; %rootlayout.attrib;
      %Core.attrib;
      %I18n.attrib;
      %BackgroundColor-deprecated.attrib;
      %common-layout-attrs;
>


<!-- ================= AudioLayout ===================== -->
<!ENTITY % AudioLayout.module "IGNORE">
<![%AudioLayout.module;[
  <!-- ================== AudioLayout Entities =========== -->
  <!ENTITY % audio-attrs "
      soundLevel                         CDATA    '100&#37;'
  ">

  <!-- ================= AudioLayout Elements ============== -->
  <!-- ================ Add soundLevel to region element == -->
  <!ATTLIST %region.qname; %audio-attrs;>
]]> <!-- end AudioLayout.module -->


<!-- ================ MultiWindowLayout =================== -->
<!ENTITY % MultiWindowLayout.module "IGNORE">
<![%MultiWindowLayout.module;[
  <!-- ============== MultiWindowLayout Profiling Entities = -->
  <!ENTITY % topLayout.attrib    "">
  <!ENTITY % topLayout.content   "EMPTY">

  <!-- ============== MultiWindowLayout Elements ========= -->
  <!--================= topLayout element ================= -->
  <!ENTITY % topLayout.qname "topLayout">
  <!ELEMENT %topLayout.qname; %topLayout.content;>
  <!ATTLIST %topLayout.qname; %topLayout.attrib;
      %Core.attrib;
      %I18n.attrib;
      %common-layout-attrs;
    close              (onRequest|whenNotActive) 'onRequest'
    open               (onStart|whenActive)      'onStart'
  >
]]> <!-- end MultiWindowLayout.module -->
```

Continued

Listing 26-8 *(continued)*

```
    <!-- ===================== HierarchicalLayout ============ -->
<!ENTITY % HierarchicalLayout.module "IGNORE">
<![%HierarchicalLayout.module;[
    <!-- ========== HierarchicalLayout Profiling Entities === -->
    <!ENTITY % regPoint.attrib      "">
    <!ENTITY % regPoint.content    "EMPTY">

    <!-- ============ HierarchicalLayout Elements =========== -->
    <!ENTITY % regPoint.qname "regPoint">
    <!ELEMENT %regPoint.qname; %regPoint.content;>
    <!ATTLIST %regPoint.qname; %regPoint.attrib;
        %Core.attrib;
        %I18n.attrib;
        %RegAlign.attrib;
        bottom            CDATA    'auto'
        left              CDATA    'auto'
        right             CDATA    'auto'
        top               CDATA    'auto'
    >
]]> <!-- end HierarchicalLayout.module -->


<!-- end of SMIL-layout.mod -->
```

This DTD fragment is divided into two parts. The first part contains the elements absolutely required for any SMIL implementation: Basic Layout Elements, the Region element, and the Root-layout elements. These are declared straight away, without being wrapped in any INCLUDE or IGNORE blocks. There is no easy way to turn them off. That's a pretty big hint that these elements are essential.

The next several sections — Audio Layout, Multi Window Layout, and Hierarchical Layout — are wrapped in INCLUDE/IGNORE blocks. That's your first clue that the elements declared here aren't essential. The second, even bigger clue, is that all three of these are set to IGNORE by default. As usual, if you want to include them you can simply redefine the HierarchicalLayout.module, MultiWindowLayout.module and AudioLayout.module parameter entities to INCLUDE instead. Indeed, the full SMIL 2.0 Language Profile does this.

The Linking Module

The Linking Module, Listing 26-9, defines all SMIL elements related to hypertext, specifically a, area, and anchor. These are required elements but they're not as absolutely essential as the layout, region, and root-layout elements in the previous module. You can conceive of a SMIL document that doesn't use any of

these. Consequently their declarations are wrapped in an INCLUDE/IGNORE block
with parameter entity references determining whether they're included or ignored.
However, they are included by default.

Listing 26-9: SMIL-link.mod: The SMIL Linking Module DTD

```
<!-- ========================================================= -->
<!-- SMIL Linking Module  ==================================== -->
<!-- file: SMIL-link.mod

     This is SMIL 2.0.
     Copyright 2000 W3C (MIT, INRIA, Keio), All Rights
     Reserved.

     Author: Jacco van Ossenbruggen, Lloyd Rutledge, Aaron Cohen
     Revision:   $Id: SMIL-link.mod,v 1.17 2000/10/23 11:55:51
                     jvanoss Exp $

     This DTD module is identified by the PUBLIC and SYSTEM
     identifiers:

         PUBLIC "-//W3C//ELEMENTS SMIL 2.0 Linking//EN"
         SYSTEM "SMIL-link.mod"


     ========================================================= -->

<!-- ======================= LinkingAttributes Entities == -->
<!ENTITY % linking-attrs "
     sourceLevel            CDATA              '100&#37;'
     destinationLevel       CDATA              '100&#37;'
     sourcePlaystate        (play|pause|stop)  #IMPLIED
     destinationPlaystate   (play|pause|stop)  'play'
     show                   (new|pause|replace) 'replace'
     accesskey              %Character.datatype; #IMPLIED
     target                 CDATA              #IMPLIED
     external               (true|false)       'false'
     actuate                (onRequest|onLoad) 'onRequest'
     %Tabindex.attrib;
">



<!-- ======================= BasicLinking Elements ====== -->
<!ENTITY % BasicLinking.module "IGNORE">
<![%BasicLinking.module;[

  <!-- ======================= BasicLinking Entities ====== -->
  <!ENTITY % Shape "(rect|circle|poly|default)">
  <!ENTITY % Coords "CDATA">
```

Continued

Listing 26-9 *(continued)*

```
    <!-- comma separated list of lengths -->

  <!ENTITY % a.attrib   "">
  <!ENTITY % a.content "EMPTY">
  <!ENTITY % a.qname    "a">
  <!ELEMENT %a.qname; %a.content;>
  <!ATTLIST %a.qname; %a.attrib;
    %linking-attrs;
    href                       %URI.datatype;     #IMPLIED
    %Core.attrib;
    %I18n.attrib;
  >

  <!ENTITY % area.attrib   "">
  <!ENTITY % area.content "EMPTY">
  <!ENTITY % area.qname    "area">
  <!ELEMENT %area.qname; %area.content;>
  <!ATTLIST %area.qname; %area.attrib;
    %linking-attrs;
    shape                      %Shape;            'rect'
    coords                     %Coords;           #IMPLIED
    href                       %URI.datatype;     #IMPLIED
    nohref                     (nohref)           #IMPLIED
    %Core.attrib;
    %I18n.attrib;
  >

  <!ENTITY % anchor.attrib   "">
  <!ENTITY % anchor.content "EMPTY">
  <!ENTITY % anchor.qname   "anchor">
  <!ELEMENT %anchor.qname; %anchor.content;>
  <!ATTLIST %anchor.qname; %anchor.attrib;
    %linking-attrs;
    shape                      %Shape;            'rect'
    coords                     %Coords;           #IMPLIED
    href                       %URI.datatype;
#IMPLIED
    nohref                     (nohref)           #IMPLIED
    %Core.attrib;
    %I18n.attrib;
  >
]]> <!-- end of BasicLinking -->

<!-- ======================= ObjectLinking =============== -->
<!ENTITY % ObjectLinking.module "IGNORE">
<![%ObjectLinking.module;[

  <!ENTITY % Fragment "
    fragment                   CDATA              #IMPLIED
  ">
```

```
<!-- ======================= ObjectLinking Elements ====== -->
<!-- add fragment attribute to area, and anchor elements -->
<!ATTLIST %area.qname;
    %Fragment;
>

<!ATTLIST %anchor.qname;
    %Fragment;
>
]]>
<!-- ======================= End ObjectLinking =========== -->

<!-- end of SMIL-link.mod -->
```

There's also an optional section called ObjectLinking Elements. This section is ignored by default, but can be turned on by setting ObjectLinking.module to INCLUDE. Interestingly this section does not declare any new elements. However, it does add one attribute, fragment, to the three elements declared previously in this module.

Although all elements and most attributes here and in other modules are defined using parameter entity references, there are a few attributes that are defined with string literals so their names and content models cannot be easily changed. For example, the shape, coords, href and nohref attributes of both the area and anchor attributes are defined using direct names. The types of the shape, coords, and href attributes are specified using the parameter entity references %Shape;, %Coords;, and %URI.datatype;. However, these are almost constant data types. They are not easily overridden entities like %shape.type;, %coords.type;, or %href.type;. The nohref attribute in both cases has the literal fixed value nohref. Even more telling is that although these four attributes are declared identically in both the area and anchor attribute declarations, an extra parameter entity reference such as %link.attribs; is not used to separate out the commonality. While doing so would be more maintainable, it would also incorrectly suggest that these attribute lists could be changed. In fact, they are required to be exactly as they are given here. Thus the DTD deliberately avoids adding extra levers by which an author could move the vocabulary in a non-conformant way. If you want to use the area and anchor attributes at all, you have to use them with these attributes.

The Media Object Module

Listing 26-10 shows the SMIL Media Object Module DTD. This module declares the different elements used to point to non XML media files like video clips, sound files, and images.

Listing 26-10: SMIL-media.mod: The SMIL Media Object Module DTD

```
<!-- ======================================================= -->
<!-- SMIL 2.0 Media Objects Modules ======================== -->
<!-- file: SMIL-media.mod

     This is SMIL 2.0.
     Copyright 2000 W3C (MIT, INRIA, Keio), All Rights
     Reserved.

     Author:      Rob Lanphier, Jacco van Ossenbruggen
     Revision:    $Id: SMIL-media.mod,v 1.33 2000/11/20 18:40:51
                  jvanoss Exp $

     This DTD module is identified by the PUBLIC and SYSTEM
     identifiers:

     PUBLIC "-//W3C//ELEMENTS SMIL 2.0 Media Objects//EN"
     SYSTEM "SMIL-media.mod"

     ======================================================= -->

<!-- ================== Profiling Entities ================ -->

<!ENTITY % MediaClipping.module "IGNORE">
<![%MediaClipping.module;[
  <!ENTITY % mo-attributes-MediaClipping "
    %MediaClip.attrib;
  ">
]]>
<!ENTITY % mo-attributes-MediaClipping "">

<!ENTITY % MediaClipping.deprecated.module "IGNORE">
<![%MediaClipping.module;[
  <!ENTITY % mo-attributes-MediaClipping-deprecated "
    %MediaClip.attrib.deprecated;
  ">
  ]]>
<!ENTITY % mo-attributes-MediaClipping-deprecated "">

<!ENTITY % MediaParam.module "IGNORE">
<![%MediaParam.module;[
  <!ENTITY % mo-attributes-MediaParam "
      erase        (whenDone|never)      'whenDone'
      mediaRepeat  (preserve|strip)      'preserve'
  ">
  <!ENTITY % param.qname "param">
  <!ELEMENT %param.qname; EMPTY>

  <!ATTLIST %param.qname; %param.attrib;
    %Core.attrib;
```

```
    %I18n.attrib;
    name          CDATA             #IMPLIED
    value         CDATA             #IMPLIED
    valuetype     (data|ref|object) "data"
    type          %ContentType.datatype;  #IMPLIED
  >
]]>
<!ENTITY % mo-attributes-MediaParam "">

<!ENTITY % MediaAccessibility.module "IGNORE">
<![%MediaAccessibility.module;[
  <!ENTITY % mo-attributes-MediaAccessibility "
       readIndex    CDATA             #IMPLIED
  ">
]]>
<!ENTITY % mo-attributes-MediaAccessibility "">

<!ENTITY % BasicMedia.module "INCLUDE">
<![%BasicMedia.module;[
  <!ENTITY % media-object.content "EMPTY">
  <!ENTITY % media-object.attrib "">

  <!-- ================ Media Objects Entities ============ -->

  <!ENTITY % mo-attributes-BasicMedia "
       src             CDATA   #IMPLIED
       type            CDATA   #IMPLIED
  ">

  <!ENTITY % mo-attributes "
       %Core.attrib;
       %I18n.attrib;
       %Description.attrib;
       %mo-attributes-BasicMedia;
       %mo-attributes-MediaParam;
       %mo-attributes-MediaAccessibility;
       %media-object.attrib;
  ">

  <!--
     Most info is in the attributes, media objects are empty or
     have children defined at the language integration level:
  -->

  <!ENTITY % mo-content "%media-object.content;">

  <!-- ================ Media Objects Elements ============ -->
  <!ENTITY % ref.qname        "ref">
  <!ENTITY % audio.qname      "audio">
  <!ENTITY % img.qname        "img">
  <!ENTITY % video.qname      "video">
  <!ENTITY % text.qname       "text">
```

Continued

Listing 26-10 *(continued)*

```
<!ENTITY % textstream.qname "textstream">
<!ENTITY % animation.qname  "animation">

<!ENTITY % ref.content           "%mo-content;">
<!ENTITY % audio.content         "%mo-content;">
<!ENTITY % img.content           "%mo-content;">
<!ENTITY % video.content         "%mo-content;">
<!ENTITY % text.content          "%mo-content;">
<!ENTITY % textstream.content "%mo-content;">
<!ENTITY % animation.content  "%mo-content;">

<!ELEMENT %ref.qname;            %ref.content;>
<!ELEMENT %audio.qname;          %audio.content;>
<!ELEMENT %img.qname;            %img.content;>
<!ELEMENT %video.qname;          %video.content;>
<!ELEMENT %text.qname;           %text.content;>
<!ELEMENT %textstream.qname;     %textstream.content;>
<!ELEMENT %animation.qname;      %animation.content;>

<!ATTLIST %img.qname;
     %mo-attributes;
>
<!ATTLIST %text.qname;
     %mo-attributes;
>
<!ATTLIST %ref.qname;
        %mo-attributes-MediaClipping;
        %mo-attributes-MediaClipping-deprecated;
        %mo-attributes;
>
<!ATTLIST %audio.qname;
        %mo-attributes-MediaClipping;
        %mo-attributes-MediaClipping-deprecated;
        %mo-attributes;
>
<!ATTLIST %video.qname;
        %mo-attributes-MediaClipping;
        %mo-attributes-MediaClipping-deprecated;
        %mo-attributes;
>
<!ATTLIST %textstream.qname;
        %mo-attributes-MediaClipping;
        %mo-attributes-MediaClipping-deprecated;
        %mo-attributes;
>
<!ATTLIST %animation.qname;
        %mo-attributes-MediaClipping;
        %mo-attributes-MediaClipping-deprecated;
        %mo-attributes;
>
]]>
```

```
<!ENTITY % mo-attributes-BasicMedia "">

<!-- BrushMedia -->
<!ENTITY % BrushMedia.module "IGNORE">
<![%BrushMedia.module;[
  <!ENTITY % brush.attrib "">
  <!ENTITY % brush.content "%mo-content;">
  <!ENTITY % brush.qname "brush">
  <!ELEMENT %brush.qname; %brush.content;>
  <!ATTLIST %brush.qname; %brush.attrib;
        %Core.attrib;
        %I18n.attrib;
        %Description.attrib;
        %mo-attributes-MediaAccessibility;
        %mo-attributes-MediaParam;
        %media-object.attrib;
        color          CDATA              #IMPLIED
  >
]]>

<!-- end of SMIL-media.mod -->
```

This module begins with some ignored declarations for deprecated attributes from SMIL 1.0. If you've got legacy documents you can turn them on. Otherwise, just leave them off. What's interesting here is what happens to the entities if they're ignored. The entities are still dereferenced later in the file, so they have to be defined to be something. INCLUDE/IGNORE unfortunately does not provide a means of saying INCLUDE A or if not A then INCLUDE B. However, because XML allows you to declare entities multiple times, we can take advantage of that. Unlike most programming languages, it's the first declaration (setting of a variable if you prefer) that counts, not the last. Consider this, for example:

```
<![%MediaClipping.module;[
  <!ENTITY % mo-attributes-MediaClipping "
        %MediaClip.attrib;
  ">
]]>
<!ENTITY % mo-attributes-MediaClipping "">
```

If MediaClipping.module is set to INCLUDE, then mo-attributes-MediaClipping is set to %MediaClip.attrib; (or whatever its replacement text is). The last line that attempts to set mo-attributes-MediaClipping to the empty string has no effect.

However, if MediaClipping.module is set to IGNORE, then the first declaration is skipped, and mo-attributes-MediaClipping is set to an empty string, but it does have a value and it can be dereferenced.

Several of these ignored sections such as `mo-attributes-MediaClipping-deprecated` focus on deprecated elements and attributes from SMIL 1.0. When evolving DTDs over time, it's almost inevitable that you'll discover some mistakes in the design of the original DTD. In other cases, what once made sense may no longer be a good idea given changes to other parts of the DTD. And you may simply discover better or more precise ways of describing something. Therefore you may wish to eliminate certain elements from your DTD. However, if you still have documents that use the old version of the vocabulary, you may want the new DTD to be able to validate the old elements as well. Therefore it's best to deprecate them rather than remove them from the new DTD completely. At the same time, you want to allow people to validate their documents against a strict version of the DTD that doesn't allow the deprecated elements and attributes. To this end, the deprecated elements can be moved into a transitional module. This module may or may not be included by default. However, whatever the default is, the user should be provided with a simple means of changing it, typically by redefining a single parameter entity that resolves to either `IGNORE` or `INCLUDE`.

I'd also like to point out another interesting use of double indirection in this module. Here it's not being used as a hackish workaround to allow setting different namespace prefixes. Instead it's being used to share a common content model between different elements while still allowing the content models of particular elements to be customized. The section in question are the declarations of the content models for the media object elements like `audio` and `img` which go something like this:

```
<!ENTITY % mo-content "%media-object.content;">

<!ENTITY % ref.content        "%mo-content;">
<!ENTITY % audio.content      "%mo-content;">
<!ENTITY % img.content        "%mo-content;">
<!ENTITY % video.content      "%mo-content;">
<!ENTITY % text.content       "%mo-content;">
<!ENTITY % textstream.content "%mo-content;">
<!ENTITY % animation.content  "%mo-content;">

<!ELEMENT %ref.qname;        %ref.content;>
<!ELEMENT %audio.qname;      %audio.content;>
<!ELEMENT %img.qname;        %img.content;>
<!ELEMENT %video.qname;      %video.content;>
<!ELEMENT %text.qname;       %text.content;>
<!ELEMENT %textstream.qname; %textstream.content;>
<!ELEMENT %animation.qname;  %animation.content;>
```

Each element 's content model is declared using the form `%elementName.content;`; e.g. `%ref.content;`, `%audio.content;`, etc. Thus they all appear to have different content models; and indeed these are potentially different. However, all of these resolve back to simply `%mo-content;` so they all do have the same content by default. If you want to change the content model for all of them, you can adjust `%mo-content;`. If you want to change the content for just one, you can do that too. More indirection provides more customizability.

The Structure Module

The Structure module, shown in Listing 26-11, is a very straight-forward module that declares the document root element smil and its immediate children, head and body.

Listing 26-11: SMIL-struct.mod: The SMIL Structure Module DTD

```
<!-- ========================================================= -->
<!-- SMIL Structure Module   ================================= -->
<!-- file: SMIL-struct.mod

     This is SMIL 2.0.
     Copyright 2000 W3C (MIT, INRIA, Keio), All Rights
     Reserved.

     This DTD module is identified by the PUBLIC and SYSTEM
     identifiers:

     PUBLIC "-//W3C//ELEMENTS SMIL 2.0 Document Structure//EN"
     SYSTEM "SMIL-struct.mod"

     Author: Warner ten Kate, Jacco van Ossenbruggen
     Revision: $Id: SMIL-struct.mod,v 1.17 2000/10/23 11:57:40
               jvanoss Exp $


     ========================================================= -->

<!-- ================== SMIL Document Root ================ -->
<!ENTITY % smil.attrib   "" >
<!ENTITY % smil.content "EMPTY" >
<!ENTITY % smil.qname    "smil" >

<!ELEMENT %smil.qname; %smil.content;>
<!ATTLIST %smil.qname; %smil.attrib;
        %Core.attrib;
        %I18n.attrib;
        xmlns %URI.datatype; #REQUIRED
>

<!-- ================== The Document Head ================== -->
<!ENTITY % head.content "EMPTY" >
<!ENTITY % head.attrib   "" >
<!ENTITY % head.qname    "head" >

<!ELEMENT %head.qname; %head.content;>
<!ATTLIST %head.qname; %head.attrib;
```

Continued

Listing 26-11 *(continued)*

```
        %Core.attrib;
        %I18n.attrib;
>

<!--==================== The Document Body - Timing Root === -->
<!ENTITY % body.content "EMPTY" >
<!ENTITY % body.attrib  "" >
<!ENTITY % body.qname   "body" >

<!ELEMENT %body.qname; %body.content;>
<!ATTLIST %body.qname; %body.attrib;
        %Core.attrib;
        %I18n.attrib;
>
<!-- end of SMIL-struct.mod -->
```

There's not a lot new here. You've seen all these techniques in previous modules. Since these are all required elements, there's not much opportunity to turn particular parts on or off. You can add attributes to these elements by redefining the smil.attrib, head.attrib, and body.attrib parameter entities.

One thing that's a little striking about these declarations. The content models for all three elements are declared as EMPTY:

```
<!ENTITY % smil.content "EMPTY" >
<!ENTITY % head.content "EMPTY" >
<!ENTITY % body.content "EMPTY" >
```

Of course none of these elements should be empty. The smil element contains a head and a body. The head contains a layout, and the body contains par or seq elements (at a minimum). These entity definitions are just placeholders. By the time the parser gets this far it's already read the document model module, which has already defined these entities thusly:

```
<!ENTITY % smil.content "(head?,body?)">
<!ENTITY % head-layout.content     "layout">
<!ENTITY % head.content "(%head-layout.content;)?">
<!ENTITY % body.content "(%timecontainer.class|%media-object;|
        %content-control;|a)*)">
```

The redeclaration here does not override or replace the previous declaration. This module is not designed to be used in isolation. A document model that properly defines these entities must be loaded first.

The Timing and Synchronization Module

Listing 26-12 shows the SMIL Timing and Synchronization Module DTD. This module defines the par, seq, excl and priorityClass elements used to specify when media files are displayed and played.

Listing 26-12: SMIL-timing.mod: The SMIL Timing and Synchronization Module DTD

```
<!-- ======================================================= -->
<!-- SMIL Timing and Synchronization Modules ============== -->
<!-- file: SMIL-timing.mod

     This is SMIL 2.0.
     Copyright 2000 W3C (MIT, INRIA, Keio), All Rights
     Reserved.

     Author:     Jacco van Ossenbruggen.
     Revision:   $Id: SMIL-timing.mod,v 1.15 2000/10/09
                 09:44:44 jvanoss Exp $

     This DTD module is identified by the PUBLIC and SYSTEM
     identifiers:

     PUBLIC "-//W3C//ELEMENTS SMIL 2.0 Timing//EN"
     SYSTEM "SMIL-timing.mod"

     ======================================================= -->


<!-- ================= Timing Elements ================== -->
<!ENTITY % BasicTimeContainers.module "IGNORE">
<![%BasicTimeContainers.module;[
  <!ENTITY % par.content "EMPTY">
  <!ENTITY % seq.content "EMPTY">
  <!ENTITY % par.attrib  "">
  <!ENTITY % seq.attrib  "">
  <!ENTITY % seq.qname   "seq">
  <!ENTITY % par.qname   "par">

  <!ELEMENT %seq.qname; %seq.content;>
  <!ATTLIST %seq.qname; %seq.attrib;
   %Core.attrib;
   %I18n.attrib;
   %Description.attrib;
  >
```

Continued

Listing 26-12 *(continued)*

```
    <!ELEMENT %par.qname; %par.content;>
    <!ATTLIST %par.qname; %par.attrib;
     %Core.attrib;
     %I18n.attrib;
     %Description.attrib;
    >
]]>  <!-- End of BasicTimeContainers.module -->


<!ENTITY % ExclTimeContainers.module "IGNORE">
<![%ExclTimeContainers.module;[
  <!ENTITY % excl.content          "EMPTY">
  <!ENTITY % priorityClass.content "EMPTY">
  <!ENTITY % excl.attrib           "">
  <!ENTITY % priorityClass.attrib  "">
  <!ENTITY % excl.qname            "excl">
  <!ENTITY % priorityClass.qname   "priorityClass">

  <!ELEMENT %excl.qname; %excl.content;>
  <!ATTLIST %excl.qname; %excl.attrib;
   %Core.attrib;
   %I18n.attrib;
   %Description.attrib;
  >

  <!ELEMENT %priorityClass.qname; %priorityClass.content;>
  <!ATTLIST %priorityClass.qname; %priorityClass.attrib;
   peers        (stop|pause|defer|never) "stop"
   higher       (stop|pause)             "pause"
   lower        (defer|never)            "defer"
   pauseDisplay (disable|hide|show )     "show"
   %Description.attrib;
   %Core.attrib;
   %I18n.attrib;
  >
]]>  <!-- End of ExclTimeContainers.module -->

<!-- end of SMIL-timing.mod -->
```

Here I want to look at the custom attributes of the par and seq elements. To be blunt, there aren't any. These elements have some common attributes like id, but none that are unique to them. Nonetheless, the attribute declarations for these elements do use the %seq.attrib; and %par.attrib; parameter entity references to offer the possibility of them having special attributes:

```
    <!ATTLIST %seq.qname; %seq.attrib;
     %Core.attrib;
     %I18n.attrib;
```

```
 %Description.attrib;
>

<!ATTLIST %par.qname; %par.attrib;
 %Core.attrib;
 %I18n.attrib;
 %Description.attrib;
>
```

However, these entities are defined as empty:

```
<!ENTITY % par.attrib   "">
<!ENTITY % seq.attrib   "">
```

Why go to this effort for no effect? Because it allows the DTD to more easily be customized. Standard SMIL may not need to add any non-common attributes to par and seq, but other applications using this DTD might. A good DTD provides hooks for expansion and extensions, even if it doesn't need to use those hooks itself.

The Content Control Module

Listing 26-13 shows the SMIL Content Control Module DTD that defines the switch, customTest, customAttributes, and prefetch elements. What unifies these different attributes and elements is that they all in some way defer decisions about what to show when until the content is actually displayed. In some cases, the decision may rest on use preferences.

Listing 26-13: SMIL-control.mod: The SMIL Content Control Module DTD

```
<!-- ========================================================= -->
<!-- SMIL Content Control Module  ========================== -->
<!-- file: SMIL-control.mod

     This is SMIL 2.0.
     Copyright 2000 W3C (MIT, INRIA, Keio), All Rights
     Reserved.

     Author:     Jacco van Ossenbruggen, Aaron Cohen
     Revision:   $Id: SMIL-control.mod,v 1.19 2001/02/01
                 17:48:43 jvanoss Exp $

     This DTD module is identified by the PUBLIC and SYSTEM
     identifiers:

     PUBLIC "-//W3C//ELEMENTS SMIL 2.0 Content Control//EN"
```

Continued

Listing 26-13 *(continued)*

```
      SYSTEM "SMIL-control.mod"

      ======================================================== -->

<!ENTITY %  BasicContentControl.module "INCLUDE">
<![%BasicContentControl.module;[
  <!ENTITY % switch.attrib "">
  <!ENTITY % switch.content "EMPTY">
  <!ENTITY % switch.qname "switch">

  <!ELEMENT %switch.qname; %switch.content;>
  <!ATTLIST %switch.qname; %switch.attrib;
        %Core.attrib;
        %I18n.attrib;
  >
]]>

<!-- ========================== CustomTest Elements ======== -->
<!ENTITY %  CustomTestAttributes.module "IGNORE">
<![%CustomTestAttributes.module;[

  <!ENTITY % customTest.attrib "">
  <!ENTITY % customTest.qname "customTest">
  <!ENTITY % customTest.content "EMPTY">
  <!ELEMENT %customTest.qname; %customTest.content;>
  <!ATTLIST %customTest.qname; %customTest.attrib;
        defaultState (true|false)                   'false'
        override     (visible|hidden)               'hidden'
        uid           %URI.datatype;                #IMPLIED
        %Core.attrib;
        %I18n.attrib;
  >
  <!ENTITY % customAttributes.attrib "">
  <!ENTITY % customAttributes.qname "customAttributes">
  <!ENTITY % customAttributes.content "(customTest+)">
  <!ELEMENT %customAttributes.qname;
    %customAttributes.content;>
  <!ATTLIST %customAttributes.qname; %customAttributes.attrib;
        %Core.attrib;
        %I18n.attrib;
  >

]]> <!-- end of CustomTestAttributes -->

<!-- ========================== PrefetchControl Elements === -->
<!ENTITY % PrefetchControl.module "IGNORE">
<![%PrefetchControl.module;[
  <!ENTITY % prefetch.attrib "">
  <!ENTITY % prefetch.qname "prefetch">
```

```
<!ENTITY % prefetch.content "EMPTY">
<!ELEMENT %prefetch.qname; %prefetch.content;>
<!ATTLIST %prefetch.qname; %prefetch.attrib;
      src              %URI.datatype;    #IMPLIED
      mediaSize        CDATA             #IMPLIED
      mediaTime        CDATA             #IMPLIED
      bandwidth        CDATA             #IMPLIED
      %Core.attrib;
      %I18n.attrib;
>
]]>
```

Notice here how the content models and attribute lists for elements are given as locally declared entities that don't actually contain very much. For example,

```
<!ENTITY % switch.attrib "">
<!ENTITY % switch.content "EMPTY">
<!ENTITY % switch.qname "switch">

<!ELEMENT %switch.qname; %switch.content;>
<!ATTLIST %switch.qname; %switch.attrib;
      %Core.attrib;
      %I18n.attrib;
>
```

Why not simply declare them without the extra parameter entity reference like this?

```
<!ELEMENT %switch.qname; EMPTY>
<!ATTLIST %switch.qname;
      %Core.attrib;
      %I18n.attrib;
>
```

The reason is simple: using the parameter entity reference allows other modules to override this content model. These aren't necessarily modules used here, but ones that may be merged with the existing modules to form new XML applications.

Also notice the grouping into IGNORE and INCLUDE blocks. The switch and prefetch elements can be turned on or off independently of the other three elements. However, the customTest and customAttributes elements come as a pair that cannot be broken up. You have both or neither, not one or the other. In this case, this is because they depend on each other; a customTest element contains customAttributes elements and every customAttributes element is always contained in a customTest element. It's quite common to have elements that depend on each other as here. In this case those elements should be placed in a single INCLUDE/IGNORE block to allow for unified control over their presence or absence.

The SMIL 2.0 Language Profile

The SMIL 2.0 Language Profile is intended for general purpose computers with a reasonable amount of CPU power that can display essentially any media type. The SMIL 2.0 Language Profile DTD (SMIL20.dtd), shown in Listing 26-14, is structured very similarly to the Basic Language Profile of Listing 26-2. Indeed, that DTD was created by modifying this one. However the full DTD adds three more modules for meta information, transitions between media, and an optional Streaming Media Object Module. Rather than using the basic document model of Listing 26-7, it uses the full language profile of Listing 26-15 below. The modules that are shared (Content Control, Layout, Linking, Media Object, Structure and Timing) are exactly the same modules used for the basic profile. However, because the full profile defines different values for certain entity references these same modules can have different effects and turn on more elements and attributes from those modules than are turned on in the basic DTD. This is the power of modularization and parameter entity references.

Listing 26-14: **SMIL20.dtd: The SMIL Language Profile Driver DTD**

```
<!-- .............................................. -->
<!-- SMIL 2.0 DTD  ...................................... -->
<!-- file: SMIL20.dtd
-->
<!-- SMIL 2.0 DTD

     This is SMIL 2.0.

     Copyright 1998-2000 World Wide Web Consortium
        (Massachusetts Institute of Technology, Institut
         National de Recherche en Informatique et en
         Automatique, Keio University).
         All Rights Reserved.

     Permission to use, copy, modify and distribute the SMIL
     2.0 DTD and its accompanying documentation for any purpose
     and without fee is hereby granted in perpetuity, provided
     that the above copyright notice and this paragraph appear
     in all copies.  The copyright holders make no
     representation about the suitability of the DTD for any
     purpose.

     It is provided "as is" without expressed or implied
     warranty.

        Author:    Jacco van Ossenbruggen
        Revision:  $Id: SMIL20.dtd,v 1.5 2000/08/08 11:40:53
                   jvanoss Exp $
```

```
-->
<!-- This is the driver file for the SMIL 2.0 DTD.

     This DTD module is identified by the PUBLIC and SYSTEM
     identifiers:

     PUBLIC "-//W3C//DTD SMIL 2.0//EN"
     SYSTEM "http://www.w3.org/2001/SMIL20/WD/SMIL20.dtd"
-->

<!ENTITY % NS.prefixed "IGNORE" >
<!ENTITY % SMIL.prefix "" >

<!-- Define the Content Model -->
<!ENTITY % smil-model.mod
     PUBLIC "-//W3C//ENTITIES SMIL 2.0 Document Model 1.0//EN"
            "smil-model-1.mod" >

<!-- Modular Framework Module
............................. -->
<!ENTITY % smil-framework.module "INCLUDE" >
<![%smil-framework.module;[
<!ENTITY % smil-framework.mod
   PUBLIC "-//W3C//ENTITIES SMIL 2.0 Modular Framework 1.0//EN"
            "smil-framework-1.mod" >
%smil-framework.mod;]]>

<!-- The SMIL 2.0 Profile includes the following sections:
                 C. The SMIL Animation Module
                 D. The SMIL Content Control Module
                 G. The SMIL Layout Module
                 H. The SMIL Linking Module
                 I. The SMIL Media Object Module
                 J. The SMIL Metainformation Module
                 K. The SMIL Structure Module
                 L. The SMIL Timing and Synchronization Module
                 M. Integrating SMIL Timing into other XML-Based
Languages
                 P. The SMIL Transition effects Module

                 The SMIL Streaming Media Object Module is optional.
-->

<!ENTITY % streamingmedia.model "IGNORE">
<![%streamingmedia.model;[
  <!ENTITY % streaming-mod
 PUBLIC "-//W3C//ELEMENTS SMIL 2.0 Streaming Media Objects//EN"
    "SMIL-streamingmedia.mod">
  %streaming-mod;
```

Continued

Listing 26-14 *(continued)*

```
        ]]>
<!ENTITY % anim-mod
  PUBLIC "-//W3C//ELEMENTS SMIL 2.0 Animation//EN"
  "SMIL-anim.mod">
<!ENTITY % control-mod
  PUBLIC "-//W3C//ELEMENTS SMIL 2.0 Content Control//EN"
  "SMIL-control.mod">
<!ENTITY % layout-mod
  PUBLIC "-//W3C//ELEMENTS SMIL 2.0 Layout//EN"
  "SMIL-layout.mod">
<!ENTITY % link-mod
  PUBLIC "-//W3C//ELEMENTS SMIL 2.0 Linking//EN"
  "SMIL-link.mod">
<!ENTITY % media-mod
  PUBLIC "-//W3C//ELEMENTS SMIL 2.0 Media Objects//EN"
  "SMIL-media.mod">
<!ENTITY % meta-mod
  PUBLIC "-//W3C//ELEMENTS SMIL 2.0 Document
Metainformation//EN"
  "SMIL-metainformation.mod">
<!ENTITY % struct-mod
  PUBLIC "-//W3C//ELEMENTS SMIL 2.0 Document Structure//EN"
  "SMIL-struct.mod">
<!ENTITY % timing-mod
  PUBLIC "-//W3C//ELEMENTS SMIL 2.0 Timing//EN"
  "SMIL-timing.mod">
<!ENTITY % transition-mod
  PUBLIC "-//W3C//ELEMENTS SMIL 2.0 Transition//EN"
  "SMIL-transition.mod">

%struct-mod;
%anim-mod;
%control-mod;
%meta-mod;
%layout-mod;
%link-mod;
%media-mod;
%timing-mod;
%transition-mod;
```

This DTD is organized along the same lines as the basic language profile DTD. First, there is an intellectual property notice that tells you it's OK to use this DTD. Then there are some comments that tell you how to use this DTD. Next come entity declarations that will be important for the imported modules. Finally, the various modules are imported. The difference between the basic and the full DTDs lies in which modules are imported.

There's one module that stands out though, and its illustrates some important principles of modular DTD design. This is the streaming media module. Rather than being imported directly, it's first wrapped in an IGNORE block like this:

```
<!ENTITY % streamingmedia.model "IGNORE">
<![%streamingmedia.model;[
  <!ENTITY % streaming-mod
 PUBLIC "-//W3C//ELEMENTS SMIL 2.0 Streaming Media Objects//EN"
    "SMIL-streamingmedia.mod">
  %streaming-mod;
]]>
```

By default, the streaming media module is not imported. If you want to include streaming media in your SMIL documents, you need to redefine streamingmedia. model to INCLUDE. You'll also need to provide the SMIL-streamingmedia.mod file. SMIL 2.0 doesn't have it. This block is in essence a placeholder. Different companies and developers that use SMIL such as RealNetworks and Intel can provide their own and point to it here. Eventually the W3C Synchronized Multimedia Working group may define a standard for streaming media, but until they do this is essentially anything goes. Nonetheless, all these different experiments can still fit cleanly into the existing framework of SMIL 2.0.

Listing 26-15 shows the document model for the full language profile. Where the driver DTD makes fairly large scale adjustments by including or not including particular modules, the new document model makes more surgical adjustments by turning off or on individual sections of particular modules. It does this by defining parameter entity references as either IGNORE or INCLUDE. Furthermore, it defines the content models and attribute types for many different elements.

Listing 26-15: **smil-model-1.mod: The SMIL 2.0 Full Language Profile document model**

```
<!-- ======================================================= -->
<!-- SMIL 2.0 Document Model Module ====================== -->
<!-- file: smil-model-1.mod

     This is SMIL 2.0.
     Copyright 1998-2000 W3C (MIT, INRIA, Keio), All Rights
     Reserved.

     This DTD module is identified by the PUBLIC and SYSTEM
     identifiers:

     PUBLIC "-//W3C//ENTITIES SMIL 2.0 Document Model 1.0//EN"
     SYSTEM "smil-model-1.mod"

   Author: Warner ten Kate, Jacco van Ossenbruggen, Aaron Cohen
```

Continued

Listing 26-15 *(continued)*

```
        Revision: $Id: smil-model-1.mod,v 1.56 2001/02/01 09:09:24
                  jvanoss Exp $
        ======================================================== -->

<!--
        This file defines the SMIL 2.0 Language Document Model.
        All attributes and content models are defined in the
        second half of this file.  We first start with some
        utility definitions.  These are mainly used to simplify
        the use of Modules in the second part of the file.

-->

<!-- ================== Util: Head ========================= -->
<!ENTITY % head-meta.content        "metadata">
<!ENTITY % head-layout.content      "layout|switch">
<!ENTITY % head-control.content     "customAttributes">
<!ENTITY % head-transition.content "transition+">

<!--================== Util: Body - Content Control ====== -->
<!ENTITY % content-control "switch|prefetch">
<!ENTITY % content-control-attrs "%Test.attrib;
%CustomTest.attrib; %SkipContent.attrib;">

<!--================== Util: Body - Animation =========== -->
<!ENTITY % animation.elements
"animate|set|animateMotion|animateColor">

<!--================== Util: Body - Media ============== -->

<!ENTITY % media-object
         "audio|video|animation|text|img|textstream|ref|brush
                         |%animation.elements;">

<!--================== Util: Body - Timing ============== -->
<!ENTITY % BasicTimeContainers.class "par|seq">
<!ENTITY % ExclTimeContainers.class "excl">
<!ENTITY % timecontainer.class
 "%BasicTimeContainers.class;|%ExclTimeContainers.class;">
<!ENTITY % timecontainer.content
 "%timecontainer.class;|%media-object;|%content-control;|a">

<!ENTITY % smil-basictime.attrib "
 %BasicInlineTiming.attrib;
 %BasicInlineTiming-deprecated.attrib;
 %MinMaxTiming.attrib;
">

<!ENTITY % timecontainer.attrib "
 %BasicInlineTiming.attrib;
 %BasicInlineTiming-deprecated.attrib;
```

```
 %MinMaxTiming.attrib;
 %RestartTiming.attrib;
 %RestartDefaultTiming.attrib;
 %SyncBehavior.attrib;
 %SyncBehaviorDefault.attrib;
 %FillDefault.attrib;
">


<!-- ========================================================= -->
<!-- ========================================================= -->
<!-- ========================================================= -->

<!--
     The actual content model and attribute definitions for
     each module sections follow below.
-->

<!-- ================== Content Control ==================== -->
<!ENTITY % BasicContentControl.module  "INCLUDE">
<!ENTITY % CustomTestAttributes.module "INCLUDE">
<!ENTITY % PrefetchControl.module      "INCLUDE">
<!ENTITY % SkipContentControl.module   "INCLUDE">

<!ENTITY % switch.content "((%timecontainer.class;|
    %media-object;|%content-control;|a|area|anchor)*|layout*)">

<!ENTITY % switch.attrib   "%Test.attrib; %CustomTest.attrib;">
<!ENTITY % prefetch.attrib "
 %timecontainer.attrib;
 %MediaClip.attrib;
 %MediaClip.attrib.deprecated;
 %Test.attrib;
 %CustomTest.attrib;
 %SkipContent.attrib;
">

<!ENTITY % customAttributes.attrib  "%Test.attrib;
%SkipContent.attrib;">
<!ENTITY % customTest.attrib        "%SkipContent.attrib;">

<!-- ================== Animation ========================== -->
<!ENTITY % BasicAnimation.module "INCLUDE">

<!-- choose targetElement or XLink: -->
<!ENTITY % animation-targetElement "INCLUDE">
<!ENTITY % animation-XLinkTarget   "IGNORE">

<!ENTITY % animate.content "EMPTY">
<!ENTITY % animateColor.content "EMPTY">
<!ENTITY % animateMotion.content "EMPTY">
```

Continued

Listing 26-15 *(continued)*

```
<!ENTITY % set.content "EMPTY">

<!ENTITY % animate.attrib        "%SkipContent.attrib;
%CustomTest.attrib;">
<!ENTITY % animateColor.attrib   "%SkipContent.attrib;
%CustomTest.attrib;">
<!ENTITY % animateMotion.attrib  "%SkipContent.attrib;
%CustomTest.attrib;">
<!ENTITY % set.attrib            "%SkipContent.attrib;
%CustomTest.attrib;">

<!-- ================== Layout ============================= -->
<!ENTITY % BasicLayout.module        "INCLUDE">
<!ENTITY % AudioLayout.module        "INCLUDE">
<!ENTITY % MultiWindowLayout.module  "INCLUDE">
<!ENTITY % HierarchicalLayout.module "INCLUDE">

<!ENTITY % layout.content "(region|topLayout|root-
layout|regPoint)*">
<!ENTITY % region.content "(region)*">
<!ENTITY % topLayout.content "(region)*">
<!ENTITY % rootlayout.content "EMPTY">
<!ENTITY % regPoint.content "EMPTY">

<!ENTITY % layout.attrib            "%Test.attrib;
%CustomTest.attrib;">
<!ENTITY % rootlayout.attrib        "%content-control-attrs;">
<!ENTITY % topLayout.attrib         "%content-control-attrs;">
<!ENTITY % region.attrib            "%content-control-attrs;">
<!ENTITY % regPoint.attrib          "%content-control-attrs;">

<!-- ================== Linking =========================== -->
<!ENTITY % LinkingAttributes.module "INCLUDE">
<!ENTITY % BasicLinking.module      "INCLUDE">
<!ENTITY % ObjectLinking.module     "INCLUDE">

<!ENTITY % a.content      "(%timecontainer.class;|%media-object;|
                          %content-control;)*">
<!ENTITY % area.content   "(animate|set)*">
<!ENTITY % anchor.content "(animate|set)*">

<!ENTITY % a.attrib       "%smil-basictime.attrib; %Test.attrib;
%CustomTest.attrib;">
<!ENTITY % area.attrib    "%smil-basictime.attrib; %content-
control-attrs;">
<!ENTITY % anchor.attrib "%smil-basictime.attrib; %content-
control-attrs;">

<!-- ================== Media  ============================= -->
<!ENTITY % BasicMedia.module                   "INCLUDE">
<!ENTITY % MediaClipping.module                "INCLUDE">
```

```
<!ENTITY % MediaClipping.deprecated.module         "INCLUDE">
<!ENTITY % MediaClipMarkers.module                 "INCLUDE">
<!ENTITY % MediaParam.module                       "INCLUDE">
<!ENTITY % BrushMedia.module                       "INCLUDE">
<!ENTITY % MediaAccessibility.module               "INCLUDE">

<!ENTITY % media-object.content "(%animation.elements;|switch
                                 |anchor|area|param)*">
<!ENTITY % media-object.attrib "
  %BasicInlineTiming.attrib;
  %BasicInlineTiming-deprecated.attrib;
  %MinMaxTiming.attrib;
  %RestartTiming.attrib;
  %RestartDefaultTiming.attrib;
  %SyncBehavior.attrib;
  %SyncBehaviorDefault.attrib;
  %Endsync.media.attrib;
  %Fill.attrib;
  %FillDefault.attrib;
  %Test.attrib;
  %CustomTest.attrib;
  %Region.attrib;
  %Transition.attrib;
  %BackgroundColor.attrib;
  %BackgroundColor-deprecated.attrib;
  %Sub-region.attrib;
  %RegistrationPoint.attrib;
  %Fit.attrib;
  %Tabindex.attrib;
">

<!ENTITY % brush.attrib       "%SkipContent.attrib;">
<!ENTITY % param.attrib       "%content-control-attrs;">

<!-- ================== Metadata =========================== -->
<!ENTITY % meta.content       "EMPTY">
<!ENTITY % meta.attrib        "%SkipContent.attrib;">

<!ENTITY % metadata.content "EMPTY">
<!ENTITY % metadata.attrib  "%SkipContent.attrib;">

<!-- ================== Structure =========================== -->
<!ENTITY % Structure.module "INCLUDE">
<!ENTITY % smil.content "(head?,body?)">
<!ENTITY % head.content "(
        meta*,
        ((%head-control.content;),    meta*)?,
        ((%head-meta.content;),       meta*)?,
        ((%head-layout.content;),     meta*)?,
        ((%head-transition.content;),meta*)?
)">
<!ENTITY % body.content "(%timecontainer.class;|%media-object;|
```

Continued

Listing 26-15 *(continued)*

```
                            %content-control;|a)*">

<!ENTITY % smil.attrib "%Test.attrib;">
<!ENTITY % body.attrib "
      %timecontainer.attrib;
      %Description.attrib;
      %Fill.attrib;
">

<!-- ================== Transitions ===================== -->
<!ENTITY % BasicTransitions.module       "INCLUDE">
<!ENTITY % TransitionModifiers.module    "INCLUDE">
<!ENTITY % InlineTransitions.module      "IGNORE">

<!ENTITY % transition.content "EMPTY">
<!ENTITY % transition.attrib "%content-control-attrs;">

<!-- ================== Timing ========================== -->
<!ENTITY % BasicInlineTiming.module      "INCLUDE">
<!ENTITY % SyncbaseTiming.module         "INCLUDE">
<!ENTITY % EventTiming.module            "INCLUDE">
<!ENTITY % WallclockTiming.module        "INCLUDE">
<!ENTITY % MultiSyncArcTiming.module     "INCLUDE">
<!ENTITY % MediaMarkerTiming.module      "INCLUDE">
<!ENTITY % MinMaxTiming.module           "INCLUDE">
<!ENTITY % BasicTimeContainers.module    "INCLUDE">
<!ENTITY % ExclTimeContainers.module     "INCLUDE">
<!ENTITY % PrevTiming.module             "INCLUDE">
<!ENTITY % RestartTiming.module          "INCLUDE">
<!ENTITY % SyncBehavior.module           "INCLUDE">
<!ENTITY % SyncBehaviorDefault.module    "INCLUDE">
<!ENTITY % RestartDefault.module         "INCLUDE">
<!ENTITY % FillDefault.module            "INCLUDE">

<!ENTITY % par.attrib "
      %Endsync.attrib;
      %Fill.attrib;
      %timecontainer.attrib;
      %Test.attrib;
      %CustomTest.attrib;
      %Region.attrib;
">
<!ENTITY % seq.attrib "
      %Fill.attrib;
      %timecontainer.attrib;
      %Test.attrib;
      %CustomTest.attrib;
      %Region.attrib;
```

```
">
<!ENTITY % excl.attrib "
        %Endsync.attrib;
        %Fill.attrib;
        %timecontainer.attrib;
        %Test.attrib;
        %CustomTest.attrib;
        %Region.attrib;
        %SkipContent.attrib;
">
<!ENTITY %  par.content "(%timecontainer.content;)*">
<!ENTITY %  seq.content "(%timecontainer.content;)*">
<!ENTITY % excl.content
"((%timecontainer.content;)*|priorityClass+)">

<!ENTITY % priorityClass.attrib  "%content-control-attrs;">
<!ENTITY % priorityClass.content "(%timecontainer.content;)*">
```

Syntactically, there's nothing new here. You've seen all these techniques before. However, I do want to look at one comment in particular:

```
<!--
    The actual content model and attribute definitions for
    each module sections follow below.
-->
```

Do you see the error? This sentence is grammatically incorrect. It should be either "each module section" (singular) or "the module sections" (plural). However "each module sections" is just wrong. Admittedly this is not a major problem, and is not likely to confuse anyone. Nonetheless it should be fixed. Fortunately, this only appeared in the Proposed Recommendation draft when there was still time to fix it before the final recommendation. Most importantly, this draft was published to the world for interested parties to pour over and comment on. During that process, many mistakes and misconceptions were found and fixed. These ranged from quite trivial mistakes like this minor grammatical error to major flaws of syntax and semantics.

Outside review is crucial here. Even though many very intelligent developers wrote the SMIL 2.0 specification, a lot of problems would have slipped through the cracks if not for the interested eyes of outsiders. When only the people developing a DTD look at it, it's very easy for them to become so accustomed to the mistakes that they don't see problems that would be obvious to a third party. Do not expect that you can spring your XML application on the world fully grown like Athena out of Zeus's head. You will have to publish multiple intermediate drafts, and aggressively seek out commentary on those drafts before you can be confident you have a clean, useful, correct specification.

The Metainformation Module

Listing 26-16 shows the SMIL Metainformation Module DTD. This is a very basic module that declares just two elements, meta and metadata. Both are used only in the full language profile, not in the basic profile. The meta element is very similar to the meta element in HTML. It has name and value attributes that allow you to associate any sort of meta-information with a particular SMIL document. The metadata element is intended to contain more complete Resource Description Framework (RDF) metadata for the document.

Cross-Reference   RDF is described in Chapter 24.

Listing 26-16: **SMIL-metainformation.mod: The SMIL Metainformation Module DTD**

```
<!-- ======================================================= -->
<!-- SMIL Metainformation Module  ========================== -->
<!-- file: SMIL-metainformation.mod

     This is SMIL 2.0.
     Copyright 2000 W3C (MIT, INRIA, Keio), All Rights
     Reserved.

     This module declares the meta and metadata elements types
     and its attributes, used to provide declarative document
     metainformation.

     Author: Thierry Michel, Jacco van Ossenbruggen
     Revision: $Id: SMIL-metainformation.mod,v 1.6 2000/10/09
               09:44:21 jvanoss Exp $

     This DTD module is identified by the PUBLIC and SYSTEM
     identifiers:

     PUBLIC "-//W3C//ELEMENTS SMIL 2.0 Document Metadata//EN"
     SYSTEM "SMIL-metainformation.mod"

     ======================================================= -->


<!-- ================== Profiling Entities ================ -->

<!ENTITY % meta.content      "EMPTY">
<!ENTITY % meta.attrib       "">
<!ENTITY % meta.qname        "meta">

<!ENTITY % metadata.content  "EMPTY">
<!ENTITY % metadata.attrib   "">
<!ENTITY % metadata.qname    "metadata">
```

```
<!-- ================== meta element ====================== -->

<!ELEMENT %meta.qname; %meta.content;>
<!ATTLIST %meta.qname; %meta.attrib;
  %Core.attrib;
  %I18n.attrib;
  content CDATA #IMPLIED
  name CDATA #REQUIRED
  >

<!-- ================== metadata element ================== -->

<!ELEMENT %metadata.qname; %metadata.content;>
<!ATTLIST %metadata.qname; %metadata.attrib;
  %Core.attrib;
  %I18n.attrib;
>

<!-- end of SMIL-metadata.mod -->
```

There's no rule that says DTD modules have to be big. This one most certainly isn't, declaring as it does only two elements and a couple of attributes. If it makes sense to use very small modules declaring individual elements that are independent of each other, then do so. More modular systems with more parts are easier to maintain, understand, and extend.

This DTD module declares that the metadata element is empty. However, that's not the intent. According to the prose specification, the metadata element is meant to hold a complete RDF description of the content. This would naturally require a complete DTD for RDF. Furthermore, since RDF is normally used only in conjunction with an additional vocabulary such as the Dublin Core, you'd also need a DTD for that as well. The modular framework makes it possible to import all these and insert them where necessary. For example, suppose you want to say that the metadata element can contain exactly one rdf:RDF element. Then you would redefine the metadata.content entity like this:

```
<!ENTITY % metadata.content "( rdf:RDF )">
```

You would have to have already imported a DTD for RDF before you used this parameter entity. The W3C has not published one, and indeed most RDF documents are invalid. However, it's not hard to write one for your own use if you know the vocabulary you'll be intermixing with the RDF markup.

Tip   Although the SYMM Working Group intends the metadata element to be used specifically for RDF, there's no reason you can't use it for an alternative metadata XML application such as topic maps. Whichever vocabulary you choose, you'll still need to redefine the metadata.content parameter entity.

The Transition Module

Listing 26-17 shows the SMIL Transition Module DTD. This module defines elements to specify different kinds of wipes and transitions as one image or clip fades into another. This module is only used in the full language profile, not in the basic profile.

Listing 26-17: SMIL-transition.mod: The SMIL Transition Module DTD

```
<!-- ========================================================= -->
<!-- SMIL Transition Module  ============================== -->
<!-- file: SMIL-transition.mod

     This is SMIL 2.0
     Copyright 2000 W3C (MIT, INRIA, Keio), All Rights
     Reserved.

     Revision:   $Id: smil-DTD.html,v 1.1 2001/06/05 09:16:20
                 jigsaw Exp $

     This DTD module is identified by the PUBLIC and SYSTEM
     identifiers:

     PUBLIC "-//W3C//ELEMENTS SMIL 2.0 Transition//EN"
     SYSTEM "SMIL-transition.mod"

     ========================================================= -->

<!ENTITY % TransitionModifiers.module "IGNORE">
<![%TransitionModifiers.module;[
 <!ENTITY % transition-modifiers-attrs '
    horzRepeat    CDATA                  "0"
    vertRepeat    CDATA                  "0"
    borderWidth   CDATA                  "0"
    borderColor   CDATA                  "black"
 '>
]]> <!-- End of TransitionModifiers.module -->
<!ENTITY % transition-modifiers-attrs "">

<!ENTITY %  BasicTransitions.module "INCLUDE">
<![%BasicTransitions.module;[

 <!ENTITY % transition-types "(barWipe|boxWipe|fourBoxWipe|
   barnDoorWipe|diagonalWipe|bowTieWipe|miscDiagonalWipe|
   veeWipe|barnVeeWipe|zigZagWipe|barnZigZagWipe|irisWipe|
   triangleWipe|arrowHeadWipe|pentagonWipe|hexagonWipe|
   ellipseWipe|eyeWipe|roundRectWipe|starWipe|miscShapeWipe|
   clockWipe|pinWheelWipe|singleSweepWipe|fanWipe|doubleFanWipe|
   doubleSweepWipe|saloonDoorWipe|windshieldWipe|snakeWipe|
   spiralWipe|parallelSnakesWipe|boxSnakesWipe|waterfallWipe|
```

```
  pushWipe|slideWipe|fade)"
>

<!ENTITY % transition-subtypes "(bottom
  |bottomCenter|bottomLeft|bottomLeftClockwise|
  bottomLeftCounterClockwise|bottomLeftDiagonal|bottomRight|
  bottomRightClockwise|bottomRightCounterClockwise|
  bottomRightDiagonal|centerRight|centerTop|circle|
  clockwiseBottom|clockwiseBottomRight|clockwiseLeft|
  clockwiseNine|clockwiseRight|clockwiseSix|clockwiseThree|
  clockwiseTop|clockwiseTopLeft|clockwiseTwelve|cornersIn|
  cornersOut|counterClockwiseBottomLeft|
  counterClockwiseTopRight|crossfade|diagonalBottomLeft|
  diagonalBottomLeftOpposite|diagonalTopLeft|
  diagonalTopLeftOpposite|diamond|doubleBarnDoor|doubleDiamond|
  down|fadeFromColor|fadeToColor|fanInHorizontal|fanInVertical|
  fanOutHorizontal|fanOutVertical|fivePoint|fourBlade|
  fourBoxHorizontal|fourBoxVertical|fourPoint|fromBottom|
  fromLeft|fromRight|fromTop|heart|horizontal|horizontalLeft|
  horizontalLeftSame|horizontalRight|horizontalRightSame|
  horizontalTopLeftOpposite|horizontalTopRightOpposite|keyhole|
  left|leftCenter|leftToRight|oppositeHorizontal|
  oppositeVertical|parallelDiagonal|parallelDiagonalBottomLeft|
  parallelDiagonalTopLeft|parallelVertical|rectangle|right|
  rightCenter|sixPoint|top|topCenter|topLeft|topLeftClockwise|
  topLeftCounterClockwise|topLeftDiagonal|topLeftHorizontal|
  topLeftVertical|topRight|topRightClockwise|
  topRightCounterClockwise|topRightDiagonal|topToBottom|
  twoBladeHorizontal|twoBladeVertical|twoBoxBottom|twoBoxLeft|
  twoBoxRight|twoBoxTop|up|vertical|verticalBottomLeftOpposite|
  verticalBottomSame|verticalLeft|verticalRight|
  verticalTopLeftOpposite|verticalTopSame)"
>

<!ENTITY  % transition-attrs '
    type          %transition-types;      #IMPLIED
    subtype       %transition-subtypes;   #IMPLIED
    fadeColor     CDATA                   "black"
    %transition-modifiers-attrs;
 '>

<!ENTITY % transition.attrib  "">
<!ENTITY % transition.content "EMPTY">
<!ENTITY % transition.qname   "transition">
<!ELEMENT %transition.qname; %transition.content;>
<!ATTLIST %transition.qname; %transition.attrib;
    %Core.attrib;
    %I18n.attrib;
    %transition-attrs;
    dur           %TimeValue.datatype; #IMPLIED
    startProgress CDATA                 "0.0"
    endProgress   CDATA                 "1.0"
```

Continued

Listing 26-17 *(continued)*

```
    direction      (forward|reverse)  "forward"
 >
]]> <!-- End of BasicTransitions.module -->

<!ENTITY %  InlineTransitions.module "IGNORE">
<![%InlineTransitions.module;[

 <!ENTITY % transitionFilter.attrib   "">
 <!ENTITY % transitionFilter.content "EMPTY">
 <!ENTITY % transitionFilter.qname   "transitionFilter">
 <!ELEMENT %transitionFilter.qname; %transitionFilter.content;>
 <!ATTLIST %transitionFilter.qname; %transitionFilter.attrib;
    %Core.attrib;
    %I18n.attrib;
    %transition-attrs;
    %BasicInlineTiming.attrib;
    %BasicAnimation.attrib;
    calcMode   (discrete|linear|paced) 'linear'
 >
]]> <!-- End of InlineTransitions.module -->

<!-- end of SMIL-transition.mod -->
```

Rolling Your Own Language Profiles

Sometimes neither the basic nor the full profile is exactly what you need. In these cases it is permissible to pick and choose those modules you want from SMIL by creating your own master DTD. This DTD should follow the general structure of the two DTDs provided with SMIL 2.0. In particular, you can normally just start with the full DTD and delete those sections you don't want. For instance, Listing 26-18 is similar to the basic driver DTD shown earlier. However, it omits the linking module and adds the meta module.

Listing 26-18: A customized SMIL DTD

```
<!-- ..................................................  -->
<!-- SMIL 2.0 Custom DTD  ..............................  -->
<!-- file: 26-18.dtd -->
<!-- SMIL 2.0 DTD

    Copyright 1998-2000 World Wide Web Consortium
    (Massachusetts Institute of Technology, Institut National
     de Recherche en Informatique et en Automatique, Keio
     University). All Rights Reserved.
```

Permission to use, copy, modify and distribute the SMIL
2.0 DTD and its accompanying documentation for any purpose
and without fee is hereby granted in perpetuity, provided
that the above copyright notice and this paragraph appear
in all copies. The copyright holders make no
representation about the suitability of the DTD for any
purpose.

It is provided "as is" without expressed or implied
warranty.

    Author: Elliotte Rusty Harold derived from the work
                     of Jacco van Ossenbruggen
    Revision: 2001/05/14

This is a revised version of the SMIL 2.0 DTD used as an
example of customizing a DTD in the XML Bible, Gold
Edition.

-->

<!ENTITY % NS.prefixed "IGNORE" >
<!ENTITY % SMIL.prefix "" >

<!-- Define the Content Model -->
<!ENTITY % smil-model.mod
    PUBLIC "-//W3C//ENTITIES SMIL 2.0 Document Model 1.0//EN"
           "smil-model-1.mod" >

<!-- Modular Framework Module
.... -->
<!ENTITY % smil-framework.module "INCLUDE" >
<![%smil-framework.module;[
<!ENTITY % smil-framework.mod
    PUBLIC "-//W3C//ENTITIES SMIL 2.0 Modular Framework
1.0//EN"
           "smil-framework-1.mod" >
%smil-framework.mod;]]>

<!-- This is a variation of the SMIL 2.0 Profile
     that includes the following sections:
             D. The SMIL Content Control Module
             G. The SMIL Layout Module
             I. The SMIL Media Object Module
             J. The SMIL Metainformation Module
             K. The SMIL Structure Module
             L. The SMIL Timing and Synchronization Module
             M. Integrating SMIL Timing into other XML-Based
Languages

     -->

Continued

Listing 26-18 (continued)

```
<!ENTITY % control-mod
  PUBLIC "-//W3C//ELEMENTS SMIL 2.0 Content Control//EN"
  "SMIL-control.mod">
<!ENTITY % layout-mod
  PUBLIC "-//W3C//ELEMENTS SMIL 2.0 Layout//EN"
  "SMIL-layout.mod">
<!ENTITY % media-mod
  PUBLIC "-//W3C//ELEMENTS SMIL 2.0 Media Objects//EN"
  "SMIL-media.mod">
<!ENTITY % meta-mod
  PUBLIC "-//W3C//ELEMENTS SMIL 2.0 Document
Metainformation//EN"
  "SMIL-metainformation.mod">
<!ENTITY % struct-mod
  PUBLIC "-//W3C//ELEMENTS SMIL 2.0 Document Structure//EN"
  "SMIL-struct.mod">
<!ENTITY % timing-mod
  PUBLIC "-//W3C//ELEMENTS SMIL 2.0 Timing//EN"
  "SMIL-timing.mod">

%struct-mod;
%control-mod;
%meta-mod;
%layout-mod;
%media-mod;
%timing-mod;
```

You can make further changes and customizations by changing the document model module. More minor changes can be made simply by redefining particular parameter entities in the internal DTD subsets of your instance documents.

Not all SMIL based systems need every piece of SMIL. Depending on your needs you may well be able to omit transitions, links, particular media types, animation, metadata, and other advanced features of SMIL. In addition it's easy to mix in other modules to this basic set as you desire. For example, as already mentioned you could develop your own vocabulary for streaming media and add it as just one more module.

Going in the other direction you can include some parts of SMIL in other applications you develop. For instance, if you just need to describe timing you can import the timing module. This will also require you to pull in some of the other framework modules like qualified names, and perhaps to define a new document model; but you won't need to invent everything from scratch. You can't call the resulting application SMIL, but it does provide a neat way to add some multimedia savvy to a more domain-specific DTD without going overboard and pulling in the full multimedia smorgasbord that is SMIL 2.0. Indeed there's an ongoing effort at the W3C to integrate SMIL 2.0 with XHTML 1.1 through the modularity features of both of these XML applications.

Techniques to Imitate

Pablo Picasso is often quoted as saying, "Good artists copy. Great artists steal." Part of the reason the SMIL 2.0 DTD is broken up into so many parts is precisely so that you can steal from it. If you need basic timing as part of an XML application you're developing, you don't need to invent your own. You can simply import the necessary modules. This has the added advantage that document authors who have to use your XML application are possibly already familiar with this markup from SMIL. Nonetheless, let's go ahead and look at some techniques you can borrow from the SMIL DTD for your own DTDs without out-and-out stealing the DTDs themselves.

Comments

The SMIL DTDs are profusely commented. Every single file has a comment that gives a title, the relevant copyright notice, and an abstract of what's in the file, before there's even one single declaration. Every section of the file is separated off by a new comment that specifies the purpose of the section. And almost every declaration features a comment discussing what that declaration means. These comments make the file **much** easier to read and understand.

This still isn't perfect, however. Many of the attribute declarations are not sufficiently commented. For example, consider this declaration from the content control module:

```
<!ATTLIST %prefetch.qname; %prefetch.attrib;
    src             %URI.datatype;    #IMPLIED
    mediaSize       CDATA             #IMPLIED
    mediaTime       CDATA             #IMPLIED
    bandwidth       CDATA             #IMPLIED
    %Core.attrib;
    %I18n.attrib;
>
```

There's no indication of what the value of all these attributes should be. An additional comment like this would be helpful:

```
<!-- ATTLIST prefetch
    src        The URI of the media file to be fetched before
               it is needed
```

```
mediaSize How much of the resource to fetch;
          specified as a number of bytes (e.g. 100000)
          or a percentage of the total size of the resource
          (e.g. 10%). 100% is the default.
mediaTime How long of the resource to fetch;
          specified as a clock-value (e.g. 00:05:30)
          or a percentage of the total duration of the
          resource (e.g. 10%). 100% is the default.
bandwidth The amount of available network bandwidth
          that should be devoted to fetching this
          resource.
          Can be specified as the number of bits per
          second (e.g. 34000)
          or a percentage (e.g. 25%). 100% is the default.
-->
```

Of course you could find all of this out simply by reading the specification for SMIL 2.0. However, many times when complete documentation is left to a later, prose document, that prose document never gets written. It certainly doesn't hurt to include extra commentary when you're writing the DTD for the first time.

Copyright Notices in DTDs

If you're designing a DTD solely for your use on your own Web site or for printed documentation within a single company, feel free to place any copyright notice you want on it. However, if you're designing a DTD for an entire industry or area of study, please consider any copyright notice very carefully. A simple, ordinary copyright notice like "Copyright 2001 MyCorp" immediately makes the DTD unusable for many people because by default it means the DTD can't be copied onto a different Web server or into a new document without explicit permission. While many people and companies will simply ignore these restrictions (which the authors never intended anyway), I don't think many people will be comfortable relying on this in our overly litigious world.

The whole point of XML is to allow broad, standardized documents. To this end, any markup language that's created, whether described in a DTD, a schema, or something else, must explicitly allow itself to be reused and reprinted without prior permission. My preference is that these DTDs be placed in the public domain, because it's simplest and easiest to explain to lawyers. Open source works well too. Even a copyright statement that allows reuse but not modification is adequate for many needs.

Therefore, I implore you to think very carefully about any copyright you place on a DTD. Ask yourself, "What does this really say? What do I want people to do with this DTD? Does this statement allow them to do that?" There's very little to be gained by writing a DTD you hope an industry will adopt, if you unintentionally prohibit the industry from adopting it.

(Although this book as a whole and its prose text is copyrighted, I am explicitly placing the code examples I've written in the public domain. Please feel free to use any fragment of code or an entire DTD in any way that you like, with or without credit.)

Part of the problem is that restrictions on character data are not well expressed in DTDs; for instance that `media-size` must be a positive integer or a percentage. In the future, schemas will help address this shortcoming.

In cases of complicated attribute and element declarations, it's also often useful to provide an example in a comment. For instance:

```
<!--

  <prefetch src="http://www.example.com/images/image.png"
          mediaSize="50%"
          mediaTime="50%"
          bandwidth="34000"
  />

-->
```

Parameter entities

The SMIL DTD makes extremely heavy use of both internal and external parameter entities. Your DTDs can, too. There are many uses for parameter entities that were demonstrated in the SMIL DTD. To summarize, you can use them to:

✦ Break up long content models and attribute lists into manageable, related pieces

✦ Standardize common sets of elements and attributes

✦ Enable different DTDs to change content models and attribute lists

✦ More clearly specify element and attribute types

✦ Compress the DTD by reusing common sequences of text

✦ Split the DTD into individual, related modules

Break Up Long Content Models and Attribute Lists into Manageable, Related Pieces

A typical SMIL element like `par` can easily have several dozen possible attributes and children. Listing them all in a content model or attribute list will simply overwhelm anyone trying to read a DTD. To the extent that related elements and attributes can be grouped, it's better to separate them into several parameter entities. For example, here's SMIL's element declaration for `par`:

```
<!ELEMENT %par.qname; %par.content;>
```

It uses only a single parameter entity reference, rather than the many separate element names that the reference resolves into.

Here's SMIL's attribute list for `par`:

```
<!ATTLIST %par.qname; %par.attrib;
  %Core.attrib;
  %I18n.attrib;
  %Description.attrib;
>
```

This is a little more complex but not much. It uses four parameter entities to list the attributes, and you can quickly see that three of them are just standard sets of common attributes shared by most SMIL elements.

Standardize common sets of elements and attributes

When you're dealing with 30 or more items in a list, it's easy to miss one if you have to keep repeating the list. For instance, almost all SMIL elements can have these six attributes:

- ✦ `xml:base`
- ✦ `id`
- ✦ `class`
- ✦ `title`
- ✦ `longdesc`
- ✦ `alt`

By combining them all into one `%Core.attrib;` parameter entity reference, you avoid the chance of omitting or mistyping one of them in an attribute list. If at any point in the future, you want to add an attribute to this list, you can add it just by including it in the declaration of `Core.attrib`. You don't have to add it to each of a hundred or more element declarations.

Enable different DTDs to change content models and attribute lists

One of the neatest tricks with parameter entity references in SMIL 2.0 is how they're used to customize different DTDs from the same basic modules. The key is that each customizable item, whether a content model or an attribute list, is given as a parameter entity reference. Each DTD can then redefine the content model or attribute list by redefining the parameter entity reference. This allows particular DTDs to both add and remove items from content models and attribute lists.

For example, suppose you want to eliminate video and animation as allowed media types. These are normally represented by `video` or `animation` elements, which appear as a child of either a `par` or a `seq`. However, both `par` and `seq` are declared to have a content model of `%timeContainer.content;`:

```
<!ENTITY %  par.content "%timeContainer.content;">
<!ENTITY %  seq.content "%timeContainer.content;">
```

This, it turns out, is defined thusly:

```
<!ENTITY % timecontainer.content
    "%timecontainer.class;|%media-object;|%content-control;|a">
```

It's actually the `media-object` entity that references the different media types such as `audio`, `video` and `img`:

```
<!ENTITY % media-object
    "audio|video|animation|text|img|textstream|ref|brush|
    %animation.elements;">
```

It's straight-forward to place this entity definition in the document that imports the normal SMIL DTD:

```
<!ENTITY % media-object "audio|text|img|textstream|ref|brush">
```

This will override the declaration in smil-model-1.mod so that documents adhering to your DTD cannot include video or animation in their `par` and `seq` elements. In fact, even if you forgot to check the content model for some element besides `par` and `seq` that could have `video` or `animation` child, chances are good that it also uses these elements through the intermediary of the `%media-object;` parameter entity reference. When you redefined `%media-object;`, you redefined everything that depended on it, so your change is made everywhere you need it to be made.

More clearly specify element and attribute types

One of the most unusual tricks the XHTML DTD plays with parameter entity references is using them to replace the `CDATA` attribute type. Although `%ContentType.datatype;`, `%Character.datatype;`, `%Script.datatype;`, `%LanguageCodes.datatype;`, `%Number.datatype;`, `%LinkTypes;`, `%Text.datatype;`, and `%URI.datatype;`, are on one level just synonyms for `CDATA`, on another level they make the attribute types a lot more specific. `CDATA` can really mean almost anything. Using parameter entities in this way goes a long way toward narrowing down and documenting the actual meaning in a particular context. While such parameter entities can't enforce their meanings, simply documenting them is no small achievement.

Compress the DTD by reusing common sequences of text

The complete SMIL 2.0 DTD occupies about 60 kilobytes. That's not a huge amount, especially for applications that reside on a local drive or network, but it is non-trivial for Internet applications. It would probably be three to five times larger if all the parameter entity references were fully expanded.

Even more significant than the file size saving achieved by parameter entity references are the savings in legibility. Short files are easier to read and comprehend. A 600- kilobyte DTD, even broken up into 60-kilobyte chunks, would be too much to ask document authors to read, especially given the turgid, non-English code that makes up DTDs. (Let me put it this way: Of the much smaller modules in this chapter, how many of them did you actually read from start to finish and how many did you just skip over until the example was done? Any code module that's longer than a page is likely to thwart all but the most determined and conscientious readers.)

Split the DTD into individual, related modules

On a related note, splitting the DTD into several related modules makes it easier to grasp overall. All the transitions material is conveniently gathered in one place, as is all the animation material, all the linking material, and so forth. Furthermore, this makes the DTD easier to understand because you can take it one bite-sized piece at a time.

On the other hand, the interconnections between some of the modules do make this a little more confusing than perhaps it needs to be. In order to truly understand any one of the modules, you must at a minimum understand the modularization framework provided by the datatypes module, the common attributes module, the qualified names module, and the framework module because these provide crucial definitions for entities used in all the other modules. Furthermore, a module can only really be understood in the context of either the basic or full profile, each of which requires a document model. So there are at least six files you need to grok before you can really start to get a handle on any one. Still, the clean separation between modules is impressive, and recommends itself for imitation.

Summary

In this chapter, you learned how to read and write DTDs by exploring the SMIL 2.0 DTD. More specifically, you learned:

✦ All writers learn by reading other writers' work. XML writers should read other XML writers' work.

✦ SMIL 2.0, the Synchronized Multimedia Integration Language, is an XML application for the description of time sensitive, multimedia presentations.

✦ The SMIL 2.0 DTD is divided across many different files. This modular design allows you to pick and choose only those pieces you need.

✦ SMIL 2.0 defines two separate profiles, a basic one that only provides the minimal set of SMIL elements and attributes, and a more complete one that takes full advantage of all of SMIL's options. In addition you can create your own DTDs that fall somewhere in between these two.

✦ Nine module DTDs each describe the elements and attributes of an area of related functionality.

✦ Document models define the parameter entity references that provide the common content models and attribute types used in the modules.

✦ Good comments make DTDs much easier to read. You can never have too many comments in your DTDs.

✦ Parameter entities are extremely powerful tools for building complex yet manageable DTDs.

In the next two chapters, we'll explore another XML application, XHTML, the Extensible Hypertext Markup Language. XHTML 1.0 is an XMLized form of HTML. XHTML 1.1 is a modularized form of XHTML 1.0. Indeed, the DTD for XHTML 1.1 is structured much like the SMIL DTD explored in this chapter. However, rather than focusing on the DTD, we'll be looking at the use of the application itself.

✦　　✦　　✦

XHTML

XHTML, the Extensible Hypertext Markup Language, is
the W3C's effort to redefine HTML based on XML rather
than SGML. This requires tightening up a lot of the looseness
of traditional HTML. End tags must be added to elements that
don't normally have them, such as p and dt. Empty-element
tags, such as hr and img, must end in /> instead of just >.
Attribute values must be quoted. The names of all HTML elements and attributes are standardized in lowercase. But
XHTML goes one step further than merely requiring HTML
documents to be well-formed XML. It actually provides a document type definition (DTD) that you can use to validate your
HTML documents. In fact, it provides three:

♦ The XHTML strict DTD for new HTML documents:
`http://www.w3.org/TR/xhtml1/DTD/`
`xhtml1-strict.dtd`

♦ The XHTML transitional DTD for legacy HTML documents that still use deprecated tags such as applet:
`http://www.w3.org/TR/xhtml1/DTD/xhtml1-`
`transitional.dtd`

♦ The XHTML frameset DTD for documents that use
frames: `http://www.w3.org/TR/xhtml1/DTD/`
`xhtml1-frameset.dtd`

You can choose the one that best fits your site.

Why Validate HTML?

XHTML, the Extensible Hypertext Markup Language, is a reformulation of HTML 4.0 as well-formed and valid XML. XHTML
documents must adhere to all the rules of XML. For instance,
all start tags must have matching end tags. Tags can nest but
cannot overlap. Attribute values must be quoted. The ampersand and less-than characters can only be used to start entity
references and tags respectively; and so on.

Valid documents aren't required for HTML, but validity does make it much easier for browsers to properly display documents. A valid XHTML document is far more likely to render correctly and predictably across many different browsers than an invalid HTML document. Until recently, too much of the competition among browser vendors revolved around just how much broken HTML they could make sense of. For instance, Internet Explorer fills in a missing `</table>` end tag whereas Netscape Navigator does not. For some time, many pages on Microsoft's Web site contained missing `</table>` tags and could not be viewed in Netscape Navigator. (I'll leave it to the reader to decide whether this was unfortunate happenstance or deliberate sabotage.) In either case, if Microsoft had required valid HTML on its Web site, this would not have happened.

It is extremely difficult for even the largest Web shops to test their pages against even a small fraction of the browsers that people actually use. Even testing the latest versions of both Netscape and Internet Explorer is more than some designers manage. While I certainly won't argue that you shouldn't test your pages in as many versions of as many browsers as possible, the reality is that time and resources are finite. Validating HTML goes a long way toward ensuring that your pages render reasonably in a broad spectrum of browsers.

In addition, validating HTML helps you find your mistakes. There are a surprising number of HTML documents on the Web today with truly mistaken HTML. I've seen pages where authors have placed attributes on the wrong elements, misspelled element and attribute names, left off the closing " on an attribute or > on a tag, and more. These problems don't just cause problems in some browsers; they cause major problems in all browsers! Yet you'll find mistakes like these on some of the largest and most popular sites on the Web. All of these common problems can be easily detected if you validate your documents before publishing them.

There are also advantages to XHTML beyond the realm of browser display. First, when your documents are XHTML rather than HTML, you get to use the myriad of XML-aware tools to process your HTML documents. For example, you can use XSLT to transform XHTML documents into XSL Formatting Objects for high-quality printing.

Second, because XML is much more carefully defined and stricter in what it does and doesn't allow than classic HTML, it's much easier for your own custom programs to process XHTML than HTML. Web spiders, indexing tools, link checkers, and other programs are all much easier to write for XHTML than for HTML.

Third, it's much easier to mix other XML applications like Scalable Vector Graphics (SVG) or MathML into an XHTML document than an HTML document. XHTML's well-formedness and validity rules make it really obvious where other, non-XHTML content can be placed. Furthermore, XML namespaces make it easy for browsers to determine which parts of a page come from which XML vocabulary, so that it knows what to pass to the MathML plug-in, what to display as an SVG picture, and what to format in a normal HTML fashion.

And while it may be marginally more difficult to write XHTML by hand than traditional HTML, it's not significantly more difficult for editors such as DreamWeaver or Microsoft Word to produce XHTML than HTML. The current versions of these tools mostly produce malformed HTML, but in the future, they'll generate correct XHTML without any extra effort on the user's part.

Moving to XHTML

The XHTML 1.0 specification defines a Strictly Conforming XHTML Document as one that meets the following criteria:

1. The root element must be `html`.

2. The root element must set the default namespace to `http://www.w3.org/1999/xhtml`.

3. The document must have a `DOCTYPE` declaration that references the strict, transitional, or frameset DTD using one of the these three Formal Public Identifiers:

- `-//W3C//DTD XHTML 1.0 Strict//EN`
- `-//W3C//DTD XHTML 1.0 Transitional//EN`
- `-//W3C//DTD XHTML 1.0 Frameset//EN`

4. The document must be valid.

These requirements have certain implications. For instance, well-formedness is a prerequisite for validity. Therefore, requirement four implies that the document must be well-formed. And, of course, requirement three has all sorts of implications based on the rules found in those three DTDs. For the most part, these rules match your expectations about what an HTML document should look like. However, there are some exceptions, especially for the strict DTD. For instance, all element and attribute names must be lowercase. Nonstandard elements such as `marquee` and `layer` and nonstandard attributes such as `datafld` are strictly forbidden.

Let's explore the process you'll have to go through to convert an existing HTML document to XHTML. I'll choose as an example the Mobile Office page from *Project FREEDOM*, Web site of U.S. Representative Ron Paul, (`http://www.house.gov/paul/mobileo.htm`). I chose this page because it's a particularly egregious example of malformed, invalid, ugly, and just-plain-wrong HTML. According to the site information at `http://www.house.gov/paul/siteman.htm`, "The site is stored on the main House of Representative [*sic*] secure server and is generally created using a combination of web-design software applications and direct HTML coding. The site operates equally well on the most recent versions of Netscape and Microsoft Internet Explorer-compatible platforms, working best with a frames-enabled browser." In fact, I'd be surprised if it works well in any browser. The most common problem on Web sites today is that they've been designed to look good on only one particular browser or platform. However, this one seemed especially unsightly on every browser I tried, including IE5.5 for Windows (shown in Figure 27-1).

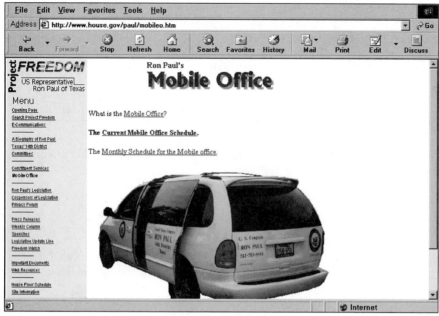

Figure 27-1: Ron Paul's Mobile Office Web page

The HTML source code is given in Listing 27-1. This is shown exactly as it appeared on the site on December 1, 2000, aside from adding a few line breaks to fit it on the printed page. Read through it carefully and see how many problems you can find.

Listing 27-1: **http://www.house.gov/paul/mobileo.htm**

```
<head><title>Mobile Office

</title></head>
<!--INSERT TITLE, INSERT TEXT-->

<body bgcolor=#ffffff text=black link=#000080 vlink=#000080
alink=#000080  leftmargin=0 topmargin=0 marginwidth=0
marginheight=0  >
<basefont size=2 face="Times New Roman">
<table border=0 valign=top align=left>
<tr><td bgcolor=#EFEFCE valign=top>
<a href=http://www.house.gov/paul/><IMG
SRC="images/pflogosm.gif" BORDER=0></a><br>
<table border=0><tr><td width=2></td><td border=1>
<font size=+1 face="MS Sans Serif, Geneva,
Verdana">Menu</font><br>
<font size=-2 face="Arial Narrow">
    <a href=display.htm>Opening Page</a><br>
<a href=search.htm>Search Project Freedom</a><br>
```

```
<a href=mail/welcome.htm>E-Communications</a><br>
-------------------<br>
<a href=bio.htm>A Biography of Ron Paul</a><br>
<a href=about14.htm>Texas' 14th District</a><br>
<a href=committeework/welcome.htm>Committees</a><br>
-------------------<br>
<a href=services14.htm>Constituent Services</a><br>
<B>Mobile Office<br></B>
-------------------<br>
<a href=legis/welcome.htm>Ron Paul's Legislation</a><br>
<a href=legis/106/cospon.htm>Cosponsors of Legislation</a><br>
<a href=privacy/display.htm>Privacy Forum</a><br>
-------------------<br>
<a href=press/welcome.htm>Press Releases</a><br>
<a href=tst/welcome.htm>Weekly Column</a><br>
<a href=congrec/welcome.htm>Speeches</a><br>
<a href=tst/lu.htm>Legislative Update Line</a><br>
<a href=fwu/welcome.htm>Freedom Watch</a><br>
-------------------<br>
<a href=impdoc.htm>Important Documents</a><br>
<a href=links.htm>Web Resources</a><br>
-------------------<br>
<a href=http://majoritywhip.house.gov/whipnotice.htm>House
Floor Schedule</a><br>
<a href=siteman.htm>Site Information<br>
</td></tr></table>
<table align=right border=1><tr><td>
<font size=1 face="Arial Narrow">
<P>
The Office of U.S. Rep. Ron Paul<br>
203 Cannon HOB<br>
Washington, DC 20515<br>
(202) 225-2831<p>
</td></tr></table>

</td>

<td valign=top align=left>
<!--PAGE TEXT INSERT HERE-->



<CENTER><img src="images/mo.gif" alt="The Mobile
Office"></CENTER>
<P>
What is the <A HREF="mobilewhatis.htm" >Mobile Office</a>?
<P>
<b>The <A HREF="mosched.htm" target=new>Current Mobile Office
Schedule</A>.</b>
<P>
<P>
The <a href=moset.htm>Monthly Schedule for the Mobile
```

Continued

Listing 27-1 (continued)

```
office</a>.<P>
<P>

<IMG SRC="images/mobileoffice.gif" BORDER=0>




<!--END OF PAGE-->
</td></tr>
</table>
<P>
```

In fact, there are more than 25 separate errors in this document, the exact number depending on how you count. Since this document is so completely broken, let's divide the task of converting it to XHTML into three parts. First, we'll convert it to well-formed XML; then we'll make it valid XHTML according to the transitional XHTML DTD; and finally, we'll upgrade it to full conformance with the XHTML strict DTD.

Making the document well-formed XML

Listing 27-1 contains numerous well-formedness errors. Let's address them in order. The first one you should have noted is that there's no root element! The `html` element that should enclose all HTML and XHTML documents is missing. The document starts with a `head`. This is followed by a `body` element. All well-formed XML documents must have exactly one root element. Therefore the first thing you need to do is add an `html` root element like this:

```
<html>
  <head><title>Mobile Office</title></head>
  <body>
  ...
</html>
```

However, the `html` root element isn't the only element with problems in this document. Many, many elements in this document, the `body` element being just the first one, have start tags but no corresponding end tags. You have to fix all these too. For instance, near the bottom of the document, you'll find these six paragraphs:

```
<P>
What is the <A HREF="mobilewhatis.htm" >Mobile Office</a>?
<P>
<b>The <A HREF="mosched.htm" target=new>Current Mobile Office
Schedule</A>.</b>
<P>
<P>
The <a href=moset.htm>Monthly Schedule for the Mobile
office</a>.<P>
<P>
```

However, these paragraphs are identified by six `<P>` start tags that are all unmatched by `</P>` end tags. This needs to be fixed wherever it occurs. For example, that section should be rewritten like this:

```
<P>
What is the <A HREF="mobilewhatis.htm" >Mobile Office</a>?
</P>
<P>
<b>The <A HREF="mosched.htm" target=new>Current Mobile Office
Schedule</A>.</b>
</P>
<P></P>
<P>
The <a href=moset.htm>Monthly Schedule for the Mobile
office</a>.
</P>
<P></P>
<P></P>
```

When matching start tags to end tags, it's also important to make sure that their cases match. A `<P>` start tag cannot be closed with a `</p>` end tag. This mistake is made in the first paragraph of this sample:

```
What is the <A HREF="mobilewhatis.htm" >Mobile Office</a>?
```

The opening uppercase `<A>` tag is closed by a lowercase `</a>` tag. The easiest way to fix mismatched case problems is to adopt a single case for all tags. The XHTML DTDs actually specify that all tags be written in lowercase, so you should change the above fragment to this:

```
<p>
What is the <a href="mobilewhatis.htm" >Mobile Office</a>?
</p>
<p>
<b>The <a HREF="mosched.htm" target=new>Current Mobile Office
Schedule</a>.</b>
</p>
<p></p>
```

```
<p>
The <a href=moset.htm>Monthly Schedule for the Mobile
office</a>.
</p>
<p></p>
<p></p>
```

Another frequent problem with elements, one of the few this document doesn't really exhibit, is overlapping tags. This is when a start tag appears inside an element but the corresponding end tag appears outside that element. This problem looks like this:

```
<b>The <a HREF="mosched.htm" target=new>Current Mobile Office
Schedule</b>.</a>
```

There are a couple of instances of this in Listing 27-1, but they're all results of omitted end tags.

The final common problem with elements is an empty element that does not use an empty-element tag. This is extremely prevalent because HTML includes many empty elements such as `br`, `img`, and `hr`. However, HTML browsers don't always recognize XML's empty-element tags, such as `<br/>` and `<hr/>`, and consequently won't always include the line break or horizontal rule you were aiming for. They seem to think that these tags represent an element named `br/` or `hr/` rather than an empty element named `br` or `hr`.

You could use start tag-end tag pairs, such as `<br></br>` and `<hr></hr>`, instead. However, these also cause problems for some browsers. In particular, you may get two line breaks or horizontal lines where you only wanted one. The solution that seems to work best in practice is to add an attribute to the empty-element tag. This pushes the / away from the element name and eliminates problems with most browsers. Conveniently, XHTML allows all elements to have a `class` attribute with any convenient value. It's normally used as a hook off which to hang CSS style rules. However, it can also be used for any purpose you like, including simply moving the `/>` away from the element name. For example, consider this fragment with four empty elements from Listing 27-1:

```
------------------<br>
<a href=impdoc.htm>Important Documents</a><br>
<a href=links.htm>Web Resources</a><br>
------------------<br>
```

You can easily make the `br` elements well formed by adding `class="empty"` attributes to their tags like this:

```
------------------<br class="empty"/>
<a href=impdoc.htm>Important Documents</a><br class="empty"/>
<a href=links.htm>Web Resources</a><br class="empty"/>
------------------<br class="empty"/>
```

The value of the `class` attribute doesn't have any particular significance here. It does not have to be the word `empty`. If you need to place a different value in the `class` attribute for some other purpose, you can. All that's required to make the empty-element tags work is that some attribute be present with some value. For this function, it doesn't really matter what the attribute is or what value it has.

The final thing that you need to do to make Listing 27-1 well formed is to quote all the attribute values. Right now, more attribute values are unquoted than quoted. For example, here's the `body` start tag:

```
<body bgcolor=#ffffff text=black link=#000080 vlink=#000080
alink=#000080  leftmargin=0 topmargin=0 marginwidth=0
marginheight=0  >
```

You can place either single or double quotes around the attribute values, whichever you prefer. Most Web browsers will accept either one, but some third-party tools, such as Web spiders, work better with double quotes. For example,

```
<body bgcolor="#ffffff" text="black" link="#000080"
      vlink="#000080" alink="#000080" leftmargin="0"
      topmargin="0" marginwidth="0" marginheight="0">
```

After all these changes are made, you now have a fully well-formed document. Listing 27-2 demonstrates. I cleaned up the white space a little too.

Listing 27-2: A well-formed version of the Mobile Office page

```
<html>
  <head><title>Mobile Office</title></head>
<!--INSERT TITLE, INSERT TEXT-->

  <body bgcolor="#ffffff" text="black" link="#000080"
      vlink="#000080" alink="#000080" leftmargin="0"
      topmargin="0" marginwidth="0" marginheight="0">
  <basefont size="2" face="Times New Roman"/>
  <table border="0" valign="top" align="left">
    <tr><td bgcolor="#EFEFCE" valign="top">
    <a href="http://www.house.gov/paul/">
    <img SRC="images/pflogosm.gif" border="0"/></a>
    <br class="empty"/>
    <table border="0"><tr><td width="2"></td><td border="1">
      <font size="+1" face="MS Sans Serif, Geneva, Verdana">
        Menu</font><br class="empty"/>
      <font size="-2" face="Arial Narrow">
    <a href="display.htm">Opening Page</a><br class="empty"/>
    <a href="search.htm">Search Project Freedom</a>
    <br class="empty"/>
    <a href="mail/welcome.htm">E-Communications</a>
```

Continued

Listing 27-2 (continued)

```
        <br class="empty"/>
        -------------------<br class="empty"/>
        <a href="bio.htm">A Biography of Ron Paul</a>
        <br class="empty"/>
        <a href="about14.htm">Texas' 14th District</a>
        <br class="empty"/>
        <a href="committeework/welcome.htm">Committees</a>
        <br class="empty"/>
        -------------------<br class="empty"/>
        <a href="services14.htm">Constituent Services</a>
        <br class="empty"/>
        <b>Mobile Office<br class="empty"/></b>
        -------------------<br class="empty"/>
        <a href="legis/welcome.htm">Ron Paul's Legislation</a>
        <br class="empty"/>
       <a href="legis/106/cospon.htm">Cosponsors of Legislation</a>
        <br class="empty"/>
        <a href="privacy/display.htm">Privacy Forum</a>
        <br class="empty"/>
        -------------------<br class="empty"/>
        <a href="press/welcome.htm">Press Releases</a>
        <br class="empty"/>
        <a href="tst/welcome.htm">Weekly Column</a>
        <br class="empty"/>
        <a href="congrec/welcome.htm">Speeches</a>
        <br class="empty"/>
        <a href="tst/lu.htm">Legislative Update Line</a>
        <br class="empty"/>
        <a href="fwu/welcome.htm">Freedom Watch</a>
        <br class="empty"/>
        -------------------<br class="empty"/>
        <a href="impdoc.htm">Important Documents</a>
        <br class="empty"/>
        <a href="links.htm">Web Resources</a><br class="empty"/>
        -------------------<br class="empty"/>
        <a href="http://majoritywhip.house.gov/whipnotice.htm">
        House Floor Schedule</a><br class="empty"/>
        <a href="siteman.htm">Site Information</a>
        <br class="empty"/>
      </font>
  </td></tr></table>
<table align="right" border="1"><tr><td>
<font size="1" face="Arial Narrow">
<p></p>
The Office of U.S. Rep. Ron Paul<br class="empty"/>
203 Cannon HOB<br class="empty"/>
Washington, DC 20515<br class="empty"/>
(202) 225-2831<p></p>
</font>
</td></tr></table>
```

```
</td>

<td valign="top" align="left">
<!--PAGE TEXT INSERT HERE-->

<center><img src="images/mo.gif" alt="The Mobile
Office"/></center>
<p>
What is the <a href="mobilewhatis.htm" >Mobile Office</a>?
</p>
<p>
<b>The <a href="mosched.htm" target="new">
Current Mobile Office Schedule</a>.</b>
</p>
<p></p>
<p>
The <a href="moset.htm">Monthly Schedule for the Mobile
office</a>.
</p>
<p></p>

<img src="images/mobileoffice.gif" border="0"/>

<!--END OF PAGE-->
</td></tr>
</table>
<p></p>
</body>
</html>
```

Well-formedness is a very picky criterion for documents to satisfy. I would never trust myself to merely eyeball the well-formedness of a document without checking it. Since XHTML is XML, and a well-formed XHTML document is a well-formed XML document, you can use all the tools you use to check the well-formedness of an XML document to check the well-formedness of an XHTML document. This includes the sax.SAXCount program from Xerces.

Cross-Reference   sax.SAXCount was introduced in Chapter 8.

For example, here are the last couple of checks I made while I was converting Listing 27-1 into Listing 27-2. The first one found an error where an opening <A> tag was closed by </a> tag, that is, a case mismatch. The last check was naturally error-free. (Otherwise, it wouldn't have been the last check.)

```
D:\books\bible2\examples\27>java sax.SAXCount 27-2.html
[Fatal Error] 27-2.html:63:57: The element type "A" must be
terminated by the matching end-tag "</A>".
org.xml.sax.SAXException: Stopping after fatal error: The
element type "A" must be terminated by the matching end-tag "</A>".
```

```
        at
org.apache.xerces.framework.XMLParser.
reportError(XMLParser.java:1040)
        at
org.apache.xerces.framework.XMLDocumentScanner.
reportFatalXMLError(XMLDocumentScanner.java:634)
        at org.apache.xerces.framework.XMLDocumentScanner
.abortMarkup(XMLDocumentScanner.java:683)
        at org.apache.xerces.framework.XMLDocumentScanner$
ContentDispatcher.dispatch(XMLDocumentScanner.java:1187)
        at
org.apache.xerces.framework.XMLDocumentScanner.parseSome(
XMLDocumentScanner.java:380)
        at
org.apache.xerces.framework.XMLParser.parse(XMLParser.java:900)
        at
org.apache.xerces.framework.XMLParser.parse(XMLParser.java:939)
        at sax.SAXCount.print(SAXCount.java:152)
        at sax.SAXCount.main(SAXCount.java:372)

D:\books\bible2\examples\27>java sax.SAXCount 27-2.html
27-2.html: 240 ms (87 elems, 90 attrs, 0 spaces, 758 chars)
```

The one thing you cannot do with an XHTML document that you can do with a normal XML document is just load it into an XML-savvy browser such as Netscape 6 to see whether or not it's well formed. If you give a Web browser a malformed XHTML document, it will probably just treat it as a normal HTML document and try to quietly fix any problems it finds rather than reporting the mistakes. This may depend on the details of the MIME media type or filename extension. However, in any case, it's not a reliable way to check XHTML documents for well-formedness.

Another common change that's required to make many documents well formed, though not this particular one, is to define your entity references. HTML predefines and authors use numerous entity references including , ©, &tm;, and more. None of these are allowed in an XML document unless they're first declared in a DTD. Fortunately, the XHTML DTD predefines all the usual HTML entity references, as well as a few new ones besides, so as soon as you add a DOCTYPE declaration pointing to one of the three XHTML DTDs these entity references are no longer a problem.

Making the document valid

A well-formed HTML document is only halfway to being a valid XHTML document. Recall that there are four conditions for XHTML validity:

1. The root element of the document must be html.

2. The root element of the document must set the default namespace to http://www.w3.org/1999/xhtml.

3. The document must have a DOCTYPE declaration that references the strict, transitional, or frameset DTD using one of the these three Formal Public Identifiers:

- -//W3C//DTD XHTML 1.0 Strict//EN
- -//W3C//DTD XHTML 1.0 Transitional//EN
- -//W3C//DTD XHTML 1.0 Frameset//EN

4. The document must be valid.

We've improved the document a great deal from its original form, but we've still only met the first of these four conditions and the prerequisite for the fourth condition.

Meeting the second condition is straightforward. Just add the necessary name-space declaration to the html root element start tag like this:

```
<html xmlns="http://www.w3.org/1999/xhtml">
```

Adding the DOCTYPE declaration is no harder. Attaching that, the beginning of the document now looks like this:

```
<!DOCTYPE html PUBLIC "-//W3C//DTD XHTML 1.0 Transitional//EN"
    "http://www.w3.org/TR/xhtml1/DTD/xhtml1-transitional.dtd">
<html xmlns="http://www.w3.org/1999/xhtml">
```

I've chosen the transitional DTD because it's the simplest one to move an existing document to. New documents should use the strict DTD instead. It would probably also be a good idea to store a local copy of the DTD on your own site rather than referencing the one on the W3C site. If you did that, the DOCTYPE declaration would look similar to this:

```
<!DOCTYPE html PUBLIC "-//W3C//DTD XHTML 1.0 Transitional//EN"
                "xhtml1-transitional.dtd">
```

If you wanted to, you could also add an XML declaration to the prolog. However, that's not absolutely required. Because a few older Web browsers will attempt to display the XML declaration as plain text at the start of the document, I prefer not to include it in XHTML documents.

After you've added the DOCTYPE declaration, you can attempt to validate the document using sax.SAXCount or some other program. The W3C provides an online validation service at http://validator.w3.org/ shown in Figure 27-2. This can check XHTML documents against the DTD they specify, as well as check normal HTML documents against the SGML DTD for HTML 4.0.

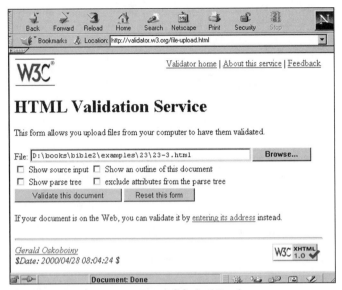

Figure 27-2: The W3C HTML Validation Service

Cross-Reference The various tools that you can use to validate XML documents are described in Chapter 8.

Here are the results of my first attempt to validate the XHTMLized Mobile Office page using the W3C validator:

✦ Line 8, column 49:

```
vlink="#000080" alink="#000080" leftmargin="0"
```

   Error: there is no attribute "leftmargin"

✦ Line 9, column 16:

```
topmargin="0" marginwidth="0" marginheight="0">
              ^
```

   Error: there is no attribute "topmargin"

✦ Line 9, column 32:

```
topmargin="0" marginwidth="0" marginheight="0">
                            ^
```

   Error: there is no attribute "marginwidth"

✦ Line 9, column 49:

```
topmargin="0" marginwidth="0" marginheight="0">
                                            ^
```

   Error: there is no attribute "marginheight"

✦ Line 11, column 27:

```
<table border="0" valign="top" align="left">
                          ^
```

Error: there is no attribute "valign"

✦ Line 14, column 13:

```
<img SRC="images/pflogosm.gif" border="0"/></a>
         ^
```

Error: there is no attribute "SRC"

✦ Line 14, column 46:

```
<img SRC="images/pflogosm.gif" border="0"/></a>
                                          ^
```

Error: required attribute "src" not specified

✦ Line 14, column 46:

```
<img SRC="images/pflogosm.gif" border="0"/></a>
                                          ^
```

Error: required attribute "alt" not specified

✦ Line 16, column 56:

```
<table border="0"><tr><td width="2"></td><td border="1">
                                                       ^
```

Error: there is no attribute "border"

✦ Line 67, column 2:

```
<p></p>
 ^
```

Error: document type does not allow element "p" here; missing one of "object", "applet", "map", "iframe", "button", "ins", "del", "noscript" start-tag

✦ Line 71, column 16:

```
(202) 225-2831<p></p>
               ^
```

Error: document type does not allow element "p" here; missing one of "object", "applet", "map", "iframe", "button", "ins", "del", "noscript" start-tag

✦ Line 94, column 46:

```
<img src="images/mobileoffice.gif" border="0"/>
                                             ^
```

Error: required attribute "alt" not specified

That's 12 separate errors that need to be dealt with. Some of them have obvious solutions; some of them don't.

The first two problems noted are of similar provenance. The DTD does not declare `leftmargin` and `topmargin` attributes for the `body` element. In fact, these are Microsoft extensions to HTML that were never supported in standard HTML or Netscape. They should be replaced by a CSS `style` attribute that sets those properties. For example,

```
<body style="leftmargin: 0; topmargin: 0"
      bgcolor="#ffffff" text="black" link="#000080"
      vlink="#000080" alink="#000080"
      marginwidth="0" marginheight="0">
```

This should work in all browsers that `leftmargin` and `topmargin` work in and quite a few more besides. This demonstrates one of the advantages of validating your XHTML: The pages you produce are much more cross-browser compatible.

The next two problems are the `marginwidth` and `marginheight` attributes on the `body` element. These are non-standard Netscape extensions to HTML that were never supported in standard HTML or Internet Explorer. They have the same effect in Netscape that `leftmargin` and `topmargin` do in Internet Explorer. However, to achieve XHTML conformance, we must delete:

```
<body style="leftmargin: 0; topmargin: 0"
      bgcolor="#ffffff" text="black" link="#000080"
      vlink="#000080" alink="#000080">
```

This demonstrates one benefit of validating your XHTML — it catches your mistakes. These can be cases in which you misremembered the name of the attribute that provides the effect you want, or they can be simple typos, `gbcolor` instead of `bgcolor`, for example. Whichever they are, these are real problems that cause real trouble for Web browsers today, not just anal-retentive rules about how code is supposed to be written. Finding and fixing these sorts of mistakes is important, even if you don't really care whether or not your document is valid.

The next error is of a similar nature. The page author placed the `valign` attribute on the `table` element. However, a `table` element isn't allowed to have a `valign` attribute, so this doesn't mean anything to a browser. It's possible that the author meant this to be an `align` attribute, which a `table` is allowed to have; but given the value of `top`, it's more likely that they were trying to set the default vertical alignment for cells within the table. It's reasonable to guess that HTML might let you do this, but in fact it doesn't. Instead, you have to place the `valign` attribute on the `tr` or `td` elements. Fortunately, it's fairly easy to fix this here because the `table` in question only contains a single row. You just move the attribute from the `table` start tag to the `tr` start tag like this:

```
<table border="0" align="left">
  <tr valign="top">
```

If the `table` contained multiple rows, you'd just copy the `valign` attribute to each `<tr>` start tag.

The next two errors are related, and both stem from this element:

```
<img SRC="images/pflogosm.gif" border="0"/>
```

The first error says, "there is no attribute 'SRC'." The second error says, "required attribute 'src' not specified." In both cases, the problem is XML's case sensitivity. In XHTML, the `SRC` attribute is not the same as the `src` attribute, although they are the same in traditional HTML. XHTML requires all attribute and element names to be typed in lowercase. This fix is easy to make. Just change the attribute names to lowercase:

```
<img src="images/pflogosm.gif" border="0"/>
```

The next error also refers to this `img` element. It says, "required attribute 'alt' not specified." In most cases, the transitional DTD lets most common, but improper, forms of HTML slip through with only a little tweaking to require well formedness. However, in this case, the W3C has decided to put its foot down in defense of accessibility. In XHTML, unlike in HTML, all images must be supplied with alternate text. This means you have to add an `alt` attribute to this element. For example, this `alt` attribute suffices:

```
<img src="images/pflogosm.gif" border="0"
     alt="Project Freedom Logo"/>
```

The next problem is a familiar one, "there is no attribute 'border'" for the `td` element. Again, the attribute was placed on the wrong element. It belongs on the `table` element, not the `td` element. However, this `table` element already has a `border` attribute with a different value. Since as written the `border` attribute on the `td` element has no effect, I'll assume that it was just a fluke and delete it completely. That will keep us as close to the original page as possible.

The tenth and eleventh errors are the nastiest. These are the long ones that state "Error: document type does not allow element 'p' here; missing one of 'object', 'applet', 'map', 'iframe', 'button', 'ins', 'del', 'noscript' start-tag." This isn't very clear, and the validator doesn't tell you which one is missing or how it should be inserted. These sorts of errors, when an element doesn't match its content model, can be some of the hardest to track down.

A different validator (`sax.SAXCount`) gave the different but equally unhelpful message, "The content of element type 'font' must match '(#PCDATA|a|br|span|bdo| object|applet|img|map|iframe|tt|i|b|big|small|u|s|strike|font|basefont|em| strong|dfn|code|q|sub|sup|samp|kbd|var|cite|abbr|acronym|input|select| textarea|label|button|ins|del|script|noscript)*'."

These are two different ways of looking at the same problem. The specific problem is that there's an element A inside an element B when elements of type B are not allowed to contain elements of type A. The W3C validator reports that as a problem with A, while sax.SAXCount reports it as a problem with B. However, in both cases the problem is the same. Neither validator tells you the whole problem, but by putting them together, you see that the problem is that there's a p element inside a font element.

Looking at the content model that's violated you should notice that, as long as it is, it does not include every element defined in XHTML. In particular, it just includes the inline elements like a and strong. It does not include any of the block-level elements like p or table. Therefore, chances are that's exactly what you're looking for: A block-level element that's a child of a font element. With that information in hand, it's not hard to locate the offender. It's this font element:

```
<font size="1" face="Arial Narrow">
  <p>
    The Office of U.S. Rep. Ron Paul<br class="empty"/>
    203 Cannon HOB<br class="empty"/>
    Washington, DC 20515<br class="empty"/>
    (202) 225-2831
  </p>
</font>
```

The solution is straightforward: Move the font tags inside the p element like this:

```
<p>
  <font size="1" face="Arial Narrow">
    The Office of U.S. Rep. Ron Paul<br class="empty"/>
    203 Cannon HOB<br class="empty"/>
    Washington, DC 20515<br class="empty"/>
    (202) 225-2831
  </font>
</p>
```

There's one final problem to be fixed, but this is one you've seen before. The img element in line 94 does not have an alt attribute. This particular image is a picture of the mobile office, so fill it in like this:

```
<img src="images/mobileoffice.gif" border="0"
     alt="Mobile Office Minivan"/>
```

Now you're done. The document validates, at least against the transitional DTD. Listing 27-3 shows the finished XHTML document.

Listing 27-3: **A valid XHTML document**

```
<!DOCTYPE html PUBLIC "-//W3C//DTD XHTML 1.0 Transitional//EN"
                      "xhtml1-transitional.dtd">
<html xmlns="http://www.w3.org/1999/xhtml">
  <head><title>Mobile Office</title></head>
<!--INSERT TITLE, INSERT TEXT-->

  <body bgcolor="#ffffff" text="black" link="#000080"
      vlink="#000080" alink="#000080"
      style="leftmargin: 0; topmargin: 0">
    <basefont size="2" face="Times New Roman"/>
    <table border="0" align="left">
      <tr valign="top"><td bgcolor="#EFEFCE" valign="top">
        <a href="http://www.house.gov/paul/">
          <img src="images/pflogosm.gif" border="0"
              alt="Project Freedom Logo"/>
        </a>
        <br class="empty"/>
        <table border="0">
          <tr>
            <td width="2"></td>
            <td>
          <font size="+1" face="MS Sans Serif, Geneva, Verdana">
                Menu
          </font><br class="empty"/>
      <font size="-2" face="Arial Narrow">
      <a href="display.htm">Opening Page</a><br class="empty"/>
      <a href="search.htm">Search Project Freedom</a>
      <br class="empty"/>
      <a href="mail/welcome.htm">E-Communications</a>
      <br class="empty"/>
      -------------------<br class="empty"/>
      <a href="bio.htm">A Biography of Ron Paul</a>
      <br class="empty"/>
      <a href="about14.htm">Texas' 14th District</a>
      <br class="empty"/>
      <a href="committeework/welcome.htm">Committees</a>
      <br class="empty"/>
      -------------------<br class="empty"/>
      <a href="services14.htm">Constituent Services</a>
      <br class="empty"/>
      <b>Mobile Office<br class="empty"/></b>
      -------------------<br class="empty"/>
      <a href="legis/welcome.htm">Ron Paul's Legislation</a>
      <br class="empty"/>
  <a href="legis/106/cospon.htm">Cosponsors of Legislation</a>
      <br class="empty"/>
      <a href="privacy/display.htm">Privacy Forum</a>
      <br class="empty"/>
```

Continued

Listing 27-3 (continued)

```
-------------------<br class="empty"/>
<a href="press/welcome.htm">Press Releases</a>
<br class="empty"/>
<a href="tst/welcome.htm">Weekly Column</a>
<br class="empty"/>
<a href="congrec/welcome.htm">Speeches</a>
<br class="empty"/>
<a href="tst/lu.htm">Legislative Update Line</a>
<br class="empty"/>
<a href="fwu/welcome.htm">Freedom Watch</a>
<br class="empty"/>
-------------------<br class="empty"/>
<a href="impdoc.htm">Important Documents</a>
<br class="empty"/>
<a href="links.htm">Web Resources</a><br class="empty"/>
-------------------<br class="empty"/>
<a href="http://majoritywhip.house.gov/whipnotice.htm">
House Floor Schedule</a><br class="empty"/>
<a href="siteman.htm">Site Information</a>
    <br class="empty"/>
  </font>
 </td></tr>
 </table>
 <table align="right" border="1">
   <tr><td>
     <p><font size="1" face="Arial Narrow">
     The Office of U.S. Rep. Ron Paul<br class="empty"/>
     203 Cannon HOB<br class="empty"/>
     Washington, DC 20515<br class="empty"/>
     (202) 225-2831
     </font></p>
   </td></tr>
 </table>
</td>

<td valign="top" align="left">
  <!--PAGE TEXT INSERT HERE-->

  <center>
    <img src="images/mo.gif" alt="The Mobile Office"/>
  </center>
  <p>
  What is the
  <a href="mobilewhatis.htm">Mobile Office</a>?
  </p>
  <p>
  <b>The <a href="mosched.htm" target="new">
  Current Mobile Office Schedule</a>.</b>
  </p>
  <p></p>
```

```
        <p>
          The <a href="moset.htm">Monthly Schedule
          for the Mobile office</a>.
        </p>
        <p></p>

          <img src="images/mobileoffice.gif" border="0"
               alt="Mobile Office Minivan"/>

    <!--END OF PAGE-->
          </td></tr>
       </table>
       <p></p>
    </body>
  </html>
```

The strict DTD

Moving to the transitional DTD is a good first step, and the easiest one to take; but new documents should use the strict DTD instead. Time and resources permitting, you should try to transition your HTML documents and XHTML transitional documents to the strict DTD as well. The very name *transitional* implies that it's not around forever, and that possibly starting with XHTML 2.0 or perhaps some later version, the strict DTD will be the only option for valid, future-looking Web pages.

The biggest difference between the strict DTD and the transitional DTD is that the strict DTD almost completely eliminates presentational elements such as `font` and `center` and presentational attributes such as `bgcolor` and `width`. Instead, these should all be replaced by CSS styles. The goal here is to return to the original plan for HTML as a semantic rather than presentational markup language.

To indicate that you want to use the strict DTD, just change the `DOCTYPE` declaration of your document as follows:

```
<!DOCTYPE html PUBLIC "-//W3C//DTD XHTML 1.0 Strict//EN"
                      "xhtml1-strict.dtd">
```

Then run it through your validation tool of choice. When I changed the document type declaration of Listing 27-3 to point to the strict DTD and passed it through the W3C validator, 19 more problems were uncovered:

✦ Line 7, column 16:
```
<body bgcolor="#ffffff" text="black" link="#000080"
              ^
```

Error: there is no attribute "bgcolor"

✦ Line 7, column 31:

```
<body bgcolor="#ffffff" text="black" link="#000080"
                              ^
```

Error: there is no attribute "text"

✦ Line 7, column 44:

```
<body bgcolor="#ffffff" text="black" link="#000080"
                                          ^
```

Error: there is no attribute "link"

✦ Line 8, column 12:

```
        vlink="#000080" alink="#000080"
               ^
```

Error: there is no attribute "vlink"

✦ Line 8, column 28:

```
        vlink="#000080" alink="#000080"
                               ^
```

Error: there is no attribute "alink"

✦ Line 10, column 19:

```
      <basefont size="2" face="Times New Roman"/>
                       ^
```

Error: there is no attribute "size"

✦ Line 10, column 28:

```
      <basefont size="2" face="Times New Roman"/>
                                ^
```

Error: there is no attribute "face"

✦ Line 10, column 46:

```
      <basefont size="2" face="Times New Roman"/>
      ^
```

Error: element "basefont" undefined

✦ Line 11, column 28:

```
      <table border="0" align="left">
                              ^
```

Error: there is no attribute "align"

✦ Line 12, column 35:

```
      <tr valign="top"><td bgcolor="#EFEFCE" valign="top">
                                    ^
```

Error: there is no attribute "bgcolor"

✦ Line 14, column 48:

```
<img src="images/pflogosm.gif" border="0"
                                       ^
```

Error: there is no attribute "border"

✦ Line 20, column 22:

```
<td width="2"></td>
           ^
```

Error: there is no attribute "width"

✦ Line 22, column 20:

```
<font size="+1" face="MS Sans Serif, Geneva, Verdana">
         ^
```

Error: there is no attribute "size"

✦ Line 22, column 30:

```
<font size="+1" face="MS Sans Serif, Geneva, Verdana">
                   ^
```

Error: there is no attribute "face"

✦ Line 22, column 62:

```
<font size="+1" face="MS Sans Serif, Geneva, Verdana">
                                                    ^
```

Error: element "font" undefined

✦ Line 25, column 41:

```
<font size="-2" face="Arial Narrow">
                                   ^
```

Error: element "font" undefined

✦ Line 74, column 48:

```
<p><font size="1" face="Arial Narrow">
                                     ^
```

Error: element "font" undefined

✦ Line 87, column 14:

```
<center>
       ^
```

Error: element "center" undefined

✦ Line 95, column 43:

```
<b>The <a href="mosched.htm" target="new">
                                        ^
```

Error: there is no attribute "target"

Each of these problems is either an element or attribute that is not available in the strict DTD. An element that's not available in the DTD will produce several error messages — one for the element itself and one for each attribute that element possesses. In every case, the forbidden item provides presentational information that can be replaced with a CSS style. For example, the first five problems all relate to color attributes on the body start tag:

```
<body bgcolor="#ffffff" text="black" link="#000080"
    vlink="#000080" alink="#000080"
    style="leftmargin: 0; topmargin: 0">
```

You can move the bgcolor and text values inside the allowed style attribute like this:

```
<body style="background-color: #ffffff; color: black;
            leftmargin: 0; topmargin: 0">
```

When moving to CSS, the bgcolor attribute becomes the background-color property and the text attribute becomes the (foreground) color property.

Background-color, color, and the other CSS properties used in this section are discussed in Chapter 16.

The three link colors are trickier. CSS doesn't provide any properties that are exact equivalents for the link, vlink, and alink attributes. Instead, you have to provide CSS rules that use the appropriate selectors to choose links, visited links, and active links, and assign the desired colors to each one. These rules can be placed in a style element in the document's head like this:

```
<head>
  <title>Mobile Office</title>
  <style type="text/css">
    a:link     {color: #000080}
    a:visited {color: #000080}
    a:active   {color: #000080}
  </style>
</head>
```

In HTML, it's customary to enclose the CSS rules in the content of the style element in a comment like this:

```
<style type="text/css">
  <!-- a:link     {color: #000080}
       a:visited {color: #000080}
       a:active   {color: #000080} -->
</style>
```

This hides the style rules from older browsers that don't recognize CSS, and that might try to display the contents of the `style` element as part of the document. However, most browsers that understand strict XHTML can handle CSS, and all of them at least recognize the `style` element. Furthermore, XML rules dictate that XHTML browsers should not pay any attention to the contents of comments. (In practice some do and some don't.) The XML parser built-in to the browser may not even provide the text of the comments to the rendering engine for display. If you do need to write pages that work well in older browsers, you should use the transitional XHTML DTD instead of the strict one.

Tip
Changing link colors is a very bad thing to do to your readers. Browsing a page that uses nonstandard link colors is a little like driving in a country where the stop signs are blue, the warning signs are green, and the directional signs are red. While the default link colors (blue, purple, and red) are hardly the ideal choices, they are the ones standardized in today's browsers, and they are the colors readers have learned to expect. If you change the link colors, many readers won't realize where the links are on the page. They certainly won't be able to tell the difference between visited and unvisited links.

The next three errors stem from the `basefont` element:

```
<basefont size="2" face="Times New Roman"/>
```

This is a standard HTML element for setting the default font on the page. The first two errors say that the `size` and `face` attributes of this element aren't defined, while the last error says that the `basefont` element itself isn't defined. It has been deleted from strict XHTML. Instead, you set default font properties for the document by attaching CSS style properties to the `body` element of the document. The `basefont`'s `size` attribute can be replaced by a CSS `font-size` property. In HTML, the `size` attribute of the `basefont` is given as a number between 1 and 7, where 3 is the browser's default font-size. Thus, the CSS equivalent is using `smaller` on `font-size`. The `basefont`'s `face` attribute can be replaced by a CSS `font-family` property. This makes the `body` start tag look like this:

```
<body style="font-size: smaller;
        font-family: 'Times New Roman';
        background-color: #ffffff; color: black;
        leftmargin: 0; topmargin: 0">
```

The next problem is the `align` attribute on the first `table`. Because this already has the default value `left`, you can just drop it out. There's no need to replace it with a CSS style.

The tenth problem is straightforward and easy to fix: The `bgcolor` attribute is not allowed on table cells (`td` elements) any more than it's allowed on the `body` element. Again, you can replace it with a CSS `background-color` property, like this:

```
<td style="background-color: #EFEFCE" valign="top">
```

Perhaps a little surprisingly, the `valign` presentational attribute is allowed here. That's because it has a special meaning for table cells that no generic CSS property can really match.

The next problem is similar. In strict XHTML, the `img` element can't have a `border` attribute. Instead, it should have a `border-width` CSS style property. Furthermore, this property can't be an absolute number such as 0 or 2; it must have units. Thus, you change this:

```
<img src="images/pflogosm.gif" border="0"
            alt="Project Freedom Logo"/>
```

to this:

```
<img src="images/pflogosm.gif" style="border-width: 0px"
            alt="Project Freedom Logo"/>
```

The next problem arises in line 20. The `td` element can't have a `width` attribute. This must be replaced by a CSS `width` property. Again, the HTML width is given in pixels, so the equivalent CSS property must specify units of pixels like this:

```
<td style="width: 2px"></td>
```

Next comes one of the most common problems with documents being converted from old-style HTML to XHTML—the `font` element. Fortunately, this is easy to change to CSS. The `font` element attributes map to CSS font properties just as they did for the `basefont` element earlier. The `size` attribute is replaced by a `font-size` property and the `face` attribute is replaced by a `font-family` property. Of course, because the `font` element itself is illegal, you need an element to hang this style on. A lot of times there's a fortuitous p or `td` or some other element in the right place to fill this need; but if there's not, you can add a `span` or `div` element instead. Use `span` for inline runs of style and `div` for styles that surround one or more block-level elements such as p and `blockquote`. For instance, in this case you can change the offending `font` element to this `span` element:

```
<span style="font-size: +1;
            font-family: 'MS Sans Serif', Geneva, Verdana">
    Menu
</span>
```

The next problem element is also a `font` element, and is changed to another `span` element:

```
<span style="font-size: -2; font-family: 'Arial Narrow'">
```

The penultimate problem is the `center` element used to center the picture of the mobile office minivan within its table cell. The `center` element has been completely deprecated. Instead, you should use a `div` element with a CSS `text-align` property; for example:

```
<div style="text-align: center">
  <img src="images/mo.gif" alt="The Mobile Office"/>
</div>
```

Although this property is named `text-align`, it will align anything contained in the `div` element including, as in this case, images.

The final problem is an unusual one: the `target` attribute of the `a` element is forbidden. There's no CSS equivalent for this attribute. It's simply gone. Consequently, you simply have to delete the `target` attribute from your strict XHTML documents, and suffer the corresponding loss in functionality.

```
<a href="mosched.htm">Current Mobile Office Schedule</a>
```

Note   The reason the W3C removed `target` from strict XHTML was that it's used to control link behavior. In particular, `target` determines which window or frame the document is displayed in. For instance, by setting `target` to `_blank` you can specify that the document will open in a new window rather than the current one. The W3C feels that link behavior is outside the scope of HTML. This is, in my opinion, a flaw in strict XHTML. It's not presentational information, and I certainly don't see any reason for link behavior to be ruled out of bounds for a *Hypertext* Markup Language. XLink does provide equivalent functionality through the `xlink:show` attribute, but XHTML 1.0 doesn't support XLink.

Cross-Reference   XLinks and the `xlink:show` attribute are discussed in Chapter 20.

That's the last error the validator reported. Listing 27-4 is the complete, fixed document with all the changes described above.

Listing 27-4: The fixed XHTML document

```
<!DOCTYPE html PUBLIC "-//W3C//DTD XHTML 1.0 Strict//EN"
                      "xhtml1-strict.dtd">
<html xmlns="http://www.w3.org/1999/xhtml">
  <head>
    <title>Mobile Office</title>
    <style type="text/css">
      a:link     {color: #000080}
      a:visited  {color: #000080}
      a:active   {color: #000080}
    </style>
  </head>
<!--INSERT TITLE, INSERT TEXT-->

  <body style="font-size: smaller;
               font-family: 'Times New Roman';
```

Continued

Listing 27-4 (continued)

```
                background-color: #ffffff; color: black;
                leftmargin: 0; topmargin: 0">
    <table border="0">
      <tr valign="top">
        <td style="background-color: #EFEFCE" valign="top">
          <a href="http://www.house.gov/paul/">
       <img src="images/pflogosm.gif" style="border-width: 0px"
              alt="Project Freedom Logo"/>
          </a>
          <br class="empty"/>
          <table border="0">
            <tr>
              <td style="width: 2px"></td>
              <td>
          <span style="font-size: +1;
                font-family: 'MS Sans Serif', Geneva, Verdana">
                Menu
          </span><br class="empty"/>
          <span style="font-size: -2;
                      font-family: 'Arial Narrow'">
      <a href="display.htm">Opening Page</a><br class="empty"/>
      <a href="search.htm">Search Project Freedom</a>
      <br class="empty"/>
      <a href="mail/welcome.htm">E-Communications</a>
      <br class="empty"/>
      ------------------<br class="empty"/>
      <a href="bio.htm">A Biography of Ron Paul</a>
      <br class="empty"/>
      <a href="about14.htm">Texas' 14th District</a>
      <br class="empty"/>
      <a href="committeework/welcome.htm">Committees</a>
      <br class="empty"/>
      ------------------<br class="empty"/>
      <a href="services14.htm">Constituent Services</a>
      <br class="empty"/>
      <b>Mobile Office<br class="empty"/></b>
      ------------------<br class="empty"/>
      <a href="legis/welcome.htm">Ron Paul's Legislation</a>
      <br class="empty"/>
  <a href="legis/106/cospon.htm">Cosponsors of Legislation</a>
      <br class="empty"/>
      <a href="privacy/display.htm">Privacy Forum</a>
      <br class="empty"/>
      ------------------<br class="empty"/>
      <a href="press/welcome.htm">Press Releases</a>
      <br class="empty"/>
      <a href="tst/welcome.htm">Weekly Column</a>
      <br class="empty"/>
      <a href="congrec/welcome.htm">Speeches</a>
      <br class="empty"/>
      <a href="tst/lu.htm">Legislative Update Line</a>
```

```
<br class="empty"/>
<a href="fwu/welcome.htm">Freedom Watch</a>
<br class="empty"/>
-------------------<br class="empty"/>
<a href="impdoc.htm">Important Documents</a>
<br class="empty"/>
<a href="links.htm">Web Resources</a><br class="empty"/>
-------------------<br class="empty"/>
<a href="http://majoritywhip.house.gov/whipnotice.htm">
House Floor Schedule</a><br class="empty"/>
<a href="siteman.htm">Site Information</a>
    <br class="empty"/>
  </span>
 </td></tr>
 </table>
 <table align="right" border="1">
   <tr><td>
     <p><font size="1" face="Arial Narrow">
     The Office of U.S. Rep. Ron Paul<br class="empty"/>
     203 Cannon HOB<br class="empty"/>
     Washington, DC 20515<br class="empty"/>
     (202) 225-2831
     </font></p>
   </td></tr>
 </table>
</td>

<td valign="top" align="left">
  <!--PAGE TEXT INSERT HERE-->

  <div style="text-align: center">
    <img src="images/mo.gif" alt="The Mobile Office"/>
  </div>
  <p>
  What is the
  <a href="mobilewhatis.htm">Mobile Office</a>?
  </p>
  <p>
  <b>The <a href="mosched.htm">
  Current Mobile Office Schedule</a>.</b>
  </p>
  <p></p>
  <p>
    The <a href="moset.htm">Monthly Schedule
    for the Mobile office</a>.
  </p>
  <p></p>

   <img src="images/mobileoffice.gif" border="0"
        alt="Mobile Office Minivan"/>
```

Continued

Listing 27-4 (continued)

```
<!--END OF PAGE-->
      </td></tr>
    </table>
    <p></p>
  </body>
</html>
```

Listing 27-4 fixes all the errors that the validator found. Are you done? Is this now a valid XHTML document? Unfortunately, the answer is still no. If you read Listing 27-4, you should have noticed that it still contains a number of illegal presentational elements such as `font` and presentational attributes such as `border`. In fact, if you rerun Listing 27-4 through the W3C validator, it spits out these five additional error messages:

✦ Line 79, column 20:

```
    <table align="right" border="1">
                   ^
```

Error: there is no attribute "align"

✦ Line 81, column 25:

```
        <p><font size="1" face="Arial Narrow">
                        ^
```

Error: there is no attribute "size"

✦ Line 81, column 34:

```
        <p><font size="1" face="Arial Narrow">
                                 ^
```

Error: there is no attribute "face"

✦ Line 81, column 48:

```
        <p><font size="1" face="Arial Narrow">
                                           ^
```

Error: element "font" undefined

✦ Line 112, column 50:

```
        <img src="images/mobileoffice.gif" border="0"
                                                  ^
```

Error: there is no attribute "border"

Fortunately, all these errors are ones you've seen before, and they're relatively easy to fix. Listing 27-5 makes the necessary corrections. Still there's a deeper question. Why didn't the validator detect these problems the first time through? The reason is that some problems can mask other problems. In particular, the validator will not check anything inside an undefined element. For instance, if a font element contains a center element, the validator will only report the font element as being a problem. It does not look inside the font element, so it won't find the center element or any other illegal elements or attributes that might be hidden there. Therefore, when you think you're done, you need to run the finished document through the validator to make sure that no hidden problems have been revealed (or even created) by your edits. In some cases, you may even need to make four or five or more passes through the validator before you have finally eliminated all the problems. This, however, is not one of those times. It turns out that Listing 27-5 is indeed valid strict XHTML, and no further edits are required.

Listing 27-5: **The valid XHTML document**

```
<!DOCTYPE html PUBLIC "-//W3C//DTD XHTML 1.0 Strict//EN"
                      "xhtml1-strict.dtd">
<html xmlns="http://www.w3.org/1999/xhtml">
  <head>
    <title>Mobile Office</title>
    <style type="text/css">
      a:link    {color: #000080}
      a:visited {color: #000080}
      a:active  {color: #000080}
    </style>
  </head>
<!--INSERT TITLE, INSERT TEXT-->

  <body style="font-size: smaller;
               font-family: 'Times New Roman';
               background-color: #ffffff; color: black;
               leftmargin: 0; topmargin: 0">
    <table border="0">
      <tr valign="top">
        <td style="background-color: #EFEFCE" valign="top">
          <a href="http://www.house.gov/paul/">
        <img src="images/pflogosm.gif" style="border-width: 0px"
             alt="Project Freedom Logo"/>
          </a>
          <br class="empty"/>
          <table border="0">
            <tr>
              <td style="width: 2px"></td>
              <td>
          <span style="font-size: +1;
                font-family: 'MS Sans Serif', Geneva, Verdana">
                Menu
          </span><br class="empty"/>
        <span style="font-size: -2; font-family: 'Arial Narrow'">
        <a href="display.htm">Opening Page</a><br class="empty"/>
        <a href="search.htm">Search Project Freedom</a>
```

Continued

Listing 27-5 (continued)

```
<br class="empty"/>
<a href="mail/welcome.htm">E-Communications</a>
<br class="empty"/>
------------------<br class="empty"/>
<a href="bio.htm">A Biography of Ron Paul</a>
<br class="empty"/>
<a href="about14.htm">Texas' 14th District</a>
<br class="empty"/>
<a href="committeework/welcome.htm">Committees</a>
<br class="empty"/>
------------------<br class="empty"/>
<a href="services14.htm">Constituent Services</a>
<br class="empty"/>
<b>Mobile Office<br class="empty"/></b>
------------------<br class="empty"/>
<a href="legis/welcome.htm">Ron Paul's Legislation</a>
<br class="empty"/>
<a href="legis/106/cospon.htm">Cosponsors of Legislation</a>
<br class="empty"/>
<a href="privacy/display.htm">Privacy Forum</a>
<br class="empty"/>
------------------<br class="empty"/>
<a href="press/welcome.htm">Press Releases</a>
<br class="empty"/>
<a href="tst/welcome.htm">Weekly Column</a>
<br class="empty"/>
<a href="congrec/welcome.htm">Speeches</a>
<br class="empty"/>
<a href="tst/lu.htm">Legislative Update Line</a>
<br class="empty"/>
<a href="fwu/welcome.htm">Freedom Watch</a>
<br class="empty"/>
------------------<br class="empty"/>
<a href="impdoc.htm">Important Documents</a>
<br class="empty"/>
<a href="links.htm">Web Resources</a><br class="empty"/>
------------------<br class="empty"/>
<a href="http://majoritywhip.house.gov/whipnotice.htm">
House Floor Schedule</a><br class="empty"/>
<a href="siteman.htm">Site Information</a>
    <br class="empty"/>
  </span>
</td></tr>
</table>
<table border="1">
  <tr><td>
  <p style="font-size: -2; font-family: 'Arial Narrow'">
    The Office of U.S. Rep. Ron Paul<br class="empty"/>
    203 Cannon HOB<br class="empty"/>
```

```
                    Washington, DC 20515<br class="empty"/>
                    (202) 225-2831
                  </p>
                </td></tr>
              </table>
            </td>

            <td valign="top" align="left">
              <!--PAGE TEXT INSERT HERE-->

              <div style="text-align: center">
                <img src="images/mo.gif" alt="The Mobile Office"/>
              </div>
              <p>
              What is the
              <a href="mobilewhatis.htm">Mobile Office</a>?
              </p>
              <p>
              <b>The <a href="mosched.htm">
              Current Mobile Office Schedule</a>.</b>
              </p>
              <p></p>
              <p>
                The <a href="moset.htm">Monthly Schedule
                for the Mobile office</a>.
              </p>
              <p></p>

               <img src="images/mobileoffice.gif"
                    style="border-width: 0"
                    alt="Mobile Office Minivan"/>
      <!--END OF PAGE-->
            </td></tr>
          </table>
          <p></p>
      </body>
    </html>
```

The disadvantage of this approach is that many browsers don't support all of the CSS style properties used here, although they do support the equivalent presentational elements and attributes. For example, when I loaded Listing 27-5 into Netscape Navigator 4.6.1 for Windows, as shown in Figure 27-3, the picture of the Mobile Office minivan had moved to the top of the page for no apparent reason. However, Internet Explorer 5.5 did place the picture in the right place on the page. Because of problems such as this, it may be advisable to stick with the transitional DTD and the presentational attributes for a while longer until all your users have upgraded to browsers that fully support CSS and XHTML.

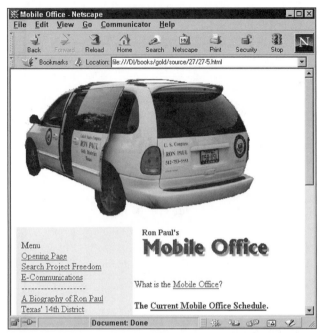

Figure 27-3: A browser exhibiting incorrect and unexplained rendering of an XHTML plus CSS document

The frameset DTD

The transitional DTD omits one popular feature of HTML—frames. The W3C has never liked frames, and with good reason—they're a user interface disaster that consistently irritate and bewilder readers. Nonetheless, many Web designers like them, and many existing Web sites use them.

Although I agree with the W3C and suggest that you avoid frames on all new pages you create, there are times when an existing site design makes that impossible, at least without an excessive investment of resources. Consequently, if you must use frames but you still want to move to XHTML and validate your documents, you can use the frameset DTD. This is very close to the transitional DTD, but adds all the necessary declarations for `frame`, `iframe`, `frameset`, and other frame-related elements and attributes. The document type declaration for a page built on top of the frameset DTD looks like this:

```
<!DOCTYPE html PUBLIC "-//W3C//DTD XHTML 1.0 Frameset//EN"
    "http://www.w3.org/TR/xhtml1/DTD/xhtml1-frameset.dtd">
```

As with the other two XHTML DTDs, it's probably a good idea to store a local copy of the frameset DTD and identify it by a relative URL rather than relying on the official copy at the W3C. Then the document type declaration would look like this instead:

```
<!DOCTYPE html PUBLIC "-//W3C//DTD XHTML 1.0 Frameset//EN"
                      "xhtml1-frameset.dtd">
```

HTML Tidy

Converting malformed HTML documents to valid XHTML by hand, as I've done in this chapter, can be a tedious and time-consuming job. Fortunately, Dave Raggett of the W3C has published HTML Tidy, an open source tool that can do much of the work for you. Tidy is a character-mode program written in ANSI C that can be compiled and run on most platforms including Windows, Unix, BeOS, and the Mac.

On the CD-ROM Tidy is on the CD-ROM in the directory utilities/tidy. Binaries are included for Windows. Portable source code is included for other platforms. The latest version is available from http://www.w3.org/People/Raggett/tidy/.

In its default mode Tidy tends to remove unnecessary (for HTML, but not for XML) end tags such as `</li>` and to make other modifications that break well-formedness. However, you can use the `--output-xhtml` switch to specify that you want valid XHTML output. For example, to convert the file mobile_office.html to valid XHTML, you would type this command from a DOS window or shell prompt:

```
C:\> tidy --output-xhtml true mobile_office.html
```

By default Tidy just prints its output on the stdout (the console or DOS window from which you ran it) as well as messages about any problems it couldn't fix. You'll probably want to redirect the corrected HTML into a file using the > redirection operator like this:

```
C:\>tidy --output-xhtml true mobile_office.html>27-6.html

Tidy (vers 30th April 2000) Parsing "mobile_office.html"
line 9 column 30 - Warning: <img> lacks "alt" attribute
line 68 column 4 - Warning: <img> lacks "alt" attribute

"mobile_office.html" appears to be HTML 3.2
2 warnings/errors were found!

The alt attribute should be used to give a short description
of an image; longer descriptions should be given with the
longdesc attribute which takes a URL linked to the description.
These measures are needed for people using non-graphical
browsers.
```

```
For further advice on how to make your pages accessible
see "http://www.w3.org/WAI/GL". You may also want to try
"http://www.cast.org/bobby/" which is a free Web-based
service for checking URLs for accessibility.

You are recommended to use CSS to specify the font and
properties such as its size and color. This will reduce
the size of HTML files and make them easier to maintain
compared with using <FONT> elements.

HTML & CSS specifications are available from http://www.w3.org/
To learn more about Tidy see
http://www.w3.org/People/Raggett/tidy/
Please send bug reports to Dave Raggett care of
<html-tidy@w3.org>
Lobby your company to join W3C, see
http://www.w3.org/Consortium
```

Listing 27-6 shows the XHTML document Tidy produced. As the above message indicates, it's not actually a valid XHTML document. In this case, the problem is that two img elements are missing alt attributes. While Tidy could insert an empty alt attribute, that wouldn't really serve any purpose. It has to rely on a human being (you) to fill in a reasonable value for the alternate text. Otherwise, the document is well formed. In general, whatever Tidy leaves out is not too difficult to fix by hand.

Listing 27-6: The well-formed, almost-valid XHTML document produced by Tidy

```
<!DOCTYPE html PUBLIC "-//W3C//DTD XHTML 1.0 Transitional//EN"
    "http://www.w3.org/TR/xhtml1/DTD/xhtml1-transitional.dtd">
<html xmlns="http://www.w3.org/1999/xhtml">
<head>
<meta name="generator" content="HTML Tidy, see www.w3.org" />
<title>Mobile Office</title>
<!--INSERT TITLE, INSERT TEXT-->
</head>
<body>
<basefont size="2" face="Times New Roman" />
<table border="0" valign="top" align="left">
<tr>
<td bgcolor="#EFEFCE" valign="top"><a
href="http://www.house.gov/paul/"><img
src="images/pflogosm.gif"
border="0" /></a><br />
<table border="0">
<tr>
<td width="2"></td>
<td border="1"><font size="+1"
face="MS Sans Serif, Geneva, Verdana">Menu</font><br />
```

```
  <font size="-2" face="Arial Narrow"><a
href="display.htm">Opening
Page</a><br />
<a href="search.htm">Search Project Freedom</a><br />
<a href="mail/welcome.htm">E-Communications</a><br />
------------------<br />
<a href="bio.htm">A Biography of Ron Paul</a><br />
<a href="about14.htm">Texas' 14th District</a><br />
<a href="committeework/welcome.htm">Committees</a><br />
------------------<br />
<a href="services14.htm">Constituent Services</a><br />
<b>Mobile Office<br />
</b> ------------------<br />
<a href="legis/welcome.htm">Ron Paul's Legislation</a><br />
<a href="legis/106/cospon.htm">Cosponsors of Legislation</a><br
/>
<a href="privacy/display.htm">Privacy Forum</a><br />
------------------<br />
<a href="press/welcome.htm">Press Releases</a><br />
<a href="tst/welcome.htm">Weekly Column</a><br />
<a href="congrec/welcome.htm">Speeches</a><br />
<a href="tst/lu.htm">Legislative Update Line</a><br />
<a href="fwu/welcome.htm">Freedom Watch</a><br />
------------------<br />
<a href="impdoc.htm">Important Documents</a><br />
<a href="links.htm">Web Resources</a><br />
------------------<br />
<a href="http://majoritywhip.house.gov/whipnotice.htm">House
Floor
Schedule</a><br />
<a href="siteman.htm">Site Information<br />
</a></font> </td>
</tr>
</table>

<table align="right" border="1">
<tr>
<td><font size="1" face="Arial Narrow"></font>

<p><font size="1" face="Arial Narrow">The Office of U.S. Rep.
Ron
Paul<br />
203 Cannon HOB<br />
Washington, DC 20515<br />
(202) 225-2831</font></p>

<p><font size="1" face="Arial Narrow"></font></p>
</td>
</tr>
</table>
</td>
<td valign="top" align="left"><!--PAGE TEXT INSERT HERE-->
```

Continued

Listing 27-6 (continued)

```
<center><img src="images/mo.gif" alt="The Mobile Office" />
</center>

<p>What is the <a href="mobilewhatis.htm">Mobile
Office</a>?</p>

<p><b>The <a href="mosched.htm" target="new">Current Mobile
Office
Schedule</a>.</b></p>

<p>The <a href="moset.htm">Monthly Schedule for the Mobile
office</a>.</p>

<p><img src="images/mobileoffice.gif" border="0" />
<!--END OF PAGE--></p>
</td>
</tr>
</table>
</body>
</html>
```

Tidy also missed a couple of problems as well. When I ran this document through the W3C validator, in addition to the aforementioned missing alt attributes, these two problems were found:

✦ Line 11, column 25:

```
<table border="0" valign="top" align="left">
                   ^
```

   Error: there is no attribute "valign"

✦ Line 19, column 11:

```
<td border="1"><font size="+1"
     ^
```

   Error: there is no attribute "border"

Still, all of these issues are easy enough to resolve once they're noticed. Tidy may not do everything for you, but it does do a lot.

Tidy is limited to converting documents to transitional XHTML. It isn't yet smart enough to handle the more difficult task of converting a document to strict XHTML. However, even if you need strict XHTML, you can still save a lot of time by first converting the document to transitional XHTML using Tidy, and then finishing the conversion by hand. Just remember to change the document type declaration to point to the strict DTD before validating.

What's New in XHTML

For the most part XHTML just tightens up existing HTML syntax. In the strict version, it even throws out some familiar elements and attributes such as `font` and `bgcolor`. However, besides the stick of validity, XHTML proffers a few carrots as well. Browsers that understand XHTML can use the full panoply of XML syntax that isn't available in classic HTML. This includes:

✦ Character references

✦ Custom entity references defined in the DTD

✦ CDATA sections

✦ Encoding declarations

✦ The `xml:lang` attribute

On the other hand, these constructs are quite near the bleeding edge since almost all of them cause problems for many browsers people are still using. Nonetheless, they can be viable in certain controlled environments and will become more useful as time passes and more people upgrade their browsers to full XHTML support. This section explores a few of the advantages of using fully XHTML-aware browsers.

Character references

XML documents are Unicode. By implication, that means XHTML documents are Unicode, too. You can present an XHTML browser with a document containing mixed English, Greek, Arabic, and Japanese, and expect it to do something reasonable with it. The browser may not have the necessary fonts to render the non-Latin text, but at least it should not try to pretend that Arabic, Japanese, or Greek is just a funny form of Latin-1 as many browsers do now.

Even if the browser can display text written in unusual character sets, it may still not be easy to write such a document using existing editors. However, when writing XHTML, you can use decimal or hexadecimal character references to produce the full range of Unicode characters. A Unicode decimal character reference consists of the two characters `&#` followed by the character code, followed by a semicolon. For instance, the capital Greek letter Σ has Unicode value 931, so it may be inserted in an XML file as `&#931;`. To use hexadecimal instead, just put an x after the `#`. For example, Σ has hexadecimal value 3A3, so it may be inserted in an XML file as `&#x03A3;`. Because two bytes always produce exactly four hexadecimal digits and because most current Unicode characters occupy two bytes, it's customary (though not required) to include leading zeros in hexadecimal character references so that they are rounded out to four digits. Listing 27-7 shows an XHTML document containing a few lines from Plato's *Gorgias* that use a mix of ASCII characters and decimal and hexadecimal character references.

Listing 27-7: An XHTML document that uses character references

```
<!DOCTYPE html PUBLIC "-//W3C//DTD XHTML 1.0 Strict//EN"
                      "xhtml1-strict.dtd">
<html xmlns="http://www.w3.org/1999/xhtml">
<head>
  <title>Gorgias 447a from Plato</title>
</head>
<body>
<h1>Plato, <cite>Gorgias 447a</cite></h1>
<p>
<span style="font-weight: bold">
&#922;&#945;&#955;&#955;&#953;&#x301;&#954;&#955;&#951;&#962;
</span>:
&#960;&#959;&#955;&#949;&#x301;&#956;&#959;&#965;
&#954;&#945;&#953;&#x300;
&#956;&#945;&#x301;&#967;&#951;&#962;
&#966;&#945;&#963;&#953;&#x300;
&#967;&#961;&#951;&#x302;&#957;&#945;&#953;;,
&#969;&#x313;&#x302;
&#931;&#969;&#x301;&#954;&#961;&#945;&#964;&#949;&#962;;,
&#959;&#965;&#x314;&#x301;&#964;&#969;
&#956;&#949;&#964;&#945;&#955;&#945;&#947;&#967;&#945;&#x301;
&#957;&#949;&#953;&#957;;.
</p>
<p>
<span style="font-weight: bold">
&#931;&#969;&#954;&#961;&#945;&#x301;&#964;&#951;&#962;</span>:
&#945;&#x313;&#955;&#955;'
&#951;&#x313;&#x302;;, &#964;&#959;&#x300;
&#955;&#949;&#947;&#959;&#x301;&#956;&#949;&#957;&#959;&#957;;,
&#954;&#945;&#964;&#959;&#x301;&#960;&#953;&#957;
&#949;&#x314;&#959;&#961;&#964;&#951;&#x302;&#962;
&#951;&#x314;&#x301;&#954;&#959;&#956;&#949;&#957;
&#954;&#945;&#953;&#x300;
&#965;&#x314;&#963;&#964;&#949;&#961;&#959;&#965;&#x302;&#956;
&#949;&#957;;;
</p>
<p>
<span style="font-weight: bold">
&#922;&#945;&#955;&#955;&#953;&#x301;&#954;&#955;&#951;&#962;
</span>:
&#954;&#945;&#953;&#x300; &#956;&#945;&#x301;&#955;&#945;
&#947;&#949;
&#945;&#x313;&#963;&#964;&#949;&#953;&#953;&#x301;&#945;&#962;
&#949;&#x314;&#959;&#961;&#964;&#951;&#x302;&#962;::
&#960;&#959;&#955;&#955;&#945;&#x300;
&#947;&#945;&#x300;&#961; &#954;&#945;&#953;&#x300;
&#954;&#945;&#955;&#945;&#x300;
&#915;&#959;&#961;&#947;&#953;&#x301;&#945;&#962;
```

```
&#951;&#x314;&#956;&#953;&#x302;&#957;&#959;&#x313;&#955;&#953;
&#x301;&#947;&#959;&#957;
&#960;&#961;&#959;&#x301;&#964;&#949;&#961;&#959;&#957;&#949;
&#x313;&#960;&#949;&#948;&#949;&#953;&#x301;&#958;&#945;&#964;
&#959;.
</p>
<p><span style="font-weight: bold">
&#931;&#969;&#954;&#961;&#945;&#x301;&#964;&#951;&#962;</span>:
&#964;&#959;&#965;&#x301;&#964;&#969;&#957;
&#956;&#949;&#x301;&#957;&#964;&#959;&#953;,
&#969;&#x313;&#x302;
&#922;&#945;&#955;&#955;&#953;&#x301;&#954;&#955;&#949;&#953;
&#962;,
&#945;&#953;&#x313;&#x301;&#964;&#953;&#959;&#962;
&#967;&#945;&#953;&#961;&#949;&#966;&#969;&#x302;&#957;
&#959;&#x314;&#x301;&#948;&#949;,
&#949;&#x313;&#957;
&#945;&#x313;&#947;&#959;&#961;&#945;&#x302;&#x345;
&#945;&#x313;&#957;&#945;&#947;&#954;&#945;&#x301;&#963;&#945;
&#962;
&#951;&#x314;&#956;&#945;&#x302;&#962;
&#948;&#953;&#945;&#964;&#961;&#953;&#x302;&psi;&#945;&#953;
</p>
</body>
</html>
```

Figure 27-4 shows this document loaded into the XHTML-savvy Mozilla. However, this document doesn't work nearly so well in non-XHTML-aware browsers such as Netscape 4.6, as Figure 27-5 shows.

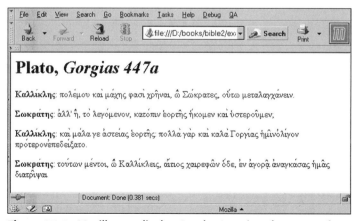

Figure 27-4: Mozilla can display Greek text using character references.

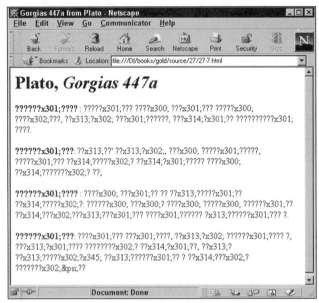

Figure 27-5: Legacy browsers such as Netscape 4.6 don't know what to do with character references.

There's also a middle ground. Some browsers understand character references but either don't have or don't know how to use the fonts needed to display those characters. Opera 4.0 and 5.0 just display boxes for most of the characters in Listing 27-7, as shown in Figure 27-6. Internet Explorer 5.5 can handle the Greek letters, and some of the accents, but is thrown by the breathing marks, as shown in Figure 27-7. Mozilla is actually the first browser I've found that can really handle classical Greek, regardless of how it's encoded. Support for other typographically challenging languages such as Arabic and Chinese also varies a great deal from browser to browser.

Cross-Reference Character references and browser support for various character sets are discussed in more detail in Chapter 7.

Custom entity references defined in DTD

Most Web browsers understand a very basic set of predefined entity references including `&lt;`, `&amp;`, `&quot;`, `&copy;`, ` `, and so on. HTML 4.0 expanded this set to several hundred entity references, including characters from the upper half of the Latin-1 character set such as ñ (`&ntilde;`) and Ü (`&Uuml;`), mathematical symbols such as ∂ (`&part;`) and √ (`&radic;`), Greek letters such as θ (`&theta;`) and Ω (`&Omega;`), and a few others besides. All of these are available to you in XHTML documents as well. All three XHTML DTDs define these entities so that you can use them.

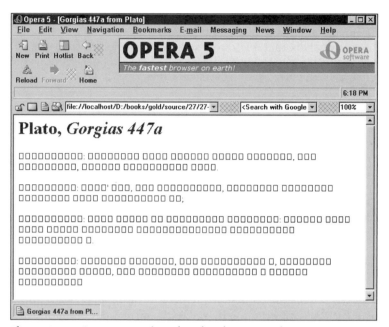

Figure 27-6: Opera recognizes that the character references are not Roman letters, but can't display them.

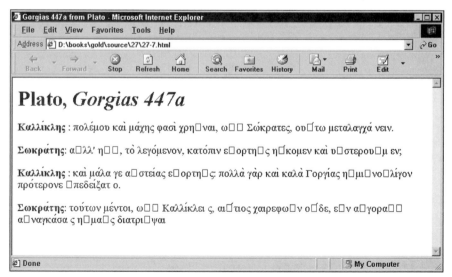

Figure 27-7: Internet Explorer 5.5 can handle the Greek letters but not the breathing marks.

In addition, you can define other entity references in the internal or external DTD subsets of your document, just as you might for any XML document. These can either point to individual characters, to text strings, to elements, or to groups of elements. For example, Listing 27-8 is a DTD fragment that defines several combining diacritical marks frequently used in classical Greek.

Listing 27-8: greek_accents.ent: A DTD subset defining Greek diacritical marks

```
<!ENTITY varia           "&#x300;"> <!-- grave accent -->
<!ENTITY oxia            "&#x301;"> <!-- acute accent -->
<!ENTITY circumflex      "&#x302;">
<!ENTITY psili           "&#x313;"> <!-- smooth breathing -->
<!ENTITY dasia           "&#x314;"> <!-- rough breathing -->
<!ENTITY iota_subscript  "&#x345;">
```

Listing 27-9 is a more intelligible version of Listing 27-7. It imports this entity set and uses the five general entities found there for the accent and breathing marks instead of numeric character references. For the Greek letters, it uses general entity references defined in the XHTML strict DTD. Finally, it defines three general entities in the internal DTD subset for the names of Socrates, Gorgias, and Kallikles.

Listing 27-9: An XHTML document that uses entity references

```
<!DOCTYPE html PUBLIC "-//W3C//DTD XHTML 1.0 Strict//EN"
                      "xhtml1-strict.dtd" [

  <!ENTITY % greek_accents SYSTEM "greek_accents.ent">
  %greek_accents;

  <!ENTITY Socrates
   "&Sigma;&omega;&kappa;&rho;&alpha;&oxia;&tau;&eta;&sigmaf;">
  <!ENTITY Gorgias
   "&Gamma;&omicron;&rho;&gamma;&iota;&oxia;&alpha;&sigmaf;">
  <!ENTITY Kallikles
"&Kappa;&alpha;&lambda;&lambda;&iota;&oxia;&kappa;&lambda;&eta;
&sigmaf;"
>

]>
<html xmlns="http://www.w3.org/1999/xhtml">
<head>
  <title>Gorgias 447a from Plato</title>
</head>
<body>
```

```
<h1>Plato, <cite>Gorgias 447a</cite></h1>
<p>
<span style="font-weight: bold">&Kallikles;</span>:
&pi;&omicron;&lambda;&epsilon;&oxia;&mu;&omicron;&upsilon;
&kappa;&alpha;&iota;&varia;
&mu;&alpha;&oxia;&chi;&eta;&sigmaf;
&phi;&alpha;&sigma;&iota;&varia;
&chi;&rho;&eta;&circumflex;&nu;&alpha;&iota;,
&omega;&psili;&circumflex;
&Sigma;&omega;&oxia;&kappa;&rho;&alpha;&tau;&epsilon;&sigmaf;,
&omicron;&upsilon;&dasia;&oxia;&tau;&omega;
&mu;&epsilon;&tau;&alpha;&lambda;&alpha;&gamma;&chi;
&alpha;&oxia;&nu;&epsilon;&iota;&nu;.
</p>
<p>
<span style="font-weight: bold">&Socrates;</span>:
&alpha;&psili;&lambda;&lambda;'
&eta;&psili;&circumflex;, &tau;&omicron;&varia;
&lambda;&epsilon;&gamma;&omicron;&oxia;&mu;&epsilon;&nu;
&omicron;&nu;,
&kappa;&alpha;&tau;&omicron;&oxia;&pi;&iota;&nu;
&epsilon;&dasia;&omicron;&rho;&tau;&eta;&circumflex;&sigmaf;
&eta;&dasia;&oxia;&kappa;&omicron;&mu;&epsilon;&nu;
&kappa;&alpha;&iota;&varia;
&upsilon;&dasia;&sigma;&tau;&epsilon;&rho;&omicron;
&upsilon;&circumflex;&mu;&epsilon;&nu;;
</p>
<p>
<span style="font-weight: bold">
&Kallikles;</span>:
&kappa;&alpha;&iota;&varia;
&mu;&alpha;&oxia;&lambda;&alpha;
&gamma;&epsilon;
&alpha;&psili;&sigma;&tau;&epsilon;&iota;&oxia;&alpha;&sigmaf;
&epsilon;&dasia;&omicron;&rho;&tau;&eta;&circumflex;&sigmaf;:
&pi;&omicron;&lambda;&lambda;&alpha;&varia;
&gamma;&alpha;&varia;&rho; &kappa;&alpha;&iota;&varia;
&kappa;&alpha;&lambda;&alpha;&varia; &Gorgias;
&eta;&dasia;&mu;&iota;&circumflex;&nu;&omicron;&psili;&lambda;
&iota;&oxia;&gamma;&omicron;&nu;
&pi;&rho;&omicron;&oxia;&tau;&epsilon;&rho;&omicron;&nu;
&epsilon;&psili;&pi;&epsilon;&delta;&epsilon;&iota;&oxia;&xi;
&alpha;&tau;&omicron;.
</p>
<p><span style="font-weight: bold">
&Socrates;</span>:
&tau;&omicron;&upsilon;&oxia;&tau;&omega;&nu;
&mu;&epsilon;&oxia;&nu;&tau;&omicron;&iota;,
&omega;&psili;&circumflex;
&Kappa;&alpha;&lambda;&lambda;&iota;&oxia;&kappa;&lambda;
&epsilon;&iota;&sigmaf;,
```

Continued

Listing 27-9 (continued)

```
&alpha;&iota;&psili;&oxia;&tau;&iota;&omicron;&sigmaf;
&Chi;&alpha;&iota;&rho;&epsilon;&phi;&omega;&circumflex;&nu;
&omicron;&dasia;&oxia;&delta;&epsilon;, &epsilon;&psili;&nu;
&alpha;&psili;&gamma;&omicron;&rho;
&alpha;&circumflex;&iota;_subscript;
&alpha;&psili;&nu;&alpha;&gamma;&kappa;&alpha;&oxia;&sigma;
&alpha;&sigmaf;
&eta;&dasia;&mu;&alpha;&circumflex;&sigmaf;
&delta;&iota;&alpha;&tau;&rho;&iota;&circumflex;&psi;&alpha;
&iota;
</p>
</body>
</html>
```

Unfortunately, this document requires a level of XHTML-savvy that none of the browsers I was able to test possessed. Even Mozilla 0.9 was not able to recognize the nonpredefined entities. Therefore, the use of author-defined entity references in XHTML documents is likely to remain theoretical for some time to come.

 Cross-Reference Entity references are discussed in more detail in Chapter 10.

Encoding declarations

Web servers are supposed to identify the character set and encoding of documents they send in the Content-type field of the HTTP header they prefix to each document. For example, this HTTP header specifies the UTF-8 encoding of the Unicode character set:

```
HTTP/1.1 200 OK
Date: Thu, 07 Dec 2000 21:09:53 GMT
Server: Apache/1.3.6 Ben-SSL/1.36 (Unix)
Last-Modified: Tue, 21 Dec 1999 03:04:51 GMT
Content-Length: 5201
Content-Type: text/html; charset=utf-8
```

In practice, however, most servers fail to do this. Furthermore, it's difficult to configure a Web server to understand that particular documents are in some encoding other than the most common one on that particular system. Therefore HTML authors who use a character set that goes beyond simple ASCII normally identify the set they're using with a meta element and an http-equiv attribute in the HTML head, like this:

```
<meta
  http-equiv="Content-Type" content="text/html; charset=UTF-8"
/>
```

To make matters worse, whereas most Web browsers assume a document uses Latin-1 when faced with an unidentified character set, XML processors are required to assume that documents are written in UTF-8 unless they're told otherwise. While some browsers (though not all) will recognize a charset parameter passed in an HTTP header, none will notice a meta element similar to this one.

Of course, XML documents have a different means of specifying character sets using an encoding declaration inside the XML declaration. For example:

```
<?xml version="1.0" encoding="UTF-8"?>
```

Unfortunately, some browsers that don't recognize this construct as an XML declaration or explicitly support XHTML will try to display it, so you want to avoid including it if possible. The most broadly compatible option is to author your documents in UTF-8 so that you can omit the XML declaration, and use a meta element to tell HTML browsers what they're dealing with. If UTF-8 is too sophisticated for your installed base of browsers, then you should stick to pure ASCII (a subset of UTF-8) and the predefined entity references.

Cross-Reference   The encoding declaration, UTF-8, and Unicode are covered in much more detail in Chapter 7.

The xml:lang attribute

The xml:lang attribute contains a code identifying which language the content of that element is written in. For example, these opening lines from Marcel Proust's *Du cote de chez Swann* are written in French, *naturellement*:

```
<q xml:lang="fr-FR"
 cite="ftp://movie0.archive.org/pub/etext/etext01/swann10h.htm"
>
Longtemps, je me suis couché de bonne heure. Parfois, ♪ peine
ma bougie éteinte, mes yeux se fermaient si vite que je n'avais
pas le temps de me dire: "Je m'endors."
</q>
```

In HTML, language identification is normally handled by the lang attribute instead, but otherwise the syntax is the same. For example,

```
<q lang="fr-FR"
 cite="ftp://movie0.archive.org/pub/etext/etext01/swann10h.htm"
>
Longtemps, je me suis couché de bonne heure. Parfois, ♪ peine
ma bougie éteinte, mes yeux se fermaient si vite que je n'avais
pas le temps de me dire: "Je m'endors."
</q>
```

For XHTML, the W3C recommends using both the `lang` and `xml:lang` attributes, like this:

```
<q lang="fr-FR" xml:lang="fr-FR"
 cite="ftp://movie0.archive.org/pub/etext/etext01/swann10h.htm"
>
Longtemps, je me suis couché de bonne heure. Parfois, ♪ peine
ma bougie éteinte, mes yeux se fermaient si vite que je n'avais
pas le temps de me dire: "Je m'endors."
</q>
```

HTML-aware tools will use the `lang` attribute to determine the language. XML-aware tools will use the `xml:lang` attribute. In the event of a conflict between the two, the value of the `xml:lang` attribute should take precedence, though this may depend more on which attribute the tool in question expects to read than on the official rules for disambiguation.

Cross-Reference

The `xml:lang` attribute was first introduced in Chapter 11.

CDATA sections

Before there were any books about HTML, many people, the author of this book included, learned HTML from the NCSA's *A Beginner's Guide to HTML*, which is itself written in HTML and published on the Web at `http://www.ncsa.uiuc.edu/General/Internet/WWW/HTMLPrimer.html`. Over the years, many other online tutorials about HTML and other new markup languages have been written in HTML and published on the Web. Today, many people are writing and reading online tutorials about SVG, WML, schemas, XHTML, and other cutting-edge topics. Indeed, I read a few of these while preparing to write the book you're reading now.

If you've ever written such a tutorial, you've noticed a problem. It's extremely inconvenient to write about HTML or anything that looks remotely like HTML in HTML. The problem is that all the examples of markup are interpreted by the browser as markup and disappear from the rendered document. For example, if I were writing about the `pre` element in HTML, I might write something like this:

```
<p>
HTML normally answers the question of whether white space is
significant or not by predefining the meaning of white space in
particular elements. For instance, white space is significant
inside <code><pre></code> and <code></pre></code> tags.
It's not significant almost everywhere else. This means that if
you want to preserve line breaks without using a monospaced
font, you need to insert a lot of <code><br></code> tags as in
this first stanza from William Blake's poem <cite>The
Tyger</cite>:
```

```
</p>
<pre><code><p>
Tyger! Tyger! burning bright<br class="empty"/>
In the forests of the night<br class="empty"/>
What immortal hand or eye<br class="empty"/>
Could frame thy fearful symmetry?<br class="empty"/>
</p></code></pre>
```

Of course, when this was displayed in a browser you'd see something like this:

HTML normally answers the question of whether white space is significant or not by predefining the meaning of white space in particular elements. For instance, white space is significant inside

```
and
```

tags. It's not significant almost everywhere else. This means that if you want to preserve line breaks without using a monospaced font, you need to insert a lot of tags as in this first stanza from William Blake's poem *The Tyger*:

```
Tyger! Tyger! burning bright

In the forests of the night

What immortal hand or eye

Could frame thy fearful symmetry?
```

This is not what you wanted at all! Of course, you know the solution. I should have escaped all the less-than signs from the markup I wanted to appear in the rendered document using entity references such as <, and if there were any raw amper-sands in this sample, they'd need to be escaped too. The result looks like this:

```
<p>
HTML normally answers the question of whether white space is
significant or not by predefining the meaning of white space in
particular elements. For instance, white space is significant
inside <code>&lt;pre></code> and <code>&lt;/pre></code> tags.
It's not significant almost everywhere else. This means that if
you want to preserve line breaks without using a monospaced
font, you need to insert a lot of <code>&lt;br></code> tags as
in this first stanza from William Blake's poem <cite>The
Tyger</cite>:
</p>
<pre><code>&lt;p>
Tyger! Tyger! burning bright&lt;br class="empty"/>
In the forests of the night&lt;br class="empty"/>
What immortal hand or eye&lt;br class="empty"/>
Could frame thy fearful symmetry?&lt;br class="empty"/>
&lt;/p></code></pre>
```

While adequate for occasional illegal characters, this is very tedious to do for large examples. XML, by contrast, offers a very neat solution: Just wrap the entire example in a CDATA section and then use the markup as you normally would. You can still use < and & for the smaller pieces where the example markup is intermingled with real markup. For example,

```
<p>
HTML normally answers the question of whether white space is
significant or not by predefining the meaning of white space in
particular elements. For instance, white space is significant
inside <code>&lt;pre></code> and <code>&lt;/pre></code> tags.
It's not significant almost everywhere else. This means that if
you want to preserve line breaks without using a monospaced
font, you need to insert a lot of <code>&lt;br></code> tags as
in this first stanza from William Blake's poem <cite>The
Tyger</cite>:
</p>
<pre><code><![CDATA[<p>
Tyger! Tyger! burning bright<br class="empty"/>
In the forests of the night<br class="empty"/>
What immortal hand or eye<br class="empty"/>
Could frame thy fearful symmetry?<br class="empty"/>
</p>]]></code></pre>
```

This is much easier to write, much easier to debug, and much easier to read. Unfortunately, current browsers don't reliably support CDATA sections; but when they do, they'll make writing online tutorials for the next generation of markup languages much easier.

Caution
Of the allegedly XHTML-aware browsers I tested, only Amaya 4.1 correctly recognized and handled CDATA sections as shown in Figure 27-8. Mozilla 0.9 completely omitted the content of the CDATA section, treating it as an unrecognized tag. Opera 4.0.1, 5.0, and 5.11 and Internet Explorer 5.5 left out the <[CDATA[but included everything else, as shown in Figure 27-9. They treated the tags inside the CDATA section as markup rather than the plain text they actually are.

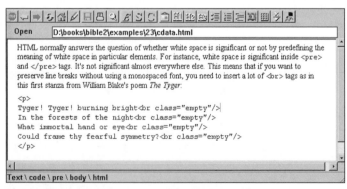

Figure 27-8: Amaya 4.1 recognizes CDATA sections in XHTML documents.

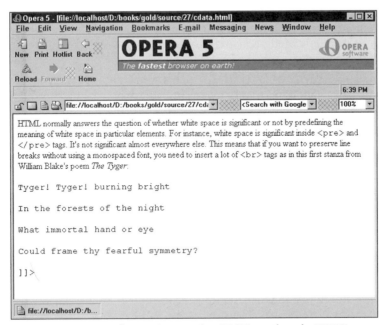

Figure 27-9: Opera does not recognize CDATA sections in XHTML documents.

Cross-Reference CDATA sections are discussed in more detail in Chapter 6.

Summary

In this chapter, you learned that:

✦ XHTML is a reformulation of HTML as an XML application. Among other changes, this requires making your HTML documents well formed.

✦ When converting an existing HTML document into well-formed XML, you have to make sure all attribute values are quoted, all entity references are declared, all start tags have matching end tags, that there is a single root element, and that elements do not overlap.

✦ XHTML documents must be valid according to one of three DTDs.

✦ The XHTML transitional DTD allows most standard HTML and XHTML elements and attributes defined in HTML 4.0 and earlier except for frames.

✦ The XHTML frameset DTD allows everything the transitional DTD allows, and adds the elements and attributes needed to work with frames.

✦ The XHTML strict DTD disallows frame elements such as `frame`, presentational elements such as `center` and `bgcolor`, and deprecated elements such as `applet`. The eliminated presentational attributes and elements are replaced by CSS styles.

✦ When converting an existing HTML document into valid XHTML, you have to repeatedly use a validation tool to make sure you're only using allowed elements and attributes and only in the ways the DTD allows them to be used.

✦ Dave Raggett's HTML Tidy is a very useful tool for automating a lot of the grunt work involved in converting existing HTML documents to XHTML; but you'll still need to do some work by hand when Tidy is through with a document.

✦ XHTML lets you use character references in your Web pages, though the browser still needs a font it can use to draw those characters.

✦ XHTML lets you define entity references in the DTD to use in your Web pages, but current browsers often don't recognize these.

✦ XML parsers determine the character set from an encoding declaration. HTML parsers determine the character set from the charset parameter of the Content-type field of an HTTP header. XHTML documents use the encoding declaration, but only if the browser specifically knows about XHTML.

✦ XML's `xml:lang` attribute and HTML's `lang` attribute should both be used to identify the language of an element.

✦ Theoretically XHTML allows you to use CDATA sections in your Web pages, but browser support for this feature is lacking.

This chapter described XHTML 1.0. The next chapter takes up Modular XHTML and XHTML 1.1. While the basic vocabulary is the same between XHTML 1.0 and 1.1, Modular XHTML divides the XHTML DTD into many separate parts that can be mixed and matched with other applications such as MathML and SMIL to create unique combinations of functionality. Different profiles of XHTML offer different combinations of functionality suitable for different needs.

✦   ✦   ✦

Modular XHTML

XHTML 1.0 is still, by and large, HTML. The syntax has changed a little, but the same elements and attributes are present, and they mean pretty much the same things in XHTML that they mean in HTML 4.0. You can do pretty much the same things with XHTML 1.0 that you're already doing with HTML. Officially, the acronym XHTML stands for *Extensible Hypertext Markup Language*, but in truth its extensibility is limited. You get to pick the transitional, strict, or frameset DTDs, but that's the limit of your freedom. You can't mix in Scalable Vector Graphics (SVG) or MathML or take out tables without violating the DTDs, and thus producing invalid XHTML.

XHTML 1.1, by contrast, is much more practically extensible. It is divided into abstract modules, each covering a specific area of functionality, such as tables, forms, images, structure, and text. The individual modules are instantiated as particular DTD or schema components. The DTD components are connected by parameter entity references. By overriding particular parameter entity references, you can pick and choose which modules you want to include in your own applications. Furthermore, you can mix in DTD modules from other XML applications such as SVG or the Resource Directory Description Language (RDDL). As well as the full XHTML 1.1 profile, the W3C has published a stripped-down version called XHTML Basic and duded-up versions that add Synchronized Multimedia Integration Language (SMIL) and MathML (Mathematical Markup Language). Alternately, you can embed XHTML or particular parts of it into your own XML applications.

The Modules of XHTML

Modular XHTML does not define any new elements or attributes not already present in HTML 4.0 and XHTML 1.0. However, it does organize all the elements and attributes of standard HTML into 28 *modules*, each of which defines a different subset of the elements and attributes used in XHTML. Most of these subsets are disjoint, though there are a few places where they overlap. Table 28-1 lists the 28 modules and specifies which elements each declares.

Table 28-1
XHTML Modules

Module	Purpose	Defines
Structure	organization of the XML document	`body`, `head`, `html`, and `title`
Text	basic text markup	`abbr`, `acronym`, `address`, `blockquote`, `br`, `cite`, `code`, `dfn`, `div`, `em`, `h1`, `h2`, `h3`, `h4`, `h5`, `h6`, `kbd`, `p`, `pre`, `q`, `samp`, `span`, `strong`, and `var`
Hypertext	linking	the `a` element and its unique attributes: `accesskey`, `charset`, `href`, `hreflang`, `rel`, `rev`, `tabindex`, and `type`
List	three different kinds of lists	`dl`, `dt`, `dd`, `ul`, `ol`, and `li`.
Applet	Java applets	the `applet` and `param` elements, as well as their unique attributes
Presentation	Elements that are solely about appearance rather than meaning	`b`, `big`, `hr`, `i`, `small`, `sub`, `sup`, and `tt`
Edit	Revision tracking	`del` and `ins`, as well as their unique attributes, `cite` and `datetime`
Bi-directional Text	elements used to indicate a shift from left-to-right to right-to-left text and vice versa	the `bdo` element and its `dir` attribute
Basic Forms	forms as defined in HTML 3.2 and earlier	`form`, `input`, `label`, `select`, `option`, and `textarea` elements
Forms	forms as defined in HTML 4.0 and later	`form`, `input`, `label`, `select`, `option`, `textarea`, `button`, `fieldset`, `label`, `legend`, and `optgroup`
Basic Tables	a limited group of table elements	`table`, `td`, `th`, `tr`, and `caption`
Tables	all the table elements	`table`, `td`, `th`, `tr`, `col`, `colgroup`, `tbody`, `thead`, `tfoot`, and `caption`

Module	Purpose	Defines
Image	images	the `img` element and its unique attributes `alt`, `width`, `height`, `longdesc`, and `src`
Client-side Image Map	image maps resolved by the client	`area` and `map`; also adds some attributes to the `a`, `img`, `input`, and `object` elements to support their use in image maps
Server-side Image Map	image maps interpreted by the server	the `ismap` attribute of the `img` and `input` elements
Object	embedded non-HTML content like Flash pictures and Shockwave animations	`object` and `param`
Frames	frame-related elements and attributes	`frame`, `frameset`, and `noframes`
Iframe	internal frames	`iframe`
Target	which frame to load a selection in	the `target` attribute of the `a`, `area`, `base`, `link`, and `form` elements
Intrinsic Events	JavaScript event handlers	`onblur`, `onfocus`, `onload`, `onunload`, `onreset`, `onsubmit`, `onchange`, and `onselect` attributes
Scripting	scripts	the `script` and `noscript` elements
Metainformation	information about the document	the `meta` element along with its `content`, `http-equiv`, `name`, and `scheme` attributes
Style Sheet	elements used for CSS styles	the `style` element and its `media`, `title`, and `type` attributes
Style Attribute	attributes used for CSS styles	the `style` attribute
Link	related resources	the `link` element used in HTML headers along with its `charset`, `href`, `hreflang`, `media`, `rel`, `rev`, and `type` attributes

Continued

Table 28-1 *(continued)*

Module	Purpose	Defines
Base	used to identify the URL against which relative URLs in the document should be resolved	the `base` element and its `href` attribute
Name Identification	intradocument linking	the deprecated `name` attribute of the `a`, `applet`, `form`, `frame`, `iframe`, `img` and `map` elements
Legacy	very deprecated presentational elements and attributes you really don't need to use in 2001	`basefont`, `center`, `dir`, `font`, `isindex`, `menu`, `s`, `strike`, and `u` as well as deprecated presentational attributes such as `bgcolor` and `align`

Within some limits you can use these modules independently of each other and pick and choose those you want. For example, if you just want to add simple lists to your application, you only have to load the list module, the modules that define what a list item can contain (mostly the text module), and the framework modules on which all the other XHTML modules depend. (I'll get to that shortly.) However, you don't have to use tables, frames, applets, and all the other complicated parts of HTML if you don't need them.

Some modules are used in almost all variations of XHTML. For example, the structure, text, hypertext, and list modules are the core on which XHTML documents are built. To some extent they correspond to the functionality that's been present since HTML 1.0. Other modules are used quite rarely. For instance, the legacy module declares deprecated elements such as `font`, `center`, and `dir` that you shouldn't use in new documents but might need to validate in older ones. In a few cases, modules are alternatives to each other. For example, you can choose either the Basic Tables module, which includes only the `table`, `caption`, `th`, `td`, and `tr` elements, or the full tables module, which includes `col`, `colgroup`, `tbody`, `thead`, and `tfoot` as well. However, you wouldn't choose both.

For the most part, however, standard HTML pages require most of the modules. It's when you begin mixing XHTML into your own applications that you can take advantage of smaller subsets of functionality. For instance, in a collection of movie reviews, each review might contain elements for the title of the movie, the year, the actors in the movie, and so forth. However, because the review itself is a more-or-less free-form narrative text with no particular structure, each review could also contain a `description` element that contained XHTML. If you wanted only simple reviews you might choose to leave out the forms and tables and applet modules, and indeed omit everything except the core modules.

A Sample DTD Module

Listing 28-1 shows the List module, one of the four core modules required for a minimal implementation of XHTML. This defines the definition, unordered, and ordered lists represented by the dl, dt, dd, ul, ol, and li elements.

Like all modules in XHTML, it has a standard public identifier, -//W3C//ELEMENTS XHTML Lists 1.0//EN. It also has a suggested system identifier, http://www.w3.org/TR/xhtml-modularization/DTD/xhtml-list-1.mod. However, this can be changed if you want to point to a different copy of the DTD in a different location, for instance, if you wanted to store a copy on your local hard drive rather than relying on the official version at the W3C Web site.

xhtml-list-1.mod and all the other DTD modules for XHTML 1.1 can be found on the CD-ROM in the directory specs/xhtml-modularization/DTD.

Listing 28-1: **xhtml-list-1.mod: The list module DTD**

```
<!-- ............................................ -->
<!-- XHTML Lists Module  ............................ -->
<!-- file: xhtml-list-1.mod

     This is XHTML, a reformulation of HTML as a modular XML
     application.
     Copyright 1998-2001 W3C (MIT, INRIA, Keio), All Rights
     Reserved.
     Revision: $Id: xhtml-list-1.mod,v 4.0 2001/04/02 22:42:49
     altheim Exp $ SMI

     This DTD module is identified by the PUBLIC and SYSTEM
     identifiers:

PUBLIC "-//W3C//ELEMENTS XHTML Lists 1.0//EN"
SYSTEM "http://www.w3.org/TR/xhtml-modularization/DTD/xhtml-
list-1.mod"

     Revisions:
     (none)
     ............................................... -->

<!-- Lists

      dl, dt, dd, ol, ul, li

     This module declares the list-oriented element types
     and their attributes.
-->
```

Continued

Listing 28-1 *(continued)*

```
<!ENTITY % dl.qname   "dl" >
<!ENTITY % dt.qname   "dt" >
<!ENTITY % dd.qname   "dd" >
<!ENTITY % ol.qname   "ol" >
<!ENTITY % ul.qname   "ul" >
<!ENTITY % li.qname   "li" >

<!-- dl: Definition List ............................. -->

<!ENTITY % dl.element  "INCLUDE" >
<![%dl.element;[
<!ENTITY % dl.content  "( %dt.qname; | %dd.qname; )+" >
<!ELEMENT %dl.qname;  %dl.content; >
<!-- end of dl.element -->]]>

<!ENTITY % dl.attlist  "INCLUDE" >
<![%dl.attlist;[
<!ATTLIST %dl.qname;
     %Common.attrib;
>
<!-- end of dl.attlist -->]]>

<!-- dt: Definition Term ............................. -->

<!ENTITY % dt.element  "INCLUDE" >
<![%dt.element;[
<!ENTITY % dt.content
     "( #PCDATA | %Inline.mix; )*"
>
<!ELEMENT %dt.qname;  %dt.content; >
<!-- end of dt.element -->]]>

<!ENTITY % dt.attlist  "INCLUDE" >
<![%dt.attlist;[
<!ATTLIST %dt.qname;
     %Common.attrib;
>
<!-- end of dt.attlist -->]]>

<!-- dd: Definition Description ....................... -->

<!ENTITY % dd.element  "INCLUDE" >
<![%dd.element;[
<!ENTITY % dd.content
     "( #PCDATA | %Flow.mix; )*"
>
<!ELEMENT %dd.qname;  %dd.content; >
<!-- end of dd.element -->]]>

<!ENTITY % dd.attlist  "INCLUDE" >
<![%dd.attlist;[
```

```
<!ATTLIST %dd.qname;
      %Common.attrib;
>
<!-- end of dd.attlist -->]]>

<!-- ol: Ordered List (numbered styles) ............... -->

<!ENTITY % ol.element   "INCLUDE" >
<![%ol.element;[
<!ENTITY % ol.content   "( %li.qname; )+" >
<!ELEMENT %ol.qname;   %ol.content; >
<!-- end of ol.element -->]]>

<!ENTITY % ol.attlist   "INCLUDE" >
<![%ol.attlist;[
<!ATTLIST %ol.qname;
      %Common.attrib;
>
<!-- end of ol.attlist -->]]>

<!-- ul: Unordered List (bullet styles) ............... -->

<!ENTITY % ul.element   "INCLUDE" >
<![%ul.element;[
<!ENTITY % ul.content   "( %li.qname; )+" >
<!ELEMENT %ul.qname;   %ul.content; >
<!-- end of ul.element -->]]>

<!ENTITY % ul.attlist   "INCLUDE" >
<![%ul.attlist;[
<!ATTLIST %ul.qname;
      %Common.attrib;
>
<!-- end of ul.attlist -->]]>

<!-- li: List Item ................................. -->
<!ENTITY % li.element   "INCLUDE" >
<![%li.element;[
<!ENTITY % li.content
     "( #PCDATA | %Flow.mix; )*"
>
<!ELEMENT %li.qname;   %li.content; >
<!-- end of li.element -->]]>

<!ENTITY % li.attlist   "INCLUDE" >
<![%li.attlist;[
<!ATTLIST %li.qname;
      %Common.attrib;
>
<!-- end of li.attlist -->]]>

<!-- end of xhtml-list-1.mod -->
```

Entity references are used throughout the module for element and attribute names, for content models, and for conditional section markers that allow you to turn particular declarations on or off. This is a common pattern in modular DTDs that allows a great deal of customizability. The key idea is that entity declarations can be overridden by an earlier declaration, especially one in the internal DTD subset of document.

Modularization of DTDs in general is discussed in great detail in Chapter 26. Identical techniques are being used here.

Element names

The names of the elements are all defined by entities that follow the pattern *elementName*.qname. Thus, the name of the dl element is defined by the parameter entity reference %dl.qname;. The name of the dt element is defined by the parameter entity reference %dt.qname;. The name of the dd element is defined by the parameter entity reference %dd.qname;, and so on. Suppose for some reason you wanted to change these to uppercase. To do this, you'd place the following declarations in your internal DTD subset:

```
<!ENTITY % dl.qname   "DL" >
<!ENTITY % dt.qname   "DT" >
<!ENTITY % dd.qname   "DD" >
<!ENTITY % ol.qname   "OL" >
<!ENTITY % ul.qname   "UL" >
<!ENTITY % li.qname   "LI" >
```

Because other modules also use these parameter entity references to define the content models of elements that can contain lists, these changes also change the definitions used in the other modules. Thus, all the elements that contain lists are redefined to contain DL, UL, and OL elements instead of dl, ol, and ul elements. In fact, direct element names are used almost nowhere. This indirection through parameter entity references is used throughout the modular XHTML DTDs.

Element-specific content models

Content models are also defined by parameter entity references. It is easy enough to say that a dl element must contain matched dt dd pairs, or that a %dl.qname; element must contain matched %dt.qname; %dd.qname; pairs. Instead, however, a dl.content parameter entity is first defined liked this:

```
<!ENTITY % dl.content  "( %dt.qname; | %dd.qname; )+" >
```

The %dl.content; parameter entity reference is then used to define the dl element like this:

```
<!ELEMENT %dl.qname;   %dl.content; >
```

If for some reason you decide that you want dl elements to contain definition elements, each of which contains a dt dd pair, rather than having the dl element contain the dt dd pair directly, you simply define the new definition element and override the declaration of the dl.content entity like this:

```
<!ELEMENT definition  "( %dt.qname; | %dd.qname; )+" >
<!ENTITY % dl.content  "( definition )+" >
```

Of course if you do change the name or content models of the dl element, or of any other element, you should not expect off-the-shelf Web browsers to understand your revised elements.

Generic content models

The default content models for dl, ul, and ol elements are defined completely in terms of other elements defined in Listing 28-1. However, that isn't true for the elements they contain: dt, dd, and li. These are defined like this:

```
<!-- dt: Definition Term ............................. -->

<!ENTITY % dt.element  "INCLUDE" >
<![%dt.element;[
<!ENTITY % dt.content
    "( #PCDATA | %Inline.mix; )*"
>
<!ELEMENT %dt.qname;  %dt.content; >
<!-- end of dt.element -->]]>

<!-- dd: Definition Description ....................... -->

<!ENTITY % dd.element  "INCLUDE" >
<![%dd.element;[
<!ENTITY % dd.content
    "( #PCDATA | %Flow.mix; )*"
>
<!ELEMENT %dd.qname;  %dd.content; >
<!-- end of dd.element -->]]>

<!-- li: List Item ................................. -->

<!ENTITY % li.element  "INCLUDE" >
<![%li.element;[
<!ENTITY % li.content
    "( #PCDATA | %Flow.mix; )*"
>
<!ELEMENT %li.qname;  %li.content; >
<!-- end of li.element -->]]>
```

This can be simplified by resolving the parameter entity references defined close by (assuming that no previously loaded module is redefining any of these parameter entity references), deleting the comments, and including everything that can be included. The result looks like this:

```
<!ELEMENT dt  ( #PCDATA | %Inline.mix; )* >
<!ELEMENT dd  ( #PCDATA | %Flow.mix; )* >
<!ELEMENT li  ( #PCDATA | %Flow.mix; )* >
```

Perhaps surprisingly, there are still three parameter entity references for two different parameter entities left: %Inline.mix; and %Flow.mix;. These are not defined anywhere in Listing 28-1. Instead they must be defined before Listing 28-1 is loaded. Although you could define them in your own DTDs, they are normally defined in the document model module. I get to this later. In the meantime, what you need to know is that there are three main parameter entity references used to define common content models shared among many different types of elements:

✦ Inline.mix: a choice containing all inline elements such as a, abbr, acronym, br, img, kbd, object, span, em, strong, dfn, cite, code, q, samp, strong, var, input, select, textarea, and label

✦ Block.mix: a choice containing all block-level elements such as p, div, h1, h2, h3, h4, h5, h6, ul, ol, dl, table, form, pre, blockquote, and address

✦ Flow.mix: a choice containing all of the above inline and block-level elements

Generic attribute models

The document model also defines a number of common attribute sets that can be applied to most elements. For example, the li element is declared to possess the common attributes:

```
<!ATTLIST %li.qname;
    %Common.attrib;
>
```

Common.attrib is a parameter entity defined in another part of the framework, the common attributes module, xhtml-attribs-1.mod. I discuss it below in Table 28-3. For now, what you need to know is that %Common.attrib; has the necessary replacement text so that the id, class, title, and other attributes that apply to almost all HTML elements get applied to this element.

INCLUDE and IGNORE blocks

Another use of parameter entity references is to remove particular elements from content models. For example, let's suppose you just don't like definition lists and want to forbid the dl, dt, and dd elements completely. All the declarations for these elements and their attributes are enclosed in blocks like these:

```
<!ENTITY % dl.element  "INCLUDE" >
<![%dl.element;[
<!ENTITY % dl.content  "( %dt.qname; | %dd.qname; )+" >
<!ELEMENT %dl.qname;  %dl.content; >
<!-- end of dl.element -->]]>

<!ENTITY % dl.attlist  "INCLUDE" >
<![%dl.attlist;[
<!ATTLIST %dl.qname;
     %Common.attrib;
>
<!-- end of dl.attlist -->]]>
```

Normally, %dl.element; and %dl.attlist; have the replacement text INCLUDE. Consequently, the above fragment resolves to this, and the dl element is included:

```
<![INCLUDE[
<!ENTITY % dl.content  "( %dt.qname; | %dd.qname; )+" >
<!ELEMENT %dl.qname;  %dl.content; >
<!-- end of dl.element -->]]>

<![INCLUDE[
<!ATTLIST %dl.qname;
     %Common.attrib;
>
<!-- end of dl.attlist -->]]>
```

However, if you redefine dl.element and dl.attlist to IGNORE, then those declarations are omitted, and the dl element is effectively forbidden. The same trick can be used for any element and attribute in XHTML. For example, to drop out the blockquote element define blockquote.element and blockquote.attlist as IGNORE like this:

```
<!ENTITY % blockquote.element  "IGNORE" >
<!ENTITY % blockquote.attlist  "IGNORE" >
```

To omit the cite element, define cite.element and cite.attlist as IGNORE like this:

```
<!ENTITY % cite.element  "IGNORE" >
<!ENTITY % cite.attlist  "IGNORE" >
```

Note   Actually, since you are allowed to declare attributes for elements that don't exist, all you absolutely have to do is redeclare *elementName*.content as IGNORE. However, I find it more aesthetically complete to drop both out.

Using XHTML entities in other applications

You can also use the entity references defined here in your own XML applications. For example, suppose you have a DICTIONARY element that you want to allow to contain a definition list, but not all the other XHTML elements. You would simply import the XHTML DTD and then declare your element as possessing a content model of %dl.qname; like this:

```
<!ENTITY % xhtml SYSTEM "xhtml-basic10.dtd">
%xhtml;
<!ELEMENT DICTIONARY (%dl.qname;)>
```

Even though you aren't using the whole of XHTML in your own application you still need to import it all because the lists module you are using relies on it.

Or suppose you want to say that in your definition list the dt and dd elements can only contain parsed character data, no child elements. Then before you imported it, you'd redefine the dt and dd content models as #PCDATA like this:

```
<!ENTITY % dt.content "(#PCDATA)">
<!ENTITY % dd.content "(#PCDATA)">
<!ENTITY % xhtml SYSTEM "xhtml-basic10.dtd">
%xhtml;
<!ELEMENT DICTIONARY (%dl.qname;)>
```

Another useful trick is to declare that one of your elements contains the same content as one of the standard XHTML elements. For example, suppose your XML application contains a LIST element, and you want to say that this has the same content as XHTML's ul element. Simply import the XHTML DTD and use the %ul.content; parameter entity reference like this:

```
<!ELEMENT LIST %ul.content;>
```

Depending on context, the parameter entity references that are most useful are:

✦ %span.content;: for inline elements

✦ %div.content;: for block-level elements that can contain other block-level elements

✦ %p.content;: for block-level elements that cannot contain other block-level elements

✦ %body.content;: for entire documents

The Framework

By themselves the 28 modules are incomplete. They rely on a number of parameter entity references, such as %Common.attrib; and %Flow.mix;, that must be defined before the modules can be used. These are defined by a driver DTD. More specifically, they are defined by other framework modules that the driver DTD imports.

The framework is provided by the XHTML Modular Framework Module, xhtml-framework-1.mod. This module loads the other modules that lay the foundation for the 28 XHTML modules by defining notations, datatypes, namespaces, common attributes, the document model, and character entities. Until the framework module is loaded, none of the other modules can be used.

Listing 28-2 shows the XHTML 1.1 framework module. It does not declare any elements or attributes itself. It just gathers together all the pieces of the framework and loads them. None of these pieces declare any elements or attributes either. They all just define entity references that will be used to actually declare elements and attributes in the 28 modules.

Listing 28-2: xhtml-framework-1.mod: The XHTML framework module DTD

```
<!-- ............................................ -->
<!-- XHTML Modular Framework Module  ..................... -->
<!-- file: xhtml-framework-1.mod

     This is XHTML, a reformulation of HTML as a modular XML
     application.
     Copyright 1998-2001 W3C (MIT, INRIA, Keio), All Rights
     Reserved.
     Revision: $Id: xhtml-framework-1.mod,v 4.0 2001/04/02
     22:42:49 altheim Exp $ SMI

     This DTD module is identified by the PUBLIC and SYSTEM
     identifiers:

       PUBLIC "-//W3C//ENTITIES XHTML Modular Framework 1.0//EN"
       SYSTEM "http://www.w3.org/TR/xhtml-modularization/DTD/
       xhtml-framework-1.mod"

     Revisions:
     (none)
     ............................................ -->

<!-- Modular Framework

     This required module instantiates the modules needed
     to support the XHTML modularization model, including:

         +  notations
         +  datatypes
         +  namespace-qualified names
         +  common attributes
         +  document model
```

Continued

Listing 28-2 *(continued)*

```
            +   character entities

        The Intrinsic Events module is ignored by default but
        occurs in this module because it must be instantiated
        prior to Attributes but after Datatypes.
-->

<!ENTITY % xhtml-arch.module "IGNORE" >
<![%xhtml-arch.module;[
<!ENTITY % xhtml-arch.mod
        PUBLIC "-//W3C//ELEMENTS XHTML Base Architecture 1.0//EN"
               "xhtml-arch-1.mod" >
%xhtml-arch.mod;]]>

<!ENTITY % xhtml-notations.module "INCLUDE" >
<![%xhtml-notations.module;[
<!ENTITY % xhtml-notations.mod
        PUBLIC "-//W3C//NOTATIONS XHTML Notations 1.0//EN"
               "xhtml-notations-1.mod" >
%xhtml-notations.mod;]]>

<!ENTITY % xhtml-datatypes.module "INCLUDE" >
<![%xhtml-datatypes.module;[
<!ENTITY % xhtml-datatypes.mod
        PUBLIC "-//W3C//ENTITIES XHTML Datatypes 1.0//EN"
               "xhtml-datatypes-1.mod" >
%xhtml-datatypes.mod;]]>

<!-- placeholder for XLink support module -->
<!ENTITY % xhtml-xlink.mod "" >
%xhtml-xlink.mod;

<!ENTITY % xhtml-qname.module "INCLUDE" >
<![%xhtml-qname.module;[
<!ENTITY % xhtml-qname.mod
        PUBLIC "-//W3C//ENTITIES XHTML Qualified Names 1.0//EN"
               "xhtml-qname-1.mod" >
%xhtml-qname.mod;]]>

<!ENTITY % xhtml-events.module "IGNORE" >
<![%xhtml-events.module;[
<!ENTITY % xhtml-events.mod
        PUBLIC "-//W3C//ENTITIES XHTML Intrinsic Events 1.0//EN"
               "xhtml-events-1.mod" >
%xhtml-events.mod;]]>

<!ENTITY % xhtml-attribs.module "INCLUDE" >
<![%xhtml-attribs.module;[
<!ENTITY % xhtml-attribs.mod
        PUBLIC "-//W3C//ENTITIES XHTML Common Attributes 1.0//EN"
               "xhtml-attribs-1.mod" >
```

```
%xhtml-attribs.mod;]]>

<!-- placeholder for content model redeclarations -->
<!ENTITY % xhtml-model.redecl "" >
%xhtml-model.redecl;

<!ENTITY % xhtml-model.module "INCLUDE" >
<![%xhtml-model.module;[
<!-- instantiate the Document Model module declared in the DTD
driver
-->
%xhtml-model.mod;]]>

<!ENTITY % xhtml-charent.module "INCLUDE" >
<![%xhtml-charent.module;[
<!ENTITY % xhtml-charent.mod
     PUBLIC "-//W3C//ENTITIES XHTML Character Entities 1.0//EN"
            "xhtml-charent-1.mod" >
%xhtml-charent.mod;]]>

<!-- end of xhtml-framework-1.mod -->
```

This module potentially loads as many as ten other modules:

✦ The architecture module is ignored by default, but if `xhtml-arch.module` is redefined to `INCLUDE`, then it adds declarations that allow XHTML to become an architectural forms base architecture.

✦ The notations module declares a number of notations that can be used to type unparsed entities and element content.

✦ The datatypes module defines parameter entities that can be used as aliases for attribute types that would otherwise have type `CDATA`, `NMTOKEN`, or `NMTO-KENS`.

✦ The XLink module doesn't exist yet, but `xhtml-xlink.mod` holds its place for a future addition or extension.

✦ The qualified names module defines the namespace URIs and prefixes used in XHTML.

✦ The events module declares entities that can be used in attribute declarations for attributes such as `onfocus`, `onblur`, and `onclick`. It is ignored by default because the definitions of these events are expected to change in the future as a result of work on the Document Object Model. However, if `xhtml-events.module` is defined as `INCLUDE` instead, then this module is included.

✦ The common attributes module defines entities that can be used in attribute declarations for attributes shared by many XHTML elements such as `id`, `xml:lang`, and `class`.

✦ The content model module defines entities such as `Inline.mix` that can be used inside element declaration content models for many elements.

✦ The redeclaration module is loaded before the normal content model module. You define entities here before they get defined in the content model module to adjust the normal rules of XHTML.

✦ The character entities module defines general entities such as `&alpha;` and `&copy;` that can be used in XHTML instance documents.

In nine of the ten cases, the framework module defines the location of the module it's loading and then loads it. The tenth case is the document model. It merely loads this from the parameter entity reference `%xhtml-model.mod;`. However, it does not define that parameter entity. It assumes that `%xhtml-model.mod;` has already been defined in the DTD that loaded the framework module. The framework module itself depends on the document model. The document model is defined in the driver DTD. The driver DTD is the one file that is referenced from the instance document's `DOCTYPE` declaration. The driver DTD defines the document model and loads the framework, which then loads the document model and the individual modules.

The notations framework module

The notations module, `xhtml-notations.module`, defines a number of XML notations for unparsed data. For example, this declaration from the notations module defines a notation for dates and times:

```
<!-- date and time information. ISO date format -->
<!NOTATION datetime
    PUBLIC "-//W3C//NOTATION XHTML Datatype: Datetime//EN" >
```

Table 28-2 summarizes the notations declared here, but overall this module doesn't have a lot of practical impact on HTML documents.

Table 28-2
Notations Declared in Modular XHTML

Name	Public Identifier	Type
w3c-xml	ISO 8879//NOTATION Extensible Markup Language (XML) 1.0//EN	XML document
cdata	-//W3C//NOTATION XML 1.0: CDATA//EN	XML CDATA
fpi	ISO 8879:1986//NOTATION Formal Public Identifier//EN	SGML Formal Public Identifier
pixels	-//W3C//NOTATION XHTML Datatype: Pixels//EN	integer representing length in pixels

Name	Public Identifier	Type
length	-//W3C//NOTATION XHTML Datatype: Length//EN	nn for pixels or nn% for percentage length
multiLength	-//W3C//NOTATION XHTML Datatype: MultiLength//EN	pixel, percentage, or relative length
linkTypes	-//W3C//NOTATION XHTML Datatype: LinkTypes//EN	a space-separated list of link types
mediaDesc	-//W3C//NOTATION XHTML Datatype: MediaDesc//EN	single or comma-separated list of media descriptors
number	-//W3C//NOTATION XHTML Datatype: Number//EN	one or more digits
script	-//W3C//NOTATION XHTML Datatype: Script//EN	script expression
text	-//W3C//NOTATION XHTML Datatype: Text//EN	textual content
character	-//W3C//NOTATION XHTML Datatype: Character//EN	a single Unicode character
charset	-//W3C//NOTATION XHTML Datatype: Charset//EN	a MIME character encoding
charsets	-//W3C//NOTATION XHTML Datatype: Charsets// ENcharacter encodings	a space separated list of MIME
contentType	-//W3C//NOTATION XHTML Datatype: ContentType//EN	a MIME media type
contentTypes	-//W3C//NOTATION XHTML Datatype: ContentTypes//EN	a comma-separated list of MIME media types
datetime	-//W3C//NOTATION XHTML Datatype: Datetime//EN	ISO 8601 date and time
languageCode	-//W3C//NOTATION XHTML Datatype: LanguageCode//EN	an RFC 3066 language code
uri	-//W3C//NOTATION XHTML Datatype: URI//EN	a Uniform Resource Identifier (URI)
uris	-//W3C//NOTATION XHTML Datatype: URIs//EN	a space-separated list of URIs

Cross-Reference   Notations are discussed in Chapter 12.

The data-types framework module

The datatypes module defines parameter entity references that can be used as alternate names for attribute types that would otherwise have type CDATA, NMTOKEN, or NMTOKENS. For example, this declaration defines a number type:

```
<!-- one or more digits (NUMBER) -->
<!ENTITY % Number.datatype "CDATA" >
```

XML parsers can't enforce these types, but they do make the DTD a little clearer about what kind of data is expected where. Table 28-3 lists the data types defined in modular XHTML. You'll notice there's a considerable amount of overlap with the notations in Table 28-2. That's not an accident. These are for attribute types and those are for unparsed entities, but the basic types are the same.

Table 28-3
Data Types Defined by Modular XHTML

Parameter Entity Reference	Required Type	XML Type
%Length.datatype;	nn for pixels or nn% for percentage length	CDATA
%LinkTypes.datatype;	A space-separated list of link types	NMTOKENS
%MediaDesc.datatype;	A comma-separated list of media descriptors	CDATA
%MultiLength.datatype;	Pixel, percentage, or relative length	CDATA
%Number.datatype;	One or more digits	CDATA
%Pixels.datatype;	An integer representing a length in pixels	CDATA
%Script.datatype;	A script expression	CDATA
%Text.datatype;	A Unicode string	CDATA
%Character.datatype;	A single Unicode character	CDATA
%Charset.datatype;	A MIME character encoding	CDATA
%Charsets.datatype;	A space separated list of MIME character encodings	CDATA
%Color.datatype;	Color specification using color name or sRGB (#RRGGBB) values	CDATA
%ContentType.datatype;	A MIME media type	CDATA
%ContentTypes.datatype;	A comma-separated list of MIME media types	CDATA
%Datetime.datatype;	An ISO 8601 format date and time	CDATA

Parameter Entity Reference	Required Type	XML Type
`%FPI.datatype;`	An ISO 8879 formal public identifier	CDATA
`%LanguageCode.datatype;`	An RFC 3066 language code	NMTOKEN
`%URI.datatype;`	A Uniform Resource Identifier (URI)	CDATA
`%URIs.datatype;`	A space-separated list of URIs	CDATA

Schema-aware parsers can enforce these data types, which makes schema-validated XHTML somewhat stronger and more robust than DTD-validated XML.

The namespace-qualified names module

The namespace-qualified names module, `xhtml-qname-1.mod`, is divided into two sections. Section A declares the namespace URIs and prefixes used for XHTML. By redefining the entities in this part of the module you can choose which namespace prefix to use or to use no prefix at all (the default). This is normally done in the driver DTD, as you'll see shortly.

Table 28-4 lists the various parameter entity references declared in Section A, their default values, and their purposes. The two most important entities are `%XHTML.prefixed;` and `%XHTML.prefix`. To use namespace prefixes on all elements, define `%XHTML.prefixed;` as `INCLUDE` and `%XHTML.prefix` as the prefix you want to use, such as `html`.

Table 28-4
Parameter Entities Defined in the Qualified Names Module

Parameter Entity Reference	Purpose	Default value
`%NS.prefixed;`	whether or not to use namespace prefixes, as inherited from the driver DTD	IGNORE
`%XHTML.prefixed;`	whether or not to use namespace prefixes	`%NS.prefixed;`
`%XHTML.xmlns;`	the namespace for all XHTML elements	`http://www.w3.org/1999/xhtml`
`%XHTML.prefix`	the namespace prefix	the empty string (i.e. no prefix)
`%XHTML.pfx;`	the prefix used when prefixing is active	the empty string (i.e. no prefix)

Continued

Table 28-4 *(continued)*

Parameter Entity Reference	Purpose	Default value
`%xhtml-qname-extra.mod;`	the name of the module from which to load additional qualified names	the empty string (no such module is loaded)
`%XHTML.xmlns.extra.attrib;`	namespace declaration attributes for non-XHTML applications that are embedded in XHTML such as MathML or SVG	the empty string (only XHTML elements are included)
`%NS.decl.attrib;`	all namespace declarations used in the DTD, including the namespace declaration for XHTML	`xmlns:%XHTML.prefix;` `%URI.datatype;` `#FIXED` `'%XHTML.xmlns;'` `%XHTML.xmlns.extra.attrib;`
`%XLINK.xmlns.attrib;`	a placeholder for future XLink support	the empty string (XLink is not supported yet)
`%XHTML.xmlns.attrib;`	all namespace declarations used in the DTD including the namespace declarations for XHTML and XLink	`xmlns %URI.datatype; #FIXED` `'%XHTML.xmlns;'` `%XLINK.xmlns.attrib;`
`% xhtml-qname.redecl;`	the module from which to load replacements for the standard qualified names	the empty string (do not change the normal names of XHTML elements)

Section B of the qualified names module declares the prefixed names for all the different elements used in XHTML. The actual name of each element is the lowercase name of the element followed by `.qname`. For example, this section defines the names of the block structural elements:

```
<!-- module:  xhtml-blkstruct-1.mod -->
<!ENTITY % div.qname     "%XHTML.pfx;div" >
<!ENTITY % p.qname       "%XHTML.pfx;p" >
```

There are declarations like this for all the standard HTML elements.

The common attributes module

The common attributes module, `xhtml-attribs-1.mod`, declares parameter entities that represent parts of `ATTLIST` declarations for attributes that apply to all or most HTML elements such as `id`, `class`, and `lang`. For instance, this is the entity declaration for the `title` attribute:

```
<!ENTITY % title.attrib
    "title        %Text.datatype;              #IMPLIED"
>
```

These are then grouped into collections of attributes. For example, this is the declaration for the core attributes entity:

```
<!ENTITY % Core.attrib
    "%XHTML.xmlns.attrib;
    %id.attrib;
    %class.attrib;
    %title.attrib;
    %Core.extra.attrib;"
>
```

Finally all the different collections are grouped into one master collection called %Common.attrib; that includes all of them. Table 28-5 summarizes the different parameter entities defined in this module and the attributes they represent.

Table 28-5
Common Attributes and Attribute Groups Defined in Modular XHTML

Parameter entity Reference	Attributes Included
%id.attrib;	id
%class.attrib;	class
%title.attrib;	title
%Core.extra.attrib;	
%Core.attrib;	xmlns, id, class, title
%lang.attrib;	xml:lang
%dir.attrib;	dir
%I18n.attrib;	dir, xml:lang
%Common.extra.attrib;	
%Events.attrib;	
%Common.attrib;	xmlns, id, class, title, dir, xml:lang

This table is not the final word on what attributes belong to which parameter entities. Many of these can be redefined. For instance, three of them, Core.extra.attrib, Common.extra.attrib, and Events.attrib, have empty replacement text by default. They only exist so that other modules can redefine them.

Furthermore, some of these attributes can be controlled by other parameter entities that determine whether to `INCLUDE` or `IGNORE` a particular set. For example, the internationalization attributes are controlled by the definition of `%XHTML.bidi;`.

```
<![%XHTML.bidi;[
<!ENTITY % dir.attrib
    "dir          ( ltr | rtl )              #IMPLIED"
>

<!ENTITY % I18n.attrib
    "%dir.attrib;
     %lang.attrib;"
>

]]>
<!ENTITY % I18n.attrib
    "%lang.attrib;"
>
```

If `%XHTML.bidi;` is set to `INCLUDE`, then `I18n.attrib` includes the `dir` attribute. If `%XHTML.bidi;` resolves to `IGNORE`, then `I18n.attrib` includes only the `xml:lang` attribute.

The character entity modules

The character entities module, `xhtml-charent-1.mod`, loads the three entity set modules that define all of HTML's standard entities such as `&copy;` for the copyright sign © or `&Omega;` for the capital Greek letter omega Ω. There are three of these entity sets modules, each containing a different collection of characters:

✦ `xhtml-lat1.ent`: characters 160 through 255 of Latin-1

✦ `xhtml-special.ent`: assorted useful characters and punctuation marks from outside the Latin-1 set such as the Euro sign and the em dash

✦ `xhtml-symbol.ent`: the Greek alphabet and assorted symbols commonly used for math like ∞ and ∫

The filenames of the entity modules are distinguished from the usual modules because they all end in `.ent` rather than in `.mod`.

For example, these are the lines from `xhtml-symbol.ent` that declare the `&infin;` and `&ang;` entities:

```
<!ENTITY infin    "&#8734;" ><!-- infinity, U+221E ISOtech -->
<!ENTITY ang      "&#8736;" ><!-- angle, U+2220 ISOamso -->
```

The Driver DTD

The modules discussed so far all provide parts of XHTML, but none of them are suitable for use as the DTD of an actual XHTML document. None of them can be referenced from a document type declaration like this:

```
<!DOCTYPE html SYSTEM "xhtml-framework-1.mod">
```

The DTD that puts them all together so that it can be referenced in a document type declaration is called the *driver DTD*, and in fact there's more than one. One of the advantages of modular XHTML is that you can easily customize a driver DTD to meet the needs of your own documents. Sometimes this may mean deleting modules that you don't use such as the table module. At other times it may mean adding in extra pieces, such as MathML equations, that aren't part of standard HTML.

Driver DTDs are customized by redefining the parameter entity references that control particular modules. Each driver DTD is responsible for:

✦ Deciding whether to use namespace prefixes or the default namespace by setting the NS.prefixed entity to IGNORE (no prefixes) or INCLUDE (use prefixes)

✦ Specifying what namespace prefix to use by setting the XHTML.prefix entity

✦ Locating the document model by setting the xhtml-model.mod entity

✦ Loading all the modules the instance documents will use

In addition, the driver DTD may choose to predefine some of the entity references used in the modules to customize the content or attributes of various elements. Alternately, this can be done in a custom document model module or in a redeclaration module.

For example, Listing 28-3 contains the XHTML Basic driver DTD. This is a simple DTD suitable for uncomplicated Web pages. It does not use namespace prefixes (NS.prefixed is set to IGNORE) and thus the XHTML.prefix entity is set to the empty string. It uses the document model found at the relative URL xhtml-basic10-model-1.mod. It loads the structural, text, hypertext, list, image, tables, forms, link, metainformation, base, object, and param element modules, and ignores the rest.

Listing 28-3: **xhtml-basic10.dtd: The XHTML Basic Driver DTD**

```
<!-- XHTML Basic 1.0 DTD  .............................. -->
<!-- file: xhtml-basic10.dtd -->

<!-- XHTML Basic 1.0 DTD

     This is XHTML Basic, a proper subset of XHTML.

The Extensible HyperText Markup Language (XHTML)
Copyright 1998-2000 World Wide Web Consortium
(Massachusetts Institute of Technology, Institut National de
Recherche en Informatique et en Automatique, Keio University).
All Rights Reserved.

Permission to use, copy, modify and distribute the XHTML Basic
DTD and its accompanying documentation for any purpose and
without fee is hereby granted in perpetuity, provided that the
above copyright notice and this paragraph appear in all
copies.  The copyright holders make no representation about
the suitability of the DTD for any purpose.

It is provided "as is" without expressed or implied warranty.

Editors: Murray M. Altheim <mailto:altheim@eng.sun.com>
         Peter Stark        <mailto:Peter.Stark@ecs.ericsson.se>
      Revision:   $Id: xhtml-basic10.dtd,v 2.13 2000/12/18
                  12:56:23 mimasa Exp $ SMI

-->
<!-- This is the driver file for version 1.0 of the XHTML Basic
     DTD.

   This DTD is identified by the PUBLIC and SYSTEM identifiers:

     PUBLIC: "-//W3C//DTD XHTML Basic 1.0//EN"
   SYSTEM: "http://www.w3.org/TR/xhtml-basic/xhtml-basic10.dtd"
-->
<!ENTITY % XHTML.version  "-//W3C//DTD XHTML Basic 1.0//EN" >

<!-- Use this URI to identify the default namespace:

        "http://www.w3.org/1999/xhtml"

     See the Qualified Names module for information
     on the use of namespace prefixes in the DTD.
-->
<!ENTITY % NS.prefixed "IGNORE" >
<!ENTITY % XHTML.prefix  "" >

<!-- Reserved for use with the XLink namespace:
-->
```

```
<!ENTITY % XLINK.xmlns "" >
<!ENTITY % XLINK.xmlns.attrib "" >

<!-- For example, if you are using XHTML Basic 1.0 directly,
     use the FPI in the DOCTYPE declaration, with the xmlns
     attribute on the document element to identify the default
     namespace:

         <?xml version="1.0"?>
         <!DOCTYPE html PUBLIC "-//W3C//DTD XHTML Basic 1.0//EN"
          "http://www.w3.org/TR/xhtml-basic/xhtml-basic10.dtd" >
         <html xmlns="http://www.w3.org/1999/xhtml"
               xml:lang="en" >
          ...
          </html>
-->

<!-- reserved for future use with document profiles -->
<!ENTITY % XHTML.profile  "" >

<!-- Bidirectional Text features
     This feature-test entity is used to declare elements
     and attributes used for bidirectional text support.
-->
<!ENTITY % XHTML.bidi  "IGNORE" >

<?doc type="doctype" role="title" { XHTML Basic 1.0 } ?>

<!-- :::::::::::::::::::::::::::::::::::::::::::::::::::::::: -->

<!ENTITY % xhtml-events.module    "IGNORE" >
<!ENTITY % xhtml-bdo.module       "%XHTML.bidi;" >

<!ENTITY % xhtml-model.mod
     PUBLIC
      "-//W3C//ENTITIES XHTML Basic 1.0 Document Model 1.0//EN"
      "xhtml-basic10-model-1.mod" >

<!ENTITY % xhtml-framework.mod
     PUBLIC "-//W3C//ENTITIES XHTML Modular Framework 1.0//EN"
             "xhtml-framework-1.mod" >
%xhtml-framework.mod;

<!ENTITY % pre.content
     "( #PCDATA
      | %InlStruct.class;
      %InlPhras.class;
      %Anchor.class;
      %Inline.extra; )*"
```

Continued

Listing 28-3 *(continued)*

```
>

<!ENTITY % xhtml-text.mod
    PUBLIC "-//W3C//ELEMENTS XHTML Text 1.0//EN"
           "xhtml-text-1.mod" >
%xhtml-text.mod;

<!ENTITY % xhtml-hypertext.mod
    PUBLIC "-//W3C//ELEMENTS XHTML Hypertext 1.0//EN"
           "xhtml-hypertext-1.mod" >
%xhtml-hypertext.mod;

<!ENTITY % xhtml-list.mod
    PUBLIC "-//W3C//ELEMENTS XHTML Lists 1.0//EN"
           "xhtml-list-1.mod" >
%xhtml-list.mod;

<!-- :::::::::::::::::::::::::::::::::::::::::::::::::::::::::: -->

<!-- Image Module  ........................................ -->
<!ENTITY % xhtml-image.module "INCLUDE" >
<![%xhtml-image.module;[
<!ENTITY % xhtml-image.mod
    PUBLIC "-//W3C//ELEMENTS XHTML Images 1.0//EN"
           "xhtml-image-1.mod" >
%xhtml-image.mod;]]>

<!-- Tables Module
........................................ -->
<!ENTITY % xhtml-table.module "INCLUDE" >
<![%xhtml-table.module;[
<!ENTITY % xhtml-table.mod
    PUBLIC "-//W3C//ELEMENTS XHTML Basic Tables 1.0//EN"
           "xhtml-basic-table-1.mod" >
%xhtml-table.mod;]]>

<!-- Forms Module  ........................................ -->
<!ENTITY % xhtml-form.module "INCLUDE" >
<![%xhtml-form.module;[
<!ENTITY % xhtml-form.mod
    PUBLIC "-//W3C//ELEMENTS XHTML Basic Forms 1.0//EN"
           "xhtml-basic-form-1.mod" >
%xhtml-form.mod;]]>

<!-- Link Element Module
........................................ -->
<!ENTITY % xhtml-link.module "INCLUDE" >
<![%xhtml-link.module;[
<!ENTITY % xhtml-link.mod
    PUBLIC "-//W3C//ELEMENTS XHTML Link Element 1.0//EN"
           "xhtml-link-1.mod" >
```

```
%xhtml-link.mod;]]>

<!-- Document Metainformation Module
.......................... -->
<!ENTITY % xhtml-meta.module "INCLUDE" >
<![%xhtml-meta.module;[
<!ENTITY % xhtml-meta.mod
     PUBLIC "-//W3C//ELEMENTS XHTML Metainformation 1.0//EN"
            "xhtml-meta-1.mod" >
%xhtml-meta.mod;]]>

<!-- Base Element Module
.................................. -->
<!ENTITY % xhtml-base.module "INCLUDE" >
<![%xhtml-base.module;[
<!ENTITY % xhtml-base.mod
     PUBLIC "-//W3C//ELEMENTS XHTML Base Element 1.0//EN"
            "xhtml-base-1.mod" >
%xhtml-base.mod;]]>

<!-- Param Element Module
................................. -->
<!ENTITY % xhtml-param.module "INCLUDE" >
<![%xhtml-param.module;[
<!ENTITY % xhtml-param.mod
     PUBLIC "-//W3C//ELEMENTS XHTML Param Element 1.0//EN"
            "xhtml-param-1.mod" >
%xhtml-param.mod;]]>

<!-- Embedded Object Module
................................. -->
<!ENTITY % xhtml-object.module "INCLUDE" >
<![%xhtml-object.module;[
<!ENTITY % xhtml-object.mod
     PUBLIC "-//W3C//ELEMENTS XHTML Embedded Object 1.0//EN"
            "xhtml-object-1.mod" >
%xhtml-object.mod;]]>

<!ENTITY % xhtml-struct.mod
     PUBLIC "-//W3C//ELEMENTS XHTML Document Structure 1.0//EN"
            "xhtml-struct-1.mod" >
%xhtml-struct.mod;

<!-- end of XHTML Basic 1.0 DTD ......................... -->
```

However, this is not the only possible DTD for modular XHTML. There are others, and you can create your own as well. For example, Listing 28-4 is a minimal driver DTD that does use the namespace prefix html. It refers to the document model xhtml-minimal-model.mod, and it loads only the framework, structural, and text modules. It omits links, tables, forms, images, and a lot more. An HTML variant like this might be suitable for embedding a little marked-up narrative text inside a larger, non-HTML application. This is not part of any W3C specification. It's just something I created for this book because it seemed useful to me. You're equally free to make your own drivers to meet your needs.

Listing 28-4: xhtml-minimal.dtd: A Minimal XHTML driver DTD

```
<!-- XHTML Minimal DTD  .............................. -->
<!-- file: xhtml-minimal.dtd -->

<!-- XHTML Minimal DTD

This is XHTML Minimal, a proper subset of XHTML.

The Extensible HyperText Markup Language (XHTML)
Copyright 1998-2000 World Wide Web Consortium
(Massachusetts Institute of Technology, Institut National de
Recherche en Informatique et en Automatique, Keio University).
All Rights Reserved.

Permission to use, copy, modify and distribute the XHTML Basic
DTD and its accompanying documentation for any purpose and
without fee is hereby granted in perpetuity, provided that the
above copyright notice and this paragraph appear in all
copies.  The copyright holders make no representation about
the suitability of the DTD for any purpose.

This is an even smaller version of the XHTML Basic DTD
developed by Elliotte Rusty Harold for the XML Bible,
Gold Edition.

It is provided "as is" without expressed or implied warranty.

Editors: Elliotte Rusty Harold <mailto:elharo@metalab.unc.edu>
Revision:   2001/05/14

-->
<!ENTITY % NS.prefixed "INCLUDE" >
<!ENTITY % XHTML.prefix  "html" >

<!-- Reserved for use with the XLink namespace:
-->
<!ENTITY % XLINK.xmlns "" >
<!ENTITY % XLINK.xmlns.attrib "" >

<!-- reserved for future use with document profiles -->
<!ENTITY % XHTML.profile  "" >
```

```
<!-- Bidirectional Text features
     This feature-test entity is used to declare elements
     and attributes used for bidirectional text support.
-->
<!ENTITY % XHTML.bidi  "IGNORE" >

<!-- :::::::::::::::::::::::::::::::::::::::::::::::::::::::: -->

<!ENTITY % xhtml-events.module    "IGNORE" >
<!ENTITY % xhtml-bdo.module       "%XHTML.bidi;" >

<!ENTITY % xhtml-model.mod
      PUBLIC
        "-//ERH//ENTITIES XHTML Minimal Document Model 1.0//EN"
        "xhtml-minimal-model.mod" >

<!ENTITY % xhtml-framework.mod
      PUBLIC "-//W3C//ENTITIES XHTML Modular Framework 1.0//EN"
             "xhtml-framework-1.mod" >
%xhtml-framework.mod;

<!ENTITY % xhtml-text.mod
      PUBLIC "-//W3C//ELEMENTS XHTML Text 1.0//EN"
             "xhtml-text-1.mod" >
%xhtml-text.mod;

<!ENTITY % xhtml-struct.mod
      PUBLIC "-//W3C//ELEMENTS XHTML Document Structure 1.0//EN"
             "xhtml-struct-1.mod" >
%xhtml-struct.mod;

<!-- end of XHTML Minimal 1.0 DTD  ...................... -->
```

You can also add things to the driver DTD. For instance, if you wanted to add MathML to XHTML Basic you could simply put this at the end of the normal XHTML Basic DTD:

```
<!ENTITY % mathml.dtd
      PUBLIC "-//W3C//DTD MathML 2.0//EN"
             "http://www.w3.org/TR/MathML2/dtd/mathml2.dtd" >
%mathml.dtd;
```

However, you'd also have to change the document model to enable MathML math elements to appear where you wanted them. I take this up in the next section.

The Document Model

In XHTML, the document model is primarily responsible for defining the permissible contents of elements. It accomplishes this by defining three parameter entity references:

- ✦ %Block.mix;
- ✦ %Flow.mix;
- ✦ %Inline.mix;

Many XHTML elements have content models specified almost completely by one of these content models. For instance, the inline code element defined in the Text module declares its content model like this:

```
<!ENTITY % code.element  "INCLUDE" >
<![%code.element;[
<!ENTITY % code.content
    "( #PCDATA | %Inline.mix; )*"
>
<!ENTITY % code.qname  "code" >
<!ELEMENT %code.qname;  %code.content; >
<!-- end of code.element -->]]>
```

When most of the entities and INCLUDE blocks are resolved what's left is this:

```
<!ELEMENT code ( #PCDATA | %Inline.mix; )* >
```

In fact, more than a dozen elements use exactly this content model. The innards of a code element are pretty much the same as the innards of an em element, a strong element, a kbd element, and more.

This isn't true of all elements, though. Some elements have unique content models. For instance, a table can only contain caption, col, colgroup, thead, tbody, tr, and tfoot elements. Because this content model is unique to tables it is defined completely within the tables module like this:

```
<!ENTITY % table.element  "INCLUDE" >
<![%table.element;[
<!ENTITY % table.content
    "( %caption.qname;?, ( %col.qname;* | %colgroup.qname;* ),
    (( %thead.qname;?, %tfoot.qname;?, %tbody.qname;+ ) |
    ( %tr.qname;+ )))"
>
<!ELEMENT %table.qname;  %table.content; >
<!-- end of table.element -->]]>
```

It is still written using parameter entity references, and these could be predefined in the document model. However, that would be rare. Most of the time, only the cross-module parameter entity references like %Block.mix; are predefined in the document model.

The td element, by contrast, can contain almost any nonstructural HTML element, and thus its content model is specified using the common content model %Flow.mix; like this:

```
<!ENTITY % td.element   "INCLUDE" >
<![%td.element;[
<!ENTITY % td.content
     "( #PCDATA | %Flow.mix; )*"
>
<!ELEMENT %td.qname;  %td.content; >
<!-- end of td.element -->]]>
```

The XHTML Basic document model

Listing 28-5 shows the XHTML Basic document model module, xhtml-basic10-model-1.mod. This is a straightforward and simple model that supports most of the nondeprecated features of HTML.

Listing 28-5: **xhtml-basic10-model-1.mod: The XHTML Basic Document Model DTD**

```
<!-- .............................................. -->
<!-- XHTML Basic 1.0 Document Model Module  .............. -->
<!-- file: xhtml-basic10-model-1.mod

     This is XHTML Basic, a proper subset of XHTML.
     Copyright 1998-2000 W3C (MIT, INRIA, Keio), All Rights
     Reserved.
     Revision: $Id: xhtml-basic10-model-1.mod,v 2.8 2000/11/03
     14:28:25 mimasa Exp $ SMI

     This DTD module is identified by the PUBLIC and SYSTEM
     identifiers:

PUBLIC
   "-//W3C//ENTITIES XHTML Basic 1.0 Document Model 1.0//EN"
SYSTEM
   "http://www.w3.org/TR/xhtml-basic/xhtml-basic10-model-1.mod"

     Revisions:
```

Continued

Listing 28-5 *(continued)*

```
    (none)
    .............................................. -->

<!-- XHTML Basic Document Model

    This module describes the groupings of elements that make
    up common content models for XHTML elements.
-->

<!-- Optional Elements in head  .............. -->

<!ENTITY % HeadOpts.mix
    "( %meta.qname; | %link.qname; | %object.qname; )*" >

<!-- Miscellaneous Elements  ................ -->

<!ENTITY % Misc.class "" >

<!-- Inline Elements  ...................... -->

<!ENTITY % InlStruct.class "%br.qname; | %span.qname;" >

<!ENTITY % InlPhras.class
    "| %em.qname; | %strong.qname; | %dfn.qname; | %code.qname;
     %samp.qname; | %kbd.qname; | %var.qname; | %cite.qname;
     %abbr.qname; | %acronym.qname; | %q.qname;" >

<!ENTITY % InlPres.class "" >

<!ENTITY % I18n.class "" >

<!ENTITY % Anchor.class "| %a.qname;" >

<!ENTITY % InlSpecial.class "| %img.qname; | %object.qname;" >

<!ENTITY % InlForm.class
    "| %input.qname; | %select.qname; | %textarea.qname;
     | %label.qname;"
>

<!ENTITY % Inline.extra "" >

<!ENTITY % Inline.class
    "%InlStruct.class;
     %InlPhras.class;
     %Anchor.class;
     %InlSpecial.class;
     %InlForm.class;
     %Inline.extra;"
>
```

```
<!ENTITY % InlNoAnchor.class
    "%InlStruct.class;
     %InlPhras.class;
     %InlSpecial.class;
     %InlForm.class;
     %Inline.extra;"
>

<!ENTITY % InlNoAnchor.mix
    "%InlNoAnchor.class;
     %Misc.class;"
>

<!ENTITY % Inline.mix
    "%Inline.class;
     %Misc.class;"
>

<!-- Block Elements  ...................... -->

<!ENTITY % Heading.class
    "%h1.qname; | %h2.qname; | %h3.qname;
     | %h4.qname; | %h5.qname; | %h6.qname;"
>
<!ENTITY % List.class  "%ul.qname; | %ol.qname; | %dl.qname;" >

<!ENTITY % Table.class "| %table.qname;" >

<!ENTITY % Form.class  "| %form.qname;" >

<!ENTITY % BlkStruct.class "%p.qname; | %div.qname;" >

<!ENTITY % BlkPhras.class
    "| %pre.qname; | %blockquote.qname; | %address.qname;"
>

<!ENTITY % BlkPres.class "" >

<!ENTITY % BlkSpecial.class
    "%Table.class;
     %Form.class;"
>

<!ENTITY % Block.extra "" >

<!ENTITY % Block.class
    "%BlkStruct.class;
     %BlkPhras.class;
     %BlkSpecial.class;
     %Block.extra;"
>
```

Continued

Listing 28-5 *(continued)*

```
<!ENTITY % Block.mix
    "%Heading.class;
    | %List.class;
    | %Block.class;
    %Misc.class;"
>

<!-- All Content Elements  ................. -->

<!-- declares all content except tables
-->
<!ENTITY % FlowNoTable.mix
    "%Heading.class;
    | %List.class;
    | %BlkStruct.class;
    %BlkPhras.class;
    %Form.class;
    %Block.extra;
    | %Inline.class;
    %Misc.class;"
>

<!ENTITY % Flow.mix
    "%Heading.class;
    | %List.class;
    | %Block.class;
    | %Inline.class;
    %Misc.class;"
>

<!-- end of xhtml-basic10-model-1.mod -->
```

This module progressively builds larger collections out of smaller pieces. For instance, the Flow.mix entity comprises five other entities: Heading.class, List.class, Block.class, Inline.class, and Misc.class. Each of these entities is built from still other pieces. Table 28-6 lists the parameter entities and their customary replacement text as given in XHTML Basic, assuming the standard element names are used without namespace prefixes. You'll find these same parameter entities in the document models for XHTML 1.1 and XHTML 1.1 plus MathML. However, in those cases, the replacement text will be a little larger and contain a few more elements.

Table 28-6
Document Model Parameter Entities Defined in XHTML Basic

Parameter Entity	Replacement Text
%HeadOpts.mix;	(meta | link | object)*
%Misc.class;	
%InlStruct.class;	br | span
%InlPhras.class;	| em | strong | dfn | code | samp | kbd | var | cite | abbr | acronym | q
%InlPres.class;	
%I18n.class;	
%Anchor.class;	| a
%InlSpecial.class;	| img | object
%InlForm.class;	| input | select | textarea | label
%Inline.extra ;	
%Inline.class;	br | span | em | strong | dfn | code | samp | kbd | var | cite | abbr | acronym | q | a | img | object | input | select | textarea | label
%InlNoAnchor.class;	br | span | em | strong | dfn | code | samp | kbd | var | cite | abbr | acronym | q | img | object | input | select | textarea | label
%InlNoAnchor.mix;	br | span | em | strong | dfn | code | samp | kbd | var | cite | abbr | acronym | q | img | object | input | select | textarea | label
%Inline.mix;	br | span | em | strong | dfn | code | samp | kbd | var | cite | abbr | acronym | q | a | img | object | input | select | textarea | label
%Heading.class;	h1 | h2 | h3 | h4 | h5 | h6
%List.class;	ul | ol | dl
%Table.class;	| table
%Form.class;	| form
%BlkStruct.class;	p | div
%BlkPhras.class;	| pre | blockquote | address
%BlkPres.class;	

Continued

Table 28-6 *(continued)*

Parameter Entity	Replacement Text
%BlkSpecial.class;	| table | form
%Block.extra;	
%Block.class;	p | div | pre | blockquote | address | table | form
%Block.mix;	h1 | h2 | h3 | h4 | h5 | h6 | ul | ol | dl | p | div | pre | blockquote | address | table | form
%FlowNoTable.mix;	h1 | h2 | h3 | h4 | h5 | h6 | ul | ol | dl | p | div | pre | blockquote | address | form | br | span | em | strong | dfn | code | samp | kbd | var | cite | abbr | acronym | q | a | img | object | input | select | textarea | label
%Flow.mix;	h1 | h2 | h3 | h4 | h5 | h6 | ul | ol | dl | p | div | pre | blockquote | address | table | form | br | span | em | strong | dfn | code | samp | kbd | var | cite | abbr | acronym | q | a | img | object | input | select | textarea | label

A number of the entities in Table 28-6 are empty by default. There are two reasons for this. Some of them, such as %InlPres.class; and %Blockpres.class;, hold elements XHTML Basic does not allow. For instance, InlPres.class represents inline presentational elements such as i and b. These are included in XHTML 1.1 but not in XHTML Basic. In XHTML 1.1, %InlPres.class; and %Blockpres.class; are not empty.

The other category of empty parameter entities are the extra entities such as %Inline.extra; and %Block.extra;. By redefining these, you can add elements to the content models of many elements. For instance, to allow the MathML math element to appear wherever a block level element can appear, you simply redefine %Block.extra; like this:

```
<!ENTITY % Block.extra "| math" >
```

Of course, you also have to load the MathML DTD that defines the math element.

When you're mixing XHTML markup into your own applications, you may want to use these parameter entity references to define the content models for your own elements. For instance, a NOTE element in a PATIENT_RECORD might be allowed to contain essentially any XHTML block-level elements. In this case, you'd import the XHTML Basic DTD into your own DTD and then declare the NOTE element like this:

```
<!ENTITY % xhtml-basic SYSTEM "xhtml-basic10.dtd">
%xhtml_basic
<!ELEMENT NOTE ((%Block.mix;)*)>
```

Because of interdependencies among the different XHTML modules, it is necessary to pull in the full XHTML Basic DTD rather than just the document model or the block-level elements you actually want. Still, the extra elements won't get in your way. They're defined but they're not allowed anywhere inside the DTD for the PATIENT_RECORD.

This is a case in which you might want to use a prefix for the XHTML elements rather than rely on the default namespace, especially if the NOTE and PATIENT_RECORD elements themselves use the default namespace. In this case, you'd just predefine the NS.prefixed and XHTML.prefix entities somewhere in the patient record DTD before you load the XHTML driver DTD. For example,

```
<!ENTITY % NS.prefixed "INCLUDE" >
<!ENTITY % XHTML.prefix  "html" >
<!ENTITY % xhtml-basic SYSTEM "xhtml-basic10.dtd">
%xhtml_basic
<!ELEMENT NOTE ((%Block.mix)*)>
```

Now all the NOTE elements will contain prefixed HTML. You'll still need to declare the XHTML namespace with an xmlns:html attribute on each NOTE element or one of its ancestors in the PATIENT_RECORD documents. One possibility is to make the declaration a fixed attribute of the root PATIENT_RECORD element in its DTD, like this:

```
<!ATTLIST PATIENT_RECORD
        xmlns:html CDATA #FIXED "http://www.w3.org/1999/xhtml">
```

A minimal document model

If you define your own subsets of XHTML, you'll probably need to define your own document models as well. Listing 28-6 is a minimal XHTML document for use with the minimal XHTML driver DTD seen previously in Listing 28-4. It's based on the XHTML Basic document model module, but it removes forms, tables, images, lists, and more from the entity references defined here. The end result is a very Spartan vocabulary.

> ### Listing 28-6: **xhtml-minimal-model.mod: A Minimal XHTML Document Model DTD**

```
<!-- ...................................................... -->
<!-- XHTML Minimal Document Model Module  ................. -->
<!-- file: xhtml-minimal-model.mod

    This is XHTML Minimal, a proper subset of XHTML, derived
    from XHTML Basic for the XML Bible Gold Edition.

    This DTD module is identified by the PUBLIC and SYSTEM
    identifiers:

    PUBLIC
     "-//ERH//ENTITIES XHTML Basic 1.0 Document Model 1.0//EN"
    SYSTEM "xhtml-minimal-model.mod"

    ...................................................... -->

<!-- XHTML Minimal Document Model

    This module describes the groupings of elements that make
    up common content models for XHTML elements.
-->

<!-- Optional Elements in head  .............. -->

<!ENTITY % HeadOpts.mix "( )*" >

<!-- Miscellaneous Elements  ................. -->

<!ENTITY % Misc.class "" >

<!-- Inline Elements  ....................... -->

<!ENTITY % InlStruct.class "%br.qname; | %span.qname;" >

<!ENTITY % InlPhras.class
    "| %em.qname; | %strong.qname; | %dfn.qname; | %code.qname;
     | %samp.qname; | %kbd.qname; | %var.qname; | %cite.qname;
     | %abbr.qname; | %acronym.qname; | %q.qname;" >

<!ENTITY % InlPres.class "" >

<!ENTITY % I18n.class "" >

<!ENTITY % Anchor.class "" >

<!ENTITY % InlSpecial.class "" >

<!ENTITY % InlForm.class "" >
```

```
<!ENTITY % Inline.extra "" >

<!ENTITY % Inline.class
     "%InlStruct.class;
      %InlPhras.class;
      %Anchor.class;
      %InlSpecial.class;
      %InlForm.class;
      %Inline.extra;"
>

<!ENTITY % InlNoAnchor.class
     "%InlStruct.class;
      %InlPhras.class;
      %InlSpecial.class;
      %InlForm.class;
      %Inline.extra;"
>

<!ENTITY % InlNoAnchor.mix
     "%InlNoAnchor.class;
      %Misc.class;"
>

<!ENTITY % Inline.mix
     "%Inline.class;
      %Misc.class;"
>

<!-- Block Elements  ........................ -->

<!ENTITY % Heading.class
     "%h1.qname; | %h2.qname; | %h3.qname;
      | %h4.qname; | %h5.qname; | %h6.qname;"
>
<!ENTITY % List.class  "" >

<!ENTITY % Table.class "" >

<!ENTITY % Form.class  "" >

<!ENTITY % BlkStruct.class "%p.qname; | %div.qname;" >

<!ENTITY % BlkPhras.class
    "| %pre.qname; | %blockquote.qname; | %address.qname;"
>

<!ENTITY % BlkPres.class "" >

<!ENTITY % BlkSpecial.class
     "%Table.class;
      %Form.class;"
```

Continued

Listing 28-6 *(continued)*

```
>

<!ENTITY % Block.extra "" >

<!ENTITY % Block.class
     "%BlkStruct.class;
      %BlkPhras.class;
      %BlkSpecial.class;
      %Block.extra;"
>

<!ENTITY % Block.mix
     "%Heading.class;
      | %List.class;
      | %Block.class;
      %Misc.class;"
>

<!-- All Content Elements  .................. -->

<!-- declares all content except tables
-->
<!ENTITY % FlowNoTable.mix
     "%Heading.class;
      | %List.class;
      | %BlkStruct.class;
      %BlkPhras.class;
      %Form.class;
      %Block.extra;
      | %Inline.class;
      %Misc.class;"
>

<!ENTITY % Flow.mix
     "%Heading.class;
      | %List.class;
      | %Block.class;
      | %Inline.class;
      %Misc.class;"
>

<!-- end of xhtml-minimal-model.mod -->
```

An alternate approach is to keep the normal XHTML Basic document model, but to add a new module that predefines the various entity references that you want to change. To do this, you'd point the parameter entity reference %xhtml-model. redecl; at your module containing the redeclarations, as shown in Listing 28-7.

Listing 28-7: xhtml-minimal-redecl.mod: A Content Model Redeclaration Module for Minimal XHTML

```
<!-- .............................................. -->
<!-- XHTML Minimal Redeclarations Module  ................ -->
<!-- file: xhtml-minimal-redecl.mod

    This is XHTML Minimal, a proper subset of XHTML, derived
    from XHTML Basic for the XML Bible Gold Edition.

    This DTD module is identified by the PUBLIC and SYSTEM
    identifiers:

    PUBLIC
     "-//ERH//ENTITIES XHTML Minimal 1.0 Redeclarations 1.0//EN"
    SYSTEM "xhtml-minimal-redecl.mod"

    .......................................... -->

<!-- XHTML Minimal Document Model

    This module describes the groupings of elements that make
    up common content models for XHTML elements.
-->

<!-- Optional Elements in head  ............. -->

<!ENTITY % HeadOpts.mix "( )*" >

<!ENTITY % I18n.class "" >

<!ENTITY % Anchor.class "" >

<!ENTITY % InlSpecial.class "" >

<!ENTITY % InlForm.class "" >

<!-- Block Elements  ........................ -->

<!ENTITY % List.class  "" >

<!ENTITY % Table.class "" >

<!ENTITY % Form.class  "" >

<!-- end of xhtml-minimal-redecl.mod -->
```

This module is much smaller than the module in Listing 28-6 because it only has to change a few entity references. In many cases, it can just accept the defaults.

A Sample Schema Module

The schema implementation of XHTML modularization is not nearly as complete as the DTD implementation, mostly because the W3C Schema Language took a lot longer to finish than was expected. Nonetheless, version 1.0 is now more or less complete, and work has begun on schema implementations of the various XHTML modules. Listing 28-8 demonstrates the schema version of the list module, as defined in the March 22, 2001, Working Draft of *Modularization of XHTML in XML Schema*. As you can see this is based on the October 24, 2000, candidate recommendation of the W3C XML Schema Language rather than the final recommendation syntax from May 2, 2001, described in Chapter 23. However, aside from the namespace URIs, this is essentially as it should be in the final draft.

Listing 28-8: **The List Module Schema**

```
<?xml version="1.0" encoding="UTF-8"?>
<xsd:schema xmlns:xsd="http://www.w3.org/2000/10/XMLSchema"
            targetNamespace="http://www.w3.org/1999/xhtml"
         xmlns:xsi="http://www.w3.org/2000/10/XMLSchema-instance"
         xsi:schemaLocation="http://www.w3.org/2000/10/XMLSchema
                      http://www.w3.org/2000/10/XMLSchema.xsd"
            elementFormDefault="unqualified"
            version="1.1"
>
<xsd:annotation>
     <xsd:documentation>
/**
* This is the XML Schema Lists module for XHTML
*   Please use this formal public identifier to identify it:
*           "-//W3C//ELEMENTS XHTML Lists 1.0//EN"
*
*/
  </xsd:documentation>

     <xsd:documentation>
/**
*
* Versioning block

* Author: Daniel Austin
* $RCSfile: xhtml-list-1.xsd,v $
* $Revision: 1.6 $
* $Date: 2001/03/21 22:19:48 $
* $Author: daustin $
* (remove the NO below to see the full revision log)
* Log: $NOLog: $
*
*/
  </xsd:documentation>
```

```
   <xsd:documentation>
/**
* Lists
*
*        dl, dt, dd, ol, ul, li
*
*     This module declares the list-oriented element types
*     and their attributes.
*
*/
   </xsd:documentation>

<xsd:documentation source="xhtml-copyright-1.txt"/>

</xsd:annotation>

  <!-- definition lists -->
  <!-- dt: Definition Term  -->
  <xsd:attributeGroup name="dt.attlist">
    <xsd:attributeGroup ref="Common.attrib"/>
    <xsd:anyAttribute namespace="##other"/>
  </xsd:attributeGroup>

  <xsd:complexType name="dt.type" mixed="true">
    <xsd:group ref="Inline.mix"/>
    <xsd:attributeGroup ref="dt.attlist"/>
  </xsd:complexType>

  <xsd:element name="dt" type="dt.type"/>

  <!-- dd: Definition Description  -->
  <xsd:attributeGroup name="dd.attlist">
    <xsd:attributeGroup ref="Common.attrib"/>
    <xsd:anyAttribute namespace="##other"/>
  </xsd:attributeGroup>

  <xsd:complexType name="dd.type" mixed="true">
    <xsd:group ref="Flow.mix"/>
    <xsd:attributeGroup ref="dd.attlist"/>
  </xsd:complexType>

  <xsd:element name="dd" type="dd.type"/>

  <!-- dl: Definition List  -->
  <xsd:attributeGroup name="dl.attlist">
    <xsd:attributeGroup ref="Common.attrib"/>
    <xsd:anyAttribute namespace="##other"/>
  </xsd:attributeGroup>
  <!-- content model? -->
  <xsd:group name="dl.content">
    <xsd:sequence minOccurs="1" maxOccurs="unbounded">
      <xsd:element ref="dt"/>
```

Continued

Listing 28-8 *(continued)*

```
      <xsd:element ref="dd"/>
    </xsd:sequence>
</xsd:group>

<xsd:complexType name="dl.type" mixed="true">
  <xsd:group ref="dl.content"/>
  <xsd:attributeGroup ref="dl.attlist"/>
</xsd:complexType>

<xsd:element name="dl" type="dl.type"/>

<!-- li: List Item -->
<xsd:attributeGroup name="li.attlist">
  <xsd:attributeGroup ref="Common.attrib"/>
  <xsd:anyAttribute namespace="##other"/>
</xsd:attributeGroup>

<xsd:complexType name="li.type" mixed="true">
  <xsd:group ref="Flow.mix"/>
  <xsd:attributeGroup ref="li.attlist"/>
</xsd:complexType>

<xsd:element name="li" type="li.type"/>

<!-- ol: Ordered List (numbered styles) -->
<xsd:attributeGroup name="ol.attlist">
  <xsd:attributeGroup ref="Common.attrib"/>
  <xsd:anyAttribute namespace="##other"/>
</xsd:attributeGroup>

<xsd:complexType name="ol.type">
  <xsd:sequence minOccurs="1">
    <xsd:element ref="li"/>
  </xsd:sequence>
  <xsd:attributeGroup ref="ol.attlist"/>
</xsd:complexType>

<xsd:element name="ol" type="ol.type"/>

<!-- ul: Unordered List -->
<xsd:attributeGroup name="ul.attlist">
  <xsd:attributeGroup ref="Common.attrib"/>
  <xsd:anyAttribute namespace="##other"/>
</xsd:attributeGroup>

<xsd:complexType name="ul.type">
  <xsd:sequence minOccurs="1">
    <xsd:element ref="li"/>
  </xsd:sequence>
  <xsd:attributeGroup ref="ul.attlist"/>
```

```
    </xsd:complexType>

    <xsd:element name="ul" type="ul.type"/>

  </xsd:schema>
```

A complete schema implementation of modular XHTML also requires schema versions of all the underlying framework modules such as the common attributes module and the data types module, as well as schemas for the document model. Instead of a driver DTD, the schema implementation of XHTML 1.1 uses a hub document. All of these are currently under development and may be available by the time you're reading this. Consult `http://www.w3.org/TR/xhtml-m12n-schema` for the latest information.

Summary

In this chapter, you learned about modular XHTML, a W3C recommendation for organizing XHTML as a set of semi-independent DTDs that are easy to mix and match with other XML applications. In particular, you learned that:

✦ Modular XHTML divides the different parts of HTML into 28 modules, each defining a related group of elements.

✦ These 28 modules depend on a framework module that defines entities all the modules use to specify element names, namespace URIs and prefixes, content models, and attribute types.

✦ A driver module integrates all the different parts of both the framework and the abstract modules.

✦ A document model module defines the common content models shared among the different modules.

✦ The abstract modules have concrete implementations as both DTDs and schemas.

✦ You can use your own driver modules and document model modules to integrate your own XML applications into XHTML or to subsume XHTML into your own applications.

The next chapter investigates an application that's built on top of XHTML Basic and modular XHTML — the Resource Directory Description Language (RDDL). RDDL adds a single `resource` element to XHTML Basic. The `resource` element is an XLink that can locate a resource associated with a particular namespace URI.

✦   ✦   ✦

The Resource Directory Description Language

If you've read Chapter 13, you know that there isn't a DTD or schema at the end of a namespace URI. In fact, there may well be no page there at all. Even though almost all namespace URIs are URLs, they do not actually locate anything. Namespace URLs are simply formal identifiers. This has proven to be completely counterintuitive and has led to many repetitions of the very frequently asked question, "What's at the end of a namespace URL?" on xml-dev and other XML mailing lists and newsgroups.

After answering this question for about the three thousandth time, Tim Bray and Jonathan Borden decided to turn the problem on its head. If they couldn't convince developers that a namespace URL didn't actually locate anything, then maybe they should convince document authors to use namespace URLs that did locate things instead. In particular, they decided to invent a new XML application for documents located at the end of a namespace URL. This application is called the Resource Directory Description Language, or simply RDDL (pronounced "riddle"). RDDL is a combination of XHTML Basic, XLink, and one new `resource` element. A RDDL document lists various documents that are related to an XML application identified by a particular namespace URL including but not limited to schemas, DTDs, specifications, style sheet, logos, software, and more. RDDL was carefully designed to be easily viewed in existing Web browsers by humans and to be straightforwardly machine readable to enable automated resource lookup by software.

The Problem

XSLT 1.0 is identified by the namespace URL `http://www.w3.org/1999/XSL/Transform`. After teaching numerous XSLT classes, I've learned that as soon as I introduce this, a student — almost inevitably — asks, "Does this mean I need to be connected to the Internet to use XSLT?" In other words, does an XSLT processor actually need to load whatever page is at the URL `http://www.w3.org/1999/XSL/Transform` in order to continue? The short answer to this question is no, the namespace URL is just a formal identifier that's built into all XSLT 1.0 processors. An XSLT 1.0 processor looks for that URL in the style sheets it processes, but it does not at any time connect to `www.w3.org`.

Nonetheless, it's quite natural to look at a URL such as `http://www.w3.org/1999/XSL/Transform` and expect that there must be something there. Novice developers routinely type these URLs into their browsers just to see what might be there. For a long time, when loading `http://www.w3.org/1999/XSL/Transform` and other official W3C namespace URLs into their browsers, developers simply got a 404 Not Found error. HTTPD error logs at the W3C were filling up with the failed requests from people who typed in namespace URIs to see what they would get. In some cases, DNS servers were overloaded with attempts to resolve nonexistent hostnames that were nonetheless used inside namespace URLs. Eventually the W3C got tired of all the extra messages these URLs added to their error logs and began putting up pages similar to the one shown in Figure 29-1.

Figure 29-1: The HTML page at the XSLT namespace URL

However, this page was just a quick hack to avoid unnecessarily confusing developers. It was never intended as more than that, or as a suggestion that pages like this should be put at the end of namespace URLs. In fact, the Namespaces in XML specification specifically disavows the notion that a namespace URI can be resolved. ("The namespace name, to serve its intended purpose, should have the characteristics of uniqueness and persistence. It is not a goal that it be directly usable for retrieval of a schema (if any exists).") Nonetheless, many developers expect that they can find some sort of schema, whether a DTD, a W3C XML Schema Language schema, an RDF schema, or some other kind of schema at the end of a namespace URL.

The reason the inventors of namespaces decided not to require namespace URLs to be resolved was manyfold. However, it really boils down to the fact that there was no obvious and unique choice of what to actually put at the end of a namespace URL. For instance, they could have required a DTD; but that would have caused problems for XML applications that used schemas. They could have required a schema or a DTD and used MIME media types to tell which one was there, but that would have required parsers to be able to read both DTDs and schemas. More importantly, it wouldn't have handled at all well the common case where the document using the namespace is merely well formed and not valid. For instance, all XSLT style sheets use namespaces, but almost none of them use DTDs.

Another possibility was to put a specification for the XML application at the namespace URL. However, not all XML applications have formal specifications identifiable with a URL. For instance, the baseball statistics example used in the early chapters of this book was developed ad hoc and is not formally documented anywhere. That's a perfectly legal use of XML. Another problem with placing specifications at the namespace URLs is that the specifications often change faster than the namespace URI does. For instance, XSLT 1.0, XSLT 2.0, and a now withdrawn proposal for XSLT 1.1 all use the same `http://www.w3.org/1999/XSL/Transform` namespace URL, even though they have three different specification documents.

Because the W3C couldn't decide what to place at the end of a namespace URL, they decided not to require anything to be there. However, they also decided not to disallow documents from being there either, or to make any restrictions on what sort of documents could be there. They deliberately chose not to decide. This allowed specific XML applications to add additional requirements beyond the minimal set mandated by Namespaces in XML. For example, the Resource Description Framework (RDF) requires that an RDF schema be found at the end of a namespace URI for an RDF property.

The Solution

By the time Tim Bray, Jonathan Borden, and the xml-dev mailing list revisited the problem of what to put at the end of a namespace URL in late 2000, it had become obvious that the W3C's nondecision was confusing many developers, and that a solution was needed. Clearly putting nothing there wasn't working, and leaving the decision about what to put there to individual XML application developers wasn't much better.

Bray, Borden, and the xml-dev mailing list attacked the problem using an old programmer's adage: every problem can be solved by adding an additional level of indirection. Instead of choosing one possible thing to put at a namespace URL such as a DTD, a schema, a specification document, or something else, they decided to put a list of pointers to all different kinds of related resources. For any given namespace URL, a single document could provide a pointer to a DTD, a pointer to a schema, a pointer to a specification, a pointer to a style sheet, a pointer to software to process the XML, and more. In fact it could even have pointers to more than one of each. Of course, since this was the Web, the pointers would be URLs. Since this was XML, the URLs would be embedded in XLinks. And since the document containing the list would have to make sense to a human being loading the URL in a traditional, non-XML-aware Web browser, the XLinks would be placed in an XHTML Basic document.

The resource Element

A RDDL document is a well-formed XHTML document with one extra element — `resource`. This element may appear anywhere a `div` element can appear and can contain anything a `div` element can contain. To distinguish this from XHTML elements, it is placed in the `http://www.rddl.org/` namespace. The prefix `rddl` is customary, but as always, this can be changed as long as the URI remains the same. Naturally, if you actually try to resolve that URL, you'll see a RDDL document describing RDDL itself as shown in Figure 29-2. To a casual user this looks just like any other Web page, which is the beauty of RDDL. If a developer types a namespace URL into a Web browser location bar to see what's there, they should see something they can read.

Each `rddl:resource` element identifies one resource that is somehow related to the XML application denoted by a particular namespace URL. This related resource may be a DTD, a schema, a style sheet, a specification, software that can be used to read documents written in that XML vocabulary, or something else. For example, here's a typical `rddl:resource` element for the URL `http://www.cafeconleche.org/namespaces/baseball/` that says a DTD for the XML application identified by that namespace URI can be found at the URL `http://ibiblio.org/xml/dtds/season.dtd`:

```
<rddl:resource xmlns:rddl="http://www.rddl.org/"
  xlink:type="simple"
  xlink:href="http://ibiblio.org/xml/dtds/season.dtd"
  xlink:role="http://www.isi.edu/in-
notes/iana/assignments/media-types/application/xml-dtd"
>
  XHTML can go here...
</rddl:resource>
```

`rddl:resource` elements are simple XLinks, as indicated here by the `xlink:type="simple"` attribute. The `xlink:href` attribute contains a URL pointing to the location of the related resource. The `xlink:role` attribute contains a URL identifying exactly what the related resource is. In this case, that URL indicates the specific MIME media type registered for DTDs by pointing to the official registration page for the DTD MIME type at the Institute for Information Sciences at the University of Southern California. XLink requires that the value of an `xlink:role` attribute contain a URL, not just a simple MIME media type such as application/xml-dtd. The `rddl:resource` element does not specify the namespace URL of the resource this resource is related to. That's provided by the URL of the page containing the `rddl:resource` element.

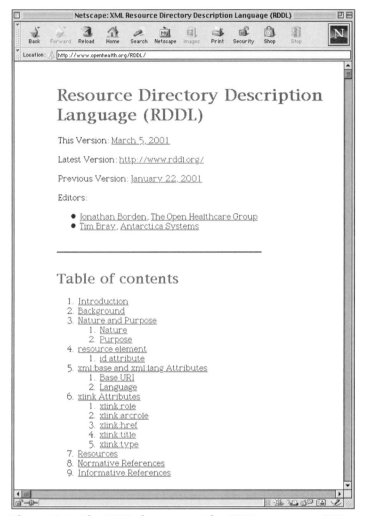

Figure 29-2: The RDDL document at the RDDL namespace URL

The RDDL DTD declares the `rddl:resource` element like this:

```
<!ELEMENT rddl:resource (#PCDATA | %Flow.mix;)*>
```

If you recall the `%Flow.mix;` parameter entity reference from the last chapter, you realize that this means a `rddl:resource` element can contain essentially anything the HTML `body` element can contain: block-level elements such as `p` and `div`, inline elements such as `span` and `em`, unmarked-up text, or mixed content. Well-written RDDL documents take advantage of this by putting a full description of the resource being linked to inside each `rddl:resource` element. For example,

```
<rddl:resource xmlns:rddl="http://www.rddl.org/"
  xlink:type="simple"
  xlink:href="http://ibiblio.org/xml/dtds/season.dtd"
  xlink:role="http://www.isi.edu/in-
notes/iana/assignments/media-types/application/xml-dtd" >

    <p>
      A <a href="http://ibiblio.org/xml/dtds/season.dtd">
      Document Type Definition (<abbr>DTD</abbr>)
      for baseball statistics</a> is available.
      This DTD is developed and described in Chapters 9 and 10
      of the <cite>XML Bible, Gold Edition</cite>
      by <a href="mailto:elharo@metalab.unc.edu">Elliotte
      Rusty Harold</a>.
    </p>

</rddl:resource>
```

The rest of a RDDL document is just XHTML. Listing 29-1 demonstrates. Notice in particular how this page is designed to provide a human-readable description of the resource. Novices who naively type namespace URLs into the location bars of their Web browsers will no longer find themselves staring at 404 Not Found errors.

Listing 29-1: A Simple RDDL Document that Points to the DTD for the http://www.cafeconleche.org/ namespaces/baseball/ XML Application

```
<!DOCTYPE html PUBLIC "-//XML-DEV//DTD XHTML RDDL 1.0//EN"
                      "http://www.rddl.org/rddl-xhtml.dtd">
<html xmlns="http://www.w3.org/1999/xhtml"
      xmlns:xlink="http://www.w3.org/1999/xlink"
      xmlns:rddl="http://www.rddl.org/">
<head>
  <title>An XML Application for Baseball Statistics</title>
</head>
<body>
<h1>An XML Application for Baseball Statistics</h1>

<div class="head">
<p>This Version: <a
href="http://www.cafeconleche.org/namespaces/baseball/200100505
/">May 5, 2001</a></p>
<p>Latest Version: <a
href="http://www.cafeconleche.org/namespaces/baseball/">http://
www.cafeconleche.org/namespaces/baseball/</a></p>
<p>Previous Version: <a
href="http://www.cafeconleche.org/namespaces/baseball/200100505
/">May 5, 2001</a></p>
<p>Authors:</p>
<ul>
```

```
<li><a href="mailto:elharo@metalab.unc.edu">Elliotte Rusty
Harold</a></li>
</ul>
</div>

<p>
This document describes the an XML application for baseball
statistics used as an example in the Gold edition of the
<cite>XML Bible</cite> by <a
href="mailto:elharo@metalab.unc.edu">Elliotte Rusty Harold</a>.
</p>

<p>This document has no official standing and has not been
considered or approved by any organization.</p>

<rddl:resource xmlns:rddl="http://www.rddl.org/"
  xlink:type="simple"
  xlink:href="http://ibiblio.org/xml/dtds/season.dtd"
  xlink:role="http://www.isi.edu/in-
notes/iana/assignments/media-types/application/xml-dtd" >

    <p>
       A <a href="http://ibiblio.org/xml/dtds/season.dtd">
       Document Type Definition (<abbr>DTD</abbr>)
       for baseball statistics</a> is available.
       This DTD is developed and described in Chapters 9 and 10
       of the <cite>XML Bible, Gold Edition</cite>.
    </p>

</rddl:resource>

</body>
</html>
```

Figure 29-3 shows this document loaded into Netscape Navigator 4. As far as Netscape knows, this is just an HTML document, and it can display it. Netscape does not recognize the `<rddl:resource>` tags or `xmlns` attributes, so it ignores them. In all other respects, it treats this as a regular HTML document.

RDDL documents are free to use any part of XHTML Basic that seems useful, including tables, forms, links, and CSS style sheets. The only major things missing are deprecated presentational elements such as `i` and `b`, frames, and bidirectional text.

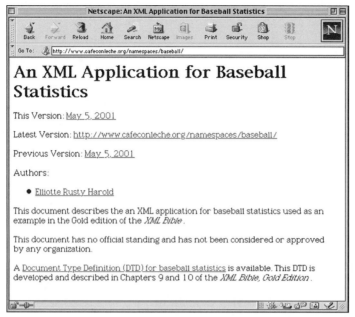

Figure 29-3: Listing 29-1 displayed in a Web browser

You can write anything that seems appropriate in the XHTML parts of your document. In Listing 29-1, I placed information about the version at the top of the document, but if I preferred to put it at the bottom, I could. I can make the document as long or short as it needs to be. I could even include the complete text of Chapters 4, 5, 9, 10, and 11 if that seemed useful. There are no more limits on a RDDL document than on any other HTML document. You are free to let your imagination and creativity run wild.

That having been said, don't forget the ultimate purpose of a RDDL page. It's technical documentation for a specific XML application. It should be clear, concise, and straightforward. It should not include extraneous fluff or be overdesigned. For the most part, a simple, top-to-bottom presentation of just the facts is what users will appreciate most. You're not trying to win Cool Site of the Year with this page; you're just explaining to curious users what the application is and where they can learn more about it.

Software that reads the page will ignore the XHTML markup completely. It can quickly search the page for `rddl:resource` elements and extract all the information it needs from those elements' start tags.

Of course, the point of RDDL is that there's often more than one resource related to any given XML application. Thus, a RDDL document can contain as many `rddl:resource` elements as there are related resources. Listing 29-2 adds `rddl:resource` elements that point to the CSS style sheets and XSLT style sheets developed for baseball earlier in this book.

Listing 29-2: A RDDL Document that Locates Multiple Related Resources for the http://www.cafeconleche.org/ namespaces/baseball/ XML Application

```
<!DOCTYPE html PUBLIC "-//XML-DEV//DTD XHTML RDDL 1.0//EN"
                      "http://www.rddl.org/rddl-xhtml.dtd">
<html xmlns="http://www.w3.org/1999/xhtml"
      xmlns:xlink="http://www.w3.org/1999/xlink"
      xmlns:rddl="http://www.rddl.org/">
<head>
  <title>An XML Application for Baseball Statistics</title>
</head>
<body>
<h1>An XML Application for Baseball Statistics</h1>

<div class="head">
<p>This Version: <a
href="http://www.cafeconleche.org/namespaces/baseball/200100505
/">May 5, 2001</a></p>
<p>Latest Version: <a
href="http://www.cafeconleche.org/namespaces/baseball/">http://
www.cafeconleche.org/namespaces/baseball/</a></p>
<p>Previous Version: <a
href="http://www.cafeconleche.org/namespaces/baseball/200100505
/">May 5, 2001</a></p>
<p>Authors:</p>
<ul>
<li><a href="mailto:elharo@metalab.unc.edu">Elliotte Rusty
Harold</a></li>
</ul>
</div>

<p>
This document describes the an XML application for baseball
statistics used as an example in the Gold edition of the
<cite>XML Bible</cite>.
</p>

<p>This document has no official standing and has not been
considered or approved by any organization.</p>

<h2>Document Type Definition</h2>

<rddl:resource xmlns:rddl="http://www.rddl.org/"
  xlink:type="simple"
  xlink:href="http://ibiblio.org/xml/dtds/season.dtd"
  xlink:role="http://www.isi.edu/in-
notes/iana/assignments/media-types/application/xml-dtd" >
```

Continued

Listing 29-2 *(continued)*

```
    <p>
       A <a href="http://ibiblio.org/xml/dtds/season.dtd">
       Document Type Definition (<abbr>DTD</abbr>)
       for baseball statistics</a> is available.
       This DTD is developed and described in Chapters 9 and 10
       of the <cite>XML Bible, Gold Edition</cite>.
    </p>

</rddl:resource>

<h2>CSS Style Sheet</h2>

<rddl:resource xmlns:rddl="http://www.rddl.org/"
  xlink:type="simple"
  xlink:href="http://ibiblio.org/xml/styles/baseball.css"
  xlink:role="http://www.isi.edu/in-
notes/iana/assignments/media-types/text/css" >

    <p>
       A <a href="http://ibiblio.org/xml/styles/baseball.css">
       CSS style sheet for baseball statistics</a> is
       available. This style sheet was developed and described
       in Chapter 4 of the <cite>XML Bible, Gold
       Edition</cite>.
    </p>

</rddl:resource>

<h2>XSLT Style Sheet</h2>

<rddl:resource xmlns:rddl="http://www.rddl.org/"
  xlink:type="simple"
  xlink:href="http://ibiblio.org/xml/styles/baseball.xsl"
  xlink:role="http://www.isi.edu/in-
notes/iana/assignments/media-types/application/xml+xslt" >

    <p>
       An <a href="http://ibiblio.org/xml/styles/baseball.xsl">
       XSLT style sheet for baseball statistics</a> is
       available. This style sheet was developed and described
       in Chapter 5 of the <cite>XML Bible, Gold
       Edition</cite>.
    </p>

</rddl:resource>

</body>
</html>
```

Natures

In a `rddl:resource` element, the `xlink:role` attribute defines the *nature* of the related resource. The nature tells you what kind of document you'll find on the other end of the `xlink:href` attribute for that resource. Examples of natures include CSS style sheets, W3C Schema Language schemas, Schematron schemas, HTML specification documents, Java applets, and more. RDDL does not place any limits on what kinds of resources a RDDL document can point to. If it's useful to you, you can refer to it from a RDDL document.

However, RDDL does specify that certain URLs identify particular natures. For instance, the URL `http://www.isi.edu/in-notes/iana/assignments/media-types/application/xml-dtd` always means that the nature is an XML DTD. The URL `http://www.w3.org/TR/xhtml1/DTD/xhtml1-strict` always means that the nature is strict XHTML 1.0.

Using standard URLs for standard natures allows software to find and apply style sheets, schemas, DTDs, and other useful resources without human intervention. For example, suppose a browser reads an XML document using a vocabulary it's never seen before, and it doesn't immediately know how to display it. It needs to find a style sheet that can display documents using that vocabulary. It sees that the namespace URL for the document's root element is `http://www.cafeconleche.org/namespaces/baseball/` so it silently loads that URL. (The browser would not show the page it loaded to the reader in this scenario.) The browser then scans the RDDL document at `http://www.cafeconleche.org/namespaces/baseball/` looking for a `rddl:resource` element whose nature indicates that it's a CSS style sheet. According to the RDDL specification, this is indicated by the URL `http://www.isi.edu/in-notes/iana/assignments/media-types/text/css`, so that's the URL the browser looks for. When it finds a `rddl:resource` with this nature, it loads the URL in the `xlink:href` attribute of that element to get the style sheet. It can then apply the newly found style sheet to the original document.

The same technique can be used anytime a browser or other tool needs to find a resource that's somehow related to the current document. By searching for different natures, it can locate different kinds of related resources. Well-known natures in RDDL include:

✦ `http://www.isi.edu/in-notes/iana/assignments/media-types/text/css`: a CSS style sheet

✦ `http://www.isi.edu/in-notes/iana/assignments/media-types/application/xml-dtd`: a document type definition (DTD)

✦ `http://www.rddl.org/natures#mailbox`: a UNIX mailbox

✦ `http://www.isi.edu/in-notes/iana/assignments/media-types/text/html`: an HTML document

✦ `http://www.w3.org/TR/html4/`: an HTML 4.0 document

✦ `http://www.w3.org/TR/html4/strict`: an HTML 4 strict document

✦ `http://www.w3.org/TR/html4/transitional`: an HTML 4 transitional document

✦ `http://www.w3.org/TR/html4/frameset`: an HTML 4 frameset document

✦ `http://www.w3.org/1999/xhtml`: an XHTML document

✦ `http://www.w3.org/TR/xhtml1/DTD/xhtml1-strict`: an XHTML 1.0 strict document

✦ `http://www.w3.org/TR/xhtml1/DTD/xhtml1-transitional`: an XHTML 1.0 transitional document

✦ `http://www.w3.org/2000/01/rdf-schema#`: an RDF schema

✦ `http://www.xml.gr.jp/xmlns/relaxCore`: a RELAX Core grammar

✦ `http://www.xml.gr.jp/xmlns/relaxNamespace`: a RELAX namespace

✦ `http://www.ascc.net/xml/schematron`: a Schematron schema

✦ `http://www.rddl.org/natures#SOCAT`: an OASIS Open Catalog

✦ `http://www.w3.org/2000/10/XMLSchema`: a W3C XML Schema Language schema

✦ `http://www.w3.org/TR/REC-xml.html#dt-chardata`: character data

✦ `http://www.w3.org/TR/REC-xml.html#dt-escape`: character data in which left angle brackets, ampersands, and possibly other characters have been escaped with general entity or character references such as & and &

✦ `http://www.w3.org/TR/REC-xml.html#dt-unparsed`: an unparsed entity

✦ `http://www.rddl.org/natures/software#language`: software written in an unspecified programming language

✦ `http://www.rddl.org/natures/software#python`: software written in Python

✦ `http://www.rddl.org/natures/software#java`: software written in Java

✦ `http://www.ietf.org/rfc/rfc2026.txt`: an IETF Request For Comment (RFC)

✦ `http://www.iso.ch/`: an ISO standard

This is not a definitive list, and these are not the only allowed natures. In the future more may be published at http://www.rddl.org/natures/. Most importantly you can use any reasonable URL to identify new kinds of natures that you choose for your own needs. There are some conventional ways to pick these nature URIs, as demonstrated by the above list:

✦ A nature with a standard MIME media type can be identified by a URL to the official registration for the type at the Internet Assigned Numbers Authority (IANA) registry at `http://www.isi.edu/in-notes/iana/assignments/media-types/`.

✦ A nature that is an XML document written in a standard vocabulary can be identified by that vocabulary's namespace URI.

✦ Standard, well-known natures that don't have namespace URIs or registered MIME media types can be identified by pointing to a part of a page on the RDDL site at `http://www.rddl.org/`.

However, if none of these work for your resources, you're free to identify natures with some other kind of URL. Just make sure that the URL is actually resolvable.

Natures alone are not enough. For example, you may know that an HTML 4.0 document is somehow related to a particular application but you may not know how. Is it the specification for the application? A tutorial for the vocabulary? The biography of the person who invented it? Something else? Indeed, there may be multiple related HTML 4.0 resources, one for each of these possibilities. To further expand on the relationship between the original XML application and the related resource, you can add a purpose in an `xlink:arcrole` attribute.

Purposes

There's often more than one resource of a given nature associated with an XML application. For instance, separate CSS style sheets might be provided for the different environments such as aural, braille, handheld, print, projection, screen, tty, and tv. XHTML 1.0 has one namespace URL but three different DTDs depending on whether you want to use strict, transitional, or frameset XHTML. XHTML 1.1 adds several more possible variations on the DTD while keeping the namespace URL the same.

In cases like this, it's clear the RDDL document needs to provide more than one resource for each given nature. The different *purposes* of these resources with the same *natures* can be distinguished by an optional `xlink:arcrole` attribute. As with `xlink:role`, the XLink specification requires that the value of the `xlink:arcrole` attribute be a URI.

Once again, the RDDL specification defines a number of URIs for well-known purposes. For instance, the URL `http://www.rddl.org/purposes#entities` would be used on a document with the nature `http://www.isi.edu/in-notes/iana/assignments/media-types/application/xml-dtd` to signify that the purpose of this DTD is to define entities. Here's the complete list of well-known purposes as of May 2001:

✦ http://www.rddl.org/purposes#validation: this resource should be used for classic XML or SGML DTD validation before the document is parsed

✦ http://www.rddl.org/purposes#schema-validation: this resource should be used for validation via some sort of schema after the document is parsed; the type of schema would normally be identified by the nature

✦ http://www.rddl.org/purposes#module: a file that is only part of a complete DTD and that is typically used in modularized DTDs such as XHTML 1.1 and SMIL 2.0

✦ http://www.rddl.org/purposes#schema-module: a module used in a schema

✦ http://www.rddl.org/purposes#entities: a DTD fragment containing only entity definitions such as xhtml-special.ent in modular XHTML

✦ http://www.rddl.org/purposes#notations: a DTD fragment containing only notation declarations such as xhtml-notations-1.mod in modular XHTML

✦ http://www.rddl.org/purposes/software#xslt-extension: software implementing an extension function or element for XSLT

✦ http://www.rddl.org/purposes/software#software-package: a grouping of software resources

✦ http://www.rddl.org/purposes/software#software-project: a collection of resources related to a software package

✦ http://www.rddl.org/purposes#JAR: a zip file with the extension .jar containing Java classes

✦ http://www.rddl.org/purposes/software#reference: documentation for the resource

✦ http://www.rddl.org/purposes/software#normative-reference: the definitive specification of the resource's syntax and semantics

✦ http://www.rddl.org/purposes/software#non-normative-reference: a useful but nonauthoritative description of the resource's syntax and semantics

✦ http://www.rddl.org/purposes#prior-version: documentation for a previous version of the resource's vocabulary; for example, the XHTML 1.0 specification relative to XHTML 1.1

✦ http://www.rddl.org/purposes#definition: the definition of a term

✦ http://www.rddl.org/purposes#icon: an image that represents the resource

✦ http://www.rddl.org/purposes#directory: another RDDL document whose resources should be merged with this document's resources

✦ http://www.rddl.org/purposes#alternate: an alternative for a resource with the same nature as this one

Currently all well-known purpose URLs begin with `http://www.rddl.org/purposes#`. However, this may change in the future, and you are allowed to add to this list to create new purposes that suit your applications.

Summary

In this chapter, you learned about RDDL, the Resource Directory Description Language. In particular, you learned that:

✦ RDDL documents are placed at the end of namespace URLs to allow both human readers and automated software to locate resources associated with the XML application identified by the namespace URL.

✦ RDDL documents are essentially XHTML Basic documents with one extra element — `rddl:resource`.

✦ The `rddl:resource` element is a simple XLink. The `xlink:href` attribute of each `rddl:resource` element points to the related resource.

✦ The `xlink:role` attribute of the `rddl:resource` element identifies the nature of the related resource. Natures are identified by well-known URLs.

✦ The `xlink:arcrole` attribute of the `rddl:resource` element identifies the purpose of the related resource. Purposes are also identified by well-known URLs.

The next chapter explores yet another HTML-like XML application, WML, the Wireless Markup Language. WML is used to write Web pages that are displayed on cell phones and other bandwidth-limited devices with small screens, rather than on computers with relatively large monitors and fast connections.

✦ ✦ ✦

The Wireless Markup Language

The Wireless Markup Language (WML) is an XML application designed for delivering Web content to cell phones, pagers, personal digital assistants (PDAs), and similar bandwidth-, display-, and memory-challenged devices. It uses a mix of HTML-like elements such as p, em, a, and strong, along with WML-unique elements such as go, do, card, and onevent. WML is being used today to provide services that pass small nuggets of information to consumers including weather reports, flight schedules, traffic reports, stock prices, and sports scores.

WML is just one part of the Wireless Application Protocol (WAP). As well as WML, WAP includes specifications for WMLC, a binary compression format for WML; WBMP, a bitmapped format for black and white images embedded in WML decks; WMLScript, a scripting language for WML; WSP, the protocol by which cell phones talk to WAP gateways; and a lot more. If WML is like HTML, then WAP is like HTML plus HTTP, CGI, JavaScript, SOCKS, gzip, and PNG.

WML is the only part of WAP implemented in XML. Fortunately, WML is the only one of these a content provider needs to be intimately familiar with — at least at the start. As you graduate to more complex documents and to more sophisticated sites, you might want to learn about WMLScript and WBMP. The remaining protocols and formats only really need to be understood by cell phone manufacturers and service providers. This is similar to how you can learn to write and publish HTML pages without knowing very much, if anything, about HTTP. Consequently, this chapter focuses exclusively on WML with brief nods at WBMP and WMLScript.

What Is WML?

WML, the Wireless Markup Language, is an XML application designed to deliver Web content to cell phones, pagers, and personal digital assistants. These devices have several things in common, most notably a very small black-and-white screen and very limited bandwidth. Screens can be as tiny as 4 rows by 10 columns; that is, 40 total characters. In other words, the single sentence you're reading right now could not be displayed on some cell phones without scrolling. Most phones can only display text and perhaps 1-bit black-and-white images; very few have any sort of scripting language built-in. A cell phone may have more CPU power and memory than a 1960s-era multimillion dollar IBM mainframe, but it is still quite weak when compared to even the slowest of today's PCs. Bandwidth may be equivalent to a 14.4K modem or slower. Latency may be even worse, averaging five seconds or more per request. These devices are not really suitable for browsing the everyday Web and require special pages designed especially for very constricted environments. These pages are written in WML.

Because of the innate limitations of the devices on which WML documents are read, WML uses a different metaphor than HTML. Where HTML presents sites of scrollable pages, WML offers decks of flippable cards. A single document is transmitted as a unit but displayed as multiple cards. Each card contains a small amount of XML markup and text using an HTML-like vocabulary. Rather than viewing the entire document at once, and perhaps scrolling, users move forward and backward in the deck by flipping cards. The deck author inserts hypertext links in the deck to allow the user to jump to particular cards or to other decks completely.

Different cell phones have widely varying WML support. Most phones that can browse the wireless Web at all support WML 1.1 or later. Most of the markup discussed in this chapter is identical from WML 1.1 on. WML 1.2 and 1.3 differ from earlier versions in support for advanced features such as WMLScript, but are pretty much the same with respect to their document type definitions (DTDs). Unfortunately, many phones implement different subsets of WML 1.1. For instance, some phones can make text bold; others can't. Some phones can center text; others can't. However, as long as you don't tie your applications too closely to the detailed presentational capabilities of one phone or another, most phones will happily ignore the markup they can't handle and still present the basic information you serve to the user.

Hello WML

Listing 30-1 is about the simplest WML document imaginable. It is an XML document, as you can plainly see. It has an XML declaration. It has a document type declaration, and it is valid. It does not use namespaces. It will probably be stored in a file called something like hello.wml or 30-1.wml, although it could also be stored in a file called hello.xml or even hello.txt. The root element is `wml`. The `wml` element contains a single `card` element. The `card` element contains a single p element that represents a paragraph of text. This text is "Hello WML!"

Listing 30-1: **Hello WML**

```
<?xml version="1.0"?>
<!DOCTYPE wml PUBLIC "-//WAPFORUM//DTD WML 1.1//EN"
                     "http://www.wapforum.org/DTD/wml_1.1.xml">
<wml>
  <card>
    <p>Hello WML!</p>
  </card>
</wml>
```

You can place this document on a normal Web server. It's served over HTTP like any other file. Before a cell phone can load it, it's actually downloaded to one of the cell phone company's proxy servers first; but that's pretty much transparent to both the client and the page author.

Tip

Some cell phones let you omit the document type declaration. However, I strongly recommend that you include one and validate your WML documents. WML browsers are much less forgiving of poor markup than traditional HTML browsers such as Netscape. For instance, if you merely left out the `<p>` and `</p>` tags in Listing 30-1, but otherwise wrote a well-formed document, most WML browsers would not be able to display it. Validation is a very important tool for debugging WML documents.

The WML MIME media type

The main thing you need to worry about on the server side is that the server assigns the file the correct MIME media type, text/vnd.wap.wml. Consult your server documentation to determine exactly how to set up a mapping between .wml files and that MIME type. If you're using Apache (and if you're not, you should be), then all you need to do is add this line to the httpd.conf file:

```
addtype text/vnd.wap.wml wml
```

Some WML documents also use other unusual file formats, including .wbmp (wireless Bitmap Images), .wmls (WMLScript), and .wmlc (a brain-damaged, non-XML, compiled binary form of WML). You might as well add mappings for these:

```
addtype text/vnd.wap.wmlscript      wmls
addtype image/vnd.wap.wbmp          wbmp
addtype text/vnd.wap.si             si
addtype text/vnd.wap.sl             sl
addtype application/vnd.wap.wbxml   wbxml
addtype application/vnd.wap.wmlc    wmlc
addtype application/vnd.wap.wmlscriptc wmlsc
```

Note
The fundamental flaw in WML is that it doesn't support the one media type that actually makes sense for cell phones — audio.

If you don't want to set these mappings for the entire server, or if you don't have write access to httpd.conf but you are using Apache, then you can simply put these directives in a file named .htaccess in the directory that contains your WML files.

An alternative that you can use on a file-by-file basis with some browsers is to add a `meta` tag to the deck's head. An `http-equiv` attribute can specify the content type. Listing 30-2 demonstrates.

Listing 30-2: A WML document that specifies its MIME media type

```
<?xml version="1.0"?>
<!DOCTYPE wml PUBLIC "-//WAPFORUM//DTD WML 1.1//EN"
                     "http://www.wapforum.org/DTD/wml_1.1.xml">
<wml>
  <head>
    <meta http-equiv="Content-Type"
          content='text/vnd.wap.wml; charset="ISO-8859-1"'/>
  </head>
  <card>
    <p>Hello WML!</p>
  </card>
</wml>
```

However, this only works for WML documents, not for WMLScript programs, WBMP images, or any of the other media types that may be used on a WAP site. Furthermore, not all WML browsers recognize this, so it should be used only as a last resort.

Browsing the Web from your phone

Listing 30-1 file can be accessed from any browser that understands WML, which basically means the browser built into your cell phone. (Opera 5.0 also has experimental WML support.) You'll need to select Access the Internet, or the equivalent on your cell phone's menu. Next select Go to... to tell the phone you want to type in a URL. Then use the cell phone's keypad to type in the URL. You'll have to press each key multiple times until it cycles to the letter that you want. This is not an easy operation for even the simplest URLs. If the URL is something like `http://www.ibiblio. org/xml/books/biblegold/examples/30/30-1.wml`, it's almost hopeless. The state of user interfaces on the Web today is bad. The state of user interfaces in the wireless world is a thousand times worse. Once you've succeeded, you should see something like Figure 30-1, details depending on which phone you're using of course.

Note Not all cell phones and not all providers support WAP and WML. In particular, VoiceStream claimed that the Ericsson phone they sold me would support WAP, but in fact it did not work on their network, and they couldn't provide me with one that did. If you buy a cell phone to use with WAP, be sure to try it out in the store before signing any contracts.

Cell phone simulators

If you don't like developing cross-browser Web sites for multiple versions of Internet Explorer and Netscape, as well as for various other browsers, you're going to hate WML. Although only two programs account for almost all the browsers built into most cell phones, the different screen sizes and capabilities of different phones make the same browsers behave very differently on different phones. To test across all the different possible combinations of phones that users might own, you'd need to buy dozens of phones — and more are being released every month. Of course, while you were testing these phones, you'd likely be paying exorbitant prices for the air time.

Fortunately, you can run WAP simulator software to make your PC pretend that it's a cell phone. Better yet, you can download skins for this software that will make it take on the appearance of different phones on the market. Several different developer kits are available with these phone simulators, including:

✦ Phone.com's UP.SDK developer kit for Windows, `http://developer.phone.com/`

✦ The Ericsson WAP IDE, `http://www.ericsson.com/developerszone/`

✦ The Nokia WAP Toolkit, `http://www.nokia.com/corporate/wap/sdk.html`

You'll need to fill in some pointless registration forms to get any of these. I routinely lie on these forms.

Caution All of these products have bugs ranging from minor annoyances to major hassles. Version 2.0 of the Nokia WAP Toolkit completely incapacitated my normally stable Windows NT 4.0 PC to the point where I had to switch the power off to restart the machine. It is definitely not my first choice. As of January 2001, Phone.com's UP.SDK 4.0 seems to be the least buggy of a bad lot, so I used it for most of the screenshots in this chapter.

Figure 30-2 shows a phone simulator loaded with a Motorola Timeport P7389 skin, which I had to download separately. However, not all cell phones and not all simulators support the same set of features or behave the same way. To get screen shots of some of the less-supported WML features for this chapter, I had to test multiple simulators and skins before I found one that worked. On the other hand, if you're developing your own wireless services, you'll want to test your decks in as many different phones as possible and ruthlessly eliminate any features that don't at least degrade gracefully on phones where they're not supported.

Figure 30-1: Hello WML on a cell phone. Photo courtesy of Reggie Dablo.

Figure 30-2: Hello WML on
a cell phone simulator

One advantage to using a simulator instead of a real phone is that a simulator can
show you a lot more details about just what the cell phone is sending and what it's
getting back. Figure 30-3 shows the Information Window from Phone.com's
UP.Simulator. This is invaluable for debugging and is particularly useful for diagnos-
ing problems with forms and misconfigured servers. It can also let you know when
you're getting something out of the cache rather than from the Web site. WAP gateways cache much more aggressively than most HTTP proxy servers. It's essential to
clear the cache before reloading a changed WML document.

Caution   There's a danger in using the simulator instead of a real phone to test: it's too
easy! First, the simulator lets you use a real keyboard to type in the URLs. Don't! If
you do this, you'll get a totally false picture of how easy or difficult WML is to use.
In fact, it's extremely difficult. If you avail yourself of crutches that your customers
with real cell phones won't have (like keyboards), you won't find out how much
trouble it is to access your site. Second, the simulator will load content a lot faster
than a real phone will. For a more accurate measure, disconnect your normal
Internet connection and replace it with an old 9600 bps modem.

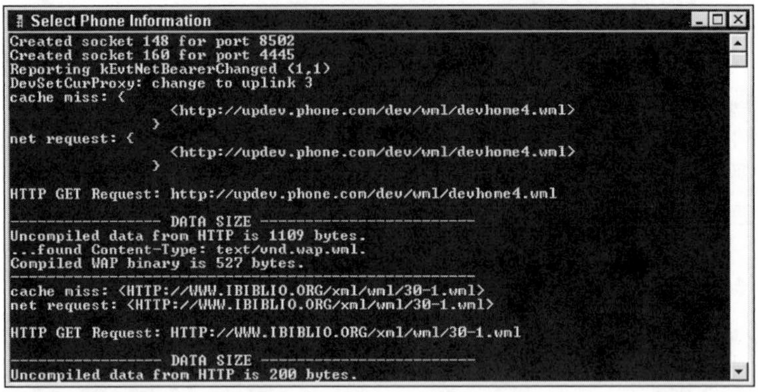

Figure 30-3: The tracing console

Basic Text Markup

The text inside a WML `card` is divided into paragraphs, each of which is represented by a p element. This is very similar to the p element you know from HTML, and indeed many of the tags and attributes you use inside paragraphs are also adapted from HTML. However when using these, you must keep in mind that you only have between 4 and 8 lines of 10 to 20 characters each. This is not nearly enough to write HTML like you're accustomed to. You probably shouldn't even write full sentences when fragments will do.

Elements that WML 1.1 and later adopt from HTML include:

head	a	u	td
meta	em	big	select
p	strong	small	option
br	b	table	input
img	i	tr	

WML 1.2, which is supported by relatively few phones as of early 2001, adds one more element, `pre`. WML 1.3, which is not yet supported by any phones as of January 2001, does not add any elements to this list.

These elements all mean more or less the same things they mean in standard HTML, although they often don't allow all the attributes that they can have in HTML. Since WML is well formed and potentially valid XML, these tags must always be written in lowercase. Every start tag must have a matching end tag. Attribute values must be quoted, and all other well-formedness rules must be followed.

Listing 30-3 shows a simple WML deck. The root element is `wml` instead of `html`. Instead of a `body` element, there's a `card` element. Otherwise, this could easily be HTML. The card contains six `p` elements, signifying six paragraphs. Each paragraph exhibits a different character style.

Listing 30-3: **Text Styles in WML**

```
<?xml version="1.0"?>
<!DOCTYPE wml PUBLIC "-//WAPFORUM//DTD WML 1.1//EN"
                     "http://www.wapforum.org/DTD/wml_1.1.xml">
<wml>
  <card>
    <p>Normal</p>
    <p><strong>Strong</strong></p>
    <p><em>Emphasized</em></p>
    <p><big>Big</big></p>
    <p><u>Underline</u></p>
    <p><i>Italic</i></p>
  </card>
</wml>
```

Figure 30-4 shows Listing 30-3 in a phone simulator. Different WML browsers have varying levels of support for the various styles. For instance, in this particular browser `strong`, `em`, and `big` all have the same effect, making the text bold. This browser can't underline anything, so instead it makes the underlined element italic. Other browsers may do a better or worse job, but I wouldn't count on any great fidelity to the designer's intent. Existing phones are just too limited.

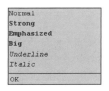

Figure 30-4: Paragraphs with normal, strong, emphasized, big, underlined, and italic text

The `p` element has two optional attributes that affect its presentation:

✦ `align` with the values `left`, `right`, and `center`

✦ `mode` with the values `wrap` and `nowrap`

Listing 30-4 demonstrates these attributes. Figure 30-5 shows this document in a simulator that does support all these features. However, you should be aware that many real phones can't handle these attributes and will simply ignore them. Don't write cards that depend on proper presentation of these attributes.

Listing 30-4: Paragraph attributes in WML

```
<?xml version="1.0"?>
<!DOCTYPE wml PUBLIC "-//WAPFORUM//DTD WML 1.1//EN"
                  "http://www.wapforum.org/DTD/wml_1.1.xml">
<wml>
  <card>
    <p align="center">
      <strong>Titles Are Often Centered</strong>
    </p>
    <p align="left" mode="wrap">
      Left-aligned, wrapped text is the default.
    </p>
    <p align="right">Right aligned</p>
    <p mode="nowrap">
      This text should extend across one
      line with some form of horizontal
      scrolling, possibly automatic;
      but many phones will wrap it anyway.
    </p>
  </card>
</wml>
```

Figure 30-5: Left-aligned, right-aligned, and centered, wrapped and unwrapped paragraphs

Tables

WML provides very limited table support, just the `table`, `tr`, and `td` elements. For example, Listing 30-5 demonstrates a very simple stock quote table. The left column contains the stock symbol. The right column contains the price. This example is merely a static WML file, but cards such as this are customarily produced on-the-fly by a CGI program that fills in the table with the latest prices.

Listing 30-5: A stock quote table

```
<?xml version="1.0"?>
<!DOCTYPE wml PUBLIC "-//WAPFORUM//DTD WML 1.1//EN"
                  "http://www.wapforum.org/DTD/wml_1.1.xml">
<wml>
  <card>
```

```
     <p>
     <table columns="2" title="Your Portfolio">
       <tr><td>Symbol</td><td>Price</td></tr>
       <tr><td>RHAT</td><td>8.69</td></tr>
       <tr><td>COVD</td><td>2.81</td></tr>
       <tr><td>NPNT</td><td>0.75</td></tr>
     </table>
     </p>
   </card>
</wml>
```

Figure 30-6 shows the rendered table. If a portfolio contains more than three or four stocks, the user will probably have to scroll down to see the whole table.

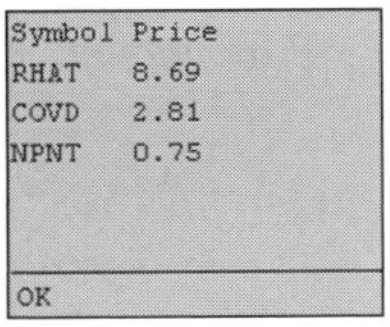

Figure 30-6: A stock quote table

Despite the superficial similarities, there are a number of differences between WML and HTML tables that you should keep in mind:

✦ A WML table element must have a columns attribute that specifies the number of columns in this table. Each table row (tr element) must have exactly this number of table cells (td elements).

✦ A WML table element can have a title attribute instead of HTML's caption element. However, many browsers choose not to display table titles.

✦ The table element can have an optional align attribute. However, this has a very different meaning than the align attribute of HTML's table. In particular, it indicates how the text in each column is aligned rather than how the table is aligned relative to the element that contains it. The value of this attribute is a white space-separated list of letters from the set C (centered), R (right-aligned), L (left-aligned), and D (default), one letter for each column in the table. For example, align="L R" means that the first column is left-aligned and the second column is right-aligned.

✦ A td element can only contain inline elements such as a, img, em, and strong. It cannot contain paragraphs or other tables.

✦ WML tables don't allow you to set the borders, background colors, spacing, padding, or other presentational properties of each cell.

WML table support is very rudimentary compared to HTML. Even within these limitations, not all WML browsers support tables; and those that do support tables don't necessarily support every detail such as alignment.

Images

WML cards can contain simple bitmapped images. Each image must be black and white. It should be no larger than 127 pixels by 127 pixels, and preferably about a quarter of that. Furthermore, you cannot use a standard GIF, JPEG, or PNG image. Instead, you have to convert your image into a special *Wireless Bitmap* format. These files should have the four-letter extension .wbmp and be served with the MIME media type image/vnd.wap.wbmp.

Standard graphics programs such as Adobe Photoshop and Macromedia Freehand don't support this format yet, but a Google search for WBMP will turn up several tools for creating WBMP images, including:

✦ WAPTiger, an open source BMP to WBMP command line conversion program for Linux and Windows that you can download from `http://www.waptiger.de/download.html`

✦ The TeraFlops online converter form for GIF, JPEG, and BMP images at `http://www.teraflops.com/wbmp/`

✦ Laurent Charbonnel's $10 shareware Adobe Photoshop plug-in for the Macintosh that you can download from `http://www.creationflux.com/laurent/wbmp.html`

After you've converted your image to the WBMP format, you use an `img` element to place it on a card. This is very much like HTML's `img` element. The `src` attribute contains an absolute or relative URL locating the external image file. The `alt` attribute contains text to be displayed if the browser can't load the image (and many WML browsers can't load images at all). The `height` and `width` attributes contain the number of pixels in the image vertically and horizontally. Listing 30-6 demonstrates with a deck that loads a simple WBMP image I use as a logo on one of my Web sites.

Listing 30-6: **A WML card that loads a WBMP image**

```
<?xml version="1.0" encoding="ISO-8859-1"?>
<!DOCTYPE wml PUBLIC "-//WAPFORUM//DTD WML 1.1//EN"
                    "http://www.wapforum.org/DTD/wml_1.1.xml">
<wml>
  <card>
    <p><img src="cup.wbmp" alt="Cafe au Lait logo"
            height="39" width="69"/></p>
    <p><strong>Cafe au Lait</strong></p>
  </card>
</wml>
```

Caution Not all cell phones and WML browsers support images. In fact, I'd venture to say most don't. In my tests, only the Nokia simulator and Opera 5.0 displayed the WBMP images instead of the `alt` text. It's probably too early yet to use images on your WML cards.

Entity references

The WML DTD defines seven entity references that you can use. These are the five standard predefined XML entity references and two new ones:

✦ `&quot;` the straight double quotation mark "

✦ `&amp;` the ampersand &

✦ `&apos;` the straight single quote '

✦ `&lt;` the less than sign <

✦ `&gt;` the greater than sign >

✦ ` ` the non-breaking space

✦ `&shy;` the optional "soft" hyphen

The soft hyphen is particularly useful because a typical cell phone screen is so narrow that it's very helpful to allow lines to break in the middle of words. This lets you make use of more of the limited screen size. Listing 30-7 demonstrates.

Listing 30-7: **Soft hyphens to help split text up**

```
<?xml version="1.0"?>
<!DOCTYPE wml PUBLIC "-//WAPFORUM//DTD WML 1.1//EN"
                     "http://www.wapforum.org/DTD/wml_1.1.xml">
<wml>
  <card>
    <p>
      An ex&shy;cep&shy;tion&shy;al&shy;ly grand&shy;i&shy;ose
      vo&shy;cab&shy;u&shy;lar&shy;y is&shy;n't to be
      com&shy;mend&shy;ed when pro&shy;duc&shy;ing WML.
    </p>
  </card>
</wml>
```

Caution Soft hyphens don't work in a lot of WML browsers. For instance, Opera 5.0 doesn't use them to break words. Other browsers do even worse and display them as hard hyphens, whether they're used to break words or not. Figure 30-7 demonstrates.

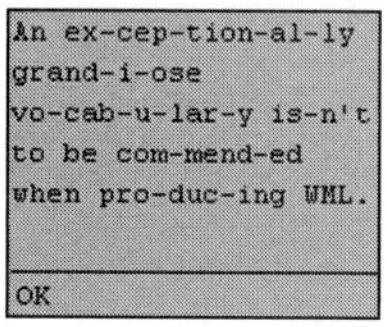

An ex-cep-tion-al-ly
grand-i-ose
vo-cab-u-lar-y is-n't
to be com-mend-ed
when pro-duc-ing WML.

OK

Figure 30-7: Phone.com's UP.Simulator 4.0 doesn't handle soft hyphens properly.

Cards and Links

Despite superficial similarities in text formatting, WML is not HTML. The biggest difference is that WML documents are divided into decks of cards. Although the deck is stored on the server in a single file and the browser (that is, the phone) retrieves the entire deck in a single download, the user only sees one card at a time. Each card customarily contains links to the next card, and perhaps other related cards elsewhere in the deck or to cards in other decks.

Multicard decks

Imagine a WML service that drills users on their foreign language vocabulary. A bored traveler stuck at LaGuardia Airport waiting for a delayed flight to Quebec City could dial up the service and load a deck to practice their French. Each deck contains several foreign words interspersed with their English translations. The first card contains a foreign word; the second card contains the English translation; the third card contains a foreign word; the fourth card contains the English translation; and so on. At the end of the deck the user is given the option to download a new batch of words. Listing 30-8 shows one such deck of six cards.

Listing 30-8: A WML deck with six cards

```
<?xml version="1.0" encoding="ISO-8859-1"?>
<!DOCTYPE wml PUBLIC "-//WAPFORUM//DTD WML 1.1//EN"
                     "http://www.wapforum.org/DTD/wml_1.1.xml">
<wml>
  <card xml:lang="fr-CA">
    <p>Bonjour</p>
  </card>
  <card xml:lang="en-US">
    <p>Hello</p>
  </card>
  <card xml:lang="fr-CA">
    <p>monde</p>
  </card>
  <card xml:lang="en-US">
    <p>world</p>
```

```
    </card>
    <card xml:lang="fr-CA">
      <p>rédiger</p>
    </card>
    <card xml:lang="en-US">
      <p>write, draw up, edit</p>
    </card>
  </wml>
```

It's straightforward to load this deck into the cell-phone browser as shown in Figure 30-8. However, this only shows the first card in the deck. The answer card and the other four cards are nowhere to be seen. Furthermore, no matter how you punch the buttons on the phone, they're not going to appear.

Figure 30-8: The first card of the WML deck in Listing 30-8

The do element

What's needed is a means of navigating from one card to the next. The word "OK" in the lower-right corner of the screen and the OK button below it looks promising, but hitting it just brings up the phone's default menu. It does not load the next card.

You'd like to remap the OK button so that it jumps to the next card rather than to the default menu. Fortunately, that's not hard to do. First, you need to give each card its own id attribute so that it can be linked to separately from the entire deck. Number the French cards f1 through f3 and the English cards e1 through e3, like this:

```
<card id="f1" xml:lang="fr-CA">
  <p>Bonjour</p>
</card>
<card id="e1" xml:lang="en-US">
  <p>Hello</p>
</card>
```

Next, you want to make the OK button jump to a particular named card. You do this with a do element like this one:

```
<do type="accept">
  <go href="#e1"/>
</do>
```

The type attribute of the do element specifies the user action that triggers the contents of the do element. In this case, the action is accept, which corresponds to the OK button on this particular phone. It may correspond to a different button on different phones — on some phones the user might even say the word "OK" into the handset — but there should be an accept button somewhere. An action can be attached to any of these six types:

✦ accept

✦ prev

✦ help

✦ reset

✦ options

✦ delete

These are abstract, semantic types. In general, there won't be a key on the phone marked accept or delete or prev. However, the phone should provide the user with some obvious means of taking each of these actions, and you should use it. For instance, if you provide a help card, it should be activated by the help action, not by the accept action.

The contents of the do element tell the browser what to do when the user presses the OK button. In this case, a go element says to jump to the URL specified by its href attribute. In this case, that URL is the fragment identifier #e1, which means jump to the card in the same deck with the ID e1. However, it could also be a full URL telling the browser to jump to a different deck completely. Furthermore, instead of a go element, you could use any of the elements in Table 30-1 to map a key to a different kind of action.

Table 30-1
Action Elements

Label	Corresponds to
go	Go to the URL identified by the `href` attribute
prev	Go the previous card, like the Back button in a Web browser
noop	Short for "no operation;" do nothing at all; useful for eliminating default behavior
refresh	Resets variables as specified by the `refresh` element's `setvar` child elements

Listing 30-9 is a complete vocabulary deck that lets you navigate from one card to the next.

Listing 30-9: **A WML deck with six linked cards**

```
<?xml version="1.0" encoding="ISO-8859-1"?>
<!DOCTYPE wml PUBLIC "-//WAPFORUM//DTD WML 1.1//EN"
                      "http://www.wapforum.org/DTD/wml_1.1.xml">
<wml>
  <card id="f1" xml:lang="fr-CA">
    <p>Bonjour</p>
    <do type="accept">
      <go href="#e1"/>
    </do>
  </card>
  <card id="e1" xml:lang="en-US">
    <p>Hello</p>
    <do type="accept">
      <go href="#f2"/>
    </do>
  </card>
  <card id="f2" xml:lang="fr-CA">
    <p>monde</p>
    <do type="accept">
      <go href="#e2"/>
    </do>
  </card>
  <card id="e2" xml:lang="en-US">
    <p>world</p>
    <do type="accept">
      <go href="#f3"/>
    </do>
  </card>
```

Continued

Listing 30-9 *(continued)*

```
<card id="f3" xml:lang="fr-CA">
  <p>rédiger</p>
  <do type="accept">
    <go href="#e3"/>
  </do>
</card>
<card id="e3" xml:lang="en-US">
  <p>write, draw up, edit</p>
</card>
</wml>
```

Anchors

Suppose instead of drilling users on vocabulary you want to quiz them. You can set up a single card with one foreign word and three possible translations, one right and two wrong, like this:

```
<card id="q1">
  <p><strong>raconter</strong>:</p>
  <p>tell about</p>
  <p>resemble</p>
  <p>sail</p>
</card>
```

You then provide cards for the right answer and the wrong answer, like this:

```
<card id="right">
  <p><strong>Correct!</strong></p>
</card>
<card id="wrong">
  <p>
    <strong>Wrong!</strong>
    Try again.
  </p>
</card>
```

You can use the same a tag you're familiar with from HTML to link between the cards. Its href attribute contains a URL pointing to a different deck or a fragment identifier pointing to a different card in the same deck. Listing 30-10 shows the completed quiz using links.

Listing 30-10: A simple quiz using the a element to connect cards

```
<?xml version="1.0" encoding="ISO-8859-1"?>
<!DOCTYPE wml PUBLIC "-//WAPFORUM//DTD WML 1.1//EN"
                     "http://www.wapforum.org/DTD/wml_1.1.xml">
<wml>
  <card id="q1">
    <p><strong>raconter</strong>:</p>
    <p><a href="#right">tell about</a></p>
    <p><a href="#wrong">resemble</a></p>
    <p><a href="#wrong">sail</a></p>
  </card>
  <card id="right">
    <p><strong>Correct!</strong></p>
  </card>
  <card id="wrong">
    <p>
        <strong>Wrong!</strong>
        Try again.
    </p>
  </card>
</wml>
```

Figure 30-9 shows the first card in this deck. The phone in this picture indicates links by placing them inside square brackets. Other phones may use a different visual metaphor such as underlining the link, or showing it in reverse video. When color phones become available, they may even color links blue just like most Web browsers do. WML browsers exercise a lot more leeway in user interface than typical Web browsers.

The user can navigate from link to link by using the arrow keys. When the cursor is positioned at a link, the status indicator at the bottom left of the display changes from OK to Link. A user activates a link by pressing the accept button. On most phones, one of the keys also serves as a Back button so users can go back to the previous card without explicitly following a link.

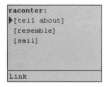

Figure 30-9: Links

Caution It doesn't really matter for this simple, ungraded quiz, but there are some security implications here. If this were a more serious test, or even a competitive trivia game, you would not want to send the user the answers at the same time you send them the question. You'd wait until they sent their response back to the server before uploading the answers to their browser. Otherwise, there are several ways a cheater could peek at the answers before they answered the question.

Instead of an a link, you can use an anchor element with a go action. For example,

```
<card id="q1">
  <p><strong>raconter</strong>:</p>
  <p><anchor><go href="#right"/>tell about</anchor></p>
  <p><anchor><go href="#wrong"/>resemble</anchor></p>
  <p><anchor><go href="#wrong"/>sail</anchor></p>
</card>
```

The advantage of this is that you can also use a prev or refresh action. For example, Listing 30-11 features a back link to the original question from the wrong answer card and an a link from the correct answer card that loads a new question from the server.

Listing 30-11: A simple quiz using anchor elements to connect cards and decks

```
<?xml version="1.0" encoding="ISO-8859-1"?>
<!DOCTYPE wml PUBLIC "-//WAPFORUM//DTD WML 1.1//EN"
                     "http://www.wapforum.org/DTD/wml_1.1.xml">
<wml>
  <card id="q1">
    <p><strong>raconter</strong>:</p>
    <p><anchor><go href="#right"/>tell about</anchor></p>
    <p><anchor><go href="#wrong"/>resemble</anchor></p>
    <p><anchor><go href="#wrong"/>sail</anchor></p>
  </card>
  <card id="right">
    <p><strong>Correct!</strong></p>
    <p><a href="q2.wml">Next question</a></p>
  </card>
  <card id="wrong">
    <p>
      <strong>Wrong!</strong><br/>
      <anchor><prev/>Try again.</anchor>
    </p>
  </card>
</wml>
```

Figure 30-10 shows the wrong answer card with the link back to the card the user came from. This is one place where WML is actually more powerful than HTML. HTML doesn't let you link back to the last card the user saw without knowing which card that was; but WML does.

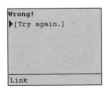

Figure 30-10: The wrong answer card

Selections

Making choices from lists of options, as in the French quiz examples, is one of the few user interfaces that works at all on cell phones. Anything that requires displaying more text, or asking the user to type in any word longer than four letters, is hopeless. WML provides special support for such lists of choices using the `select` element and its `option` children. The hierarchy is like this:

1. A `card` contains a p.

2. A p contains a `select` that has a `title` attribute.

3. A `select` contains one or more `option` elements.

4. Each `option` contains parsed character data.

5. Each `option` has an `onpick` attribute specifying which card to jump to when the option is selected.

Listing 30-12 uses a `select` group for the quiz of Listing 30-10. Each answer is encoded as an `option` element.

Listing 30-12: A simple quiz using a select group for question answers

```
<?xml version="1.0" encoding="ISO-8859-1"?>
<!DOCTYPE wml PUBLIC "-//WAPFORUM//DTD WML 1.1//EN"
                     "http://www.wapforum.org/DTD/wml_1.1.xml">
<wml>
  <card id="q1">
    <p>
      <strong>raconter:</strong>
      <select>
        <option onpick="#right">tell about</option>
```

Continued

Listing 30-12 *(continued)*

```
            <option onpick="#wrong">resemble</option>
            <option onpick="#wrong">sail</option>
        </select>
    </p>
</card>
<card id="right">
    <p><strong>Correct!</strong></p>
</card>
<card id="wrong">
    <p>
        <strong>Wrong!</strong>
        Try again.
    </p>
</card>
</wml>
```

Figure 30-11 shows the resulting quiz page. It's very similar to Figure 30-10. The user interface is a little different, and as always may vary from phone to phone. Here, the user can either use the arrow keys and the OK button to make their choice, or simply press 1, 2, or 3 on the keypad.

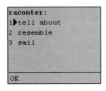

Figure 30-11: A select-based quiz

Tip   Never place more than nine options in a menu. There are only nine usable digits on the phone's keypad, after all.

The Options Menu

HTML documents often have menus of related pages down the right- or left-hand-side of the page. This allows the user to easily navigate to different sections of the site. Cell phones don't have the space to waste on such gewgaws, but it's still a useful feature. Thus, WML allows you to build an *options menu* into cards and decks that is normally hidden, but which the user can access by pressing the appropriate key. (As usual, exactly which key this is varies from phone to phone.)

Options menus are built from multiple do elements at the top-level of the card, outside of any p elements. Each such do element should have a type attribute with the value options and a label attribute giving the text of the menu item. For example, suppose the entrance to the foreign language WML service offers quizzes in French, Latin, and Greek. To let the user pick one, you would specify three do elements, each one linking to a different quiz with a go child. The deck in Listing 30-13 demonstrates.

Listing 30-13: **An options menu for choosing a quiz language**

```
<?xml version="1.0" encoding="ISO-8859-1"?>
<!DOCTYPE wml PUBLIC "-//WAPFORUM//DTD WML 1.1//EN"
                     "http://www.wapforum.org/DTD/wml_1.1.xml">
<wml>
  <card id="front_door">
    <do type="options" label="French">
      <go href="french.wml"/>
    </do>
    <do type="options" label="Latin">
      <go href="latin.wml"/>
    </do>
    <do type="options" label="Greek">
      <go href="greek.wml"/>
    </do>
    <p>
      <strong>Please choose a language from the menu</strong>:
    </p>
  </card>
</wml>
```

The browser initially presents just the card's paragraphs as shown in Figure 30-12. The phone clues in the user that an options menu is available for this card by placing the word Menu, Options, or some localized equivalent in its status bar. The user can access the menu from the Menu button on the phone, or their phone's equivalent. Again the exact phrasing and button placement can vary from phone to phone. However, once the menu has been activated it will look similar to Figure 30-13, with a number next to each menu option. Users can select options using the arrow keys and the accept button; or they can simply press the corresponding number on the phone's keypad for one-touch access.

Figure 30-12: The first screen for Listing 30-11

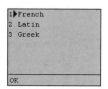

Figure 30-13: The options menu for Listing 30-11

Templates

You often want the same options menu to appear on each and every card. In this case, rather than placing the same batch of do elements on each card, you can place them all in a top-level template child element of the wml element. This element is optional, but if it's present it must be placed between the head and the first card element. For example, Listing 30-14 uses a template to allow the user to switch languages at any time in the vocabulary drill deck.

Listing 30-14: An options menu for multiple cards based on a template

```
<?xml version="1.0" encoding="ISO-8859-1"?>
<!DOCTYPE wml PUBLIC "-//WAPFORUM//DTD WML 1.1//EN"
                     "http://www.wapforum.org/DTD/wml_1.1.xml">
<wml>
  <template>
    <do type="options" label="French">
      <go href="french.wml"/>
    </do>
    <do type="options" label="Latin">
      <go href="latin.wml"/>
    </do>
    <do type="options" label="Greek">
      <go href="greek.wml"/>
    </do>
  </template>
  <card xml:lang="fr-CA">
    <p>Bonjour</p>
  </card>
  <card xml:lang="en-US">
    <p>Hello</p>
  </card>
  <card xml:lang="fr-CA">
    <p>monde</p>
  </card>
  <card xml:lang="en-US">
    <p>world</p>
  </card>
  <card xml:lang="fr-CA">
    <p>rédiger</p>
```

```
    </card>
    <card xml:lang="en-US">
      <p>write, draw up, edit</p>
    </card>
</wml>
```

If you put an options menu in both an individual card and in a template at the top level of the deck, then the one on the card overrides the one defined in the template on that card. On other cards without their own options menus, the one from the template is used.

WML templates are not parameterized. You cannot change the contents of the options menu from card to card or use more than one template in a deck. If you need to provide different options menus on different cards, then you need to use individual do elements on each card, even if there's a lot of duplication from card to card.

Events

WML operates in a much more limited environment than does HTML. However, it does have considerably more built-in interactivity. Some of the features that HTML needs additional technologies to implement, such as Flash, JavaScript, and HTML+Time, are a standard part of WML. In particular, you can install event handlers that respond to particular occurrences such as:

✦ A fixed amount of time elapsing (ontimer)

✦ A user loading the page from a URL (onenterforward)

✦ A user moving back to a page that they previously visited (onenterbackward)

An event handler is represented by an onevent child element of a card. The type attribute of the onevent element specifies what kind of event (ontimer, onenterforward, onenterbackward) the handler responds to. Each onevent element has a single child element that specifies what action to take when the event occurs. This should be one of the action elements listed in Table 30-1 and used previously for do actions: go, prev, refresh, or noop.

An onenterforward event occurs anytime the user follows a link to a card or types in the URL for a card. An onenterbackward event occurs anytime the user presses the back button to go to a card they've seen before. These events can be intercepted to prevent the user from seeing or returning to a card, for instance by responding to an onenterbackward event with a jump to a different card.

ontimer events do not naturally occur as the user navigates a deck. To create an ontimer event you must first add a timer element to the card. Each timer element has a value attribute that gives the number of tenths of seconds that elapse between when the card is first loaded and when the event is fired. Thus a value of 10 equals 1 second, a value of 20 equals 2 seconds, and so forth. Fractional values (that is, better than a tenth of a second precision) are not allowed.

The typical response to an ontimer event is to jump to a different card without a specific user request. For instance, you might use it to scroll large amounts of text one screen a second without requiring the user to continuously press the down-arrow key. (Unfortunately, there's no way to pause a screen.)

For example, let's suppose that you want to give the user no more than 10 seconds to answer a question in a quiz, and you only want to give them one shot at the question. First, you'd add a timer to the question card with a value of 100. If the timer expired before the user chose an answer, you'd go to a time-expired card. Then you'd add an onevent handler for onenterbackward events that jumped to an error card immediately if the user tried to go back to a question that the user had already seen. Listing 30-15 demonstrates.

Listing 30-15: **A timed quiz question**

```
<?xml version="1.0" encoding="ISO-8859-1"?>
<!DOCTYPE wml PUBLIC "-//WAPFORUM//DTD WML 1.1//EN"
                     "http://www.wapforum.org/DTD/wml_1.1.xml">
<wml>
  <card id="q1">
    <onevent type="onenterbackward">
      <go href="#one_chance"/>
    </onevent>
    <onevent type="ontimer">
      <go href="#time_expired"/>
    </onevent>
    <timer value="100"/>
    <p>
      <strong>raconter:</strong>
      <select>
        <option onpick="#right">tell about</option>
        <option onpick="#wrong">resemble</option>
        <option onpick="#wrong">sail</option>
      </select>
    </p>
  </card>
  <card id="right">
    <p><strong>Correct!</strong></p>
  </card>
  <card id="wrong">
    <p>
      <strong>Wrong!</strong>
    </p>
```

```
    </card>
    <card id="time_expired">
      <p>
        Sorry. You must answer in ten seconds or less.
      </p>
    </card>
    <card id="one_chance">
      <p>
        You only get one chance to answer each question.
      </p>
    </card>
</wml>
```

Using timers to automatically jump from one card to the next is so common that there's a shortcut for it. Instead of having a separate onevent element for the timer, you can just add an ontimer attribute to the parent card element. The value of this attribute is the URL of the card to jump to when the timer expires. You still have to include the timer child element itself, though. For example, by using this shortcut, the first card in Listing 30-15 could be rewritten like this:

```
    <card id="q1" ontimer="#time_expired">
      <onevent type="onenterbackward">
        <go href="#one_chance"/>
      </onevent>
      <timer value="100"/>
      <p>
        <strong>raconter:</strong>
        <select>
          <option onpick="#right">tell about</option>
          <option onpick="#wrong">resemble</option>
          <option onpick="#wrong">sail</option>
        </select>
      </p>
    </card>
```

The Header

WML documents can be spidered, searched, and indexed just like HTML and XML documents. Current spiders don't pay a lot of attention to WML; but if WML achieves broad adoption, this is likely to change. You can make your decks friendlier to search-engine robots, Web spiders, and intelligent agents by including metadata in your WML pages.

Just as in HTML, this metadata is customarily placed in a single head element at the start of the document. This element can have one access child and any number of meta children. The access element specifies which other decks are allowed to link to this one. The meta element can be used to specify values for arbitrary quantities for any purpose.

The access element

By default, any card in any WML deck at any Web site can link to your own decks and cards. The `access` element lets you control which other decks are allowed to link to this deck. You can limit access to a particular domain, to a particular host, or to a particular directory, subdirectory, or file on a particular host. Remember that what's being limited is where users are allowed to come to your deck from, not where users are allowed to go to from your deck.

Note　The `access` element is completely new to WML. HTML has nothing like it, although it can be simulated in JavaScript. If HTML did have such an element, problems such as the Ticketmaster-Microsoft lawsuit probably wouldn't have arisen in the first place.

The `access` element has two attributes: `domain` and `path`. The value of the `domain` attribute is a string such as `edu`, `fordham.edu`, or `www.fordham.edu`. Only decks somewhere in the specified domain will be allowed to link to your deck. The value of the `path` attribute is a partial path such as `/mll` or `/mll/ModLangs`. Only decks whose path begins with the specified string will be allowed to link to your deck.

For example, if the French quiz were developed at Fordham University, and you wanted to limit incoming links to other pages and sites at Fordham, you might place this `access` element in the `head`:

```
<access domain="fordham.edu"/>
```

If you wanted to limit access to links from other university sites, you might use this `access` element:

```
<access domain="edu"/>
```

However, if you wanted to limit access to surfers being referred from the Modern Languages department at Fordham University, you'd have to set the `path` attribute as well, like this:

```
<access domain="www.fordham.edu" path="/mll/ModLangs"/>
```

Remember that the `access` element only controls which other pages and decks are allowed to refer to your deck. It has nothing to do with where the user is or what domain they're in. I can be surfing the Internet from spy.cia.gov and still read decks that are restricted to fordham.edu as long as I get to your decks by going through a link from a fordham.edu Web page or WML deck.

Caution　Because access control is enforced on the client side, and can easily be subverted by customized client software, this is not secure. Do not rely it on for anything more important than one-player games.

Meta

WML meta elements have the same general syntax and purpose as HTML meta elements. To provide arbitrary meta-information you use the name and content attributes instead of name and value attributes. For example, if you want to specify that robots are not allowed to index or follow the links in a page, you'd place this meta tag in your head element:

```
<meta name="robots" content="noindex,nofollow"/>
```

To identify the author of the page, you could use a meta element like this one:

```
<meta name="author" content="Elliotte Rusty Harold"/>
```

To set the value of one of the HTTP headers that's sent by the server before the WML document, use the http-equiv attribute instead of name. For example, to specify that the document is written in the ISO-8859-1 character set, you could use this meta element:

```
<meta http-equiv="Content-Type"
      content='text/vnd.wap.wml; charset="ISO-8859-1"'/>
```

On some Web servers, this may also be a more convenient way of specifying the proper MIME media type for WML files than reconfiguring the server to recognize the .wml extension.

WML does add one new attribute to the meta element that HTML doesn't have. This is forua, which stands for "for user agent." WML documents are normally served through a WAP gateway, and the gateway normally takes the action requested by the meta element, and then strips it out of the file it sends to the client. However, if you set forua to true, the gateway will pass the meta element along to the client unchanged.

Variables

HTML browsers use cookies to maintain state as users move from page to page within the site. WML browsers use *variables*. The good news is that variables are a lot easier to configure and use than HTML cookies because variables were designed into WML from the start, rather than being bolted on after the fact like cookies.

Caution   The bad news is that the privacy implications of WML variables are just as bad as with cookies, though different. Any site that knows the name of a variable can read its value, not just the site that sent it to you. This means users can be tracked across sites, and that secure information such as passwords and credit card numbers should not be stored in variables. On the other hand, cookies can live forever so that users can be tracked over time by a single site. All WML variables are erased when the phone is turned off. There are efforts under way to add persistent cookie support to WAP so that cell phone users will have the worst of both worlds. If that's not scary enough, advertisers and law enforcement agencies are salivating over the prospect of cell phones that can tell them your physical location within a few meters at any given time. The next time you're walking past the local adult bookshop, don't be surprised if you get a call on your cell phone telling you that Ryan Idol videos are on sale this week.

Reading and writing variables

Each WML variable has a name and a value. Both of these are strings. WML does not have any integer, floating point, char, array, object, or other variable types.

The `setvar` element assigns a value to a variable. If the variable does not exist, it is created. If it does exist, its old value is overwritten. For example, this `setvar` element gives the variable `username` the value `armaup`:

```
<setvar name="username" value="armaup"/>
```

The `setvar` element is only allowed inside `go`, `prev`, `refresh`, and `postfield` elements. This means the user must take some action or an event must occur before a variable can be set.

Variable names must be composed exclusively of the English letters A through Z and a through z, the digits 0 through 9, and the underscore _. Each variable must begin with an underscore or a letter. There is no limit to the number of characters that you can use in a variable value, as long as the normal rules of XML are followed. The length of both variable names and values is unlimited. A variable that is set to the empty string (for example, `<setvar name="username" value=""/>`) is considered to be *unset*; that is, it does not have a value.

To use a variable, you include its name in the text of your WML document, preceded by a dollar sign. For example, `$username` refers to the variable named username. The name is sometimes enclosed in parentheses, like `$(username)`, if the variable name is not immediately followed by white space. The browser will replace the variable reference with the variable value before displaying the card to the user. Variables may be used in the text of a card, and in the values of `href`, `title`, `label`, `name`, `value`, `iname`, `ivalue`, and `alt` attributes. However, variables cannot be used to substitute for tags or entire elements. They are not entity references, in other words.

Listing 30-16 is a simple WML deck in which the first card asks the user whether they prefer apples or oranges. Users indicate their choice by clicking a link. If they choose the first link, then `fruit` is set to apples. If they choose the second link, then `fruit` is set to oranges. Simultaneously with their choice, they go to the second card, which displays this value, as shown in Figure 30-15. This requires that the user come to the first card before the second card. If the user reaches the second card before the first card, then `fruit` will not have been set. Judicious use of the `onenterforward` and `onenterbackward` events can sometimes prevent this from happening. However, it's not easily possible to check whether a variable has a value or what that value is before displaying it.

Listing 30-16: **A deck that uses variables**

```
<?xml version="1.0" encoding="ISO-8859-1"?>
<!DOCTYPE wml PUBLIC "-//WAPFORUM//DTD WML 1.1//EN"
                     "http://www.wapforum.org/DTD/wml_1.1.xml">
<wml>
  <card id="c1">
    <p>
      Do you prefer
      <anchor>
        apples
        <go href="#c2">
          <setvar name="fruit" value="apples"/>
        </go>
      </anchor>
      or
      <anchor>
        oranges?
        <go href="#c2">
          <setvar name="fruit" value="oranges"/>
        </go>
      </anchor>
    </p>
  </card>
  <card id="c2">
    <p>You prefer $(fruit).</p>
  </card>
</wml>
```

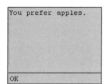

Figure 30-14: The user can't tell that the value came from a variable.

WMLScript

Normally variables go hand-in-hand with a programming language such as C, Basic, or JavaScript. Indeed, WML does have a programming language called WMLScript, and WMLScript programs can access and work with WML variables created by `setvar`, `input`, or `select` elements. WMLScript is essentially JavaScript with a few extra functions for working with WML documents in particular. Thus, it provides all the arithmetic, logic, string manipulation, and other functionality that you'd expect from a traditional programming language.

However, traditional procedural programming language syntax doesn't map well into XML's element- and attribute-based hierarchy. Therefore, WMLScript is not written in XML. Instead, WMLScripts are placed in separate files, generally with the four-letter extension .wmls. They can be linked to from `go`, `a`, and `do` elements just like regular WML decks and cards. The URL part specifies the WMLScript file, and the fragment identifier provides the name and arguments of the function to call in that file. When such a link is activated, the script is executed.

However, as of early 2001, WMLScript is supported by relatively few actual cell phones, so it's not a good idea to build your WML services around it. Furthermore, because WMLScript is not XML (unlike WML) and requires some experience with JavaScript, it's doubly outside the scope of this book. If you want to know more, the WAP Forum at `http://www.wapforum.org/what/technical.htm` provides the WMLScript language and library specifications in PDF format.

A single dollar sign in WML content always represents the start of a variable reference. If you just want to include a dollar sign as a dollar sign, in a price for example, then you have to replace each single dollar sign with a double dollar sign. For example, if you wanted to add dollar signs to the quotes in the stock portfolio example, as shown in Figure 30-15, you have to use double dollar signs, as shown in Listing 30-17. If you used single dollar signs, the browser would report an error.

Listing 30-17: **A deck that includes dollars signs in the parsed character data**

```
<?xml version="1.0"?>
<!DOCTYPE wml PUBLIC "-//WAPFORUM//DTD WML 1.1//EN"
                     "http://www.wapforum.org/DTD/wml_1.1.xml">
<wml>
  <card>
    <p>
    <table columns="2" title="Your Portfolio">
      <tr><td>Symbol</td><td>Price</td></tr>
      <tr><td>RHAT</td><td>$$8.69</td></tr>
      <tr><td>COVD</td><td>$$2.81</td></tr>
```

```
       <tr><td>NPNT</td><td>$$0.75</td></tr>
     </table>
     </p>
   </card>
</wml>
```

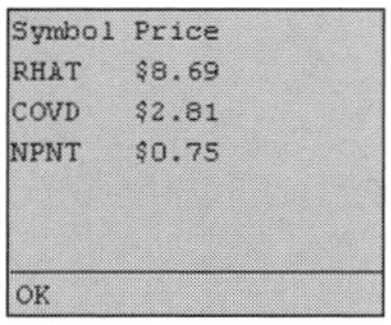

```
Symbol Price
RHAT    $8.69
COVD    $2.81
NPNT    $0.75


OK
```

Figure 30-15: Dollar signs in #PCDATA must be doubled in the source document.

Input fields

One of the main uses for variables in WML is to hold input from the user. The input element, which is very similar to the input element in HTML, allows you to collect a small amount of information from the user and display it on cards or send it back to the server. The name attribute of the input element gives the name of the variable being input. For example, Listing 30-18 asks the user for their name and then gives them a personalized greeting.

Listing 30-18: Hello you

```
<?xml version="1.0" encoding="ISO-8859-1"?>
<!DOCTYPE wml PUBLIC "-//WAPFORUM//DTD WML 1.1//EN"
                  "http://www.wapforum.org/DTD/wml_1.1.xml">
<wml>
  <card id="c1">
    <p>
      <strong>Please tell me your name:</strong>
      <input name="username"/>
      <do type="accept">
        <go href="#c2"/>
      </do>
    </p>
  </card>
  <card id="c2">
    <p>Hello $username</p>
  </card>
</wml>
```

Figure 30-16 shows the input field as shown on the phone. Figure 30-17 shows the personalized message.

Figure 30-16: An input field

Figure 30-17: The variable $username has been set by the input field.

Use input fields **VERY** sparingly. While it's straightforward to type in a name using the keyboard in a simulator, it is extremely difficult to enter even a few letters from an actual cell phone keypad. In fact, many WML providers actually have users customize their menus and services online at a real Web site from their desktop PCs rather than from their cell phones because it's just too hard to enter data on a phone. The most I'd ask users to enter from their keypad would be a three-letter airport code or a four-letter stock symbol.

Besides the required name attribute, the input element can have any of these optional attributes:

✦ type: If the type attribute has the value password, then only dots are echoed on the screen when the user types into the field.

✦ value: A default value for the input field that is shown before the user starts typing.

✦ format: A mask specifying which characters the user is allowed to type where; for instance, the format string NN\/NN\/NNNN specifies that the user must input a date in the form 01/19/2001.

✦ emptyok: This either has the value true — the field is allowed to be empty — or false — the field is not allowed to be empty. The default is false.

✦ size: An integer indicating how many letters the browser should set aside space for.

✦ maxlength: The maximum number of characters allowed in the value; for instance in a credit card number this might be 16.

✦ title: A label for the field which the browser may or may not choose to show.

Select

The select element can also be used to set variables. The name attribute specifies the variable to set. The value attribute specifies the default value for the variable in case the user doesn't make a selection. Each of the option child elements also has a value attribute that gives the value to assign to the variable if the user chooses that option.

Listing 30-19 demonstrates with a card that asks the user whether they want to drill on nouns, verbs, or adjectives. The default choice is nouns. Users are sent to different decks depending on their choice.

Listing 30-19: The select element sets the part_of_speech variable

```
<?xml version="1.0" encoding="ISO-8859-1"?>
<!DOCTYPE wml PUBLIC "-//WAPFORUM//DTD WML 1.1//EN"
                     "http://www.wapforum.org/DTD/wml_1.1.xml">
<wml>
  <card>
    <p>
      <strong>Drill on:</strong>
      <select name="part_of_speech" value="noun">
        <option value="nouns">Nouns</option>
        <option value="verbs">Verbs</option>
        <option value="adjectives">Adjectives</option>
      </select>
      <do type="accept">
        <go href="$(part_of_speech).wml"/>
      </do>
    </p>
  </card>
</wml>
```

If it's more convenient you can set a variable to the integer index of the selection such as 1, 2, or 3. In this case, use the iname attribute of the select element to hold the variable name and the ivalue attribute to hold the default value. You can use name and value and iname and ivalue at the same time to set two different variables, although it's rarely necessary to do so.

Setting a new context for variables

WML variables are global. A variable set on one card or site still exists on all other cards and sites visited by the browser until it's overwritten. Because variables aren't segregated by the sites that create them, another site's variables can overwrite yours; and that other site's variables can provide confusing information to your site. If you use variables with common names such as x or username, this is especially likely. If you're going to use variables in your decks and sites to track the progress of users, the first thing you need to do when a user enters your site is wipe out existing variables that might conflict with yours. You do this by giving the card a newcontext attribute with the value true. For example,

```
<card id="entrance_card" newcontext="true">
  <p>...</p>
</card>
```

Unfortunately, this has the side effect of wiping out the user's history so they won't be able to go back to any card they came from prior to entering your site. Furthermore, if the user ever comes back to this card while in the process of navigating your site, all the variables they've set and their navigation history through your site will also be lost. You can make this problem less likely by using events. For example, consider these two cards:

```
<card>
  <!-- This must be the first card in the deck -->
  <onevent type="onenterforward">
    <go href="#wipeout"/>
  </onevent>
  <p>...</p>
</card>
<card id="wipeout" newcontext="true">
  <onevent type="onenterforward"><prev/></onevent>
  <onevent type="onenterbackward"><prev/></onevent>
</card>
```

Users initially go to the main card by following a link to the entire deck with no fragment identifier. They are then immediately redirected to the wipeout card, which sets a new context and thereby erases all existing variables and history. The wipeout card then redirects them back to the card they came from using the prev action and an onenterforward event. (The same thing happens through an onenterbackward event if somehow a user backs into the wipeout card, though this is unlikely.) There should be no direct links to the entrance card from anywhere else in the deck, which its lack of an id attribute enforces. If the user uses the Back button to return to the entrance card, only an onenterbackward event occurs, which does not result in a jump to the wipeout card, so all variables are maintained. Frankly, this is a big hack and is not perfectly reliable. Nonetheless, this is the best you can do given the brain-damaged way variables are implemented in WML.

Talking Back to the Server

Until now, all the WML document examples have been static files, which make nice, simple book examples. In the real world, however, most WML sites, even more than HTML sites, rely on databases, CGI, servlets, ASP, JSP, PHP, ColdFusion, Zope,

Enhydra, and other server-side technologies. Many WML pages are dynamically generated out of databases. For example, the various foreign language drill-and-quiz examples might use randomly chosen words from large dictionaries.

If you're familiar with any of these server-side environments, writing the code to dynamically or randomly generate the decks is not at all hard. However, with all this powerful server machinery you'd like to do more. You'd like to store quiz scores on the server. You might want to adjust the difficulty of questions according to a student's prior performance. You might want more secure quizzes that don't send students the correct answers until they've submitted their answer. All of this and a lot more requires that the cell phone browser be able to send information back to the server.

There are two main ways that the WML client can send information back to the server:

✦ By encoding the data in a request for a URL. For instance, a server might interpret the URL `http://www.wmlstocks.com/getQuote.wml?symbol=RHAT` as a request for the current stock price of Red Hat. This is called the GET method. I've already implicitly used this approach several times in this chapter.

✦ By submitting form data after the request for a URL. This is called the POST method.

The GET method is very straightforward. You simply build the URL in the form the server expects to receive it. If you use a variable to hold the query string values, then the WML browser will even automatically encode it in the x-www-form-url-encoded syntax required by the CGI specification. For example, this card collects a stock symbol from the user, attaches it to a relative URL, and sends the whole thing to a server.

```
<card>
  <p>
    <strong>Please enter stock symbol and press OK:</strong>
    <input name="symbol"/>
    <do type="accept">
      <go href="prices.cgi?stock=$(symbol)"/>
    </do>
  </p>
</card>
```

Almost all the effort here is in writing the server-side program that receives and responds to the request. For details on that end, consult any good book on CGI programming (or servlets, JSP, ASP, PHP, or similar technologies).

POST is only slightly more complicated. To indicate that you want to use POST instead of GET, you add a `method` attribute with the value `post` to the `go` element. The `go` element must still have an `href` attribute that specifies the URL to post the data to. You place the name-value pairs the server-side program expects to receive in `postfield` elements, one such element for each CGI variable. The `postfield` element has `name` and `value` attributes providing the value to post.

For example, a couple of times in this chapter I've warned you that the quizzes weren't secure because the questions and answers were sent to the browser at the same time. Now I'm going to show you how to fix that. Listing 30-20 uses the same question you've seen several times in this chapter. However, this time the answers aren't included. Instead, when the user makes a selection and presses the Accept button, their answer is sent to the server. Some program running on the server must inspect that answer and decide which page to send back. It can also keep track of a user's answers to provide a final grade when the quiz is finished.

Listing 30-20: A secure quiz

```
<?xml version="1.0" encoding="ISO-8859-1"?>
<!DOCTYPE wml PUBLIC "-//WAPFORUM//DTD WML 1.1//EN"
                     "http://www.wapforum.org/DTD/wml_1.1.xml">
<wml>
  <card id="q1">
    <p>
      <strong>raconter:</strong>
      <select name="answer" value="">
        <option value="tell about">tell about</option>
        <option value="resemble">resemble</option>
        <option value="sail">sail</option>
      </select>
      <do type="accept">
        <go href="answer.wml" method="post">
          <postfield name="response" value="$(answer)"/>
          <postfield name="username" value="armaup"/>
        </go>
      </do>
    </p>
  </card>
</wml>
```

What does the server do when it receives this data? That's up to you. You'll need to write some sort of servlet, CGI, or other server-side program that receives and responds to the data.

There is a speed penalty to this strategy. The browser has to go back to the server for each card. That could be alleviated in part by feeding all the question cards as one deck but leaving the answers on the server. Overall, though, the server is a much more secure and convenient place to store state and other information than the client.

Summary

In this chapter, you learned that:

✦ The Wireless Markup Language (WML) is an XML application for serving Web content to cell phones, PDAs, and other display-, CPU-, memory-, and bandwidth-limited devices.

✦ The root element of WML documents is wml.

✦ The wml element contains an optional head, an optional template, and one or more card elements.

✦ The head element can contain a single access element that specifies which other sites and decks are allowed to link to this one.

✦ The head element can also contain meta elements that set HTTP headers, control robots, add keywords and abstracts for search engines, or perform other behind-the-scenes jobs.

✦ The template element defines an options menu for every card in the deck. Each option is a do element with a type="options" attribute.

✦ Each card element represents one screenful of data.

✦ The text of a card is contained inside p elements, which represent paragraphs.

✦ Text can be formatted using familiar HTML-like elements such as u, b, strong, em, i, and br. However, not all WML browsers can display all possible styles.

✦ Hypertext links can be inserted into text with the familiar a element from HTML or an anchor element with a go child.

✦ The img element lets you add black-and-white images in a special Wireless Bitmap (WBMP) format to your cards.

✦ The do element lets you define an action to be taken at user option. Its type attribute specifies what the user has to do to take the specified action.

✦ The onevent element lets you take action when a timer expires, the user views a card for the first time, or the user returns to a card.

✦ Actions you can take include going to a new card with go, returning to the previous card with prev, or resetting the variables with refresh.

   ✦ The `setvar` element defines a variable using `name` and `value` attributes.

   ✦ The `input` element defines a variable using its `name` attribute and text the user types in from the keypad.

   ✦ The `select` element defines a variable using its `name` attribute and a choice the user makes from a menu.

   ✦ The `postfield` element lets you send data to server-side programs that expect their input to come via the POST method.

In the next chapter, we explore a standard XML application from the W3C — Scalable Vector Graphics (SVG). SVG is a W3C Recommendation for an XML format for line art. Unlike most XML applications that describe text of some kind or another, or perhaps numeric data, SVG documents describe pictures. SVG goes a long way toward proving just how versatile XML really is.

✦   ✦   ✦

Scalable Vector Graphics

The world has several well-understood, well-supported formats for photographs, painted art, and other bitmapped graphics including GIF, JPEG, and, most recently, PNG. These have all achieved broad adoption on the Web and elsewhere. However, a standard format for line art, such as flowcharts, blueprints, technical diagrams, and other sorts of drawings, has been sorely lacking. Scalable Vector Graphics (SVG) is the first realistic candidate to fill this hole.

SVG is a W3C-endorsed XML application for line art. It defines elements that represent polygons, rectangles, ellipses, lines, curves, and more. New shapes can be defined using a simple path language. Color schemes and patterns can be applied to shapes through clipping, masking, compositing, fills, and gradients. Furthermore, the shapes on the page can move. JavaScript can make shapes respond to user input. SVG is a complete format for detailed descriptions of dynamic vector graphics. For static graphics, SVG is almost on a par with Adobe's EPS (Encapsulated PostScript) format, and considerably more powerful than CGM (Computer Graphics Metafile). For animated pictures, it's as powerful as the proprietary SWF format used by Macromedia Flash.

SVG documents can be embedded in Web pages. Browser plug-ins exist that enable Netscape and Internet Explorer (IE) to display SVG graphics. Eventually, SVG support will be built directly into browsers so that you can include SVG drawings in your Web pages with no more effort than you expend today to add a GIF or JPEG picture to a page. However, SVG's significance extends far past the limited domain of Web sites. SVG will eventually become the standard exchange medium for drawings produced by all sorts of vector graphics software on any platform.

A Word of Caution about SVG

SVG is still under development. The SVG language has changed in the past, and will change again in the future. This chapter is based on the July 19, 2001 SVG Proposed Recommendation. By the time you read this book, the final version of SVG will probably have been released and a few details will have changed. If you do encounter something that doesn't seem to work quite right, please compare the examples in this book against the final specification.

To make matters worse, at the time of this writing no software implemented all of the July 19, 2001 SVG Proposed Recommendation. In fact, so far there are only a few standalone programs and browser plug-ins that can understand SVG documents. None of the major Web browsers (Netscape, IE, Opera) know how to interpret and display an SVG picture embedded in an HTML page without a plug-in. Eventually, of course, this should be straightened out as SVG evolves toward its final incarnation and more vendors implement it in their software.

What Is SVG?

There are two primary types of computer graphics: bitmapped and vector. A bitmapped graphic contains a list of the colors of individual pixels in a normally rectangular area. Examples include the GIF, JPEG, and PNG images used on most Web pages. If a bitmapped graphic is 3 inches by 4 inches and has a resolution of 90 pixels per inch, then it contains $90 \times 3 \times 90 \times 4$ pixels, that is, 97,000 pixels. If the image is stored in 24-bit color, then each pixel occupies 3 bytes, so this image uses 2,332,800 bits, or about 285KB of memory. The actual file may use a variety of lossy and nonlossy compression algorithms to reduce this size somewhat, but bitmapped images still get very big very quickly. This is why Web pages with lots of pictures are so slow to load.

By contrast, a vector graphic does not store several bytes of data for each pixel in the image. Instead it stores a list of instructions for drawing the image. These instructions may say to draw a black line between the upper-left corner and the lower-right corner of the page, place a purple circle with a 2-inch radius in the middle of the page, and draw the text "Delicious, delicious. Oh how boring!" 12 points high in the Palatino font on top of the circle. As a general rule, the space required for these instructions is much less than the space required for a bitmapped equivalent. Vector graphics are much smaller and more efficient than bitmapped images. Vector formats aren't suitable for all graphics — for instance, they don't work well for photographs — but they are much better for graphics that were drawn on a computer by a human being rather than being copied from nature using a camera, digital or otherwise.

There are many vector graphics formats in the world today including PICT, EPS, and CGM; but for historical and political reasons, there really hasn't been a standard format everyone could use. PICT files are based on the Macintosh's native

QuickDraw software and algorithms. They are mostly limited to the Macintosh and don't port well to other platforms. EPS documents require a full-blown PostScript interpreter, which, while potentially cross-platform, is too big a task for many graphic software vendors. CGM was probably the closest to a vendor-neutral, standard, vector graphics format, especially in its WebCGM incarnation; but CGM lacks complex fills, image clipping, image manipulation, detailed color control, and other high-end features that graphic designers need. Furthermore, CGM is a binary file format, with all the concurrent disadvantages of binary file formats. In fact, all three of these formats are so difficult to implement that few Web browsers (and none of the major ones) have included built-in support for them. It seems probable that SVG will be the first successful effort to define a truly open, cross-platform standard for vector graphics.

SVG is an XML application for describing drawings. SVG elements represent two-dimensional shapes: rectangles, ovals, circles, triangles, clouds, spirals, trapezoids, and so forth. Each shape is described as a path formed from a series of lines and curves. SVG uses elements and attributes to describe the position, size, and outline of each shape. CSS styles are used to attach colors, fonts, and other details to the abstract geometric shapes.

XSL also integrates very nicely with SVG. Because SVG documents are well-formed XML documents, an XSLT processor can convert SVG documents into other SVG documents or into other XML applications. More commonly, an existing XML document can be converted into SVG. For example, a file full of numbers might be converted into a bar graph, a pie chart, or even a bar code. The resulting SVG document might then be embedded in an XSL Formatting Objects document. SVG merges very nicely with XSL-FO. The XSL-FO can describe the general text-based page layout, while SVG describes all the graphics.

Most SVG documents are drawn using a GUI (graphical user interface), and only saved into SVG form. Consequently, you don't need to know the detailed syntax of each and every SVG element and attribute. However, if you know a little, you can sometimes do some surprising tricks with the SVG file that may prove impossible with a graphical editor. For example, you can search for all the blue elements, and change them to red. SVG is also a much easier graphics format to generate from programs you write than binary formats such as TIFF, PICT, or CGM.

Scalability

The *S* in SVG stands for *Scalable*. That means a given SVG picture is not tied to a single resolution or size. The same picture can be expanded or compressed. The same SVG document can become a very small picture on a Palm Pilot, a medium-sized picture on a Web page, or a very large picture projected on a movie screen. An SVG picture can even be zoomed in or out at full resolution on the same display. SVG pictures do not have absolute sizes.

Scalable also means that the same picture can be displayed at different resolutions. I can print a full-page picture on my Apple Personal LaserWriter NTR, and the picture will be printed at the printer's full resolution of 300 dots per inch. I can show the same picture on my Silicon Graphics 1600SW flat panel monitor, and it will use the monitor's lesser resolution of 110 dots per inch. If I used a higher-resolution printer or a lower-resolution monitor, the picture would adjust accordingly. Unlike bitmapped formats such as TIFF, JPEG, and GIF, SVG pictures don't require you to choose between size and resolution.

Scalable also means that SVG can scale to very large projects where documents are built up out of thousands of individual pictures. For instance, an architectural diagram for a new campus of a large corporation might include separate SVG documents representing each room. Floor documents would be built up by combining the room documents. Buildings would be created by combining the floor documents. The campus would be created by combining the individual building documents and adding a few pieces to represent the tunnels and roads and green spaces that connected them. Similar buildings and floors might be described by annotating small changes on top of basic templates. Different architects could work on different parts of the campus at the same time; then combine all the pieces together.

Caution

In my opinion, this definition of scalability isn't well met by SVG 1.0. There are two problems. First, the ability to build one SVG document out of multiple component parts is based on some other specifications, such as XInclude and XLink, that aren't finished yet. Second, SVG documents don't carry any notion of the real-world sizes of what they describe, just a scalable local coordinate space. This means that there's no standard way of making sure that the water fountain I design will fit through the door of the building you design.

Vector versus bitmapped graphics

Since the demise of daisy-wheel printers, all modern computer rendering devices have used bitmapped graphics. They divide the canvas on which they draw into a grid of pixels of varying colors. The basic algorithms for rendering raster graphics are the same whether you're talking about a 72-dpi color CRT monitor or a 1200-dpi black-and-white printer. This means that when a vector document such as an SVG picture is drawn, it must first be converted into a bitmap. The real difference, therefore, between finite precision bitmapped pictures and infinitely precise vector graphics is in where the conversion to the bitmap, and subsequent loss of information, takes place. With a bitmapped image, the information is lost when the document is first created at a particular resolution. With a vector image, all information is maintained perfectly until the document is actually drawn on the screen or printed on paper.

Because SVG graphics will eventually be rendered as a bitmap, the W3C Scalable Vector Graphics Working Group decided that it might as well take advantage of that fact. Consequently, they added a number of fundamentally bitmapped features to SVG that are applied to SVG pictures on the client side when the document is rendered. For example, you can place bitmapped JPEG and PNG images in an SVG document using the `image` element. For another example, infinitely precise vector text doesn't need antialiasing but bitmapped text does. SVG renderers can apply a variety of antialiasing algorithms to both text and lines before drawing them on the screen. SVG documents can also request bitmap filter effects such as blurring and drop shadows.

A Simple SVG Document

Listing 31-1 is an SVG document that describes a red circle. This document should be saved in a file named something like circle.svg or 31-1.svg. The three-letter extension .svg is customary, although not always required. This is an XML document so it could be saved as circle.xml or as circle.txt. The MIME media type of this document should be set to image/svg+xml in environments that support MIME types. Figure 31-1 shows the document displayed in the Apache XML Project's Batik.

On the CD-ROM Batik is an open source program included on the CD-ROM in the directory utilities/batik. The most recent version can be downloaded from the Web at `http://xml.apache.org/batik/`. Batik requires Java 1.2 or later. Once you've unzipped the zip file, you can run the Batik SVGViewer by double-clicking the batik-svgbrowser.jar file. Alternately, you can run it at the command line from inside the batik directory like this:

```
C:\batik-1.0>java -jar batik-svgviewer.jar
```

Figure 31-1: An SVG document

Listing 31-1: An SVG document that represents a red circle with a blue outline

```
<?xml version="1.0" encoding="UTF-8" standalone="yes"?>
<svg xmlns="http://www.w3.org/2000/svg"
     width="3.5in" height="1in">
  <title>Listing 31-1 from the XML Bible</title>
  <circle  r="30" cx="34" cy="34"
           style="fill: red; stroke: blue; stroke-width: 2" />
</svg>
```

This is an XML document, so it begins with an XML declaration like all good XML documents should. This particular document doesn't have a document type declaration, so it's only well formed, not valid. However, the SVG specification does include a DTD that you can use to validate SVG documents, and you could reference it if it seemed useful to do so. You could even provide an `xml-stylesheet` processing instruction that connected this document to a CSS or XSL style sheet.

The root element of this and all SVG documents is `svg`. This element is in the `http://www.w3.org/2000/svg` namespace. Sometimes, as here, this is the default namespace. Other times, it's mapped to a prefix. The prefix `svg` is customary. As usual, the specific prefix (or lack thereof) doesn't matter as long as the URI is correct.

Note   This chapter uses the `http://www.w3.org/2000/svg` URI from the July 19, 2001, SVG Proposed Recommendation exclusively. However, earlier working drafts of the SVG specification used different URIs, and it's possible that the final release version of SVG 1.0 will use a different namespace.

The `svg` element has `width` and `height` attributes that specify the size of the canvas on which the picture is drawn. Here it's a 3.5-inch wide by 1-inch high rectangle. These attributes aren't required, but some versions of Batik don't seem to work properly if they aren't included.

The root `svg` element also contains two child elements: a `title` and a `circle`. The `title` contains a string of text that's displayed in the title bar of the SVG browser. The `circle` is a shape to be drawn. This circle has a radius of 30. "30 what?" you may be asking. Is that 30 pixels? 30 inches? 30 parsecs? It's actually 30 units in the nondimensional local coordinate space. Remember that SVG graphics are scalable. The real size of a radius 30 circle can change from one environment to another. By default, it maps to 30 pixels on the local display so the circle will be smaller on higher-resolution monitors. However, you can use transforms and other markup to change the actual size, as you'll see soon.

The center of the circle is placed at position x=34, y=34. This is 34 units down from and 34 units to the right of the upper-left corner of the window. Standard computer graphics coordinates are used. That is, the upper-left corner of this rectangle is point 0, 0. X coordinates increase to the right; Y coordinates increase down. Figure 31-2 diagrams this coordinate system. You can use floating-point numbers such as 7.5 to place shapes anywhere on this grid. You are not limited to placing shapes at the actual pixels of the display. An SVG document represents an abstract, infinitely precise, almost Platonic ideal of a two-dimensional plane.

The `style` attribute assigns CSS properties to this circle. In particular, it sets the fill color to red and the stroke color to blue. Furthermore it makes the stroke two units wide.

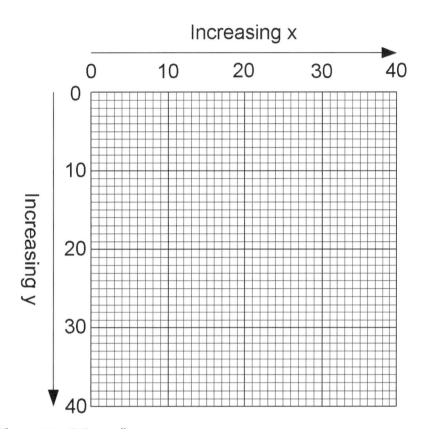

Figure 31-2: SVG coordinate system

 Caution In my opinion, this is one of the flakier aspects of SVG. CSS defines a color property, but it doesn't define any fill, stroke, or stroke-width properties. SVG has adopted the CSS syntax as an optional feature, but applied it to its own set of properties. The same circle could equally well have been written like this:

```
<circle r="30" cx="34" cy="34"
        fill="red" stroke="blue" stroke-width="2" />
```

For inline styles, I prefer to use the more explicit attributes. However, you can also attach external CSS style sheets to SVG documents that set various properties for different elements. This is perhaps a little more useful.

SVG elements and attribute names only use the ASCII character set, so any normal text editor can produce and save an SVG document. However, if the drawing content itself contains non-ASCII text (for example, a Russian billboard) then you'd have to save it in some other character set and use the appropriate encoding declaration to identify it. Of course, as you'll see at the end of this chapter, you don't have to use a text editor to create or save an SVG document at all. In fact, most of the time, you'll probably use a graphics program such as Adobe Illustrator that offers a standard user interface for drawing pictures. You'll just save the finished result as SVG.

Embedding SVG Pictures in Web Pages

It's very easy to include SVG pictures in Web pages for browsers that natively understand SVG. You don't even have to use valid XHTML. Just paste the SVG source code into the HTML document where you want the picture to appear. Listing 31-2 demonstrates by embedding Listing 31-1 in a simple HTML document.

Listing 31-2: An HTML document in which Listing 31-1 is embedded

```
<HTML>
  <HEAD>
    <TITLE>Circles are my friends</TITLE>
  </HEAD>
  <BODY>
  <H1>Rectangles are the Enemy!</H1>

  <svg xmlns="http://www.w3.org/2000/svg"
       style="width: 3.5in; height: 1in">
    <title>Listing 31-1 from the XML Bible</title>
    <circle r="30" cx="34" cy="34"
            style="fill: red; stroke: blue; stroke-width: 2" />
  </svg>

  <HR>
  Last Modified May 30, 2001<BR>
  Copyright 2001
  <A HREF="mailto:elharo@metalab.unc.edu">
    Elliotte Rusty Harold
  </A>

  </BODY>
</HTML>
```

At the time of this writing, only the Amaya browser from the W3C natively supports SVG included in this fashion. Figure 31-3 shows Amaya displaying Listing 31-2.

On the CD-ROM Amaya is on the CD-ROM in the directory browsers/amaya. You can download the latest version from http://www.w3.org/Amaya/. This chapter was written using Amaya 4.3.2.

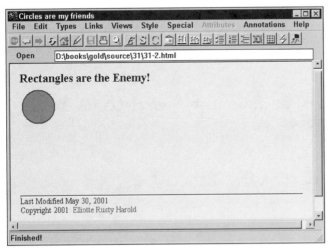

Figure 31-3: An SVG document included in a Web page

Although they're text, SVG documents are no more part of HTML than are the binary GIF, JPEG, and PNG formats. Therefore most browsers don't support SVG pictures that are pasted into HTML source code, as in Listing 31-2. Instead, you have to save the picture in a separate document and link to it from the HTML using the EMBED element. This is very much like the normal IMG element you're familiar with from HTML. It has WIDTH, HEIGHT, ALT, ALIGN, and SRC attributes that mean more or less the same as they mean for IMG. The only difference is that IMG is used for image formats the browser natively supports, while EMBED is used for data formats that require a separate plug-in. Most EMBED elements also have a PLUG-INSPAGE attribute whose value is a URL where the browser can download the plug-in it needs to display the embedded content. I recommend the Adobe SVG Viewer plug-in, which is available for Netscape and Internet Explorer on both Windows and MacOS. For example, this EMBED element could be used to place Listing 31-1 in a 100-pixel by 100-pixel rectangle on the page:

```
<EMBED WIDTH="100" HEIGHT="100" SRC="31-1.svg"
       ALT="A red circle with a blue border"
       ALIGN="LEFT"
       PLUGINSPAGE="http://www.adobe.com/svg/viewer/install/">
```

The SVG picture will be left-aligned so that text flows around it on the right. If the browser can't handle this type of content, it will display the alternate text "A red circle with a blue border" instead. And if the user does not have the necessary plug-in to load this document, then it will ask them if they want to go to the Adobe Web site to get it. Figure 31-4 shows the final result after the plug-in is installed and Listing 31-3 is loaded into Netscape Navigator.

Caution You need version 2.0 or later of the Adobe SVG Plug-In to view the SVG documents in this chapter. Version 1.0 of the Adobe SVG Plug-In only supports an older, out-of-date, working draft of SVG from March 2000. This chapter describes the more current Proposed Recommendation of SVG from July 2001. The latest version should be available from `http://www.adobe.com/svg/viewer/install`.

Listing 31-3: An HTML document in which Listing 31-1 is embedded

```
<HTML>
  <HEAD>
    <TITLE>Circles are my friends</TITLE>
  </HEAD>
  <BODY>
  <H1>Rectangles are the Enemy!</H1>

  <EMBED WIDTH="100" HEIGHT="100" SRC="31-1.svg"
         ALT="A red circle with a blue border"
         ALIGN="LEFT"
         PLUGINSPAGE="http://www.adobe.com/svg/viewer/install/">

  <P>
    You need version 2.0 or later of the Adobe SVG plug-in
    for this to work. Version 1.0 of the Adobe SVG plug-in only
    supports an older, out-of-date working draft of SVG from
    March 2000. This chapter describes the more current
    Candidate Recommendation of SVG from November 2000.
  </P>


  <HR>
  Last Modified May 30, 2001<BR>
  Copyright 2001
  <A HREF="mailto:elharo@metalab.unc.edu">
    Elliotte Rusty Harold
  </A>

  </BODY>
</HTML>
```

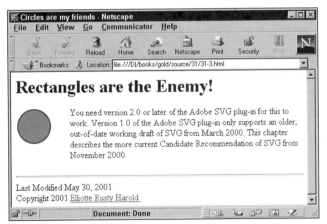

Figure 31-4: An SVG document embedded in a Web page

Simple Shapes

SVG defines six simple shape elements that you can use to place particular kinds of shapes on the page. These are:

- ✦ `rect`
- ✦ `circle`
- ✦ `ellipse`
- ✦ `line`
- ✦ `polygon`
- ✦ `polyline`

You're not limited to these shapes, however. You can also define arbitrary one- and two-dimensional shapes using paths. But let's begin with the basic shapes.

The rect element

The `rect` element represents a rectangle aligned with the two coordinate axes. In other words, it represents rectangles like the one on the left side of Figure 31-5 but not the one on the right side.

Figure 31-5: SVG rect elements represent rectangles like the one on the left, not the one on the right.

Given the constraint of axis alignment, each rectangle can be fully specified by the coordinates of its upper-left corner, its width, and its height. These are given by four attributes on the rect element:

✦ x: the x coordinate of the upper-left corner of the rectangle

✦ y: the y coordinate of the upper-left corner of the rectangle

✦ width: the extent of the rectangle parallel to the x-axis

✦ height: the extent of the rectangle parallel to the y-axis

For example, this rect element represents a 10-by-10 square whose upper-left corner is aligned with the upper-left corner of the picture:

```
<rect x="0" y ="0" width="10" height="10"/>
```

Listing 31-4 draws part of a checkerboard by alternating red and black squares, each 25 units square. Figure 31-6 shows the rendered document.

Listing 31-4: **A partial checkerboard made up out of rects**

```
<?xml version="10" encoding="UTF-8" standalone="yes"?>
<svg xmlns="http://www.w3.org/2000/svg"
     width="3.5in" height="1.0in">
  <title>Listing 31-4 from the XML Bible</title>
  <rect x="0"  y="0"  width="25" height="25" fill="red"/>
  <rect x="25" y="0"  width="25" height="25" fill="black"/>
  <rect x="50" y="0"  width="25" height="25" fill="red" />
  <rect x="0"  y="25" width="25" height="25" fill="black"/>
  <rect x="25" y="25" width="25" height="25" fill="red" />
  <rect x="50" y="25" width="25" height="25" fill="black"/>
  <rect x="0"  y="50" width="25" height="25" fill="red" />
  <rect x="25" y="50" width="25" height="25" fill="black"/>
  <rect x="50" y="50" width="25" height="25" fill="red" />
</svg>
```

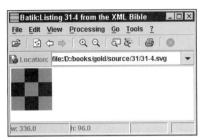

Figure 31-6: A piece of a checkerboard arranged with nine rect elements

You can make rounded rectangles by setting the rx and ry attributes of the rectangle to a positive length. The larger this number, the more rounded the corners will be. The maximum rounding is half the width of the rectangle for rx and half the length of the rectangle for ry. This much rounding turns the rectangle into an ellipse. Anything beyond that is ignored. For example, Listing 31-5 adds five units of rounding to each of the rectangles from Listing 31-4. Figure 31-7 shows the results of adding this rounding.

Listing 31-5: A pattern of nine rounded rects

```
<?xml version="10" encoding="UTF-8" standalone="yes"?>
<svg xmlns="http://www.w3.org/2000/svg"
     width="3.5in" height="1.0in">
  <title>Listing 31-5 from the XML Bible</title>
  <rect x="0"  y="0"  width="25" height="25" rx="5" ry="5"
        fill="red"/>
  <rect x="25" y="0"  width="25" height="25" rx="5" ry="5"
        fill="black"/>
  <rect x="50" y="0"  width="25" height="25" rx="5" ry="5"
        fill="red" />
  <rect x="0"  y="25" width="25" height="25" rx="5" ry="5"
        fill="black"/>
  <rect x="25" y="25" width="25" height="25" rx="5" ry="5"
        fill="red" />
  <rect x="50" y="25" width="25" height="25" rx="5" ry="5"
        fill="black"/>
  <rect x="0"  y="50" width="25" height="25" rx="5" ry="5"
        fill="red" />
  <rect x="25" y="50" width="25" height="25" rx="5" ry="5"
        fill="black"/>
  <rect x="50" y="50" width="25" height="25" rx="5" ry="5"
        fill="red" />
</svg>
```

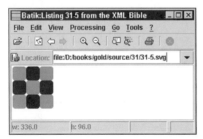

Figure 31-7: A pattern of rounded rects

The circle element

The circle element represents a circle. The position of the circle is determined by the coordinates of its center. The size of the circle is determined by its radius. These are specified by three attributes of the circle element:

✦ cx: the x coordinate of the center of the circle

✦ cy: the y coordinate of the center of the circle

✦ r: the length of the radius

For example, this circle element has a 31-unit radius. Its center is positioned at the upper-left corner of the picture. Thus, only the lower-right quarter (fourth quadrant) of the circle will be shown. The other three-quarters of the circle are off the screen.

```
<circle cx="0" cy="0" r="25" />
```

Listing 31-6 uses circle elements to draw a bull's-eye on the screen. The circles in a bull's-eye are concentric so that the center coordinates are the same for each circle. Only the radius changes. This example takes advantage of the implicit z-ordering of SVG shapes. Each shape is drawn on top of its previous sibling. That is, the first circle element is drawn first, the second circle element is drawn on top of the first, the third circle is drawn on top of the second, and so forth. Without this ordering, the largest circle might be drawn on top of all the others, obscuring them. Figure 31-8 shows the result.

Listing 31-6: **An SVG bull's-eye**

```
<?xml version="1.0" encoding="UTF-8" standalone="yes"?>
<svg xmlns="http://www.w3.org/2000/svg"
     width="3.5in" height="2.0in">
  <title>Listing 31-6 from the XML Bible</title>
  <circle cx="90" cy="90" r="70"
      fill="red" stroke="black" stroke-width="2" />
  <circle cx="90" cy="90" r="60"
```

```
              fill="white" stroke="black" stroke-width="2" />
    <circle cx="90" cy="90" r="50"
           fill="red" stroke="black" stroke-width="2" />
    <circle cx="90" cy="90" r="40"
           fill="white" stroke="black" stroke-width="2" />
    <circle cx="90" cy="90" r="30"
           fill="red" stroke="black" stroke-width="2" />
    <circle cx="90" cy="90" r="20"
           fill="white" stroke="black" stroke-width="2"/>
    <circle cx="90" cy="90" r="10"
           fill="red" stroke="black" stroke-width="2" />
</svg>
```

Figure 31-8: An SVG bull's-eye

The ellipse element

Ellipses are a little like squashed circles, or, reversing the perspective, circles are degenerate ellipses. Whereas circles have perfect rotational symmetry, ellipses do have definite x and y axes. Like SVG rectangles, SVG ellipses line up their axes parallel to the coordinate axes. Thus, like rectangles, you only need four numbers to specify an ellipse:

- ✦ cx: the x coordinate of the center of the ellipse
- ✦ cy: the y coordinate of the center of the ellipse
- ✦ rx: the length of the radius of the ellipse parallel to the x-axis
- ✦ ry: the length of the radius of the ellipse parallel to the y-axis

For example, this ellipse is four times as long as it is high:

```
<ellipse cx="45" cy="20" rx="40" ry="10" />
```

Listing 31-7 places two very eccentric ellipses more or less perpendicular to each other to form a simple four-pointed star. These use the default fill color (black) and stroke (none). Figure 31-9 shows the result.

Listing 31-7: **Two ellipses perpendicular to each other**

```
<?xml version="1.0" encoding="UTF-8" standalone="yes"?>
<svg xmlns="http://www.w3.org/2000/svg"
     width="3.5in" height="1.0in">
  <title>Listing 31-7 from the XML Bible</title>
  <ellipse cx="45" cy="45" rx="40" ry="10" />
  <ellipse cx="45" cy="45" rx="10" ry="40" />
</svg>
```

Figure 31-9: Two ellipses perpendicular to each other

The line element

The line element represents a straight-line segment between two points. It is identified by the x and y coordinates of its end points as specified in these attributes:

- ✦ x1: The x-coordinate of the start point
- ✦ y1: The y-coordinate of the start point
- ✦ x2: The x-coordinate of the end point
- ✦ y2: The y-coordinate of the end point

For example, this is a 100-unit horizontal line:

```
<line x1="0" y1="100" x2="100" y2="100"/>
```

This is a 100-unit vertical line:

```
<line x1="0" y1="100" x2="0" y2="0"/>
```

This line runs at a 45-degree angle between the end points of the two previous lines:

```
<line x1="0" y1="0" x2="100" y2="100"/>
```

Listing 31-8 puts them all together to form a right triangle. However, as currently written these lines won't actually be visible. To display them, you need to at least set the stroke color to something other than white. Listing 31-8 also expands the stroke width to two pixels. Figure 31-10 shows the result.

Listing 31-8: **A right triangle formed from three lines**

```
<?xml version="1.0" encoding="UTF-8" standalone="yes"?>
<svg xmlns="http://www.w3.org/2000/svg"
    width="3.5in" height="2.0in">
  <title>Listing 31-8 from the XML Bible</title>
  <line x1="0" y1="100" x2="100" y2="100"
      stroke-width="2px" stroke="black"/>
  <line x1="0" y1="100" x2="0" y2="0"
      stroke-width="2px" stroke="black"/>
  <line x1="0" y1="0" x2="100" y2="100"
      stroke-width="2px" stroke="black"/>
</svg>
```

Figure 31-10: A right triangle formed from three lines

Polygons and polylines

A polygon is a closed curve formed by straight-line segments between a sequence of three or more points. The first point is connected to the second point, the second to the third, the third to the fourth, and so on, until the last point, which is connected back to the first point. Thus, a polygon with N points has N line segments. A polyline is similar except that the last point is not connected back to the first point. A polyline with N points has only N-1 line segments. Polygons include not only the usual convex polygons like triangles and concave polygons like stars, but also considerably stranger items such as polygons with self-intersecting edges. Figure 31-11 shows the three major kinds. SVG polygons include all these cases. Rectangles are special cases of polygons, but circles are not because they don't use straight lines.

Figure 31-11: A convex polygon, a concave polygon, and a complex polygon, each formed from eight points

The points forming a polygon are listed in order in the `polygon` element's `points` attribute. The first point is connected to the second point, the second point is connected to the third point, the third point is connected to the fourth point, and so on. The last point is connected back to the first point. All points are given as pairs of dimensionless numbers in the local coordinate space separated by a comma. Points are separated from each other by white space. For example, the right triangle of Listing 31-8 could instead be written as this polygon:

```
<polygon points="0,100 100,100 0,0"/>
```

Figure 31-11 was actually created using `polygon` elements in the SVG document shown in Listing 31-9.

Listing 31-9: **Three polygons**

```
<?xml version="1.0" encoding="UTF-8" standalone="yes"?>
<svg xmlns="http://www.w3.org/2000/svg"
     width="3.5in" height="1.5in">
  <title>Listing 31-9 from the XML Bible</title>
  <polygon points="0,30 30,0 80,0 110,30 110,80 80,110
                   30,110 0,80"/>
  <polygon points="120,55 160,40 180,0 200,40 240,55 200,80
                   180,120 160,80"/>
  <polygon points="240,30 270,45 312,80 270,110 268,82
                   272,23 267,71 311,17 "/>
</svg>
```

The `polyline` element is almost identical to the `polygon` element except that the last point listed in the `points` attribute is *not* connected back to the first point. However, the last point can repeat the first point, so that the path is connected. For example, the right triangle of Listing 31-8 could instead be written as this `polyline`:

```
<polyline points="0,100 100,100 0,0 0,100"/>
```

It's necessary to repeat the first point as the last point to get the polyline to close up. On the other hand, polylines are filled by default, so adding the last point is only really necessary if you turn the fill off using `style="fill: none"`.

Paths

The `path` element represents an arbitrary two-dimensional curve. Paths can be stroked so that they look like lines. They can be filled so they appear as solid shapes. They can even be used as masks or clipping regions. You can think of a path as the curve a pen draws as it moves across the paper. Often paths are connected, but occasionally the artist may pick up the pen and put it down at a different point on the page and continue drawing from there. However, the pen draws in a single-color ink (possibly invisible) and the tip of the pen has a fixed thickness. To change the color or size of the line the artist must change pens.

There are ten basic operations the artist can perform with a pen:

✦ Move to: Pick the pen up and put it down at a specified point on the paper.

✦ Line to: Draw a straight line from the current pen position to a specified point.

✦ Horizontal line to: Draw a straight line from the current pen position across to a specified x coordinate, keeping the y coordinate the same.

✦ Vertical line to: Draw a straight line from the current pen position up or down to a specified y coordinate, keeping the x coordinate the same.

✦ Arc: Draw an elliptical or circular arc from the current pen position to a specified point.

✦ Curve to: Draw a cubic Bézier curve from the current pen position to a specified point.

✦ Smooth curve to: Draw a "smooth" cubic Bézier curve from the current pen position to a specified point.

✦ Quadratic curve to: Draw a quadratic Bézier curve from the current pen position to a specified point.

✦ Smooth quadratic curve to: Draw a "smooth" quadratic Bézier curve from the current pen position to a specified point.

✦ Close path: Draw a straight line from the current pen position back to the first point in the path.

An SVG document represents a path with a `path` element. The d (for data) attribute of the path contains the instructions for drawing the path. The instructions are each represented by single letters:

✦ M and m for move to

✦ L and l for line to

✦ H and h for draw a horizontal line to

✦ V and v for draw a vertical line to

✦ A and a for draw an elliptical arc to

✦ C and c for draw a cubic Bézier curve to

✦ S and s for draw a smooth cubic Bézier curve to

✦ Q and q for draw a quadratic Bézier curve to

✦ T and t for draw a smooth quadratic Bézier curve to

✦ Z and z for close path

The uppercase letters give the points as absolute coordinates. The lowercase letters give the points as positive or negative offsets from the current pen position.

Every path begins with an M or m to set the initial point. Paths must end with a Z or z. Each M and L instruction is followed by the coordinates of the point to go to. For example, here's a `path` element that draws an isosceles triangle:

```
<path d="M 0,200 L 100,0 L 200,200 Z" />
```

Don't worry if it isn't obvious to you that this is an isosceles triangle. In fact, I'd be surprised if it were even obvious that this is a triangle. Here's how this `path` element is interpreted:

1. M 0,200: Move the pen to the point x=0, y=200. This is where the path begins.

2. L 100,0: Draw a straight line from the current pen location (x=0, y=200) to x=100, y=0.

3. L 200,200: Draw a straight line from the current pen location (x=100, y=0) to x=200, y=200.

4. Z: Close the path; that is, draw a straight line from the last point (x=200, y=200) back to the first point (x=0, y=200).

There's often more than one way to define a given path. For instance, this `path` element represents that same triangle but uses lowercase, relative units after establishing the initial point:

```
<path d="m 0,200 l 100,-200 l 100,200 z" />
```

Here's how this `path` attribute is interpreted:

1. `m 0,200`: Because this move to command is the first point in the path, the relative coordinates are treated as absolute coordinates, and the pen is moved to the point x=0, y=200. This is where the path begins.

2. `l 100,-200`: Draw a line from the current pen location (x=0, y=200) that goes 100 pixels to the right and 200 pixels down; that is, draw a line to (x=100, y=0).

3. `l 100,200`: Draw a line from the current pen location (x=100, y=0) that goes 100 pixels to the right and 200 pixels down; that is, draw a line to (x=200, y=200).

4. `z`: Close the shape; that is, draw a line from the current point (x=200, y=200) back to the first point (x=0, y=200).

There are a variety of other forms path data can take, although the meaning is the same. For instance you can use a space to separate the x and y coordinates in a point rather than a comma, and you can provide several coordinates after a line-to command to indicate that you want multiple lines drawn. For instance, the above path could equally easily have been written like this:

```
<path d="m0 200l100 -200 100 200z" />
```

One reason not to write your coordinates this way is that although this form is equally easy to write, it is far from equally easy to read. For instance, is it obvious to you where the second command is in the above path? (Hint: be sure to distinguish between the letter *l* and the digit *1*).

Listing 31-10 shows a tic-tac-toe board drawn as one single, long, self-intersecting path. Because a tic-tac-toe grid is made up exclusively of horizontal and vertical lines, this document uses the `V` and `H` operators heavily. Also note the use of the `M` command to move the pen around the board without drawing a line. Finally, because paths are filled by default, CSS styles are used to turn off filling and to turn on stroking. Figure 31-12 shows the finished board.

Listing 31-10: **Tic-tac-toe**

```
<?xml version="1.0" encoding="UTF-8" standalone="yes"?>
<svg xmlns="http://www.w3.org/2000/svg"
     width="3.6in" height="3.4in">
  <title>Listing 31-10 from the XML Bible</title>
  <path d="M 100,0 V 300
           M 200,0 V 300
           M 0,100 H 300
           M 0,200 H 300 Z"
           fill="none" stroke="black" stroke-width="2px" />
</svg>
```

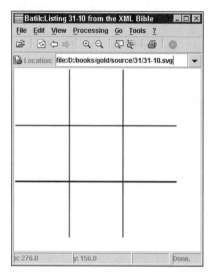

Figure 31-12: A tic-tac-toe board formed from a single path element

Arcs

Arcs are more complex than straight lines. You have to specify seven separate numbers to determine which arc will be drawn from the current point. These seven numbers are:

1. The x coordinate of the point to draw the arc to

2. The y coordinate of the point to draw the arc to

3. The radius of the arc along the x axis; the larger the radius the less curved the arc will be

4. The radius of the arc along the y axis; equal x and y radii produce a circular arc

5. The orientation of the ellipse with respect to the x axis, in clockwise degrees

6. Whether the arc should subtend an angle greater than or less than 180 degrees; 1 for more than 180 degrees, 0 for less than 180 degrees

7. Whether the arc should be drawn with an increasing or decreasing angle; 1 for an increasing angle, 0 for a decreasing angle

Here's a `path` that uses an arc to draw a piece of pie with a 30-degree arc centered on the y axis:

```
<path d="M 100,100
         L 74.11809548975, 3.40741737109
         A 100 100 0 0 1 125.8819045103 3.40741737109
         L 100, 100 Z"
      style="fill: none; stroke: black; stroke-width: 1px" />
```

Determining the correct coordinates for the above path required trigonometry, a hand calculator, and some experimentation. The end points of the arc were calculated like this:

1. Make the radius of the circle 100 units.

2. Place the center of the circle at x=100, y=100.

3. Start the arc at the position x = 100 − 100 sin (30/2), y = 100 − 100 cos (30/2).

4. Finish the arc at the position x = 100 + 100 sin (30/2), y = 100 − 100 cos (30/2).

If that seems a little involved, that's because it is. And this example is simpler than many because:

1. Only circular arcs were used, not elliptical ones

2. The coordinates and radius were deliberately chosen to make the math as simple as possible

Many arcs will be considerably worse than this. Arcs are really beginning to hit the limit of what you can plausibly work with by hand. Listing 31-11 draws a complete pie with eight 45-degree pieces. Figure 31-13 shows the result. Forty-five-degree increments are marginally easier to work with than 30-degree increments, but the coordinates were still quite burdensome to calculate. The bottom line is that arc paths are really intended for computers to calculate. Humans should use some sort of reasonable GUI to describe them.

Listing 31-11: **A pie formed by eight arc paths**

```
<?xml version="1.0" encoding="UTF-8" standalone="yes"?>
<svg xmlns="http://www.w3.org/2000/svg"
     width="3.6in" height="2.4in">
  <title>Listing 31-11 from the XML Bible</title>
  <path d="M 100,100
           L 100, 0
           A 100 100 0 0 1 170.7106781187 29.28932188135
           L 100, 100 Z"
        fill="brown" stroke="black" stroke-width="1px" />
  <path d="M 100,100
           L 170.7106781187 29.28932188135
           A 100 100 0 0 1 200 100
           L 100, 100 Z"
        fill="brown" stroke="black" stroke-width="1px" />
```

Continued

Listing 31-11 *(continued)*

```
<path d="M 100,100
        L 200, 100
        A 100 100 0 0 1 170.7106781187   170.7106781187
        L 100, 100 Z"
        fill="brown" stroke="black" stroke-width="1px" />
<path d="M 100,100
        L 170.7106781187,170.7106781187
        A 100 100 0 0 1 100 200
        L 100, 100 Z"
        fill="brown" stroke="black" stroke-width="1px" />
<path d="M 100,100
        L 100,200
        A 100 100 0 0 1 29.28932188135 170.7106781187
        L 100, 100 Z"
        fill="brown" stroke="black" stroke-width="1px" />
<path d="M 100,100
        L 29.28932188135 170.7106781187
        A 100 100 0 0 1 0 100
        L 100, 100 Z"
        fill="brown" stroke="black" stroke-width="1px" />
<path d="M 100,100
        L 0, 100
        A 100 100 0 0 1 29.28932188135 29.28932188135
        L 100, 100 Z"
        fill="brown" stroke="black" stroke-width="1px" />
<path d="M 100,100
        L 29.28932188135 29.28932188135
        A 100 100 0 0 1 100 0
        L 100, 100 Z"
        fill="brown" stroke="black" stroke-width="1px" />
</svg>
```

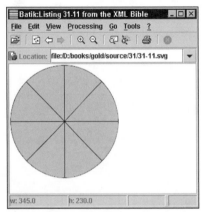

Figure 31-13: A pie formed by eight arc paths

Curves

You now have the tools needed to produce essentially any two-dimensional shape that can be formed from straight lines, as well as circles, ellipses, and pieces thereof. But that still leaves a lot unaccounted for. Figure 31-14 shows just a few of the things that you can't really describe with the shapes and paths discussed so far.

Figure 31-14: Figures drawn with Bézier curves

Paths like those in Figure 31-14, and many more, can be modeled by *Bézier curves*. A Bézier curve is defined by a start point and an end point, as well as one or more control points that define lines tangent to the curve through the start and end points. One control point produces a quadratic Bézier curve. Two control points produce a cubic Bézier curve. Smooth Bézier curves mirror one coordinate point off the preceding coordinate point.

If you thought arcs were bad, Bézier curves are even worse. Where trigonometry sufficed for arcs, Bézier curves require differential calculus. Fortunately, no one expects you to calculate the coordinates for curves like this by hand. In a few cases, a computer program might calculate them. For instance, the spiral in Figure 31-14 is straightforward to generate algorithmically. However, most Bézier curves are produced by a human artist in conjunction with a graphics program like Adobe Illustrator. Indeed that is exactly how Figure 31-14 was drawn. Thus, I'll spare you all the details of exactly how Bézier coordinates are specified in SVG. Instead, in Listing 31-12 I'll merely show you the SVG source code for the first shape in Figure 31-14.

This was produced by Adobe Illustrator, and cleaned up a little by hand for printing in the book. The SVG source code for the last three pictures in Figure 31-14 would take too much space to show here, but is on the CD-ROM and Web site. I suggest that you use a drawing program that can export SVG when you need to draw complicated paths like these.

Listing 31-12: **Bézier curves**

```
<?xml version="1.0" encoding="utf-8"?>
<!-- Generator: Adobe Illustrator 9.0, SVG Export Plug-In  -->
<svg xml:space="preserve" xmlns="http://www.w3.org/2000/svg">
 <g id="Layer_x0020_1"
    style="fill-rule:nonzero; clip-rule:nonzero; fill:#FFFFFF;
        stroke:#000000; stroke-width:0.25;
        stroke-miterlimit:4;">
  <path style="stroke-width:1;"
      d="M99.233,22.5c0,27.614-22.386,50-50,50c-22.091,
        0-40-17.909-40-40c0-17.673,14.327-32,
        32-32c14.139,0,25.6,11.461,25.6,25.6c0,
        11.311-9.169,20.48-20.48,20.48c-9.049,
        0-16.384-7.335-16.384-16.384 c0-7.239,
        5.869-13.107,13.107-13.107c5.791,0,10.486,4.694,
        10.486,10.486c0,4.633-3.756,8.389-8.389,
        8.389c-3.707,0-6.711-3.005-6.711-6.711"/>
 </g>
</svg>
```

Bézier curves can also handle the simpler cases of straight lines, arcs, circles, and more. Adobe Illustrator is a Bézier-based program and consequently uses Bézier curves like the ones shown here for almost all shapes when it exports an SVG document, even for straighter shapes that could have been encoded as rectangles, polygons, or lines.

Text

Picture books are fine for three-year-olds, but most vector graphics meant for adults include text. Sometimes, this text can be part of the Web page or an XSL-FO document in which the SVG is embedded. However, it's also useful to be able to make text part of the picture. Sometimes you want a single line of text placed at a particular position, and other times you want to wrap text around a curving path. SVG provides all of these features; and, of course, it lets you choose the font family, weight, and style. Furthermore, you can treat text as just another shape or path. This means that you can apply coordinate transformations to skew or rotate text, paint the text, clip and mask it, and do anything else to text that you could do to a circle or a rectangle or a polygon. Finally, because XML documents are Unicode, you aren't just limited to standard Latin text. If the necessary fonts are installed, SVG can handle text in right-to-left languages such as Arabic and ideographic languages such as Chinese.

The one thing that SVG really can't do with text is wrap it. There's no `textBox` element in SVG. You can't define a rectangle, assign some text to the rectangle, and expect it to wrap every time a line reaches the right edge of the box. All line breaks have to be inserted manually. The reason is that many languages, such as Tibetan, Arabic, and Chinese, have relatively complex, context-sensitive rules about how and where to break lines, and SVG implementers couldn't be expected to be familiar with all of them.

Strings

The `text` element places a single line of text on the canvas at the position indicated by its x and y attributes. These are the coordinates of the lower-left corner of the string. The text to place is simply the content of the `text` element. For example, this `text` element places the string Hello SVG! at the coordinates x=50, y=50 in the default font and size.

```
<text x="50" y="50">Hello SVG!</text>
```

Listing 31-13 is a nursery rhyme in SVG. Figure 31-15 shows the displayed text.

Listing 31-13: **Four text elements, one for each line of a poem**

```
<?xml version="1.0" encoding="utf-8"?>
<svg xmlns="http://www.w3.org/2000/svg"
     width="3.6in" height="1.0in">
  <title>Listing 31-13 from the XML Bible</title>
  <text x="50" y="20">Mary had a little lamb</text>
  <text x="50" y="40">whose fleece was white as snow</text>
  <text x="50" y="60">and everywhere that Mary went</text>
  <text x="50" y="80">the lamb was sure to go</text>
</svg>
```

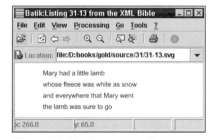

Figure 31-15: Four text strings

Notice that the poem begins on the line with y=20. Y coordinates increase down. The y attribute of the text element specifies the position of the baseline of the string; that is the bottom of the string. Therefore, if you set y to 0, then most of the string, aside from the descenders in letters like *y* and *g*, would be positioned at negative coordinates, outside the visible range.

The text element does not consider line breaks. Each line should be a separate text element with a different y coordinate. For example, suppose you were to use this single text element instead of the four in Listing 31-13:

```
<text x="50" y="20">  Mary had a little lamb
   whose fleece was white as snow
   and everywhere that Mary went
   the lamb was sure to go
</text>
```

Then SVG would just place all four verses on the same line as shown in Figure 31-16, even if that means some of the text runs off the right-hand-side of the visible area and gets truncated.

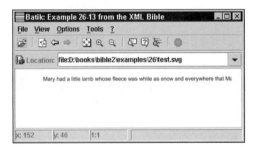

Figure 31-16: One text string

Normally, the XML parser compresses all runs of white space to a single space. You can change this behavior by adding an xml:space attribute with the value preserve to the text element like this:

```
<text x="50" y="20" xml:space="preserve">
   Mary had a little lamb
   whose fleece was white as snow
   and everywhere that Mary went
   the lamb was sure to go
</text>
```

However, while this will add some extra space between words at the ends of the verses like *lamb* and *whose*, it still won't preserve the line breaks.

Text on a path

Suppose instead of a nursery rhyme that neatly divides into small lines with well-defined line breaks, you have a much larger run of prose, like the text of this paragraph for example. You normally want to place that inside a box of fixed width and fixed position, but unlimited height, and allow the formatter to decide where to break the lines. SVG can't quite do that, but it can get close.

SVG allows you to place text along a path other than a straight line. You can wrap text along a triangle, a spiral, a cloud, Abraham Lincoln's beard, or just about any other path you can imagine. This is accomplished by placing a textpath element inside a text element. The textpath element contains the text to draw and an xlink:href attribute pointing to the path along which to draw it.

For example, to wrap the prose of a paragraph along five parallel lines, you first need a path element that describes five parallel lines. This one will do.

```
<path id="para5"
      d="M 10,20 L 200,20 M 10,40 L 200,40
         M 10,60 L 200,60 M 10,80 L 200,80
         M 10,100 L 200,100
         M 10, 20 Z"
      fill="none" stroke="none"/>
```

Notice the use of the M commands to jump from one line to the next without including the jumps in the path. In particular, notice the last one that moves the pen back to the beginning of the path. Without this, the last line of text might get drawn across a diagonal line connecting the last point to the first point. Also notice that this path element has an id attribute so that it can be linked to.

The text element that writes along this path is given like this:

```
<text>
  <textPath xlink:href="#para5"
            xmlns:xlink="http://www.w3.org/1999/xlink">
    The text to be wrapped along the path goes here
  </textPath>
</text>
```

Don't forget to map the xlink prefix to the http://www.w3.org/1999/xlink URI. If you use this in multiple places in the document, it might be more convenient to declare it on the root svg element.

Listing 31-14 is a complete SVG document that wraps a paragraph of text around a path composed of horizontal lines.

Listing 31-14: Text on a path

```
<?xml version="1.0" encoding="utf-8"?>
<svg xmlns="http://www.w3.org/2000/svg"
     width="4.0in" height="1.5in">

  <title>Listing 31-14 from the XML Bible</title>

  <path id="para5"
        d="M 10,20 L 360,20 M 10,40 L 360,40
           M 10,60 L 360,60 M 10,80 L 360,80
           M 10,100 L 360,100 M 10, 120 L 360, 120
           M 10,20 Z"
        fill="none" stroke="black"/>/>

  <text>
    <textPath xlink:href="#para5"
              xmlns:xlink="http://www.w3.org/1999/xlink">
      Suppose instead of a nursery rhyme that neatly divides
      into small lines with well-defined line breaks, you have
      a much larger run of prose, like the text of this
      paragraph for example. You normally want to place that
      inside a box of fixed width and fixed position, but
      unlimited height, and allow the formatter to decide where
      to break the lines. SVG can't quite do that yet, but it
      can get close.
    </textPath>
  </text>

</svg>
```

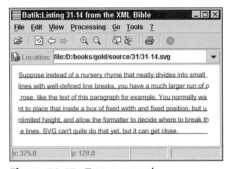

Figure 31-17: Text on a path

Figure 31-17 shows this example in Batik. You'll notice that SVG is not very smart about deciding where to break lines. In fact, it doesn't even try. It just fills up to the end of the line with text, and then starts at the next point on the path. Part of the problem here is that SVG needs to be internationalizable. A good line-breaking algorithm is highly language dependent. Hebrew and Chinese, for example, break very differently than do English and French.

Fonts and text styles

SVG adopts CSS text and font properties more or less in toto. You set the font family, font weight, font style, font size, text decoration, color, and so forth by using CSS Level 2 text properties. For example, this paragraph is written in 12-point Times New Roman. If you were to encode it in SVG, it would look something like this:

```
<text x="20" y="20" font-size="12pt;
  font-family="Times, 'Times New Roman', 'New York', serif">
  SVG adopts CSS text and font properties more or less in
  toto. You set the font family, font weight, font style,
  font size, ...
</text>
```

If you prefer, you can use the text element's style attribute like this:

```
<text x="20" y="20"
  style="font-size: 12pt;
   font-family: Times, 'Times New Roman', 'New York', serif">
  SVG adopts CSS text and font properties more or less in
  toto. You set the font family, font weight, font style,
  font size, ...
</text>
```

Cross-Reference

CSS text and font properties are covered in great detail in Chapter 16. A big advantage to SVG adopting CSS for such properties is that you don't need to learn, and I don't have to write about, two different syntaxes that describe pretty much the same thing. As large as this book is, it would have been even larger without such economical reuse of syntax.

Text spans

The tspan element lets you apply styles to pieces of a text element. It's similar to the span element in HTML, that is, a convenient hook off of which to hang CSS styles or other properties. For example, tspan enables you to format the first sentence of this paragraph with only the word *tspan* and *text* in Courier. Here's how:

```
<text x="20" y="20" font-size="12pt"
      font-family="Times, 'Times New Roman', serif">
  The <tspan font-family="Courier, monospace">tspan</tspan>
  element lets you apply styles to pieces of a
  <tspan font-family="Courier, monospace">text</tspan> element.
</text>
```

Bitmapped Images

SVG is a format for vector graphics. Nonetheless, it's very often useful or necessary to place bitmapped images in line art. For example, you might want to start with a photograph and then overlay text and arrows on that photograph calling out individual parts. Or perhaps a calendar includes both vector graphics for functionality and a photograph of a nature scene to make the calendar pretty to look at. In fact, almost anywhere you look in printed matter, you're likely to find art that combines bitmapped images and vector graphics.

SVG allows you to place bitmapped images in documents in a straightforward fashion. As with the IMG element in HTML, the actual bitmap data is not included in the SVG document. Instead it is linked in from a URL. Also as in HTML, exactly which bitmapped graphic formats are supported depends on what software you're using. All SVG processors can handle JPEG and PNG. GIF is problematical because of patent problems.

The image element contains a link to the file containing the bitmapped data. The URL where the image data can be found is read from the xlink:href attribute, where the xlink prefix is mapped to the standard XLink URI, http://www.w3.org/1999/xlink. The x and y attributes specify where in the local coordinate system the upper-left-hand corner of the image should be placed. As with any SVG shape, the chosen position may cause the image to lay on top of or beneath other items on the canvas. The width and height attributes determine the size of the box in which the image is placed. If the actual image is too large or too small for the box, then it will be scaled as necessary to fit the box, perhaps even disproportionately exactly like the IMG element in HTML. For example, Listing 31-15 is a complete SVG document that contains a picture of one of my cats, Marjorie. SVG text elements layer the phrases "This is my cat Marjorie." and "She likes to have her picture taken." on top of the picture. Figure 31-18 shows the results.

Listing 31-15: **Placing a JPEG image in an SVG picture**

```
<?xml version="1.0" encoding="UTF-8" standalone="yes"?>
<svg xmlns="http://www.w3.org/2000/svg"
     xmlns:xlink="http://www.w3.org/1999/xlink"
     width="360px" height="310px">
  <title>Listing 31-15 from the XML Bible</title>

  <image xlink:href="marjorie.jpg"
    x="20px" y="5px" width="260px" height="297px"/>

  <text x="25px" y="240px"
      font-size="14pt" font-weight="bold"
      font-family="Helvetica, Arial, sans">
    This is my cat Marjorie.
  </text>
```

```
<text x="25px" y="255px"
        font-size="14pt" font-weight="bold"
        font-family="Helvetica, Arial, sans">
    She likes to have her picture taken.
</text>

</svg>
```

Figure 31-18: Text laid on top of an image

The image element can also be used to load another SVG document into the current one. The XML for the loaded SVG document is not merged into the existing document, as it might be with XInclude. Instead, it's just treated as another picture with a certain size at a certain set of coordinates, possibly with some filters applied to it.

Coordinate Systems and Viewports

So far, we've worked in nondimensional units that map to screen pixels. However, SVG supports all the units of length defined in CSS, including inches, centimeters, millimeters, points, picas, pixels, and even percentages. For instance, you can say that a rectangle is two inches wide by three inches high like this:

```
<rect x="0in" y="0in" width="2in" height="3in"/>
```

When an SVG renderer such as Batik displays this rectangle, it will ask its environment how many pixels there are in an inch. On most computer displays, it would get an answer back that is somewhere between 68 and 200 pixels per inch. It would then convert the requested length in inches to the equivalent length in pixels before drawing the picture on the screen. Depending on the resolution of the monitor and the capabilities of both the renderer and the host operating system, the actual sizes may be a little more or a little less than what you asked for. For instance, if you draw a circle with a 10-inch radius on your display, then measure it with a ruler (not an onscreen ruler, but a real physical ruler made out of wood), it should be approximately 10 inches, maybe 8, maybe 12, depending on the resolution of the monitor, but something in the ballpark of 10 inches. And if the circle is 20 percent off of its expected size, then all the other shapes drawn on that display will also be 20 percent off.

Not all SVG lengths can be specified in real-world units like inches and points. In particular, only rectangles, circles, ellipses, and lines can be specified this way. Polygons and polylines must use nondimensional local units for the coordinates given in their `points` attributes. Paths must also use nondimensional local units for the coordinates given in their d attributes. This makes real-world units less useful than they might otherwise be.

However, if you prefer to design your drawings in inches or feet or centimeters rather than pixels, there is a work-around. You can assign a width and a height to your `svg` element to specify how much space it occupies on the page. Then you can set the `viewBox` attribute to define a local coordinate system within that `svg` element. The combination of the actual, onscreen width and height with the view box can define a mapping between the actual pixels and any units of length you desire, from nanometers to parsecs.

The viewport

SVG pictures are drawn on an infinite, two-dimensional plane with infinitely precise coordinates. Of course, when such a picture is actually shown on the screen, you only see a finite rectangular region of limited precision called the *viewport*. This viewport has a certain width and height that can be determined in several ways.

The first possibility applies when an SVG document is included in an HTML page using an `EMBED` element as in Listing 31-3. In this case, the `WIDTH` and `HEIGHT` attributes of the `EMBED` element establish the size of the canvas. Alternately, if the `svg` element is pasted right into the HTML document as in Listing 31-2, then it can have CSS height and width properties that set its size, even if this results in the image being clipped. Listing 31-16 demonstrates.

Listing 31-16: **Using CSS properties to set the size of an embedded SVG picture**

```
<HTML>
  <HEAD>
    <TITLE>Circles are my friends</TITLE>
  </HEAD>
  <BODY>
  <H1>Rectangles are the Enemy!</H1>

  <svg xmlns="http://www.w3.org/2000/svg"
       style="width: 100px; height: 100px">
    <title>Listing 31-16 from the XML Bible</title>
    <circle  r="30" cx="34" cy="34"
             fill="red" stroke="blue" stroke-width="2"/>
  </svg>

  <HR>
  Last Modified May 25, 2001<BR>
  Copyright 2001
  <A HREF="mailto:elharo@metalab.unc.edu">
    Elliotte Rusty Harold
  </A>

  </BODY>
</HTML>
```

If the svg element is not embedded in HTML in one fashion or another, or if the external document in which it is embedded does not set its width and height, then the height is set by the width and height attributes of the svg element itself. For example, this svg element has a viewport that's ten inches by five inches:

```
<svg xmlns="http://www.w3.org/2000/svg"
     width="10in" height="5in">
  <circle r="30" cx="34" cy="34"/>
</svg>
```

Alternately, the width and the height can be given in user coordinates, in which case the real units are pixels. This svg element has a viewport that's 144 pixels by 72 pixels:

```
<svg xmlns="http://www.w3.org/2000/svg"
     width="144" height="72">
  <circle r="30" cx="34" cy="34"/>
</svg>
```

Remember that this only changes the size of the viewport on the screen. It has no effect on the size of the shapes that the svg element contains. If the shapes are too big for the viewport, then they'll be truncated; but the plane on which the shapes are rendered is still infinitely large.

Coordinate systems

There are many reasons why you might want to adjust the local coordinate system. For example, if you were drawing a map, it might be convenient to have each local coordinate unit represent a mile. Furthermore, you'd like one mile to map to one inch, approximately 72 pixels. Or perhaps you want to draw a blueprint of a house on which the local coordinate units reflect the actual size of the rooms in feet. For instance, the room in which I'm typing this is 10 feet by 12 feet, so I might represent it as this `rect` element:

```
<rect x="0" y="0" width="10" height="12"/>
```

However, I do want the room to appear larger than 10 pixels by 12 pixels on the display. So, I need to use a local coordinate system that is not so tightly locked to the size of a pixel.

You can both scale and translate the local coordinate system by attaching a `viewBox` attribute to the `svg` element. This changes the local coordinate system inside the viewport by specifying four characteristics of the local coordinate system:

1. The x coordinate of the upper-left corner of the viewport
2. The y coordinate of the upper-left corner of the viewport
3. The width of the viewport in local coordinates
4. The height of the viewport in local coordinates

These four numbers are given in this order in the `viewBox` attribute of the SVG element. For example, let's suppose you have a four-inch by four-inch space to work with on the screen. However, your arithmetic would be simplified if you could use a 1000 by 1000 unit square. Then you would set up your `svg` element like this:

```
<svg xmlns="http://www.w3.org/2000/svg"
     width="4in" height="4in" viewBox="0 0 1000 1000">
  <!-- SVG shapes -->
</svg>
```

The upper-left corner is still at point x=0, y=0. The width and height in the local coordinate space are now 1000 each. Dividing 1000 units by 4 inches, you find that 250 local units equal one inch on the screen. For example, consider the `svg` element in Listing 31-17. This is 100 pixels by 100 pixels square. A large (radius=500) circle is placed at x=400, y=400. Figure 31-19 shows the result. Most of the circle is cut off both below and to the right because most of the circle is outside the viewport. You only see a small part of the upper-left quadrant of the circle.

Listing 31-17: **A circle that doesn't fit in its viewport**

```
<?xml version="1.0" encoding="UTF-8" standalone="yes"?>
<svg xmlns="http://www.w3.org/2000/svg"
     width="100px" height="100px">
  <title>Listing 31-17 from the XML Bible</title>
  <circle cx="400" cy="400" r="500" />
</svg>
```

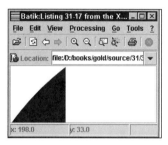

Figure 31-19: A radius 500 circle at 400,400 displayed in a 100-pixel square viewport.

Now suppose you add a `viewBox` attribute to this `svg` element that sets the width of the viewport to 1000 pixels by 1000 pixels. This is shown in Listing 31-18. This effectively shrinks the circle by a factor of 10 to 1, as shown in Figure 31-20. However, because the radius of the circle is 500 and the circle's center is positioned at x=400, y=400, the leftmost and topmost parts of the circle extend into the negative coordinate space and are truncated.

Listing 31-18: **Using a viewBox attribute to adjust the local coordinate system**

```
<?xml version="1.0" encoding="UTF-8" standalone="yes"?>
<svg xmlns="http://www.w3.org/2000/svg"
     width="100px" height="100px"
     viewBox="0 0 1000 1000">
  <title>Listing 31-18 from the XML Bible</title>
  <circle cx="400" cy="400" r="500" />
</svg>
```

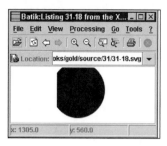

Figure 31-20: A radius 500 circle at 400,400 displayed in a 100-pixel square viewport and a 1000-unit square view box

You can fix the truncation by using the view box to shift the coordinate system 100 units left and up. To do this set the first two numbers in the viewBox attribute to –100. Then the local coordinate system extends from –100 to 899 instead of 0 to 999. Listing 31-19 demonstrates, and Figure 31-21 shows the result.

Listing 31-19: **Using a viewBox attribute to adjust the local coordinate system**

```
<?xml version="1.0" encoding="UTF-8" standalone="yes"?>
<svg xmlns="http://www.w3.org/2000/svg"
     width="100px" height="100px"
     viewBox="-100 -100 1000 1000">
  <title>Listing 31-19 from the XML Bible</title>
  <circle cx="400" cy="400" r="500" />
</svg>
```

Figure 31-21: A radius 500 circle at 400,400 displayed in a 100-pixel square viewport and a 1000-unit square view box shifted down and to the right by 100 units

Suppose the viewport is three inches wide by four inches high, and you want 100 local units to equal one inch on the screen. You'd multiply the actual width and height by 100/inch to get a 300 width and a 400 height. Then you'd use this svg element:

```
<svg xmlns="http://www.w3.org/2000/svg"
     width="3in" height="4in" viewBox="0 0 300 400">
  <!-- SVG shapes -->
</svg>
```

You can even scale the x and y axes independently. For example, suppose you want 100 units per inch resolution on the y axis, but 300 units per inch resolution on the x axis, and the viewport is four inches square. You could use this svg element:

```
<svg xmlns="http://www.w3.org/2000/svg"
     width="4in" height="4in" viewBox="0 0 1200 400">
  <!-- SVG shapes -->
</svg>
```

However, by default SVG will attempt to maintain the aspect ratio of the picture. In this case, it will expand the y coordinate to fit the x coordinates. You can change this behavior by setting the preserveAspectRatio attribute of the svg element to none, in which case, using different scale factors on the x and y axes can lead to pictures that seem squeezed along the more precise dimension. For example, you'd normally think this rect element was a square:

```
<rect x="200" y="200" width="100" height="100"/>
```

However, if you place this rect element in the above nonuniform coordinate system and set preserveAspectRatio to none as shown in Listing 31-20, then you get the rectangle shown in Figure 31-22.

Listing 31-20: Nonuniform coordinate systems squeeze shapes if the aspect ratio isn't preserved

```
<?xml version="1.0" encoding="UTF-8" standalone="yes"?>
<svg xmlns="http://www.w3.org/2000/svg"
     width="4in" height="4in" viewBox="0 0 1200 400"
     preserveAspectRatio="none">
  <title>Listing 31-20 from the XML Bible</title>
  <rect x="200" y="200" width="100" height="100"/>
</svg>
```

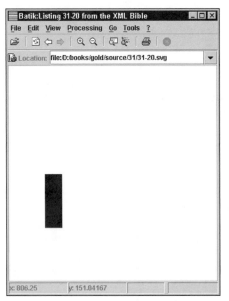

Figure 31-22: Nonuniform coordinate systems squeeze shape

Grouping Shapes

The g (for group) element combines shapes so they can be treated as a single entity. The g can have its own local coordinate space in which its child shapes are placed. This entire collection of shapes can then be moved, positioned, styled, and copied as a unit. For example, suppose you need a shape that is a star inside a circle. You can create it by combining a circle with a polygon in a g element like this:

```
<g width="6cm" height="6cm" viewBox="0 0 250 250">
  <circle cx="115" cy="115" r="100" fill="red" />
  <polygon fill="blue"
    points="33,90 97,90 117,36 137,90 199,90 147,125
            167,180 117,146 67,180 85,125">
  </polygon>
</g>
```

The width and height attributes define the dimensions of the containing block. The viewBox attribute defines the local coordinate system of the elements contained in the group. This is an abstract system, not one based on any sort of physical units such as inches, pixels, or ems. The conversion between the local units and the global units depends on the height and the width of the group. For instance, in the above example the group's actual height and width is 6 cm by 6 cm, but its local width and height is 250 by 250. Thus, each local unit is 0.024 cm (6 cm/250). As the height and width of the group change, the sizes of the contents of the group scale proportionately. Furthermore, as you'll see in the next section, the group can be copied by use elements that can adjust the actual height and width. In this case, the contents scale proportionately.

Referencing Shapes

Almost any shape, path, or group in an SVG document can be copied into multiple different places in the document. The use element refers to an element defined elsewhere in the document. For example, suppose you defined red and white squares, like this:

```
<rect id="RedSquare"
      width="1in" height="1in"
      fill="red"/>
<rect id="WhiteSquare"
      width="1in" height="1in"
      fill="white"/>
```

Now suppose you want to place a copy of the red square at coordinates x=3in, y=3in. This use element does that:

```
<use x="3in" y="3in" xlink:href="#RedSquare"/>
```

For this to work, the xlink prefix has to be mapped to the standard XLink namespace URI, http://www.w3.org/1999/xlink. This is normally done on the root element.

It's customary to put the referenced elements inside a defs element. This hides them so they won't be drawn until they're referenced by a use element. For example,

```
<defs>
  <rect id="RedSquare"
        width="1in" height="1in"
        fill="red"/>
  <rect id="WhiteSquare"
        width="1in" height="1in"
        fill="white"/>
</defs>
```

Referencing elements is especially useful if you have many different copies of the same styled element at different positions. For example, designing a checkerboard in SVG would normally require 64 different shapes, one for each square on the board. However, with use and g, you can reduce that to just 2 rectangles, 2 groups of rectangles, and 24 use elements. Listing 31-21 demonstrates. Note especially the nesting of the references. That is, the board uses the rows that use the squares. Figure 31-23 shows the result of Listing 31-21.

Listing 31-21: A checkerboard

```
<?xml version="1.0" encoding="utf-8"?>
<svg xmlns="http://www.w3.org/2000/svg"
     xmlns:xlink="http://www.w3.org/1999/xlink"
     width="8in" height="8in">

  <title>Listing 31-21 from the XML Bible</title>

  <defs>

    <rect id="RedSquare"
          width="1in" height="1in"
          fill="red"/>
    <rect id="BlackSquare"
          width="1in" height="1in"
          fill="black"/>

    <g id="RowA">
      <use x="0in" xlink:href="#RedSquare"/>
      <use x="1in" xlink:href="#BlackSquare"/>
      <use x="2in" xlink:href="#RedSquare"/>
      <use x="3in" xlink:href="#BlackSquare"/>
      <use x="4in" xlink:href="#RedSquare"/>
      <use x="5in" xlink:href="#BlackSquare"/>
      <use x="6in" xlink:href="#RedSquare"/>
      <use x="7in" xlink:href="#BlackSquare"/>
    </g>

    <g id="RowB">
      <use x="0in" xlink:href="#BlackSquare"/>
      <use x="1in" xlink:href="#RedSquare"/>
      <use x="2in" xlink:href="#BlackSquare"/>
      <use x="3in" xlink:href="#RedSquare"/>
      <use x="4in" xlink:href="#BlackSquare"/>
      <use x="5in" xlink:href="#RedSquare"/>
      <use x="6in" xlink:href="#BlackSquare"/>
      <use x="7in" xlink:href="#RedSquare"/>
    </g>

  </defs>

  <use y="0in" xlink:href="#RowA"/>
  <use y="1in" xlink:href="#RowB"/>
  <use y="2in" xlink:href="#RowA"/>
  <use y="3in" xlink:href="#RowB"/>
  <use y="4in" xlink:href="#RowA"/>
  <use y="5in" xlink:href="#RowB"/>
  <use y="6in" xlink:href="#RowA"/>
  <use y="7in" xlink:href="#RowB"/>

</svg>
```

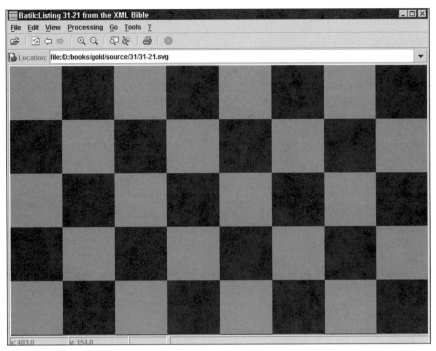

Figure 31-23: A checkerboard

This is actually not the most compact solution possible. You could build double rows of two rows each, and then quadruple rows of two double rows each. However, this is the most straightforward solution.

One thing SVG does not give you, which would be very useful in cases such as this, is any sort of iterative structure that would let you simply say, "Give me eight rows of four black squares each spaced two inches apart." Tasks like this can sometimes be accomplished with JavaScript and the SVG Document Object Model (DOM).

Transformations

There are two ways to travel to Jupiter. The first is to get in a rocket ship and fly yourself there. The second is to pick up the entire universe, and drag everything in the universe except yourself a few hundred million miles so that Jupiter arrives where you are, with everything else having moved the same amount in the same direction. Needless to say, one of these solutions is considerably easier to accomplish than the other. However, in the abstract, massless world of SVG, that's not true. It is just as easy, sometimes even easier, to move the entire universe to where you want it to be as it is to move a shape or path or group to where it needs to go.

The process of moving the SVG universe is called a *coordinate system transformation*, and the engine that powers the move is the `transform` attribute of the g element.

The coordinate system transformation that moves the universe so that you end up on Jupiter is called a translation, but this is not the only kind of transformation available in SVG. In fact, there are six kinds of transformation, each represented by a different function that can be used in the value of a `transform` attribute:

✦ `translate(dx dy)`: Add dx to all x coordinates and dy to all y coordinates.

✦ `rotate(Θ x y)`: Rotate the coordinate system by Θ degrees around a z-axis passing through the point x, y.

✦ `scale(sx sy)`: Multiply the x coordinates by sx and the y coordinates by sy.

✦ `skewX(Θ)`: Skew the y-axis relative to the x-axis by Θ degrees.

✦ `skewY(Θ)`: Skew the x-axis relative to the y-axis by Θ degrees.

✦ `matrix(a b c d e f)`: Multiply all coordinate vectors (x, y, 1) by this translation matrix:

$$\begin{bmatrix} a & c & e \\ b & d & f \\ 0 & 0 & 1 \end{bmatrix}$$

Translations and rotations are *rigid transformations*; that is, they preserve the distance between points. If a line is 70 units long before a translation or a rotation, then it is still 70 units long after a translation or rotation. For that matter, it is still 70 units long after any combination of translations and rotations. A scaling, by contrast, may change the sizes of various objects, though their relative sizes will be the same. A skew can change both objects' absolute and relative sizes. Finally, a matrix is a fairly arbitrary transformation that can combine any or all of the other four transforms, as well as add a few things those can't do, such as a flip.

Coordinate transforms are important tools in SVG and allow you to easily perform tasks that are otherwise quite difficult; particularly because you don't have to make these transformations on the entire canvas at once. Instead you make it one group at a time. In each group you use the coordinate space that's most appropriate for it. The change from the original coordinate space to the new coordinate space is defined by the g element's `transform` attribute.

For example, consider the pie made up of 45-degree arcs from Listing 31-11. It was relatively difficult to do all the trigonometry to calculate the proper end points of each of the eight arcs. However some arcs are easier than others. And once you've got one arc, you can copy it to different positions and rotate each copy. Listing 31-22 is exactly the same pie as Listing 31-11, but it only required one bout with the calculator and is a smaller document over all.

Listing 31-22: **A pie formed by eight rotated copies of one wedge**

```xml
<?xml version="1.0" encoding="UTF-8" standalone="yes"?>
<svg xmlns="http://www.w3.org/2000/svg"
     xmlns:xlink="http://www.w3.org/1999/xlink">
  <title>Listing 31-22 from the XML Bible</title>
  <defs>
    <path id="piece"
          d="M 100,100
             L 100, 0
             A 100 100 0 0 1 170.7106781187 29.28932188135
             L 100, 100 Z"
          fill="brown" stroke="black" stroke-width="1px" />
  </defs>

  <g transform="rotate(0 100 100)">
    <use xlink:href="#piece"/>
  </g>
  <g transform="rotate(45 100 100)">
    <use xlink:href="#piece"/>
  </g>
  <g transform="rotate(90 100 100)">
    <use xlink:href="#piece"/>
  </g>
  <g transform="rotate(135 100 100)">
    <use xlink:href="#piece"/>
  </g>
  <g transform="rotate(180 100 100)">
    <use xlink:href="#piece"/>
  </g>
  <g transform="rotate(225 100 100)">
    <use xlink:href="#piece"/>
  </g>
  <g transform="rotate(270 100 100)">
    <use xlink:href="#piece"/>
  </g>
  <g transform="rotate(315 100 100)">
    <use xlink:href="#piece"/>
  </g>

</svg>
```

Suppose you want to split the pie apart so that there are gaps between the pieces, as in an exploded drawing. This is relatively difficult to do by manually calculating the coordinates of each piece. However, it's very straightforward to do with a translation. First, you translate the entire picture down and to the right, because as originally written it butts up against the top and left edges. Then you rotate each piece and translate it four units to the right and ten up. Listing 31-23 demonstrates. Figure 31-24 shows the result.

Listing 31-23: **An exploded pie**

```
<?xml version="1.0" encoding="UTF-8" standalone="yes"?>
<svg xmlns="http://www.w3.org/2000/svg"
     xmlns:xlink="http://www.w3.org/1999/xlink"
     width="3.6in" height="2.8in">
  <title>Listing 31-23 from the XML Bible</title>
  <defs>
    <path id="piece"
          d="M 100,100
             L 100, 0
             A 100 100 0 0 1 170.7106781187 29.28932188135
             L 100, 100 Z"
          fill="brown" stroke="black" stroke-width="1px" />
  </defs>

  <g transform="translate(50 50)">
    <g transform="rotate(0 100 100) translate(4 -10)">
     <use xlink:href="#piece"/>
    </g>
    <g transform="rotate(45 100 100) translate(4 -10)">
     <use xlink:href="#piece"/>
    </g>
    <g transform="rotate(90 100 100) translate(4 -10)">
     <use xlink:href="#piece"/>
    </g>
    <g transform="rotate(135 100 100) translate(4 -10)">
     <use xlink:href="#piece"/>
    </g>
    <g transform="rotate(180 100 100) translate(4 -10)">
     <use xlink:href="#piece"/>
    </g>
    <g transform="rotate(225 100 100) translate(4 -10)">
     <use xlink:href="#piece"/>
    </g>
    <g transform="rotate(270 100 100) translate(4 -10)">
     <use xlink:href="#piece"/>
    </g>
    <g transform="rotate(315 100 100) translate(4 -10)">
     <use xlink:href="#piece"/>
    </g>
  </g>

</svg>
```

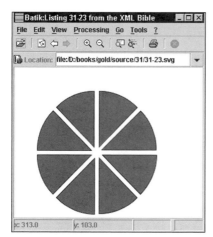

Figure 31-24: An exploded diagram of a pie

In this case each transformation consists of a rotation followed by a translation. You can string as many of these together as you like. However, transformations are not, in general, commutative. Order matters in transformations.

Scaling is a very straightforward operation in which the size of everything is multiplied by a fixed factor. You can provide different scales for the x and y axes, or just one scale for both. For example, Listing 31-24 defines several pie pieces, each one and a half times the size of the previous one. In this example, notice how the coordinate system of the largest piece is actually the product of the multiple groups it's enclosed in and the transformations each imposes. Figure 31-25 shows the result.

Listing 31-24: **Scaled pie**

```
<?xml version="1.0" encoding="UTF-8" standalone="yes"?>
<svg xmlns="http://www.w3.org/2000/svg"
     xmlns:xlink="http://www.w3.org/1999/xlink">
  <title>Listing 31-24 from the XML Bible</title>
  <defs>
    <path id="piece"
          d="M 100,100
             L 100, 0
             A 100 100 0 0 1 170.7106781187 29.28932188135
             L 100, 100 Z"
          fill="brown" stroke="black" stroke-width="1px" />
  </defs>
```

Continued

Listing 31-24 *(continued)*

```
<g transform="translate(-100 0)">
  <use xlink:href="#piece"/>
  <g transform="translate(0 50) scale(1.5)">
    <use xlink:href="#piece"/>
    <g transform="translate(0 50) scale(1.5)">
      <use xlink:href="#piece"/>
      <g transform="translate(0 50) scale(1.5)">
        <use xlink:href="#piece"/>
      </g>
    </g>
  </g>
</g>

</svg>
```

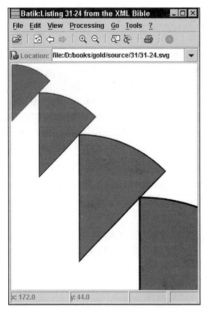

Figure 31-25: Scaled pieces of pie

Skewing rotates one axis of the coordinate system, either x or y, but not both. Lines that appear perpendicular to each other before skewing no longer appear so after skewing. Figures tend to get squashed and pushed over in one direction or another.

You can skew either the x axis relative to the y axis with skewY() or the y axis relative to the x axis with skewX(). Each takes as an argument the number of degrees to skew the axis by. This is sometimes used for text effects as demonstrated in Listing 31-25 and shown in Figure 31-26. The text normally runs along the x axis whereas the letters are oriented parallel to the y axis. Thus skewing with respect to the x axis (skewX()) merely slants the text within a line. However, skewing with respect to the y axis (skewY()) changes the baseline of the text but keeps all non-italic text pretty much perpendicular to the baseline.

Listing 31-25: **Skewed text**

```
<?xml version="1.0" encoding="UTF-8" standalone="yes"?>
<svg xmlns="http://www.w3.org/2000/svg"
     width="4.6in" height="4.6in">
  <title>Listing 31-25 from the XML Bible</title>

    <g transform="skewX(45)">
      <text x="10" y="72"
            font-size="24pt" font-weight="bold"
            font-family="Helvetica, Arial, sans">
        X Skewed 45 Degrees
      </text>
    </g>

    <g transform="skewY(45)">
      <text x="10" y="72"
            font-size="24pt" font-weight="bold"
            font-family="Helvetica, Arial, sans">
        Y Skewed 45 Degrees
      </text>
    </g>

</svg>
```

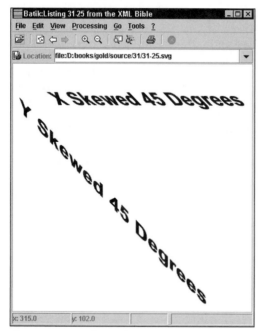

Figure 31-26: Skewed text

All of these transformations — translations, skews, and rotations — are defined mathematically as multiplications of vectors by matrixes. An arbitrary two-dimensional rigid transformation, as well as the nonrigid scales and skews, can be defined in terms of multiplying the coordinate vector by a particular matrix. Furthermore, any combinations of translations, scales, skews, and rotations can be defined as multiplication by a matrix that is the product of the matrixes for each of the individual transformations. However, the reverse is not true. Not all matrix transformations can be decomposed into sequences of rotations, translations, scales, and skews. In particular, a matrix allows you to flip the coordinate system; that is, map negative coordinates into positive coordinates and vice versa; or, another way of thinking about it, flip the entire plane over through the third dimension. The matrix for flipping the coordinate system around the y axis looks like this:

$$\begin{bmatrix} -1 & 0 & 0 \\ 0 & 1 & 0 \\ 0 & 0 & 1 \end{bmatrix}$$

If you're familiar with linear algebra, it should be obvious that this simple diagonal matrix multiplies the x coordinates by –1 and leaves the y coordinates untouched. In other words, it transforms vectors such as [x y 1] to [–x y 1]. If you're not familiar with linear algebra, just take my word for it. In SVG, this matrix is written as [–1 0 0 1 0 0]. (The last row of the transformation matrix is always (0 0 1) in SVG.) Thus, to flip the coordinate system, you can use this transform:

```
<g transform="matrix(-1 0 0 1 0 0)">
  <!-- SVG elements here -->
</g>
```

To flip the y axis around the x axis, and thus get a coordinate system in which increasing y is up, you'd use this transform:

```
<g transform="matrix(1 0 0 -1 0 0)">
  <!-- SVG elements here -->
</g>
```

There are also matrixes for flips about other axes.

Linking

Because SVG graphics are meant to be used on the Web, it shouldn't come as any great surprise that they can contain simple hypertext links. This allows SVG pictures to be used as image maps on Web pages without separate map files.

The a element indicates that its contents are a link. This is very similar to the a element in HTML and XHTML, and behaves almost identically. However, instead of using an href attribute, it uses an xlink:href attribute in which the xlink prefix is mapped to the http://www.w3.org/1999/xlink URI. For example, Listing 31-26 draws nine circles in a three by three grid. Each circle element is enclosed in an element that links to a news site such as CNN or the *New York Times*. When the user clicks on a circle, they're transported to the home page of a different news site.

Listing 31-26: **Nine circles linked to different sites**

```
<?xml version="1.0" encoding="UTF-8" standalone="yes"?>
<svg xmlns="http://www.w3.org/2000/svg"
    xmlns:xlink="http://www.w3.org/1999/xlink"
    width="3.6in" height="3.6in"
    viewBox="0 0 300 300">
  <title>Listing 31-26 from the XML Bible</title>

  <a xlink:href="http://www.cnn.com/">
   <circle r="20" cx="25"  cy="25" fill="yellow"/>
  </a>
  <a xlink:href="http://www.msnbc.com/">
   <circle r="20" cx="75"  cy="25" fill="blue"/>
  </a>
  <a xlink:href="http://www.news.com/">
    <circle r="20" cx="125" cy="25" fill="green"/>
  </a>
  <a xlink:href="http://www.cnn.com/">
```

Continued

Listing 31-26 *(continued)*

```
    <circle r="20" cx="25"  cy="75" fill="red"/>
  </a>
  <a xlink:href="http://news.altavista.com/">
    <circle r="20" cx="75"  cy="75" fill="orange"/>
  </a>
  <a xlink:href="http://www.nytimes.com/">
    <circle r="20" cx="125" cy="75" fill="violet"/>
  </a>
  <a xlink:href="http://www.abcnews.com/">
    <circle r="20" cx="25"  cy="125" fill="indigo"/>
  </a>
  <a xlink:href="http://www.csmonitor.com/">
    <circle r="20" cx="75"  cy="125" fill="pink"/>
  </a>
  <a xlink:href="http://news.bbc.co.uk/">
    <circle r="20" cx="125" cy="125" fill="purple"/>
  </a>

</svg>
```

The a element may also have all the other attributes of a simple Xlink, including
xlink:role, xlink:arcrole, xlink:title, xlink:type, xlink:show, and
xlink:actuate. xlink:type must have the value simple. xlink:actuate is limited to onRequest. xlink:show is limited to new and replace. (To embed content
in an SVG document you have to use image rather than a.) These attributes have
the same meaning and behavior as for any other XLink.

**Cross-
Reference**   XLinks are discussed in Chapter 20.

Metadata

Graphics, even ones written in XML, can be rather opaque to anyone who can't see
very well. This class of users includes not only visually impaired people, but also
computer programs such as Web spiders, indexers, spell checkers, and so forth. To
make the information normally encoded in graphics more accessible to this class of
users, most of the elements in an SVG document can contain title, desc, and
metadata elements. SVG places no restrictions on the contents of these elements,
except that:

1. The content must be well-formed XML

2. The content can use any XML vocabulary provided you use a namespace to
   distinguish its elements from SVG's elements

The main difference between these three elements (title, desc, and metadata) is the rough semantic meaning they imply. In particular:

✦ The title element is a short string of generally unmarked-up text. It can be placed in the title bar of the window showing the picture, as Batik does, or in a tool tip when the user places the mouse over the titled element.

✦ The metadata element often contains indexing information in some formal vocabulary such as RDF (Resource Description Framework), topic maps, and/or the Dublin Core.

✦ The desc element often contains marked-up text intended for humans to read, particularly well-formed HTML.

However, in practice they're pretty much equivalent. Feel free to use whichever elements seem right to you. For instance, a metadata element might contain XHTML or RDF. The information in the metadata element is intended for non-SVG processors that need to try to make sense out of the picture. For example, Listing 31-27 adds some metadata describing the picture of my cat Marjorie originally seen in Listing 31-15. The title element says this is Listing 31-27 from the XML Bible. The desc element describes Marjorie with a little HTML. The metadata element contains an RDF description of this picture. However, when loaded into a browser, the picture hasn't changed at all. Metadata is for almost anything except an SVG renderer.

Listing 31-27: **RDF and XHTML metadata embedded in an SVG document**

```
<?xml version="1.0" encoding="UTF-8" standalone="yes"?>
<svg xmlns="http://www.w3.org/2000/svg"
     xmlns:xlink="http://www.w3.org/1999/xlink"
     width="300px" height="320px">
  <title>Listing 31-27 from the XML Bible</title>

  <desc>
    <body xmlns="http://www.w3.org/1999/xhtml">
      <p>
        <i>Marjorie</i> is a 9-pound blue British shorthair.
        She's about three years old, loves cameras,
        and hates people. She tolerates Beth and me,
        <em>barely</em>, but hides in the back of the
        bedroom closet anytime company comes over.
      </p>

      <p>
        She's definitely something of a wimp.
        The other cat in our household, <i>Charm</i>, is
        constantly attacking her; and, even though she's a
```

Continued

Listing 31-27 *(continued)*

```
         couple of pounds heavier than him, her only real
         defense is to lay down and wait until he gets bored
         and runs away. When we got her, we hoped she'd bite
         back and teach Charm that biting hurts, but no such
         luck. Charm still bites anything and anyone he can
         catch: mice, cats, dogs, people, furniture, paper,
         computers, household appliances, etc.
         If he can catch it, he will bite it.
      </p>
    </body>
  </desc>

  <metadata>
    <rdf:RDF
       xmlns:rdf="http://www.w3.org/1999/02/22-rdf-syntax-ns#"
       xmlns:dc="http://purl.org/dc/elements/1.1/">

       <rdf:Description about="#marjorie picture">
         <dc:title>Marjorie the Kitten</dc:title>
         <dc:creator
           rdf:resource="mailto:elharo@metalab.unc.edu"/>
         <dc:description>
           A photo of a grey cat standing on a table
           looking into the camera.
         </dc:description>
         <dc:date>2000-12-21</dc:date>
         <dc:type>Photograph</dc:type>
         <dc:format>image/jpeg</dc:format>
         <dc:rights>
           Copyright 2000 Elliotte Rusty Harold
         </dc:rights>
       </rdf:Description>

       <rdf:Description about="mailto:elharo@metalab.unc.edu">
         <dc:title>Elliotte Rusty Harold</dc:title>
       </rdf:Description>

    </rdf:RDF>
  </metadata>

  <image id="marjorie_picture" xlink:href="marjorie.jpg"
    x="20px" y="5px" width="260px" height="297px"/>

  <text x="25px" y="240px"
       font-size="14pt" font-weight="bold"
       font-family="Helvetica, Arial, sans">
    This is my cat Marjorie.
  </text>
```

```
<text x="25px" y="255px"
      font-size="14pt" font-weight="bold"
      font-family="Helvetica, Arial, sans">
  She likes to have her picture taken.
</text>

</svg>
```

Cross-Reference RDF and the Dublin Core Vocabulary used here are discussed in Chapter 24.

Although the most common place to put `title`, `desc`, and `metadata` elements is at the top level, as immediate children of the root `svg` element, they can appear essentially anywhere in the SVG document. For instance, if one SVG document contained multiple `image` elements, you could give each `image` element a `metadata` child to describe the element.

SVG Editors

Drawing pictures with a keyboard is more than a little like hammering a nail with a sponge. A keyboard simply isn't the right tool with which to draw. A mouse is better, and a graphics tablet is best of all. Fortunately, you can use more traditional graphics tools such as Adobe Illustrator and CorelDRAW to produce SVG documents. Graphics programs that support SVG to some extent include:

✦ Adobe Illustrator 9.0 and later can export graphics as SVG, though it cannot yet open and edit documents saved as SVG. It's available for both Macintosh and Windows.

✦ Version 4.3.2 of the W3C's Amaya Web browser and editor has a very rudimentary drawing tool that produces SVG. However, it's really little more than a proof of concept, and thoroughly inadequate for real work. Future versions may improve on it though.

✦ JASC Software, best known for PaintShop Pro, also publishes WebDraw, a native SVG editor for Windows 95/98/Me/NT4/2000.

✦ CorelDRAW 10 for Windows can both import and export SVG documents. As time passes, many other traditional graphics tools will add SVG to their repertoire, and programs that already support it will improve their support. Within a few years, SVG should be as ubiquitous in vector drawing programs as GIF and JPEG are today in bitmapped paint programs.

Summary

In this chapter, you learned about SVG, an XML application for vector graphics recommended by the W3C. In particular, you learned that:

✦ SVG provides a standard XML format for vector drawings.

✦ SVG pictures can be included directly in HTML documents for browsers that understand SVG natively such as Amaya.

✦ For browsers that don't understand SVG natively, you can link to SVG pictures from HTML using EMBED elements and render them with the Adobe SVG Plug-in.

✦ All SVG elements are in the http://www.w3.org/2000/svg namespace.

✦ The root element of an SVG picture is svg.

✦ Rectangles are defined by their upper-left corner, width, and height. They are parallel to the coordinate axes and are represented by rect elements.

✦ Circles are defined by their center point and radius. They are represented by circle elements.

✦ Ellipses are defined by their center point, x radius, and y radius. They are parallel to the coordinate axes and are represented by ellipse elements.

✦ Line segments are defined by their end points. They are represented by line elements.

✦ Polygons are defined by a list of the points of the corners of the polygon. This list is stored in the points attribute of a polygon element.

✦ Polylines are just like polygons except that the last point is not automatically connected back to the first point.

✦ Paths are defined by a path element. The d attribute of a path element contains a list of commands for the path and coordinates for those commands including move to, line to, arc to, curve to, and close path.

✦ Each path command is represented by a single letter; uppercase if the coordinates are absolute, lowercase if the coordinates are relative.

✦ Shapes and paths can be combined into a single unit called a group and represented by a g element.

✦ The use element copies a shape, path, or group defined elsewhere in the document. An xlink:href attribute containing an XPointer identifies the shape to draw.

✦ The defs element prevents its contents from being drawn until they're referenced by a use element.

✦ CSS styles are used to define the colors, fonts, and other details of the abstract geometric shapes defined by the SVG elements. These are attached to shapes, paths, and groups using a `style` attribute.

✦ The `viewBox` attribute of the `svg` element maps a local coordinate space onto the actual rectangular canvas where the picture will be drawn.

✦ The `transform` attribute of the `g` element can rotate, translate, scale, skew, and flip SVG shapes.

✦ You can annotate your SVG documents and elements with non-SVG information using `title`, `metadata` and `desc` elements.

✦ Graphics programs such as CoralDRAW are often a better way to produce SVG documents than drawing in a text editor.

In the next chapter, you explore VML, the Vector Markup Language, an alternative XML format for vector graphics. VML was invented by Microsoft and is used in Office 2000 and Internet Explorer 5.x

✦　　✦　　✦

The Vector Markup Language

Microsoft's Vector Markup Language (VML) is an XML application for vector graphics that can be embedded in Web pages in place of the bitmapped GIF and JPEG images loaded by HTML's IMG element. Vector graphics take up less space and thus display much faster over slow network connections than traditional GIF and JPEG bitmap images. VML is supported by the various components of Microsoft Office 2000 (Word, PowerPoint, Excel), as well as by Internet Explorer 5.0 and later. When you save a Word 2000, PowerPoint 2000, or Excel 2000 document as HTML, graphics created in those programs are converted to VML.

What Is VML?

VML elements represent shapes: rectangles, ovals, circles, triangles, clouds, trapezoids, and so forth. Each shape is described as a path formed from a series of connected lines and curves. VML uses elements and attributes to describe the outline, fill, position, and other properties of each shape. Cascading Style Sheet (CSS) styles are used to position the individual VML elements on the Web page, alongside the usual HTML elements such as P and IMG.

Listing 32-1 is an HTML document. Embedded in this HTML file is the VML code to draw a five-pointed blue star and a red circle. Figure 32-1 shows the document displayed in Internet Explorer.

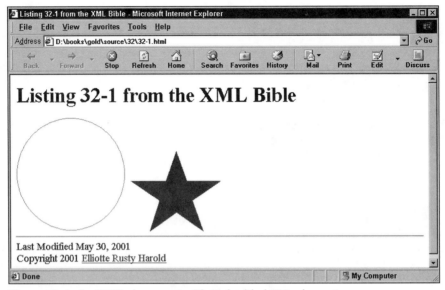

Figure 32-1: An HTML document with embedded VML elements

Listing 32-1: An HTML document with VML code that draws a five-pointed blue star and a red circle

```
<html xmlns:vml="urn:schemas-microsoft-com:vml">

  <head>
    <title>Listing 32-1 from the XML Bible</title>
    <object id="VMLRender"
      classid="CLSID:10072CEC-8CC1-11D1-986E-00A0C955B42E">
    </object>
    <style>
      vml\:* { behavior: url(#VMLRender) }
    </style>
  </head>

  <body>
    <h1>Listing 32-1 from the XML Bible</h1>

    <div>
      <vml:oval
        style="width:200px; height: 200px"
        strokecolor="red"
        strokeweight="2">
      </vml:oval>
```

```
      <vml:polyline
        style="width: 200px; height: 200px"
        stroked="false"
        filled="true"
        fillcolor="blue"
        points="8, 65, 72, 65, 92, 11, 112, 65,
                174, 65, 122, 100, 142, 155, 92,
                121, 42, 155, 60, 100">
      </vml:polyline>
    </div>
    <hr></hr>
    Last Modified May 30, 2001<br />
    Copyright 2001
    <a href="http://www.macfaq.com/personal.html">
      Elliotte Rusty Harold
    </a>
  </body>

</html>
```

Listing 32-1 obviously isn't an ordinary HTML document, even though it contains some standard HTML elements. First, the `html` root element binds the namespace prefix `vml` to the URI `urn:schemas-microsoft-com:vml`. As usual, the prefix can change as long as the URI stays the same. In fact, Microsoft uses the single-letter prefix `v` in most of its examples. In this chapter, I assume that the prefix `vml` is bound to `urn:schemas-microsoft-com:vml` without further comment.

The `head` element contains an `object` child with the `id` VMLRender. (VMLRender is a program installed with Internet Explorer 5.) There's also a CSS `style` element that specifies that all elements in the `urn:schemas-microsoft-com:vml` namespace (that is, all elements that begin with `vml:`) should have the `behavior` property `url(#VMLRender)`. This is a relative URL that points to the aforementioned `object` element. This tells the Web browser to pass all elements in the VML namespace to the object with the ID VMLRender for display.

The `body` element contains several of the usual HTML elements, including `div`, `h1`, `hr`, and `a`. However, it also contains `vml:oval` and `vml:polyline` elements. The `vml:oval` element has a red border (stroke) two pixels wide. In addition, the `style` attribute sets the CSS width and height properties of this oval to 200 pixels each. The `vml:polyline` element is filled in blue, and also has an area of 200 pixels by 200 pixels. A five-pointed star has 10 vertices. Therefore, the `points` attribute provides 10 pairs of x-y coordinates, one for each vertex.

Drawing with a Keyboard

Writing VML pictures by typing raw XML code in a text editor is not easy, but it can be done. I suggest that you start any attempt to program vector images with some graph paper, and draw the images with a pencil the way you wish to see them on the screen. You can then use the images from the graph paper to determine coordinates for various VML elements, such as shape, oval, and polyline.

The shape element

The fundamental VML element is vml:shape. This describes an arbitrary closed curve in two dimensions. Most shapes have a path that defines the outline of the shape. The outline may or may not have a stroke with a particular color and width — that is, the outline may or may not be visible. The shape may or may not be filled with a particular color. For example, in Figure 32-1 the circle has a red stroke but no fill, whereas the star has a blue fill but no stroke.

The properties of a shape are defined in three ways:

✦ By the attributes of the vml:shape element

✦ By the CSS styles of the vml:shape element, which are normally set inside a style attribute on the vml:shape element

✦ By the child elements of the vml:shape element

At a minimum, each shape must have these three properties:

✦ The height of the element defined by a CSS height property

✦ The width of the element defined by a CSS width property

✦ A path for the outline of the shape, defined either by a path attribute or a vml:path child element

For example, here's a vml:shape element that draws an isosceles triangle.

```
<vml:shape
  style="height: 200px; width: 200px"
  path="M 0,200 L 100,0, 200,200 X E">
</vml:shape>
```

The bounding box of the shape, that is, the rectangle that contains the shape and that will be positioned on the page in the midst of the HTML elements, is 200 pixels wide by 200 pixels high. This is established by the CSS `height` and `width` properties, which the `style` attribute provides.

The `path` attribute contains the instructions that draw an isosceles triangle. Don't worry if it isn't obvious to you that this is an isosceles triangle. In fact, I'd be surprised if it were even obvious that this is a triangle. Most VML elements (including this one) are drawn using a GUI and only saved into VML form. Consequently, you don't need to know the detailed syntax of each and every VML element and attribute. However, if you know a little, you can sometimes do some surprising tricks with the VML file that may prove impossible with a graphical editor. For example, you can search for all the blue elements, and change them to red.

Here's how the value of this `path` attribute is interpreted. Each command is represented by a letter such as `M` or `L`. (Microsoft uses lowercase letters in their examples, but I prefer uppercase letters because it's hard to tell the difference between the lowercase letter `l` and the digit `1` in most fonts.) The command is followed by zero or more coordinate points. Each point is given as an x coordinate and a y coordinate, separated by a comma. The commands used here, and their arguments are:

1. `M 0,200`: Move the pen to the point x = 0, y = 200.
2. `L 100,0, 200,200`: Draw a line from the current pen location (x = 0, y = 200) to x = 100, y = 0. Then draw a line from there to the point x = 200, y = 200.
3. `X`: Close the shape; that is, draw a line from the last point back to the first point.
4. `E`: End the path.

Note that all coordinates are given in the standard computer graphics coordinates in which x increases to the right and y increases down. Figure 32-2 demonstrates.

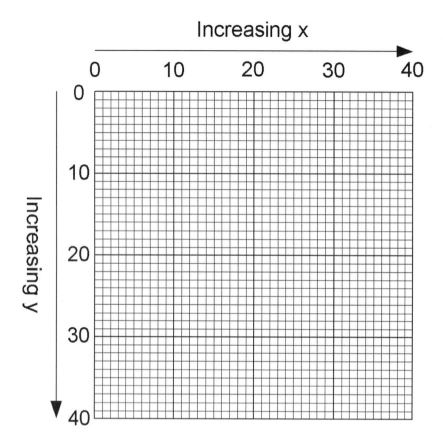

Figure 32-2: VML uses a left-handed coordinate system with the origin in the upper-left corner of the window.

Other shape attributes

Additional attributes can be added to a vml:shape element to set its color, stroke color, alternate text, and more. Table 32-1 summarizes the standard set of these attributes.

Table 32-1
Standard Attributes of the vml:shape Element

Attribute Name	Attribute Value	Default
adj	A comma-delimited string of up to eight integers that provides input parameters for vml:formulas child elements	None
alt	Alternate text shown if the shape can't be drawn for any reason; similar to the ALT attribute of HTML's IMG element	None
class	The class of the shape; used to attach CSS styles to groups of elements in the same class	None
coordorigin	The local coordinates of the upper-left corner of the shape's box	0, 0
coordsize	The width and height of the shape's box in the local coordinate space	Same as the width and height of the entire shape
fillcolor	The color the shape is filled with; for example, red or #66FF33	White
filled	A boolean specifying whether the shape is filled	False
href	The URL to jump to when the shape is clicked	None
id	A unique XML name for the element (same as any other XML ID type attribute)	None
path	Commands that define the shape's path	None
strokecolor	The color used to draw the outline of the shape	Black
stroked	A boolean specifying whether the path (outline) of the shape should be drawn	True
strokeweight	The width of the line outlining the shape's path	1px
style	The CSS properties applied to this shape	None
target	The name of the frame or window that a URL loaded when the shape is clicked will be displayed in	None
title	The name of the shape; displayed when the mouse pointer moves over the shape	None
type	A reference to the ID of a vml:shapetype element	None

Note   Microsoft Office 2000 adds a number of extension attributes as well. Apparently Microsoft can't even resist embracing and extending those standards they themselves created.

Shape child elements

Some properties of shapes are more convenient to set with child elements than with attributes. Furthermore, using child elements allows finer control of some aspects of shapes. Table 32-2 lists the possible child elements of a shape. If a child element conflicts with an attribute, then the value specified by the child element is used.

Table 32-2
Shape Child Elements

Element Name	Purpose
extrusion	A three-dimensional extruded effect
fill	Specifies how and with what the shape is filled
formulas	Formulas used to calculate the path of the shape
handles	Handles by which the shape can be manipulated
imagedata	A bitmapped picture from an external source rendered on top of the shape
path	Commands specifying how to draw the shape's outline
shadow	The shadow effect for the shape
skew	An angle by which to skew the shape
stroke	The visible outline of the shape
textbox	Text inside the shape
textpath	A path along which the text is drawn

Predefined shapes

Because working with paths manually isn't very convenient, VML predefines a number of common shapes with different syntax that can be more naturally specified. For instance, you could define a rectangle using a path like this:

```
<vml:shape style="height: 200px; width: 100px"
  path="M 0,0 L 100,0, 100,200, 0,200 X E">
</vml:shape>
```

However it's easier to specify it by giving the coordinates of its corners, or one corner and the width and the height; indeed, VML let's you do this by using a `vml:rect` element instead of a `vml:shape` element like this:

```
<vml:rect style="height: 200; width: 100; top: 0; left: 0">
</vml:rect>
```

The rectangle is completely specified by the CSS styles. VML predefines eight shapes, all listed in Table 32-3.

Table 32-3
Predefined Shapes

Element	Shape
arc	A curved line defined by the arc of a circle between two points through a specified number of degrees
curve	A curved line defined by a cubic Bézier curve
image	A bitmapped image loaded from an external source
line	A straight line between two points
oval	The largest oval that can fit in a rectangular box of specified size
polyline	A series of straight lines drawn between successive pairs of points
rect	A rectangle oriented parallel to the coordinate axes defined by one corner and a height and a width
roundrect	A rectangle with rounded edges

Each of these child elements can have all the attributes that `vml:shape` has and that are shown in Table 32-1: `fill`, `fillcolor`, `stroke`, and so on. In addition, each has some unique attributes that allow its path to be specified in a more convenient way. For instance, `vml:line`, one of the simplest, has `from` and `to` attributes that define the end points of the line. The value of each of these attributes is a 2D coordinate in the local coordinate space, such as `0, 5` or `32, 10`. Detailed syntax is on the Microsoft Web site at `http://msdn.microsoft.com/workshop/author/vml/`.

The shapetype element

The `vml:shapetype` element defines a shape that can be reused multiple times, by referencing it at a later point within a document using a `vml:shape` element. The `vml:shapetype` element itself is never drawn. A `vml:shape` element references a `vml:shapetype` element using a `type` attribute whose value is a relative URL pointing to the `id` of the `vml:shapetype` element. The syntax of the `vml:shapetype` element is almost identical to the syntax of the `vml:shape` element except that a `vml:shapetype` generally does not give an explicit width and height because it is not actually drawn on the page. Instead, a `coordsize` attribute defines an abstract coordinate system that is mapped to the width and height of the actual shapes that reference it.

For example, Listing 32-2 includes a `vml:shapetype` element that defines a blue right triangle. It also includes three shape elements that merely reference this `vml:shapetype`. Thus, there are three right triangles in Figure 32-3, even though it's only defined once. Each of these triangles has a different size as set in the individual `shape` elements, even though they're all calculated from the same formulas.

Listing 32-2: **Multiple shape elements copy a single shapetype**

```
<html xmlns:vml="urn:schemas-microsoft-com:vml">

  <head>
    <title>Listing 32-2 from the XML Bible</title>
    <object id="VMLRender"
      classid="CLSID:10072CEC-8CC1-11D1-986E-00A0C955B42E">
    </object>
    <style>
      vml\:* { behavior: url(#VMLRender) }
    </style>
  </head>

  <body>
    <h1>Listing 32-2 from the XML Bible</h1>

    <vml:shapetype id="fred"
      coordsize="500,500"
      fillcolor="blue"
      path="m 0,0 l 0,400, 300,400 x e">
    </vml:shapetype>

    <vml:shape type="#fred" style="width:50px; height:50px" />
    <vml:shape type="#fred" style="width:100px; height:100px"/>
    <vml:shape type="#fred" style="width:150px; height:150px"/>

    <hr></hr>
    Last Modified May 30, 2001<br />
    Copyright 2001
    <a href="http://www.macfaq.com/personal.html">
      Elliotte Rusty Harold
    </a>
  </body>

</html>
```

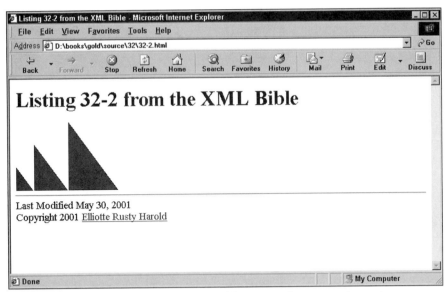

Figure 32-3: Three triangle shapes copied from one shapetype element.

When a vml:shape element references a vml:shapetype element, vml:shape may duplicate some of the attributes applied to the vml:shapetype element. In this case, the values associated with vml:shape override those of vml:shapetype.

The group element

The group top-level element combines shapes and other top-level elements. The group has its own local coordinate space in which its child shapes are placed. This entire collection of shapes can then be moved and positioned as a unit. The only attributes the group can have are the core attributes that a shape can have (that is, id, class, style, title, href, target, alt, coordorigin, and coordsize). For example, suppose you need a shape that is a star inside a circle. You can create it by combining an oval with a polyline in a group element like this:

```
<vml:group style="width: 6cm; height: 6cm"
   coordorigin="0,0" coordsize="250,250">
   <vml:oval style="position: absolute; top: 15; left: 15;
                   width: 200; height: 200"
     filled="true" fillcolor="red">
   </vml:oval>

   <vml:polyline style="position: absolute; top: 25; left: 25;
                       width: 200; height: 200"
     filled="true" fillcolor="blue"
     points="8, 65, 72, 65, 92, 11, 112, 65, 174, 65, 122,
             100, 142, 155, 92, 121, 42, 155, 60, 100">
   </vml:polyline>
</vml:group>
```

The `coordsize` and `coordorigin` attributes define the local coordinate system of the elements contained in the group. The `coordsize` attribute defines the dimensions of the containing block. The `coordorigin` attribute defines the coordinate of the top-left corner of the containing block.

This is an abstract system, not a system based on any sort of physical units such as inches, pixels, or ems. The conversion between the local units and the global units depends on the height and the width of the group. For instance, in the above example, the group's actual height and width is 6 cm by 6 cm, and its `coordsize` is 250,250. Thus, each local unit is 0.024 cm (6 cm/250). As the height and width of the `group` change, the sizes of the contents of the `group` scale proportionately.

Inside a `group`, all the CSS properties used to position VML, such as `left` and `width`, are given as nondimensional numbers in the local coordinate space. In other words, unlike normal CSS properties, they do not use units and are only pure numbers, not real lengths. All children of the `group` are positioned and sized according to the local coordinate system. For example, consider this `group`:

```
<vml:group style="width: 400px; height: 400px"
        coordsize="100,100"
        coordorigin="-50,-50">
</vml:group>
```

The containing block is 400 pixels wide by 400 pixels high. The `coordsize` property specifies that there are 100 units both horizontally and vertically within this `group`. Each of the local units is four pixels long. The coordinate system inside the containing block ranges from –50.0 to 50.0 along the x-axis and –50.0 to 50.0 along the y-axis with 0.0, 0.0 at the center of the rectangle. Shapes positioned outside this region will not be truncated, but they are likely to fall on top of or beneath HTML elements and other VML shapes on the page.

Positioning VML Shapes with CSS Properties

VML elements fit directly into the CSS Level 2 visual-rendering model, exactly like HTML elements. This means that each VML element is contained in an implicit box, which is placed at a certain point on the Web page. The following standard CSS properties place the box at particular absolute or relative positions on the page:

✦ `display`

✦ `position`

✦ `float`

✦ `clear`

✦ `height`

✦ `width`

✦ `top`

- ✦ bottom
- ✦ left
- ✦ right
- ✦ border
- ✦ margin
- ✦ visibility
- ✦ z-index

Cross-Reference

Chapter 15 discusses the syntax and semantics of these properties.

In addition to supporting the standard CSS2 visual-rendering model, VML adds four new properties so that shapes can be rotated, flipped, and positioned:

- ✦ rotation
- ✦ flip
- ✦ center-x
- ✦ center-y

Note

Personally, I think adding nonstandard CSS properties to the style attribute is a very bad idea. I would much prefer that these properties simply be additional attributes on the various VML shape elements. The center-x and center-y properties are particularly annoying because they do nothing the left and right properties don't already do.

VML elements use a style attribute to set these properties, just like HTML elements. This has the same syntax as the HTML style attribute. For example, this VML oval uses its style attribute to set its position, border, and margin properties:

```
<vml:oval style="top: 15; left: 15; width: 200; height: 100;
    margin: 10; border-style: solid; border-right-width: 2;
    border-left-width: 2; border-top-width: 1.5;
    border-bottom-width: 1.5"
    stroked="false" filled="true" fillcolor="green">
</vml:oval>
```

VML shapes are positioned on the page using the CSS position, left, right, width, and height properties. If the position property has the value absolute, the invisible rectangular box that contains the shape is placed at particular coordinates relative to the window that displays the shape, regardless of what else appears on the page. This means that shapes and HTML elements can overlap. VML uses the z-index CSS property to layer the first (lowest) to the last (highest) layer, with the latest elements obscuring the earlier elements. This allows you to stack elements on top of each other. If elements don't have z-index properties, then elements that come later in the document are placed on top of elements that come earlier in the document.

Listing 32-3 uses absolute positioning to place the blue star on top of the red circle, which is itself on top of the h1 header and the signature block. Figure 32-4 shows the result.

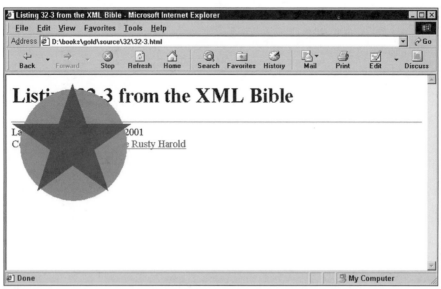

Figure 32-4: A blue star on top of a red circle on top of the body of the page

---

Listing 32-3: VML code that draws a five-pointed blue star on top of a red circle

```
<html xmlns:vml="urn:schemas-microsoft-com:vml">

  <head>
    <title>Listing 32-3 from the XML Bible</title>
    <object id="VMLRender"
      classid="CLSID:10072CEC-8CC1-11D1-986E-00A0C955B42E">
    </object>
    <style>
      vml\:* { behavior: url(#VMLRender) }
    </style>
  </head>

  <body>
    <h1>Listing 32-3 from the XML Bible</h1>
```

```
<div>
  <vml:polyline
    style="position:absolute; top:0px; left:0px;
           width: 250px; height: 250px; z-index: 1"
    stroked="false"
    filled="true"
    fillcolor="blue"
    points="8pt, 65pt, 72pt, 65pt, 92pt, 11pt, 112pt, 65pt,
            174pt, 65pt, 122pt, 100pt, 142pt, 155pt, 92pt,
            121pt, 42pt, 155pt, 60pt, 100pt">
  </vml:polyline>

  <vml:oval style="position:absolute; top:25px; left:25px;
                   width:200px; height: 200px; z-index: 0"
    stroked="false"
    filled="true"
    fillcolor="red">
  </vml:oval>

</div>
<hr></hr>
Last Modified May 30, 2001<br />
Copyright 1999, 2001
<a href="http://www.macfaq.com/personal.html">
  Elliotte Rusty Harold
</a>
</body>

</html>
```

The default value of the `position` property is `static`, which simply means that both HTML elements and VML shapes are laid out one after the other, each taking as much space as it needs, but none laying on top of another.

The `position` property can also be set to `relative`, which begins by placing the box where it would normally be, and then offsetting it from that position by the amount specified in the `top`, `bottom`, `left`, and `right` properties.

The rotation property

The `rotation` property does not exist in standard CSS, but it can be used as a CSS property of VML shapes. The `rotation` property specifies the number of degrees a shape is rotated in a clockwise direction about an axis passing through the center of the shape. Negative values rotate the shape counterclockwise. Values are specified in the format `45deg`, `90deg`, `-30deg`, and so forth. Listing 32-4 rotates Listing 32-1's star by 120 degrees. Figure 32-5 shows the result.

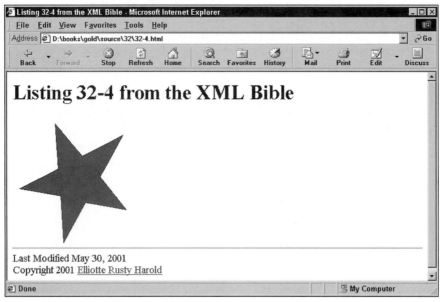

Figure 32-5: A star rotated by 120 degrees

Listing 32-4: **A star rotated by 120 degrees**

```
<html xmlns:vml="urn:schemas-microsoft-com:vml">

  <head>
    <title>Listing 32-4 from the XML Bible</title>
    <object id="VMLRender"
      classid="CLSID:10072CEC-8CC1-11D1-986E-00A0C955B42E">
    </object>
    <style>
      vml\:* { behavior: url(#VMLRender) }
    </style>
  </head>

  <body>
    <h1>Listing 32-4 from the XML Bible</h1>

    <div>

      <vml:polyline
        style="width: 250px; height: 250px; rotation: 120deg"
        stroked="true"
        strokecolor="black"
        strokeweight="5"
        filled="true"
        fillcolor="blue"
```

```
            points="8pt, 65pt, 72pt, 65pt, 92pt,11pt, 112pt, 65pt,
                    174pt, 65pt, 122pt,100pt, 142pt, 155pt, 92pt,
                    121pt, 42pt, 155pt, 60pt, 100pt, 8pt, 65pt">
        </vml:polyline>
    </div>
    <hr></hr>
    Last Modified May 30, 2001<br />
    Copyright 2001
    <a href="http://www.macfaq.com/personal.html">
        Elliotte Rusty Harold
    </a>
  </body>

</html>
```

The flip property

The flip property also does not exist in standard CSS, but it can be used as a CSS property of VML shapes. It flips a shape around either its x- or y-axis, or both. This is given as a CSS property on the style attribute of a VML shape element. To flip the y coordinates about the x-axis, set flip to y. To flip the x coordinates about the y-axis, set flip to x. The flip property specifies which coordinates are flipped, not which axis they're flipped about. Listing 32-5 flips the shape about its x-axis. Figure 32-6 shows the result.

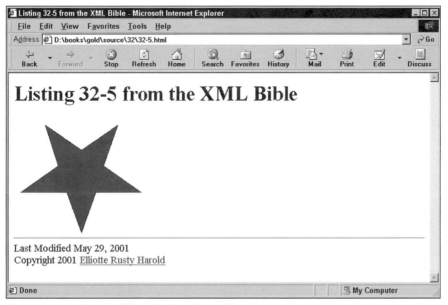

Figure 32-6: The star flipped about its x-axis

Listing 32-5: A star flipped about its *x*-axis

```
<html xmlns:vml="urn:schemas-microsoft-com:vml">

  <head>
    <title>Listing 32-5 from the XML Bible</title>
    <object id="VMLRender"
      classid="CLSID:10072CEC-8CC1-11D1-986E-00A0C955B42E">
    </object>
    <style>
      vml\:* { behavior: url(#VMLRender) }
    </style>
  </head>

  <body>
    <h1>Listing 32-5 from the XML Bible</h1>

    <div>

      <vml:polyline
        style="width: 250px; height: 250px; flip: y"
        stroked="true"
        strokecolor="black"
        strokeweight="5"
        filled="true"
        fillcolor="blue"
        points="8pt, 65pt, 72pt, 65pt, 92pt,11pt, 112pt, 65pt,
                174pt, 65pt, 122pt,100pt, 142pt, 155pt, 92pt,
                121pt, 42pt, 155pt, 60pt, 100pt, 8pt, 65pt">
      </vml:polyline>
    </div>
    <hr></hr>
    Last Modified May 29, 2001<br />
    Copyright 2001
    <a href="http://www.macfaq.com/personal.html">
      Elliotte Rusty Harold
    </a>
  </body>

</html>
```

The center-x and center-y properties

The center-x and center-y properties locate the center of the box that contains the shape. These properties offer alternatives to the left and right CSS properties and ultimately convey the same information. Because center-x and left are alternatives for each other as are `center-y` and `right`, you should not specify them both. If you do specify both, then the value associated with `center-x` and `center-y` is used.

VML in Microsoft Office

Drawing pictures with a keyboard is more than a little like hammering a nail into wood with a sponge. A keyboard simply isn't the right tool with which to draw. A mouse is better, and a graphics tablet is best of all. In this section, you'll learn how to use more traditional graphics tools such as PowerPoint to produce VML documents. Microsoft Word, Excel, and PowerPoint 2000 and later support VML by converting graphics drawn in these programs into VML markup on HTML pages.

Settings

VML is not turned on by default in Office 2000. Before you can create VML documents with any of the Office products, you have to adjust your settings. These are in essentially the same location in each of the three Office programs that can create VML. To set VML as the default graphics type, perform these steps as shown in Figure 32-7:

1. From within Microsoft PowerPoint/Word/Excel, open the Tools menu and select Options....

2. Select the General tab.

3. Click the Web Options... button.

4. Select the Pictures tab from the Web Options dialog window.

5. Check the option that reads Rely on VML for displaying graphics in browsers, as shown in Figure 32-7.

6. Click OK in the Web Options window, and then OK again in the Options window. PowerPoint/Word/Excel is now configured to use VML graphics whenever you save a presentation in Web format.

Office 2000 will only convert to VML those images that you draw in their documents using their drawing tools. All other pictures will be saved as bitmapped GIF or PNG files. This means that you cannot use PowerPoint or Word as a conversion utility for other graphics that you have embedded in Office documents.

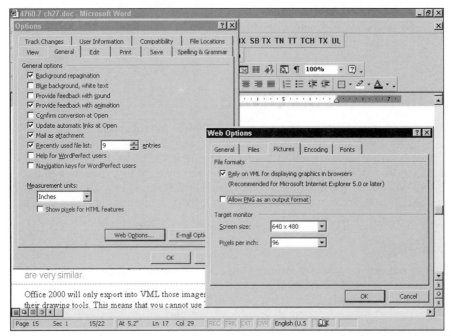

Figure 32-7: Setting VML as the default graphic type is very similar in Microsoft Word, PowerPoint, and Excel.

Drawing a house

Office 2000 may not have all the power of Macromedia Free Hand or CorelDRAW, but it does make drawing simple graphics easy—much easier than drawing with the keyboard. PowerPoint is the most graphically oriented of the Office components, so let's demonstrate by using PowerPoint to draw a little house. By employing the following steps, it's as simple as drawing a few squares, circles, and triangles.

1. Choose New... from the File menu.

2. In the dialog that appears, select Blank Presentation, and then click OK.

3. In the New Slide window, select the slide with only a title bar at the top, as shown in Figure 32-8, and then click OK.

4. Click in the Title bar area, and give your slide a name, for example, My VML House.

5. On the drawing toolbar at the bottom of the window, click the Rectangle tool. Use this tool to draw the foundation for the house.

6. On the drawing toolbar, click the AutoShapes button, select the Basic Shapes option, and then select the Isosceles triangle.

7. Use the Isosceles triangle to draw a roof over the house.

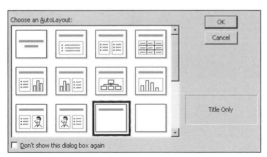

Figure 32-8: Selecting a template for the slide

8. Use the Rectangle tool to draw windows and doors on your house, until your image looks something like the one shown in Figure 32-9.

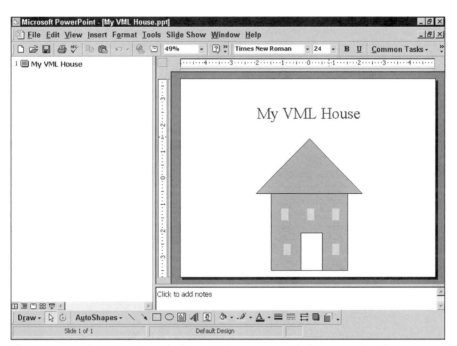

Figure 32-9: The VML House in PowerPoint 2000, ready for conversion into VML text

9. Open the File menu, and select Save As Web Page. Type the name of the page, for example, VMLHouse.html, and then click Save.

10. Close PowerPoint and open the file you just created using Internet Explorer 5.0 or 5.5. Figure 32-10 shows the resulting Web page.

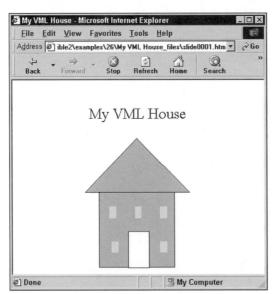

Figure 32-10: The VML House, shown as a Web page in Internet Explorer 5.0

The HTML and VML code created by PowerPoint to display this slide is shown in Listing 32-6. It's pretty messy because it's not really meant to be seen by humans or edited by hand. It's intended purely for Web browsers and authoring tools to read.

Note   The VML house will only display in Internet Explorer 5.0 or later. Other browsers will only see the embedded images, not the VML.

Listing 32-6: A PowerPoint slide converted to HTML with embedded VML

```
<html xmlns:v="urn:schemas-microsoft-com:vml"
xmlns:o="urn:schemas-microsoft-com:office:office"
xmlns:p="urn:schemas-microsoft-com:office:powerpoint"
xmlns="http://www.w3.org/TR/REC-html40">

<head>
<meta http-equiv=Content-Type content="text/html;
  charset=windows-1252">
<meta name=ProgId content=PowerPoint.Slide>
<meta name=Generator content="Microsoft PowerPoint 9">
<link id=Main-File rel=Main-File
      href="../My%20VML%20House.htm">
<link rel=Preview href=preview.wmf>
<!--[if !mso]>
<style>
```

```
v\:* {behavior:url(#default#VML);}
o\:* {behavior:url(#default#VML);}
p\:* {behavior:url(#default#VML);}
.shape {behavior:url(#default#VML);}
v\:textbox {display:none;}
</style>
<![endif]-->
<title>My VML House</title>
<meta name=Description content="17-Feb-01: My VML House">
<link rel=Stylesheet href="master03_stylesheet.css">
<![if !ppt]>
<style media=print>
<!--.sld
  {left:0px !important;
 width:6.0in !important;
 height:4.5in !important;
 font-size:146% !important;}
-->
</style>
<script src=script.js></script><!--[if vml]><script>g_vml = 1;
</script><![endif]--><script for=window event=onload><!--
LoadSld( gId );
MakeSldVis(0);
//-->
</script><![endif]><o:shapelayout v:ext="edit">
 <o:idmap v:ext="edit" data="2"/>
</o:shapelayout>
</head>

<body lang=EN-US style='margin:0px;background-color:white'
onresize="_RSW()">

<div id=SlideObj class=sld
style='position:absolute;top:0px;left:0px;
width:394px;height:295px;font-size:16px;
background-color:white;clip:rect(0%, 101%, 101%, 0%);
visibility:hidden'><p:slide coordsize="720,540"
 colors="#FFFFFF,#000000,#808080,#000000,#00CC99,#3333CC,
#CCCCFF,#B2B2B2"
 masterhref="master03.xml">
 <p:shaperange href="master03.xml#_x0000_s1026"/>
<![if !ppt]><p:shaperange
  href="master03.xml#_x0000_s1028"/><p:shaperange
  href="master03.xml#_x0000_s1029"/><![endif]><p:shaperange
  href="master03.xml#_x0000_m1026"/>
<v:shape id="_x0000_s2050" type="#_x0000_m1026"
  style='position:absolute;left:54pt;top:48pt;width:612pt;
height:90pt'>
  <v:fill o:detectmouseclick="f"/>
  <v:stroke o:forcedash="f"/>
  <o:lock v:ext="edit" text="f"/>
  <p:placeholder type="title"/></v:shape>
```

Continued

Listing 32-6: *(continued)*

```
<v:rect id="_x0000_s2051" style='position:absolute;
  left:252pt;top:312pt;width:3in;height:210pt;
mso-wrap-style:none;
  v-text-anchor:middle' fillcolor="#0c9 [4]"
strokecolor="black [1]">
  <v:fill color2="white [0]"/>
  <v:shadow color="gray [2]"/>
 </v:rect><v:shapetype id="_x0000_t5"
coordsize="21600,21600" o:spt="5" adj="10800"
  path="m@0,0l0,21600,21600,21600,21600xe">
  <v:stroke joinstyle="miter"/>
  <v:formulas>
   <v:f eqn="val #0"/>
   <v:f eqn="prod #0 1 2"/>
   <v:f eqn="sum @1 10800 0"/>
  </v:formulas>
  <v:path gradientshapeok="t" o:connecttype="custom"
o:connectlocs=
"@0,0;@1,10800;0,21600;10800,21600;21600,21600;@2,10800"
textboxrect="0,10800,10800,18000;5400,10800,16200,18000;10800,
10800,21600,18000;0,7200,7200,21600;7200,7200,14400,21600;
14400,7200,21600,21600"/>
  <v:handles>
   <v:h position="#0,topLeft" xrange="0,21600"/>
  </v:handles>
 </v:shapetype>
<v:shape id="_x0000_s2052" type="#_x0000_t5"
style='position:absolute;
  left:210pt;top:162pt;width:300pt;height:150pt;
mso-wrap-style:none;
  v-text-anchor:middle' fillcolor="#0c9 [4]"
 strokecolor="black [1]">
  <v:fill color2="white [0]"/>
  <v:shadow color="gray [2]"/>
 </v:shape><v:rect id="_x0000_s2053"
style='position:absolute;left:336pt;top:420pt;
  width:60pt;height:102pt;mso-wrap-style:none;
v-text-anchor:middle'
  fillcolor="white [0]" strokecolor="black [1]">
  <v:shadow color="gray [2]"/>
 </v:rect><v:rect id="_x0000_s2054"
style='position:absolute;left:282pt;top:354pt;
  width:18pt;height:30pt;mso-wrap-style:none;
```

```
v-text-anchor:middle' fillcolor="#ccf [6]"
  strokecolor="#ccf [6]">
  <v:shadow color="gray [2]"/>
 </v:rect><v:rect id="_x0000_s2055"
style='position:absolute;left:354pt;top:354pt;
  width:18pt;height:30pt;mso-wrap-style:none;
v-text-anchor:middle' fillcolor="#ccf [6]"
  strokecolor="#ccf [6]">
  <v:shadow color="gray [2]"/>
 </v:rect><v:rect id="_x0000_s2056"
style='position:absolute;left:426pt;top:354pt;
  width:18pt;height:30pt;mso-wrap-style:none;
v-text-anchor:middle' fillcolor="#ccf [6]"
  strokecolor="#ccf [6]">
  <v:shadow color="gray [2]"/>
 </v:rect><v:rect id="_x0000_s2057"
 style='position:absolute;left:426pt;top:450pt;
  width:18pt;height:30pt;mso-wrap-style:none;
v-text-anchor:middle' fillcolor="#ccf [6]"
  strokecolor="#ccf [6]">
  <v:shadow color="gray [2]"/>
 </v:rect><v:rect id="_x0000_s2058"
 style='position:absolute;left:4in;top:450pt;
  width:18pt;height:30pt;mso-wrap-style:none;
v-text-anchor:middle' fillcolor="#ccf [6]"
  strokecolor="#ccf [6]">
  <v:shadow color="gray [2]"/>
 </v:rect>
 <div v:shape="_x0000_s2050"
class=T style='position:absolute;top:12.88%;
 left:8.62%;width:83.24%;height:9.49%'>My VML House</div>
</p:slide></div>

</body>

</html>
```

As well as a lot of standard HTML and VML code, Listing 32-6 contains a number of elements in the urn:schemas-microsoft-com:office:office and urn:schemas-microsoft-com:office:powerpoint namespaces. These contain information that most Web browsers won't use, but that PowerPoint will if the HTML file is opened in PowerPoint. The purpose of these elements is to enable a document to make a roundtrip from PowerPoint to HTML and back again without losing anything along the way.

Summary

In this chapter, you learned about Microsoft's Vector Markup Language, an XML application for vector graphics used in Internet Explorer 5.0 and Office 2000. In particular, you learned:

✦ What VML can do for Web graphics

✦ The various elements and attributes associated with VML shapes, and how to use them to create the visual images that you need

✦ How to configure Microsoft Office 2000 applications to use VML when creating graphics for Web documents and presentations

✦ How to draw VML figures using PowerPoint 2000

In the next chapter, we explore another nonstandardized XML application from Microsoft, the Channel Definition Format (CDF). CDF is used to push content to subscribers through their Web browsers.

✦   ✦   ✦

The Channel Definition Format

This chapter discusses Microsoft's Channel Definition Format (CDF), an XML application for defining channels. A *channel* is a set of Web pages that can be pushed to a subscriber automatically. A CDF document lists the pages to be pushed, the frequency with which they're pushed, and similar information. As well as Web pages, channels can use Dynamic HTML, Java, and JavaScript to create interactive, continually updated stock tickers, sports score boxes, and the like. Subject to security restrictions, channels can even push software updates to registered users and install them automatically. Readers can subscribe to channels using Internet Explorer 4.0 and later.

What Is the Channel Definition Format?

CDF is an XML application developed by Microsoft to add push capabilities to Internet Explorer. Channels allow Web sites to automatically notify readers of changes to critical information. This method is sometimes called *Webcasting* or *push*. Currently, Internet Explorer (IE) is the only major browser that implements CDF, and broader adoption seems unlikely. The World Wide Web Consortium (W3C) has not done more than formally acknowledge receipt of the CDF specification.

A CDF file is an XML document, separate from, but linked to, the HTML documents on a site. The CDF document defines the parameters for a connection between the readers and the content on the site. The data can be transferred through *push*—sending notifications, or even entire Web sites to registered readers—or through *pull*—readers choosing to load the page in their Web browser and get the update information.

You do not need to substantially rearchitect your Web site or rewrite your existing pages to take advantage of CDF. You simply have to add one CDF file to your site and make a link to it, probably from the main page of the site. When the reader follows this link, IE will download a copy of the channel index in the CDF document to the reader's machine and put an icon for the site in the Favorites list. Later, the reader can click this icon to load the current contents of the channel.

Creating Channels

There are three steps to creating a channel:

1. Decide what content to include in the channel
2. Write the channel definition file that identifies this content
3. Link from the home page of the Web site to the channel definition file

Determining channel content

Before you get bogged down in the nitty-gritty technical details of creating a channel with CDF, you first need to decide what content belongs in the channel and how it should be delivered.

Your first consideration when converting existing sites to channels is how many and which pages to include. Human interface factors suggest that no channel should have more than eight items for readers to choose from. Otherwise, readers become confused and have trouble finding what they need. However, channels can be arranged hierarchically. Additional levels of content can be added as subchannels. For example, a newspaper channel might have sections for business, science, entertainment, sports, international news, national news, and local news. The entertainment section might be divided into subchannels for television, movies, books, music, and art.

The organization and hierarchy you choose may or may not match the organization and hierarchy of your existing Web site, just as the organization and hierarchy of your Web site does not necessarily match the organization and hierarchy of the files on the server hard drive. However, matching the hierarchy of the channel to the hierarchy of the Web site will make the channel easier to maintain. Nonetheless, you can certainly select particular pages out of the site and then arrange them in a hierarchy specific to the channel if it seems sensible to do so.

Your second consideration is the way new content will be delivered to subscribers. When subscribing to a channel, readers are offered three options:

1. The channel can be added to the channel bar and subscribers can check in when they feel like it.

2. Subscribers can be notified of new content via e-mail and then load the channel when they feel like it.

3. The browser can periodically check the site for updates and download the changed content automatically.

Your content should be designed to work well with whichever of these three options the reader chooses.

Creating CDF files and documents

After you've decided what content will be in your channel, and how that content will be organized and delivered, you're ready to write the CDF document that implements these decisions. A CDF document specifies the contents, schedule, and logos for the channel. All of this information is marked up using a particular set of XML tags. This document will be placed on the Web server where clients can download it.

Note

While it would be almost trivial to design a DTD for CDF, and while I suspect Microsoft has one internally, they have not yet published it for the current version of CDF. A DTD for a much earlier and obsolete version of CDF can be found in a W3C note at http://www.w3.org/TR/NOTE-CDFsubmit.html. However, this really doesn't come close to describing the current version of CDF. Consequently, CDF documents can be at most well formed, but not valid.

A CDF document begins with an XML declaration because a CDF document is an XML document and follows the same rules as all XML documents. The root and only required element of a CDF document is CHANNEL. The CHANNEL element must have an HREF attribute that specifies the page being monitored for changes. The root CHANNEL element usually identifies the key page in the channel. Listing 33-1 is a simple CDF document that points to a page that is updated more or less daily.

Listing 33-1: **The simplest possible CDF document for a page**

```
<?xml version="1.0"?>
<CHANNEL HREF="http://www.ibiblio.org/xml/index.html">
</CHANNEL>
```

Note Most Microsoft documentation for CDF is based on a prerelease of the XML specification that used the uppercase `<?XML version="1.0"?>` instead of the now
current lowercase `<?xml version="1.0"?>`. However, both case conventions
seem to work with Internet Explorer, so in this chapter I use the lowercase `xml`
that conforms to standard XML usage.

As well as the main page, most channels contain a collection of other pages identified by ITEM children. Each ITEM has an HREF attribute pointing to the page. Listing
33-2 demonstrates a channel that contains a main page
(`http://www.ibiblio.org/xml/index.html`) with three individual subpages in
ITEM elements. Channels are often shown in a collapsible outline view that allows
the user to show or hide the individual items in the channel as they choose. Figure
33-1 shows this channel expanded in Internet Explorer 5.0's Favorites bar.

Listing 33-2: A CDF channel with ITEM children

```
<?xml version="1.0"?>
<CHANNEL HREF="http://www.ibiblio.org/xml/index.html">
  <ITEM HREF="http://www.ibiblio.org/xml/books.html">
  </ITEM>
  <ITEM HREF="http://www.ibiblio.org/xml/tradeshows.html">
  </ITEM>
  <ITEM HREF="http://www.ibiblio.org/xml/mailinglists.html">
  </ITEM>
</CHANNEL>
```

Linking the Web page to the channel

The third and final step is to make the CDF file available to the reader. The simplest
way to accomplish this is with a standard HTML A element that readers click to
load the CDF file. Generally, the contents of this element will be some text or an
image asking the reader to subscribe to the channel. For example:

```
<A HREF="cafeconleche.cdf">Subscribe to Cafe con Leche</A>
```

When the reader activates this link in a CDF-enabled browser (which is just a fancy
way of saying Internet Explorer 4.0 and later), the browser downloads the CDF file
named in the HREF attribute and adds the channel to its list of subscriptions. Other
browsers that don't support CDF will probably ask the user to save the document
as shown in Figure 33-2.

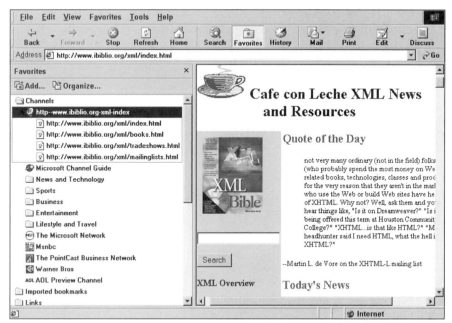

Figure 33-1: The open channels folder in Internet Explorer 5.0's Favorites bar with three sub-pages displayed

Figure 33-2: Netscape Navigator does not support CDF nor does it understand CDF files.

After the CDF file has been downloaded, the browser will ask the user how they wish to be notified of future changes to the channel as shown in Figure 33-3. The user has three choices:

✦ The channel can be added to the browser and active desktop channel bars. The subscriber must manually select the channel to get the update. This isn't all that different from a bookmark, except that when the user opens the "channel mark," all pages in the channel are refreshed rather than just one.

✦ The browser periodically checks the channel for updates and notifies the subscriber of any changes via e-mail. The user must still choose to download the new content.

✦ The browser periodically checks the channel for updates and notifies the subscriber of any changes via e-mail. However, when a change is detected, the browser automatically downloads and caches the new content so that it's immediately available for the user to view, even if they aren't connected to the Internet when they check the channel site.

Listing 33-2 only makes the first choice available because this particular channel doesn't provide a schedule for updates. We'll add that soon.

Figure 33-3: Internet Explorer asks the user to choose how they wish to be notified of changes at the site.

Describing the Channel

The channel itself and each item in the channel can have a title, an abstract, and up to three logos of different sizes. These are established by giving the CHANNEL and ITEM elements TITLE, ABSTRACT, and LOGO children.

Title

The title of the channel is not the same as the title of the Web page. Rather, the channel title appears in the channel guide, the channel list, and the channel bar, as shown in Figure 33-1 where the title is http--www.ibiblio.org-xml-index (although the subscriber did have the option to customize it by typing a different title as shown in Figure 33-3). You can provide a more descriptive default title for each CHANNEL and ITEM element by giving it a TITLE child. Each TITLE element can contain only character data, no markup. Listing 33-3 adds titles to the individual pages in the Cafe con Leche channel as well as to the channel itself. Figure 33-4 shows how this affects the individual items in the channel list.

> **Listing 33-3: A CDF channel with titles**
>
> ```xml
> <?xml version="1.0"?>
> <CHANNEL HREF="http://www.ibiblio.org/xml/index.html">
>   <TITLE>Cafe con Leche</TITLE>
>   <ITEM HREF="http://www.ibiblio.org/xml/books.html">
>     <TITLE>Books about XML</TITLE>
>   </ITEM>
>   <ITEM HREF="http://www.ibiblio.org/xml/tradeshows.html">
>     <TITLE>Trade shows and conferences about XML</TITLE>
>   </ITEM>
>   <ITEM HREF="http://www.ibiblio.org/xml/mailinglists.html">
>     <TITLE>Mailing Lists dedicated to XML</TITLE>
>   </ITEM>
> </CHANNEL>
> ```

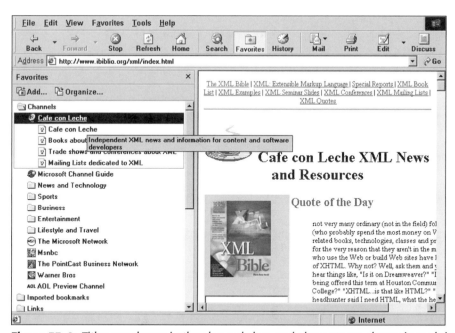

Figure 33-4: Titles are shown in the channels bar, and abstracts are shown in tool-tips.

Abstract

Titles may be sufficient for a channel with a well-established brand such as Disney or MSNBC; but for the rest of us lesser lights in the news firmament, it probably doesn't hurt to tell subscribers a little more about what they can expect to find at a given site. To this end, each CHANNEL and ITEM element can contain a single ABSTRACT child element. The ABSTRACT element should contain a short (200 characters or less) block of text describing the item or channel. Generally, this description will appear in a tool-tip as shown in Figure 33-4, which is based on Listing 33-4.

Listing 33-4: **A CDF channel with titles and abstracts**

```xml
<?xml version="1.0"?>
<CHANNEL HREF="http://www.ibiblio.org/xml/index.html">
  <TITLE>Cafe con Leche</TITLE>
  <ABSTRACT>
    Independent XML news and information for content
    and software developers
  </ABSTRACT>

  <ITEM HREF="http://www.ibiblio.org/xml/books.html">
    <TITLE>Books about XML</TITLE>
    <ABSTRACT>
      A comprehensive list of books about XML
      with capsule reviews and ratings
    </ABSTRACT>
  </ITEM>


  <ITEM HREF="http://www.ibiblio.org/xml/tradeshows.html">
    <TITLE>Trade shows and conferences about XML</TITLE>
    <ABSTRACT>
      Upcoming conferences and shows with an XML focus
    </ABSTRACT>
  </ITEM>

  <ITEM HREF="http://www.ibiblio.org/xml/mailinglists.html">
    <TITLE>Mailing Lists dedicated to XML</TITLE>
    <ABSTRACT>
      Mailing lists where you can discuss XML
    </ABSTRACT>
  </ITEM>
</CHANNEL>
```

Logos

CDF documents can provide logos for channels. These logos appear on the reader's machine, either on the desktop or in the browser's channel list. Logos can be used in a number of different ways within the channel: icons on the desktop, icons in the program launcher, and logos in the channel guide and channel bar. Each CHANNEL and ITEM element can have up to three logos: one for the desktop, one for the program launcher, and one for the channel bar.

A particular logo is attached to a channel with the LOGO element. This element is a child of the CHANNEL it represents. The HREF attribute of the LOGO element is an absolute or relative URL where the graphic file containing the logo is found. Internet Explorer supports GIF, JPEG, and ICO format images for logos — but not animated GIFs. Because logos may appear against a whole range of colors and patterns on the desktop, GIFs with a transparent background that limit themselves to the Windows halftone palette work best.

The LOGO element also has a required STYLE attribute that specifies the size of the image. The value of the STYLE attribute must be one of the three keywords ICON, IMAGE, or IMAGE-WIDE. These are different sizes of images, as given in Table 33-1. Figure 33-5 shows the logos used for Cafe con Leche in the three different sizes.

Table 33-1
Values for the STYLE Attribute of the LOGO Element

Image Size	Description
ICON	A 16-pixel-wide by 16-pixel-high icon displayed in the file list and in the channel bar next to the page and site titles
IMAGE	An 80-pixel-wide by 32-pixel-high image displayed in the desktop channel bar
IMAGE-WIDE	A 194-pixel-wide by 32-pixel-high image displayed in the browser's channel bar

Figure 33-5: The Cafe con Leche channel icons in three different sizes

Listing 33-5 is a CDF document that provides various sizes of logos. Figure 33-6 shows the Internet Explorer 5.0 favorites bar with the new Cafe con Leche logo.

Listing 33-5: **A CDF channel with logos in various sizes**

```
<?xml version="1.0"?>
<CHANNEL HREF="http://www.ibiblio.org/xml/index.html">
  <LOGO HREF="cup_ICON.gif"       STYLE="ICON"/>
  <LOGO HREF="cup_IMAGE.gif"      STYLE="IMAGE"/>
  <LOGO HREF="cup_IMAGE-WIDE.gif" STYLE="IMAGE-WIDE"/>
  <TITLE>Cafe con Leche</TITLE>
  <ABSTRACT>
    Independent XML news and information for content
    and software developers
  </ABSTRACT>

  <ITEM HREF="http://www.ibiblio.org/xml/books.html">
    <TITLE>Books about XML</TITLE>
    <ABSTRACT>
      A comprehensive list of books about XML
      with capsule reviews and ratings
    </ABSTRACT>
  </ITEM>

  <ITEM HREF="http://www.ibiblio.org/xml/tradeshows.html">
    <TITLE>Trade shows and conferences about XML</TITLE>
    <ABSTRACT>
      Upcoming conferences and shows with an XML focus
    </ABSTRACT>
  </ITEM>

  <ITEM HREF="http://www.ibiblio.org/xml/mailinglists.html">
    <TITLE>Mailing Lists dedicated to XML</TITLE>
    <ABSTRACT>
      Mailing lists where you can discuss XML
    </ABSTRACT>
  </ITEM>
</CHANNEL>
```

When the content in the channel changes, the browser places a highlight gleam in the upper-left corner of the logo image. This gleam hides anything in that corner. Also, if a reader stretches the window width beyond the recommended 194 pixels, the browser uses the top-right pixel to fill the expanded logo. Consequently, you need to pay special attention to the upper-left and upper-right corners of the logo.

Figure 33-6: The favorites bar now contains the Cafe con Leche icon instead of the generic channel icon.

Scheduling Updates

The CHANNEL, TITLE, ABSTRACT, and LOGO elements are enough to build a working channel, but all they provide is a bookmark that readers can use to quickly load your site. They aren't enough to push content to the readers. Passive channels — that is, channels such as Listings 33-1 through 33-5 that don't have an explicit push schedule — don't do very much.

To actually push the contents to subscribers, you have to include a schedule for updates. You can schedule a download for the entire channel or schedule individual items in the channel separately. This is accomplished by adding a SCHEDULE child element to the channel. For example:

```
<SCHEDULE STARTDATE="2001-03-29" STOPDATE="2002-03-29"
  TIMEZONE="-0500">
  <INTERVALTIME DAY="7"/>
  <EARLIESTTIME DAY="1" HOUR="0" MIN="0"/>
  <LATESTTIME  DAY="2" HOUR="12" MIN="0"/>
</SCHEDULE>
```

The SCHEDULE element has three attributes: STARTDATE, STOPDATE, and TIMEZONE. STARTDATE indicates when the schedule begins. STOPDATE indicates when it ends. Target the period between your usual site overhauls. If you change the structure of your Web site on a regular interval, use that interval. STARTDATE and STOPDATE use the same date format: full numeric year, two-digit numeric month, and two-digit day of month, separated by hyphens; for example, 1999-12-31.

The TIMEZONE attribute shows the difference in hours between the server's time zone and Greenwich Mean Time. If the tag does not include the TIMEZONE attribute, the scheduled update occurs according to the reader's time zone — not the server's. In the continental U.S., Eastern Standard Time is –0500, Central Standard Time is –0600, Mountain Standard Time is –0700, and Pacific Standard Time is –0800. Hawaii and Alaska are –1000.

SCHEDULE can have between one and three child elements. INTERVALTIME is a required, empty element that specifies how often the browser should check the channel for updates (assuming the user has asked the browser to do so). INTERVALTIME has DAY, HOUR, and MIN attributes that determine the amount of time that is allowed to elapse between updates. As long as one is present, the other two can be omitted.

EARLIESTTIME and LATESTTIME are optional elements that specify times between which the browser should check for updates. The updates and resulting server load are distributed over the interval between the earliest and latest times. If you don't specify these, the browser simply checks in at its convenience. EARLIESTTIME and LATESTTIME have DAY and HOUR attributes that specify when updates take place. DAY ranges from 1 (Sunday) to 7 (Saturday). HOUR ranges from 0 (midnight) to 23 (11:00 p.m.). For instance, the above example says that the browser should update the channel once a week (<INTERVALTIME DAY="7"/>) between Sunday midnight (<EARLIESTTIME DAY="1" HOUR="0" MIN="0"/>) and noon Monday (<LATESTTIME DAY="2" HOUR="12" MIN="0"/>).

EARLIESTTIME and LATESTTIME may also have a TIMEZONE attribute that specifies the time zone in which the earliest and latest times are calculated. If a time zone isn't specified, the reader's time zone is used to determine the earliest and latest times. To specify the update times in a particular time zone rather than client's local time, include the optional TIMEZONE attribute in the EARLIESTTIME and LATESTTIME tags. For example:

```
<EARLIESTTIME DAY="1" HOUR="0"  TIMEZONE="-0500"/>
<LATESTTIME   DAY="2" HOUR="12" TIMEZONE="-0500"/>
```

Listing 33-6 expands the Cafe con Leche channel to include scheduled updates. Because content is updated daily, INTERVALTIME is set to one day. Most days the update takes place between 7:00 a.m. and 12:00 noon Eastern time. Consequently, it sets EARLIESTTIME to 10:00 a.m. EST and LATESTTIME to 12:00 noon EST. There's no particular start or end date for the changes to this content, so the STARTDATE and STOPDATE attributes are omitted from the schedule.

Listing 33-6: A CDF channel with scheduled updates

```xml
<?xml version="1.0"?>
<CHANNEL HREF="http://www.ibiblio.org/xml/index.html">

  <TITLE>Cafe con Leche</TITLE>
  <ABSTRACT>
    Independent XML news and information for content
    and software developers
  </ABSTRACT>
  <LOGO HREF="cup_ICON.gif" STYLE="ICON"/>
  <LOGO HREF="cup_IMAGE.gif" STYLE="IMAGE"/>
  <LOGO HREF="cup_IMAGE-WIDE.gif" STYLE="IMAGE-WIDE"/>

  <SCHEDULE TIMEZONE="-0500">
    <INTERVALTIME DAY="1"/>
    <EARLIESTTIME HOUR="10" TIMEZONE="-0500"/>
    <LATESTTIME HOUR="12" TIMEZONE="-0500"/>
  </SCHEDULE>

  <ITEM HREF="http://www.ibiblio.org/xml/books.html">
    <TITLE>Books about XML</TITLE>
    <ABSTRACT>
      A comprehensive list of books about XML
      with capsule reviews and ratings
    </ABSTRACT>
  </ITEM>

  <ITEM HREF="http://www.ibiblio.org/xml/tradeshows.html">
    <TITLE>Trade shows and conferences about XML</TITLE>
    <ABSTRACT>
      Upcoming conferences and shows with an XML focus
    </ABSTRACT>
  </ITEM>

  <ITEM HREF="http://www.ibiblio.org/xml/mailinglists.html">
    <TITLE>Mailing Lists dedicated to XML</TITLE>
    <ABSTRACT>
      Mailing lists where you can discuss XML
    </ABSTRACT>
  </ITEM>
</CHANNEL>
```

Precaching and Web Crawling

If the subscriber has chosen to download the channel's contents automatically, then the site owner has the option of allowing subscribers to view the pages offline and even to download more than merely those pages identified in the CDF document. In particular, you can allow the browser to spider through your site, downloading additional pages between one and three levels deep from the specified pages.

Precaching

By default, browsers precache the pages listed in a channel for offline browsing if the user has requested that they do so. However, the author can prevent a page from being precached by including a PRECACHE attribute in the CHANNEL or ITEM element with the value NO. For example:

```
<CHANNEL PRECACHE="NO"
         HREF="http://www.ibiblio.org/xml/index.html">
...
</CHANNEL>
```

If the value of PRECACHE is NO, then the content will not be precached regardless of user settings. If the value of PRECACHE is YES (or if there is no explicit PRECACHE attribute) *and* the user requested precaching when they subscribed, then the content will be downloaded automatically. However, if the user has not requested precaching, then the site channel will not be precached regardless of the value of the PRECACHE attribute.

When you design a channel, you must remember that some readers will view content offline almost exclusively. As a result, any links in the channel contents are effectively dead. If you are pushing documents across an intranet, the cache option doesn't make a lot of sense, as you'll be duplicating the same files on disks across the corporation. If you are delivering content to readers who pay for online time, you may want to organize it so that it can be cached and easily browsed offline.

Web crawling

Browsers are not limited to loading only the Web pages specified in CHANNEL and ITEM elements. If a CHANNEL or ITEM element has a LEVEL attribute with a value higher than zero, the browser will Web crawl during updates. Web crawling lets the browser collect more pages than are listed in the channel. For example, if the page listed in a channel contains a number of links to related topics, it may be easier to let the browser load them all rather than list them in individual ITEM elements. If the site has a fairly even hierarchy, you can safely add a LEVEL attribute to the topmost channel tag and allow the Web crawl to include all of the pages at the subsequent levels. LEVEL can range from zero (the default) to three. This specifies how far down into the site hierarchy you want the browser to dig when caching the content. The hierarchy is the abstract hierarchy defined by the document links, not the hierarchy defined by the directory structure of files on the Web server. Framed pages are considered to be at the same level as the frameset page, even though an additional link is required for the former. The LEVEL attribute really only has meaning if precaching is enabled.

Listing 33-7 sets the LEVEL of the Cafe con Leche channel to three. This goes deep enough to reach most pages on the site. Because the pages previously referenced in ITEM children are only one level down from the main page, there's not as much need to list them separately. However, Web crawling this deep may not be such a good idea Most of the pages on the site don't change daily. Nonetheless, they'll still be checked each and every update.

Listing 33-7: A CDF channel that precaches three levels deep

```
<?xml version="1.0"?>
<CHANNEL LEVEL="3"
         HREF="http://www.ibiblio.org/xml/index.html">

  <TITLE>Cafe con Leche</TITLE>
  <ABSTRACT>
    Independent XML news and information for content
    and software developers
  </ABSTRACT>
  <LOGO HREF="logo_icon.gif" STYLE="ICON"/>
  <LOGO HREF="corp_logo_regular.gif" STYLE="IMAGE"/>
  <LOGO HREF="corp_logo_wide.gif" STYLE="IMAGE-WIDE"/>

  <SCHEDULE TIMEZONE="-0500">
    <INTERVALTIME DAY="1"/>
    <EARLIESTTIME HOUR="10" TIMEZONE="-0500"/>
    <LATESTTIME   HOUR="12" TIMEZONE="-0500"/>
  </SCHEDULE>

</CHANNEL>
```

The Reader Access Log

One disadvantage of channels compared to traditional Web browsing is that the server does not necessarily know which pages the reader actually saw. This can be important for tracking advertisements, among other things. Internet Explorer can track the reader's passage through a site cached offline and report it back to the Web server. However, the user always has the option to disable this behavior if they feel it's a privacy violation.

To collect statistics about the offline browsing of a site, add LOG and LOGTARGET child elements to the CHANNEL element. During a channel update, the server sends the new channel contents to the browser; and the browser sends the log file to the server. The LOG element always has this form, though other possible values of the VALUE attribute may be added in the future:

```
<LOG VALUE="document:view"/>
```

The LOGTARGET element has an HREF attribute that identifies the URL it will be sent to, a METHOD attribute that identifies the HTTP method like POST or PUT that will be used to upload the log file, and a SCOPE attribute that has one of the three values — ALL, ONLINE, or OFFLINE — indicating which page views should be counted. The LOGTARGET element may have a PURGETIME child with an HOUR attribute that specifies the number of hours for which the logging information is considered valid. It may also have any number of HTTP-EQUIV children used to set particular key-value pairs in the HTTP header. Listing 33-8 demonstrates a channel with a reader-access log.

Listing 33-8: **A CDF channel with log reporting**

```
<?xml version="1.0"?>
<CHANNEL HREF="http://www.ibiblio.org/xml/index.html">

  <TITLE>Cafe con Leche</TITLE>
  <ABSTRACT>
    Independent XML news and information for content
    and software developers
  </ABSTRACT>
  <LOGO HREF="logo_icon.gif"          STYLE="ICON"/>
  <LOGO HREF="corp_logo_regular.gif" STYLE="IMAGE"/>
  <LOGO HREF="corp_logo_wide.gif"     STYLE="IMAGE-WIDE"/>

  <LOG VALUE="document:view"/>
  <LOGTARGET METHOD="POST" SCOPE="ALL"
   HREF="http://www.ibiblio.org/xml/cgi-bin/getstats.pl" >
    <PURGETIME HOUR="12"/>
    <HTTP-EQUIV NAME="ENCODING-TYPE" VALUE="text"/>
  </LOGTARGET>

  <SCHEDULE TIMEZONE="-0500">
    <INTERVALTIME DAY="1"/>
    <EARLIESTTIME HOUR="10" TIMEZONE="-0500"/>
    <LATESTTIME HOUR="12"   TIMEZONE="-0500"/>
  </SCHEDULE>

  <ITEM HREF="http://www.ibiblio.org/xml/books.html">
    <TITLE>Books about XML</TITLE>
```

```
    <ABSTRACT>
      A comprehensive list of books about XML
      with capsule reviews and ratings
    </ABSTRACT>
    <LOG VALUE="document:view"/>
  </ITEM>

  <ITEM HREF="http://www.ibiblio.org/xml/tradeshows.html">
    <TITLE>Trade shows and conferences about XML</TITLE>
    <ABSTRACT>
      Upcoming conferences and shows with an XML focus
    </ABSTRACT>
    <LOG VALUE="document:view"/>
  </ITEM>

  <ITEM HREF="http://www.ibiblio.org/xml/mailinglists.html">
    <TITLE>Mailing Lists dedicated to XML</TITLE>
    <ABSTRACT>
      Mailing lists where you can discuss XML
    </ABSTRACT>
  </ITEM>
</CHANNEL>
```

Only elements with LOG children will be noted in the log file. For instance, in Listing 33-8, hits to http://www.ibiblio.org/xml/index.html, http://www.ibiblio.org/xml/books.html, and http://www.ibiblio.org/xml/tradeshows.html will be logged. However hits to http://www.ibiblio.org/xml/mailinglists.html will not be.

The CDF logging information is stored in the Extended File Log format used by most modern Web servers. However, the Web server must be configured, most commonly through a CGI program, to accept the log file that the client sends and to merge it into the main server log.

The LOGTARGET element should appear as a child of the top-level CHANNEL tag and describes log file handling for all items it contains. However, each CHANNEL and ITEM element that you want included in the log must have its own LOG child.

The BASE Attribute

The previous examples have all used absolute URLs for CHANNEL and ITEM elements. However, absolute URLs are inconvenient. For one thing, they're often long and easy to mistype. For another, they make site maintenance difficult when pages are moved from one directory to another, or from one site to another. You can use relative URLs instead if you add a BASE attribute to the CHANNEL element.

The value of the BASE attribute is a URL to which relative URLs in the channel are relative. For instance, if the BASE is set to "http://www.ibiblio.org/xml/", then an HREF attribute can simply be "books.html" instead of "http://www.ibiblio.org/xml/books.html". Listing 33-9 demonstrates.

Listing 33-9: **A CDF channel with a BASE attribute**

```
<?xml version="1.0"?>
<CHANNEL BASE="http://www.ibiblio.org/xml/">
  <TITLE>Cafe con Leche</TITLE>
  <ABSTRACT>
    Independent XML news and information for content
    and software developers
  </ABSTRACT>
  <LOGO HREF="cup_ICON.gif" STYLE="ICON"/>
  <LOGO HREF="cup_IMAGE.gif" STYLE="IMAGE"/>
  <LOGO HREF="cup_IMAGE-WIDE.gif" STYLE="IMAGE-WIDE"/>
  <ITEM HREF="books.html">
    <TITLE>Books about XML</TITLE>
    <ABSTRACT>
      A comprehensive list of books about XML
      with capsule reviews and ratings
    </ABSTRACT>
  </ITEM>

  <ITEM HREF="tradeshows.html">
    <TITLE>Trade shows and conferences about XML</TITLE>
    <ABSTRACT>
      Upcoming conferences and shows with an XML focus
    </ABSTRACT>
  </ITEM>

  <ITEM HREF="mailinglists.html">
    <TITLE>Mailing Lists dedicated to XML</TITLE>
    <ABSTRACT>
      Mailing lists where you can discuss XML
    </ABSTRACT>
  </ITEM>
</CHANNEL>
```

Whichever location you use for the link to the content, you can use a relative URL in the child elements if you specify a BASE attribute in the parent CHANNEL element.

The LASTMOD Attribute

When a browser requests a document from a Web server, the server sends an HTTP response header before with the requested file. This header includes various pieces of information, such as the MIME media type of the file, the length of the file, the current date and time, and the time the file was last modified. For example:

```
HTTP/1.1 200 OK
Date: Wed, 27 Jun 1999 21:42:31 GMT
Server: Stronghold/2.4.1 Apache/1.3.3 C2NetEU/2409 (Unix)
Last-Modified: Tue, 20 Oct 1998 13:15:36 GMT
ETag: "4b94d-c70-362c8cf8"
Accept-Ranges: bytes
Content-Length: 3184
Connection: close
Content-Type: text/html
```

If a browser sends a HEAD request instead of the more common GET request, only the header is returned. The browser can then inspect the Last-Modified field to determine whether a file that was previously loaded from the channel needs to be reloaded or not. However, although HEAD requests are quicker than GET requests, a lot of them still eat up server resources.

To cut down on the load that frequent channel updates place on your server, you can add LASTMOD attributes to all CHANNEL and ITEM tags. The browser will only have to check back with the server for modification times for those items and channels that don't provide LASTMOD attributes.

The value of the LASTMOD attribute is a date and time in a *year-month-day*T*hour:minutes* form such as 2001-05-23T21:42. This says when the page referenced by the HREF attribute was last changed. The browser detects and compares the LASTMOD date given in the CDF file with the last modified date provided by the Web server. When the content on the Web server has changed, the cache is updated with the current content. This way the browser only needs to check one file, the CDF document, for modification times rather than every file that's part of the channel. Listing 33-10 demonstrates.

Listing 33-10: **A CDF channel with LASTMOD attributes**

```
<?xml version="1.0"?>
<CHANNEL BASE="http://www.ibiblio.org/xml/"
         LASTMOD="1999-01-27T12:16" >
  <TITLE>Cafe con Leche</TITLE>
  <ABSTRACT>
    Independent XML news and information for content
    and software developers
```

Continued

Listing 33-10 *(continued)*

```
  </ABSTRACT>
  <LOGO HREF="cup_ICON.gif" STYLE="ICON"/>
  <LOGO HREF="cup_IMAGE.gif" STYLE="IMAGE"/>
  <LOGO HREF="cup_IMAGE-WIDE.gif" STYLE="IMAGE-WIDE"/>
  <ITEM HREF="books.html" LASTMOD="1999-01-03T16:25">
    <TITLE>Books about XML</TITLE>
    <ABSTRACT>
      A comprehensive list of books about XML
      with capsule reviews and ratings
    </ABSTRACT>
  </ITEM>

  <ITEM HREF="tradeshows.html" LASTMOD="1999-01-10T11:40">
    <TITLE>Trade shows and conferences about XML</TITLE>
    <ABSTRACT>
      Upcoming conferences and shows with an XML focus
    </ABSTRACT>
  </ITEM>

  <ITEM HREF="mailinglists.html" LASTMOD="1999-01-06T10:50">
    <TITLE>Mailing Lists dedicated to XML</TITLE>
    <ABSTRACT>
      Mailing lists where you can discuss XML
    </ABSTRACT>
  </ITEM>
</CHANNEL>
```

In practice, this is way too much trouble to do manually, especially for frequently changed documents (and the whole point of channels and push is that they provide information that changes frequently). However, you might be able to write the CDF document as a file full of server-side includes that automatically incorporate LAST-MOD values in the appropriate format or devise some other programmatic solution rather than manually adjusting the LASTMOD attribute every time you edit a file.

The USAGE Element

A CHANNEL or ITEM element may contain an optional USAGE child element that extends the presence of the channel on the subscriber's desktop. The meaning of the USAGE element is determined by its VALUE attribute. Possible values for the VALUE attribute are:

✦ Channel

✦ DesktopComponent

✦ Email

✦ NONE

✦ ScreenSaver

✦ SoftwareUpdate

Most of the time USAGE is an empty element. For example:

```
<USAGE VALUE="ScreenSaver" />
```

The default value for USAGE is Channel. Items with channel usage appear in the browser channel bar. All the CHANNEL and ITEM elements you've seen until now have had Channel usage, even though they didn't have an explicit USAGE element. Other values for USAGE change the way the reader sees channel content.

Desktop components

Desktop components are small Web pages or images that are displayed directly on the user's desktop. Because a Web page can contain a Java applet, fancy DHTML, or an ActiveX control, a desktop component can actually be a program (assuming the subscriber has abandoned all semblance of caution and installed Active Desktop).

The desktop component is installed on the subscriber's desktop with a separate CDF document containing an ITEM element that points to the document to be displayed on the user's desktop. As well as the usual child elements, this ITEM must contain a nonempty USAGE element whose VALUE is DesktopComponent. This USAGE element may contain OPENAS, HEIGHT, WIDTH, and CANRESIZE children.

The VALUE attribute of the OPENAS element specifies the type of file at the location in the ITEM element's HREF attribute. This should either be HTML or Image. If no OPENAS element is present, Internet Explorer assumes it is an HTML file.

The VALUE attributes of the HEIGHT and WIDTH elements specify the number of pixels the item occupies on the desktop.

The VALUE attribute of the CANRESIZE element indicates whether the reader can change the height and width of the component on the fly. Its possible values are Yes and No. Yes is the default. You can also allow or disallow horizontal or vertical resizing independently with CANRESIZEX and CANRESIZEY elements.

Listing 33-11 is a simple desktop component that displays a real-time image of the Sun as provided by the friendly folks at the National Solar Observatory in Sunspot, New Mexico. The image is 640 pixels high and 480 pixels wide. The image is refreshed every minute between 6:00 a.m. MST and 7:00 p.m. MST. (There's no point refreshing the image at night!)

Listing 33-11: **A desktop component channel**

```xml
<?xml version="1.0"?>
<CHANNEL HREF="http://www.sunspot.noao.edu/DSTWWW/sunpic.html">
  <TITLE>
    Hydrogen Alpha Image of the Sun Desktop Component
  </TITLE>
  <ABSTRACT>
   This desktop component shows a picture of the Sun
   as it appears this very minute from the top of
   Sacramento Peak in New Mexico. The picture is taken
   in a single color at the wavelength of the Hydrogen
   alpha light (6563 Angstroms) using a monochrome
   camera which produces a grayscale image in
   which the red light of Hydrogen alpha appears white.
  </ABSTRACT>

  <ITEM HREF=
"ftp://ftp.sunspot.noao.edu/realtime-images/live-
sun/sunnow.gif"
   >
    <TITLE>Hydrogen Alpha Image of the Sun</TITLE>

    <SCHEDULE TIMEZONE="-0700">
      <INTERVALTIME MIN="1"/>
      <EARLIESTTIME HOUR="6"/>
      <LATESTTIME HOUR="19"/>
    </SCHEDULE>

    <USAGE VALUE="DesktopComponent">
      <WIDTH VALUE="640"/>
      <HEIGHT VALUE="480"/>
      <CANRESIZE VALUE="Yes"/>
      <OPENAS VALUE="Image"/>
    </USAGE>
  </ITEM>
</CHANNEL>
```

E-mail

Normally, when a site sends a subscriber e-mail to notify them of a change to a channel, it sends along the main page of the channel as the text of the e-mail message. However, you can specify that a different e-mail message be sent by including an ITEM in the channel whose USAGE element has the value email.

Listing 33-12 specifies that the file at `http://www.ibiblio.org/xml/whatsnew.html` is sent to notify subscribers of content changes. If the first `ITEM` were not present, then `http://www.ibiblio.org/xml/` from the `HREF` attribute of the `CHANNEL` would be sent instead. This gives you an opportunity to send a briefer message specifying what has changed, rather than sending the entire changed page. Often "What's new" information is easier for readers to digest than the entire page, especially when the changes are relatively minor.

Listing 33-12: A channel that e-mails notification of changes

```xml
<?xml version="1.0"?>
<CHANNEL BASE="http://www.ibiblio.org/xml/">
  <TITLE>Cafe con Leche</TITLE>
  <ABSTRACT>
    Independent XML news and information for content
    and software developers
  </ABSTRACT>
  <LOGO HREF="cup_ICON.gif"       STYLE="ICON"/>
  <LOGO HREF="cup_IMAGE.gif"      STYLE="IMAGE"/>
  <LOGO HREF="cup_IMAGE-WIDE.gif" STYLE="IMAGE-WIDE"/>

  <ITEM HREF="whatsnews.html">
    <USAGE VALUE="Email"/>
  </ITEM>

  <ITEM HREF="books.html">
    <TITLE>Books about XML</TITLE>
    <ABSTRACT>
      A comprehensive list of books about XML
      with capsule reviews and ratings
    </ABSTRACT>
  </ITEM>

  <ITEM HREF="tradeshows.html">
    <TITLE>Trade shows and conferences about XML</TITLE>
    <ABSTRACT>
      Upcoming conferences and shows with an XML focus
    </ABSTRACT>
  </ITEM>

  <ITEM HREF="mailinglists.html">
    <TITLE>Mailing Lists dedicated to XML</TITLE>
    <ABSTRACT>
      Mailing lists where you can discuss XML
    </ABSTRACT>
  </ITEM>
</CHANNEL>
```

Precaching

Items whose USAGE value is NONE don't appear anywhere; not in the channel bar, not on the Active Desktop, not in the favorites menu, nowhere. However, such items are precached and are thus more quickly available when the reader follows a link to them later.

Precaching channel content moves items such as sound and video clips to the reader's machine for later use by channel pages. You can precache a single item or a series of items by defining a channel that includes the set of precached items, as is demonstrated in this example:

```
<ITEM HREF="welcome.wav">   <USAGE VALUE="NONE"/> </ITEM>
<ITEM HREF="spacemusic.au"> <USAGE VALUE="NONE"/> </ITEM>
```

This example includes two sound files used at the site when the browser downloads the channel contents for offline viewing. These two files won't be displayed in the channel bar, but if a file in the channel bar does use one of these sound files then it will be immediately available, already loaded when the page is viewed offline. The reader won't have to wait for them to be downloaded from a remote Web site, an important consideration when dealing with relatively large multimedia files.

Screen savers

Items whose USAGE value is ScreenSaver point to an HTML page that replaces the normal desktop after a user-specified period of inactivity. Generally, a screen saver will be written as a completely separate CDF document from the normal channel and will require a separate download and install link. For example:

```
<A HREF="ccl_screensaver.cdf">
  Download and install the Cafe con Leche Screen Saver!
</A>
```

Unless the subscriber has already selected the Channel Screen Saver as the system screen saver in the Display control panel as shown in Figure 33-7, the browser will ask the user whether they want to use the Channel Screen Saver or the currently selected screen saver. Assuming they choose the Channel Screen Saver, the next time the screen is saved, the document referenced in the screen saver channel will be loaded and displayed. If the user has subscribed to more than one screen saver channel, the browser will rotate through the subscribed screen saver channels every 30 seconds. The user can change this interval and a few other options (whether screen savers play sounds, for instance) using the screen saver settings in the Display control panel.

Listing 33-13 is a simple screen saver channel. The actual document displayed when the screen is saved is pointed to by the ITEM element's HREF attribute. This page will generally make heavy use of Dynamic HTML, JavaScript, and other tricks to animate the screen. A static screen saver page is a bad idea.

Listing 33-13: **A screen saver channel**

```xml
<?xml version="1.0"?>
<CHANNEL BASE="http://www.ibiblio.org/xml/">

  <ITEM HREF="http://www.ibiblio.org/screensaver.html">
    <USAGE VALUE="ScreenSaver"/>
  </ITEM>

</CHANNEL>
```

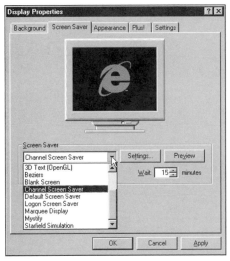

Figure 33-7: The Screen Saver tab of the Display
Properties control panel in Windows NT 4.0

Two things you should keep in mind when designing screen savers:

✦ Presumably the user is doing something else when the screen is saved. After all, inactivity activates the screen saver. Therefore, don't go overboard or expect a lot of user attention or interaction with your screen saver.

✦ Although almost no modern monitor really needs its screen saved, screen savers should save the screen nonetheless. Thus, most of the screen should be dark most of the time, and no pixel on the screen should ever be continuously on. Most importantly, no pixel should continuously be one non-black color, especially white.

Software update

The final possible value of the USAGE element is SoftwareUpdate. Channels aren't limited to delivering news and Web pages. They can send software, too. Software update channels can both notify users of updates to software and deliver the product across the Internet. Given a sufficiently trusting (perhaps insufficiently paranoid is more accurate) user, they can even automatically install the software.

To create a software push channel, write a CDF file with a root CHANNEL element whose USAGE element has the value SoftwareUpdate. This channel can have a title, abstract, logos, and schedule, just like any other channel. Listing 33-14 is a fake software update channel.

Listing 33-14: A software update channel

```
<?xml version="1.0"?>
<CHANNEL HREF="http://www.whizzywriter.com/updates/2001.html">
  <TITLE>WhizzyWriter 2001 Update</TITLE>
  <ABSTRACT>
    WhizzyWriter 2001 offers the same kitchen sink approach
    to word processing that WhizzyWriter 2000 was infamous for,
    but now with tint control! plus many more six-legged
    friends to delight and amuse! Don't worry though. All the
    old arthropods you've learned to love and adore in the
    last 2000 versions are still here!
  </ABSTRACT>

  <USAGE VALUE="SoftwareUpdate"/>
  <SOFTPKG NAME="WhizzyWriter 2001 with tint control 2.1EA3"
    HREF="http://www.whizzywriter.com/updates/2001.cab"
    VERSION="2001,0,d,3245" STYLE="ActiveSetup">

    <!-- other OSD elements can go here -->

  </SOFTPKG>

</CHANNEL>
```

Besides the VALUE of the USAGE element, the key to a software update channel is its SOFTPKG child element. The HREF attribute of the SOFTPKG element provides a URL from which the software can be downloaded and installed. The URL should point to a compressed archive of the software in Microsoft's cabinet (CAB) format. This archive must carry a digital signature from a certificate authority. Furthermore, it must also contain an OSD file describing the software update. OSD, the Open

Software Description format, is an XML application for describing software updates invented by Microsoft and Marimba. The OSD file structure and language is described on the Microsoft Web site at `http://msdn.microsoft.com/work-shop/delivery/download/overview/entry.asp`.

Cross-Reference

OSD is discussed briefly in Chapter 2.

The `SOFTPKG` element must also have a `NAME` attribute that contains up to 260 characters describing the application. For example, WhizzyWriter 2100 with tint control 2.1EA3.

The `SOFTPKG` element must also have a `STYLE` attribute with one of two values — `ActiveSetup` or `MSICD` (Microsoft Internet Component Download), which determines how the software is downloaded and installed.

There are several optional attributes on `SOFTPKG` as well. The `SOFTPKG` element may have a `PRECACHE` attribute with either the value `Yes` or `No`. This has the same meaning as other `PRECACHE` attributes; that is, determining whether the package will be downloaded before the user decides whether they want it. The `VERSION` attribute is a comma-separated list of major, minor, custom, and build version numbers, such as 6,2,3,3124. Finally, setting the `AUTOINSTALL` attribute to `Yes` tells the browser to download the software package automatically as soon as the CDF document is loaded. The value `No` instructs the browser to wait for a specific user request and is the default if the `AUTOINSTALL` attribute is not included.

These child elements can go inside the `SOFTPKG` element:

✦ `TITLE`

✦ `ABSTRACT`

✦ `LANGUAGE`

✦ `DEPENDENCY`

✦ `NATIVECODE`

✦ `IMPLEMENTATION`

However these elements are not part of CDF. Rather they're part of OSD. (Technically, `SOFTPKG` is also a part of OSD.) Consequently, I only summarize them here:

✦ The `TITLE` element of the `SOFTPKG` assigns a name to the package. It contains only parsed character data.

✦ The `ABSTRACT` element describes the software and is essentially the same as the CDF `ABSTRACT` element.

✦ The LANGUAGE element defines the language supported by this update using a VALUE attribute whose value is an ISO 639/RFC 1766 two-letter language code such as EN for English. If multiple languages are supported, the different codes are separated by semicolons.

✦ DEPENDENCY is an empty element with a single attribute, ACTION, which may take on one of two values — Assert or Install. Assert is the default and means that the update will only be installed if the necessary CAB file is already on the local computer. With a value of Install, the necessary files will be downloaded from the server.

✦ The NATIVECODE element holds CODE child elements. Each CODE child element points to the distribution files for a particular architecture, such as Windows 98 on X86 or Windows NT on alpha.

✦ The IMPLEMENTATION element describes the configuration required for the software package. If the requirements are not met by the reader's machine, the download and installation do not proceed. The IMPLEMENTATION element is an optional element with child elements CODEBASE, LANGUAGE, OS, and PROCESSOR.

  • The CODEBASE element has FILENAME and HREF attributes that say where the files for the update can be found.

  • The LANGUAGE element is the same as the LANGUAGE child element of SOFTPKG.

  • The OS element has a VALUE attribute whose value is Mac, Win95, or Winnt, thereby identifying the operating system required for the software. This element can have an empty child element called OSVERSION with a VALUE attribute that identifies the required release.

  • The PROCESSOR element is an empty element whose VALUE attribute can have the value Alpha, MIPS, PPC, or x86. This describes the CPU architecture the software supports.

For more details about OSD, you can consult the OSD specification at http://msdn.microsoft.com/workshop/delivery/osd/reference/reference.asp.

Summary

In this chapter, you learned that:

✦ The Channel Definition Format (CDF) is a Microsoft XML application used to describe data pushed from Web sites to Web browsers.

✦ CDF support is limited to Internet Explorer 4.0 and later.

✦ CDF files are XML documents, although they customarily have the three-letter extension .cdf instead of .xml.

✦ The root element of a CDF file is CHANNEL.

✦ Each CHANNEL element must contain an HREF attribute identifying the pushed page.

✦ A CHANNEL element may contain additional ITEM child elements whose HREF attributes contain URLs of additional pages to be pushed.

✦ Each CHANNEL and ITEM element may contain TITLE, ABSTRACT, and LOGO children that describe the content of the page the element references.

✦ The SCHEDULE element specifies when and how often the browser should check the server for updates.

✦ The LOG element identifies items whose viewing is reported back to the Web server, though the subscriber can disable this reporting.

✦ The LOGTARGET element defines how logging information from a channel is reported back to the server.

✦ The BASE attribute provides a starting point from which relative URLs in child element HREF attributes can be calculated.

✦ The LASTMOD attribute specifies the last time a page was changed so the browser can tell whether or not it needs to be downloaded.

✦ The USAGE attribute allows you to use Web pages as channels, precached content, Active Desktop components, screen savers, and software updates.

The last few chapters, including this one, looked at a variety of XML applications designed by third parties that are ready for you to use today. In the next chapter, we change gears and design a new XML application from scratch that covers genealogy.

✦　　✦　　✦

Designing a New XML Application

The last several chapters discussed XML applications that were already invented by other people and showed you how to use them. This chapter shows you how to develop an XML application from scratch. This chapter builds an XML application and associated document type definitions (DTDs) for genealogical data from the ground up.

Organization of the Data

When developing a new XML application, you need to organize, either in your head or on paper, the data you're describing. There are three basic steps in this process:

1. List the elements

2. Identify the fundamental elements

3. Relate the elements to each other

An easy way to start the process is to explore the forms and reports that are already available from other formats that describe this data. Genealogy is a fairly well established discipline, and genealogists have a fairly good idea of what information is and is not useful and how it should be arranged. This is often included in a family group sheet, a sample of which is shown in Figure 34-1.

You'll need to duplicate and organize the fields from the standard reports in your DTD to the extent that they match what you want to do. You can, of course, supplement or modify them to fit your specific needs.

Family Group Sheet

Name	Samuel English Anderson	
Birth	25 Aug 1871	Sideview
Death	10 Nov 1919	Mt. Sterling, KY
Father	Thomas Corwin Anderson (1845-1889)	
Mother	LeAnah (Lee Anna, Annie) DeMint English (1843-1898)	
Other spouses: Cavanaugh		

Misc. Notes

Samuel English Anderson was known in Montgomery County for his red hair and the temper that went with it. He did once kill a man, but the court found that it was in self-defense. He was shot by a farm worker whom he had fired the day before for smoking in a tobacco barn.

Hamp says this may have been self-defense, because he threatened to kill the workers for smoking in the barn. He also says old-time rumors say they mashed his head with a fencepost.

Beth heard he was cut to death with machetes in the field, but Hamp says they wouldn't be cutting tobacco in Nov., only stripping it in the barn.

Marriage	15 Jul 1892	Cincinnati, Ohio, Central Christian Church

Spouse	Cora Rucker (Blevins?) McDaniel	
Birth	1 Aug 1873	
Death	21 Jul 1909	Sideview, bronchial trouble TB
Burial		Machpelah Cemetery, Mt. Sterling KY , Sideview
Father	Judson McDaniel (1834-1905)	
Mother	Mary E. Blevins (1847-1886)	

Misc. Notes

She was engaged to General Hood of the Confederacy, but she was seeing Mr. Anderson on the side. A servant was posted to keep Mr. Anderson away. However the girl fell asleep, and Cora eloped with Mr. Anderson.

Children

1 M	Judson McDaniel Anderson	
Birth	19 Jul 1894	Montgomery County, KY, 1893
Death	27 Apr 1941	Mt. Sterling, KY
Spouse	Mary Elizabeth Hart	
Marriage	16 Dec 1914	
Spouse	Zelda (Zorah?) Mefford	
2 M	Thomas Corwin Anderson	
Birth	16 Jan 1898	
Death		Probably Australia
3 M	Rodger French Anderson	
Birth	26 Nov 1899	
Death		Birmingham, AL
Spouse	Ruby McDaniel	
4 F	Mary English Anderson	
Birth	8 Apr 1902	August 4, 1902? , Sideview, KY
Death	19 Dec 1972	Mt. Sterling, KY
Spouse	Clark Hagan (Hazen?) Mitchell Major	
Marriage	4 Dec 1939	Fort Knox, KY
Spouse	Carl Edwin (Cully) Berg	
Marriage	1921	
Spouse	Burton Prewitt	

Figure 34-1: A family group sheet

Note　Object-oriented programmers will note many similarities between what's described in this section and the techniques they use to gather user requirements. This is partly the result of my own experience and prejudices as an object-oriented programmer, but more of it is due to the similarity of the tasks involved. Gathering user requirements for software is not that different from gathering user requirements for markup languages. Database designers may also notice a lot of similarity between what's done here and what they do when designing a new database.

Listing the elements

The first step in developing an XML application for a domain is to decide what the elements are. This isn't hard. It mostly involves brainstorming to determine what may appear in the domain. As an exercise, write down everything you can think of that may be genealogical information. To keep the problem manageable, include only genealogical data. Assume you can use XHTML for standard text information such as paragraphs, page titles, and so forth. Again, include only elements that specifically apply to genealogy.

 Cross-Reference   XHTML is discussed in Chapters 27 and 28.

Don't be shy. It's easy to remove information later if there's too much of it or something doesn't prove useful. At this stage, expect to have redundant elements or elements that you'll throw away after further thought.

Here's the list I came up with. Your list will be at least a little different. Of course, you may have used different names for the same things. That's okay. There's no one right answer (which is not to say that all answers are created equal or that some answers aren't better than others).

father	gender	uncle
parent	source	daughter
baptism	grandparent	marriage
note	family	date
aunt	birthday	middle name
mother	burial	nephew
child	surname	husband
adoption	grandmother	wife
gravesite	son	spouse
niece	death date	ancestor
person	grandfather	descendant
baby	given name	

Identifying the fundamental elements

The list in the last section has some effective duplicates and some elements that aren't really necessary. It's probably missing a few elements as well, which you'll discover as you continue. This is normal. Developing an XML application is an iterative process that takes some time before you feel comfortable with the result.

What you really need to do at this stage is determine the fundamental elements of the domain. These are likely to be those elements that appear as immediate children of the root, rather than contained in some other element. There are two real possibilities here: family and person. Most of the other items in the list are either characteristics of a person or family (occupation, birthday, marriage) or they're a kind of family or person (uncle, parent, baby).

At this stage, most people's instinct is to say that family is the only fundamental element, and that families contain people. This is certainly consistent with the usage of the terms *parent* and *child* to describe the relationships of XML elements (a usage I eschew in this chapter to avoid confusion with the human parents and children being modeled). For example, you might imagine that a family looks like this:

```
<FAMILY>
  <HUSBAND>Samuel English Anderson</HUSBAND>
  <WIFE>Cora Rucker McDaniel</WIFE>
  <CHILD>Judson McDaniel Anderson</CHILD>
  <CHILD>Thomas Corwin Anderson</CHILD>
  <CHILD>Rodger French Anderson</CHILD>
  <CHILD>Mary English Anderson</CHILD>
</FAMILY>
```

However, there's a problem with this approach. A single person likely belongs to more than one family. I am both the child of my parents and the husband of my wife. That's two different families. Perhaps you can think of this as one extended family, but how far back does this go? Are my grandparents part of the same family? My great-grandparents? My in-laws? Genealogists generally agree that for the purposes of keeping records, a family is a mother, a father, and their children.

Of course, the real world isn't that simple. Some people have both adoptive and biological parents. Many people have more than one spouse over a lifetime. My father-in-law, Sidney Hart Anderson, was married 15 separate times to 12 different women. Admittedly, Sidney is an extreme case. When he died, he was only four marriages away from tying the world record for serial marriage. (Since then, former Baptist minister Glynn Wolfe pushed the record to 29 consecutive marriages, but he lived almost 40 years longer than Sidney did.) Nonetheless, you do need to account for the likelihood that the same people belong to different families.

The standard family group sheets used by the Mormons, a variation of which was shown in Figure 34-1, account for this by repeating the same people and data on different sheets. But for computer applications it's better not to store the same information more than once. Among other things, this avoids problems where data stored in one place is updated while data stored in another is not. Instead, you can make connections between different elements by using ID and IDREF attributes.

Thus, it is not enough to have only a single fundamental family element. There must be at least one other fundamental element — the person. Each person is unique. Each has a single birthday, a single death date, most of the time (though not always) a single name, and various other data. Families are composed of different collections of persons. By defining the persons who make up a family, as well as their roles inside the family, you define the family.

| Note | We often think of our family as an extended family including grandparents, daughters-in-law, uncles, aunts, and cousins, and perhaps biologically unrelated individuals who happen to live in the same house. However, in the context of genealogy, a family is a single pair of parents and their children. In some cases, the names of these people may be unknown, and in many cases there may be no children or no husband or wife (a single individual qualifies as a family of one). However, a family does not include more distant relationships. A large part of genealogy is the establishment of the actual biological or adoptive relationships between people. It's not uncommon to discover in the course of one's research that the Cousin Puss or Aunt Moot referred to in old letters was in fact no relation at all! Such people should certainly be included in your records, but failure to keep their actual connections straight can only lead to confusion farther down the road. |

There's one more key element that may or may not be a direct child of the root. That's the source for information. A source is like a bibliographical footnote, specifying where each piece of information came from. The source may be a magazine article such as "Blaise Pradel, Man At Arms, May/June 1987, pp. 26–31"; a book like "*A Sesquicentennial History of Kentucky* by Frederik A. Wallis & Hambleon Tapp, 1945, The Historical Record Association, Hopkinsville, KY"; a family bible such as "English-Demint Anderson Bible, currently held by Beth Anderson in Brooklyn"; or simply word of mouth such as "Anne Sandusky, interview, 6-12-1995."

Tracking the source for a particular datum is important because different sources often disagree. It's not uncommon to see birth and death dates that differ by a day or a year, plus or minus. Less common, but still too frequent, are confusions between parents and grandparents, aunts and cousins, names of particular people, and more. When you uncover information that disputes information you've already collected, it's important to make a reasonable judgment about whether the new information is more reliable than the old. Not all sources are equally reliable. In my own research I've found a document claiming to trace my wife's lineage back to Adam and Eve through assorted biblical figures and various English royalty from the Middle Ages. Needless to say, I don't take this particular source very seriously.

I can think of plausible reasons to make the source a child of the individual elements it documents, but ultimately I think the source is not part of a person or a family in the same way that a birth date or marriage date belongs to a particular person. Rather, it is associated information that should be stored separately and referenced through an ID. The main reason is that a single source, such as an old family bible, may well contain data about many different people and families. In keeping with principles of data normalization, I'd prefer not to repeat the information about the source more than once in the document. If you like, think of this as akin to using endnotes rather than footnotes.

Establishing relationships among the elements

The third and final step before actually designing the application and writing the DTD is to identify how the different pieces of information you want to track are connected and what they contain. You've determined that the three fundamental elements are the person, the family, and the source. Now you must decide what you want to include in these fundamental elements.

Family

A family is generally composed of a husband, a wife, and zero or more children. Either the husband or the wife is optional. If you wish to account for same-sex marriages (something most genealogy software couldn't do until recently), simply require one or two parents or spouses without specifying gender. Gender may then be included as an attribute of a person, which is where it probably belongs anyway.

There's some question about the proper names for these elements. Husband and wife may not be exactly the right words for unmarried couples, or for single people who never married. Many genealogists prefer father and mother instead, although, again, that's not really accurate when describing either couples or single people who never had children. You could be excessively clinical and call them the male and the female, or perhaps man and woman, but that doesn't really identify the relationship. For purposes of this book, I'm going to choose husband and wife; but you should be aware that the proper choice of names can be somewhat fraught and highly emotional.

Is there other information associated with a family, as opposed to individuals in the family? I can think of one thing that is important to genealogists: marriage information. The date and place a couple was married (if any) and the date and place a couple was divorced (again, if any) are important information. Although you could include such dates as part of each married individual, it really makes sense to make it part of the family. Given that, a family looks something like this:

```
<FAMILY>
  <MARRIAGE>
    <DATE>...</DATE>
    <PLACE>...</PLACE>
  </MARRIAGE>
  <DIVORCE>
    <DATE>...</DATE>
    <PLACE>...</PLACE>
  </DIVORCE>
  <HUSBAND>...</HUSBAND>
  <WIFE>...</WIFE>
  <CHILD>...</CHILD>
  <CHILD>...</CHILD>
  <CHILD>...</CHILD>
</FAMILY>
```

Information can be omitted if it isn't relevant (for instance, you wouldn't include a DIVORCE element for a couple that never divorced) or if you don't know it.

Person

The PERSON element is likely to be more complex. Let's review the standard information you'd want to store about a person:

- ✦ Name
- ✦ Gender
- ✦ Birth date
- ✦ Baptism date
- ✦ Death date
- ✦ Burial date and place
- ✦ Father
- ✦ Mother

Of these, name, birth, baptism, death, and burial are likely to be elements contained inside a person. Gender is probably best modeled as an optional attribute with a fixed value list. Father and mother are likely to be attributes of the person that refer back to the person elements for those people. Furthermore, a person needs an ID attribute so he or she can be referred to by family and other person elements.

Caution   Father and mother seem to be borderline cases where you might get away with using attributes, but there is the potential to run into trouble. Although everyone has exactly one biological mother and one biological father, many people have adoptive parents that may also need to be connected to the person.

Names are generally divided into family name and given name. This allows you to do things like write a style sheet that boldfaces all people with the last name Harold.

Birth, death, burial (and possibly baptism — sometimes a baptismal record is all that's available for an individual) can all be divided into a date (possibly including a time) and a place. Again, the place may simply be CDATA, or it can even be a full address element. However, in practice, full street addresses that the post office could deliver mail to are not available. Much more common are partial addresses such as Mount Sterling, Kentucky, or the name of an old family farm.

Dates can either be stored as text or broken up into day, month, and year. In general, it's easier to break them into day, month, and year than to stick to a common format for dates. On the other hand, allowing arbitrary text inside a date element also allows for imprecise dates such as 1919-20, before 1753, or about 1800.

That may seem like everything, but we've left out one of the most interesting and important pieces of all — notes. A note about a person may contain simple data such as "first Eagle Scout in Louisiana," or it may contain a complete story, such as how Sam Anderson was killed in the field. This may be personal information such as religious affiliation, or it may be medical information like which ancestors died of stomach cancer. If you've got a special interest in particular information like religion or medical history, you can make that a separate element of its own, but you should still include some element that can hold arbitrary information of interest that you dig up during your research.

There are other things that you could include in a PERSON element, photographs for instance, but I'll stop here so that this chapter remains manageable. Let's move on to the SOURCE element.

Source

The third and final top-level element is SOURCE. A source is bibliographic information that says where you learned a particular fact. It can be a standard citation to a published article or book such as *Collin's History of Kentucky*, Volume II, p. 325, 1840, 1875. Sources such as this have a lot of internal structure that could be captured with elements like BOOK, AUTHOR, VOLUME, PAGE_RANGE, YEAR, and so forth.

Several efforts are currently underway to produce DTDs for generic bibliographies. The one that seems furthest along is BiblioML (http://www.culture.fr/ BiblioML/) from France's Ministère de la culture et de la communication Mission de la recherche et de la technologie. BiblioML is based on the international standard Unimarc Bibliographic Format. Unfortunately, this isn't finished as of mid-2001.

Furthermore, sources in genealogy tend to be a lot messier than in the typical term paper. For instance, one of the most important sources in genealogy can be the family bible with records of births, dates, and marriages. In such a case, it's not the edition, translation, or the publisher of the bible that's important; it's the individual copy that resides in Aunt Doodie's house. For another example, exactly how do you cite an obituary you found in a 50-year-old newspaper clipping in a deceased relative's purse? Chances are the information in the obituary is accurate, but it's not easy to figure out exactly what page of what newspaper on what date it came from.

Because developing an XML application for bibliographies could easily be more than a chapter of its own, and is a task best left to professional informaticians, I will satisfy myself with making the SOURCE element contain only character data. It will also have an ID attribute in the form s1, s2, s3, and so forth, so that each source can be referred to by different elements. Let's move on to writing the DTD that documents this XML application.

Choosing a Namespace

Although not all XML applications need to use namespaces, most public ones should probably use them. Namespaces are the standard way to identify which elements belong with which software when multiple XML vocabularies get mixed together. Even if you plan to keep your documents simple and not mix them with any outside vocabulary, there's no guarantee that other people who use your application will not mix them. For example, even though you think of a genealogy document as an indivisible whole, somebody else might make it a part of a SOAP request.

The namespace URI you pick should be a URL and should be resolvable, because you're eventually going to want to put a Resource Directory Description Language (RDDL) document there. It should probably use the http protocol unless you've got a really good reason to pick something else. Most importantly, the URL should be persistent. It needs to be in a domain name that will remain stable. Thus it really needs to be in a domain you own. You should not use URLs at free hosts like GeoCities or ISP user accounts. If you change your ISP for any reason, the namespace URL should still be usable. I have an account at IBiblio so I could use the namespace URL `http://ibiblio.org/xml/namespaces/genealogy/`. However, IBiblio has changed its name several times since I started there. It used to be metalab.unc.edu and before that it was sunsite.unc.edu. This sort of instability is not acceptable in a host responsible for namespace resolution. Consequently, I will pick a host in a domain I own, cafeconleche.org. Furthermore I'm going to dedicate a specific host just to namespaces, ns.cafeconleche.org, so that the namespace URI will begin `http://ns.cafeconleche.org/`. However, it's equally feasible, and indeed more common, just to set up a special directory on my main web server; for example, `http://www.cafeconleche.org/namespaces/`.

> **Tip**
>
> If you don't have your own domain name, one alternative is to use a persistent Uniform Resource Locator, or PURL. A PURL is a URL such as `http://purl.oclc.org/DC/`. However, when the user tries to retrieve that URL, they're automatically redirected to another site, presumably one you control. You can change the site that users are redirected to without changing the namespace URL. The Dublin Core uses PURL for namespace URLs, as you saw in Chapter 24. The PURL service is provided by the Online Computer Library Center's Office of Research (`http://www.oclc.org/research/`) or by anybody else who wants to run a PURL server. Of course, using a PURL makes you dependent on the stability of whoever is running your PURL server.

For the sake of convenience, the namespace URL should probably point to a directory rather than to a specific file. You can put the RDDL document in the index file for this directory. The name of this directory should reflect the name of the application you're developing. I'm writing about genealogy so my full namespace URL will be `http://ns.cafeconleche.org/genealogy/`.

If I wanted to, I could pick a standard prefix at this point, but I'm not going to do that. I expect that most of my genealogy documents will reside in their own files, so I'm not going to need any prefix. The default namespace will do fine. However, I will be careful to design the application in such a way that if someone else wants to add a prefix at a later point, it's straightforward for them to do so.

Persons

By using external entity references or XInclude, it's possible to store individual people in separate files, and then pull them together into families and family trees later. So, let's begin by working on an XML application for a single person. We'll merge this into a larger XML application for families and family trees in the next sections.

A sample person

To develop a DTD or schema, it's often useful to work backwards — that is, first write out the XML markup you'd like to see using a real example or two, then write the DTD that matches the data. I'm going to use my great-grandfather-in-law Samuel English Anderson as an example, because I have enough information about him to serve as a good example, and also because he's been dead long enough that no one should get upset over anything I say about him. (You'd be amazed at the scandals and gossip you dig up when doing genealogical research.) Here's the information I have about Samuel English Anderson, more or less as it appears in a standard genealogy database:

Name: Samuel English Anderson[29, 43]

Birth: 25 Aug 1871   Sideview

Death: 10 Nov 1919   Mt. Sterling, KY

Father: Thomas Corwin Anderson (1845-1889)

Mother: LeAnah (Lee Anna, Annie) DeMint English (1843-1898)

Misc. Notes[219]

Samuel English Anderson was known in Montgomery County for his red hair and the temper that went with it. He did once *kill a man*, but the court found that it was in self-defense.

He was shot by a farm worker whom he had fired the day before for smoking in a tobacco barn. Hamp says this may have been self-defense, because he threatened to kill the workers for smoking in the barn. Hamp also claims that old-time rumors say they mashed his head with a fence post. Beth heard he was cut to death with machetes in the field, but Hamp says they wouldn't be cutting tobacco in November, only stripping it in the barn.

Now let's reformat this into XML as shown in Listing 34-1:

Listing 34-1: **An XML document for Samuel English Anderson**

```xml
<?xml version="1.0"?>
<PERSON ID="p37" SEX="M"
   xmlns="http://ns.cafeconleche.org/genealogy/">
  <REFERENCE SOURCE="s29"/>
  <REFERENCE SOURCE="s43"/>
  <NAME>
    <GIVEN>Samuel English</GIVEN>
    <SURNAME>Anderson</SURNAME>
  </NAME>
  <BIRTH>
    <PLACE>Sideview</PLACE>
    <DATE>25 Aug 1871</DATE>
  </BIRTH>
  <DEATH>
    <PLACE>Mt. Sterling, KY</PLACE>
    <DATE>10 Nov 1919</DATE>
  </DEATH>
  <SPOUSE PERSON="p1099"/>
  <SPOUSE PERSON="p2660"/>
  <FATHER PERSON="p1035"/>
  <MOTHER PERSON="p1098"/>
  <NOTE>
    <REFERENCE SOURCE="s219"/>
    <body xmlns="http://www.w3.org/1999/xhtml">
      <p>
        Samuel English Anderson was known in Montgomery County
        for his red hair and the temper that went with it. He
        did once <strong>kill a man</strong>, but the court
        found that it was in self-defense.
      </p>

      <p>
        He was shot by a farm worker whom he had
        fired the day before for smoking in a tobacco barn.
        Hamp says this may have been self-defense, because he
        threatened to kill the workers for smoking in the barn.
        Hamp also says old-time rumors say they mashed his head
        with a fence post. Beth heard he was cut to death with
        machetes in the field, but Hamp says they wouldn't be
        cutting tobacco in November, only stripping it in the
        barn.
      </p>
    </body>
  </NOTE>
</PERSON>
```

The information about other people has been removed and replaced with references to them. The ID numbers are provided by the database I use to store this information (Reunion 5.0 for the Mac from Leister Productions, `http://www.leisterpro.com`). The endnote numbers become `SOURCE` attributes of `REFERENCE` elements. HTML tags are used to mark up the note.

Eventually we may need to add a document type declaration, schema location attributes, and `xml-stylesheet` processing instructions to this document. However, that can wait. For now we just need a basic example from which we can work when writing the DTD. Exactly what we put in the document type declaration and/or the schema location attributes will depend on exactly what we come up with when we write the DTD, schema, and style sheet.

The person DTD

Now let's see what a DTD for Listing 34-1 would look like. I'm going to begin with the simplest DTD just to get started. Once the DTD is finished, I'll use the modularization techniques you learned about in Chapters 26 and 28 to allow users to adjust the namespace prefix. However, it's certainly easier to begin with a less indirect approach until the basic application is debugged.

The first element is `PERSON`. This element may contain names, references, births, deaths, burials, baptisms, notes, spouses, fathers, and mothers. I'm going to allow zero or more of each in any order.

```
<!ELEMENT PERSON (NAME | REFERENCE | BIRTH | DEATH | BURIAL
    | BAPTISM | NOTE | SPOUSE | FATHER | MOTHER )*>
```

At first glance it may seem strange not to require a `BIRTH` or some of the other elements. After all, everybody has exactly one birthday. However, keep in mind that what's being described here is more your knowledge of the person than the person him- or herself. You often know about a person without knowing the exact day or even year they were born. Similarly, you may sometimes have conflicting sources that give different values for birthdays or other information. Therefore, it may be necessary to include extra data.

The `PERSON` element has three attributes: `xmlns`, which I'll make fixed, `ID`, which I'll require, and a `SEX`, which I'll make optional. (Old records often contain children of unspecified gender, sometimes named, sometimes not. Even photographs can be unclear about gender, especially when children who died very young are involved.)

```
<!ATTLIST PERSON
    xmlns  CDATA  #FIXED "http://ns.cafeconleche.org/genealogy/"
    ID     ID     #REQUIRED
    SEX    (M | F) #IMPLIED>
```

Next the child elements must be declared. Four of them — BIRTH, DEATH, BURIAL, and BAPTISM — consist of a place and a date, and are otherwise the same. This is a good place for a parameter entity reference:

```
<!ENTITY % event    "(REFERENCE*, PLACE?, DATE?)*">
<!ELEMENT  BIRTH    %event;>
<!ELEMENT  BAPTISM %event;>
<!ELEMENT  DEATH    %event;>
<!ELEMENT  BURIAL   %event;>
```

I've also added one or more optional REFERENCE elements at the start, even though this example doesn't have a SOURCE for any event information. Sometimes, you'll have different sources for different pieces of information about a person. In fact, I'll add REFERENCE elements as potential children of almost every element in the DTD. I declare REFERENCE like this, along with a comment in case it isn't obvious from glancing over the DTD exactly what's supposed to be found in the reference:

```
<!-- The ID number of a SOURCE element
     that documents this entry -->
<!ELEMENT  REFERENCE EMPTY>
<!ATTLIST  REFERENCE SOURCE NMTOKEN #REQUIRED>
```

Here the SOURCE attribute merely contains the number of the corresponding source. When actual SOURCE elements are added to the DTD below, this can become the ID of the SOURCE element.

A PLACE contains only text. A DATE contains a date string. I decided against requiring a separate year, date, and month to allow for less-certain dates that are common in genealogy such as "about 1876" or "sometime before 1920".

```
<!ELEMENT  PLACE (#PCDATA)>
<!ELEMENT  DATE  (#PCDATA)>
```

The SPOUSE, FATHER, and MOTHER attributes each contain a link to the ID of a PERSON element via a PERSON attribute. Again, this is a good opportunity to use a parameter entity reference:

```
<!ENTITY % personref "PERSON NMTOKEN #REQUIRED">
<!ELEMENT  SPOUSE  EMPTY>
<!ATTLIST  SPOUSE  %personref;>
<!ELEMENT  FATHER  EMPTY>
<!ATTLIST  FATHER  %personref;>
<!ELEMENT  MOTHER  EMPTY>
<!ATTLIST  MOTHER  %personref;>
```

Ideally, the PERSON attribute would have type IDREF. However, as long as the person being identified may reside in another file, the best you can do is require a name token type.

The NAME element may contain any number of REFERENCE elements and zero or one SURNAME and GIVEN elements. Each of these may contain text.

```
<!ELEMENT  NAME    (REFERENCE*, GIVEN?, SURNAME?)>
<!ELEMENT  GIVEN   (#PCDATA)>
<!ELEMENT  SURNAME (#PCDATA)>
```

The NOTE element may contain an arbitrary amount of text. Some standard markup would be useful here. The easiest solution is to adopt XHTML Basic. Simply use a parameter entity reference to import the XHTML Basic DTD. I'll allow each NOTE to contain zero or more REFERENCE elements and a single body element.

```
<!ENTITY % xhtml PUBLIC "-//W3C//DTD XHTML Basic 1.0//EN"
                        "xhtml-basic10.dtd">
%xhtml;
<!ELEMENT  NOTE    (REFERENCE*, body)>
```

Those three little lines get you all the markup you need for simple narratives. There's no need to invent your own. You can use the already familiar and well-supported HTML tags. I chose to use only body because adding a header here seemed a little superfluous, but if you want to include complete HTML documents, it's easy to do — just replace body with html in the above. This does assume that the file xhtml-basic10.dtd and all the files it depends on can be found in the same directory as this DTD, although that's easy to adjust if you want to put it somewhere else. You could even use the absolute URL at the W3C Web site, http://www.w3.org/TR/xhtml-basic/xhtml-basic10.dtd, although I prefer not to make my documents dependent on the availability of a Web site I don't control. Listing 34-2 shows the complete person DTD.

Listing 34-2: **person.dtd: The complete PERSON DTD**

```
<!ELEMENT PERSON ( NAME | REFERENCE | BIRTH | DEATH | BURIAL
                 | BAPTISM | NOTE | FATHER | MOTHER | SPOUSE )* >
<!ATTLIST PERSON
   xmlns  CDATA   #FIXED "http://ns.cafeconleche.org/genealogy/"
   ID     ID      #REQUIRED>

<!ATTLIST PERSON SEX (M | F) #IMPLIED>

<!-- The ID number of a SOURCE element that documents
     this entry -->
<!ELEMENT  REFERENCE  EMPTY>
<!ENTITY % sourceref "SOURCE NMTOKEN #REQUIRED">
<!ATTLIST  REFERENCE %sourceref;>

<!ENTITY % event    "(REFERENCE*, PLACE?, DATE?)">
<!ELEMENT  BIRTH   %event;>
<!ELEMENT  BAPTISM %event;>
<!ELEMENT  DEATH   %event;>
<!ELEMENT  BURIAL  %event;>
```

```
<!ELEMENT  PLACE    (#PCDATA)>
<!ELEMENT  DATE     (#PCDATA)>

<!ENTITY % personref "PERSON NMTOKEN #REQUIRED">
<!ELEMENT  SPOUSE   EMPTY>
<!ATTLIST  SPOUSE   %personref;>
<!ELEMENT  FATHER   EMPTY>
<!ATTLIST  FATHER   %personref;>
<!ELEMENT  MOTHER   EMPTY>
<!ATTLIST  MOTHER   %personref;>

<!ELEMENT  NAME     (GIVEN?, SURNAME?)>
<!ELEMENT  GIVEN    (#PCDATA)>
<!ELEMENT  SURNAME (#PCDATA)>

<!ENTITY % xhtml PUBLIC "-//W3C//DTD XHTML Basic 1.0//EN"
                        "xhtml-basic10.dtd">
%xhtml;

<!ELEMENT  NOTE    (REFERENCE*, body)>
```

Listing 34-2 is a complete DTD for PERSON elements. It's straightforward and reasonably easy to understand. Or is it? Perhaps it only seems so to me because I wrote it. If it's obvious to you, that may only be because before you looked at Listing 34-2 you were treated to several pages of exposition and development. What will it look like to someone just staring at the DTD cold? In general, I haven't overly commented the examples in this book because the prose text explains what's going on. However, most real-world DTDs don't come attached to a 1500+ page printed book. Thus, actual DTDs need a lot more exposition inside the DTD itself. This normally takes the form of XML comments. Listing 34-3 demonstrates. The DTD is almost twice as long, but correspondingly much easier to understand.

Listing 34-3: **commented_person.dtd: The PERSON DTD with comments**

```
<!-- ..........................................  -->
<!-- Genealogy Person DTD  .........................  -->
<!-- file: person.dtd

     This DTD describes a PERSON element intended for use
     in family tree documents. It was developed as an example
     for Chapter 34 of the XML Bible, Gold Edition, by
     Elliotte Rusty Harold (elharo@metalab.unc.edu)
     Published by Hungry Minds 2001. ISBN 0-7645-4819-0.
```

Continued

Listing 34-3: *(continued)*

```
        This schema is placed in the public domain. Please
        feel free to use it or adapt it in any way you like.

        This DTD is identified by the PUBLIC and SYSTEM
        identifiers:

        PUBLIC "-//ERH//Genealogy Person DTD 1.0//EN"
        SYSTEM "person.dtd"

        All the elements declared in this DTD are in the
        http://ns.cafeconleche.org/genealogy/ namespace.
        No prefix is used. The attributes are in no namespace.

        It is not a formal standard, and has not been considered
        or approved by any standards body.

        .............................................. -->

<!-- PERSON is the root element of documents that use this
     DTD. However, it is more intended to be used as a part
     of larger XML applications which would contain multiple
     PERSON elements in a single document. -->
<!ELEMENT PERSON ( NAME | REFERENCE | BIRTH | DEATH | BURIAL
               | BAPTISM | NOTE | FATHER | MOTHER | SPOUSE )* >
<!ATTLIST PERSON
   xmlns  CDATA  #FIXED "http://ns.cafeconleche.org/genealogy/"
   ID     ID     #REQUIRED>

<!ATTLIST PERSON
   xmlns:xsi CDATA #FIXED
     "http://www.w3.org/2001/XMLSchema-instance"
   xsi:schemaLocation CDATA #IMPLIED
>

<!--M means male, F means female -->
<!ATTLIST PERSON SEX (M | F) #IMPLIED>

<!-- The ID number of a SOURCE element that documents
     this entry -->
<!ELEMENT  REFERENCE  EMPTY>
<!ENTITY % sourceref "SOURCE NMTOKEN #REQUIRED">
<!ATTLIST  REFERENCE %sourceref;>

<!-- Events are occurrences at a certain
     time and place, though the exact time and place may
     not be known for certain. Events include marriages,
     births, deaths, baptisms, and burials.  -->
<!ENTITY % event   "(REFERENCE*, PLACE?, DATE?)">
<!ELEMENT  BIRTH   %event;>
<!ELEMENT  BAPTISM %event;>
```

```
<!ELEMENT    DEATH    %event;>
<!ELEMENT    BURIAL   %event;>

<!ELEMENT    PLACE    (#PCDATA)>
<!ELEMENT    DATE     (#PCDATA)>

<!-- A person reference is a pointer to another person
     encoded in a PERSON element. The pointer is the ID
     of the PERSON pointed to. -->
<!ENTITY % personref "PERSON NMTOKEN #REQUIRED">
<!ELEMENT    SPOUSE   EMPTY>
<!ATTLIST    SPOUSE   %personref;>
<!ELEMENT    FATHER   EMPTY>
<!ATTLIST    FATHER   %personref;>
<!ELEMENT    MOTHER   EMPTY>
<!ATTLIST    MOTHER   %personref;>

<!-- Middle names should be encoded as part of the
     given name; e.g.
     <NAME>
       <GIVEN>Elliotte Rusty</GIVEN>
       <SURNAME>Harold</SURNAME>
     </NAME>
 -->
<!ELEMENT    NAME     (GIVEN?, SURNAME?)>
<!ELEMENT    GIVEN    (#PCDATA)>
<!ELEMENT    SURNAME  (#PCDATA)>

<!-- The NOTE element contains an XHTML Basic body element
     holding the text of the note. This allows you to write
     essentially anything you care to write in a note.
 -->
<!ENTITY % xhtml PUBLIC "-//W3C//DTD XHTML Basic 1.0//EN"
                        "xhtml-basic10.dtd">
%xhtml;

<!ELEMENT    NOTE     (REFERENCE*, body)>
```

There are a number of useful bits of information in the comments that are not found in the element and attribute declarations:

✦ Copyright information so that users know how and where they can use it (any way they please in this case)

✦ An e-mail address to write to if the user has questions

✦ The public identifier and the suggested filename and system identifier

✦ What abbreviations stand for

✦ What the text content of some elements should look like

This isn't the limit either. You could certainly add a lot more detail in the comments, up to and including the complete prose specification for the application. Validators can easily skip over the comments. Human readers may find well-written comments more useful than the declarations.

The person schema

Now that the DTD is finished, let's see what a schema for Listing 34-1 would look like. The key element is PERSON. This is an element with complex content, and it is the root element of the document. Therefore, it must be declared with a top-level xsd:element element. The big question for this, and other elements with author-defined types, is whether it should be declared with a named type or an anonymous type. Generally, a named type should be used if you expect the element or the type to be used in many different contexts and you want to reuse the type. Although the PERSON element and type are only used in one context in Listing 34-1, it's clear it will be used as a nonroot element in the full family tree document. Thus, it's best to define it as a type of its own.

The application is the same as it was in the DTD, so we don't need to revisit all the questions about what makes up a person. We can just translate the existing declaration of the PERSON element in the DTD into a schema. In the DTD, this declaration is:

```
<!ELEMENT PERSON (NAME | REFERENCE | BIRTH | DEATH | BURIAL
    | BAPTISM | NOTE | SPOUSE | FATHER | MOTHER )*>
```

Translating into an xsd:complexType element, this becomes:

```
<xsd:complexType name="PersonType">
  <xsd:choice minOccurs="0" maxOccurs="unbounded">
    <xsd:element name="NAME"      type="NameType"/>
    <xsd:element name="REFERENCE" type="ReferenceType"/>
    <xsd:element name="BIRTH"     type="BirthType"/>
    <xsd:element name="DEATH"     type="DeathType"/>
    <xsd:element name="BURIAL"    type="BurialType"/>
    <xsd:element name="BAPTISM"   type="BaptismType"/>
    <xsd:element name="NOTE"      type="NoteType"/>
    <xsd:element name="SPOUSE"    type="SpouseType"/>
    <xsd:element name="FATHER"    type="FatherType"/>
    <xsd:element name="MOTHER"    type="MotherType"/>
  </xsd:choice>
</xsd:complexType>
```

However, this does raise some new questions about the type of each of the child elements of the PERSON that the DTD does not answer. All of these elements, at least potentially, have either child elements or attributes, so they're all complex types. However, is each of them really a different type? The answer is no. For instance, BURIAL, BAPTISM, BIRTH, and DEATH all contain the same child elements and should share a content model. In the DTD, this was indicated by parameter entity references. In a schema, the same effect is achieved by defining one EventType and assigning it to all the elements that share that type:

```
<xsd:complexType name="EventType">
  <xsd:sequence>
    <xsd:element name="REFERENCE" type="ReferenceType"
                 minOccurs="0"    maxOccurs="unbounded"/>
    <xsd:element name="PLACE" type="xsd:string" minOccurs="0"/>
    <xsd:element name="DATE"  type="xsd:string" minOccurs="0"/>
  </xsd:sequence>
</xsd:complexType>
```

I chose to make PLACE and DATE strings rather than dates for the same reasons they were made #PCDATA in the DTD. In this particular application, dates tend to be quite fuzzy.

Similarly FATHER, MOTHER, and SPOUSE are all just instances of some kind of PersonRefType, an empty element with a PERSON NMTOKEN attribute:

```
<xsd:complexType name="PersonRefType">
  <xsd:attribute name="PERSON" type="xsd:NMTOKEN"/>
</xsd:complexType>
```

Eventually, of course, we'll want to change the type of the PERSON attribute from xsd:NMTOKEN to xsd:IDREF when we build the full family tree schema by overriding the definition of PersonRefType given here.

This still leaves NameType, ReferenceType, and NoteType. These do need their own declarations. The NAME element is only used here, so it might as well use an anonymous type declaration:

```
<xsd:element name="NAME">
  <xsd:complexType>
    <xsd:sequence>
      <xsd:element name="REFERENCE" type="ReferenceType"
                   minOccurs="0" maxOccurs="unbounded"/>
      <xsd:element name="GIVEN" type="xsd:string"
                   minOccurs="0" />
      <xsd:element name="SURNAME" type="xsd:string"
                   minOccurs="0" />
    </xsd:sequence>
  </xsd:complexType>
</xsd:element>
```

The reference type will be used in many places in the schema, so it should have a named type:

```
<xsd:complexType name="ReferenceType">
  <xsd:attribute name="SOURCE" type="xsd:NMTOKEN"/>
</xsd:complexType>
```

The note type will also be used in multiple places so it too has a named type. However its declaration is much trickier because one of the elements it contains, body, comes from a different namespace. Thus, you first have to import the schema for XHTML to retrieve the necessary declarations for that namespace:

```
<xsd:import namespace="http://www.w3.org/1999/xhtml"
            schemaLocation="xhtml1.1.xsd"/>
```

I'm using the full schema for XHTML here only because a schema for XHTML Basic wasn't available at the time of this writing. It would be easy enough to adjust this when one does become available. The relative URL used here assumes that the file xhtml1.1.xsd and all the files it depends on can be found in the same directory as this schema.

Since the body element is declared in a different schema, I declare it here by reference rather than by name and type. Since the default namespace in this schema is already mapped to http://ns.cafeconleche.org/genealogy/, I also have to put a prefix on the body element and declare that prefix with an xmlns:html attribute:

```
<xsd:complexType name="NoteType"
                 xmlns:html="http://www.w3.org/1999/xhtml">
  <xsd:sequence>
    <xsd:element name="REFERENCE" type="ReferenceType"
                 minOccurs="0" />
    <xsd:element ref="html:body"/>
  </xsd:sequence>
</xsd:complexType>
```

However, none of this means that you have to use such prefixes in your instance documents. Schemas validate against namespace URIs, not prefixes. The prefixes used here are chosen purely for convenience inside the schema. They do not apply in the instance documents.

The PERSON element also has three attributes: xmlns, which doesn't have to be declared in a schema, ID, which I'll require, and SEX, which I'll make optional:

```
<xsd:attribute name="ID"  xsd:type="ID" use="required"/>
<xsd:attribute name="SEX">
  <xsd:simpleType>
    <xsd:restriction base="xsd:string">
      <xsd:enumeration value="M"/>
      <xsd:enumeration value="F"/>
    </xsd:restriction>
  </xsd:simpleType>
</xsd:attribute>
```

After adding all these pieces and putting them together, the completed person schema is shown in Listing 34-4:

Listing 34-4: **person.xsd: The complete PERSON schema**

```xml
<?xml version="1.0"?>
<xsd:schema xmlns:xsd="http://www.w3.org/2001/XMLSchema"
  xmlns="http://ns.cafeconleche.org/genealogy/"
  targetNamespace="http://ns.cafeconleche.org/genealogy/"
  elementFormDefault="qualified"
  attributeFormDefault="unqualified"
>

  <xsd:import namespace="http://www.w3.org/1999/xhtml"
              schemaLocation="xhtml1.1.xsd"/>

  <xsd:complexType name="EventType">
    <xsd:sequence>
      <xsd:element name="REFERENCE" type="ReferenceType"
                   minOccurs="0" maxOccurs="unbounded"/>
      <xsd:element name="PLACE" type="xsd:string"
                   minOccurs="0"/>
      <xsd:element name="DATE"  type="xsd:string"
                   minOccurs="0"/>
    </xsd:sequence>
  </xsd:complexType>

  <xsd:complexType name="PersonRefType">
    <xsd:attribute name="PERSON" type="xsd:NMTOKEN"/>
  </xsd:complexType>

  <xsd:complexType name="ReferenceType">
    <xsd:attribute name="SOURCE" type="xsd:NMTOKEN"/>
  </xsd:complexType>

  <xsd:complexType name="ReferenceType">
    <xsd:attribute name="SOURCE" type="xsd:NMTOKEN"/>
  </xsd:complexType>

  <xsd:complexType name="NoteType"
                    xmlns:html="http://www.w3.org/1999/xhtml">
    <xsd:sequence>
      <xsd:element name="REFERENCE" type="ReferenceType"
                   minOccurs="0" />
      <xsd:element ref="html:body"/>
    </xsd:sequence>
  </xsd:complexType>


  <xsd:complexType name="PersonType">
    <xsd:choice minOccurs="0" maxOccurs="unbounded">
      <xsd:element name="NAME">
        <xsd:complexType>
```

Continued

Listing 34-4: *(continued)*

```
        <xsd:sequence>
          <xsd:element name="REFERENCE" type="ReferenceType"
                       minOccurs="0"   maxOccurs="unbounded"/>
          <xsd:element name="GIVEN"      type="xsd:string"
                       minOccurs="0" />
          <xsd:element name="SURNAME"    type="xsd:string"
                       minOccurs="0" />
        </xsd:sequence>
      </xsd:complexType>
    </xsd:element>
    <xsd:element name="REFERENCE" type="ReferenceType"/>
    <xsd:element name="BIRTH"     type="EventType"/>
    <xsd:element name="DEATH"     type="EventType"/>
    <xsd:element name="BURIAL"    type="EventType"/>
    <xsd:element name="BAPTISM"   type="EventType"/>
    <xsd:element name="NOTE"      type="NoteType"/>
    <xsd:element name="SPOUSE"    type="PersonRefType"/>
    <xsd:element name="FATHER"    type="PersonRefType"/>
    <xsd:element name="MOTHER"    type="PersonRefType"/>
  </xsd:choice>
  <xsd:attribute name="ID"  type="xsd:ID" use="required"/>
  <xsd:attribute name="SEX">
    <xsd:simpleType>
      <xsd:restriction base="xsd:string">
        <xsd:enumeration value="M"/>
        <xsd:enumeration value="F"/>
      </xsd:restriction>
    </xsd:simpleType>
  </xsd:attribute>
</xsd:complexType>

<xsd:element name="PERSON" type="PersonType"/>

</xsd:schema>
```

Before you can validate the sample document against this schema, you need to add the necessary schema location and namespace declaration attributes to the root element of the instance document like this:

```
<xsd:schema xmlns:xsd="http://www.w3.org/2001/XMLSchema"
  xmlns="http://ns.cafeconleche.org/genealogy/"
  targetNamespace="http://ns.cafeconleche.org/genealogy/"
  elementFormDefault="qualified"
  attributeFormDefault="unqualified"
>
```

Having done that, if you still want to be able to validate against the DTD, you need to add declarations for those attributes to the DTD, like this:

```
<!ATTLIST PERSON
    xmlns:xsi CDATA #FIXED
              "http://www.w3.org/2001/XMLSchema-instance"
    xsi:schemaLocation CDATA #IMPLIED
>
```

Caution

Schemas are still very bleeding edge technology. Very few parsers actually support the final recommendation of XML Schemas. Of those that do, there are a lot of gaps in the support, outright bugs, and incompatibilities between implementations. Please don't assume that just because you need schemas you can rely on them. Stable systems are going to need the more proven technology of DTDs for a long time to come. You can use schemas if they're useful to you. Just don't think you can throw out DTDs just yet.

Listing 34-4 does provide a complete content model for PERSON elements. It's short, simple, fairly straightforward, and reasonably easy to follow. Or is it? I think it is because I wrote it, and one's own code always seems more obvious to one's self than to anyone else. Furthermore, as I type these words I just wrote that code so it's very fresh in my mind. It's probably also fairly obvious to you, too, because before you looked at Listing 34-4 you were treated to several pages of exposition and development. Nonetheless, it's almost certain that this schema won't be nearly as clear to anyone who's just picking it up without reading this book. Most schemas can be improved substantially by adding numerous comments and annotations that describe exactly what is going on in the schema and why. Listing 34-5 does exactly this. The schema is longer but much clearer to someone reading this schema for the first time.

Listing 34-5: **annotated_person.xsd: The annotated PERSON schema**

```
<?xml version="1.0"?>
<xsd:schema xmlns:xsd="http://www.w3.org/2001/XMLSchema"
  xmlns="http://ns.cafeconleche.org/genealogy/"
  targetNamespace="http://ns.cafeconleche.org/genealogy/"
  elementFormDefault="qualified"
  attributeFormDefault="unqualified"
>

  <xsd:annotation>
    <xsd:documentation>

      This schema describes a PERSON element intended for use
      in family tree documents. It was developed as an example
      for Chapter 34 of the XML Bible, Gold Edition, by
      Elliotte Rusty Harold (elharo@metalab.unc.edu)
      Published by Hungry Minds 2001. ISBN 0-7645-4819-0.
```

Continued

Listing 34-5: *(continued)*

```
    This schema is placed in the public domain. Please
    feel free to use it or adapt it in any way you like.

    It is not a formal standard, and has not been considered
    or approved by any standards body.

  </xsd:documentation>
</xsd:annotation>

<xsd:complexType name="EventType">
  <xsd:annotation>
    <xsd:documentation>
      The EventType describes occurrences at a certain
      time and place, though the exact time and place may
      not be known for certain. Events include marriages,
      births, deaths, baptisms, and burials.
    </xsd:documentation>
  </xsd:annotation>
  <xsd:sequence>
    <xsd:element name="REFERENCE" type="ReferenceType"
                 minOccurs="0" maxOccurs="unbounded"/>
    <xsd:element name="PLACE" type="xsd:string"
                 minOccurs="0"/>
    <xsd:element name="DATE"  type="xsd:string"
                 minOccurs="0"/>
  </xsd:sequence>
</xsd:complexType>

<xsd:complexType name="PersonRefType">
  <xsd:annotation>
    <xsd:documentation>
      The PersonRefType contains a pointer to a person
      encoded in a PERSON element somewhere in this document.
      The pointer is the ID of the PERSON pointed to.
    </xsd:documentation>
  </xsd:annotation>
  <xsd:attribute name="PERSON" type="xsd:NMTOKEN"/>
</xsd:complexType>

<xsd:complexType name="ReferenceType">
  <xsd:annotation>
    <xsd:documentation>
      The ReferenceType contains a pointer to a SOURCE
      element somewhere in this document. The pointer
      is the ID of the SOURCE element pointed to.
    </xsd:documentation>
  </xsd:annotation>
  <xsd:attribute name="SOURCE" type="xsd:NMTOKEN"/>
</xsd:complexType>
```

```
<xsd:complexType name="NoteType"
                 xmlns:html="http://www.w3.org/1999/xhtml">
  <xsd:annotation>
    <xsd:documentation>
      The NoteType is used for NOTE elements that contain
      mostly narrative text discussing whatever seems
      interesting about or relevant to a particular element.
      The contents of the note are marked up in XHTML Basic.
      (http://www.w3.org/TR/xhtml-basic)
    </xsd:documentation>
  </xsd:annotation>
  <xsd:sequence>
    <xsd:element name="REFERENCE" type="ReferenceType"
                 minOccurs="0" />
    <xsd:element ref="html:body"/>
  </xsd:sequence>
</xsd:complexType>

<xsd:complexType name="PersonType">
  <xsd:annotation>
    <xsd:documentation>
      The PersonType is used for PERSON elements. It
      describes one unique individual, with a name,
      a birthday, and so on. However, some or all of the
      information about this individual may be unknown
      and hence omitted.
    </xsd:documentation>
  </xsd:annotation>
  <xsd:choice minOccurs="0" maxOccurs="unbounded">
    <xsd:element name="NAME">
      <xsd:complexType>
        <xsd:sequence>
          <xsd:element name="REFERENCE" type="ReferenceType"
                       minOccurs="0"  maxOccurs="unbounded"/>
          <xsd:element name="GIVEN"     type="xsd:string"
                       minOccurs="0" />
          <xsd:element name="SURNAME"   type="xsd:string"
                       minOccurs="0" />
        </xsd:sequence>
      </xsd:complexType>
    </xsd:element>
    <xsd:element name="REFERENCE" type="ReferenceType"/>
    <xsd:element name="BIRTH"     type="EventType"/>
    <xsd:element name="DEATH"     type="EventType"/>
    <xsd:element name="BURIAL"    type="EventType"/>
    <xsd:element name="BAPTISM"   type="EventType"/>
    <xsd:element name="NOTE"      type="NoteType"/>
    <xsd:element name="SPOUSE"    type="PersonRefType"/>
    <xsd:element name="FATHER"    type="PersonRefType"/>
    <xsd:element name="MOTHER"    type="PersonRefType"/>
```

Continued

Listing 34-5: *(continued)*

```
    </xsd:choice>
    <xsd:attribute name="ID"  type="xsd:ID" use="required"/>
    <xsd:attribute name="SEX">
      <xsd:simpleType>
        <xsd:restriction base="xsd:string">
          <xsd:enumeration value="M"/>
          <xsd:enumeration value="F"/>
        </xsd:restriction>
      </xsd:simpleType>
    </xsd:attribute>
  </xsd:complexType>

  <xsd:element name="PERSON" type="PersonType">
    <xsd:annotation>
      <xsd:documentation>
        PERSON elements may be used as the root element of a
        document. No other element declared in this
        schema may be so used.
      </xsd:documentation>
    </xsd:annotation>
  </xsd:element>

</xsd:schema>
```

Here I've used mostly xsd:annotation elements to describe what's happening. You could also use XML comments. Generally, I prefer annotations for larger blocks of text that describe an entire type or schema, whereas I use comments for smaller notes about individual lines of code or something below the level of an entire schema or top-level element. Listing 34-5 does this when explaining about the values of a particular enumeration that M represents male and F represents female.

Using xsd:annotation elements also makes it easier to automatically generate documentation for a schema using XSLT or other XML tools. All the processor needs to do is extract the contents of all the xsd:documentation elements. Although here I've only placed plain text in those elements, they are allowed to contain any well-formed markup. For instance each xsd:documentation element could contain one or more complete XHTML documents or parts of a whole document that would be assembled automatically when the documentation was desired.

Families

Now that we know what a person looks like, the next step is to design a family. Let's begin with a sample family XML document, as shown in Listing 34-6:

Listing 34-6: An XML document for Samuel English Anderson's family

```
<?xml version="1.0" standalone="no"?>
<FAMILY ID="f25"
        xmlns="http://ns.cafeconleche.org/genealogy/">
  <HUSBAND PERSON="p37"/>
  <WIFE    PERSON="p1099"/>
  <CHILD   PERSON="p23"/>
  <CHILD   PERSON="p36"/>
  <CHILD   PERSON="p1033"/>
  <CHILD   PERSON="p1034"/>
  <MARRIAGE>
    <PLACE>Cincinnati, OH</PLACE>
    <DATE>15 Jul 1892</DATE>
  </MARRIAGE>
</FAMILY>
```

All that's needed here are references to the members of the family, not the actual family members themselves. The reference PERSON IDs are again provided from the database where this information is stored. Their exact values aren't important as long as they're reliably unique and stable.

The family DTD

Now that you've got a sample family, you have to prepare the DTD for all families, similar to the one shown in Listing 34-7. Don't forget to include items that are needed for some families — even if not for this example — such as a divorce. A parameter entity reference will pull in the declarations from the person DTD of Listing 34-3. We'll need this to define the %personref; and %event; entity references.

Listing 34-7: family.dtd: A DTD that describes a family

```
<!-- ................................................. -->
<!-- Genealogy Family DTD ............................ -->
<!-- file: family.dtd

     This DTD describes a FAMILY element intended for use
     in family tree documents. It was developed as an example
     for Chapter 34 of the XML Bible, Gold Edition, by
     Elliotte Rusty Harold (elharo@metalab.unc.edu)
     Published by Hungry Minds 2001. ISBN 0-7645-4819-0.
```

Continued

Listing 34-7: *(continued)*

```
This DTD is placed in the public domain. Please
feel free to use it or adapt it in any way you like.

This DTD is identified by the PUBLIC and SYSTEM
identifiers:

PUBLIC "-//ERH//Genealogy Family DTD 1.0//EN"
SYSTEM "family.dtd"

All the elements declared in this DTD are in the
http://ns.cafeconleche.org/genealogy/ namespace.
No prefix is used. The attributes are in no namespace.

It is not a formal standard, and has not been considered
or approved by any standards body.

..................................................... -->

<!-- FAMILY is the root element of documents that use this
     DTD. However, it is more intended to be used as a part
     of larger XML applications which would contain multiple
     FAMILY elements in a single document. -->

<!-- The person DTD defines the %personref; and %event;
     parameter entity references used here -->

<!ENTITY % person SYSTEM "person.dtd">
%person;

<!-- A FAMILY can consist of as little as one person  -->
<!ELEMENT FAMILY (REFERENCE*, HUSBAND?, WIFE?, CHILD*,
                  MARRIAGE*, DIVORCE*, NOTE*)>
<!ATTLIST FAMILY ID ID #REQUIRED>

<!-- HUSBAND and WIFE are used here for legacy reasons.
     They should not be taken to imply anything about
     marital state of the parties.  -->
<!-- HUSBAND, WIFE, and CHILD are all EMPTY elements that
     point to a PERSON element by matching its ID.  -->
<!ELEMENT  HUSBAND  EMPTY>
<!ATTLIST  HUSBAND  %personref;>
<!ELEMENT  WIFE     EMPTY>
<!ATTLIST  WIFE     %personref;>
<!ELEMENT  CHILD    EMPTY>
<!ATTLIST  CHILD    %personref;>
<!ELEMENT  DIVORCE  %event;>
<!ELEMENT  MARRIAGE %event;>
```

I'm assuming no more than one HUSBAND or WIFE per FAMILY element. This is a fairly standard assumption in genealogy, even in cultures where plural marriages are common, because it helps to keep the children sorted out. When documenting genealogy in a polygamous society, the same HUSBAND may appear in multiple FAM-ILY elements. When documenting genealogy in a polyandrous society, the same WIFE may appear in multiple FAMILY elements. Aside from overlapping dates, this is essentially the same procedure that's followed when documenting serial marriages. Of course, there's nothing in the DTD that actually requires people to be married in order to have children, any more than there's anything in biology that requires it.

Overall, this scheme is very flexible, much more so than if a FAMILY element had to contain individual PERSON elements rather than merely pointers to them. That would almost certainly require duplication of data across many different elements and files. The only thing this DTD doesn't handle well are same-sex marriages, and that could easily be fixed by changing the FAMILY declaration to the following:

```
<!ELEMENT FAMILY (((HUSBAND, WIFE) | (HUSBAND, HUSBAND?)
                | (WIFE, WIFE?)), MARRIAGE*, DIVORCE*, CHILD*)>
```

Allowing multiple marriages and divorces in a single family may seem a little strange, but it does happen. My mother-in-law married and divorced my father-in-law three separate times. Remarriages to the same person aren't common, but they do happen.

The Family Schema

The schema for families is not much more complicated than the DTD. It declares a top-level FAMILY element with a family type. All the other types defined here can be anonymous because they only appear inside FAMILY elements. There's no reason to pollute the type space with extraneous definitions. Keeping everything as local as possible is a standard principle of good design. Listing 34-8 demonstrates.

Listing 34-8: **family.xsd: A schema that describes a family**

```
<?xml version="1.0"?>
<xsd:schema xmlns:xsd="http://www.w3.org/2001/XMLSchema"
  xmlns="http://ns.cafeconleche.org/genealogy/"
  targetNamespace="http://ns.cafeconleche.org/genealogy/"
  elementFormDefault="qualified"
  attributeFormDefault="unqualified"
>

  <xsd:annotation>
    <xsd:documentation>
      This schema describes a FAMILY element intended for use
      in family tree documents. It was developed as an example
```

Continued

Listing 34-8: *(continued)*

```
      for Chapter 34 of the XML Bible, Gold Edition, by
      Elliotte Rusty Harold (elharo@metalab.unc.edu)
      Published by Hungry Minds 2001. ISBN 0-7645-4819-0.

      This schema is placed in the public domain. Please
      feel free to use it or adapt it in any way you like.
    </xsd:documentation>
  </xsd:annotation>

  <xsd:include schemaLocation="person.xsd"/>

  <xsd:complexType name="FamilyType">
    <xsd:annotation>
      <xsd:documentation>
        The FamilyType is used exclusively for FAMILY elements.
        Each such element can contain one father
        (represented by a HUSBAND element for legacy reasons,
        although no marriage is implied), one mother
        (represented by a WIFE element for legacy reasons,
        although no marriage is implied), and any number of
        children represented by CHILD elements. All of these
        elements reference PERSON elements elsewhere in the
        document and any or all of them may be omitted.

        Family membership is not exclusive. A single person may
        be a member of multiple families.
      </xsd:documentation>
    </xsd:annotation>
    <xsd:sequence>
      <xsd:element name="REFERENCE" type="ReferenceType"
                   minOccurs="0" maxOccurs="unbounded"/>
      <xsd:element name="HUSBAND" type="PersonRefType"
                   minOccurs="0" />
      <xsd:element name="WIFE"    type="PersonRefType"
                   minOccurs="0" />
      <xsd:element name="CHILD"   type="PersonRefType"
                   minOccurs="0"  maxOccurs="unbounded"/>
      <xsd:element name="MARRIAGE" type="EventType"
                   minOccurs="0"  maxOccurs="unbounded"/>
      <xsd:element name="DIVORCE" type="EventType"
                   minOccurs="0"  maxOccurs="unbounded"/>
      <xsd:element name="NOTE"    type="NoteType"
                   minOccurs="0" maxOccurs="unbounded"/>
    </xsd:sequence>
    <xsd:attribute name="ID"  xsd:type="ID" use="required"/>
  </xsd:complexType>

  <xsd:element name="FAMILY" type="FamilyType"/>

</xsd:schema>
```

This schema uses the `PersonRefType`, `EventType`, and `NoteType` types defined in Listing 34-4. To get access to them, we simply include person.xsd using `xsd:include`. This element differs from `xsd:import` in that the included schema covers the same namespace. If you're using two different namespaces (such as HTML), use `xsd:import`; if you're using the same namespace, use `xsd:include`.

Sources

The third and final top-level element is `SOURCE`. I'm using a watered-down `SOURCE` element with little internal structure. However, storing the DTD in a separate file makes it easy to add structure to it later. Some typical `SOURCE` elements look like this:

```
<SOURCE ID="s218">Hamp Hoskins interview, 11-38-1996</SOURCE>
<SOURCE ID="s29">English-Demint Anderson Bible</SOURCE>
<SOURCE ID="s43">Anderson Bible</SOURCE>
<SOURCE ID="s43">
  Letter from R. Foster Adams to Beth Anderson, 1972
</SOURCE>
<SOURCE ID="s66">
  Collin's History of Kentucky, Volume II, p. 325, 1840, 1875
</SOURCE>
```

A `SOURCE` element has a lot of internal structure. Work is ongoing in several places to produce a generic DTD for bibliographic information with elements for articles, authors, pages, publication dates, and more. However, this is quite a complex topic when considered in its full generality; and, as previously mentioned, it doesn't work quite the same for genealogy as it does for most fields. The individual copy of a family bible or newspaper clipping with handwritten annotations may be more significant than the more generic, standard author, title, publisher data used in most bibliographies.

Because developing an XML application for bibliographies could easily be more than a chapter of its own, and is a task best left to experts in the field, I will satisfy myself with making the `SOURCE` element contain only character data. It will also have an `ID` attribute in the form s1, s2, s3, and so forth, so that each source can be referred to by different elements. Listing 34-9 shows the extremely simple DTD for sources.

Listing 34-9: **source.dtd: A simple SOURCE DTD**

```
<!-- ............................................... -->
<!-- Genealogy Source DTD  ................................. -->
<!-- file: source.dtd
```

Continued

Listing 34-9: *(continued)*

```
            This DTD describes a SOURCE element intended for use
            in family tree documents. It was developed as an example
            for Chapter 34 of the XML Bible, Gold Edition, by
            Elliotte Rusty Harold (elharo@metalab.unc.edu)
            Published by Hungry Minds 2001. ISBN 0-7645-4819-0.

            This schema is placed in the public domain. Please
            feel free to use it or adapt it in any way you like.

            This DTD is identified by the PUBLIC and SYSTEM
            identifiers:

            PUBLIC "-//ERH//Genealogy Source DTD 1.0//EN"
            SYSTEM "source.dtd"

            All the elements declared in this DTD are in the
            http://ns.cafeconleche.org/genealogy/ namespace.
            No prefix is used. The attributes are in no namespace.

            It is not a formal standard, and has not been considered
            or approved by any standards body.

            .............................................. -->

<!-- SOURCE is the root element of documents that use this
     DTD. However, it is more intended to be used as a part
     of larger XML applications which would contain multiple
     SOURCE elements in a single document. -->

<!-- The character data of the DTD contains a bibliographic
     citation for the source -->
<!ELEMENT  SOURCE  (#PCDATA)>
<!ATTLIST  SOURCE ID ID #REQUIRED>
```

Listing 34-10 shows the almost equally simple source schema. This is an example of a schema that only defines types. It does not actually declare any elements and cannot be used on its own to validate a document. However, it can be included in another schema that does declare elements of type SourceType.

Listing 34-10: source.xsd: A simple SOURCE schema

```
<?xml version="1.0"?>
<xsd:schema xmlns:xsd="http://www.w3.org/2001/XMLSchema"
  xmlns="http://ns.cafeconleche.org/genealogy/"
  targetNamespace="http://ns.cafeconleche.org/genealogy/"
  elementFormDefault="qualified"
```

```
      attributeFormDefault="unqualified"
 >

   <xsd:annotation>
     <xsd:documentation>
       This schema describes a REFERENCE element intended for
       use in family tree documents. It was developed as an
       example for Chapter 34 of the XML Bible, Gold Edition, by
       Elliotte Rusty Harold (elharo@metalab.unc.edu)
       Published by Hungry Minds 2001. ISBN 0-7645-4819-0.

       This schema is placed in the public domain. Please
       feel free to use it or adapt it in any way you like.
     </xsd:documentation>
   </xsd:annotation>

   <xsd:complexType name="SourceType">
     <xsd:annotation>
       <xsd:documentation>
         The SourceType is used exclusively for REFERENCE
         elements. Each such element has a unique ID attribute
         by which it can be referred to, and PCDATA content
         identifying the source of the information; e.g.,
         a document, an interview, personal recollection, etc.
       </xsd:documentation>
     </xsd:annotation>
     <xsd:simpleContent>
       <xsd:extension base="xsd:string">
         <xsd:attribute name="ID" type="xsd:ID" use="required"/>
       </xsd:extension>
     </xsd:simpleContent>
   </xsd:complexType>

   <xsd:element name="SOURCE" type="SourceType"/>

 </xsd:schema>
```

The Family Tree

It's now possible to combine the various people, families, and sources into a single grouping that includes everyone. I'll call the root element of this document FAM-ILY_TREE. It will include PERSON, FAMILY, and SOURCE elements in no particular order. Listing 34-11 shows a complete family tree document that includes 11 people, three families, and seven sources. The necessary document type declaration and schema location attributes have been attached in the right places.

Listing 34-11: **An XML document of a complete family tree**

```
<?xml version="1.0" standalone="no"?>
<!DOCTYPE FAMILY_TREE SYSTEM "family_tree.dtd">
<FAMILY_TREE xmlns="http://ns.cafeconleche.org/genealogy/"
   xmlns:xsi="http://www.w3.org/2001/XMLSchema-instance"
   xsi:schemaLocation =
       "http://ns.cafeconleche.org/genealogy/ family_tree.xsd
        http://www.w3.org/1999/xhtml xhtml1.1.xsd">

  <PERSON ID="p23" SEX="M">
    <REFERENCE SOURCE="s44"/>
    <FATHER PERSON="p37"/>
    <MOTHER PERSON="p1099"/>
    <NAME>
      <GIVEN>Judson McDaniel</GIVEN>
      <SURNAME>Anderson</SURNAME>
    </NAME>
    <BIRTH>
      <PLACE>Montgomery County, KY, 1893</PLACE>
      <DATE>19 Jul 1894</DATE>
    </BIRTH>
    <DEATH>
      <PLACE>Mt. Sterling, KY</PLACE>
      <DATE>27 Apr 1941</DATE>
    </DEATH>
    <NOTE>
      <body xmlns="http://www.w3.org/1999/xhtml">
      <p>Agriculture College in Iowa</p>
      <p>Farmer</p>
      <p>32nd degree Mason</p>
      <p>
        He shot himself in the pond in the back of Sideview
        when he found that he was terminally ill. It has also
        been claimed that he was having money and wife
        troubles. (He and Zelda did not get along and he was
        embarrassed to have married her.) It has further been
        claimed that this was part of the Anderson family
        curse.
      </p>
    </body>
    </NOTE>
  </PERSON>

  <PERSON ID="p36" SEX="F">
    <REFERENCE SOURCE="s43"/>
    <FATHER PERSON="p37"/>
    <MOTHER PERSON="p1099"/>
    <NAME>
      <GIVEN>Mary English</GIVEN>
      <SURNAME>Anderson</SURNAME>
```

```
    </NAME>
    <BIRTH>
      <PLACE>August 4, 1902?, Sideview, KY</PLACE>
      <DATE>8 Apr 1902</DATE>
    </BIRTH>
    <DEATH>
      <PLACE>Mt. Sterling, KY</PLACE>
      <DATE>19 Dec 1972</DATE>
    </DEATH>
  </PERSON>

  <PERSON ID="p37" SEX="M">
    <REFERENCE SOURCE="s29"/>
    <REFERENCE SOURCE="s43"/>
    <FATHER PERSON="p1035"/>
    <MOTHER PERSON="p1098"/>
    <NAME>
      <GIVEN>Samuel English</GIVEN>
      <SURNAME>Anderson</SURNAME>
    </NAME>
    <BIRTH>
      <PLACE>Sideview</PLACE>
      <DATE>25 Aug 1871</DATE>
    </BIRTH>
    <DEATH>
      <PLACE>Mt. Sterling, KY</PLACE>
      <DATE>10 Nov 1919</DATE>
    </DEATH>
    <NOTE>
      <body xmlns="http://www.w3.org/1999/xhtml">
        <p>
          Samuel English Anderson was known in Montgomery
          County for his red hair and the temper that went
          with it. He did once <strong>kill a man</strong>,
          but the court found that it was in self-defense.
        </p>

        <p>
          He was shot by a farm worker whom he had
          fired the day before for smoking in a tobacco barn.
          Hamp says this may have been self-defense, because he
          threatened to kill the workers for smoking in the
          barn. Hamp also says old-time rumors say they mashed
          his head with a fence post. Beth heard he was cut to
          death with machetes in the field, but Hamp says they
          wouldn't be cutting tobacco in November, only
          stripping it in the barn.
        </p>
      </body>
    </NOTE>

  </PERSON>
```

Continued

Listing 34-11: *(continued)*

```
<PERSON ID="p1033" SEX="M">
  <REFERENCE SOURCE="s43"/>
  <FATHER PERSON="p37"/>
  <MOTHER PERSON="p1099"/>
  <NAME>
    <GIVEN>Thomas Corwin</GIVEN>
    <SURNAME>Anderson</SURNAME>
  </NAME>
  <BIRTH>
    <DATE>16 Jan 1898</DATE>
  </BIRTH>
  <DEATH>
    <PLACE>Probably Australia</PLACE>
  </DEATH>
  <NOTE>
    <body xmlns="http://www.w3.org/1999/xhtml">
      <p>
      Corwin fought with his father and then left home.
      His last letter was from Australia.
      </p>
    </body>
  </NOTE>
</PERSON>

<PERSON ID="p1034" SEX="M">
  <REFERENCE SOURCE="s43"/>
  <FATHER PERSON="p37"/>
  <MOTHER PERSON="p1099"/>
  <NAME>
    <GIVEN>Rodger French</GIVEN>
    <SURNAME>Anderson</SURNAME>
  </NAME>
  <BIRTH>
    <DATE>26 Nov 1899</DATE>
  </BIRTH>
  <DEATH>
    <PLACE>Birmingham, AL</PLACE>
  </DEATH>
  <NOTE>
    <body xmlns="http://www.w3.org/1999/xhtml">
      <p>
      Killed when the car he was driving hit a pig in the
      road. Despite the many suicides in the family, this is
      the only known sowicide.
      </p>
    </body>
  </NOTE>
</PERSON>
```

```
<PERSON ID="p1035" SEX="M">
  <NAME>
    <GIVEN>Thomas Corwin</GIVEN>
    <SURNAME>Anderson</SURNAME>
  </NAME>
  <BIRTH>
    <DATE>24 Aug 1845</DATE>
  </BIRTH>
  <DEATH>
    <PLACE>Mt. Sterling, KY</PLACE>
    <DATE>18 Sep 1889</DATE>
  </DEATH>
  <NOTE>
    <body xmlns="http://www.w3.org/1999/xhtml">
      <p>Yale 1869 (did not graduate)</p>
      <p>Breeder of short horn cattle</p>
      <p>He was named after an Ohio senator. The name Corwin
        is from the Latin <span xml:lang="la">corvinus</span>
        which means raven and is akin
        to <em>corbin</em>/<em>corbet</em>.
        In old French it was <span xml:lang="la">cord</span>
        and in Middle English <em>Corse</em> which meant raven
        or cow.
      </p>
      <p>Attended Annapolis for one year, possibly to
        avoid service in the Civil War.</p>
      <p>
        He farmed the old Mitchell farm
        and became known as a leading short horn breeder.
        He suffered from asthma and wanted to move to
        Colorado in 1876 to avoid the Kentucky weather, but
        he didn't.
      </p>
    </body>
  </NOTE>
</PERSON>

<PERSON ID="p1098" SEX="F">
  <REFERENCE SOURCE="s29"/>
  <NAME>
    <GIVEN>LeAnah (Lee Anna, Annie) DeMint</GIVEN>
    <SURNAME>English</SURNAME>
  </NAME>
  <BIRTH>
    <PLACE>Louisville, KY</PLACE>
    <DATE>1 Mar 1843</DATE>
  </BIRTH>
  <DEATH>
    <REFERENCE SOURCE="s16"/>
    <PLACE>acute Bright's disease, 504 E. Broadway</PLACE>
    <DATE>31 Oct 1898</DATE>
```

Continued

Listing 34-11: *(continued)*

```
    </DEATH>
    <NOTE>
      <body xmlns="http://www.w3.org/1999/xhtml">
        <p>Writer (pseudonymously) for Louisville Herald</p>
        <p>Ann or Annie was from Louisville. She wrote under
          an assumed name for the Louisville Herald.</p>
      </body>
    </NOTE>
  </PERSON>

  <PERSON ID="p1099" SEX="F">
    <REFERENCE SOURCE="s39"/>
    <FATHER PERSON="p1100"/>
    <MOTHER PERSON="p1101"/>
    <NAME>
      <GIVEN>Cora Rucker (Blevins?)</GIVEN>
      <SURNAME>McDaniel</SURNAME>
    </NAME>
    <BIRTH>
      <DATE>1 Aug 1873</DATE>
    </BIRTH>
    <DEATH>
      <REFERENCE SOURCE="s41"/>
      <REFERENCE SOURCE="s60"/>
      <PLACE>Sideview, bronchial trouble TB</PLACE>
      <DATE>21 Jul 1909</DATE>
    </DEATH>
    <NOTE>
      <body xmlns="http://www.w3.org/1999/xhtml">
        <p>She was engaged to General Hood of the Confederacy,
        but she was seeing Mr. Anderson on the side. A servant
        was posted to keep Mr. Anderson away. However the girl
        fell asleep, and Cora eloped with Mr. Anderson.</p>
      </body>
    </NOTE>
  </PERSON>

  <PERSON ID="p1100" SEX="M">
    <NAME>
      <GIVEN>Judson</GIVEN>
      <SURNAME>McDaniel</SURNAME>
    </NAME>
    <BIRTH>
      <DATE>21 Feb 1834</DATE>
    </BIRTH>
    <DEATH>
      <DATE>9 Dec 1905</DATE>
    </DEATH>
  </PERSON>
```

```
<PERSON ID="p1101" SEX="F">
  <NAME>
    <GIVEN>Mary E.</GIVEN>
    <SURNAME>Blevins</SURNAME>
  </NAME>
  <BIRTH>
    <DATE>1847</DATE>
  </BIRTH>
  <DEATH>
    <DATE>1886</DATE>
  </DEATH>
  <BURIAL>
    <PLACE>Machpelah Cemetery, Mt. Sterling KY</PLACE>
  </BURIAL>
</PERSON>

<PERSON ID="p1102" SEX="M">
  <REFERENCE SOURCE="s29"/>
  <NAME>
    <GIVEN>John Jay (Robin Adair)</GIVEN>
    <SURNAME>Anderson</SURNAME>
  </NAME>
  <BIRTH>
    <REFERENCE SOURCE="s43"/>
    <PLACE>Sideview</PLACE>
    <DATE>13 May 1873</DATE>
  </BIRTH>
  <DEATH>
    <DATE>18 Sep 1889</DATE>
  </DEATH>
  <NOTE>
    <body xmlns="http://www.w3.org/1999/xhtml">
      <p>
        Died of flux. Rumored to have been killed by his
        brother.
      </p>
    </body>
  </NOTE>
</PERSON>

<FAMILY ID="f25">
  <HUSBAND PERSON="p37"/>
  <WIFE PERSON="p1099"/>
  <CHILD PERSON="p23"/>
  <CHILD PERSON="p36"/>
  <CHILD PERSON="p1033"/>
  <CHILD PERSON="p1034"/>
</FAMILY>
```

Continued

Listing 34-11: *(continued)*

```
<FAMILY ID="f732">
  <HUSBAND PERSON="p1035"/>
  <WIFE PERSON="p1098"/>
  <CHILD PERSON="p1102"/>
  <CHILD PERSON="p37"/>
</FAMILY>

<FAMILY ID="f779">
  <HUSBAND PERSON="p1102"/>
</FAMILY>

<SOURCE ID="s16">newspaper death notice in purse</SOURCE>
<SOURCE ID="s29">English-Demint Anderson Bible</SOURCE>
<SOURCE ID="s39">
  Judson McDaniel &amp; Mary E. Blevins Bible
</SOURCE>
<SOURCE ID="s41">
  Cora McDaniel obituary, clipping from unknown newspaper
</SOURCE>
<SOURCE ID="s43">Anderson Bible</SOURCE>
<SOURCE ID="s44">
  A Sesquicentennial History of Kentucky
  Frederik A. Wallis &amp; Hambleon Tapp, 1945,
  The Historical Record Association, Hopkinsville, KY
</SOURCE>
<SOURCE ID="s60">
  Interview with Ann Sandusky, May 1996
</SOURCE>

</FAMILY_TREE>
```

The Family Tree DTD

FAMILY_TREE is the one new element in Listing 34-10. It can contain any number of PERSON, FAMILY, and SOURCE elements in any order. This is indicated with a choice:

```
<!ELEMENT FAMILY_TREE (PERSON | FAMILY | SOURCE)*>
```

It's not necessary to redeclare the PERSON, FAMILY, and SOURCE elements and their children. Instead, these can be imported by importing the family and source DTDs with external parameter entity references. The family DTD then imports the person DTD:

```
<!ENTITY % family SYSTEM "family.dtd">
%family;
<!ENTITY % source SYSTEM "source.dtd">
%source;
```

One thing you want to do at this point is switch from using NMTOKEN types for spouses, parents, and references to actual ID types. This is because a FAMILY element that's part of a FAMILY_TREE should include all necessary PERSON elements. You can do that by overriding the personref and sourceref parameter entity declarations in the DTD for the family tree:

```
<!ENTITY % personref "PERSON IDREF #REQUIRED">
<!ENTITY % sourceref "SOURCE IDREF #REQUIRED">
```

That's all you need. Everything else is contained in the imported person and family DTDs. Listing 34-12 shows the family tree DTD.

Listing 34-12: **familytree.dtd: The family tree DTD**

```
<!-- ............................................. -->
<!-- Genealogy Family Tree DTD  ...................... -->
<!-- file: family_tree.dtd

     This DTD describes a FAMILY_TREE element intended for use
     as the root element in family tree documents. It was
     developed as an example for Chapter 34 of the
     XML Bible, Gold Edition,
     by Elliotte Rusty Harold (elharo@metalab.unc.edu)
     Published by Hungry Minds 2001. ISBN 0-7645-4819-0.

     This DTD is placed in the public domain. Please
     feel free to use it or adapt it in any way you like.

     This DTD is identified by the PUBLIC and SYSTEM
     identifiers:

     PUBLIC "-//ERH//Genealogy Family Tree DTD 1.0//EN"
     SYSTEM "family_tree.dtd"

     All the elements declared in this DTD are in the
     http://ns.cafeconleche.org/genealogy/ namespace.
     No prefix is used. The attributes are in no namespace.

     It is not a formal standard, and has not been considered
     or approved by any standards body.

     ............................................. -->

<!-- Predefine the %personref; and %sourceref; parameter entity
     references so that they'll have type IDREF instead
     of NMTOKEN -->
<!ENTITY % personref "PERSON IDREF #REQUIRED">
<!ENTITY % sourceref "SOURCE IDREF #REQUIRED">
```

Continued

Listing 34-12: *(continued)*

```
<!-- Import the family and source DTDs. The family DTD imports
     the person DTD. -->
<!ENTITY % family SYSTEM "family.dtd">
%family;

<!ENTITY % source SYSTEM "source.dtd">
%source;

<!-- A family tree consists of any number of SOURCE, PERSON,
and
     FAMILY elements in any order. These are all top-level
     elements that refer to each other by ID attributes
     and references. None of them contain any of the others.
-->
<!ELEMENT FAMILY_TREE (SOURCE | PERSON | FAMILY )*>
```

The family tree schema

The family tree schema is similar in general structure to the family tree DTD. It defines one new element, FAMILY_TREE, and uses most of the existing definitions of the other elements. However, now that we have all the FAMILY and PERSON and SOURCE elements in one document, it would be good to change the various reference attributes from type NMTOKEN to type IDREF. In the DTD, this was done by predefining certain parameter entity references. In the schema, we use the xsd:redefine element instead. This behaves like the xsd:include element except that you can place type definitions inside xsd:redefine that override the type definitions made in the included schemas. For example, this xsd:redefine element imports most of the family schema (which itself includes the person schema) but overrides the definitions of PersonRefType and SourceRefType:

```
<xsd:redefine schemaLocation="person.xsd">
  <!-- Because all referenced persons will now be included
       in this document, we can switch the pointer attributes
       from name tokens to ID references. -->

  <xsd:complexType name="PersonRefType">
    <xsd:complexContent>
      <xsd:restriction base="PersonRefType">
        <xsd:attribute name="PERSON" type="xsd:IDREF"/>
      </xsd:restriction>
    </xsd:complexContent>
  </xsd:complexType>
```

```
    <xsd:complexType name="ReferenceType">
      <xsd:complexContent>
        <xsd:restriction base="ReferenceType">
          <xsd:attribute name="SOURCE" type="xsd:IDREF"/>
        </xsd:restriction>
      </xsd:complexContent>
    </xsd:complexType>

  </xsd:redefine>
```

Listing 34-13 shows the complete family tree schema.

Listing 34-13: **familytree.xsd: The family tree schema**

```
<?xml version="1.0"?>
<xsd:schema xmlns:xsd="http://www.w3.org/2001/XMLSchema"
  xmlns="http://ns.cafeconleche.org/genealogy/"
  targetNamespace="http://ns.cafeconleche.org/genealogy/"
  elementFormDefault="qualified"
  attributeFormDefault="unqualified"
>

  <xsd:annotation>
    <xsd:documentation>
      This schema describes a FAMILY_TREE element intended for
      use as the root element genealogy documents. It was
      developed as an example for Chapter 34 of the XML Bible,
      Gold Edition, by Elliotte Rusty Harold
      (elharo@metalab. unc.edu)
      Published by Hungry Minds 2001. ISBN 0-7645-4819-0.

      This schema is placed in the public domain. Please
      use it or adapt it in any way you like.
    </xsd:documentation>
  </xsd:annotation>

  <xsd:include schemaLocation="source.xsd"/>

  <xsd:include schemaLocation="family.xsd"/>

  <xsd:redefine schemaLocation="person.xsd">
    <!-- Because all referenced persons will now be included
         in this document, we can switch the pointer attributes
         from name tokens to ID references. -->

    <xsd:complexType name="PersonRefType">
      <xsd:complexContent>
        <xsd:restriction base="PersonRefType">
          <xsd:attribute name="PERSON" type="xsd:IDREF"/>
```

Continued

> **Listing 34-13:** *(continued)*

```
        </xsd:restriction>
      </xsd:complexContent>
    </xsd:complexType>

    <xsd:complexType name="ReferenceType">
      <xsd:complexContent>
        <xsd:restriction base="ReferenceType">
          <xsd:attribute name="SOURCE" type="xsd:IDREF"/>
        </xsd:restriction>
      </xsd:complexContent>
    </xsd:complexType>

  </xsd:redefine>

  <xsd:complexType name="FamilyTreeType">
    <xsd:choice minOccurs="0" maxOccurs="unbounded">
      <xsd:element ref="PERSON"/>
      <xsd:element ref="FAMILY"/>
      <xsd:element ref="SOURCE"/>
    </xsd:choice>
  </xsd:complexType>

  <xsd:element name="FAMILY_TREE" type="FamilyTreeType"/>

</xsd:schema>
```

Modularizing the DTDs

As written, the genealogy DTD is already partially modular. It is divided into separate files for the PERSON, FAMILY, SOURCE, and FAMILYTREE elements. It does use parameter entity references for some content models and attribute lists. It does use the DTDs for Modular XHTML and XHTML Basic. However, it's not nearly as modular as the SMIL 2.0 DTD explored in Chapter 28 or the modular XHTML DTDs explored in Chapter 30.

This is not unusual at this point. Modular DTDs can be hard to read and hard to follow as compared to monolithic DTDs. When designing a new XML application, it's easiest to make everything explicit, at least at the start. However, after the basic application is designed, it's time to ask yourself if there are any ways in which you can restructure the DTD to make it more extensible in the future without changing what is and is not allowed now.

I'm not sure we really need that much modularity here. For one thing, in a data-oriented application such as this, you may well want to limit the permissible content models and attributes of elements and not allow them to be so easily modified. However, at the very least, you should allow the author to choose whether and which namespace prefix the author wants to use. To do this, you have to define the prefix and all element names as parameter entity references rather than directly. You saw this technique previously in Chapters 28 and 30. Let's begin by creating a new DTD module that does nothing but define parameter entity references for the namespace URI and prefix. Listing 34-14 demonstrates.

Listing 34-14: **genealogy-namespace.mod: The namespace DTD module**

```
<!-- .............................................. -->
<!-- Genealogy Namespace Module  ........................ -->
<!-- file: genealogy-namespace.mod

     This DTD is in the public domain.

     This DTD module is identified by the PUBLIC and SYSTEM
     identifiers:

     PUBLIC "-//ERH//Genealogy Namespace Parts 1.0//EN"
     SYSTEM "genealogy-namespace.mod"

     .............................................. -->

<!-- Genealogy Namespace

     This module declares parameter entities to support
     namespace-qualified names, namespace declarations, and
     name prefixing for the genealogy application developed
     in Chapter 34 of the XML Bible Gold Edition.

-->

<!-- 1. Declare the parameter entity containing
        the namespace URI for the genealogy namespace: -->

<!ENTITY % GENEALOGY.xmlns
"http://ns.cafeconleche.org/genealogy/" >

<!-- 2. Declare the parameter entity containing
        the default namespace prefix string to use when
        prefixing is enabled. This may be overridden. -->
```

Continued

Listing 34-14: *(continued)*

```
<!ENTITY % SMIL.prefix   "" >

<!-- 3. Declare a %GENEALOGY.prefixed; conditional section
        keyword, used to activate namespace prefixing. The
        default is not to use prefixing. -->
<!ENTITY % GENEALOGY.prefixed "IGNORE" >

<!-- 4. Declare parameter entities containing the
        prefix used when prefixing is active, an empty
        string when it is not.
-->
<![%GENEALOGY.prefixed;[
<!ENTITY % GENEALOGY.pfx   "%GENEALOGY.prefix;:" >
]]>
<!ENTITY % GENEALOGY.pfx   "" >
```

Next, you need a DTD that declares the qualified names of all the elements in terms of these parameter entity references. Listing 34-15 is this module. The double indirection of parameter entity references for the element names is really necessary here only to prevent parsers from inserting extra white space into the middle of element names, but it does make this DTD a little more adaptable.

Listing 34-15: genealogy-qname.mod: The namespace DTD module

```
<!-- .......................................... -->
<!-- Genealogy Qualified Names Module  ................. -->
<!-- file: genealogy-qname.mod

     This DTD is in the public domain.

This DTD module is identified by the PUBLIC and SYSTEM
identifiers:

     PUBLIC "-//ERH//Genealogy Qualified Names 1.0//EN"
     SYSTEM "genealogy-qname.mod"

     ........................................... -->

<!-- Genealogy Qualified Names

     This module declares parameter entities to support
     namespace-qualified names for the genealogy application
     developed in Chapter 34 of the XML Bible Gold Edition.
```

```
-->

<!-- module: person.mod -->
<!ENTITY % PERSON.qname    "%GENEALOGY.pfx;PERSON" >
<!ENTITY % REFERENCE.qname "%GENEALOGY.pfx;REFERENCE" >
<!ENTITY % BIRTH.qname     "%GENEALOGY.pfx;BIRTH" >
<!ENTITY % BAPTISM.qname   "%GENEALOGY.pfx;BAPTISM" >
<!ENTITY % DEATH.qname     "%GENEALOGY.pfx;DEATH" >
<!ENTITY % PLACE.qname     "%GENEALOGY.pfx;PLACE" >
<!ENTITY % DATE.qname      "%GENEALOGY.pfx;DATE" >
<!ENTITY % SPOUSE.qname    "%GENEALOGY.pfx;SPOUSE" >
<!ENTITY % FATHER.qname    "%GENEALOGY.pfx;FATHER" >
<!ENTITY % MOTHER.qname    "%GENEALOGY.pfx;MOTHER" >
<!ENTITY % NAME.qname      "%GENEALOGY.pfx;NAME" >
<!ENTITY % GIVEN.qname     "%GENEALOGY.pfx;GIVEN" >
<!ENTITY % SURNAME.qname   "%GENEALOGY.pfx;SURNAME" >
<!ENTITY % NOTE.qname      "%GENEALOGY.pfx;NOTE" >

<!-- module: family.mod -->
<!ENTITY % HUSBAND.qname   "%GENEALOGY.pfx;HUSBAND" >
<!ENTITY % WIFE.qname      "%GENEALOGY.pfx;WIFE" >
<!ENTITY % CHILD.qname     "%GENEALOGY.pfx;CHILD" >
<!ENTITY % DIVORCE.qname   "%GENEALOGY.pfx;DIVORCE" >
<!ENTITY % MARRIAGE.qname  "%GENEALOGY.pfx;MARRIAGE" >

<!-- module: source.mod -->
<!ENTITY % SOURCE.qname    "%GENEALOGY.pfx;SOURCE" >

<!-- module: family_tree.mod -->
<!ENTITY % FAMILY_TREE.qname "%GENEALOGY.pfx;FAMILY_TREE" >

<!-- end of genealogy-qname-1.mod -->
```

Next, we rewrite the person, source, and family DTDs to use the parameter entities defined in Listing 34-15. These DTDs are shown in Listings 34-16 through 34-19:

Listing 34-16: **person.mod: The person module**

```
<!-- ............................................ -->
<!-- Genealogy Person DTD module ................ -->
<!-- file: person.mod

     This DTD module describes a PERSON element intended for
     use in family tree documents. It was developed as part of
     a genealogy example in Chapter 34 of the
     XML Bible, Gold Edition, by
```

Continued

Listing 34-16: *(continued)*

```
    Elliotte Rusty Harold (elharo@metalab.unc.edu)
    Published by Hungry Minds 2001. ISBN 0-7645-4819-0.

    This DTD is placed in the public domain. Please
    feel free to use it or adapt it in any way you like.

    This DTD is identified by the PUBLIC and SYSTEM
    identifiers:

    PUBLIC "-//ERH//Genealogy Person Module 1.0//EN"
    SYSTEM "person.mod"

    It is not a formal standard, and has not been considered
    or approved by any standards body.

    ........................................................ -->

<!ELEMENT %PERSON.qname; ( %NAME.qname;    | %REFERENCE.qname; |
                           %BIRTH.qname;   | %DEATH.qname;     |
                           %BURIAL.qname;  | %BAPTISM.qname;   |
                           %NOTE.qname;    | %FATHER.qname;    |
                           %MOTHER.qname;  | %SPOUSE )* >

<!ATTLIST %PERSON.qname;
   xmlns   CDATA  #FIXED "http://ns.cafeconleche.org/genealogy/"
   ID      ID     #REQUIRED>

<!ATTLIST %PERSON.qname;
   xmlns:xsi CDATA #FIXED "http://www.w3.org/2001/XMLSchema-
instance"
   xsi:schemaLocation CDATA #IMPLIED
>

<!--M means male, F means female -->
<!ATTLIST %PERSON.qname; SEX (M | F) #IMPLIED>

<!-- The ID number of a SOURCE element that documents
     this entry -->
<!ELEMENT %REFERENCE.qname;  EMPTY>
<!ENTITY % sourceref "SOURCE NMTOKEN #REQUIRED">
<!ATTLIST %REFERENCE.qname; %sourceref;>

<!-- Events are occurrences at a certain
     time and place, though the exact time and place may
     not be known for certain. Events include marriages,
     births, deaths, baptisms, and burials.  -->
<!ENTITY % event   "(%REFERENCE.qname;*, %PLACE.qname;?,
%DATE.qname;?)">
```

```
<!ELEMENT  %BIRTH.qname;    %event;>
<!ELEMENT  %BAPTISM.qname;  %event;>
<!ELEMENT  %DEATH.qname;    %event;>
<!ELEMENT  %BURIAL.qname;   %event;>

<!ELEMENT  %PLACE.qname;    (#PCDATA)>
<!ELEMENT  %DATE.qname;     (#PCDATA)>

<!-- A person reference is a pointer to another person
     encoded in a PERSON element. The pointer is the ID
     of the PERSON pointed to. -->
<!ENTITY % personref "PERSON NMTOKEN #REQUIRED">
<!ELEMENT  %SPOUSE.qname;   EMPTY>
<!ATTLIST  %SPOUSE.qname;   %personref;>
<!ELEMENT  %FATHER.qname;   EMPTY>
<!ATTLIST  %FATHER.qname;   %personref;>
<!ELEMENT  %MOTHER.qname;   EMPTY>
<!ATTLIST  %MOTHER.qname;   %personref;>

<!-- Middle names should be encoded as part of the
     given name; e.g.,
     <NAME>
       <GIVEN>Elliotte Rusty</GIVEN>
       <SURNAME>Harold</SURNAME>
     </NAME>
 -->
<!ELEMENT  %NAME.qname;     (%GIVEN.qname;?, %SURNAME.qname;?)>
<!ELEMENT  %GIVEN.qname;    (#PCDATA)>
<!ELEMENT  %SURNAME.qname;  (#PCDATA)>

<!ELEMENT  NOTE    (REFERENCE*, body)>
```

Listing 34-17: **family.mod: The family module**

```
<!-- .............................................. -->
<!-- Genealogy Family DTD  ............................ -->
<!-- file: family.mod

    This DTD module describes a FAMILY element intended for
    use in family tree documents. It was developed as an
    example for Chapter 34 of the XML Bible, Gold Edition, by
    Elliotte Rusty Harold (elharo@metalab.unc.edu)
    Published by Hungry Minds 2001. ISBN 0-7645-4819-0.

    This DTD is placed in the public domain. Please
    feel free to use it or adapt it in any way you like.
```

Continued

Listing 34-17: *(continued)*

```
         This DTD is identified by the PUBLIC and SYSTEM
         identifiers:

         PUBLIC "-//ERH//Genealogy Family Module 1.0//EN"
         SYSTEM "family.mod"

         All the elements declared in this DTD are in the
         http://ns.cafeconleche.org/genealogy/ namespace.
         No prefix is used. The attributes are in no namespace.

         It is not a formal standard, and has not been considered
         or approved by any standards body.

         .............................................. -->

<!-- FAMILY is the root element of documents that use this
     DTD. However, it is more intended to be used as a part
     of larger XML applications which would contain multiple
     FAMILY elements in a single document. -->

<!-- A FAMILY can consist of as little as one person  -->
<!ELEMENT %FAMILY.qname; (%REFERENCE.qname;*, %HUSBAND.qname;?,
   %WIFE.qname;?, %CHILD.qname;*, MARRIAGE.qname;*,
   %DIVORCE.qname;*, %NOTE.qname;*)>
<!ATTLIST  %FAMILY.qname; ID ID #REQUIRED>

<!-- HUSBAND and WIFE are used here for legacy reasons.
     They should not be taken to imply anything about
     marital state of the parties.  -->
<!-- HUSBAND, WIFE, and CHILD are all EMPTY elements that
     point to a PERSON element by matching its ID.  -->
<!ELEMENT   %HUSBAND.qname;   EMPTY>
<!ATTLIST   %HUSBAND.qname;   %personref;>
<!ELEMENT   %WIFE.qname;      EMPTY>
<!ATTLIST   %WIFE.qname;      %personref;>
<!ELEMENT   %CHILD.qname;     EMPTY>
<!ATTLIST   %CHILD.qname;     %personref;>
<!ELEMENT   %DIVORCE.qname;   %event;>
<!ELEMENT   %MARRIAGE.qname;  %event;>
```

Listing 34-18: **source.mod: The source module**

```
<!-- .............................................. -->
<!-- Genealogy Source Module  ........................... -->
<!-- file: source.mod
```

This DTD describes a SOURCE element intended for use
in family tree documents. It was developed as an example
for Chapter 34 of the XML Bible, Gold Edition, by
Elliotte Rusty Harold (elharo@metalab.unc.edu)
Published by Hungry Minds 2001. ISBN 0-7645-4819-0.

This DTD is placed in the public domain. Please
feel free to use it or adapt it in any way you like.

This DTD is identified by the PUBLIC and SYSTEM
identifiers:

PUBLIC "-//ERH//Genealogy Source Module 1.0//EN"
SYSTEM "source.mod"

It is not a formal standard, and has not been considered
or approved by any standards body.

.... -->

```
<!-- SOURCE is the root element of documents that use this
     DTD. However, it is more intended to be used as a part
     of larger XML applications, which would contain multiple
     SOURCE elements in a single document. -->

<!-- The character data of the DTD contains a bibliographic
     citation for the source -->
<!ELEMENT  %SOURCE.qname; (#PCDATA)>
<!ATTLIST  %SOURCE.qname; ID ID #REQUIRED>
```

Listing 34-19: **family_tree.mod: The family tree module**

```
<!-- ................................................. -->
<!-- Genealogy Family Tree Module  ...........................
-->
<!-- file: family_tree.mod
```

This DTD describes a FAMILY_TREE element intended for use
as the root element in family tree documents. It was
developed as an example for Chapter 34 of the
XML Bible, Gold Edition,
by Elliotte Rusty Harold (elharo@metalab.unc.edu)
Published by Hungry Minds 2001. ISBN 0-7645-4819-0.

This schema is placed in the public domain. Please
feel free to use it or adapt it in any way you like.

Continued

Listing 34-19: *(continued)*

```
        This DTD is identified by the PUBLIC and SYSTEM
        identifiers:

        PUBLIC "-//ERH//Genealogy Family Tree Module 1.0//EN"
               "family_tree.mod"

        SYSTEM "family_tree.mod"

        It is not a formal standard, and has not been considered
        or approved by any standards body.

        .................................................. -->

<!-- A family tree consists of any number of SOURCE, PERSON,
     and FAMILY elements in any order. These are all top-level
     elements that refer to each other by ID attributes
     and references. None of them contain any of the others.
-->
<!ELEMENT %FAMILY_TREE.qname; (
  %SOURCE.qname; | %PERSON.qname; | %FAMILY.qname;
  )*
>
```

Finally, we write the complete driver DTD for family trees that imports all five DTDs, as well as XHTML Basic. Listing 34-20 demonstrates.

Listing 34-20: **FamilyTree_driver.dtd: The driver DTD**

```
<!-- .................................................. -->
<!-- Genealogy Family Tree Driver DTD  .................... -->
<!-- file: FamilyTree_driver.dtd

     This DTD describes a FAMILY_TREE element intended for use
     as the root element in family tree documents. It was
     developed as an example for Chapter 34 of the
     XML Bible, Gold Edition,
     by Elliotte Rusty Harold (elharo@metalab.unc.edu)
     Published by Hungry Minds 2001. ISBN 0-7645-4819-0.

     This DTD is placed in the public domain. Please
     feel free to use it or adapt it in any way you like.

     This DTD is identified by the PUBLIC and SYSTEM
```

```
        identifiers:

        PUBLIC "-//ERH//Genealogy Family Tree DTD 1.0//EN"
               "family_tree.dtd"

        SYSTEM "family_tree.dtd"

        It is not a formal standard, and has not been considered
        or approved by any standards body.

        ............................................... -->
<!-- Define namespaces and qualified names -->
<!ENTITY % namespaces SYSTEM "genealogy-namespaces.mod">
%namespaces;
<!ENTITY % qnames SYSTEM "genealogy-qname.mod">
%qnames;

<!-- Import XHTML Basic -->
<!ENTITY % xhtml PUBLIC "-//W3C//DTD XHTML Basic 1.0//EN"
                        "xhtml-basic10.dtd">
%xhtml;

<!ENTITY % personref "PERSON IDREF #REQUIRED">
<!ENTITY % sourceref "SOURCE IDREF #REQUIRED">

<!ENTITY % source PUBLIC
    "-//ERH//Genealogy Source Module 1.0//EN"
    "source.mod">
%source;

<!ENTITY % person PUBLIC
    "-//ERH//Genealogy Person Module 1.0//EN"
    "person.mod"
>
%person;

<!ENTITY % family PUBLIC
    "-//ERH//Genealogy Family Module 1.0//EN"
    "family.mod"
>
%family;

<!ENTITY % family_tree PUBLIC
    "-//ERH//Genealogy Family Tree Module 1.0//EN"
    "family_tree.mod">
%family_tree;
```

As written, Listings 34-16 through 34-19 can only be used in conjunction with Listing 34-20 because they don't import the namespace and qualified names modules that declare the parameter entities that they use. However, if it were important that they be able to be used independently, it would not be hard to import the namespace and qualified names modules in a different driver DTD.

No further work is necessary to modularize the schemas. The schemas are already as modular as they need to be. Since schemas only consider namespace URIs and not prefixes, no special tricks are needed to allow authors to change the prefix. Furthermore, schemas allow new types to be derived from existing types, and allow existing types to be redefined in new schemas by using `xsd:redefine` in place of `xsd:include`. All the modularity and extensibility that takes so much work to set up in a DTD comes almost for free with schemas. That's one of the big advantages schemas have over DTDs.

Designing a Style Sheet for Family Trees

The family tree document is organized as a data file rather than as a narrative. To get a reasonably pleasing view of the document, you need to reorder and reorganize the contents before displaying them. CSS really isn't powerful enough for this task. Consequently, an XSLT style sheet is called for.

The input document uses multiple namespaces, `http://ns.cafeconleche.org/genealogy/` and `http://www.w3.org/1999/xhtml`. In the input document, both of these are the default namespace on their respective sections. I want to output regular HTML instead of XHTML for better compatibility with legacy browsers, so I need to make sure my output elements are not in any namespace at all. And, of course, there's the XSLT namespace, too. Thus, the style sheet itself needs to distinguish between four different namespaces. This would be far too difficult to do if I had to use the same prefix (or lack thereof) in the style sheet as in the input document. Fortunately, I don't. Instead, I can choose to use prefixes in my style sheet even where I didn't in the input document. Specifically, I will choose:

✦ `xsl` for `http://www.w3.org/1999/XSL/Transform`

✦ `gen` for `http://ns.cafeconleche.org/genealogy/`

✦ `xhtml` for `http://www.w3.org/1999/xhtml`

The resulting `xsl:stylesheet` root element will declare all these namespaces like this:

```
<xsl:stylesheet version="1.0"
  xmlns:xsl="http://www.w3.org/1999/XSL/Transform"
  xmlns:gen="http://ns.cafeconleche.org/genealogy/"
  xmlns:html="http://www.w3.org/1999/xhtml">
```

The default namespace is not explicitly mapped so any element names without prefixes will be in no namespace at all.

Now we're ready to start writing template rules that match the nodes in the input document. It's best to begin with the root node. That way you can apply the style sheet to the document after you write each template to make sure you're getting what you expect. Here the root node is merely replaced by the standard html, head, and body elements. Templates are applied to the FAMILY_TREE root element to continue processing. Note, however, that I have to use the gen namespace prefix on FAMILY_TREE to make sure that I'm selecting the FAMILY_TREE element in the http://ns.cafeconleche.org/genealogy/ namespace and not the FAMILY_TREE element in no namespace.

```
<xsl:template match="/">
  <html>
    <head>
      <title>Family Tree</title>
    </head>
    <body>
      <xsl:apply-templates select="gen:FAMILY_TREE"/>
    </body>
  </html>
</xsl:template>
```

The template rule for the FAMILY_TREE element divides the document into three parts, one each for the families, people, and sources. Templates are applied to each separately. Again, prefixes are used to sort the different elements into the right namespaces.

```
<xsl:template match="gen:FAMILY_TREE">

  <h1>Family Tree</h1>

  <h2>Families</h2>
  <xsl:apply-templates select="gen:FAMILY"/>

  <h2>People</h2>
  <xsl:apply-templates select="gen:PERSON"/>

  <h2>Sources</h2>
  <ul>
    <xsl:apply-templates select="gen:SOURCE"/>
  </ul>

</xsl:template>
```

The SOURCE rule is quite simple. Each source is wrapped in a li element. Furthermore, its ID is attached using the name attribute of the HTML a element. This allows for cross-references directly to the source, as shown below:

```
<xsl:template match="gen:SOURCE">

  <li>
    <xsl:element name="a">
      <xsl:attribute name="name">
        <xsl:value-of select="@ID"/>
      </xsl:attribute>
      <xsl:value-of select="."/>
    </xsl:element>
  </li>

</xsl:template>
```

The PERSON element is much more complex, so I'll break it up into several template rules. The PERSON template rule selects the individual parts, and formats those that aren't too complex. It applies templates to the rest. The name is placed in an h3 header. This is surrounded with an HTML anchor whose name is the person's ID. The BIRTH, DEATH, BAPTISM, and BURIAL elements are formatted as list items, as demonstrated here:

```
<xsl:template match="gen:PERSON">

    <h3>
      <xsl:element name="a">
        <xsl:attribute name="name">
          <xsl:value-of select="@ID"/>
        </xsl:attribute>
      <xsl:value-of select="gen:NAME"/>
      </xsl:element>
    </h3>

    <ul>
      <xsl:if test="gen:BIRTH">
        <li>Born: <xsl:value-of select="gen:BIRTH"/></li>
      </xsl:if>
      <xsl:if test="gen:DEATH">
        <li>Died: <xsl:value-of select="gen:DEATH"/></li>
      </xsl:if>
      <xsl:if test="gen:BAPTISM">
        <li>Baptism: <xsl:value-of select="gen:BAPTISM"/></li>
      </xsl:if>
      <xsl:if test="gen:BURIAL">
        <li>Burial: <xsl:value-of select="gen:BURIAL"/></li>
      </xsl:if>
      <xsl:apply-templates select="gen:FATHER"/>
      <xsl:apply-templates select="gen:MOTHER"/>
```

```
    </ul>

    <xsl:apply-templates select="gen:NOTE"/>

  </xsl:template>
```

The FATHER and MOTHER elements are also list items, but they need to be linked to their respective people. These two template rules do that:

```
    <xsl:template match="gen:FATHER">
      <li>
        <xsl:element name="a">
          <xsl:attribute name="href">#<xsl:value-of
            select="@PERSON"/></xsl:attribute>
          Father
        </xsl:element>
      </li>
    </xsl:template>

    <xsl:template match="gen:MOTHER">
      <li>
        <xsl:element name="a">
          <xsl:attribute name="href">#<xsl:value-of
            select="@PERSON"/></xsl:attribute>
          </xsl:attribute>
          Mother
        </xsl:element>
      </li>
    </xsl:template>
```

I want to comment on a couple of elements that are indented in an unusual fashion — the xsl:attribute elements. These were originally written in a more standard form like this:

```
  <xsl:attribute name="href">
    #<xsl:value-of select="@PERSON"/></xsl:attribute>
  </xsl:attribute>
```

The problem with this approach is that the XSLT processor will consider the extra white space between <xsl:attribute name="href"> and # to be significant and include it, encoded line breaks and all, in the attribute values it produces. The attributes come out looking like this:

```
  <a href="%0A          #p1099">
    Mother
  </a>
```

However, what I want is this:

```
  <a href="#p1099">
    Mother
  </a>
```

XSLT processors normally strip nodes that contain nothing but white space. However, they do not trim nodes of leading and trailing white space if the node contains something other than white space, the sharp sign in this example. The solution is straightforward, simply trim the extra white space yourself; but it does tend to leave the style sheet looking less than pretty.

The final thing you need to do to format PERSON elements is to copy the contents of the NOTE into the finished document. This requires replacing the body element with a div element, because a genealogy document may contain multiple body elements but an HTML document may not. However, all the contents should be moved over verbatim. This rule does that by using xsl:for-each to iterate through the children and attributes of the body, copying each one using xsl:copy-of:

```
<xsl:template match="xhtml:body">
  <div>
    <xsl:for-each select="node()|@*">
      <xsl:copy-of select="."/>
    </xsl:for-each>
  </div>
</xsl:template>
```

The template rule for FAMILY elements will list the name and role of each member of the family as a list item in an unordered list. Each member will be linked to the description of that individual. The rules to do this look like the following:

```
<xsl:template match="FAMILY">
  <ul>
    <xsl:apply-templates select="HUSBAND"/>
    <xsl:apply-templates select="WIFE"/>
    <xsl:apply-templates select="CHILD"/>
  </ul>
</xsl:template>

<xsl:template match="HUSBAND">
  <li>Husband: <a href="#{@PERSON}">
    <xsl:value-of select="id(@PERSON)/NAME"/>
  </a></li>
</xsl:template>

<xsl:template match="WIFE">
  <li>Wife: <a href="#{@PERSON}">
    <xsl:value-of select="id(@PERSON)/NAME"/>
  </a></li>
</xsl:template>

<xsl:template match="CHILD">
  <li>Child: <a href="#{@PERSON}">
    <xsl:value-of select="id(@PERSON)/NAME"/>
  </a></li>
</xsl:template>
```

The trickiest thing about these rules is the insertion of data from one element (the PERSON) in a template that matches a different element (HUSBAND, WIFE, CHILD). The ID of the PERSON stored in the HUSBAND/WIFE/CHILD's PERSON attribute is used to locate the right PERSON element; then its NAME child is selected.

Listing 34-21 is the finished family tree style sheet. Figure 34-2 shows the beginning of the document after it's been converted into HTML and loaded into Netscape Navigator.

Listing 34-21: **The complete family tree style sheet**

```
<?xml version="1.0"?>
<xsl:stylesheet version="1.0"
  xmlns:xsl="http://www.w3.org/1999/XSL/Transform"
  xmlns:gen="http://ns.cafeconleche.org/genealogy/"
  xmlns:xhtml="http://www.w3.org/1999/xhtml">

  <xsl:template match="/">
    <html>
      <head>
        <title>Family Tree</title>
      </head>
      <body>
        <xsl:apply-templates select="gen:FAMILY_TREE"/>
      </body>
    </html>
  </xsl:template>

  <xsl:template match="gen:FAMILY_TREE">

    <h1>Family Tree</h1>

    <h2>Families</h2>
    <xsl:apply-templates select="gen:FAMILY"/>

    <h2>People</h2>
    <xsl:apply-templates select="gen:PERSON"/>

    <h2>Sources</h2>
    <ul>
     <xsl:apply-templates select="gen:SOURCE"/>
    </ul>

  </xsl:template>

  <xsl:template match="gen:PERSON">
```

Continued

Listing 34-21: *(continued)*

```
<h3>
  <xsl:element name="a">
    <xsl:attribute name="name">
      <xsl:value-of select="@ID"/>
    </xsl:attribute>
  <xsl:value-of select="gen:NAME"/>
  </xsl:element>
</h3>

<ul>
  <xsl:if test="gen:BIRTH">
    <li>Born: <xsl:value-of select="gen:BIRTH"/></li>
  </xsl:if>
  <xsl:if test="gen:DEATH">
    <li>Died: <xsl:value-of select="gen:DEATH"/></li>
  </xsl:if>
  <xsl:if test="gen:BAPTISM">
    <li>Baptism: <xsl:value-of select="gen:BAPTISM"/></li>
  </xsl:if>
  <xsl:if test="BURIAL">
    <li>Burial: <xsl:value-of select="gen:BURIAL"/></li>
  </xsl:if>
  <xsl:apply-templates select="gen:FATHER"/>
  <xsl:apply-templates select="gen:MOTHER"/>
</ul>

<xsl:apply-templates select="gen:NOTE"/>

</xsl:template>

<xsl:template match="gen:FATHER">
  <li>
    <xsl:element name="a">
      <xsl:attribute name="href">#<xsl:value-of
        select="@PERSON"/></xsl:attribute>
      Father
    </xsl:element>
  </li>
</xsl:template>

<xsl:template match="gen:MOTHER">
  <li>
    <xsl:element name="a">
      <xsl:attribute name="href">#<xsl:value-of
        select="@PERSON"/></xsl:attribute>
      Mother
    </xsl:element>
  </li>
</xsl:template>
```

```xml
<xsl:template match="xhtml:body">
  <div>
    <xsl:for-each select="node()|@*">
      <xsl:copy-of select="."/>
    </xsl:for-each>
  </div>
</xsl:template>

<xsl:template match="gen:SOURCE">

  <li>
    <xsl:element name="a">
      <xsl:attribute name="name">
        <xsl:value-of select="@ID"/>
      </xsl:attribute>
      <xsl:value-of select="."/>
    </xsl:element>
  </li>

</xsl:template>

<xsl:template match="gen:FAMILY">
  <ul>
    <xsl:apply-templates select="gen:HUSBAND"/>
    <xsl:apply-templates select="gen:WIFE"/>
    <xsl:apply-templates select="gen:CHILD"/>
  </ul>
</xsl:template>

<xsl:template match="gen:HUSBAND">
  <li>Husband: <a href="#{@PERSON}">
    <xsl:value-of select="id(@PERSON)/gen:NAME"/>
  </a></li>
</xsl:template>

<xsl:template match="gen:WIFE">
  <li>Wife: <a href="#{@PERSON}">
    <xsl:value-of select="id(@PERSON)/gen:NAME"/>
  </a></li>
</xsl:template>

<xsl:template match="gen:CHILD">
  <li>Child: <a href="#{@PERSON}">
    <xsl:value-of select="id(@PERSON)/gen:NAME"/>
  </a></li>
</xsl:template>

</xsl:stylesheet>
```

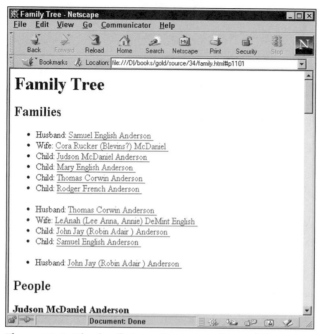

Figure 34-2: The family tree after conversion to HTML

A RDDL Document for Family Trees

The XML application and its style sheet, DTDs, and schemas are now complete. However, one more thing needs to be done before I can say that I'm finished. I've been using the namespace URL http://ns.cafeconleche.org/genealogy/. Now, I should put something there. Specifically, I should put a RDDL document listing all the related resources for this application. The related resources described in this chapter are:

- ✦ A DTD
- ✦ A modularized DTD
- ✦ A schema
- ✦ An XSLT style sheet

A DTD resource has the nature http://www.isi.edu/in-notes/iana/ assignments/media-types/application/xml-dtd. We actually developed multiple DTDs in this chapter, one for the PERSON, one for the FAMILY, one for the SOURCE, and one for the FAMILY_TREE. The driver DTD has the validation purpose identified by the well-known URL http://www.rddl.org/purposes#validation. The other three DTDs have the DTD module purpose identified by the well-known URL http://www.rddl.org/purposes#module. The family tree DTD depends on the source and family DTDs. The family DTD depends on the person DTD. When I wrote the RDDL document, this dependency seemed to naturally point to embedding one RDDL resource element inside another, which is perfectly OK.

```
<rddl:resource xmlns:rddl="http://www.rddl.org/"
  xlink:type="simple"
  xlink:href="http://ibiblio.org/xml/dtds/family_tree.dtd"
  xlink:role=
   "http://www.isi.edu/in-notes/iana/assignments/media-
types/application/xml-dtd"
  xlink:arcrole="http://www.rddl.org/purposes#validation"
>
   <p>
   The
   <a href="http://ibiblio.org/xml/dtds/family_tree.dtd">
      family tree DTD
   </a> describes an XML application for basic
   genealogical data. It's designed to validate documents
   with the root element <code>FAMILY_TREE</code> in the
   http://ns.cafeconleche.org/genealogy/ namespace.
   It depends on two DTD modules:
   </p>

   <ul>
     <li>
       <rddl:resource xlink:type="simple"
          xlink:href="http://ibiblio.org/xml/dtds/source.dtd"
          xlink:role="http://www.isi.edu/in-
notes/iana/assignments/media-types/application/xml-dtd"
          xlink:arcrole="http://www.rddl.org/purposes#module"
       >
         <p>
         The source DTD describes <code>REFERENCE</code>
         elements in the http://ns.cafeconleche.org/genealogy/
         namespace.
         </p>
       </rddl:resource>
     </li>
     <li>
       <rddl:resource xlink:type="simple"
          xlink:href="http://ibiblio.org/xml/dtds/family.dtd"
          xlink:role="http://www.isi.edu/in-
notes/iana/assignments/media-types/application/xml-dtd"
          xlink:arcrole="http://www.rddl.org/purposes#module"
       >
         <p>
         The family DTD describes <code>FAMILY</code>
         elements in the http://
         ns.cafeconleche.org/ genealogy/namespace.
```

```
                        This in turn depends on the
                        <rddl:resource xlink:type="simple"
                        xlink:href="http://ibiblio.org/xml/dtds/person.dtd"
                        xlink:role="http://www.isi.edu/in-
           notes/iana/assignments/media-types/application/xml-dtd"
                        xlink:arcrole="http://www.rddl.org/purposes#module"
                        >
                          person DTD. This DTD describes a single
                          <code>PERSON</code> element in the
                          http://ns.cafeconleche.org/genealogy/ namespace.
                        </rddl:resource>
                      </p>
                    </rddl:resource>
                  </li>
                </ul>

          </rddl:resource>
```

The resource describing the modularized DTD is similar, although a little longer because it needs to point to a few more DTD fragments. You can see it in Listing 34-22 later in this chapter.

A schema resource has the nature http://www.w3.org/2001/XMLSchema. There are several schema files here, each of which can be thought of as a separate resource. The FAMILY_TREE schema has the purpose http://www.rddl.org/purposes#schema-validation. The other three schema documents have the purpose http://www.rddl.org/purposes#schema-module. The modular structure of these schemas is the same so it isn't surprising that nesting the rddl:resource elements seemed the most natural way to describe them. This rddl:resource elements describes all four schemas:

```
<rddl:resource xmlns:rddl="http://www.rddl.org/"
  xlink:type="simple"
  xlink:href="http://ibiblio.org/xml/dtds/family_tree.xsd"
  xlink:role="http://www.w3.org/2001/XMLSchema"
  xlink:arcrole="http://www.rddl.org/purposes#schema-validation"
>
  <p>
  The
  <a href="http://ibiblio.org/xml/dtds/family_tree.xsd">
     family tree W3C XML Schema Language schema
  </a> describes an XML application for basic
  genealogical data. It's designed to validate documents with
  the root element <code>FAMILY_TREE</code> in the
  http://ns.cafeconleche.org/genealogy/ namespace. It
  depends on two DTD modules:
  </p>

  <ul>
    <li>
      <rddl:resource xlink:type="simple"
          xlink:href="http://ibiblio.org/xml/dtds/source.xsd"
          xlink:role="http://www.w3.org/2001/XMLSchema"
```

```
            xlink:arcrole="http://www.rddl.org/purposes#schema-module"
              >
              <p>
                 The source W3C XML Schema Language schema
                 describes <code>REFERENCE</code> elements
                 in the http://ns.cafeconleche.org/genealogy/
                 namespace.
              </p>
              </rddl:resource>
         </li>
         <li>
           <rddl:resource xlink:type="simple"
              xlink:href="http://ibiblio.org/xml/dtds/family.xsd"
              xlink:role="http://www.w3.org/2001/XMLSchema"
            xlink:arcrole="http://www.rddl.org/purposes#schema-module"
              >
              <p>
                 The family W3C XML Schema Language schema
                 describes FAMILY elements in the
                 http://ns.cafeconleche.org/genealogy/ namespace.
                 This in turn depends on the
                 <rddl:resource xlink:type="simple"
                 xlink:href="http://ibiblio.org/xml/dtds/person.xsd"
                 xlink:role="http://www.w3.org/2001/XMLSchema"
               xlink:arcrole="http://www.rddl.org/purposes#schema-module"
                   >
                    person schema. This schema describes a single
                    PERSON element in the
                    http://ns.cafeconleche.org/genealogy/ namespace.
                 </rddl:resource>
              </p>
              </rddl:resource>
         </li>
       </ul>

    </rddl:resource>
```

I don't think it's necessary to include `rddl:resource` elements here that describe the XHTML schemas or DTDs. Those are part of a different namespace and should be described by a RDDL document at that URL, `http://www.w3.org/1999/xhtml`. There isn't one there yet, but that's the W3C's responsibility, not mine.

The next resource is the XSLT style sheet. This has the nature `http://www.isi.edu/in-notes/iana/assignments/media-types/application/xml+xslt` based on its MIME media type. There's only one so a purpose isn't needed. The `rddl:resource` element describing it is straightforward:

```
<rddl:resource xmlns:rddl="http://www.rddl.org/"
  xlink:type="simple"
  xlink:href="http://ibiblio.org/xml/styles/familytree.xsl"
  xlink:role="http://www.isi.edu/in-
notes/iana/assignments/media-types/application/xml+xslt"
```

```
>
    <p>An <a href="http://ibiblio.org/xml/styles/familytree.xsl">
    XSLT 1.0 style sheet for genealogy data</a> is available.
    This does not work with Internet Explorer 5.5 and earlier
    because of Microsoft's nonconforming implementation of
    XSLT.</p>
</rddl:resource>
```

Is there anything else? I can think of one more thing, this book itself. After all, where else are you going to find the complete description of the genealogy application? The problem is that this book isn't easily resolvable because it doesn't live on the Internet anywhere. Nonetheless, it does have a URI based on its ISBN number, if not a URL. This URI is urn:isbn:0764548190. We can use this to set up one more rddl:resource element identifying a reference for this application (purpose http://www.rddl.org/purposes/software#reference).

```
<rddl:resource xmlns:rddl="http://www.rddl.org/"
   xlink:type="simple"
   xlink:href="urn:isbn:0764548190"
 xlink:arcrole="http://www.rddl.org/purposes/software#reference"
 >
   <p>
      Chapter 34 of the XML Bible, Gold Edition, describes and
      explains this XML application in much greater detail. You
      should be able to find it in any bookstore that stocks
      computer books including <a href=
      "http://www.bookpool.com/">Bookpool</a> and
      <a href="http://www.fatbrain.com/">FatBrain</a>.
      The list price is $69.99,
      but it's often discounted. If you need to special order
      it, the
      ISBN number is 0-7645-4819-0 and the author is
      <a href="http://www.macfaq.com/personal.html">Elliotte
      Rusty Harold</a>
   </p>
</rddl:resource>
```

Listing 34-22 and Figure 34-3 show the completed RDDL document for the family tree application. This should be placed at the actual namespace URI, http://ns.cafeconleche.org/genealogy/. Unfortunately, because of the recent Northpoint bankruptcy that URL no longer exists. :(I'm hopeful that I'll have it running again by the time you read this.

Listing 34-22: **The RDDL document for the family tree XML application developed in this chapter**

```
<!DOCTYPE html PUBLIC "-//XML-DEV//DTD XHTML RDDL 1.0//EN"
                    "http://www.rddl.org/rddl-xhtml.dtd">
```

```
<html xmlns="http://www.w3.org/1999/xhtml"
      xmlns:xlink="http://www.w3.org/1999/xlink"
      xmlns:rddl="http://www.rddl.org/">
<head>
  <title>An XML Application for Genealogy</title>
</head>
<body>
<h1>An XML Application for Genealogy</h1>

<div class="head">
<p>This Version: <a
href="http://ns.cafeconleche.org/genealogy/200100525/">May 25,
2001</a></p>
<p>Latest Version: <a
href="http://ns.cafeconleche.org/genealogy/">http://ns.cafeconl
eche.org/genealogy/</a></p>
<p>Previous Version: <a
href="http://ns.cafeconleche.org/genealogy/200100505/">May 25,
2001</a></p>
<p>Authors:</p>
<ul>
<li><a href="mailto:elharo@metalab.unc.edu">Elliotte Rusty
Harold</a></li>
</ul>
</div>

<p>
This document describes the an XML application for genealogy
statistics used as an example in the Gold edition of the
<cite>XML Bible</cite>.
</p>

<p>Available related resource include:</p>

<ul>
  <li><a href="#DTD">A DTD</a></li>
  <li><a href="#Modularized">A Modularized DTD</a></li>
  <li><a href="#schema">A schema</a></li>
  <li><a href="#xslt">An XSLT stylesheet</a></li>
</ul>

<rddl:resource xmlns:rddl="http://www.rddl.org/"
  xlink:type="simple"
  xlink:href="urn:isbn:0764548190"
xlink:arcrole="http://www.rddl.org/purposes/software#reference"
>
  <p>
    Chapter 34 of the <cite>XML Bible, Gold Edition</cite>,
    describes and explains this XML application in much
    greater detail. You should be able to find it in any
    bookstore that stocks computer books including <a href=
```

Continued

Listing 34-22: *(continued)*

```
       "http://www.bookpool.com/">Bookpool</a> and
       <a href="http://www.fatbrain.com/">FatBrain</a>.
       The list price is $69.99,
       but it's often discounted. If you need to special order
       it, the
       ISBN number is 0-7645-4819-0 and the author is
       <a href="http://www.macfaq.com/personal.html">Elliotte
       Rusty Harold</a>
    </p>
 </rddl:resource>


 <p>This document has no official standing and has not been
 considered or approved by any organization.</p>

 <h2 id="DTD">Document Type Definition</h2>

 <rddl:resource xmlns:rddl="http://www.rddl.org/"
   xlink:type="simple"
   xlink:href="http://ibiblio.org/xml/dtds/family_tree.dtd"
   xlink:role=
    "http://www.isi.edu/in-notes/iana/assignments/media-
 types/application/xml-dtd"
   xlink:arcrole="http://www.rddl.org/purposes#validation"
 >
    <p>
    The
    <a href="http://ibiblio.org/xml/dtds/family_tree.dtd">
       family tree DTD
    </a> describes an XML application for basic
    genealogical data. It's designed to validate documents
    with the root element <code>FAMILY_TREE</code> in the
    http://ns.cafeconleche.org/genealogy/ namespace.
    It depends on two DTD modules:
    </p>

    <ul>
      <li>
       <rddl:resource xlink:type="simple"
          xlink:href="http://ibiblio.org/xml/dtds/source.dtd"
          xlink:role="http://www.isi.edu/in-
 notes/iana/assignments/media-types/application/xml-dtd"
          xlink:arcrole="http://www.rddl.org/purposes#module"
       >
        The
        <a href="http://ibiblio.org/xml/dtds/source.dtd">source
        DTD</a> describes <code>SOURCE</code> elements in the
        http://ns.cafeconleche.org/genealogy/ namespace.
```

```
        </rddl:resource>
      </li>
      <li>
        <rddl:resource xlink:type="simple"
            xlink:href="http://ibiblio.org/xml/dtds/family.dtd"
            xlink:role="http://www.isi.edu/in-
  notes/iana/assignments/media-types/application/xml-dtd"
            xlink:arcrole="http://www.rddl.org/purposes#module"
        >
          The <a href="http://ibiblio.org/xml/dtds/family.dtd">
          family DTD</a> describes <code>FAMILY</code>
          elements in the http://ns.cafeconleche.org/genealogy/
          namespace. This in turn depends on the
          <rddl:resource xlink:type="simple"
            xlink:href="http://ibiblio.org/xml/dtds/person.dtd"
            xlink:role="http://www.isi.edu/in-
  notes/iana/assignments/media-types/application/xml-dtd"
            xlink:arcrole="http://www.rddl.org/purposes#module"
          >
            <a href="http://ibiblio.org/xml/dtds/person.dtd">
            person DTD</a>. This DTD describes a single
            <code>PERSON</code> element in the
            http://ns.cafeconleche.org/genealogy/ namespace.
          </rddl:resource>
        </rddl:resource>
      </li>
    </ul>

</rddl:resource>


<h2 id="Modularized">A Modularized DTD</h2>

<rddl:resource xmlns:rddl="http://www.rddl.org/"
  xlink:type="simple"

xlink:href="http://ibiblio.org/xml/dtds/FamilyTree_driver.dtd"
  xlink:role=
   "http://www.isi.edu/in-notes/iana/assignments/media-
types/application/xml-dtd"
  xlink:arcrole="http://www.rddl.org/purposes#validation"
>
  <p>
  The
  <a href="http://ibiblio.org/xml/dtds/FamilyTree_driver.dtd">
    modularized family tree DTD
  </a> describes the same XML application for basic
  genealogical data as the previous DTD. However, it's
  designed to allow document authors to modify the namespace
  prefix by overriding the <code>%GENEALOGY.prefix;</code> and
  <code>%GENEALOGY.prefixed;</code> parameter entity
  references.
```

Continued

Listing 34-22: *(continued)*

```
If you wish to turn on prefixing, set
<code>%GENEALOGY.prefixed;</code> to <code>INCLUDE</code>
and <code>%GENEALOGY.prefix;</code> to the prefix you want
to use.
</p>

<p>
  It is composed of six modules and one driver DTD:
</p>

<ul>
  <li>
    <rddl:resource xlink:type="simple"
        xlink:href="http://ibiblio.org/xml/dtds/source.dtd"
        xlink:role="http://www.isi.edu/in-
notes/iana/assignments/media-types/application/xml-dtd"
          xlink:arcrole="http://www.rddl.org/purposes#module"
    >
      The <a href="http://ibiblio.org/xml/dtds/source.mod">
      source module</a> describes <code>SOURCE</code>
      elements in the http://ns.cafeconleche.org/genealogy/
      namespace.
    </rddl:resource>
  </li>
  <li>
    <rddl:resource xlink:type="simple"
        xlink:href="http://ibiblio.org/xml/dtds/family.mod"
        xlink:role="http://www.isi.edu/in-
notes/iana/assignments/media-types/application/xml-dtd"
        xlink:arcrole="http://www.rddl.org/purposes#module"
    >
      The <a href="http://ibiblio.org/xml/dtds/family.mod">
      family module</a> describes <code>FAMILY</code>
      elements in the http://ns.cafeconleche.org/genealogy/
      namespace.
    </rddl:resource>
  </li>
  <li>
    <rddl:resource xlink:type="simple"
        xlink:href="http://ibiblio.org/xml/dtds/person.mod"
        xlink:role="http://www.isi.edu/in-
notes/iana/assignments/media-types/application/xml-dtd"
        xlink:arcrole="http://www.rddl.org/purposes#module"
    >
      The <a href="http://ibiblio.org/xml/dtds/person.mod">
      person module</a> describes <code>PERSON</code>
      elements in the http://ns.cafeconleche.org/genealogy/
      namespace.
    </rddl:resource>
```

```
      </li>
      <li>
        <rddl:resource xlink:type="simple"
            xlink:href="http://ibiblio.org/xml/dtds/person.mod"
            xlink:role="http://www.isi.edu/in-
notes/iana/assignments/media-types/application/xml-dtd"
            xlink:arcrole="http://www.rddl.org/purposes#module"
        >
          The <a href=
          "http://ibiblio.org/xml/dtds/family_tree.mod">
          family tree module</a> describes
          <code>FAMILY_TREE</code> elements in the
          http://ns.cafeconleche.org/genealogy/ namespace.
        </rddl:resource>
      </li>
      <li>
        <rddl:resource xlink:type="simple"
            xlink:href="http://ibiblio.org/xml/dtds/genealogy-
namespace.mod"
            xlink:role="http://www.isi.edu/in-
notes/iana/assignments/media-types/application/xml-dtd"
            xlink:arcrole="http://www.rddl.org/purposes#module"
        >
          The <a href=
          "http://ibiblio.org/xml/dtds/genealogy-namespace.mod">
          namespaces module</a> defines the namespace URI
          and prefix used in this application.
        </rddl:resource>
      </li>
      <li>
        <rddl:resource xlink:type="simple"
            xlink:href="http://ibiblio.org/xml/dtds/genealogy-
qname.mod"
            xlink:role="http://www.isi.edu/in-
notes/iana/assignments/media-types/application/xml-dtd"
            xlink:arcrole="http://www.rddl.org/purposes#module"
        >
          The <a href=
          "http://ibiblio.org/xml/dtds/genealogy-qname.mod">
          qualified names module</a> defines parameter entity
          references that resolve to the prefixed names of the
          different elements in this application.
        </rddl:resource>
      </li>
      <li>
        <rddl:resource xlink:type="simple"

xlink:href="http://ibiblio.org/xml/dtds/FamilyTree_driver.dtd"
            xlink:role="http://www.isi.edu/in-
notes/iana/assignments/media-types/application/xml-dtd"
            xlink:arcrole="http://www.rddl.org/purposes#module"
        >
```

Continued

Listing 34-22: *(continued)*

```
        The <a href=
        "http://ibiblio.org/xml/dtds/FamilyTree_driver.dtd">
        driver DTD</a> loads all the modules in the correct
        order.
      </rddl:resource>
    </li>
  </ul>

</rddl:resource>

<h2 id="schema">Schema</h2>

<rddl:resource xmlns:rddl="http://www.rddl.org/"
  xlink:type="simple"
  xlink:href="http://ibiblio.org/xml/dtds/family_tree.xsd"
  xlink:role="http://www.w3.org/2001/XMLSchema"
 xlink:arcrole="http://www.rddl.org/purposes#schema-validation"
>
  <p>
  The
  <a href="http://ibiblio.org/xml/dtds/family_tree.xsd">
    family tree W3C XML Schema Language schema
  </a> describes an XML application for basic
  genealogical data. It's designed to validate documents with
  the root element <code>FAMILY_TREE</code> in the
  http://ns.cafeconleche.org/genealogy/ namespace. It
  depends on two DTD modules:
  </p>

  <ul>
    <li>
      <rddl:resource xlink:type="simple"
        xlink:href="http://ibiblio.org/xml/dtds/source.xsd"
        xlink:role="http://www.w3.org/2001/XMLSchema"
   xlink:arcrole="http://www.rddl.org/purposes#schema-module"
      >
        The <a href="http://ibiblio.org/xml/dtds/source.xsd">
        source W3C XML Schema Language schema</a>
        describes <code>SOURCE</code> elements
        in the http://ns.cafeconleche.org/genealogy/
        namespace.
      </rddl:resource>
    </li>
    <li>
      <rddl:resource xlink:type="simple"
        xlink:href="http://ibiblio.org/xml/dtds/family.xsd"
        xlink:role="http://www.w3.org/2001/XMLSchema"
```

```
          xlink:arcrole="http://www.rddl.org/purposes#schema-module"
        >
          The <a href="http://ibiblio.org/xml/dtds/family.xsd">
          family W3C XML Schema Language schema</a>
          describes <code>FAMILY</code> elements in the
          http://ns.cafeconleche.org/genealogy/ namespace.
          This in turn depends on the
          <rddl:resource xlink:type="simple"
             xlink:href="http://ibiblio.org/xml/dtds/person.xsd"
             xlink:role="http://www.w3.org/2001/XMLSchema"
      xlink:arcrole="http://www.rddl.org/purposes#schema-module"
          >
            <a href="http://ibiblio.org/xml/dtds/person.xsd">
            person schema</a>. This schema describes a single
            <code>PERSON</code> element in the
            http://ns.cafeconleche.org/genealogy/ namespace.
          </rddl:resource>
        </rddl:resource>
      </li>
    </ul>

</rddl:resource>


<h2 id="xslt">XSLT Style Sheet</h2>

<rddl:resource xmlns:rddl="http://www.rddl.org/"
  xlink:type="simple"
  xlink:href="http://ibiblio.org/xml/styles/familytree.xsl"
  xlink:role="http://www.isi.edu/in-
notes/iana/assignments/media-types/application/xml+xslt"
>
  <p>An <a href="http://ibiblio.org/xml/styles/familytree.xsl">
  XSLT 1.0 style sheet for genealogy data</a> is available.
  This does not work with Internet Explorer 5.5 and earlier
  because of Microsoft's nonconforming implementation of
  XSLT.</p>
</rddl:resource>

</body>
</html>
```

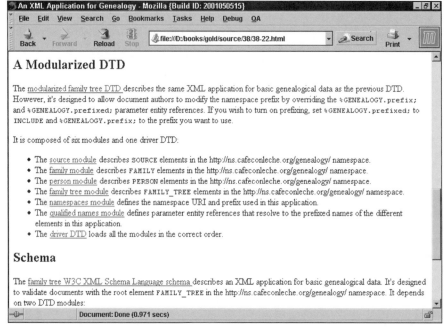

Figure 34-3: The RDDL document for the genealogy application

Summary

In this chapter, you saw an XML application for genealogy developed from scratch. Along the way you learned to:

◆ Always begin a new XML application by considering the domain you're describing.

◆ Try to identify the fundamental elements of the domain. Everything else is likely to either be contained in or to be an attribute of one of these.

◆ Try to avoid including the same data in more than one place. Instead, use ID and IDREF attributes to establish pointers from one element to another.

◆ Be sure to consider special cases. Don't base your entire design on the most obvious cases.

◆ Use parameter entities to merge the DTDs for each piece of the XML application into one complete DTD.

✦ Use `xsd:include` and `xsd:import` to merge the schemas for each piece of the XML application into one complete schema.

✦ Don't get hung up on what your data will look like when you're designing the application. You can always reorganize it with XSLT.

✦ Make your namespace URIs resolvable URLs, and place a RDDL document at the end of each namespace URL.

This concludes the main body of *The XML Bible, Gold Edition*. Go forth and write your own XML applications! The following appendixes provide a variety of useful reference information and the official XML 1.0 Specification.

✦   ✦   ✦

What's on the CD-ROM

The CD that comes with this book should be readable on a Mac, Solaris, Linux, and Windows 95/98/Me/NT/2000/XP. Just put the CD in the drive, and mount it using whatever method you normally use to load a CD on your platform, probably filemanager in Solaris, and just stick it in the drive if you're using a Mac, Linux or Windows. There's no fancy installer. You can browse the directories as you would a hard drive.

All CD-ROM files are read-only. Therefore, if you open a file from the CD-ROM and make any changes to it, you'll need to save it to your hard drive. If you copy a file from the CD-ROM to your hard drive on Windows, the file retains its read-only attribute. To change this attribute after copying a file, right-click the file name or icon and select Properties from the shortcut menu. In the Properties dialog box, click the General tab and remove the checkmark from the Read-only checkbox.

The CD is divided into seven main directories:

- ◆ Browsers
- ◆ Parsers
- ◆ Specifications
- ◆ Examples
- ◆ Source Code
- ◆ Utilities
- ◆ PDFs

Browsers

This directory contains a number of Web browsers that support XML to a greater or lesser extent including:

+ Microsoft Internet Explorer for Windows
+ Microsoft Internet Explorer for MacOS
+ Mozilla (various platforms)
+ Amaya (various platforms)

Parsers

This directory contains a variety of open source XML parsers including:

+ The Xerces-J XML parser for Java
+ The Xerces-C XML parser for C++
+ The Xerces.pm XML parser for Perl
+ The expat parser for C++

Most of the examples in this book that have used a specific parser have used Xerces Java, in particular, the sax.SAXCount program, To install it, just copy the xerces.jar and xercesSamples.jar archives to your jre\lib\ext directory. You'll need the Java Runtime Environment (JRE) 1.2 or later, which you can download from http://java.sun.com/. If you've installed the Java Development Kit (JDK) instead of the JRE on Windows, you may have two ext directories, one somewhere like C:\jdk1.3\jre\lib\ext and the other somewhere like C:\Program Files\Javasoft\jre\1.3\lib\ext. You need to copy the jar archive into both ext directories. Putting one copy in one directory and an alias into the other directory does not work. You must place complete, actual copies into each ext directory.

Specifications

This directory contains the XML Specifications from the World Wide Web Consortium (W3C) including:

+ XML 1.0, second edition
+ Namespaces in XML
+ CSS Level 1
+ CSS Level 2
+ XSLT 1.0

◆ XPath 1.0

◆ HTML 4.0

◆ XHTML 1.0

◆ MathML 2.0

◆ The Resource Description Framework

◆ Modularization of XHTML

◆ XHTML 1.1 — Module-based XHTML

◆ XHTML Basic

◆ XML Schema Part 0: Primer

◆ XML Schema Part 1: Structures

◆ XML Schema Part 2: Datatypes

◆ Canonical XML Version 1.0

◆ SMIL 2.0

These are all included in HTML format, and most are available in XML as well. Some are also provided in additional formats such as PDF or plain text. Many technologies discussed in this book are not yet finalized (for example, XPointers). You can find the current draft specifications for these on the World Wide Web Consortium (W3C) Web site at `http://www.w3.org/TR/`.

Examples

This directory contains several examples of large XML files and large collections of XML documents. Some (but not all) of these are based on smaller examples printed in the book. For instance, you'll find complete statistics for the 1998 Major League Baseball season including all players and teams. Examples include:

◆ The 1998 Major League Baseball season

◆ The complete works of Shakespeare (courtesy of Jon Bosak)

◆ The Old Testament (courtesy of Jon Bosak)

◆ The New Testament (courtesy of Jon Bosak)

◆ The Koran (courtesy of Jon Bosak)

◆ The Book of Mormon (courtesy of Jon Bosak)

◆ The periodic table of the elements

Source Code

All complete numbered code listings from this book are on the CD-ROM in a directory called source. They are organized by chapter. Very simple HTML indexes are provided for the examples in each chapter. However, because most of the examples are raw XML files and because most don't have style sheets, some Web browsers won't display them very well. Internet Explorer 5.x probably does the best job with most of these files. Otherwise, you're probably better off just opening the directories in Windows Explorer, the Finder or the equivalent on your platform of choice, and reading the files with a text editor.

Most of the files are named according to the listing number in the book (for example, 6-1.xml, 27-1.cdf). However, in a few cases in which a specific name is used in the book, such as family.dtd or family.xml, then that name is also used on the CD. The files on the CD appear exactly as they do in the book's listings.

Utilities

The utilities directory contains assorted programs that will be useful for processing XML documents of one type or another. These include:

 ✦ Dave Raggett's HTML Tidy, compiled for a variety of platforms. Tidy can clean up most HTML files so that they become well-formed XML. Tidy can correct many common problems and warn you about the ones you need to fix yourself. The latest version can be found at `http://www.w3.org/People/Raggett/tidy`

 ✦ The Xalan-J XSLT Processor from the XML Apache Project

 ✦ Michael Kay's SAXON XSLT Processor

 ✦ The Batik SVG Viewer from the XML Apache Project

 ✦ FOP, an XSL formatting objects to PDF converter from the XML Apache Project

PDF

The pdf directory contains Acrobat PDF files for this entire book. To read them, you'll need the free Acrobat Reader software included on the CD-ROM. Feel free to put them on your local hard disk for easy access. I don't really care if you loan the CD-ROM to some cash-strapped undergrad who finds it cheaper to tie up a school printer for a few hours printing all 1500+ pages rather than spend $69.99 for a printed copy. (If you're using your own printer, toner, and paper, it's much cheaper to buy the book.) However, I would very much appreciate it if you do not place these files on Web, FTP, Gnutella, Publius, or any other servers. This includes intranet servers, password-protected sites, and other things that aren't meant for the public at large. Most local sites and intranets are far more exposed to the broader Internet than most people think. Today's search engines are very good at locating content that is supposed to be hidden. Putting mirror copies of these files around the Web makes it extremely difficult to keep all the files up to date and to make sure that search engines find the right copies.

✦   ✦   ✦

XML Reference Material

This appendix contains XML reference material. It is divided into three main parts:

1. XML BNF grammar
2. Well-formedness constraints
3. Validity constraints

The XML BNF grammar reference section shows you how to read a BNF grammar and includes the BNF rules for XML 1.0, second edition, and examples of the productions. The well-formedness constraints reference section explains what a well-formedness constraint is. Then it lists and explains all 12 well-formedness constraints. The validity constraints reference section explains what a validity constraint is and lists and explains the 25 validity constraints in XML 1.0, second edition.

XML BNF Grammar

According to the XML 1.0 specification, an XML document is well formed if:

1. Taken as a whole it matches the production-labeled document.
2. It meets all the well-formedness constraints given in this specification.
3. Each parsed entity that is referenced directly or indirectly within the document is well formed.

This section is designed to help you understand the first of those requirements and to more quickly determine whether your documents meet that requirement.

Reading a BNF grammar

BNF is an abbreviation for Backus-Naur Form. BNF grammars are an outgrowth of compiler theory. A BNF grammar defines what is and is not a syntactically correct program or, in the case of XML, a syntactically correct document. It is possible to compare a document to a BNF grammar and determine precisely whether it does or does not meet the conditions of that grammar. There are no borderline cases. BNF grammars, properly written, have the advantage of leaving no room for interpretation. The advantage of this should be obvious to anyone who's had to struggle with HTML documents that display in one browser but not in another.

Note Technically, XML uses an Extended-Backus-Naur-Form (EBNF) grammar, which adds a few pieces not normally found in traditional, compiler-oriented BNF grammars.

Syntactical correctness is a necessary but not sufficient condition for XML documents. A document may strictly adhere to the BNF grammar and yet fail to be well formed or valid. For a document to be well formed, it must also meet all the well-formedness constraints of the XML 1.0 specification. Well-formedness is the minimum level that a document must achieve to be parsed. To be valid, a document must also meet all the validity constraints of the XML 1.0 specification. The well-formedness and validity constraints are discussed in the next two sections of this appendix.

BNF grammar parts

A BNF grammar has three parts:

1. A set of literal strings called *terminals*. For example, `CDATA`, `</`, `<`, `>`, `#REQUIRED`, and `<!ENTITY` are all terminals used in the XML 1.0 grammar.

2. A set of *nonterminals* that will ultimately be replaced by terminals.

3. A list of *productions* or rules that map nonterminals to particular sequences of terminals and other nonterminals, including one specially identified as the *start* or *document* production.

If you're not a compiler theorist, that list probably could have been written in ancient Etruscan and made about as much sense. Let's see if we can make things clearer with a simple example before we dive into the complexities of the XML 1.0 grammar.

Consider strings composed of nonnegative, single-digit integers added to or subtracted from each other, such as these:

```
9+8+1+2+3
8-1-2-4-5
9+8-9-0+5+3
4
4+3
```

Notice a few things that are not in the list, and that we want to forbid in our grammar:

- ✦ Any character except the digits 0 through 9 and the plus (+) and the minus (−) signs
- ✦ White space
- ✦ A string that begins with a + or a −
- ✦ Numbers less than 0 or greater than 9
- ✦ The empty string

Here's a BNF grammar that defines precisely those strings that we want, and none of those strings that we don't want:

```
[1] string ::= digit
[2] digit  ::= '0' | '1' | '2' | '3' | '4' | '5' | '6' | '7'
             | '8' | '9'
[3] string ::= string '+' digit
[4] string ::= string '-' digit
```

Suppose you want to determine whether the string "9+3-2" satisfies this grammar. You begin by looking at the first production. This says that a string is the nonterminal digit. So, you move to Production [2], which defines digit. Indeed, 9 is one of the terminals listed as a digit. Thus, the string "9" is a legitimate string. Production [3] says that a string followed by the plus sign and another digit is also a legitimate string. Thus "9+3" satisfies the grammar. Furthermore, it itself is a string. Production [4] says that a string followed by the minus sign and another digit is a legitimate string. Thus "9+3–2" is a legitimate string and satisfies the grammar.

Now consider the string "–9+1". According to Production [1], a string must begin with a digit. This string doesn't begin with a digit, so it's illegal. Or consider the string "99+100". This begins with a digit. However, no production allows a digit to be followed by a digit. Therefore, this is also an illegal string.

The XML 1.0 grammar is much larger and more complicated than this simple grammar. The next section lists its 83 productions. The following section elaborates on each of these productions in detail.

> **Note** The 83 productions are numbered from 1 to 89. Productions 33 through 38 and Production 79 were not reachable from the start production and thus never actually used. They have been deleted from the second edition of XML. Furthermore, production 28a was added between production 28 and 29 in the second edition, resulting in 83 productions.

BNF symbols

In XML's EBNF grammar, the following basic symbols are used on the right-hand sides of productions:

#xN	N is a hexadecimal integer, and #xN is the Unicode character at code point N
[a-zA-Z]	Matches any character in the specified range
[#xN-#xN]	Matches any character in the specified range where N is the hexadecimal value of a Unicode character
[^a-z]	Matches any character not in the specified range
[^#xN-#xN]	Matches any character not in the specified range where N is the hexadecimal value of a Unicode character
[^abc]	Matches any character not in the list
[^#xN#xN#xN]	Matches any character whose hexadecimal value is not in the list
'string'	Matches the literal string inside the single quotes
"string"	Matches the literal string inside the double quotes

These nine basic patterns may be grouped to match more complex expressions:

(*contents*)	The contents of the parentheses are treated as a unit
A?	Matches zero or one occurrences of A
A B	Matches A followed by B
A	B	Matches A or B, but not both
A - B	Matches any string that matches A and does not match B
A+	Matches one or more occurrences of A
A*	Matches zero or more occurrences of A

The XML specification also uses three forms that you probably won't encounter in non-XML–related specifications:

/* *text of comment* */	This is a comment, and any text inside the comment is ignored.
[WFC: *name*]	This names a well-formedness constraint associated with this production that documents must meet in order to qualify as well formed. Well-formedness constraints are a necessary part of the XML specification, but they are not part of the BNF grammar. They state rules that are difficult to impossible to describe in BNF form.

[VC: *name*]   This names a validity constraint associated with this production that documents must meet in order to qualify as valid. Validity constraints are an optional part of the XML specification, but they are also not part of the BNF grammar.

The BNF rules for XML 1.0

The complete BNF grammar for XML is given in the XML 1.0 specification, which you'll find in Appendix C of this book. However, if you're merely trying to match up your markup against productions in the grammar, it can be inconvenient to flip through the pages hunting for the necessary rules. For that purpose, the BNF rules, and only the BNF rules for XML 1.0, are reproduced here.

Document

```
[1] document ::= prolog element Misc*
```

Character range

```
[2] Char ::= #x9 | #xA | #xD | [#x20-#xD7FF] | [#xE000-#xFFFD]
             | [#x10000-#x10FFFF]
```

White space

```
[3] S ::= (#x20 | #x9 | #xD | #xA)+
```

Names and tokens

```
[4] NameChar ::= Letter | Digit | '.' | '-' | '_' | ':'
                 | CombiningChar | Extender
[5] Name     ::= (Letter | '_' | ':') (NameChar)*
[6] Names    ::= Name (S Name)*
[7] Nmtoken  ::= (NameChar)+
[8] Nmtokens ::= Nmtoken (S Nmtoken)*
```

Literals

```
[9]  EntityValue   ::= '"' ([^%&"] | PEReference | Reference)*
                       '"' | "'" ([^%&'] | PEReference
                       | Reference)* "'"
[10] AttValue      ::= '"' ([^<&"] | Reference)* '"'
                       | "'" ([^<&'] | Reference)* "'"
[11] SystemLiteral ::= ('"' [^"]* '"') | ("'" [^']* "'")
[12] PubidLiteral  ::= '"' PubidChar* '"'
                       | "'" (PubidChar - "'")* "'"
[13] PubidChar     ::= #x20 | #xD | #xA | [a-zA-Z0-9]
                       | [-'()+,./:=?;!*#@$_%]
```

Character data

```
[14] CharData ::= [^<&]* - ([^<&]* ']]>' [^<&]*)
```

Comments

```
[15] Comment   ::= '<!--' ((Char - '-')
                   | ('-' (Char - '-')))* '-->'
```

Processing instructions

```
[16] PI        ::= '<?' PITarget
                   (S (Char* - (Char* '?>' Char*)))? '?>'
[17] PITarget ::= Name - (('X' | 'x') ('M' | 'm') ('L' | 'l'))
```

CDATA sections

```
[18] CDSect    ::= CDStart CData CDEnd
[19] CDStart   ::= '<![CDATA['
[20] CData     ::= (Char* - (Char* ']]>' Char*))
[21] CDEnd     ::= ']]>'
```

Prolog

```
[22] prolog      ::= XMLDecl? Misc* (doctypedecl Misc*)?
[23] XMLDecl     ::= '<?xml' VersionInfo EncodingDecl? SDDecl?
                     S? '?>'
[24] VersionInfo ::= S 'version' Eq ('"' VersionNum '"'
                     | '"' VersionNum '"')
[25] Eq          ::= S? '=' S?
[26] VersionNum  ::= ([a-zA-Z0-9_.:] | '-')+
[27] Misc        ::= Comment | PI |  S
```

Document type definition

```
[28] doctypedecl ::= '<!DOCTYPE' S Name (S ExternalID)? S?
                     ('[' (markupdecl | DeclSep)* ']' S?)? '>'
                        [VC: Root Element Type]
                        [WFC: External Subset]
[28a] DeclSep    ::= PEReference | S
                        [WFC: PE Between Declarations]
[29] markupdecl  ::= elementdecl | AttlistDecl | EntityDecl
                     | NotationDecl | PI | Comment
                        [ VC: Proper Declaration/PE Nesting ]
                        [ WFC: PEs in Internal Subset ]
```

External subset

```
[30] extSubset    ::=   TextDecl? extSubsetDecl
[31] extSubsetDecl ::= ( markupdecl | conditionalSect |
                         DeclSep)*
```

Standalone document declaration

```
[32] SDDecl ::= S 'standalone' Eq (("'" ('yes' | 'no')
                "'") | ('"' ('yes' | 'no') '"'))
                          [ VC: Standalone Document Declaration ]
```

Element

```
[39] element ::= EmptyElemTag | STag content ETag
                        [ WFC: Element Type Match ]
                        [ VC: Element Valid ]
```

Start tag

```
[40] STag ::= '<' Name (S Attribute)* S? '>'
                        [ WFC: Unique Att Spec ]
[41] Attribute ::= Name Eq AttValue
                        [ VC: Attribute Value Type ]
                        [ WFC: No External Entity References ]
                        [ WFC: No < in Attribute Values ]
```

End tag

```
[42] ETag ::= '</' Name S? '>'
```

Content of elements

```
[43] content ::= CharData?
                 ((element | Reference | CDSect | PI | Comment)
                 CharData?)*
```

Tags for empty elements

```
[44] EmptyElemTag ::= '<' Name (S Attribute)* S? '/>'
                        [ WFC: Unique Att Spec ]
```

Element type declaration

```
[45] elementdecl ::= '<!ELEMENT' S Name S contentspec S? '>'
                                 [ VC: Unique Element Type Declaration ]
[46] contentspec ::= 'EMPTY' | 'ANY' | Mixed | children
```

Element-content models

```
[47] children ::= (choice | seq) ('?' | '*' | '+')?
[48] cp       ::= (Name | choice | seq) ('?' | '*' | '+')?
[49] choice   ::= '(' S? cp ( S? '|' S? cp )+ S? ')'
                                 [ VC: Proper Group/PE Nesting ]
[50] seq      ::= '(' S? cp ( S? ',' S? cp )* S? ')'
                                 [ VC: Proper Group/PE Nesting ]
```

Mixed-content declaration

```
[51] Mixed ::= '(' S? '#PCDATA' (S? '|' S? Name)* S? ')*'
             | '(' S? '#PCDATA' S? ')'
                                 [ VC: Proper Group/PE Nesting ]
                                 [ VC: No Duplicate Types ]
```

Attribute-list declaration

```
[52] AttlistDecl ::= '<!ATTLIST' S Name AttDef* S? '>'
[53] AttDef      ::= S Name S AttType S DefaultDecl
```

Attribute types

```
[54] AttType ::= StringType | TokenizedType | EnumeratedType
[55] StringType ::= 'CDATA'
[56] TokenizedType ::= 'ID' | 'IDREF' | 'IDREFS' | 'ENTITY'
                     | 'ENTITIES' | 'NMTOKEN' | 'NMTOKENS'
                     [ VC: ID ]
                     [ VC: One ID per Element Type ]
                     [ VC: ID Attribute Default ]
                     [ VC: IDREF ]
                     [ VC: Entity Name ]
                     [ VC: Name Token ]
```

Enumerated attribute types

```
[57] EnumeratedType ::= NotationType | Enumeration
[58] NotationType   ::= 'NOTATION' S '(' S? Name (S? '|' S?
                        Name)* S? ')'
                        [ VC: Notation Attributes ]
                        [ VC: One Notation Per Element Type]
                        [ VC: No Notation on Empty Element]
[59] Enumeration ::= '(' S? Nmtoken (S? '|' S? Nmtoken)* S? ')'
                        [ VC: Enumeration ]
```

Attribute defaults

```
[60] DefaultDecl ::= '#REQUIRED' | '#IMPLIED'
                   | (('#FIXED' S)? AttValue)
                       [ VC: Required Attribute ]
                       [ VC: Attribute Default Legal ]
                       [ WFC: No < in Attribute Values ]
                       [ VC: Fixed Attribute Default ]
```

Conditional section

```
[61] conditionalSect ::=  includeSect | ignoreSect
[62] includeSect      ::= '<![' S? 'INCLUDE' S? '['
                            extSubsetDecl ']]>'
                  [VC: Proper Conditional Section/PE Nesting]
[63] ignoreSect       ::= '<![' S? 'IGNORE' S? '['
                            ignoreSectContents* ']]>'
                  [VC: Proper Conditional Section/PE Nesting]
[64] ignoreSectContents ::= Ignore ('<![' ignoreSectContents
                            ']]>' Ignore)*
[65] Ignore           ::= Char* - (Char* ('<![' | ']]>') Char*)
```

Character reference

```
[66] CharRef ::= '&#' [0-9]+ ';' | '&#x' [0-9a-fA-F]+ ';'
                     [ WFC: Legal Character ]
```

Entity reference

```
[67] Reference  ::= EntityRef | CharRef
[68] EntityRef  ::= '&' Name ';'
                     [ WFC: Entity Declared ]
                     [ VC: Entity Declared ]
                     [ WFC: Parsed Entity ]
                     [ WFC: No Recursion ]
[69] PEReference ::= '%' Name ';'
                     [ VC: Entity Declared ]
                     [ WFC: No Recursion ]
                     [ WFC: In DTD ]
```

Entity declaration

```
[70] EntityDecl ::= GEDecl | PEDecl
[71] GEDecl     ::= '<!ENTITY' S Name S EntityDef S? '>'
[72] PEDecl     ::= '<!ENTITY' S '%' S Name S PEDef S? '>'
[73] EntityDef  ::= EntityValue | (ExternalID NDataDecl?)
[74] PEDef      ::= EntityValue | ExternalID
```

External entity declaration

```
[75] ExternalID ::= 'SYSTEM' S SystemLiteral
               | 'PUBLIC' S PubidLiteral S SystemLiteral
[76] NDataDecl  ::= S 'NDATA' S Name
                    [ VC: Notation Declared ]
```

Text declaration

```
[77] TextDecl ::= '<?xml' VersionInfo? EncodingDecl S? '?>'
```

Well-formed external parsed entity

```
[78] extParsedEnt ::= TextDecl? content
```

Encoding declaration

```
[80] EncodingDecl ::= S 'encoding' Eq ('"' EncName '"'
                    | "'" EncName "'" )
[81] EncName      ::= [A-Za-z] ([A-Za-z0-9._] | '-')*
```

Notation declarations

```
[82] NotationDecl  ::= '<!NOTATION' S Name S (ExternalID
                     | PublicID) S? '>'
                     [VC: Unique Notation Name]
[83] PublicID      ::= 'PUBLIC' S PubidLiteral
```

Characters

```
[84] Letter   ::= BaseChar | Ideographic
[85] BaseChar ::= [#x0041-#x005A] | [#x0061-#x007A]
              | [#x00C0-#x00D6] | [#x00D8-#x00F6]
              | [#x00F8-#x00FF] | [#x0100-#x0131]
              | [#x0134-#x013E] | [#x0141-#x0148]
              | [#x014A-#x017E] | [#x0180-#x01C3]
              | [#x01CD-#x01F0] | [#x01F4-#x01F5]
              | [#x01FA-#x0217] | [#x0250-#x02A8]
              | [#x02BB-#x02C1] | #x0386 | [#x0388-#x038A]
              | #x038C | [#x038E-#x03A1] | [#x03A3-#x03CE]
              | [#x03D0-#x03D6] | #x03DA | #x03DC | #x03DE
              | #x03E0 | [#x03E2-#x03F3] | [#x0401-#x040C]
              | [#x040E-#x044F] | [#x0451-#x045C]
              | [#x045E-#x0481] | [#x0490-#x04C4]
              | [#x04C7-#x04C8] | [#x04CB-#x04CC]
              | [#x04D0-#x04EB] | [#x04EE-#x04F5]
              | [#x04F8-#x04F9] | [#x0531-#x0556] | #x0559
              | [#x0561-#x0586] | [#x05D0-#x05EA]
              | [#x05F0-#x05F2] | [#x0621-#x063A]
              | [#x0641-#x064A] | [#x0671-#x06B7]
              | [#x06BA-#x06BE] | [#x06C0-#x06CE]
```

```
|  [#x06D0-#x06D3] |  #x06D5  |  [#x06E5-#x06E6]
|  [#x0905-#x0939] |  [#x093D] |  [#x0958-#x0961]
|  [#x0985-#x098C] |  [#x098F-#x0990]
|  [#x0993-#x09A8] |  [#x09AA-#x09B0]
|  #x09B2 |  [#x09B6-#x09B9] |  [#x09DC-#x09DD]
|  [#x09DF-#x09E1] |  [#x09F0-#x09F1]
|  [#x0A05-#x0A0A] |  [#x0A0F-#x0A10]
|  [#x0A13-#x0A28] |  [#x0A2A-#x0A30]
|  [#x0A32-#x0A33] |  [#x0A35-#x0A36]
|  [#x0A38-#x0A39] |  [#x0A59-#x0A5C]
|  #x0A5E |  [#x0A72-#x0A74] |  [#x0A85-#x0A8B]
|  #x0A8D |  [#x0A8F-#x0A91] |  [#x0A93-#x0AA8]
|  [#x0AAA-#x0AB0] |  [#x0AB2-#x0AB3]
|  [#x0AB5-#x0AB9] |  #x0ABD |  #x0AE0
|  [#x0B05-#x0B0C] |  [#x0B0F-#x0B10]
|  [#x0B13-#x0B28] |  [#x0B2A-#x0B30]
|  [#x0B32-#x0B33] |  [#x0B36-#x0B39]
|  #x0B3D |  [#x0B5C-#x0B5D] |  [#x0B5F-#x0B61]
|  [#x0B85-#x0B8A] |  [#x0B8E-#x0B90]
|  [#x0B92-#x0B95] |  [#x0B99-#x0B9A] |  #x0B9C
|  [#x0B9E-#x0B9F] |  [#x0BA3-#x0BA4]
|  [#x0BA8-#x0BAA] |  [#x0BAE-#x0BB5]
|  [#x0BB7-#x0BB9] |  [#x0C05-#x0C0C]
|  [#x0C0E-#x0C10] |  [#x0C12-#x0C28]
|  [#x0C2A-#x0C33] |  [#x0C35-#x0C39]
|  [#x0C60-#x0C61] |  [#x0C85-#x0C8C]
|  [#x0C8E-#x0C90] |  [#x0C92-#x0CA8]
|  [#x0CAA-#x0CB3] |  [#x0CB5-#x0CB9] |  #x0CDE
|  [#x0CE0-#x0CE1] |  [#x0D05-#x0D0C]
|  [#x0D0E-#x0D10] |  [#x0D12-#x0D28]
|  [#x0D2A-#x0D39] |  [#x0D60-#x0D61]
|  [#x0E01-#x0E2E] |  #x0E30 |  [#x0E32-#x0E33]
|  [#x0E40-#x0E45] |  [#x0E81-#x0E82] |  #x0E84
|  [#x0E87-#x0E88] |  #x0E8A |  #x0E8D
|  [#x0E94-#x0E97] |  [#x0E99-#x0E9F]
|  [#x0EA1-#x0EA3] |  #x0EA5 |  #x0EA7
|  [#x0EAA-#x0EAB] |  [#x0EAD-#x0EAE] |  #x0EB0
|  [#x0EB2-#x0EB3] |  #x0EBD |  [#x0EC0-#x0EC4]
|  [#x0F40-#x0F47] |  [#x0F49-#x0F69]
|  [#x10A0-#x10C5] |  [#x10D0-#x10F6] |  #x1100
|  [#x1102-#x1103] |  [#x1105-#x1107] |  #x1109
|  [#x110B-#x110C] |  [#x110E-#x1112] |  #x113C
|  #x113E |  #x1140 |  #x114C |  #x114E |  #x1150
|  [#x1154-#x1155] |  #x1159 |  [#x115F-#x1161]
|  #x1163 |  #x1165 |  #x1167 |  #x1169
|  [#x116D-#x116E] |  [#x1172-#x1173] |  #x1175
|  #x119E |  #x11A8 |  #x11AB |  [#x11AE-#x11AF]
|  [#x11B7-#x11B8] |  #x11BA |  [#x11BC-#x11C2]
|  #x11EB |  #x11F0 |  #x11F9 |  [#x1E00-#x1E9B]
```

```
                      | [#x1EA0-#x1EF9] | [#x1F00-#x1F15]
                      | [#x1F18-#x1F1D] | [#x1F20-#x1F45]
                      | [#x1F48-#x1F4D] | [#x1F50-#x1F57] | #x1F59
                      #x1F5B | #x1F5D | [#x1F5F-#x1F7D]
                      | [#x1F80-#x1FB4] | [#x1FB6-#x1FBC] | #x1FBE
                      | [#x1FC2-#x1FC4] | [#x1FC6-#x1FCC]
                      | [#x1FD0-#x1FD3] | [#x1FD6-#x1FDB]
                      | [#x1FE0-#x1FEC] | [#x1FF2-#x1FF4]
                      | [#x1FF6-#x1FFC] | #x2126 | [#x212A-#x212B]
                      #x212E | [#x2180-#x2182] | [#x3041-#x3094]
                      | [#x30A1-#x30FA] | [#x3105-#x312C]
                      | [#xAC00-#xD7A3]
   [86] Ideographic    ::= [#x4E00-#x9FA5] | #x3007
                      | [#x3021-#x3029]
   [87] CombiningChar ::= [#x0300-#x0345] | [#x0360-#x0361]
                      | [#x0483-#x0486] | [#x0591-#x05A1]
                      | [#x05A3-#x05B9] | [#x05BB-#x05BD]
                      | #x05BF | [#x05C1-#x05C2] | #x05C4
                      | [#x064B-#x0652] | #x0670
                      | [#x06D6-#x06DC] | [#x06DD-#x06DF]
                      | [#x06E0-#x06E4] | [#x06E7-#x06E8]
                      | [#x06EA-#x06ED] | [#x0901-#x0903]
                      | #x093C | [#x093E-#x094C] | #x094D
                      | [#x0951-#x0954] | [#x0962-#x0963]
                      | [#x0981-#x0983] | #x09BC | #x09BE
                      | #x09BF | [#x09C0-#x09C4]
                      | [#x09C7-#x09C8] | [#x09CB-#x09CD]
                      | #x09D7 | [#x09E2-#x09E3] | #x0A02
                      | #x0A3C | #x0A3E | #x0A3F
                      | [#x0A40-#x0A42] | [#x0A47-#x0A48]
                      | [#x0A4B-#x0A4D] | [#x0A70-#x0A71]
                      | [#x0A81-#x0A83] | #x0ABC
                      | [#x0ABE-#x0AC5] | [#x0AC7-#x0AC9]
                      | [#x0ACB-#x0ACD] | [#x0B01-#x0B03]
                      | #x0B3C | [#x0B3E-#x0B43]
                      | [#x0B47-#x0B48] | [#x0B4B-#x0B4D]
                      | [#x0B56-#x0B57] | [#x0B82-#x0B83]
                      | [#x0BBE-#x0BC2] | [#x0BC6-#x0BC8]
                      | [#x0BCA-#x0BCD] | #x0BD7
                      | [#x0C01-#x0C03] | [#x0C3E-#x0C44]
                      | [#x0C46-#x0C48] | [#x0C4A-#x0C4D]
                      | [#x0C55-#x0C56] | [#x0C82-#x0C83]
                      | [#x0CBE-#x0CC4] | [#x0CC6-#x0CC8]
                      | [#x0CCA-#x0CCD] | [#x0CD5-#x0CD6]
                      | [#x0D02-#x0D03] | [#x0D3E-#x0D43]
                      | [#x0D46-#x0D48] | [#x0D4A-#x0D4D]
                      | #x0D57 | #x0E31 | [#x0E34-#x0E3A]
```

```
                          | [#x0E47-#x0E4E] | #x0EB1
                          | [#x0EB4-#x0EB9] | [#x0EBB-#x0EBC]
                          | [#x0EC8-#x0ECD] | [#x0F18-#x0F19]
                          | #x0F35 | #x0F37 | #x0F39 | #x0F3E
                          | #x0F3F | [#x0F71-#x0F84]
                          | [#x0F86-#x0F8B] | [#x0F90-#x0F95]
                          | #x0F97 | [#x0F99-#x0FAD]
                          | [#x0FB1-#x0FB7] | #x0FB9
                          | [#x20D0-#x20DC] | #x20E1
                          | [#x302A-#x302F] | #x3099 | #x309A
    [88] Digit ::=          [#x0030-#x0039] | [#x0660-#x0669]
                          | [#x06F0-#x06F9] | [#x0966-#x096F]
                          | [#x09E6-#x09EF] | [#x0A66-#x0A6F]
                          | [#x0AE6-#x0AEF] | [#x0B66-#x0B6F]
                          | [#x0BE7-#x0BEF] | [#x0C66-#x0C6F]
                          | [#x0CE6-#x0CEF] | [#x0D66-#x0D6F]
                          | [#x0E50-#x0E59] | [#x0ED0-#x0ED9]
                          | [#x0F20-#x0F29]
    [89] Extender ::=      #x00B7 | #x02D0 | #x02D1 | #x0387
                          | #x0640 | #x0E46 | #x0EC6 | #x3005
                          | [#x3031-#x3035] | [#x309D-#x309E]
                          | [#x30FC-#x30FE]
```

Examples of the XML 1.0 productions

This section shows you some instances of the productions to give you a better idea
of what each one means.

Document

[1] document ::= prolog element Misc*

This rule says that an XML document is composed of a prolog (Production [22]),
followed by a single root element (Production [39]), followed by any number of miscellaneous items (Production [27]). In other words, a typical document looks like
this:

```
<?xml version="1.0"?>
<!-- a DTD might go here -->
<ROOT_ELEMENT>
  Content
</ROOT_ELEMENT>
<!-- comments can go here -->
<?Reader processing instructions can also go here?>
```

In practice, it's rare for anything to follow the close of the root element.

Production [1] rules out documents with more than one root element like this:

```
<?xml version="1.0"?>
<ELEMENT1>
  Content
</ELEMENT1>
<ELEMENT2>
  Content
</ELEMENT2>
<ELEMENT1>
  Content
</ELEMENT1>
```

Character range

[2] Char ::= #x9 | #xA | #xD | [#x20-#xD7FF] | [#xE000-#xFFFD] | [#x10000-#x10FFFF]

Production [2] defines the subset of Unicode characters that may appear in an XML document. The main items of interest here are the characters not included. Specifically, these are the nonprinting ASCII control characters of which the most common are the bell, vertical tab, and form feed; the surrogates block; and the noncharacters #xFFFE and #xFFFF. The control characters are not needed in XML and may cause problems in files displayed on old terminals or passed through old terminal servers and software.

The surrogates block between #xD800 to #xDFFF is used to extend Unicode to support over one million different characters. However, when processed, each surrogate pair is converted into a single character in the range #x10000 to #x10FFFF. The parser should do this before checking the document for well formedness (just as it would convert any other character encoding), so that an application receiving data from the parser never sees surrogates.

The noncharacters #xFFFE and #xFFFF are not defined in Unicode. The appearance of xFFFE, especially at the start of a document, indicates that you're reading the document with the wrong byte order; that is, little endian instead of big endian, or vice versa.

Not all the code points used in this production are actually defined in Unicode. You should avoid undefined code points in your documents. However, these undefined characters are allowed to support future developments of Unicode. For instance, when the first edition of XML 1.0 was released in February 1998, the current version of Unicode was 2.0 with 38,885 characters. Today, in April 2001, the current version of Unicode is 3.1 with 94,140 characters. XML parsers accept the 55,255 new characters added since Unicode 2.0 without any complaint. Although these characters can't be used in XML names and name tokens like the Unicode 2.0 characters can be used, they can be used in the character data of the document. This makes it possible to write XML documents in scripts such as Cherokee, Deseret, Gothic, Tengwar, and Ethiopic that weren't included in Unicode 2.0 but were added to Unicode 3.0.

White space

[3] S ::= (#x20 | #x9 | #xD | #xA)+

Production [3] defines white space as a run of one or more space characters (#x20), the horizontal tab (#x9), the carriage return (#xD), and the linefeed (#xA). Because of the +, 20 of these characters in a row are treated exactly the same as one.

Other ASCII white space characters such as the vertical tab (#xB) are prohibited by Production [2]. Other non-ASCII, Unicode white space characters, such as the non-breaking space (#xA0), are not considered white space for the purposes of XML.

Names and tokens

[4] NameChar ::= Letter | Digit | '.' | '-' | '_' | ':' | CombiningChar | Extender

Production [4] defines the characters that may appear in an XML name. XML names may only contain letters (Production [84]), digits (Production [88]), periods, hyphens, underscores, colons, combining characters (Production [87]), and extenders (Production [89]).

Although the XML 1.0 BNF grammar allows names to contain colons, the second edition adds the following note:

> The Namespaces in XML Recommendation [XML Names] assigns a meaning to names containing colon characters. Therefore, authors should not use the colon in XML names except for namespace purposes, but XML processors must accept the colon as a name character.

[5] Name ::= (Letter | '_' | ':') (NameChar)*

Production [5] says an XML name must begin with a letter (Production [84]), an underscore, or a colon. It may not begin with a digit, a period, or a hyphen. Subsequent characters in an XML name may include any XML name character (Production [4]) including digits, periods, and hyphens. The following are acceptable XML names:

```
airplane
text.encoding
r
SEAT
Pilot
Pilot1
OscarWilde
BOOK_TITLE
_8ball
ετνους
```

These are unacceptable XML names:

```
air plane
.encoding
-r
Wilde,Oscar
BOOK TITLE
8ball
AHA!
```

Although this rule allows names to begin with colons, the Namespaces in XML Recommendation does not. You should not use names that begin with colons.

[6] Names ::= Name (S Name)*

Production [6] defines a group of names as one or more XML names (Production [5]) separated by white space. This is a valid group of XML names:

```
BOOK AUTHOR TITLE PAGE EDITOR CHAPTER
```

This is not a valid group of XML names:

```
BOOK, AUTHOR, TITLE, PAGE, EDITOR, CHAPTER
```

[7] Nmtoken ::= (NameChar)+

Production [7] defines a name token as any sequence of one or more name characters (Production [4]). Unlike an XML name, a name token has no restrictions on what the first character is as long as it is a valid name character. In other words, XML name tokens may begin with a digit, a period, or a hyphen, whereas an XML name may not. All XML names are XML name tokens, but not all name tokens are XML names.

The following are acceptable name tokens:

```
airplane
text.encoding
r
SEAT
Pilot
Pilot1
OscarWilde
BOOK_TITLE
:TITLE
_8ball
ετνους
.encoding
-r
8ball
```

The following are unacceptable name tokens:

```
air plane
Wilde,Oscar
BOOK TITLE
AHA!
```

[8] Nmtokens ::= Nmtoken (S Nmtoken)*

Production [8] says a group of name tokens is one or more XML name tokens (Production [7]) separated by white space. This is a valid group of XML name tokens:

```
1POTATO 2POTATO 3POTATO 4
```

This is not a valid group of XML name tokens:

```
1POTATO, 2POTATO, 3POTATO, 4
```

Literals

[9] EntityValue ::= '"' ([^%&"] | PEReference | Reference)* '"' | "'" ([^%&'] | PEReference | Reference)* "'"

Production [9] defines an entity value as any string of characters enclosed in double quotes or single quotes except for %, &, and the quote character (single or double) used to delimit the string. % and & may be used, however, if and only if they're the start of a parameter entity reference (Production [69]), a general entity reference (Production [67]), or a character reference (Production [66]). If you really need to include % and & in your entity values, you can escape them with the character references % and &, respectively.

These are legal entity values:

```
"This is an entity value"
'This is an entity value'
"75&#37; off"
"Ben &amp; Jerry's New York Super Fudge Chunk Ice Cream"
<YEAR>2001</YEAR>
```

These are illegal entity values:

```
"This is an entity value'
'This is an entity value"
"75% off"
"Ben & Jerry's New York Super Fudge Chunk Ice Cream"
'Ben &amp; Jerry's New York Super Fudge Chunk Ice Cream
```

[10] AttValue ::= '"' ([^<&"] | Reference)* '"' | "'" ([^<&'] | Reference)* "'"

Production [10] says that an attribute value may consist of any characters except <, &, and " enclosed in double quotes, or any characters except <, &, and ' enclosed in single quotes. The & may appear, however, only if it's used as the start of a reference (Production [67]) (either general or character).

These are legal attribute values:

```
"This is an attribute value"
'This is an attribute value'
'#FFCC33'
"75% off"
"Ben &amp; Jerry's New York Super Fudge Chunk Ice Cream"
"i &lt; j"
```

These are illegal attribute values:

```
"This is an attribute value'
'This is an attribute value"
"Ben & Jerry's New York Super Fudge Chunk Ice Cream"
'Ben and Jerry's New York Super Fudge Chunk Ice Cream'
"i < j"
```

[11] SystemLiteral ::= ('"' [^"]* '"') | ("'" [^']* "'")

Production [11] defines a system literal as any string of text that does not contain the double quote mark enclosed in double quotes. Alternately, a system literal may be any string of text that does not contain the single quote mark enclosed in single quotes. These are grammatical system literals:

```
"spec.dtd"
"http://www.w3.org/XML/1998/06/xmlspec-v21.dtd"
"Jimmy's Bar"
" Hello there! "
' Hello
  there!'
"Embedded markup is <OK/> in system literals"
```

These are ungrammatical system literals:

```
" He said, "Get out of here!""
'Bailey's Cove'
```

Although this production is extremely liberal in what it accepts, non-BNF considerations require that all system literals be relative or absolute Uniform Resource Identifiers (URIs). In particular, system-literal URIs are used to locate a document's DTD in the document type declaration, and to locate the source of an external entity reference. URIs have much stricter rules, including that all non-ASCII characters (and quite a few ASCII characters as well) must be escaped using a percent sign and the hexadecimal form of their encoding in UTF-8.

[12] PubidLiteral ::= '"' PubidChar* '"' | "'" (PubidChar - "'")* "'"

Production [12] says that a public ID literal is either zero or more public ID characters (Production [13]) enclosed in double quotes, or zero or more public ID characters except the single quote mark enclosed in single quotes.

These are grammatical public ID literals:

```
"-//IETF//NONSGML Media Type application/pdf//EN"
'-//IETF//NONSGML Media Type application/pdf//EN'
"-//W3C//DTD XHTML 1.0 Strict + Math//EN"
```

These are ungrammatical public ID literals:

```
"{-//IETF//NONSGML Media Type application/pdf//EN}"
"-//IETF//NONSGML Media Type application/πΔΦ//GR}"
```

XML 1.0 does not provide any additional hints about what a proper public ID string should look like or how it is resolved. This is left up to the parser. For this reason, some people have suggested that public IDs should be deprecated in favor of system IDs that contain a well-understood standard form of a URI.

[13] PubidChar ::= #x20 | #xD | #xA | [a-zA-Z0-9] | [-'()+,./:=?;!*#@$_%]

Production [13] lists the permissible public ID characters, essentially, the ASCII space, carriage return, and linefeed, the letters *a* through *z* and *A* through *Z*, the digits *0* through *9*, and the punctuation characters *-'()+,./:=?;!*#@$_%*.

Character data
[14] CharData ::= [^<&]* - ([^<&]* ']]>' [^<&]*)

Production [14] defines character data as any number of any characters except for < and &. Furthermore, the CDEnd string]]> may not appear as part of the character data. Character data may contain as few as zero characters.

Comments
[15] Comment ::= '<!-' ((Char - '-') | ('-' (Char - '-')))* '->'

Production [15] defines a comment as any string of text enclosed between <!-- and --> marks with the single exception of the double hyphen --. These are all valid comments:

```
<!--Hello-->
<!--Hello there!-->
<!-- Hello there! -->
<!-- Hello
     there! -->
<!--<Hello/> <there/>!-->
<!-- Grade: B- -->
```

These are illegal comments:

```
<!-- Hello--there! -->
<!-- Grade: A--->
```

Processing instructions

[16] PI ::= '<?' PITarget (S (Char* - (Char* '?>' Char*)))? '?>'

Production [16] says that a processing instruction starts with the literal <?, followed by the name of the processing instruction target (Production [17]), optionally followed by white space, followed by any number of characters except ?>. Finally, the literal ?> closes the processing instruction.

These are all legal processing instructions:

```
<?gcc version="2.9.5" options="-04"?>
<?Terri Do you think this is a good example?>
```

These are illegal processing instructions:

```
<? I have to remember to fix this next part?>
<?Terri This is a good example!>
```

[17] PITarget ::= Name - (('X' | 'x') ('M' | 'm') ('L' | 'l'))

Production [17] says that a processing instruction target may be any XML name (Production [5]) except the string *XML* (in any combination of case). Thus, these are all acceptable processing instruction targets:

```
gcc
acrobat
Acrobat
Joshua
Acrobat_301
xml-stylesheet
XML_Whizzy_Writer_2000
```

These are unacceptable processing instruction targets:

```
xml
XML
xmL
-renfield
123
Terri,
```

CDATA sections

[18] CDSect ::= CDStart CData CDEnd

Production [18] states that a CData section is composed of a CDStart (Production [19]), CData (Production [20]), and a CDEnd (Production [21]), in that order.

[19] CDStart ::= '<![CDATA['

Production [19] defines a CDStart as the literal string `<![CDATA[` and nothing else.

[20] CData ::= (Char* - (Char* ']]>' Char*))

Production [20] says that a CData section may contain absolutely any characters except the CDEnd string `]]>`.

[21] CDEnd ::= ']]>'

Production [21] defines a CDEnd as the literal string `]]>` and nothing else.

These are correct CDATA sections:

```
<![CDATA[ The < character starts a tag in XML ]]>
<![CDATA[ CDATA sections begin with the literal <![CDATA[ ]]>
```

This is an illegal CDATA section:

```
<![CDATA[
  The three characters ]]> terminate a CDATA section
]]>
```

Prolog

[22] prolog ::= XMLDecl? Misc* (doctypedecl Misc*)?

Production [22] says that a prolog consists of an optional XML declaration, followed by zero or more miscellaneous items (Production [27]), followed by an optional document type declaration (Production [28]), followed by zero or more miscellaneous items. For instance, this is a legal prolog:

```
<?xml version="1.0"?>
```

This is also a legal prolog:

```
<?xml version="1.0" standalone="yes"?>
<?xml-stylesheet type="text/css" href="greeting.css"?>
<!DOCTYPE greeting [
  <!ELEMENT greeting (#PCDATA)>
]>
```

This is also a legal prolog:

```
<!--This strange document really doesn't have anything
    in its prolog! -->
```

This is an illegal prolog because a comment precedes the XML declaration:

```
<!--This is from the example in Chapter 8 -->
<?xml version="1.0" standalone="yes"?>
<?xml-stylesheet type="text/css" href="greeting.css"?>
<!DOCTYPE greeting [
  <!ELEMENT greeting (#PCDATA)>
]>
```

[23] XMLDecl ::= '<?xml' VersionInfo EncodingDecl? SDDecl? S? '?>'

Production [23] defines an XML declaration as the literal string `<?xml` followed by a mandatory version info string (Production [24]), optionally followed by an encoding declaration (Production [80]), optionally followed by a stand-alone document declaration (Production [32]), optionally followed by white space, followed by the literal string `?>`. These are legal XML declarations:

```
<?xml version="1.0"?>
<?xml version="1.0" encoding="Big5"?>
<?xml version="1.0" encoding="ISO-8859-1" standalone="yes"?>
<?xml version="1.0" standalone="no"? >
<?xml version="1.0" encoding="ISO-8859-5"?>
```

These are illegal XML declarations:

```
<?xml?>
<?xml version=1.0 encoding=Big5?>
<?xml encoding="Big5"?>
<?xml version="1.0" standalone="yes"? encoding="ISO-8859-1" ?>
<?xml version="1.0" standalone="no"? stylesheet="poems.css"?>
```

[24] VersionInfo ::= S 'version' Eq ("'" VersionNum "'" | '"' VersionNum '"')

Production [24] defines the version info string as white space followed by the literal string `version`, followed by an equals sign (Production [25]), followed by a version number enclosed in either single or double quotes. These are legal version info strings:

```
version="1.0"
version='1.0'
version = '1.0'
```

These are ungrammatical version info strings:

```
version=1.0
version='1.0"
"1.0"=version
```

[25] Eq ::= S? '=' S?

Production [25] defines the string `Eq` in the grammar as a stand-in for the equals sign (=) in documents. White space (Production [3]) may or may not appear on either side of the equals sign. The reason for this production is to say that white space around equals signs is always optional without having to repeat that in every production that uses an equals sign.

[26] VersionNum ::= ([a-zA-Z0-9_.:] | '-')+

Production [26] says that a version number consists of one or more of the letters *a* through *z*, the capital letters *A* through *Z*, the underscore, the period, and the hyphen. The following are grammatically correct version numbers:

```
1.0
1.x
1.1.3
1.5EA2
v1.5
EA_B
```

The following are ungrammatical version numbers:

```
version 1.5
1,5
1!1
1 5 3
v 1.5
—
```

Note The only version number currently used in XML documents is 1.0. Parsers are allowed but not required to signal an error if some other value is used. For now, this production might as well read:

```
VersionNum ::= "1.0"
```

[27] Misc ::= Comment | PI | S

Production [27] defines the miscellaneous items in an XML document as comments (Production [15]), processing instructions (Production [16]), and white space (Production [3]).

Document type definition

[28] doctypedecl ::= '<!DOCTYPE' S Name (S ExternalID)? S? ('[' (markupdecl | DeclSep)* ']' S?)? '>'

Production [28] says that a document type declaration consists of the literal string `<!DOCTYPE`, followed by white space (Production [3]), followed by an XML name (Production [5]), optionally followed by white space and an external ID (Production [75]), optionally followed by more white space, followed by a left square bracket (`[`), followed by zero or more markup declarations (Production [29]) and/or declaration separators (Production [28a]), followed by a right square bracket (`]`) and white space, followed by a closing angle bracket.

These are all legal document type declarations:

```
<!DOCTYPE SEASON SYSTEM "baseball.dtd">
<!DOCTYPE smil PUBLIC
  "-//W3C//ENTITIES SMIL 2.0 Modular Framework 1.0//EN"
  "smil-framework-1.mod">
<!DOCTYPE DOCUMENT SYSTEM "greeting.dtd" [
    <!ELEMENT DOCUMENT (GREETING, DATE)>
    <!ELEMENT DATE (#PCDATA)>
]>
<!DOCTYPE GREETING [
  <!ELEMENT GREETING (#PCDATA)>
]>
```

This is an illegal document type declaration:

```
<!DOCTYPE smil PUBLIC
  "-//W3C//ENTITIES SMIL 2.0 Modular Framework 1.0//EN">
```

[28a] DeclSep ::= PEReference | S

Production [28a] defines a declaration separator as either a parameter entity reference (Production [69]) or white space (Production [3]). The unusual number is because it was necessary to add this production between the existing productions 28 and 29 in the second edition of the XML 1.0 specification.

[29] markupdecl ::= elementdecl | AttlistDecl | EntityDecl | NotationDecl | PI | Comment

Production [29] says that a markup declaration may be either an element declaration (Production [45]), an attribute list declaration (Production [52]), an entity declaration (Production [70]), a notation declaration (Production [82]), a processing instruction (Production [16]), or a comment (Production [15]).

External subset

[30] extSubset ::= TextDecl? extSubsetDecl

Production [30] says that an external subset consists of an optional text declaration (Production [77]), followed by an external subset declaration (Production [31]).

[31] extSubsetDecl ::= (markupdecl | conditionalSect | DeclSep)

Production [31] says the external subset declaration contains any number of markup declarations (Production [29]), conditional sections (Production [61]), or declaration separators (Production [28a]) in any order. In essence, the external subset can contain everything that the internal DTD can contain plus conditional sections (INCLUDE and IGNORE blocks). The internal DTD subset may not contain conditional sections.

Standalone document declaration

[32] SDDecl ::= S 'standalone' Eq (("'" ('yes' | 'no') "'") | ('"' ('yes' | 'no') '"'))

Production [32] says that the standalone document declaration consists of the literal standalone, followed by an equals sign (which may be surrounded by white space), followed by either yes or no enclosed in single or double quotes. Legal standalone document declarations include:

```
standalone="yes"
standalone="no"
standalone='yes'
standalone='no'
standalone = "yes"
standalone= "no"
```

Language identification

Productions [33] through [38] were included in the first edition of XML 1.0. However, they were unreachable; that is, they were not start productions and they were not referenced by any other production. Nonetheless, some parsers (incorrectly) chose to implement them to specify the format for language codes used in xml:lang attribute values. To clarify matters, these productions have been deleted from the second edition of the XML 1.0 specification.

Element

[39] element ::= EmptyElemTag | STag content ETag

Production [39] defines an element as either an empty element tag (production [44]) or a start tag (production [40]), followed by content (production [43]), followed by an end tag (production [42]).

These are legal elements:

```
<P>Hello!</P>
<P><EM>Hello</EM>!</P>
<P/>
<P></P>
```

These are illegal elements:

```
<P>Hello!</p>
<P>
</Q>
```

This production does not actually require that the name in an end tag match the name in the corresponding start tag. That actually proves to be impossible to do using only BNF. Therefore, this constraint is instead imposed by a well-formedness constraint.

Start tag

[40] STag ::= '<' Name (S Attribute)* S? '>'

Production [40] says that a start tag begins with a < followed by an XML name (Production [5]), followed by any number of attributes (Production [41]) separated by white space, followed by a closing >. These are legal start tags:

```
<DOCUMENT>
<ДОКУМЕНТ>
<DOCUMENT  >
<DOCUMENT TITLE="The Red Badge of Courage" >
<DOCUMENT TITLE="The Red Badge of Courage" PAGES="129">
```

These are illegal start tags:

```
< DOCUMENT>
<>
<12091998>
```

[41] Attribute ::= Name Eq AttValue

Production [41] says that an attribute consists of an XML name (Production [5]), followed by an equals sign (which may be encased in white space) followed by an attribute value (Production [10]). Grammatical attributes include:

```
TITLE="The Red Badge of Courage"
PAGES="129"
TITLE = "The Red Badge of Courage"
PAGES = "129"
TITLE='The Red Badge of Courage'
PAGES='129'
SENTENCE='Jim said, "I didn&apos;t expect to see you here."'
```

Ungrammatical attributes include:

```
TITLE="The Red Badge of Courage'
PAGES=129
SENTENCE='Jim said, "I didn't expect to see you here."'
```

End tag
[42] ETag ::= '</' Name S? '>'

Production [42] defines an end tag as the literal string </ immediately followed by an XML name, optionally followed by white space, followed by the > character. For example, these are grammatical XML end tags:

```
</PERSON>
</PERSON >
</AbrahamLincoln>
<ДОКУМЕНТ>
```

These are ungrammatical XML end tags:

```
</ PERSON>
</Abraham Lincoln>
</PERSON NAME="Abraham Lincoln">
</>
```

Content of elements
[43] content ::= CharData? ((element | Reference | CDSect | PI | Comment) CharData?)*

Production [43] defines content as optional character data (Production [14]), followed by elements (Production [39]), references (Production [67]), CDATA sections (Production [18]), processing instructions (Production [16]), and comments (Production [15]) optionally interspersed with more character data in any order. This production lists everything that can appear inside an element.

Tags for empty elements
[44] EmptyElemTag ::= '<' Name (S Attribute)* S? '/>'

Production [44] defines an empty-element tag as the character <, followed by an XML name, followed by white space, followed by zero more attributes separated from each other by white space, optionally followed by white space, followed by the literal />. These are grammatical empty–Element tags:

```
<PERSON/>
<PERSON />
<Person/>
<person />
<AbrahamLincoln/>
<ДОКУМЕНТ>
```

These are ungrammatical empty-element tags:

```
< PERSON/>
<PERSON>
</Person>
</person/>
</>
```

(The second and third are grammatical start and end tags, respectively.)

Element type declaration

[45] elementdecl ::= '<!ELEMENT' S Name S contentspec S? '>'

Production [45] says that an element declaration consists of the literal <!ELEMENT, followed by white space, followed by an XML name (Production [5]), followed by a content specification (Production [46]), optionally followed by white space, followed by the > character.

Grammatical element declarations include:

```
<!ELEMENT DOCUMENT ANY>
<!ELEMENT HR EMPTY>
<!ELEMENT DOCUMENT (#PCDATA | P | H)>
```

[46] contentspec ::= 'EMPTY' | 'ANY' | Mixed | children

Production [46] defines a content specification as either the literals EMPTY or ANY, a list of children (Production [47]), or mixed content (Production [51]).

Element-content models

[47] children ::= (choice | seq) ('?' | '*' | '+')?

Production [47] says that a list of children consists of either a choice (Production [49]) or a sequence (Production [50]) optionally followed by one of the characters ?, *, or +.

[48] cp ::= (Name | choice | seq) ('?' | '*' | '+')?

Production [48] defines a content particle as an XML name (Production [5]), choice, (Production [49]), or sequence (Production [50], optionally suffixed with a ?, *, or +.

[49] choice ::= '(' S? cp (S? '|' S? cp)+ S? ')'

Production [49] says that a choice is one or more content particles (Production [48]) enclosed in parentheses and separated from each other by vertical bars and optional white space. Grammatical choices include:

```
(P | UL | H1 | H2 | H3 | H4 | H5 | BLOCKQUOTE | PRE | HR | DIV)
(P|UL|H1|H2|H3|H4|H5|H6|BLOCKQUOTE|PRE|HR|DIV)
(SON | DAUGHTER)
( SON | DAUGHTER )
(ADDRESS | (NAME, STREET, APT, CITY, STATE, ZIP))
```

[50] seq ::= '(' S? cp (S? ',' S? cp)* S? ')'

Production [50] says that a sequence is one or more content particles (Production [48]) enclosed in parentheses and separated from each other by commas and optional white space. Grammatical sequences include:

```
(NAME, STREET, APT, CITY, STATE, ZIP)
(NAME , STREET , APT , CITY , STATE , ZIP)
(NAME,STREET,APT,CITY,STATE,ZIP)
( NAME,STREET,APT, CITY,STATE,ZIP )
(NAME, (STREET|BOX), (APT|SUITE), CITY, STATE, ZIP, COUNTRY?)
(NAME)
```

Mixed-content declaration

[51] Mixed ::= '(' S? '#PCDATA' (S? '|' S? Name)* S? ')*' | '(' S? '#PCDATA' S? ')'

Production [51] says that mixed content is either the literal (#PCDATA) (with allowances for optional white space) or a choice that includes the literal #PCDATA as its first content particle and is suffixed by an asterisk. These are grammatical mixed-content models:

```
(#PCDATA)
(#PCDATA)*
( #PCDATA )
(#PCDATA | PERSON)*
( #PCDATA | PERSON )*
( #PCDATA | TITLE | JOURNAL | MONTH | YEAR | SERIES | VOLUME )*
```

These are ungrammatical mixed-content models:

```
(PERSON | #PCDATA)*
(#PCDATA | PERSON)
(#PCDATA, TITLE, #PCDATA, JOURNAL, MONTH, YEAR, #PCDATA)*
(#PCDATA | (NAME, STREET, APT, CITY, STATE, ZIP))*
```

Attribute list declaration

[52] AttlistDecl ::= '<!ATTLIST' S Name AttDef* S? '>'

Production [52] says that an attribute list declaration consists of the literal <!ATTLIST, followed by white space, followed by an XML name (Production [5]),

followed by zero or more attribute definitions (Production [53]), optionally followed by white space, followed by the > character.

Grammatical attribute list declarations include:

```
<!ATTLIST IMG ALT    CDATA   #REQUIRED
              WIDTH  NMTOKEN #REQUIRED
              HEIGHT NMTOKEN #REQUIRED
>
<!ATTLIST REC WIDTH NMTOKEN #REQUIRED HEIGHT NMTOKEN #REQUIRED>
<!ATTLIST AUTHOR EXTENSION CDATA #IMPLIED>
<!ATTLIST AUTHOR COMPANY   CDATA #FIXED "TIC">
<!ATTLIST P VISIBLE (TRUE | FALSE) "TRUE">
<!ATTLIST ADDRESS STATE NMTOKEN #REQUIRED>
<!ATTLIST ADDRESS STATES NMTOKENS #REQUIRED>
<!ATTLIST P PNUMBER ID #REQUIRED>
<!ATTLIST PERSON FATHER IDREF #IMPLIED>
<!ATTLIST SLIDESHOW SOURCES ENTITIES #REQUIRED>
<!ATTLIST SOUND PLAYER NOTATION (MP) #REQUIRED>
```

[53] AttDef ::= S Name S AttType S DefaultDecl

Production [53] defines an attribute definition as white space, an XML name (Production [5]), more white space, an attribute type (Production [54]), more white space, and a default declaration (Production [60]). Grammatical attribute definitions include:

```
IMG ALT CDATA #REQUIRED
AUTHOR EXTENSION CDATA #IMPLIED
AUTHOR COMPANY   CDATA #FIXED "TIC"
P VISIBLE (TRUE | FALSE) "TRUE"
ADDRESS STATE  NMTOKEN #REQUIRED
ADDRESS STATES NMTOKENS #REQUIRED
P PNUMBER ID #REQUIRED
PERSON FATHER IDREF #IMPLIED
SLIDESHOW SOURCES ENTITIES #REQUIRED
SOUND PLAYER NOTATION (MP) #REQUIRED
```

Attribute types

[54] AttType ::= StringType | TokenizedType | EnumeratedType

Production [54] defines an attribute type as either a string type (Production [55]), a tokenized type (Production [56]), or an enumerated type (Production [57]).

[55] StringType ::= 'CDATA'

Production [55] defines a string type as the literal CDATA.

[56] TokenizedType ::= 'ID' | 'IDREF' | 'IDREFS' | 'ENTITY' | 'ENTITIES' | 'NMTOKEN' | 'NMTOKENS'

Production [56] defines a tokenized type as any one of these seven literals:

```
ID
IDREF
IDREFS
ENTITY
ENTITIES
NMTOKEN
NMTOKENS
```

Enumerated attribute types

[57] EnumeratedType ::= NotationType | Enumeration

Production [57] defines an enumerated type as either a notation type (Production [58]) or an enumeration (Production [59]).

[58] NotationType ::= 'NOTATION' S '(' S? Name (S? '|' S? Name)* S? ')'

Production [58] defines a notation type as the literal NOTATION, followed by white space, followed by one or more XML names (Production [5]), separated by vertical bars, and enclosed in parentheses. These are grammatical notation types:

```
NOTATION (MP)
NOTATION (MP | PDF)
NOTATION (mp | gcc | xv)
NOTATION (A | B | C)
```

These are ungrammatical notation types:

```
NOTATION ("MP")
NOTATION (MP PDF)
NOTATION (mp, gcc, xv)
NOTATION ("A" | "B" | "C")
```

[59] Enumeration ::= '(' S? Nmtoken (S? '|' S? Nmtoken)* S? ')'

Production [59] defines an enumeration as one or more XML name tokens (Production [7]) separated by vertical bars and enclosed in parentheses. These are grammatical enumerations:

```
(airplane)
(airplane | train | car | horse)
( airplane | train | car | horse )
(cavalo | carro | trem |avi o)
```

The following are ungrammatical enumerations:

```
( )
(airplane train car horse)
(airplane, train, car, horse)
airplane | train | car | horse
```

Attribute defaults
[60] DefaultDecl ::= '#REQUIRED' | '#IMPLIED' | (('#FIXED' S)? AttValue)

Production [60] defines the default declaration as one of these four things:

+ The literal #REQUIRED

+ The literal #IMPLIED

+ The literal #FIXED followed by white space (Production [3]), followed by an attribute value (Production [10])

+ An attribute value (Production [10])

Conditional section
[61] conditionalSect ::= includeSect | ignoreSect

Production [61] defines a conditional section as either an include section (Production [62]) or an ignore section (Production [63]).

[62] includeSect ::= '<![' S? 'INCLUDE' S? '[' extSubsetDecl ']]>'

Production [62] defines an include section as an external subset declaration (Production [31]) sandwiched between <![INCLUDE[ ]]>, modulo white space. These are grammatical include sections:

```
<![ INCLUDE [ ]]>
<![INCLUDE[ ]]>
<![ INCLUDE[ ]]>
```

[63] ignoreSect ::= '<![' S? 'IGNORE' S? '[' ignoreSectContents* ']]>'

Production [63] defines an ignore section as ignore section contents (Production [64]) sandwiched between <![IGNORE[ ]]>, modulo white space. These are grammatical ignore sections:

```
<![ IGNORE [ ]]>
<![IGNORE[ ]]>
<![ IGNORE[ ]]>
```

[64] ignoreSectContents ::= Ignore ('<![' ignoreSectContents ']]>' Ignore)*

Production [64] defines an ignore section's contents as an ignore block (Production [65]), optionally followed by a block of text sandwiched between <![and]]> literals, followed by more text. This may be repeated as many times as desired. This allows ignore sections to nest.

[65] Ignore ::= Char* - (Char* ('<![' | ']]>') Char*)

Production [65] defines an ignore block as any run of text that contains neither the <![nor the]]> literals. This prevents any possible confusion about where an ignore block ends.

Character reference
[66] CharRef ::= '&#' [0-9]+ ';' | '&#x' [0-9a-fA-F]+ ';'

Production [66] defines two forms for character references. The first is the literal &# followed by one or more of the ASCII digits 0 through 9. The second form is the literal &#x followed by one or more of the hexadecimal digits 0 through F. The digits representing 10 through 16 (A through F) may be either lowercase or uppercase.

Entity reference
[67] Reference ::= EntityRef | CharRef

Production [67] defines a reference as either an entity reference (Production [68]) or a character reference (Production [66]).

[68] EntityRef ::= '&' Name ';'

Production [68] defines an entity reference as an XML name (Production [5]) sandwiched between the ampersand character and a semicolon. These are grammatical entity references:

```
&amp;
&agrave;
&my_abbreviation;
```

These are ungrammatical entity references:

```
&amp
& agrave ;
& my_abbreviation;
```

[69] PEReference ::= '%' Name ';'

Production [69] defines a parameter entity reference as an XML name (Production [5]) sandwiched between the percent character and a semicolon. These are grammatical parameter entity references:

```
%inlines;
%mathml;
%MyElements;
```

These are ungrammatical parameter entity references:

```
%inlines
% mathml ;
%my elements;
```

Entity declaration

[70] EntityDecl ::= GEDecl | PEDecl

Production [70] defines an entity declaration as either a general entity declaration (Production [71]) or a parameter entity declaration (Production [71]).

[71] GEDecl ::= '<!ENTITY' S Name S EntityDef S? '>'

Production [71] defines a general entity declaration as the literal `<!ENTITY` followed by white space (Production [3]), followed by an XML name (Production [5]), followed by an entity definition (Production [73]), optionally followed by white space, followed by the > character. These are grammatical general entity declarations:

```
<!ENTITY alpha "&#945;">
<!ENTITY Alpha "&#913;">
<!ENTITY SPACEMUSIC SYSTEM "/sounds/space.wav" NDATA MP >
<!ENTITY LOGO SYSTEM "logo.gif">
<!ENTITY COPY01 "Copyright 2001 %erh;">
```

These are ungrammatical general entity declarations:

```
<!ENTITY alpha &#945;>
<!ENTITY Capital Greek Alpha "&#913;">
<!ENTITY LOGO SYSTEM logo.gif>
```

[72] PEDecl ::= '<!ENTITY' S '%' S Name S PEDef S? '>'

Production [72] defines a parameter entity declaration as the literal `<!ENTITY` followed by white space (Production [3]), followed by a percent sign and more white space, followed by an XML name (Production [5]), followed by an entity definition (Production [73]), optionally followed by white space, followed by the > character.

In essence, this says that parameter entity declarations are the same as general entity declarations except for the % between the `<!ENTITY` and the name. These are grammatical parameter entity declarations:

```
<!ENTITY % fulldtd "IGNORE">
<!ENTITY % ERH "Elliotte Rusty Harold">
<!ENTITY % inlines
  "(person | degree | model | product | animal | ingredient)*">
```

These are ungrammatical parameter entity declarations:

```
<!ENTITY %fulldtd; "IGNORE">
<!ENTITY % ERH  Elliotte Rusty Harold>
<!ENTITY % inlines
  "(person | degree | model | product | animal | ingredient)*'>
```

[73] EntityDef ::= EntityValue | (ExternalID NDataDecl?)

Production [73] says that an entity definition is either an entity value (Production [9]) or an external ID (Production [75]) optionally followed by an NData declaration (Production [76]).

[74] PEDef ::= EntityValue | ExternalID

Production [74] says that the definition of a parameter entity may be either an entity value (Production [9]) or an external ID (Production [75]).

External entity declaration

[75] ExternalID ::= 'SYSTEM' S SystemLiteral | 'PUBLIC' S PubidLiteral S SystemLiteral

Production [75] defines an external ID as either the keyword SYSTEM followed by white space and a system literal (Production [11]) or the keyword PUBLIC followed by white space, a public ID literal (Production [12]), more white space, and a system literal (Production [11]). These are grammatical external IDs:

```
SYSTEM "logo.gif"
SYSTEM "/images/logo.gif"
SYSTEM "http://www.idgbooks.com/logo.gif"
SYSTEM "../images/logo.gif"

PUBLIC "-//IETF//NONSGML Media Type image/gif//EN"
"http://www.isi.edu/in-notes/iana/assignments/
mediatypes/image/gif"
```

These are ungrammatical external IDs:

```
SYSTEM logo.gif
SYSTEM "/images/logo.gif'
SYSTEM http://www.idgbooks.com/logo.gif
PUBLIC "-//IETF//NONSGML Media Type image/gif//EN"
PUBLIC "http://www.isi.edu/in-notes/iana/assignments/media-
types/image/gif"
```

[76] NDataDecl ::= S 'NDATA' S Name

Production [76] defines an NData declaration as white space (Production [3]), followed by the NDATA literal, followed by white space, followed by an XML name (Production [5]). For example:

```
NDATA PDF
NDATA MIDI
```

Text declaration

[77] TextDecl ::= '<?xml' VersionInfo? EncodingDecl S? '?>'

Production [77] says that a text declaration looks almost like an XML declaration (Production [23]) except that it may not have a standalone document declaration (Production [32]) and it must have an encoding declaration. These are grammatical text declarations:

```
<?xml version="1.0" encoding="Big5"?>
<?xml version="1.0" encoding="ISO-8859-5"?>
<?xml encoding="Big5"?>
```

These are ungrammatical text declarations:

```
<?xml version="1.0"?>
<?xml encoding="Big5" version="1.0" ?>
<?xml version="1.0" standalone="yes"? encoding="ISO-8859-1" >
<?xml version="1.0" styles="poems.css">
<?xml version="1.0" encoding="ISO-8859-1" standalone="yes"?>
<?xml version="1.0" standalone="no"? >
```

Well-formed external parsed entity

[78] extParsedEnt ::= TextDecl? content

Production [78] says that an external general parsed entity consists of an optional text declaration followed by content (Production [43]). The main point of this production is that the content may not include a document type declaration.

Production [79] was removed from the second edition of the XML 1.0 specification.

Encoding declaration

[80] EncodingDecl ::= S 'encoding' Eq ('"' EncName '"' | "'" EncName "'")

Production [80] defines an encoding declaration as white space (Production [3]), followed by the string "encoding", followed by an equals sign (Production [25]), followed by the name of the encoding (Production [81]) enclosed in either single or double quotes. These are all legal encoding declarations:

```
encoding="Big5"
encoding="ISO-8859-5"
encoding = "Big5"
encoding = "ISO-8859-5"
encoding= 'Big5'
encoding= 'ISO-8859-5'
```

These are illegal encoding declarations:

```
encoding "Big5"
encoding="ISO-8859-51'
encoding = "Big5
encoding = 'ISO-8859-5"
```

[81] EncName ::= [A-Za-z] ([A-Za-z0-9._] | '-')*

Production [81] says the name of an encoding begins with one of the ASCII letters *A* through *Z* or *a* through *z*, followed by any number of ASCII letters, digits, periods, underscores, and hyphens. These are legal encoding names:

```
ISO-8859-8
Big5
GB2312
```

These are illegal encoding names:

```
ISO 8859-8
Big5 Chinese
GB 2312
ελοτ 851
```

Notation declarations

[82] NotationDecl ::= '<!NOTATION' S Name S (ExternalID | PublicID) S? '>'

Production [82] defines a notation declaration as the literal string "<!NOTATION", followed by white space (Production [3]), followed by an XML name (Production[5]) for the notation, followed by white space, followed by either an

external ID (Production [75]) or a public ID (Production [83]), optionally followed by white space, followed by the literal string ">". These are grammatical notation declarations:

```
<!NOTATION GIF SYSTEM "image/gif">
<!NOTATION GIF SYSTEM "image/gif" >
<!NOTATION GIF PUBLIC
   "-//IETF//NONSGML Media Type image/gif//EN"
"http://www.isi.edu/in-notes/iana/assignments/media-types/
image/gif">
```

These are ungrammatical notation declarations:

```
<! NOTATION GIF SYSTEM "image/gif" >
< !NOTATION GIF SYSTEM "image/gif" >
<!NOTATION GIF "image/gif">
<!NOTATION GIF SYSTEM image/gif>
<!NOTATION GIF PUBLIC
"http://www.isi.edu/in-notes/iana/assignments/media-types/
image/gif">
```

[83] PublicID ::= 'PUBLIC' S PubidLiteral

Production [83] defines a public ID as the literal string PUBLIC, followed by white space (Production [3]), followed by a public ID literal (Production [12]). These are grammatical public IDs:

```
PUBLIC "-//IETF//NONSGML Media Type image/gif//EN"
PUBLIC "ISO 8879:1986//ENTITIES Added Latin 1//EN//XML"
```

These are ungrammatical public IDs:

```
PUBLIC -//IETF//NONSGML Media Type image/gif//EN
PUBLIC 'ISO 8879:1986//ENTITIES Added Latin 1//EN//XML"
```

Characters
[84] Letter ::= BaseChar | Ideographic

Production [84] defines a letter as either a base character or an ideographic character.

[85] BaseChar ::= [#x0041-#x005A] | [#x0061-#x007A] | [#x00C0-#x00D6] | [#x00D8-#x00F6] | [#x00F8-#x00FF] | [#x0100-#x0131] | [#x0134-#x013E] | [#x0141-#x0148] | [#x014A-#x017E] | [#x0180-#x01C3] | [#x01CD-#x01F0] | [#x01F4-#x01F5] | [#x01FA-#x0217] | [#x0250-#x02A8] | [#x02BB-#x02C1] | #x0386 | [#x0388-#x038A] | #x038C | [#x038E-#x03A1] | [#x03A3-#x03CE] | [#x03D0-#x03D6] | #x03DA | #x03DC | #x03DE | #x03E0 | [#x03E2-#x03F3] |

[#x0401-#x040C] | [#x040E-#x044F] | [#x0451-#x045C] | [#x045E-#x0481] |
[#x0490-#x04C4] | [#x04C7-#x04C8] | [#x04CB-#x04CC] | [#x04D0-#x04EB] |
[#x04EE-#x04F5] | [#x04F8-#x04F9] | [#x0531-#x0556] | #x0559 | [#x0561-
#x0586] | [#x05D0-#x05EA] | [#x05F0-#x05F2] | [#x0621-#x063A] | [#x0641-
#x064A] | [#x0671-#x06B7] | [#x06BA-#x06BE] | [#x06C0-#x06CE] |
[#x06D0-#x06D3] | #x06D5 | [#x06E5-#x06E6] | [#x0905-#x0939] | #x093D |
[#x0958-#x0961] | [#x0985-#x098C] | [#x098F-#x0990] | [#x0993-#x09A8] |
[#x09AA-#x09B0] | #x09B2 | [#x09B6-#x09B9] | [#x09DC-#x09DD] | [#x09DF-
#x09E1] | [#x09F0-#x09F1] | [#x0A05-#x0A0A] | [#x0A0F-#x0A10] | [#x0A13-
#x0A28] | [#x0A2A-#x0A30] | [#x0A32-#x0A33] | [#x0A35-#x0A36] |
[#x0A38-#x0A39] | [#x0A59-#x0A5C] | #x0A5E | [#x0A72-#x0A74] | [#x0A85-
#x0A8B] | #x0A8D | [#x0A8F-#x0A91] | [#x0A93-#x0AA8] | [#x0AAA-#x0AB0] |
[#x0AB2-#x0AB3] | [#x0AB5-#x0AB9] | #x0ABD | #x0AE0 | [#x0B05-#x0B0C] |
[#x0B0F-#x0B10] | [#x0B13-#x0B28] | [#x0B2A-#x0B30] | [#x0B32-#x0B33] |
[#x0B36-#x0B39] | #x0B3D | [#x0B5C-#x0B5D] | [#x0B5F-#x0B61] | [#x0B85-
#x0B8A] | [#x0B8E-#x0B90] | [#x0B92-#x0B95] | [#x0B99-#x0B9A] | #x0B9C |
[#x0B9E-#x0B9F] | [#x0BA3-#x0BA4] | [#x0BA8-#x0BAA] | [#x0BAE-#x0BB5] |
[#x0BB7-#x0BB9] | [#x0C05-#x0C0C] | [#x0C0E-#x0C10] | [#x0C12-#x0C28] |
[#x0C2A-#x0C33] | [#x0C35-#x0C39] | [#x0C60-#x0C61] | [#x0C85-#x0C8C] |
[#x0C8E-#x0C90] | [#x0C92-#x0CA8] | [#x0CAA-#x0CB3] | [#x0CB5-#x0CB9] |
#x0CDE | [#x0CE0-#x0CE1] | [#x0D05-#x0D0C] | [#x0D0E-#x0D10] | [#x0D12-
#x0D28] | [#x0D2A-#x0D39] | [#x0D60-#x0D61] | [#x0E01-#x0E2E] | #x0E30 |
[#x0E32-#x0E33] | [#x0E40-#x0E45] | [#x0E81-#x0E82] | #x0E84 | [#x0E87-
#x0E88] | #x0E8A | #x0E8D | [#x0E94-#x0E97] | [#x0E99-#x0E9F] | [#x0EA1-
#x0EA3] | #x0EA5 | #x0EA7 | [#x0EAA-#x0EAB] | [#x0EAD-#x0EAE] | #x0EB0 |
[#x0EB2-#x0EB3] | #x0EBD | [#x0EC0-#x0EC4] | [#x0F40-#x0F47] | [#x0F49-
#x0F69] | [#x10A0-#x10C5] | [#x10D0-#x10F6] | #x1100 | [#x1102-#x1103] |
[#x1105-#x1107] | #x1109 | [#x110B-#x110C] | [#x110E-#x1112] | #x113C |
#x113E | #x1140 | #x114C | #x114E | #x1150 | [#x1154-#x1155] | #x1159 |
[#x115F-#x1161] | #x1163 | #x1165 | #x1167 | #x1169 | [#x116D-#x116E] |
[#x1172-#x1173] | #x1175 | #x119E | #x11A8 | #x11AB | [#x11AE-#x11AF] |
[#x11B7-#x11B8] | #x11BA | [#x11BC-#x11C2] | #x11EB | #x11F0 | #x11F9 |
[#x1E00-#x1E9B] | [#x1EA0-#x1EF9] | [#x1F00-#x1F15] | [#x1F18-#x1F1D] |
[#x1F20-#x1F45] | [#x1F48-#x1F4D] | [#x1F50-#x1F57] | #x1F59 | #x1F5B |
#x1F5D | [#x1F5F-#x1F7D] | [#x1F80-#x1FB4] | [#x1FB6-#x1FBC] | #x1FBE |
[#x1FC2-#x1FC4] | [#x1FC6-#x1FCC] | [#x1FD0-#x1FD3] | [#x1FD6-#x1FDB] |
[#x1FE0-#x1FEC] | [#x1FF2-#x1FF4] | [#x1FF6-#x1FFC] | #x2126 | [#x212A-
#x212B] | #x212E | [#x2180-#x2182] | [#x3041-#x3094] | [#x30A1-#x30FA] |
[#x3105-#x312C] | [#xAC00-#xD7A3]

Production [85] lists the base characters. These are the characters that Unicode *2.0* defines as alphabetic. It does not include punctuation marks or digits. It does not include new alphabetic characters added in Unicode 3.0 and later. For instance, A-Z and a-z are base characters but 0-9 and !, ", #, $, and so forth are not. This list is so long because it contains characters from not only the English alphabet but also from the Greek, Hebrew, Arabic, Cyrillic, and all the other alphabetic scripts that Unicode 2.0 supports.

[86] Ideographic ::= [#x4E00-#x9FA5] | #x3007 | [#x3021-#x3029]

Production [86] lists the ideographic characters. #x4E00-#x9FA5 are Unicode 2.0's Chinese-Japanese-Korean unified ideographs. #x3007 is the ideographic number zero. Characters #x3021 through #x3029 are the Hangzhou style numerals.

[87] CombiningChar ::= [#x0300-#x0345] | [#x0360-#x0361] | [#x0483-#x0486] | [#x0591-#x05A1] | [#x05A3-#x05B9] | [#x05BB-#x05BD] | #x05BF | [#x05C1-#x05C2] | #x05C4 | [#x064B-#x0652] | #x0670 | [#x06D6-#x06DC] | [#x06DD-#x06DF] | [#x06E0-#x06E4] | [#x06E7-#x06E8] | [#x06EA-#x06ED] | [#x0901-#x0903] | #x093C | [#x093E-#x094C] | #x094D | [#x0951-#x0954] | [#x0962-#x0963] | [#x0981-#x0983] | #x09BC | #x09BE | #x09BF | [#x09C0-#x09C4] | [#x09C7-#x09C8] | [#x09CB-#x09CD] | #x09D7 | [#x09E2-#x09E3] | #x0A02 | #x0A3C | #x0A3E | #x0A3F | [#x0A40-#x0A42] | [#x0A47-#x0A48] | [#x0A4B-#x0A4D] | [#x0A70-#x0A71] | [#x0A81-#x0A83] | #x0ABC | [#x0ABE-#x0AC5] | [#x0AC7-#x0AC9] | [#x0ACB-#x0ACD] | [#x0B01-#x0B03] | #x0B3C | [#x0B3E-#x0B43] | [#x0B47-#x0B48] | [#x0B4B-#x0B4D] | [#x0B56-#x0B57] | [#x0B82-#x0B83] | [#x0BBE-#x0BC2] | [#x0BC6-#x0BC8] | [#x0BCA-#x0BCD] | #x0BD7 | [#x0C01-#x0C03] | [#x0C3E-#x0C44] | [#x0C46-#x0C48] | [#x0C4A-#x0C4D] | [#x0C55-#x0C56] | [#x0C82-#x0C83] | [#x0CBE-#x0CC4] | [#x0CC6-#x0CC8] | [#x0CCA-#x0CCD] | [#x0CD5-#x0CD6] | [#x0D02-#x0D03] | [#x0D3E-#x0D43] | [#x0D46-#x0D48] | [#x0D4A-#x0D4D] | #x0D57 | #x0E31 | [#x0E34-#x0E3A] | [#x0E47-#x0E4E] | #x0EB1 | [#x0EB4-#x0EB9] | [#x0EBB-#x0EBC] | [#x0EC8-#x0ECD] | [#x0F18-#x0F19] | #x0F35 | #x0F37 | #x0F39 | #x0F3E | #x0F3F | [#x0F71-#x0F84] | [#x0F86-#x0F8B] | [#x0F90-#x0F95] | #x0F97 | [#x0F99-#x0FAD] | [#x0FB1-#x0FB7] | #x0FB9 | [#x20D0-#x20DC] | #x20E1 | [#x302A-#x302F] | #x3099 | #x309A

Production [87] lists the combining characters. These are characters that are generally combined with the preceding character to form the appearance of a single character. For example, character ̀ is the combining accent grave. The letter a (a) followed by a combining accent grave would generally be rendered as à and occupy only a single character width, even in a monospaced font.

[88] Digit ::= [#x0030-#x0039] | [#x0660-#x0669] | [#x06F0-#x06F9] | [#x0966-#x096F] | [#x09E6-#x09EF] | [#x0A66-#x0A6F] | [#x0AE6-#x0AEF] | [#x0B66-#x0B6F] | [#x0BE7-#x0BEF] | [#x0C66-#x0C6F] | [#x0CE6-#x0CEF] | [#x0D66-#x0D6F] | [#x0E50-#x0E59] | [#x0ED0-#x0ED9] | [#x0F20-#x0F29]

Production [88] lists the characters that are considered to be digits. These include not only the usual European numerals 0, 1, 2, 3, 4, 5, 6, 7, 8, and 9, but also the Arabic-Indic digits used primarily in Egyptian Arabic, the Eastern Arabic Indic digits used in Persian and Urdu, and many more.

[89] Extender ::= #x00B7 | #x02D0 | #x02D1 | #x0387 | #x0640 | #x0E46 | #x0EC6 | #x3005 | [#x3031-#x3035] | [#x309D-#x309E] | [#x30FC-#x30FE]

Production [89] lists the characters that are considered to be extenders. In order, these characters are the middle dot; the modifier letter triangular colon; the modifier letter half-triangular colon; the Greek middle dot; the Arabic tatweel; the Thai maiyamok; the Lao ko la; the ideographic iteration mark; five Japanese Kana repeat marks; the Japanese Hiragana iteration mark and voiced iteration mark; and the Japanese Katakana and Hiragana sound mark and prolonged sound mark. An extender is a character that's neither a letter nor a combining character but that is nonetheless included in words as part of the word. The closest equivalent in English is perhaps the hyphen used in words such as *mother-in-law* and *well-off*. However, the hyphen is not considered to be an extender in XML.

Note #x0387, the triangular colon, was removed from the extender class in a Unicode erratum sheet, but this change has not yet trickled down into XML.

Well-Formedness Constraints

According to the XML 1.0 specification, an XML document is well formed if:

1. Taken as a whole it matches the production-labeled document.

2. It meets all the well-formedness constraints given in this specification.

3. Each parsed entity that is referenced directly or indirectly within the document is well formed.

This reference section is designed to help you understand the second of those requirements and to more quickly determine whether your documents meet that requirement.

What is a well-formedness constraint?

As you read the XML specification, you'll notice that some BNF productions have associated well-formedness constraints, abbreviated WFC. For example, here's production [40]:

```
[40] STag ::= '<' Name (S Attribute)* S? '>'
                                    [ WFC: Unique Att Spec ]
```

What follows `WFC:` is the name of the well-formedness constraint, `Unique Att Spec` in this example. Generally, if you look a little below the production you'll find the constraint with the given name. For example, looking below Production [40] you'll find this:

Well-Formedness Constraint: Unique Att Spec
No attribute name may appear more than once in the same start tag or empty-element tag.

This says that a given attribute may not appear more than once in a single element. For example, the following tag violates well-formedness:

```
<P COLOR="red" COLOR="blue">
```

Well-formedness constraints are used for requirements such as this that are difficult or impossible to state in the form of a BNF grammar. As XML parsers read a document, they must not only check that the document matches the document production of the BNF grammar; they must also check that it satisfies all well-formedness constraints.

Note There are also validity constraints that must be satisfied by valid documents. XML processors are not required to check validity constraints if they do not wish to, however. Most validity constraints deal with declarations in the DTD. Validity constraints are discussed later in this appendix.

Productions associated with well-formedness constraints

This section lists the productions associated with well-formedness constraints and explains those constraints. Most productions don't have any well-formedness constraints, so most productions are not listed here. The complete list of productions is found in the BNF Grammar portion of this appendix.

Document type definition

[28] doctypedecl ::= '<!DOCTYPE' S Name (S ExternalID)? S? ('[' (markupdecl | DeclSep)* ']' S?)? '>'

[Well-formedness Constraint: External Subset]

This well-formedness constraint states that if the DTD has one or more external DTD subsets, then each of those subsets must independently match Production [30], external subset.

[28a] DeclSep ::= PEReference | S

[Well-formedness Constraint: PE Between Declarations]

This well-formedness constraint states that the replacement text of a parameter entity used between markup declarations (rather than inside markup declarations) must match Production [31] for external subset declarations. In effect, this says that replacing the parameter entity with its replacement text should not produce a malformed document.

[29] markupdecl ::= elementdecl | AttlistDecl | EntityDecl | NotationDecl | PI | Comment

[Well-formedness Constraint: PEs in Internal Subset]

This well-formedness constraint states that parameter entity references defined in the *internal* DTD subset cannot be used inside a markup declaration. For example, the following is illegal inside the internal DTD subset:

```
<!ENTITY % INLINES SYSTEM "(I | EM | B | STRONG | CODE)*">
<!ELEMENT P %INLINES; >
```

On the other hand, the above would be legal in the *external* DTD subset.

[39] element ::= EmptyElemTag | STag content ETag

[Well-Formedness Constraint: Element Type Match]

This well-formedness constraint simply says that the name of the start tag must match the name of the corresponding end tag. For instance, these elements are well formed:

```
<TEST>content</TEST>
<test>content</test>
```

However, these elements are not well formed:

```
<TEST>content</test>
<Fred>content</Ethel>
```

[40] STag ::= '<' Name (S Attribute)* S? '>'

[Well-formedness Constraint: Unique Att Spec]

This constraint says that a given attribute may not appear more than once in a single element. For example, the following tags violate well-formedness:

```
<P COLOR="red" COLOR="blue">
<P COLOR="red" COLOR="red">
```

The problem is that the COLOR attribute appears twice in the same tag. In the second case, it doesn't matter that the value is the same both times. It's still malformed. The following two tags are well-formed because the attributes have slightly different names:

```
<P COLOR1="red" COLOR2="blue">
<P COLOR1="red" COLOR2="red">
```

[41] Attribute ::= Name Eq AttValue

[Well-formedness Constraint: No External Entity References]

This constraint says that attribute values may not contain entity references that point to data in other documents. For example, consider this attribute:

```
<BOX COLOR="&RED;" />
```

Whether this is well formed depends on how the entity RED is defined. If it's completely defined in the DTD, either in the internal or external subset, this tag is acceptable. For example:

```
<!ENTITY RED "#FF0000">
```

However, if the RED entity is defined as an external entity whose replacement text comes from a separate file, then it's not well defined. In that case, the ENTITY declaration would look something like this:

```
<!ENTITY RED SYSTEM "red.txt" NDATA COLOR>
```

This constraint only applies to parsed entities. It does not apply to unparsed entities given as the value of an attribute of type ENTITY or ENTITIES. For example, the following is legal even though RED is an external entity used as an attribute value.

```
<?xml version="1.0"?>
<!DOCTYPE EXAMPLE [
  <!ELEMENT EXAMPLE (#PCDATA)>
  <!NOTATION COLOR SYSTEM "x-color">
  <!ENTITY RED SYSTEM "red.txt" NDATA COLOR>
  <!ATTLIST EXAMPLE HUE ENTITY #REQUIRED>
]>
<EXAMPLE HUE="RED">
testing 1 2 3
</EXAMPLE>
```

[Well-formedness Constraint: No < in Attribute Values]

This constraint is very simple. The less than sign (<) cannot be part of an attribute value. For example, the following tags are malformed:

```
<BOX COLOR="<6699FF>" />
<HALFPLANE REGION="X < 8" />
```

Technically, these tags are already forbidden by Production [10]. The real purpose of this constraint is to make sure that a < doesn't slip in through an internal entity reference. The correct way to embed a < in an attribute value is to use the < entity reference like this:

```
<BOX COLOR="&lt;6699FF>" />
<HALFPLANE REGION="X &lt; 8" />
```

[44] EmptyElemTag ::= '<' Name (S Attribute)* S? '/>'

[Well-formedness Constraint: Unique Att Spec]

This is the same constraint as seen in Production [40]. This constraint says that a given attribute may not appear more than once in a single, empty-element tag. For example, the following tags violate well-formedness:

```
<P COLOR="red" COLOR="blue" />
<P COLOR="red" COLOR="red" />
```

Look at the second example. Even the purely redundant attribute violates well-formedness.

[60] DefaultDecl ::= '#REQUIRED' | '#IMPLIED' | (('#FIXED' S)? AttValue)

[Well-formedness Constraint: No < in Attribute Values]

This is the same constraint as seen in Production [41]. This merely states that you can't place a < in a default attribute value in a <!ATTLIST> declaration. For example, these are malformed attribute declarations:

```
<!ATTLIST RECTANGLE COLOR  CDATA "<330033>">
<!ATTLIST HALFPLANE REGION CDATA "X < 0" />
```

[66] CharRef ::= '&#' [0-9]+ ';' | '&#x' [0-9a-fA-F]+ ';'

[Well-formedness Constraint: Legal Character]

This constraint says that characters referred to by character references must be legal characters if they were simply typed in the document. Character references are convenient for inputting legal characters that are difficult to type on a particular system. They are not a means to input otherwise forbidden characters.

The definition of a legal character is given by Production [2]:

```
[2] Char ::= #x9 | #xA | #xD | [#x20-#xD7FF]
               | [#xE000-#xFFFD] | [#x10000-#x10FFFF]
```

The main items of interest here are the characters not included. Specifically, these are the nonprinting ASCII control characters of which the most common are the bell, vertical tab, and form feed; the surrogates block from #xD800 to #xDFFF, and the noncharacters #xFFFE and #xFFFF.

[68] EntityRef ::= '&' Name ';'

[Well-formedness Constraint: Entity Declared]

The intent of this well-formedness constraint is to make sure that all entities used in the document are declared in the DTD using `<!ENTITY>`. However, there are two loopholes:

1. The five predefined entities — `&lt;`, `&apos;`, `&gt;`, `&quot;`, and `&amp;` — are not required to be declared, although they may be.

2. A nonvalidating processor can allow undeclared entities if it's possible that they may have been declared in the external DTD subset (which a nonvalidating processor is not required to read). Specifically, it's possible that entities were declared in an external DTD subset if:

   a. The standalone document declaration does not have `standalone="yes"`.

   b. The DTD contains at least one parameter entity reference.

If either of these conditions is violated, then undeclared entities (other than the five in loophole 1) are not allowed.

This constraint also specifies that if entities are declared, they must be declared before they're used in a default value in an `ATTLIST` declaration.

[Well-formedness Constraint: Parsed Entity]

This constraint states that entity references may only contain the names of parsed entities. Unparsed entity names are only contained in attribute values of type `ENTITY` or `ENTITIES`. For example, this is a malformed document:

```
<?xml version="1.0" standalone="no"?>
<!DOCTYPE DOCUMENT [
  <!ELEMENT DOCUMENT (IMAGE)>
  <!ENTITY LOGO SYSTEM "http://www.ibiblio.org/xml/logo.gif"
    NDATA GIF>
<!NOTATION GIF SYSTEM "image/gif">
]>
<DOCUMENT>
  &LOGO;
</DOCUMENT>
```

This is the correct way to embed the unparsed entity `LOGO` in the document:

```
<?xml version="1.0" standalone="no"?>
<!DOCTYPE DOCUMENT [

  <!ELEMENT DOCUMENT (IMAGE)>
  <!ENTITY LOGO SYSTEM "http://www.ibiblio.org/xml/logo.gif"
    NDATA GIF>
  <!NOTATION GIF SYSTEM "image/gif">
  <!ELEMENT IMAGE EMPTY>
  <!ATTLIST IMAGE SOURCE ENTITY #REQUIRED>
```

```
]>
<DOCUMENT>
  <IMAGE SOURCE="LOGO" />
</DOCUMENT>
```

[Well-formedness Constraint: No Recursion]

This well-formedness constraint states that a parsed entity cannot refer to itself.
For example, this free software classic is malformed:

```
<!ENTITY GNU "&GNU;'s not Unix!">
```

Circular references are a little trickier to spot, but are equally illegal:

```
<!ENTITY LEFT  "Left &RIGHT; Left!">
<!ENTITY RIGHT "Right &LEFT; Right!">
```

Note that it's only the recursion that's malformed, not the mere use of one entity
reference inside another. The following is legal because although the COPY01 entity
depends on the ERH entity, the ERH entity does not depend on the COPY01 entity.

```
<!ENTITY ERH    "Elliotte Rusty Harold">
<!ENTITY COPY01 "Copyright 2001 &ERH;">
```

[69] PEReference ::= '%' Name ';'

[Well-formedness Constraint: No Recursion]

This is the same constraint that applies to Production [68]. Parameter entities can't
recurse any more than general entities can. For example, this entity declaration is
malformed:

```
<!ENTITY % GNU "%GNU;'s not Unix!">
```

And this entity declaration is illegal:

```
<!ENTITY % LEFT  "Left  %RIGHT; Left!">
<!ENTITY % RIGHT "Right %LEFT; Right!">
```

[Well-formedness Constraint: In DTD]

This well-formedness constraint requires that parameter entity references can only
appear in the DTD. They may not appear in the content of the document or anywhere else that's not the DTD.

This constraint is a little funny because it's not actually an error to include something that looks like a parameter entity reference and even has the same name as a
parameter entity in the document content. However, that will simply be interpreted
as raw character data. It is not treated as a parameter entity reference.

Validity Constraints

This reference section is designed to help you understand what is required in order for an XML document to be *valid*. Validity is often useful but is not always required. You can do a lot with simply well-formed documents, and such documents are often easier to write because there are fewer rules to follow. For valid documents, you must follow the BNF grammar, the well-formedness constraints, *and* the validity constraints discussed in this section.

What is a validity constraint?

A validity constraint is a rule that must be adhered to by a valid document. Not all XML documents are, or need to be, valid. It is not necessarily an error for a document to fail to satisfy a validity constraint. Validating processors have the option of reporting violations of these constraints as errors, but they do not have to. All syntax (BNF) errors and well-formedness violations must still be reported, however.

Only documents with DTDs may be validated. Almost all the validity constraints deal with the relationships between the content of the document and the declarations in the DTD.

Validity constraints in XML 1.0

This section lists and explains all of the validity constraints in the XML 1.0 standard. These are organized according to the BNF rule each applies to.

[28] doctypedecl ::= '<!DOCTYPE' S Name (S ExternalID)? S? ('[' (markupdecl | PEReference | S)* ']' S?)? '>'

Validity Constraint: Root Element Type

This constraint simply states that the name given in the DOCTYPE declaration must match the name of the root element. In other words, the bold parts below all have to be the same.

```
<?xml version="1.0"?>
<!DOCTYPE ROOTNAME [
  <!ELEMENT ROOTNAME (#PCDATA)>
]>
<ROOTNAME>
  content
</ROOTNAME>
```

It's also true that the root element must be declared—that's done by the line in italic; however, that declaration is required by a different validity constraint, not this one.

[29] markupdecl ::= elementdecl | AttlistDecl | EntityDecl | NotationDecl | PI | Comment

Validity Constraint: Proper Declaration/PE Nesting

This constraint requires that a markup declaration contain or be contained in one or more parameter entities, but that it may not be split across a parameter entity. For example, consider this element declaration:

```
<!ELEMENT PARENT ( FATHER | MOTHER )>
```

The parameter entity declared by the following entity declaration is a valid substitute for the content model, because the parameter entity contains both the < and the >:

```
<!ENTITY % PARENT_DECL "<!ELEMENT PARENT ( FATHER | MOTHER )>">
```

Given that entity, you can rewrite the element declaration like this:

```
%PARENT_DECL;
```

This is valid because the parameter entity contains both the < and the >. Another option is to include only part of the element declaration in the parameter entity. For example, if you had many elements whose content model was (FATHER | MOTHER), then it might be useful to do something like this:

```
<!ENTITY % PARENT_TYPES "( FATHER | MOTHER )">
<!ELEMENT PARENT %PARENT_TYPES;>
```

Here, neither the < or > is included in the parameter entity. You cannot enclose one of the angle brackets in the parameter entity without including its mate. The following, for example, is invalid, even though it appears to expand into a legal element declaration:

```
<!ENTITY % PARENT_TYPES "( FATHER | MOTHER )>">
<!ELEMENT PARENT %PARENT_TYPES;
```

Note that the problem is *not* that the parameter entity's replacement text contains a > character. That's legal. The problem is how the > character is used to terminate an element declaration that began in another entity.

[32] SDDecl ::= S 'standalone' Eq (("'" ('yes' | 'no') "'") | ('"' ('yes' | 'no') '"'))

Validity Constraint: Standalone Document Declaration

In short, this constraint says that a document must have a standalone document declaration with the value no (`standalone="no"`) if any other files are required to process this file and determine its validity. Mostly this affects external DTD subsets linked in through parameter entities. This is the case if any of the following are true:

✦ An entity used in the document is declared in an external DTD subset.

✦ The external DTD subset provides default values for attributes that appear in the document without values.

✦ The external DTD subset changes how attribute values in the document may be normalized.

✦ The external DTD subset declares elements whose children are only elements (no character data or mixed content) when those children may themselves contain white space.

Only if none of these are true may `standalone` have the value `yes`. However, it always acceptable to give `standalone` the value `no`, even if these constraints are satisfied and the document could stand alone.

[39] element ::= EmptyElemTag | STag content ETag

Validity Constraint: Element Valid

This constraint simply states that this element matches an element declaration in the DTD. More precisely, one of the following conditions must be true:

1. The element has no content and the element declaration declares the element `EMPTY`.

2. The element contains only child elements that match the regular expression in the element's content model.

3. The element is declared to have mixed content, and the element's content contains character data and child elements that are declared in the mixed-content declaration.

4. The element is declared `ANY`, and all child elements are declared.

[41] Attribute ::= Name Eq AttValue

Validity Constraint: Attribute Value Type

This constraint simply states that the attribute's name must have been declared in an `ATTLIST` declaration for the element the attribute is attached to in the DTD. Furthermore, the attribute value must match the declared type in the `ATTLIST` declaration.

[45] elementdecl ::= '<!ELEMENT' S Name S contentspec S? '>'

Validity Constraint: Unique Element Type Declaration

An element cannot be declared more than once in the DTD, whether the declarations are compatible or not. For example, this is valid:

```
<!ELEMENT EM (#PCDATA)>
```

This, however, is invalid:

```
<!ELEMENT EM (#PCDATA)>
<!ELEMENT EM (#PCDATA | B)>
```

And this is also invalid:

```
<!ELEMENT EM (#PCDATA)>
<!ELEMENT EM (#PCDATA)>
```

This is most likely to cause problems when merging external DTD subsets from different sources that both declare some of the same elements. To a limited extent, namespaces can help resolve this.

[49] choice ::= '(' S? cp (S? '|' S? cp)* S? ')'

Validity Constraint: Proper Group/PE Nesting

This constraint states that a choice may contain or be contained in one or more parameter entities, but that it may not be split across a parameter entity. For example, consider this element declaration:

```
<!ELEMENT PARENT ( FATHER | MOTHER )>
```

The parameter entity declared by the following entity declaration is a valid substitute for the content model because the parameter entity contains both the (and the):

```
<!ENTITY % PARENT_TYPES "( FATHER | MOTHER )">
```

That is, you can rewrite the element declaration like this:

```
<!ELEMENT PARENT %PARENT_TYPES;>
```

This is valid because the parameter entity contains both the (and the). Another option is to include only the child elements, and leave out both parentheses. For example:

```
<!ENTITY % PARENT_TYPES " FATHER | MOTHER ">
<!ELEMENT PARENT ( %PARENT_TYPES; )>
```

The advantage here is that you can easily add additional elements not defined in the parameter entity. For example:

```
<!ELEMENT PARENT ( UNKNOWN | %PARENT_TYPES; ) >
```

What you cannot do, however, is enclose one of the parentheses in the parameter entity without including its mate. The following, for example, is invalid, even though it appears to expand into a legal element declaration.

```
<!ENTITY % FATHER " FATHER )">
<!ENTITY % MOTHER " ( MOTHER | ">
<!ELEMENT PARENT %FATHER; %MOTHER; ) >
```

The problem in this example is the ELEMENT declaration, not the ENTITY declarations. It is valid to declare the entities as done here; it's their use in the context of a choice that makes them invalid.

[50] seq ::= '(' S? cp (S? ',' S? cp)* S? ')'

Validity Constraint: Proper Group/PE Nesting

This is exactly the same constraint as in Production [49], except that it's being applied to sequences rather than to choices. It requires that a sequence may contain or be contained in one or more parameter entities, but it may not be split across a parameter entity. For example, consider this element declaration:

```
<!ELEMENT ADDRESS ( NAME, STREET, CITY, STATE, ZIP )>
```

The parameter entity declared by the following entity declaration is a valid substitute for the content model because the replacement text contains both the (and the):

```
<!ENTITY % SIMPLE_ADDRESS "( NAME, STREET, CITY, STATE, ZIP )">
```

That is, you can rewrite the element declaration like this:

```
<!ELEMENT ADDRESS %SIMPLE_ADDRESS;>
```

This is valid because the parameter entity contains both the (and the). Another option is to include only the child elements, but leave out both parentheses. For example:

```
<!ENTITY % SIMPLE_ADDRESS " NAME, STREET, CITY, STATE, ZIP ">
<!ELEMENT ADDRESS( %SIMPLE_ADDRESS; )>
```

The advantage here is that you can easily add additional elements not defined in the parameter entity. For example:

```
<!ENTITY % INTERNATIONAL_ADDRESS " NAME, STREET, CITY,
  PROVINCE?, POSTAL_CODE?, COUNTRY ">
```

```
<!ELEMENT ADDRESS ( (%SIMPLE_ADDRESS;)
                   | (%INTERNATIONAL_ADDRESS;) ) >
```

What you cannot do, however, is enclose one of the parentheses in the parameter entity without including its mate. The following, for example, is invalid, even though it appears to expand into a legal element declaration:

```
<!ENTITY % SIMPLE_ADDRESS_1 "( NAME, STREET, ">
<!ENTITY % SIMPLE_ADDRESS_2 "CITY, STATE, ZIP)">
<!ELEMENT ADDRESS %SIMPLE_ADDRESS_1; %SIMPLE_ADDRESS_2; >
```

The problem in this example is the ELEMENT declaration, not the ENTITY declarations. It is valid to declare the entities like this; it's their use in the context of a sequence that makes them invalid.

[51] Mixed ::= '(' S? '#PCDATA' (S? '|' S? Name)* S? ')'* | '(' S? '#PCDATA' S? ')'

Validity Constraint: Proper Group/PE Nesting

This is exactly the same constraint as in the two previous productions, except that it's being applied to mixed content rather than to choices or sequences. It requires that a mixed-content model may contain or be contained in a parameter entity, but that the mixed-content model may not be split across a parameter entity. For example, consider this element declaration:

```
<!ELEMENT P ( #PCDATA | I | EM | B | STRONG )>
```

The parameter entity declared by the following entity declaration is a valid substitute for the content model because the replacement text contains both the (and the):

```
<!ENTITY % INLINES "( #PCDATA | I | EM | B | STRONG )">
```

That is, you can rewrite the element declaration like this:

```
<!ELEMENT P %INLINES;>
```

This is valid because the parameter entity contains both the (and the). Another option is to include only the content particles, but leave out both parentheses. For example:

```
<!ENTITY % INLINES " #PCDATA | I | EM | B | STRONG ">
<!ELEMENT P ( %INLINES; ) >
```

The advantage here is that you can easily add additional elements not defined in the parameter entity. For example:

```
<!ELEMENT QUOTE ( %INLINES; | SPEAKER ) >
```

What you cannot do, however, is enclose one of the parentheses in the parameter entity without including its mate. The following, for example, is invalid, even though it appears to expand into a legal element declaration:

```
<!ENTITY % INLINES1 " ( #PCDATA | SPEAKER | ">
<!ENTITY % INLINES2 " I | EM | B | STRONG )">
<!ELEMENT QUOTE %INLINES1; %INLINES2; >
```

The problem in this example is the ELEMENT declaration, not the ENTITY declarations. It is valid to declare the entities as is done here. It's their use in the context of a mixed content declaration that makes them invalid.

Validity Constraint: No Duplicate Types

No element can be repeated in a mixed-content declaration. For example, the following is invalid:

```
( #PCDATA | I | EM | I | EM )
```

There's really no reason to write a mixed-content declaration like this, but at the same time, it's not obvious what the harm is. Interestingly, pure choices do allow content models like this:

```
( I | EM | I | EM )
```

It only becomes a problem when #PCDATA is mixed in.

Caution This choice is ambiguous; that is, when the parser encounters an I or an EM, it doesn't know whether it matches the first or the second instance in the content model. So, although legal, some parsers will report it as an error, and it should be avoided if possible.

[56] TokenizedType ::= 'ID' | 'IDREF' | 'IDREFS' | 'ENTITY' | 'ENTITIES' | 'NMTOKEN' | 'NMTOKENS'

Validity Constraint: ID

Attribute values of ID type must be valid XML names (Production [5]). Furthermore, a single name cannot be used more than once in the same document as the value of an ID type attribute. For example, this is invalid given that ID is declared to be of type ID:

```
<BOX ID="B1" WIDTH="50"  HEIGHT="50" />
<BOX ID="B1" WIDTH="250" HEIGHT="250" />
```

This is also invalid because XML names cannot begin with numbers:

```
<BOX ID="1276" WIDTH="50" HEIGHT="50" />
```

This is valid if `NAME` does not have type `ID`:

```
<BOX ID="B1"    WIDTH="50"  HEIGHT="50" />
<BOX NAME="B1"  WIDTH="250" HEIGHT="250" />
<BOX NAME="1276" WIDTH="50"  HEIGHT="50" />
```

On the other hand, this example is invalid if `NAME` does have type `ID`, even though the `NAME` attribute is different from the `ID` attribute. Furthermore, the following is invalid if `NAME` has type `ID`, even though two different elements are involved:

```
<BOX    NAME="FRED" WIDTH="50" HEIGHT="50" />
<PERSON NAME="FRED" />
```

`ID` attribute values must be unique across all elements and ID type attributes, not just a particular class of elements or attributes.

Validity Constraint: One ID per Element Type

Each element can have at most one attribute of type `ID`. For example, the following is invalid:

```
<!ELEMENT PERSON (ANY) >
<!ATTLIST PERSON SS_NUMBER   ID #REQUIRED>
<!ATTLIST PERSON EMPLOYEE_ID ID #REQUIRED>
```

Validity Constraint: ID Attribute Default

All attributes of ID type must be declared `#IMPLIED` or `#REQUIRED`. `#FIXED` is not allowed. For example, the following is invalid:

```
<!ATTLIST PERSON SS_NUMBER ID #FIXED "SS123-45-6789">
```

The problem is that if there's more than one `PERSON` element in the document, the ID validity constraint will automatically be violated.

Validity Constraint: IDREF

The IDREF validity constraint specifies that an attribute value of an `IDREF` type attribute must be the same as the value of an `ID` type attribute of an element in the document. Multiple `IDREF` attributes in the same or different elements may point to a single element. `ID` attribute values must be unique (at least among other `ID` attribute values in the same document), but `IDREF` attributes do not need to be.

Additionally, attribute values of type `IDREFS` must be a white space-separated list of `ID` attribute values from elements in the document.

Validity Constraint: Entity Name

The value of an attribute whose declared type is ENTITY must be the name of an unparsed general (nonparameter) entity declared in the DTD, whether in the internal or external subset.

The value of an attribute whose declared type is ENTITIES must be a whitespace–separated list of the names of unparsed general (nonparameter) entities declared in the DTD, whether in the internal or external subset.

Validity Constraint: Name Token

The value of an attribute whose declared type is NMTOKEN must be a name token. That is, it must be composed of one or more name characters.

The value of an attribute whose declared type is NMTOKENS must be a whitespace–separated list of name tokens. For example, this is a valid element with a COLORS attribute of type NMTOKENS:

```
<BOX WIDTH="50" HEIGHT="50" COLORS="red green blue" />
```

This is an invalid element with a COLORS attribute of type NMTOKENS:

```
<BOX WIDTH="50" HEIGHT="50" COLORS="red, green, blue" />
```

[58] NotationType ::= 'NOTATION' S '(' S? Name (S? '|' S? Name)* S? ')'

Validity Constraint: Notation Attributes

The value of an attribute whose declared type is NOTATION must be the name of a notation that's been declared in the DTD.

Validity Constraint: One Notation Per Element Type

An element cannot have more than one attribute with the notation type. A notation describes the type of an element's content. This constraint limits each element to one notation type.

Validity Constraint: No Notation on Empty Element

An element that must be empty — that is, an element with the content model EMPTY, not merely an element which in a particular instance happens to be empty — may not have an attribute with the notation type. The reason for this constraint is that the notation is supposed to describe the type of the content of an element. If the element has no content, then it can't have a type.

[59] Enumeration ::= '(' S? Nmtoken (S? '|' S? Nmtoken)* S? ')'

Validity Constraint: Enumeration

The value of an attribute whose declared type is ENUMERATION must be a white-space–separated list of name tokens. These name tokens do not necessarily have to be the names of anything declared in the DTD or elsewhere. They simply have to match the NMTOKEN production (Production [7]). For example, this is an invalid enumeration because commas, rather than white space, are used to separate the name tokens:

```
( red, green, blue)
```

This is an invalid enumeration because the name tokens are enclosed in quote marks:

```
( "red" "green" "blue")
```

Neither commas nor quote marks are valid name characters, so there's no possibility for these common mistakes to be misinterpreted as a white-space–separated list of unusual name tokens.

[60] DefaultDecl ::= '#REQUIRED' | '#IMPLIED' | (('#FIXED' S)? AttValue)

Validity Constraint: Required Attribute

If an attribute of an element is declared to be #REQUIRED, then it is a validity error for any instance of the element not to provide a value for that attribute.

Validity Constraint: Attribute Default Legal

This common-sense validity constraint merely states that any default attribute value provided in an ATTLIST declaration must satisfy the constraints for an attribute of that type. For example, the following is invalid because the default value, UNKNOWN, is not one of the choices given by the content model.

```
<!ATTLIST CIRCLE VISIBLE (TRUE | FALSE) "UNKNOWN">
```

UNKNOWN would be invalid for this attribute whether it was provided as a default value or in an actual element like the following:

```
<CIRCLE VISIBLE="UNKNOWN" />
```

Validity Constraint: Fixed Attribute Default

This common sense validity constraint merely states that if an attribute is declared #FIXED in its ATTLIST declaration, then that same ATTLIST declaration must also provide a default value. For example, the following is invalid:

```
<!ATTLIST AUTHOR COMPANY CDATA #FIXED>
```

This is a corrected declaration:

```
<!ATTLIST AUTHOR COMPANY CDATA #FIXED "TIC">
```

[62] includeSect ::= '<![' S? 'INCLUDE' S? '[' extSubsetDecl ']]>'

Validity Constraint: Proper Conditional Section/PE Nesting

This constraint states that if a parameter entity contains the start of an include section, `<![`, or the second `[` in an include section, then it must also contain the end of the same include section, `]]>`, and vice versa. A parameter entity may contain only some pieces of the include section, for instance the included markup declarations or the word `INCLUDE`, in which case the include section is assembled from multiple entities. However, if it provides any one of the `<![`, `[`, or `]]>`, then it has to provide the other two as well.

[63] ignoreSect ::= '<![' S? 'IGNORE' S? '[' ignoreSectContents* ']]>'

Validity Constraint: Proper Conditional Section/PE Nesting

This constraint states that if a parameter entity contains the start of an ignore section, `<![`, or the second `[` in an ignore section, then it must also contain the end of the same ignore section, `]]>`, and vice versa. A parameter entity may contain only some pieces of the ignore section, for instance the included markup declarations or the literal `IGNORE`, in which case the ignore section is assembled from multiple entities. However, if it provides any one of the `<![`, `[`, or `]]>`, then it has to provide the other two as well.

[68] EntityRef ::= '&' Name ';'

Validity Constraint: Entity Declared

This constraint expands on the well-formedness constraint of the same name. In a valid document, all referenced entities must be defined by `<!ENTITY>` declarations in the DTD. Definitions must precede any use of the entity they define in default attribute values.

The loophole for `standalone="no"` documents that applies to merely well-formed documents is no longer available. The loophole for the five predefined entities — `&lt;`, `&apos;`, `&gt;`, `&quot;`, and `&amp;` — is still available. However, it is recommended that you declare them, even though you don't absolutely have to. Those declarations would look like this:

```
<!ENTITY lt   "&#38;#60;">
<!ENTITY gt   "&#62;">
<!ENTITY amp  "&#38;#38;">
<!ENTITY apos "&#39;">
<!ENTITY quot "&#34;">
```

[69] PEReference ::= '%' Name ';'

Validity Constraint: Entity Declared

This is the same constraint as the previous one, merely applied to parameter entity references instead of to general entity references.

[76] NDataDecl ::= S 'NDATA' S Name

Validity Constraint: Notation Declared

The name used in a notation data declaration (which is, in turn, used in an entity definition for an unparsed entity) must be the name of a notation declared in the DTD. For example, the following document is valid. However, if you take away the line declaring the GIF notation (shown in bold) it becomes invalid.

```
<?xml version="1.0" standalone="yes"?>
<!DOCTYPE DOCUMENT [
  <!ELEMENT DOCUMENT (IMAGE)>
  <!ELEMENT IMAGE EMPTY>
  <!ATTLIST IMAGE SOURCE ENTITY #REQUIRED>
  <!NOTATION GIF SYSTEM "image/gif">
  <!ENTITY LOGO SYSTEM "http://www.ibiblio.org/xml/logo.gif"
     NDATA GIF>
]>
<DOCUMENT>
  <IMAGE SOURCE="LOGO"/>
</DOCUMENT>
```

✦   ✦   ✦

The XML 1.0 Specification, Second Edition

This appendix contains the complete second edition of the XML 1.0 specification as published by the World Wide Web Consortium (W3C). This document has been reviewed by W3C Members and other interested parties and has been endorsed by the Director as a W3C Recommendation. It is a stable document and may be used as reference material or cited as a normative reference from another document.

This document isn't always easy reading. Precision is preferred over clarity. However, when you're banging your head against the wall, and trying to decide whether the problem is with your XML processor or with your XML code, this is the deciding document. Therefore, it's important to have at least a cursory familiarity with it, and to be able to find things in it when you need to.

What's New in the Second Edition

The second edition of XML does not change the allowed syntax of XML documents in any way. Therefore, this is still XML 1.0. The changes are mostly editorial. A number of points that proved confusing have been clarified. Some examples that didn't show what they were supposed to show have been fixed. Unreachable, and therefore irrelevant, rules in the BNF grammar have been deleted. And the writing has been tightened up considerably.

However, all documents that were well formed with respect to the first edition are still well formed. All documents that were not well formed with respect to the first edition are still not well formed. Almost all documents that were valid with respect to the first edition are still valid, and all documents that were invalid with respect to the first edition are still invalid.

In a few cases, the second edition clarifies points which particular parsers got wrong in the past. For instance, the rules that led some parser vendors to incorrectly believe that three-letter language codes in `xml:lang` attributes were illegal have been deleted. Therefore, a few documents that XML first-edition parsers reported as malformed may now seem to have become well formed when checked with a newer version of the parser. However, in these cases, it was the parser that was giving incorrect information. These documents were always well formed. The parser misinterpreted the specification and therefore gave faulty results. The second edition of the specification leaves much less room for misinterpretation.

Extensible Markup Language (XML) 1.0 (Second Edition)

W3C Recommendation 6 October 2000

This version:

`http://www.w3.org/TR/2000/REC-xml-20001006` (XHTML, XML, PDF, XHTML review version with color-coded revision indicators)

Latest version:

`http://www.w3.org/TR/REC-xml`

Previous versions:

`http://www.w3.org/TR/2000/WD-xml-2e-20000814`

`http://www.w3.org/TR/1998/REC-xml-19980210`

Editors:

Tim Bray, Textuality and Netscape <tbray@textuality.com>

Jean Paoli, Microsoft <jeanpa@microsoft.com>

C. M. Sperberg-McQueen, University of Illinois at Chicago and Text Encoding Initiative <cmsmcq@uic.edu>

Eve Maler, Sun Microsystems, Inc. <eve.maler@east.sun.com> - Second Edition

Copyright © 2000 W3C® (MIT, INRIA, Keio), All Rights Reserved. W3C liability, trademark, document use, and software licensing rules apply.

Abstract

The Extensible Markup Language (XML) is a subset of SGML that is completely described in this document. Its goal is to enable generic SGML to be served, received, and processed on the Web in the way that is now possible with HTML. XML has been designed for ease of implementation and for interoperability with both SGML and HTML.

Status of this Document

This document has been reviewed by W3C Members and other interested parties and has been endorsed by the Director as a W3C Recommendation. It is a stable document and may be used as reference material or cited as a normative reference from another document. W3C's role in making the Recommendation is to draw attention to the specification and to promote its widespread deployment. This enhances the functionality and interoperability of the Web.

This document specifies a syntax created by subsetting an existing, widely used international text processing standard (Standard Generalized Markup Language, ISO 8879:1986(E) as amended and corrected) for use on the World Wide Web. It is a product of the W3C XML Activity, details of which can be found at `http://www.w3.org/XML`. The English version of this specification is the only normative version. However, for translations of this document, see `http://www.w3.org/XML/#trans`. A list of current W3C Recommendations and other technical documents can be found at `http://www.w3.org/TR`.

This second edition is *not* a new version of XML (first published 10 February 1998); it merely incorporates the changes dictated by the first-edition errata (available at `http://www.w3.org/XML/xml-19980210-errata`) as a convenience to readers. The errata list for this second edition is available at `http://www.w3.org/XML/xml-V10-2e-errata`.

Please report errors in this document to xml-editor@w3.org; archives are available.

 Note C. M. Sperberg-McQueen's affiliation has changed since the publication of the first edition. He is now at the World Wide Web Consortium, and can be contacted at cmsmcq@w3.org.

Table of Contents

1 Introduction

Extensible Markup Language, abbreviated XML, describes a class of data objects called XML documents and partially describes the behavior of computer programs which process them. XML is an application profile or restricted form of SGML, the Standard Generalized Markup Language [ISO 8879]. By construction, XML documents are conforming SGML documents.

XML documents are made up of storage units called entities, which contain either parsed or unparsed data. Parsed data is made up of characters, some of which form character data, and some of which form markup. Markup encodes a description of the document's storage layout and logical structure. XML provides a mechanism to impose constraints on the storage layout and logical structure.

[Definition: A software module called an **XML processor** is used to read XML documents and provide access to their content and structure.] [Definition: It is assumed that an XML processor is doing its work on behalf of another module, called the **application**.] This specification describes the required behavior of an XML processor in terms of how it must read XML data and the information it must provide to the application.

1.1 Origin and Goals

XML was developed by an XML Working Group (originally known as the SGML Editorial Review Board) formed under the auspices of the World Wide Web Consortium (W3C) in 1996. It was chaired by Jon Bosak of Sun Microsystems with the active participation of an XML Special Interest Group (previously known as the SGML Working Group) also organized by the W3C. The membership of the XML Working Group is given in an appendix. Dan Connolly served as the WG's contact with the W3C.

The design goals for XML are:

1. XML shall be straightforwardly usable over the Internet.
2. XML shall support a wide variety of applications.
3. XML shall be compatible with SGML.
4. It shall be easy to write programs which process XML documents.
5. The number of optional features in XML is to be kept to the absolute minimum, ideally zero.
6. XML documents should be human-legible and reasonably clear.
7. The XML design should be prepared quickly.
8. The design of XML shall be formal and concise.
9. XML documents shall be easy to create.
10. Terseness in XML markup is of minimal importance.

This specification, together with associated standards (Unicode and ISO/IEC 10646 for characters, Internet RFC 1766 for language identification tags, ISO 639 for language name codes, and ISO 3166 for country name codes), provides all the information necessary to understand XML Version 1.0 and construct computer programs to process it.

This version of the XML specification may be distributed freely, as long as all text and legal notices remain intact.

1.2 Terminology

The terminology used to describe XML documents is defined in the body of this specification. The terms defined in the following list are used in building those definitions and in describing the actions of an XML processor:

may

[Definition: Conforming documents and XML processors are permitted to but need not behave as described.]

must

[Definition: Conforming documents and XML processors are required to behave as described; otherwise they are in error.]

error

[Definition: A violation of the rules of this specification; results are undefined. Conforming software may detect and report an error and may recover from it.]

fatal error

[Definition: An error which a conforming XML processor must detect and report to the application. After encountering a fatal error, the processor may continue processing the data to search for further errors and may report such errors to the application. In order to support correction of errors, the processor may make unprocessed data from the document (with intermingled character data and markup) available to the application. Once a fatal error is detected, however, the processor must not continue normal processing (i.e., it must not continue to pass character data and information about the document's logical structure to the application in the normal way).]

at user option

[Definition: Conforming software may or must (depending on the modal verb in the sentence) behave as described; if it does, it must provide users a means to enable or disable the behavior described.]

validity constraint

[Definition: A rule which applies to all valid XML documents. Violations of validity constraints are errors; they must, at user option, be reported by validating XML processors.]

well-formedness constraint

[Definition: A rule which applies to all well-formed XML documents. Violations of well-formedness constraints are fatal errors.]

match

[Definition: (Of strings or names:) Two strings or names being compared must be identical. Characters with multiple possible representations in ISO/IEC 10646 (e.g. characters with both precomposed and base+diacritic forms) match only if they have the same representation in both strings. No case folding is performed. (Of strings and rules in the grammar:) A string matches a grammatical production if it belongs to the language generated by that production. (Of content and content models:) An element matches its declaration when it conforms in the fashion described in the constraint **[VC: Element Valid]**.]

for compatibility

[Definition: Marks a sentence describing a feature of XML included solely to ensure that XML remains compatible with SGML.]

for interoperability

[Definition: Marks a sentence describing a non-binding recommendation included to increase the chances that XML documents can be processed by the existing installed base of SGML processors which predate the WebSGML Adaptations Annex to ISO 8879.]

2 Documents

[Definition: A data object is an **XML document** if it is well-formed, as defined in this specification. A well-formed XML document may in addition be valid if it meets certain further constraints.]

Each XML document has both a logical and a physical structure. Physically, the document is composed of units called entities. An entity may refer to other entities to cause their inclusion in the document. A document begins in a "root" or document entity. Logically, the document is composed of declarations, elements, comments, character references, and processing instructions, all of which are indicated in the document by explicit markup. The logical and physical structures must nest properly, as described in **4.3.2 Well-Formed Parsed Entities**.

2.1 Well-Formed XML Documents

[Definition: A textual object is a **well-formed** XML document if:]

1. Taken as a whole, it matches the production labeled document.

2. It meets all the well-formedness constraints given in this specification.

3. Each of the parsed entities which is referenced directly or indirectly within the document is well-formed.

Document

```
[1] document ::= prolog element Misc*
```

Matching the document production implies that:

1. It contains one or more elements.

2. [Definition: There is exactly one element, called the **root**, or document element, no part of which appears in the content of any other element.] For all other elements, if the start-tag is in the content of another element, the end-tag is in the content of the same element. More simply stated, the elements, delimited by start- and end-tags, nest properly within each other.

[Definition: As a consequence of this, for each non-root element C in the document, there is one other element P in the document such that C is in the content of P, but is not in the content of any other element that is in the content of P. P is referred to as the **parent** of C, and C as a **child** of P.]

2.2 Characters

[Definition: A parsed entity contains **text**, a sequence of characters, which may represent markup or character data.] [Definition: A **character** is an atomic unit of text as specified by ISO/IEC 10646 [ISO/IEC 10646] (see also [ISO/IEC 10646-2000]). Legal characters are tab, carriage return, line feed, and the legal characters of Unicode and ISO/IEC 10646. The versions of these standards cited in **A.1 Normative References** were current at the time this document was prepared. New characters may be added to these standards by amendments or new editions. Consequently, XML processors must accept any character in the range specified for Char. The use of "compatibility characters", as defined in section 6.8 of [Unicode] (see also D21 in section 3.6 of [Unicode3]), is discouraged.]

Character Range

```
[2] Char ::= #x9 | #xA | #xD | [#x20-#xD7FF]    /* any Unicode
             | [#xE000-#xFFFD] | [#x10000-#x10FFFF]   character,
                                                      excluding the
                                                      surrogate
                                                      blocks, FFFE,
                                                      and FFFF. */
```

The mechanism for encoding character code points into bit patterns may vary from entity to entity. All XML processors must accept the UTF-8 and UTF-16 encodings of 10646; the mechanisms for signaling which of the two is in use, or for bringing other encodings into play, are discussed later, in **4.3.3 Character Encoding in Entities**.

2.3 Common Syntactic Constructs

This section defines some symbols used widely in the grammar.

S (white space) consists of one or more space (#x20) characters, carriage returns, line feeds, or tabs.

White Space

```
[3] S ::= (#x20 | #x9 | #xD | #xA)+
```

Characters are classified for convenience as letters, digits, or other characters. A letter consists of an alphabetic or syllabic base character or an ideographic character. Full definitions of the specific characters in each class are given in **B Character Classes**.

[Definition: A **Name** is a token beginning with a letter or one of a few punctuation characters, and continuing with letters, digits, hyphens, underscores, colons, or full stops, together known as name characters.] Names beginning with the string "xml", or any string which would match ((('X'|'x') ('M'|'m') ('L'|'l')), are reserved for standardization in this or future versions of this specification.

| Note | The Namespaces in XML Recommendation [XML Names] assigns a meaning to names containing colon characters. Therefore, authors should not use the colon in XML names except for namespace purposes, but XML processors must accept the colon as a name character. |

An Nmtoken (name token) is any mixture of name characters.

Names and Tokens

```
[4] NameChar ::= Letter | Digit | '.' | '-' | '_' | ':' |
                 CombiningChar | Extender
[5] Name     ::= (Letter | '_' | ':') (NameChar)*
[6] Names    ::= Name (S Name)*
[7] Nmtoken  ::= (NameChar)+
[8] Nmtokens ::= Nmtoken (S Nmtoken)*
```

Literal data is any quoted string not containing the quotation mark used as a delimiter for that string. Literals are used for specifying the content of internal entities (EntityValue), the values of attributes (AttValue), and external identifiers (SystemLiteral). Note that a SystemLiteral can be parsed without scanning for markup.

Literals

```
[9]  EntityValue   ::= '"' ([^%&"] | PEReference | Reference)* '"'
                     | "'" ([^%&'] | PEReference | Reference)* "'"
[10] AttValue      ::= '"' ([^<&"] | Reference)* '"'
                     | "'" ([^<&'] | Reference)* "'"
[11] SystemLiteral ::= ('"' [^"]* '"') | ("'" [^']* "'")
[12] PubidLiteral  ::= '"' PubidChar* '"'
                     | "'" (PubidChar - "'")* "'"
[13] PubidChar ::= #x20 | #xD | #xA | [a-zA-Z0-9]
                 | [-'()+,./:=?;!*#@$_%]
```

Note   Although the EntityValue production allows the definition of an entity consisting of a single explicit < in the literal (e.g. <!ENTITY mylt "<">), it is strongly advised to avoid this practice since any reference to that entity will cause a well-formedness error.

2.4 Character Data and Markup

Text consists of intermingled character data and markup. [Definition: **Markup** takes the form of start-tags, end-tags, empty-element tags, entity references, character references, comments, CDATA section delimiters, document type declarations, processing instructions, XML declarations, text declarations, and any white space that is at the top level of the document entity (that is, outside the document element and not inside any other markup).]

[Definition: All text that is not markup constitutes the **character data** of the document.]

The ampersand character (&) and the left angle bracket (<) may appear in their literal form *only* when used as markup delimiters, or within a comment, a processing instruction, or a CDATA section. If they are needed elsewhere, they must be escaped using either numeric character references or the strings "&" and "<" respectively. The right angle bracket (>) may be represented using the string ">", and must, for compatibility, be escaped using ">" or a character reference when it appears in the string "]]>" in content, when that string is not marking the end of a CDATA section.

In the content of elements, character data is any string of characters which does not contain the start-delimiter of any markup. In a CDATA section, character data is any string of characters not including the CDATA-section-close delimiter, "]]>".

To allow attribute values to contain both single and double quotes, the apostrophe or single-quote character (') may be represented as "'", and the double-quote character (") as """.

Character Data
```
[14] CharData ::= [^<&]* - ([^<&]* ']]>' [^<&]*)
```

2.5 Comments

[Definition: **Comments** may appear anywhere in a document outside other markup; in addition, they may appear within the document type declaration at places allowed by the grammar. They are not part of the document's character data; an XML processor may, but need not, make it possible for an application to retrieve the text of comments. For compatibility, the string "--" (double-hyphen) must not occur within comments.] Parameter entity references are not recognized within comments.

Comments
```
[15] Comment ::= '<!--' ((Char - '-')|('-' (Char - '-')))*'-->'
```

An example of a comment:

```
<!-- declarations for <head> & <body> -->
```

Note that the grammar does not allow a comment ending in --->. The following example is *not* well-formed.

```
<!-- B+, B, or B--->
```

2.6 Processing Instructions

[Definition: **Processing instructions** (PIs) allow documents to contain instructions for applications.]

Processing Instructions
```
[16] PI ::= '<?' PITarget
             (S (Char* - (Char* '?>' Char*)))? '?>'
[17] PITarget ::= Name - (('X' | 'x') ('M' | 'm') ('L' | 'l'))
```

PIs are not part of the document's character data, but must be passed through to the application. The PI begins with a target (PITarget) used to identify the application to which the instruction is directed. The target names "XML", "xml", and so on are reserved for standardization in this or future versions of this specification. The XML Notation mechanism may be used for formal declaration of PI targets. Parameter entity references are not recognized within processing instructions.

2.7 CDATA Sections

[Definition: **CDATA sections** may occur anywhere character data may occur; they are used to escape blocks of text containing characters which would otherwise be recognized as markup. CDATA sections begin with the string "<![CDATA[" and end with the string "]]>":]

CDATA Sections

```
[18] CDSect  ::= CDStart CData CDEnd
[19] CDStart ::= '<![CDATA['
[20] CData   ::= (Char* - (Char* ']]>' Char*))
[21] CDEnd   ::= ']]>'
```

Within a CDATA section, only the CDEnd string is recognized as markup, so that left angle brackets and ampersands may occur in their literal form; they need not (and cannot) be escaped using "<" and "&". CDATA sections cannot nest.

An example of a CDATA section, in which "<greeting>" and "</greeting>" are recognized as character data, not markup:

```
<![CDATA[<greeting>Hello, world!</greeting>]]>
```

2.8 Prolog and Document Type Declaration

[Definition: XML documents should begin with an **XML declaration** which specifies the version of XML being used.] For example, the following is a complete XML document, well-formed but not valid:

```
<?xml version="1.0"?> <greeting>Hello, world!</greeting>
```

and so is this:

```
<greeting>Hello, world!</greeting>
```

The version number "1.0" should be used to indicate conformance to this version of this specification; it is an error for a document to use the value "1.0" if it does not conform to this version of this specification. It is the intent of the XML working group to give later versions of this specification numbers other than "1.0", but this intent does not indicate a commitment to produce any future versions of XML, nor if any are produced, to use any particular numbering scheme. Since future versions are not ruled out, this construct is provided as a means to allow the possibility of automatic version recognition, should it become necessary. Processors may signal an error if they receive documents labeled with versions they do not support.

The function of the markup in an XML document is to describe its storage and logical structure and to associate attribute-value pairs with its logical structures. XML provides a mechanism, the document type declaration, to define constraints on the logical structure and to support the use of predefined storage units. [Definition: An XML document is **valid** if it has an associated document type declaration and if the document complies with the constraints expressed in it.]

The document type declaration must appear before the first element in the document.

Prolog

```
[22] prolog  ::= XMLDecl? Misc* (doctypedecl Misc*)?
[23] XMLDecl ::= '<?xml' VersionInfo EncodingDecl?
                 SDDecl? S? '?>'
[24] VersionInfo ::= S 'version' Eq ("'" VersionNum "'"
                 | '"' VersionNum '"')/* */
[25] Eq ::= S? '=' S?
[26] VersionNum ::= ([a-zA-Z0-9_.:] | '-')+
[27] Misc ::= Comment | PI | S
```

[Definition: The XML **document type declaration** contains or points to markup declarations that provide a grammar for a class of documents. This grammar is known as a document type definition, or **DTD**. The document type declaration can point to an external subset (a special kind of external entity) containing markup declarations, or can contain the markup declarations directly in an internal subset, or can do both. The DTD for a document consists of both subsets taken together.]

[Definition: A **markup declaration** is an element type declaration, an attribute-list declaration, an entity declaration, or a notation declaration.] These declarations may be contained in whole or in part within parameter entities, as described in the well-formedness and validity constraints below. For further information, see **4 Physical Structures**.

Document Type Definition

```
[28] doctypedecl ::= '<!DOCTYPE' S Name (S ExternalID)?
                     S? ('[' (markupdecl | DeclSep)* ']'
                     S?)? '>'
                     [VC: Root Element Type]
                     [WFC: External Subset] /* */
[28a] DeclSep ::= PEReference | S
                     [WFC: PE Between Declarations] /* */
[29] markupdecl ::= elementdecl | AttlistDecl | EntityDecl |
                     NotationDecl | PI | Comment
                     [VC: Proper Declaration/PE Nesting]
                     [WFC: PEs in Internal Subset]
```

Note that it is possible to construct a well-formed document containing a doctypedecl that neither points to an external subset nor contains an internal subset.

The markup declarations may be made up in whole or in part of the replacement text of parameter entities. The productions later in this specification for individual nonterminals (elementdecl, AttlistDecl, and so on) describe the declarations *after* all the parameter entities have been included.

Parameter entity references are recognized anywhere in the DTD (internal and external subsets and external parameter entities), except in literals, processing instructions, comments, and the contents of ignored conditional sections (see **3.4 Conditional Sections**). They are also recognized in entity value literals. The use of parameter entities in the internal subset is restricted as described below.

Validity constraint: Root Element Type

The Name in the document type declaration must match the element type of the root element.

Validity constraint: Proper Declaration/PE Nesting

Parameter-entity replacement text must be properly nested with markup declarations. That is to say, if either the first character or the last character of a markup declaration (markupdecl above) is contained in the replacement text for a parameter-entity reference, both must be contained in the same replacement text.

Well-formedness constraint: PEs in Internal Subset

In the internal DTD subset, parameter-entity references can occur only where markup declarations can occur, not within markup declarations. (This does not apply to references that occur in external parameter entities or to the external subset.)

Well-formedness constraint: External Subset

The external subset, if any, must match the production for extSubset.

Well-formedness constraint: PE Between Declarations

The replacement text of a parameter entity reference in a DeclSep must match the production extSubsetDecl.

Like the internal subset, the external subset and any external parameter entities referenced in a DeclSep must consist of a series of complete markup declarations of the types allowed by the non-terminal symbol markupdecl, interspersed with white space or parameter-entity references. However, portions of the contents of the external subset or of these external parameter entities may conditionally be ignored by using the conditional section construct; this is not allowed in the internal subset.

External Subset

```
[30] extSubset ::= TextDecl? extSubsetDecl
[31] extSubsetDecl ::= ( markupdecl | conditionalSect |
                         DeclSep)* /* */
```

The external subset and external parameter entities also differ from the internal subset in that in them, parameter-entity references are permitted *within* markup declarations, not only *between* markup declarations.

An example of an XML document with a document type declaration:

```
<?xml version="1.0"?> <!DOCTYPE greeting SYSTEM "hello.dtd">
<greeting>Hello, world!</greeting>
```

The system identifier "hello.dtd" gives the address (a URI reference) of a DTD for the document.

The declarations can also be given locally, as in this example:

```
<?xml version="1.0" encoding="UTF-8" ?>
<!DOCTYPE greeting [
  <!ELEMENT greeting (#PCDATA)>
]>
<greeting>Hello, world!</greeting>
```

If both the external and internal subsets are used, the internal subset is considered to occur before the external subset. This has the effect that entity and attribute-list declarations in the internal subset take precedence over those in the external subset.

2.9 Standalone Document Declaration

Markup declarations can affect the content of the document, as passed from an XML processor to an application; examples are attribute defaults and entity declarations. The standalone document declaration, which may appear as a component of the XML declaration, signals whether or not there are such declarations which appear external to the document entity or in parameter entities. [Definition: An **external markup declaration** is defined as a markup declaration occurring in the external subset or in a parameter entity (external or internal, the latter being included because non-validating processors are not required to read them).]

Standalone Document Declaration

```
[32] SDDecl ::= S 'standalone' Eq (("'" ('yes' | 'no') "'")
                                  | ('"' ('yes' | 'no') '"'))
                       [VC: Standalone Document Declaration]
```

In a standalone document declaration, the value "yes" indicates that there are no external markup declarations which affect the information passed from the XML processor to the application. The value "no" indicates that there are or may be such external markup declarations. Note that the standalone document declaration only denotes the presence of external *declarations*; the presence, in a document, of references to external *entities*, when those entities are internally declared, does not change its standalone status.

If there are no external markup declarations, the standalone document declaration has no meaning. If there are external markup declarations but there is no standalone document declaration, the value "no" is assumed.

Any XML document for which standalone="no" holds can be converted algorithmically to a standalone document, which may be desirable for some network delivery applications.

Validity constraint: Standalone Document Declaration

The standalone document declaration must have the value "no" if any external markup declarations contain declarations of:

- ✦ attributes with default values, if elements to which these attributes apply appear in the document without specifications of values for these attributes, or

- ✦ entities (other than amp, lt, gt, apos, quot), if references to those entities appear in the document, or

- ✦ attributes with values subject to *normalization*, where the attribute appears in the document with a value which will change as a result of normalization, or

- ✦ element types with element content, if white space occurs directly within any instance of those types.

An example XML declaration with a standalone document declaration:

```
<?xml version="1.0" standalone='yes'?>
```

2.10 White Space Handling

In editing XML documents, it is often convenient to use "white space" (spaces, tabs, and blank lines) to set apart the markup for greater readability. Such white space is typically not intended for inclusion in the delivered version of the document. On the other hand, "significant" white space that should be preserved in the delivered version is common, for example in poetry and source code.

An XML processor must always pass all characters in a document that are not markup through to the application. A validating XML processor must also inform the application which of these characters constitute white space appearing in element content.

A special attribute named xml:space may be attached to an element to signal an intention that in that element, white space should be preserved by applications. In valid documents, this attribute, like any other, must be declared if it is used. When declared, it must be given as an enumerated type whose values are one or both of "default" and "preserve". For example:

```
<!ATTLIST poem  xml:space (default|preserve) 'preserve'>

<!-- -->
<!ATTLIST pre xml:space (preserve) #FIXED 'preserve'>
```

The value "default" signals that applications' default white-space processing modes are acceptable for this element; the value "preserve" indicates the intent that applications preserve all the white space. This declared intent is considered to apply to all elements within the content of the element where it is specified, unless overridden with another instance of the xml:space attribute.

The root element of any document is considered to have signaled no intentions as regards application space handling, unless it provides a value for this attribute or the attribute is declared with a default value.

2.11 End-of-Line Handling

XML parsed entities are often stored in computer files which, for editing convenience, are organized into lines. These lines are typically separated by some combination of the characters carriage-return (#xD) and line-feed (#xA).

To simplify the tasks of applications, the characters passed to an application by the XML processor must be as if the XML processor normalized all line breaks in external parsed entities (including the document entity) on input, before parsing, by translating both the two-character sequence #xD #xA and any #xD that is not followed by #xA to a single #xA character.

2.12 Language Identification

In document processing, it is often useful to identify the natural or formal language in which the content is written. A special attribute named xml:lang may be inserted in documents to specify the language used in the contents and attribute values of any element in an XML document. In valid documents, this attribute, like any other, must be declared if it is used. The values of the attribute are language identifiers as defined by [IETF RFC 1766], *Tags for the Identification of Languages*, or its successor on the IETF Standards Track.

Note   [IETF RFC 1766] tags are constructed from two-letter language codes as defined by [ISO 639], from two-letter country codes as defined by [ISO 3166], or from language identifiers registered with the Internet Assigned Numbers Authority [IANA-LANGCODES]. It is expected that the successor to [IETF RFC 1766] will introduce three-letter language codes for languages not presently covered by [ISO 639].

(Productions 33 through 38 have been removed.)

For example:

```
<p xml:lang="en">The quick brown fox jumps over the lazy
dog.</p>
<p xml:lang="en-GB">What colour is it?</p>
<p xml:lang="en-US">What color is it?</p>
<sp who="Faust" desc='leise' xml:lang="de">
  <l>Habe nun, ach! Philosophie,</l>
  <l>Juristerei, und Medizin</l>
  <l>und leider auch Theologie</l>
  <l>durchaus studiert mit heißem Bemüh'n.</l>
</sp>
```

The intent declared with xml:lang is considered to apply to all attributes and content of the element where it is specified, unless overridden with an instance of xml:lang on another element within that content.

A simple declaration for xml:lang might take the form

```
xml:lang NMTOKEN #IMPLIED
```

but specific default values may also be given, if appropriate. In a collection of French poems for English students, with glosses and notes in English, the xml:lang attribute might be declared this way:

```
<!ATTLIST poem    xml:lang NMTOKEN 'fr'>
<!ATTLIST gloss   xml:lang NMTOKEN 'en'>
<!ATTLIST note    xml:lang NMTOKEN 'en'>
```

3 Logical Structures

[Definition: Each XML document contains one or more **elements**, the boundaries of which are either delimited by start-tags and end-tags, or, for empty elements, by an empty-element tag. Each element has a type, identified by name, sometimes called its "generic identifier" (GI), and may have a set of attribute specifications.] Each attribute specification has a name and a value.

Element

```
[39] element ::= EmptyElemTag | STag content ETag
                                    [WFC: Element Type Match]
                                    [VC: Element Valid]
```

This specification does not constrain the semantics, use, or (beyond syntax) names of the element types and attributes, except that names beginning with a match to (('X'|'x')('M'|'m')('L'|'l')) are reserved for standardization in this or future versions of this specification.

Well-formedness constraint: Element Type Match

The Name in an element's end-tag must match the element type in the start-tag.

Validity constraint: Element Valid

An element is valid if there is a declaration matching elementdecl where the Name matches the element type, and one of the following holds:

1. The declaration matches **EMPTY** and the element has no content.

2. The declaration matches children and the sequence of child elements belongs to the language generated by the regular expression in the content model, with optional white space (characters matching the nonterminal S) between the start-tag and the first child element, between child elements, or between the last child element and the end-tag. Note that a CDATA section containing only white space does not match the nonterminal S, and hence cannot appear in these positions.

3. The declaration matches Mixed and the content consists of character data and child elements whose types match names in the content model.

4. The declaration matches **ANY**, and the types of any child elements have been declared.

3.1 Start-Tags, End-Tags, and Empty-Element Tags

[Definition: The beginning of every non-empty XML element is marked by a **start-tag**.]

Start-tag

```
[40] STag ::= '<' Name (S Attribute)* S? '>'
                              [WFC: Unique Att Spec]
[41] Attribute ::= Name Eq AttValue
                              [VC: Attribute Value Type]
                              [WFC: No External Entity References]
                              [WFC: No < in Attribute Values]
```

The Name in the start- and end-tags gives the element's **type**. [Definition: The Name-AttValue pairs are referred to as the **attribute specifications** of the element], [Definition: with the Name in each pair referred to as the **attribute name**] and [Definition: the content of the AttValue (the text between the ' or " delimiters) as the **attribute value**.] Note that the order of attribute specifications in a start-tag or empty-element tag is not significant.

Well-formedness constraint: Unique Att Spec

No attribute name may appear more than once in the same start-tag or empty-element tag.

Validity constraint: Attribute Value Type

The attribute must have been declared; the value must be of the type declared for it. (For attribute types, see **3.3 Attribute-List Declarations**.)

Well-formedness constraint: No External Entity References

Attribute values cannot contain direct or indirect entity references to external entities.

Well-formedness constraint: No < in Attribute Values

The replacement text of any entity referred to directly or indirectly in an attribute value must not contain a <.

An example of a start-tag:

```
<termdef id="dt-dog" term="dog">
```

[Definition: The end of every element that begins with a start-tag must be marked by an **end-tag** containing a name that echoes the element's type as given in the start-tag:]

End-tag
```
[42] ETag ::= '</' Name S? '>'
```

An example of an end-tag:

```
</termdef>
```

[Definition: The text between the start-tag and end-tag is called the element's **content**:]

Content of Elements
```
[43] content ::= CharData? ((element | Reference | CDSect
                 | PI | Comment) CharData?)* /* */
```

[Definition: An element with no content is said to be **empty**.] The representation of an empty element is either a start-tag immediately followed by an end-tag, or an empty-element tag. [Definition: An **empty-element tag** takes a special form:]

Tags for Empty Elements
```
[44] EmptyElemTag ::= '<' Name (S Attribute)* S? '/>'
                                        [WFC: Unique Att Spec]
```

Empty-element tags may be used for any element which has no content, whether or not it is declared using the keyword **EMPTY**. For interoperability, the empty-element tag should be used, and should only be used, for elements which are declared EMPTY.

Examples of empty elements:

```
<IMG align="left"
 src="http://www.w3.org/Icons/WWW/w3c_home" />
<br></br>
<br/>
```

3.2 Element Type Declarations

The element structure of an XML document may, for validation purposes, be constrained using element type and attribute-list declarations. An element type declaration constrains the element's content.

Element type declarations often constrain which element types can appear as children of the element. At user option, an XML processor may issue a warning when a declaration mentions an element type for which no declaration is provided, but this is not an error.

[Definition: An **element type declaration** takes the form:]

Element Type Declaration

```
[45] elementdecl ::= '<!ELEMENT' S Name S contentspec S? '>'
                                 [VC: Unique Element Type Declaration]
[46] contentspec ::= 'EMPTY' | 'ANY' | Mixed | children
```

where the Name gives the element type being declared.

Validity constraint: Unique Element Type Declaration

No element type may be declared more than once.

Examples of element type declarations:

```
<!ELEMENT br EMPTY>
<!ELEMENT p (#PCDATA|emph)* >
<!ELEMENT %name.para; %content.para; >
<!ELEMENT container ANY>
```

3.2.1 Element Content

[Definition: An element type has **element content** when elements of that type must contain only child elements (no character data), optionally separated by white space (characters matching the nonterminal S).] [Definition: In this case, the constraint includes a **content model**, a simple grammar governing the allowed types of the child elements and the order in which they are allowed to appear.] The grammar is built on content particles (cps), which consist of names, choice lists of content particles, or sequence lists of content particles:

Element-content Models

```
[47] children ::= (choice | seq) ('?' | '*' | '+')?
[48] cp ::= (Name | choice | seq) ('?' | '*' | '+')?
[49] choice ::= '(' S? cp ( S? '|' S? cp )+ S? ')' /* */
                          /* */ [VC: Proper Group/PE Nesting]
[50] seq ::= '(' S? cp ( S? ',' S? cp )* S? ')' /* */
                          [VC: Proper Group/PE Nesting]
```

where each Name is the type of an element which may appear as a child. Any content particle in a choice list may appear in the element content at the location where the choice list appears in the grammar; content particles occurring in a sequence list must each appear in the element content in the order given in the list. The optional character following a name or list governs whether the element or the content particles in the list may occur one or more (+), zero or more (*), or zero or one times (?). The absence of such an operator means that the element or content particle must appear exactly once. This syntax and meaning are identical to those used in the productions in this specification.

The content of an element matches a content model if and only if it is possible to trace out a path through the content model, obeying the sequence, choice, and repetition operators and matching each element in the content against an element type in the content model. For compatibility, it is an error if an element in the document can match more than one occurrence of an element type in the content model. For more information, see **E Deterministic Content Models**.

Validity constraint: Proper Group/PE Nesting

Parameter-entity replacement text must be properly nested with parenthesized groups. That is to say, if either of the opening or closing parentheses in a choice, seq, or Mixed construct is contained in the replacement text for a parameter entity, both must be contained in the same replacement text.

For interoperability, if a parameter-entity reference appears in a choice, seq, or Mixed construct, its replacement text should contain at least one non-blank character, and neither the first nor last non-blank character of the replacement text should be a connector (| or ,).

Examples of element-content models:

```
<!ELEMENT spec (front, body, back?)>
<!ELEMENT div1 (head, (p | list | note)*, div2*)>
<!ELEMENT dictionary-body (%div.mix; | %dict.mix;)*>
```

3.2.2 Mixed Content

[Definition: An element type has **mixed content** when elements of that type may contain character data, optionally interspersed with child elements.] In this case, the types of the child elements may be constrained, but not their order or their number of occurrences:

Mixed-content Declaration

```
[51] Mixed ::= '(' S? '#PCDATA' (S? '|' S? Name)* S? ')*'
             | '(' S? '#PCDATA' S? ')'
                                     [VC: Proper Group/PE Nesting]
                                     [VC: No Duplicate Types]
```

where the Names give the types of elements that may appear as children. The keyword **#PCDATA** derives historically from the term "parsed character data."

Validity constraint: No Duplicate Types

The same name must not appear more than once in a single mixed-content declaration.

Examples of mixed content declarations:

```
<!ELEMENT p (#PCDATA|a|ul|b|i|em)*>
<!ELEMENT p (#PCDATA | %font; | %phrase; | %special; | %form;)*>
<!ELEMENT b (#PCDATA)>
```

3.3 Attribute-List Declarations

Attributes are used to associate name-value pairs with elements. Attribute specifications may appear only within start-tags and empty-element tags; thus, the productions used to recognize them appear in **3.1 Start-Tags, End-Tags, and Empty-Element Tags**. Attribute-list declarations may be used:

- ✦ To define the set of attributes pertaining to a given element type.
- ✦ To establish type constraints for these attributes.
- ✦ To provide default values for attributes.

[Definition: **Attribute-list declarations** specify the name, data type, and default value (if any) of each attribute associated with a given element type:]

Attribute-list Declaration
```
[52] AttlistDecl ::= '<!ATTLIST' S Name AttDef* S? '>'
[53] AttDef      ::= S Name S AttType S DefaultDecl
```

The Name in the AttlistDecl rule is the type of an element. At user option, an XML processor may issue a warning if attributes are declared for an element type not itself declared, but this is not an error. The Name in the AttDef rule is the name of the attribute.

When more than one AttlistDecl is provided for a given element type, the contents of all those provided are merged. When more than one definition is provided for the same attribute of a given element type, the first declaration is binding and later declarations are ignored. For interoperability, writers of DTDs may choose to provide at most one attribute-list declaration for a given element type, at most one attribute definition for a given attribute name in an attribute-list declaration, and at least one attribute definition in each attribute-list declaration. For interoperability, an XML processor may at user option issue a warning when more than one attribute-list declaration is provided for a given element type, or more than one attribute definition is provided for a given attribute, but this is not an error.

3.3.1 Attribute Types

XML attribute types are of three kinds: a string type, a set of tokenized types, and enumerated types. The string type may take any literal string as a value; the tokenized types have varying lexical and semantic constraints. The validity constraints noted in the grammar are applied after the attribute value has been normalized as described in **3.3 Attribute-List Declarations**.

Attribute Types

```
[54] AttType      ::= StringType | TokenizedType | EnumeratedType
[55] StringType ::= 'CDATA'
[56] TokenizedType ::= 'ID'          [VC: ID]
                                     [VC: One ID per Element Type]
                                     [VC: ID Attribute Default]
                   | 'IDREF'    [VC: IDREF]
                   | 'IDREFS'   [VC: IDREF]
                   | 'ENTITY'   [VC: Entity Name]
                   | 'ENTITIES' [VC: Entity Name]
                   | 'NMTOKEN'  [VC: Name Token]
                   | 'NMTOKENS' [VC: Name Token]
```

Validity constraint: ID

Values of type **ID** must match the Name production. A name must not appear more than once in an XML document as a value of this type; i.e., ID values must uniquely identify the elements which bear them.

Validity constraint: One ID per Element Type

No element type may have more than one ID attribute specified.

Validity constraint: ID Attribute Default

An ID attribute must have a declared default of **#IMPLIED** or **#REQUIRED**.

Validity constraint: IDREF

Values of type **IDREF** must match the Name production, and values of type **IDREFS** must match Names; each Name must match the value of an ID attribute on some element in the XML document; i.e., **IDREF** values must match the value of some ID attribute.

Validity constraint: Entity Name

Values of type **ENTITY** must match the Name production, values of type **ENTITIES** must match Names; each Name must match the name of an unparsed entity declared in the DTD.

Validity constraint: Name Token

Values of type **NMTOKEN** must match the Nmtoken production; values of type **NMTOKENS** must match Nmtokens.

[Definition: **Enumerated attributes** can take one of a list of values provided in the declaration]. There are two kinds of enumerated types:

Enumerated Attribute Types

```
[57] EnumeratedType ::= NotationType | Enumeration
[58] NotationType    ::= 'NOTATION' S '(' S? Name
                          (S? '|' S? Name)* S? ')'
                          [VC: Notation Attributes]
                          [VC: One Notation Per Element Type]
                          [VC: No Notation on Empty Element]
[59] Enumeration ::= '(' S? Nmtoken ( S? '|' S? Nmtoken)*
                      S? ')' [VC: Enumeration]
```

A **NOTATION** attribute identifies a notation, declared in the DTD with associated system and/or public identifiers, to be used in interpreting the element to which the attribute is attached.

Validity constraint: Notation Attributes

Values of this type must match one of the *notation* names included in the declaration; all notation names in the declaration must be declared.

Validity constraint: One Notation Per Element Type

No element type may have more than one **NOTATION** attribute specified.

Validity constraint: No Notation on Empty Element

For compatibility, an attribute of type **NOTATION** must not be declared on an element declared **EMPTY**.

Validity constraint: Enumeration

Values of this type must match one of the Nmtoken tokens in the declaration.

For interoperability, the same Nmtoken should not occur more than once in the enumerated attribute types of a single element type.

3.3.2 Attribute Defaults

An attribute declaration provides information on whether the attribute's presence is required, and if not, how an XML processor should react if a declared attribute is absent in a document.

Attribute Defaults

```
[60] DefaultDecl ::= '#REQUIRED' | '#IMPLIED'
                   | (('#FIXED' S)? AttValue)
                               [VC: Required Attribute]
                               [VC: Attribute Default Legal]
                               [WFC: No < in Attribute Values]
                               [VC: Fixed Attribute Default]
```

In an attribute declaration, **#REQUIRED** means that the attribute must always be provided, **#IMPLIED** that no default value is provided. [Definition: If the declaration is neither **#REQUIRED** nor **#IMPLIED**, then the AttValue value contains the declared **default** value; the **#FIXED** keyword states that the attribute must always have the default value. If a default value is declared, when an XML processor encounters an omitted attribute, it is to behave as though the attribute were present with the declared default value.]

Validity constraint: Required Attribute

If the default declaration is the keyword **#REQUIRED**, then the attribute must be specified for all elements of the type in the attribute-list declaration.

Validity constraint: Attribute Default Legal

The declared default value must meet the lexical constraints of the declared attribute type.

Validity constraint: Fixed Attribute Default

If an attribute has a default value declared with the **#FIXED** keyword, instances of that attribute must match the default value.

Examples of attribute-list declarations:

```
<!ATTLIST termdef
          id      ID       #REQUIRED
          name    CDATA    #IMPLIED>
<!ATTLIST list
          type    (bullets|ordered|glossary)   "ordered">
<!ATTLIST form
          method  CDATA    #FIXED "POST">
```

3.3.3 Attribute-Value Normalization

Before the value of an attribute is passed to the application or checked for validity, the XML processor must normalize the attribute value by applying the algorithm below, or by using some other method such that the value passed to the application is the same as that produced by the algorithm.

1. All line breaks must have been normalized on input to #xA as described in **2.11 End-of-Line Handling**, so the rest of this algorithm operates on text normalized in this way.

2. Begin with a normalized value consisting of the empty string.

3. For each character, entity reference, or character reference in the unnormalized attribute value, beginning with the first and continuing to the last, do the following:

   - For a character reference, append the referenced character to the normalized value.

   - For an entity reference, recursively apply step 3 of this algorithm to the replacement text of the entity.

   - For a white space character (#x20, #xD, #xA, #x9), append a space character (#x20) to the normalized value.

   - For another character, append the character to the normalized value.

If the attribute type is not CDATA, then the XML processor must further process the normalized attribute value by discarding any leading and trailing space (#x20) characters, and by replacing sequences of space (#x20) characters by a single space (#x20) character.

Note that if the unnormalized attribute value contains a character reference to a white space character other than space (#x20), the normalized value contains the referenced character itself (#xD, #xA or #x9). This contrasts with the case where the unnormalized value contains a white space character (not a reference), which is replaced with a space character (#x20) in the normalized value and also contrasts with the case where the unnormalized value contains an entity reference whose replacement text contains a white space character; being recursively processed, the white space character is replaced with a space character (#x20) in the normalized value.

All attributes for which no declaration has been read should be treated by a non-validating processor as if declared **CDATA**.

Following are examples of attribute normalization. Given the following declarations:

```
<!ENTITY d  "&#xD;">
<!ENTITY a  "&#xA;">
<!ENTITY da "&#xD;&#xA;">
```

the attribute specifications in the left column below would be normalized to the character sequences of the middle column if the attribute a is declared **NMTOKENS** and to those of the right columns if a is declared **CDATA**.

Attribute specification	a is NMTOKENS	a is CDATA
a="		
xyz"	x y z	#x20 #x20 x y z
a="&d;&d;A&a;&a;B&da;"	A #x20 B	#x20 #x20 A #x20 #x20 B #x20 #x20
a=		
"A

B
"	#xD #xD A #xA #xA B #xD #xA	#xD #xD A #xA #xA B #xD #xD

Note that the last example is invalid (but well-formed) if a is declared to be of type **NMTOKENS**.

3.4 Conditional Sections

[Definition: **Conditional sections** are portions of the document type declaration external subset which are included in, or excluded from, the logical structure of the DTD based on the keyword which governs them.]

Conditional Section

```
[61] conditionalSect ::= includeSect | ignoreSect
[62] includeSect     ::= '<![' S? 'INCLUDE' S?
                         '[' extSubsetDecl ']]>'  /* */
                 [VC: Proper Conditional Section/PE Nesting]
[63] ignoreSect      ::= '<![' S? 'IGNORE' S? '['
                         ignoreSectContents* ']]>' /* */
                 [VC: Proper Conditional Section/PE Nesting]
[64] ignoreSectContents ::= Ignore ('<![' ignoreSectContents
                            ']]>' Ignore)*
[65] Ignore ::= Char* - (Char* ('<![' | ']]>') Char*)
```

Validity constraint: Proper Conditional Section/PE Nesting

If any of the "<![", "[", or "]]>" of a conditional section is contained in the replacement text for a parameter-entity reference, all of them must be contained in the same replacement text.

Like the internal and external DTD subsets, a conditional section may contain one or more complete declarations, comments, processing instructions, or nested conditional sections, intermingled with white space.

If the keyword of the conditional section is **INCLUDE**, then the contents of the conditional section are part of the DTD. If the keyword of the conditional section is **IGNORE**, then the contents of the conditional section are not logically part of the

DTD. If a conditional section with a keyword of **INCLUDE** occurs within a larger conditional section with a keyword of **IGNORE**, both the outer and the inner conditional sections are ignored. The contents of an ignored conditional section are parsed by ignoring all characters after the "[" following the keyword, except conditional section starts "<![" and ends "]]>", until the matching conditional section end is found. Parameter entity references are not recognized in this process.

If the keyword of the conditional section is a parameter-entity reference, the parameter entity must be replaced by its content before the processor decides whether to include or ignore the conditional section.

An example:

```
<!ENTITY % draft 'INCLUDE' >
<!ENTITY % final 'IGNORE' >

<![%draft;[
<!ELEMENT book (comments*, title, body, supplements?)>
]]>
<![%final;[
<!ELEMENT book (title, body, supplements?)>
]]>
```

4 Physical Structures

[Definition: An XML document may consist of one or many storage units. These are called **entities**; they all have **content** and are all (except for the document entity and the external DTD subset) identified by entity **name**.] Each XML document has one entity called the document entity, which serves as the starting point for the XML processor and may contain the whole document.

Entities may be either parsed or unparsed. [Definition: A **parsed entity's** contents are referred to as its replacement text; this text is considered an integral part of the document.]

[Definition: An **unparsed entity** is a resource whose contents may or may not be text, and if text, may be other than XML. Each unparsed entity has an associated notation, identified by name. Beyond a requirement that an XML processor make the identifiers for the entity and notation available to the application, XML places no constraints on the contents of unparsed entities.]

Parsed entities are invoked by name using entity references; unparsed entities by name, given in the value of **ENTITY** or **ENTITIES** attributes.

[Definition: **General entities** are entities for use within the document content. In this specification, general entities are sometimes referred to with the unqualified term *entity* when this leads to no ambiguity.] [Definition: **Parameter entities** are parsed entities for use within the DTD.] These two types of entities use different forms of reference and are recognized in different contexts. Furthermore, they occupy different namespaces; a parameter entity and a general entity with the same name are two distinct entities.

4.1 Character and Entity References

[Definition: A **character reference** refers to a specific character in the ISO/IEC 10646 character set, for example one not directly accessible from available input devices.]

Character Reference

```
[66] CharRef ::= '&#' [0-9]+ ';'   | '&#x' [0-9a-fA-F]+ ';'
                                            [WFC: Legal Character]
```

Well-formedness constraint: Legal Character

Characters referred to using character references must match the production for Char.

If the character reference begins with "&#x", the digits and letters up to the terminating ; provide a hexadecimal representation of the character's code point in ISO/IEC 10646. If it begins just with "&#", the digits up to the terminating ; provide a decimal representation of the character's code point.

[Definition: An **entity reference** refers to the content of a named entity.] [Definition: References to parsed general entities use ampersand (&) and semicolon (;) as delimiters.] [Definition: **Parameter-entity references** use percent-sign (%) and semi-colon (;) as delimiters.]

Entity Reference

```
[67] Reference ::= EntityRef | CharRef
[68] EntityRef ::= '&' Name ';'   [WFC: Entity Declared]
                                  [VC: Entity Declared]
                                  [WFC: Parsed Entity]
                                  [WFC: No Recursion]
[69] PEReference ::= '%' Name ';' [VC: Entity Declared]
                                  [WFC: No Recursion]
                                  [WFC: In DTD]
```

Well-formedness constraint: Entity Declared

In a document without any DTD, a document with only an internal DTD subset which contains no parameter entity references, or a document with "standalone='yes'", for an entity reference that does not occur within the external subset or a parameter entity, the Name given in the entity reference must match that in an *entity declaration* that does not occur within the external subset or a parameter entity, except that well-formed documents need not declare any of the following entities: amp, lt, gt, apos, quot. The declaration of a general entity must precede any reference to it which appears in a default value in an attribute-list declaration.

Note that if entities are declared in the external subset or in external parameter entities, a non-validating processor is *not obligated to* read and process their declarations; for such documents, the rule that an entity must be declared is a well-formedness constraint only if *standalone='yes'*.

Validity constraint: Entity Declared

In a document with an external subset or external parameter entities with "standalone='no'", the Name given in the entity reference must match that in an *entity declaration*. For interoperability, valid documents should declare the entities amp, lt, gt, apos, quot, in the form specified in **4.6 Predefined Entities**. The declaration of a parameter entity must precede any reference to it. Similarly, the declaration of a general entity must precede any attribute-list declaration containing a default value with a direct or indirect reference to that general entity.

Well-formedness constraint: Parsed Entity

An entity reference must not contain the name of an unparsed entity. Unparsed entities may be referred to only in attribute values declared to be of type **ENTITY** or **ENTITIES**.

Well-formedness constraint: No Recursion

A parsed entity must not contain a recursive reference to itself, either directly or indirectly.

Well-formedness constraint: In DTD

Parameter-entity references may only appear in the DTD.

Examples of character and entity references:

```
Type <key>less-than</key> (&#x3C;) to save options.
This document was prepared on &docdate; and
is classified &security-level;.
```

Example of a parameter-entity reference:

```
<!-- declare the parameter entity "ISOLat2"... -->
<!ENTITY % ISOLat2
         SYSTEM "http://www.xml.com/iso/isolat2-xml.entities" >
<!-- ... now reference it. -->
%ISOLat2;
```

4.2 Entity Declarations

[Definition: Entities are declared thus:]

Entity Declaration

```
[70] EntityDecl ::= GEDecl | PEDecl
[71] GEDecl     ::= '<!ENTITY' S Name S EntityDef S? '>'
[72] PEDecl     ::= '<!ENTITY' S '%' S Name S PEDef S? '>'
[73] EntityDef  ::= EntityValue | (ExternalID NDataDecl?)
[74] PEDef      ::= EntityValue | ExternalID
```

The Name identifies the entity in an entity reference or, in the case of an unparsed entity, in the value of an **ENTITY** or **ENTITIES** attribute. If the same entity is declared more than once, the first declaration encountered is binding; at user option, an XML processor may issue a warning if entities are declared multiple times.

4.2.1 Internal Entities

[Definition: If the entity definition is an EntityValue, the defined entity is called an **internal entity**. There is no separate physical storage object, and the content of the entity is given in the declaration.] Note that some processing of entity and character references in the literal entity value may be required to produce the correct replacement text: see **4.5 Construction of Internal Entity Replacement Text**.

An internal entity is a parsed entity.

Example of an internal entity declaration:

```
<!ENTITY Pub-Status "This is a pre-release of the
  specification.">
```

4.2.2 External Entities

[Definition: If the entity is not internal, it is an **external entity**, declared as follows:]

External Entity Declaration

```
[75] ExternalID ::= 'SYSTEM' S SystemLiteral
                  | 'PUBLIC' S PubidLiteral S SystemLiteral
[76] NDataDecl ::= S 'NDATA' S Name [VC: Notation Declared]
```

If the NDataDecl is present, this is a general unparsed entity; otherwise it is a parsed entity.

Validity constraint: Notation Declared

The Name must match the declared name of a notation.

[Definition: The SystemLiteral is called the entity's **system identifier**. It is a URI reference (as defined in [IETF RFC 2396], updated by [IETF RFC 2732]), meant to be dereferenced to obtain input for the XML processor to construct the entity's replacement text.] It is an error for a fragment identifier (beginning with a # character) to be part of a system identifier. Unless otherwise provided by information outside the scope of this specification (e.g. a special XML element type defined by a particular DTD, or a processing instruction defined by a particular application specification), relative URIs are relative to the location of the resource within which the entity declaration occurs. A URI might thus be relative to the document entity, to the entity containing the external DTD subset, or to some other external parameter entity.

URI references require encoding and escaping of certain characters. The disallowed characters include all non-ASCII characters, plus the excluded characters listed in Section 2.4 of [IETF RFC 2396], except for the number sign (#) and percent sign (%) characters and the square bracket characters re-allowed in [IETF RFC 2732]. Disallowed characters must be escaped as follows:

1. Each disallowed character is converted to UTF-8 [IETF RFC 2279] as one or more bytes.

2. Any octets corresponding to a disallowed character are escaped with the URI escaping mechanism (that is, converted to *%HH*, where HH is the hexadecimal notation of the byte value).

3. The original character is replaced by the resulting character sequence.

[Definition: In addition to a system identifier, an external identifier may include a **public identifier**.] An XML processor attempting to retrieve the entity's content may use the public identifier to try to generate an alternative URI reference. If the processor is unable to do so, it must use the URI reference specified in the system literal. Before a match is attempted, all strings of white space in the public identifier must be normalized to single space characters (#x20), and leading and trailing white space must be removed.

Examples of external entity declarations:

```
<!ENTITY open-hatch
  SYSTEM "http://www.textuality.com/boilerplate/OpenHatch.xml">
<!ENTITY open-hatch PUBLIC
     "-//Textuality//TEXT Standard open-hatch boilerplate//EN"
     "http://www.textuality.com/boilerplate/OpenHatch.xml">
<!ENTITY hatch-pic
        SYSTEM "../grafix/OpenHatch.gif"
        NDATA gif >
```

4.3 Parsed Entities

4.3.1 The Text Declaration

External parsed entities should each begin with a **text declaration**.

Text Declaration
```
[77] TextDecl ::= '<?xml' VersionInfo? EncodingDecl S? '?>'
```

The text declaration must be provided literally, not by reference to a parsed entity. No text declaration may appear at any position other than the beginning of an external parsed entity. The text declaration in an external parsed entity is not considered part of its replacement text.

4.3.2 Well-Formed Parsed Entities

The document entity is well-formed if it matches the production labeled document. An external general parsed entity is well-formed if it matches the production labeled extParsedEnt. All external parameter entities are well-formed by definition.

Well-Formed External Parsed Entity
```
[78] extParsedEnt ::= TextDecl? content
```

An internal general parsed entity is well-formed if its replacement text matches the production labeled content. All internal parameter entities are well-formed by definition.

A consequence of well-formedness in entities is that the logical and physical structures in an XML document are properly nested; no start-tag, end-tag, empty-element tag, element, comment, processing instruction, character reference, or entity reference can begin in one entity and end in another.

4.3.3 Character Encoding in Entities

Each external parsed entity in an XML document may use a different encoding for its characters. All XML processors must be able to read entities in both the UTF-8 and UTF-16 encodings. The terms "UTF-8" and "UTF-16" in this specification do not apply to character encodings with any other labels, even if the encodings or labels are very similar to UTF-8 or UTF-16.

Entities encoded in UTF-16 must begin with the Byte Order Mark described by Annex F of [ISO/IEC 10646], Annex H of [ISO/IEC 10646-2000], section 2.4 of [Unicode], and section 2.7 of [Unicode3] (the ZERO WIDTH NO-BREAK SPACE character, #xFEFF). This is an encoding signature, not part of either the markup or the character data of the XML document. XML processors must be able to use this character to differentiate between UTF-8 and UTF-16 encoded documents.

Although an XML processor is required to read only entities in the UTF-8 and UTF-16 encodings, it is recognized that other encodings are used around the world, and it may be desired for XML processors to read entities that use them. In the absence of external character encoding information (such as MIME headers), parsed entities which are stored in an encoding other than UTF-8 or UTF-16 must begin with a text declaration (see **4.3.1 The Text Declaration**) containing an encoding declaration:

Encoding Declaration

```
[80] EncodingDecl ::= S 'encoding' Eq ('"' EncName '"'
                      | "'" EncName "'" )
[81] EncName ::= [A-Za-z] ([A-Za-z0-9._] | '-')*
        /* Encoding name contains only Latin characters */
```

In the document entity, the encoding declaration is part of the XML declaration. The EncName is the name of the encoding used.

In an encoding declaration, the values "UTF-8", "UTF-16", "ISO-10646-UCS-2", and "ISO-10646-UCS-4" should be used for the various encodings and transformations of Unicode/ISO/IEC 10646, the values "ISO-8859-1", "ISO-8859-2", ... "ISO-8859-*n*" (where *n* is the part number) should be used for the parts of ISO 8859, and the values "ISO-2022-JP", "Shift_JIS", and "EUC-JP" should be used for the various encoded forms of JIS X-0208-1997. It is recommended that character encodings registered (as *charset*s) with the Internet Assigned Numbers Authority [IANA-CHARSETS], other than those just listed, be referred to using their registered names; other encodings should use names starting with an "x-" prefix. XML processors should match character encoding names in a case-insensitive way and should either interpret an IANA-registered name as the encoding registered at IANA for that name or treat it as unknown (processors are, of course, not required to support all IANA-registered encodings).

In the absence of information provided by an external transport protocol (e.g. HTTP or MIME), it is an error for an entity including an encoding declaration to be presented to the XML processor in an encoding other than that named in the declaration, or for an entity which begins with neither a Byte Order Mark nor an encoding declaration to use an encoding other than UTF-8. Note that since ASCII is a subset of UTF-8, ordinary ASCII entities do not strictly need an encoding declaration.

It is a fatal error for a TextDecl to occur other than at the beginning of an external entity.

It is a fatal error when an XML processor encounters an entity with an encoding that it is unable to process. It is a fatal error if an XML entity is determined (via default, encoding declaration, or higher-level protocol) to be in a certain encoding but contains octet sequences that are not legal in that encoding. It is also a fatal error if an XML entity contains no encoding declaration and its content is not legal UTF-8 or UTF-16.

Examples of text declarations containing encoding declarations:

```
<?xml encoding='UTF-8'?>
<?xml encoding='EUC-JP'?>
```

4.4 XML Processor Treatment of Entities and References

The table below summarizes the contexts in which character references, entity references, and invocations of unparsed entities might appear and the required behavior of an XML processor in each case. The labels in the leftmost column describe the recognition context:

Reference in Content

as a reference anywhere after the start-tag and before the end-tag of an element; corresponds to the nonterminal content.

Reference in Attribute Value

as a reference within either the value of an attribute in a start-tag, or a default value in an AttValue.

Occurs as Attribute Value

as a Name, not a reference, appearing either as the value of an attribute which has been declared as type ENTITY, or as one of the space-separated tokens in the value of an attribute which has been declared as type ENTITIES.

Reference in Entity Value

as a reference within a parameter or internal entity's literal entity value in the entity's declaration; corresponds to the nonterminal EntityValue.

Reference in DTD

as a reference within either the internal or external subsets of the DTD, but outside of an EntityValue, AttValue, PI, Comment, SystemLiteral, PubidLiteral, or the contents of an ignored conditional section (see 3.4 Conditional Sections).

	Entity Type				Character
	Parameter	Internal General	External Parsed General	Unparsed	
Reference in Content	*Not recognized*	*Included*	*Included if validating*	*Forbidden*	*Included*
Reference in Attribute Value	*Not recognized*	*Included in literal*	*Forbidden*	*Forbidden*	*Included*
Occurs as Attribute Value	*Not recognized*	*Forbidden*	*Forbidden*	*Notify*	*Not recognized*
Reference in EntityValue	*Included in literal*	*Bypassed*	*Bypassed*	*Forbidden*	*Included*
Reference in DTD	*Included as PE*	*Forbidden*	*Forbidden*	*Forbidden*	*Forbidden*

4.4.1 Not Recognized

Outside the DTD, the % character has no special significance; thus, what would be parameter entity references in the DTD are not recognized as markup in content. Similarly, the names of unparsed entities are not recognized except when they appear in the value of an appropriately declared attribute.

4.4.2 Included

[Definition: An entity is **included** when its replacement text is retrieved and processed, in place of the reference itself, as though it were part of the document at the location the reference was recognized.] The replacement text may contain both character data and (except for parameter entities) markup, which must be recognized in the usual way. (The string "AT&T;" expands to "AT&T;" and the remaining ampersand is not recognized as an entity-reference delimiter.) A character reference is **included** when the indicated character is processed in place of the reference itself.

4.4.3 Included If Validating

When an XML processor recognizes a reference to a parsed entity, in order to validate the document, the processor must include its replacement text. If the entity is external, and the processor is not attempting to validate the XML document, the processor may, but need not, include the entity's replacement text. If a non-validating processor does not include the replacement text, it must inform the application that it recognized, but did not read, the entity.

This rule is based on the recognition that the automatic inclusion provided by the SGML and XML entity mechanism, primarily designed to support modularity in authoring, is not necessarily appropriate for other applications, in particular document browsing. Browsers, for example, when encountering an external parsed entity reference, might choose to provide a visual indication of the entity's presence and retrieve it for display only on demand.

4.4.4 Forbidden
The following are forbidden, and constitute fatal errors:

✦ the appearance of a reference to an unparsed entity.

✦ the appearance of any character or general-entity reference in the DTD except within an EntityValue or AttValue.

✦ a reference to an external entity in an attribute value.

4.4.5 Included in Literal
When an entity reference appears in an attribute value, or a parameter entity reference appears in a literal entity value, its replacement text is processed in place of the reference itself as though it were part of the document at the location the reference was recognized, except that a single or double quote character in the replacement text is always treated as a normal data character and will not terminate the literal. For example, this is well-formed:

```
<!--  -->
<!ENTITY % YN '"Yes"' >
<!ENTITY WhatHeSaid "He said %YN;" > .
```

while this is not:

```
<!ENTITY EndAttr "27'" >
<element attribute='a-&EndAttr;>
```

4.4.6 Notify
When the name of an unparsed entity appears as a token in the value of an attribute of declared type **ENTITY** or **ENTITIES**, a validating processor must inform the application of the system and public (if any) identifiers for both the entity and its associated notation.

4.4.7 Bypassed
When a general entity reference appears in the EntityValue in an entity declaration, it is bypassed and left as is.

4.4.8 Included as PE
Just as with external parsed entities, parameter entities need only be *included if validating*. When a parameter-entity reference is recognized in the DTD and included, its replacement text is enlarged by the attachment of one leading and one following

space (#x20) character; the intent is to constrain the replacement text of parameter entities to contain an integral number of grammatical tokens in the DTD. This behavior does not apply to parameter entity references within entity values; these are described in **4.4.5 Included in Literal**.

4.5 Construction of Internal Entity Replacement Text

In discussing the treatment of internal entities, it is useful to distinguish two forms of the entity's value. [Definition: The **literal entity value** is the quoted string actually present in the entity declaration, corresponding to the non-terminal EntityValue.] [Definition: The **replacement text** is the content of the entity, after replacement of character references and parameter-entity references.]

The literal entity value as given in an internal entity declaration (EntityValue) may contain character, parameter-entity, and general-entity references. Such references must be contained entirely within the literal entity value. The actual replacement text that is included as described above must contain the *replacement text* of any parameter entities referred to, and must contain the character referred to, in place of any character references in the literal entity value; however, general-entity references must be left as-is, unexpanded. For example, given the following declarations:

```
<!ENTITY % pub     "&#xc9;ditions Gallimard" >
<!ENTITY    rights "All rights reserved" >
<!ENTITY    book   "La Peste: Albert Camus,
&#xA9; 1947 %pub;. &rights;" >
```

then the replacement text for the entity "book" is:

```
La Peste: Albert Camus,
(c) 1947 ∞ditions Gallimard. &rights;
```

The general-entity reference "&rights;" would be expanded should the reference "&book;" appear in the document's content or an attribute value.

These simple rules may have complex interactions; for a detailed discussion of a difficult example, see **D Expansion of Entity and Character References**.

4.6 Predefined Entities

[Definition: Entity and character references can both be used to **escape** the left angle bracket, ampersand, and other delimiters. A set of general entities (amp, lt, gt, apos, quot) is specified for this purpose. Numeric character references may also be used; they are expanded immediately when recognized and must be treated as character data, so the numeric character references "<" and "&" may be used to escape < and & when they occur in character data.]

All XML processors must recognize these entities whether they are declared or not. For interoperability, valid XML documents should declare these entities, like any others, before using them. If the entities lt or amp are declared, they must be declared as internal entities whose replacement text is a character reference to the respective character (less-than sign or ampersand) being escaped; the double escaping is required for these entities so that references to them produce a well-formed result. If the entities gt, apos, or quot are declared, they must be declared as internal entities whose replacement text is the single character being escaped (or a character reference to that character; the double escaping here is unnecessary but harmless). For example:

```
<!ENTITY lt     "&#38;#60;">
<!ENTITY gt     "&#62;">
<!ENTITY amp    "&#38;#38;">
<!ENTITY apos   "&#39;">
<!ENTITY quot   "&#34;">
```

4.7 Notation Declarations

[Definition: **Notations** identify by name the format of unparsed entities, the format of elements which bear a notation attribute, or the application to which a processing instruction is addressed.]

[Definition: **Notation declarations** provide a name for the notation, for use in entity and attribute-list declarations and in attribute specifications, and an external identifier for the notation which may allow an XML processor or its client application to locate a helper application capable of processing data in the given notation.]

Notation Declarations
```
[82] NotationDecl ::= '<!NOTATION' S Name S (ExternalID
                        | PublicID) S? '>'
                                            [VC: Unique Notation Name]
[83] PublicID ::= 'PUBLIC' S PubidLiteral
```

Validity constraint: Unique Notation Name

Only one notation declaration can declare a given Name.

XML processors must provide applications with the name and external identifier(s) of any notation declared and referred to in an attribute value, attribute definition, or entity declaration. They may additionally resolve the external identifier into the system identifier, file name, or other information needed to allow the application to call a processor for data in the notation described. (It is not an error, however, for XML documents to declare and refer to notations for which notation-specific applications are not available on the system where the XML processor or application is running.)

4.8 Document Entity

[Definition: The **document entity** serves as the root of the entity tree and a starting-point for an XML processor.] This specification does not specify how the document entity is to be located by an XML processor; unlike other entities, the document entity has no name and might well appear on a processor input stream without any identification at all.

5 Conformance

5.1 Validating and Non-Validating Processors

Conforming XML processors fall into two classes: validating and non-validating.

Validating and non-validating processors alike must report violations of this specification's well-formedness constraints in the content of the document entity and any other parsed entities that they read.

[Definition: **Validating processors** must, at user option, report violations of the constraints expressed by the declarations in the DTD, and failures to fulfill the validity constraints given in this specification.] To accomplish this, validating XML processors must read and process the entire DTD and all external parsed entities referenced in the document.

Non-validating processors are required to check only the document entity, including the entire internal DTD subset, for well-formedness. [Definition: While they are not required to check the document for validity, they are required to **process** all the declarations they read in the internal DTD subset and in any parameter entity that they read, up to the first reference to a parameter entity that they do *not* read; that is to say, they must use the information in those declarations to *normalize* attribute values, *include* the replacement text of internal entities, and supply *default attribute values*.] Except when `standalone="yes"`, they must not process entity declarations or attribute-list declarations encountered after a reference to a parameter entity that is not read, since the entity may have contained overriding declarations.

5.2 Using XML Processors

The behavior of a validating XML processor is highly predictable; it must read every piece of a document and report all well-formedness and validity violations. Less is required of a non-validating processor; it need not read any part of the document other than the document entity. This has two effects that may be important to users of XML processors:

  ✦ Certain well-formedness errors, specifically those that require reading external entities, may not be detected by a non-validating processor. Examples include the constraints entitled *Entity Declared*, *Parsed Entity*, and *No Recursion*, as well as some of the cases described as *forbidden* in **4.4 XML Processor Treatment of Entities and References**.

✦ The information passed from the processor to the application may vary, depending on whether the processor reads parameter and external entities. For example, a non-validating processor may not *normalize* attribute values, *include* the replacement text of internal entities, or supply *default attribute values*, where doing so depends on having read declarations in external or parameter entities.

For maximum reliability in interoperating between different XML processors, applications which use non-validating processors should not rely on any behaviors not required of such processors. Applications which require facilities such as the use of default attributes or internal entities which are declared in external entities should use validating XML processors.

6 Notation

The formal grammar of XML is given in this specification using a simple Extended Backus-Naur Form (EBNF) notation. Each rule in the grammar defines one symbol, in the form

```
symbol ::= expression
```

Symbols are written with an initial capital letter if they are the start symbol of a regular language, otherwise with an initial lower case letter. Literal strings are quoted.

Within the expression on the right-hand side of a rule, the following expressions are used to match strings of one or more characters:

```
#xN
```

where N is a hexadecimal integer, the expression matches the character in ISO/IEC 10646 whose canonical (UCS-4) code value, when interpreted as an unsigned binary number, has the value indicated. The number of leading zeros in the #xN form is insignificant; the number of leading zeros in the corresponding code value is governed by the character encoding in use and is not significant for XML.

```
[a-zA-Z], [#xN-#xN]
```

matches any Char with a value in the range(s) indicated (inclusive).

```
[abc], [#xN#xN#xN]
```

matches any Char with a value among the characters enumerated. Enumerations and ranges can be mixed in one set of brackets.

```
[^a-z], [^#xN-#xN]
```

matches any Char with a value ***outside*** the range indicated.

[^abc], [^#xN#xN#xN]

matches any Char with a value not among the characters given. Enumerations and ranges of forbidden values can be mixed in one set of brackets.

"string"

matches a literal string matching that given inside the double quotes.

'string'

matches a literal string matching that given inside the single quotes.

These symbols may be combined to match more complex patterns as follows, where A and B represent simple expressions:

(expression)

expression is treated as a unit and may be combined as described in this list.

A?

matches A or nothing; optional A.

A B

matches A followed by B. This operator has higher precedence than alternation; thus A B | C D is identical to (A B) | (C D).

A | B

matches A or B but not both.

A - B

matches any string that matches A but does not match B.

A+

matches one or more occurrences of A.Concatenation has higher precedence than alternation; thus A+ | B+ is identical to (A+) | (B+).

A*

matches zero or more occurrences of A. Concatenation has higher precedence than alternation; thus A* | B* is identical to (A*) | (B*).

Other notations used in the productions are:

`/* ... */`

comment.

`[ wfc: ... ]`

well-formedness constraint; this identifies by name a constraint on well-formed documents associated with a production.

`[ vc: ... ]`

validity constraint; this identifies by name a constraint on valid documents associated with a production.

A References

A.1 Normative References
IANA-CHARSETS

(Internet Assigned Numbers Authority) ***Official Names for Character Sets***, ed. Keld Simonsen et al. See ftp://ftp.isi.edu/in-notes/iana/assignments/character-sets.

IETF RFC 1766

IETF (Internet Engineering Task Force). ***RFC 1766: Tags for the Identification of Languages***, ed. H. Alvestrand. 1995. (See `http://www.ietf.org/rfc/rfc1766.txt`.)

ISO/IEC 10646

ISO (International Organization for Standardization). ***ISO/IEC 10646-1993 (E). Information technology -- Universal Multiple-Octet Coded Character Set (UCS) -- Part 1: Architecture and Basic Multilingual Plane.*** [Geneva]: International Organization for Standardization, 1993 (plus amendments AM 1 through AM 7).

ISO/IEC 10646-2000

ISO (International Organization for Standardization). ***ISO/IEC 10646-1:2000. Information technology -- Universal Multiple-Octet Coded Character Set (UCS) -- Part 1: Architecture and Basic Multilingual Plane.*** [Geneva]: International Organization for Standardization, 2000.

Unicode

The Unicode Consortium. *The Unicode Standard, Version 2.0.* Reading, Mass.: Addison-Wesley Developers Press, 1996.

Unicode3

The Unicode Consortium. *The Unicode Standard, Version 3.0.* Reading, Mass.: Addison-Wesley Developers Press, 2000. ISBN 0-201-61633-5.

A.2 Other References

Aho/Ullman

Aho, Alfred V., Ravi Sethi, and Jeffrey D. Ullman. *Compilers: Principles, Techniques, and Tools*. Reading: Addison-Wesley, 1986, rpt. corr. 1988.

Berners-Lee et al.

Berners-Lee, T., R. Fielding, and L. Masinter. *Uniform Resource Identifiers (URI): Generic Syntax and Semantics*. 1997. (Work in progress; see updates to RFC1738.)

Brüggemann-Klein

Brüggemann-Klein, Anne. Formal Models in Document Processing. Habilitationsschrift. Faculty of Mathematics at the University of Freiburg, 1993. (See ftp://ftp.informatik.uni-freiburg.de/documents/papers/brueggem/habil.ps.)

Brüggemann-Klein and Wood

Brüggemann-Klein, Anne, and Derick Wood. *Deterministic Regular Languages*. Universität Freiburg, Institut für Informatik, Bericht 38, Oktober 1991. Extended abstract in A. Finkel, M. Jantzen, Hrsg., STACS 1992, S. 173-184. Springer-Verlag, Berlin 1992. Lecture Notes in Computer Science 577. Full version titled *One-Unambiguous Regular Languages* in Information and Computation 140 (2): 229-253, February 1998.

Clark

James Clark. Comparison of SGML and XML. See `http://www.w3.org/TR/NOTE-sgml-xml-971215`.

IANA-LANGCODES

(Internet Assigned Numbers Authority) *Registry of Language Tags*, ed. Keld Simonsen et al. (See `http://www.isi.edu/in-notes/iana/assignments/languages/`.)

IETF RFC2141

IETF (Internet Engineering Task Force). *RFC 2141: URN Syntax*, ed. R. Moats. 1997.
(See `http://www.ietf.org/rfc/rfc2141.txt`.)

IETF RFC 2279

IETF (Internet Engineering Task Force). *RFC 2279: UTF-8, a transformation format of ISO 10646*, ed. F. Yergeau, 1998.
(See `http://www.ietf.org/rfc/rfc2279.txt`.)

IETF RFC 2376

IETF (Internet Engineering Task Force). *RFC 2376: XML Media Types*. ed. E. Whitehead, M. Murata. 1998. (See `http://www.ietf.org/rfc/rfc2376.txt`.)

IETF RFC 2396

IETF (Internet Engineering Task Force). *RFC 2396: Uniform Resource Identifiers (URI): Generic Syntax*. T. Berners-Lee, R. Fielding, L. Masinter. 1998.
(See `http://www.ietf.org/rfc/rfc2396.txt`.)

IETF RFC 2732

IETF (Internet Engineering Task Force). *RFC 2732: Format for Literal IPv6 Addresses in URL's*. R. Hinden, B. Carpenter, L. Masinter. 1999.
(See `http://www.ietf.org/rfc/rfc2732.txt`.)

IETF RFC 2781

IETF (Internet Engineering Task Force). *RFC 2781: UTF-16, an encoding of ISO 10646*, ed. P. Hoffman, F. Yergeau. 2000.
(See `http://www.ietf.org/rfc/rfc2781.txt`.)

ISO 639

(International Organization for Standardization). *ISO 639:1988 (E). Code for the representation of names of languages.* [Geneva]: International Organization for Standardization, 1988.

ISO 3166

(International Organization for Standardization). ISO 3166-1:1997 (E). Codes for the representation of names of countries and their subdivisions — Part 1: Country codes [Geneva]: International Organization for Standardization, 1997.

ISO 8879

ISO (International Organization for Standardization). ***ISO 8879:1986(E).
Information processing – Text and Office Systems – Standard Generalized
Markup Language (SGML).*** First edition — 1986-10-15. [Geneva]: International
Organization for Standardization, 1986.

ISO/IEC 10744

ISO (International Organization for Standardization). ISO/IEC 10744-1992 (E).
Information technology — Hypermedia/Time-based Structuring Language (HyTime).
[Geneva]: International Organization for Standardization, 1992. Extended Facilities
Annexe. [Geneva]: International Organization for Standardization, 1996.

WEBSGML

ISO (International Organization for Standardization). ***ISO 8879:1986 TC2.
Information technology – Document Description and Processing Languages.***
[Geneva]: International Organization for Standardization, 1998.
(See `http://www.sgmlsource.com/8879rev/n0029.htm`.)

XML Names

Tim Bray, Dave Hollander, and Andrew Layman, editors. ***Namespaces in XML***.
Textuality, Hewlett-Packard, and Microsoft. World Wide Web Consortium, 1999.
(See `http://www.w3.org/TR/REC-xml-names/`.)

B Character Classes

Following the characteristics defined in the Unicode standard, characters are
classed as base characters (among others, these contain the alphabetic characters
of the Latin alphabet), ideographic characters, and combining characters (among
others, this class contains most diacritics). Digits and extenders are also distinguished.

Characters

```
[84] Letter   ::= BaseChar | Ideographic
[85] BaseChar ::= [#x0041-#x005A] | [#x0061-#x007A]
                | [#x00C0-#x00D6] | [#x00D8-#x00F6]
                | [#x00F8-#x00FF] | [#x0100-#x0131]
                | [#x0134-#x013E] | [#x0141-#x0148]
                | [#x014A-#x017E] | [#x0180-#x01C3]
                | [#x01CD-#x01F0] | [#x01F4-#x01F5]
                | [#x01FA-#x0217] | [#x0250-#x02A8]
                | [#x02BB-#x02C1] | #x0386 | [#x0388-#x038A]
```

```
| #x038C | [#x038E-#x03A1] | [#x03A3-#x03CE]
| [#x03D0-#x03D6] | #x03DA | #x03DC | #x03DE
| #x03E0 | [#x03E2-#x03F3] | [#x0401-#x040C]
| [#x040E-#x044F] | [#x0451-#x045C]
| [#x045E-#x0481] | [#x0490-#x04C4]
| [#x04C7-#x04C8] | [#x04CB-#x04CC]
| [#x04D0-#x04EB] | [#x04EE-#x04F5]
| [#x04F8-#x04F9] | [#x0531-#x0556] | #x0559
| [#x0561-#x0586] | [#x05D0-#x05EA]
| [#x05F0-#x05F2] | [#x0621-#x063A]
| [#x0641-#x064A] | [#x0671-#x06B7]
| [#x06BA-#x06BE] | [#x06C0-#x06CE]
| [#x06D0-#x06D3] | #x06D5 | [#x06E5-#x06E6]
| [#x0905-#x0939] | #x093D | [#x0958-#x0961]
| [#x0985-#x098C] | [#x098F-#x0990]
| [#x0993-#x09A8] | [#x09AA-#x09B0]
| #x09B2 | [#x09B6-#x09B9] | [#x09DC-#x09DD]
| [#x09DF-#x09E1] | [#x09F0-#x09F1]
| [#x0A05-#x0A0A] | [#x0A0F-#x0A10]
| [#x0A13-#x0A28] | [#x0A2A-#x0A30]
| [#x0A32-#x0A33] | [#x0A35-#x0A36]
| [#x0A38-#x0A39] | [#x0A59-#x0A5C]
| #x0A5E | [#x0A72-#x0A74] | [#x0A85-#x0A8B]
| #x0A8D | [#x0A8F-#x0A91] | [#x0A93-#x0AA8]
| [#x0AAA-#x0AB0] | [#x0AB2-#x0AB3]
| [#x0AB5-#x0AB9] | #x0ABD | #x0AE0
| [#x0B05-#x0B0C] | [#x0B0F-#x0B10]
| [#x0B13-#x0B28] | [#x0B2A-#x0B30]
| [#x0B32-#x0B33] | [#x0B36-#x0B39]
| #x0B3D | [#x0B5C-#x0B5D] | [#x0B5F-#x0B61]
| [#x0B85-#x0B8A] | [#x0B8E-#x0B90]
| [#x0B92-#x0B95] | [#x0B99-#x0B9A] | #x0B9C
| [#x0B9E-#x0B9F] | [#x0BA3-#x0BA4]
| [#x0BA8-#x0BAA] | [#x0BAE-#x0BB5]
| [#x0BB7-#x0BB9] | [#x0C05-#x0C0C]
| [#x0C0E-#x0C10] | [#x0C12-#x0C28]
| [#x0C2A-#x0C33] | [#x0C35-#x0C39]
| [#x0C60-#x0C61] | [#x0C85-#x0C8C]
| [#x0C8E-#x0C90] | [#x0C92-#x0CA8]
| [#x0CAA-#x0CB3] | [#x0CB5-#x0CB9] | #x0CDE
| [#x0CE0-#x0CE1] | [#x0D05-#x0D0C]
| [#x0D0E-#x0D10] | [#x0D12-#x0D28]
| [#x0D2A-#x0D39] | [#x0D60-#x0D61]
| [#x0E01-#x0E2E] | #x0E30 | [#x0E32-#x0E33]
| [#x0E40-#x0E45] | [#x0E81-#x0E82] | #x0E84
| [#x0E87-#x0E88] | #x0E8A | #x0E8D
```

```
                          | [#x0E94-#x0E97] | [#x0E99-#x0E9F]
                          | [#x0EA1-#x0EA3] | #x0EA5 | #x0EA7
                          | [#x0EAA-#x0EAB] | [#x0EAD-#x0EAE] | #x0EB0
                          | [#x0EB2-#x0EB3] | #x0EBD | [#x0EC0-#x0EC4]
                          | [#x0F40-#x0F47] | [#x0F49-#x0F69]
                          | [#x10A0-#x10C5] | [#x10D0-#x10F6] | #x1100
                          | [#x1102-#x1103] | [#x1105-#x1107] | #x1109
                          | [#x110B-#x110C] | [#x110E-#x1112] | #x113C
                          | #x113E | #x1140 | #x114C | #x114E | #x1150
                          | [#x1154-#x1155] | #x1159 | [#x115F-#x1161]
                          | #x1163 | #x1165 | #x1167 | #x1169
                          | [#x116D-#x116E] | [#x1172-#x1173] | #x1175
                          | #x119E | #x11A8 | #x11AB | [#x11AE-#x11AF]
                          | [#x11B7-#x11B8] | #x11BA | [#x11BC-#x11C2]
                          | #x11EB | #x11F0 | #x11F9 | [#x1E00-#x1E9B]
                          | [#x1EA0-#x1EF9] | [#x1F00-#x1F15]
                          | [#x1F18-#x1F1D] | [#x1F20-#x1F45]
                          | [#x1F48-#x1F4D] | [#x1F50-#x1F57] | #x1F59
                          | #x1F5B | #x1F5D | [#x1F5F-#x1F7D]
                          | [#x1F80-#x1FB4] | [#x1FB6-#x1FBC] | #x1FBE
                          | [#x1FC2-#x1FC4] | [#x1FC6-#x1FCC]
                          | [#x1FD0-#x1FD3] | [#x1FD6-#x1FDB]
                          | [#x1FE0-#x1FEC] | [#x1FF2-#x1FF4]
                          | [#x1FF6-#x1FFC] | #x2126 | [#x212A-#x212B]
                          | #x212E | [#x2180-#x2182] | [#x3041-#x3094]
                          | [#x30A1-#x30FA] | [#x3105-#x312C]
                          | [#xAC00-#xD7A3]
[86] Ideographic    ::= [#x4E00-#x9FA5] | #x3007
                          | [#x3021-#x3029]
[87] CombiningChar ::= [#x0300-#x0345] | [#x0360-#x0361]
                          | [#x0483-#x0486] | [#x0591-#x05A1]
                          | [#x05A3-#x05B9] | [#x05BB-#x05BD]
                          | #x05BF | [#x05C1-#x05C2] | #x05C4
                          | [#x064B-#x0652] | #x0670
                          | [#x06D6-#x06DC] | [#x06DD-#x06DF]
                          | [#x06E0-#x06E4] | [#x06E7-#x06E8]
                          | [#x06EA-#x06ED] | [#x0901-#x0903]
                          | #x093C | [#x093E-#x094C] | #x094D
                          | [#x0951-#x0954] | [#x0962-#x0963]
                          | [#x0981-#x0983] | #x09BC | #x09BE
                          | #x09BF | [#x09C0-#x09C4]
                          | [#x09C7-#x09C8] | [#x09CB-#x09CD]
                          | #x09D7 | [#x09E2-#x09E3] | #x0A02
                          | #x0A3C | #x0A3E | #x0A3F
                          | [#x0A40-#x0A42] | [#x0A47-#x0A48]
                          | [#x0A4B-#x0A4D] | [#x0A70-#x0A71]
```

```
                              | [#x0A81-#x0A83] | #x0ABC
                              | [#x0ABE-#x0AC5] | [#x0AC7-#x0AC9]
                              | [#x0ACB-#x0ACD] | [#x0B01-#x0B03]
                              | #x0B3C | [#x0B3E-#x0B43]
                              | [#x0B47-#x0B48] | [#x0B4B-#x0B4D]
                              | [#x0B56-#x0B57] | [#x0B82-#x0B83]
                              | [#x0BBE-#x0BC2] | [#x0BC6-#x0BC8]
                              | [#x0BCA-#x0BCD] | #x0BD7
                              | [#x0C01-#x0C03] | [#x0C3E-#x0C44]
                              | [#x0C46-#x0C48] | [#x0C4A-#x0C4D]
                              | [#x0C55-#x0C56] | [#x0C82-#x0C83]
                              | [#x0CBE-#x0CC4] | [#x0CC6-#x0CC8]
                              | [#x0CCA-#x0CCD] | [#x0CD5-#x0CD6]
                              | [#x0D02-#x0D03] | [#x0D3E-#x0D43]
                              | [#x0D46-#x0D48] | [#x0D4A-#x0D4D]
                              | #x0D57 | #x0E31 | [#x0E34-#x0E3A]
                              | [#x0E47-#x0E4E] | #x0EB1
                              | [#x0EB4-#x0EB9] | [#x0EBB-#x0EBC]
                              | [#x0EC8-#x0ECD] | [#x0F18-#x0F19]
                              | #x0F35 | #x0F37 | #x0F39 | #x0F3E
                              | #x0F3F | [#x0F71-#x0F84]
                              | [#x0F86-#x0F8B] | [#x0F90-#x0F95]
                              | #x0F97 | [#x0F99-#x0FAD]
                              | [#x0FB1-#x0FB7] | #x0FB9
                              | [#x20D0-#x20DC] | #x20E1
                              | [#x302A-#x302F] | #x3099 | #x309A
[88] Digit ::=                [#x0030-#x0039] | [#x0660-#x0669]
                              | [#x06F0-#x06F9] | [#x0966-#x096F]
                              | [#x09E6-#x09EF] | [#x0A66-#x0A6F]
                              | [#x0AE6-#x0AEF] | [#x0B66-#x0B6F]
                              | [#x0BE7-#x0BEF] | [#x0C66-#x0C6F]
                              | [#x0CE6-#x0CEF] | [#x0D66-#x0D6F]
                              | [#x0E50-#x0E59] | [#x0ED0-#x0ED9]
                              | [#x0F20-#x0F29]
[89] Extender ::=             #x00B7 | #x02D0 | #x02D1 | #x0387
                              | #x0640 | #x0E46 | #x0EC6 | #x3005
                              | [#x3031-#x3035] | [#x309D-#x309E]
                              | [#x30FC-#x30FE]
```

The character classes defined here can be derived from the Unicode 2.0 character database as follows:

Name start characters must have one of the categories Ll, Lu, Lo, Lt, Nl.

- ✦ Name characters other than Name-start characters must have one of the categories Mc, Me, Mn, Lm, or Nd.

- ✦ Characters in the compatibility area (i.e. with character code greater than #xF900 and less than #xFFFE) are not allowed in XML names.

✦ Characters which have a font or compatibility decomposition (i.e. those with a "compatibility formatting tag" in field 5 of the database — marked by field 5 beginning with a "<") are not allowed.

✦ The following characters are treated as name-start characters rather than name characters, because the property file classifies them as Alphabetic: [#x02BB-#x02C1], #x0559, #x06E5, #x06E6.

✦ Characters #x20DD-#x20E0 are excluded (in accordance with Unicode 2.0, section 5.14).

✦ Character #x00B7 is classified as an extender, because the property list so identifies it.

✦ Character #x0387 is added as a name character, because #x00B7 is its canonical equivalent.

✦ Characters ':' and '_' are allowed as name-start characters.

✦ Characters '-' and '.' are allowed as name characters.

C XML and SGML (Non-Normative)

XML is designed to be a subset of SGML, in that every XML document should also be a conforming SGML document. For a detailed comparison of the additional restrictions that XML places on documents beyond those of SGML, see [Clark].

D Expansion of Entity and Character References (Non-Normative)

This appendix contains some examples illustrating the sequence of entity- and character-reference recognition and expansion, as specified in **4.4 XML Processor Treatment of Entities and References**.

If the DTD contains the declaration

```
<!ENTITY example "<p>An ampersand (&#38;#38;) may be escaped
numerically (&#38;#38;#38;) or with a general entity
(&amp;amp;).</p>" >
```

then the XML processor will recognize the character references when it parses the entity declaration, and resolve them before storing the following string as the value of the entity "example":

```
<p>An ampersand (&#38;) may be escaped
numerically (&#38;#38;) or with a general entity
(&amp;amp;).</p>
```

A reference in the document to "&example;" will cause the text to be reparsed, at which time the start- and end-tags of the p element will be recognized and the three references will be recognized and expanded, resulting in a p element with the following content (all data, no delimiters or markup):

```
An ampersand (&) may be escaped
numerically (&#38;) or with a general entity
(&amp;).
```

A more complex example will illustrate the rules and their effects fully. In the following example, the line numbers are solely for reference.

```
1 <?xml version='1.0'?>
2 <!DOCTYPE test [
3 <!ELEMENT test (#PCDATA) >
4 <!ENTITY % xx '&#37;zz;'>
5 <!ENTITY % zz '&#60;!ENTITY tricky "error-prone" >' >
6 %xx;
7 ]>
8 <test>This sample shows a &tricky; method.</test>
```

This produces the following:

✦ in line 4, the reference to character 37 is expanded immediately, and the parameter entity "xx" is stored in the symbol table with the value "%zz;". Since the replacement text is not rescanned, the reference to parameter entity "zz" is not recognized. (And it would be an error if it were, since "zz" is not yet declared.)

✦ in line 5, the character reference "<" is expanded immediately and the parameter entity "zz" is stored with the replacement text "<!ENTITY tricky "error-prone" >", which is a well-formed entity declaration.

✦ in line 6, the reference to "xx" is recognized, and the replacement text of "xx" (namely "%zz;") is parsed. The reference to "zz" is recognized in its turn, and its replacement text ("<!ENTITY tricky "error-prone" >") is parsed. The general entity "tricky" has now been declared, with the replacement text "error-prone".

✦ in line 8, the reference to the general entity "tricky" is recognized, and it is expanded, so the full content of the test element is the self-describing (and ungrammatical) string *This sample shows a error-prone method.*

E Deterministic Content Models (Non-Normative)

As noted in **3.2.1 Element Content**, it is required that content models in element type declarations be deterministic. This requirement is for compatibility with SGML (which calls deterministic content models "unambiguous"); XML processors built using SGML systems may flag non-deterministic content models as errors.

For example, the content model ((b, c) | (b, d)) is non-deterministic, because given an initial b the XML processor cannot know which b in the model is being matched without looking ahead to see which element follows the b. In this case, the two references to b can be collapsed into a single reference, making the model read (b, (c | d)). An initial b now clearly matches only a single name in the content model. The processor doesn't need to look ahead to see what follows; either c or d would be accepted.

More formally: a finite state automaton may be constructed from the content model using the standard algorithms, e.g. algorithm 3.5 in section 3.9 of Aho, Sethi, and Ullman [Aho/Ullman]. In many such algorithms, a follow set is constructed for each position in the regular expression (i.e. each leaf node in the syntax tree for the regular expression); if any position has a follow set in which more than one following position is labeled with the same element type name, then the content model is in error and may be reported as an error.

Algorithms exist which allow many but not all non-deterministic content models to be reduced automatically to equivalent deterministic models; see Brüggemann-Klein 1991 [Brüggemann-Klein].

F Autodetection of Character Encodings (Non-Normative)

The XML encoding declaration functions as an internal label on each entity, indicating which character encoding is in use. Before an XML processor can read the internal label, however, it apparently has to know what character encoding is in use — which is what the internal label is trying to indicate. In the general case, this is a hopeless situation. It is not entirely hopeless in XML, however, because XML limits the general case in two ways: each implementation is assumed to support only a finite set of character encodings, and the XML encoding declaration is restricted in position and content in order to make it feasible to autodetect the character encoding in use in each entity in normal cases. Also, in many cases other sources of information are available in addition to the XML data stream itself. Two cases may be distinguished, depending on whether the XML entity is presented to the processor without, or with, any accompanying (external) information. We consider the first case first.

F.1 Detection Without External Encoding Information

Because each XML entity not accompanied by external encoding information and not in UTF-8 or UTF-16 encoding *must* begin with an XML encoding declaration, in which the first characters must be '<?xml', any conforming processor can detect, after two to four octets of input, which of the following cases apply. In reading this list, it may help to know that in UCS-4, '<' is "#x0000003C" and '?' is "#x0000003F", and the Byte Order Mark required of UTF-16 data streams is "#xFEFF". The notation ## is used to denote any byte value except that two consecutive ##s cannot be both 00.

With a Byte Order Mark:

00 00 FE FF	UCS-4, big-endian machine (1234 order)
FF FE 00 00	UCS-4, little-endian machine (4321 order)
00 00 FF FE	UCS-4, unusual octet order (2143)
FE FF 00 00	UCS-4, unusual octet order (3412)
FE FF ## ##	UTF-16, big-endian
FF FE ## ##	UTF-16, little-endian
EF BB BF	UTF-8

Without a Byte Order Mark:

00 00 00 3C	UCS-4 or other encoding with a 32-bit code unit and ASCII characters encoded as ASCII values, in respectively big-endian (1234), little-endian (4321) and two unusual byte orders (2143 and 3412). The encoding declaration must be read to determine which of UCS-4 or other supported 32-bit encodings applies.
3C 00 00 00 00 00 3C 00 00 3C 00 00 00 3C 00 3F	UTF-16BE or big-endian ISO-10646-UCS-2 or other encoding with a 16-bit code unit in big-endian order and ASCII characters encoded as ASCII values (the encoding declaration must be read to determine which).
3C 00 3F 00	UTF-16LE or little-endian ISO-10646-UCS-2 or other encoding with a 16-bit code unit in little-endian order and ASCII characters encoded as ASCII values (the encoding declaration must be read to determine which).
3C 3F 78 6D	UTF-8, ISO 646, ASCII, some part of ISO 8859, Shift-JIS, EUC, or any other 7-bit, 8-bit, or mixed-width encoding which ensures that the characters of ASCII have their normal positions, width, and values; the actual encoding declaration must be read to detect which of these applies, but since all of these encodings use the same bit patterns for the relevant ASCII characters, the encoding declaration itself may be read reliably.
4C 6F A7 94	EBCDIC (in some flavor; the full encoding declaration must be read to tell which code page is in use).
Other	UTF-8 without an encoding declaration, or else the data stream is mislabeled (lacking a required encoding declaration), corrupt, fragmentary, or enclosed in a wrapper of some kind.

Note In cases above which do not require reading the encoding declaration to determine the encoding, section 4.3.3 still requires that the encoding declaration, if present, be read and that the encoding name be checked to match the actual encoding of the entity. Also, it is possible that new character encodings will be invented that will make it necessary to use the encoding declaration to determine the encoding, in cases where this is not required at present.

This level of autodetection is enough to read the XML encoding declaration and parse the character-encoding identifier, which is still necessary to distinguish the individual members of each family of encodings (e.g. to tell UTF-8 from 8859, and the parts of 8859 from each other, or to distinguish the specific EBCDIC code page in use, and so on).

Because the contents of the encoding declaration are restricted to characters from the ASCII repertoire (however encoded), a processor can reliably read the entire encoding declaration as soon as it has detected which family of encodings is in use. Since in practice, all widely used character encodings fall into one of the categories above, the XML encoding declaration allows reasonably reliable in-band labeling of character encodings, even when external sources of information at the operating-system or transport-protocol level are unreliable. Character encodings such as UTF-7 that make overloaded usage of ASCII-valued bytes may fail to be reliably detected.

Once the processor has detected the character encoding in use, it can act appropriately, whether by invoking a separate input routine for each case, or by calling the proper conversion function on each character of input.

Like any self-labeling system, the XML encoding declaration will not work if any software changes the entity's character set or encoding without updating the encoding declaration. Implementors of character-encoding routines should be careful to ensure the accuracy of the internal and external information used to label the entity.

F.2 Priorities in the Presence of External Encoding Information

The second possible case occurs when the XML entity is accompanied by encoding information, as in some file systems and some network protocols. When multiple sources of information are available, their relative priority and the preferred method of handling conflict should be specified as part of the higher-level protocol used to deliver XML. In particular, please refer to [IETF RFC 2376] or its successor, which defines the `text/xml` and `application/xml` MIME types and provides some useful guidance. In the interests of interoperability, however, the following rule is recommended.

If an XML entity is in a file, the Byte Order Mark and encoding declaration are used (if present) to determine the character encoding.

G W3C XML Working Group (Non-Normative)

This specification was prepared and approved for publication by the W3C XML Working Group (WG). WG approval of this specification does not necessarily imply that all WG members voted for its approval. The current and former members of the XML WG are:

Jon Bosak, Sun (*Chair*)

James Clark (*Technical Lead*)

Tim Bray, Textuality and Netscape (*XML Co-editor*)

Jean Paoli, Microsoft (*XML Co-editor*)

C. M. Sperberg-McQueen, U. of Ill. (*XML Co-editor*)

Dan Connolly, W3C (*W3C Liaison*)

Paula Angerstein, Texcel

Steve DeRose, INSO

Dave Hollander, HP

Eliot Kimber, ISOGEN

Eve Maler, ArborText

Tom Magliery, NCSA

Murray Maloney, SoftQuad, Grif SA, Muzmo and Veo Systems

MURATA Makoto (FAMILY Given), Fuji Xerox Information Systems

Joel Nava, Adobe

Conleth O'Connell, Vignette

Peter Sharpe, SoftQuad

John Tigue, DataChannel

H W3C XML Core Group (Non-Normative)

The second edition of this specification was prepared by the W3C XML Core Working Group (WG). The members of the WG at the time of publication of this edition were:

Paula Angerstein, Vignette

Daniel Austin, Ask Jeeves

Tim Boland

Allen Brown, Microsoft

Dan Connolly, W3C (*Staff Contact*)

John Cowan, Reuters Limited

John Evdemon, XMLSolutions Corporation

Paul Grosso, Arbortext (*Co-Chair*)

Arnaud Le Hors, IBM (*Co-Chair*)

Eve Maler, Sun Microsystems (*Second Edition Editor*)

Jonathan Marsh, Microsoft

MURATA Makoto (FAMILY Given), IBM

Mark Needleman, Data Research Associates

David Orchard, Jamcracker

Lew Shannon, NCR

Richard Tobin, University of Edinburgh

Daniel Veillard, W3C

Dan Vint, Lexica

Norman Walsh, Sun Microsystems

François Yergeau, Alis Technologies (*Errata List Editor*)

Kongyi Zhou, Oracle

I Production Notes (Non-Normative)

This Second Edition was encoded in the XMLspec DTD (which has documentation available). The HTML versions were produced with a combination of the xmlspec.xsl, diffspec.xsl, and REC-xml-2e.xsl XSLT stylesheets. The PDF version was produced with the html2ps facility and a distiller program.

Errata for Extensible Markup Language (XML) 1.0 (Second Edition)

No document is perfect. The second edition of the XML 1.0 specification was published to correct errors and misinterpretations of the first edition. And within the less-than-a-year since the second edition was published, errors have been spotted in the second edition as well. Indeed, Richard H. Adin, the copy editor for this book, found one while he was editing this appendix! (It's erratum E13 below.) Eventually, there'll have to be a third edition of the XML 1.0 specification that corrects the errors in the second edition, and a fourth edition that corrects the errors in the third, and a fifth edition that corrects the errors in the fourth, and so on, at least until XML 1.0 is replaced by something better.

In the meantime, the W3C has published a list of known errata in the second edition. Due to copyright problems, we were not allowed to correct the mistakes in the specification itself. Instead, we reproduce the complete list of acknowledged errata here. This list is current as of June 16, 2001. For the most up-to-date list, see http://www.w3.org/XML/xml-V10-2e-errata

XML 1.0 Second Edition Specification Errata

Abstract

This document records all known errors in the *Second Edition of the Extensible Markup Language (XML) 1.0 Specification*; for updates see the latest version.

The errata are numbered, classified as Substantive, Editorial or Clarification and listed in reverse chronological order of their date of publication.

Please email error reports to xml-editor@w3.org.

Known Errors

Errata as of 2001-06-13
E21 *Substantive*

Section 2.8

Add a new production [28b] and modify production [28] to refer to it:

```
[28] doctypedecl ::= '<!DOCTYPE' S Name (S ExternalID)? S?
                     ('[' intSubset ']' S?)? '>'
                     [VC: Root Element Type]
                     [WFC: External Subset]
[28a] DeclSep     ::= PEReference | S
                     [WFC: PE Between Declarations]
[28b] intSubset   ::= (markupdecl | DeclSep)*
[29] markupdecl   ::= elementdecl | AttlistDecl | EntityDecl |
                     NotationDecl | PI | Comment
                     [VC: Proper Declaration/PE Nesting]
                     [WFC: PEs in Internal Subset]
```

Rationale

Clarify what internal subset means, in particular that it doesn't include the enclosing square brakets "[...]".

Errata as of 2001-05-24
E20 *Substantive*

Obsoletes erratum E108 to first edition

Section 2.3

Change productions [6] Names and [8] Nmtokens to use #x20 (a single-space character) instead of S:

```
[6] Names ::= Name (#x20 Name)*
[8] Nmtokens ::= Nmtoken (#x20 Nmtoken)*
```

Add a note after production 8:

> Note: The Names and Nmtokens productions are used to define the validity of tokenized attribute values after normalization (see 3.3.1 Attribute Types).

Rationale

This restores first edition erratum E62, which was rescinded by E108. It seems likely that when E108 was adopted the productions were incorrectly thought to apply to unnormalized attribute values, which would have prevented the use of non-#x20 white space (tabs and newlines) as separators in tokenized attribute values. In fact, it only prohibits the use of character references to these characters.

This change restores SGML compatibility (*cf.* the "name list" and "name token list" productions in SGML).

E19 *Clarification*

Section 4.5

Modify the third sentence of the first paragraph, so that it reads:

> The actual replacement text that is included (or included in literal) as described above must contain the replacement text of any parameter entities referred to, and must contain the character referred to, in place of any character references in the literal entity value; however, general-entity references must be left as-is, unexpanded.

Errata as of 2001-04-24
E18 *Clarification*

Section 4.2.2

To the sentence:

> Unless otherwise provided by information outside the scope of this specification (e.g. a special XML element type defined by a particular DTD, or a processing instruction defined by a particular application specification), relative URIs are relative to the location of the resource within which the entity declaration occurs.

(inside the paragraph following the Notation declared VC), append the following:

> This is defined to be the external entity containing the '<' which starts the declaration, at the point when it is parsed as a declaration.

Rationale

This clarifies exactly where a declaration occurs, for purposes of determining the base for relative URIs. Given the example:

```
example.xml:

<!DOCTYPE foo [
<!ENTITY % pe SYSTEM "subdir1/pe">
%pe;
%intpe;
]>
<foo>&ent;</foo>
```

```
subdir1/pe:

<!ENTITY % extpe SYSTEM "../subdir2/extpe">
<!ENTITY % intpe "%extpe;">

subdir2/extpe

<!ENTITY ent SYSTEM 'entfile'>
```

Though the characters making up the declaration of `ent` appear in `subdir2/extpe`, they are not parsed as a declaration there. They are just treated as characters making up the replacement text of `intpe`. They are not parsed as a declaration until `intpe` is parsed, at which point the containing external entity is the document entity, so the relevant base URI is that of `example.xml`.

The fact that it is the containing *external* entity that is used may be summed up by saying that internal entities do not carry any base URI with them; indeed, they consist only of their replacement text.

If `example.xml` contained `%extpe;` instead of `%intpe;` the situation would be different: the contents of `subdir2/extpe` would be parsed as a declaration, and the relevant base URI would be that of `subdir2`

Errata as of 2001-04-11
E17 *Editorial*

Section 6

From the definition for "A | B", delete "but not both":

A | B

matches A or B `but not both`.

Rationale

"but not both" was found misleading by some and was in fact useless.

E16 *Substantive*

Appendix A

Move the entries for [IETF RFC 2396] and [IETF RFC 2732] from A.2 (informative) to A.1 (normative).

Rationale

In 4.2.2, immediately after the Notation Declared VC, there is a definition of **system identifier** which clearly depends normatively on those RFCs.

Errata as of 2001-03-27
E15 *Clarification*

Section 3

Rewrite the **Element valid** VC as follows:

Validity constraint: Element Valid
An element is valid if there is a declaration matching elementdecl where the Name matches the element type, and one of the following holds:

1. The declaration matches EMPTY and the element has no content (not even entity references, comments, PIs or white space).

2. The declaration matches children and the sequence of child elements (after replacing any entity references with their replacement text) belongs to the language generated by the regular expression in the content model, with optional white space ~~(characters matching the nonterminal S)~~, comments and PIs (i.e. markup matching production [27] Misc) between the start-tag and the first child element, between child elements, or between the last child element and the end-tag. Note that a CDATA section containing only white space or a reference to an entity whose replacement text is character references expanding to white space do not match the nonterminal S, and hence cannot appear in these positions; however, a reference to an internal entity with a literal value consisting of character references expanding to white space does match S, since its replacement text is the white space resulting from expansion of the character references.

3. The declaration matches Mixed and the content (after replacing any entity references with their replacement text) consists of character data, comments, PIs and child elements whose types match names in the content model.

4. The declaration matches ANY, and the types of any child elements (after replacing any entity references with their replacement text) have been declared.

Section 3.1

In the paragraph just after production [43] `content`, amend the definition of empty element so that the word "content" within the definition is a link to production [43].

Errata as of 2001-03-07
E14 *Clarification*

Section 4.3.2

Amend the last paragraph so that it reads:

> A consequence of well-formedness in general entities is that the logical and physical structures in an XML document are properly nested; no start-tag, end-tag, empty-element tag, element, comment, processing instruction, character reference, or entity reference can begin in one entity and end in another.

Rationale

"General" is added because:

- ✦ since all parameter entities are (now) well-formed by definition, there can't be any interesting consequences of their well-formedness;
- ✦ the list of properly-nested structures notably does not include declarations.

This clarifies that the following from the OASIS test suite:

```
xmltest/invalid/001.xml:
<!DOCTYPE doc SYSTEM "001.ent">
<doc></doc>

with 001.ent:
<!ELEMENT doc EMPTY>
<!ENTITY % e "<!--">
%e; -->
```

is well-formed but violates a validity constraint.

Errata as of 2001-03-05
E13 *Editorial*

Section 2.10

In the first paragraph after the example, replace "overriden" with "overridden" (two d's) in the sentence "This declared intent is considered to apply to all elements within the content of the element where it is specified, unless overridden with another instance of the xml:space attribute."

Errata as of 2001-02-22
E12 *Substantive*

Appendix F.2

Change the [IETF RFC 2376] reference to [IETF RFC 3023] (keeping the same #RFC2376 fragment identifier in order not to break existing links).

Appendix A.2

Change the IETF RFC 2376 entry to:

IETF RFC 3023

IETF (Internet Engineering Task Force). *RFC 3023: XML Media Types*. eds. M. Murata, S. St.Laurent, D. Kohn. 2001. (See http://www.ietf.org/rfc/rfc3023.txt.)

Rationale

RFC 3023 updates and obsoletes RFC 2376.

E11 *Substantive*

Section 1.1

Amend the next to last paragraph so that it reads:

> This specification, together with associated standards (Unicode and ISO/IEC 10646 for characters, Internet RFC 3066 for language identification tags, ISO 639 for language name codes, and ISO 3166 for country name codes), provides all the information necessary to understand XML Version 1.0 and construct computer programs to process it.

[The only change is that "RFC 1766" becomes "RFC 3066".]

Everywhere

Change all [IETF RFC 1766] references to [IETF RFC 3066] (keeping the same #RFC1766 fragment identifier in order not to break existing links).

Section 2.12

Remove the last sentence of the Note: "It is expected that the successor to [IETF RFC 1766] will introduce three-letter language codes for languages not presently covered by [ISO 639]."

Appendix A.1

Change the IETF RFC 1766 entry to:

IETF RFC 3066

IETF (Internet Engineering Task Force). RFC 3066: Tags for the Identification of Languages, ed. H. Alvestrand. 2001. (See http://www.ietf.org/rfc/rfc3066.txt.)

Rationale

RFC 3066 updates and obsoletes RFC 1766.

E10 *Substantive*

Section 3.3.3

Just after the paragraph beginning "All attributes for which no declaration has been read…" (just before the examples), append the following paragraph:

> It is an error if an attribute refers to an entity when there is a declaration for that entity which the processor has not read. This can happen only when a non-validating processor is being used.

Errata as of 2001-01-25
E9 *Clarification*

Section 3.3.2

Change the title and the text of *Attribute Default Legal* Validity Constraint to:

Validity Constraint: Attribute Default Value Syntactically Correct

> The declared default value must meet the syntactic constraints of the declared attribute type.

> Note that only the syntactic constraints of the type are required here; other constraints (e.g. that the value be the name of a declared unparsed entity, for an attribute of type ENTITY) may come into play if the declared default value is actually used (an element without a specification for this attribute occurs).

Rationale

This clarification was prompted by the "sun/invalid/attr11.xml" test file in the OASIS test suite. The interpretation is that the default value of an attribute only needs to be syntactically correct unless it is actually used (i.e an element occurs without a specification for that attribute), in which case the default value must also meet the constraints bearing on this use. This is believed to be required for SGML compatibility and to be what the XML 1.0 spec currently says.

E8 *Clarification*

Section 4.1

Change the first sentence of the second paragraph of the *Entity Declared* **WFC** (not the VC of the same name) to read:

> Note that non-validating processors are not obligated to read and process entity declarations occurring in parameter entities or in the external subset.

Rationale

The note was inconsistent with the normative text, as it read "external parameter entities" whereas internal parameter entities are also not necessarily processed.

E7 *Clarification*

Section 4.5

Remove the word "internal" from the title of the section.

Change the first paragraph, in particular removing the word "internal", so that it reads:

> In discussing the treatment of internal entities, it is useful to distinguish two forms of the entity's value. [Definition: For an internal entity, the **literal entity value** is the quoted string actually present in the entity declaration, corresponding to the non-terminal EntityValue.] [Definition: For an external entity, the **literal entity value** is the exact text contained in the entity.] [Definition: For an internal entity, the **replacement text** is the content of the entity, after replacement of character references and parameter-entity references.] [Definition: For an external entity, the **replacement text** is the content of the entity, after stripping the text declaration (leaving any surrounding whitespace) if there is one but without any replacement of character references or parameter-entity references.]

Rationale

The concept of an entity's replacement text is used throughout the spec, but was defined anywhere for external entities. Also, it was not clear whether the replacement text of an external entity is the content after replacement of character references and parameter-entity references, as for internal entities.

Errata as of 2000-12-06
E6 *Editorial*

Section 3.3.3

Modify the second example in the table at the end of the section to read as follows (add a   in the middle):

a="&d;&d;A&a;&a;B&da;"	A #x20 B	#x20 #x20 A #x20 #x20 #x20 B #x20 #x20

Rationale

Illustrate how space characters (#x20) get normalized no matter whether they come from a character reference or not.

Errata as of 2000-12-01
E5 *Editorial*

Section 4.2.2

In the numbered list explaining the escaping of disallowed characters in URI references, changes "octets" to "bytes".

Rationale

For consistency. We had "octets" and "bytes" meaning the same thing, but apparently suggesting that they were different. "bytes" won by majority rule.

Errata as of 2000-11-22
E4 *Clarification*

Section 4.2.2

Replace the last sentence of the paragraph beginning with "URI references require encoding and escaping of certain characters." with the following: "The XML processor must escape disallowed characters as follows:"

Rationale

The fact that the XML processor is responsible for escaping disallowed characters when resolving URI references was lost in the modifications of the 2nd edition.

E3 *Clarification*

Section 4.2.2

After the sentence reading "A URI might thus be relative to the document entity, to the entity containing the external DTD subset, or to some other external parameter entity.", which follows the definition of SystemLiteral, add the following:

Attempts to retrieve the resource identified by a URI may be redirected at the parser level (for example, in an entity resolver) or below (at the protocol level, for example, via an HTTP Location: header). In the absence of additional information outside the scope of this specification within the resource, the base URI of a resource is always the URI of the actual resource returned. In other words, it is the URI of the resource retrieved after all redirection has occurred.

Errata as of 2000-11-16
E2 *Substantive*

Section 3.3.1

Add a validity constraint applying to productions [58] NotationType and [59] Enumeration as follows:

Validity constraint: No duplicate tokens
The notation names in a single NotationType attribute declaration, as well as the NmTokens in a single Enumeration attribute declaration, must all be distinct.

Rationale

Necessary to maintain compatibility with SGML.

Errata as of 2000-11-02
E1 *Editorial*

Section 3.3.3

In the set of examples at the end of the section, change the last character of the 3rd column of the last example from "#xD" to "#xA". The change makes the third column identical to the second column (for that third example).

Rationale

"#xD" was a typo.

Last updated $Date: 2001/06/13 15:13:58 $ by $Author: fyergeau $
xml-editor

✦   ✦   ✦

Index

Continued

Continued

Continued

Hungry Minds, Inc.
End-User License Agreement

READ THIS. You should carefully read these terms and conditions before opening the software packet(s) included with this book ("Book"). This is a license agreement ("Agreement") between you and Hungry Minds, Inc. ("HMI"). By opening the accompanying software packet(s), you acknowledge that you have read and accept the following terms and conditions. If you do not agree and do not want to be bound by such terms and conditions, promptly return the Book and the unopened software packet(s) to the place you obtained them for a full refund.

1. **License Grant.** HMI grants to you (either an individual or entity) a nonexclusive license to use one copy of the enclosed software program(s) (collectively, the "Software") solely for your own personal or business purposes on a single computer (whether a standard computer or a workstation component of a multi-user network). The Software is in use on a computer when it is loaded into temporary memory (RAM) or installed into permanent memory (hard disk, CD-ROM, or other storage device). HMI reserves all rights not expressly granted herein.

2. **Ownership.** HMI is the owner of all right, title, and interest, including copyright, in and to the compilation of the Software recorded on the disk(s) or CD-ROM ("Software Media"). Copyright to the individual programs recorded on the Software Media is owned by the author or other authorized copyright owner of each program. Ownership of the Software and all proprietary rights relating thereto remain with HMI and its licensers.

3. **Restrictions On Use and Transfer.**

   (a) You may only (i) make one copy of the Software for backup or archival purposes, or (ii) transfer the Software to a single hard disk, provided that you keep the original for backup or archival purposes. You may not (i) rent or lease the Software, (ii) copy or reproduce the Software through a LAN or other network system or through any computer subscriber system or bulletin-board system, or (iii) modify, adapt, or create derivative works based on the Software.

   (b) You may not reverse engineer, decompile, or disassemble the Software. You may transfer the Software and user documentation on a permanent basis, provided that the transferee agrees to accept the terms and conditions of this Agreement and you retain no copies. If the Software is an update or has been updated, any transfer must include the most recent update and all prior versions.

4. **Restrictions on Use of Individual Programs.** You must follow the individual requirements and restrictions detailed for each individual program in Appendix A of this Book. These limitations are also contained in the individual license agreements recorded on the Software Media. These limitations may include a requirement that after using the program for a specified period of time, the user must pay a registration fee or discontinue use. By opening the

Software packet(s), you will be agreeing to abide by the licenses and restrictions for these individual programs that are detailed in Appendix A and on the Software Media. Except as expressly provided herein, none of the material on this Software Media or listed in this Book may ever be redistributed, in original or modified form, for commercial purposes.

5. Limited Warranty.

(a) HMI warrants that the Software and Software Media are free from defects in materials and workmanship under normal use for a period of sixty (60) days from the date of purchase of this Book. If HMI receives notification within the warranty period of defects in materials or workmanship, HMI will replace the defective Software Media.

(b) HMI AND THE AUTHOR OF THE BOOK DISCLAIM ALL OTHER WARRANTIES, EXPRESS OR IMPLIED, INCLUDING WITHOUT LIMITATION IMPLIED WARRANTIES OF MERCHANTABILITY AND FITNESS FOR A PARTICULAR PURPOSE, WITH RESPECT TO THE SOFTWARE, THE PROGRAMS, THE SOURCE CODE CONTAINED THEREIN, AND/OR THE TECHNIQUES DESCRIBED IN THIS BOOK. HMI DOES NOT WARRANT THAT THE FUNCTIONS CONTAINED IN THE SOFTWARE WILL MEET YOUR REQUIREMENTS OR THAT THE OPERATION OF THE SOFTWARE WILL BE ERROR FREE.

(c) This limited warranty gives you specific legal rights, and you may have other rights that vary from jurisdiction to jurisdiction.

6. Remedies.

(a) HMI's entire liability and your exclusive remedy for defects in materials and workmanship shall be limited to replacement of the Software Media, which may be returned to HMI with a copy of your receipt at the following address: Software Media Fulfillment Department, Attn.: *XML Bible, Gold Edition*, Hungry Minds, Inc., 10475 Crosspoint Blvd., Indianapolis, IN 46256, or call 1-800-762-2974. Please allow four to six weeks for delivery. This Limited Warranty is void if failure of the Software Media has resulted from accident, abuse, or misapplication. Any replacement Software Media will be warranted for the remainder of the original warranty period or thirty (30) days, whichever is longer.

(b) In no event shall HMI or the author be liable for any damages whatsoever (including without limitation damages for loss of business profits, business interruption, loss of business information, or any other pecuniary loss) arising from the use of or inability to use the Book or the Software, even if HMI has been advised of the possibility of such damages.

(c) Because some jurisdictions do not allow the exclusion or limitation of liability for consequential or incidental damages, the above limitation or exclusion may not apply to you.

7. **U.S. Government Restricted Rights.** Use, duplication, or disclosure of the Software for or on behalf of the United States of America, its agencies and/or instrumentalities (the "U.S. Government") is subject to restrictions as stated in paragraph (c)(1)(ii) of the Rights in Technical Data and Computer Software clause of DFARS 252.227-7013, or subparagraphs (c) (1) and (2) of the Commercial Computer Software - Restricted Rights clause at FAR 52.227-19, and in similar clauses in the NASA FAR supplement, as applicable.

8. **General.** This Agreement constitutes the entire understanding of the parties and revokes and supersedes all prior agreements, oral or written, between them and may not be modified or amended except in a writing signed by both parties hereto that specifically refers to this Agreement. This Agreement shall take precedence over any other documents that may be in conflict herewith. If any one or more provisions contained in this Agreement are held by any court or tribunal to be invalid, illegal, or otherwise unenforceable, each and every other provision shall remain in full force and effect.

CD-ROM Installation Instructions

The CD-ROM is divided into several directories that contain source code, examples, browsers, a PDF version of this book, and other tools and utilities.

To install the software and source code, mount the CD-ROM using whatever method you normally use on your platform, probably filemanager in Solaris, and just put it in the drive on Mac or Windows. There isn't a fancy installer. You can browse the directories directly from the CD, or copy them onto your local drive. The root directory contains an index.html file you can load into your Web browser of choice to provide a simple HTML interface for the CD-ROM.